21ST-CENTURY OXFORD AUTHORS

GENERAL EDITOR

SEAMUS PERRY

This volume in the 21st Century Oxford Authors series offers students and readers an authoritative, comprehensive selection of the work of Sir Thomas Browne (1605–1682). Accompanied by full scholarly apparatus, the edition demonstrates the breadth of the author of some of the most brilliant and delirious prose in English Literature.

Lauded by writers ranging from Coleridge to Virginia Woolf, from Borges to W.G. Sebald, Browne's distinct style and the musicality of his phrasing have long been seen as a pinnacle of early modern prose. However, it is Browne's range of subject matter that makes him truly distinct. His writings include the hauntingly meditative *Urn-Burial*, and the elaborate *The Garden of Cyrus*, a work that borders on a madness of infinite pattern. Religio Medici, probably Browne's most famous work, is at once autobiography, intricate religious-scientific paradox, and a monument of tolerance in the era of the English civil war. This volume also includes his *Pseudodoxia Epidemica*, an encyclopaedia of error which contains within its vast remit the entire intellectual landscape of the seventeenth century-its science, its natural history, its painting, its history, its geography and its biblical oddities. The volume enables students to experience the ways in which Browne brings his lucid, baroque and stylish prose to bear across this range of diverse material, together with a carefully poised wit. This volume contains almost all of the author's work that was published in his lifetime, as well as a selection of writings published after his death.

Explanatory notes and commentary are included, to enhance the study, understanding, and enjoyment of these works, and the edition includes an Introduction to the life and works of Browne.

Kevin Killeen is Senior Lecturer in English and Related Literature at the University of York. He has written extensively on Thomas Browne and the intellectual culture of the seventeenth century, as well as the history of science and religion. Among his books is the prize winning *Biblical Scholarship, Science and Politics in Early Modern Culture: Thomas Browne and The Thorny Place of Knowledge* (2009).

Seamus Perry is the General Editor of the 21st-Century Oxford Authors series. He is Professor of English Literature at the University of Oxford and a Fellow of Balliol College. His publications include *Coleridge and the Uses of Division and Coleridge's Notebooks: A Selection*, and, co-edited with Robert Douglas-Fairhurst, *Tennyson Among the Poets* (all OUP).

FIG. 1 Thomas Browne—Engraving from 1672 works.

Dedication

To Molly Rose Killeen

ACKNOWLEDGEMENTS

I have had great support in putting this volume together. The Department of English and Related Literatures at the University of York has provided me with funding for editorial assistants and I'm very grateful to David Atwell and Helen Fulton for help with this. I would like to thank Tamsin Badcoe, Rachel Willie, and Amritesh Singh for their excellent editorial skills. Particular thanks to Tania Demetriou, who checked and stabilized the Greek, to Christine Phillips, Elizabeth Tyler, Michele Campopiano, and Henry Stead, who provided me with information and translations that saved me from some wilder mis-rendering of the text, and to Hannah DeGroff for indexing. Thanks also to my colleagues in the Centre for Renaissance and Early Modern Studies, Brian Cummings, Tania Demetriou, Mark Jenner, John Roe, Richard Rowland, Bill Sherman, and Helen Smith, as well as staff in the Old Palace Library at York Minster, University of York library, the British Library, and the Brotherton Library.

This one-volume edition of Browne puts all his major published work into a single volume, and is to be followed over the coming years by a major eight-volume *Complete Works of Sir Thomas Browne* from Oxford University Press, bringing a full scholarly treatment to his writings. Such a large and international venture has meant that I have benefitted from a group of scholars working on all aspects of Browne, and I would particularly like to thank Claire Preston, the general editor of the edition, as well as Katherine Murphy and Reid Barbour. Previous editors of Browne have provided superb models of scholarship and I have made full use of their unwaveringly reliable source-referencing to guide me to the appropriate places. I have tried on the whole to amplify their references into description or direct quotation of the passages, though this could not be a uniform policy in a one-volume edition.

I have made frequent use of the complete editions of Browne, by Simon Wilkin (4 vols., London: Pickering, 1835–6) and Geoffrey Keynes' four-volume *Works* (London: Faber, 1964), and earlier selections of his work including, L. C. Martin, *Religio Medici and Other Works* (Oxford: Clarendon Press, 1964), Norman Endicott, *The Prose of Sir Thomas Browne* (New York University Press, 1968), Robin Robbins, *Religio Medici, Hydriotaphia and the Garden of Cyrus* (Oxford: Clarendon Press, 1972), and C. A. Patrides, *Sir Thomas Browne: The Major Works* (London: Penguin, 1977). Among the single-work volumes that have been particularly useful, it is worth noting the following: *Religio Medici*, ed. Jean-Jacques Denonain (Cambridge University Press, 1953), *Hydriotaphia*, ed. W. Murison (Cambridge University Press, 1933), and *Pseudodoxia Epidemica*, ed. Robin Robbins (Oxford University Press, 1981). We are perhaps at the tipping point where it is no longer possible to suppose that the internet is just a passing fad that will not really take off, but despite its ephemera, it is worth noting LacusCurtius, whose online bilingual editions of out-of-copyright Loeb editions has been a wonderful tool, as has Tufts University Perseus Project, with its searchable classics, and the online editions of Browne by James Eason, based at the University of Chicago. Thanks are also due for the excellent editorial support from Oxford University Press, in particular, Jacqueline Baker, Seamus Perry, Rachel Platt, Rosie Chambers, Elizabeth Chadwick, and also to Malcolm Todd.

Thanks mostly to Molly Killeen, and to the wonderful Sharon Holm.

CONTENTS

LIST OF ILLUSTRATIONS

INTRODUCTION

G. K. Chesterton, comparing Thomas Browne with Oliver Cromwell, remarks that, all things considered, it was 'highly probably that the religious ideals of Oliver Cromwell were infinitely inferior to those of Sir Thomas Browne'. He explains that whatever Cromwell's policy genius, 'his religious ideals practically united him with the meanest drummer in his army'. In contrast, 'we should laugh at the mere idea of Browne's archaeological emotions and mystical charity being shared by his butler or keeping his gardener awake at night'. Though Chesterton strangely underestimates the numinous gardeners who occupy Browne's work, and though it is both unrecorded and unlikely that an early modern physician employed a butler, his point is the particular religious finery of an author who so steeped himself in the ineffable, who in an age of ardent religiosity, saw the paradox of the divine unknowability everywhere.

Chesterton's comments occur in a review of Edward Dowden's *Puritan and Anglican*, who, in speaking about Browne, 'is just and sympathetic, but not frantic with admiration, as he ought to be'. This is not, of course, frantic in the Cromwellian manner or that of his mean drummer, but rather with the zeal of a crusading literary critic, whose task is to recognize in Browne a writer in whom, quite singularly, style was the conduit of mysticism:

> Style, in his sense, did not merely mean sound, but an attempt to give some twist of wit or symbolism to every clause or parenthesis: when he went over his work again he did not merely polish brass, he fitted in gold. This habit of working with a magnifying glass, this turning and twisting of minor words, is the true parent of mysticism, for the mystic is not . . . a man who reverences large things so much as a man who reverences small ones, who reduces himself to a point, without parts or magnitude, so that to him the grass is really a forest and the grasshopper a dragon. Little things please great minds.[1]

This account of Browne's style, intricate, opulent, performed with tweezers and microscope, describes a malleable prose, in whose minutiae, every object, and each twist of the pen has theological purpose. But he is less mystical jeweller than mystical anatomist, who finds in his

[1] G. K. Chesterton, *The Speaker: The Liberal Review*, December 15, 1900, p. 301, reviewing Edward Dowden, *Puritan and Anglican* (London: Kegan Paul, 1900).

relentless microcosmic manoeuvres all creation reiterated in the form of the body, natural philosophy yielding natural theology. It is as a physician rather than knight that Browne—Dr Browne—was known, the knighthood being an apparently accidental conferment towards the end of his life, when the mayor of Norwich turned down a no doubt affronted Charles II, who sought a nearby alternative.[2] Browne's work is saturated with the medical—with the body, and its unfathomable complexity, with plants, and the impalpable dynamics of growth, with death, and the poetics of rebirth.

Browne was a significant, if perplexing, natural philosopher and scholar, a figure whose experimental acumen could be trusted by Robert Boyle and whose amalgams of knowledge in *Pseudodoxia Epidemica* (1646) were widely admired.[3] An emergent generation of natural philosophers in the 1650s and 1660s—Joseph Glanville, Henry Power, Henry More, and Robert Boyle himself—all derive something of their tendency to theological and scientific amalgamation from Browne, though not without some reserve.[4] His writing, proposing, as it so often did, the dislocation of reason at the vital moment of submerging itself into the divine, was at odds with the direction of science as it was represented in the pages of the Royal Society's *Philosophical Transactions*. His mannered rhetoric and his humanist habits of reference were increasingly alien to the more terse and functional prose of scientific writing. But Browne's supposition that both soul and body were the proper objects of natural philosophy was the working presumption of many if not most contemporaries. *Religio Medici* (1643) had announced Browne as a writer of some importance in this respect. Though later readers have focused on its tolerance and his habits of dazzling paradox, the immediate responses to Browne's first work were as interested in its depiction of the soul.[5]

[2] Francis Blomefield, *An Essay towards a Topographical History of the County of Norfolk*, 10 vols. (1805), vol. 3, p. 414.

[3] Robert Boyle, *Certain Physiological Essays* in Michael Hunter and Edward B. Davis (eds.), *The Works of Robert Boyle*, 14 vols. (London: Pickering and Chatto, 2000), vol. 2, p. 78.

[4] Comment on Browne's scientific acumen is found in Walter Charleton, *A Ternary of Paradoxes* (1650), sig. B3r; Henry Power, *Experimental philosophy, in Three Books* (1664), p. 58; Nehemiah Grew, *The Anatomy of Plants with an Idea of a Philosophical History of Plants* (1682), p. 31; John Ray, *The Ornithology of Francis Willughby* (1678), preface; Thomas Vaughan, *A Brief Natural History* (1669), p. 94.

[5] Browne's account of the soul is given detailed attention in Kenelm Digby, *Observations Upon Religio Medici* (1643); Alexander Ross, *Medicus Medicatus* (1645).

However, it was Browne's later works, *Hydriotaphia* and *The Garden of Cyrus*, that earned him his reputation in the eighteenth and nineteenth century as a writer of the sublime, whose texts were both luminous and opaque, nugatory and all-encompassing, moving to and fro between the local and the universal. This sometimes exuberant admiration is illustrated in miniature by a volume of Browne's works, which served as a much-sought-after autograph book for the Romantics. Owned by Samuel Taylor Coleridge, who annotated Browne extensively, it has 'Mr Wordsworth, Rydal Mount' inscribed on the title page of *Pseudodoxia Epidemica*, while the flyleaf contains the note 'C. Lamb 9th March 1804, bought for S. T. Coleridge'. Under this, in Coleridge's hand are the words 'Given by S.T.C to S. Hutchinson March 1804', followed by the note 'N.B. It was the 10th, on which day I dined and punched at Lamb's—& exulted in his having procured the Hydriotaphia & all the rest lucro posito'.[6]

The basis of such admiration was, according to a letter sent to Sara Hutchinson, because Browne 'has brains in his Head, which is all the more interesting for a *Little Twist* in the Brains'. The twist was that identified also by Chesterton, Browne's habitual and vertiginous shifts in scale, moving from the tiny to the infinite. Praising *Hydriotaphia or Urne-Buriall* for its 'Sir Thomas Browne-ness', Coleridge goes on to define this as an impulse to totality, that 'we wonder at and admire his *entireness* in every subject which is before him—he is totus in illo . . . for whatever happens to be his subject, he metamorphoses all Nature into it'.[7] Commenting on *The Garden of Cyrus*, Coleridge continues, 'There is the same attention to oddities, to the remotenesses and *minutiae* of vegetable terms—the same entireness of subject.'

In these two strangest of works, *Hydriotaphia* and *The Garden of Cyrus*, Browne moves from intricate scholarship to a delirium of fact upon fact piled up, but it is a delirium in perfect rhetorical order, never for a moment missing the solemn pace that the decorum of his subject matter enjoins, but never entirely, in its impulse to draw

[6] This Folio *Works* is in the Berg Collection of the New York Public Library. Reproduced in Coleridge, *Marginalia*, ed. George Whalley (London: Routledge, 1980), vol. 1, p. 761. We can, I think, presume this to be drinking punch rather than fighting.

[7] Letter to Sarah Hutchinson, *Coleridge on the Seventeenth Century*, ed. Roberta Florence Brinkley (Duke University Press, 1955), pp. 447–8. A version of this letter appears in *Blackwood's Magazine*, 6:32 (Nov 1819), 197–8; Coleridge, *Marginalia*, pp. 762–4.

everything into its orbit, being free from the madness of infinite pattern. These are works of elaborate architecture, both in relation to each other and in their own construction. But it is an Escheresque architecture, whose singular quality is its geometric impossibility—they are works that could not exist in the real world.

Browne's writings cover a vast terrain, from the earthy mineral underworld and its airs to angels, from the Aristotelian to the Platonic, from the fantastical Plinyesque to the meticulous Baconian. His is a landscape of knowledge that is vast, complicated, and fragile—that takes its extensive biblical learning as unimpeachable and yet also poetically flexible, that views its manner of enquiry as faithful to classical traditions in natural philosophy and at the same time as the embodiment of all things new, of anatomical and experimental daring. Few subjects escape Browne's pen, and as such, his writings constitute a field-guide to what was worth knowing in the seventeenth century. If he is a repository of ideas and an ossuary of knowledge, however, he is also the most poetic and playful of writers. His liquefying prose provokes the suspicion that the subject matter is mere fodder for style, and yet this is not the case—when he is an antiquarian, he does not stint in full-bookish antiquarianism, just as Browne the enquiring doctor-scientist can weigh his dragms and grains experimentally with scrupulous attention.

Browne inhabits and characterizes an era in which knowledge was not quite fissured in the ways it was to become in the following centuries, when natural philosophy, religion, classicism, and meditative flight settled into their divided and distinct areas. His writings have that quality of poetry that they are immune to paraphrase, that their meaning is embodied in their tone, form, and pace. Such a claim is true (but differently true) of all his major writings. Tone is everything in *Religio Medici*. The subject matter is protean, formless, and ephemeral, while all the time, the under-hum of Browne's voice maintains the quasi-autobiographical unity, whether deemed soft and flexible or, as others will have it, slippery and cunningly uncommitted. But it is in Browne's paired enigmas, *Hydriotaphia* and *The Garden of Cyrus*, where tone as content is raised to its highest pitch. In what follows, this introduction gives something of a survey of works, with an eye to Browne's amalgams of knowledge, then, more briefly, a biographical note, though introductions are, of course, there to be skipped for the works themselves.

WORKS OF BROWNE

(i) The Garden of Cyrus

The Garden of Cyrus is a work animated by an obsessive and capacious seeking of the quincunx (the shape of a domino five), in nature, in design, in universal pattern. Quincuncial forms are found everywhere, in orchards and fish scales, in brick-wedgings and diamond windows, in crucifixions and the webbing of beds, military formations and doctors' forceps, even before coming to the stuff of nature, the webs of spiders or the seeds of sunflowers as they sit podded on their flower. This for Browne is the 'fundamental figure', prompting Samuel Johnson's comment 'so that a reader, not watchful against the power of his infusions, would imagine that decussation was the great business of the world, and that nature and art had no other purpose than to exemplify and imitate a Quincunx'.[8] Garden design is very briefly the subject, though gardeners on a mythological scale: the vineyards of Noah, the Babylonian designs of Nebuchadnezzar, and the eponymous Cyrus the Elder. What might be a treatise on gardens, however, turns out to be a work of 'arithmetical divinity', whose sweep takes in its collateral subject matter by the merest of connections, some more and some less tangible. It might be suspected that given the right prompt, three or six or seven would serve Browne as well. He cheats on his geometrical rules, twisting and bending shapes so that they qualify as quincuncial—lozenge or rhomboid, dissected, sliced, and 'decussated' half-shapes, anything strung crossways will serve his compulsive gorging on geometry and figure.

Always, with *The Garden of Cyrus*, we are mid-enquiry, this being the dynamic of a work in which everything is digression and whose numerous instances of five-foldedness exist almost without syntax, strung together with trick grammar. Browne builds his text via long instances of *occupatio* (describing what will be omitted, in the process of which, it is discussed), or long paragraphs of *problemata* (thought-lists of things to be investigated later).

For to omit the position of squared stones, cuneatim or wedgwise in the walls of Roman and Gothick buildings; and the lithostrata or figured pavements of the ancients, which consisted not all of square stones, but were divided into

[8] Samuel Johnson's 'Life of Browne' prefaces his edition of *Christian Morals* (1756), p. xxv. Similarly, Coleridge, *Marginalia*, p. 764.

triquetrous segments, honey-combs, and sexangular figures, according to Vitruvius.

The detailing of what one is forced to omit is a standard rhetorical and oratorical trick in the Renaissance, but in *The Garden of Cyrus*, it comes to seem almost an epistemological necessity—that pattern occurs fleetingly and the knowledge of fives comes to mean anything only when it is shown to be multiplied throughout nature and human design. Similarly, *problemata* served as a way of thinking and a mode of enquiry: Browne uses them as a wall of questions, in which they come to seem the very structure of nature, a universe constructed in question form:

> whether seminall nebbes hold any sure proportion unto seminall enclosures, why the form of the germe doth not answer the figure of the enclosing pulp, why the nebbe is seated upon the solid, and not the channeld side of the seed as in grains, why since we often meet with two yolks in one shell, and sometimes one egge within another, we do not oftener meet with two nebbes in one distinct seed.

There is a breathlessness in this, the truncated first clause of the grammatically unfinished sentence never meeting any answering second part, and the paragraph continues for some span before allowing any syntactical rest, these being 'quæries which might enlarge but must conclude this digression'. This is not unfamiliar Brownean territory. Indeed it is not unfamiliar in Renaissance thought, rooted in Aristotle's *Problemata* for speculative, sometimes scientific enquiry, a way of coordinating queries for investigation. Browne's notebooks are filled with such conjectural questions-in-waiting, a distant relative of the scholastic *quaestio disputata*, whose form seems to propose a suspension of enquiry, the description of the natural world by the questions that might be asked of it.

The Garden of Cyrus depends for its strategies of accumulation upon an intricate knowledge of natural philosophy in its many forms, along with mathematics, natural history, and anatomy, so much so that it has been seen as Browne's most scientifically astute, if obtuse, work.[9] It is meticulous in its observation and its habits of discovery, finding the quincunx in the forms of plants, 'the pendulous excrescences of several trees', in leaves and the textures of the vegetable world, in

[9] The amorphous philosophical purposes of the text are best explored in Claire Preston, *Thomas Browne and the Writing of Early Modern Science* (Cambridge University Press, 2005), pp. 175–210.

pine-cones, and in the movement of plant generation, the proscribed order by which nature produces leaves on the stalk, and in the plastic, propulsive power or 'fructifying principle' that generates plant-growth. Scientific precision, for Browne, was underlain by theological purposes. It provided a reprise and reproductive image of the original creation, a slow-motion glimpse of divine explication, the layer-by-layer unfolding of the world in process. Likewise, in the search for the quasi-theological, quasi-philosophical imprint of God, the animal world provided quincuncial fodder for mysticism, from honeycombs to anatomical structures, from the multiple stomachs of cows to the dynamics of limbs in motion, from Vetruvian figures inscribed in a circle to Platonic hermaphrodites divided in two, all of which contribute to a polyformous and protean theology of shape.

For long stretches of Chapters 3 and 4, the job of preserving the ubiquity of decussation in nature is mathematical: the tapering cylindricality of trees, Archimedes on conic shapes, squaring the circle, and the pyramids of light through the aperture of the eye. If *The Garden of Cyrus* is an almost mathematical work, suffused in the Euclidean pleasures of number and form, Browne also dwells on the near-tactility and texture of his geometrical vocabulary, 'helicall or spirall roundles, volutas, conicall sections, circular Pyramids, and frustums of Archimedes', before closing, in his final chapter, on the number 5 itself, magically, mystically, even magnetically considered, bowing in passing acknowledgement to Plutarch's *De E Apud Delphos* (*The E at Delphi*), which may be the one work which could be considered in its skittishness the generic predecessor of *Cyrus*.

If *The Garden of Cyrus* is a work of natural philosophy, however, it also stretches any definition of science. It is latticed with humanist and historical reference, with a poetics of creation and an aesthetic of endemic digression. Its observational science of plants is at the same time precise and deranged. Browne imagines, in diagrammatic form, how a tree extending above ground is mirrored under the earth by its roots, thus forming a quincunx in profile. But it goes further. The tree-tops exude an effluvia to meet with the rays of sun, stretching out beyond their uppermost leaves, while underneath there is a corresponding rooty effluvia, and together these constitute the light and dark of growth. Exploring throughout the chapter how shadow and light alternate, Browne moves from the example of a forest with its 'intercolumniations' of trees, whose canopy protects against the light, onto a parallel with the hand cupped above the eye, and Browne's discovery that optics encapsulates the working of the quincunx, in the diagrammatically figured crossing of the rays of light as they pass through the pupil:

for all things are seen quincuncially; for at the eye the pyramidal rayes from the object, receive a decussation, and so strike a second base upon the retina or hinder coat, the proper organ of vision; wherein the pictures from objects are represented, answerable to the paper, or wall in the dark chamber.

Browne's remarkable claim here is that the design of light, in its rays rather than its general effusion, makes reference to the great quincuncial pattern of the world, that the quincunx occurs in every act of sight. Rarely can the anatomy of the eye have been put to such irrelevant purpose. Reference to shadow and light also serves theology, and what is true for physical light is equally so for an allegorical light of the soul:

life it self is but the shadow of death, and souls departed but the shadows of the living: all things fall under this name. The sunne it self is but the dark simulachrum, and light but the shadow of God.

Rosalie Colie called upon Browne for the title of her study of the Renaissance paradox tradition, *Paradoxia Epidemica*, though he is only an honorary presence there in the more formal traditions of literary paradox.[10] *The Garden of Cyrus*, however, might seem wholly imbricated in the era's palpable interest in verbal illusion and paradox, a discussion of optics becoming, by a typological trick, an account of the fugitive presence of the divine. Browne's design is to represent, as Frank Huntley put it, a passing glimpse of the 'mind of the Infinite Geometrician',[11] the unknowable shadowed forth dimly by the profusion of the natural world. In doing so, *The Garden of Cyrus* superimposes on its relentless pattern a delirious variety, as disorderly a text as can be imagined, whose argument is endless order.

(ii) Hydriotaphia or Urne-Buriall

Hydriotaphia, or Urne-Buriall was published together with *The Garden of Cyrus*, and that they bear some relationship, that the one is in concert with the other, is very probable, but is it a fleeting and

[10] Rosalie L. Colie, *Paradoxia Epidemica, The Renaissance Tradition of Paradox* (Princeton University Press, 1966).

[11] Frank L. Huntley, 'Sir Thomas Browne: The Relationship of "Urn Burial" and "The Garden of Cyrus"', *Studies in Philology*, 53:2 (1956): 204–19 (205).

elusive relationship. We might suppose, for instance, the fecundity of *Cyrus*, its immense and irresponsible profusion of life multiplied by a virus of quincuncial geometry to have its counterpart in the proliferation of death, through the ages of burial practices, multiplied till death seems as profuse and animate as life. We might see the five-part structures in conversation with each other. The prose of both is rich and both texts are fugal, depending upon the delirious modulation of their initial theme, their rhetorical effect achieved by the sheer bulk of atonal song, in augmentation and cacophony, which, when it resolves and its wave of sound ceases, closes in a monumental calm.

Hydriotaphia (with the 'taph' as in 'Cenotaph') is about burial, and the ceremonies of death, opening with an almost antiquarian account of comparative burial, in earth, fire, air, or water—almost, but not quite antiquarian. *Hydriotaphia* is driven as much by its musical qualities, its particular measure of lament—restrained in tone, long in the phrasing of its prosody, with something of the funeral sermon about it. It can be seen among the era's many experiments in the form and formality of mourning, whether the literary and exegetical weave that went into orations for the dead at the hands of Lancelot Andrewes, Joseph Hall, or Edward Reynolds, or the unprecedented emergence and outpouring of poetic elegy: Henry King producing his formally-perfect, guttural wail of strewn verses upon the grave of his wife; John Donne's revisiting the grave of Elizabeth Drury in the holy and gruesome autopsy of his *Anniversaries*, or Milton's *Lycidas*, where the formal pastoral elegy melts into a vatic swell of political prophecy. Browne's dead, however, are long gone, and while it borrows something from the dynamics of elegy, this is a collective dead and philosophical mourning. Its sources are those of scholarly antiquarianism, such as Johannes Kirchmann's *de Funeribus Romanorum* (1625) or Antonio Bosio's *Roma Sotteranea* (1632). Browne's work remains *sui generis*, however, with its own and remarkable digressive manoeuvres across its five chapters.

It takes its cue, initially at least, from a capaciously anthropological tour of the dead and habits of burial—Indian 'Brachmans', Chaldeans, 'Persees', Egyptians, and Scythians—cultures whose distance lent them a quality of the mythological and lost. The cataloguing of nations divides them by what element they rely upon to best obliterate the dead. While English and Western customs of earthy burials ('centrall interrment') are taken to be the oldest and biblical manner of disposing of bodies, the animating motive of the work is the profusion in the ceremonies of death: 'men have been most phantasticall in the singular contrivances of their corporall dissolution'. Trojan, Roman, and Norse accounts of cremation vie with those who attempt to dispose of the dead by water or by dissolution in the air, or, in the case of the Balearians, by the fossilizing weight of having heaps of wood press the body to dissolution. Christian cultures, he notes, may disdain the burning of the dead, but are less concerned with immolating the living: 'though they stickt not to give their bodies to be burnt in their lives, detested that mode after death'.

This tour is at once scholarly and mournful. It moves from its account of the historical and long-gone dead to the newly discovered 'field of old Walsingham' full of urns, occasioning an account of Roman Norfolk—the Saxon Urns wrongly attributed to the long imperial occupation—and their relations in passing with Druids, Danes, and ancient Britons. Browne notices the necks of urns to resemble wombs 'making our last bed like our first' and how, connoisseur of death that he is, the brick covering of Yarmouth Urns differs from the 'Homericall urne of Patroclus' wrapped in its 'purple peece of silk'. There are lamps to consider and 'lachrymatories'—bottles to fill with the tears of the mourners. There are the ceremonies and monuments to ephemera, hills heaped upon the dead, inscriptions and anonymity. Nor are the dead insulated from humiliation—whether dissection, the 'provocatives of mirth from anatomies', or 'tricks with skeletons' performed by jugglers. The opportunities are multiple: 'To be gnawed out of our graves, to have our sculs made drinking-bowls, and our bones tuned into pipes'. Some nations burn better and some rot better than others—he reports upon an 'hydropicall body' from a churchyard which had coagulated into the consistency of 'the hardest castle-soap'.

Dying, in early modern thought, was as much to do with the soul as the body and their philosophically baffling division and promise of reunion. Funeral rites had the task of emblematically representing and prefiguring resurrection, while pagan rites served for what meagre comfort they could manage. At the death of a child in Roman culture, 'mourning without hope, they had an happy fraud against excessive lamentation, by a common opinion that deep sorrows disturbed their ghosts'. The state of the soul in the 'Hades of Homer' and 'Latin Hell' is one of terrifying ghostly suspension, retaining only confused half-connections to the earth, in a thronging and unhappy crowd of souls, the hell of it being not a Dantesque afterlife, but rather a state of bodiless eternal senility. This is Browne's Pascalian Wager—Christian death being better to believe in and, after all, there being nothing to lose. If at times, the voice is that of an antiquarian, studying with precision the widely disparate cultures of death and the archaeology of disturbed urns, *Hydriotaphia* imperceptibly shifts, through the documentary to the ethical and onto an epistemology of oblivion.

Browne's final chapters take paradoxes of time, eternity, and immortality to task. The urns may have survived, but the manner of life and the mode of death that they memorialize are beyond our knowledge: 'wrapt up in the bundle of time, they fall into indistinction'. 'The long habit of living indisposeth us for dying', Browne explains, even while some might wish themselves unborn, like the 'male-content of Job', who 'lived here but in an hidden state of life, and as it were an abortion'. There can be few such misanthropic descriptions of life that match Browne's sense here of one's years as a deferred and long miscarriage. Urns lack names and names alone mean little: 'who cares to subsist like Hippocrates patients, or Achilles horses in Homer, under naked nominations... who had not rather have been the good theef, then Pilate?' But individual extinction is little compared with the incalculable mass of those dying, whose names pass unrecorded. 'The iniquity of oblivion blindely scattereth her poppy', Browne muses, in considering the unbalanced 'arithmetique' whereby 'The number of the dead long exceedeth all that shall live'. *Hydriotaphia* is a rising lament to the dissolution of memory, the vanity of 'pyramids, arches, obelisks' against the loss, and the unknown moment of the apocalypse, to which Browne brings the hope of an almost creedal nothingness: 'annihilation, extasis, exolution, liquefaction, transformation, the kisse of the spouse, gustation of God, and ingression into the divine shadow'.

(iii) Religio Medici

Browne's late paired works are like little else, at once abstruse and moving, pedantic and orotund, works of spectacular pointlessness, nit-pickingly precise and lavishly meditative. *Religio Medici*, Browne's first work, shares something of this elusive impulse, but attracts admiration and reservation, for quite different reasons. It is similarly difficult to characterize by subject matter, is digressive and diffuse, self-regarding and impressively tolerant, politically tetchy and philosophically capacious. It is a work often thought of as autobiographical, though biography as life-writing is only fitfully present. Its version of the self is rather a responsive style: put what you will in front of the author—be it foreign food or Platonic mystery, a piece of music or a passing beggar—and he will respond with a torrent of magnanimity.

Structurally speaking, this is a boneless text, oozing between religion, doctrine, body and soul, snippets of the self, the bible, and philosophy. Its logic is less a progression of ideas than a relative tonal unity and emotional equanimity in response to its vast range of subject matter. It embodies the kind of philosophical theology that so characterizes the era, the compendious attention to the microcosm and 'cosmography of [the] selfe' (sec 1.15), the conceit of the two books of Scripture and nature in antiphonal relationship to each other (sec. 1.12), God as a 'skillful geometrician' of the world (sec. 1.16), who in artfulness produced time as a miniature model, to replicate eternity, in which there is 'no distinction of tenses' (sec. 1.11), the latter borrowing Plato's dictum, that Time is 'a moving image of Eternity' (*Timaeus*, 37d).

Religio Medici is neither a work of philosophy or theology if by those we mean systematic exposition. But, in its thoroughgoing attention to the fleeting presence of the invisible in the visible and natural world, it is both Platonic and Pauline. The value of what can be scrutinized, the purview of the physician and the natural philosopher, is, firstly, its use as the shadow and type of that which is unthinkable and unknowable, evoked only via the transitory—time instead of eternity, object instead of Form—our natures being such that we see 'but asquint upon reflex or shadow' (1.13). Browne's endemically protean text catches sight, again and again, of what is there, if at all, for a mere instant: the angelic diffused and melted in light, or what happens on the cusp of creation and the soul *in potentia* awaiting 'the opportunity of objects' (1.39), or the moment the soul sloughs off its body. Browne's rhetorical throb is such that we never encounter more than a glimpse of his subject matter before the text shifts again. Angels, whose absence from the creation narrative of Genesis is often noted, are 'the best part of nothing' (1.34), brought into existence *ex nihilo*, and yet barely seeming to have ascended from that state, only to be conceived as a particular kind of light, whose quality is that it is unseeable: 'conceive light invisible, and that is a spirit' (1.33).

Browne's cascade of the ethereal into the earthy has it that the medial point of existence is the human: 'we are onely that amphibious piece between a corporall and spirituall essence, that middle forme that linkes those two together' (1.34).[12] The intellectual ripples of

[12] The glancing biblical references here being to Hebrews 2:7 and Psalm 8:5, humans being 'a little below the angels'.

this human position as epitome of the world are everywhere in *Religio Medici*, that 'there is all Africa, and her prodigies in us; we are that bold and adventurous piece of nature, which he that studies, wisely learnes in a compendium, what others labour at in a divided piece and endlesse volume' (1.15). The shrinkage of everything being in everything, folded up and reiterated—Coleridge's 'entireness in every subject'—produces Browne's most ambitious statement of the ineffable:

> In the seed of a plant to the eyes of God, and to the understanding of man, there exists, though in an invisible way, the perfect leaves, flowers, and fruit thereof: (for things that are in posse to the sense, are actually existent to the understanding.) Thus God beholds all things, who contemplates as fully his workes in their epitome, as in their full volume, and beheld as amply the whole world in that little compendium of the sixth day, as in the scattered and dilated pieces of those five before. (1.50)

To note an ingrained Platonism in Browne's work speaks to no more than a passing alliance with contemporaries' use of Plato, that of Henry More, Nathaniel Culverwell, and the others in the loose grouping who came to be known as Cambridge Platonists, whose works deploy a philosophical register and rhetoric that is wholly impersonal. Browne's first work, by contrast, is all *credo*: I believe, I concede, I confess, I hold, I wonder. Given that it is so endemically fleeting a text—ranging across doctrinal fideism and nascent scepticism, from iconoclasm to the role of fate in wealth, from the whiff of heresy to the chemistry of the resurrection—it is a work that revels in its chief paradox: in what way can such a conglomerate of questions and statements of the unthinkable be subject to the impress of *credo*?

Belief, in *Religio Medici*, is less a matter of positive assent than a capacity for and indeed a revelling in bafflement, a succumbing to inevitably fragmentary glimpses of truth. Belief only comes into play at the point beyond which we cannot know things, and Browne courts this sacred ignorance and nescience, not constituted by lack of enquiry, but by a surfeit of questions, the close and experimental scrutiny of the natural world. Browne takes it upon himself, for instance, to think through (and get lost in) the physics of the final and post-apocalyptic resurrection. The dissolute and meandering particles of each human, 'scattered in the wilderness of forms', must resolve themselves into their original state—this much may be theology, but study of the natural world, for Browne, provides a model for how this will happen. He considers, in turn, the 'artificiall resurrection and revivification of

Mercury' that rolls itself up into 'its numericall selfe' (1.48), and that when a leaf is burnt to ashes, it may seem utterly gone. But Browne insists that its fundamental forms remain, 'withdrawne into their incombustible part', and moreover, that natural philosophy can model the resurrection in palingenesis: 'This is made good by experience, which can from the ashes of a plant revive the plant, and from its cinders recall it into its stalk and leaves againe' (1.48). The burden of such experiments is that the ability of things to revive and return to their original state gives a hint of the resurrection. It is not the case that in exploring the mechanics of this, Browne aims to make last things more comprehensible, but rather to augment its unintelligibility, and confound the mind. Miracles are mere baubles in comparison with the bafflement that can be garnered from careful and scientific study of the world: 'Those strange and mysticall transmigrations that I have observed in silkewormes, turn'd my philosophy into divinity' (1.39), he explains, as a summary of his creedal unknowing: '*certum est quia impossibile est*', he quotes from Tertullian. It is certain because it is impossible (1.9).

Browne is not consistently the philosopher-in-mysticism that he sometimes appears. For all that he vaunts his own openness to the multiplicity of humanity, he recoils with horror from its political and monstrous actuality: 'that great enemy of reason, vertue and religion, the multitude, that numerous piece of monstrosity, which taken asunder seeme men, and the reasonable creatures of God; but confused together, make but one great beast' (2.1). *Religio Medici* is on the one hand a work of mystical latitude, lavish with its seeing the divine everywhere, and on the other, a work that is peevish about the capacity of others to do so. He complains about the vulgar's unlearned appreciation of beauty: 'The wisedome of God receives small honour from those vulgar heads, that rudely stare about, and with a grosse rusticity admire his workes' (1.13). But the rude and wrong-headed staring of some is balanced by the near infernal knack of others, the 'master mendicants', who discern and target those whose dispositions are generous, whose natural inclination to charity is written, inscribed like signatures, on their faces:

> whereby they instantly discover a mercifull aspect, and will single out a face, wherein they spy the signatures and markes of mercy: for there are mystically in our faces certaine characters which carry in them the motto of our Soules, wherein he that cannot read *A.B.C.* may read our natures. (2.2)

Browne's beggar is a masterly rhetorical creature, a Quintilian upon misery, deciphering the shadowed languages of the face and the marks of mercy and weakness there. In the first part of *Religio Medici*, the reader of signatures in nature is engaged in an act of theology, 'to joyne and reade these mysticall letters... these common hieroglyphicks' (1.16). Here, the hieroglyphical reader is reduced to picking out the likely candidate from whom to beg alms, like some Faustus who, though he might penetrate all the secrets of nature, exercises his talent on lowbrow slapstick. There is an august history of suspicion about *Religio Medici*—from Kenelm Digby's complaint about its autobiographical intrusions, to Samuel Johnson's account of its 'self-love', and on, more mischievously and recently, to Stanley Fish's doubting of its sincerity, or Michael Wildings' withering account of its politics.[13] However, the longer and labyrinthine first part of the work remains remarkable, as an epitome of seventeenth-century tropes of thought and in its theology of nescience that seems quite alien to an era that so battled over its rival interpretations of right religion.

(iv) Pseudodoxia Epidemica

Browne's habits of incongruity are at work across his writings. The most elaborate of these is the vast miscellany that is *Pseudodoxia Epidemica* (1646), a work of breathtaking scope, intricate scholarship, and hyperbolic irrelevance, a Plinyesque assortment of things that are not true. Nobody, it is probable, has ever considered *Pseudodoxia* to be Browne's masterpiece. When set alongside the mesmerizing fugues of *Urne-Buriall* or *The Garden of Cyrus*, it can appear an ungainly patchwork, rhythm-less, and staccato in comparison to the torrential walls of sound in the later works. After *Religio Medici*, it can seem mundane in its eschewing the mystical and the poetics of paradox. But any such response misses its very particular (and very entertaining) understanding of the miscellaneous, its vast orchestral annals of ignorance. It is a cornucopia of all things early modern. The contents list reads, to modern ears at least, like a vast and ironic tissue of formal nonsense—that 'a diamond is made soft, or broke by the blood of a goate', 'that a badger hath the legs of one side shorter then of the other', 'of the pissing of toads', 'that storkes will onely live in

[13] Stanley Fish, *Self Consuming Artifacts: The Experience of Seventeenth Century Literature* (Berkeley: University of California Press, 1972); Michael Wilding, *Dragon's Teeth: Literature in the English Revolution* (Oxford: Clarendon Press, 1987), pp. 89–114.

republicks and free states'. It takes and inverts the long lists of imponderable and unknowable events, many of which were listed in *Religio Medici* as characterizing futility in knowledge—scriptural 'stories that doe exceed the fable of poets' (1.21) and which are here subjected to improbably serious scrutiny: whether Adam had a navel, how the animals fitted and were peaceful in the ark at the deluge, the antediluvian population of the world, all, as he puts it in the earlier work, 'a catalogue of doubts... a bundle of curiosities... not worthy our vacant houres, much lesse our serious studies' (1.21). It is hard to tell if Browne is being serious in his vast second work, or if serious, whether pedantic, and if pedantry, whether parodic. *Pseudodoxia* takes error to be encyclopaedic, and proceeds with scrupulous precision across many hundreds of instances, in natural philosophy, in natural history, in anatomy, in biblical painting, in geographical and historical and anthropological minutiae.

It is by far Browne's longest and most learned work and the book that established him among his contemporaries as a figure of some scholarly weight. Though it has the running header of 'vulgar errors', it is not primarily designed to correct simple falsehood, or those of the 'vulgar' per se, any more than *Urne-Buriall* is designed as an archaeological account of Norfolk shards. Neither is it a guide to what the benighted and pre-enlightenment seventeenth century believed in its poor and huddled superstition, even if at times it suggests the chronic gullibility of its own and past ages. *Pseudodoxia* exercises its sometimes censorious, sometimes indulgent eye on errors that arrive, by and large, already corrected. The criterion for inclusion is less that something is merely and straightforwardly wrong, but rather that a belief demonstrates and is the occasion of poor interpretation, when symbolic, poetic, or hieroglyphic ideas come to be believed in a literal sense. This practice of poor exegesis is, for Browne, endemic across every area of learning and, if there can be a unifying principle in a work of such encyclopaedic form, it is that error stems from interpretative practice, receiving 'precepts in a different sense from his intention, converting metaphors into proprieties, and receiving as litterall expressions, obscure and involved truths', as Browne puts it in partial defence of Pythagoras (1.4). Browne's typically cavernous rhetoric works in *Pseudodoxia* on a smaller and more precise scale in its many and miscellaneous chapters, but his majestic habits of phrasing remain, together with a cabinet of curious vocabulary. There is grandeur also in its design, bordering on hubris, that it aims to trace a repeated dynamic of error across all creation, from the mineral, plant and animal worlds and on to a political and cultural encyclopaedia of pictures, history, and geography.

Somewhere between a third and a half of this large work is concerned with natural philosophy, natural history and scientific truth, and its investigations throughout are shot through with the concerns of Browne the physician, the compulsive anatomist and observer of the natural world. Contemporaries place him almost unanimously as a figure of scientific repute, and the roll-call of references to his 'ingenious' explorations in error is impressive: Robert Boyle, Walter Charleton, Henry Power, John Ray, John Evelyn, Nehemiah Grew all respond to him as a figure of some intellectual authority, and he corresponds at the edges of the Royal Society.[14] But for all the admiration, Browne is never quite part of the same conversation in which such figures engage. *Pseudodoxia* is a work with its own peculiar rhetorical and literary sweep, with its idiosyncratic writing of natural philosophy and its rag-bag of tools: forensic logic, philology, Aristotelian first principles, Augustinian seminal principles, together with its deep-rooted habits of experimental logic. If there is a Baconian heart to the work, it is perhaps less in any shared practices of austere empiricism than it is in a shared magpie impulse, the Bacon who, as Graham Rees characterized it, 'raided disparate natural philosophical traditions for attractive titbits which he refashioned and spatchcocked together to form a curious hybrid which embodied, even by the standards of the early seventeenth century, some very peculiar alliances of ideas indeed'.[15] Bacon rivets his philosophical universe together with breathtaking metaphor, where Browne (rhetorically speaking) deploys sumptuous oratory as the strategy by which to hide the awkward philosophical seams.

Browne is not distinct from his contemporaries in his insistence that the demands of truth, such as they are, remain rooted in the theological, or that God acts as the ultimate guarantor that the world is reasonable. This is not the manoeuvre of the mystic we encounter in *Religio Medici*, where philosophy encounters the pleasure of paradox too dark to fathom, too deep to entertain. In *Pseudodoxia*, God and devil battle over every syllogism. The kinds and criteria of truth we encounter in *Pseudodoxia* are various. At times empirical and mere fact

[14] See notes 3 and 5.

[15] Graham Rees, 'Bacon's Speculative Philosophy' in *The Cambridge Companion to Bacon* (Cambridge University Press, 2006), p. 122.

is enough, but there are other dynamics at work as well, in which God is the daunting yardstick of truth:

In briefe, there is nothing infallible but God, who cannot possibly erre. For things are really true as they correspond unto his conception, and have so much of verity, as they hold of conformity unto that intellect, in whose Idea they had their first determinations: And therefore being the rule he cannot bee irregular, nor being truth it selfe conceiveably admit the impossible society of error. (1.1)

How the phenomena of the natural world should be applied to and measured against the ineffable mind of God is Browne's not inconsiderable task, and he provides, in his opening book ('The General Part') a toolkit of seventeenth-century thought on the perusal of truth. Some of these tools are scholastic—that error emerges from such verbal and logical fallacies as 'æquivocation and amphibologie'; some are the commonplace decrying of dependence on authority and testimony, 'supinity or neglect of enquiry' (1.5). The book is framed, however, around the delusive and ubiquitous 'endeavours of Satan . . . the first contriver of error, and professed opposer of Truth, the Divell' (1.10). Browne's devil is hardly Miltonic or Marlovian, but Browne takes him seriously nevertheless, as almost synonymous with error itself. Browne's devil makes one think askew, 'distorting the order and theorie of causes perpendicular to their effects'. He is content to work away on the tiniest of error, 'maligning the tranquility of truth' (1.11), in the manner of a Cartesian demon, all the time aiming merely to disturb the somewhat mysterious attribute of God that is uppermost in *Pseudodoxia*, divine oneness. Muddying this essential unity, 'the inseparable and essentiall attribute of Deitie', is the chief Satanic purpose, to blur one's belief into atheism or polytheism, which, 'were to make Euclide beleeve there were more then one Center in a Circle, or one right Angle in a Triangle'. (1.10). This devil's temptations are epistemological rather than ethical.

As the books open onto their wide vistas of individual errors, however, the pulse of the work changes, theology recedes and Browne begins to engage with the whole of the world and all its error. At times the individual topic can be the mere springboard from which to leap, having collected together the necessary classical, patristic, and contemporary precedents for the question. It is rare that Browne moves directly to empirical disproof, though experiment, or testimony of experiment, is generally a part of his armoury. As a rule, he wants firstly to reason his way out of error, but wants equally to swill its delicious waters first. In disproving that crystal is concreted ice (2.1), Browne embarks upon a theory of mineral origin and the growth of stones. The intellectual pedigree of such theory can be traced, via figures such as the Belgian Boëtius de Boodt and the German Georgius Agricola, back to Aristotelian understandings of mineral exhalations, but *Pseudodoxia* remains only briefly with its sources. It is, rather, an elaborate lecture on changes of physical state, and the chemistry of flux. A collateral pleasure of his study is the wallowing in a quasi-tactile language of natural philosophy, the 'lapidificall principles of . . . conglaceation', the 'salinous spirits, concretive juyces, and causes circumjacent', the 'exsiccation . . . humectation . . . fiery siccity' and 'colliquation' of earth. The natural world demands, for Browne, its own poetics. Crystal, he concludes, is formed from its inner impulsive form, forcing itself into shape and stone by its own stony principle. It is:

> made of a lentous colament of earth, drawne from the most pure and limpid juyce thereof, owing unto the coldnesse of the earth some concurrence or coadjuvancy, but not its immediate determination and efficiency, which are wrought by the hand of its concretive spirit, the seeds of petrification and Gorgon within it selfe. (2.1)

The Gorgon of the earth hardens, if not frightens, its liquid self into petrified form, an Ovidian metamorphosis as much as a raw process of nature, the poetics and theology of which prove indistinguishable from the scientific. Browne's scope and purpose becomes evident as the work proceeds, and the endlessly variegated forms of error begin to replicate themselves across not only what might be encompassed in the term 'natural philosophy', but in the medical and anthropological, the pictorial and the scriptural, the chronological and geographical, though for many readers, it is his third book on animals that best exemplifies Browne's practice in *Pseudodoxia*, a collection of errors so preposterous that their intricate disproof seems itself to be an act of mockery and spoof, but without ever revealing itself to be so.

(v) Posthumous Works

Browne's remaining works, quite considerable in length and variable in quality, were published posthumously. *Certain Miscellany Tracts* (1683), *A Letter to a Friend* (1690), and *Christian Morals* (1716) are included in full here, though the 1712 antiquarian *Miscellanies*—including Repertorium and Brampton Urns—are not. Browne's earlier *Miscellany Tracts* share the sense of monumental irrelevance that characterizes his best work (such as 'Of the fishes eaten by our saviour'), and has Browne assuming the role of letter-writing agony-aunt for tortuous queries in scholarship and natural philosophy. *A Letter to a Friend*, containing advice on a good death, has a good deal of direct overlap and borrowing from *Christian Morals*, which is among the most neglected of Browne's writings, in large part because is a work of relentless didactic intent. However, the work also contains some wholly Brownean and dizzying prose, even if accumulated *sententiae* and gathered aphorisms tend to pale quickly as a form. Neither is it a commonplace notebook, however, being far too stagey for that, composed with stylized antiquarian forms of 'thee' and 'thou', and a narrator who comes to seem a kind of baroque Polonius. This volume, then, contains the vast majority of Browne's published writing.

BIOGRAPHY

Biographical information on Browne is relatively slender, and much of what there is to say of his life comes from amplifying these few and limited sources, and producing a life by proxy, in concert with the biography of institutions—schools, universities, professions—he was associated with, but it is worth saying something of his early life.[16] He was born in 1605, trained as a doctor, and lived most of his adult life in Norwich. Where knowledge of his later years grows thin, it can of course be added to from his works, which contain a degree of autobiographical material and intellectual autobiography, and we have a good stock of letters from after 1660, particularly to his sons. The picture of Browne we might derive from his work, all even-keel and calm of temper, is not necessarily the product of early familial tranquillity, his childhood being (at its most dramatic) a tale of financial and military skulduggery—and we might choose to add maternal abandonment. He spent his early years in Cheapside, the broad, chaotic, opulent centre of London's market life, where wealth and poverty vied in ostentation. His father was a mercer, was taken into livery in the company in 1604, but died in December 1613, with probate granted

[16] See the definitive biography by Reid Barbour, *Sir Thomas Browne: A Life* (Oxford University Press, 2013).

to his wife, Anne.[17] As executrix, she was required to present an inventory of property, debts, and business affairs to the Court of Orphans, the body of the City of London that administered the will of a freeman with minor children. This she did in March 1614, with debts of £11,209 4*s.* 1*d.* and a set of roughly equivalent 'doubtful and desperate debts' owed in turn to the estate of Browne, leaving it valued, initially, at £5,722 7*s.* 7½*d.*[18]

However, this accounting of affairs was brought into question by the brother of the deceased, Edward, and the Court of Aldermen was called to investigate, a matter both hindered and fuelled by Anne's marriage, with Hamletesque hastiness, to the soldier Sir Thomas Dutton. The court expressed concern at the profligate spending that had occurred in the brief period between the marriage and the hearing and, moreover, concern with Dutton's putting himself beyond the jurisdiction of the court, in his foreign activities. Dame Anne, as she now was, was forced to relinquish her part, and not have 'any further meddling or dealing' with the affairs of the estate, though in August 1614 Anne protested the costs of her lying-in, having given birth to a daughter, Thomas's sister, Ellen.[19] According to an account by John Whitefoot, prefacing the 1712 *Posthumous Works*, 'He was likewise very much defrauded by his guardians', which Johnson describes as the 'common fate of orphans'. Such nefarious tales are the bare remains of his early childhood.

However, Browne's stepfather, the impressively scurrilous Sir Thomas Dutton, provides his own dark interest, as a brawler and skinflint, on the edges of Browne's childhood. The story is told by Arthur Wilson, in his interregnum annals of the reign of James I, how in 1610, a truce in the Low Countries left a restless English army of some four thousand soldiers without immediate action, and in the twitchy lull between fighting a quarrel arose between Sir Hatton Cheke, next in command to Edward Cecil, and Thomas Dutton, the latter 'a man of crabbed temper', but with enough control not to break rank by attacking his superior officer. 'Instantly quitting his command' instead, Dutton returned to England and began his defamatory

[17] Mercers' Company, Acts of Court, 159501629, f. 57v.

[18] Corporation of London Records Office (CLRO), Repertory 31 (2), f. 224v; Orphanage, Common Serjeant's Book 1, f. 417v. See Trevor Hughes, 'The Childhood of Sir Thomas Browne: Evidence from the Court of Orphans', *London Journal*, 23 (1998): 21–9 (23).

[19] CLRO, Rep. 31 (2), ff. 372v–375, 386v–387.

venting against Cheke, 'both in court and city'. Cheke, hearing of this, called Dutton 'to account the large expence of his tongue against him', giving Browne's now decommissioned stepfather the opportunity he sought to duel on Calais Sands, dramatically related by Wilson:

> Cheek ran Dutton into the neck with his Rapier, and stab'd him in the neck back ward with his Dagger, miraculously missing his windpipe; And at the same instant, like one motion, Dutton ran Cheek through the body, and stab'd him into the back with his left hand, locking themselves together thus with four bloody keys.[20]

Despite, or perhaps because of this outrage against his military superior, Dutton received the post of Scoutmaster-General in Ireland in April 1610. Before his departure, however, the matter came to the attention of James I and according to the State Papers 'The King said Sir Thomas was to be punished according to a maxim in his Basilicon Doron, that "faults in war are of all others straightest to be looked into." Dutton arrived at the Court to excuse himself, but was arrested', the report continues.[21] In 1611, writing to Lord Salisbury he 'begs favour for his offence in killing his foe in self-defence'.[22] Apparently forgiven, Dutton appears regularly over the following two decades in the State Papers, and in the Correspondence of the Commissioners for Irish affairs, engaged in a seemingly relentless haggling over money, and new sources of income in Ireland, where he was living with Browne's mother. The King seeks advice in relation to Dutton's Gogolesque suit for the wages of the army dead, in which he 'seeks an increase of his pay by being granted one dead pay out of every company of horse and foot in the list of the army there'.[23] There are ongoing disputes over the fees for entertainments he was required to bear as army General, wrangling over the income from forts, with Dutton attempting to claim rights to inland as well as sea-forts.[24] In 1619, his problems were at least temporarily eased by the granting of a plantation of seized land in Longford, though this came back to haunt the family.

[20] Arthur Wilson, *The history of Great Britain: being the life and reign of King James the First* (1653), pp. 49–50.

[21] SP 63/240/2, f. 18, 25 April 1610.

[22] SP 14/64, f. 61, 17 June 1611.

[23] The King to Sir Arthur Chichester, in Calendar of State Papers relating to Ireland, Entry 413, p. 239, Jan. 1612.

[24] PC 2/32, f. 83, 23 July 1623 'A letter to the Lord Deputie of Irelande'.

Browne seems likely to have visited Ireland in mid 1629, in the company of his stepfather, when according to Whitefoot he made 'a visitation of the forts and castles of that Kingdom'.[25] The State Papers contain 'A Passe for Sir Thomas Dutton, knight, one of his Majesties Counsell in Irelande, to retourne into Irelande with his whole family and retinue', and Browne makes occasional, if unrevealing reference to his brief travels to Ireland at this time.[26] Dutton seems not to have absorbed the generally benign attitude to religious tolerance that his son-in-law later shows, but religion did impinge upon his money-raising strategies, around the time of Browne's visit, with his letters to the king in 1629–30 raising the spectre of 'Jesuits and schoolmen' in every Irish barn, with a particularly rich crop, as he explains, in Wexford, Longford, and Leitrim, a claim that segues effortlessly into financial affairs:[27]

> Unless the Papists and seminary schools are rooted out and destroyed, it will be impossible to plant the Gospel here... The admitting of recusants to be justices and captains weakens the Government greatly. These Papists forswear themselves in juries and sway all causes throughout the Kingdom. I hope I may still have my company. When I left England my debts were 2,500l, which I hope your Majesty will confer on me.[28]

Browne's connections with his mother in Ireland are obscure, though he maintained contact with his sisters, the younger two of whom lived in Longford. The lack of letters documenting this period means we have no record of his response to the dramatic affairs of the early 1640s, by which time Browne himself was in Norwich. Dutton had been awarded possession of the confiscated lands of the Farrell family in Longford, to create a 2,000-acre plantation and, at the rebellion of 1641, some time after Thomas Dutton's death, a general revenge upon the English enveloped Anne, Browne's mother. The uprising was of unparalleled enormity, and the enquiry into it sought out some 8,000 mostly Protestant statements. According to the 1641 deposition by John Stibbs, the Longford rebellion resulted in the lynching of the English guard and the ousting of Anne Dutton from her estate by Oliver Fitzgarrett and Lishagh Farrell: 'ladie Ann Dutton, and her

25 Whitefoot, *Life*, in *Posthumous Works* (1712), p. ii.

26 Acts of the Privy Council of England: A.D. 1542–June 1631, Vol. 45: 1629 May–1630 May; Vol. V (P.C. 2/39), 289a; f.365, 19 July 1629.

27 Sir Thomas Dutton to the King. SP 63/249, f. 296, 20 Dec. 1629.

28 SP 63/250, f. 170, 4 April 1630.

daughter *&* Mris Elenor Browne, her man her mayd and this deponents wiffe were threatened to be putt to death: & the warrant was signed to that purpose by those of the Cabinett Counsell & by them sent to Captaine ffergus fferrall to see them executed'. They were saved, however, by Sir James Dillon, who took the 'said lady Duttons & divers other poore English protestants from those parts to his owne howse, and from thence sent them all saffe to Athlone'.[29] The Roscommon deposition of Edward Peirson likewise blames Fitzgarret 'whoe hanged 16 of the English there: & stript the lady Dutton of all her goodes and clothes'. The apparent trauma of this does not, however, find any corresponding ripple in Browne's writing, who mentions only some observations of spiders and burnt trees, along with a sea-sickness he endured coming from Ireland, though he does tell his daughter, late in his life, the dramatic story: 'I came once from Dublin to Chester at Michaelmas and was so tossed, that nothing but milk and Possets would goe down with me 2 or 3 days after.'[30]

It may be that Browne, brought up in England, had little connection, emotional or otherwise, with his mother and stepfamily in Ireland. The brief facts of Browne's younger life, as we have them, are that he was 'educated in Grammar Learning, in Wykeham's School near Winchester; he was entred a Commoner of Broadgates Hall (soon after, known by the Name of Pembroke College) in the Beginning of the Year 1623'.[31] In Oxford, he was tutored by Thomas Lushington, mathematician, churchman, and reputed Socinian, and who would be instrumental in Browne's move to Norwich.[32] Lushington translated the philosophical and mathematical commentaries of Proclus on Euclid, and involved himself in a notorious attack on the

[29] Deposition of John Stibbs, MS 817, ff. 203r–206v (f. 204r), Trinity College Dublin, MSS 1641, TCD, 1641 Depositions Project, online transcript: <http://1641.tcd.ie/deposition.php?depID <?php echo 817203r162?>; Deposition of Suzan Steele, MS 817, ff. 203r–206v (f. 204r) <http://1641.tcd.ie/deposition.php?depID<?php echo 817213r169?>. Deposition of Edward Peirson, MS 830, ff. 012r–013v <http://1641.tcd.ie/deposition.php?depID<?php echo 830012r016?>]. See also Hughes, 'Childhood of Thomas Browne', p. 26; N. J. Endicott, '*Sir Thomas Browne as "Orphan"*, with Some Account of his Stepfather, Sir Thomas Dutton', *University of Toronto Quarterly*, 30 (1961): 180–210 (191–201).

[30] 15 Sept. 1681, in *Works*, ed. Keynes, 4.200.

[31] Whitefoot, *Life*, in *Posthumous Works* (1712), p. ii. The date was in fact 5 Dec. 1623.

[32] Frank Huntley, 'Dr. Thomas Lushington (1590–1661), Sir Thomas Browne's Oxford Tutor', *Modern Philology*, 81:1 (1983): 14, *Procli Elementa & Prologica* (BL Sloan 1838), Anthony à Wood, *Athenae Oxonienses* (1691), v. 2, p. 535.

typical parliamentary 'peasant' who 'under pretence of his privilege in parliament . . . would dispose of kings and commonwealths', this being a response to parliament's pressing the new King, who had for some years been attempting a much despised Spanish Match, to involve himself in the Continental wars.[33] The other key Oxford figure for Browne was Thomas Clayton, Regius Professor of Physic, on whose shoulders most of the teaching of medicine fell.

Oxford had a relatively unimpressive reputation for medical training, however, and Browne's visit to Ireland, after receiving his MA in 1629, was the beginning of some extensive travel, following the not uncommon path of prospective physicians to the more prestigious European universities.[34] If his purpose was, in addition to training as a physician, an early version of the Grand Tour, his travels were constrained by the tides of the Thirty Years War, which limited travel in central Europe, at least, but the medical fraternities of the Continent remained mobile. He spent time in three important centres of European medicine—Montpellier, Padua, and Leiden—each of which had its distinct traditions and priorities in medical training, and whose variety was in large part responsible for Browne's elaborate interlacing of the humanist, the theological, and the scientific. Browne did not produce any specifically medical writings, for all that *Religio Medici* suggests the presiding presence of a physician over its theological stew, but medicine and anatomy pervade his voluminous notes and more obliquely underwrite all his work.

Montpellier, Browne's first destination, was among the preeminent medical schools of France and Europe. It maintained, quite staunchly, its independence from the university and its theological faculty, and had inherited the richest stock of medical knowledge from Muslim and Jewish Spain, and hence from the classical world.[35] Montpellier was a formerly Huguenot city and broadly receptive to Protestants. His studies would have centred on the botanical gardens, established in 1593, which were particularly impressive and central to a rapidly shifting landscape of pharmacological ideas, out of which was

[33] Lushington, *The Resurrection of our Saviour Vindicated* (1741); Huntley, pp. 14–15; Wood, *Athenae Oxonienses* (1691), v. 2, p. 172.

[34] Robert G. Frank, in *The History of the University of Oxford*, vol. 4: *The Seventeenth Century*, ed. Nicolas Tyacke (Oxford University Press, 1997), pp. 516–18.

[35] Jack Goody, *Renaissances: The One or the Many?* (Cambridge University Press, 2010); H. Bonnet, *La Faculté de Médecine de Montpellier: huit siècles d'histoire et d'éclat* (Montpellier: Sauramps, 1992).

produced Lazare Rivière's influential *Praxis Medica* (1640).[36] Various traditions of medical theory had to be mastered by the aspiring physician—the Galenic, Hippocratic, and Arabian inheritance of medical care, along with more practical, sometimes domestic, sometimes military and surgical traditions, buttressed by an increasing knowledge of pharmacology, anatomy, and occasional surges of interest in physiognomy. There was, on the whole, no stark division or conflict between approaches, though the stirring polemic of Paracelsus against classical traditions did temporarily raise the rhetorical stakes.

Padua, which Browne arrived at in 1632, was the most important Italian centre of medical studies, home to the anatomical theatricality of Andreas Vesalius (1514–64) and a host of impressive medical writers, including the figure of Hieronymus Fabricus of Aquapendente (1533–1619), whose practices of 'philosophical anatomy' sought the relationship of the body to the soul.[37] Anatomy became something of a philosophical spectator sport, occasionally even accompanied by music, and with the border between body and metaphysics becoming ever more blurred.[38] In a retrospective critical comment on the practices of Paduan anatomy, Johann Veslingus (1598–1649), who was appointed to the medical faculty in 1632, complained that the philosophizing around the body had turned its study of anatomy into a practice like 'contemplating the siege of Troy'.[39] If Browne does not quite describe the body in terms of its Homeric themes, he was certainly concerned to seek its associative meanings and metaphysics.

Browne finished his studies at Leiden, whose reputation centred on its chemical medicine, under Jan Baptista van Helmont (*c.*1579–1644), but which had its own and independent traditions of anatomy,

[36] Charles Coury, 'The Teaching of Medicine in France from the Beginning of the Seventeenth Century', in C. D. O'Malley, *The History of Medical Education* (Berkeley: University of California Press, 1970), pp. 121–72; Anna Pavord, *The Naming of Names: The Search for Order in the World of Plants* (London: Bloomsbury, 2009).

[37] Andrew Cunningham, 'Fabricius and the "Aristotle Project"', in Andrew Wear, Roger French, and I. M. Lonie (eds.), *The Medical Renaissance of the Sixteenth Century* (Cambridge University Press, 1985), pp. 195–222.

[38] Cynthia Klestinec, 'Medical Education in Padua: Students, Faculty and Faculties', in Ole Peter Grell, Andrew Cunningham, and Jon Arrizabalaga (eds.), *Centres of Medical Excellence?: Medical Travel and Education in Europe, 1500–1789* (Farnham: Ashgate, 2010), p. 214.

[39] Johann Veslingus, *Syntagma Anatomicum* (Padua, 1647), to the reader, cited in Klestinec, p. 219.

developed under Petrus Paaw (1564–1617), who was succeeded in the professorship of anatomy in Browne's time by the curious pairing of Otho Heurnius (van Herne, 1577–1652) and Adrianus Valckenburg. Hernius proved a reluctant anatomist, but flamboyant collector and orchestrator of Leiden's impressive assemblage of anatomical curiosities, while the phlegmatic Valckenburg, forgoing the theatricalism that had come to be expected of anatomy, petitioned the university to be allowed bodies for private anatomy, without ever producing the promised illustrated book that he had claimed would derive from it.[40] Heurnius' contribution to the practicalities of anatomy and its teaching may have been relatively slight, but his design of and additions to the emblematics of the anatomy theatre were splendid—rarities, paintings and engravings, skeletons, embalmed bodies of animals and children, Japanese tea-sets, the winding linens of mummy—all contributing to a moral, philosophical, and theological montage, in counterpoint to the practice of dissection.[41] If Browne could take relatively little from his short stay in Leiden, one thing that would emerge was its concern with the emblematics of the body, as a correlate to medicine, a theme that proves so constant a presence in *Pseudodoxia Epidemica*.

Browne matriculated and then graduated MD in quick succession at the end of 1633, having undergone a doctoral process involving a private examination on the fundamentals of medicine, a public viva, in which a defence of Hippocratic aphorisms would be demanded of the candidate against questions put by members of faculty, followed by a presentation of his doctoral thesis on smallpox.[42] He is noted in the Leiden Archives as 'Thomas Braun, Anglus Londinensis, apud Ricardum Monck in Sonneveltsteeg', the latter being the English tobacconist, Richard Monck, with whom Browne lodged and who was affiliated to the Separatist movement that constituted a large

[40] Tim Huisman, *The Finger of God: Anatomical Practice in 17th-Century Leiden* (o: Primavera Pers, 2009), pp. 43–9.

[41] Harold J. Cook, *Matters of Exchange: Commerce, Medicine, and Science in the Dutch Golden* Age (New Haven, CT: Yale University Press, 2007), pp. 168–9; Huisman, *The Finger of God*, p. 45.

[42] Reid Barbour, 'Discipline and Praxis: Thomas Browne in Leiden', in Kathryn Murphy and Richard Todd (eds.), *"A man very well studyed": New Contexts for Thomas Browne* (Leiden: Brill, 2009), pp. 21–9; Reid Barbour, 'The Topic of Sir Thomas Browne's Dissertation', *Notes & Queries*, 252 (2007): 38–9.

proportion of the exiled English community in Holland.[43] So Browne's European travels ended and he returned to England, probably early in 1634.

He may have begun his medical practice in Oxfordshire, according at least to Anthony à Wood and after him Samuel Johnson, though he settled in Shibden Vale, Halifax, where it is likely he wrote the first draft of *Religio Medici*.[44] Browne was incorporated as a doctor of physic on 10 July 1637 and moved to Norwich in 1637, where he remained for the rest of his life. He married Dorothy Mileham (1621–85) and they had eleven children, four of whom survived beyond childhood. Fame and admiration arrived after the 1643 publication of *Religio Medici* and the 1646 *Pseudodoxia Epidemica*, although our knowledge of Browne's life from this point on recedes. His young medical practice and his young family no doubt occupied his time and his notebooks make clear his ongoing habits of home-anatomy and botany, experiment and labyrinthine reading.

In part through his marriage, and in part via his role as physician, Browne was acquainted with many of the gentry, politically active and wealthy families of Norfolk. Over the years, he tended to and was friends with the Hobarts, Pastons, Tenisons, and Astleys, as well as successive Bishops of Norwich, including most closely Joseph Hall, the brilliant satirist and scholar, whose bishopric in Norwich before his ejection was brief, but who remained in the area for many years after the sequestering of his property. Norwich itself held broadly parliamentarian sympathies and sided against the king during the simmering years of the civil war. Browne attended the parish of St George Tombland, and from 1650 St Peter Mancroft (where his portrait now hangs), both of which were subjected to intermittent acts of iconoclasm, with echoes, oblique and direct, in Browne's writing on pictures.[45] Though both *Religio Medici* and *Pseudodoxia* can be seen in relationship to events of the 1640s, Browne was not a

[43] University Library Leiden, Archief Senaat en Faculteiten 9, Volumen inscriptionum 1631–1645, in Harm Beukers, 'Studying Medicine in Leiden in the 1630s', in Murphy and Todd (eds.), *"A man very well studyed"*. On Monck, C. W. Schoneveld, *Sea-Changes: Studies in Three Centuries of Anglo-Dutch Cultural Transmission* (Amsterdam: 1996), p. 340; Barbour, 'Discipline and Praxis', p. 40.

[44] Anthony à Wood, *Athenae Oxonienses*, vol. 2 (1691), p. 535; W. Rye, 'What Brought Sir Thomas Browne to Norwich', *Norfolk Antiquarian Miscellany*, 2nd ser., 1 (1906): 33–5.

[45] Kevin Killeen, *Biblical Scholarship, Science and Politics: Thomas Browne and the Thorny Place of Knowledge* (Aldershot: Ashgate,2009), pp. 202–3.

writer who addressed the quotidian and the contemporary, except by implicit and circuitous routes. His later works, *Hydriotaphia* and *The Garden of Cyrus*, with their arcane and scholarly flights, have often been taken to indicate a retreat from the world, melancholic, but abstractly so, unallied to particular circumstance, though in their searing rhetoric, knowledge becomes lament that can hardly be separated from the upheaval of the times.

Our knowledge of Browne at this time comes primarily from the intellectual life of his books, though it can be augmented by a reasonably rich stock of letters, from exchanges with Kenelm Digby and Henry Power on natural philosophy, on to correspondence with John Evelyn, Hamon L'Estrange, William Dugdale, Henry Oldenburg, and John Aubrey, through to, most extensively, his letters to his sons, Thomas and Edward. These are on the whole domestic, with occasional news, much advice, and detailed discussion of medical matters with Edward, who, after his travels in Europe, became a successful physician and member of the Royal College of Physicians. Thus, Browne's later life seems relatively quiet. All we can be sure of was his interest in bowls, Browne being listed among the benefactors of the 'Great Ward of Mancroft', on the curious condition that the city did not revoke the licence for his bowling-green: 'Thom Browne sealed a bond to the curst, to pay 12*d*. a week to the overseers, to be laid out in bread for the poor, so long as the city continue to license a certain house and bowling-green of the said Thomas, which was then occupied by one Lancelot Rigsby.'[46] He died in 1682 and reporting his death, Horatio Townsend wrote: 'Sr. Tho: Browne is dead & as hee lived in an eaven temper without deep concerne with how the world went & was therein very happy so hee died like a wise old philosopher . . . All scholars allow him to have the most curious Learning of all sorts & that his fellow is not left.'[47]

[46] Blomefield, *Topographical History of the County of Norfolk*, vol. 4, p. 165.

[47] Geoffrey Keynes, *A Bibliography of Sir Thomas Browne* (Oxford: Clarendon Press, 1963), epigram.

NOTES ON TEXT AND ANNOTATION

The primary texts used in this book are, in all cases, the first authorized edition: *Religio Medici* (1643), *Pseudodoxia Epidemica* (1646), *Hydriotaphia or Urne-Buriall* and *The Garden of Cyrus* (1658), and for the posthumous works, *Certain Miscellany Tracts* (1683), *Letter to a Friend* (1690), *Christian Morals* (1716). In the case of *Pseudodoxia*, some chapters of particular interest from later editions are also included—Browne responds to developments in European natural philosophy—and the first date of such chapters is given in the textual notes. Textual variations are noted in *Religio Medici*—based on manuscript and the first two editions—and in *Hydriotaphia* and *The Garden of Cyrus*, based on the uncorrected *errata*. The original does not present any significant difficulties and changes are made only where it seemed to be intrusive upon the meaning, in which case there is some light modernization; u/v and i/j have been regularized, to reflect modern orthography; in cases where an ambiguity is created by early modern spelling, punctuation or apostrophe-use in plurals, I have regularized them, but on the whole, I have preferred to let the original remain, even when spelling is inconsistent within a particular chapter, so we can encounter Plinie and Pliny, Atheneus or Athenæus, crystall and chrystall, wee or we, without any ambiguity. One change that has been made is a standardization of the somewhat arbitrary capitalization and italics. Endnote references are collected at the end of the sentence or after the colons and semi-colons that serve, frequently, as syntactical stops, except where it is one of Browne's notes or a textual matter or the length of the phrase makes for a lack of clarity.

The style and purpose of the annotations differ from text to text, however, and it is worth explaining the rationale. Browne's writing is symphonic and does not bear well the interruption and necessary pedantry of footnotes. It is very much dependant on its surge-force. However, his writing is also consummately learned and, with its habits of half-reference or its embedded quotes, it is demanding material and requires extensive annotation. However, each of Browne's works is scholarly in a different way, which has necessitated for each a particular mode of endnoting. The notes gloss, firstly, unfamiliar language—and given his frequent invention and adoption of orphan Latin words, there is a fairly large volume of such annotation. Second, the glosses note what I take to be unfamiliar ideas and the many points of reference, classical or biblical, that inhabit the text. The notes are not primarily interpretative, however, and do not necessarily seek buried references too fully.

Beyond this, there is a specificity to the notes on each of his works. The history of reading *Religio Medici* has frequently involved a parallel engagement with his early commentators—Kenelm Digby's *Observations upon Religio Medici* (1643), Alexander Ross's *Medicus medicatus* (1645), and Thomas Keck's *Annotations upon Religio Medici* (1654), published with the 1672 edition—so it has seemed worthwhile to feature their comments in reasonable detail. Given that they all work as section-by-section animadversions to particular passages, their comments appear in the endnotes. This has bulked up considerably what is intended, in general, to be glossatory material and this differentiates the editorial involvement with *Religio Medici* from that given to Browne's other works. The text of *Religio Medici* is the 1643 first authorized version, which announces itself a hastily constructed correction of a pirated 1642 version. There are some interesting and important changes between these that are tracked in the notes when they seem significant to the meaning, but by no means exhaustively—most significant is the addition of several sections (8, 28, 43, and 56). There is no authorial manuscript of *Religio Medici* as such, but eight non-authoritative manuscript versions in other hands, with variations, as well as two slightly different printed editions of the 1642 pirated and sectionless edition. The 1643 text has various errors, either Browne's or the printers, lending it a complex textual history, traced in superlative detail in Jean-Jacques Denonain's 1953 edition of the work. Denonain proposed a good number of textual changes, based on the manuscript variations (chiefly the Pembroke MS, but keyed to the other seven), to produce an excellent, if patchwork text. These variations are useful, but not authoritative and are included as textual notes.[48]

On *Hydriotaphia*, the kind of annotation needed is different. Browne's margins in this work are thick with notes supplementing the main text. This is very much part of a textual polyphony and they are included on the page as marginalia (see illustration on p. 518). The

[48] On Browne's revisions, see also Brooke Conti, 'Sir Thomas Browne's Annotated Copy of His 1642 *Religio Medici*', *Princeton University Library Chronicle*, 67:3 (2006): 594–610.

level and indeed the obscurity of reference is important, in a work about the fleeting nature not so much of life as of death. I have annotated the origins of stories, of names and emperors, of burial and cremation ceremonies alluded to in the writing. However, there is every possibility that the oblivion into which they so quickly pass in the text is the very point—the prose in torrent sweeps aside the individual and their circumstances—and to delay their passing in the form of endnotes may be merely the accumulation of dust. The text itself is (relatively) straightforward. First published in a 1658 octavo edition by Henry Brome, it was reprinted with *Pseudodoxia* (in quarto) in the same year, though there are some differences in the marginalia between the two texts, and additions from the quarto are included in square brackets. It was reprinted in 1659 and 1669. A list of *errata* (either 18 or 24 lines) was added to some copies of the first edition, but these were not corrected in subsequent editions. Such errata, when adopted, are glossed in the textual notes, preceded by (Er). References to the 1658 octavo are noted by (58). Obvious and minor printer's errors are silently corrected, with reference to L. C. Martin's 1964 edition of Browne's works, as well as Keynes (1964), Robbins (1972), and Patrides (1977), who is more sparing in the emendations he adopts. There is also an additional set of *errata*, in the quarto 1658 edition, correcting both new errors and errors not corrected in the octavo. Where significant, these are noted. Following Martin, these are designated (Er2). In addition, there are some authorial handwritten corrections in a number of printed copies, collated first in John Carter's 1932 edition of *Hydriotaphia* and *Cyrus*, and these are also gathered into the textual notes under (C).

The Garden of Cyrus is particularly luscious in its vocabulary and its syntax, the sheer foliage of verbal texture that the work creates. The general intention behind the annotations is to gloss those words and terms which may not be familiar to a reader coming to the text for the first time, or to elucidate terms that may have variant early modern meanings. This extends also to clarifying how we might parse the sentence, on occasion. Here too, there is rhetorical purpose in the fabric of the dense prose, the unaccommodating sentence and the dazzling barrage of things and stories that constitute the text, and Browne's endemic practices of half-reference are traced as far as possible. *Errata* are incorporated, as with *Hydriotaphia*. One variant upon the 1658 edition is that the dedicatory letter to Nicholas Bacon, which prefaces *The Garden of Cyrus*, has been moved to that prefatory position, whereas, in the original, it is placed before *Hydriotaphia*.

Pseudodoxia Epidemica is a work too little known, and is included almost, but not quite, in full. Browne's vocabulary in this work is heavily idiosyncratic and the OED is awash with obscure words whose definitions are exemplified (if not deduced) from *Pseudodoxia*. This conscious obscurity is mitigated somewhat by Browne's frequently incorporating doublet-phrasing, whereby the Latin form is paired with its own English equivalent, 'eructation or belching', 'tollutation or ambling'. This is very much part of the rhythm and prosody of *Pseudodoxia*, which aims to create, or animate a vocabulary for the sciences, naturalizing Latin roots, but also luxuriating in their verbal textures. Such a stylistic habit, the continual invention and manipulation of words, is not to all tastes: 'The style of Sir Thomas Browne is not English,' complained Noah Webster, the lexographer, in lambasting Samuel Johnson's frequent reference to Browne.[49] In referencing Browne's sources for *Pseudodoxia*, I have taken much more of a light touch, noting the source, by and large, only of works directly mentioned. Browne quotes a bewildering range of classical and patristic authorities in *Pseudodoxia*, along with medical, travel, and philosophical writing. He is not averse to citing contemporary authors, but the longevity of the errors is in large part his point, and it is the classical manifestations of error that tend to preface the chapters. It is also true that in many cases these have been collated elsewhere and he makes ample use, for instance, of de Boodt on gems or Aldrovandi on animals. The dizzyingly full notes of Robbins, *Pseudodoxia* (1981) pursue these in glorious detail. The size of *Pseudodoxia* is such that some excisions had to be made, largely from the long sixth book on chronology and the origin of the world, and two chapters from book 4, though I quote at least a part of every chapter. The 1646 edition of *Pseudodoxia* was, according to Keynes, 'very accurately printed' though the tale in subsequent editions was one of increasing debasement, until the 1672 compositor who 'surpassed all his predecessors in villainy . . . was stupid, careless and impertinent' (1964, vii). This is somewhat harsh, and that the 1646 edition was so accurate may be questioned,[50] but there is only minimal tracing here of the changes. Printer's errors, caught in later editions, are corrected without comment. Variants from later editions are included on the basis of their

[49] Noah Webster: 'Letter to Dr David Ramsay' (Oct. 1807) in James Boulton (ed.), *Samuel Johnson: The Critical Heritage* (London: Routledge, 1971), p. 129.

[50] Endicott, *Prose of Sir Thomas Browne*, p. 516; and in Robbins' textual notes.

intellectual interest. Books 2 and 3, for instance, with their more scientific subject matter, clearly respond to Browne's reading in natural philosophy, and so some passages that replace the 1646 text are included in the notes.

Christian Morals is edited from its first edition of 1716, overseen by Browne's daughter, Elizabeth Lyttleton, and John Jeffrey, Archdeacon of Norwich, but the notes include a good selection from Samuel Johnson's second edition of 1756. *A Letter to a Friend* (1690) shares a number of passages with *Christian Morals*. *Certain Miscellany Tracts* (1712) is included in full, but annotated very lightly.

Classical references, by default, follow Loeb translations, and use English titles. Exceptions to this are Aristotle, *Complete Works of* Aristotle, ed. Jonathan Barnes, 2vols. (Princeton, 1984); Plato, *Complete Works*, ed. John Cooper (Hackett, 1997) and Galen, *On the Usefulness of the Parts of the Body*, trans. Margaret Tallmadge May (Cornell, 1969). Albertus Magnus is cited from *On Animals*, trans. Kenneth F. Kitchell Jr. and Irven Michael Resnick, 2 vols. (Baltimore: Johns Hopkins, 1999). Biblical references are taken, except where there is a reason not to, from the King James Bible. Early modern works, where possible, are referenced to the Sales Catalogue of Browne (1711), which contained the libraries of Browne and his son, Edward, rather than first editions of works, though if it is merely a generalized reference, the original publication date seems more useful. The standard points of reference for Patristic writings are: J.P. Migne, *Patrologiae Cursus Completus, Series Latina* (*PL*, 1862–5); J.P. Migne, *Patrologiae Cursus Completus, Series Graeca* (*PG*, 1857–66), though particularly with the latter, I have also used the *Ante-Nicene Fathers*, ed. Alexander Roberts (Edinburgh: T & T Clark, 1867–73) and the *Nicene and Post-Nicene Fathers*, ed. Phillip Schaff (Edinburgh: T & T Clark, 1886–1900).

RELIGIO MEDICI

FIG. 2 Title page from *Religio Medici* (1642).

To the Reader

Certainly that man were greedy of life, who should desire to live when all the world were at an end; and he must needs be very impatient, who would repine at death in the societie of all things that suffer under it.[1] Had not almost every man suffered by the presse; or were not the tyranny thereof become universall; I had not wanted reason for complaint:[2] but in times wherein I have lived to behold the highest perversion of that excellent invention; the name of his Majesty defamed, the honour of Parliament depraved, the writings of both depravedly, anticipatively, counterfeitly imprinted;[3] complaints may seeme ridiculous in private persons, and men of my condition may be as incapable of affronts, as hopelesse of their reparations.[4] And truly had not the duty I owe unto the importunitie of friends,[5] and the allegeance I must ever acknowledge unto truth prevayled with me; the inactivitie of my disposition might have made these sufferings continuall, and time that brings other things to light, should have satisfied me in the remedy of its oblivion. But because things evidently false are not onely printed, but many things of truth most falsly set forth; in this latter I could not but thinke my selfe engaged: for though we have no power to redresse the former, yet in the other the reparation being within our selves, I have at present represented unto the world a full and intended copy of that piece which was most imperfectly and surreptitiously published before.

This I confesse about seven yeares past,[6] with some others of affinitie thereto, for my private exercise and satisfaction, I had at leisurable houres composed; which being communicated unto one, it became common unto many, and was by transcription successively corrupted untill it arrived in a most depraved copy at the presse. He that shall peruse that worke, and shall take notice of sundry particularities and personall expressions therein, will easily discerne the intention was not publik: and being a private exercise directed to my selfe, what is delivered therein was rather a memoriall unto me then an example or rule unto any other: and therefore if there bee any singularitie therein correspondent unto the private conceptions of any man, it doth not advantage them; or if dissentaneous thereunto, it no way overthrowes them.[7] It was penned in such a place and with such disadvantage, that (I protest) from the first setting of pen unto paper, I had not the assistance of any good booke, whereby to promote my invention or relieve my memory; and therefore there might be many reall lapses therein, which others might take notice of, and more than I suspected my selfe. It was set downe many yeares past, and was the sense of my conceptions at that time, not an immutable law unto my advancing judgement at all times, and therefore there might be many things therein plausible unto my passed apprehension, which are not agreeable unto my present selfe. There are many things delivered rhetorically, many expressions therein meerely tropicall, and as they best illustrate my intention;[8] and therefore also there are many things to be taken in a soft and flexible sense, and not to be called unto the rigid test of reason. Lastly all that is contained therein is in submission unto maturer discernments, and as I have declared shall no further father them then the best and learned judgements shall authorize them;[9] under favour of which considerations I have made its secrecie publike and committed the truth thereof to every ingenuous reader.

Thomas Browne.

Religio Medici

SECTION 1

For my religion, though there be severall circumstances that might perswade the world I have none at all, as the generall scandall of my profession, the naturall course of my studies, the indifferency of my behaviour, and discourse in matters of religion, neither violently defending one, nor with that common ardour and contention opposing another;[10] yet in despight hereof I dare, without usurpation, assume the honorable stile of a Christian:[11] not that I meerely owe this title to the font, my education, or clime wherein I was borne, as being bred up either to confirme those principles my parents instilled into my unwary understanding;[12] or by a generall consent proceed in the religion of my countrey: but having, in my riper yeares, and confirmed judgement, seene and examined all, I finde my selfe obliged by the principles of grace, and the law of mine owne reason, to embrace no other name but this;[13] neither doth herein my zeale so farre make me forget the generall charitie I owe unto humanity, as rather to hate then pity Turkes, infidels, and (what is worse) Jewes, rather contenting my selfe to enjoy that happy stile, then maligning those who refuse so glorious a title.

SECTION 2

But because the name of a Christian is become too generall to expresse our faith, there being a geography of religions as well as lands, and every clime distinguished not onely by their lawes and limits, but circumscribed by their doctrines and rules of faith; to be particular, I am of that reformed new-cast religion, wherein I dislike nothing but the name,[14] of the same beliefe our saviour taught, the Apostles disseminated, the fathers authorised, and the martyrs confirmed;[15] but by the sinister ends of princes, the ambition and avarice of prelates, and the fatall corruption of times, so decaied, impaired, and fallen from its native beauty, that it required the carefull and charitable hand of these times to restore it to its primitive integrity:[16] now the accidentall occasion whereon, the slender meanes whereby, the low and abject condition of the person by whom so good a worke was set on foot,[17] which in our adversaries beget contempt and scorn, fills me with wonder, and is the very same objection the insolent Pagans first cast at Christ and his Disciples.

SECTION 3

Yet have I not so shaken hands with those desperate resolutions, who had rather venture at large their decaied bottome, then bring her in to be new trim'd in the dock;[18] who had rather promiscuously retaine all, then abridge any, and obstinately be what they are, then what they have beene, as to stand in diameter and swords point with them:[19] we have reformed from them, not against them;[20] for omitting those improperations and termes of scurrility betwixt us, which onely difference our affections,[21] and not our cause, there is between us one common name and appellation, one faith, and necessary body of principles common to us both; and therefore I am not scrupulous to converse and live with them,[22] to enter their churches in defect of ours, and either pray with them, or for them: I could never perceive any rationall consequence from those many texts which prohibite the children of Israel to pollute themselves with the temples of the heathens;[23] we being all Christians, and not divided by such detested impieties as might prophane our prayers, or the place wherein we make them; or that a resolved conscience may not adore her Creator any where, especially in places devoted to his service;[24] where if their devotions offend him, mine may please him, if theirs prophane it, mine may hallow it; holy water and crucifix (dangerous to the common people) deceive not my judgement, nor abuse my devotion at all:[25] I am, I confesse, naturally inclined to that, which misguided zeale termes superstition; my common conversation I do acknowledge austere, my behaviour full of rigour, sometimes not without morosity; yet at my devotion I love to use the civility of my knee, my hat, and hand, with all those outward and sensible motions, which may expresse, or promote my invisible devotion.[26] I should violate my owne arme rather then a church, nor willingly deface the memory of saint or martyr.[27] At the sight of a crosse or crucifix I can dispence with my hat, but scarce with the thought or memory of my saviour; I cannot laugh at but rather pity the fruitlesse journeys of pilgrims, or contemne the miserable condition of friers; for though misplaced in circumstance, there is something in it of devotion: I could never heare the *Ave Marie* bell* without an elevation, or thinke it a sufficient warrant, because they erred in one circumstance, for me to erre in all, that is in silence and dumbe contempt;[28] whilst therefore they directed their devotions to her, I offered mine to God, and rectified the errours of their prayers by rightly ordering mine owne; at a solemne procession I have wept abundantly, while my consorts, blinde with opposition and prejudice, have fallen into an accesse of scorne and laughter:[29] There are questionlesse both in Greek, Roman, and African churches, solemnities, and ceremonies, whereof the wiser zeales doe make a Christian use, and stand condemned by us; not as evill in themselves, but as allurements and baits of superstition to those vulgar heads that looke asquint on the face of truth, and those unstable judgements that cannot consist in the narrow point and centre of vertue without a reele or stagger to the circumference.

* A Church Bell that tolls every day at 6. and 12. of the Clocke, at the hearing whereof every one in what place soever either of house or street betakes him to his prayer, which is commonly directed to the Virgin.

SECTION 4

As there were many reformers, so likewise many reformations; every countrey proceeding in a particular way and method, according as their nationall interest together with their constitution and clime inclined them, some angrily and with extremitie, others calmely, and with mediocrity, not rending, but easily dividing the community, and leaving an honest possibility of a reconciliation, which though peaceable spirits doe desire, and may conceive that revolution of time, and the mercies of God may effect; yet that judgement that shall consider the present antipathies between the two extreames, their contrarieties in condition, affection and opinion, may with the same hopes expect an union in the poles of Heaven.

SECTION 5

But to difference my self neerer,[30] and draw into a lesser circle: there is no church whose every part so squares unto my conscience, whose articles, constitutions, and customes seeme so consonant unto reason, and as it were framed to my particular devotion, as this whereof I hold my beliefe, the Church of England, to whose faith I am a sworne subject, and therefore in a double obligation, subscribe unto her articles, and endeavour to observe her Constitutions:[31] whatsoever is beyond, as points indifferent,[32] I observe according to the rules of my private reason, or the humour and fashion of my devotion, neither believing this, because Luther affirmed it, or disproving that, because Calvin hath disavouched it.[33] I condemne not all things in the Councell of Trent, nor approve all in the Synod of Dort.[34] In briefe, where the Scripture is silent, the church is my text; where that speakes, 'tis but my comment; where there is a joynt silence of both, I borrow not the rules of my religion from Rome or Geneva, but the dictates of my own reason. It is an unjust scandall of our adversaries, and a gross error in our selves, to compute the nativity of our religion from Henry the eight,[35] who though he rejected the Pope, refus'd not the faith of Rome, and effected no more then what his owne predecessors desired and assayed in ages past, and was conceived the state of Venice would have attempted in our dayes.[36] It is as uncharitable a point in us to fall upon those popular scurrilities and opprobrious scoffes of the Bishop of Rome, whom as a temporall prince, we owe the duty of good language;[37] I confesse there is cause of passion between us; by his sentence I stand excommunicated, Heretick is the best language he affords me; yet can no eare witnesse I ever returned to him the name of Antichrist, man of sin, or whore of Babylon;[38] It is the method of charity to suffer without reaction: those usuall satyrs,[39] and invectives of the pulpit may perchance produce a good effect on the vulgar, whose eares are opener to rhetorick then logick, yet doe they in no wise confirme the faith of wiser beleevers, who know that a good cause needs not to be patron'd by a passion, but can sustaine it selfe upon a temperate dispute.

SECTION 6

I could never divide my selfe from any man upon the difference of an opinion, or be angry with his judgement for not agreeing with mee in that, from which perhaps within a few dayes I should dissent my selfe:[40] I have no genius to disputes in religion, and have often thought it wisedome to decline them, especially upon a disadvantage, or when the cause of truth might suffer in the weakenesse of my patronage:[41] where we desire to be informed, 'tis good to contest with men above our selves; but to confirme and establish our opinions, 'tis best to argue with judgements below our own, that the frequent spoyles and victories over their reasons may settle in our selves an esteeme, and confirmed opinion of our owne. Every man is not a proper champion for truth, nor fit to take up the gauntlet in the cause of veritie:[42] many from the ignorance of these maximes, and an inconsiderate zeale unto truth, have too rashly charged the troopes of error, and remaine as trophees unto the enemies of truth: a man may be in as just possession of truth as of a city, and yet bee forced to surrender: 'tis therefore farre better to enjoy her with peace, then to hazzard her on a battell: If therefore there rise any doubts in my way, I doe forget them, or at least defer them, till my better settled judgement, and more manly reason be able to resolve them; for I perceive every mans owne reason is his best Oedipus, and will upon a reasonable truce, find a way to loose those bonds wherewith the subtilties of errour have enchained our more flexible and tender judgements.[43] In philosophy where truth seemes double-faced, there is no man more paradoxicall then my self; but in divinity I love to keepe the road, and though not in an implicite, yet an humble faith, follow the great wheele of the church, by which I move, not reserving any proper poles or motion from the epicycle of my own braine;[44] by this meanes I leave no gap for heresies, schismes, or errors, of which at present, I hope I shall not injure truth, to say, I have no taint or tincture; I must confesse my greener studies have beene polluted with two or three, not any begotten in the latter centuries, but old and obsolete, such as could never have been revived, but by such extravagant and irregular heads as mine; for indeed heresies perish not with their authors, but like the river Arethusa, though they lose their currents in one place, they rise up againe in another:[45] one generall councell is not able to extirpate one single heresie, it may be cancelled for the present, but revolution of time and the like aspects from Heaven, will restore it, when it will flourish till it be condemned againe;[46] for as though there were a metempsychosis, and the soule of one man passed into another, opinions doe finde after certaine revolutions, men and mindes like those that first begat them.[47] To see our selves againe we neede not looke for Plato's yeare*;[48] every man is not onely himselfe; there have beene many Diogenes, and as many Timons, though but few of

* A revolution of certaine thousand yeares when all things should returne unto their former estate and he be teaching againe in his schoole as when he delivered this opinion.

that name;[49] men are lived over againe, the world is now as it was in ages past, there was none then, but there hath been some one since that parallels him, and is as it were his revived selfe.

SECTION 7

Now the first of mine was that of the Arabians, that the soules of men perished with their bodies, but should yet bee raised againe at the last day; not that I did absolutely conceive a mortality of the soule; but if that were, which faith, not philosophy hath yet thoroughly disproved, and that both entred the grave together, yet I held the same conceit thereof that we all doe of the body, that it should rise againe.[50] Surely it is but the merits of our unworthy natures, if we sleepe in darkenesse, untill the last alarum:[51] a serious reflex upon my owne unworthinesse did make me backward from challenging this prerogative of my soule;[52] so I might enjoy my Saviour at the last, I could with patience be nothing almost unto eternity. The second was that of Origen, that God would not persist in his vengeance for ever, but after a definite time of his wrath hee would release the damned soules from torture;[53] which error I fell into upon a serious contemplation of the great attribute of God his mercy, and did a little cherish it in my selfe, because I found therein no malice, and a ready weight to sway me from the other extreme of despaire, whereunto melancholy and contemplative natures are too easily disposed. A third there is which I did never positively maintaine or practice, but have often wished it had been consonant unto truth, and not offensive to my religion, and that is the prayer for the dead;[54] whereunto I was inclined from some charitable inducements, whereby I could scarce containe my prayers for a friend at the ringing of a bell, or behold his corpse without an oraison for his soule: 'twas a good way me thought to be remembered by posterity, and farre more noble then an history. These opinions I never maintained with pertinacity, or endeavoured to enveagle any mans beliefe unto mine, nor so much as ever revealed or disputed them with my dearest friends;[55] by which meanes I neither propagated them in others, nor confirmed them in my selfe, but suffering them to flame upon their own substance, without addition of new fuell, they went out insensibly of themselves; therefore these opinions, though condemned by lawfull Councels, were not heresies in me, but bare errors, and single lapses of my understanding, without a joynt depravity of my will:[56] those have not only depraved understandings but diseased affections, which cannot enjoy a singularity without a heresie, or be the author of an opinion, without they be of a sect also; this was the villany of the first schisme of Lucifer, who was not content to erre alone, but drew into his faction many legions of spirits;[57] and upon this experience hee tempted only Eve, as well understanding the communicable nature of sin, and that to deceive but one, was tacitely and upon consequence to delude them both.

SECTION 8[58]

That heresies should arise we have the prophecy of Christ, but that old ones should be abolished we hold no prediction.[59] That there must be heresies, is true, not onely in our church, but also in any other: even in doctrines hereticall there will be super-heresies, and Arians not onely divided from their church, but also among themselves:[60] for heads that are disposed unto schisme and complexionally propense to innovation, are naturally disposed for a community, nor will ever be confined unto the order or œconomy of one body;[61] and therefore when they separate from others they knit but loosely among themselves; nor contented with a generall breach or dichotomie with their church, do subdivide and mince themselves almost into atomes.[62] 'Tis true, that men of singular parts and humors have not beene free from singular opinions and conceits in all ages; retaining something not onely beside the opinion of his own church or any other, but also any particular author: which notwithstanding a sober judgement may doe without offence or heresie; for there is yet after all the decrees of counsells and the niceties of the schooles, many things untouch'd, unimagin'd, wherein the libertie of an honest reason may play and expatiate with security and farre without the circle of an heresie.[63]

SECTION 9

As for those wingy mysteries in divinity, and ayery subtilties in religion, which have unhindg'd the braines of better heads, they never stretched the *Pia Mater* of mine;[64] methinkes there be not impossibilities enough in religion for an active faith; the deepest mysteries ours containes, have not only been illustrated, but maintained by syllogisme, and the rule of reason: I love to lose my selfe in a mystery to pursue my reason to an *oh altitudo*.[65] 'Tis my solitary recreation to pose my apprehension with those involved ænigmas and riddles of the Trinity, with incarnation and resurrection.[66] I can answer all the objections of Satan, and my rebellious reason, with that odde resolution I learned of Tertullian, *certum est quia impossibile est*.[67] I desire to exercise my faith in the difficultest point, for to credit ordinary and visible objects is not faith, but perswasion. Some beleeve the better for seeing Christ his sepulchre, and when they have seene the Red Sea, doubt not of the miracle.[68] Now contrarily I blesse my selfe, and am thankefull that I lived not in the dayes of miracles, that I never saw Christ nor his Disciples; I would not have beene one of those Israelites that passed the Red Sea, nor one of Christ's patients, on whom he wrought his wonders;[69] then had my faith beene thrust upon me, nor should I enjoy that greater blessing pronounced to all that believe and saw not.[70] 'Tis an easie and necessary beliefe to credit what our eye and sense hath examined: I believe he was dead, and buried, and rose againe; and desire to see him in his glory, rather then to contemplate him in his cenotaphe, or sepulchre. Nor is this much to beleeve, as we have reason, we owe this faith unto history: they only had the advantage of a bold and noble faith, who lived before his coming, who upon obscure prophesies and mysticall types could raise a beliefe, and expect apparent impossibilities.[71]

SECTION 10

'Tis true, there is an edge in all firme beliefe, and with an easie metaphor we may say the sword of faith; but in these obscurities I rather use it, in the adjunct the Apostle gives it, a Buckler;[72] under which I perceive a wary combatant may lie invulnerable. Since I was of understanding to know we knew nothing, my reason hath beene more pliable to the will of faith; I am now content to understand a mystery without a rigid definition in an easie and Platonick description.[73] That allegoricall description of Hermes*,[74] pleaseth mee beyond all the

* *Sphæra, cujus centrum ubique, circumferentia nullibi.*

metaphysicall definitions of divines; where I cannot satisfie my reason, I love to humour my fancy; I had as leive you tell me that *anima est angelus hominis, est Corpus Dei*, as *Entelechia*; *Lux est umbra Dei*, as *actus perspicui*:[75] where there is an obscurity too deepe for our reason, 'tis good to set downe with a description, periphrasis, or adumbration;[76] for by acquainting our reason how unable it is to display the visible and obvious effect of nature, it becomes more humble and submissive unto the subtilties of faith: and thus I teach my haggard and unreclaimed reason to stoope unto the lure of faith. I believe there was already a tree whose fruit our unhappy parents tasted, though in the same chapter, when God forbids it, 'tis positively said, the plants of the field were not yet growne; for God had not caused it to raine upon the earth.[77] I beleeve that the serpent (if we shall literally understand it) from his proper forme and figure, made his motion on his belly before the curse.[78] I find the triall of the pucellage and virginity of women, which God ordained the Jewes, is very fallible.[79] Experience, and history informes me, that not onely many particular women, but likewise whole nations have escaped the curse of childbirth, which God seemes to pronounce upon the whole sex; yet doe I beleeve that all this is true, which indeed my reason would perswade me to be false;[80] and this I think is no vulgar part of faith to believe a thing not only above, but contrary to reason, and against the arguments of our proper senses.

SECTION 11

In my solitary and retired imagination, (*neque enim cum porticus aut me lectulus accepit, desum mihi*) I remember I am not alone, and therefore forget not to contemplate him and his attributes who is ever with mee, especially those two mighty ones, his wisedome and eternitie;[81] with the one I recreate, with the other I confound my understanding: for who can speake of eternitie without a solecisme, or thinke thereof without an extasie?[82] Time we may comprehend, 'tis but five days elder then our selves, and hath the same horoscope with the world;[83] but to retire so farre backe as to apprehend a beginning, to give such an infinite start forward, as to conceive an end in an essence that we affirme hath neither the one nor the other; it puts my reason to Saint Pauls sanctuary;[84] my philosophy dares not say the angells can doe it; God hath not made a creature that can comprehend him, 'tis the priviledge of his owne nature; *I am that I am*, was his owne definition unto Moses;[85] and 'twas a short one, to confound mortalitie, that durst question God, or aske him what hee was; indeed he only is, all others have and shall be, but in eternity there is no distinction of tenses; and therefore that terrible terme *predestination*, which hath troubled so many weake heads to conceive, and the wisest to explaine, is in respect to God no prescious determination of our estates to come, but a definitive blast of his will already fulfilled, and at the instant that he first decreed it; for to his eternitie which is indivisible, and altogether, the last trumpe is already sounded, the reprobates in the flame, and the blessed in Abrahams bosome. Saint Peter speakes modestly, when hee saith, a thousand yeares to God are but as one day:[86] for to speake like a philosopher, those continued instances of time which flow into thousand yeares, make not to him one moment; what to us is to come, to his eternitie is present, his whole duration being but one permanent point without succession, parts, flux, or division.

SECTION 12

There is no attribute that adds more difficulty to the mystery of the Trinity, where though in a relative way of Father and Son, we must deny a priority.[87] I wonder how Aristotle could conceive the world eternall, or how hee could make good two eternities:[88] his similitude of a triangle, comprehended in a square, doth somewhat illustrate the Trinity of our soules, and that the triple unity of God;[89] for there is in us not three, but a Trinity of soules, because there is in us, if not three distinct soules, yet differing faculties, that can, and doe subsist apart in different subjects, and yet in us are so united as to make but one soule and substance;[90] if one soule were so perfect as to informe three distinct bodies, that were a petty Trinity: conceive the distinct number of three, not divided nor separated by the intellect, but actually comprehended in its unity, and that is a perfect Trinity. I have often admired the mysticall way of Pythagoras, and the secret magicke of numbers;[91] beware of philosophy, is a precept not to be received in too large a sense;[92] for in this masse of nature there is a set of things that carry in their front, though not in capitall letters, yet in stenography,[93] and short characters, something of divinitie, which to wiser reasons serve as luminaries in the abysse of knowledge,[94] and to judicious beliefes, as scales and roundles to mount the pinnacles and highest pieces of divinity. The severe schooles shall never laugh me out of the philosophy of Hermes, that this visible world is but a picture of the invisible, wherein as in a pourtract, things are not truely, but in equivocall shapes; and as they counterfeit some more reall substance in that invisible fabrick.[95]

SECTION 13

That other attribute wherewith I recreate my devotion, is his wisedome, in which I am happy; and for the contemplation of this onely, do not repent me that I was bred in the way of study: The advantage I have of the vulgar, with the content and happinesse I conceive therein, is an ample recompence for all my endeavours, in what part of knowledg soever. Wisedome is his most beauteous attribute, no man can attaine unto it, yet Solomon pleased God when hee desired it.[96] Hee is wise because hee knowes all things, and hee knoweth all things because he made them all, but his greatest knowledg is in comprehending that he made not, that is himselfe. And this is also the greatest knowledge in man. For this do I honour my own profession and embrace the counsell even of the Devill himselfe: had he read such a lecture in paradise as hee did at Delphos, we had better knowne our selves, nor had we stood in feare to know him*.[97] I know he is wise in all, wonderfull in what we conceive, but far more in what we comprehend not, for we behold him but asquint upon reflex or shadow; our understanding is dimmer than Moses' eye, we are ignorant of the backparts, or lower side of his divinity;[98] therefore to pry into the maze of his counsels, is not onely folly in man, but presumption even in angels;[99] like us, they are his servants, not his senators; he holds no Councell, but that mysticall one of the Trinity, wherein though there be three persons, there is but one minde that decrees, without contradiction; nor needs he any, his actions are not begot with deliberation, his wisedome naturally knowes what's best; his intellect stands ready fraught with the superlative and purest Ideas of goodnesse; consultation and election, which are two motions in us, make but one in him; his actions springing from his power, at the first touch

* γνῶθι σεαυτὸν, *nosce teipsum*.

of his will. These are contemplations metaphysicall, my humble speculations have another method, and are content to trace and discover those expressions hee hath left in his creatures, and the obvious effects of nature;[100] there is no danger to profound these mysteries, no *sanctum sanctorum* in philosophy:[101] the world was made to be inhabited by beasts, but studied and contemplated by man: 'tis the debt of our reason we owe unto God, and the homage we pay for not being beasts; without this the world is still as though it had not been, or as it was before the sixt day when as yet there was not a creature that could conceive, or say there was a world. The wisedome of God receives small honour from those vulgar heads, that rudely stare about, and with a grosse rusticity admire his workes; those highly magnifie him whose judicious enquiry into his acts, and deliberate research into his creatures, returne the duty of a devout and learned admiration.

Therefore,[102]

Search while thou wilt, and let thy reason goe
To ransome truth even to the abysse below.
Rally the scattered causes, and that line
Which nature twists, be able to untwine.[103]
It is thy makers will, for unto none
But unto reason can he ere be knowne.
The devills doe know thee, but those damned meteours
Build not thy glory, but confound thy creatures.
Teach my endeavours so thy workes to read,
That learning them, in thee I may proceed.
Give thou my reason that instructive flight,
Whose weary wings may on thy hands still light.
Teach me to soare aloft, yet ever so,
When neare the sunne, to stoope againe below.[104]
Thus shall my humble feathers safely hover,
And though neere earth, more then the Heavens discover.
And then at last, when homeward I shall drive
Rich with the spoyles of nature to my hive,
There will I sit, like that industrious flye,
Buzzing thy prayses, which shall never die
Till death abrupts them, and succeeding glory
Bid me goe on in a more lasting story.

And this is almost all wherein an humble creature may endeavour to requite, and someway to retribute unto his creator; for if not he that sayeth *Lord, Lord; but he that doth the will of the*

Father shall be saved;[105] certainely our wills must be our performances, and our intents make out our actions; otherwise our pious labours shall finde anxiety in their graves, and our best endeavours not hope, but feare a resurrection.

SECTION 14

There is but one first cause, and foure second causes of all things; some are without efficient, as God, others without matter, as angels, some without forme, as the first matter, but every essence, created or uncreated, hath its finall cause, and some positive end both of its essence and operation;[106] this is the cause I grope after in the workes of nature, on this hangs the providence of God; to raise so beauteous a structure, as the world and the creatures thereof, was but his art, but their sundry and divided operations with their predestinated ends, are from the treasury of his wisedome. In the causes, nature, and affections of the eclipse of sunne and moone, there is most excellent speculation; but to profound farther,[107] and to contemplate a reason why his providence hath so disposed and ordered their motions in that vast circle, as to conjoyne and obscure each other, is a sweeter piece of reason, and a diviner point of philosophy; therefore sometimes, and in some things there appeares to mee as much divinity in Galen his books *De usu partium*, as in Suarez' Metaphysicks:[108] had Aristotle beene as curious in the enquiry of this cause as he was of the other, hee had not left behinde him an imperfect piece of philosophy, but an absolute tract of divinity.

SECTION 15

Natura nihil agit frustra, is the onely indisputable axiome in philosophy;[109] there are no grotesques in nature; nor any thing framed to fill up empty cantons, and unnecessary spaces; in the most imperfect creatures, and such as were not preserved in the Arke, but having their seeds and principles in the wombe of nature, are every-where where the power of the sun is;[110] in these is the wisedome of his hand discovered: out of this ranke Solomon chose the object of his admiration, indeed what reason may not goe to schoole to the wisedome of bees, ants, and spiders?[111] What wise hand teacheth them to doe what reason cannot teach us? Ruder heads stand amazed at those prodigious pieces of nature, whales, elephants, dromidaries, and camels; these I confesse, are the Colossus and majestick pieces of her hand; but in these narrow engines there is more curious mathematicks, and the civilitie of these little citizens more neatly set forth the wisedome of their Maker;[112] who admires not *Regio-Montanus* his fly beyond his eagle, or wonders not more at the operation of two soules in those little bodies, than but one in the trunck of a cedar?[113] I could never content my contemplation with those generall pieces of wonders, the flux and reflux of the sea, the encrease of Nile, the conversion of the needle to the north,[114] and have studied to match and parallel those in the more obvious and neglected pieces of nature, which without further travell I can doe in the cosmography of my selfe;[115] we carry with us the wonders, we seeke without us: there is all Africa, and her prodigies in us; we are that bold and adventurous piece of nature, which he that studies, wisely learnes in a compendium, what others labour at in a divided piece and endlesse volume.[116]

SECTION 16

Thus there are two bookes from whence I collect my divinity; besides that written one of God, another of his servant nature, that universall and publik manuscript, that lies expans'd unto the eyes of all;[117] those that never saw him in the one, have discovered him in the other: this was the Scripture and theology of the heathens; the naturall motion of the sun made them more admire him, than its supernaturall station did the children of Israel;[118] the ordinary effect of nature wrought more admiration in them, than in the other all his miracles; surely the heathens knew better how to joyne and reade these mysticall letters, than we Christians, who cast a more carelesse eye on these common hieroglyphicks, and disdain to suck divinity from the flowers of nature.[119] Nor do I so forget God, as to adore the name of nature; which I define not with the schooles, the principle of motion and rest, but, that streight and regular line, that setled and constant course the wisedome of God hath ordained the actions of his creatures, according to their severall kinds.[120] To make a revolution every day is the nature of the sun, because that necessary course which God hath ordained it, from which it cannot swerve, but by a faculty from that voyce which first did give it motion. Now this course of nature God seldom, alters or perverts, but like an excellent artist hath so contrived his worke, that with the selfe same instrument, without a new creation hee may effect his obscurest designes. Thus he sweetneth the water with a wood, preserveth the creatures in the Arke, which the blast of his mouth might have as easily created:[121] for God is like a skillful geometrician, who when more easily, and with one stroke of his compasse, he might describe, or divide a right line, had yet rather doe this in a circle or longer way, according to the constituted and forelaid principles of his art:[122] yet this rule of his hee doth sometimes pervert, to acquaint the world with his prerogative, lest the arrogancy of our reason should question his power, and conclude he could not; and thus I call the effects of nature the works of God, whose hand and instrument she only is; and therefore to ascribe his actions unto her, is to devolve the honor of the principall agent, upon the instrument;[123] which if with reason we may doe, then let our hammers rise up and boast they have built our houses, and our pens receive the honour of our writings. I hold there is a generall beauty in the works of God, and therefore no deformity in any kind or species of creature whatsoever: I cannot tell by what logick we call a toad, a beare, or an elephant, ugly, they being created in those outward shapes and figures which best expresse the actions of their inward formes.[124] And having past that generall visitation of God,[125] who saw that all that he had made was good, that is, conformable to his will, which abhors deformity, and is the rule of order and beauty; there is no deformity but in monstrosity, wherein notwithstanding there is a kind of beauty, nature so ingeniously contriving the irregular parts, as they become sometimes more remarkable than the principall fabrick.[126] To speake yet more narrowly, there was never any thing ugly, or misshapen, but the chaos;[127] wherein notwithstanding to speake strictly, there was no deformity, because no forme, nor was it yet impregnate by the voyce of God: now nature is not at variance with art, nor art with nature; they being both the servants of his providence: art is the perfection of nature: were the world now as it was the sixt day, there were yet a chaos: nature hath made one world, and art another.[128] In briefe, all things are artificiall, for nature is the art of God.

SECTION 17

This is the ordinary and open way of his providence, which art and industry have in a good part discovered, whose effects we may foretell without an oracle; to foreshew these is not prophesie, but prognostication. There is another way full of meanders and labyrinths, whereof the Devill and spirits have no exact Ephemerides, and that is a more particular and obscure method of his providence, directing the operations of individualls and single essences;[129] this we call Fortune, that serpentine and crooked line, whereby he drawes those actions his wisedome intends in a more unknowne and secret way; this cryptick and involved method of his providence have I ever admired, nor can I relate the history of my life, the occurrences of my dayes, the escapes of dangers, and hits of chance with a *Bezo las Manos*, to fortune, or a bare Gramercy to my good starres:[130] Abraham might have thought the ram in the thicket came thither by accident; humane reason would have said that meere chance conveyed Moses in the Arke to the sight of Pharaohs daughter; what a labyrinth is there in the story of Joseph, able to convert a Stoick?[131] Surely there are in every mans life certaine rubs, doublings, and wrenches which passe a while under the effects of chance, but at the last, well examined, prove the meere hand of God:[132] 'twas not dumbe chance, that to discover the Fougade or Powder Plot, contrived a miscarriage in the letter.[133] I like the victory of 88. the better for that one occurrence which our enemies imputed to our dishonour, and the partiality of Fortune, to wit, the tempests, and contrarietie of winds.[134] King Philip did not detract from the nation, when he said, he sent his Armado to fight with men, and not to combate with the winds. Where there is a manifest disproportion between the powers and forces of two severall agents, upon a maxime of reason we may promise the victory to the superiour; but when unexpected accidents slip in, and unthought of occurrences intervene, these must proceed from a power that owes no obedience to those axioms: where, as in the writing upon the wall, we behold the hand, but see not the spring that moves it.[135] The successe of that pety Province of Holland (of which the Grand Seignieur proudly said, that if they should trouble him as they did the Spaniard, hee would send his men with shovels and pick-axes and throw it into the sea) I cannot altogether ascribe to the ingenuity and industry of the people, but to the mercy of God, that hath disposed them to such a thriving genius; and to the will of his providence, that disposeth her favour to each countrey in their preordinate season.[136] All cannot be happy at once, for because the glory of one state depends upon the ruine of another, there is a revolution and vicissitude of their greatnesse, and must obey the swing of that wheele, not moved by intelligences, but by the hand of God, whereby all estates arise to their zenith and verticall points, according to their predestinated periods. For the lives not onely of men, but of commonweales, and the whole world, run not upon an helix that still enlargeth, but on a circle, where arriving to their meridian, they decline in obscurity, and fall under the horizon againe.[137]

SECTION 18

These must not therefore bee named the effects of fortune, but in a relative way, and as we terme the workes of nature. It was the ignorance of mans reason that begat this very name, and by a carelesse terme miscalled the providence of God: for there is no liberty for causes to operate in a loose and stragling way, nor any effect whatsoever, but hath its warrant from some universall or superiour cause. 'Tis not a ridiculous devotion, to say a prayer before a game at tables; for even in sortilegies and matters of greatest uncertainty, there is a setled and preordered course of effects;[138] 'tis we that are blind, not fortune: because our eye is too dim to discover the mystery of her effects, we foolishly paint her blind, and hoodwink the providence of the Almighty.[139] I cannot justifie that contemptible proverb, *that fooles onely are fortunate*; or that insolent paradox, *that a wise man is out of the reach of fortune*; much lesse those opprobrious epithets of poets, *whore*, *baud*, and *strumpet*:[140] 'tis I confesse the common fate of men of singular gifts of mind, to be destitute of those of fortune; which doth not any way deject the spirit of wiser judgements, who throughly understand the justice of this proceeding; and being enriched with higher donatives, cast a more carelesse eye on these vulgar parts of felicity. 'Tis a most unjust ambition, to desire to engrosse the mercies of the Almighty, nor to be content with the goods of mind, without a possession of those of body or fortune: and 'tis an errour worse than heresie, to adore these complementall and circumstantiall pieces of felicity, and undervalue those perfections and essentiall points of happinesse, wherin we resemble our Maker. To wiser desires 'tis satisfaction enough to deserve, though not to enjoy the favours of fortune; let providence provide for fooles: 'tis not partiality, but equity in God, who deales with us but as our naturall parents; those that are able of body and mind, he leaves to their deserts; to those of weaker merits hee imparts a larger portion, and pieces out the defect of one by the excesse of the other. Thus have wee no just quarrell with nature, for leaving us naked, or to envie the hornes, hoofs, skins, and furs of other creatures, being provided with reason, that can supply them all. Wee need not labour with so many arguments to confute judiciall astrology;[141] for if there be a truth therein, it doth not injure divinity; if to be born under Mercury disposeth us to be witty, under Jupiter to be wealthy, I doe not owe a knee unto these, but unto that mercifull hand that hath ordered my indifferent and uncertaine nativity unto such benevolous aspects. Those that hold that all things were governed by fortune had not erred, had they not persisted there: the Romans that erected a temple to Fortune, acknowledged therein, though in a blinder way, somewhat of divinity; for in a wise supputation all things begin and end in the Almighty.[142] There is a neerer way to heaven than Homers chaine;[143] an easie logick may conjoyne heaven and earth in one argument, and with lesse than a sorites resolve all things into God.[144] For though we christen effects by their most sensible and nearest causes, yet is God the true and infallible cause of all, whose concourse though it be generall, yet doth it subdivide it selfe into the particular actions of every thing, and is that spirit, by which each singular essence not onely subsists, but performes its operation.

SECTION 19

The bad construction and perverse comment on these paire of second causes, or visible hands of God, have perverted the devotion of many unto Atheisme;[145] who forgetting the honest advisoes of faith, have listened unto the conspiracie of passion and reason.[146] I have therefore alwayes endeavoured to compose those fewds and angry dissentions between affection, faith, and reason: for there is in our soule a kind of Triumvirate, or triple government of three competitors, which distract the peace of this our common-wealth, not lesse than did that other the State of Rome.[147]

As reason is a rebell unto faith, so passion unto reason: as the propositions of faith seeme absurd unto reason, so the theorems of reason unto passion, and both unto reason;[148] yet a moderate and peaceable discretion may so state and order the matter, that they may bee all Kings, and yet make but one monarchy, every one exercising his soveraignty and prerogative in a due time and place, according to the restraint and limit of circumstance. There is, as in philosophy, so in divinity, sturdy doubts, and boysterous objections, wherewith the unhappinesse of our knowledge too neerely acquainteth us. More of these no man hath knowne than my selfe, which I confesse I conquered, not in a martiall posture, but on my knees.[149] For our endeavours are not onely to combate with doubts, but alwayes to dispute with the Devill; the villany of that spirit takes a hint of infidelity from our studies, and by demonstrating a naturality in one way, makes us mistrust a miracle in another. Thus having perus'd the Archidoxis and read the secret sympathies of things, he would disswade my beliefe from the miracle of the brazen serpent, make me conceit that image work'd by sympathie, and was but an Ægyptian tricke to cure their diseases without a miracle.[150] Againe, having seene some experiments of Bitumen, and having read farre more of Naptha, he whispered to my curiositie the fire of the altar might be naturall, and bid me mistrust a miracle in Elias when he entrench'd the altar round with water;[151] for that inflamable substance yeelds not easily unto water, but flames in the armes of its antagonist: and thus would hee inveagle my beliefe to thinke the combustion of Sodom might be naturall, and that there was an asphaltick and bituminous nature in that lake before the fire of Gomorrha:[152] I know that manna is now plentifully gathered in Calabria, and Josephus tels me in his dayes 'twas as plentifull in Arabia;[153] the Devill therefore made the quere, where was then the miracle in the dayes of Moses? the Israelites saw but that in his time, the natives of those countries behold in ours. Thus the Devill played at chesse with mee, and yeelding a pawne, thought to gaine a queen of me, taking advantage of my honest endeavours; and whilst I labour'd to raise the structure of my reason, hee striv'd to undermine the edifice of my faith.

SECTION 20

Neither had these or any other ever such advantage of me, as to encline me to any point of infidelity or desperate positions of

Atheisme; for I have beene these many yeares of opinion there was never any. Those that held religion was the difference of man from beasts, have spoken probably, and proceed upon a principle as inductive as the other:[154] that doctrine of Epicurus, that denied the providence of God, was no Atheism, but a magnificent and high-strained conceit of his Majesty, which hee deemed too sublime to minde the triviall actions of those inferiour creatures:[155] that fatall necessitie of the Stoickes, is nothing but the immutable Law of his will. Those that heretofore denied the divinitie of the holy Ghost, have been condemned but as heretickes;[156] and those that now deny our saviour (though more than hereticks) are not so much as Atheists: for though they deny two persons in the Trinity, they hold as we do, there is but one God.

That villain and secretary of Hell, that composed that miscreant piece of the three impostors, though divided from all religions, and was neither, Jew, Turk, nor Christian, was not a positive Atheist.[157] I confesse every countrey hath its Machiavell, every age its Lucian, whereof common heads must not heare, nor more advanced judgements too rashly venture on:[158] 'tis the rhetorick of Satan and may pervert a loose or prejudicate beleefe.

SECTION 21

I confesse I have perused them all, and can discover nothing that may startle a discreet beliefe: yet are there heads carried off with the wind and breath of such motives. I remember a doctor in physick of Italy, who could not perfectly believe the immortality of the soule, because Galen seemed to make a doubt thereof.[159] With another I was familiarly acquainted in France, a divine and man of singular parts, that on the same point was so plunged and gravelled with three lines of Seneca[*],[160] that all our antidotes, drawne from both Scripture and philosophy, could not expell the poyson of his errour. There are a set of heads, that can credit the relations of mariners, yet question the testimonies of Saint Paul; and peremptorily maintaine the traditions of Ælian or Pliny, yet in histories of Scripture, raise queres and objections, beleeving no more than they can parallel in humane Authors.[161]

[*] Post mortem nihil est, ipsa; mors nihil. Mors individua est noxia corpori, Nec patiens animæ—Toti morimur, nullaq; pars manet Nostri.

I confesse there are in Scripture stories that doe exceed the fable of poets, and to a captious reader sound like Gargantua or Bevis:[162] search all the legends of times past, and the fabulous conceits of these present, and 'twill bee hard to find one that deserves to carry the buckler unto Sampson, yet is all this of an easie possibility, if we conceive a divine concourse or an influence but from the little finger of the Almighty.[163] It is impossible that either in the discourse of man, or in the infallible voyce of God, to the weakenesse of our apprehensions, there should not appeare irregularities, contradictions, and antinomies: my selfe could shew a catalogue of doubts, never yet imagined nor questioned, as I know, which are not resolved at the first hearing, not fantastick queres, or objections of ayre: for I cannot heare of atoms in divinity.[164] I can read the history of the pigeon that was sent out of the Ark, and returned no more, yet not question how shee found out her mate that was left behind: that Lazarus was raised from the dead, yet not demand where in the interim his soule awaited; or raise a law-case, whether his heire might lawfully detaine his inheritance, bequeathed unto him by his death; and he, though restored to life, have no plea or title unto his former possessions.[165] Whether Eve was framed out of the left side of Adam, I dispute not; because I stand not yet assured which is the right side of a man, or whether there be any such distinction in nature; that she was edified out of the ribbe of Adam I believe, yet raise no question who shall arise with that ribbe at the Resurrection.[166] Whether Adam was an hermaphrodite, as the Rabbines contend upon the letter of the text;[167] because it is contrary to reason, there should bee an hermaphrodite before there was a woman, or a composition of two natures, before there was a second composed. Likewise, whether the world was created in Autumne, Summer, or the Spring; because it was created in them all; for whatsoever signe the sun possesseth, those foure seasons are actually existent: it is the nature of this luminary to distinguish the severall seasons of the yeare, all which it makes at one time in the whole earth, and successive in any part thereof.[168] There are a bundle of curiosities, not onely in philosophy but in divinity, proposed and discussed by men of most supposed abilities, which indeed are not worthy our vacant houres, much lesse our serious studies; pieces onely fit to be placed in Pantagruels library*, or bound up with *Tartaretus de modo Cacandi*.[169]

* In Rabelais.

SECTION 22

These are niceties that become not those that peruse so serious a mystery. There are others more generally questioned and called to the barre, yet me thinkes of an easie, and possible truth. 'Tis ridiculous to put off, or drowne the generall flood of Noah in that particular inundation of Deucalion: that there was a deluge once, seemes not to mee so great a miracle, as that there is not one alwayes.[170] How all the kinds of creatures, not only in their owne bulks, but with a competency of food and sustenance, might be preserved in one Arke, and within the extent of three hundred cubits, to a reason that rightly examines it, will appeare very foesible.[171] There is another secret, not contained in the Scripture, which is more hard to comprehend, and put the honest Father to the refuge of a miracle;[172] and that is, not onely how the distinct pieces of the world, and divided ilands should bee first planted by men, but inhabited by tygers, panthers and beares. How America abounded with beasts of prey, and noxious animals, yet contained not in it that necessary creature, a horse, is very strange. By what passage those, not onely birds, but dangerous and unwelcome beasts came over: How there bee creatures there, which are not found in this triple continent;[173] all which must needs bee strange unto us, that hold but one Arke, and that the creatures began their progresse from the mountaines of Ararat.[174] They who to salve this would make the deluge particular, proceed upon a principle that I can no way grant;[175] not onely upon the negative of holy Scriptures, but of mine owne reason, whereby I can make it probable, that the world was as well peopled in the time of Noah as in ours, and fifteene hundred yeares to people the world, as full a time for them as foure thousand yeares since have beene to us. There are other assertions and common tenents drawn from Scripture, and generally beleeved as Scripture; whereunto, notwithstanding, I would never betray the libertie of my reason. 'Tis a paradoxe[176] to me, that Methusalem was the longest liv'd of all the children of Adam, and no man will bee able to prove it; when from the processe of the text I can manifest it may be otherwise.[177] That Judas perished by hanging himself, there is no certainety in Scripture, though in one place it seemes to affirme it, and by a doubtfull word hath given occasion to translate it; yet in another place, in a more punctuall description, it makes it improbable, and seemes to overthrow it.[178] That our fathers, after the flood, erected the tower of Babell, to preserve themselves against a second deluge, is generally opinioned and beleeved; yet is there another intention of theirs expressed in Scripture: besides, it is improbable from the circumstance of the place, that is, a plaine in the land of Shinar.[179] These are no points of faith, and therefore may admit a free dispute. There are yet others, and those familiarly concluded from the text, wherein (under favour) I see no consequence.[180] The Church of Rome confidently proves the opinion of tutelary angels, from that answer when Peter knockt at the doore, *'tis not he but his angel*;[181] that is, might some say, his messenger, or some body from him; for so the originall signifies, and is as likely to be the doubtfull families meaning. This exposition I once suggested to a young divine, that answered upon this point, to which I remember the Franciscan opponent replyed no more, but, that it was a new and no authentick interpretation.

SECTION 23

These are but the conclusions, and fallible discourses of man upon the word of God, for such I doe beleeve the holy Scriptures; yet were it of man, I could not choose but say, it was the singularest, and superlative piece that hath been extant since the creation; were I a Pagan, I should not refraine the lecture of it; and cannot but commend the judgement of Ptolomy, that thought not his library compleate without it:[182] the Alcoran of the Turks[183] (I speake without prejudice) is an ill composed piece, containing in it vaine and ridiculous errours in philosophy,[184] impossibilities, fictions, and vanities beyond laughter, maintained by evident and open sophismes, the policy of ignorance, deposition of Universities, and banishment of learning, that hath gotten foot by armes and violence; this without a blow hath disseminated it selfe through the whole earth. It is not unremarkable what Philo first observed, That the law of Moses continued two thousand yeares without the least alteration;[185] whereas, we see, the lawes of other commonweales doe alter with occasions; and even those that pretended their originall from some Divinity, to have vanished without trace or memory. I beleeve, besides Zoroaster, there were divers that writ before Moses, who notwithstanding have suffered the common fate of time.[186] Mens workes have an age like themselves; and though they out-live their authors, yet have they a stint and period to their duration: this onely is a worke too hard for the teeth of time, and cannot perish but in the generall flames, when all things shall confesse their ashes.[187]

SECTION 24

I have heard some with deepe sighs lament the lost lines of Cicero; others with as many groanes deplore the combustion of the library of Alexandria;[188] for my owne part, I thinke there be too many in the world, and could with patience behold the urne and ashes of the Vatican, could I with a few others recover the perished leaves of Solomon.[189] I would not omit a copy of Enochs pillars, had they many neerer authors than Josephus, or did not relish somewhat of the fable.[190] Some men have written more than others have spoken; Pineda[*] quotes more authors in one work, than are necessary in a whole world. Of those three great inventions in Germany, there are two which are not without their incommodities, and 'tis disputable whether they exceed not their use and commodities.[191] 'Tis not a melancholy *utinam* of mine owne, but the desires of better heads, that there were a generall Synod;[192] not to unite the incompatible difference of religion, but for the benefit of learning, to reduce it as it lay at first in a few and solid authours; and to condemne to the fire those swarms and millions of rhapsodies, begotten onely to distract and abuse the weaker judgements of scholars, and to maintaine the trade and mystery of typographers.

[*] *Pineda* in his *Monarchia Ecclesiastica* quotes one thousand and fortie Authors.

SECTION 25

I cannot but wonder with what exceptions the Samaritanes could confine their beliefe to the Pentateuch, or five books of Moses.[193] I am ashamed at the rabbinicall Interpretation of the Jews, upon the Old Testament, as much as their defection from the New:[194] and truely it is beyond wonder, how that contemptible and degenerate issue of Jacob, once so devoted to ethnick superstition,[195] and so easily seduced to the idolatry of their neighbours, should now in such an obstinate and peremptory beliefe, adhere unto their owne doctrine, expect impossibilities, and in the face and eye of the Church persist without the least hope of conversion: this is a vice in them, that were a vertue in us; for obstinacy in a bad cause, is but constancy in a good. And herein I must accuse those of my own religion; for there is not any of such a fugitive faith, such an unstable belief, as a Christian; none that do so oft transforme themselves, not unto severall shapes of Christianity and of the same species, but unto more unnaturall and contrary formes, of Jew and Mahometan, that from the name of Saviour can condescend to the bare terme of Prophet; and from an old beliefe that he is come, fall to a new expectation of his comming: it is the promise of Christ to make us all one flock;[196] but how and when this union shall be, is as obscure to me as the last day. Of those foure members of religion we hold a slender proportion;[197] there are I confesse some new additions, yet small to those which accrew to our adversaries, and those onely drawne from the revolt of Pagans, men but of negative impieties, and such as deny Christ, but because they never heard of him: but the religion of the Jew is expressly against the Christian, and the Mahometan against both; for the Turke, in the bulke hee now stands, he is beyond all hope of conversion; if hee fall asunder there may be conceived hopes, but not without strong improbabilities. The Jew is obstinate in all fortunes; the persecution of fifteene hundred yeares hath but confirmed them in their errour: they have already endured whatsoever may be inflicted, and have suffered, in a bad cause, even to the condemnation of their enemies.[198] Persecution is a bad and indirect way to plant religion; it hath beene the unhappy method of angry devotions, not onely to confirme honest religion, but wicked heresies, and extravagant opinions. It was the first stone and basis of our faith, none can more justly boast of persecutions, and glory in the number and valour of martyrs; for, to speake properly, those are true and almost onely examples of fortitude: those that are fetch'd from the field, or drawne from the actions of the campe, are not oft-times so truely precedents of valour as audacity, and at the best attaine but to some bastard piece of fortitude: if we shall strictly examine the circumstances and requisites which Aristotle requires to true and perfect valour, we shall finde the name onely in his master Alexander, and as little in that Romane worthy, Julius Cæsar;[199] and if any, in that easie and active way, have done so nobly as to deserve that name,[200] yet in the passive and more terrible piece these have surpassed, and in a more heroicall way may claime the honour of that title. 'Tis not in the power of every honest faith to proceed thus farre, or passe to Heaven through the flames; every one hath it not in that full measure, nor in so audacious and resolute a temper, as to endure those terrible tests and trialls, who notwithstanding in a peaceable way doe truely adore their saviour, and have (no doubt) a faith acceptable in the eyes of God.

SECTION 26

Now as all that die in warre are not termed souldiers, so neither can I properly terme all those that suffer in matters of religion martyrs. The Councell of Constance condemnes John Husse for an heretick, the stories of his owne party stile him a martyr;[201] he must needs offend the divinity of both, that sayes hee was neither the one nor the other: there are many (questionlesse) canonized on earth, that shall never be saints in Heaven; and have their names in Histories and Martyrologies, who in the eyes of God, are not so perfect martyrs as was that wise heathen Socrates, that suffered on a fundamentall point of religion, the unity of God.[202] I have often pitied the miserable bishop that suffered in the cause of Antipodes, yet cannot choose but accuse him of as much madnesse, for exposing his living on such a trifle, as those of ignorance and folly that condemned him.[203] I think my conscience will not give me the lie, if I say, there are not many extant that in a noble way feare the face of death lesse than my selfe, yet from the morall duty I owe to the Commandement of God, and the naturall respects that I tender unto the conservation of my essence and being, I would not perish upon a ceremony, politick points, or indifferency;[204] nor is my beleefe of that untractable temper, as not to bow at their obstacles, or connive at matters wherein there are not manifest impieties: the leaven therefore and ferment of all, not onely civill, but religious actions, is wisedome; without which, to commit our selves to the flames is homicide, and (I feare) but to passe through one fire into another.

SECTION 27

That miracles are ceased, I can neither prove, nor absolutely deny, much lesse define the time and period of their cessation;[205] that they survived Christ, is manifest upon record of Scripture; that they out-lived the Apostles also, and were revived at the conversion of nations, many yeares after, we cannot deny, if we shall not question those writers whose testimonies we doe not controvert, in points that make for our owne opinions; therefore that may have some truth in it that is reported by the Jesuites of their miracles in the Indies,[206] I could wish it were true, or had any other testimony then their owne pennes: they may easily beleeve those miracles abroad, who daily conceive a greater at home; the transmutation of those visible elements into the body and blood of our Saviour:[207] for the conversion of water into wine, which he wrought in Cana, or what the Devill would have had him done in the wildernesse, of stones into bread, compared to this, will scarce deserve the name of a miracle:[208] though indeed, to speake properly, there is not one miracle greater than another, they being the extraordinary effect of the hand of God, to which all things are of an equall facility; and to create the world as easie as one single creature. For this is also a miracle, not onely to produce effects against, or above nature, but before nature; and to create nature as great a miracle, as to contradict or transcend her. Wee doe too narrowly define the power of God, restraining it to our capacities. I hold that God can doe all things, how he should work contradictions I do not understand, yet dare not therefore deny.[209] I cannot see why the angel of God should question Esdras to recall the time past, if it were beyond his owne power;[210] or that God should pose mortalitie in that, which hee was not able to performe himselfe. I will not say God cannot, but hee will not performe many things, which we plainely affirme he cannot: this I am sure is the mannerliest proposition, wherein notwithstanding I hold no paradox. For strictly his power is the same with his will, and they both with all the rest doe make but one God.

SECTION 28[211]

Therefore that miracles have beene I doe beleeve, that they may yet bee wrought by the living I doe not deny: but have no confidence in those which are fathered on the dead; and this hath ever made me suspect the efficacy of reliques, to examine the bones, question the habits and appertinencies of saints, and even of Christ himselfe:[212] I cannot conceive why the crosse that

Helena found and whereon Christ himself died should have power to restore others unto life; I excuse not Constantine from a fall off his horse, or a mischiefe from his enemies, upon the wearing those nayles on his bridle which our Saviour bore upon the crosse in his hands:[213] I compute among your *piæ fraudes*, nor many degrees before consecrated swords and roses, that which Baldwin King of Jerusalem return'd the Genovese for their cost and paines in his warre, to wit the ashes of John the Baptist.[214] Those that hold the sanctitie of their soules doth leave behind a tincture and sacred facultie on their bodies, speake naturally of miracles, and doe not salve the doubt. Now one reason I tender so little devotion unto reliques is, I think, the slender and doubtfull respect I have alwayes held unto antiquities: for that indeed which I admire is farre before antiquity, that is eternity, and that is God himselfe; who though hee be stiled the Antient of dayes, cannot receive the adjunct of antiquity, who was before the world, and shall be after it, yet is not older then it:[215] for in his yeares there is no climacter,[216] his duration is eternity, and farre more venerable then antiquitie.

SECTION 29

But above all things, I wonder how the curiositie of wiser heads could passe that great and indisputable miracle, the cessation of oracles:[217] and in what swoun their reasons lay, to content themselves and sit downe with such far-fetch't and ridiculous reasons as Plutarch alleadgeth for it.[218] The Jewes that can beleeve the supernaturall solstice of the sunne in the dayes of Joshua, have yet the impudence to deny the eclipse, which every Pagan confessed at his death: but for this, it is evident beyond all contradiction, the Devill himselfe confessed it*.[219] Certainly it is not a warrantable curiosity, to examine the verity of Scripture by the concordance of humane history, or seek to confirme the chronicle of Hester or Daniel, by the authority of Magasthenes or Herodotus.[220] I confesse I have had an unhappy curiosity this way, till I laughed my selfe out of it with a piece of Justine, where hee delivers that the children of Israel for being scabbed were banished out of Egypt.[221] And truely since I have understood the occurrences of the world, and know in what counterfeit shapes and deceitfull vizzards time represents on the stage things past;[222] I doe beleeve them little more than things to come. Some have beene of my opinion, and endevoured to write

* In his oracle to Augustus.

the history of their own lives; wherein Moses hath outgone them all, and left not onely the story of his life, but as some will have it of his death also.[223]

SECTION 30

It is a riddle to me, how this story of oracles hath not worm'd out of the world that doubtfull conceit of spirits and witches;[224] how so many learned heads should so farre forget their metaphysicks, and destroy the ladder and scale of creatures, as to question the existence of spirits:[225] for my part, I have ever beleeved, and doe now know, that there are witches; they that doubt of these, doe not onely deny them, but spirits; and are obliquely and upon consequence a sort, not of infidels, but Atheists.[226] Those that to confute their incredulity desire to see apparitions, shall questionlesse never behold any, nor have the power to be so much as witches; the Devill hath them already in a heresie as capitall as witchcraft, and to appeare to them, were but to convert them: of all the delusions wherewith he deceives mortalitie, there is not any that puzleth mee more than the legerdemain of changelings;[227] I doe not credit those transformations of reasonable creatures into beasts, or that the Devill hath a power to transpeciate a man into a horse, who tempted Christ (as a triall of his divinitie) to convert but stones into bread.[228] I could beleeve that spirits use with man the act of carnality, and that in both sexes; I conceive they may assume, steale, or contrive a body, wherein there may be action enough to content decrepit lust, or passion to satisfie more active veneries; yet in both, without a possibility of generation: and therefore that opinion, that Antichrist should be borne of the tribe of Dan by conjunction with the Devill, is ridiculous, and a conceit fitter for a Rabbin than a Christian.[229] I hold that the Devill doth really possesse some men, the spirit of melancholy others, the spirit of delusion others; that, as the Devill is concealed and denyed by some, so God and good angels are pretended by others, whereof the late defection of the Maid of Germany hath left a pregnant example.[230]

SECTION 31

Againe, I beleeve that all that use sorceries, incantations, and spells, are not witches, or as we terme them, magicians;

I conceive there is a traditionall magicke, not learned immediately from the Devill, but at second hand from his schollers; who having once the secret betrayed, are able, and doe emperically practice without his advice, they both proceeding upon the principles of nature: where actives aptly conjoyned to disposed passives, will under any master produce their effects.[231] Thus I thinke at first a great part of philosophy was witchcraft, which being afterward derived to one another, proved but philosophy, and was indeed no more but the honest effects of nature: what invented by us is philosophy, learned from him is magicke. Wee doe surely owe the discovery of many secrets to the discovery of good and bad angels. I could never passe that sentence of Paracelsus without an asterisk or annotation; *ascendens constellatum multa revelat; quærentibus magnalia naturæ*, i.e. *opera dei*[*].[232] I doe thinke that many mysteries ascribed to our owne inventions, have beene the courteous revelations of spirits; for those noble essences in Heaven beare a friendly regard unto their fellow-natures on earth;[233] and therefore beleeve that those many prodigies and ominous prognostickes which fore-run the ruines of states, princes, and private persons, are the charitable premonitions of good angels, which more careless enquiries terme but the effects of chance and nature.

[*] Thereby is meant our good Angel appointed us from our nativity.

SECTION 32

Now besides these particular and divided spirits, there may be (for ought I know) an universall and common spirit to the whole world. It was the opinion of Plato, and it is yet of the hermeticall philosophers; if there be a common nature that unites and tyes the scattered and divided individuals into one species, why may there not bee one that unites them all?[234] However, I am sure there is a common spirit that playes within us, yet makes no part of us, and that is the spirit of God, the fire and scintillation of that noble and mighty essence, which is the life and radicall heat of spirits, and those essences that know not the vertue of the sunne, a fire quite contrary to the fire of Hell:[235] this is that gentle heate that brooded on the waters, and in six dayes hatched the world;[236] this is that irradiation that dispells the mists of Hell, the clouds of horrour, feare, sorrow, despaire; and preserves the region of the mind in serenity: whosoever feels not the warme gale and gentle ventilation of this spirit (though I feele his pulse) I dare not say he lives; for truely without this, to mee there is no heat under the tropick; nor any light, though I dwelt in the body of the sunne.

As when the labouring Sun hath wrought his track,
Up to the top of lofty Cancers back,
The ycie ocean cracks, the frozen pole
Thawes with the heat of the celestiall coale;
So when thy absent beames begin t'impart
Againe a solstice on my frozen heart,
My winters ov'r, my drooping spirits sing,
And every part revives into a Spring.
But if thy quickning beames a while decline,
And with their light blesse not this orbe of mine,
A chilly frost surpriseth every member,
And in the midst of June I feele December.
O how this earthly temper doth debase
The noble soule, in this her humble place!
Whose wingy nature ever doth aspire,
To reach that place whence first it took its fire.
These flames I feele, which in my heart doe dwell,
Are not thy beames, but take their fire from Hell:
O quench them all, and let thy light divine
Be as the sunne to this poore orbe of mine.
And to thy sacred spirit convert those fires,
Whose earthly fumes choake my devout aspires.

SECTION 33

Therefore for Spirits I am so farre from denying their existence, that I could easily beleeve, that not onely whole countries, but particular persons have their tutelary, and guardian angels: It is not a new opinion of the Church of Rome, but an old one of Pythagoras and Plato;[237] there is no heresie in it, and if not manifestly defin'd in Scripture,[238] yet is it an opinion of a good and wholesome use in the course and actions of a mans life, and would serve as an hypothesis to salve many doubts, whereof common philosophy affordeth no solution:[239] now if you demand my opinion and metaphysicks of their natures, I confesse them very shallow, most of them in a negative way, like that of God; or in a comparative, between our selves and fellow creatures; for there is in this universe a staire, or manifest scale of creatures, rising not disorderly, or in confusion, but with a comely method and proportion: between creatures of meere existence and things of life, there is a large disproportion of nature; between plants and animals or creatures of sense, a wider difference; between them and man, a farre greater: and if the proportion hold on, between man and angels there should bee yet a greater.[240] We doe not comprehend their natures, who retaine the first definition of Porphyry, and distinguish them from our selves by immortality;[241] for before his fall, man also was immortall; yet must we needs affirme that he had a different essence from the angels: having therefore no certaine knowledge of their natures, 'tis no bad method of the schooles, whatsoever perfection we finde obscurely in our selves, in a more compleate and absolute way to ascribe unto them.[242] I beleeve they have an extemporary knowledge, and upon the first motion of their reason doe what we cannot without study or deliberation; that they know things by their formes, and define by specificall difference, what we describe by accidents and properties; and therefore probabilities to us may bee demonstrations unto them; that they have knowledge not onely of the specificall, but numericall formes of individualls, and understand by what reserved difference each single hypostasis (besides the relation to its species) becomes its numericall selfe.[243] That as the soule hath a power to move the body it informes, so there's a faculty to move any, though informe none; ours upon restraint of time, place, and distance; but that invisible hand that conveyed Habakkuk to the lions den, or Philip to Azotus, infringeth this rule, and hath a secret conveyance, wherewith mortality is not acquainted;[244] if they have that intuitive knowledge, whereby as in reflexion they behold the thoughts of one another, I cannot peremptorily deny but they know a great part of ours. They that to refute the invocation of saints, have denied that they have any knowledge of our affaires below, have proceeded too farre, and must pardon my opinion, till I can thoroughly answer that piece of Scripture, *at the conversion of a sinner the angels of Heaven rejoyce.*[245] I cannot with those in that great Father securely interpret the worke of the first day, *fiat lux*, to the creation of angels,[246] though (I confesse) there is not any creature that hath so neare a glympse of their nature, as light in the sunne and elements; we stile it a bare accident, but where it subsists alone, 'tis a spirituall substance, and may bee an angel: in briefe, conceive light invisible, and that is a spirit.[247]

SECTION 34

These are certainly the magisteriall and master pieces of the creator, the flower (or as we may say) the best part of nothing,[248] actually existing, what we are but in hopes, and probabilitie, we are onely that amphibious piece between a corporall and spirituall essence,[249] that middle forme that linkes those two together, and makes good the method of God and nature, that jumps not from extreames, but unites the incompatible distances by some middle and participating natures; that we are the breath and similitude of God, it is indisputable, and upon record of holy Scripture,[250] but to call our selves a microcosme, or little world, I thought it onely a pleasant trope of rhetorick, till my neare judgement and second thoughts told me there was a reall truth therein:[251] for first we are a rude masse, and in the ranke of creatures, which only are, and have a dull kinde of being not yet priviledged with life, or preferred to sense or reason;[252] next we live the life of plants, the life of animals, the life of men, and at last the life of spirits, running on in one mysterious nature those five kinds of existences,[253] which comprehend the creatures not onely of the world, but of the universe; thus is man that great and true *Amphibium*, whose nature is disposed to live not onely like other creatures in divers elements, but in divided and distinguished worlds; for though there bee but one to sense, there are two to reason; the one visible, the other invisible, whereof Moses seemes to have left no description,[254] and of the other so obscurely, that some parts thereof are yet in controversie; and truely for the first chapters of Genesis, I must confesse a great deale of obscurity, though divines have to the power of humane reason endeavoured to make all goe in a literall meaning, yet those allegoricall interpretations are also probable, and perhaps the mysticall method of Moses bred up in the hieroglyphicall schooles of the Egyptians.[255]

SECTION 35

Now for that immateriall world, me thinkes we need not wander so farre as the first moveable,[256] for even in this materiall fabricke the spirits walke as freely exempt from the affection of time, place, and motion, as beyond the extreamest circumference;[257] doe but extract from the corpulency of bodies,[258] or resolve things beyond their first matter, and you discover the habitation of angels, which if I call the ubiquitary, and omnipresent essence of God, I hope I shall not offend divinity;[259] for before the creation of the world God was really all things. For the angels hee created no new world, or determinate mansion, and therefore they are every where where is his essence, and doe live at a distance even in himselfe: that God made all things for man, is in some sense true, yet not so farre as to subordinate the creation of those purer creatures unto ours, though as ministring spirits they doe, and are willing to fulfill the will of God in these lower and sublunary affaires of man;[260] God made all things for himself, and it is impossible hee should make them for any other end than his owne glory;[261] it is all he can receive, and all that is without himselfe; for honour being an externall adjunct, and in the honourer rather than in the person honoured, it was necessary to make a creature, from whom hee might receive this homage, and that is in the other world angels, in this, man; which when we neglect, we forget the very end of our creation, and may justly provoke God, not onely to repent that hee hath made the world, but that hee hath sworne hee would not destroy it.[262] That there is but one world, is a conclusion of faith. Aristotle with all his philosophy hath not beene able to prove it, and as weakely that the world was eternall;[263] that dispute much troubled the penne of the antient philosophers,[264] but Moses decided that question,[265] and all is salved with the new terme of a creation, that is, a production of something out of nothing; and what is that? Whatsoever is opposite to something or more exactly, that which is truely contrary unto God: for he onely is, all others have an existence, with dependency and are something but by a distinction; and herein is divinity conformant unto philosophy, and generation not onely founded on contrarieties, but also creation; God being all things is contrary unto nothing out of which were made all things, and so nothing became something, and omneity informed nullity into an essence.[266]

SECTION 36[267]

The whole creation is a mystery, and particularly that of man, at the blast of his mouth were the rest of the creatures made, and at his bare word they started out of nothing: but in the frame of man (as the text describes it) he played the sensible operator, and seemed not so much to create, as make him;[268] when hee had separated the materials of other creatures, there consequently resulted a forme and soule, but having raised the wals of man, he was driven to a second and harder creation of a substance like himselfe, an incorruptible and immortall soule. For these two affections we have the philosophy, and opinion of the heathens, the flat affirmative of Plato, and not a negative from Aristotle:[269] there is another scruple cast in by divinity (concerning its production) much disputed in the Germane auditories, and with that indifferency and equality of arguments, as leave the controversie undetermined.[270] I am not of Paracelsus minde that boldly delivers a receipt to make a man without conjunction, yet cannot but wonder at the multitude of heads that doe deny traduction, having no other argument to confirme their beliefe, then that rhetoricall sentence, and antimetathesis of Augustine, *creando infunditur, infundendo creatur*:[271] either opinion will consist well enough with religion, yet I should rather incline to this, did not one objection haunt mee, not wrung from speculations and subtilties, but from common sense, and observation, not pickt from the leaves of any author, but bred amongst the weeds and tares of mine owne braine. And this is a conclusion from the equivocall and monstrous productions in the copulation of man with beast;[272] for if the soule of man bee not transmitted and transfused in the seed of the parents, why are not those productions meerely beasts, but have also an impression and tincture of reason in as high a measure as it can evidence it selfe in those improper organs?[273] Nor truely can I peremptorily deny, that the soule in this her sublunary estate, is wholly and in all acceptions inorganicall,[274] but that for the performance of her ordinary actions, is required not onely a symmetry and proper disposition of organs, but a crasis and temper correspondent to its operations;[275] yet is not this masse of flesh and visible structure the instrument and proper corps of the soule, but rather of sense, and that the hand of reason. In our study of anatomy there is a masse of mysterious philosophy, and such as reduced the very heathens to divinitie; yet amongst all those rare discoveries, and curious pieces I finde in the fabricke of man, I doe not so much content my selfe, as in that I finde not, that is no organe or instrument for the rationall soule; for in the braine, which we tearme the seate of reason, there is not any thing of moment more than I can discover in the cranie of a beast:[276] and this is a sensible and no inconsiderable argument of the inorganity of the soule, at least in that sense we usually so receive it. Thus we are men, and we know not how, there is something in us, that can be without us, and will be after us, though it is strange that it hath no history, what it was before us, nor cannot tell how it entred in us.

SECTION 37

Now for these wals of flesh, wherein the soule doth seeme to be immured before the resurrection, it is nothing but an elementall composition, and a fabricke that must fall to ashes; *all flesh is grasse*, is not onely metaphorically, but literally true, for all those creatures we behold, are but the hearbs of the field, digested into flesh in them, or more remotely carnified in our selves.[277] Nay further, we are what we all abhorre, antropophagi and cannibals, devourers not onely of men, but of our selves;[278] and that not in an allegory, but a positive truth; for all this masse of flesh which we behold, came in at our mouths: this frame we looke upon, hath beene upon our trenchers; in briefe, we have devoured our selves. I cannot beleeve the wisedome of Pythagoras did ever positively, and in a literall sense, affirme his metempsychosis, or impossible transmigration of the soules of men into beasts:[279] of all metamorphoses or transmigrations, I beleeve onely one, that is of Lots wife, for that of Nabuchodonosor proceeded not so farre;[280] in all others I conceive there is no further verity then is contained in their implicite sense and morality: I beleeve that the whole frame of a beast doth perish, and is left in the same state after death, as before it was materialled unto life;[281] that the soules of men know neither contrary nor corruption, that they subsist beyond the body, and outlive death by the priviledge of their proper natures, and without a miracle; that the soules of the faithfull, as they leave earth, take possession of Heaven: that those apparitions, and ghosts of departed persons are not the wandring soules of men, but the unquiet walkes of Devils, prompting and suggesting us unto mischiefe, bloud, and villany, instilling, and stealing into our hearts, that the blessed spirits are not at rest in their graves, but wander solicitous of the affaires of the world; but those phantasmes appeare often, and doe frequent cemiteries, charnall houses, and churches,[282] it is because those are the dormitories of the dead, where the Devill like an insolent champion beholds with pride the spoyles and trophies of his victory in Adam.

SECTION 38

This is that dismall conquest we all deplore, that makes us so often cry (O) Adam, *quid fecisti*?[283] I thanke God I have not those strait ligaments, or narrow obligations to the world, as to dote on life, or be convulst and tremble at the name of death: not that I am insensible of the dread and horrour thereof, or by raking into the bowells of the deceased, continuall sight of anatomies, skeletons, or cadaverous reliques, like vespilloes,[284] or grave-makers, I am become stupid, or have forgot the apprehension of mortality, but that marshalling all the horrours, and contemplating the extremities thereof, I finde not any thing therein able to daunt the courage of a man, much lesse a well resolved Christian. And therefore am not angry at the errour of our first parents, or unwilling to beare a part of this common fate, and like the best of them to dye, that is, to cease to breathe, to take a farewell of the elements, to be a kinde of nothing for a moment, to be within one instant of a spirit. When I take a full view and circle of my selfe, without this reasonable moderator, and equall piece of justice, death, I doe conceive my selfe the miserablest person extant; were there not another life that I hope for, all the vanities of this world should not intreat a moments breath from me; could the Devill worke my beliefe to imagine I could never dye, I would not out-live that very thought;[285] I have so abject a conceit of this common way of existence, this retaining to the sunne and elements, I cannot thinke this is to be a man, or to live according to the dignitie of humanity; in expectation of a better, I can with patience embrace this life, yet in my best meditations doe often defie death;[286] I honour any man that contemnes it, nor can I highly love any that is afraid of it; this makes me naturally love a souldier, and honour those tattered and contemptible regiments that will die at the command of a sergeant.[287] For a Pagan there may bee some motives to bee in love with life, but for a Christian to be amazed at death, I see not how hee can escape this dilemma, that he is too sensible of this life, or hopelesse of the life to come.[288]

SECTION 39

Some divines count Adam 30 yeares old at his creation, because they suppose him created in the perfect age and stature of man;[289] and surely wee are all out of the computation of our age, and every man is some moneths elder than hee bethinkes him; for we live, move, have a being, and are subject to the actions of the elements, and the malice of diseases in that other world, the truest microcosme, the wombe of our mother; for besides that generall and common existence we are conceived to hold in our chaos, and whilst wee sleepe within the bosome of our causes,[290] wee enjoy a being and life in three distinct worlds, wherein we receive most manifest graduations: in that obscure world and wombe of our mother, our time is short, computed by the moone; yet longer than the dayes of many creatures that behold the sunne, our selves being not yet without life, sense, and reason, though for the manifestation of its actions, it awaits the opportunity of objects; and seemes to live there but in its roote and soule of vegetation: entring afterwards upon the scene of the world, we arise up and become another creature, performing the reasonable actions of man, and obscurely manifesting that part of divinity in us, but not in complement and perfection, till we have once more cast our secondine,[291] that is, this slough of flesh, and are delivered into the last world, that is, that ineffable place of Paul, that proper *ubi* of spirits.[292] The smattering I have of the philosophers stone, (which is something more then the perfect exaltation of gold)[293] hath taught me a great deale of divinity, and instructed my beliefe, how that immortall spirit and incorruptible substance of my soule may lye obscure, and sleepe a while within this house of flesh.[294] Those strange and mysticall transmigrations that I have observed in silkewormes, turn'd my philosophy into divinity. There is in these workes of nature, which seeme to puzle reason, something divine, and hath more in it then the eye of a common spectator doth discover.[295]

SECTION 40

I am naturally bashfull, nor hath conversation, age, or travell, beene able to effront, or enharden me, yet I have one part of modesty, which I have seldome discovered in another, that is (to speake truly) I am not so much afraid of death, as ashamed thereof; 'tis the very disgrace and ignominy of our natures, that in a moment can so disfigure us that our nearest friends, wife, and children stand afraid and start at us. The birds and beasts of the field that before in a naturall feare obeyed us, forgetting all allegiance begin to prey upon us. This very conceite hath in a tempest disposed and left me willing to be swallowed up in the abysse of waters; wherein I had perished unseene, unpityed, without wondring eyes, teares of pity, lectures of mortality, and none had said, *quantum mutatus ab illo*![296] Not that I am ashamed of the anatomy of my parts, or can accuse nature for playing the bungler in any part of me, or my owne vitious life for contracting any shamefull disease upon me, whereby I might not call my selfe as wholesome a morsell for the wormes as any.

SECTION 41

Some upon the courage of a fruitfull issue, wherein, as in the truest chronicle, they seem to outlive themselves, can with greater patience away with death. This conceit and counterfeit subsisting in our progenies seemes to mee a meere fallacy, unworthy the desires of a man, that can but conceive a thought of the next world;[297] who, in a nobler ambition, should desire to live in his substance in Heaven rather than his name and shadow in the earth. And therefore at my death I meane to take a totall adieu of the world, not caring for a monument, history, or epitaph, not so much as the bare memory of my name to be found any where but in the universall register of God: I am not yet so cynicall, as to approve the testament of Diogenes*,[298] nor doe I altogether allow that rodomontado of Lucan;

* Who willed his friend not to bury him, but to hang him up with a staffe in his hand to fright away the crowes.

> —*Cœlo tegitur, qui non habet urnam.*
> He that unburied lies wants not his herse,
> For unto him a tombe's the universe.[299]

But commend in my calmer judgement, those ingenuous intentions that desire to sleepe by the urnes of their fathers, and strive to goe the nearest way unto corruption. I doe not envie the temper of crowes and dawes, nor the numerous and weary dayes of our fathers before the flood.[300] If there bee any truth in astrology, I may outlive a Jubilee, as yet I have not seene one revolution of Saturne,[301] nor hath my pulse beate thirty yeares, and yet excepting one, have seene the ashes, and left under ground, all the kings of Europe, have beene contemporary to three emperours, foure grand signiours, and as many popes;[302] mee thinkes I have outlived my selfe, and begin to bee weary of the sunne, I have shaked hands with delight in my warme blood and canicular dayes,[303] I perceive I doe anticipate the vices of age, the world to mee is but a dreame, or mockshow, and we all therein but pantalones and antickes to my severer contemplations.

SECTION 42

It is not, I confesse, an unlawfull prayer to desire to surpasse the dayes of our saviour, or wish to out-live that age wherein he thought fittest to dye, yet if (as divinity affirmes) there shall be no gray hayres in Heaven, but all shall rise in the perfect state of men, we doe but out-live those perfections in this world, to be recalled unto them, by a greater miracle in the next, and run on here but to be retrograde hereafter. Were there any hopes to out-live vice, or a point to be super-annuated from sin, it were worthy our knees to implore the dayes of Methuselah.[304] But age doth not rectifie, but incurvate our natures, turning bad dispositions into worser habits, and (like diseases) brings on incurable vices;[305] for every day as we grow weaker in age, we grow stronger in sinne, and the number of our dayes doth but make our sinnes innumerable. The same vice committed at sixteene, is not the same, though it agree in all other circumstances, at forty, but swels and doubles from the circumstance of our ages, wherein besides the constant and inexcusable habit of transgressing, the maturity of our judgement cuts off pretence unto excuse or pardon: every sin, the oftner it is committed, the more it acquireth in the quality of evill; as it succeeds in time, so it precedes in degrees of badnesse, for as they proceed they ever multiply, and like figures in arithmeticke, the last stands for more than all that went before it:[306] and though I thinke no man can live well once but hee that could live twice, yet for my owne part, I would not live over my houres past, or beginne againe the thred of my dayes: not upon Cicero's ground, because I have lived them well, but for feare I should live them worse:[307] I find my growing judgement dayly instruct me how to be better, but my untamed affections and confirmed vitiosity makes mee dayly doe worse;[308] I finde in my confirmed age the same sinnes I discovered in my youth,

I committed many then because I was a child, and because I commit them still I am yet an infant. Therefore I perceive a man may bee twice a child before the dayes of dotage, and stand in need of Æsons bath before threescore.[309]

SECTION 43[310]

And truely there goes a great deale of providence to produce a mans life unto threescore; there is more required than an able temper for those yeeres; though the radicall humour containe in it sufficient oyle for seventie, yet I perceive in some it gives no light past thirty; men assigne not all the causes of long life that write whole bookes thereof.[311] They that found themselves on the radicall balsome or vitall sulphur of the parts, determine not why Abel liv'd not so long as Adam.[312] There is therefore a secret glome or bottome of our dayes;[313] 'twas his wisedome to determine them, but his perpetuall and waking providence that fulfils and accomplisheth them, wherein the spirits, our selves, and all the creatures of God in a secret and disputed way doe execute his will. Let them not therefore complaine of immaturitie that die about thirty, they fall but like the whole world, whose solid and well composed substance must not expect the duration and period of its constitution, when all things are compleated in it, its age is accomplished, and the last and generall fever may as naturally destroy it before six thousand, as me before forty:[314] there is therfore some other hand that twines the thread of life than that of nature; wee are not onely ignorant in antipathies and occult qualities,[315] our ends are as obscure as our beginnings, the line of our dayes is drawne by night, and the various effects therein by a pencill that is invisible; wherein though we confesse our ignorance, I am sure we doe not erre, if wee say, it is the hand of God.

SECTION 44

I am much taken with two verses of Lucan, since I have beene able not onely, as we doe at schoole, to construe, but understand:[316]

Victurosque Dei celant ut vivere durent,
Felix esse mori.
We're all deluded, vainely searching wayes,
To make us happy by the length of dayes;
For cunningly to make's protract this breath,
The Gods conceale the happiness of death.[317]

There be many excellent straines in that poet, wherewith his stoicall genius hath liberally supplyed him; and truely there are singular pieces in the philosophy of Zeno, and doctrine of the stoickes, which I perceive, delivered in a pulpit, passe for currant divinity:[318] yet herein are they in extreames, that can allow a man to be his own assassine, and so highly extoll the end and suicide of Cato;[319] this is indeed not to feare death, but yet to bee afraid of life. It is a brave act of valour to contemne death, but where life is more terrible than death, it is then the truest valour to dare to live, and herein religion hath taught us a noble example: for all the valiant acts of Curtius, Scevola or Codrus, do not parallel or match that one of Job;[320] and sure there is no torture to the racke of a disease, nor any poynyards in death it selfe like those in the way or prologue unto it. *Emori nolo, sed me esse mortuum nihil curo*, I would not die, but care not to be dead.[321] Were I of Cæsars religion I should be of his desires, and wish rather to goe off at one blow, then to be sawed in peeces by the grating torture of a disease.[322] Men that looke no further than their outsides thinke health an appertinance unto life, and quarrell with their constitutions for being sick; but I that have examined the parts of man, and know upon what tender filaments that fabrick hangs, doe wonder that we are not alwayes so; and considering the thousand dores that lead to death doe thanke my God that we can die but once. 'Tis not onely the mischiefe of diseases, and the villanie of poysons that make an end of us, we vainly accuse the fury of Gunnes, and the new inventions of death; 'tis in the power of every hand to destroy us, and we are beholding unto every one we meete hee doth not kill us. There is therefore but one comfort left, that though it be in the power of the weakest arme to take away life, it is not in the strongest to deprive us of death: God would not exempt himselfe from that, the misery of immortality in the flesh, he undertooke not that was in it immortall. Certainly there is no happinesse within this circle of flesh, nor is it in the opticks of these eyes to behold felicity; the first day of our jubilee is death; the Devill hath therefore fail'd of his desires; wee are happier with death than we should have beene without it: there is no misery but in himselfe where there is no end of misery; and so indeed in his own sense, the stoick is in the right. Hee forgets that hee can die who complaines of misery, wee are in the power of no calamitie while death is in our owne.

SECTION 45

Now besides this literall and positive kinde of death, there are others whereof divines make mention, and those I thinke, not meerely metaphoricall, as mortification, dying unto sin and the world; therefore, I say, every man hath a double horoscope, one of his humanity, his birth; another of his Christianity, his baptisme, and from this doe I compute or calculate my nativitie, not reckoning those *horæ combustæ*, and odde dayes, or esteeming my selfe any thing, before I was my saviours, and inrolled in the Register of Christ:[323] whosoever enjoyes not this life, I count him but an apparition, though he weare about him the sensible affections of flesh. In these morall acceptions, the way to be immortall is to die daily,[324] nor can I thinke I have the true theory of death, when I contemplate a skull, or behold a skeleton with those vulgar imaginations it casts upon us; I have therefore enlarged that common *memento mori*, into a more Christian memorandum, *memento quatuor novissima*, those foure inevitable points of us all, death, judgement, Heaven, and Hell.[325] Neither did the contemplations of the heathens rest in their graves, without a further thought of Radamanth or some judiciall proceeding after death, though in another way, and upon suggestion of their naturall reasons.[326] I cannot but marvaile from what Sibyll or Oracle they stole the prophesy of the worlds destruction by fire, or whence Lucan learned to say,

> *Communis mundo superest rogus, ossibus astra*
> *Misturus.—*
> There yet remaines to th'world one common fire,
> Wherein our bones with stars shall make one pyre.[327]

I beleeve the world growes neare its end, yet is neither old nor decayed, nor will ever perish upon the ruines of its owne principles. As the worke of creation was above nature, so is its adversary, annihilation; without which the world hath not its end, but its mutation. Now what force should bee able to consume it thus farre, without the breath of God, which is the truest consuming flame, my philosophy cannot informe me. Some beleeve[328] there went not a minute to the worlds creation, nor shal there go to its destruction; those six dayes so punctually described, make not to them one moment, but rather seem to manifest the method and idea of the great worke of the intellect of God, than the manner how hee proceeded in its operation. I cannot dreame that there should be at the last day any such judiciall proceeding, or calling to the barre, as indeed the Scripture seemes to imply, and the literall commentators doe conceive:[329] for unspeakable mysteries in the Scriptures are often delivered in a vulgar and illustrative way, and being written unto man, are delivered, not as they truely are, but as they may bee understood;[330] wherein notwithstanding the different interpretations according to different capacities may stand firme with our devotion, nor bee any way prejudiciall to each single edification.

SECTION 46

Now to determine the day and yeare of this inevitable time, is not onely convincible and statute madnesse, but also manifest impiety;[331] how shall we interpret Elias 6000 yeares, or imagine the secret communicated to a Rabbi, which God hath denyed unto his angels?[332] It had beene an excellent quære, to have posed the devill of Delphos, and must needs have forced him to some strange amphibology;[333] it hath not onely mocked the predictions of sundry astrologers in ages past, but the prophecies of many melancholy heads in these present, who neither understanding reasonably things past or present, pretend a knowledge of things to come, heads ordained onely to manifest the incredible effects of melancholy, and to fulfill old prophesies*,[334] rather than be the authors of new.[335] 'In those dayes there shall come warres and rumours of warres,' to me seemes no prophesie, but a constant truth, in all times verified since it was pronounced:[336] 'There shall bee signes in the moone and stares,' how comes he then like a theefe in the night, when he gives an item of his comming?[337] That common signe drawne from the revelation of Antichrist is as obscure as any;[338] in our common compute he hath beene come these many yeares, but for my owne part to speake freely, I am halfe of opinion that Antichrist is the

* In those dayes there shall come lyers and false prophets.

philosophers stone in divinity,[339] for the discovery and invention whereof, though there be prescribed rules, and probable inductions, yet hath hardly any man attained the perfect discovery thereof. That generall opinion that the world growes neere its end, hath possessed all ages past as neerely as ours; I am afraid that the soules that now depart, cannot escape that lingring expostulation of the saints under the altar, *Quousque Domine? How long, O Lord?* and groane in the expectation of the great Jubilee.[340]

SECTION 47

This is the day[341] that must make good that great attribute of God, his justice, that must reconcile those unanswerable doubts that torment the wisest understandings, and reduce those seeming inequalities, and respective distributions in this world, to an equality and recompensive justice in the next. This is that one day, that shall include and comprehend all that went before it, wherein as in the last scene, all the actors must enter to compleate and make up the catastrophe of this great peece. This is the day whose memory hath onely power to make us honest in the darke, and to bee vertuous without a witnesse. *Ipsa sui pretium virtus sibi*, that vertue is her owne reward, is but a cold principle, and not able to maintaine our variable resolutions in a constant and setled way of goodnesse.[342] I have practised that honest artifice of Seneca, and in my retired and solitary imaginations, to detaine me from the foulenesse of vice, have fancyed to my selfe the presence of my deare and worthiest friends, before whom I should lose my head, rather than be vitious, yet herein I found that there was nought but morall honesty, and this was not to be vertuous for his sake who must reward us at the last.[343] I have tryed if I could reach that great resolution of his, to be honest without a thought of Heaven or Hell; and indeed I found upon a naturall inclination, an inbred loyalty unto vertue, that I could serve her without a livery,[344] yet not in that resolved and venerable way, but that the frailty of my nature, upon an easie temptation, might be induced to forget her. The life therefore and spirit of all our actions, is the resurrection, and stable apprehension, that our ashes shall enjoy the fruit of our pious endeavours; without this, all religion is a fallacy, and those impieties of Lucian, Euripedes, and Julian are no blasphemies, but subtile verities, and Atheists have beene the onely philosophers.[345]

SECTION 48

How shall the dead arise, is no question of my faith;[346] to beleeve onely possibilities, is not faith, but meere philosophy; many things are true in divinity, which are neither inducible by reason, nor confirmable by sense, and many things in philosophy confirmable by sense, yet not inducible by reason. Thus it is impossible by any solid or demonstrative reasons to perswade a man to beleeve the conversion of the needle to the north;[347] though this be possible, and true, and easily credible, upon a single experiment unto the sense. I beleeve that our estranged and divided ashes shall unite againe, that our separated dust after so many pilgrimages and transformations into the parts of mineralls, plants, animals, elements, shall at the voyce of God returne into their primitive shapes; and joyne againe to make up their primary and predestinate formes.[348] As at the creation, there was a separation of that confused masse into its species, so at the destruction thereof there shall bee a separation into its distinct individuals.[349] As at the creation of the world, all the distinct species that we behold, lay involved in one masse, till the fruitfull voyce of God separated this united multitude into its severall species: so at the last day, when these corrupted reliques shall be scattered in the wildernesse of formes, and seeme to have forgot their proper habits, God by a powerfull voyce shall command them backe into their proper shapes, and call them out by their single individuals: Then shall appeare the fertilitie of Adam, and the magicke of that sperme that hath dilated into so many millions.[350] I have often beheld as a miracle, that artificiall resurrection and revivification of Mercury, how being mortified into thousand shapes, it assumes againe its owne, and returns into its numericall selfe.[351] Let us speake naturally, and like philosophers, the formes of alterable bodies in these sensible corruptions perish not; nor, as wee imagine, wholly quit their mansions, but retire and contract themselves into their secret and unaccessible parts, where they may best protect themselves from the action of their antagonist. A plant or vegetable consumed to ashes, to a contemplative and schoole philosopher seemes utterly destroyed, and the forme to have taken his leave for ever: but to a sensible Artist the formes are not perished, but withdrawne into their incombustible part, where they lie secure from the action of that devouring element.[352] This is made good by experience, which can from the ashes of a plant revive the plant, and from its cinders recall it into its stalk and leaves againe.[353] What the art of man can doe in these inferiour pieces, what blasphemy is it to affirme the finger of God cannot doe in these more perfect and sensible structures? This is that mysticall philosophy, from whence no true scholler becomes an Atheist, but from the visible effects of nature, growes up a reall divine, and beholds not in a dreame, as Ezekiel, but in an ocular and visible object the types of his resurrection.[354]

SECTION 49

Now, the necessary mansions of our restored selves are those two contrary and incompatible places we call Heaven and Hell; to define them, or strictly to determine what and where these are, surpasseth my divinity. That elegant Apostle which seemed to have a glimpse of Heaven, hath left but a negative description thereof; 'which neither eye hath seen, nor eare hath heard, nor can enter into the heart of man':[355] he was translated out of himself to behold it, but being returned into himselfe could not expresse it.[356] Saint Johns description by emeralds, chrysolites, and pretious stones, is too weake to expresse the materiall Heaven we behold.[357] Briefely therefore, where the soule hath the full measure, and complement of happinesse, where the boundlesse appetite of that spirit remaines compleatly satisfied, that it can neither desire addition nor alteration, that I thinke is truely Heaven: and this can onely be in the enjoyment of that essence, whose infinite goodnesse is able to terminate the desires of it selfe, and the unsatiable wishes of ours; where-ever God will thus manifest himselfe, there is Heaven, though within the circle of this sensible world.[358] Thus the soule of man may bee in Heaven any where, even within the limits of his own proper body, and when it ceaseth to live in the body, it may remaine in its owne soule, that is its creator. And thus we may say that saint Paul, whether in the body, or out of the body, was yet in Heaven.[359] To place it in the empyreall, or beyond the tenth spheare, is to forget the worlds destruction;[360] for when this sensible world shall bee destroyed, all shall then be here as it is now there, an empyreall Heaven, a quasi vacuitie,[361] when to aske where Heaven is, is to demand where the presence of God is, or where we have the glory of that happy vision. Moses that was bred up in all the learning of the Egyptians, committed a grosse absurdity in philosophy, when with these eyes of flesh he desired to see God, and petitioned his maker, that is truth it selfe, to a contradiction.[362] Those that imagine Heaven and Hell neighbours, and conceive a vicinity between those two extreames, upon consequence of the parable, where Dives discoursed with Lazarus in Abrahams bosome, do too grossely conceive of those glorified creatures, whose eyes shall easily out-see the sunne, and behold without a perspective, the extremist distances:[363] for if there shall be in our glorified eyes, the faculty of sight and reception of objects I could thinke the visible species there to be in as unlimitable a way as now the intellectuall. I grant that two bodies placed beyond the tenth spheare, or in a vacuity, according to Aristotles philosophy, could not behold each other, because there wants a body or medium to hand and transport the visible rayes of the object unto the sense;[364] but when there shall be a generall defect of either medium to convey, or light to prepare and dispose that medium, and yet a perfect vision, we must suspend the rules of our philosophy, and make all good by a more absolute piece of opticks.

SECTION 50

I cannot tell how to say that fire is the essence of Hell, I know not what to make of purgatory, or conceive a flame that can either prey upon, or purifie the substance of a soule; those flames of sulphure mentioned in the Scriptures,[365] I take not to be understood of this present Hell, but of that to come, where fire shall make up the complement of our tortures, and have a body or subject wherein to manifest its tyranny: some who have had the honour to be textuarie in divinity, are of opinion it shall be the same specificall fire with ours.[366] This is hard to conceive, yet can I make good how even that may prey upon our bodies, and yet not consume us: for in this materiall world, there are bodies that persist invincible in the powerfullest flames, and though by the action of fire they fall into ignition and liquation, yet will they never suffer a destruction: I would gladly know how Moses with an actuall fire calcin'd, or burnt the golden calfe into powder:[367] for that mysticall mettle of gold, whose solary and celestiall nature I admire, exposed unto the violence of fire, grows onely hot and liquifies, but consumeth not:[368] so when the consumable and volatile pieces of our bodies shall be refined into a more impregnable and fixed temper like gold, though they suffer from the action of flames, they shall never perish, but lie immortall in the armes of fire. And surely if this frame must suffer onely by the action of this element, there will many bodies escape, and not onely Heaven, but earth will not bee at an end, but rather a beginning; for at present it is not earth, but a composition of fire, water, earth, and aire; but at that time spoyled of these ingredients, it shall appeare in a substance more like it selfe, its ashes. Philosophers that opinioned the worlds destruction by fire, did never dreame of annihilation, which is beyond the power of sublunary causes; for the last and proper action of that element is but vitrification or a reduction of a body into glasse;[369] and therefore some of our chymicks facetiously affirm,[370] that at the last fire all shall be crystallized and reverberated into glasse, which is the utmost action of that element.[371] Nor need we fear this term 'annihilation' or wonder that God will destroy the workes of his creation: for man subsisting, who is, and will then truely appeare a microcosme, the world cannot bee said to be destroyed. For the eyes of God, and perhaps also of our glorified selves, shall as really behold and contemplate the world in its epitome or contracted essence, as now it doth at large and in its dilated substance.[372] In the seed of a plant to the eyes of God, and to the understanding of man, there exists, though in an invisible way, the perfect leaves, flowers, and fruit thereof: (for things that are *in posse* to the sense, are actually existent to the understanding.) Thus God beholds all things, who contemplates as fully his workes in their epitome, as in their full volume, and beheld as amply the whole world in that little compendium of the sixth day, as in the scattered and dilated pieces of those five before.[373]

SECTION 51

Men commonly set forth the torments of Hell by fire, and the extremity of corporall afflictions, and describe Hell in the same method that Mahomet doth Heaven.[374] This indeed makes a noyse, and drums in popular eares: but if this be the terrible piece thereof, it is not worthy to stand in diameter with Heaven, whose happinesse consists in that part that is best able to comprehend it, that immortall essence, that translated divinity and colony of God, the soule.[375] Surely though we place Hell under earth, the Devils walke and purlue is about it; men speake too popularly who place it in those flaming mountaines, which to grosser apprehensions represent Hell.[376] The heart of man is the place the Devill dwels in; I feele somtimes a Hell within my selfe, Lucifer keeps his court in my brest, Legion is revived in me.[377] There are as many Hells as Anaxagoras conceited worlds; there was more than one Hell in Magdalen, when there were seven Devils;[378] for every Devill is an Hell unto himselfe: hee holds enough of torture in his owne ubi, and needs not the misery of circumference to afflict him, and thus a distracted conscience here is a shadow or introduction unto Hell hereafter;[379] who can but pity the mercifull intention of those hands that doe destroy themselves? the Devill were it in his power would doe the like, which being impossible his miseries are endlesse, and he suffers most in that attribute wherein he is impassible, his immortality.[380]

SECTION 52

I thanke God, and with joy I mention it, I was never afraid of Hell, nor never grew pale at the description of that place; I have so fixed my contemplations on Heaven, that I have almost forgot the idea of Hell, and am afraid rather to lose the joyes of the one than endure the misery of the other; to be deprived of them is a perfect Hell, and needs me thinkes no addition to compleate our afflictions; that terrible terme hath never detained me from sin, nor do I owe any good action to the name thereof: I feare God, yet am not afraid of him, his mercies make me ashamed of my sins, before his judgements afraid thereof: these are the forced and secondary method of his wisedome, which he useth but as the last remedy, and upon provocation, a course rather to deterre the wicked, than incite the vertuous to his worship. I can hardly thinke there was ever any scared into Heaven, they goe the fairest way to Heaven, that would serve God without a Hell, other mercenaries that crouch unto him in feare of Hell, though they terme themselves the servants, are indeed but the slaves of the Almighty.

SECTION 53

And to be true, and speake my soule, when I survey the occurrences of my life, and call into account the finger of God, I can perceive nothing but an abysse and masse of mercies, either in generall to mankind, or in particular to my selfe; and whether out of the prejudice of my affection, or an inverting and partiall conceit of his mercies, I know not, but those which others terme crosses, afflictions, judgements, misfortunes, to me who enquire farther into them than their visible effects, they both appeare, and in event have ever proved the secret and dissembled favours of his affection. It is a singular piece of wisedome to apprehend truly, and without passion the workes of God, and so well to distinguish his justice from his mercy, as not to miscall those noble attributes; yet it is likewise an honest piece of logick so to dispute and argue the proceedings of God, as to distinguish even his judgements into mercies. For God is mercifull unto all, because better to the worst, than the best deserve, and to say he punisheth none in this world, though it be a paradox, is no absurdity. To one that hath committed murther, if the Judge should onely ordaine a fine,[381] it were a madnesse to call this a punishment, and to repine at the sentence, rather than admire the clemency of the Judge. Thus our offences being mortall, and deserving not onely death, but damnation, if the goodnesse of God be content to traverse and passe them over with a losse, misfortune, or disease, what frensie were it to terme this a punishment, rather than an extremity of mercy, and to groane under the rod of his judgements, rather than admire the scepter of his mercies? Therefore to adore, honour, and admire him, is a debt of gratitude due from the obligation of our nature, states, and conditions; and with these thoughts, he that knowes them best, will not deny that I adore him; that I obtaine Heaven, and the blisse thereof, is accidentall, and not the intended worke of my devotion, it being a felicitie I can neither thinke to deserve, nor scarce in modesty to expect. For these two ends of us all, either as rewards or punishments, are mercifully ordained and disproportionally disposed unto our actions, the one being so far beyond our deserts, the other so infinitely below our demerits.

SECTION 54

There is no salvation to those that beleeve not in Christ, that is, say some, since his nativity, and as divinity affirmeth, before also; which makes me much apprehend the end of those honest worthies and philosophers which died before his incarnation. It is hard to place those soules in Hell whose worthy lives doe teach us vertue on earth; methinks amongst those many subdivisions of Hell, there might have bin one limbo left for these:[382] what a strange vision will it be to see their poeticall fictions converted into verities, and their imagined and fancied furies, into reall Devils? How strange to them will sound the history of Adam, when they shall suffer for him they never heard of? when they derive their genealogy from the gods, shall know they are the unhappy issue of sinfull man? It is an insolent part of reason to controvert the works of God, or question the justice of his proceedings; could humility teach others, as it hath instructed me, to contemplate the infinite and incomprehensible distance betwixt the creator and the creature, or did we seriously perpend that one simile of saint Paul, *Shall the vessell say to the Potter, Why hast thou made me thus?*[383] it would prevent these arrogant disputes of reason, nor would we argue the definitive sentence of God, either to Heaven or Hell. Men that live according to the right rule and law of reason, live but in their owne kinde, as beasts doe in theirs; who justly obey the prescript of their natures, and therefore cannot reasonably demand a reward of their actions, as onely obeying the naturall dictates of their reason. It will therefore, and must at last appeare, that all salvation is through Christ; which verity I feare these great examples of vertue must confirme, and make it good, how the perfectest actions of earth have no title or claime unto Heaven.

SECTION 55

Nor truely doe I thinke the lives of these or of any other were ever correspondent, or in all points conformable unto their doctrines; it is evident that Aristotle transgressed the rule of his owne Ethicks;[384] the Stoicks that condemne passion, and command a man to laugh in Phalaris his bull, could not endure without a groane a fit of the stone or collick.[385] The Scepticks that affirmed they know nothing, even in that opinion confute themselves, and thought they knew more than all the world beside.[386] Diogenes I hold to bee the most vaineglorious man of his time, and more ambitious in refusing all honours, than Alexander in rejecting none.[387]

Vice and the Devill put a fallacie upon our reasons and provoking us too hastily to run from it, entangle and profound us deeper in it. The duke of Venice, that weds himselfe unto the sea, by a ring of Gold, I will not argue of prodigality, because it is a solemnity of good use and consequence in the state.[388] But the philosopher that threw his money into the sea to avoyd avarice, was a notorious prodigal.[389] There is no road or ready way to vertue, it is not an easie point of art to disentangle our selves from this riddle, or web of sin: To perfect vertue, as to religion, there is required a panoplia or compleat armour, that whilst we lye at close ward against one vice we lye open to the vennie of another:[390] and indeed wiser discretions that have the thred of reason to conduct them, offend without a pardon; whereas under heads may stumble without dishonour. There goe so many circumstances to piece up one good action, that it is a lesson to be good, and we are forced to be vertuous by the booke. Againe, the practice of men holds not an equall pace, yea, and often runnes counter to their theory; we naturally know what is good, but naturally pursue what is evill: the rhetoricke wherewith I perswade another cannot perswade my selfe: there is a depraved appetite in us, that will with patience heare the learned instructions of reason; but yet performe no farther than agrees to its owne irregular humour. In briefe, we all are monsters, that is, a composition of man and beast, wherein we must endeavour to be as the poets fancy that wise man Chiron, that is, to have the region of man above that of beast, and sense to sit but at the feete of reason.[391] Lastly, I doe desire with God, that all, but yet affirme with men, that few shall know salvation, that the bridge is narrow, the passage straite unto life;[392] yet those who doe confine the church of God, either to particular nations, churches, or families, have made it farre narrower than our Saviour ever meant it.

SECTION 56[393]

The vulgarity of those judgements that wrap the church of God in Strabo's cloake and restraine it unto Europe, seeme to mee as bad geographers as Alexander, who thought hee had conquer'd all the world when hee not subdued the halfe of any part thereof:[394] for wee cannot deny the church of God both in

Asia and Africa, if we doe not forget the peregrinations of the Apostles, the death of their martyrs, the sessions of many, and even in our reformed judgement lawfull councells held in those parts in the minoritie and nonage of ours:[395] nor must a few differences more remarkable in the eyes of man than perhaps in the judgement of God, excommunicate from Heaven one another, much lesse those Christians who are in a manner all martyrs, maintaining their faith in the noble way of persecution, and serving God in the fire, whereas we honour him but in the sunshine. 'Tis true we all hold there is a number of elect and many to be saved, yet take our opinions together, and from the confusion thereof there will be no such thing as salvation, nor shall any one be saved;[396] for first the Church of Rome condemneth us, wee likewise them, the sub-reformists and sectaries sentence the doctrine of our Church as damnable, the Atomist, or Familist reprobates all these, and all these them againe.[397] Thus whilst the mercies of God doth promise us Heaven, our conceits and opinions exclude us from that place. There must be therefore more than one Saint Peter, particular churches and sects usurpe the gates of Heaven, and turne the key against each other, and thus we goe to Heaven against each others wills, conceits and opinions, and with as much uncharity as ignorance, doe erre I feare in points, not onely of our own, but one anothers salvation.

SECTION 57

I beleeve many are saved who to man seeme reprobated, and many are reprobated, who in the opinion and sentence of man, stand elected;[398] there will appeare at the last day, strange, and unexpected examples, both of his justice and his mercy, and therefore to define either is folly in man, and insolency, even in the Devils; those acute and subtill spirits, in all their sagacity, can hardly divine who shall be saved, which if they could prognostick, their labour were at an end; nor need they compasse the earth, seeking whom they may devoure.[399] Those who upon a rigid application of the law, sentence Solomon unto damnation, condemne not onely him, but themselves, and the whole world;[400] for by the letter, and written Word of God,[401] we are without exception in the state of death, but there is a prerogative of God, and an arbitrary pleasure above the letter of his owne law, by which alone we can pretend unto salvation, and through which Solomon might be as easily saved as those who condemne him.

SECTION 58

The number of those who pretend unto salvation, and those infinite swarmes who thinke to passe through the eye of this needle, have much amazed me.[402] That name and compellation of *little flocke*, doth not comfort but deject my devotion, especially when I reflect upon mine owne unworthinesse, wherein, according to my humble apprehensions, I am below them all.[403] I beleeve there shall never be an anarchy in Heaven, but as there are hierarchies amongst the angels, so shall there be degrees of priority amongst the saints. Yet is it (I protest) beyond my ambition to aspire unto the first rankes, my desires onely are, and I shall be happy therein, to be but the last man, and bring up the rere in Heaven.

SECTION 59

Againe, I am confident, and fully perswaded, yet dare not take my oath of my salvation; I am as it were sure, and do beleeve, without all doubt, that there is such a city as Constantinople, yet for me to take my oath thereon, were a kinde of perjury, because I hold no infallible warrant from my owne sense to confirme me in the certainty thereof. And truely, though many pretend an absolute certainty of their salvation, yet when an humble soule shall contemplate her owne unworthinesse, she shall meete with many doubts and suddainely finde how little[404] we stand in need of the precept of saint Paul, *Worke out your salvation with feare and trembling.*[405] That which is the cause of my election, I hold to be the cause of my salvation, which was the mercy, and beneplacit of God, before I was, or the foundation of the world.[406] *Before Abraham was, I am*, is the saying of Christ,[407] yet is it true in some sense if I say it of my selfe, for I was not onely before my selfe, but Adam, that is, in the Idea of God, and the decree of that synod held from all eternity. And in this sense, I say, the world was before the creation, and at an end before it had a beginning; and thus was I dead before I was alive, though my grave be England, my dying place was Paradise, and Eve miscarried of mee before she conceiv'd of Cain.

SECTION 60

Insolent zeales that doe decry good workes and rely onely upon faith, take not away merit:[408] for depending upon the efficacy of their faith, they enforce the condition of God, and in a more sophisticall way doe seeme to challenge Heaven. It was decreed by God, that onely those that lapt in the water like dogges, should have the honour to destroy the Midianites, yet could none of those justly challenge, or imagine hee deserved that honour thereupon.[409] I doe not deny, but that true faith, and such as God requires, is not onely a marke or token, but also a meanes of our salvation, but where to finde this, is as obscure to me, as my last end. And if our Saviour could object unto his owne Disciples, and favourites, a faith, that to the quantity of a graine of mustard seed, is able to remove mountaines;[410] surely that which we boast of, is not any thing, or at the most, but a remove from nothing. This is the tenor of my beleefe, wherein, though there be many things singular, and to the humour of my irregular selfe, yet, if they square not with maturer Judgements, I disclaime them, and doe no further father them, than the learned and best judgements shall authorize them.

The second part

SECTION 1

Now for that other vertue of charity, without which faith is a meer notion,[411] and of no existence, I have ever endeavoured to nourish the mercifull disposition, and humane inclination I borrowed from my parents, and regulate it to the written and prescribed lawes of charity; and if I hold the true anatomy of my selfe, I am delineated and naturally framed to such a piece of vertue: for I am of a constitution so generall, that it consorts, and sympathizeth with all things; I have no antipathy, or rather idio-syncrasie, in dyet, humour, ayre, any thing;

I wonder not at the French, for their dishes of frogges, snailes, and toadstooles, nor at the Jewes for locusts and grasse-hoppers, but being amongst them, make them my common viands; and I finde they agree with my stomach as well as theirs; I could digest a sallad gathered in a church-yard, as well as in a garden. I cannot start at the presence of a serpent, scorpion, lizard, or salamander; at the sight of a toad, or viper, I finde in me no desire to take up a stone to destroy them. I feele not in my selfe those common antipathies that I can discover in others: those nationall repugnances doe not touch me, nor doe I behold with prejudice the French, Italian, Spaniard, or Dutch; but where I finde their actions in ballance with my countrey-mens, I honour, love, and embrace them in the same degree; I was borne in the eighth Climate, but seeme for to bee framed, and constellated unto all;[412] I am no plant that will not prosper out of a garden. All places, all ayres make unto me one country; I am in England, every where, and under any meridian; I have beene shipwrackt, yet am not enemy with the sea or winds;[413] I can study, play, or sleepe in a tempest. In briefe, I am averse from nothing,[414] my conscience would give me the lie if I should say I absolutely detest or hate any essence but the Devill, or so at least abhorre any thing but that we might come to composition. If there be any among those common objects of hatred I doe contemne and laugh at, it is that great enemy of reason, vertue and religion, the multitude, that numerous piece of monstrosity, which taken asunder seeme men, and the reasonable creatures of God; but confused together, make but one great beast, and a monstrosity more prodigious than hydra;[415] it is no breach of charity to call these fooles, it is the stile all holy writers have afforded them, set downe by Solomon in canonicall Scripture, and a point of our faith to beleeve so.[416] Neither in the name of multitude doe I onely include the base and minor sort of people; there is a rabble even amongst the gentry, a sort of plebeian heads, whose fancy moves with the same wheele as these; men in the same levell with mechanickes,[417] though their fortunes doe some-what guild their infirmities, and their purses compound for their follies. But as in casting account, three or foure men together come short in account of one man placed by himselfe below them: So neither are a troope of these ignorant dora-does,[418] of that true esteeme and value, as many a forlorne person, whose condition doth place them below their feet. Let us speake like politicians, there is a nobility without heraldry, a naturall dignity, whereby one man is ranked with another, another filed before him, according to the quality of his desert, and preheminence of his good parts. Though the corruption of these times, and the bias of present practise wheele another way,[419] thus it was in the first and primitive Common-wealths, and is yet in the integrity and cradle of well-ordered polities, till corruption getteth ground, ruder desires labouring after that which wiser considerations contemn, every one having a liberty to amasse and heape up riches, and they a license or faculty to doe or purchase any thing.

SECTION 2

This generall and indifferent temper of mine, doth more neerely dispose mee to this noble vertue. It is a happinesse to be borne and framed unto vertue, and to grow up from the seeds of nature, rather than the inoculation and forced graftes of education;[420] yet if we are directed only by our particular natures, and regulate our inclinations by no higher rule than that of our reasons, we are but moralists; divinity will still call us heathens. Therfore this great worke of charity, must have other motives, ends, and impulsions: I give no almes[421] to satisfie the hunger of my brother, but to fulfill and accomplish the will and command of my God; I draw not my purse for his sake that demands it, but his that enjoyned it;[422] I relieve no man upon the rhetorick of his miseries, nor to content mine own commiserating disposition, for this is still but morall charity, and an act that oweth more to passion than reason. Hee that relieves another upon the bare suggestion and bowels of pity, doth not this so much for his sake as for his own: for by compassion we make anothers misery our own, and so by relieving them, we relieve our selves also. It is as erroneous a conceite to redresse other mens misfortunes upon the common considerations of mercifull natures, that it may bee one day our owne case, for this is a sinister and politick kind of charity, wherby we seem to bespeak the pities of men, in the like occasions;[423] and truly I have observed that those professed eleemosynaries,[424] though in a croud or multitude, doe yet direct and place their petitions on a few and selected persons; there is surely a physiognomy,[425] which those experienced and master mendicants observe, whereby they instantly discover a mercifull aspect, and will single out a face, wherein they spy the signatures and markes of mercy:[426] for there are mystically in our faces certaine characters which carry in them the motto of our soules, wherein he that cannot read A.B.C. may read our natures. I hold moreover that there is a phytognomy, or physiognomy, not onely of men, but of plants, and vegetables; and in every one of them, some outward figures which hang as signes or bushes of their inward formes.[427] The finger of God hath left an inscription upon all his workes, not graphicall or composed of letters, but of their severall formes, constitutions, parts, and operations, which aptly joyned together doe make one word that doth expresse their natures. By these letters God cals the starres by their names, and by this alphabet Adam assigned to every creature a name peculiar to its nature.[428] Now there are besides these characters in our faces, certaine mysticall figures in our hands, which I dare not call meere dashes, strokes, *a la volee*,[429] or at randome, because delineated by a pencill, that never workes in vaine; and hereof I take more particular notice, because I carry that in mine owne hand, which I could never read of, nor discover in another. Aristotle, I confesse, in his acute, and singular booke of physiognomy, hath made no mention of chiromancy,[430] yet I beleeve the Egyptians, who were neerer[431] addicted to those abstruse and mysticall sciences, had a knowledge therein, to which those vagabond and counterfeit Egyptians did after pretend,[432] and perhaps retained a few corrupted principles, which sometimes might verifie their prognostickes.

It is the common wonder of all men, how among so many millions of faces, there should be none alike; now contrary, I wonder as much how there should be any; he that shall consider how many thousand severall words have beene carelessly and without study composed out of 24 letters;[433] withall how many hundred lines there are to be drawn in the fabrick of one man; shall easily finde that this variety is necessary: and it will bee very hard that they shall so concur as to make one portract like another.[434] Let a Painter carelessly limbe out a million of faces,[435] and you shall finde them all different, yea let him have his copy before him, yet after all his art there will remaine a sensible distinction; for the patterne or example of every thing is the perfectest in that kind, whereof wee still come short, though wee transcend or goe beyond it, because herein it is wide and agrees not in all points unto its copy.[436] Nor doth the similitude of creatures disparage the variety of nature, nor any way confound the workes of God. For even in things alike, there is diversitie, and those that doe seeme to accord, doe manifestly disagree. And thus is man like God, for in the same things that we resemble him, we are utterly different from him. There was never any thing so like another, as in all points to concurre, there will ever some reserved difference slip in, to prevent the identity, without which, two severall things would not be alike, but the same, which is impossible.

SECTION 3

But to returne from philosophy to charity, I hold not so narrow a conceit of this vertue, as to conceive that to give almes, is onely to be charitable, or thinke a piece of liberality can comprehend the totall of charity; divinity hath wisely divided the act thereof into many branches, and hath taught us in this narrow way, many pathes unto goodnesse; as many wayes as we may doe good, so many wayes we may bee charitable; there are infirmities, not onely of body, but of soule, and fortunes, which doe require the mercifull hand of our abilities. I cannot contemn a man for ignorance but behold him with as much pity as I doe Lazarus.[437] It is no greater charity to cloath his body, than apparell the nakednesse of his soule. It is an honourable object to see the reasons of other men weare our liveries, and their borrowed understandings doe homage to the bounty of ours. It is the cheapest way of beneficence, and like the naturall charity of the sunne illuminates another without obscuring it selfe. To be reserved and caitif in this part of goodnesse, is the sordidest piece of covetousnesse, and more contemptible than the pecuniary avarice.[438] To this (as calling my selfe a scholler) I am obliged by the duty of my condition, I make not therefore my head a grave, but a treasure of knowledge; I intend no monopoly, but a community in learning; I study not for my owne sake onely, but for theirs that study not for themselves. I envy no man that knowes more than my selfe, but pity them that know lesse. I instruct no man as an exercise of my knowledge, or with an intent rather to nourish and keepe it alive in mine owne head, than beget and propagate it in his; and in the midst of all my endeavours there is but one thought that dejects me, that my acquired parts must perish with my selfe, nor can bee legacyed among my honoured friends.[439] I cannot fall out or contemne a man for an errour, or conceive why a difference in opinion should divide an affection: for controversies, disputes, and argumentations, both in philosophy, and in divinity, if they meete with discreet and peaceable natures, doe not infringe the lawes of charity.[440] In all disputes, so much as there is of passion, so much there is of nothing to the purpose, for then reason like a bad hound spends upon a false sent, and forsakes the question first started. And this is one reason why controversies are never determined, for though they be amply proposed, they are scarce at all handled, they doe so swell with unnecessary digressions, and the parenthesis on the party, is often as large as the maine discourse upon the subject. The foundations of religion are already established, and the principles of salvation subscribed unto by all, there remaines not many controversies worth a passion, and yet never any disputed without, not onely in divinity, but in inferiour arts: what a *Βατραχομυομαχία* and hot skirmish is betwixt S. and T. in Lucian?[441] How doth grammarians hack and slash for the genitive case in Jupiter*.[442] How doe they breake their owne pates to salve that of Priscian?[443] *Si foret in terris, rideret Democritus.*[444] Yea, even amongst wiser militants, how many wounds have beene given, and credits slaine for the poore victory of an opinion or beggerly conquest of a distinction?[445] Schollers are men of peace, they beare no armes, but their tongues are sharper than Actius his razor, their pens carry farther, and give a lowder report than thunder;[446] I had rather stand in the shock of a basilisco than in the fury of a mercilesse pen.[447] It is not meere zeale to learning, or devotion to the muses, that wiser princes patron the arts, and carry an indulgent aspect unto schollers, but a desire to have their names eternized by the memory of their writings, and a feare of the revengefull pen of succeeding ages: for these are the men, that when they have played their parts, and had their exits, must step out and give the morall of their scenes, and deliver unto posterity an inventory of their vertues and vices. And surely there goes a great deale of conscience to the compiling of an history, there is no reproach to the scandall of a story; It is such an authenticke kinde of falsehood that with authority belies our good names to all nations and posteritie.

* Whether Jovis or Jupiteris.

SECTION 4

There is another offence unto charity, which no author hath ever written of, and few take notice of, and that's the reproach, not of whole professions, mysteries and conditions, but of whole nations, wherein by opprobrious epithets we miscall each other, and by an uncharitable logicke from a disposition in a few conclude a habit in all.

> *Le mutin Anglois, et le bravache Escossois;*
> *Le bougre Italien, et le fol Francois;*
> *Le poultron Romain, le larron de Gascongne,*
> *L'Espagnol superbe, et l' Aleman yurongne.*[448]

Saint Paul that cals the Cretians lyers, doth it but indirectly and upon quotation of their owne Poet.[449] It is as bloody a thought in one way as Neroes was in another.[450] For by a word wee wound a thousand, and at one blow assassine the honour of a nation. It is as compleate a piece of madnesse to miscall and rave against the times, or thinke to recall men to reason, by a fit of passion: Democritus that thought to laugh the times into goodnesse, seemes to me as deeply hypochondriack, as Heraclitus that bewailed them;[451] it moves not my spleene to behold the multitude in their proper humours, that is, in their fits of folly and madnesse, as well understanding that wisedome is not prophan'd unto the world, and 'tis the priviledge of a few to be vertuous.[452] They that endeavour to abolish vice destroy also vertue, for contraries, though they destroy one another, are yet the life of one another. Thus vertue (abolish vice) is an Idea; againe, the communitie of sinne doth not disparage goodnesse; for when vice gaines upon the major part, vertue, in whom it remaines, becomes more excellent, and being lost in some, multiplies its goodnesse in others which remaine untouched, and persists intire in the generall inundation.[453] I can therefore behold vice without a satyre, content onely, with an admonition, or instructive reprehension;[454] for noble natures, and such as are capable of goodnesse, are railed into vice, that might as easily bee admonished into vertue; and we should be all so farre the orators of goodnesse, as to protect her from the power of vice, and maintaine the cause of injured truth. No man can justly censure or condemne another, because indeed no man truely knowes another. This I perceive in my selfe, for I am in the darke to all the world, and my nearest friends behold mee but in a cloud, those that know mee but superficially, thinke lesse of me than I doe of my selfe; those of my neere acquaintance thinke more; God, who truely knowes me, knowes that I am nothing, for hee onely beholds me, and all the world, who lookes not on us through a derived ray, or a trajection of a sensible species, but beholds the substance without the helpes of accidents, and the formes of things, as wee their operations.[455] Further, no man can judge another, because no man knowes himselfe, for we censure others but as they disagree from that humour which wee fancy laudable in our selves, and commend others but for that wherein they seeme to quadrate and consent with us. So that in conclusion, all is but that we all condemne, selfe-love. 'Tis the generall complaint of these times, and perhaps of those past, that charity growes cold; which I perceive most verified in those which most doe manifest the fires and flames of zeale; for it is a vertue that best agrees with coldest natures, and such as are complexioned for humility: But how shall we expect charity towards others, when we are uncharitable to our selves? Charity begins at home, is the voyce of the world, yet is every man his greatest enemy, and as it were, his owne executioner. *Non occides*, is the commandement of God, yet scarce observed by any man;[456] for I perceive every man is his owne Atropos, and lends a hand to cut the thred of his owne dayes.[457] Cain was not therefore the first murtherer, but Adam, who brought in death; whereof hee beheld the practise and example in his owne sonne Abel,[458] and saw that verified in the experience of another; which faith could not perswade him in the theory of himselfe.

SECTION 5

There is I thinke no man that apprehends his owne miseries lesse than my selfe, and no man that so neerely apprehends anothers. I could lose an arme without a teare, and with few groans, mee thinkes, be quartered into pieces; yet can I weepe most seriously at a play, and receive with a true passion, the counterfeit griefes of those knowne and professed impostures.[459] It is a barbarous part of inhumanity to adde unto any afflicted parties misery, or endeavour to multiply in any man, a passion, whose single nature is already above his patience; this was the greatest affliction of Job, and those oblique expostulations of his friends a deeper injury than the downe-right blowes of the Devill.[460] It is not the teares of our owne eyes onely, but of our friends also, that doe exhaust the current of our sorrowes, which falling into many streames, runne more peaceably,[461] and is contented with a narrower channel. It is an act within the power of charity, to translate a passion out of one breast into another, and to divide a sorrow almost out of it selfe; for an affliction like a dimension may be so divided, as if not indivisible, at least to become insensible.[462] Now with my friend I desire not to share or participate, but to engrosse his sorrowes,[463] that by making them mine owne, I may more easily discusse them; for in mine owne reason, and within my selfe I can command that, which I cannot entreate without my selfe, and within the circle of another. I have often thought those noble paires and examples of friendship not so truely histories of what had beene, as fictions of what should be, but I now perceive nothing in them, but possibilities, nor any thing in the heroick examples of Damon and Pythias, Achilles and Patroclus,[464] which mee thinkes upon some grounds I could not performe within the narrow compasse of my selfe.[465] That a man should lay down his life for his friend, seemes strange to vulgar affections, and such as confine themselves within that worldly principle, charity beginnes at home. For mine owne part I could never remember the relations that I held unto my selfe, nor the respect that I owe unto mine owne nature, in the cause of God, my country, and my friends. Next to these three, I doe embrace my selfe; I confesse that I doe not observe that order that the schooles ordaine our affections, to love our parents, wifes, children, and then our friends, for excepting the injunctions of religion, I doe not find in my selfe such a necessary and indissoluble sympathy to all those of my bloud. I hope I doe not breake the fifth commandement,[466] if I conceive I may love my friend before the nearest of my bloud, even those to whom I owe the principles of life; I never yet cast a true affection on a woman, but I have loved my friend as I do vertue, my soule, my God.[467] From hence me thinkes I doe conceive how God loves man, what happinesse there is in the love of God. Omitting all other, there are three most mysticall unions; two natures in one person; three persons in one nature; one soule in two bodies.[468] For though indeed they bee really divided, yet are they so united, as they seeme but one, and make rather a duality then two distinct soules.

SECTION 6

There are wonders in true affection, it is a body of *Ænigmaes*, mysteries and riddles, wherein two so become one, as they both become two; I love my friend before my selfe, and yet me thinkes I do not love him enough; some few months hence my multiplyed affection will make me beleeve I have not loved him at all, when I am from him, I am dead till I bee with him, when I am with him, I am not satisfied, but would still be nearer him: united soules are not satisfied with embraces, but desire to be truely each other, which being impossible, their desires are infinite, and must proceed without a possibility of satisfaction. Another misery there is in affection, that whom we truely love like our owne, wee forget their lookes, nor can our memory retaine the idea of their faces; and it is no wonder, for they are our selves, and our affections makes their lookes our owne. This noble affection fals not on vulgar and common constitutions, but on such as are mark'd for vertue; he that can love his friend with this noble ardour, will in a competent degree affect all. Now if wee can bring our affections to looke beyond the body, and cast an eye upon the soule, wee have found out the true object, not onely of friendship but charity; and the greatest happinesse that wee can bequeath the soule, is that wherein we all doe place our last felicity, salvation, which though it bee not in our power to bestow, it is in our charity, and pious invocations to desire, if not procure, and further. I cannot contentedly frame a prayer for my selfe in particular, without a catalogue for my friends, nor request a happinesse wherein my sociable disposition doth not desire the fellowship of my neighbour. I never heare the toll of a passing bell, though in my mirth, without my prayers and best wishes for the departing spirit; I cannot goe to cure the body of my patient, but I forget my profession, and call unto God for his soule; I cannot see one say his prayers, but in stead of imitating him, I fall into a supplication for him, who perhaps is no more to mee than a common nature: and if God hath vouchsafed an eare to my supplications, there are surely many happy that never saw me, and enjoy the blessing of mine unknowne devotions. To pray for enemies, that is, for their salvation, is no harsh precept, but the practise of our daily and ordinary devotions. I cannot beleeve the story of the Italian, our bad wishes and uncharitable desires proceed no further than this life;[469] it is the Devill, and the uncharitable votes of Hell, that desire our misery in the world to come.

SECTION 7

To doe no injury, nor take none, was a principle, which to my former yeares, and impatient affections, seemed to containe enough of morality, but my more setled yeares and Christian constitution have fallen upon severer resolutions. I can hold there is no such thing as injury, that if there be, there is no such injury as revenge, and no such revenge as the contempt of an injury; that to hate another, is to maligne himselfe, that the truest way to love another, is to despise our selves. I were unjust unto mine owne conscience, if I should say I am at variance with any thing like my selfe, I finde there are many pieces in this one fabricke of man; this frame is raised upon a masse of antipathies:[470] I am one mee thinkes, but as the world; wherein notwithstanding there are a swarme of distinct essences, and in them another world of contrarieties; wee carry private and domesticke enemies within, publike and more hostile adversaries without. The Devill that did but buffet Saint Paul, playes mee thinkes at sharpe with me:[471] let mee be nothing if within the compasse of my selfe, I doe not find the battell of Lepanto, passion against reason, reason against faith, faith against the Devill, and my conscience against all.[472] There is another man within mee that's angry with mee, rebukes, commands, and dastards mee.[473] I have no conscience of marble to resist the hammer of more heavie offences, nor yet so soft and waxen, as to take the impression of each single peccadillo or scape of infirmity:[474] I am of a strange beliefe, that it is as easie to be forgiven some sinnes, as to commit some others. For my originall sinne, I hold it to be washed away in my baptisme; for my actuall transgressions, I compute and reckon with God, but from my last repentance, sacrament or generall absolution: and therefore am not terrified with the sinnes or madnesse of my youth. I thanke the goodnesse of God I have no sinnes that want a name, I am not singular in offences, my transgressions are epidemicall, and from the common breath of our corruption.[475] For there are certaine tempers of body, which matcht with an humorous depravity of mind, doe hatch and produce viciosities, whose newnesse and monstrosity of nature admits no name;[476] this was the temper of that lecher that carnald with a statua, and the constitution of Nero in his spintrian recreations.[477] For the Heavens are not onely fruitfull in new and unheard of starres,[478] the earth in plants and animals, but mens minds also in villany and vices; now the dulnesse of my reason, and the vulgarity of my disposition, never prompted my invention, nor sollicited my affection unto any of these; yet even those common and quotidian infirmities that so necessarily attend me,[479] and doe seeme to bee my very nature, have so dejected me, so broken the estimation that I should have otherwise of my self,[480] that I repute my selfe the most abjectest piece of mortality:[481] divines prescribe a fit of sorrow to repentance, there goes indignation, anger, sorrow, hatred, into mine, passions of a contrary nature, which neither seeme to sute with this action, nor my proper constitution. It is no breach of charity to our selves to be at variance with our vices, nor to abhorre that part of us, which is an enemy to the ground of charity, our God; wherein we doe but imitate our great selves the world,[482] whose divided antipathies and contrary faces doe yet carry a charitable regard unto the whole by their particular discords, preserving the common harmony, and keeping in fetters those powers, whose rebellions once masters, might bee the ruine of all.[483]

SECTION 8

I thanke God, amongst those millions of vices I doe inherit and hold from Adam, I have escaped one, and that a mortall enemy to charity, the first and father sin, not only of man, but of the Devil, Pride, a vice whose name is comprehended in a monosyllable, but in its nature not circumscribed with a world;[484] I have escaped it in a condition that can hardly avoid it: those petty acquisitions and reputed perfections that advance and elevate the conceits of other men, adde no feathers unto mine; I have seene a grammarian toure, and plume himselfe over a single line in Horace, and shew more pride in the construction of one ode, than the author in the composure of the whole book.[485] For my owne part, besides the jargon and patois of severall provinces, I understand no lesse then six languages,[486] yet I protest I have no higher conceit of my selfe than had our fathers before the confusion of Babel, when there was but one language in the world, and none to boast himselfe either linguist or criticke. I have not onely seene severall countries, beheld the nature of their climes, the chorography of their provinces, topography of their cities,[487] but understood their severall lawes, customes and policies; yet cannot all this perswade the dulnesse of my spirit unto such an opinion of my self, as I behold in nimbler and conceited heads, that never looked a degree beyond their nests. I know the names, and somewhat more, of all the constellations in my horizon, yet I have seene a prating mariner that could onely name the poynters and the north starre, out-talke mee, and conceit himselfe a whole spheare above mee.[488] I know most of the plants of my country and of those about mee; yet me thinkes I do not know so many as when I did but know an hundred, and had scarcely ever simpled further than Cheap-side:[489] for indeed heads of capacity, and such as are not full with a handfull, or easie measure of knowledg, thinke they know nothing, till they know all, which being impossible, they fall upon the opinion of Socrates, and onely know they know not any thing.[490] I cannot thinke that Homer pin'd away upon the riddle of the fisherman,[491] or that Aristotle, who understood the uncertainty of knowledge, and confessed so often the reason of man too weake for the workes of nature, did ever drowne himselfe upon the flux and reflux of Euripus:[492] we doe but learne to day, what our better advanced judgements will unteach to morrow: and Aristotle doth but instruct us as Plato did him; that is, to confute himselfe. I have runne through all sorts, yet finde no rest in any, though our first studies and junior endeavors may stile us Peripateticks, Stoicks, or Academicks, yet I perceive the wisest heads prove at last, almost all Scepticks, and stand like Janus in the field of knowledge.[493] I have therefore one common and authentick philosophy I learned in the schooles, whereby I discourse and satisfie the reason of other men, another more reserved and drawne from experience, whereby I content mine owne. Solomon that complained of ignorance in the height of knowledge, hath not onely humbled my conceits, but discouraged my endeavours.[494] There is yet another conceit that hath sometimes made me shut my bookes; which tels mee it is a vanity to waste our dayes in the blind pursuit of knowledge, it is but attending a little longer, and wee shall enjoy that by instinct and infusion which we endeavour at here by labour and inquisition: it is better to sit downe in a modest ignorance, and rest contented with the naturall blessing of our owne reasons, then buy the uncertaine knowledge of this life, with sweat and vexation, which death gives every foole gratis, and is an accessary of our glorification.

SECTION 9

I was never yet once, and commend not their resolutions who never marry twice,[495] not that I disallow of second marriage; as neither in all cases of polygamy, which considering some times and the unequall number of both sexes may bee also necessary. The whole world was made for man, but the twelfth part of man for woman:[496] man is the whole world and the breath of God, woman the rib and crooked piece of man.[497] I could be content[498] that we might procreate like trees, without conjunction, or that there were any way to perpetuate the world without this triviall and vulgar way of coition; it is the foolishest act a wise man commits in all his life, nor is there any thing that will more deject his imagination coold, when hee shall consider what an odde and unworthy piece of folly hee hath committed; I speake not in prejudice, nor am averse from that sweet sexe, but naturally amorous of all that is beautifull; I can looke a whole day with delight upon a handsome picture, though it be but of an horse.[499] It is my temper, and I like it the better, to affect all harmony, and sure there is musicke even in the beauty, and the silent note which Cupid strikes, farre sweeter than the sound of an instrument. For there is a musicke where-ever there is a harmony, order or proportion; and thus farre we may maintain the musick of the spheares;[500] for those well ordered motions, and regular paces, though they give no sound unto the eare, yet to the understanding they strike a note most full of harmony. Whatsoever is harmonically composed, delights in harmony; which makes me much distrust the symmetry of those heads which declaime against all church musicke.[501] For my selfe, not only from my obedience but my particular genius, I doe imbrace it; for even that vulgar and taverne musicke, which makes one man merry, another mad, strikes in mee a deepe fit of devotion, and a profound contemplation of the first composer,[502] there is something in it of divinity more than the eare discovers. It is an hieroglyphicall and shadowed lesson of the whole world, and creatures of God, such a melody to the eare, as the whole world well understood, would afford the understanding. In briefe, it is a sensible fit of that harmony,[503] which intellectually sounds in the eares of

God.[504] I will not say with Plato, the soule is an harmony, but harmonicall, and hath its neerest sympathy unto musicke:[505] thus some, whose temper of body agrees, and humours the constitution of their soules, are borne poets, though indeed all are naturally inclined unto rhythme. This made Tacitus in the very first line of his story, fall upon a verse*;[506] and Cicero, the worst of poets, but declayming for a poet, falls in the very first sentence upon a perfect Hexameter†.[507] I feele not in me those sordid, and unchristian desires of my profession,[508] I doe not secretly implore and wish for plagues, rejoyce at famines, revolve ephemerides, and almanacks, in expectation of malignant aspects, fatall conjunctions, and eclipses:[509] I rejoyce not at unwholsome springs, nor unseasonable winters; my prayer goes with the husbandmans;[510] I desire every thing in its proper season, that neither men nor the times bee out of temper. Let mee be sicke my selfe, if sometimes the malady of my patient be not a disease unto me, I desire rather to cure his infirmities than my own necessities; where I do him no good me thinkes it is scarce honest gaine, though I confesse 'tis but the worthy salary of our well-intended endeavours: I am not onely ashamed, but heartily sorry, that besides death, there are diseases incurable, yet not for my own sake, or that they be beyond my art, but for the general cause and sake of humanity whose common cause I apprehend as mine own: and to speak more generally, those three noble professions which all civil common wealths doe honour, are raised upon the fall of Adam, and are not any exempt from their infirmities; there are not onely diseases incurable in physicke, but cases indissoluble in lawes, vices incorrigible in divinity: if general councells may erre, I doe not see why particular courts should be infallible, their perfectest rules are raised upon the erroneous reasons of man, and the lawes of one, doe but condemn the rules of another; as Aristotle oft-times the opinions of his predecessours, because, though agreeable to reason, yet were not consonant to his owne rules, and the logicke of his proper principles. Againe, to speake nothing of the sinne against the Holy Ghost, whose cure not onely, but whose nature is unknowne;[511] I can cure the gout or stone in some, sooner than divinity, pride, or avarice in others. I can cure vices by physicke, when they remaine incurable by divinity, and shall obey my pils, when they contemne their precepts.[512] I boast nothing, but plainely say, we all labour against our owne cure, for death is the cure of all diseases. There is no Catholicon or

* *Urbem Romam in principio Reges habuere.*

† *In qua me non inficior mediocriter esse.*

universall remedy I know but this, which though nauseous to queasie stomachs, yet to prepared appetites is nectar and a pleasant potion of immortality.

SECTION 10

For my conversation, it is like the sunne's with all men; and with a friendly aspect to good and bad. Me thinkes there is no man bad, and the worst, best; that is, while they are kept within the circle of those qualities, wherein they are good: there is no mans minde of such discordant and jarring a temper to which a tuneable disposition may not strike a harmony. *Magnæ virtutes nec minora vitia*, it is the posie of the best natures, and may bee inverted on the worst;[513] there are in the most depraved and venemous dispositions, certaine pieces that remaine untoucht; which by an antiperistasis become more excellent,[514] or by the excellency of their antipathies are able to preserve themselves from the contagion of their enemy vices, and persist entire beyond the generall corruption. For it is also thus in natures. The greatest balsames doe lie enveloped in the bodies of most powerfull corrosives;[515] I say moreover, and I ground upon experience, that poysons containe within themselves their own antidote, and that which preserves them from the venom of themselves; without which they were not deletorious to others onely, but to themselves also.[516] But it is the corruption that I feare within me, not the contagion of commerce without me. 'Tis that unruly regiment within me that will destroy me, 'tis I that doe infect my selfe, the man without a navell yet lives in me;[517] I feele that originall canker corrode and devoure me, and therefore *defenda me Dios de me*, Lord deliver me from my selfe, is a part of my Letany, and the first voyce of my retired imaginations. There is no man alone, because every man is a microcosme, and carries the whole world about him; *nunquam minus solus quam cum solus*, though it bee the apophthegme of a wise man, is yet true in the mouth of a foole;[518] for indeed, though in a wildernesse, a man is never alone, not onely because hee is with himselfe, and his owne thoughts, but because he is with the Devill, who ever consorts with our solitude, and is that unruly rebell that musters up those disordered motions, which accompany our sequestred imaginations: and to speake more narrowly, there is no such thing as solitude, nor any thing that can be said to be alone, and by it selfe, but God, who is his owne circle, and can subsist by himselfe, all others besides their dissimilary and heterogeneous parts, which in a manner multiply their natures, cannot subsist without the concourse of God, and the society of that hand which doth uphold their natures.[519] In briefe, there can be nothing truely alone, and by its self, which is not truely one, and such is onely God: all others doe transcend an unity, and so by consequence are many.

SECTION 11

Now for my life, it is a miracle of thirty yeares, which to relate, were not a history, but a peece of poetry, and would sound to common eares like a fable; for the world, I count it not an inne, but an hospitall, and a place, not to live, but to die in. The world that I regard is my selfe, it is the microcosme of mine owne frame, that I cast mine eye on; for the other, I use it but like my globe, and turne it round sometimes for my recreation. Men that look upon my outside, perusing onely my condition, and fortunes, do erre in my altitude; for I am above Atlas his shoulders.[520] The earth is a point not onely in respect of the Heavens above us, but of that heavenly and celestiall part within us: that masse of flesh that circumscribes me, limits not my mind: that surface that tells the Heavens it hath an end, cannot perswade me I have any; I take my circle to be above three hundred and sixty, though the number of the Arke do measure my body, it comprehendeth not my minde:[521] whilst I study to finde how I am a microcosme or little world, I finde my selfe something more than the great. There is surely a piece of Divinity in us, something that was before the elements, and owes no homage unto the sun.[522] Nature tels me I am the Image of God as well as Scripture;[523] he that understands not thus much, hath not his introduction or first lesson, and is yet to begin the alphabet of man. Let me not injure the felicity of others, if I say I am as happy as any;[524] *Ruat cœlum Fiat voluntas tua*, salveth all;[525] so that whatsoever happens, it is but what our daily prayers desire. In briefe, I am content, and what should providence adde more? Surely this is it we call happinesse, and this doe I enjoy, with this I am happy in a dreame, and as content to enjoy a happinesse in a fancie as others in a more apparent truth and reality. There is surely a neerer apprehension of any thing that delights us in our dreames, than in our waked senses;[526] without this I were unhappy, for my awaked judgement discontents me, ever whispering unto me, that I am from my friend, but my friendly dreames in the night requite me, and make me thinke I am within his armes. I thanke God for my happy dreames, as I doe for my good rest, for there is a satisfaction in them unto reasonable desires, and such as can be content with a fit of happinesse; and surely it is not a melancholy conceite to thinke we are all asleepe in this world, and that the conceits of this life are as meare dreames to those of the next, as the phantasmes of the night, to the conceit of the day.[527] There is an equall delusion in both, and the one doth but seeme to bee the embleme or picture of the other; we are somewhat more than our selves in our sleepes, and the slumber of the body seemes to bee but the waking of the soule. It is the ligation of sense, but the liberty of reason, and our awaking conceptions doe not match the fancies of our sleepes. At my nativity, my ascendant was the watery signe of Scorpius;[528] I was borne in the planetary houre of Saturne, and I think I have a piece of that leaden planet in me.[529] I am no way facetious, nor disposed for the mirth and galliardize of company,[530] yet in one dreame I can compose a whole comedy, behold the action, apprehend the jests, and laugh my self awake at the conceits thereof; were my memory as faithfull as my reason is then fruitfull, I would never study but in my dreames, and this time also would I chuse for my devotions, but our grosser memories have then so little hold of our abstracted understandings, that they forget the story, and can only relate to our awaked soules, a confused and broken tale of that that hath passed. Aristotle, who hath written a singular tract of sleepe, hath not me thinkes throughly defined it, nor yet Galen, though hee seeme to have corrected it;[531] for those *noctambuloes* and night-walkers, though in their sleepe, doe yet enjoy the action of their senses: we must therefore say that there is something in us that is not in the jurisdiction of Morpheus;[532] and that those abstracted and ecstaticke soules doe walke about in their owne corps, as spirits with the bodies they assume, wherein they seeme to heare, see, and feele, though indeed the organs are destitute of sense, and their natures of those faculties that should informe them. Thus it is observed that men sometimes upon the houre of their departure, doe speake and reason above themselves. For then the soule begins to bee freed from the ligaments of the body, begins to reason like her selfe, and to discourse in a straine above mortality.

SECTION 12

We tearme sleepe a death, and yet it is waking that kils us, and destroyes those spirits that are the house of life.[533] 'Tis indeed a part of life that best expresseth death, for every man truely lives so long as hee acts his nature, or someway makes good the faculties of himselfe: Themistocles therefore that slew his souldier in his sleepe was a mercifull executioner, 'tis a kinde of punishment the mildnesse of no lawes hath invented;[534] I wonder the fancy of Lucan and Seneca did not discover it.[535] It is that death by which we may be literally said to die daily, a death which Adam died before his mortality;[536] a death whereby we live a middle and moderating point between life and death; in fine, so like death, I dare not trust it without my prayers, and an halfe adiew unto the world,[537] and take my farewell in a colloquy with God.

The night is come like to the day,
Depart not thou great God away.
Let not my sinnes, blacke as the night,
Eclipse the lustre of thy light.
Keepe still in my Horizon, for to me,
The sunne makes not the day, but thee.
Thou whose nature cannot sleepe,
On my temples centry keepe;[538]
Guard me 'gainst those watchfull foes,
Whose eyes are open while mine close.
Let no dreames my head infest,
But such as Jacobs temples blest.[539]
While I doe rest, my soule advance,
Make my sleepe a holy trance:
That I may, my rest being wrought,
Awake into some holy thought.
And with as active vigour runne
My course, as doth the nimble sunne.
Sleepe is a death, O make me try,
By sleeping what it is to die.
And as gently lay my head
On my grave, as now my bed.
How ere I rest, great God let me
Awake againe at last with thee.

And thus assur'd, behold I lie
Securely, or to wake or die.
These are my drowsie dayes, in vaine
I doe now wake to sleepe againe.
O come that houre, when I shall never
Sleepe againe, but wake for ever!

This is the dormitive I take to bedward, I need no other laudanum than this to make me sleepe;[540] after which I close mine eyes in security, content to take my leave of the sunne, and sleepe unto the resurrection.

SECTION 13

The method I should use in distributive justice, I often observe in commutative, and keepe a geometricall proportion in both, whereby becomming equable to others, I become unjust to my selfe, and supererogate in that common principle, doe unto others as thou wouldest be done unto thy selfe.[541] I was not borne unto riches, neither is it I thinke my starre to be wealthy;[542] or if it were, the freedome of my minde, and franknesse of my disposition, were able to contradict and crosse my fates: for to me avarice seemes not so much a vice, as a deplorable piece of madnesse; to conceive our selves urinals, or bee perswaded that we are dead, is not so ridiculous, nor so many degrees beyond the power of hellebore, as this.[543] The opinions of theory and positions of men are not so voyd of reason as their practised conclusion: some have held that snow is blacke, that the earth moves, that the soule is ayre, fire, water,[544] but all this is philosophy, and there is no delirium, if we doe but speculate the folly and indisputable dotage of avarice to that subterraneous Idoll, and God of the earth.[545] I doe confesse I am an atheist, I cannot perswade my selfe to honour that the world adores;[546] whatsoever vertue its prepared substance may have within my body, it hath no influence nor operation without;[547] I would not entertaine a base designe, or an action that should call mee villaine, for the Indies, and for this onely doe I love and honour my owne soule, and have mee thinkes, two armes too few to embrace my selfe. Aristotle is too severe, that will not allow us to bee truely liberall without wealth, and the bountifull hand of fortune;[548] if this be true, I must confesse I am charitable onely in my liberall intentions, and bountifull well-wishes. But if the example of the mite bee not onely an act of wonder, but an example of the noblest charity, surely poore men may also build hospitals, and the rich alone have not erected cathedralls.[549] I have a private method which others observe not, I take the opportunity of my selfe to do good, I borrow occasion of charity from mine owne necessities, and supply the wants of others, when I am in most neede my selfe;[550] for it is an honest stratagem to take advantage of our selves, and so to husband the act of vertue, that where they are defective in one circumstance, they may repay their want, and multiply their goodnesse in another. I have not Peru in my desires, but a competence, and abilitie to performe those good workes to which hee hath inclined my nature.[551] Hee is rich, who hath enough to bee charitable, and it is hard to bee so poore, that a noble minde may not finde a way to this piece of goodnesse. *Hee that giveth to the poore lendeth to the Lord*;[552] there is more rhetorick in that one sentence than in a library of sermons, and indeed if those sentences were understood by the reader, with the same emphasis as they are delivered by the author, we needed not those volumes of instructions, but might bee honest by an epitome. Upon this motive onely I cannot behold a begger without relieving his necessities with my purse, or his soule with my prayers; these scenicall and accidentall differences[553] between us cannot make mee forget that common and untoucht part of us both; there is under these *Centoes* and miserable outsides,[554] these mutilate and semi-bodies, a soule of the same alloy with our owne, whose genealogy is God as well as ours, and in as faire a way to salvation, as our selves. Statists that labour to contrive a common-wealth without poverty, take away the object of charity, not understanding only the common-wealth of a Christian, but forgetting the prophecy of Christ.[555]

SECTION 14

Now there is another part of charity, which is the basis and pillar of this, and that is the love of God, for whom we love our neighbour: for this I thinke charity, to love God for himselfe, and our neighbour for God. All that is truely amiable is God, or as it were a divided piece of him, that retaines a reflex or shadow of himselfe. Nor is it strange that we should place affection on that which is invisible, all that we truely love is thus, what we adore under affection of our senses, deserves not the honour of so pure a title. Thus wee adore vertue, though to the eyes of sense shee bee invisible. Thus that part of our noble friends that wee love, is not that part that we embrace, but that insensible part that our armes cannot embrace. God being all goodnesse, can love nothing but himselfe, hee loves us but for that part which is as it were himselfe, and the traduction of his holy spirit.[556] Let us call to assize the loves of our parents, the affection of our wives and children, and they are all dumbe showes, and dreames, without reality, truth, or constancy;[557] for first there is a strong bond of affection between us and our parents, yet how easily dissolved? We betake our selves to a woman, forgetting our mothers in a wife, and the wombe that bare us in that that shall beare our image. This woman blessing us with children, our affection leaves the levell it held before, and sinkes from our bed unto our issue and picture of posterity, where affection holds no steady mansion. They growing up in yeares desire our ends, or applying themselves to a woman, take a lawfull way to love another better than our selves. Thus I perceive a man may bee buried alive, and behold his grave in his owne issue.

SECTION 15

I conclude therefore and say, there is no happinesse under (or as Copernicus will have it, above) the sunne,[558] nor any crambe in that repeated veritie and burthen of all the wisedome of Solomon, *all is vanitie and vexation of spirit*;[559] there is no felicity in that the world adores. Aristotle whilst hee labours to refute the Ideas of Plato, fals upon one himselfe: for his *summum bonum*, is a chimæra, and there is no such thing as his felicity.[560] That wherein God himselfe is happy, the holy angels are happy, in whose defect the Devils are unhappy; that dare I call happinesse: whatsoever conduceth unto this, may with an easie metaphor deserve that name; whatsoever else the world termes happines, is to me a story out of Pliny, an apparition, or neat delusion, wherin there is no more of happinesse than the name.[561] Blesse mee in this life with but the peace of my conscience, command of my affections, the love of thy selfe and my dearest friends, and I shall be happy enough to pity Cæsar. These are O Lord the humble desires of my most reasonable ambition and all I dare call happinesse on earth: wherein I set no rule or limit to thy hand or providence, dispose of me according to the wisedome of thy pleasure. Thy will bee done, though in my owne undoing.[562]

Finis.

Prefatory Material to Religio Medici

To such as have, or shall peruse the observations upon a former corrupt copy of this booke.

There are some men that Politian speakes of, *Cui quam recta manus, tam fuit et facilis:*[563] and it seemes the authour to the observations upon this book would arrogate as much to himselfe; for they were by his owne confession, but the conceptions of one night; a hasty birth; and so it proves: for what is really controulable, he generally omitteth; and what is false upon the error of the copy, he doth not alwaies take notice of; and wherein he would contradict, he mistaketh, or traduceth the intention, and (besides a parenthesis sometimes upon the authour) onely medleth with those points from whence he takes a hint to deliver his prepar'd conceptions: but the grosse of his booke is made out by discourses collaterall, and digressions of his owne, not at all emergent from this discourse; which is easily perceptible unto the intelligent reader. Thus much I thought good to let thee understand, without the authours knowledge, who slighting the refute, hath inforcedly published (as a sufficient confutation) his owne booke; and in this I shall not make so bold with him, as the observator hath done with that noble knight, whose name he hath wrongfully prefixed, as I am informed, to his slight animadversions; but I leave him to repentance, and thee to thy satisfaction.

Farewell.

Yours, A. B.

Pſeudodoxia Epidemica:

OR,

ENQUIRIES

INTO

Very many received

TENENTS,

And commonly preſumed

TRUTHS.

By THOMAS BROVVNE Dr. of Phyſick.

IUL. SCALIG.

Ex Libris colligere quæ prodiderunt Authores longe eſt periculoſiſſimum; Rerum ipſarum cognitio vera è rebus ipſis eſt.

LONDON,

Printed by *T. H.* for *Edward Dod*, and are to be ſold in *Ivie Lane*. 1646.

FIG. 3 Title page from *Pseudodoxia Epidemica* (1646).[1]

THOMAS BROWNE, *PSEUDODOXIA EPIDEMICA, OR, ENQUIRIES INTO VERY MANY RECEIVED TENENTS AND COMMONLY PRESUMED TRUTHS.* 1646

March the 14th 1645.

I have perused these learned animadversions upon the common tenets and opinions of men in former and in these present times, entituled *Pseudodoxia Epidemica*; and finding them much transcending vulgar conceipt, and adorned with great variety of matter, and multiplicity of reading; I approve them as very worthy to be printed and published.

John Downame.

To the reader

Would truth dispense, we could be content, with Plato, that knowledge were but remembrance; that intellectuall acquisition were but reminiscentiall evocation, and new impressions but the colourishing of old stamps which stood pale in the soul before.[2] For, what is worse, knowledge is made by oblivion; and to purchase a clear and warrantable body of truth, we must forget and part with much wee know. Our tender enquiries taking up learning at large, and together with true and assured notions, receiving many, wherein our renewing judgements doe finde no satisfaction;[3] and therefore in this encyclopædie and round of knowledge, like the great and exemplary wheeles of heaven, wee must observe two circles: that while we are daily carried about, and whirled on by the swindge and rapt of the one, wee may maintaine a naturall and proper course, in the slow and sober wheele of the other.[4] And this wee shall more readily performe, if we timely survey our knowledge; impartially singling out those encroachments, which junior compliance and popular credulity hath admitted. Whereof at present wee have endeavoured a long and serious *Adviso*; proposing not onely a large and copious list, but from experience and reason, attempting their decisions.[5]

And first wee crave exceeding pardon in the audacity of the attempt; humbly acknowledging a worke of such concernment unto truth, and difficulty in it selfe, did well deserve the conjunction of many heads: and surely more advantageous had it beene unto truth, to have fallen into the endeavours of some cooperating advancers, that might have performed it to the life, and added authority thereto: which the privacie of our condition, and unequall abilities cannot expect.[6] Whereby notwithstanding wee have not beene diverted, nor have our solitary attempts beene so discouraged, as to despaire the favourable looke of learning upon our single and unsupported endeavours.

Nor have wee let fall our penne, upon discouragement of contradiction, unbeleefe, and difficulty of disswasion from radicated beliefs, and points of high prescription; although we are very sensible how hardly teaching yeares do learn;[7] what roots old age contracteth into errours, and how such as are but twigges in younger dayes,[8] grow oaks in our elder heads, and become inflexible unto the powerfullest arme of reason. Although we have also beheld, what cold requitals others have found in their severall redemptions of truth; and how their ingenuous enquiries have been dismissed with censure, and obloquie of singularities.[9]

Some consideration we hope from the course of our profession,[10] which though it leadeth us into many truths that passe undiscerned by others, yet doth it disturbe their communications, and much interrupteth the office of our pens in their well intended transmissions: and therefore surely in this worke attempts will exceed performances: it being composed by snatches of time, as medicall vacations, and the fruitlesse importunity of uroscopy* would permit us.[11] And therefore also perhaps it hath not found that regular and constant stile, those infallible experiments, and those assured determinations, which the subject sometime requireth, and might be expected from others, whose quiet doors and unmolested hours afford no such distractions. Although who shall indifferently perpend the exceeding difficulty, which either the obscurity of the subject, or unavoidable paradoxologie must often put upon the attemptor, will easily discerne, a worke of this nature is not to bee performed upon one legge, and should smell of oyle if duly and deservedly handled.[12]

* inspection of urines.

Our first intentions considering the common interest of truth, resolved to propose it unto the Latine republike and equall judges of Europe; but owing in the first place this service unto our country, and therein especially unto its ingenuous gentry, we have declared our selfe in a language best conceived.[13] Although I confesse, the quality of the subject will sometimes carry us into expressions beyond meere English apprehensions; and indeed, if elegancie still proceedeth, and English pennes maintaine that stream wee have of late observed to flow from many, wee shall within few yeares bee faine to learne Latine to understand English, and a work will prove of equall facility in either. Nor have wee addressed our penne or stile unto the people, (whom bookes doe not redresse, and are this way incapable of reduction) but unto the knowing and leading part of learning; as well understanding (at least probably hoping) except they be watered from higher regions, and fructifying meteors of knowledge, these weeds must lose their alimentall sappe and wither of themselves; whose conserving influence, could our endeavors prevent, wee should trust the rest unto the sythe of time, and hopefull dominion of truth.[14]

Wee hope it will not bee unconsidered, that wee finde no open tract, or constant manuduction in this labyrinth;[15] but are oft-times faine to wander in the America and untravelled parts of truth: for though not many years past, Dr. Primrose hath made a learned and full Discourse of Vulgar Errors in Physick, yet have we discussed but two or three thereof.[16] Laurentius Joubertus, by the same title led our expectation into thoughts of great releef; whereby notwithstanding we reaped no advantage; it answering scarce at all the promise of the inscription.[17] Nor perhaps (if it were yet extant) should wee finde any farther assistance from that ancient peece of Andreas, pretending the same title.[18] And therefore wee are often constrained to stand alone against the strength of opinion; and to meet the Goliah and Gyant of authority, with contemptible pibbles, and feeble arguments, drawne from the scrip and slender stocke of our selves.[19] Nor have wee indeed scarce named any author whose name we doe not honour; and if detraction could invite us, discretion surely would containe us from any derogatory intention, where highest pennes and friendiest eloquence must faile in commendation.

And therefore also wee cannot but hope the equitable considerations and candour of reasonable mindes. We cannot expect the frowne of theologie herein; nor can they which behold the present state of things, and controversie of points so long received in divinity, condemne our sober enquiries in the doubtfull appertinancies of arts, and receptaries of philosophy.[20] Surely philologers and criticall discoursers, who look beyond the shell and obvious exteriours of things, will not be angry with our narrower explorations. And wee cannot doubt, our brothers in physicke (whose knowledge in naturals will lead them into a nearer apprehension of many things delivered) will friendly accept, if not countenance our endeavours.[21] Nor can we conceive it may be unwelcome unto those honoured worthies, who endeavour the advancement of learning:[22] as being likely to finde a clearer progression, when so many rubbes are levelled, and many untruths taken off, which passing as principles with common beliefes, disturb the tranquility of axiomes, which otherwise might bee raysed.[23] And wise men cannot but know, that arts and learning want this expurgation: and if the course of truth bee permitted unto its selfe, like that of time and uncorrected computations, it cannot escape many errours, which duration still enlargeth.[24]

Lastly, wee are not magisteriall in opinions, nor have wee dictator-like obtruded our conceptions, but in the humility of enquiries or disquisitions, have only proposed them unto more ocular discerners.[25] And therefore opinions are free, and open it is for any to thinke or declare the contrary. And wee shall so farre encourage contradiction, as to promise no disturbance, or reoppose any penne, that shall elenchically[26] refute us, that shall onely lay hold of our lapses, single out digressions, corollaries, or ornamentall conceptions, to evidence his own in as indifferent truths.[27] And shall only take notice of such, whose experimentall and judicious knowledge shall solemnly looke upon it; not onely to destroy of ours, but to establish of his owne, not to traduce or extenuate, but to explaine, and dilucidate, to adde and ampliate, according to the laudable custome of the ancients in their sober promotions of learning.[28] Unto whom notwithstanding, wee shall not contentiously rejoyne, or onely to justifie our owne, but to applaud or confirme his maturer assertions; and shall conferre what is in us unto his name and honour. Ready to bee swallowed in any worthy enlarger: as having acquired our end, if any way, or under any name wee may obtaine a worke, so much desired, at least, desiderated of truth.[29]

T. B.

A TABLE OF THE CONTENTS.

Chap. 4. *Of bodies electricall in generall. Of jet and amber in particular, that they attract all light bodies, except basil and bodies oyled.*

Chap. 5. *Compendiously of severall other tenents.*

That a diamond is made soft, or broke by the blood of a goate.

That glasse is poyson.

Of the cordiall quality of gold in substance or decoction.

That a pot full of ashes will containe as much water as it would without them.

Of white powder that kils without report.

That corall is soft under water, but hardeneth in the ayre.

That porcellane or china dishes lye under the earth an hundred yeares in preparation, with some others.

Chap. 6. *Of sundry tenents concerning vegetables.*

That the roote of mandrakes resembleth the shape of man.

That they naturally grow under gallowes and places of execution.

That the roote gives a shreeke upon eradication.

That it is fatall or dangerous to dig them up.

That cinnamon, ginger, cloves, mace, are but the parts or fruits of the same tree.

That misseltoe is bred upon trees, from seeds which birds let fall thereon.

Of the Rose of Jerico that flowreth every yeare upon Christmas Eve.

That Sferra Cavallo hath a power to breake or loosen iron.

That bayes preserve from the mischiefe of lightning and thunder.

That bitter almonds are preservatives against ebriety, with some others.

Chap. 7: *Of some insects and the properties of several plants*

THE THIRD BOOK.

Of popular and received tenents concerning animals.

Chap. 1. *That an elephant hath no joynts.*

Chap. 2. *That an horse hath no gall.*

Chap. 3. *That a pigeon hath no gall.*
Chap. 4. *That a bever to escape the hunter bites off his testicles or stones.*
Chap. 5. *That a badger hath the legs of one side shorter then of the other.*
Chap. 6. *That a beare brings forth her cubs informous or unshaped.*
Chap. 7. *Of the basilisk.*
Chap. 8. *That a wolfe first seeing a man begets a dumbnesse in him.*
Chap. 9. *Of the long life of deere*
Chap. 10. *That a kingsfisher hanged by the bill sheweth where the winde is.*
Chap. 11. *Of gryphins.*
Chap. 12. *Of the phœnix.*
Chap. 13. *Of the pissing of toads, of the stone in their head, and of the generation of frogs.*
Chap. 14. *That a salamander lives in the fire.*
Chap. 15. *Of the amphisbæna or serpent with two heads moving either way.*
Chap. 16. *That young vipers force their way through the bowels of their dam.*
Chap. 17. *That hares are both male and female.*
Chap. 18. *That moles are blinde and have no eyes.*
Chap. 19. *That lampries have many eyes.*
Chap. 20. *That snayles have two eyes, and at the ends of their hornes.*
Chap. 21. *That the chamæleon lives onely by aire.*
Chap. 22. *That the ostridge digesteth iron.*
Chap. 23. *Of the unicornes horne.*
Chap. 24. *That all animals in the land are in their kinde in the sea.*
Chap. 25. *Concerning the common course of Diet, in making choice of some Animals and abstaining from eating others.*
Chap. 26. *Of Sperma-Ceti and the Sperma-Ceti Whale*
Chap. 27. *Compendiously of some others.*
Of the musicall note of swans before their death.
That the flesh of peacocks corrupteth not.

THE FOURTH BOOK.

Of many popular and received tenents concerning man.

THE FIFTH BOOK.

Of many things questionable as they are described in pictures.

Of the picture of sun, moone, and the winds.
Of the sun dancing on Easter day.
Of the silly howe or covering about some childrens heads.
Of being drunk once a month.
Of the appearing of the devill with a cloven hoofe.
Of Moses his rod in the discovery of mines.
Of discovering of doubtfull matters by hooke or staffe.

THE SIXTH BOOK.
Concerning sundry tenents geographicall and historicall.

Chap. 1. *Concerning the beginning of the world that the time thereof is not precisely knowne, as commonly it is presumed.*
Chap. 2. *Of mens enquiries in what season or point of the zodiack it began, that as they are generally made they are in vaine, and as particularly, incertaine.*
Chap. 3. *Of the divisions of the seasons and foure quarters of the yeare, according unto astronomers and physitians, that the common compute of the ancients, and which is still retained by some, is very questionable.*
Chap. 4. *Of some computation of dayes, and diductions of one part of the yeare unto another.*
Chap. 5. *A digression of the wisdome of God in the site and motion of the Sunne.*
Chap. 6. *Concerning the vulgar opinion that the earth was slenderly peopled before the floud.*
Chap. 7. *Of east and west, and properties respectively ascribed unto countries.*
Chap. 8. *Of the seven heads of Nile.*
Of the greatnesse of Nile.
Of its inundation and certaine time thereof.
That it never rayneth in Aegypt, etc.
Chap. 9. *Of the Red Sea.*
Chap. 10. *Of the blacknesse of Negroes.*
Chap. 11. *Of the same.*
Chap. 12. *A digression of blacknesse.*
Chap. 13. *Of Gypsies.*

THE SEVENTH BOOK.

Concerning many historicall tenents generally received, and some deduced from the history of holy Scripture.

THE FIRST BOOK: OR, GENERALL PART

CHAPTER I
Of the Causes of Common Errors

The first and father cause of common error, is the common infirmity of humane nature; of whose deceptible condition, although perhaps there should not need any other eviction, then the frequent errors, we shall our selves commit, even in the expresse declarement hereof: yet shall wee illustrate the same from more infallible constitutions, and persons presumed as farre from us in condition, as time, that is our first and ingenerated forefathers, from whom as we derive our being, and the severall wounds of constitution, so may wee in some manner excuse our infirmities in the depravity of those parts, whose traductions were pure in them, and their originalls but once removed from God.[30] Yet notwithstanding (if posterity may take leave to judge of the fact, as they are assured, to suffer in the punishment) were grossely deceived in their perfection, and so weakly deluded in the clarity of their understanding, that it hath left no small obscurity in ours, how error should gaine upon them.[31]

For first, they were deceived by Satan, and that not in an invisible insinuation, but an open and discoverable apparition; that is, in the form of a serpent; whereby although there were many occasions of suspition, and such as could not easily escape a weaker circumspection, yet did the unwary apprehension of Eve take no advantage thereof.[32] It hath therefore seemed strange unto some, shee should be deluded by a serpent, or subject her reason unto a beast of the field, which God had subjected unto hers. It hath empuzzeled the enquiries of others to apprehend, and enforced them unto strange conceptions, to make out how without feare or doubt she could discourse with such a creature, or heare a serpent speake, without suspition of imposture. The wits of others, have been so bold as to accuse her simplicity in receiving his temptation so coldly, and when such specious effects of the fruit were promised, as to make them like gods, not to desire, at least not to wonder he pursued not that benefit himselfe; and had it been their owne case would perhaps have replied, If the taste of this fruit maketh the eaters like gods, why remainest thou a beast? If it maketh us but like gods, we are so already. If thereby our eyes shall be opened hereafter, they are at present quicke enough to discover thy deceit, and we desire them no opener to behold our owne shame. If to know good and evill be our advantage, although we have free will unto both, wee desire to performe but one, we know 'tis good to obey the commandement of God, but evill if we transgresse it.

They were deceived by one another, and in the greatest disadvantage of delusion, that is the stronger by the weaker: for Eve presented the fruit, and Adam received it from her. Thus the serpent was cunning enough to begin the deceit in the weaker; and the weaker of strength, sufficient to consummate the fraud in the stronger. Art and fallacy was used unto her, a naked offer proved sufficient unto him: so his superstruction was his ruin, and the fertility of his sleep, an issue of death unto him.[33] And although the condition of sex and posterity of creation might somewhat extenuate the error of the woman: yet was it very strange and inexcusable in the man, especially if as some affirme, he was the wisest of all men since, or if as others have conceived, he was not ignorant of the fall of the angels, and had thereby example and punishment to deterre him.

They were deceived from themselves, and their owne apprehensions, for Eve either mistooke or traduced the commandement of God.[34] Of every tree of the garden thou maiest freely eat, but of the tree of knowledge of good and evill thou shalt not eat, for in the day thou eatest thereof, thou shalt surely dye.[35] Now Eve upon the question of the serpent returned the precept in different tearmes, You shall not eat of it, neither shall you touch it lest perhaps you dye. In which delivery, there were no lesse then two mistakes, or rather additionall mendacites; for the commandement forbids not the touch of the fruit, and positively said ye shall surely dye, but she extenuating replied, *ne forte moriamini*, lest perhaps ye dye.[36] For so in the vulgar translation it runneth, and so is it expressed in the Thargum or Paraphrase of Jonathan.[37] And therefore although it be said, and that very truly that the divell was a liar from the beginning, yet was the woman herein the first expresse beginner, and falsified twice before the replye of Satan, and therefore also to speak strictly, the sin of the fruit was not the first offence, they first transgressed the rule of their own reason, and after the commandement of God.

They were deceived through the conduct of their senses, and by temptations from the object it selfe, whereby although their intellectualls had not failed in the theorie of truth, yet did the inservient and brutall faculties controle the suggestion of reason: pleasure and profit already overswaying the instructions of honesty, and sensuallity perturbing the reasonable commands of vertue.[38] For so is it delivered in the text; that when the woman saw that the tree was good for food, and that it was pleasant unto the eye, and a tree to be desired to make one wise, she tooke of the fruit thereof and did eat. Now hereby it appeareth, that Eve before the fall, was by the same and beaten way of allurements inveigled, whereby her posterity hath been deluded ever since; that is those three delivered by Saint John, the lust of the flesh, the lust of the eye, and the pride of life, wherein indeed they seemed as weakly to faile as their debilitated posterity, ever after.[39] Whereof notwithstanding some in their imperfections, have resisted more powerfull temptations, and in many moralities condemned the facility of their seductions.

Againe, they might for ought we know, be still deceived in the unbeliefe of their mortality, even after they had eat of the fruit. For Eve observing no immediate execution of the curse, she delivered the fruit unto Adam, who after the taste thereof, perceiving himselfe still to live, might yet remaine in doubt, whether he had incurred death, which perhaps he did not indubitably believe, untill he was after convicted in the visible example of Abel; for he that would not believe the menace of God at first, it may be doubted whether before an ocular example hee believed the curse at last, and therefore they are not without all reason, who have disputed the fact of Cain, that is although he purposed to mischiefe, whether he intended to murther his brother, or designed that, whereof he had not beheld an example in his owne kinde, there might be somewhat in it that he would not have done, or desired undone, when he brake forth as desperately as before hee had done unmannerly, My iniquity is greater then can be forgiven me.[40]

Some nicities I confesse there are which extenuate, but many more that aggravate this delusion, which exceeding the bounds of our discourse, and perhaps our satisfaction, we shall at present passe over.[41] And therefore whether the sinne of our first parents were the greatest of any since, whether the transgression of Eve seducing, did not exceed that of Adam seduced, or whether the resistibility of his reason did not equivalence the facility of her seduction, wee shall referre it unto the schoolman.[42] Whether there were not in Eve as great injustice in deceiving her husband, as imprudence in being deceived her self,[43] we leave it unto the morallist. Whether the whole relation be not allegoricall, that is, whether the temptation of the man by the woman, bee not the seduction of the rationall, and higher parts by the inferiour and feminine faculties: or whether the tree in the middest of the garden, were not that part in the centre of the body, on which was afterward the appointment of circumcision in males, we leave it unto the Thalmudist.[44] Whether there were any policie in the devill to tempt them before conjunction, or whether the issue before tentation might in justice have suffered with those after, we leave it unto the lawyer.[45] Whether Adam foreknew the advent of Christ, or the reparation of his error by his Saviour, how the execution of the curse should have been ordered, if after Eve had eaten, Adam had yet refused.[46] Whether if they had tasted the tree of life before that of good and evill, they had yet suffered the curse of mortality; or whether the efficacie of the one had not overpowred the penalty of the other, we leave it unto God: for he alone can truly determine these and all things else, who as he hath proposed the world unto our disputation, so hath he reserved many things unto his owne resolution, whose determinations we cannot hope from flesh, but must with reverence suspend unto that great day, whose justice shall either condemne our curiosities, or resolve our disquisitions.[47]

Lastly, man was not only deceiveable in his integrity, but the Angells of light in all their clarity.[48] He that said he would bee like the highest did erre if in some way he conceived himselfe not so already; but in attempting so high an effect from himselfe, hee mis-understood the nature of God, and held a false apprehension of his owne; whereby vainly attempting not only insolencies, but impossibilities, he deceived himselfe as low as hell. In briefe, there is nothing infallible but God, who cannot possibly erre. For things are really true as they correspond unto his conception, and have so much of verity, as they hold of conformity unto that intellect, in whose Idea they had their first determinations: and therefore being the rule he cannot bee irregular, nor being truth it selfe conceiveably admit the impossible society of error.[49]

CHAPTER II
A Further Illustration of the Same

Being thus deluded before the fall, it is no wonder if their conceptions were deceitfull, and could scarce speake without an error after; for what is very remarkable (and no man I know hath yet observed) in the relation of Scripture before the flood, there is but one speech delivered by man, wherein there is not an erronious conception; and strictly examined, most hainously injurious unto truth. The penne of Moses is briefe in the account before the flood, and the speeches recorded are six.[50]

The first is that of Adam, when upon the expostulation of God, he replyed; I heard thy voice in the garden, and because I was naked, I hid my selfe: in which reply, there was included a very grosse mistake, and if with pertinacity maintained, a high and capitall errour: for thinking by this retirement to obscure himselfe from God, he infringed the omnisciency and essentiall ubiquity of his Maker; who as he created all things, so is he beyond and in them all, not onely in power, as under his subjection, or in his presence, as being in his cognition, but in his very Essence, as being the soule of their causalities, and the essentiall cause of their existences.[51] Certainely his posterity at this distance and after so perpetuated an impayrement, cannot but condemne the poverty of his conception, that thought to obscure himselfe from his Creator in the shade of the garden, who had beheld him before in the darkenesse of his Chaos, and in the obscurity of nothing; that thought to flye from God, which could not flye himselfe, or imagined that one tree should conceale his nakednesse from Gods eye, as another had revealed it unto his owne.[52] Those tormented spirits that wish the mountaines to cover them, have fallen upon desires of lesse absurdity, and chosen wayes of lesse improbable concealement; though this be also as ridiculous unto reason, as fruitlesse unto their desires; for he that laid the foundations of the earth, cannot be excluded the secrecy of the mountains, nor can there any thing escape the perspicacity of those eyes which were before light, and unto whose opticks there is no opacity.[53] This is the consolation of all good men, unto whom his ubiquity affordeth continuall comfort and security: and this is the affliction of hell, unto whom it affordeth despaire, and remedilesse calamity. For those restlesse spirits that flye the face of the Almighty, being deprived the fruition of his eye, would also avoid the extent of his hand; which being impossible, their sufferings are desperate, and their afflictions without evasion, untill they can get out of Trismegistus his circle, that is, to extend their wings above the universe, and pitch beyond ubiquity it selfe.[54]

The second is that speech of Adam unto God, the woman whom thou gavest me to be with me, she gave me of the tree, and I did eate[55]: this indeed was a very unsatisfactory reply, and therein was involved a very impious errour, as implying God the Author of sinne, and accusing his Maker of his transgression: as if he had said, If thou hadst not given me a woman I had not beene deceived: Thou promisedst to make her a help, but she hath proved destruction unto me; had I remained alone, I had not sinned, but thou gavest me a consort, and so I became seduced. This was a bold and open accusation of God, making the fountaine of good the contriver of evill, and the forbidder of the crime an abetter of the fact prohibited. Surely, his mercy was great that did not revenge the impeachment of his Justice; and his goodnesse to be admired, that it refuted not his argument in the punishment of his excusation, or onely pursued the first transgression without a penalty of this the second.[56]

The third was that of Eve. The serpent beguiled me, and I did eate.[57] In which reply there was not onely a very feeble excuse, but an erroneous translating her owne offence upon another. Extenuating her sinne from that which was an aggravation, that is to excuse the fact at all, much more upon the suggestion of a beast, which was before in the strictest termes prohibited by her God.[58] For although we now doe hope the mercies of God will consider our degenerated integrities unto some minoration of our offences, yet had not the sincerity of our first parents, so colourable expectations, unto whom the commandement was but single, and their integrities best able to resist the motions of its transgression:[59] And therefore so hainous conceptions have risen hereof, that some have seemed more angry therewith then God himselfe, being so exasperated with the offence, as to call in question their salvation, and to dispute the eternall punishment of their Maker. Assuredly with better reason may posterity accuse them, then they the serpent, or one another; and the displeasure of the Pelagians must needs be irreconcileable, who peremptorily maintaining they can fulfill the whole law, will insatisfactorily condemne the non-observation of one.[60]

The fourth was that speech of Cain upon the demand of God, Where is thy Brother? and he said, I know not.[61] In which negation, beside the open impudence, there was implyed a notable errour; for returning a lye unto his Maker, and presuming in this manner, to put off the Searcher of hearts, he denied the omnisciency of God, whereunto there is nothing concealable. The answer of Satan in the case of Job, had more of truth, wisdome and reverence, then this; Whence commest thou Satan? and he said, from compassing of the Earth.[62] For though an enemy of God, and hater of all truth, his wisdome will hardly permit him to falsifie with the Almighty: for well understanding the omniscience of his nature, he is not so ready to deceive himselfe, as to falsifie unto him whose cognition is no way deludable:[63] And therefore when in the tentation of Christ he played upon the fallacy, and thought to deceive the Author of truth, the method of this proceeding arose from the uncertainty of his divinity, whereof had he remained assured, he had continued silent, nor would his discretion attempt so unsucceedable a temptation.[64] And so againe at the last day, when our offences shall be drawne into accompt, the subtilty of that Inquisitor shall not present unto God a bundle of calumnies or confutable accusations, but will discreetly offer up unto his Omnisciencie, a sure and undeniable list of our transgressions.[65]

The fifth is another reply of Cain upon the denouncement of his curse, My iniquity is greater then can be forgiven: for so is it expressed in some translations.[66] The assertion was not onely desperate, but the conceit erroneous, overthrowing that glorious attribute of God his mercy, and conceiving the sinne of murder unpardonable; which how great soever, is not above the repentance of man, but far below the mercies of God, and was as some conceive expiated, in that punishment he suffered temporally for it.[67] There are but two examples of this errour in holy Scripture, and they both for murder, and both as it were of the same person; for Christ was mystically slaine in Abel;[68] and therefore Cain had some influence on his death, as well as Judas; but the sinne had a different effect on Cain, from that it had on Judas, and most that since have fallen into it; for they like Judas desire death, and not unfrequently pursue it: Cain on the contrary grew afraid thereof, and obtained a securement from it. Assuredly if his despaire continued, there was punishment enough in life, and justice sufficient in the mercy of his protection. For the life of the desperate equals the anxieties of death, who in uncessant inquietudes but act the life of the damned, and anticipate the desolations of hell. Tis indeed a sinne in man, but a punishment onely in the devils, who offend not God but afflict themselves, in the appointed despaire of his mercies. And as to be without all hope is the affliction of the damned, so is it the happinesse of the blessed, who having their expectations present, are not distracted with futurities. So is it also their felicity to have no faith, for enjoying the beatifical vision there is nothing unto them inevident, and in the fruition of the object of faith, they have received the full evacuation of it.[69]

The last speech was that of Lamech, I have slaine a man to my wound, and a young man to my hurt:[70] If Cain be avenged seven fold, truly Lamech seventy and seven fold. Now herein there seemes to be a very erroneous illation;[71] from the indulgence of God unto Cain, concluding an immunity unto himselfe, that is, a regular protection from a single example, and an exemption from punishment in a fact that naturally deserved it. The error of this offendor was contrary to that of Cain, whom the Rabbins conceive that Lamech at this time killed.[72] He despaired of Gods mercy in the same fact, where this presumed of it, he by a decollation of all hope annihilated his mercy, this by an immoderancy thereof destroyed his justice, though the sin were lesse, the errour was as great;[73] for as it is untrue that his mercy will not forgive offenders, or his benignity cooperate to their conversions, so is it also of no lesse falsity to affirme his Justice will not exact account of sinners, or punish such as continue in their transgressions.

And thus may we perceive, how weakely our fathers did erre before the floud, how continually and upon common discourse they fell upon errours after, it is therefore no wonder we have been erroneous ever since: and being now at greatest distance from the beginning of errour, are almost lost in its dissemination, whose wayes are boundlesse, and confesse no circumscription.[74]

CHAPTER III

Of the second cause of Popular Errors; the erroneous disposition of the People

Having thus declared the fallible nature of man even from his first production, we have beheld the generall cause of error, but as for popular errors, they are more neerely founded upon an erroneous inclination of the people;[75] as being the most deceptible part of mankind, and ready with open armes to receive the encroachments of error; which condition of theirs although deduceable from many grounds, yet shall we evidence it, but from a few, and such as most neerely and undeniably declare their natures.[76]

How unequall discerners of truth they are, and openly exposed unto errour, will first appeare from their unqualified intellectuals, unable to umpire the difficulty of its dissentions.[77] For error to speake strictly,[78] is a firme assent unto falsity. Now whether the object whereunto they deliver up their assent be true or false, they are incompetent judges.

For the assured truth of things is derived from the principles of knowledge, and causes, which determine their verities; whereof their uncultivated understandings, scarce holding any theory, they are but bad discerners of verity, and in the numerous tract of error, but casually do hit the point and unity of truth.[79]

Their understanding is so feeble in the discernement of falsities, and averting the errors of reason, that it submitteth unto the fallacies of sence, and is unable to rectifie the error of its sensations. Thus the greater part of mankinde having but one eye of sence and reason, conceive the Earth farre bigger then the Sun, the fixed stars lesser then the Moone, their figures plaine, and their spaces equidistant.[80] For thus their sence enformeth them, and herein their reason cannot rectifie them, and therefore hopelesly continuing in their mistakes, they live and dye in their absurdities; passing their dayes in perverted apprehensions, and conceptions of the world, derogatory unto God, and the wisdome of his creation.

Againe, being so illiterate in point of intellect, and their sence so incorrected, they are farther indisposed ever to attaine unto truth, as commonly proceeding in those wayes, which have most reference unto sence, and wherein there lyeth most notable and popular delusion: For being unable to weild the intellectuall armes of reason, they are faine to betake themselves unto wasters and the blunter weapons of truth; affecting the grosse and sensible wayes of doctrine, and such as will not consist with strict and subtile reason.[81] Thus unto them a piece of rhetorick is a sufficient argument of logick, an Apologue of Æsope, beyond a syllogisme in Barbara, parables then propositions, and proverbs more powerfull, then demonstrations.[82]

And therefore are they led rather by example, then precept, receiving perswasions from visible inducements, before intellectual instructions; and therefore also do they judge of humane actions by the event; for being uncapable of operable circumstances, or rightly to judge the prudenciality of affairs, they onely gaze upon the visible successe, and thereafter condemn or cry up the whole progression.[83] And so from this ground in the lecture of holy Scripture, their apprehensions, are commonly confined unto the literall sence of the text, from whence have ensued the grosse and duller sort of heresies.[84] For not attaining the deuteroscopy, and second intention of the words, they are faine to omit their superconsequencies, coherencies, figures, or tropologies and are not sometime perswaded by fire beyond their literalities.[85] And therefore also things invisible, but unto intellectuall discernments, to humor the grossenesse of their comprehensions, have been degraded from their proper forms, and God himselfe dishonoured into manuall expressions;[86] and so likewise being unprovided, or unsufficient for higher speculations, they will alwayes betake themselves, unto sensible representations, and can hardly be restrained the dulness of idolatry.[87] A sinne or folly not only derogatory unto God, but man, overthrowing their reason, as well as his divinitie. In briefe a reciprocation, or rather an inversion of the creation, making God one way, as he made us another; that is, after our image, as he made us after his owne.[88]

Moreover, their understanding thus weake in it selfe, and perverted by sensible delusions,[89] is yet farther impaired by the dominion of their appetite, that is, the irrationall and brutall part of the soule, which lording it over the soveraigne facultie, interrupts the actions of that noble part, and choakes those tender sparkes, which Adam hath left them of reason: and therefore they doe not onely swarm with errours, but vices depending thereon.[90] Thus they commonly affect no man any farther then hee deserts his reason, or complies with their aberrancies.[91] Hence they embrace not vertue for it selfe, but its reward, and the argument from pleasure or utilitie is farre more powerfull, then that from vertuous honesty; which Mahomet and his contrivers wel understood, when hee set out the felicitie of his heaven, by the contentments of flesh, and the delights of sense:[92] slightly passing over the accomplishment of the soule, and the beatitude of that part which earth and visibilities too weakly affect.[93] But the wisdom of our Saviour, and the simplicity of his truth proceeded another way, defying the popular provisions of happinesse from sensible expectations, placing his felicitie in things removed from sense, and the intellectuall enjoyment of God. And therefore the doctrine of the one was never afraid of universities, or endeavoured the banishment of learning like the other.[94] And though Galen doth sometime nibble at Moses, and beside the Apostate Christian, some heathens have questioned his philosophicall part or treatie of the Creation.[95] Yet is there surely no reasonable pagan, that will not admire the rationall and well grounded precepts of Christ, whose life as it was conformable unto his doctrine, so was that unto the highest rules of reason; and must therefore flourish in the advancement of learning, and the perfection of parts best able to comprehend it.

Againe, their individuall imperfections being great, they are moreover enlarged by their aggregation, and being erroneous in their single numbers once hudled together, they will be errour it selfe; for being a confusion of knaves and fooles, and a farraginous concurrence of all conditions, tempers, sex, and ages, it is but naturall if their determinations be monstrous, and many wayes inconsistent with truth.[96] And therefore wise men have alwayes applauded their owne judgment, in the contradiction of that of the people, and their soberest adversaries, have ever afforded them the stile of fooles and mad men; and to speak impartially, their actions have often made good these epithites.[97] Had Orestes been judge, he would not have acquitted that Lystrian rabble of madnesse, who upon a visible miracle, falling into so high a conceit of Paul and Barnabas, that they termed the one Jupiter, the other Mercurius, that they brought oxen and garlands, and were hardly restrained, from sacrificing unto them, did notwithstanding suddenly after fall upon Paul, and having stoned him, drew him for dead out of the citie.[98] It might have hazarded the sides of Democritus, had hee been present at that tumult of Demetrius, when the people flocking together in great numbers, some cryed one thing, and some another, and the assembly was confused, and the most part knew not wherefore they were come together; notwithstanding, all with one voice for the space of two houres cryed out, Great is Diana of the Ephesians.[99] It had overcome the patience of Job, as it did the meeknesse of Moses, and would surely have mastered any, but the longanimity and great sufferance of God, Had they beheld the mutiny in the wildernesse, when after tenne great miracles in Egypt, and some in the same place, they melted down their stolen ear-rings into a calf, and monstrously cryed out, These are thy gods O Israel! that brought thee out of the land of Egypt.[100] It much accuseth the impatiencie of Peter, who could not endure the staves of the multitude, and is the greatest example of lenitie in our Saviour, when he desired of God forgivenes unto those, who having one day brought him into the citie in triumph, did presently after, act all dishonour upon him, and nothing could be heard but *Crucifge* in their courts.[101] Certainely hee that considereth these things in Gods peculiar people, will easily discerne how little of truth, there is in the wayes of the multitude; and though somtimes they are flattered with that aphorisme, will hardly beleeve the voyce of the people to bee the voyce of God.[102]

Lastly, being thus divided from truth in themselves, they are yet farther removed by advenient deception.[103] For true it is, (and I hope shall not offend their vulgarities) if I say they are daily mocked into errour by subtler devisors, and have been expresly deluded, by all professions whatsoever.[104] Thus the priests of elder time, have put upon them many incredible conceits, not onely deluding their apprehensions, with ariolation, south-saying, and such oblique idolatries, but winning their credulities unto the literall and downe-right adorement of cats, lizards, and beetles;[105] and thus also in some Christian churches, wherein is presumed an irreproveable truth,[106] if all be true that is suspected, or halfe what is related, there have not wanted, many strange deceptions, and some thereof are still confessed by the name of pious fraudes. Thus Theudas an imposture was able to lead away foure thousand into the wildernesse, and the delusions of Mahomet almost the fourth part of mankinde.[107] Thus all heresies how grosse soever, have found a welcome with the people. For thus, what is scarce imaginable, many of the Jews were wrought into beliefe, that Herod was the Messias, and David George of Leyden and Arden, were not without a partie amongst the people, who maintained the same opinion of themselves almost in our dayes.[108]

Physitions (many at least that make profession thereof) beside divers lesse discoverable wayes of fraude, have made them beleeve, there is the book of fate, or the power of Aarons brest-plate in urines.[109] And therefore hereunto they have recourse as unto the oracle of life, the great determinator of virginity, conception, fertilitie, and the inscrutable infirmities of the whole body. For as though there were a seminalitie in urine, or that like the seed that carried with it the Idea of every part, they foolishly conceive wee visibly behold therein the anatomie of every particle, and can thereby indigitate their affections; [and running into any demands expect from us a sudden resolution in things wherein the devil of Delphos would demurre, and we know hath taken respite of some daies to answer easier questions].[110]

Saltimbancoes, quacksalvers, and charlatans, deceive them in lower degrees;[111] were Æsop alive the Piazza and Ponte Neufe could not but speake their fallacies, meane while there are too many, whose cryes cannot conceale their mischiefes:[112] for their impostures are full of crueltie, and worse then any other, deluding not onely unto pecuniary defraudations, but the irreparable deceit of death.

Astrologers, which pretend to be of Caballa with the starres, such I meane as abuse that worthy enquirie, have not been wanting in their deceptions, who having wonne their beliefe unto principles whereof they make great doubt themselves, have made them beleeve that arbitrary events below, have necessary causes above;[113] whereupon their credulities assent unto any prognosticks, and daily swallow the predictions of men, which besides the independency of their causes, and contingency in their events, are onely in the prescience of God.

Fortune tellers, juglers, geomancers, and the like incantatory impostors, though commonly men of inferiour ranke, and from whom without infusion[114] they can expect no more then from themselves, doe daily and professedly delude them:[115] unto whom (what is deplorable in men and Christians) too many applying themselves, betwixt jest and earnest, betray the cause of truth, and insensibly make up, the legionarie body of errour.[116]

Statistes and politicians, unto whom *Ragione di Stato*, is the first considerable, as though it were their businesse to deceive the people, as a maxime, do hold, that truth is to be concealed from them, unto whom although they reveale the visible designe, yet doe they commonly conceale the capitall intention;[117] and therefore have they alway beene the instruments of great designes, yet seldome understood the true intention of any, accomplishing the drifts of wiser heads as inanimate and ignorant agents, the generall designe of the world; who though in some latitude of sence, and in a naturall cognition performe their proper actions, yet do they unknowingly concurre unto higher ends, and blindely advance the great intention of nature.[118] Now how farre they may bee kept in ignorance, a great example there is in the people of Rome, who never knew, the true and proper name of their owne city. For beside that common appellation received by the citizens, it had a proper and secret name concealed from them: *Cujus alterum nomen dicere secretis Ceremoniarum nefas habetur*, saith Plinie.[119] The reason hereof was superstitious, lest the name thereof being discovered unto their enemies, their Penates and Patronall gods, might be called forth by charms and incantations.[120] For according unto the tradition of magitians, the tutelary spirits wil not remove at common appellations, but at the proper names of things whereunto they are protectors.[121]

Thus having beene deceived by themselves, and continually deluded by others, they must needs be stuffed with errors, and even over-runne with these inferiour falsities, whereunto whosoever shall resigne their reasons, either from the root of deceit in themselves, or inabilitie to resist such triviall ingannations from others, although their condition and fortunes may place them many spheres above the multitude, yet are they still within the line of vulgaritie, and the Democraticall enemies of truth.[122]

CHAPTER IV

Of the nearer and more immediate Causes of Popular Errours, both in the Wiser, and Common sort, Misapprehension, Fallacy, or False diduction, Credulity, Supinity, Adherence unto Antiquitie, Tradition, and Authoritie

The first is a mistake, or a conception of things, either in their first apprehensions, or secondary relations.[123] So Eve mistook the commandement, either from the immediate injunction of God, or from the secondary narration of her husband. So might the disciples mistake our Saviour, in his answer unto Peter, concerning the death of John, as is delivered, John 21. Peter seeing John, saith unto Jesus, Lord, and what shall this man doe?[124] Jesus saith, If I will, that he tarry till I come, what is that unto thee? Then went this saying abroad among the brethren, that that disciple should not die. Thus began the conceit and opinion of the Centaures, that is in the mistake of the first beholders, as is declared by Servius, when some young Thessalians on horsebacke were beheld a farre off, while their horses watered, that is, while their heads were depressed, they were conceived by their first spectators, to be but one animall, and answerable hereunto have their pictures been drawn ever since.[125]

And as simple mistakes commonly beget fallacies, so men rest not in false apprehensions, without absurd and inconsequent diductions, from fallacious foundations, and misapprehended mediums, erecting conclusions no way inferrible from their premises.[126] Now the fallacies whereby men deceive others, and are deceived themselves, the ancients, have divided into verball and reall.[127] Of the verball, and such as conclude from mistakes of the word, although there be no lesse then sixe, yet are there but two onely thereof worthy our notation: and unto which the rest may be referred: that is the fallacie of æquivocation and amphibologie, which conclude from the ambiguity of some one word, or the ambiguous sintaxis of many put together.[128] From this fallacy arose that calamitous error of the Jewes, misapprehending the prophesies of their Messias, and expounding them alwayes unto literall and temporall expectation. By this way many errors crept in and perverted the doctrine of Pythagoras, whilest men received his precepts in a different sense from his intention, converting metaphors into proprieties, and receiving as litterall expressions, obscure and involved truths.[129] Thus when he enjoyned his disciples, an abstinence from beanes, many conceived they were with severity debarred the use of that pulse; which notwithstanding could not be his meaning for as Aristoxenus who wrote his life, averreth he delighted much in that kind of food himselfe;[130] but herein as Plutarch observeth, he had no other intention, then to disswade men from magistracie, or undertaking the publike offices of state; for by beanes were the magistrates elected in some parts of Greece; and after his dayes, wee read in Thucydides, of the councell of the beane in Athens.[131] The same word also in Greeke doth signifie a testicle, and hath been thought by some an injunction only of continencie, as Aul. Gellius hath expounded, and as Empedocles may also be interpreted, *πὰν δειλοὶ κυαμῶν ἀπὸ χεῖρας ἔχεσθε*, that is *Testiculis miseri dextras subducite*, [and might be the original intention of Pythagoras, as having a notable hint hereof in Beans, from the natural signature of the venereal organs of both sexes].[132] Againe his injunction is, not to harbour swallowes in our houses:[133] whose advice notwithstanding we doe not contemne, who daily admit and cherish them; for herein a caution is only implied not to entertain ungratefull and thanklesse persons, which like the swallow are no way commodious unto us, but having made use of our habitations, and served their owne turnes, forsake us. So he commands to deface the print of a cauldron in the ashes, after it hath boyled. Which strictly to observe were most condemnable superstition: for hereby he covertly adviseth us not to persevere in anger, but after our choler hath boyled, to retaine no impression thereof. In the like sense are to be received, or they will else be misapprehended, when he adviseth his disciples to give the right hand but to few, to put no viands in a chamberpot, not to passe over a ballance, not to rake up fire with a sword, or pisse against the sunne, which enigmatical deliveries comprehended usefull verities, but being mistaken by literall expositors at the first, they have been misunderstood[134] by most since, and may bee occasion of error to verball capacities for ever.

This fallacy in the first delusion Satan did put upon Eve, and his whole tentation might be this elench continued;[135] so when he said, Yee shall not dye, that was in his equivocation, she shall not incurre a present death, or a destruction immediatly ensuing your transgression. Your eyes shall be opened, that is, not to the enlargement of your knowledge, but to the discovery of your shame and proper confusion.[136] You shall know good and evill, that is you shall have knowledge of good by its privation, but cognisance of evill by sense and visible experience. And the same fallacy or way of deceit so well succeeding in Paradise, hee continued in his oracles through all the world. Which had not men more warily understood, they might have performed many acts inconsistent with his intention: Brutus might have made haste with Tarquine to have kissed his owne mother.[137] The Athenians might have built them wooden walls, or doubled the altar at Delphos.[138]

The circle of this fallacie is very large, and herein may be comprised all ironicall mistakes;[139] for intended expressions receiving inverted significations, all deductions from metaphors, parables, allegories, unto reall and rigid interpretations.[140] Whereby have arisen not only popular errors in philosophy, but vulgar and senselesse heresies in divinity, as will be evident unto any that shall examine their foundations, as they stand related by Epiphanius, Austin, or Prateolus.[141]

Other wayes there are of deceit which consist not, in false apprehension of words, that is verball expressions or sententiall significations, but fraudulent deductions, or inconsequent illations, from a false conception of things.[142] Of these extradictionary and reall fallacies, Aristotle and logicians make in number six, but we observe that men are most commonly deceived by foure thereof: those are, *Petitio principii. A dicto secundum quid ad dictum simpliciter. A non causa pro causa.* And *fallacia consequentis.*[143]

The first is *petitio principii*, which fallacie is committed, when a question is made a medium, or we assume a medium as granted, whereof we remaine as unsatisfied as of the question.[144] Briefly where that is assumed as a principle, to prove another thing which is not conceaded as true it selfe. By this fallacie was Eve deceived, when shee took for granted, the false assertion of the devill; Yee shall not surely dye, for God doth know that in the day she shall eat thereof, your eyes shall be opened, and you shall be as gods;[145] which was but a bare affirmation of Satan without any proofe or probable inducement, contrary unto the command of God and former beliefe of herselfe; and this was the logick of the Jews, when they accused our Saviour unto Pilate, who demanding a reasonable impeachment, or the allegation of some crime worthy of condemnation; they only replyed, if he had not been worthy of death, we would not have brought him before thee;[146] wherein there was neither accusation of the person, nor satisfaction of the judge, who well understood a bare accusation was no presumption of guilt, and the clamors of the people no accusation at all. The same fallacy is sometime used in the dispute, between Job, and his friends, they often taking that for granted which afterward he denyeth and disproveth.

The second is *à dicto secundum quid ad dictum simpliciter*, when from that which is but true in a qualified sense an inconditionall and absolute verity is inferred, transferring the speciall consideration of things unto their generall acceptions, or concluding from their strict acception, unto that without all limitation. This fallacie men commit when they argue from a particular to a generall, as when we conclude the vices or qualities of a few upon a whole nation, or from a part unto the whole. Thus the divell argued with our Saviour, and by this he would perswade him he might be secure if hee cast himselfe from the pinacle: for said he, it is written, he shall give his Angels charge concerning thee, and in their hands they shall beare thee up, lest at any time thou dash thy foot against a stone.[147] But this illation was fallacious leaving out part of the text, Psalme 91. He shall keep thee in all thy wayes; that is, in the wayes of righteousnesse, and not of rash attempts: so he urged a part for the whole, and inferred more in the conclusion, then was contained in the premises. By this same fallacie we proceed, when we conclude from the signe unto the thing signified. By this incroachment idolatry first crept in, men converting the symbolicall use of idols into their proper worship, and receiving the representation of things as the substance and thing it selfe.[148] So the statue of Belus at first erected in his memory, was in after times adored as a divinity.[149] And so also in the sacrament of the Eucharist, the bread and wine which were but the signalls or visible signes, were made the things signified, and worshipped for the body of Christ. And hereby generally men are deceived that take things spoken in some latitude without any at all. Hereby the Jewes were deceived concerning the commandement of the Sabbath, accusing our Saviour for healing the sicke, and his disciples for plucking the ears of corne, upon that day.[150] And by this deplorable mistake they were deceived unto destruction, upon the assault of Pompey the great made upon that day, by whose superstitious observation they could not defend themselves, or performe any labour whatsoever.[151]

The third is *à non causâ pro causâ*, when that is pretended for a cause which is not, or not in that sense which is inferred. Upon this consequence the law of Mahomet forbids the use of wine, and his successors abolished universities:[152] by this also many Christians have condemned literature, misunderstanding the counsell of Saint Paul, who adviseth no further then to beware of philosophy.[153] On this foundation were built the conclusions of southsayers in their auguriall, and tripudiary divinations, collecting presages from voice or food of birds, and conjoyning events unto causes of no connexion.[154] Hereupon also are grounded the grosse mistakes, in the cure of many diseases, not only from the last medicine, and sympatheticall receits, but amulets charms, and all incantatory applications, deriving effects not only from inconcurring causes, but things devoid of all efficiencie whatever.

The fourth is the fallacie of the consequent, which if strictly taken, may be a fallacious illation in reference unto antecedencie, or consequencie; as to conclude from the position of the antecedent, unto the position of the consequent, or from the remotion of the consequent to the remotion of the antecedent.[155] This is usually committed, when in connexed propositions the termes adhere contingently. This is frequent in oratorie illations, and thus the Pharisees, because he conversed with publicans and sinners, accused the holinesse of Christ.[156] But if this fallacy be largely taken, it is committed in any vitious illation offending the rules of good consequence, and so it may be very large, and comprehend all false illations against the setled laws of logick;[157] but the most usuall inconsequencies[158] are from particulars, from negatives, and from affirmative conclusions in the second figure, wherein indeed offences are most frequent, and their discoveries not difficult.

CHAPTER V
Of Credulity and Supinity

A third cause of common errors is the credulity of men, that is an easie assent, to what is obtruded, or a believing at first eare what is delivered by others;[159] this is a weaknesse in the understanding, without examination assenting unto things, which from their natures and causes doe carry no perswasion; whereby men often swallow falsities for truths, dubiosities for certainties, fesibilities for possibilities, and things impossible as possibilities themselves. Which though a weaknesse of the intellect, and most discoverable in vulgar heads, yet hath it sometime fallen upon wiser braines, and great advancers of truth. Thus many wise Athenians so far forgot their philosophy, and the nature of humane production, that they descended unto beliefes, the originall of their nation was from the earth, and had no other beginning then from the seminality and wombe of their great mother.[160] Thus is it not without wonder, how those learned Arabicks so tamely delivered up their beliefe unto the absurdities of the Alcoran.[161] How the noble Geber, Avicenna and Almanzor, should rest satisfied in the nature and causes of earthquakes, delivered from the doctrine of their prophet; that is, from the motion of a great bull, upon whose hornes all the earth is poised.[162] How their faiths could decline so low, as to concede their generations in heaven, to be made by the smell of a citron, or that the felicity of their paradise should consist in a jubile of conjunction,[163] that is a coition of one act prolonged unto fifty years.[164] Thus is it almost beyond wonder, how the beliefe of reasonable creatures, should ever submit unto idolatry: and the credulity of those men scarce credible, without presumption of a second fall, who could believe a deity in the worke of their owne hands. For although in that ancient and diffused adoration of idolls, unto the priests and subtiler heads, the worship perhaps might be symbolicall, and as those images some way related unto their deities, yet was the idolatry direct and downe-right in the people, whose credulity is illimitable, who may be made believe that any thing is God, and may be made believe there is no God at all.

And as credulity is the cause of error, so incredulity oftentimes of not enjoying truth, and that not only an obstinate incredulity, whereby wee will not acknowledge assent unto what is reasonably inferred, but any academicall reservation in matters of easie truth, or rather scepticall infidelity against the evidence of reason and sense.[165] For these are conceptions befalling wise men, as absurd as the apprehensions of fooles, and the credulity of the people which promiscuously swallow any thing.[166] For this is not only derogatory unto the wisdome of God, who hath proposed the world unto our knowledge, and thereby the notion of himselfe, but also detractory unto the intellect, and sense of man expressedly disposed for that inquisition.[167] And therefore *hoc tantum scio quod nihil scio*, is not to be received in an absolute sense, but is comparatively expressed unto the number of things whereof our knowledge is ignorant;[168] nor will it acquit the insatisfaction of those which quarrell with all things, or dispute of matters concerning whose verities we have conviction from reason, or decision from the inerrable and requisite conditions of sense.[169] And therefore if any man shall affirme the earth doth move, and will not believe with us, it standeth still, because he hath probable reasons for it, and I no infallible sense nor reason against it, I will not quarrell with his assertion: but if like Zeno he shall walke about, and yet deny there is any motion in nature, surely it had been happy he had been born in Antycera, and is only fit to converse with their melancholies, who having a conceit that they are dead, cannot be convicted into the society of the living.[170]

The fourth is a supinity or neglect of enquiry, even in matters whereof we doubt, rather beleeving, as we say, then going to see, or doubting with ease and gratis, then beleeving with difficulty or purchase;[171] whereby either by a temperamentall inactivity we are unready to put in execution the suggestions or dictates of reason, or by a content and acquiescence in every species of truth we embrace the shadow thereof, or so much as may palliate its just and substantiall acquirements.[172] Had our forefathers sat downe in these resolutions, or had their curiosities been sedentary, who pursued the knowledge of things through all the corners of nature, the face of truth had been obscure unto us, whose lustre in some part their industries have revealed.[173]

Certainly the sweat of their labours was not salt unto them, and they took delight in the dust of their endeavours. For questionlesse in knowledge there is no slender difficulty, and truth which wise men say doth lye in a well, is not recoverable but by exantlation.[174] It were some extenuation of the curse, if *in sudore vultus tui*, were confineable unto corporall exercitations, and there still remained a paradise or unthorny place of knowledge;[175] but now our understandings being eclipsed, as well as our tempers infirmed, we must betake our selves to wayes of reparation, and depend upon the illumination of our endeavours; for thus we may in some measure repaire our primarie ruins, and build our selves men againe.[176] And though the attempts of some have been precipitous, and their enquiries so audacious as to come within command of the flaming swords, and lost themselves in attempts above humanity, yet have the inquiries of most defected by the way, and tyred within the sober circumference of knowledge.[177]

And this is the reason why some have transcribed any thing, and although they cannot but doubt thereof, yet neither make experiment by sence or enquiry by reason, but live in doubts of things whose satisfaction is in their owne power, which is indeed the inexcusable part of our ignorance, and may perhaps fill up the charge of the last day.[178] For not obeying the dictates of reason, and neglecting the cryes of truth, we faile not onely in the trust of our undertakings, but in the intention of man it selfe, which although more veniall unto ordinary constitutions, and such as are not framed beyond the capacity of beaten notions, yet will it inexcusably condemne some men, who having received excellent endowments, and such as will accuse the omissions of perfection, have yet sat downe by the way, and frustrated the intention of their habilities.[179] For certainely as some men have sinned, in the principles of humanity, and must answer, for not being men, so others offend if they be not more; *Magis extra vitia quam cum virtutibus*, would commend those, these are not excusable without an excellency.[180] For great constitutions, and such as are constellated unto knowledge, do nothing till they outdoe all;[181] they come short of themselves if they go not beyond others, and must not sit downe under the degree of worthies.[182] God expects no lustre from the minor stars, but if the sun should not illuminate all, it were a sin in Nature. *Ultimus bonorum*, will not excuse every man, nor is it sufficient for all to hold the common levell;[183] mens names should not onely distinguish them: a man should be something that men are not, and individuall in somewhat beside his proper nature. Thus while it exceeds not the bounds of reason, and modesty, we cannot condemne singularity. *Nos numerus sumus*, is the motto of the multitude, and for that reason are they fooles.[184] For things as they recede from unity, the more they approach to imperfection, and deformity; for they hold their perfection in their simplicities, and as they neerest approach unto God.

Now as there are many great wits to be condemned, who have neglected the increment of Arts, and the sedulous pursuit of knowledge, so are there not a few very much to be pittied, whose industry being not attended with naturall parts, they have sweat to little purpose, and roled the stone in vain:[185] which chiefly proceedeth from naturall incapacity, and geniall indisposition, at least to those particular wayes whereunto they apply their endeavours. And this is one reason why though universities bee full of men, they are oftentimes empty of learning. Why as there are some which do much without learning, so others but little with it, and few that attaine to any perfection[186] in it. For many heads that undertake it, were never squared nor timbred for it. There are not onely particular men, but whole nations indisposed for learning, whereunto is required not onely education, but a pregnant Minerva and teeming constitution.[187] For the wisdome of God hath divided the genius of men according to the different affaires of the world, and varied their inclinations according to the variety of actions to be performed therein, which they who consider not, rudely rushing upon professions and wayes of life unequall to their natures; dishonour not onely themselves and their functions, but pervert the harmony of the whole world. For if the world went on as God hath ordained it, and were every one implyed in points concordant to their natures; professions, arts and common-wealths would rise up of themselves; nor needed we a lanthorne to finde a man in Athens.[188]

CHAPTER VI
Of Adherence unto Antiquity

But the mortallest enemy unto knowledge, and that which hath done the greatest execution upon truth, hath beene a peremptory adhesion unto authority, and more especially the establishing of our beliefe upon the dictates of antiquities.[189] For (as every capacity may observe) most men of ages present, so superstitiously do look on ages past, that the authorities of the one, exceed the reasons of the other.[190] Whose persons indeed being farre removed from our times, their works which seldome with us passe uncontrouled, either by contemporaries or immediate successors, are now become out of the distance of envies.[191] And the farther removed from present times, are conceived to approach the neerer unto truth it selfe. Now hereby me thinks wee manifestly delude our selves, and widely walke out of the tracke of truth.

For first, men hereby impose a thraldome on their times, which the ingenuity of no age should endure, or indeed the presumption of any did ever yet enjoyne. Thus Hippocrates about 2000 yeare agoe, conceived it no injustice, either to examine or refute the doctrines of his predecessors: Galen the like, and Aristotle most of any;[192] yet did not any of these conceive themselves infallible, or set downe their dictates as verities irrefragable;[193] but when they either deliver their owne inventions, or rejected other mens opinions, they proceed with judgement and ingenuity, establishing their assertion, not onely with great solidity, but submitting them also unto the correction of future discovery.

Secondly, men that adore times past, consider not that those times were once present, that is, as our owne are at this instant, and wee our selves unto those to come, as they unto us at present; as wee rely on them, even so will those on us, and magnifie us hereafter, who at present condemne our selves; which very absurdity is dayly committed amongst us even in the esteeme and censure of our owne times. And to speake impartially, old men from whom wee should expect the greatest example of wisdome, do most exceede in this point of folly; commending the dayes of their youth, they scarce remember, at least well understood not; extolling those times their younger yeares have heard their fathers condemne, and condemning those times the gray heads of their posterity shall commend. And thus is it the humour of many heads to extoll the dayes of their fore-fathers, and declaime against the wickednesse of times present; which notwithstanding they cannot handsomely doe, without the borrowed helpe and satyres of times past, condemning the vices of their times, by the expressions of vices in times which they commend, which cannot but argue the community of vice in both; Horace therefore, Juvenall and Perseus were no prophets, although their lives did seeme to indigitate and point at our times.[194] There is a certaine list of vices committed in all ages, and declaimed against by all authors, which will last as long as humane nature, or digested into common places may serve for any theme, and never be out of date untill doomes day.

Thirdly, the testimonies of antiquity and such as passe oraculously amongst us, were not, if wee consider them alwayes so exact, as to examine the doctrine they delivered. For some, and those the acutest of them, have left unto us many things of falsitie, controulable, not onely by criticall and collective reason, but common and countrey observation. Hereof there want not many examples in Aristotle, through all his booke of animals; we shall instance onely in three of his problemes, and all contained under one section.[195] The first enquireth why a man doth cough, but not an oxe or cow? Whereas notwithstanding the contrary is often observed by husbandmen, and stands confirmed by those who have expresly treated *de re Rustica*, and have also delivered diverse remedies for it.[196] Why Juments, as horses, oxen and asses, have no eructation or belching, whereas indeed the contrary is often observed, and also delivered by Columella.[197] And thirdly, *cur solus homo*, why man alone hath gray hayres?[198] whereas it cannot escape the eyes, and ordinary observation of all men, that horses, dogs, and foxes, wax gray with age in our countries, and in colder regions many other animals without it.

Other authors write often dubiously, even in matters wherein is expected a strict and definitive truth, extenuating their affirmations, with *aiunt*, *ferunt*, *fortasse*, as Dioscorides, Galen, Aristotle, and many more.[199] Others by heare say, taking upon trust most they have delivered, whose volumes are meer collections, drawne from the mouthes or leaves of other authours; as may bee observed in Plinie, Ælian, Athenæus, and many others.[200] Not a few transcriptively, subscribing their names unto other mens endeavours, and meerely transcribing almost all they have written. The Latines transcribing the Greekes, the Greekes and Latines each other. Thus hath Justine borrowed all from Trogus Pompeius, and Julius Solinus in a manner transcribed Plinie, thus have Lucian and Apuleius served Lucius Pratensis, men both living in the same time, and both transcribing the same authour, in those famous bookes, entituled Lucius by the one, and Aureus Asinus by the other.[201] In the same measure hath Simocrates in his tract *De Nilo*, dealt with Diodorus Siculus, as may be observed, in that worke annexed unto Herodotus, and translated by Jungermannus.[202] Thus Eratosthenes wholy translated Timotheus *De Insulis*, not reserving the very preface.[203] The very same doth Strabo report of Edorus and Ariston in a treatise entituled *De Nilo*.[204] Clemens Alexandrinus hath also observed many examples hereof among the Greekes, and Plinie speaketh very plainely in his Preface, that conferring his authors, and comparing their workes together, hee generally found those that went before *verbatim* transcribed, by those that followed after, and their originalls never so much as mentioned.[205] [To omit how much the wittiest peece of Ovid is beholding unto Parhenius Chius;] even the magnified Virgil hath borrowed almost all his works: his Eclogues from Theocritus, his Georgicks from Hesiod and Aratus, his Æneads from Homer, the second booke thereof containing the exploit of Sinon and the Trojan horses, (as Macrobius observeth) he hath *verbatim* derived from Pisander.[206] Our own profession is not excusable herein. Thus Oribasius, Ætius and Ægineta have in a manner transcribed Galen.[207] But Marcellus Empericus who hath left a famous worke *De medicamentis*, hath word for word, transcribed all Scriboneus Largus, *De compositione medicamentorum*, and not left out his very peroration.[208] And thus may we perceive the ancients were but men, even like our selves. The practise of transcription in our dayes was no monster in theirs: plagiarie had not its nativitie with printing, but began in times when thefts were difficult, and the paucity of bookes scarce wanted that invention.

Fourthly, while we so eagerly adhear unto antiquity, and the accounts of elder times, we are to consider the fabulous condition thereof;[209] and that wee shall not deny if wee call to minde the mendacity of Greece,[210] from whom we have received most relations, and that a considerable part of ancient times, was by the Greeks themselves termed *μύθικον*, that is made up or stuffed out with fables, and surely the fabulous inclination of those dayes, was greater then any since, which swarmed so with fables, and from such slender grounds, tooke hyntes for fictions, poysoning the world ever after; wherein how far they exceeded, may be exemplified from Palæphatus, in his book of fabulous narrations.[211] That fable of Orpheus, who by the melody of his musick, made woods and trees to follow him, was raised upon a slender foundation; for there were a crew of mad women, retyred unto a mountain, from whence being pacifyed by his musicke, they descended with boughs in their hands, which unto the fabulositie of those times, proved a sufficient ground to celebrate unto all posteritie the magick of Orpheus harpe, and its power to attract the senselesse trees about it.[212] That Medea the famous Sorceresse could renue youth, and make old men young againe, was nothing else but that from the knowledge of simples shee had a receipt to make white haire black, and reduce old heads into the tincture of youth againe.[213] The fable of Gerion and Cerberus with three heads was this: Gerion was of the city Tricarinia, that is of three heads, and Cerberus of the same place was one of his dogs, which running into a cave upon pursuit of his masters oxen, Hercules perforce drew him out of that place, from whence the conceits of those dayes affirmed no lesse, then that Hercules descended into hell, and brought up Cerberus into the habitation of the living.[214] Upon the like grounds was raised the figment of Briareus, who dwelling in a city called Hecatonchiria, the fancies of those times assigned him an hundred hands.[215] Twas ground enough to fancy wings unto Daedalus, in that he stole out of a window from Minos, and sailed away with his son Icarus, who steering his cours wisely, escaped, but his son carrying too high a saile was drowned. That Niobe weeping over her children was turned into a stone, was nothing else but that during her life, she erected over their sepultures, a marble tombe of her owne. When Acteon had undone himselfe with dogs, and the prodigall attendance of hunting, they made a solemne story how he was devoured by his hounds. And upon the like grounds was raised the anthropophagie of Diomedes his horses.[216] Upon as slender foundation was built, the fable of the Minotaure; for one Taurus a servant of Minos begat his mistresse Pasiphae with childe, from whence the infant was named Minotaurus.[217] Now this unto the fabulositie of those times was thought sufficient to accuse Pasiphae of beastialitie, or admitting conjunction with a bull, and in succeeding ages gave a hynte of depravity unto Domitian to act the fable into realitie.[218]

Fiftly, we applaude many things delivered by the ancients, which are in themselves but ordinarie, and come short of our own conceptions. Thus we usually extoll, and our orations cannot escape the sayings of the wisemen of Greece. *Nosce teipsum* of Thales: *Nosce tempus* of Pittacus:[219] *Nihil nimis* of Cleobulus; which notwithstanding to speake indifferently, are but vulgar precepts in morality, carrying with them nothing above the lyne, or beyond the extemporall sententiosity of common conceits with us.[220] Thus we magnifie the apothegmes, or reputed replyes of wisdome, whereof many are to be seen in Laertius, more in Lycosthenes, not a few in the second booke of Macrobius, in the salts of Cicero, Augustus, and the comicall wits of those times:[221] in most whereof there is not much of admiration, and are me thinkes exceeded, not only in the replyes of wise men, but the passages of societie and daily urbanities of our times. And thus we extoll their adages or proverbs; and Erasmus hath taken great pains to make collections of them, whereof notwithstanding the greater part will, I beleeve, unto indifferent judges be esteemed no such rarities, and may be paralelled, if not exceeded, by those of more unlearned nations, and many of our own.[222]

Sixtly, wee urge authorities, in points that need not, and introduce the testimony of ancient writers, to confirm things evidently beleeved, and whereto no reasonble hearer but would assent without them, such as are; *Nemo mortalium omnibus horis sapit*; *Virtute nil præstantius, nil pulchrius*; *Omnia vincit amor*; *Præclarum quiddam veritas*,[223] all which, although things knowne and vulgar, are frequently urged by many men, and though triviall verities in our mouthes, yet noted from Plato, Ovid, or Cicero, they receive immediate additions, and become reputed elegancies. For many hundred to instance but in one we meet with while we are writing. Antonius Guevara that elegant Spaniard, in his book intituled, *The Diall of Princes*, beginneth his epistle thus:[224] Apolonius Thyaneus disputing with the schollers of Hiarchas, said, that among all the affections of nature, nothing was more naturall, then the desire all have to preserve life; which being a confessed truth, and a veritie acknowledged by all, it was a superstuous affectation, to derive its authoritie from Apolonius, or seeke a confirmation thereof as farre as India, and the learned schollers of Hiarchus;[225] which whether it be not all one to strengthen common dignities and principles known by themselves, with the authoritie of mathematicians; or thinke a man should beleeve; the whole is greater then its parts, rather upon the authoritie of Euclide, then if it were propounded alone, I leave unto the second and wiser cogitations of all men.[226] Tis sure a practise that savours much of pedantery, a reserve of puerilitie wee have not shaken off from schoole, where being seasoned with minor sentences, by a neglect of higher enquiries, they prescribe upon our riper cares, and are never worne out but with our memories.

Lastly, while we so devoutly adhere unto antiquity in some things, we doe not consider we have deserted them in severall other; for they indeed have not only been imperfect, in the conceit of many things, but either ignorant or erroneous in divers other. They understood not the motion of the eight spheare from west to east, and so conceived the longitude of the starres invariable. They conceived the torrid zone unhabitable, and so made frustrate the goodliest part of the earth.[227] But we now know 'tis very well empeopled, and the habitation thereof esteemed so happy, that some have made it the proper seat of Paradise, and beene so farre from judging it unhabitable that they have made it the first habitation of all.[228] Many of the ancients denyed the Antipodes, and some unto the penalty of contrary affirmations;[229] but the experience of our enlarged navigations, can now assert them beyond all dubitation.[230] Having thus totally relinquisht them in some things, it may not be presumptuous, to examine them in others, but surely most unreasonable to adhere to them in all, as though they were infallible or could not erre in any.

CHAPTER VII
Of Authority

Nor is only a resolved prostration unto antiquity a powerfull enemy unto knowledge, but also a confident adherence unto any authority, or resignation of our judgements upon the testimony of any age or author whatsoever.[231]

For first,[232] to speake generally an argument from authority to wiser examinations, is but a weaker kinde of proofe, it being no other but a topicall probation, and as we terme it, an inartificiall argument, depending upon a naked asseveration: wherein neither declaring the causes, affections or adjuncts of what we believe,[233] it carrieth not with it the reasonable inducements of knowledge, and therefore *contra negantem principia*, *Ipse dixit*, or *oportet discentem credere*,[234] although they may be postulates, very accomodable unto junior indoctrinations, yet are their authorities but temporary, and not to be imbraced beyond the minority of our intellectuals.[235] For our advanced beliefs are not to be built upon dictates, but having received the probable inducements of truth, we become emancipated from testimoniall engagements, and are to erect upon the surer base of reason.

Secondly, unto reasonable perpensions it hath no place in some sciences, small in others, and suffereth many restrictions, even where it is most admitted.[236] It is of no validity in the mathematicks, especially the mother part thereof arithmetick and geometry:[237] For these sciences concluding from dignities and principles knowne by themselves, they receive not satisfaction from probable reasons, much lesse from bare and peremptory asseverations.[238] And therefore if all Athens should decree, that in every triangle, two sides which soever be taken are greater then the side remaining, or that in rectangle triangles the square which is made of the side that subtendeth the right angle, is equall to the squares which are made of the sides containing the right angle: although there be a certaine truth therein, would geometritians notwithstanding, receive a satisfaction without demonstration thereof?[239] 'Tis true by the vulgarity of philosophers, there are many points beleeved without probation, and if a man affirme from Ptolomy, that the Sun is bigger then the Earth, shall he probably meet with any contradiction herein, whereunto notwithstanding astronomers will not assent without some convincing argument or demonstrative proofe thereof?[240] And therefore certainly of all men a philosopher should be no swearer: for an oath which is the end of controversies in law cannot determine any here, nor are the deepest sacraments or desperate imprecations of any force to perswade where reason only, and necessary mediums must induce.[241]

In naturall philosophy, and which is more generally pursued amongst us, it carryeth but slender consideration, for that also proceeding from setled principles, therein is expected a satisfaction from scientificiall progressions, and such as beget, a sure and rationall beleefe. For if authority might have made out the assertions of philosophy, wee might have held, that snow was blacke, that the sea was but the sweat of the earth, and many of the like absurdities.[242] Then was Aristotle injurious to fall upon Melissus, and to reject the assertions of

Anaxagoras, Anaximander, and Empedocles, and then were we also ungratefull unto himselfe, from whom our junior endeavours embracing many things by his authority, our mature and secondary enquiries, are forced to quit those receptions, and to adhere unto the nearest accounts of reason.[243] And although it be not unusuall, even in philosophicall tractates to make enumeration of authors, yet are there reasons usually introduced, and to ingenuous readers doe carry the stroake in the perswasion.[244] And surely if we account it reasonable among our selves, and not injurious unto rationall authors, no farther to abet their opinions then as they are supported by solid reason; certainly with more excusable reservation may we shrink at their bare testimonies, whose argument is but precarious and subsists upon the charity of our assentments.

In morality, rhetorick, law and history, there is I confesse a frequent and allowable use of testimony, and yet herein I perceive, it is not unlimitable, but admitteth many restrictions. Thus in law both civill and divine, that is only esteemed *legitimum testimonium*, or a legall testimony, which receives comprobation from the mouths of at least two witnesses;[245] and that not onely for prevention of calumny, but assurance against mistake, whereas notwithstanding the solid reason of one man, is as sufficient as the clamor of a whole nation;[246] and within imprejudicate apprehensions begets as firm a beleef as the authoritie or aggregated testimony of many hundreds: for reason being the very root of our natures, and the principles thereof common unto all, what is against the lawes of true reason, or the undeceived[247] understanding of any one, if rightly apprehended must be disclaimed by all nations, and rejected even by mankinde.

Againe, a testimony is of small validity if deduced from men out of their owne profession; so if Lactantius affirme the figure of the earth is plaine, or Austin himselfe deny there are Antipodes;[248] though venerable Fathers of the Church, and ever to be honoured, yet will not their authorities prove sufficient to ground a beleefe thereon?[249] Whereas notwithstanding the solid reason or confirmed experience of any man, is very approveable in what profession soever. So Raymund Sebund, a physitian of Tholouze, besides his learned Dialogues, *De natura humana*, hath written a naturall theologie, demonstrating therein the attributes of God, and attempting the like in most points of religion.[250] So Hugo Grotius a civilian, did write an excellent tract in Dutch of the verity of Christian religion, and hath since contracted the same into six bookes in Latine, wherein most rationally delivering themselves, their works will be embraced by most that understand them, and their reasons enforce beliefe even from prejudicate readers.[251] Neither indeed have the authorities of men bin ever so awfull, but that by some they have beene rejected, even in their owne professions. Thus Aristotle affirming the birth of the infant or time of its gestation, extendeth sometimes unto the eleventh month, but Hippocrates averring that it exceedeth not the tenth. Adrian the Emperour in a solemne processe, determined for Aristotle, but Justinian many yeares after, tooke in with Hippocrates and reversed the decree of the other.[252] Thus have councels not onely condemned private men, but the decrees and acts of one another. So Galen after all his veneration of Hippocrates, in some things hath fallen from him. Avicen in many from Galen, and others succeeding from him: and although the singularity of Paracelsus be intollerable, who sparing onely Hippocrates, hath reviled not onely the authors, but almost all the learning that went before him;[253] yet is it not much lesse injurious unto knowledge obstinately and inconvincibly to side with any one: which humour unhappily possessing many men, they have by prejudice withdrawne themselves into parties, and contemning the soveraignty of truth, seditiously abetted the private divisions of error.

Moreover a testimony in points historicall, and where it is of unavoydable use, is of no illation in the negative, nor is it of consequence that Herodotus writing nothing of Rome, there was therefore no such city in his time; or because Dioscorides hath made no mention of unicornes horne, there is therefore no such thing in nature.[254] Indeed intending an accurate enumeration of medicall materials, the omission hereof affords some probability; it was not used by the ancients, but will not conclude the nonexistence thereof. For so may we annihilate many simples unknowne to his enquiries, as senna, rhabarbe, bezoar, ambregris, and divers others.[255] Whereas indeed the reason of man hath no such restraint, concluding not onely affirmatively but negatively, not onely affirming there is no magnitude beyond the last heavens, but also denying there is any vacuity within them: although it be confessed the affirmative hath the prerogative illation, and Barbara engrosseth the powerfull demonstration.[256]

Lastly, the strange and unimaginable relations made by authors, may sufficiently discourage our adherence unto authority, and which if we beleeve we must be apt to swallow any thing. Thus Basil will tell us, the serpent went erect like man, and that that beast could speake before the fall.[257] Tostatus would make us beleeve that Nilus encreaseth every new moone.[258] Leonardo Fioravanti an Italian physitian, beside many other secrets assumeth unto himselfe the discovery of one concerning pellitory of the wall; that is, that it never groweth in the sight of the North Star.[259] *Dove si possa vedere la stella Tramontana*, wherein how wide he is from truth is easily discoverable unto every one, who hath but astronomy enough to know that starre.[260] Franciscus Sanctius in a laudable comment of his upon Alciats Emblems, affirmeth and that from experience, a nightingale hath no tongue. *Avem Philomelam lingua carere pro certo affirmare possum, nisi me oculi fallunt.*[261] Which if any man for a while shall beleeve upon his experience, he may at his leasure refute it by his owne. What foole almost would beleeve, at least, what wise man would rely upon that Antidote delivered by Pierius in his Hieroglyphicks against the sting of a scorpion? That is, to sit upon an asse with ones face toward his taile; for so the paine, from its sting leaveth the man, and passeth into the beast.[262] It were me thinks but an uncomfortable receite for a quartane ague, and yet as good perhaps as many others used, to have recourse unto the remedy of Sammonicus, that is, to lay the fourth book of Homers Iliads under ones head, according to the precept of that physitian and poet, *Mœoniae Iliados quartum suppone trementi*. There are surely few that have beliefe to swallow, or hope enough to experiment the Collyrium of Albertus, which promiseth a strange effect, and such as thieves would count inestimable; that is, to make one see in the darke: yet thus much, according unto his receit, will the right eye of an hedgehog boyled in oyle and preserved in a brasen vessell effect.[263] As strange it is, and unto vicious inclinations were worth a nights lodging with Lais, what is delivered in Kiranides, that the left stone of a weesell, wrapt up in the skin of a she mule, is able to secure incontinency from conception.[264]

These with swarmes of others have men delivered in their writings, whose verities are onely supported by their authorities: but being neither consonant unto reason, nor correspondent unto experiment, their affirmations are unto us no axiomes, wee esteeme thereof as things unsaid, and account them but in the list of nothing. I wish herein the chymistes had beene more sparing, who overmagnifying their preparations, inveigle the curiosity of many, and delude the security of most.[265] For if their experiments would answer their encomiums, the stone and quartane agues, were not opprobrious unto physitians; And we might contemne that first, and most uncomfortable aphorisme of Hippocrates; *Ars Longa, Vita Brevis*, for surely that art were soone attained, that hath so generall remedies, and life could not be short, were there such to prolong it.[266]

CHAPTER VIII
A Briefe Enumeration of Authors

Now for as much as we have discoursed of authority, and there is scarce any tradition or popular error but stands also delivered by some good author; we shall endeavour a short discovery of such as for the major part have given authority hereto: who although excellent and usefull authors, yet being either transcriptive, or following the common relations of things, their accounts are not to be swallowed at large, or entertained without a prudent circumspection.[267] In whom the *ipse dixit*, although it be no powerfull argument in any, is yet lesse authentick then in many other, because they deliver not their owne experiences, but others affirmations, and write from others as we our selves from them.

1. The first in order as also in time, shall be Herodotus of Halicarnassus, an excellent and very elegant historian, whose books of history were so well received in his owne dayes, that at their rehearsall in the Olympick games, they obtained the names of the nine muses, and continued in such esteeme unto descending ages, that Cicero termed him *Historiarum parens*.[268] And Dionysius his countreyman, in an epistle to Pompey, after an expresse comparison, affords him the better of Thucydides;[269] all which notwithstanding, he hath received from some, the stile of *Mendaciorum pater*; his authority was much infringed by Plutarch, who being offended with him, as Polybius had bin with Philarcus, for speaking too coldly of his countreymen, hath left a particular tract, *De Malignitate Herodoti*.[270] But in this latter century, Camerarius and Stephanus have stepped in, and by their witty apologies, effectually endeavoured to frustrate the arguments of Plutarch, or any other.[271] Now in this author, as may be observed in our ensuing discourse, and is better discernable in the perusall of

himselfe, there are many things fabulously delivered, and not to be accepted as truthes: whereby neverthelesse if any man be deceived, the author is not so culpable as the believer. For he indeed imitating the father poet, whose life he hath also written, and as Thucydides observeth, as well intending the delight as benefit of his reader, hath besprinkled his worke with many fabulosities, whereby if any man be led into errour, he mistaketh the intention of the author, who plainly confesseth hee writeth many things by hearesay, and forgetteth a very considerable caution of his, that is, *Ego quæ fando cognovi, exponere narratione mea debeo omnia; credere autem esse vera omnia, non debeo.*[272]

2. In the second place is Ctesias the Cnidian, physitian unto Artaxerxes King of Persia, his books are often cited by ancient writers; and by the industry of Stephanus and Rodomanus, there are extant some fragments thereof in our dayes; he wrote the History of Persia, and many narrations of India.[273] In the first as having a fair oportunity to know the truth: and as Diodorus affirmeth the perusall of Persian records, his testimony is acceptable; in his Indiary relations, wherein are contained strange and incredible accounts, he is surely to be read with suspension;[274] and these were they which weakned his authority with former ages, and made him contemptible unto most. For as we may observe, he is seldome mentioned, without a derogatory parenthesis in any author; Aristotle besides the frequent undervaluing of his authority, in his bookes of animals gives him the lie no lesse then twice, concerning the seed of elephants.[275] Strabo in his eleventh booke hath left a harder censure of him. *Equidem facilius Hesiodo et Homero, aliquis fidem adhibuerit, itemque Tragicis Poetis, quam Ctesiæ Herodoto, Hellanico et eorum similibus.*[276] But Lucian hath spoken more plainly then any. *Scripsit Ctesias de Indorum regione, deque iis quæ apud illos sunt, ea quæ nec ipse vidit, neque ex ullius sermone audivit.*[277] Yet were his relations taken up by most succeeding writers, and many thereof revived by our country-man, Sir John Mandevell Knight and Doctor in Physicke, who after thirty years peregrination dyed at Leige, and was there honourably interred.[278] He left behinde him a booke of his travells, which hath been honoured with the translation of many languages, and hath now continued above three hundred years; herein he often attesteth the fabulous relations of Ctesias, and seems to confirme the refuted accounts of antiquity: all which may still be received in some acceptions

of morality, and to a pregnant invention, may afforde commendable mythologie, but in a naturall and proper exposition, it containeth impossibilities and things inconsistent with truth.[279]

3. There is a book *De mirandis auditionibus*, ascribed unto Aristotle, another *De mirabilibus narrationibus*, written long after by Antigonus, another also of the same title by Plegon Trallianus translated by Xilander, and with the annotations of Meursius;[280] all whereof make good the promise of their titles and may be read with caution; which if any man shall likewise observe in the Lecture of Philostratus, concerning the life of Apolonius, or not only in ancient writers, but shall carry a wary eye, on Paulus Venetus, Jovius, Olaus Magnus, Nierembergius, and many other, I thinke his circumspection is laudable, and he may thereby decline occasion of error.[281]

4. Dioscorides Anazarbeus, hee wrote many bookes in physicke, but six thereof *De Materia Medica*, have found the greatest esteeme;[282] hee is an author of good antiquity, and better use, preferred by Galen before Cratevas, Pamphilus, and all that attempted the like description before him;[283] yet all hee delivereth therein is not to be conceived oraculous: for beside that, following the warres under Anthony, the course of his life would not permit a punctuall examen in all; there are many things concerning the nature of simples, traditionally delivered, and to which I beleeve he gave no assent himselfe. It had been an excellent receit, and in his time when sadles were scarce in fashion of very great use, if that were true, which he delivers, that Vitex, or Agnus Castus held only in the hand, preserveth the rider from galling.[284] It were a strange effect, and whores would forsake the experiment of Savine, if that were a truth which hee delivereth of brake or femall fearne, that only treading over it, it causeth a sudden abortion.[285] It were to be wished true, and women would idolize him, could that be made out which he recordeth of phyllon, mercury, and other vegetables, that the juice of the masle plant drunke, or the leaves but applied unto the genitalls, determines their conceptions unto males.[286] In these relations although he be more sparing, his predecessours were very numerous; and Galen hereof most sharply accuseth Pamphilus: many of the like nature we meet sometimes in Oribasius, Ætius, Trallianus, Serapion, Evax, and Marcellus, whereof some containing no colour of verity, we may at first sight reject them, others which seem to carry some face of truth, we may reduce unto experiment.[287] And herein we shall

rather peforme good offices unto truth, then any disservice unto their relators, who have well deserved of succeeding ages, from whom having received the conceptions of former times, we have the readier hint of their conformity with ours, and may accordingly explore their verities.

5. Plinius Secundus of Verona, a man of great eloquence, and industry indefatigable, as may appeare by the number of the writings, especially those now extant, and which are never like to perish, but even with learning it selfe, that is, his naturall Historie comprised in 36 bookes;[288] hee was the greatest collector or rhapsodist of all the Latines, and as Suetonius *De viris Illustribus* observeth, hee collected this piece out of 2000 Latine and Greeke authors.[289] Now what is very strange, there is scarce a popular errour passant in our dayes, which is not either directly expressed, or diductively contained in this worke, which being in the hands of most men, hath proved a powerfull occasion of their propogation; wherein notwithstanding the credulitie of the reader, is more condemnable then the curiositie of the authour. For commonly he nameth the authors, from whom he received those accounts, and writes himselfe by heare say, as in his preface unto Vespasian he acknowledgeth.[290]

6. Claudius Ælianus, who flourished not long after in the raigne of Trajan, unto whom he dedicated his Tacticks, an elegant and miscellaneous author, he hath left two bookes which are in the hands of every one, his History of Animals, and his *Varia historia*, wherein are contained many things supicious, not a few false, some impossible;[291] hee is much beholding unto Ctesias, and in many subjects writes more confidently then Plinie.

7. Julius Solinus, who lived also about his time: he left a work entituled *Polyhistor*, containing great varietie of matter, and is with most in good request at this day:[292] but to speake freely what cannot bee concealed, it is but Plinie varied, or a transcription of his naturall historie; nor is it without all wonder it hath continued so long, but is now likely, and deserves indeed to live for ever; not so much for the elegancy of the text, as the excellency of the comment, lately performed by Salmasius, under the name of Plinian exercitations.[293]

8. Athenæus a delectable author, and very various, and as Causabone in his Epistle stiles him *Græcorum Plinius*: there is extant of his, a famous piece under the name of *Deipnosophista*, or *Cœna sapientum*, containing the discourse of many learned men, at

a feast provided by Laurentius.[294] It is a laborious collection out of many authors, and some whereof are mentioned no where else.[295] It containeth strange and singular relations, not without some spice or sprinckling of all learning. The author was probably a better gramarian then philosopher, dealing but hardly with Aristotle and Plato, and betrayeth himselfe much in his chapter *de curiositate Aristotelis*;[296] in briefe, he is an author of excellent use, and may with discretion, be read unto great advantage: and hath therefore well deserved, the comments of Causabon and Dalecampius:[297] but being miscellaneous in many things, he is to be received with suspicion; for such as amasse all relations, must erre in some, and may without offence be unbeleeved in many.

9. Wee will not omit the workes of Nicander, a poet of good antiquity, that is, his Theriaca, and Alexipharmaca, translated and commented by Gorræus:[298] for therein are contained severall traditions, and popular conceits, of venemous beasts, which only deducted, the worke is ever to be embraced, as containing the first description of poysons, and their Antidotes, whereof Dioscorides, Pliny, and Galen, have made especiall use in elder times; and Ardoynus, Grevinus and others, in times more neere our owne.[299] Wee might perhaps let passe Oppianus, that famous Cilician poet.[300] There are extant of his in Greeke, foure bookes of Cynegeticks or venation, five of Halieuticks or piscation, commented and published by Ritterhusius, wherein describing beasts of venerie, and fishes, hee hath indeed but sparingly inserted the vulgar conceptions thereof:[301] so that abating onely the annuall mutation of sexes in the hyæna, the single sex of the rhinoceros, the antipathy betweene two drummes, of a lambe and a wolfes skinne, the informity of cubbes, the venation of centaures, the copulation of the murena and the viper, with some few others, hee may bee read with great delight and profit.[302] It is not without some wonder, his elegant lines are so neglected. Surely hereby wee reject one of the best epick poets, and much condemn the judgement of Antoninus, whose apprehensions so honoured his poems, that as some report, for every verse, hee assigned him a stater of gold.[303]

10. More warily are we to receive the relations of Philes, who in Greeke iambicks delivered the proprieties of animals, for herein hee hath amassed the vulgar accounts recorded by the ancients, and hath therein especially followed Ælian, and likewise Johannes Tzetzes, a gramarian, who besides a comment upon Hesiod and Homer, hath left us Chiliads *de varia Historia*, wherein delivering the accounts of Ctesias, Herodotus,

and most of the ancients, he is to be embraced with caution, and as a transcriptive relator.[304]

11. Wee cannot without partialitie omit all caution even of holy writers, and such whose names are venerable unto all posterity, not to meddle at all with miraculous authours, or any legendary relators:[305] Wee are not without circumspection to receive some bookes even of authentick and renowned fathers. So are we to read the leaves of Basil and Ambrose in their bookes, entituled *Hexameron*, or *The description of the Creation*;[306] wherein delivering particular accounts of all the creatures, they have left us relations sutable to those of Ælian, Plinie and other naturall writers; whose authorities herein they followed, and from whom most probably, they desumed their narrations.[307] And the like hath been committed by Epiphanius, in his Phisiologie, that is, a booke he hath left concerning the nature of animals.[308] With no lesse caution must we looke on Isidor, Bishop of Sevill, who having left in 25 bookes, an accurate worke *De Originibus*, hath to the etymologie of words, superadded their received natures; wherein most generally hee consents with common opinions and authors which have delivered them.[309]

12. Albertus Bishop of Ratisbone, for his great learning and latitude of knowledge sirnamed Magnus, besides divinitie, he hath written many tracts in philosophie;[310] what we are chiefly to receive with caution, are his naturall tractates, more especially those of mineralls, vegetables, and animals, which are indeed chiefly collections out of Aristotle, Ælian, and Plinie, and respectively containe many of our popular errors. A man who hath much advanced these opinions by the authoritie of his name, and delivered most conceits, with strickt enquirie into few. In the same classis, may well be placed Vincentius Belluacensis, or rather he from whom he collected his *Speculum naturale*, that is, Gulielmus de Conchis, as also Hortus Sanitatis, and Bartholomeus Glanvill, sirnamed Anglicus, who writ *De Proprietatibus rerum*. Hither also may be referred Kiranides, which is a collection of Harpocration the Greek, and sundry Arabick writers;[311] delivering not onely the naturall but magicall proprietie of things, a worke as full of vanitie, as varietie, containing many relations, whose invention is as difficult as their beliefes, and their experiments sometime as hard as either.

13. We had almost forgot Jeronymus Cardanus that famous physition of Milan a great enquirer of truth, but too greedy a receiver of it, he hath left many excellent discourses, medicall,

naturall, and astrologicall; the most suspicious are those two he wrote by admonition in a dream, that is, *de subtilitate et varietate rerum.*[312] Assuredly this learned man hath taken many things upon trust, and although examined some, hath let slip many others. He is of singular use unto a prudent reader, but unto him that desireth hoties, or to replenish his head with varieties, like many others before related, either in the originall or confirmation, he may become no small occasion of error.[313]

14. Lastly, those authors are also suspicious, nor greedily to be swallowed, who pretend to write of secrets, to deliver antipathies, sympathies, and the occult abstrucities of things, in the list whereof may be accounted, Alexis Pedimont, Antonius Mizaldus, Trinum Magicum, and many others;[314] not omitting that famous philosopher of Naples, Baptista Porta, in whose workes, although there be contained many excellent things, and verified upon his owne experience; yet are there many also receptary, and such as will not endure the test: who although he have delivered many strange relations in other peices, as his Phylognomy, and his Villa; yet hath he more remarkeably expressed himselfe in his Naturall Magick, and the miraculous effects of nature:[315] which containing a various and delectable subject, with all promising wondrous and easie effects, they are entertained by readers at all hands, whereof the major part sit downe in his authority, and thereby omit not onely the certainty of truth, but the pleasure of its experiment.[316]

And thus have we made a briefe enumeration of these learned men, not willing any to decline their workes, (without which it is not easie to attaine any measure of generall knowledge) but to apply themselves with caution thereunto. And seeing the lapses of these worthy pens, we are to cast a wary eye on those diminutive, and pamphlet treaties dayly published amongst us, pieces maintaining rather typography then verity.[317] Authors presumably writing by common places, wherein for many yeares promiscuously amassing all that makes for their subject, they break forth at last in trite and fruitlesse rhapsodies, doing thereby not onely open injury unto learning, but committing a secret treachery upon truth.[318] For their relations falling generally upon credulous readers, they meet with prepared beliefes, whose supinities had rather assent unto all, then adventure the triall of any.

Thus, I say, must these authors be read, and thus must we be read our selves, for discoursing of matters dubious, and many controvertible truths, we cannot without arrogancy entreate a credulity, or implore any farther assent, then the probability of our reasons, and verity of experiments induce.

CHAPTER IX
Of the Same

There are beside these authors and such as have positively promoted errors, diverse other which are in some way accessory, whose verities although they do not directly assert, yet doe they obliquely concurre unto their beliefes. In which account are many holy writers, preachers, moralists, rhetoricians, orators and poets; for they depending upon invention deduce their mediums from all things whatsoever, and playing much upon the simile, or illustrative argumentation, induce their enthymemes unto the people, they take up popular conceits, and from traditions unjustifiable or really false, illustrate matters, though not of consequence, yet undeniable truths.[319] Wherein although their intention be sincere, and that course not much condemnable, yet are the effects thereof unwarrantable, in as much as they strengthen common errors, and confirme as veritable those conceits, which verity cannot allow.

Thus have some divines drawne into argument the fable of the phænix, made use of that of the salamander, pellican, basilisk, and divers relations of Pliny, deducing from thence most worthy morals, and even upon our Saviour.[320] Now although this be not prejudicial unto wiser judgements, who are indeed but weakly moved with such kind of argument, yet is it oftentimes occasion of error unto vulgar heads, who expect in the fable as equall a truth as in the morall, and conceive that infallible philosophy, which is in any sence delivered by divinity. But wiser discerners do well understand, that every art hath its owne circle, that the effects of things are best examined, by sciences wherein are delivered their causes, that strict and definitive expressions, are alway required in philosophy, but a loose and popular delivery will serve oftentimes in divinity;[321] as may be observed even in holy Scripture, which often omitteth the exact account of things, describing them rather to our apprehensions, then leaving doubts in vulgar minds, upon their unknowne and philosophicall descriptions. Thus it termeth the Sun and the Moone, the two great lights of heaven.[322] Now if any man shall from hence conclude, the

Moone is second in magnitude unto the Sun, he must excuse my beliefe; and I thinke it cannot be taken for heresie,[323] if I herein rather adhere unto the demonstration of Ptolomy, then the popular description of Moses.[324] Thus is it said, Chronicles 2.4, That Solomon made a molten sea of ten cubits, from brim to brim round in compasse, and five cubits the height thereof, and a line of thirty cubits did compasse it round about. Now in this description, the circumference is made just treble unto the diameter, that is, ten to thirty, or seven to twenty one. But Archimedes demonstrates in his *Cyclometria* that the proportion of the diameter, unto the circumference, is as 7 unto almost 22, which will occasion a sensible difference that is almost a cubit.[325] Now if herein I adhere unto Archimedes who speaketh exactly rather then the sacred text which speaketh largely, I hope I shall not offend divinity.[326] I am sure I shall have reason and experience of every circle to support me.

Thus morall writers, rhetoricians and orators make use of severall relations which will not consist with verity. Aristotle in his Ethicks takes up the conceit of the bever, and the divulsion of his testicles.[327] The tradition of the beare, the viper, and divers others are frequent amongst orators.[328] All which although unto the illiterate, and undiscerning hearers may seem a confirmation of their reallities; yet is this no reasonable establishment unto others, who will not depend hereon other-wise then common apologues, which being of impossible fal-sities do notwithstanding include wholesome moralities, and such as do expiate the trespasse of their absurdities.[329]

The hieroglyphicall doctrine of the Egyptians (which in their four hundred yeares cohabitation, some conjecture they learned from the Hebrewes) hath much advanced many popu-lar conceits, for using an alphabet of things, and not of words, through the image and pictures thereof, they endeavoured to speak their hidden conceits, in the letters and language of nature;[330] in pursuit whereof, although in many things, they exceeded not their true, and reall apprehensions, yet in some other they either framing the story, or taking up the tradition, conduceable unto their intentions, obliquely confirmed many falsities, which as authentick and conceded truths did after passe unto the Greeks, from them unto other nations, are still retained by symbolicall writers, emblematistes, heraldes and others, whereof some are strictly maintained for truths, as naturally making good their artificiall representations; others symbolically intended are literally received, and swallowed in the first sense, without all gust of the second.[331] Famous in this doctrine in former ages were Heraiscus, Cheremon, and Epius, especially Orus Apollo Niliacus, who lived in the reigne of Theodosius and in Ægyptian language left two bookes of hieroglyphicks, translated into Greek by Philippus, in Latine published by Hoschelius, and a full collection of all made lately by Pierius.[332]

Painters who are the visible representers of things, and such as by the learned sense of the eye endeavour to informe the understanding, are not inculpable herein, who either describing naturalls as they are, or actions as they have been, have oftentimes erred in their delineations, which being the bookes that all can read, are fruitfull advancers of these conceptions, especially in common and popular apprehensions, who being unable for farther enquiry must rest in the text, and letter of their descriptions.[333]

Lastly, poets and poeticall writers have in this point exceeded others, leaving unto us the notions of harpies, centaurs, gryphins, and divers others. Now how ever to make use of fictions, apologues and fables be not unwarrantable, and the intent of these inventions might point at laudable ends: yet doe they afford to our junior capacities a frequent occasion of error, setling impressions in our tender memories, which our advanced judgements, doe generally neglect to expunge. This way the vaine and idle fictions of the Gentils, did first insinuate into the heads of Christians, and thus are they continued even unto our dayes:[334] our first and literary apprehensions being commonly instructed in authors which handle nothing else;[335] wherewith our memories being stuffed, our inventions become pedantick, and cannot avoid their allusions, driving at these as at the highest elegancies, which are but the frigidities of wit, and become not the genius of our more manly ingenuities.[336] It were therefore no losse like that of Galens study, if these had found the same fate, and would in some way requite the neglect of solid authors, if they were lesse pursued.[337] For surely were a pregnant wit educated in ignorance hereof, receiving only impressions from realities, from such solid foundations, it must needs raise more substantiall superstructions, and fall upon very many excellent straynes, which have been jusled off by their intrusions.[338]

CHAPTER X

Of the Last and Common Promoter of False Opinions, the Endeavours of Satan

But beside the infirmities of humane nature, the seed of error within our selves, and the severall wayes of delusion from each other, there is an invisible agent, and secret promoter without us, whose activity is undiscerned, and playes in the darke upon us, and that is the first contriver of error, and professed opposer of truth, the Divell. For though permitted unto his proper principles, Adam perhaps would have sinned, without the suggestion of Satan, and from the transgressive infirmities of himselfe might have erred alone, as well as the angels before him.[339] And although also there were no divell at all, yet is there now in our natures a confessed sufficiency unto corruption; and the frailty of our owne oeconomie, were able to betray us out of truth;[340] yet wants there not another agent, who taking advantage hereof, proceedeth to obscure the diviner part, and efface all tract of its traduction; to attempt a particular of all his wiles, is too bold an arithmetick for man, what most considerably concerneth his popular, and practised wayes of delusion, he first deceiveth mankinde in five maine points concerning God and himselfe.[341]

And first his endeavours have ever been, and they cease not yet to instill a beleefe in the minde of man, there is no God at all; and this he specially labours to establish in a direct and literall apprehension, that is, that there is no such reallity existent, that the necessity of his entity dependeth upon ours, and is but a politicall chymera;[342] that the naturall truth of God is an artificiall erection of man, and the Creator himselfe but a subtile invention of the creature. Where hee succeeds not thus high, he labours to introduce a secondary and deductive atheisme, that although they concede there is a God, yet should they deny his providence, and therefore assertions have flown about, that he intendeth only the care of the species or common natures, but letteth loose the guard of individualls, and single essences therein:[343] that hee looks not below the moone, but hath designed the regiment of sublunary affaires unto inferiour deputations;[344] to promote which apprehensions or empuzzell their due conceptions, he casteth in the notions of fate, destiny, fortune, chance and necessity; tearms commonly misconceived by vulgar heads, and their propriety sometime perverted by the wisest. Whereby extinguishing in mindes the compensation of vertue and vice, the hope and feare of heaven or hell, they comply in their actions unto the drift of his delusions, and live like creatures below the capacity of either.

Now hereby he not only undermineth the base of religion, and destroyeth the principle preambulous unto all beliefe, but puts upon us the remotest error from truth.[345] For Atheisme is the greatest falsity, and to affirme there is no God the highest lie in nature: and therefore strictly taken, some men will say his labour is in vaine; For many there are, who cannot concive there was ever any absolute Atheist, or such as could determine there was no God, without all checke from himselfe, or contradiction from his own opinions;[346] and therefore those few so called by elder times, might be the best of pagans, suffering that name rather, in relation to the gods of the Gentiles, then the true Creatour of all. A conceit that cannot befall his greatest enemy, or him that would induce the same in us, who hath a sensible apprehension hereof, for he beleeveth with trembling. To speake yet more strictly and conformably unto some opinions, no creature can wish thus much, nor can the will which hath a power to runne into velleities, and wishes of impossibilities, have any *utinam* of this.[347] For to desire there were no God, were plainly to unwish their owne being, which must needes be anihilated in the substraction of that essence, which substantially supporteth them, and restraines them from regression into nothing. And if as some contend, no creature can desire his owne anihilation, that nothing is not appetible, and not to be at all, is worse then to bee in the miserable condition of something;[348] the divell him selfe could not embrace that motion, nor would the enemy of God be freed by such a redemption.

But coldly thriving in this designe, as being repulsed by the principles of humanity, and the dictates of that production, which cannot deny its originall, he fetcheth a wider cirle, and when he cannot make men conceive there is no God at all, hee endeavours to make them beleeve, there is not one but many; wherein he hath been so successefull with common heads, that hee hath led their beliefe thorow all the workes of nature.

Now in this latter attempt, the subtilty of his circumvension, hath indirectly obtained the former.[349] For although to opinion there be many gods, may seem an excesse in religion, and such as cannot at all consist with Atheisme, yet doth it diductively and upon inference include the same: for unity is the inseparable and essentiall attribute of deitie; and if there be more then one God, it is no Atheisme to say there is no God at all. And herein though Socrates onely suffered, yet were Plato and Aristotle guilty of the same truth, who demonstratively understanding the simplicity of perfection, and the indivisible condition of the first causator, it was not in the power of earth, or Areopagy of hell to work them from it*.[350] For holding an apodicticall knowledge, and assured science of its verity, to perswade their apprehensions unto a plurality of gods in the world, were to make Euclide beleeve there were more then one center in a circle, or one right angle in a triangle;[351] which were indeed a fruitlesse attempt, and inferreth absurdities beyond the evasion of hell. For though mechanicke and vulgar heads ascend not unto such comprehensions, who live not commonly unto halfe the advantage of their principles, yet did they not escape the eye of wiser Minervaes, and such as made good the genealogie of Jupiters braines, who although they had divers styles for God, yet under many appellations acknowledged one divinity:[352] rather conceiving thereby the evidence or acts of his power in severall wayes and places, then a multiplication of essence, or reall distraction of unity in any one.

* Areopagus *the severe Court of Athens.*

Againe, to render our errors more monstrous, (and what unto miracle sets forth the patience of God) hee hath endeavored to make the world beleeve, that he was God himselfe, and fayling of his first attempt to be but like the highest in heaven, he hath obtained with men to be the same on earth, and hath accordingly assumed the annexes of divinity, and the prerogatives of the Creator, drawing into practise the operation of miracles, and the prescience of things to come.[353] Thus hath he in a specious way wrought cures upon the sick: played over the wondrous acts of prophets, and counterfeited many miracles of Christ and his Apostles. Thus hath he openly contended with God; and to this effect his insolency was not ashamed to play a solemne prize with Moses, wherein although his performance was very specious, and beyond the common apprehension of any power below a Deitie, yet was it not such as could make good his omnipotency.[354] For he was wholly confounded in the conversion of dust into lice. An act philosophy can scarce deny to be above the power of nature, nor upon a requisite predisposition beyond the efficacy of the sun.[355] Wherein notwithstanding the head of the old serpent was confessedly too weak for Moses hand, and the arm of his magicians too short for the finger of God.[356]

Thus hath he also made men beleeve that he can raise the dead, that he hath the key of life and death, and a prerogative above that principle which makes no regression from privations. The Stoicks that opinioned the soules of wise men, dwelt about the moone, and those of fooles wandred about the earth, advantaged the conceit of this effect, wherein the Epicureans, who held that death was nothing, nor nothing after death, must contradict their principles to be deceived. Nor could the Pythagorian or such as maintained the transmigration of souls give easie admittance hereto:[357] for holding that separated soules, successively supplyed other bodies, they could hardly allow the raising of soules from other worlds, which at the same time, they conceived conjoyned unto bodies in this. More inconsistent with these opinions, is the error of Christians, who holding the dead doe rest in the Lord, doe yet beleeve they are at the lure of the divell; that he who is in bonds himself commandeth the fetters of the dead, and dwelling in the bottomlesse lake, the blessed from Abrahams bosome.[358] That can beleeve the resurrection of Samuel, or that there is any thing but delusion, in the practise of necromancy and popular conception of ghosts.[359]

He hath moreover endeavoured the opinion of deitie, by the delusion of dreames, and the discovery of things to come, in sleepe above the prescience of our waked senses.[360] In this expectation he perswaded the credulity of elder times to take up their lodging before his temple, in skinnes of their owne sacrifices, till his reservednesse had contrived answers, whose accomplishments were in his power, or not beyond his presagement.[361] Which way although it hath pleased Almightie God, sometimes to reveale himself, yet was their proceeding very different. For the revelations of heaven are conveied by new impressions, and the immediate illumination of the soule; whereas the deceaving spirit, by concitation of humors, produceth his conceited phantasmes, or by compounding the species already residing, doth make up words which mentally speake his intentions.[362]

But above all other hee most advanced his deitie in the solemne practise of oracles, wherein in severall parts of the world, he publikely professed his divinity;[363] but how short they flew, of that spirit, whose omniscience they would resemble, their weaknesse sufficiently declared. What jugling there was therein, the oratour plainely confessed, who being good at the same game himselfe, could say that Pythia Phillippised: who can but laugh at the carriage of Ammon unto Alexander, who addressing unto him as God, was made to beleeve, hee was a god himself?[364] How openly did he betray his indivinity unto Cræsus, who being ruined by his amphibologie, and expostulating with him for so ungratefull a deceit, received no higher answer, then the excuse of his impotency upon the contradiction of fate, and the setled law of powers beyond his power to controle;[365] what more then sublunary directions, or such as might proceed from the oracle of humane reason, was in his advice unto the Spartans in the time of a great plague; when for the cessation thereof, he wisht them to have recourse unto a fawn, that is in open tearms unto one Nebrus, a good physition of those dayes*.[366] From no diviner a spirit came his reply unto Caracalla, who requiring a remedy for his gout, received no other counsell then to refraine cold drinke, which was but a dieteticall caution, and such as without a journey unto Æsculapius, culinary prescription and kitchin aphorismes, might have afforded at home.[367] Nor surely if any truth there were therein of more then naturall activity was his counsell unto Democritus, when for the falling sicknesse he commended the maggot in a goats head; for many things secret are very true, sympathyes and antipathyes are safely authenticke unto us, who ignorant of their causes may yet acknowledge their effects.[368] Beside being a naturall magician he may performe many acts in wayes above our knowledge, though not transcending our naturall power, when our knowledge shall direct it;[369] part hereof hath been discovered by himselfe, and some by humane indagation which though magnified as fresh inventions unto us, are stale unto his cognition:[370] I hardly beleeve, he hath from elder times unknowne the verticity of the loadstone; surely his perspicacity discerned it to respect the north, when ours beheld it indeterminately.[371] Many secrets there are in nature of difficult discovery unto man, of naturall knowledge unto Satan, whereof some his vainglory cannot conceale, others his envy will never discover.

* Nebros *in Greek, a Fawne.*

Againe, such is the mystery of his delusion, that although he labour to make us beleeve that he is God, and supremest nature whatsoever, yet would he also perswade our beleefes that he is lesse then angels or men, and his condition not only subjected unto rationall powers, but the action of things which have no efficacy on our selves; thus hath hee inveigled no small part of the world into a credulity of artificiall magick.[372] That there is an art, which without compact commandeth the powers of hell, whence some have delivered the policy of spirits, and left an account even to their provinciall dominions, that they stand in awe of charmes, spells and conjurations, that he is afraid of letters and characters of notes and dashes, which set together doe signifie nothing; and not only in the dictionary of man, but the subtiler vocabulary of Satan.[373] That there is any power in bitumen, pitch or brimstone, to purifie the aire from his uncleannesse, that any vertue there is in Hipericon to make good the name of *fuga Demonis*, any such magick as is ascribed unto the root baaras by Josephus or Cynospastus by Ælianus, it is not easie to beleeve, nor is it naturally made out what is delivered of Tobias, that by the fume of a fishes liver, he put to flight Asmodeus.[374] That they are afraid of the pentangle of Solomon, though so set forth with the body of man, as to touch and point out the five places wherein our Saviour was wounded.[375] I know not how to assent if perhaps he hath fled from holy water, if he cares not to heare the sound of Tetragrammaton, if his eye delight not in the signe of the crosse, and that sometimes he will seem to be charmed with words of holy Scripture, and to flye from the letter and dead verbality, who must only start at the life and animated interiors thereof.[376] It may be feared they are but Parthian flights, ambuscado retreats, and elusory tergiversations, whereby to confirme our credulities, he will comply with the opinion of such powers which in themselves have no activities, whereof having once begot in our mindes an assured dependence, he makes us relye on powers which he but precariously obeyes, and to desert those true and only charmes which hell cannot withstand.[377]

Lastly, to lead us farther into darknesse, and quite to lose us in this maze of error, he would make men beleeve there is no such creature as himselfe, and that hee is not onely subject unto inferiour creatures but in the ranke of nothing: insinuating into mens mindes there is no divell at all and contriveth accordingly, many wayes to conceale or indubitate his existency:[378] wherein beside that hee anihilates the blessed angels and spirits in the ranke of his creation, hee begets a security of himselfe and a carelesse eye unto the last remunerations.[379] And therefore hereto he inveigleth, not only the Sadduces and such as retaine unto the Church of God, but is also content that Epicurus, Democritus or any of the heathen should hold the same.[380] And to this effect he maketh men beleeve that apparitions, and such as confirme his existence are either deceptions of sight, or melancholy depravements of phancy: thus when he had not only appeared but spake unto Brutus, Cassius the Epicurian was ready at hand to perswade him it was but a mistake in his weary imagination, and that indeed there were no such realities in nature.[381] Thus he endeavours to propagate the unbelief of witches, whose concession infers his coexistency, and by this means also he advanceth the opinion of totall death, and staggereth the immortality of the soul:[382] for those which deny there are spirits subsistent without bodies, will with more difficulty affirme the separated existence of their own.

Now to induce and bring about these falsities he hath laboured to destroy the evidence of truth, that is the revealed verity and written word of God. To which intent he hath obtained with some to repudiate the books of Moses, others those of the Prophets, and some both: to deny the Gospell and authentick histories of Christ, to reject that of John, and receive that of Judas, to disallow all and erect another of Thomas.[383] And when neither their corruption by Valentinus and Arrian, their mutilation by Marcion, Manes and Ebion could satisfie his designe, he attempted the ruine and totall destruction thereof, as he sedulously endeavoured, by the power and subtilty of Julian, Maximinus and Dioclesian.[384]

But the longevity of that peece, which hath so long escaped the common fate, and the providence of that Spirit which ever waketh over it, may at last discourage such attempts; and if not, make doubtfull its mortality, at least indubitably declare, this is a stone too bigge for Saturnes mouth, and a bit indeed oblivion cannot swallow.[385]

And thus how strangely hee possesseth us with errors may clearely be observed, deluding us into contradictory and inconsistent falsities, whilest he would make us beleeve: That there is no God. That there are many. That he himselfe is God. That he is lesse then angels or men. That he is nothing at all.

Nor hath hee onely by these wiles depraved the conception of the Creator, but with such riddles hath also entangled the nature of our Redeemer. Some denying his humanity, and that he was one of the angels, as Ebion; that the Father and Sonne were but one person, as Sabellius. That his body was phantasticall, as Manes, Basilides, Priscillian, Jovinianus; that hee onely passed through Mary, as Eutichus and Valentinus.[386] Some deny his divinity, that he was begotten of humane principles, and the seminall sonne of Joseph, as Carpocras, Symmachus,

Photinus.[387] That hee was Seth the sonne of Abraham,[388] as the Sethians. That hee was lesse then angells, as Cherinthus.[389] That hee was inferiour unto Melchisedech, as Theodotus.[390] That he was not God, but God dwelt in him, as Nicolaus. And some embroyled them both. So did they which converted the Trinity into a quaternity, and affirmed two persons in Christ, as Paulus Samosatenus;[391] that held he was man without a soul, and that the word performed that office in him, as Apollinaris.[392] That he was both Sonne and Father, as Montanus.[393] That Jesus suffered, but Christ remained impatible, as Cherinthus. And thus he endeavours to entangle truths: and when he cannot possibly destroy its substance he cunningly confounds its apprehensions, that from the inconsistent and contrary determinations thereof, collective[394] impieties, and hopefull conclusion may arise, there's no such thing at all.

CHAPTER XI
A Further Illustration

Now although these wayes of delusions, most Christians have escaped, yet are there many other whereunto we are dayly betrayed; and these we meet with in visible and obvious occurrents of the world, wherein he induceth us, to ascribe effects unto causes of no cognation, and distorting the order and theorie of causes perpendicular to their effects, he drawes them aside unto things whereto they runne parallel, and in their proper motions would never meet together.[395]

Thus doth he sometime delude us in the conceits of starres and meteors, beside their allowable actions ascribing effects thereunto of independent causations. Thus hath he also made the ignorant sort beleeve that naturall effects immediatly and commonly proceed from supernaturall powers, and these he usually derives from heaven; and his owne principality the ayre, and meteors therein, which being of themselves, the effects of naturall and created causes, and such as upon a due conjunction of actives and passives, without a miracle must arise unto what they appeare, are alwayes looked on by the ignorant spectators as supernaturall spectacles, and made the causes or signs of most succeeding contingencies.[396] To behold a rainbow in the night, is no prodigie unto a philosopher.[397] Then eclipses of Sun or Moon, nothing is more naturall. Yet with what superstition they have been beheld since the tragedy of Niceas, and his army, many examples declare.[398]

True it is, and we will not deny it, that although these being naturall productions from second and setled causes, we need not alway looke upon them as the immediate hand of God, or of his ministring spirits, yet doe they sometimes admit a respect therein, and even in their naturalls, the indifferencie of their existences contemporised unto our actions, admits a farther consideration.[399]

That two or three suns or moons appeare in any mans life or reign, it is not worth the wonder, but that the same should fall out at a remarkable time, or point of some decisive action, that the contingencie of its appearance should be confined unto that time.[400] That those two should make but one line in the booke of fate, and stand together in the great Ephemerides of God, beside the philosophical assignment of the cause, it may admit a Christian apprehension in the signality.[401]

But above all he deceiveth us when wee ascribe the effects of things unto evident and seeming causalities which arise from the secret and undiscerned action of himself. Thus hath he deluded many nations in his auguriall and extispicious inventions, from casuall and uncontrived contingences divining events succeeding.[402] Which Tuscan superstition first ceasing upon Rome hath since possessed all Europe.[403] When Augustus found two galls in his sacrifice, the credulity of the city concluded a hope of peace with Anthony, and the conjunctions of persons in choler with each other.[404] Because Brutus and Cassius met a blackmore, and Pompey had on a darke or sad coloured garment at Pharsalia;[405] these were presages of their overthrow, which notwithstanding are scarce rhetoricall sequells, concluding metaphors from realities, and from conceptions metaphoricall inferring realities again.

Now these divinations concerning events being in his power, to force, contrive, prevent or further, they must generally fall out conformably unto his predictions. When Graceus was slaine, the same day the chickens refused to come out of the coope.[406] And Claudius Pulcher underwent the like successe, when he contemned the Tripudiary Augurations.[407] They dyed not because the pullets would not feed, but because the devill foresaw their death, he contrived that abstinence in them. So was there no naturall dependance of the event upon the signe, but an artificall contrivance of the signe unto the event. An unexpected way of delusion, and whereby he more easily led away the incircumspection of their beliefe.[408] Which fallacy he might excellently have acted, before the death of Saul, which being in his power to foretell, was not beyond his ability to foreshew, and might have contrived signes thereof through all the creatures, which visibly confirmed by the event, had proved authentick unto those times, and advanced the art ever after.[409]

He deludeth us also by philters, ligatures, charmes, ungrounded amulets, characters, and many superstitious wayes in the cure of common diseases, seconding herein the expectation of men with events of his owne contriving:[410] which while some unwilling to fall directly upon magick, impute unto the power of imagination, or the efficacy of hidden causes, he obtaines a bloody advantage; for thereby he begets not onely a false opinion, but such as leadeth the open way of destruction; in maladies admitting naturall reliefes, making men rely on remedies, neither of reall operation in themselves, nor more then seeming efficacy in his concurrence, which whensoever he pleaseth to withdraw, they stand naked unto the mischiefe of their diseases, and revenge the contempt of the medicines of the earth which God hath created for them.[411] And therefore when neither miracle is expected, nor connexion of cause unto effect from naturall grounds concluded; however it be sometime successefull, it cannot be safe to rely on such practises, and desert the knowne and authentick provisions of God. In which ranke of remedies, if nothing in our knowledge or their proper power be able to relieve us, wee must with patience submit unto that restraint, and expect the will of the restrainer.

Now in these effects although he seeme oft times to imitate, yet doth hee concurre unto their productions in a different way from that spirit which sometime in naturall meanes produceth effects above nature; for whether he worketh by causes which have relation or none unto the effect, he maketh it out by secret and undiscerned wayes of nature. So when Caius the blinde, in the reigne of Antonius, was commanded to passe from the right side of the altar unto the left, to lay five fingers of one hand thereon, and five of the other upon his eyes, although the cure succeeded and all the people wondered, there was not any thing in the action which did produce it, nor any thing in his power that could enable it thereunto.[412] So for the same infirmity, when Aper was counselled by him to make a collyrium or ocular medicine with the bloud of a white cock, and honey, and apply it to his eyes for three dayes.[413] When Julian for his hæmoptysis or spitting of bloud, was cured by hony and pine nuts taken from his altar: when Lucius for the paine in his side, applyed thereto the ashes from his altar with wine, although the remedies were somewhat rationall, and not without a naturall vertue unto such intentions, can we beleeve that by their proper faculties they produced these effects?[414]

But the effects of powers divine flow from another operation, who either proceeding by visible meanes, or not, unto visible effects, is able to conjoyne them by his cooperation. And therefore those sensible wayes which seeme of indifferent natures, are not idle ceremonies, but may be causes by his command, and arise unto productions beyond their regular activities. If Nahaman the Syrian had washed in Jordan without the command of the prophet, I beleeve he had beene cleansed by them no more then by the waters of Damascus.[415] I doubt if any beside Elisha had cast in salt, the waters of Jericho had not bin made wholesome thereby.[416] I know that a decoction of wilde gourd or Colocynthis, though somewhat qualified, will not from every hand be dulcified unto aliment by an addition of flower or meale.[417] There was some naturall vertue in the plaster of figs applyed unto Ezechias;[418] we finde that gall is very mundificative, and was a proper medicine to cleere the eyes of Tobit;[419] which carrying in themselves some action of their owne, they were additionally promoted by that power which can extend their natures unto the production of effects beyond their created efficiencies.[420] And thus may he operate also from causes of no power unto their visible effects; for he that hath determined their actions unto certaine effects, hath not so emptied his own but that he can make them effectuall unto any other.

Againe, although his delusions run highest in points of practise, whose errors draw on offensive or penall enormities, yet doth he also deale in points of speculation, and things whose knowledge terminates in themselves, whose cognition although it seemes independent,[421] and therefore its aberration directly to condemne no man; yet doth he hereby preparatively dispose us unto errors, and deductively deject us into destructive conclusions.

That the sun, moone and stars are living creatures, endued with soule and life, seemes an innocent error, and a harmelesse digression from truth;[422] yet hereby he confirmed their idolatry, and made it more plausibly embraced. For wisely mistrusting that reasonable spirits would never firmely be lost in the adorement of things inanimate, and in the lowest forme of nature, he begat an opinion that they were living creatures, and could not decay for ever.

That spirits are corporeall, seemes at first view a conceit derogative unto himselfe, and such as he should rather labour to overthrow; yet hereby he establisheth the doctrine of lustrations, amulets and charmes, as we have declared before.[423]

That there are two principles of all things, one good, and another evill; from the one proceeding vertue, love, light, and unity; from the other division, discord, darknesse and deformity, was the speculation of Pythagoras, Empedocles, and many ancient philosophers, and was no more then Oromasdes and Arimanius of Zoroaster;[424] yet hereby he obtained the advantage of adoration, and as the terrible principle became more dreadfull then his maker, and therefore not willing to let it fall, he furthered the conceit in succeeding ages, and raised the faction of Manes to maintaine it.[425]

That the feminine sex have no generative emission, affording rather place then principles of conception, was Aristotles opinion of old, maintained still by some, and will be countenanced by him for ever.[426] For hereby he disparageth the fruit of the Virgin, and frustrateth the fundamentall prophesie, nor can the seed of the woman then breake the head of the serpent.[427]

Nor doth he onely sport in speculative errors, which are of consequent impieties, but the unquietnesse of his malice hunts after simple lapses· and such whose falsities do onely condemne our understandings. Thus if Xenophanes will say there is an other world in the moone; if Heraclitus with his adherents will hold the sunne is no bigger then it appeareth; If Anaxagoras affirme that snow is black; if any other opinion there are no Antipodes, or that the stars do fall, shall he not want herein the applause or advocacy of Satan.[428] For maligning the tranquility of truth, he delighteth to trouble its streames, and being a professed enemy unto God, (who is truth it selfe) he promoteth any error as derogatory to his nature, and revengeth himselfe in every deformity from truth. If therefore at any time he speake or practise truth it is upon designe, and a subtile inversion of the precept of God, to doe good that evill may come of it. And therefore sometimes wee meet with wholesome doctrines from hell, *Nosce teipsum*: the

Motto of Delphos was a good precept in morality, that a just man is beloved of the gods, an uncontroulable verity.[429] Twas a good deed, though not well done, which he wrought by Vespasian, when by the touch of his foot he restored a lame man, and by the stroake of his hand another that was blinde; but the intention hereof drived at his owne advantage, for hereby hee not onely confirmed the opinion of his power with the people, but his integrity with princes, in whose power he knew it lay to overthrow his oracles, and silence the practise of his delusions.[430]

But indeed of such a diffused nature, and so large is the empire of truth, that it hath place within the walles of hell, and the divels themselves are dayly forced to practise it; not only as being true themselves in a metaphysicall verity, that is, as having their essence conformable unto the intellect of their maker, but making use of morall and logicall verities, that is, whether in the conformity of words unto things, or things unto their owne conceptions, they practise truth in common among themselves. For although without speech they intuitively conceive each other, yet doe their apprehensions proceed through realities, and they conceive each other by species, which carry the true and proper notions of things conceived.[431] And so also in morall verities, although they deceive us, they lye not unto each other; as well understanding that all community is continued by truth, and that of hell cannot consist without it.

To come yet nearer to the point and draw into a sharper angle; they doe not onely speake and practise truth, but may bee said well-wisher thereunto, and in some sense doe really desire its enlargement. For many things which in themselves are false, they doe desire were true; hee cannot but wish hee were as he professeth, that hee had the knowledge of future events, were it in his power, the Jewes should be in the right, and the Messias yet to come. Could his desires effect it, the opinion of Aristotle should be true, the world should have no end, but be as immortall as himselfe.[432] For thereby hee might evade the accomplishment of those afflictions, he now but gradually endureth, for comparatively unto those flames hee is but yet in Balneo, then begins his *Ignis Rotæ*, and terrible fire, which will determine his disputed subtiltie, and hazard his immortality.[433]

But to speake strictly, hee is in these wishes no promoter of verity, but if considered some wayes injurious unto truth, for (besides that if things were true, which now are false, it were but an exchange of their natures, and things must then be false, which now are true) the setled and determined order of the world would bee perverted, and that course of things disturbed, which seemed best unto the wise[434] contriver. For whilest they murmure against the present disposure of things, regulating their determined realityes unto their private optations, they rest not in their established natures, but unwishing their unalterable verities, doe tacitely desire in them a difformitie from the primitive rule, and the Idea of that minde that formed all things best. And thus hee offended truth even in his first attempt; for not content with his created nature, and thinking it too low, to be the highest creature of God, he offended the ordainer thereof, not onely in the attempt, but in the wish and simple volition thereof.

THE SECOND BOOK

Of sundry popular tenents concerning minerall, and vegetable bodies, generally held for trueth, which examined, prove either false, or dubious.

CHAPTER I
Of Crystall

Hereof the common opinion hath been, and still remaineth amongst us, that crystall is nothing else, but ice or snow concreted, and by duration of time, congealed beyond liquation. Of which assertion, if the prescription of time, and numerositie of assertors, were a sufficient demonstration, we might sit downe herein, as an unquestionable truth; nor should there need ulterior disquisition.[1] For indeed, few opinions there are, which have found so many friends, or been so popularly received, through all professions and ages. And first, Plinie is positive in this opinion: *Crystallus fit gelu vehementius concreto*: the same is followed by Seneca, and elegantly described by Claudian, not denyed by Scaliger, and some way affirmed by Albertus, Brasavolus, and directly by many others.[2] The venerable Fathers of the Church have also assented hereto; as Basil in his Hexameron, Isidore in his Etymologies, and not onely Austin a Latine Father, but Gregory the Great, and Jerom upon occasion of that terme, expressed in the first of Ezekiel.[3]

All which notwithstanding upon a strict enquiry, we finde the matter controvertible, and with much more reason denyed then is as yet affirmed. For first, though many have passed it over with easie affirmatives; yet are there also many authors that deny it, and the exactest mineralogists have rejected it. Diodorus in his eleventh booke denyeth it, if crystall be there taken in its proper acception, as Rhodiginus hath used it, and not for a diamond, as Salmatius hath expounded it; for in that place he affirmeth, *Crystallum esse lapidem ex aqua pura concretum, non tamen frigore sed divini caloris vi.*[4] Solinus who transcribed Plinie, and therefore in almost all subscribed unto him, hath in this point dissented from him.[5] *Putant quidam glaciem coire, et in Crystallum corporari, sed frustra.* Mathiolus in his comment upon Dioscorides, hath with confidence and not without reason rejected it.[6] The same hath been performed by Agricola *de Natura Fossilium*; by Cardan, Boetius de Boot, Cæsius Bernardus, Sennertus, and many more.[7]

Now besides authoritie against it, there may be many reasons deduced from their severall differences which seeme to overthrow it. And first, a difference is probable in their concretion.[8] For if crystall be a stone, (as in the number thereof it is confessedly received) it is not immediatly concreted by the efficacy of cold, but rather by a minerall spirit, and lapidificall principles of its owne, and therefore while it lay *in solutis principiis*, and remained in a fluid body, it was a subject very unapt for proper conglaceation; for minerall spirits, doe generally resist and scarce submit thereto.[9] So wee observe that many waters and springs will never freeze, and many parts in rivers and lakes, where there are minerall eruptions, will still persist without congelation; as we also visibly observe, in *aqua fortis*, or any minerall solution, either of vitrioll, alum, salpeter, ammoniac, or tartar;[10] which although to some degree exhaled and placed in cold conservatories, will crystallise and shoot into white and glacious bodyes; yet is not this a congelation primarily effected by cold, but an intrinsecall induration from themselves, and a retreat into their proper solidityes, which were absorbed by the licour, and lost in a full imbibition thereof before.[11] And so also when wood and many other bodies doe petrifie, either by the sea, other waters, or earths abounding in such spirits, doe wee not usually ascribe their induration to cold,[12] but rather unto salinous spirits, concretive juyces, and causes circumjacent, which doe assimilate all bodyes not indisposed for their impressions.[13]

But ice is only water congealed by the frigidity of the ayre, whereby it acquireth no new forme, but rather a consistence or determination of its diffluency, and amitteth not its essence, but its condition of fluidity;[14] neither doth there any thing properly conglaciate but water, or watery humidity; for the determination of quick-silver is properly fixation, that of milke coagulation, and that of oyle and unctious bodies onely incrassation;[15] and therefore Aristotle makes a triall of the fertility of humane seed, from the experiment of congelation, for that sayth hee, which is not watery and improlificall will not conglaciate, which perhaps must not be taken strictly, but in the germe and spirited particles:[16] for egges I observe will freeze, in the generative and albuginous part thereof.[17] And upon this ground Paracelsus in his Archidoxis, extracteth the magistery of wine, after foure moneths digestion in horse-dunge, exposing it unto the extremity of cold, whereby the aqueous parts will freeze, but the spirit retyre and be found uncongealed in the center.[18]

[But[19] whether this congelation be simply made by cold, or also by cooperation of any nitrous coagulum, or spirit of salt the principle of concretion; whereby we observe that ice may be made with salt and snowe by the fire side; as is also observable from ice made by saltpater and water, duly mixed and strongly agitated at any time of the year, were a very considerable enquiry. For thereby we might cleer the generation of snow, haile, and hoary frosts, the piercing qualities of some winds, the coldnesse of cavernes, and some cells. We might more sensibly conceive how saltpeter fixeth the flying spirits of minerals in chymicall preparations, and how by this congealing quality it becomes an usefull medicine in fevers.]

Againe, the difference of their concretion is not without reason, collectible from their dissolution, which being many wayes performable in ice, is not in the same manner effected in crystall. Now the causes of liquation are contrary to those of concretion, and as the atoms and indivisible parcels are united, so are they in an opposite way disjoyned. That which is concreted by exsiccation or expression of humidity, will be resolved by humectation, as earth, dirt, and clay; that which is coagulated by a fiery siccity, will suffer colliquation from an aqueous humidity, as salt and sugar, which are easily dissoluble in water, but not without difficulty in oyle, and well rectified spirits of wine.[20] That which is concreated by cold, will dissolve by a moist heat, if it consist of watery parts, as gums, arabick, tragacanth, ammoniac, and others, in an ayrie heat or oyle, as all resinous bodies, turpentine, pitch, and frankincense; in both as gummy resinous bodies, masticke, camphire, and storax; in neither, as neutralls and bodies anomalous hereto, as bdellium, myrrhe and others.[21] Some by a violent dry heat, as mettalls, which although corrodible by waters, yet will they not suffer a liquation from the powerfullest heat, communicable unto that element. Some will dissolve by this heat although their ingredients be earthy, as glasse, whose materialls are fine sand, and the ashes of chali or fearne; and so will salt runne with fire, although it bee concreated by heat, and this way alone may bee effected a liquation in crystall, but not without some difficulty; that is, calcination or reducing it by arte, into a subtile powder, by which way and a vitreous commixture, glasses are sometime made hereof, and it becomes the chiefest ground for artificiall and factitious gemmes;[22] but the same way of solution is common also unto many stones, and not only berylls and cornelians, but flints and pebbles, are subject unto fusion, and will runne like glasse in fire.[23]

But ice will dissolve in any way of heat, for it will dissolve with fire, it will colliquate in water, or warme oyle;[24] nor doth it only submit to an actuall heat, but not endure the potentiall calidity of many waters;[25] for it will presently dissolve in *Aqua fortis*, spirit of vitrioll, salt or tartar, nor will it long continue its fixation in spirits of wine, as may be observed in ice injected therein.

Againe, the concretion of ice will not endure a dry attrition without liquation; for if it be rubbed long with a cloth it melteth, but crystall will calefy unto electricity, that is a power to attract strawes or light bodies, and convert the needle freely placed;[26] which is a declarement of very different parts, wherein wee shall not at present inlarge, as having discoursed at full concerning such bodies in the chapter of electricks.

They are differenced by supernatation or floating upon water, for chrystall will sinke in water as carrying in its owne bulke a greater ponderosity, then the space in any water it doth occupy, and will therefore only swim in molten mettall, and quicksilver.[27] But ice will swim in water of what thinnesse soever; and though it sinke in oyle, will float in spirits of wine or *aqua vitae.* And therefore it may swim in water, not only as being water it selfe, and in its proper place, but perhaps as weighing no more then the water it possesseth. And therefore as it will not sinke unto the bottome, so will it neither float above like lighter bodies, but being neare, or in equality of weight, lye superficially or almost horizontally unto it. And therefore also an ice or congelation of salt or sugar, although it descend not unto the bottome, yet will it abate, and decline below the surface in thin water, but very sensibly in spirits of wine.[28] For ice although it seemeth as transparent and compact as chrystall, yet is it short in either, for its atoms are not concreted into continuity, which doth diminish its translucency; it is also full of spumes and bubbles, which may abate its gravity. And therefore waters frozen in pans, and open glasses, after their dissolution do commonly leave a froth, and spume upon them; [which[29] are caused by the airy parts diffused in the congealable mixture which uniting themselves and finding no passage at the surface, doe elevate the masse, and make the liquor take up a greater place then before: as may be observed in glasses filled with water, which being frozen, will seem to swell above the brim. So that if in this condensation any one affirmeth there is also some rarefaction, experience may assert it].

They are distinguisht into substance of parts and the accidents thereof, that is in colour and figure;[30] for ice is a similary body, and homogeneous concretion, whose materiall is properly water, and but accidentally exceeding the simplicity of that element;[31] but the body of crystall is mixed, its ingredients many, and sensibly containeth those principles into which mixt bodies are reduced;[32] for beside the spirit and mercuriall principle, it containeth a sulphur or inflamable part, and that in no small quantity; for upon collision with steele, it will actually send forth its sparkes, not much inferior unto a flint. Now such bodies only strike fire as have a sulphur or ignitible parts within them. For as we elsewhere declare, these scintillations are not the accension of the ayre, upon the collision of two hard bodies, but rather the inflamable effluencies discharged from the bodies collided.[33] For diamonds, marbles, heliotropes, and agaths, though hard bodies, will not strike fire, nor one steele easily with another, nor a flint easily with a steele, if they both be wet, for then the sparkes are quenched in their eruption.[34]

It containeth also a salt, and that in some plenty which may occasion its fragility, as is also observable in corall.[35] This by the art of chymistry is separable unto the operations whereof it is lyable, with other concretions, as calcination, reverberation, sublimation, distillation:[36] And in the preparation of crystall, Paracelsus hath made a rule for that of gemms, as he declareth in his first *de Præparationibus*.[37] Briefly, it consisteth of such parts so far from an icie dissolution that powerfull menstruums are made for its emolition, whereby it may receive the tincture of minerals, and so resemble gemms, as Boetius hath declared in the distillation of urine, spirits of wine, and turpentine, and is not onely triturable, and reduceable into powder, by contrition, but will subsist in a violent fire, and endure a vitrification: wherby are testified its earthy and fixed parts.[38] For vitrification is the last worke of fire,[39] and when that arriveth, humidity is exhaled, for powdered glasse emits no fume or exhalation although it bee laid upon a red hot iron.[40] And therefore when some commend the powder of burnt glasse against the stone, they fall not under my comprehension, who cannot conceive how a body should be farther burned, which hath already passed the extreamest teste of fire.[41]

As for colour although crystall in his pellucide body seems to have none at all, yet in its reduction into powder, it hath a vaile and shadow of blew, and in its courser peeces, is of a sadder hue, then the powder of Venice glasse, which complexion it will maintaine although it long endure the fire; which notwithstanding needs not move us unto wonder, for vitrified and pellucide bodyes, are of a clearer complexion in their continuities, then in their powders and atomicall divisions.[42] So *stibium* or glasse of antimony, appears somewhat red in glasse, but in its powder yellow; so painted glasse of a sanguine red will not ascend in powder above a murrey.[43]

As for the figure of crystall (which is very strange, and forced Plinie to the despaire of resolution) it is for the most part hexagonall or six cornerd, being built upon a confused matter from whence as it were from a root angular figures arise, as in the amethists and basaltes, which regular figuration hath made some opinion, it hath not its determination from circumscription or as conforming unto contiguities, but rather from a seminall root, and formative principle of its owne, even as we observe in severall other concretions.[44] So the stones which are sometime found in the gall of a man, are most triangular, and pyramidall, although the figure of that part seems not to cooperate thereto. So the *asteria* or *lapis stellaris*, hath on it the figure of a starre, and so *lapis Judaicus*, that famous remedy for the stone, hath circular lines in length all downe its body, and equidistant, as though they had been turned by art. So that we call a fayrie stone, and is often found in gravell pits amongst us, being of an hemisphericall figure, hath five double lines arising from the center of its basis, which if no accretion distract them doe commonly concur and meet in the pole thereof. The figures are regular in many other stones, as in the belemnites, *lapis anguinus*, *cornu ammonis*, and divers beside, as by those which have not the experience hereof may be observed in their figures expressed by mineralogistes. But ice receiveth its figure according unto the surface, wherein it concreteth or the circumambiency which conformeth it.[45] So is it plaine upon the surface of water, but round in hayle, (which is also a glaciacion) and figured in its guttulous descent from the ayre.[46] And therefore Aristotle[47] in his Meteors concludeth that haile which is not round is congealed nearer the earth, for that which falleth from an high, is by the length of its journey corraded, and descendeth therefore in a lesser magnitude, but greater rotundity unto us.[48]

They are also differenced in the places of their generation; for though crystall be found in cold countries, and where ice remaineth long, and the ayre exceedeth in cold, yet is it also found in regions, where ice is seldome seen or soon dissolved, as Plinie and Agricola relate of Cyprus, Caramania and an island in the Red-sea; it is also found in the veynes of mineralls, in rocks, and sometime in common earth.[49] But as for ice it will not concrete but in the approachment of the ayre, as we have made tryall in glasses of water, covered halfe an inche with oyle, which will not easily freeze in the hardest frosts of our climate; for water concreteth first in its surface, and so conglaciates downward, and so will it doe although it be exposed in the coldest mettall of lead; which well accordeth with that expression of God, Job 38. The waters are hid as with a stone, and the face of the deep is frozen.[50] [But whether water which hath boiled or heated doth sooner receive this congelation, as commonly is delivered, we rest in the experiment of Cabeus; who hath rejected the same in his excellent discourse of Meteors.]

They have contrary qualities elementall, and uses medicinall; for ice is cold and moyst, of the quality of water: But crystall is cold and dry, according to the condition of earth, the use of ice is condemned by most physitians; that of chrystall commended by many. For although Dioscorides and Galen, have left no mention thereof; yet hath Mathiolus, Agricola, and many other commended it in disenteries and fluxes; all for the encrease of milke, most chymistes for the stone, and some as Brassavolus and Boetius, as an antidote against poyson:[51] Which occult and specificall operations, are not expectible from ice; for being but water congealed, it can never make good such qualities, nor will it reasonably admit of secret proprieties, which are the affections of formes, and compositions at distance from their elements.

Having thus declared what chrystall is not, it may afford some satisfaction to manifest what it is. To deliver therefore what with the judgement of approved authors, and best reason consisteth, it is a minerall body in the difference of stones, and reduced by some unto that subdivision, which comprehendeth gemmes;[52] transparent and resembling glasse or ice, made of a lentous colament of earth, drawne from the most pure and limpid juyce thereof, owing unto the coldnesse of the earth some concurrence or coadjuvancy, but not its immediate determination and efficiency, which are wrought by the hand of its concretive spirit, the seeds of petrification and Gorgon within it selfe;[53] as we may conceive in stones and gems, as diamonds, beryls, saphires and the like, whose generation we cannot with satisfaction confine unto the remote activity of the sun, or the common operation of coldnesse in the earth, but may more safely referre it unto a lapidificall succity, and congelitive principle which determines prepared materials unto specificall concretions.[54]

And therefore I feare we commonly consider subterranities not in contemplations sufficiently respective unto the creation. For though Moses have left no mention of minerals, nor made any other description then sutes unto the apparent and visible creation; yet is there unquestionably, a very large classis of creatures in the earth farre above the condition of elementarity: And although not in a distinct and indisputable way of vivency, or answering in all points the properties or affections of plants, yet in inferiour and descending constitutions, they do like these containe specificall distinctions, and are determined by seminalities; that is created, and defined seeds committed unto the earth from the beginning.[55] Wherein although they attaine not the indubitable requisites of animation, yet have they a neere affinity thereto. And though we want a proper name and expressive appellation, yet are they not to be closed up in the generall name of concretions, or lightly passed over as onely elementary, and subterraneous mixtions.

The principle and most gemmary affection is its tralucency; as for irradiancy or sparkling which is found in many gems it is not discoverable in this, for it commeth short of their compactnesse and durity: and therefore it requireth not the emery, as diamonds or topaze, but will receive impression from steele, more easily then the turchois.[56] As for its diaphanity or perspicuity, it enjoyeth that most eminently, and the reason thereof is its continuity, as having its earthly and salinous parts so exactly resolved, that its body is left imporous and not discreted by atomicall terminations.[57] For, that continuity of parts, is the cause of perspicuity, is made perspicuous by two wayes of experiment, that is either in effecting transparency in those bodyes which were not so before, or at least far short of the additionall degree. So snow becomes transparent upon liquation, so hornes and bodyes resolveable into continued parts or gelly. The like is observable in oyled paper, wherein the interstitial divisions being continuated by the accession of oyle, it becommeth more transparent, and admits the visible rayes with lesse umbrosity.[58] Or else by rendring those bodies opacus which were before pellucide and perspicuous.[59] So glasse which was before diaphanous, being by powder reduced into multiplicity of superficies, becomes an opacus body, and will not transmit the light:[60] and so it is in crystall powdered, and so it is also evident before; for if it be made hot in a crusible, and presently projected upon water, it will grow dim, and abate its diaphanity, for the water entring, the body begets a division of parts, and a termination of atoms united before unto continuity.[61]

The ground of this opinion might be, first the conclusions of some men from experience, for as much as crystall is found sometimes in rockes, and in some places not much unlike the stirious or stillicidious dependencies of ice;[62] which notwithstanding may happen either in places which have been forsaken or left bare by the earth, or may be petrifications, or minerall indurations, like other gemmes proceeding from percolations of the earth disposed unto such concretions.

The second and most common ground is from the name *crystallus*, whereby in Greeke, both ice and crystall are expressed, which many not duly considering, have from their community of name, conceived a community of nature, and what was ascribed unto the one, not unfitly appliable unto the other. But this is a fallacy of Æquivocation, from a society in name inferring an identity in nature. By this fallacy was he deceived that drank *aqua fortis* for strong water: By this are they deluded, who conceive *sperma cœti* (which is a bituminous superfluitance on the sea) to be the spawne of the whale;[63] or take *sanguis draconis*, (which is the gumme of a tree) to be the blood of a dragon. By the same logick we may inferre, the crystalline humor of the eye, or rather the crystalline heaven above, to be of the substance of crystall below;[64] or that almighty God sendeth downe crystall, because it is delivered in the vulgar translation, Psalm 47. *Mittit Crystallum suum sicut Buccellas*:[65] which translation although it literally expresse the Septuagint, yet is there no more meant thereby, then what our translation in plaine English expresseth;[66] that is, hee casteth forth his ice like morsels, or what Tremellius and Junius as clearly deliver, *Dejicit gelu suum sicut frusta, coram frigore eius quis consistet?*[67] which proper and Latine expressions, had they been observed in ancient translations, elder expositers had not beene misguided by the synonomy, nor had they afforded occasion unto Austen, the Glosse, Lyranus, and many others, to have taken up the common conceit, and spoke of this text conformably unto the opinion rejected.[68]

CHAPTER II

Concerning the Loadstone Of things particularly spoken thereof evidently or probably true. Of things generally beleeved, or particularly delivered, manifestly or probably false. In the first of the magneticall vertue of the earth, of the foure motions of the stone, that is, its verticity or direction, its attraction or coition, its declination, its variation, and also of its antiquity. In the second a rejection of sundry opinions and relations thereof, naturall, medicall, historicall, magicall.

And first we conceive the earth to be a magneticall body. A magnetical body, we term not only that which hath a power attractive, but that which seated in a convenient medium naturally disposeth it self to one invariable and fixed situation.[69] And such a magnetical vertue we conceive to be in the globe of the earth;[70] whereby as unto its naturall points and proper terms it disposeth it self unto the poles, being so framed, constituted and ordered unto these points, that those parts which are now at the poles, would not naturally abide under the æquator, nor Green-land remain in the place of

Magellanica;[71] and if the whole earth were violently removed, yet would it not forgoe its primitive points, nor pitch in the east or west, but return unto its polary position again. For though by compactnesse or gravity it may acquire the lowest place, and become the center of the universe, yet that it makes good that point, not varying at all by the accession of bodyes upon, or secession thereof, from its surface perturbing the equilibration of either hemispheare (whereby the altitude of the starres might vary) or that it strictly maintaines the north and southerne points, that neither upon the motions of the heavens, ayre and winds without, large eruptions and division of parts within, its polar parts should never incline or veere unto the æquator (whereby the latitude of places should also vary) it cannot so well be salved from gravity as a magneticall verticity.[72] This is probably that foundation the wisdome of the Creator hath laid unto the earth, and in this sense we may more nearly apprehend, and sensibly make out the expressions of holy Scripture, as that of Psalm 93.1. *Firmavit orbem terræ qui non commovebitur*, he hath made the round world so sure that it cannot be moved:[73] as when it is said by Job, *Extendit Aquilonem super vacuo, etc.* Hee stretcheth forth the north upon the empty place, and hangeth the earth upon nothing.[74] And this is the most probable answer unto that great question, Job 38. whereupon are the foundations of the earth fastened, or who laid the corner stone thereof?[75] Had they been acquainted with this principle, Anaxagoras, Socrates and Democritus had better made out the ground of this stability:[76] Xenophanes had not been faine to say it had no bottome, and Thales Milesius to make it swim in water.[77] Now whether the earth stand still, or moveth circularly, we may concede this magneticall stability: For although it move, in that conversion the poles and center may still remaine the same, as is conceived in the magneticall bodies of heaven, especially Jupiter and the Sunne; which according to Galileus, Kepler, and Fabricius, are observed to have dineticall motions and certaine revolutions about their proper centers; and though the one in about the space of ten dayes, the other in lesse then one, accomplish this revolution, yet do they observe a constant habitude unto their poles and firme themselves thereon in their gyration.[78]

Nor is the vigour of this great body included only in its selfe, or circumferenced by its surface, but diffused at indeterminate distances through the ayre, water and bodyes circumjacent; exciting and impregnating magneticall bodyes within its surface or without it, and performing in a secret and invisible way what we evidently behold effected by the loadstone. For these effluxions penetrate all bodyes, and like the species of visible objects are ever ready in the medium, and lay hold on all bodyes proportionate or capable of their action; those bodyes likewise being of a congenerous nature doe readily receive the impressions of their motor; and if not fettered by their gravity, conforme themselves to situations, wherein they best unite unto their animator.[79] And this will sufficiently appeare from the observations that are to follow, which can no better way bee made out then this wee speake of the magneticall vigour of the earth. Now whether these effluviums do flye by streated atomes and winding particles as Renatus des Cartes conceaveth, or glide by streames attracted from either pole and hemispheare of the earth unto the æquator, as Sir Kenelme Digby excellently declareth, it takes not away this vertue of the earth, but more distinctly sets downe the gests and progresse thereof, and are conceits of eminent use to salve magneticall phenomenas.[80] And as in astronomy those hypotheses though never so strange are best esteemed which best do salve apparencies, so surely in philosophy those principles (though seeming monstrous) may with advantage be embraced, which best confirme experiment, and afford the readiest reason of observation. And truly the doctrine of effluxions, their penetrating natures, their invisible paths, and insuspected effects, are very considerable; for besides this magneticall one of the earth, severall effusions there may be from divers other bodies, which invisibly act their parts at any time, and perhaps through any medium, a part of philosophy but yet in discovery, and will I feare prove the last leafe to be turned over in the booke of nature.

First, therefore it is evidently true and confirmable by every experiment, that steele and good iron never excited by the loadstone, discover in themselves a verticity; that is, a directive or polary faculty, whereby conveniently they do septentrionate at one extreme, and Australize at another;[81] and this is manifestible in long and thin plates of steel perforated in the middle and equilibrated, or by an easier way in long wires equiponderate with untwisted silke and soft wax; for in this manner pendulous they will conforme themselves meridionally, directing one extreame unto the north, another to the south.[82] The same is also manifest in steele wires thrust through little spheres or globes of corke and floated on the water, or in naked needles gently let fall thereon, for so disposed they will not rest untill they have found out the meridian, and as neere as they can lye parallell unto the axis of the earth: sometimes the eye, sometimes the point northward in divers needles, but the same point alwayes in most, conforming themselves unto the whole earth, in the same manner as they doe unto every loadstone; for if a needle untoucht be hanged above a loadstone, it will convert into a parallel position thereto; for in this situation it can best receive its verticity and be excited proportionably at both extremes: now this direction proceeds not primitively from themselves, but is derivative and contracted from the magneticall effluxions of the earth, which they have winded in their hammering and formation, or else by long continuance in one position, as wee shall declare hereafter.

It is likewise true what is delivered of irons heated in the fire, that they contract a verticity in their refrigeration; for heated red hot and cooled in the meridian from north to south, they presently contract a polary power, and being poysed in ayre or water convert that part unto the north which respected that point in its refrigeration; so that if they had no sensible verticity before it may be acquired by this way, or if they had any, it might be exchanged by contrary position in the cooling: for by the fire they omit not onely many drossie and scorious parts, but whatsoever they had received either from the earth or loadstone, and so being naked and despoiled of all verticity, the magneticall atomes invade their bodies with more effect and agility.[83]

Neither is it onely true what Gilbertus first observed, that irons refrigerated north and south acquire a directive faculty, but if they be cooled upright and perpendicularly they will also obtaine the same; that part which is cooled toward the north on this side the æquator, converting it selfe unto the north, and attracting the south point of the needle; the other and highest extreme respecting the south, and attracting the northerne according unto the laws magneticall:[84] for (what must be observed) contrary poles or faces attract each other, as the north the south, and the like decline each other, as the north the north. Now on this side of the æquator, that extreme which is next the earth is animated unto the north, and the contrary unto the south; so that in coition it applyes it selfe quite oppositely, the coition or attraction being contrary to the verticity or direction.[85] Contrary if wee speake according unto common use, yet alike if we conceave the virtue of the North pole to diffuse it self and open at the south, and the south at the north againe.

This polarity from refrigeration[86] upon extremity and in defect of a loadstone might serve to invigorate and touch a needle any where; and this, allowing variation, is also the truest way at any season to discover the north or south; and surely farre more certaine then what is affirmed of the graines and circles in trees, or the figure in the roote of ferne.[87] For if we erect a red hot wire untill it coole, then hang it up with wax and untwisted silke, where the lower end and that which cooled next the earth doth rest, that is the northerne point; and this we affirme will still be true, whether it be cooled in the ayre or extinguished in water, oyle of vitrioll, aqua fortis, or quicksilver. And this is also evidenced in culinary utensils and irons that often feele the force of fire, as tongs, fireshovels, prongs and andirons; all which acquire a magneticall and polary condition, and being suspended, convert their lower extremes unto the north, with the same attracting the southerne point of the needle. For easier experiment if wee place a needle touched at the foote of tongues or andirons, it will obvert or turne aside its lyllie or north point, and conforme its cuspis or south extreme unto the andiron.[88] The like verticity though more obscurely is also contracted by brickes and tiles, as wee have made triall in some taken out of the backs of chimneys. Now to contract this direction, there needs not a totall ignition, nor is it necessary the irons should bee red hot all over. For if a wire be heated onely at one end, according as that end is cooled upward or downeward, it respectively acquires a verticity, as we have declared before in wires totally candent. Nor is it absolutely requisite they should be exactly cooled perpendicularly, or strictly lye in the meridian, for whether they be refrigerated inclinatorily or somewhat æquinoxially, that is toward the easterne or westerne points though in a lesser degree, they discover some verticity.

Nor is this onely true in irons but in the loadstone it selfe; for if a loadstone be made red hot in the fire it amits the magneticall vigour it had before in it selfe, and acquires another from the earth in its refrigeration; for that part which cooleth toward the earth will acquire the respect of the north, and attract the southerne point or cuspis of the needle.[89] The experiment hereof we made in a loadstone of a parallelogram or long square figure, wherein only inverting the extremes as it came out of the fire, wee altered the poles or faces thereof at pleasure.

It is also true what is delivered of the direction and coition of irons that they contract a verticity by long and continued position; that is, not onely being placed from north to south, and lying in the meridian, but respecting the zenith and perpendicular unto the center of the earth, as is most manifest in barres of windowes, casements, hindges and the like; for if we present the needle unto their lower extremes, it wheeles about it and turnes its southerne point unto them. The same condition in long time doe bricks contract which are placed in walls, and therefore it may be a fallible way to finde out the meridian by placing the needle on a wall for some bricks therein which by a long and continued position, are often magnetically enabled to distract the polarity of the needle.[90] [And therefore those irons which are said to have been converted into loadstones; whether they were real conversions, or onely attractive augmentations, might be much promoted by this position: as the iron cross of an hundred weight upon the Church of St. John in Ariminum, or that loadston'd iron of Cæsar Moderatus, set down by Aldrovandus.]

Lastly, irons doe manifest a verticity not only upon refrigeration and constant situation, but (what is wonderfull and advanceth the magneticall hypothesis) they evidence the same by meer position according as they are inverted, and their extreams disposed respectively unto the earth. For if an iron or steele not formerly excited, be held perpendicularly or inclinatorily unto the needle, the lower end thereof will attract the *cuspis* or southerne point; but if the same extream be inverted and held under the needle, it will then attract the lilly or northerne point; for by inversion it changeth its direction acquired before, and receiveth a new and southerne polarity from the earth as being the upper extreame. Now if an iron be touched before, it varyeth not in this manner, for then it admits not this magneticall impression, as being already informed by the loadstone and polarily determined by its preaction.[91]

And from these grounds may we best determine why the northern pole of the loadstone attracteth a greater weight then the southerne on this side the equator, why the stone is best preserved in a naturall and polary situation; and why as Gilbertus observeth, it respecteth that pole out of the earth which it regarded in its minereall bed and subterraneous position.

It is likewise true and wonderfull what is delivered of the inclination or declination of the loadstone; that is, the descent of the needle below the plaine of the horizon: for long needles which stood before upon their axis parallell unto the horizon, being vigorously excited, incline and bend downeward, depressing the north extreame below the horizon; that is the north on this, the south on the other side of the equator, and at the very lyne or middle circle of the Earth stand parallell, and deflecteth neither. And this is evidenced not only from observations of the needle in severall parts of the earth, but sundry experiments in any part thereof, as in a long steele wire, equilibrated or evenly ballanced in the ayre; for excited by a vigorous loadstone it will somewhat depresse its animated extreme, and intersect the horizontall circumference. It is also manifest in a needle pierced through a globe of cork so cut away and pared by degrees that it will swim under water, yet sinke not unto the bottome, which may be well effected; for if the corke bee a thought too light to sinke under the surface, the body of the water may be attenuated with spirits of wine; if too heavy, it may be incrassated with salt;[92] and if by chance too much be added, it may againe be thinned by a proportionable addition of fresh water: if then the needle be taken out, actively touched and put in againe, it will depresse and bow down its northerne head toward the bottome, and advance its southerne extremity toward the brim. This way invented by Gilbertus may seem of difficulty; the same with lesse labour may be observed in a needled sphere of corke equally contiguous unto the surface of the water; for if the needle be not exactly equiponderant, that end which is a thought too light, if touched becommeth even; that needle also which will but just swim under water if forcibly touched will sinke deeper, and sometime unto the bottome. If likewise that inclinatory vertue be destroyed by a touch from the contrary pole, that end which before was elevated will then decline; and this perhaps might be observed in some scales exactly ballanced, and in such needles which for their bulke can hardly be supported by the water. For if they be powerfully excited and equally let fall, they commonly sink down and break the water at that extream wherat they were septentrionally excited, and by this way it is conceived there may be some fraud in the weighing of precious commodities, and such as carry a value in quarter grains, by placing a powerfull loadstone above or below, according as we intend to depres or elevate one extrem.

Now if these magneticall emissions bee only qualities, and the gravity of bodyes incline them only unto the earth; surely that which moveth other bodyes to descent carryeth not the stroak in this, but rather the magneticall alliciency of the earth, unto which with alacrity it applyeth it selfe, and in the very same way unto the whole earth, as it doth unto a single loadstone:[93] for if an untouched needle be at a distance suspended over a loadstone, it will not hang parallel, but decline at the north extreme, and at that part will first salute its director. Again, what is also wonderfull, this inclination is not invariable; for as it is observed just under the line the needle lyeth parallel with the horizon, but sayling north or south it beginneth to incline, and increaseth according as it approacheth unto either pole, and would at last endeavour to erect it selfe; and this is no more then what it doth upon the loadstone, and that more plainly upon the Terrella or sphericall magnet geographically set out with circles of the globe.[94] For at the æquator thereof the needle will stand rectangularly, but approaching northward toward the tropick it will regard the stone obliquely; and when it attaineth the pole directly, and if its bulk be no impediment, erect it self and stand perpendicularly thereon. And therefore upon strict observation of this inclination in severall latitudes and due records preserved, instruments are made whereby without the help of sun or star, the latitude of the place may be discovered; and yet it appears the observations of men have not as yet been so just and equall as is desirable, for of those tables of declination which I have perused, there are not any two that punctually agree, though som have been thought exactly calculated, especially that which Ridley received from Mr. Brigs in our time geometry professor in Oxford.[95]

It is also probable what is delivered concerning the variation of the compasse that is the cause and ground thereof, for the manner as being confirmed by observation we shall not at all dispute. The variation of the compasse is an arch of the horizon intercepted between the true and magneticall meridian, or more plainly, a deflexion and siding east and west from the true meridian. The true meridian is a major circle passing through the poles of the world, and the zenith or vertex of any place, exactly dividing the east from the west.[96] Now on this lyne the needle exactly lyeth not, but diverts and varieth its point, that is the north point on this side the æquator, the south on the other; sometimes unto the east, sometime toward the west, and in some few places varieth not at all. First, therfore it is observed that betwixt the shore of Ireland, France, Spaine, Guinie and the Azores, the north point varieth toward the east, and that in some variety; at London it varieth eleven degrees, at Antwerpe nine, at Rome but five, at some parts of the Azores it deflecteth not, but lyeth in the true meridian; on the other side of the Azores and this side the equator the north point of the needle wheeleth to the west, so that in the latitude of 36. neare the shore, the variation is about eleven degrees; but on the other side the equator, it is quite otherwise: for about Capo Frio in Brasilia, the south point varieth twelve degrees unto the west, and about the mouth of the Straites of Magellan five or six; but elongating from the coast of Brasilia toward the shore of Africa it varyeth eastward, and ariving at Capo de las Agullas, it resteth in the meridian, and looketh neither way.

Now the cause of this variation may be the inequalitie of the earth, variously disposed, and differently intermixed with the sea: withall the different disposure of its magneticall vigor in the eminencies and stronger parts thereof; for the needle naturally endeavours to conforme unto the meridian, but being distracted driveth that way where the greater and most powerfuller part of the earth is placed, which may be illustrated from what hath been delivered before, and may be conceived by any that understands the generalities of geographie. For whereas on this side the meridian, or the Isles of Azores, where the first meridian is placed, the needle varieth eastward, it may be occasioned by that vast tract of earth, that is, Europe, Asia, and Africa, seated toward the east, and disposing the needle that way: for arriving at some part of the Azores, or islands of Saint Michaels, which have a middle situation betweene these continents, and that vast and almost answerable tract of America, it seemeth equally distracted by both, and diverting unto neither, doth parallell and place it self upon the true meridian.[97] But sayling farther it veers its lilly to the west, and regardeth that quarter wherein the land is nearer or greater; and in the same latitude as it approacheth the shoare augmenteth its variation. And therefore as some observe, if Columbus or whosoever first discovered America, had apprehended the cause of this variation, having passed more then halfe the way, he might have been confirmed in the discovery, and assuredly foretold there lay a vast and mighty continent toward the west.[98] The reason I confesse, and inference is good, but the instance perhaps not so. For Columbus knew not the variation of the compasse, whereof Sebastian Cabot first took notice, who after made discovery in the northern parts of that continent.[99] And it happened indeed that part of America was first discovered, which was on this side farthest distant, that is Jamaica, Cuba, and the isles in the Bay of Mexico. And from this variation do some new discoverers deduce a probability in the attempts of the northerne passage toward the Indies.[100]

Now because where the greater continents are joyned, the action and effluence is also greater, therefore those needles do suffer the greatest variation which are in countreys which most do feel that action. And therefore hath Rome far lesse variation then London; for on the west side of Rome, are seated the great continents of France, Spaine, Germany, which take of the exuperance and in some way ballance the vigour of the eastern parts; but unto England there is almost no earth west, but the whole extent of Europe and Asia, lyeth eastward, and therfore at London it varieth eleven degrees, that is almost one *rhomb*.[101] Thus also by reason of the great continent of Brasilia, Peru, and Chili, the needle deflecteth toward the land twelve degrees; but at the straits of Magellan where the land is narrowed, and the sea on the other side, it varyeth but five or six. And so likewise, because the Cape de las Agullas hath sea on both sides near it, and other land remote and as it were æquidistant from it, therefore at that point the needle conforms unto the true meridian, and is not distracted by the vicinity of adjacencyes.[102] And this is the generall and great cause of variation. But if in certaine creekes and valleys the needle prove irregular, and vary beyond expectance, it may be imputed unto some vigorous part of the earth, or magneticall eminence not far distant. And this was the invention of Dr. Gilbert not many yeeres past, a physition in London. And therefore although some assume the invention of its direction, and others have had the glory of the carde, yet in the experiments, grounds, and causes thereof, England produced the father philosopher, and discovered more in it, then Columbus or Americus did ever by it.[103]

It is also probable what is conceived of its antiquity, that the knowledge of its polary power and direction unto the north was unknowne unto the ancients, and though Levinus Lemnius, and Cælius Calcagninus, are of another beliefe, is justly placed with new inventions by Pancirollus;[104] for their Achilles and strongest argument is an expression in Plautus, a very ancient author, and contemporary unto Ennius. *Hic ventus jam secundus est cape modo versoriam.*[105] Now this *versoriam* they construe to be the compasse, which notwithstanding according unto Pineda, who hath discussed the point, Turnebus, Cabeus, and divers others, is better interpreted the rope that helps to turne the ship; or as we say, doth make it tack about; the compasse, declaring rather the ship is turned, then conferring unto its conversion. As for the long expeditions and sundry voiages of elder times, which might confirm the antiquity of this invention, it is not improbable they were performed by the helpe of starres; and so might the Phænicean navigators, and also Ulysses saile about the Mediterranean, by the flight of birds, or keeping near the shore, and so might Hanno coast about Africa, or by the helpe of oares as is expressed in the voyage of Jonah.[106] And whereas it is contended that this verticity was not unknowne unto Salomon, in whom is presumed a universality of knowledge, it will as forcibly follow he knew the arte of typography, powder and gunnes, or had the Philosophers stone, yet sent unto Ophir for gold.[107] It is not to be denyed, that beside his politicall wisdome; his knowledge in philosophie was very large, and perhaps from his workes therein, the ancient philosophers especially Aristotle, who had the assistance of Alexanders acquirements, collected great observables, yet if he knew the use of the compasse, his ships were surely very slow, that made a three yeares voyage from Eziongeber in the Red Sea unto Ophir, which is supposed to be Taprobana or Malaca in the Indies, not many moneths sayle, and since in the same or lesser time, Drake and Candish performed their voyage about the earth.[108]

And as the knowledge of its verticity is not so old as some conceive, so is it more ancient then most beleeve; nor had its discovery with gunnes, printing, or as many thinke, some yeers before the discovery of America; for it was not unknowne unto Petrus Peregrinus a French man, who two hundred yeeres since hath left a Tract of the Magnet and a perpetual motion to be made thereby preserved by Gasserus.[109] Paulus Venetus and about five hundred yeers past, Albertus Magnus, make mention hereof, and quoteth for it a book of Aristotle *de lapide*, which book although we find in the catalogue of Laertius, yet with Cabeus I rather judge it to be the work of some Arabick writer, not many years before the dayes of Albertus.[110]

Lastly, it is likewise true what some have delivered of *crocus martis*, that is, steele corroded with vineger, sulphur, or otherwise, and after reverberated by fire. For the loadstone will not at all attract it, nor will it adhere, but lye therein like sand. This is to be understood of *crocus martis* well reverberated, and into a violet colour: for common *chalybs præparatus*, or corroded and powdered steele, the loadstone attracts like ordinary filings of iron, and many times most of that which passeth for *crocus martis.*[111] So that this way may serve as a test of its preparation, after which it becommeth a very good medicine in fluxes. The like may be affirmed of flakes of iron that are rusty and begin to tend unto earth; for their cognation then expireth, and the loadstone will not regard them.

CHAPTER III

Concerning the Loadstone; therein of sundry common Opinions, and received several relations: Naturall, Historicall, Medicall, Magicall

And first not onely a simple heterodox, but a very hard paradox, it will seeme, and of great absurdity unto obstinate ears, if wee say, attraction is unjustly appropriated unto the loadstone, and that perhaps we speake not properly, when we say vulgarly and appropriately the loadstone draweth iron; and yet herein we should not want experiment and great authority. The words of Renatus des Cartes in his Principles of Philosophy are very plain: *Præterea magnes trahet ferrum, sive potius magnes & ferrum ad invicem accedunt, neque enim ulla ibi tractio est.*[112] The same is solemnly determined by Cabeus. *Nec magnes trahit proprie ferrum, nec ferrum ad se magnetem provocat, sed ambo pari conatu ad invicem confluunt.*[113] Concordant hereto is the assertion of Doctor Ridley, physitian unto the Emperour of Russia, in his tract of Magnetical Bodies, defining magneticall attraction to be a naturall incitation and disposition conforming unto contiguitie, an union of one magneticall body with an other, and no violent haling of the weak unto the stronger.[114] And this is also the doctrine of Gilbertus, by whom this motion is termed coition, and that not made by any faculty attractive of one, but a syndrome and concourse of each;[115] a coition alway of their vigours, and also of their bodies, if bulk or impediment prevent not, and therefore those contrary actions which flow from opposite poles or faces, are not so properly expulsion and attraction, as *sequela* and *fuga*, a mutuall flight and following. [Consonant whereto are also the determinations of Helmontius, Kircherus, and Licetus.[116]]

The same is also confirmed by experiment; for if a piece of iron be fastened in the side of a bowle or bason of water, a loadstone swimming freely in a boat of cork, will presently make unto it. So if a steele or knife untouched, be offered toward the needle that is touched, the needle nimbly moveth toward it, and conformeth unto union with the steele that moveth not. Againe, if a loadstone be finely filed, the atoms or dust thereof will adheare unto iron that was never touched, even as the powder of iron doth also unto the loadstone. And lastly, if in two skiphs of cork, a loadstone and steele be placed within the orbe of their activities, the one doth not move, the other standing still, but both hoise sayle and steer unto each other;[117] so that if the loadstone attract, the steele hath also its attraction; for in this action the alliciency is reciprocall, which joyntly felt, they mutually approach and run into each others armes.[118]

And therefore surely more moderate expressions become this action, then what the ancients have used; which some have delivered in the most violent terms of their language; so Austin calls it *Mirabilem ferri raptorem*: Hippocrates, *λίθος ὅτι τὸν σίδηρον ἁρπάζει*, *Lapis qui ferrum rapit.*[119] Galen disputing against Epicurus useth the term *ἕλκειν*, but this also is too violent:[120] among the ancients Aristotle spake most warily, *λίθος ὅστις τὸν σίδηρον κινεῖ*, *Lapis qui ferrum movet*: and in some tolerable acception do runne the expressions of Aquinas, Scaliger, and Cusanus.[121]

Many relations are made, and great expectations are raised from the *magnes carneus*, or a loadstone, that hath a faculty to attract not onely iron but flesh; but this upon enquiry, and as *Cabeus* also observed, is nothing else but a weake and inanimate kind of loadstone, veined here and there with a few magnetical and ferreous lines, but chiefly consisting of a bolary and clammy substance, whereby it adheres like hæmatites, or terra lemnia, unto the lipps,[122] and this is that stone which is to be understood, when physitians joyn it with *Ætites*, or the eagle stone, and promise therein a vertue against abortion.

There is sometime a mistake concerning the variation of the compass, and therein one point is taken for another. For beyond the æquator some men account its variation by the diversion of the northerne point, whereas beyond that circle the southerne point is soveraign, and the north submits his preheminency. For in the southerne coast either of America or Africa; the souterne point deflects and varieth toward the land, as being disposed and spirited that way by the meridionall and proper hemisphere. And therefore on that side of the earth the varying point is best accounted by the south. And therefore also the writings of some, and maps of others, are to be enquired, that make the needle decline unto the east twelve degrees at Capo Frio, and sixe at the straits of Magellan; accounting hereby one point for another, and preferring the north in the liberties and province of the south.

But certainely false it is what is commonly affirmed and believed, that garlick doth hinder the attraction of the loadstone, which is notwithstanding delivered by grave and worthy writers, by Pliny, Solinus, Ptolomy, Plutarch, Albertus, Mathiolus, Rueus, Langius, and many more.[123] An effect as strange as that of Homers moly, and the garlick the gods bestowed upon Ulysses.[124] But that it is evidently false, many experiments declare. For an iron wire heated red hot and quenched in the juyce of garlick, doth notwithstanding contract a verticity from the earth, and attracteth the southerne point of the needle. If also the tooth of a loadstone be covered or stuck in garlick, it will notwithstanding attract and animate any needles excited and fixed in garlick until they begin to rust, doe yet retain their attractive and polary respects.

Of the same stampe is that which is obtruded upon us by authors ancient and modern, that an adamant or diamond prevents or suspends the attraction of the loadstone: as is in open terms delivered by Pliny. *Adamas dissidet cum Magnete lapide, ut juxta positus ferrum non patiatur abstrahi, aut si admotus magnes apprehenderit, rapiat atque auferat.*[125] For if a diamond be placed betweene a needle and a loadstone, there will nevertheless ensue a coition even over the body of the diamond. And an easie matter it is to touch or excite a needle through a diamond, by placing it at the tooth of a loadstone; and therefore the relation is false, or our estimation of these gems untrue; nor are they diamonds which carry that name amongst us.

It is not suddenly to be received what Paracelsus in his booke *De generatione rerum*, affirmeth, that if a loadstone be anointed with mercuriall oyl, or onely put into quicksilver, it omitteth its attraction for ever.[126] For we have found that Loadstones and touched needles which have laid long time in quicksilver have not amitted their attraction, and we also find that red hot needles or wires extinguished in quicksilver, do yet acquire a verticity according to the laws of position in extinction. Of greater repugnancy unto reason is that which he delivers concerning its graduation, that heated in fire and often extinguished in oyle of Mars or iron, it acquires an ability to extract or draw forth a naile fastened in a wall; for, as we have declared before, the vigor of the loadstone is destroyed by fire, nor will it be re-impregnated by any other magnete then the earth.

True it is, and we shall not deny, that besides fire some other wayes there are of its destruction, as age, ruste and what is least dreamt on, an unnaturall or contrary situation. For being impolarily adjoyned unto a more vigorous loadstone, it will in a short time exchange its poles; or being kept in undue position, that is, not lying on the meridian, or with its poles inverted, it receives in longer time impaire in activity, exchange of faces; and is more powerfully preserved by position then by the dust of steele. But the sudden and surest way is fire; that is, fire not onely actuall but potentiall; the one surely and suddenly, the other slowly and imperfectly; the one changing, the other destroying the figure. For if distilled vinegar or *aqua fortis* be poured upon the powder of loadstone, the subsiding powder dryed, retaines some magneticall vertue, and will be attracted by the loadstone; but if the menstruum or dissolvent be evaporated to a consistence, and afterward doth shoote into icycles or crystals, the loadstone hath no power upon them; and if in a full dissolution of steele a separation of parts be made by precipitation or exhalation, the exsiccated powder hath lost its wings and ascends not unto the loadstone.[127] And though a loadstone fired do presently omit its proper vertue, and according to the position in cooling contracts a new verticity from the Earth; yet if the same be laid awhile in *aqua fortis* or other corrosive water, and taken out before a considerable corrosion, it still reserves its attraction, and will convert the needle according to former polarity.[128] [And that duly preserved from violent corrosion, or the natural disease of rust, it may long conserve its vertue, beside the magneticall vertue of the earth, which hath lasted since the creation, a great example we have from the observation of our learned friend Mr. Graves, in an Ægyptian idoll cut out of loadstone, and found among the *mummies*; which still retains its attraction, though probably taken out of the mine about two thousand years agoe.]

It is improbable what Pliny affirmeth concerning the object of its attraction, that it attracts not only ferreous bodies, but also *liquorem vitri*, for in the body of glasse there is no ferreous or magneticall nature which might occasion attraction.[129] For of the glasse we use, the purest is made of the finest sand and the ashes of chali or glaswort, and the courser or greene sort of the ashes of brake or other plants.[130] Beside, vitrification is the last or utmost fusion of a body vitrifiable, and is performed by a strong and violent fire, which keeps the melted glasse red hot. Now certaine it is, and we have shewed it before, that the loadstone will not attract even steele it selfe that is candent, much lesse the incongenerous body of glasse being fired. For fire destroyes the loadstone, and therefore it declines it in its owne defence, and seekes no union with it. But that the magnet attracteth more then common iron, we can affirme. It attracteth the smyris or emery in powder, it draweth the shining or glassie powder brought from the Indies, and usually implyed in writing dust. There is also in smiths cinders by some adhesion of iron whereby they appeare as it were glazed, sometime to bee found a magneticall operation, for some thereof applyed have power to move the needle.[131] [But whether the ashes of vegetables which grow over iron mines contract a magneticall quality, as containing some minerall particles, which by sublimation ascend unto their roots, and are attracted together with their nourishment; according as some affirm from the like observations upon the mines of silver, quick silver, and gold; we must refer unto further experiment.]

It is also improbable and something singular what some conceive, and Eusebius Nierembergius, a learned Jesuit of Spain delivers, that the body of man is magneticall, and being placed in a boate, the vessell will never rest untill the head respecteth the north;[132] if this be true, the bodies of Christians doe lye unnaturally in their graves, and the Jews have fallen upon the natural position, who in the reverence of their temple, do place their beds from north to south. This opinion confirmed would much advance the microcosmicall conceit, and commend the geography of Paracelsus, who according to the cardinall points of the world, divideth the body of man; and therefore working upon humane ordure, and by long preparation rendring it odiferous, he terms it *zibeta occidentalis*, westerne civet;[133] making the face the east, but the posteriours the America or westerne part of his microcosm. The verity hereof might easily be tried in Wales, where there are portable boats, and made of leather, which would convert upon the impulsion of any verticity; and seeme to bee the same whereof in his description of Britain, Cæsar hath left some mention.

Another kinde of verticity, is that which *Angelus doce mihi jus*, *alias*, Michael Sundevogis, in a tract *de sulphure*, discovereth in vegetables, from sticks let fall or depressed under water*;[134] which equally framed and permitted unto themselves, will ascend at the upper end, or that which was verticall in their vegetation; wherein notwithstanding, as yet, we have not found satisfaction. Although perhaps too greedy of magnalities, we are apt to make but favourable experiments concerning welcome truths, and such desired verities.

* *alias*, i.e. anagrammatically.

It is also wondrous strange what Lælius Bisciola reporteth, that if unto ten ounces of loadstone one of iron be added, it encreaseth not unto eleven, but weighs ten ounces still: a relation inexcusable in the title of his work, *horæ subsecivæ*, or leasurable howres: the examination being as ready as the relation, and the falsity tryed as easily as delivered. Nor is it to be omitted what is taken up by the Cæsius Bernardus a late Mineralogist, and originally confirmed by Porta, that needles touched with a diamond contract a verticity, even as they doe with a loadstone, which will not consist with experiment.[135] And therefore, as Gilbertus observeth, he might be deceived, in touching such needles with diamonds, which had a verticity before, as we have declared most needles to have; and so had he touched them with gold or silver, he might have concluded a magneticall vertue therein.

In the same form may we place Frascatorius his attraction of silver, Philostratus his Pantarbes; Apollodorus and Beda his relation of the loadstone that attracted onely in the night: but most inexcusable is Franciscus Rueus, a man of our own profession; who in his discourse of gemmes mentioned in the Apocalyps, undertakes a chapter of the loadstone; wherein substantially and upon experiment he scarce delivereth any thing: making enumeration of its traditionall qualities, whereof he seemeth to beleeve many, and some of those above convicted by experience, he is fain to salve as impostures of the Devil. But Boetius de Boot physitian unto Rodulphus the second, hath recompenced this defect; and in his tract, *de lapidibus & gemmis*, speaks very materially hereof; and his discourse is consonant unto experience and reason.[136]

As for relations historicall, though many there be of lesse account, yet two alone deserve consideration: the first concerneth magneticall rocks, and attractive mountains in severall parts of the earth. The other the tombe of Mahomet and bodies suspended in the air. Of rocks magneticall there are likewise two relations; for some are delivered to be in the Indies, and some in the extremity of the north, and about the very pole. The northerne account is commonly ascribed unto Olaus Magnus Archbishop of Upsale, who out of his predecessour Joannes, Saxo, and others, compiled a history of some northerne nations;[137] but this assertion we have not discovered in that worke of his which passeth amongst us, and should beleeve his geographie herein no more then that in the first line of his book; when he affirmeth that Biarmia (which is not seventy degrees in latitude) hath the pole for its zenith, and equinoctiall for the horizon.

Now upon this foundation, how uncertain soever men have erected mighty illations, ascribing thereto the cause of the needles direction, and conceiving the effluxions from these mountaines and rocks invite the lilly toward the north; which conceit though countenanced by learned men, is not made out either by experience or reason, for no man hath yet attained or given a sensible account of the pole by some degrees; it is also observed the needle doth very much vary as it approacheth the pole; whereas were there such direction from the rocks, upon a nearer approachment it would more directly respect them. Beside, were there such magneticall rocks under the pole, yet being so far removed they would produce no such effect; for they that sail by the Isle of Ilua now called Elba in the Thuscan Sea which abounds in veynes of loadstone, observe no variation or inclination of the needle, much less may they expect a direction from rocks at the end of the earth. And lastly, men that ascribe thus much unto rocks of the north must presume or discover the like magneticalls at the south: for in the southern seas and far beyond the æquator, variations are large, and declinations as constant as in the northerne ocean.

The other relation of loadstone, mines and rocks, in the shore of India is delivered of old by Plinie;[138] wherein, saith he, they are so placed both in abundance and vigour, that it proves an adventure of hazard to passe those coasts in a ship with iron nailes. Serapion the Moor, an author of good esteeme and reasonable antiquity, confirmeth the same, whose expression in the word *magnes* is this.[139] The mine of this stone is in the sea-coast of India, whereto when ships approach, there is no iron in them which flies not like a bird unto those mountains; and therefore their ships are fastened not with iron but wood, for otherwise they would bee torne to peeces. But this assertion, how positive soever, is contradicted by all navigators that passe that way; which are now many, and of our own nation, and might surely have been controuled by Nearchus the admiral of Alexander;[140] who not knowing the compasse, was fain to coast that shore.

For the relation concerning Mahomet, it is generally beleeved his tombe at Medina Talnabi, in Arabia, without any visible supporters hangeth in the air betweene two loadstones artificially contrived both above and below; which conceit is fabulous and evidently false from the testimony of ocular testators, who affirme his tombe is made of stone, and lyeth upon the ground; as besides others the learned Vossius observeth from Gabriel Sionita, and Joannes Hesronita, two Maronites in their relations hereof. Of such intentions and attempt by Mahometans we read in some relators, and that might be the occasion of the fable, which by tradition of time and distance of place enlarged into the story of being accomplished: and this hath been promoted by attempts of the like nature; for we read in Plinie that one Dinocrates began to arch the Temple of Arsinoe in Alexandria with loadstone, that so her statue might be suspended in the ayre to the amazement of the beholders; and to lead on our credulity herein, confirmation may be drawn from history and writers of good authority; so is it reported by Ruffinus, that in the Temple of Serapis there was an iron chariot suspended by loadstones in the ayre, which stones removed, the chariot fell and dashed into peeces. The like doth Beda report of Bellerophons horse, which framed of iron, placed between two loadstones, with wings expansed, hung pendulous in the ayre.

The verity of these stories we shall not further dispute, their possibility we may in some way determine; if we conceive what no man will deny, that bodies suspended in the aire have this suspension from one or many loadstones placed both above and below it; or else by one or many placed only above it. Likewise the body to be suspended in respect of the loadstone above, is placed first at a pendulous distance in the medium, or else attracted unto that site by the vigor of the loadstone; and so we first affirm that possible it is a body may be suspended between two loadstones; that is, it being so equally attracted unto both, that it determineth it selfe unto neither; but surely this position will be of no duration; for if the ayre be agitated or the body waved either way, it omits the equilibration, and disposeth it selfe unto the nearest attractor. Again, it is not impossible (though hardly feisible) by a single loadstone to suspend an iron in the ayre, the iron being artificially placed and at a distance guided toward the stone, untill it find the newtral point, wherein its gravity just equals the magneticall quality, the one exactly extolling as much as the other depresseth. And lastly, impossible it is that if an iron rest upon the ground, and a loadstone be placed over it, it should ever so arise as to hang in the way or medium; for that vigor which at a distance is able to overcome the resistance of its gravity and to lift from the Earth, will as it approacheth nearer be still more able to attract it; and it will never remaine in the middle that could not abide in the extreams: now the way of *Baptista Porta* that by a thred fastneth a needle to a table, and then so guides and orders the same, that by the attraction of the loadstone it abideth in the aire, infringeth not this reason; for this is a violent retention, and if the thred be loosened, the needle ascends and adheres unto the attractor.[141]

The third consideration concerneth relations medicall; wherein what ever effects are delivered, they are derived from its mineral and ferreous condition, or else magneticall operation. Unto the ferreous and mineral quality pertaineth what Dioscorides an ancient writer and souldier under Anthony and Cleopatra affirmeth, that half a dram of loadstone given with honey and water, proves a purgative medicine, and evacuateth grosse humours;[142] but this is a quality of great incertainty; for omitting the vehicle of water and honey, which is of a laxative power it self, the powder of some loadstones in this dose doth rather constipate and binde, then purge and loosen the belly. And if sometimes it cause any laxity, it is probably in the same way with iron and steele unprepared, which will disturb some bodies, and work by purge and vomit. And therefore, whereas it is delivered in a booke ascribed unto Galen, that it is a good medicine in dropsies, and evacuates the waters of persons so affected: it may I confess by siccity and astriction afford a confirmation unto parts relaxed, and such as be hydropically disposed, and by these qualities it may be useful in hernias or ruptures, and for these it is commended by Ætius, Ægineta, and Oribasius;[143] who only affirme that it contains the vertue of hæmatites, and being burnt was sometimes vended for it.[144] To this minerall condition belongeth what is delivered by some, that wounds which are made with weapons excited by the loadstone, contract a malignity, and become of more difficult cure; which nevertheless is not to be found in the incision of chyrurgions with knives and lancets touched; which leave no such effect behinde them. Hitherto must we also referre that affirmative, which sayes the loadstone is poyson, and therefore in the lists of poysons we find it in many authors; but this our experience cannot confirm, and the practice of the King of Zeilan clearly contradicteth; who as Garcias ab Horto, physitian unto the Spanish Viceroy delivereth, hath all his meat served up in dishes of loadstone, and conceives thereby he preserveth the vigor of youth.[145]

But surely from a magneticall activity must be made out what is let fall by Ætius, that a loadstone held in the hand of one that is podagricall, doth either cure or give great ease in the gout.[146] Or what Marcellus Empericus affirmeth, that as an amulet, it also cureth the head-ach, which are but additions unto its proper nature, and hopefull enlargements of its allowed attraction;[147] for perceiving its secret power to draw unto it selfe magneticall bodies, men have invented a new attraction, to draw out the dolour and pain of any part. And from such grounds it surely became a philter, and was conceived a medicine of some venereall attraction;[148] and therefore upon this stone they graved the image of Venus, according unto that of Claudian, *venerem magnetica gemma figurat*.[149] Hither must wee also referre what is delivered concerning its power to draw out of the body bullets and heads of arrows, and for the like intention is mixed up in plaisters; which course, although as vain and ineffectuall it be rejected by many good authors, yet is it not methinks so readily to be denyed, nor the practice of many ages and physicians which have thus compounded plaisters, thus suddenly to be condemned, as may be observed in the *emplastrum divinum Nicolai*, the *Emplastrum nigrum* of Augspurge, the Opodeldoch and Attractivum of Parcelsus, with several more in the Dispensatory of Wecker, and practise of Sennertus;[150] the cure also of heurnias, or ruptures in Pareus: and the method also of curation lately delivered by Daniel Beckherus, and approved by the professors of Leyden in his tract *de Cultrivoro Prussiaco*, that is, of a young man of Spruceland that casually swallowed downe a knife about ten inches long, which was cut out of his stomach, and the wound healed up.[151] In which cure to attract the knife to a convenient situation, there was applied a plaister made up with the powder of loadstone. Now this kind of practice Libavius, Gilbertus, and lately Swickardus condemn, as vain, and altogether unusefull; and their reason is, because a loadstone in powder hath no attractive power; for in that form it omits his polary respects, and looseth those parts which are the rule of attraction; wherein to speak compendiously, if experiment hath not deceived us, we first affirme that a loadstone in powder omits not all attraction. For if the powder of a rich vein be in a reasonable quantity presented toward the needle freely placed, it will not appear to be void of all activity, but will be able to stir it; nor hath it only a power to move the needle in powder and by it selfe, but this will it also do, if incorporated and mixed with plaisters; as we have made triall in the *emplastrum de minio*; with half an ounce of the masse, mixing a dram of loadstone, for applying the magdaleon or roale unto the needle, it would both stir and attract it;[152] not equally in all parts, but more vigorously in some, according unto the mine of the stone more plentifully dispersed in the masse. And lastly, in the loadstone powdered, the polary respects are not wholly destroyed; for those diminutive particles are not atomicall or meerly indivisible, but consist of dimensions sufficient for their conditions, though in obscure effects. Thus if unto the powder of loadstone or iron we admove the north pole of the loadstone, the powders or small divisions will erect and conform themselves thereto; but if the south pole approach, they will subside, and inverting their bodies respect the loadstone with the other extreame. And this will happen not only in a body of powder together, but in any particle or dust divided from it.

Now though we affirme not these plaisters wholly ineffectuall, yet shall we not omit two cautions in their use, that therein the stone be not too subtily powdered; for it will better manifest its attraction in a more sensible dimension; that where is desired a speedy effect, it may be considered whether it were not better to relinquish the powdered plaisters, and to apply an entyre loadstone unto the part: And though the other be not wholly ineffectuall, whether this way be not more powerfull, and so might have been in the cure of the young man delivered by Beckerus.

The last consideration concerneth magicall relations; in which account we comprehend effects derived and fathered upon hidden qualities, specifical forms, antipathies, and sympathies, whereof from received grounds of art, no reasons are derived. Herein relations are strange and numerous; men being apt in all ages to multiply wonders, and philosophers dealing with admirable bodies, as historians have done with excellent men, upon the strength of their great atcheivements, ascribing acts unto them not only false but impossible; and exceeding truth as much in their relations, as they have others in their actions. Hereof we shall briefly mention some delivered by authors of good esteem, whereby we may discover the fabulous inventions of some, the credulous supinity of others, and the great disservice unto truth by both: multiplying obscurities in nature, and authorising hidden qualities that are false: whereas wise men are ashamed there are so many true.

And first, Dioscorides puts a shrewd quality upon it, and such as men are apt enough to experiment, who therewith discovers the incontinencie of a wife, by placing the loadstone under her pillow, for then shee will not be able to remain in bed with her husband.[153] The same he also makes a help unto theevery; for theeves saith he, having a designe upon a house, doe make a fire at the four corners thereof, and cast therein the fragments of loadstone: whence ariseth a fume that so disturbeth the inhabitants, that they forsake the house and leave it to the spoyl of the robbers. This relation, how ridiculous soever, hath Albertus taken up above a thousand years after, and Marbodeus the Frenchman hath continued the same in Latine verse, which with the notes of Pictorius is currant unto our dayes. As strange must be the lithomancy or divination from this stone, whereby as Tzetzes delivers, Helenus the Prophet foretold the destruction of Troy: and the magick thereof not safely to be beleeved, which was delivered by Orpheus, that sprinkled with water it will upon a question emit a voyce not much unlike an infant. But surely the loadstone of Laurentius Guascus the Physitian is never to be matched; wherewith, as Cardane delivereth, whatsoever needles or bodies were touched, the wounds and punctures made thereby, were never felt at all.[154] And yet as strange is that which is delivered by some, that a loadstone preserved in the salt of a remora, acquires a power to attract gold out of the deepest wells. Certainly a studied absurdity, not casually cast out, but plotted for perpetuity: for the strangenesse of the effect ever to bee admired, and the difficulty of the tryall never to be convicted.

These conceits are of that monstrosity that they refute themselves in their recitements. There is another of better notice, and whispered thorow the world with some attention; credulous and vulgar auditors readily beleeving it, and more judicious and distinctive heads, not altogether rejecting it. The conceit is excellent, and if the effect would follow, somewhat divine; whereby we might communicate like spirits, and confer on earth with Menippus in the moone;[155] which is pretended from the sympathy of two needles touched with the same loadstone, and placed in the center of two Abecedary circles or rings, with letters described round about them, one friend keeping one, and another the other, and agreeing upon an houre wherein they will communicate. For then saith tradition, at what distance of place soever, when one needle shall be removed unto any letter; the other by a wonderfull sympathy will move unto the same. But herein I confess my experience can find no truth; for having expressly framed two circles of wood, and according to the number of the Latine letters divided each into twenty three parts, placing therein two stiles or needles composed of the same steele, touched with the same loadstone, and at the same point: of these two, whensoever I removed the one, although but at the distance of halfe a spanne, the other would stand like Hercules pillars, and if the earth stand still, have surely no motion at all. Now as it is not possible that any body should have no boundaryes, or sphear of its activity, so it is improbable it should effect that at distance, which nearer hand it cannot at all performe.

Again, the conceit is ill contrived, and one effect inferred, whereas the contrary will ensue. For if the removing of one of the needles from A to B, should have any action or influence on the other, it would not intice it from A to B, but repell it from A to Z: for needles excited by the same point of the stone, doe not attract, but avoyd each other, even as those also do, when their invigorated extreams approach unto one another.

Lastly, were this conceit assuredly true, yet were it not a conclusion at every distance to be tryed by every head: it being no ordinary or almanack businesse, but a problem mathematicall, to finde out the difference of houres in different places; nor do the wisest exactly satisfie themselves in all. For the houres of severall places anticipate each other, according unto their longitudes, which are not exactly discovered of every place; and therefore the triall hereof at a considerable intervall, is best performed at the distance of the *Antæci*; that is, such habitations as have the same meridian and equal parallell, on different sides of the æquator; or more plainly, the same longitude and the same latitude unto the south, which we have in the north. For unto such situations it is noone and midnight at the very same time.

And therefore the sympathie of these needles is much of the same mould with that intelligence which is pretended from the flesh of one body transmuted by incision into another. For if by the Art of Taliacotius, *de curtorum chyurgia per incisionem*, a permutation of flesh, or transmutation be made from one man's body into another, as if a piece of flesh be exchanged from the bicipitall muscle of either parties arme, and about them both, an alphabet circumscribed; upon a time appointed as some conceptions affirme, they may communicate at what distance soever.[156] For if the one shall prick himself in A, the other at the same time will have a sense thereof in the same part: and upon inspection of his arme perceive what letters the other points out in his owne; which is a way of intelligence very strange: and would require the lost art of *Pythagoras*, who could read a reverse in the moone.

Now this magneticall conceit how strange soever, might have some originall in reason; for men observing no solid body whatsoever did interrupt its action, might be induced to beleeve no distance would terminate the same; and most conceiving it pointed unto the pole of heaven, might also opinion that nothing between could restrain it. Whosoever was the author, the Æolus that blew it about, was Famianus Strada, that elegant Jesuit, in his rhetoricall prolusions, who chose out this subject to express the stile of Lucretius.[157] But neither Baptista Porta, *de furtivis literarum notis*; Trithemius in his Steganography, Silenus in his Cryptography, or Nuncius *inanimatus* written of late yeers by Dr Godwin Bishop of Hereford, make any consideration hereof, although they deliver many wayes to communicate thoughts at distance.[158] And this we will not deny may in some manner be effected by the Loadstone; that is, from one room into another; by placing a table in the wall common unto both, and writing thereon the same letters one against another: for upon the approach of a vigorous Loadstone unto a letter on this side, the needle will move unto the same on the other; But this is a very different way from ours at present; and hereof there are many ways delivered, and more may be discovered which contradict not the rule of its operations.

As for *unguentum armarium*, called also *magneticum*, it belongs not to this discourse, it neither having the Loadstone for its ingredient, nor any one of its actions:[159] but supposeth other principles, as common and universall spirits, which convey the action of the remedy unto the part, and conjoins the vertue of bodies far disjoyned. But perhaps the cures it doth, are not worth so mighty principles; it commonly healing but simple wounds, and such as mundified and kept clean, doe need no other hand then that of nature, and the balsam of the proper part. Unto which effect there being fields of medicines sufficient, it may bee a hazardous curiosity to relie on this; and because men say the effect doth generally follow, it might be worth the experiment to try, whether the same will not ensue, upon the same method of cure, by ordinary balsams, or common vulnerary plasters.[160]

[Many other magnetisms may be pretended,[161] and the like attractions through all the creatures of nature. Whether the same be verified in the action of the sun upon inferiour bodies, whether there be *Æolian* magnets, whether the flux and reflux of the sea be caused by any magnetisme from the moon; whether the like be really made out, or rather metaphorically verified in the sympathies of plants and animals, might afford a large dispute; and Kircherus in his *Catena Magnetica* hath excellently discussed the same; which work came late unto our hand, but might have much advantaged this discourse.]

Other discourses there might be made of the loadstone: as morall, mysticall, theologicall; and some have handsomely done them; as Ambrose, Austine, Gulielmus Parisiensis, and many more, but these fall under no rule, and are as boundlesse as mens inventions; and though honest minds do glorifie God hereby, yet do they most powerfully magnifie him, and are to be looked on with another eye, who demonstratively set forth its magnalities; who not from postulated or precarious inferences, entreate a courteous assent, but from experiments and undeniable effects, enforce the wonder of its Maker.

CHAPTER IV
Of Bodies Electrical

Having thus spoken of the loadstone and bodies magneticall, I shall in the next place deliver somewhat of electricall, and such as may seeme to have attraction like the other; and hereof wee shall also deliver what particularly spoken or not generally knowne is manifestly or probably true, what generally beleeved is also false or dubious. Now by electricall bodies, I understand not such as are metallical, mentioned by Pliny, and the ancients; for their electrum was a mixture made of gold, with the addition of a fifth part of silver; a substance now as unknowne as true aurichaleum, or Corinthian brasse, and set down among things lost by Pancirollus.[162] Nor by electrick bodies do I conceive such onely as take up shavings, strawes, and light bodies, in which number the ancients only placed jet and amber; but such as conveniently placed unto their objects attract all bodies palpable whatsoever. I say conveniently placed, that is, in regard of the object, that it be not too ponderous, or any way affixed; in regard of the agent, that it be not foule or sullied, but wiped, rubbed, and excitated; in regard of both, that they be conveniently distant, and no impediment interposed. I say, all bodies palpable, thereby excluding fire, which indeed it will not attract, nor yet draw through it; for fire consumes its effluxions by which it should attract.

Now although in this ranke but two were commonly mentioned by the ancients, Gilbertus discovereth many more; as diamonds, saphyres, carbuncles, iris, opalls, amethistes, berill, chrystall, bristoll stones, sulphur, mastick, hard wax, hard rosin, arsenic, sal-gemme, roch-alume, common glasse, stibium, or glasse of antimony;[163] unto these Cabeus addeth white wax, gum elemi, gum guaici, pix Hispanica, and gipsum.[164] And unto these we add gum anime, benjamin, talcum, Chyna dishes, sandaraca, turpentine, styrax liquida, and caranna dryed into a hard consistence. And the same attraction we find, not onely in simple bodies, but such as are much compounded; as in the oxicroceum plaster, and obscurely that *ad herniam*, and *Gratia Dei*;[165] all which smooth and rightly prepared, will discover a sufficient power to stirre the needle, setled freely upon a well-pointed pinne; and so as the electrick may be applied unto it without all disadvantage.

But the attraction of these electricks we observe to be very different. Resinous or unctuous bodies, and such as will flame, attract most vigorously, and most thereof without frication, as anime, benjamin, and most powerfully good hard wax, which will convert the needle almost as actively as the loadstone; and wee beleeve that all or most of this substance if reduced to hardenesse, tralucency or cleerenesse, would have some attractive quality; but juyces concrete, or gums easily dissolving in water, draw not at all: as aloe, opium, sanguis draconis, lacca, galbanum, sagapenum. Many stones also both precious and vulgar, although terse and smooth, have not this power attractive: as emeralds, pearl, jaspis, corneleans, agathe, heliotropes, marble, alablaster, touchstone, flint, and bezoar. Glasse attracts but weakely, though cleere; some slick stones and thick glasses indifferently: arsenic but weakely, so likewise glasse of antimony, but crocus metallorum not at all. Saltes generally but weakely, as sal gemma, alum, and also talke; nor very discoverably by any frication, but if gently warmed at the fire, and wiped with a dry cloth, they will better discover their electricities.

No mettall attracts, nor any concretian animall wee know, although polite and smoothe; as we have made triall in elkes hooves, hawkes talons, the sword of a sword-fish, tortoyse shells, sea-horse, and elephants teeth, in bones, in harts horne, and what is usually conceived unicornes horne; no wood though never so hard and polished, although out of some thereof electrick bodies proceed; as ebony, box, lignum vitæ, cedar, &c. And although jet and amber be reckoned among bitumens, yet neither doe we find asphaltus, that is bitumens of Judea, nor seacole, nor camphire, nor mummia to attract, although we have tried in large and polished pieces. Now this attraction have wee tried in straws and paleous bodies, in needles of iron equilibrated, powders of wood and iron, in gold and silver foliate; and not onely in solid but fluent and liquid bodies, as oyles made both by expression and distillation; in water, in spirits of wine, vitriol and aqua fortis.

But how this attraction is made, is not so easily determined; that 'tis performed by effluviums is plaine, and granted by most; for electricks will not commonly attract, except they grow hot or become perspicable.[166] For if they be foule and obnubilated, it hinders their effluxion;[167] nor if they be covered, though but with linen or sarsenet, or if a body be interposed, for that intercepts the effluvium. If also a powerful and broad electrick of wax or anime be held over fine powder, the atomes or small particles will ascend most numerously unto it; and if the electrick be held unto the light, it may be observed that many thereof will flye, and be as it were discharged from the electrick to the distance sometime of two or three inches, which motion is performed by the breath of the effluvium issuing with agility; for as the electrick cooleth, the projection of the atomes ceaseth.

The manner hereof Cabeus wittily attempteth, affirming that this effluvium attenuateth and impelleth the neighbour ayre, which returning home in a gyration, carrieth with it the obvious bodies unto the electrick,[168] and this he labours to confirm by experiments; for if the strawes be raised by a vigorous electrick, they doe appear to wave and turne in their ascents; if likewise the electrick be broad, and the strawes light and chaffy, and held at a reasonable distance, they will not arise unto the middle, but rather adhere toward the verge or borders thereof. And lastly, if many strawes be laid together, and a nimble electrick approach, they will not all arise unto it, but some will commonly start aside, and be whirled a reasonable distance from it. Now that the ayre impelled returns unto its place in a gyration or whirling, is evident from the atomes or moates in the sun. For when the sunne so enters a hole or window, that by its illumination the atomes or moates become perceptible, if then by our breath the ayre bee gently impelled, it may be perceived, that they will circularly return and in a gyration unto their places againe.

Another way of their attraction is also delivered, that it is made by a tenuous emanation or continued effluvium, which after some distance retracteth into it self; as is observable in drops of syrups, oyle, and seminal viscosities, which spun at length, retire into their former dimensions. Now these effluviums advancing from the body of the electrick, in their return do carry back the bodies whereon they have laid hold within the spheare or circle of their continuities; and these they do not onely attract, but with their viscous armes hold fast a good while after. And if any shall wonder why these effluviums issuing forth impell and protrude not the straw before they can bring it back; it is because the effluvium passing out in a smaller thred and more enlengthened filament, it stirreth not the bodies interposed, but returning unto its originall, it falls into a closer substance, and carrieth them back unto it selfe. And this way of attraction is best received, embraced by Sir Kenelm Digby in his excellent Treaty of bodies, allowed by Des Cartes in his principles of Philosophy, as farre as concerneth fat and resinous bodies, and with exception of glasse, whose attraction he also deriveth from the recess of its effluxion.[169] And this in some manner the words of Gilbertus will beare: *Effluvia illa tenuiora concipiunt & amplectuntur corpora, quibus uniuntur, & electris tanquam extensis brachiis, & ad fontem propinquitate invalescentibus effluviis, deducuntur.*[170] And if the ground were true, that the earth were an electrick body, and the ayre but the effluvium thereof, we might have more reason to beleeve that from this attraction, and by this effluxion, bodies tended to the earth, and could not remaine above it.

Our other discourse of Electricks concerneth a generall opinion touching jet and amber, that they attract all light bodies, except ocymum or basil, and such as be dipped in oyle or oyled; and this is urged as high as Theophrastus: but Scaliger acquitteth him;[171] And had this bin his assertion, Pliny would probably have taken it up, who herein stands out, and delivereth no more but what is vulgarly known.[172] But Plutarch speaks positively in his Symposiacks, that Amber attracteth all bodies, excepting basil and oyled substances.[173] With Plutarch consent many authors both ancient and modern; but the most inexcusable are Lemnius and Rueus, whereof the one delivering the nature of minerals mentioned in Scripture, the infallible fountain of truth, confirmeth their vertues with erroneous traditions;[174] the other undertaking the occult and hidden miracles of nature, accepteth this for one; and endeavoureth to alledge a reason of that which is more then occult, that is, not existent.

Now herein, omitting the authority of others, as the doctrine of experiment hath informed us, we first affirm, that amber attracts not basil, is wholly repugnant unto truth; for if the leaves thereof or dryed stalks be stripped into small straws, they arise unto amber, wax, and other electrics, no otherwise then those of wheate and rye: nor is there any peculiar fatnesse or singular viscosity in that plant that might cause adhesion, and so prevent its ascension. But that jet and amber attract not strawes oyled, is in part true and false, for if the strawes be much wet or drenched in oyle, true it is that amber draweth them not, for then the oyle makes the strawes to adhere unto the part whereon they are placed, so that they cannot rise unto the attractor; and this is true, not onely if they be soaked in oyle, but spirits of wine or water. But if we speak of strawes or festucous divisions lightly drawn over oyle, and so that it causeth no adhesion, or if we conceive an antipathy between oyle and amber, the doctrine is not true; for amber will attract strawes thus oyled, it will convert the needles of dials made either of brass or iron, although they be much oyled; for in these needles consisting free upon their center, there can be no adhesion; it will likewise attract oyle it selfe, and if it approacheth unto a drop thereof, it becommeth conicall and ariseth up unto it, for oyle taketh not away his attraction, although it be rubbed over it. For if you touch a piece of wax already excitated with common oyle, it will notwithstanding attract, though not so vigorously as before. But if you moysten the same with any chymicall oyle, water, or spirits of wine, or onely breath upon it, it quite omits its attraction, for either its effluencies cannot get through, or will not mingle with those substances.

It is likewise probable the ancients were mistaken concerning its substance and generation; they conceiving it a vegetable concretion made of the gums of trees, especially pine and poplar falling into the water, and after indurated or hardened, whereunto accordeth the fable of Phaetons sisters: but surely the concretion is minerall, according as is delivered by Boetius; for either it is found in mountains and mediterraneous parts; and so it is a fat and unctuous sublimation in the earth, concreted and fixed by salt and nitrous spirits wherewith it meeteth; or else, which is most usuall, it is collected upon the sea-shore; and so it is a fat and bituminous juyce coagulated by the saltnesse of the sea. Now that salt spirits have a power to congeal and coagulate unctuous bodies, is evident in chymicall operations; in the distillations of arsenick, sublimate and antimony, in the mixture of oyle of juniper, with the salt and acide spirit of sulphur, for thereupon ensueth a concretion unto the consistence of birdlime; as also in spirits of salt, or aqua fortis poured upon oyle of olive, or more plainly in the manufacture of soape. And many bodies will coagulate upon commixture, whose separated natures promise no concretion. Thus upon a solution of tinne by aqua fortis, there will ensue a coagulation, like that of whites of egges. Thus the volatile salt of urine will coagulate aqua vitæ, or spirits of wine; and thus perhaps (as Helmont excellently declareth) the stones or calculous concretions in kidney or bladder may be produced:[175] the spirits or volatile salt of urine conjoyning with the aqua vitæ potentially lying therein; as he illustrateth from the distillation of fermented urine. From whence ariseth an aqua vitæ or spirit, which the volatile salt of the same urine will congele; and finding an earthy concurrence, strike into a lapideous substance.

Lastly, we will not omit what Bellabonus upon his own experiment writ from Dantzich unto Mellichius, as hee hath left recorded in his chapter, *de succino*, that the bodies of flies, pismires, and the like, which are said oft-times to be included in amber, are not reall but representative, as he discovered in severall pieces broke for that purpose;[176] if so, the two famous epigrams hereof in Martial are but poeticall, the pismire of Brassavolus imaginary, and Cardans mousoleum for a flye, a meere phancy. But hereunto we know not how to assent in the generall, as having met with some whose reals made good their representations.

CHAPTER V
Compendiously of sundry other common Tenents, concerning Minerall and Terreous Bodies, which examined, prove either false or dubious

1. And first we hear it in every mans mouth, and in many good authors reade it, that a diamond, which is the hardest of stones, not yielding unto steele, emery, or any thing but its own powder, is yet made soft, or broke by the bloud of a goat. Thus much is affirmed by Pliny, Solinus, Albertus, Cyprian, Austin, Isidore, and many Christian writers; alluding herein unto the heart of man and the precious bloud of our Saviour, who was typified by the goat that was slaine, and the scape-goat in the wilderness; and at the effusion of whose bloud, not only the hard hearts of his enemies relented, but the stony rocks and vaile of the Temple were shattered. But this I perceive is easier affirmed then proved. For Lapidaries, and such as professe the art of cutting this stone, doe generally deny it, and they that seem to countenance it, have in their deliveries so qualified it, that little from thence of moment can be inferred for it. For first, the holy Fathers, without a further enquiry did take it for granted, and rested upon the authority of the first deliverers. As for Albertus, he promiseth this effect, but conditionally, not except the goat drink wine, and be fed with *siler montanum*, *petroselinum*, and such hearbes as are conceived of power to breake the stone in the bladder.[177] But the words of Pliny, from whom most likely the rest at first derived it, if strictly considered, doe rather overthrow, then any way advantage this effect. His words are these: *Hircino rumpitur sanguine, nec aliter quam recenti, calidoque macerata, & sic quoque multis ictibus, tunc etiam præterquam eximias incudes malleosque ferreos frangens.* That is, it is broken with goats blood, but not except it bee fresh and warm, and that not without many blows, and then also it will

breake the best anvills and hammers of iron.[178] And answerable hereto, is the assertion of Isidore and Solinus. By which account, a diamond steeped in goats bloud, rather increaseth in hardness, then acquireth any softness by the infusion; for the best we have are comminuible without it; and are so far from breaking hammers, that they submit unto pistillation, and resist not an ordinary pestle.[179]

Upon this conceit arose perhaps the discovery of another; that the bloud of a goat was soveraign for the stone, as it stands commended by many good writers, and brings up the composition in the Lithontripticke powder of Nicolaus, or rather because it was found an excellent medicine for the stone, and its ability commended by some to dissolve the hardest thereof;[180] it might be conceived by amplifying apprehensions, to be able to break a diamond; and so it came to be ordered that the Goat should be fed with saxifragous herbes, and such as are conceived of power to breake the stone.[181] However it were, as the effect is false in the one, so is it surely very doubtfull in the other. For although inwardly received it may be very diuretick, and expulse the stone in the kidneys; yet how it should dissolve or break that in the bladder, will require a further dispute; and perhaps would be more reasonably tryed by a warm injection thereof, then as it is commonly used. Wherein notwithstanding, we should rather relie upon the urine in a castlings bladder, a resolution of crabs eyes, or the second distillation of urine, as Helmont hath commended;[182] or rather, if any such might be found, a chylifactory menstruum or digestive preparation drawn from species or individualls, whose stomacks peculiarly dissolve lapideous bodies.[183]

2. *That glasse is poyson*, according unto common conceit, I know not how to grant, not only from the innocency of its ingredients, that is, fine sand, and the ashes of glass-wort or fearn, which in themselves are harmless and usefull; or because I find it by many commended for the stone, but also from experience, as having given unto dogs above a dram thereof, subtilly powdered in butter and paste, without any visible disturbance. And the tryall thereof we the rather did make in that animall, because Grevinus in his Treaty of poysons, affirmeth that dogges are inevitably destroyed thereby.

The conceit is surely grounded upon the visible mischief of glasse grossely or coursely powdered, for that indeed is mortally noxious, and effectually used by some to destroy myce and rats; for by reason of its acuteness and angularity, it commonly excoriates the parts through which it passeth, and sollicits them unto a continuall expulsion. Whereupon there ensues fearfull symptomes, not much unlike those which attend the action of poyson. From whence notwithstanding, we cannot with propriety impose upon it that name, either by occult or elementary quality; which he that concedeth will much enlarge the catalogue or listes of poysons; for many things, neither deleterious by substance or quality, are yet destructive by figure, or some occasionall activity. So are leeches destructive, and by some accounted poyson; not properly, that is by temperamentall contrariety, occult form, or so much as elementall repugnancy; but because being inwardly taken they fasten upon the veines, and occasion an effusion of bloud, which cannot be easily stanched. So a Sponge is mischievous, not in it selfe, for in its powder it is harmlesse; but because being received into the stomach it swelleth, and occasioning a continuall distension, induceth a strangulation. So pins, needles, ears of rye or barley may be poyson. So Daniel destroyed the dragon by a composition of three things, whereof neither was poyson alone, nor properly all together, that is, pitch, fat, and haire, according as is expressed in the History. Then Daniel took pitch, and fat, and haire, and did seeth them together, and made lumps thereof, these he put in the dragons mouth, and so he burst asunder;[184] that is, the fat and pitch being cleaving bodies, and the haire continually extimulating the parts: by the action of the one, nature was provoked to expell, but by the tenacity of the other forced to retain:[185] so that there being left no passage in or out, the dragon brake in peeces. It must therefore bee taken of grossely-powdered glass, what is delivered by Grevinus: and from the same must that mortall dissentery proceed which is related by Sanctorius,[186] and in the same sense shall we onely allow a diamond to be poyson; and whereby as some relate Paracelsus himself was poysoned. And so also even the precious fragments and cordiall gems which are of frequent use in physicke, and in themselves confessed of usefull faculties; received in grosse and angular powders, may so offend the bowells, as to procure desperate languors, or cause most dangerous fluxes.[187]

[That glasse may be rendred malleable and pliable unto the hammer, many conceive, and some make little doubt, when they read in Dio, Pliny, and Petronius, that one unhappily effected it for Tiberius. Which notwithstanding must needs seem strange unto such as consider, that bodies are ductile from a tenacious humidity, which so holdeth the parts together; that though they dilate or extend, they part not from each other. That bodies runne into glasse, when the volatile parts are exhaled, and the continuating humour separated: the salt and earth, that is, the fixed parts remaining. And therefore vitrification maketh bodies brittle, as destroying the viscous humours which hinder the disruption of parts. Which may be verified even in the bodies of mettalls. For glasse of lead or tinne is fragile, when that glutinous sulphur hath been fired out, which made their bodies ductile.

He that would most probably attempt it, must experiment upon gold. Whose fixed and flying parts are so conjoined, whose sulphur and continuating principle is so united unto the salt, that some may be hoped to remain to hinder fragility after vitrification. But how to proceed, though after frequent corrosion, as that upon the agency of fire, it should not revive into its proper body, before it comes to vitrifie, will prove no easie discovery.]

3. That gold inwardly taken, and that either in substance, infusion, decoction or extinction, is a special cordiall of great efficacy, in sundry medicall uses, although a practice much used is also much questioned, and by no man determined beyond dispute. There are hereof I perceive two extream opinions; some excessively magnifying it, and probably beyond its deserts; others extreamly vilifying it, and perhaps below its demerits. Some affirming it is a powerful medicine in many diseases, others averring that so used, it is effectual in none: and in this number are very eminent physicians, Erastus, Duretus, Rondeletius, Brassavolus, and many other; who beside the strigments and sudorous adhesions from mens hands, acknowledge that nothing proceedeth from gold in the usuall decoction thereof.[188] Now the capitall reason that led men unto this opinion, was their observation of the inseparable nature of gold: it being excluded in the same quantity as it was received, without alteration of parts, or diminution of its gravity.

Now herein to deliver somewhat which in a middle way may be entertained; we first affirm & few I beleeve will deny it, that the substance of gold is indeed invincible by the powerfullest action of naturall heat; and that not only alimentally in a substantiall mutation, but also medicamentally in any corporeall conversion; as is very evident, not only in the swallowing of golden bullets but in the lesser and foliate divisions thereof:

passing the stomach and guts even as it doth the throat, that is, without abatement of weight or consistence; so that it entereth not the veynes with those electuaries, wherein it is mixed, but taketh leave of the permeant parts, at the mouths of the meseraicks, or lacteal vessels, and accompanieth the inconvertible portion unto the siege;[189] nor is its substantiall conversion expectible in any composition or aliment wherein it is taken. And therefore that was truly a starving absurdity, which befell the wishes of Midas.[190] And little credit there is to be given to the golden Hen, related by Wendlerus.[191] And so likewise in the extinction of gold, we must not conceive it parteth with any of its salt or dissoluble principle thereby, as we may affirme of iron; for the parts thereof are fixed beyond division, nor will they separate upon the strongest test of fire. And this we affirme of pure gold, for that which is currant and passeth in stampe amongst us, by reason of its allay, which is a proportion of copper mixed therewith, it is actually dequantitated by fire, and possibly by frequent extinction.[192]

Secondly, although the substance of gold be not sensibly immuted or its gravity at all decreased, yet that from thence some vertue may proceed either in substantiall reception or infusion, we cannot safely deny. For possible it is that bodies may emit vertue and operation without abatement of weight, as is most evident in the loadstone, whose effluencies are continuall, and communicable without a minoration of gravity. And the like is observable in bodies electricall, whose emissions are lesse subtile. So will a diamond or saphire emit an effluvium sufficient to move the needle or a straw, without diminution of weight. Nor will polished amber although it send forth a grosse and corporall exhalement, be found a long time defective upon the exactest scales.

Thirdly, if amulets doe worke by aporrhoias or emanations from their bodies, upon those parts whereunto they are appended, and are not yet observed to abate their weight; if they produce visible and reall effects by imponderous and invisible emissions, it may be unjust to deny all efficacie of gold in the non-omission of weight, or deperdition of any ponderous particles.

Lastly, since stibium or glasse of antimony, since also its Regulus will manifestly communicate unto water or wine, a purging and vomitory operation; and yet the body it selfe, though after iterated infusions, cannot be found to abate either vertue or weight; I dare not deny but gold may doe the like;

that is, impart some effluences unto the infusion, which carry with them the subtiler nature, and separable conditions of its body.

That therefore this mettall thus received, hath any undeniable effect upon the body either from experience in others or my selfe, I cannot satisfactorily affirm. That possibly it may have I wil not at all deny. But from power unto act, from a possible unto an actuall operation, the inference is not reasonable. And therefore since the point is dubious, and not yet authentically decided, it will be discretion not to depend on disputable remedies; but rather in cases of knowne danger, to have recourse unto medicines of knowne and approved activity; for beside the benefit accruing unto the sicke, hereby may be avoyded a grosse and frequent error, commonly committed in the use of doubtfull remedies, conjoyntly with those which are of approved vertue. That is, to impute the cure unto the conceited remedy, or place it on that whereon they place their opinion, whose operation although it be nothing, or its concurrence not considerable, yet doth it obtaine the name of the whole cure, and carryeth often the honour of the capitall energie, which had no finger in it.[193]

[Herein exact and criticall triall should be made by publike enjoinment, whereby determination might be setled beyond debate: for since thereby, not only the bodies of men, but great treasures might be preserved, it is not only an errour of physick, but folly of state, to doubt thereof any longer.]

4. That a pot full of ashes, will still contain as much water as it would without them, although by Aristotle in his Problems taken for granted, and so received by most, is surely very false, and not effectable upon the strictest experiment I could ever make.[194] For when the ayery intersticies are filled, and as much of the salt of the ashes as the water will imbibe is dissolved, there remains a grosse and terreous portion at the bottom, which will possess a space by it selfe, according whereto there will remain a quantity of water not receivable, and so will it come to passe in a pot of salt, although decrepitated;[195] and so also in a pot of snow. For so much it will want in reception, as its solution taketh up, according unto the bulke whereof, there will remain a portion of water not to be admitted. So a glasse stuffed with peeces of spunge, will want about a sixth part of what it would receive without it. So sugar will not dissolve beyond the capacity of the water, nor a mettall in aqua fortis bee corroded beyond its reception. And so a pint of salt

of tartar exposed unto a moist air untill it dissolve, will make far more liquor, or as some term it oyle, then the former measure will contain.

Nor is it only the exclusion of ayre by water, or repletion of cavities possessed thereby which causeth a pot of ashes to admit so great a quantity of water, but also the solution of the salt of the ashes into the body of the dissolvent; so a pot of ashes will receive somewhat more of hot water then of cold, for the warme water imbibeth more of the salt; and a vessell of ashes more then one of pindust or filings of iron; and a glasse full of water, will yet drink in a proportion of salt or sugar without overflowing.

5. Of white powder and such as is discharged without report, there is no small noise in the world: but how far agreeable unto truth, few I perceive are able to determine. Herein therefore to satisfie the doubts of some, and amuse the credulity of others, we first declare; that gun-powder consisteth of three ingredients, that is, salt-peter, smal-coale, and brimstone. Salt-peter, although it be also naturall and found in severall places, yet is that of common use an artificiall salt, drawn from the infusion of salt earth, as that of stals, stables, dovehouses, cellers, and other covered places, where the raine can neither dissolve, nor the sunne approach to resolve it. Brimstone is a minerall body of fat and inflamable parts, and this is used crude, and called sulphur vive, and is of a sadder colour; or after depuration, such as we have in magdeleons or rolls, of a lighter yellow:[196] Smal-coale is commonly known unto all, and for this use is made of sallow, willow, alder, hasell, and the like, which three proportionably mixed, tempered and formed into granulary bodies, doe make up that powder which is in use for gunnes.

Now all these although they bear a share in the discharge, yet have they distinct intentions, and different offices in the composition: from brimstone proceedeth the continued and durable firing, for small-coal and peter together will onley spit, nor easily continue the ignition. From small-coale ensueth the black colour and quicke accension; for neither brimstone nor peter, although in powder, will take fire like small-coale, nor will they easily kindle upon the sparks of a flint, as neither will Camphire a body very inflamable, but small-coal is equivalent to tinder, and serveth to light the sulphur: from salt-peter proceedeth the force and the report, for sulphur and small-coale mixed will not take fire with noise, or exilition, and powder which is made of impure, and greasie peter, hath but a weake emission, and giveth a faint report, and therefore in the three sorts of powder, the strongest containeth most salt-peter, and the proportion thereof is at the least ten parts of peter, unto one of coale and sulphur.[197]

But the immediate cause of the report, is the vehement commotion of the ayre upon the sudden and violent eruption of the powder; for that being suddenly fired, and almost altogether, being thus ratified it requireth by many degrees a greater space then before its body occupied; but finding resistance, it actively forceth out his way, and by concussion of the aire, occasioneth the report. Now with what vigour and violence it forceth upon the aire, may easily be conceived, if wee admit what Cardan affirmeth, that the powder fired doth occupie a hundred times a greater space then its own bulke, or rather what Snellius more exactly accounteth; that it exceedeth its former space no lesse then 12000 and 500 times.[198] And this is the reason not onely of this tonnitrous and fulminating report of gunnes, but may resolve the cause of those terrible cracks, and affrighting noise of heaven;[199] that is, the nitrous and sulphureous exhalations, set on fire in the cloudes, whereupon requiring a larger place, they force out their way, not only with the breaking of the cloud, but the laceration of the ayre about it. When if the matter be spirituous, and the cloud compact, the noise is great and terrible: If the cloud be thinne, and the materials weake, the eruption is languide, and ending in corruscations without any noyse, although but at the distance of two miles, which is esteemed the remotest distance of clouds;[200] and therefore such lightnings doe seldome any harme. And therefore also it is prodigious to have thunder in a cleare skye, as is observably recorded in some histories.

[From the like cause may also proceed subterraneous thunders and earthquakes;[201] when sulphureous and nitrous veins being fired, upon rarefaction doe force their way through bodies that resist them. Where if the kindled matter be plentifull, and the mine close and firm about it, subversion of hils and towns doth sometimes follow: If scanty, weak, and the earth hollow or porous, there only ensueth some faint concussion or tremulous and quaking motion. Surely, a main reason why the ancients were so imperfect in the doctrine of meteors, was their ignorance of gun-powder and fire-works, which best discover the causes of many thereof.]

Now therefore, he that would destroy the report of powder, must worke upon the peter, he that would exchange the colour, must thinke how to alter the small coale. For the one, that is, to make white powder, it is surely many wayes feasible: the best I know is by the powder of rotten willowes, spunck, or touchwood prepared, might perhaps make it russet: and some as Beringuccio in his Pyrotechny affirmeth, have promised to make it red.[202] All which notwithstanding doth little concerne the report: for that as wee have shewed depends on an other ingredient; and therefore also under the colour of blacke; this principle is very variable, for it is made not onely by willow, aller, hazell, &c. but some above all commend the coales of flaxe and rushes, and some also contend the same may bee effected with tinder.

As for the other, that is, to destroy the report, it is reasonably attempted but two wayes; that is, either by quite leaving out, or else by silencing the salt-peter. How to abate the vigour thereof, or silence its bombulation, a way is promised by Porta, and that not onely in generall termes by some fat bodies, but in particular by borax and butter mixed in a due proportion;[203] which sayeth he, will so goe off as scarce to be heard by the discharger; and indeed plentifully mixed, it will almost take off the report, and also the force of the charge. That it may be thus made without salt-peter, I have met with but one example, that is, of Alphonsus Duke of Ferrara, who in the relation of Brassavolus and Cardan invented such a Powder, as would discharge a bullet without report.[204]

That therefore white powder there may be, there is therein no absurdity, that also such a one as may give no report, wee will not deny a possibility. But this however, contrived either with or without salt-peter, will surely be of little force, and the effects thereof no way to be feared: for as it omits of report, so will it of effectuall exclusion; for seeing as we have delivered the strength and report, do necessarily depend upon the violent exclusion, where there is no report there will be no violent exclusion, and so the charge of no force which is excluded. For thus much is reported of that famous powder of Alphonsus, which was not of force enough to kill a chicken, according to the delivery of Brassavolus. *Iamque pulvis inventus est qui glandem sine bombo projicit, nec tamen vehementer ut vel pullum interficere possit.*[205]

It is very true and not to bee denyed, there are wayes to discharge a bullet, not only with powder that makes no noise, but without any powder at all, as is done by water and wind-gunnes; but these afford no fulminating report, and depend on single principles, and even in ordinary powder there are pretended other wayes, to alter the noise and strength of the discharge, and the best, if not onely way consists in the quality of the nitre: for as for other wayes which make either additions or alterations in the powder, or charge, I finde therein no effect. That unto every pound of sulphur, an adjection of one ounce of Quicksilver, or unto every pound of peter, one ounce of sal armoniac will much intend the force, and cosequently report, as Beringuccio hath delivered, I find no verity therein. That a piece of opium will dead the force, and blow as some have promised, I finde herein no such peculiarity, no more then in any gumme or viscose body, and as much effect there is to be found from scammonie. That a bullet dipped in oyle by preventing the transpiration of ayre, will carry farther, and pierce deeper, as Porta affirmeth, my experience cannot with satisfaction discerne. That quicksilver is more distructive then shot is surely not to be made out; for it will scarce make any penetration, and discharged from a pistoll, will hardly pierce thorow a parchment. That vineger, spirits of wine, or the distilled water of orange pilles, wherewith the powder is tempored, are more effectuall unto the report then common water, as some doe promise, I shall not affirme, but may assuredly be more conduceable unto the preservation and durance of the powder, as Cataneo hath well observed.

[That the heads of arrows and bullets have been discharged with that force,[206] as to melt or grow red hot in their flight, though commonly received, and taken up by Aristotle in his Meteors, is not so easily allowable by any, who shall consider, that a bullet of wax will mischief without melting; that an arrow or bullet discharged against linen or paper doe not set them on fire; and hardly apprehend how an iron should grow red hot, since the swiftest motion at hand will not keep one red that hath been made red by fire; as may be observed in swinging a red hot iron about, or fastening it into a wheel; which under that motion will sooner grow cold then without it. That a bullet also mounts upward upon the horizontall or point blank discharge, many artists doe not allow: who contend that it describeth a parabolicall and bowing line, by reason of its naturall gravity inclining it alwaies downward.]

But beside the prevalent report from salt-peter by some antipathie, or incummiscibility therewith upon the approach of fire, sulphur may hold a greater use in the composition and further activitie in the exclusion then is by most conceived;[207] for sulphur vive makes better powder then common sulphur, which neverthelesse is of as quicke accension as the other; for small-coale, salt-peter and camphire made into powder will bee of little force, wherein notwithstanding there wants not the accending ingredient; for camphire though it flame well, yet will not flush so lively, or defecate salt-peter, if you inject it thereon like sulphur, as in the preparation of *sal prunellæ*. And lastly, though many wayes may be found to light this powder, yet is there none I know to make a strong and vigorous powder of salt-peter, without the admixion of sulphur. Arsenick red and yellow, that is, orpement and sandarach may perhaps doe something, as being inflamable and containing sulphur in them, but containing also a salt, and hydragyrus mixtion, they will be of little effect;[208] and white or cristaline arsenick of lesse, for that being artficiall, and sublimed with salt, will not endure flamation.

And this antipathy or contention between saltpeter and sulphur upon an actuall fire, and in their compleat & distinct bodies, is also manifested in their preparations, and bodies which invisibly containe them. Thus is the preparation of crocus metallorum, the matter kindleth and flusheth like gunpowder, wherein notwithstanding, there is nothing but antimony and saltpeter, but this proceedeth from the sulphur of antimony, not enduring the society of saltpeter; for after three or foure accensions, through a fresh addition of peter, the powder will flush no more; for the sulphur of the antimony is quite exhaled. Thus iron in aqua fortis will fall into ebullition, with noise and emication, as also a crasse and fumide exhalation, which are caused from this combat of the sulphur of iron, with the acide and nitrous spirits of aqua fortis.[209] So is it also in *aurum fulminans*, or powder of gold dissolved in *aqua regis*, and precipitated with oyle of tartar, which will kindle without an actuall fire, and afford a report like gunpowder, that is, not as Crollius affirmeth from any antipathy betweene *sal armoniac* and tartar, but rather betweene the nitrous spirits of *aqua regis*, commixed *per minima* with the sulphur of gold, as in in his last, *de consensu chymicorum &c.* Sennertus hath well observed.

6. That Corall (which is a lithophyton or stone plant, and groweth at the bottome of the Sea) is soft under water, but waxeth hard as soone as it arriveth unto the ayre, although the

assertion of Dioscorides, Pliny, and consequently Solinus, Isidore, Rueus, and many others, and stands believed by most, we have some reason to doubt, not onely from so sudden a petrifaction and strange induration, not easily made out from the qualities of ayre, but because we finde it rejected by experimentall enquirers.[210] Johannes Beguinus in his chapter of the tincture of corall, undertakes to cleere the world of this errour, from the expresse experiment of John Baptista de Nicole, who was overseer of the gathering of coral upon the Kingdome of Thunis*.[211] This gentleman, saith he, desirous to finde the nature of corall, and to be resolved how it groweth at the bottome of the sea, caused a man to goe downe no lesse then a hundred fathom into the sea, with expresse to take notice whether it were hard or soft in the place where it groweth, who returning brought in each hand a branch of corall, affirming it was as hard at the bottome, as in the ayre where he delivered it. The same was also confirmed by a triall of his owne, handling it a fathome under water before it felt the ayre. Boetius de Boote in his accurate Tract *de Gemmis*, is of the same opinion, not ascribing its concretion unto the ayre, but the coagulating spirits of salt, and lapidificall juyce of the sea, which entring the parts of that plant, overcomes its vegetability, and converts it into a lapideous substance, and this, saith he, doth happen when the plant is ready to decay;[212] for all Corall is not hard, and in many concreted plants some parts remaine unpetrified, that is, the quick and livelier parts remaine as wood, and were never yet converted. Now that plants and ligneous bodies may indurate under water without approachment of ayre, we have experiment in coralline, with many coralloidall concretions, and that little stony plant which Mr. Johnson nameth, *hippuris coralloides*, and Gesner *foliis mansu arenosis*;[213] we have our selfe found in fresh water, which is the lesse concretive portion of that element. We have also with us the visible petrification of wood in many waters, whereof so much as if covered with water converteth into stone, as much as is above it and in the ayre retaineth the forme of wood, and continueth as before.

* In the french Copy.

7. We are not thorowly resolved concerning porcellane or chyna dishes, that according to common beliefe they are made of earth, which lyeth in preparation about an hundred yeares under ground, for the relations thereof are not onely divers, but contrary, and authors agree not herein. Guido Pancirollus will have them made of egge shells, lobster shells, and gypsum layed up in the earth the space of 80. yeeres: of the same

affirmation is Scaliger, and the common opinion of most.[214] Ramuzius in his Navigations is of a contrary assertion, that they are made out of earth, not laid under ground, but hardened in the Sunne and winde, the space of fourty yeeres.[215] But Gonzales de Mendoza, a man employed into Chyna, and with an honourable present, sent from Phillip the second King of Spain, hath upon ocular experience, delivered a way different from all these.[216] For enquiring into the artifice thereof, hee found they were made of a chalky earth, which beaten and steeped in water, affoordeth a cream or fatnesse on the top, and a grosse subsidence at the bottome; out of the cream or superfluitance, the finest dishes, saith he, are made; out of the residence thereof the courser; which being formed, they gild or paint, and not after an hundred yeares, but presently commit unto the furnace: and this, saith he, is knowne by experience, and more probable then what Odoardus Barbosa hath delivered, that they are made of shels, and buried under earth of hundred yeares: and answerable unto all points hereto, is the relation of Linschotten, a very diligent enquirer in his Orientall Navigations.[217] [Later confirmation may be had from Alvarez the Jesuit, who lived long in those parts, in his relations of China. That porcellane vessels were made but in one town of the province of Chiamsi: that the earth was brought out of other provinces, but for the advantage of water, which makes them more polite and perspicuous, they were only made in this. That they were wrought and fashioned like those of other countries, whereof some were tincted blew, some red, others yellow, of which colour only they presented unto the King.

The latest account hereof may be found in the voyage of the Dutch Embassadors sent from Batavia unto the Emperour of China, printed in French 1665, which plainly informeth, that the earth whereof porcellane dishes are made, is brought from the mountains of Hoang, and being formed into square loaves, is brought by water, and marked with the Emperours seal: that the earth it self is very lean, fine, and shining like sand: and that it is prepared and fashioned after the same manner which the Italians observe in the fine earthen vessels of Faventia or Fuenca: that they are so reserved concerning that artifice, that 'tis only revealed from father unto son: that they are painted with *indico* baked in a fire for fifteen days together, and with very dry and not smoaking wood: which when the author had seen he could hardly contain from laughter at the common opinion above rejected by us.]

Now if any man enquire, why being so commonly made, and in so short a time, they are become so scarce, or not at all to be had, the answer is given by these last relators, that under great penalties it is forbidden to carry the first sort out of the countrey. And of those surely the properties must be verified, which by Scaliger and others are ascribed to China dishes, that they admit no poyson, that they strike fire, that they will grow hot no higher then the liquor in them ariseth. For such as passe amongst us, and under the name of the finest, will onely strike fire, but not discover aconite, mercury, or arsenick, but may be usefull in dissenteries, and fluxes beyond the other.

8. Lastly, he must have more heads then Janus, that makes out half of those vertues ascribed unto stones, and their not onely medicall, but magicall proprieties, which are to be found in Authors of great name. In Psellus, Serapion, Evax, Albertus, Alcazar, Marbodeus; in Maiolus, Rueus; Mylius, and many other.[218]

That lapis lazuli hath in it a purgative faculty we know, that bezoar is antidotall, lapis Judaicus diureticall, corall antipilepticall, we will not deny*.[219] That cornelians, jaspis, heliotropes, and bloudstones, may be of vertue to those intentions they are implyed, experience and visible effects will make us doubt. But that an Amethist prevents inebriation, that an emerald will breake if worne in copulation; that a diamond laid under the pillow, will betray the incontinency of a wife; that a saphyre is preservative against enchantments; that the fume of an agath will avert a tempest, or the wearing of a crysoprase make one out of love with gold, as some have delivered, we are yet, I confesse, to believe, and in that infidelity are likely to end our dayes. And therefore, they which in the explication of the two beryls upon the ephod, or the twelve stones in the Rationall or breast-plate of Aaron, or those twelve which garnished the wall of the holy City in the Apocalyps, have drawne their significations from such as these, or declared their symbolicall verities from such traditionall falsities, have surely corrupted the sincerity of their analogies, or misunderstood the mystery of their intentions.[220]

* Against the falling sicknesse.

CHAPTER VI

Of sundry tenents concerning vegetables or plants, which examined, prove either false or dubious

1. Many molas and false conceptions there are of mandrakes, the first from great antiquity, conceiveth the roote thereof resembleth the shape of man, which is a conceit not to be made out by ordinary inspection, or any other eyes, then such as regarding the clouds, behold them in shapes conformable to preapprehensions.[221]

Now what ever encouraged the first invention, there have not bin wanting many wayes of its promotion. The first a catacresticall and farre derived similitude, it holds with man;[222] that is, in a byfurcation or division of the roote into two parts, which some are content to call thighes, whereas notwithstanding they are oft times three, and when but two commonly so complicated and crossed, that men for this deceit, are faine to effect their designe into other plants; And as faire a resemblance is often found in carrots, parsenips, bryony, and many others. There are, I confesse, divers plants which carry about them, not onely the shape of parts, but also of whole animals, but surely not all thereof, unto whom this conformity is imputed. Whoever shall peruse the signatures of Crollius, or rather the phytognomy of Porta, and strictly observes how vegetable realities, are commonly forced into animall representations, may easily perceive in very many, the semblance is but postulatory, and must have a more assimilating phancy then mine to make good many thereof.[223]

Illiterate heads have bin led on by the name, which in the first sillable expresseth its representation; but others have better observed the laws of etymology, and deduced it from a word of the same language, that is, μάνδρα, *Spelunca*, because it delighteth to grow in obscure and shady places, which derivation, although we shall not stand to maintaine, yet is the other openly absurd, answerable unto the etymologies of many authors, who often confound such nominall notations. Not to enquire beyond our owne profession, the Latine physitians, which most adheared unto the Arabick way, have often failed herein, particularly Valescus de Taranta a received physitian, in whose philonium or medicall practice these may be observed; *Diarhæa* saith he, *quia pluries venit in die. Herisepela, quasi hærens pilis, emorrohois, ab emach sanguis & morrhois quod est cadere. Lithargia à Litos quod est oblivio & Targus morbus, Scotomia à Scotos quod est videre & mias musca, Opthalmia ab opus Græce quod est succus, & Talmon quod est occulus, Paralisis, quasi læsio partis, Fistula à fos sonus & stolon quod est emissio, quasi emissio soni vel vocis:*[224] which are derivations as strange indeed as the other, and hardly to be paralleld elsewhere, confirming not onely the words of one language with another, but creating such as were never yet in any.

The received distinction and common notation by sexes, hath also promoted the conceit; for true it is, that Herbalists from ancient times, have thus distinguished them; naming that the masle, whose leaves are lighter, and fruit and apples rounder, but this is properly no generative division, but rather some note of distinction in colour, figure or operation.[225] For though Empedocles affirme, there is a mixt, and undivided sex in vegetables; and Scaliger upon Aristotle *de plantis*, doth favourably explain that opinion, yet will it not consist with the common and ordinary acception, nor yet with Aristotles definition:[226] for if that be masle which generates in another, that female which procreates in it selfe; if it be understood of sexes conjoyned, all plants are female, and if of disjoyned, and congressive generation, there is no male or female in them at all.

But the Atlas or maine axis, which supported this opinion, was daily experience, and the visible testimony of sense; for many there are in severall parts of Europe who carry about, and sell rootes unto ignorant poeple, which hansomely make out the shape of man or woman, but these are not productions of Nature, but contrivances of Art, as divers have noted, and Mathiolus plainly detected, who learned this way of trumpery from a vagabond cheator lying under his cure for the French disease; his words are these, and may determine the point, *Sed profecto vanum & fabulosum, &c.*[227] But that is vaine and fabulous which ignorant people, and simple women beleeve; for the roots which are carried about by impostors to deceive unfruitfull women, are made of the roots of canes, bryony, and other plants, for in these yet fresh and virent, they carve out the figures of men and women, first sticking, therein the graines of barley or millet, where they intend the haire should grow, then bury them in sand, untill the grains shoot forth their roots, which at the longest will happen in twenty dayes; afterward clip and trim those tender strings in the fashion of beard and other hayrie teguments. All which like other impostures once discovered is easily effected, and in the root of white bryony may be practised every Spring.

What is therefore delivered in favour hereof, by authors ancient or moderne, must have its roots in tradition, imposture, or farre derived similitude; so may we admit of the epithyte of Pythagoras who calls it *Anthropomorphus* and that of Columella, who tearms it *semihomo*, otherwise Albertus Magnus is not to be received when he affirmeth that Mandrakes so represent mankinde, that distinction of sex and other accidents are manifest therein. And under these tearms may those authors bee admitted, which for this opinion are introduced by Drusius, as David Camius, Moses filius Namanis, and Abenezra Hispanus.[228]

The second assertion concerneth its production, that it naturally groweth under gallowses and places of execution, arising from fat or urine that drops from the body of the dead; a story somewhat agreeable unto the fable of the Serpents teeth sowed in the earth by Cadmus, or rather the birth of Orion from the urine of Jupiter, Mercurie, and Neptune:[229] Now this opinion seems grounded on the former, that is a conceived similitude it hath with man; and therefore from him in some way they would make out its production. Which conceit is not only erroneous in the foundation, but injurious unto philosophy in the superstruction, making putrifactive generations, correspondent unto seminall productions, and conceiving in equivocall effects an univocall conformity unto the efficient; which is so far from being verified of animalls in their corruptive mutations into plants, that they maintaine not this similitude in their nearer translation into animalls. So when the oxe corrupteth into bees, or the horses into hornets, they come not forth in the image of their originalls. So the corrupt and excrementous humors in man are animated into lyce; and we may observe that hogs, sheep, goats, hawkes, hens, and divers other, have one peculiar and proper kind of vermine, not resembling themselves according to seminall conditions, it carrying a setled and confined habitude unto their corruptive originalls; and therefore come not forth in generations erraticall, or different from each other, but seem specifically and in regular shapes to attend the corruption of their bodyes, as doe more perfect conceptions, the rule of seminall productions.

The third affirmeth the roots of mandrakes doe make a noyse or give a shreeke upon eradication, which is indeed ridiculous, and false below confute; arising perhaps from a small and stridulous noyse, which being firmely rooted, it maketh upon divulsion of parts.[230] A slender foundation for such a vast conception: for such a noyse we sometime observe in other plants, in parsenips, liquorish, eringium, flags, and others.

The last concerneth the danger ensuing, that there followes an hazard of life to them that pull it up, that some evill fate pursues them, and they live not very long after; therefore the attempt hereof among the ancients, was not in ordinary way, but as Pliny informeth, when they intended to take up the root of this plant, they tooke the wind thereof, and with a sword describing three circles about it they digged it up, looking toward the West, a conceit not only injurious unto truth, and confutable by dayly experience, but somewhat derogatory unto the providence of God, that is not only to impose so destructive a quality on any plant, but conceive a vegetable whose parts are usefull unto many, should in the only taking up prove mortall unto any.[231] To think he suffereth the poyson of Nubia to be gathered, napellus, aconite and thora to be eradicated, yet this not to be moved.[232] That hee permitteth arsenick and minerall poysons to be forced from the bowells of the earth, yet not this from the surface thereof. This were to introduce a second forbidden fruit, and inhance the first malediction; making it not only mortall for Adam to taste the one, but capitall unto his posterity to eradicate or dig up the other.

Now what begot, at least promoted so strange conceptions might be the magicall opinion hereof; this being conceived the plant so much in use with Circe, and therefore named Circea, as Dioscorides and Theophrastus have delivered;[233] which being the eminent soceres of elder story, and by the magicke of simples beleeved to have wrought many wonders, some men were apt to invent, others to beleeve any tradition or magicall promise thereof.

Analogus relations concerning other plants, and such as are of neare affinity unto this, have made its currant smooth, and passe more easily among us; for the same effect is also delivered by Josephus, concerning the root Baaras, by Ælian of Cynospastus, and we read in Homer the very same opinion concerning Moly.

Μῶλυ δέ μιν καλέουσι θεοί, χαλεπὸν δέ τ᾽ὀρύσσειν
Ἀνδράσι γε θνητοῖσι, θεοὶ δέ τε πάντα δύνανται
The Gods it Moly call, whose root to dig away,
Is dangerous unto man, but Gods they all things may.[234]

Now parallels or like relations alternately releeve each other; when neither will passe asunder, yet are they plausible together, and by their mutuall concurrences support their solitary instablilities.

Signaturists have somewhat advanced it, who seldome omitting what ancients delivered, drawing into inference received distinctions of sex, not willing to examine its humane resemblance, and placing it in the forme of strange and magicall simples, have made men suspect there was more therein, then ordinary practice allowed, and so became apt to embrace what ever they heard or read conformable unto such conceptions.

Lastly, the conceit promoteth it selfe: for concerning an effect whose triall must cost so deare, it fortifies it selfe in that invention, and few there are whose experiment it need to fear. For (what is most contemptible) although not only the reason of any head, but experience of every hand may well convict it, yet will it not by divers bee rejected, for prepossessed heads will ever doubt it, and timorous beliefes will never dare to try it. So these traditions how low and ridiculous soever, will finde in some suspition, doubt in others, and serve as tests or trialls of melancholy, and superstitious tempers for ever.

2. That cinamon, ginger, clove, mace and nutmeg, are but the severall parts and fruits of the same tree, is the common beliefe of those which daily use them; whereof to speak distinctly, ginger is the root of neither tree nor shrub, but of an herbaceous plant, resembling the water flower, de luce, as Garcias first described, or rather the common reed, as Lobelius since affirmed, very common in many parts of India, growing either from root or seed, which in December and January they take up, and gently dryed, role it up in earth, whereby occluding the pores, they conserve the naturall humidity, and so prevent corruption.[235]

Cinnamon is the inward barke of a cinnamon tree, whereof the best is brought from Zeilan; this freed from the outward barke, and exposed unto the sun, contracts into those folds wherein we commonly receive it. If it have not a sufficient insolation it looketh pale, and attaines not its laudable colour, if it be sunned too long it suffereth a torrefaction, and descendeth somewhat below it.[236]

Clove is the rudiment or beginning of a fruit growing upon the clove tree, to be found but in few countries. The most commendable is that of Isles of Molucca; it is first white, afterward green, which beaten downe, and dryed in the sun becommeth blacke, and in the complexion we receive it.[237]

Nutmeg is the fruit of a tree differing from all these, and as Garcias describeth it, somewhat like a peach, growing in divers places, but fructifying in the Isle of Banda.[238] The fruit hereof, consisteth of foure parts; the first or outward part is a thick and carnous covering like that of a walnut. The second a dry and flosculous coat, commonly called mace.[239] The third a harder tegument or shell, which lyeth under the mace. The fourth a kernell included in the shell, which is the same we call nutmeg; all which both in their parts and order of disposure, are easily discerned in those fruits, which are brought in preserves unto us.

Now if because mace and nutmegs proceed from one tree, the rest must beare them company, or because they are all from the East-Indies, they are all from one plant, the inference is precipitous, nor will there such a plant be found in the herball of nature.

3. That viscus arboreus or misseltoe is bred upon trees, from seeds which birds, especially thrushes and ringdoves let fall thereon, was the creed of the ancients, and is still beleeved among us, is the account of its production, set downe by Pliny, delivered by Virgil, and subscribed by many more.[240] If so, some reason must be assigned, why it groweth onely upon certaine trees, and not upon many whereon these birds do light. For as exotick observers deliver, it groweth upon almond trees, chesnut, apples, oakes, and pine trees, as wee observe in England, very commonly upon apple, holly, bayes, crabs, and white thorne, sometimes upon sallow, hasell, and oake, never upon bayes, holly, ashes, elmes, and many others.[241] Why it groweth not in all countries and places where these birds are found, for so Brassavolus affirmeth, it is not to be found in the territorie of Ferrara, and was faine to supply himselfe from other parts of Italy.[242] Why if it ariseth from a seed, if sowne it will not grow againe, as Pliny affirmeth, and as by setting the berryes thereof, wee have in vaine attempted its production; why if it commeth from seed that falleth upon the tree, it groweth often downewards and puts forth under the bough,

where seed can neither fall, nor yet remaine. Hereof beside some others, the Lord Verulam hath taken notice.[243] And they surely speake probably who make it an arboreous excrescence, or rather superplant, bred of a viscous and superfluous sappe the tree it selfe cannot assimilate, and therefore sprouteth not forth in boughs and surcles of the same shape and similary unto the tree that beareth it, but in a different forme, and secondary unto its specificall intention, wherein once fayling, another forme succeedeth, and in the first place that of misseltoe, in plants and trees disposed to its production.[244] And therefore also where ever it groweth, it is of constant shape, and maintaines a regular figure like other supercrescenses, and such as living upon the stock of others, are termed parasiticall plants, as polypody, mosse, the smaller capillaries, and many more.

Now what begot this conceit, might be the enlargement of that part of truth conteined in its story. For certaine it is, that some birdes doe feed upon the berries of this vegetable, and we meet in Aristotle with one kind of thrush called ’ιξοβόρος, the missell thrush or feeder upon misseltoe. But that which hath most promoted it, is a received proverb. *Turdus sibi malum cacat*;[245] appliable unto such men as are authors of their owne misfortune: For according unto ancient tradition and Plinies relation, the bird not able to digest the fruit whereon shee feedeth, from her inconverted muting, ariseth this plant, of the berries whereof birdlime is made, wherewith she is after entangled. Now although proverbs bee popular principles, yet is not all true that is proverbiall; and in many thereof there being one thing delivered, and another intended, though the verball expression be false, the proverbe is true enough in the veritie of its intention.

As for the magicall vertues in this plant, and conceived efficacie unto veneficiall intentions, it seemeth unto me a pagan relique derived from the ancient Druides, the great admirers of the oake, especially the misseltoe that grew thereon; which according unto the particular of Plinie, they gathered with great solemnitie.[246] For after sacrifice the priest in a white garment, ascended the tree, cut downe the misseltoe with a golden hooke, and received it in a white coat, the vertue whereof was to resist all poysons, and make fruitfull any that used it. Vertues not expected from classicall practise; and did they answer their promise which are so commended, in epilepticall intentions, wee would abate these qualities.[247]

Countrey practise hath added another, to provoke the after-birth, and in that case the decoction is given unto Cowes. That the berries are poison as some conceive, we are so far from averring, that we have safely given them inwardly, and can confirme the experiment of Brassavolus, that they have some purgative quality.

4. The rose of Jerico, that flourishes every yeer just upon Christmas Eve is famous in Christian reports, which notwithstanding wee have some reason to doubt; and we are plainely informed by Bellonius, it is but a monasticall imposture, as hee hath delivered in his observations, concerning the plants in Jericho.[248] That which promoted the conceit, or perhaps begot its continuance, was a proprietie in this plant. For though it bee dry, yet will it upon imbibition of moisture dilate its leaves, and explicate its flowers contracted, and seemingly dryed up. And this is to bee effected not onely in the plant yet growing, but in some manner also in that which is brought exuccous and dry unto us. Which quality being observed, the subtilty of contrivers did commonly play this shew upon the eve of our Saviours nativitie, and by drying the plant againe, it closed the next day, and so pretended a double mystery. That is the opening and closing of the wombe of Mary.

There wanted not a specious confirmation from a text in Ecclesiasticus, chap. 24. *Quasi palma exaltata sum in Cades & quasi plantatio Rosæ in Iericho:* I was exalted like a palme tree in Engaddi, and as a rose in Jericho.[249] The sound whereof in common eares, begat an extraordinary opinion of the rose of that denomination. But herein there seemeth a great mistake; for by the rose in the text, is implyed the true and proper rose, *φυτὸν τοῦ ῥόδου* sayth the Greek, and ours accordingly rendreth it. But that which passeth under this name, and by us is commonly called the Rose of Jericho, is properly no rose, but a small thorny shrub or kinde of heath, bearing little white flowers, far differing from the rose, whereof Bellonius a very inquisitive herbalist could not finde any in his travells thorow Jericho. A plant so unlike a rose, it hath been mistaken by some good simplist for amomum, which truely understood is so unlike a rose, that as Dioscorides delivers, the flowers thereof, are like the white violet, and its leaves resemble bryonie;[250] sutable unto this relation almost in all points is that of the thorne at Glassenbury, and perhaps the daughter thereof; herein our endeavours as yet have not attained satisfaction, and cannot therefore enlarge.[251] Thus much in generall we may observe, that strange effects, are naturally taken for miracles by weaker heads, and artificially improved to that apprehension by wiser.

5. That *ferrum equinum*, or *sferra cavallo* hath a vertue attractive of iron, a power to breake lockes, and draw off the shooes of a horse that passeth over it. Whether you take it for one kinde of secuidaca, or will also take in lunaria, we know it to be false; and cannot but wonder at Mathiolus, who upon a parallell in Plinie was staggered into suspension;[252] who notwithstanding in the imputed vertue to open things, close and shut up, could laugh himselfe at that promise from Æthiopis, and condemne the judgement of Scipio, who having such a picklock, would spend so many years in battering the gates of Carthage. Which strange and magicall conceit, seemes unto me to have no deeper root in reason, then the figure of its seed; for therein indeed it somewhat resembles an horseshooe, which notwithstanding Baptista Porta hath thought too low a signation, and raised the same unto a lunarie representation.

6. That Bayes will protect from the mischief of lightning and thunder, is a qualitie ascribed thereto, common with the figtree, ægle, and skin of a seale. Against so famous a quality, Vicomereatus produceth experiment of a bay tree blasted in Italy, and therefore although Tiberius for this intent, did weare a laurell about his temples,[253] yet did Augustus take a more probable course, who fled under arches and hollow vautes for protection.[254] And though Porta conceive, because in a streperous eruption, it riseth against fire, it doth therefore resist lightning, yet is that no emboldning illation: and if wee consider the threefold effect of Jupiters trisulke, to burne, discusse and terebrate;[255] and if that be true which is commonly delivered, that it will melt the blade, yet passe the scabbard, kill the childe, yet spare the mother, dry up the wine, yet leave the hogshead intire; though it favour the amulet it may not spare us; it will be unsure to rely on any preservative, tis no security to be dipped in Styx, or clad in the armour of Ceneus.[256] Now that beer, wine, and other liquors, are spoyled with lightning and thunder, we conceive it proceeds not onely from noyse and concussion of the ayre, but also noxious spirits, which mingle therewith, and draw them to corruption, whereby they become not onely dead themselves, but sometime deadly unto others, as that which Seneca mentioneth, whereof whosoever dranke, either lost his life, or else his wits upon it.

7. It hath much deceived the hopes of good fellowes, what is commonly expected of bitter almonds, and though in Plutarch confirmed from the practise of Claudius his physitian, that antidote against ebriety hath commonly failed.[257] Surely men much verst in the practice doe erre in the theory of inebriation, conceaving in that disturbance the braine doth onely suffer from exhalations and vaporous ascentions from the stomack, which fat and oylie substances may suppresse, whereas the prevalent intoxication is from the spirits of drink dispersed into the veynes and arteries, from whence by common conveyances they creep into the braine, insinuate into its ventricles, and beget those vertigoes, accompanying that perversion. And therefore the same effect may be produced by a glister, the head may be intoxicated by a medicine at the heele.[258] And so the poysonous bytes of serpents, although on parts at distance from the head, yet having entered the veynes, disturbe the animall faculties, and produce the effects of drink, or poyson swallowed. And so as the head may bee disturbed by the skin, it may the same way be relieved, as is observable in balneations, washings, and fomentations, either of the whole body, or of that part alone.

CHAPTER VII
Of some Insects, and the properties of several Plants[259]

[1. Few ears have escaped the noise of the dead-watch, that is, the little clickling sound heard often in many rooms, somewhat resembling that of a watch; and this is conceived to be of an evil omen or prediction of some persons death: wherein notwithstanding there is nothing of rational presage or just cause of terrour unto melancholy and meticulous heads. For this noise is made by a little sheath-winged gray insect found often in wainscot, benches, and wood-work, in the Summer. We have taken many thereof, and kept them in thin boxes, wherein I have heard and seen them work and knack with a little proboscis or trunk against the side of the box, like a *picus martius*, or woodpecker against a tree. It worketh best in warm weather, and for the most part, giveth not over under nine or eleven stroaks at a time. He that could extinguish the terrifying apprehensions hereof, might prevent the passions of the heart, and many cold sweats in grandmothers and nurses, who in the sickness of children, are so startled with these noises.

2. The presage of the year succeeding, which is commonly made from insects or little animals in oak apples, according to the kinds thereof, either maggot, flue, or spider; that is, of famine, warre, or pestilence; whether we mean that wooddy excrescence, which shooteth from the branch about May, or that round and apple-like accretion which groweth under the leaf about the later end of Summer, is I doubt too distinct, nor verifiable from event.

For flies and maggots are found every year, very seldom spiders: And Helmont affirmeth he could never find the spider and the flye upon the same trees, that is the signs of war and pestilence, which often go together. Beside, that the flies found were at first maggots, experience hath informed us; for keeping these excrescencies, we have observed their conversions, beholding in magnifying glasses the daily progression thereof. As may be also observed in other vegetable excretions, whose maggots do terminate in flies of constant shapes; as in the nutgalls of the outlandish oake, and the mossie tuft of the wilde briar; which having gathered in November we have found the little maggots which lodged in wooden cels all Winter, to turn into flies in June.

We confesse the opinion may hold some verity in the analogy, or emblematicall phancy. For pestilence is properly signified by the spider, whereof some kinds are of a very venemous nature. Famine by maggots, which destroy the fruits of the earth. And warre not improperly by the flye; if we rest in the phancy of Homer, who compares the valiant Grecian unto a flye.

Some verity it may also have in it self, as truly declaring the corruptive constitution in the present sap and nutrimentall juice of the tree; and may consequently discover the disposition of that year, according to the plenty or kindes of these productions. For if the putrifying juices of bodies bring forth plenty of flies and maggots, they give forth testimony of common corruption, and declare that the elements are full of the seeds of putrefaction, as the great number of caterpillars, gnats, and ordinary insects doe also declare. If they runne into spiders, they give signs of higher putrefaction, as plenty of vipers and scorpions are confessed to doe; the putrefying materials producing animals of higher mischiefs, according to the advance and higher strain of corruption.

3. Whether all plants have seed, were more easily determinable, if we could conclude concerning harts-tongue, ferne, the capillaries, lunaria, and some others. But whether those little dusty particles, upon the lower side of the leaves, be seeds and seminall parts; or rather, as it is commonly conceived, excrementall separations; we have not as yet been able to determine by any germination or univocall production from them. Thus much we observe, that they seem to renew yearly, and come not fully out till the plant be in its vigour: and by the help of magnifying glasses we find these dusty atomes to be round at first, and fully representing seeds, out of which at last proceed little mites almost invisible; so that such as are old stand open, as being emptied of some bodies formerly included; which though discernable in harts-tongue, is more notoriously discoverable in some differencies of brake or ferne.

But exquisite microscopes and magnifying glasses have at last cleared this doubt, whereby also long ago the noble Federicus Cæsius beheld the dusts of polypody as bigg as pepper corns; and as Johannes Faber testifieth, made draughts on paper of such kind of seeds, as bigg as his glasses represented them: and set down such plants under the classis of *herbæ tergifœtæ*, as may be observed in his notable botanical tables.[260]

4. Whether the sap of trees runnes down to the roots in Winter, whereby they become naked and grow not: or whether they do not cease to draw any more, and reserve so much as sufficeth for conservation, is not a point indubitable. For we observe, that most trees, as though they would be perpetually green, doe bud at the fall of the leaf, although they sprout not much forward untill the Spring, and warmer weather approacheth; and many trees maintain their leaves all Winter, although they seem to receive very small advantage in their growth. But that the sap doth powerfully rise in the Spring, to repair that moisture whereby they barely subsisted in the Winter, and also to put the plant in a capacity of fructification: he that hath beheld how many gallons of water may in a small time be drawn from a birch-tree in the Spring, hath slender reason to doubt.

5. That camphire eunuchates or begets in men an impotency unto venery, observation will hardly confirm; and we have found it to fail in cocks and hens, though given for many daies; which was a more favourable triall then that of Scaliger, when he gave it unto a bitch that was proud.[261] For the instant turgescence is not to be taken off, but by medicines of higher

natures; and with any certainty but one way that we know, which notwithstanding, by suppresing that naturall evacuation, may incline unto madnesse, if taken in the Summer.

6. In the history of prodigies we meet with many showers of wheat; how true or probable, we have not room to debate: only this much we shall not omit to inform, that what was this year found in many places, and almost preached for wheat rained from the clouds, was but the seed of ivy-berries, which somewhat represent it; and though it were found in steeples and high places, might be conveyed thither, or muted out by birds: for many feed thereon, and in the crops of some we have found no less then three ounces.

7. That every plant might receive a name according unto the disease it cureth, was the wish of Paracelsus; a way more likely to multiply empericks then herbalists;[262] yet what is practised by many is advantagious unto neither; that is, relinquishing their proper appellations to re-baptize them by the name of saints, apostles, patriarchs, and martyrs, to call this the herbe of John, that of Peter, this of James or Joseph, that of Mary or Barbara, for hereby apprehensions are made additional unto their proper natures; whereon superstitious practises ensue; and stories are framed accordingly to make good their foundations.

8. We cannot omit to declare the gross mistake of many in the nominal apprehension of plants; to instance but in few. An herbe there is commonly called Betonica Pauli, or Pauls betony; hereof the people have some conceit in reference to St. Paul; whereas indeed that name is derived from Paulus Ægineta, an ancient physitian of Ægina, and is no more then speed-well, or fluellen. The like expectations are raised from *herba trinitatis*; which notwithstanding obtaineth that name from the figure of its leaves, and is one kind of liverwort, or hepatica. In *milium solis*, the epithete of the sun hath enlarged its opinion; which hath indeed no reference thereunto, it being no more then lithospermon, or grummell, or rather *milium soler*; which as Serapion from Aben Juliel hath taught us, because it grew plentifully in the mountains of Soler, received that appellation.[263] In Jews-ears something is conceived extraordinary from the name, which is in propriety but *fungus sambucinus*, or an excrescence about the roots of elder, and concerneth not the nation of the Jews, but Judas Iscariot, upon a conceit, he hanged on this tree; and is become a famous medicine in quinsies, sore throats, and strangulations ever

since. And so are they deceived in the name of the horse-raddish, horse-mint, bull-rush, and many more: conceiving therein some prenominall consideration, whereas indeed that expression is but a Grecisme, by the prefix of Hippos and Bous, that is, horse and bull, intending no more then great. According whereto the great dock is called Hippolapathum; and hee that calls the horse of Alexander, Great-head, expresseth the same which the Greeks doe in Bucephalus.

9. Lastly, many things are delivered and beleeved of other plants, wherein at least we cannot but suspend. That there is a property in basil to propagate scorpions, and that by the smell thereof they are bred in the braines of men, is much advanced by Hollerius, who found this insect in the braines of a man that delighted much in this smel.[264] Wherein beside that wee finde no way to conjoyne the effect unto the cause assigned; herein the moderns speak but timorously, and some of the ancients quite contrarily. For, according unto Oribasius, physitian unto Julian, the Affricans, men best experienced in poysons, affirm whosoever hath eaten basil, although he be stung with a scorpion, shall feel no pain thereby:[265] which is a very different effect, and rather antidotally destroying, then seminally promoting its production.

That the leaves of cataputia or spurge, being plucked upward or downeward, respectively perform their operations by purge or vomit, as some have written, and old wives still do preach, is a strange conceit, ascribing unto plants positionall operations, and after the manner of the loadstone; upon the pole whereof if a knife be drawn from the handle unto the poynt, it will take up a needle; but if drawn again from the point to the handle, it will attract it no more.

That cucumbers are no commendable fruits, that being very waterish, they fill the veins with crude and windy serosities; that containing little salt or spirit, they may also debilitate the vitall acidity, and fermentall faculty of the stomack, we readily concede. But that they should be so cold, as be almost poison by that quality, it will be hard to allow, without the contradiction of Galen;[266] who accounteth them cold but in the second degree, and in that classis have most physitians placed them.

That elder berries are poison, as we are taught be tradition, experience will unteach us. And beside the promises of Blochwitius, the healthful effects thereof daily observed will convict us.

That an ivy cup will separate wine from water, if filled with both, the wine soaking through, but the water still remaining, as after Pliny many have averred, wee know not how to affirm;[267] who making triall thereof, found both the liquors to soak indistinctly through the bowle.

That Ros solis which rotteth sheep, hath any such cordiall virtue upon us, we have some reason to doubt.

That Flos Affricanus is poison, and destroyeth dogs, in two experiments we have not found.

That yew and the berries thereof are harmless, we know.

That a snake will not endure the shade of an ash, we can deny.

That cats have such delight in the herb nepeta, called therefore cattaria, our experience cannot discover. Nor is it inconsiderable what is affirmed by Bellonius;[268] for if his assertion be true in the first of his observations, our apprehension is oftentimes wide in ordinary simples, and in common use we mistake one for another. We know not the true thyme; the savourie in our gardens, is not that commended of old; and that kind of hysop the ancients used, is unknown unto us, who make great use of another.

We omit to recite the many vertues, and endlesse faculties ascribed unto plants, which sometime occure in grave and serious authors; and we shall make a bad transaction for truth to concede a verity in half. To reckon up all, it were imployment for Archimedes, who undertook to write the number of the sands. Swarms of others there are, some whereof our future endeavours may discover; common reason I hope will save us a labour in many: whose absurdities stand naked unto every eye; errours not able to deceive the embleme of justice, and need no Argus to decry them. Herein there surely wants expurgatory animadversions, whereby we might strike out great numbers of hidden qualities; and having once a serious and conceded list, we might with more encouragement and safety, attempt their reasons.]

THE THIRD BOOK

Of divers popular and received tenents concerning animals, which examined, prove either false or dubious

CHAPTER I
Of the Elephant

The first shall be of the elephant, whereof there generally passeth an opinion it hath no joynts; and this absurdity is seconded with another, that being unable to lye downe, it sleepeth against a tree, which the hunters observing doe saw almost asunder; whereon the beast relying, by the fall of the tree falls also down it selfe, and is able to rise no more; which conceit is not the daughter of latter times, but an old and gray-headed errour, even in the dayes of Aristotle, as he delivereth in his booke, *de incessu animalium*, and stands successively related by severall other authors, by Diodorus Siculus, Strabo, Ambrose, Cassiodore, Solinus, and many more:[1] now herein me thinks men much forget themselves, not well considering the absurditie of such assertions.

For first, they affirme it hath no joynts, and yet concede it walks and moves about; whereby they conceive there may be a progression or advancement made in motion without the inflexion of parts:[2] now all progression or animall locomotion being (as Aristotle teacheth) performed *tractu* and *pulsu*; that is by drawing on, or impelling forward some part which was before in station, or at quiet; where there are no joynts or flexures neither can there be these actions; and this is true, not only in quadrupedes, volatills and fishes, which have distinct and prominent organs of motion, legs, wings, and fins; but in such also as performe their progression by the truncke, as serpents, wormes and leeches;[3] whereof though some want bones, and all extended articulations, yet have they arthriticall analogies, and by the motion of fibrous and musculous parts, are able to make progression;[4] which to conceive in bodies inflexible, and without all protrusion of parts, were to expect a race from Hercules his pillars, or hope to behold the effects of Orpheus his harpe, when trees found legges, and danced after his musicke.[5]

Againe, while men conceive they never lye downe, and enjoy not the position of rest, ordained unto all pedestrious animalls whatsoever, hereby they imagine (what reason cannot conceive) that an animall of the vastest dimension and longest duration should live in a continuall motion, without that alternity and vicissitude of rest whereby all others continue; and yet must thus much come to passe, if wee opinion they lye not downe and enjoy no decumbence at all;[6] for station is properly no rest, but one kinde of motion, relating unto that which physitians (from Galen) doe name extensive or tonicall, that is an extension of the muscles and organs of motion maintaining the body at length or in its proper figure, wherein although it seem to be immoved is neverthelesse not without all motion,[7] for in this position the muscles are sensibly extended, and labour to support the body, which permitted unto its proper gravity would suddenly subside and fall unto the earth, as it happeneth in sleep, diseases and death; from which occult action and invisible motion of the muscles in station (as Galen declareth) proceed more offensive lassitudes then from ambulation;[8] and therefore the tyranny of some have tormented men, with long and enforced station, and though Ixion and Sisiphus which alwaies moved, doe seem to have the hardest measure, yet was not Titius favoured, that lay extended upon Caucasus, and Tantalus suffered somewhat more then thirst, that stood perpetually in hell;[9] and thus Mercurialis in his Gymnasticks justly makes standing one kinde of exercise, and Galen when we lye downe, commends unto us middle figures; that is, not to lye directly, or at length, but somewhat inflected, that the muscles may be at rest; for such as he termeth Hypobolemaioi or figures of excesse, either shrinking up or stretching out, are wearisome positions, and such as perturbe the quiet of those parts.[10] [Now various parts doe variously discover these indolent and quiet positions, some in right lines, as the wrists: some at right angles, as the cubit: others at oblique angles, as the fingers and the knees: all resting satisfied in postures of moderation, and none enduring the extremity of flexure and extension.[11]]

Moreover men herein doe strangely forget the obvious relations of history, affirming they have no joynts, whereas they dayly read of severall actions which are not performable without them. They forget what is delivered by Xiphilinus, and also by Suetonius in the lives of Nero and Galba, that elephants have been instructed to walke on ropes, and that in publicke shews before the people;[12] which is not easily performed by man, and requireth not only a broad foot, but a plyable flexure of joynts, and commandible disposure of all parts of progression; they passe by that memorable place in Curtius, concerning the elephant of King Porus, *Indus qui Elephantem regebat, descendere eum ratus, more solito procumbere jussit in genua, cæteri quoque (ita enim instituti erant) demisere corpora in terram*;[13] they remember not the expression of Osorius, *de rebus gestis Emanuelis*, when he speakes of the elephant presented to Leo the tenth, *Pontificem ter genibus flexis, et demisso corporis habitu venerabundus salutavit*:[14] but above all, they call not to minde that memorable shew of Germanicus, wherein twelve elephants danced unto the sound of musick, and after laid them down in the tricliniums, or places of festivall recumbency.[15]

[They forget the etymologie of the knee*, approved by some grammarians.[16] They disturb the position of the young ones in the wombe: which upon extension of legs is not easily conceivable; and contrary unto the general contrivance of nature. Nor do they consider the impossible exclusion thereof, upon extension and rigour of the legges.]

* γόνυ from γωνία.

Lastly, they forget or consult not experience, whereof not many yeares past, we have had the advantage in England, by an elephant shewne in many parts thereof, not only in the posture of standing, but kneeling and lying downe; whereby although the opinion at present be reasonable well suppressed, yet from the strings of tradition and fruitfull recurrence of error, it is not improbable, it may revive in the next generation againe; for this was not the first that hath been seen in England, for (besides some others since) as Polydore Virgil relateth, Lewis the French King sent one to Henry the third; and Emanuel of Portugall another unto Leo the tenth into Italy, where notwithstanding the errour is still alive and epidemicall, as with us.[17]

The hint and ground of this opinion might be the grosse and somewhat cylindricall composure of the legs, the equality and lesse perceptible disposure of the joynts, especially in the fore legs of this animall, they appearing when he standeth like pillars of flesh, without any evidence of articulation: the different flexure and order of the joynts might also countenance the same, being not disposed in the elephant, as they are in other quadrupedes, but carry a nearer conformity into those of man, that is the bought of the fore legs not directly backward, but laterally and somewhat inward, but the hough or suffraginous flexure behinde rather outward,[18] contrary unto many other quadrupedes, and such as can scratch the eare with the hinder foot, as horses, camells, deere, sheep and dogs, for their fore legs bend like our legs, and their hinder legs like our armes, when we move them to our shoulders; but quadrupedes oviparous, as frogs, lizards, crocodiles, have their joynts and motive flexures more analogously framed unto ours; and some among viviparous, that is such thereof as can bring their forefeet and meat therein into their mouths, as most can doe that have the clavicles or coller-bones, whereby their breasts are broader, and their shoulders more asunder, as the ape, the monkey, the squirrell, and some others: if therefore any shall affirme the joynts of elephants are differently framed from most of other quadrupedes, and more obscurely and grossely almost then any, he doth herein no injury unto truth; but if *à dicto secundum quid ad dictum simpliciter*, he affirmeth also they have no articulations at all, he incurs the controlment of reason, and cannot avoid the contradiction of sense.[19]

As for the manner of their venation, if we consult historicall experience, we shall find it to be otherwise then as is commonly presumed, by sawing away of trees; the accounts whereof are to be seen at large in Johannes Hugo, Edwardus Lopez, Garcias ab Horto, Cadamustus, and many more:[20] other concernments there are of the elephant, which might admit of discourse, and if we should question the teeth of elephants, that is whether they be properly so termed, or might not rather be called hornes, it were no new enquiry of mine, but a paradox as old as Oppianus:[21] whether as Pliny and divers since affirme, that elephants are terrified, and make away upon the grunting of swine, Garcias ab Horto may decide, who affirmeth upon experience they enter their stalles, and live promiscuously in the woods of Malavar;[22] that the situation of the genitalls is averse, and their copulation like that of camells, as Pliny hath also delivered, is neither to be received, for we have beheld that part in a different position, and their coition is made by supersaliency like that of horses, as we are informed by some who have beheld them in that act.[23] That some elephants have not only written whole sentences, as Ælian ocularly testifieth, but have also spoken, as Oppianus delivereth, and Christophorus a Costa particularly relateth, although it sound like that of

Achilles horse in Homer, wee doe not conceive impossible;[24] nor beside the affinity of reason in this animall any such intolerable incapacity in the organs of divers other quadrupedes, whereby they might not be taught to speake, or become imitators of speech like birds; and indeed strange it is how the curiosity of men that have been active in the instruction of beasts, have never fallen upon this artifice, and among those many paradoxicall and unheard of imitations, should not attempt to make one speak; the serpent that spake unto Eve, the dogs and cats, that usually speak unto witches, might afford some encouragement, and since broad and thick chops are required in birds that speake, since lips and teeth are also organs of speech;[25] from these there is also an advantage in quadrupedes, and a proximity of reason in elephants and apes above them all. [Since also an echo will speak without any mouth at all,[26] articulately returning the voice of man, by only ordering the vocall spirit in concave and hollow places; whether the musculous and motive parts about the hollow mouths of beasts, may not dispose the passing spirit into some articulate notes, seems a querie of no great doubt.]

CHAPTER II
Of the Horse

The second assertion, that an horse hath no gall, is very generall, nor onely swallowed by the people, and common farriers, but also received by good veterinarians, and some who have laudably discoursed upon horses. It seemeth also very ancient; for it is plainly set downe by Aristotle, an horse and all solipeds have no gall; and the same is also delivered by Plinie, which notwithstanding we finde repugnant unto experience and reason;[27] for first, it calls in question the providence or wise provision of nature, who not abounding in superfluities, is neither deficient in necessities, wherein neverthelesse there would be a maine defect, and her improvision justly accusable, if such a feeding animall, and so subject unto diseases from bilious causes, should want a proper conveyance for choler, or have no other receptacle for that humor, then the veynes, and generall masse of bloud.

It is againe controulable by experience; for we have made some search and enquiry herein, encouraged by Absyrtus a Greek author, in the time of Constantine, who in his

Hippiatricks, obscurely assigneth the gall a place in the liver; but more especially by Ruino the Bononian, who in his *Anatomia del Cavallo*, hath more plainly described it, and in a manner as I found it;[28] for in the dissections of horses, and particular enquiry into that part, in the concave or simous part of the liver, whereabout the gall is usually seated in quadrupeds, I discover an hollow, long and membranous substance of a yellow colour without, and lined with choler and gall within;[29] which part is by branches diffused into the lobes and severall parcells of the liver, from whence receiving the firie superfluity, or cholericke remainder, upon the second concoction by a manifest and open passage, it conveyeth it into the duodenum or upper gut, thence into the lower bowells, which is the manner of its derivation in man and other animalls; and therefore although there be no eminent and circular follicle, no round bagge or vesicle which long containeth this humor, yet is there a manifest receptacle and passage of choler, from the liver into the guts; which being not so shut up, or at least not so long detained, as it is in other animalls, procures that frequent excretion, and occasions the horse to dung more often then many other; for choler is the naturall glister, or one excretion whereby nature excludeth another, which descending daily into the bowells, extimulates those parts, and excites them unto expulsion;[30] and so when this humor aboundeth or corrupteth, there succeeds ofttimes a *cholerica passio*, that is a sudden and vehement purgation upward and downward; and so when the passage of gall becomes obstructed, the body grows costive, and the excrements of the belly white, as it happeneth oft-times in the jaundice.[31]

If any therefore affirme an horse hath no gall, that is, no receptacle, or part ordained for the separation of choller, or not that humour at all, he hath both sence and reason to oppose him; but if he saith it hath no bladder of gall, and such as is observed in many other animals, we shall oppose our sense if we gainesay him; and thus must Aristotle be made out when he denyeth this part, and by this distinction wee may relieve Pliny of a contradiction; who in one place affirming an horse hath no gall, delivereth yet in another, that the gall of an horse was accounted poyson, and therefore at the sacrifices of horses in Rome, it was unlawfull for the flamen but to touch it;[32] but with more difficulty, or hardly at all is that reconcilable which is delivered by our countreyman, and received veterinarian, whose words in his master-piece, and chapter of diseases from the gall, are somewhat too strict, and scarce admit a reconciliation.[33] The fallacy therefore of this conceit is not unlike the former, *A dicto secundum quid ad dictum simpliciter*, because they have not a bladder of gall, like those we usually observe in others, they have no gall at all; which is a paralogisme not admittible, a fallacy that dwels not in a cloud, and needs not the sun to scatter it.

CHAPTER III
Of the Dove

The third assertion is somewhat like the second, that a dove or pigeon hath no gall, which is affirmed from very great antiquity; for as Pierius observeth, from this consideration the Ægyptians did make it the hieroglyphick of meekenesse;[34] it hath beene averred by many holy writers, commonly delivered by postillers and commentators, who from the frequent mention of the dove in the Canticles, the precept of our Saviour to bee wise as serpents, and innocent as doves, and especially the appearance of the holy Ghost in the similitude of this animall, have taken occasion to set downe many affections of the dove, and what doth most commend it, is that it hath no gall; and hereof have made use not onely inferiour and minor divines, but Cyprian, Austin, Isidore, Beda, Rupertus, Jansenius, and many more.[35]

Whereto notwithstanding we know not how to assent, it being repugnant unto the authority and positive determination of ancient philosophy; the affirmative of Aristotle in his history of animals is very plaine, *Fel aliis ventri, aliis intestino jungitur*; some have the gall adjoyned to the guts, as the crow, the swallow, sparrow, and the dove, the same is also attested by Pliny, and not without some passion by Galen, who in his booke *de atra bile*, accounts him ridiculous that denyes it.[36]

It is not agreeable to the constitution of this animall, nor can we so reasonably conceive there wants a gall; that is, the hot and fiery humour in a body so hot of temper, which phlegme or melancholy could not effect: now of what complexion it is, Julius Alexandrinus declareth, when he affirmeth, that some upon the use thereof, have fallen into feavers and quinsies;[37] the temper also of their dung and intestinall excretions do also confirme the same, which topically applyed become a phænigmus or rubifying medicine, and are of such fiery parts, that as we reade in Galen, they have of themselves conceived fire, and burnt a house about them, and therefore when in the famine of Samaria, (wherein the fourth part of a cab of pigeons dung was sold for five pieces of silver) it is delivered by Josephus, that men made use hereof instead of common salt, although the exposition seeme strange, it is more probable then many other, for that it containeth very much salt;[38] beside the effects before expressed, it is discernable by taste, and the earth of columbaries or dovehouses, so much desired in the artifice of saltpeter; and to speake generally, the excrements of birds which want both bladder and kidneys, hath more of salt and acrimony, then that of other animals, who beside the guts have also those conveyances; for whereas in these, the salt and lixiviated serosity with some portion of choler, is divided betweene the guts and bladder, it remaines undivided in birds, and hath but a single descent, by the guts, with the exclusions of the belly.[39] Now if because the dove is of a milde and gentle nature, wee cannot conceive it should be of an hot temper, our apprehensions are not distinct in the measure of constitutions, and the several parts which evidence such conditions: for the irascible passions doe follow the temper of the heart, but the concupiscible distractions the crasis of the liver;[40] now many have not livers, which have but coole and temperate hearts, and this was probably the temper of Paris, a contrary constitution to that of Ajax, and in both but short of Medea, who seemed to exceed in either.[41]

Lastly, it is repugnant to experience, for anatomicall enquirie discovereth in them a gall, and that according to the determination of Aristotle, not annexed unto the liver, but adhering unto the guts; nor is the humour contained in smaller veines, or obscure capillations, but in a vesicle or little bladder, though some affirme it hath no cystis or bag at all, and therefore the hieroglyphick of the Ægyptians, though allowable in the sence, is weake in the foundation, who expressing meeknesse and lenity by the portract of a dove with the taile erected, affirmed it had no gall in the inward parts, but onely in the rumpe, and as it were out of the body, and therefore if they conceived their gods were pleased with the sacrifice of this animall, as being without gall, the ancient heathen were surely mistaken in the reason, and in the very oblation, whereas in the holocaust or burnt offerings of Moses the gall was cast away;[42] for as Ben Maimon instructeth, the inwards whereto the gall adhereth were taken out with the crop, according unto the

Law, which the priest did not burne, but cast unto the east, that is, behinde his back, and readiest place to be carried out of the sanctuary.[43] And if they also conceived that for this reason, they were the birds of Venus, and wanting the furious and discording part, were more acceptable unto the deity of love; they surely added unto the conceit, which was at first venereall, and in this animall may be sufficiently made out from that conception.[44]

The ground of this conceit is partly like the former, that is, the obscure situation of the gall, and out of the liver, wherein it is commonly enquired, but this is a very injust illation, not well considering with what variety this part is seated in birds;[45] in some both at the stomack and the liver, as in the capriceps, in some at the liver only, as in cocks, turkeys, and phasiants, in others at the guts and liver, as in hawkes and kites; in some at the guts alone, as crowes, doves, and many more, and these perhaps may take up all the wayes of situation, not onely in birds, but also other animals, for what is said of the anchovy, that answerable unto its name, it carrieth the gall in the head, is further to be enquired; and though the discoloured particles in the skin of an heron, be commonly termed galls, yet is not this animall deficient in that part; and thus when it is conceived that the eyes of Tobias were cured by the gall of the fish callyonimus or *scorpius marinus*, commended to that effect by Dioscorides, although that part were not in the liver, were there reason to doubt that probability, and whatsoever animall it was, it may be received without exception when 'tis delivered, the married couple as a testimony of future concord, did cast the gall of the sacrifice behinde the altar?[46]

A strict and literall acception of a loose and tropicall expression was a second ground hereof; for while some affirmed it had no gall, intending onely thereby no evidence of anger or fury, others have construed it anatomically, and denied that part at all; by which illation we may inferre, and that from sacred text, a pigeon hath no heart, according to that expression, Hosea 7. *Factus est Ephraim sicut Columba seducta non habens cor*;[47] and so from the letter of Scripture wee may conclude it is no milde, but a fiery and furious animall, according to that of Jeremy, chapter 25. *Facta est terra in desolationem à facie iræ columbæ*:[48] and againe, chapter 46. *Revertamur ad terram nativitatis nostræ à facie gladii columbæ*, where notwithstanding the dove is not literally intended, but thereby are implyed the Babylonians whose Queene Semiramis was called by that name, and whose successors did beare the dove in their standard:[49] so is it proverbially said, *Formicæ sua bilis inest, habet et musca splenem*, whereas wee all know philosophy denyeth these parts, nor hath anatomy discovered them in insects.[50]

If therefore any shall affirme a pigeon hath no gall, implying no more thereby then the lenity of this animall, wee shall not controvert his affirmation; and thus may wee make out the assertions of ancient writers, and safely receive the expressions of those great divines and worthy fathers; but if by a transition from rhetorick to logick, hee shall contend, it hath no such part, or humour, he committeth an open fallacy, and such as was probably first committed concerning Spanish mares, whose swiftnesse tropically expressed from their generation by the wind, might after be grosly taken, and a reall truth conceived in that conception.[51]

CHAPTER IV
Of the Bever

That a bever to escape the hunter, bites off his testicles or stones, is a tenent very ancient, and hath had thereby advantage of propagation; for the same we finde in the hieroglyphicks of the Ægyptians, in the apologue of Æsope, an author of great antiquity, who lived in the beginning of the Persian Monarchy, and in the time of Cyrus; the same is touched by Aristotle in his Ethicks, but seriously delivered by Ælian, Plinie and Solinus, with the same we meet with in Juvenal, who by an handsome and metricall expression more welcomely engrafts it in our junior memories,

—imitatus Castora, qui se
Eunuchum ipse facit, cupiens evadere damno
Testiculorum, adeo medicatum intelligit inguen,

It hath been propagated by Emblems, and some have been so bad gramarians, as to be deceived by the name, deriving *Castor à castrando*; whereas, the proper Latine word is *Fibor*, and *Castor*, but borrowed from the Greeke so called *quasi* γάστωρ, that is, *Animal ventricosum*, from his swaggy and prominent belly.[52]

Herein therefore to speake compendiously, wee first presume to affirme, that from a strict enquiry, we cannot maintaine the evulsion or biting of any parts, and this is declareable from the best and most professed writers, for though some have made use hereof in a morall or tropicall way, yet have the professed discoursers by silence deserted, or by experience rejected this assertion.[53] Thus was it in ancient times discovered, and experimentally refuted by one Sestius a physitian, as it stands related by Plinie; by Dioscorides, who plainely affirmes that this tradition is false, by the discoveries of moderne authors, who have expresly discoursed hereon, as Aldrovandus, Mathiolus, Gesnerus, Bellonius; by Olaus Magnus, Peter Martyr and divers others, who have described the manner of their venations in America, they generally omitting this way of their escape, and have delivered severall other, by which they are daily taken.[54]

The originall of the conceit was probably hieroglyphicall, which after became mythologicall unto the Greeks, and so set down by Æsop, and by processe of tradition, stole into a totall verity, which was but partially true, that is in its covert sense and morallity. Now why they placed this invention upon the bever, (beside the medicall and merchantable commodity of *castoreum* or parts conceived to be bitten away) might be the sagacitie and wisedome of that animall, which indeed from the workes it performes, and especially its artifice in building is very strange, and surely not to be matched by any other, omitted by Plutarch *de solertia animalium*, but might have much advantaged the drift of that discourse.[55]

If therefore any affirme a wise man should demeane himselfe like the bever, who to escape with his life, contemneth the losse of his genitalls; that is, in case of extremity, not strictly to endeavour the preservation of all, but to sit downe in the enjoyment of the greater good, though with the detriment and hazzard of the lesser; wee may hereby apprehend a reall and usefull truth; and in this latitude of beliefe, wee are content to receive the fable of Hippomanes who redeemed his life, with the losse of a golden ball;[56] and whether true or false, we reject not the tragedy of Absyrtus, and the dispersion of his members by Medea to perplex the pursuit of her father;[57] but if he shall positively affirme this act, and cannot beleeve the morall, unlesse hee also credit the fable, hee is surely greedy of delusion, and will hardly avoide deception in theories of this nature. The error therefore and alogie in this opinion, is worse then in the last, that is not to receive figures for realities, but expect a verity in apologues, and beleeve, as serious affirmations, confessed and studied fables.[58]

Againe, if this were true, and that the bever in chase make some divulsion of parts, as that which we call *Castoreum*;[59] yet are not these parts avelled to be termed testicles or stones, for these cods or follicles are found in both sexes, though somewhat more protuberant in the male;[60] there is hereto no derivation of the seminall parts, nor any passage from hence, unto the vessels of ejaculations; some perforations onely in the part it selfe, through which the humor included doth exudate;[61] as may be observed in such as are fresh, and not much dryed with age; and lastly, the testicles properly so called, are of a lesser magnitude and seated inwardly upon the loynes; and therefore it were not only a fruitlesse attempt, but impossible act, to eunuchate or castrate themselves, and might bee an hazardous practise of arte, if at all attempted by others.

Now all this is confirmed from the experimentall testimony of five very memorable authors; Bellonius, Gesnerus, Amatus, Rondeletius, and Mathiolus,[62] who receiving the hint hereof from Rondeletius in the anatomie of two bevers, did finde all true that had been delivered by him, whose words are these in his learned book *De Piscibus: Fibri in inguinibus geminos tumores habent, utrinque unicum, ovi Anserini magnitudine, inter hos est mentula in maribus, in fœminis pudendum, hi tumores testes non sunt, sed folliculi membranâ contecti, in quorum medio singuli sunt meatus è quibus exudat liquor pinguis et cerosus, quem ipse Castor sæpe admoto ore lambit et exugit, postea veluti oleo, corporis partes oblinit; Hos tumores testes non esse hinc maxime colligitur, quod ab illis nulla est ad mentulam via neque ductus quo humor in mentulæ meatum derivetur, et foras emittatur; præterea quod testes intus reperiuntur, eosdem tumores Moscho animali inesse puto, è quibus odoratum illud pus emanat*;[63] then which words there can be none plainer, nor more evidently discover the improprietie of this appellation: that which is included in the cod or visible bagge about the groine, being not the testicle, or any spermaticall part, but rather a collection of some superfluous matter deflowing from the body, especially the parts of nutrition as unto their proper emunctories, and as it doth in musck and civet cats, though in a different and offensive odour, proceeding partly from its food, that being especially fish, whereof this humor may be a garous excretion, or a raucide and olidous separation.[64]

Most therefore of the modernes before Rondeletius, and all the antients excepting Sestius, have misunderstood this part, as conceiving *Castoreum* for the testicles of the bever, as Dioscorides, Galen, Ægineta, Ætius, and others have pleased to name it.[65] The Egyptians also failed in the ground of their hieroglyphick, when they expressed the punishment of adultery by the bever depriving himself of his testicles, which was amongst them the penalty of such incontinencie. Nor is Ætius perhaps, too strictly to be observed, when he prescribeth the stones of the otter, or river-dog, as succedaneous unto *Castoreum*:[66] but most inexcusable of all is Plinie, who having before him in one place the experiment of Sestius against it, sets downe in another, that the bevers of Pontus bite off their testicles, and in the same place affirmeth the like of the hyena.[67]

Now the ground of this mistake might be the resemblance and situation of these tumors about those parts, wherein we observe the testicles in other animalls; which notwithstanding is no well founded illation; for the testicles are defined by their office, and not determined by place or situation;[68] they having one office in all, but different seats in many; for beside that no serpent or fishes oviparous, have any stones at all; that neither biped nor quadruped oviparous have any exteriorly, or prominent in the groyne, some also that are viviparous contain these parts within, as beside this animall the elephant, and the hedge-hog.

If any therefore shall terme these, testicles, intending metaphorically, and in no strict acception, his language is tolerable and offends our ears no more then the tropicall names of plants, when we read in herballs in the severall kindes of orchis of dogs, fox, and goat-stones;[69] but if he insist thereon, and maintaine a propriety in this language, our discourse hath overthrowne his assertion, nor will logicke permit his illation; that is, from things alike, to conclude a thing the same, and from an accidentall convenience that is a similitude in place or figure, to infer a specificall congruity or substantiall concurrence in nature.

CHAPTER V
Of the Badger

That a brock or badger hath his legs of one side shorter then of the other, though an opinion perhaps not very ancient, is yet very generall, received not only by theorists and unexperienced beleevers, but assented unto by most who have the opportunity to behold and hunt them dayly; which notwithstanding upon enquiry I finde repugnant unto the three determinators of truth, authority, sense and reason: for first, Albertus Magnus speaks dubiously, confessing he could not confirme the verity hereof, but Aldrovand affirmeth plainly, there can be no such inequality observed;[70] and for my own part, upon indifferent enquiry, I cannot discover this difference, although the regardible side be defined, and the brevity by most imputed unto the left.

Againe, it seems no easie affront unto reason, and generally repugnant unto the course of nature; for if we survey the totall set of animals, we may in their legs, or organs of progression, observe an equality of length, and parity of numeration;[71] that is, not any to have an odde leg, or the supporters and movers of one side not exactly answered by the other; although the hinder may be unequall unto the fore and middle legs, as in frogs, locusts and grashoppers, or both unto the middle, as in some beetles, and spiders, as is determined by Aristotle, *de incessu animalium*;[72] perfect and viviparous quadrupeds, so standing in their position of pronenesse, that the opposite joynts of neighbour legs consist in the same plaine, and a line descending from their navell intersects at right angles the axis of the earth: it happeneth often I confesse that a lobster hath the chely or great claw of one side longer then the other, but this is not properly their leg, but a part of apprehension, and whereby they hold or seize upon their prey;[73] for in them the legs and proper parts of progression are inverted backward, and stand in a position opposite unto these.

Lastly, the monstrosity is ill contrived, and with some disadvantage, the shortnesse being affixed unto the legs of one side, which might have been more tolerably placed upon the thwart or diagoniall movers; for the progression of quadrupeds being performed *per Diametrum*, that is the crosse legs moving or resting together, so that two are alwayes in motion, and two in station at the same time, the brevity had been more tolerable in the crosse legs; for then the motion and station had beene performed by equall legs, whereas herein they are both performed by unequall organs, and the imperfection becomes discoverable at every hand.

CHAPTER VI
Of the Beare

That a bear brings forth her young informous and unshapen, which she fashioneth after by licking them over, is an opinion not only vulgar, and common with us at present, but hath been of old delivered by ancient writers; upon this foundation, it was a hieroglyphicke among the Ægyptians; Aristotle seems to countenance it, Solinus, Plinie and Ælian directly affirme it, and Ovid smoothly delivereth it,

Nec catulus partu quem reddidit ursa recenti
Sed male viva caro est, lambendo mater in artus
Ducit et in formam qualem cupit ipsa reducit.[74]

Which opinion notwithstanding is not only repugnant unto the sense of every one that shall with diligence enquire into it, but the exact and deliberate experiment of three authenticke philosophers; the first of Mathiolus in his comment on Dioscorides, whose words are to this effect. In the valley of Anania about Trent, in a beare which the hunters eventerated, I beheld the young ones with all their parts distinct, and not without shape, as many conceive, giving more credit unto Aristotle and Plinie, then experience and their proper senses.[75] Of the same assurance was Julius Scaliger in his Exercitations, *Ursam fœtus informes potius ejicere, quam parere, si vera dicunt, quos postea linctu effingat; Quid hujusce fabulæ authoribus fidei habendum ex hac historia cognosces; In nostris Alpibus venatores fœtam ursam cepere, dissecta ea fœtus plane formatus intus inventus est*:[76] and lastly, Aldrovandus who from the testimony of his owne eyes affirmeth, that in the cabinet of the Senate of Bononia, there was preserved in a glasse a cub dissected out of a beare perfectly formed, and compleat in every part.[77]

It is moreover injurious unto reason, and much impugneth the course and providence of nature, to conceive a birth should be ordained before there is a formation; for the conformation of parts is necessarily required not only unto the prerequisites and previous conditions of birth, as motion and animation, but also unto the parturition or very birth it selfe; wherein not only the dam, but the younglings play their parts, and the cause and act of exclusion proceedeth from them both: for the exclusion of animals is not meerly passive like that of egges, nor the totall action of delivery to be imputed unto the mother; but the first attempt beginneth from the infant, which at the accomplished period attempteth to change his mansion, and strugling to come forth, dilacerates and breaks those parts which restrained him before.[78]

Beside (what few take notice of) men hereby doe in a high measure vilifie the workes of God, imputing that unto the tongue of a beast, which is the strangest artifice in all the acts of nature, that is the formation of the infant in the womb, not only in mankind, but all viviparous animals whatsoever, wherin the plastick or formative faculty, from matter appearing homogeneous, and of a similary substance erecteth bones, membranes, veynes and arteries, and out of these contriveth every part in number, place and figure, according to the law of its species, which is so far from being fashioned by any outward agent, that once omitted or perverted by a slip of the inward Phidias, it is not reducible by any other whatsoever;[79] and therefore, *mirè me plasmaverunt manus tuæ*, though it originally respected the generation of man, yet is it applyable unto that of other animalls, who entring the wombe in indistinct and simple materialls, returne with distinction of parts, and the perfect breath of life;[80] he that shall consider these alterations without, must needs conceive there have been strange operations within, which to behold it were a spectacle almost worth ones being, a sight beyond all, except that man had been created first, and might have seen the shew of five dayes after.[81]

Now as the opinion is repugnant both unto sense and reason, so hath it probably been occasioned from some slight ground in either; thus in regard the cub comes forth involved in the chorion, a thick and tough membrane obscuring the formation, and which the dam doth after bite, and teare asunder, the beholder at first sight conceives it a rude and informous lumpe of flesh, and imputes the ensuing shape unto the mouthing of the dam; which addeth nothing thereunto, but onely drawes the curtaine, and takes away that vaile which concealed the piece before; and thus have some endeavoured to enforce the same from reason; that is, the small and slender time of the beares gestation, or going with her young, which lasting but few dayes (a month some say) the exclusion becomes precipitous, and the young ones consequently informous; according to that of Solinus, *Trigesimus dies uterum liberat ursæ, unde evenit ut præcipitata fæcunditas informes creet partus*;[82] but this will overthrow the generall method of nature, in the works of generation; for therein the conformation is not only antecedent, but proportionall unto the exclusion, and if the period of the birth be short, the terme of conformation will be as sudden also; there may I confesse from this narrow time of gestation ensue a minority or smalnesse in the exclusion, but this however inferreth no informity, and it still receiveth the name of a naturall and legitimate birth; whereas if we affirme a totall informity, it cannot admit so forward a terme as an abortment; for that supposeth conformation, and so wee must call this constant and intended act of nature, a slip, or effluxion, that is an exclusion before conformation, before the birth can beare the name of the parent, or be so much as properly called an embryon.

CHAPTER VII
Of the Basilisk

Many opinions are passant concerning the basiliske or little king of serpents, commonly called the cockatrice, some affirming, others denying, most doubting the relations made hereof;[83] what therefore in these incertainties we may more surely determine, that such an animall there is, if we evade not the testimony of Scripture, and humane writers, we cannot safely deny: so is it said, Psalm 91. *Super aspidem et Basiliscum ambulabis*, wherein the vulgar translation retaineth the word of the Septuagint, using in other places the Latine expression *Regulus*, as Proverbs 23. *Mordebit ut coluber, et sicut Regulus venena diffundet*, and Jeremy 8. *Ecce ego mittam vobis serpentes Regulos, etc.*[84] That is, as ours translate it, Behold I will send serpents, cockatrices among you which will not be charmed, and they shall bite you; and as for humane authors, or such as have discoursed of animals, or poysons, it is to be found almost in all, as Dioscorides, Galen, Pliny, Solinus, Ælian, Ætius, Avicen, Ardoynus, Grevinus, and many more;[85] in Aristotle I confesse we finde no mention, but Scaliger in his comment and enumeration of serpents, hath made supply, and in his Exercitations delivereth that a basilisk was found in Rome, in the dayes of Leo the fourth, and the like is reported by Sigonius, and some are so farre from denying one, that they have made severall kinds thereof, for such is the Catoblepas of Pliny, conceived by some, and the Dryinus of Ætius by others.[86]

But although we deny not the existence of the basilisk, yet whether we do not commonly mistake in the conception hereof, and call that a basilisk which is none at all, is surely to be questioned; for certainely that which from the conceit of its generation we vulgarly call a cockatrice, and wherein (but under a different name) we intend a formall identity and adequate conception with the basilisk, is not the basilisk of the ancients, whereof such wonders are delivered. For this of ours is generally described with legs, wings, a serpentine and winding taile, and a crist or combe somewhat like a cock; but the basilisk of elder times was a proper kinde of serpent, not above three palmes long, as some account, and differenced from other serpents by advancing his head, and some white markes or coronary spots upon the crowne, as all authentick writers have delivered.[87]

Nor is this cockatrice onely unlike the basiliske, but of no reall shape in nature, and rather an hieroglyphicall fancy, to expresse their different intentions, set forth in different fashions; sometimes with the head of a man, sometimes with the head of an hawke, as Pierius hath delivered, and as with addition of legs the heralds and painters still describe it;[88] nor was it onely of old a symbolicall and allowable invention, but is now become a manuall contrivance of art, and artificiall imposture, whereof besides others, Scaliger hath taken notice: *Basilisci formam mentiti sunt vulgo Gallinaceo similem, et pedibus binis, neque enim absimiles sunt cæteris serpentibus, nisi maculâ quasi in vertice candidâ, unde illi nomen Regium*, that is, men commonly counterfeit the forme of a basilisk, with another like a cock, and with two feet, whereas they differ not from other serpents, but in a white speck upon their crowne; now although in some manner it might be counterfeited in Indian cocks, and flying serpents, yet is it commonly contrived out of the skins of thornebacks, scaites or maids, as Aldrovand hath observed, and also graphically described in his excellent booke of fishes;[89] [and for satisfaction of my own curiousity I have caused some to be thus contrived out of the same fishes].[90]

Nor is onely the existency of this animall considerable, but many things delivered thereof, particularly its poyson, and its generation. Concerning the first, according to the doctrine of the ancients, men still affirme, that it killeth at a distance, that it poysoneth by the eye, and that by priority of vision;[91] now that deleterious it may bee at some distance and destructive without a corporall contaction, what uncertainty soever there be in the effect, there is no high improbability in the relation;[92] for if plagues or pestilentiall atomes have beene conveyed in the ayre from different regions, if men at a distance have infected each other; if the shaddowes of some trees be noxious, if torpedoes deliver their opium at a distance, and stupifie beyond themselves;[93] we cannot reasonably deny, that, beside our grosse and restrained poysons requiring contiguity unto their actions, there may proceed from subtiler seeds, more agile emanations, which will contemne those laws, and invade at distance unexpected.

That this venenation shooteth from the eye, and that this way a basilisk may empoyson, although thus much be not agreed upon by authors, some imputing it unto the breath, others unto the bite, it is not a thing impossible;[94] for eyes receive offensive impressions, from their objects, and may have influences destructive to each other; for the visible species of things strike not our senses immaterally, but streaming in corporall rayes, do carry with them the qualities of the object from whence they flow, and the medium through which they passe: thus through a greene or red glasse all things wee behold appeare of the same colours; thus sore eyes affect those which are sound, and themselves also by reflection, as will happen to an inflamed eye that beholds it selfe long in a glasse; thus is fascination made out, and thus also it is not impossible, what is affirmed of this animall, the visible rayes of their eyes carrying forth the subtilest portion of their poyson, which received by the eye of man, or beast, infecteth first the braine, and is from thence communicated unto the heart.

But lastly, that this destruction should be the effect of the first beholder, or depend upon priority of aspection, is a point not easily to be granted, and very hardly to be made out upon the principles of Aristotle, Alhazen, Vitello, and others;[95] who hold that sight is made by reception, and not by extramission, by receiving the rayes of the object into the eye, and not by sending any out; for hereby although he behold a man first, the basilisk should rather be destroyed, in regard he first receiveth the rayes of his antipathy and venemous emissions which objectively move his sense; but how powerfull soever his owne poyson be, it invadeth not the sence of man, in regard he beholdeth him not: and therefore this conceit was probably first begot by such as held the contrary opinion of sight by extramission, as did Pythagoras, Plato, Empedocles, Hipparchus, Galen, Macrobius, Proclus, Simplicius, with most of the ancients, and is the postulate of Euclide in his Opticks:[96] and of this opinion might they be, who from this antipathy of the Basilisk and man, expressed first the enmity of Christ and Sathan, and their mutuall destruction thereby; when Satan being elder then his humanity, beheld Christ first in the flesh, and so he was destroyed by the serpent, but elder then Sathan in his divinity, and so beholding him first he destroyed the old basilisk, and overcame the effects of his poyson, sin, death, and hell.

As for the generation of the basilisk, that it proceedeth from a cocks egge hatched under a toad or serpent, it is a conceit as monstrous as the brood it selfe: for if wee should grant that cocks growing old, and unable for emission, amasse within themselves some seminall matter, which may after conglobate into the forme of an egge, yet will this substance be unfruitfull, as wanting one principle of generation, and a commixture of the seed of both sexes, which is required unto production, as may be observed in the egges of hens not trodden, and as we have made triall in some which are termed cocks egges;[97] it is not indeed impossible that from the sperme of a cock, hen, or other animall being once in putrescence, either from incubation, or otherwise, some generation may ensue, not univocall and of the same species, but some imperfect or monstrous production; even as in the body of man from putred humours, and peculiar wayes of corruption, there have succeeded strange and unseconded shapes of wormes, whereof we have beheld some our selves, and reade of others in medicall observations:[98] and so may strange and venemous serpents be severall wayes engendered; but that this generation should be regular, and alway produce a basilisk, is beyond our affirmation, and we have good reason to doubt.

Againe, it is unreasonable to ascribe the equivocacy of this forme unto the hatching of a toade, or imagine that diversifies the production; for incubation alters not the species, nor if wee observe it so much as concurres either to the sex or colour, as evidently appeares in the eggs of ducks or partridges hatched under a hen, there being required unto their exclusion, onely a gentle and continued heate, and that not particular or confined unto the species or parent; so have I knowne the seed of silkewormes hatched on the bodies of women, and so Pliny reports that Livia the wife of Augustus hatched an egge in her bosome;[99] nor is onely an animall heate required hereto, but an elementall and artificiall warmth will suffice; for as Diodorus delivereth, the Ægyptians were wont to hatch their eggs in ovens, and many eye witnesses confirme that practise unto this day:[100] and therefore this generation of the basilisk, seemes like that of Castor and Helena, he that can credit the one, may easily beleeve the other; that is, that these two were hatched out of the egge, which Jupiter in the forme of a swan, begat on his mistris Leda.[101]

The occasion of this conceit might be an Ægyptian tradition concerning the bird ibis, which after became transferred unto cocks; for an old opinion it was of that nation, that the ibis feeding upon serpents, that venemous food so inquinated their ovall conceptions, or egges within their bodies, that they sometimes came forth in serpentine shapes, and therefore they alwayes brake their egges, nor would they endure the bird to sit upon them;[102] but how causelesse their feare was herein, the daily incubation of ducks, peahens, and many other testifie, and the storke might have informed them, which bird they honoured and cherished, to destroy their serpents.

That which much promoted it, was a misapprehension in holy Scripture upon the Latine translation in Esay 59. *Ova aspidum ruperunt, et telas Aranearum texuerunt, qui comedent de ovis eorum morietur, et quod confotum est, erumpet in Regulum*, from whence notwithstanding, beside the generation of serpents from egges there can be nothing concluded;[103] but what kind of serpents are meant not easie to be determined, for translations are very different: Tremellius rendring the asp *hæmorrhous*, and the regulus or basilisk a viper, and our translation for the aspe, sets down a cockatrice in the text, and an adder in the margine.

Another place of Esay doth also seeme to countenance it, chapter. 14. *Ne Læteris Philistæa quoniam diminuta est virga percussoris tui, de radice enim colubri egredietur Regulus, et semen eius absorbens volucrem*, which ours somewhat favourably rendreth, out of the serpents root shall come forth a cockatrice, and his fruit shall be a fierie flying serpent:[104] but Tremellius, *è radice Serpentis prodit Hæmorrhous, et fructus illius Præster volans*, wherein the words are different, but the sense is still the same;[105] for therein are figuratively intended Uzziah and Ezechias, for though the Philistines had escaped the minor serpent Uzziah, yet from his stock, a fiercer snake should arise, that would more terribly sting them, and that was Ezechias.[106]

CHAPTER VIII
Of the Wolfe

Such a story as the basilisk is that of the wolfe concerning prioritie of vision, that a man becomes hoarse or dumb, if a wolfe have the advantage first to eye him, and this is in plaine language affirmed by Plinie: *In Italia ut creditur, Luporum visus est noxius, vocemque homini, quem prius contemplatur adimere*;[107] so is it made out what is delivered by Theocritus, and after him by Virgil,

—Vox quoque Mœrim
Iam fugit ipsa, Lupi Mœrim videre priores.[108]

And thus is the proverbe to be understood, when during the discourse the partie or subject interveneth, and there ensueth a sudden silence, it is usually said, *Lupus est in fabulâ*: which conceit being already convicted, not only by Scaliger, Riolanus and others, but daily confutable almost every where out of England, we shall not further refute.[109]

The ground or occasional original hereof was probably the amazement and sudden silence, the unexpected appearance of wolves do often put upon travellers; not by a supposed vapour, or venemous emanation, but a vehement fear which naturally produceth obmutescence, and sometimes irrecoverable silence:[110] thus birds are silent in presence of an hawk, and Plinie saith that dogs are mute in the shadow of an hyaena; but thus could not the spirits of worthy martyrs be silenced, who being exposed not onely unto the eyes, but the mercilesse teeth of wolves, gave lowd expressions of their faith, and their holy clamours were heard as high as heaven.[111]

That which much promoted it beside the common proverb, was an expression in Theocritus, a very ancient poet, *Edere non poteris vocem, Lycus est tibi visus*; which Lycus was rivall unto another, and suddenly appearing stopped the mouth of his corrivall:[112] now Lycus signifying also a wolf, occasioned this apprehension; men taking that appellatively, which was to be understood properly, and translating the genuine acception;[113] which is a fallacy of æquivocation, and in some opinions begat the like conceit concerning Romulus and Remus, that they were fostered by a wolfe, the name of the nurse being *Lupa*; and founded the fable of Europa, and her carryage over sea by a bull, because the ship or pilots name was Taurus;[114] and thus have some been startled at the proverb *Bos in linguâ* confusedly apprehending how a man should be said to have an oxe in his tongue, that would not speake his minde; which was no more then that a piece of money had silenced him: for by the oxe was onely implyed a piece of coine stamped with that figure, first currant with the Athenians, and after among the Romanes.

CHAPTER IX
Of Deere

The common opinion concerning the long life of animals, is very ancient, especially of crowes, chaughes and deere;[115] in moderate accounts exceeding the age of man, in some the dayes of Nestor, and in others surmounting the yeares of Artephius, or Methuselah;[116] from whence antiquity hath raised proverbiall expressions, and the reall conception of their duration, hath been the hyperbolicall expression of others. From all the rest we shall single out the deere, upon concession a long lived animal, and in longævity by many conceived to attaine unto hundreds; wherein permitting every man his owne beliefe, we shall our selves crave libertie to doubt, and our reasons are these ensuing.

The first is that of Aristole, drawne from the increment and gestation of this animal, that is, its sudden arrivance unto growth and maturitie, and the small time of its remainder in the wombe;[117] his words in the translation of Scaliger, are these; *De ejus vitæ longitudine fabulantur, neque enim aut gestatio aut incrementum hinnulorum eiusmodi sunt, ut præstent argumentum longævi animalis*, that is, fables are raised concerning the vivassity of deere; for neither are their gestation or increment, such as may afford an argument of long life; and these saith Scaliger, are good mediums conjunctively taken, that is, not one without the other; for of animalls viviparous such as live long, goe long with young, and attaine but slowly to their maturitie and stature;[118] so the horse that liveth about thirty, arriveth unto his stature about six years, and remaineth above nine moneths in the wombe;[119] so the camell that liveth unto fifty, goeth with young no lesse then ten moneths, and ceaseth not to grow before seaven; and so the elephant that liveth an hundred, beareth its young above a yeare, and arriveth unto perfection at twenty; on the contrary, the sheep and goat, which live but eight or ten yeares, goe but five moneths, and attaine to their perfection at two yeares; and the like is observable in cats, hares, and conies;[120] and so the deere that endureth the wombe but eight moneths, and is compleat at six yeares, from the course of nature, wee cannot expect to live an hundred, nor in any proportionall allowance much more then thirty, as having already passed two generall motions observable in all animations, that is, its beginning and encrease, and having but two more to runne thorow, that is, its state and declination, which are proportionally set out by nature in every kinde, and naturally proceeding admit of inference from each other.

The other ground that brings its long life into suspition, is the immoderate salacity, and almost unparalleld excesse of venerie, which every September may be observed in this animall, and is supposed to shorten the lives of cockes, partridges, and sparrowes;[121] certainely a confessed and undeniable enemie unto longævitie, and that not onely as a signe in the complexionall desire, and impetuositie, but also as a cause in the frequent act, or iterated performance thereof; for though we consent not with that philosopher, who thinks a spermaticall emission unto the waight of one dragme, is æquivalent unto the effusion of sixtie ounces of blood, yet considering the resolution and languor ensuing that act in some, the extenuation and marcour in others, and the visible acceleration it maketh of age in most, wee cannot but thinke it much abridgeth our dayes:[122] although we also concede that this exclusion is naturall, that nature it selfe will finde a way hereto without either act or object; and although it be placed among the sixe non naturals, that is, such as neither naturally constitutive, nor meerly destructive, doe preserve or destroy according unto circumstance; yet do we sensibly observe an impotencie or totall privation thereof, prolongeth life, and they live longest in every kinde that exercise it not at all, and this is true not onely in eunuches by nature, but spadoes by art; for castrated animals in every species are longer lived then they which retaine their virilities: for the generation of bodies is not effected as some conceive, of soules, that is, by irradiation, or answerably unto the propagation of light, without its proper diminution;[123] but therein a transmission is made materially from some parts, and ideally from every one,[124] and the propagation of one, is in a strict acception, some minoration of another; and therefore also that axiome in philosophy, that the generation of one thing, is the corruption of another, although it be substantially true concerning the forme and matter, is also dispositively verified in the efficient or producer.

As for more sensible arguments, and such as relate unto experiment, from these we have also reason to doubt its age, and presumed vivacity; for where long life is naturall, the markes of age are late, and when they appear, the journey unto death cannot be long. Now the age of a deere (as Aristotle long agoe observed) is best conjectured, by the view of the hornes and teeth;[125] from the hornes there is a particular and annuall account unto six yeares, they arising first plaine, and so successively branching, after which the judgement of their yeares by particular markes becomes uncertaine; but when they grow old, they grow lesse branched, and first doe lose their ἀμυντῆρες, or *propugnacula*; that is, their brow antlers, or lowest furcations next the head, which Aristotle saith the young ones use in fight, and the old as needlesse have them not at all. The same may be also collected from the losse of their teeth, whereof in old age they have few or none before in either jaw. Now these are infallible markes of age, and when they appeare, wee must confesse a declination, which notwithstanding (as men informe us in England) where observations may well be made, will happen between twenty and thirty: as for the bone or rather induration of the roots of the arterial veyn, and great artery, which is thought to be found only in the heart of an old deere, and therefore becomes more precious in its rarity, it is often found in deere, much under thirty, and wee have knowne some affirme they have found it in one of halfe that age; and therefore in that account of Plinie of a deere with a collar about his necke, put on by Alexander the Great, and taken alive a hundred years after, with other relations of this nature we much suspect imposture or mistake;[126] and if we grant their verity, they are but single relations, and very rare contingencies in individualls, not affording a regular diduction upon the species: for though Ulysses his dog lived unto twenty two,[127] and the Athenian mule unto fourscore, we doe not measure their dayes by those yeares, or usually say, they live thus long, nor can the three hundred years of John of Times, or Nestor, overthrow the assertion of Moses, or afford a reasonable encouragement beyond his septuagenary determination.[128]

The ground and authority of this conceit was first hieroglyphicall, the Egyptians expressing longævitie by this animall, but upon what uncertainties, and also convincible falsities they often erected such emblems we have elsewhere delivered; and if that were true which Aristotle delivers of his time, and Plinie was not afraid to take up long after, the Ægyptians could make but weake observations herein;[129] for though it be said that Æneas feasted his followers with venison, yet Aristotle affirms that neither deer nor boar were to be found in Africa;[130] and how far they miscounted the lives and duration of animals, is evident from their conceit of the crow, which they presume to live five hundred yeares, and from the lives of hawkes which (as Ælian delivereth) the Ægyptians doe reckon no lesse then at seven hundred.[131]

The second which led the conceit unto the Grecians, and probably descended from the Ægyptians, was poeticall, and that was a passage of Hesiod, thus rendred by Ausonius,

Ter binos deciesque novem super exit in annos
Justa senescentum quos implet vita virorum.
Hos novies superat vivendo garrula cornix
Et quater egreditur cornicis sæcula cervus
Alipedem cervum ter vincit corvus.

To ninty six the life of man ascendeth,
Nine times as long that of the chough extendeth,
Foure times beyond, the life of deere doth goe,
And thrice is that surpassed by the crow.[132]

So that according to this account, allowing ninety six for the age of man, the life of a deere amounts unto three thousand, foure hundred, fifty six; a conceit so hard to be made out, that many have deserted the common and literall construction. So Theon in Aratus would have the number of nine not taken strictly, but for many yeares: in other opinions the compute so farre exceeded truth, that they have thought it more probable to take the word *genea*, that is a generation consisting of many yeares, but for one yeare, or a single revolution of the sunne, which is the remarkable measure of time, and within the compasse whereof we receive our perfection in the wombe. So that by this construction, the yeares of a deere should be but thirty six, as is discoursed at large in that tract of Plutarch, concerning the cessation of oracles, and whereto in his discourse of the crow, Aldrovandus also inclineth:[133] others not able to make it out, have rejected the whole account, as may bee observed from the words of Plinie, *Hesiodus qui primus aliquid de longævitate vitæ prodidit, fabulose (reor) multa de hominum ævo referens, cornici novem nostras attribuit ætates quadruplum ejus cervis, id triplicatum corvis et reliqua fabulosius de Phænice et nymphis*;[134] and this how slender soever, was probably the strongest ground antiquity had for this longævity of animalls, that made Theophrastus expostulate with nature concerning the long life of crows, that begat that epithite of deer in

Oppianus, and that expression of Juvenal, *Longa et cervina senectus.*[135]

The third ground was philosophicall and founded upon a probable reason in nature, and that is the defect of a gall, which part (in the opinion of Aristotle and Plinie) this animall wanted, and was conceived a cause and reason of their long life, according (say they) as it happeneth unto some few men, who have not this part at all;[136] but this assertion is first defective in the verity concerning the animall alleadged: for though it be true, a deere hath no gall in the liver like many other animalls, yet hath it that part in the guts as is discoverable by taste and colour: and therefore Plinie doth well correct himselfe, when having affirmed before, it had no gall, he afterward saith, some hold it to bee in the guts, and that for their bitternesse, dogs will refuse to eat them. It is also deficient in the verity of the induction or connumeration of other annimalls conjoyned herewith, as having also no gall;[137] that is, as Plinie accounteth, *Equi, Muli, etc.* horses, mules, asses, deer, goats, boars, camells, dolphins, have no gall; concerning horses, what truth there is herein we have declared before; as for goats wee finde not them without it, what gall the camell hath, Aristotle declareth, that hogs also have it, we can affirm, and that not in any obscure place, but in the liver, even as it is seated in man.

That therefore the deere is no short lived animall, we will acknowledge, that comparatively, and in some sense long lived wee will concede; and thus much we shall grant if we commonly account its dayes by thirty six or forty; for thereby it will exceed all other cornigerous animalls, but that it attaineth unto hundreds, or the years delivered by authors, since we have no authentick experience for it, since wee have reason and common experience against it, since the grounds are false and fabulous which doe establish it, wee know no ground to assent.[138]

Concerning the deere there also passeth another opinion, that the males thereof doe yearly lose their pizzell; for men observing the decidence of their hornes, doe fall upon the like conceit of this part that it annually rotteth away, and successively reneweth againe.[139] Now the ground hereof, was surely the observation of this part in deere after immoderate venery, and about the end of their rutt, which sometimes becomes so relaxed and pendulous, it cannot be quite retracted; and being often beset with flyes, it is conceived to rot, and at last to fall from the body; but herein experience will contradict us: for those deere which either dye or are killed at that time, or any other, are alwayes found to have that part entire; and reason also will correct us, for spermaticall parts, or such as are framed from the seminall principles of parents, although homogeneous or similary, will not admit a regeneration, much lesse will they receive an integrall restauration, which being organicall and instrumentall members, consist of many of those. Now this part, or animall of Plato,[140] containeth not only sanguineous and reparable particles, but is made up of veynes, nerves, arteries, and in some animalls of bones, whose reparation is beyond its owne fertility, and a fruit not to be expected from the fructifying part itselfe, which faculty were it communicated unto animalls, whose originalls are double, as well as unto plants, whose seed is within themselves, we might abate the art of Taliacotius, and the new inarching of noses;[141] and therefore the phansies of poets have been so modest, as not to set downe such renovations, even from the powers of their dietyes; for the mutilated shoulder of Pelops was pieced out with ivory, and that the limbs of Hyppolitus were set together, not regenerated by Æsculapius, is the utmost assertion of poetry.[142]

CHAPTER X
Of the Kingfisher

That a kingfisher hanged by the bill, sheweth in what quarter the wind is, by an occult and secret propriety, converting the breast to that point of the horizon from whence the wind doth blow, is a received opinion, and very strange; introducing naturall weathercocks, and extending magneticall conditions as far as animall natures: a conceit supported chiefly by present practice, yet not made out by reason or experience.

For unto reason it seemeth very repugnant, that a carcasse or body disanimated, should be so affected with every wind, as to carry a conformable respect and constant habitude thereto:[143] for although in sundry animalls, we deny not a kinde of naturall astrologie,[144] or innate presention both of wind and weather;[145] yet that proceeding from sense receiving impressions from the first mutation of the ayre, they cannot in reason retaine that apprehension after death, as being affections which depend on life, and depart upon disanimation, and therefore with more favourable reason may we draw the same effect, or sympathie upon the hedgehog, whose presention of winds is so exact, that it stoppeth the north or southerne hole of its nest, according to prenotion of these winds ensuing, which some men unexpectedly observing, have beene able to make predictions which way the wind would turne, and have been esteemed hereby wise men in point of weather.[146] Now this proceeding from sense in the creature alive, it were not reasonable to hang up an hedgehog dead, and to expect a conformable motion unto its living conversion:[147] and though in sundry plants their vertues doe live after death, and we know that scammonie, rhubarbe, and senna will purge without any vitall assistance;[148] yet in animals or sensible creatures, many actions are mixt, and depend upon their living forme, as well as that of mistion, and though they wholly seeme to retaine unto the body depart upon disunion:[149] thus glowewormes alive, project a lustre in the darke, which fulgour notwithstanding ceaseth after death;[150] and thus the torpedo which being alive stupifies at a distance, applied after death, produceth no such effect, which had they retained, in places where they abound, they might have supplyed opium, and served as frontalls in phrensies.[151]

As for experiment we cannot make it out by any we have attempted, for if a single kingfisher be hanged up with untwisted silke in an open roome, and where the ayre is free, it observes not a constant respect unto the mouth of the wind, but variously converting doth seldome breast it right; if two be suspended in the same roome, they will not regularly conforme their breasts, but oft-times respect the opposite points of heaven; and if we conceive that for the exact exploration they should be suspended where the ayre is quiet and unmoved, that clear of impediments, they may more freely convert upon their naturall verticity, we have also made this way of inquisition in suspending them in large and capacious glasses closely stopped; wherein neverthelesse we observed a casual station, and that they rested irregularly upon conversion, wheresoever they rested remaining inconverted, and possessing one point of the compasse, whilst the wind perhaps hath passed the two and thirty.

The ground of this popular practice might be the common opinion concerning the vertue prognosticke of these birds,* the naturall regard they have unto the winds, and they unto them againe, more especially remarkable in the time of their

* Commonly mistaken for the true Halcion.

nidulation, and bringing forth their young;[152] for at that time which happeneth about the brumall solstice, it hath beene observed even unto a proverbe, that the sea is calme, and the winds do cease, till the young ones are excluded, and forsake their nest, which floateth upon the sea, and by the roughnesse of winds might otherwise be overwhelmed;[153] but how farre hereby to magnifie their prediction we have no certaine rule, for whether out of any particular prenotion they chuse to sit at this time, or whether it be thus contrived by concurrence of causes, and the providence of nature, securing every species in their production, is not yet determined. Surely many things fall out by the designe of the generall motor and undreamt of contrivance of nature, which are not imputable unto the intention or knowledge of the particular actor. So though the seminallity of ivy be almost in every earth, yet that it ariseth and groweth not, but where it may be supported, we cannot ascribe unto the distinction of the seed, or conceive any science therein which suspends and conditionates its eruption. So if, as Pliny and Plutarch report, the crocodils of Ægypt, so aptly lay their eggs, that the natives thereby are able to know how high the floud will attaine;[154] yet is it hard to make out, how they should divine the extent of the inundation, depending on causes so many miles remote, that is, the measure of showers in Æthiopia; and whereof, as Athanasius in the life of Anthony delivers, the devill himselfe upon demand could make no cleere prediction;[155] and so are there likewise many things in nature, which are the forerunners or signes of future effects, whereto they neither concurre in causality or prenotion, but are secretly ordered by the providence of causes, and concurrence of actions collaterall to their signations.

CHAPTER XI
Of Griffons

That there are griffons in nature, that is a mixt and dubious animall, in the fore-part resembling an eagle, and behinde the shape of a lion, with erected eares, foure feet, and a long taile, many affirme, and most I perceive deny not; the same is averred by Ælian, Solinus, Mela, and Herodotus, countenanced by the name sometimes found in Scripture, and was an hieroglyphick of the Egyptians.[156]

Notwithstanding wee finde most diligent enquirers to be of a contrary assertion; for beside that Albertus and Pliny have disallowed it, the learned Aldrovand hath in a large discourse rejected it;[157] Mathias Michovius who writ of those northerne parts wherein men place these griffins, hath positively concluded against it, and if examined by the doctrine of animals, the invention is monstrous, nor much inferiour unto the figment of sphynx, chimæra, and harpies:[158] for though some species there be of a middle and participating natures, that is, of bird and beast, as we finde the bat to be, yet are their parts so conformed and set together that we cannot define the beginning or end of either, there being a commixtion of both in the whole, rather then an adaptation, or cement of the one unto the other.

Now for the word γρύψ, or Gryps, sometimes mentioned in Scripture, and frequently in humane authors, properly understood, it signifies some kinde of eagle or vulture, from whence the epithite Grypus for an hooked or aquiline nose. Thus when the Septuagint makes use of this word in the eleventh of Leviticus, Tremellius and our translation hath rendred it the ossifrage, which is one kinde of eagle, although the Vulgar translation, and that annexed unto the Septuagint retaine the word *Gryps*, which in ordinary and schoole construction is commonly rendred a griffin;[159] yet cannot the Latin assume any other sence then the Greek, from whence it is borrowed; and though the Latine *Gryphes* be altered somewhat by the addition of an h, or aspiration of the letter π, yet is not this unusuall; so what the Greeks call τρόπαιον, the Latins will call *Trophæum*, and that person which in the gospel is named Κλεόπας, the Latins will render *Cleophas*, and therefore the quarrell of Origen was injust and his conception erroneous, when he conceived the food of griffins forbidden by the law of Moses, that is, poeticall animals, and things of no existence:[160] and therefore when in the hecatombs and mighty oblations of the gentiles, it is delivered they sacrificed gryphes or griffins, hereby we may understand some stronger sort of eagles;[161] and therefore also when it said in Virgil of an improper match, or Mopsus marrying Nysa, *Iungentur jam gryhes equis*, we need not hunt after other sense, then that strange unions shall be made, and differing natures be conjoyned together.[162]

As for the testimonies of ancient writers, they are but derivative, and terminate all in one Aristeus a poet of

Proconesus; who affirmed that neere the Arimaspi, or one eyed nation, griffins defended the mines of gold: but this as Herodotus delivereth, he wrote by heresay;[163] and Michovius who hath expresly written of those parts plainly affirmeth, there is neither gold nor griffins in that countrey, nor any such animall extant, for so doth he conclude, *Ego vero contra veteres authores, Gryphes nec in illa septentrionis, nec in aliis orbis partibus inveniri affirmarim.*[164]

Lastly, concerning the hieroglyphicall authority, although it neerest approacheth the truth, it doth not inferre its existency; the conceit of the griffin properly taken being but a symbolicall phancy, in so intolerable a shape including allowable morality. So doth it well make out the properties of a guardian, or any person entrusted; the eares implying attention, the wings celerity of execution, the lion-like shape, courage and audacity, the hooked bill, reservance and tenacity.[165] It is also an embleme of valour and magnanimity, as being compounded of the eagle and lion, the noblest animals in their kinds; and so is it applyable unto princes, presidents, generals, and all heroick commanders, and so is it also borne in the coat-armes of many noble families of Europe.

CHAPTER XII
Of the Phænix

That there is but one phænix in the world, which after many hundred yeares burneth it selfe, and from the ashes thereof ariseth up another, is a conceit not new or altogether popular, but of great antiquity; not onely delivered by humane authors, but frequently expressed by holy writers, by Cyrill, Epiphanius, and others, by Ambrose in his Hexameron, and Tertullian in his poem *de Judicio Domini,* but more agreeably unto the present sence in his excellent tract, *de Resur. carnis, Illum dico alitem orientis peculiarem, de singularitate famosum, de posteritate monstruosum, qui semetipsum libenter funerans renovat, natali fine decedens, atque succedens iterum phænix, ubi jam nemo, iterum ipse, quia non jam alius idem.*[166] The Scripture also seemes to favour it, particularly that of Job 29 in the interpretation of Beda, *Dicebam in nidulo meo moriar et sicut phænix multiplicabo dies*, and Psalme 91. δίκαιος ὥσπερ φοῖνιξ ἀνθήσει, *vir justus ut Phænix florebit*, as Tertullian renders it, and so also expounds it in his booke before alledged.[167]

All which notwithstanding we cannot presume the existence of this animall, nor dare we affirme there is any phænix in nature. For, first there wants herein the definitive confirmator and test of things uncertaine, that is, the sense of man: for though many writers have much enlarged hereon, there is not any ocular describer, or such as presumeth to confirme it upon aspection;[168] and therefore Herodotus that led the story unto the Greeks, plainly saith, he never attained the sight of any, but onely in the picture.[169]

Againe, primitive authors, and from whom the streame of relations is derivative, deliver themselves very dubiously, and either by a doubtfull parenthesis, or a timorous conclusion overthrow the whole relation: thus Herodotus in his Euterpe, delivering the story hereof, presently interposeth, *ἐμοὶ μὲν οὐ πιστὰ λέγοντες*; that is, which account seemes to me improbable; Tacitus in his Annals affordeth a larger story, how the phænix was first seene at Heliopolis in the reigne of Sesostris, then in the reigne of Amasis, after in the dayes of Ptolomy, the third of the Macedonian race; but at last thus determineth, *Sed Antiquitas obscura; et nonnulli falsum esse hunc phænicem, neque Arabum è terris credidere.*[170] Pliny makes yet a fairer story, that the phænix flew into Ægypt in the consulship of Quintus Plancius, that it was brought to Rome in the censorship of Claudius, in the 800. yeare of the city, and testified also in their records; but after all concludeth, *Sed quæ falsa esse nemo dubitabit*, but that this is false no man will make doubt.[171]

Moreover, such as have naturally discoursed hereon, have so diversly, contrarily, or contradictorily delivered themselves, that no affirmative from thence can reasonably be deduced;[172] for most have positively denyed it, and they which affirme and beleeve it, assigne this name unto many, and mistake two or three in one. So hath that bird beene taken for the phænix which liveth in Arabia, and buildeth its nest with cinnamon, by Herodotus called *Cinnamulgus*, and by Aristotle *Cinnamomus*, and as a fabulous conceit is censured by Scaliger;[173] some have conceived that bird to be the phænix, which by a Persian name with the Greeks is called rhyntace; but how they made this good we finde occasion of doubt, whilst we reade in the life of Artaxerxes, that this is a little bird brought often to their tables, and wherewith Parysatis cunningly poysoned the queene.[174] The Manucodiata or bird of paradise, hath had the honour of this name, and their feathers brought from the Moluccas, doe passe for those of the phænix; which though promoted by rariety with us, the easterne travellers will hardly admit, who know they are common in those parts, and the ordinary plume of Janizaries among the Turks. And lastly, the bird semenda hath found the same appellation, for so hath Scaliger observed and refuted;[175] nor will the solitude of the phænix allow this denomination, for many there are of that species, and whose trifistulary bill and crany we have beheld our selves;[176] nor are men onely at variance in regard of the phænix it selfe, but very disagreeing in the accidents ascribed thereto: for some affirme it liveth three hundred, some five, others six, some a thousand, others no lesse then fifteene hundred yeares; some say it liveth in Æthiopia, others in Arabia, some in Ægypt, others in India, and some I thinke in Utopia, for such must that be which is described by Lactantius, that is, which neither was singed in the combustion of Phæton, or overwhelmed by the inundation of Deucalion.[177]

Lastly, many authors who have made mention hereof, have so delivered themselves, and with such intentions we cannot from thence deduce a confirmation: for some have written poetically as Ovid, Mantuan, Lactantius, Claudian, and others:[178] Some have written mystically, as Paracelsus in his booke *de Azoth*, or *de lingo et linea vitæ*;[179] and as severall hermeticall philosophers, involving therein the secret of their elixir, and enigmatically expressing the nature of their great worke: some have written rhetorically, and concessively not controverting but assuming the question, which taken as granted advantaged the illation: so have holy men made use hereof as farre as thereby to confirme the resurrection; for discoursing with heathens who granted the story of the phænix, they induced the resurrection from principles of their owne, and positions received among themselves. Others have spoken emblematically and hieroglyphically, and so did the Ægyptians, unto whom the phænix was the hieroglyphick of the sunne; and this was probably the ground of the whole relation, succeeding ages adding fabulous accounts, which laid together built up this singularity, which every pen proclaimeth.

As for the texts of Scripture, which seem to confirme the conceit duly perpended, they adde not thereunto; for whereas in that of Job, according to the Septuagint or Greeke translation we finde the word phænix, yet can it have no animall signification; for therein it is not expressed φοῖνιξ, but στέλεχος φοίνικος the truncke of the palme tree, which is also called phænix, and therefore the construction will be very hard, if not applyed unto some vegetable nature; nor can we safely insist upon the Greek expression at all: for though the Vulgar translates it *Palma*, and some retain the phænix, others do render it by a word of a different sense; for so hath Tremellius delivered it: *Dicebam quod apud nidum meum expirabo, et sicut arena multiplicabo dies*; so hath the Geneva and ours translated it, I said I shall dye in my nest, and shall multiply my dayes, as the sand: as for that in the booke of Psalmes, *Vir justus ut Phænix florebit*, as Epiphanius and Tertullian render it, it was only a mistake upon the homonymy of the Greeke word phænix, which signifies also a palme tree;[180] which is a fallacy of equivocation, from a community in name, inferring a common nature, and whereby we may as firmly conclude, that Diaphænicon a purging electuary hath some part of the phænix for its ingredient, which receiveth that name from dates, or the fruit of the palme tree, from whence as Plinie delivers, the phenix had its name.[181]

Nor doe we only arraigne the existence of this animall, but many things are questionable which are ascribed thereto, especially its unity, long life, and generation: as for its unity or conceit there should bee but one in nature, it seemeth not onely repugnant unto philosophy, but also the holy Scripture, which plainly affirmes, there went of every sort two at least into the Arke of Noah, according to the text, Genesis 7. Every fowle after his kinde, every bird of every sort, they went into the Arke, two and two of all flesh, wherein there is the breath of life, and they that went in, went in both male and female of all flesh; it infringeth the benediction of God concerning multiplication, Genesis 1. God blessed them saying, Be fruitfull and multiply, and fill the waters in the seas, and let fowl multiply in the earth; and again, Chapter 8. Bring forth with thee, every living thing that they may breed abundantly in the earth, and be fruitfull, and multiply upon the earth, which termes are not applyable unto the phænix, whereof there is but one in the world, and no more now living then at the first benediction, for the production of one, being the destruction of another, although they produce and generate, they encrease not, and must not be said to multiply, who doe not transcend an unity.

As for longævity, as that it liveth a thousand yeares, or more, beside that from imperfect observations and rarity of appearance, no confirmation can be made, there may be probably a mistake in the compute; for the tradition being very ancient and probably Ægyptian, the Greeks who dispersed the fable, might summe up the account by their owne numeration of yeares, whereas the conceit might have its originall in times of shorter compute; for if we suppose our present calculation, the phænix now in nature will be the sixt from the creation, but in the middle of its years, and if the rabbines prophesie* succeed shall conclude its dayes, not in its owne, but the last and generall flames, without all hope of reviviction.[182]

* That the world should last but six thousand years.

Concerning its generation, that without all conjunction, it begets and reseminates it selfe, hereby we introduce a vegetable production in animalls, and unto sensible natures, transferre the propriety of plants, that is to multiply among themselves, according to the law of the creation, Genesis 1.[183] Let the earth bring forth grasse, the herbe yeelding seed, and the tree yeelding fruit, whose seed is in it selfe; which way is indeed the naturall way of plants, who having no distinction of sex, and the power of the species contained in every *individuum*, beget and propagate themselves without commixtion, and therefore their fruits proceeding from simpler roots, are not so unlike, or distinguishable from each other, as are the off-springs of sensible creatures and prolifications descending from double originalls; but animall generation is accomplished by more, and the concurrence of two sexes is required to the constitution of one; and therefore such as have no distinction of sex, engender not at all, as Aristotle conceives of eeles, and testaceous animalls;[184] and though plant animalls doe multiply, they doe it not by copulation, but in a way analogous unto plants; so hermophrodites although they include the parts of both sexes, and may be sufficiently potent in either, yet unto a conception require a seperated sex, and cannot impregnate themselves; and so also though Adam included all humane nature, or was (as some opinion) an hermaphrodite, yet had hee no power to propagate himselfe; and therefore God said, It is not good that man should be alone, let us make him an help meet for him, that is, an help unto generation; for as for any other help, it had been fitter to have made another man.

Now whereas some affirme that from one phænix there doth not immediatly proceed another, but the first corrupteth into a worme, which after becommeth a phænix, it will not make probable this production; for hereby they confound the generation of perfect animalls with imperfect, sanguineous, with exanguious, vermiparous, with oviparous, and erect anomalies, disturbing the lawes of nature;[185] nor will this corruptive production be easily made out, in most imperfect generations; for although we deny not that many animals are vermiparous, begetting themselves at a distance, and as it were at the second hand, as generally insects, and more remarkably butterflies and silkwormes; yet proceeds not this generation from a corruption of themselves, but rather a specificall, and seminall diffusion, retaining still the Idea of themselves, though it act that part a while in other shapes: and this will also hold in generations equivocall, and such are not begotten from parents like themselves; so from frogs corrupting, proceed not frogs againe; so if there be anatiferous trees, whose corruption breaks forth into bernacles, yet if they corrupt, they degenerate into maggots, which produce not themselves againe;[186] for this were a confusion of corruptive and seminall production, and a frustration of that seminall power committed to animalls at the creation. The probleme might have beene spared, why wee love not our lice as well as our children, Noahs Arke had beene needlesse, the graves of animals would be the fruitfullest wombs; for death would not destroy, but empeople the world againe.

Since therefore we have so slender grounds to confirm the existence of the phænix, since there is no ocular witnesse of it, since as we have declared, by authors from whom the story is derived, it rather stands rejected, since they who have seriously discoursed hereof, have delivered themselves negatively, diversly or contrarily, since many others cannot be drawne into argument as writing poetically, rhetorically, enigmatically, hieroglyphically, since holy Scripture alleadged for it duely perpended, doth not advantage it, and lastly since so strange a generation, unity and long life hath neither experience nor reason to confirme it, how farre to rely on this tradition, wee referre unto consideration.

But surely they were not wel-wishers unto εὐπόριστα, parable physic, or remedies easily acquired, who derived medicines from the phænix, as some have done, and are justly condemned by Pliny, *Irridere est, vitæ remedia post millesimum annum reditura monstrare*;[187] it is a folly to finde out remedies that are not recoverable under a thousand yeares, or propose the prolonging of life by that which the twentieth generation may never behold; more veniable is a dependance upon the philosophers stone, potable gold, or any of those arcanas, whereby Paracelsus that dyed himselfe at forty-seven, gloried that he could make other men immortall;[188] which secrets, although extreamly difficult, and *tantum non* infesible, yet are they not impossible, nor do they (rightly understood) impose any violence on nature,[189] and therefore if strictly taken for the phænix very strange is that which is delivered by Plutarch, *de sanitate tuenda*, that the braine thereof is a pleasant bit, but that it causeth the headach;[190] which notwithstanding the luxurious emperour could never tast, though he had at his table many a phænicopterus, yet had he not one phænix; for though he expected and attempted it, wee reade not in Lampridius that he performed it;[191] and considering the unity thereof it was a vaine designe, that is, to destroy any species, or mutilate the great accomplishment of six dayes; and although some conceive, and it may seeme true, that there is in man a naturall possibility to destroy the world in one generation, that is, by a generall conspire to know no woman themselves and disable all others also; yet will this never bee effected, and therefore Cain after he had killed Abel, were there no other woman living, could not have also destroyed Eve; which although he had a naturall power to effect, yet the execution thereof, the providence of God would have resisted, for that would have imposed another creation upon him, and to have animated a second rib of Adam.

CHAPTER XIII
Frogges, Toades, and Toad-stone

Concerning the venemous urine of toads, of the stone in a toads head, and of the generation of frogges, conceptions are entertained which require consideration; and first, that a toad pisseth, and this way diffuseth its venome, is generally received, not onely with us, but also in other parts; for so hath Scaliger observed in his comment, *Aversum urinam reddere ob oculos persecutoris perniciosam ruricolis persuasum est*;[192] and Mathiolus hath also a passage, that a toad communicates its venom, not onely by urine, but by the humiditie and slaver of its mouth;[193] which notwithstanding strictly understood, will not consist with truth; for to speak properly, a toad pisseth not, nor doe they containe those urinary parts which are found in other animals, to avoid that serous excretion;[194] as may appeare unto any that exenterats or dissects them;[195] for therein will be found neither bladder, kidneyes, or ureters, any more then they are in birds, which although they eat and drink, yet for the moist and dry excretion, have but one vent and common place of exclusion; and with the same proprietie of language, we may ascribe that action unto crowes and kites; and this is verified not only in frogs and toades, but for ought I can discover, that may bee true which Aristotle affirmeth, that no oviparous animall, that is, which either spawne or lay egges doth urine, except the tortois.[196]

The ground or occasion of this expression might from hence arise, that toades are sometimes observed to exclude or spirt out a dark and liquid matter behinde, which indeed we have observed to be true, and a venemous condition there may bee perhaps therein, but it cannot bee called their urine;[197] not onely because they want those parts of secretion; but because it is emitted aversly or backward, by both sexes.

As for the stone commonly called a toad-stone, which is presumed to be found in the head of that animall, we first conceive it not a thing impossible, nor is there any substantiall reason, why in a toade, there may not be found such hard and lapideous concretions;[198] for the like we daily observe in the heads of fishes, as codds, carpes, and pearches, the like also in snailes, a soft and exosseous animall,[199] whereof in the naked and greater sort, as though she would requite the defect of a shell on their back, nature neere the head hath placed a flat white stone, or rather testaceous concretion which though Aldrovand affirms, that after dissection of many, hee found but in some few, yet of the great gray snailes, I have not met with any that wanted it, and the same is indeed so palpable, that without dissection it is discoverable by the hand.[200]

Againe, though it be not impossible, yet is it surely very rare, as we are induced to beleeve from some enquiry of our owne, from the triall of many who have beene deceived, and the frustrated search of Porta, who upon the explorement of many, could never finde one;[201] nor is it onely of rarity, but may be doubted whether it be of existency, or really any such stone in the head of a toad at all: for although lapidaries, and questuary enquirers affirme it, yet the writers of mineralls and naturall speculators, are of another beliefe conceiving the stones which beare this name, to be a minerall concretion, nor to be found in animalls, but in fields;[202] and therefore

Boetius de Boot referres it to asteria, or some kinde of *Lapis stellaris*, and plainely concludeth, *Reperiuntur in agris, quos tamen alii in annosis, ac qui diu in Arundinetis, inter rubos sentesque delituerunt bufonis capitibus generari pertinaciter affirmant.*[203]

Lastly, if any such thing there be, yet must it not for ought I see, be taken as we receive it, for a loose and moveable stone, but rather a concretion or induration of the crany it selfe;[204] for being of an earthy temper living in the earth, and as some say feeding thereon, such indurations may sometimes happen, and thus when Brassavolus after a long search had discovered one, he affirmes it was rather the forehead bone petrified, then a stone within the crany; and of this beleefe was Gesner.[205] All which considered, wee must with circumspection receive those stones, which commonly beare this name, much lesse beleeve the traditions, that in envy to mankinde they are cast out, or swallowed down by the toad, which cannot consist with anatomy, and with the rest, enforced this censure from Boetius, *Ab eo tempore pro nugis habui quod de Bufonio lapide, ejusque origine traditur.*[206]

Concerning the generation of froggs, wee shall briefly deliver that account which observation hath taught us. By frogges I understand not such as arising from putrifaction, are bred without copulation, and because they subsist not long, are called *Temporariæ*; nor doe I meane hereby the little frogge of an excellent parrat-green, that usually sits on trees and bushes, and is therefore called *Ravunculus viridis*, or *Arboreus*; but hereby I understand the aquatile or water frogge whereof in ditches and standing plashes, wee may behold many millions every Spring in England; now these doe not as Plinie conceiveth, exclude blacke pieces of flesh, which after become frogges, but they let fall their spawne in the water, which is of excellent use in physicke, and scarce unknowne unto any;[207] in this spawne of a lentous and transparent body, are to be discerned many gray specks, or little conglobations, which in a little time become of deepe blacke;[208] a substance more compacted and terrestrious then the other, for it riseth not in distillation, and affords a powder, when the white and aqueous part is exhaled. Now of this blacke or duskie substance is the frogge at last formed, as we have beheld, including the spawne with water in a glasse, and exposing it unto the sunne; for that blacke and round substance, in a few dayes began to dilate and grow ovall, after a while the head, the eyes, the taile to be discerneable, and at last to become that which the ancients called gyrinus, wee a porwigle or tadpole, and this in some weekes after, becomes a perfect frogge, the legs growing out before, and the tayle wearing away, to supply the other behinde, as may bee observed in some, which have newly forsaken the water: for in such, some part of the tayle will be seen but curtal'd and short, not long and finny as before; a part provided them a while to swim and move in the water, that is, untill such time as nature excluded legs, whereby they might be provided not only to swim in the water, but move upon the land, according to the amphibious and mixt intention of nature, that is to live in both. And because many affirme, and some deliver, that in regard it hath lungs and breatheth a frogge may bee easily drowned, though the reason be probable, I finde not the experiment answerable; for making triall, and fastning one about a span under water, it lived almost six dayes.

CHAPTER XIV
Of the Salamander

That a salamander is able to live in flames, to endure and put out fire is an assertion, not only of great antiquitie, but confirmed by frequent, and not contemptible testimonie; the Ægyptians have drawne it into their hieroglyphicks; Aristotle seemeth to embrace it, more plainely Nicander, Serenus Sammonicus, Ælian, and Plinie, who assignes the cause of this effect.[209] An animall (saith he) so cold that it extinguisheth the fire like ice; all which notwithstanding, there is on the negative authoritie and experience; Sextius a physition, as Plinie delivereth, denied this effect, Dioscorides affirmed it a point of folly to beleeve it, Galen that it endureth the fire a while, but in continuance is consumed therein;[210] for experimentall conviction Mathiolus affirmeth, he saw a salamander burnt in a very short time;[211] and of the like assertion is Amatus Lusitanus, and most plainly Pierius, whose words in his Hieroglyphicks are these; whereas it is commonly said, that a salamander extinguisheth fire, wee have found by experience, that 'tis so farre from quenching hot coales; that it dieth immediatly therein;[212] as for the contrary assertion of Aristotle, it is but by hearesay, as common opinion beleeveth, *Hæc enim (ut aiunt) ignem ingrediens eum extinguit*; and therefore there was no absurdity in Galen when as a septicall medicine he commended the ashes of a salamander, and magicians in vaine from the power of this tradition, at the burning of towns or houses expect a reliefe from salamanders.[213]

The ground of this opinion might be some sensible resistance of fire observed in the salamander, which being as Galen determineth, cold in the fourth, and moist in the third degree, and having also a mucous humidity above and under the skinne, by vertue thereof may a while endure the flame, which being consumed it can resist no more.[214] Such an humidity there is observed in newtes, or water-lizards, especially if their skinnes be prickt or perforated. Thus will frogges and snailes endure the flame, thus will whites of egges, vitreous or glassey flegme extinguish a coal, thus are unguents made which protect a while from the fire, and thus beside the Hirpini, there are later stories of men that have pass'd untoucht through fire, and therefore some trueth we allow in the tradition;[215] truth according unto Galen, that it may for a time resist a flame, or as Scaliger avers, extinguish or put out a coale; for thus much will many humide bodies performe, but that it perseveres and lives in that destructive element, is a fallacious enlargement;[216] nor doe we reasonably conclude, because for a time it endureth fire, it subdueth and extinguisheth the same, because by a cold and aluminous moisture, it is able a while to resist it, from a peculiarity of nature it subsisteth and liveth in it.[217]

It hath beene much promoted by stories of incombustible napkins and textures which endure the fire, whose materialls are call'd by the name of salamanders wooll;[218] which many too literally apprehending, conceive some investing part, or tegument of the salamander;[219] wherein beside that they mistake the condition of this animal, which is a kinde of lizard, a quadruped corticated and depilous, that is without wooll, furre, or haire, they observe not the method and generall rule of nature, whereby all quadrupeds oviparous, as lizards, froggs, tortois, chameleons, crocodiles, are without any haire, and have no covering part or hairy investment at all;[220] and if they conceive that from the skin of the salamander, these incremable pieces are composed, beside the experiments made upon the living, that of Brassavolus will step in, who in the search of this truth, did burne the skin of one dead.[221]

Nor is this salamanders wooll desumed from any animal, but a minerall substance metaphorically so called from this received opinion;[222] for beside Germanicus his heart, and Pyrrhus his great toe, there are in the number of mineralls, some bodies incombustible;[223] more remarkably that which the ancients named asbeston, and Pancirollus treats of in the chapter of *Linum vivum*:[224] whereof by art were weaved napkins, shirts, and coats inconsumable by fire, and wherein in ancient times, to preserve their ashes pure, and without commixture, they burnt the bodies of kings; a napkin hereof Plinie reports that Nero had, and the like saith Paulus Venetus, the Emperour of Tartarie sent unto Pope Alexander;[225] and affirms that in some parts of Tartarie, there were mines of iron whose filaments were weaved into incombustible cloth, which rare manufacture, although delivered for lost by Pancirollus, yet Salmuth delivereth in his comment that one Podocaterus a Cyprian, had shewed the same at Venice, and his materialls were from Cyprus, where indeed Dioscorides placeth them; the same is also ocularly confirmed by Vives upon Austin and Maiolus in his colloquies;[226] and thus in our daies do men practise to make long lasting snasts or elychinons parts for lampes, out of alumen plumosum;[227] and by the same wee read in Pausanias, that there alwayes burnt a lampe before the image of Minerva.[228]

CHAPTER XV
Of the Amphisbæna

That the amphisbæna, that is, a smaller kinde of serpent, which moveth forward and backward, hath two heads, or one at either extreame, was affirmed first by Nicander, and after by many others, by the author of the book *de Theriaca ad Pisonem*, ascribed unto Galen, more plainly Pliny, *Geminum habet caput, tanquam parum esset uno ore effundi venenum*: but Ælian most confidently, who referring the conceit of chimera and hydra unto fables, hath set downe this as an undeniable truth.[229]

Whereunto while men assent, and can beleeve a bicipitous conformation in any continued species, they admit a gemination of principall parts, which is not naturally discovered in any animall;[230] true it is that other parts in animals are not equall, for some make their progression with many legs, even to the number of an hundred, as juli, scolopendræ, or such as are termed centipedes; some flye with two wings, as birds and many insects, some with foure, as all farinaceous or mealy winged animals, as butter-flies, and moths, all vaginipennous or sheathwinged insects, as beetles and dorrs;[231] some have three testicles, as Aristotle speakes of the buzzard, and some have foure stomacks, as horned and ruminating animals;[232] but for the principall parts, the liver, heart, and especially the braine, regularly it is but one in any kinde or species whatsoever.

And were there any such species or naturall kinde of animall, it would be hard to make good those six positions of body, which according to the three dimensions are ascribed unto every animall, that is, *infra*, *supra*, *ante, retro*, *dextrorsum*, *sinistrorsum*;[233] for if (as it is determined) that be the anterior and upper part wherein the sences are placed, and that the posterior and lower part which is opposite thereunto, there is no inferiour or former part in this animall, for the senses being placed at both extreames, doe make both ends anteriour, which is impossible, the termes being relative, which mutually subsist, and are not without each other, and therefore this duplicity was ill contrived to place one head at both extreames, and had beene more tolerable to have setled three or foure at one, and therefore also poets have been more reasonable then philosophers, and Geryon or Cerberus, lesse monstrous then amphisbæna.[234]

Againe, if any such thing there were, it were not to be obtruded by the name of amphisbæna, or as an animall of one denomination; for properly that animall is not one, but multiplicious or many, which hath a duplicity or gemination of principle parts; and this doth Aristotle define, when he affirmeth a monster is to be esteemed one or many, according to its principle, which he conceived the heart, whence he derived the originall of nerves, and thereto ascribe many acts which physitians assigne unto the braine;[235] and therefore if it cannot be called one, which hath a duplicity of hearts in his sence, it cannot receive that appellation with a plurality of heads in ours; and this the practise of Christians hath acknowledged, who have baptized these geminous births, and double connascencies with severall names, as conceiving in them a distinction of soules, upon the divided execution of their functions;[236] that is, while one wept, the other laughing, while one was silent, the other speaking, while one awaked, the other sleeping, as is declared by three remarkable examples in Petrarch, Vincentius, and the Scottish history of Buchanan.[237]

It is not denyed there have beene bicipitous serpents with the head at each extreme, for an example hereof we finde in Aristotle, and in the like forme in Aldrovand wee meet with the icon of a lizzard;[238] which double formations do often happen unto multiparous generations, more especially that of serpents, whose conceptions being numerous, and their eggs in chaines or links together, (which sometime conjoyne and inoculate into each other)[239] they may unite into various shapes, and come out in mixed formations; but these are monstrous productions, and beside the intention of nature, and the statutes of generation, neither begotten of like parents, nor begetting the like againe, but irregularly produced do stand as anomalies, and make up the *quæ genus*, in the generall booke of nature; which being the shifts and forced pieces, rather then the genuine and proper effects, they afford us no illation, nor is it reasonable to conclude, from a monstrosity unto a species, or from accidentall effects, unto the regular workes of nature.[240]

Lastly, the ground of the conceit was the figure of this animall, and motion oft times both wayes; for described it is to bee like a worme, and so equally framed at both extremes, that at an ordinary distance it is no easie matter, to determine which is the head; and therefore some observing them to move both wayes, have given the appellation of heads unto both extreames, which is no proper and warrantable denomination, for many animals with one head do ordinarily performe both different and contrary motions; crabs move sideling, lobsters will swim swiftly backward, wormes and leeches wil move both wayes; and so will most of those animals, whose bodies consist of round and annulary fibers, and move by undulation, that is, like the waves of the sea, the one protruding the other, by inversion whereof they make a backward motion.

Upon the same ground hath arisen the same mistake concerning the scolopendra or hundred footed insect, as is delivered by Rhodiginus from the scholiast of Nicander: *Dicitur à Nicandro*, ἀμφικαρὴς, *id est dicepalus aut biceps, fictum vero, quoniam retrorsum (ut scribit Aristoteles) arrepit*, observed by Aldrovandus, but most plainly by Muffetus, who thus concludeth upon the text of Nicander: *Tamen pace tanti authoris dixerim, unicum illi duntaxat caput licet pari facilitate, prorsum capite, retrorsum ducente cauda, incedat, quod Nicandro aliisque imposuisse dubito*: that is, under favour of so great an author, the scolopendra hath but one head, although with equall facility it moveth forward and backward, which I suspect deceived Nicander and others.[241]

CHAPTER XVI
Of the Viper

That the young vipers force their way through the bowels of their dam, or that the female viper in the act of generation bites off the head of the male, in revenge whereof the young ones eate through the womb and belly of the female is a very ancient tradition; in this sence entertained in the hieroglyphicks of the Ægyptians, affirmed by Herodotus, Nicander, Pliny, Plutarch, Ælian, Jerome, Basil, Isidore, and seems to be countenanced by Aristotle, and his scholler Theophrastus;[242] from hence is commonly assigned the reason why the Romans punished parricides by drowning them in a sack with a viper; and so perhaps upon the same opinion the men of Melita when they saw a viper upon the hand of Paul, said presently without conceit of any other sin, No doubt this man is a murtherer, whom though he have escaped the sea, yet vengeance suffereth him not to live;[243] that is, he is now paid in his own way, the parricidous animall and punishment of murtherers is upon him; and though the tradition were currant among the Greekes to confirme the same the Latine name is introduced, *Vipera quasi vipariat*; that passage also in the Gospell, O yee generation of vipers, hath found expositions which countenance this conceit;[244] notwithstanding which authorities, transcribed relations and conjectures, upon enquiry we finde the same repugnant unto experience and reason.

And first it seemes not only injurious unto the providence of nature, to ordaine a way of production which should destroy the producer, or contrive the continuation of the species by the destruction of the continuator; but it overthrowes and frustrates the great benediction of God, which is expressed Genesis 1. God blessed them saying, Be fruitfull and multiply.[245] Now if it be so ordained that some must regularly perish by multiplication, and these be the fruits of fructifying in the viper; it cannot be said that God did blesse, but curse this animall; upon thy belly shalt thou goe, and dust shalt thou eat all thy life, was not so great a punishment unto the serpent after the fall, as encrease, be fruitfull and multiply, was before. This were to confound the maledictions of God, and translate the curse of the woman upon the serpent; that is, *in dolore paries*, in sorrow shalt thou bring forth, which being proper unto the women, is verified best in the viper, whose delivery is not only accompanied with paine, but also with death it self.[246] And lastly, it overthrows the carefull course, and parentall provision of nature, whereby the young ones newly excluded are sustained by the dam, and protected untill they grow up to a sufficiencie for themselves; all which is perverted in this eruptive generation, for the dam being destroyed, the younglings are left to their owne protection, which is not conceiveable they can at all performe, and whereof they afford us a remarkable confirmance many dayes after birth; for the young ones supposed to breake through the belly of the dam, will upon any fright for protection run into it; for then the old one receives them in at her mouth, which way the fright being past they will returne againe; which is a peculiar way of refuge; and though it seem strange is avowed by frequent experience, and undeniable testimony.

As for the experiment although we have thrice attempted it, it hath not well succeeded; for though wee fed them with milke, branne, cheese, etc. the females alwayes dyed before the young ones were mature for this eruption, but rest sufficiently confirmed in the experiements of worthy enquirers: wherein to omit the ancient conviction of Apollonius, we shall set downe some few of moderne writers:[247] the first, of Amatus Lusitanus in his comment upon Dioscorides. *Vidimus nos viperas prægnantes inclusas pyxidibus parere, quæ inde ex partu nec mortuæ, nec visceribus perforatæ manserunt*: the second is that of Scaliger, *Viperas ab impatientibus morae fœtibus numerosissimis rumpi atque interire falsum esse scimus, qui in Vincentii Camerini circulatoris lignea theca vidimus enatas viperellas, parente salva*:[248] The last and most plaine of Franciscus Bustamantinus, a Spanish physitian of Alcala de Henares, whose words in his third *de Animantibus Scripturæ* are these: *Cum vero per me et per alios hæc ipsa disquisissem servata Viperina pro genie, etc.* that is, when by my selfe and others I had enquired the truth hereof, including vipers in a glasse, and feeding them with cheese and branne, I undoubtedly found that the viper was not delivered by the tearing of her bowels, but I beheld them excluded by the passage of generation neare the orifice of the seidge.[249]

Now although the tradition be untrue, there wanted not many grounds which made it plausibly received. The first was a favourable indulgence and speciall contrivance of nature, which was the conceit of Herodotus who thus delivereth himselfe: fearfull animalls, and such as serve for food, nature hath made more fruitfull, but upon the offensive and noxious kinde, she hath not conferred fertility:[250] so the hare that becommeth a prey unto man, unto beasts, and fowles of the ayre, is fruitfull even to superfætation, but the lyon a fierce and ferocious animall hath young ones but seldome, and also but one at a time;[251] vipers indeed, although destructive, are fruitfull; but lest their number should encrease, providence hath contrived another way to abate it, for in copulation the female bites off the head of the male, and the young ones destroy the mother; but this will not consist with reason, as wee have declared before: and if wee more nearly consider the condition of vipers and noxious animalls, we shall discover another provision of nature;[252] how although in their paucity shee hath not abridged their malignity, yet hath she notoriously effected it by their secession or latitancie;[253] for not only offensive insects as hornets, waspes, and the like; but sanguineous corticated animals, as serpents, toads and lizards, do lye hid and betake themselves to coverts in the Winter;[254] whereby most countries enjoying the immunity of Ireland and Candie, there ariseth a temporall security, from their venome, and an intermission of their mischiefes, mercifully requiting the time of their activities.[255]

A second ground of this effect, was conceived the justice of nature, whereby she compensates the death of the father by the matricide or murder of the mother, and this was the expression of Nicander;[256] but the cause hereof is as improbable as the effect, and were indeed an improvident revenge in the young ones, whereby in consequence, and upon defect of provision they must destroy themselves; and whereas he expresseth this decollation of the male by so full a terme as *ἀποκόπτειν*, that is, to cut or lop off, the act is hardly conceiveable;[257] for the female viper hath but foure considerable teeth,[258] and those so disposed, so slender and needle-pointed, that they are apter for puncture then any act of incision; and if any like action there be, it may be onely some fast retention or sudden compression in the orgasmus or fury of their lust, according as that expression of Horace is construed concerning Lydia and Telephus

Sive puer furens,
Impressit memorem dente labris notam.[259]

Others ascribe this effect unto the numerous conception of the viper, and this was the opinion of Theophrastus, who though he denieth the exesion or forcing through the belly, conceiveth neverthelesse that upon a full and plentifull impletion there may perhaps succeed a disruption of the matrix, as it happeneth sometimes in the long and slender fish acus:[260] now although in hot countries, and very numerous conceptions in the viper or other animalls, there may sometimes ensue a dilaceration of the genitall parts, yet is this a rare and contingent effect, and not a naturall and constant way of exclusion;[261] for the wise Creator hath formed the organs of animalls unto their operations, and in whom hee ordaineth a numerous conception, in them he hath prepared convenient receptacles, and a sutable way of exclusion.

Others doe ground this disruption upon their continued or protracted time of delivery, presumed to last twenty dayes, whereat, excluding but one a day, the latter brood impatient, by a forcible proruption anticipate their period of exclusion, and this was the assertion of Plinie, *Cæteri tarditatis impatientes prorumpunt latera, occisâ parente*,[262] which was occasioned upon a mistake of the Greek text in Aristotle, τίκτει δ'ἐν μιᾷ ἡμέρᾳ καθ'ἕν, τίκτει δὲ πλείω ἢ εἴκοσιν, which are literally thus translated, *Paret autem una die secundum unum, parit autem plures quam viginti*, and may be thus Englished, She bringeth forth in one day one by one and sometimes more then twenty; and so hath Scaliger rendred it, *sigillatim parit, absolvit una die interdum plures quam viginti*: But Pliny whom Gaza followeth hath differently translated it, *singulos diebus singulis parit, numero fere viginti*, whereby he extends the exclusion unto twenty dayes, which in the textuary sense is fully accomplished in one.[263]

But what hath most advanced it, is a mistake in another text of Aristotle, which seemeth directly to determine this disruption, τίκτει μικρὰ ἐχίδια ἐν ὑμέσιν, αἵ περιρρήγνυνται τριταῖοι, ἐνίοτε δὲ καὶ ἔσωθεν διαφαγόντα αὐτὰ ἐξέρχεται: which Gaza hath thus translated, *Parit catulos obvolutos membranis quæ tertio die rumpuntur, evenit interdum ut qui in utero adhuc sunt abrosis membranis prorumpant.*[264] Now herein very probably Pliny, and many since have been mistaken, for the disruption of the membranes or skins, which include the young ones, conceiving a dilaceration of the matrix and belly of the viper, and concluding from a casuall dilaceration, a regular and constant disruption.

As for the Latin word *Vipera*, which in the Etymologie of Isidore promoteth this conceit, more properly it may imply *vivipera*;[265] for whereas other serpents lay egges, the viper excludeth living animalls; and though the cerastes be also viviparous, and we have found formed snakes in the belly of the cecilia or slow-worme, yet may the viper emphatically beare that name; for the notation or etymologie is not of necessity adequate unto the name; and therefore though animall be deduced from *anima*, yet are there many animations beside, and plants will challenge a right therein as well as sensible creatures.

As touching the text of Scripture, and compellation of the Pharisies, by generation of vipers, although constructions bee made hereof conformable to this tradition, and it may be plausibly expounded, that out of a viperous condition, they conspired against their prophets, and destroyed their spirituall parents;[266] yet (as Jansenius observeth) Gregory and Jerome, doe make another construction, apprehending thereby what is usually implyed by that proverb, *Mali corvi malum ovum*; that is, of evill parents, an evill generation, a posterity not unlike their majority, of mischievous progenitors, a venemous and destructive progenie.[267]

And lastly, concerning the hieroglyphicall account, according to the vulgar conception set downe by Orus Apollo, the authority thereof is only emblematicall, for were the conception true or false, to their apprehensions, it expressed filiall impiety; which strictly taken, and totally received for truth, might perhaps begin, but surely promote this conception.

[More doubtful assertions have been raised of no animal then the viper, as we have dispersedly noted:[268] and Francisco Redi hath amply discovered in his noble observations of vipers; from good reasons and iterated experiments affirming, that a viper containeth no humour, excrement, or part which either dranke or eat, is able to kill any: that the *remorsores* or dog-teeth, are not more then two in either sex: that these teeth are hollow, and though they bite and prick therewith, yet are they not venomous, but only open a way and entrance unto the poyson, which notwithstanding is not poysonous except it touch or attain unto the bloud. And that there is no other poyson in this animal, but only that almost insipid liquor like oyl of almonds, which stagnates in the sheaths and cases that cover the teeth; and that this proceeds not from the bladder of gall, but is rather generated in the head, and perhaps demitted and sent from thence into these cases by salival conducts and passages, which the head communicateth unto them.]

CHAPTER XVII
Of Hares

That hares are both male and female, beside the vulgar opinion, was the affirmative of Archelaus, of Plutarch, Philostratus, and many more.[269] [Of the same belief have been the Jewish Rabbins:[270] The same is likewise confirmed from the Hebrew word, *Arnabeth*; which as though there were no single males of that kinde, hath only obtained a name of the feminine gender; as also from the symbolicall foundation of its prohibition in the law, Levit 11, and what vices therein are figured; that is, not only pusillanimity and timidity from its temper, feneration or usury from its fecundity and superfetation, but from this mixture of sexes, unnaturall venery and denenerous effemination.] Nor are there hardly any who either treat of mutation or mixtion of sexes, who have not left some mention of this point; some speaking positively, others dubiously, and most resigning it unto the enquiry of the reader: now hereof to speake distinctly, they must be male and female by mutation and succession of sexes, or else by composition, by mixture or union thereof.

As for the mutation of sexes, or transition into one another, we cannot deny it in hares, it being observable in man: for hereof beside Empedocles or Tiresias, there are not a few examples;[271] and though very few, or rather none which have emasculated or turned women, yet very many who from an esteem or reallity of being women have infallibly proved men: some at the first point of their menstruous eruptions, some in the day of their marriage, others many yeares after, which occasioned disputes at law, and contestations concerning a restore of the dowry; and that not only mankinde, but many other animalls, may suffer this transexion, we will not deny, or hold it at al impossible; although I confesse by reason of the posticke and backward position of the feminine parts in quadrupeds, they can hardly admit the substitution of a protrusion effectuall unto masculine generation, except it be in retromingents, and such as couple backward.[272]

Nor shall we only concede the succession of sexes in some, but shall not dispute the transition of reputed species in others; that is, a transmutation, or (as Paracelsians terme it) the transplantation of one into another; hereof in perfect animalls of a congenerous seed, or neare affinity of natures, examples are not unfrequent, as horses, asses, dogs, foxes, phaisants, cocks, etc. but in imperfect kindes, and such where the discrimination of sexes is obscure, these transformations are more common:[273] and in some within themselves without commixtion, as particularly in caterpillers or silk-wormes, wherein there is visible and triple transfiguration: but in plants wherein there is no distinction of sex, these transplantations are yet more obvious then any; as that of barley into oates, of wheat into darnell, and those graines which generally arise among corne, as cockle, aracus, ægilops, and other degenerations which come up in unexpected shapes, when they want the support and maintenance of the primary and master-formes:[274] and the same do some affirm concerning other plants in lesse analogy of figures, as the mutation of mint into cresses, basill into serpoile, and turneps into radishes;[275] in all which as Severinus conceiveth there may be equivocall seeds and hermaphroditicall principles, which contain the radicality and power of different formes;[276] thus in the seed of wheat there lyeth obscurely the seminality of darnell, although in a secondary or inferiour way, and at some distance of production; which neverthelesse if it meet with convenient promotion, or a conflux and conspiration of causes more powerfull then the other, it then beginneth to edifie in chiefe, and contemning the superintendent forme, produceth the signatures of its selfe.[277]

Now therefore although we deny not these severall mutations, and doe allow that hares may exchange their sex, yet this we conceive doth come to passe but sometimes, and not in that vicissitude or annuall alternation as is presumed; that is, from imperfection to perfection, from perfection to imperfection, from female unto male, from male to female againe, and so in a circle to both without a permansion in either;[278] for beside the inconceiveable mutation of temper, which should yearly alternate the sex, this is injurious unto the order of nature, whose operations doe rest in the perfection of their intents; which having once attained, they maintaine their accomplished ends, and relapse not againe into their progressionall imperfections:

so if in the minority of naturall vigor, the parts of feminality take place, when upon the encrease or growth thereof the masculine appeare, the first designe of nature is atchieved, and those parts are after maintained.[279]

But surely it much impeacheth this iterated transexion of hares, if that be true which Cardan and other physitians affirm, that transmutation of sex is only so in opinion, and that these transfeminated persons were really men at first, although succeeding yeares produced the manifesto or evidence of their virilities;[280] which although intended and formed, was not at first excluded, and that the examples hereof have undergone no reall or new transexion, but were androgynally borne, and under some kind of hermaphrodites: for though Galen do favour the opinion, that the distinctive parts of sexes are onely different in position, that is inversion or protrusion, yet will this hardly be made out from the anatomy of those parts, the testicles being so seated in the female that they admit not of protrusion, and the necke of the matrix wanting those parts which are discoverable in the organ of virility.[281]

The second and most received acception, is, that hares are male and female by conjunction of both sexes, and such are found in mankinde, poetically called hermaphrodites, supposed to be formed from the equality, or *non victorie* of either seed, carrying about them the parts of man and woman; although with great variety in perfection, site and ability; not only as Aristotle conceived, with a constant impotencie in one;[282] but as latter observers affirme, sometimes with ability of either venery: and therefore the providence of some laws have thought good, that at the yeares of maturity, they should elect one sex, and the errors in the other should suffer a severer punishment; whereby endeavouring to prevent incontinencie, they unawares enjoyned perpetuall chastity; for being executive in both parts, and confined unto one, they restrained a naturall power, and ordained a partiall virginity. Plato and some of the Rabbines proceeded higher, who conceived the first man an hermaphrodite; and Marcus Leo the learned Jew, in some sense hath allowed it, affirming that Adam in one suppositum without division, contained both male and female;[283] and therefore whereas it is said in the text, that God created man in his owne image, in the image of God created he him, male and female created he them, applying the singular and plurall unto Adam, it might denote that in one substance, and in himselfe he included both sexes which was after divided, and the female called Woman.[284] The opinion of Aristotle extendeth farther, from whose assertion all men should be hermaphrodites; for affirming that women do not spermatize, and conferre a place or receptacle rather then essentiall principles of generation, he deductively includes both sexes in mankinde;[285] for from the father proceed not only males and females, but from him also must hermaphroditicall and masculo-feminine generations be derived, and a commixtion of both sexes arise from the seed of one: but the schoolmen have dealt with that sex more hardly then any other, who though they have not much disputed their generation, yet have they controverted their resurrection, and raysed a query whether any at the last day should arise in the sex of women, as may be observed in the supplement of Aquinas.[286]

Now as we must acknowledge this androgynall condition in man, so can we not deny the like doth happen in beasts. Thus doe we read in Plinie that Neroes chariot was drawne by foure hermaphroditicall mares, and Cardan affirmes he also beheld one at Antwerpe;[287] and thus may we also concede, that hares have been of both sexes, and some have ocularly confirmed it; but that the whole species or kinde should be bisexous we cannot affirme, who have found the parts of male and female respectively distinct and single in any wherein we have enquired; and whereas it is conceived, that being an harmlesse animall and delectable food unto man, nature hath made them with double sexes, and that actively and passively performing they might more numerously encrease; we forget an higher providence of nature whereby shee especially promotes the multiplication of hares, which is by superfetation;[288] that is, a conception upon a conception, or an improvement of a second fruit before the first be excluded, preventing hereby the usuall intermission and vacant time of generation, which is very common and frequently observable in hares, mentioned long agoe by Aristotle, Herodotus, and Pliny;[289] and we have often observed that after the first cast, there remaine successive conceptions, and other younglings very immature, and far from their terme of exclusion.[290]

Nor need any man to question this in hares, for the same wee observe doth sometime happen in women; for although it be true that upon conception, the inward orifice of the matrix exactly closeth, so that it commonly admitteth nothing after; yet falleth it out sometime, that in the act of coition, the avidity of that part dilateth it selfe, and receiveth a second burden, which if it happen to be neare in time unto the first, they commonly doe both proceed unto perfection, and have legitimate exclusions, and periodically succeed each other:[291] but if the superfetation be made with considerable intermission, the latter most commonly proves abortive; for the first being confirmed, engrosseth the aliment from the other: however therefore the project of Julia seem very plausible, and that way infallible when she received not her passengers, before she had taken in her lading, there was a fallibility therein;[292] nor indeed any absolute securitie in the policy of adultery after conception; for the matrix (which some have called another animall within us, and which is not subjected unto the law of our will) after reception of its proper tenant, may yet receive a strange and spurious inmate, as is confirmable by many examples in Plinie, by Larissæa in Hippocrates, and that merry one in Plautus urged also by Aristotle, that is of Iphicles and Hercules, the one begat by Jupiter, the other by Amphitryon upon Alcmæna;[293] as also in those superconceptions where one childe was like the father, the other like the adulterer, the one favour'd the servant, the other resembled the master.

Now the grounds that begat, or much promoted the opinion of a double sex in hares might bee some little bags or tumors, as first glance representing stones or testicles, to be found in both sexes about the parts of generation; which men observing in either sex, were induced to beleeve a masculine sex in both; but to speak properly these are no testicles or parts officiall unto generation, but glandulous substances that seeme to hold the nature of emunctories;[294] for herein may be perceived slender perforations, at which may be expressed a blacke and fœculent matter;[295] if therefore from these we shall conceive a mixtion of sexes in hares, with fairer reason we may conclude it in bevers, whereof both sexes containe a double bagge or tumor in the groine, commonly called the cod of Castor, as we have delivered before.[296]

Another ground were certaine holes or cavities observeable about the siedge; which being perceived in males, made some conceive there might be also a fæminine nature in them, and upon this very ground, the same opinion hath passed upon the hyæna, as is declared by Aristotle, and thus translated by Scaliger; *Quod autem aiunt utriusque sexus habere genitalia falsum est, quod videtur esse fœmineum sub cauda, est simile figura fœminino, verum pervium non est*;[297] and thus is it also in hares, in whom these holes, although they seeme to make a deepe cavity, yet doe they not perforate the skin, nor hold a community with any part of generation, but were (as Plinie delivereth) esteemed the marks of their age, the number of those decyding their number of yeares;[298] what verity there is herein, we shall not contend; for if in other animals there be authentick notations, if the characters of yeares be found in the hornes of cowes, or in the antlers of deere, if we conjecture the age of horses from joynts in their dockes, and undeniably presume it from their teeth;[299] we cannot affirme, there is in their conceit, any affront unto nature, although, who ever enquireth shall finde no assurance therein.

The last foundation was retromingency or pissing backward, for men observing both sexes to urine backward, or aversly between their legges, they might conceive there was a fœminine part in both; wherein they are deceived by the ignorance of the just and proper site of the pizell or part designed unto the excretion of urine, which in the hare holds not the common position, but is aversly seated, and in its distention enclines unto the coccix or scut. Now from the nature of this position, there ensueth a necessitie of retrocopulation, which also promoteth the conceit; for some observing them to couple without ascension, have not beene able to judge of male or female, or to determine the proper sex in either, and to speake generally this way of copulation, is not appropriate unto hares, nor is there one, but many wayes of coition, according to divers shapes and different conformations; for some couple laterally or sidewise as wormes, some circularly or by complication as serpents, some pronely, that is by contaction of prone parts in both, as apes, porcupines, hedgehogges, and such as are termed mollia, as the cuttlefish and the purple; some mixtly, that is, the male ascending the female, or by application of the prone parts of the one, unto the postick parts of the other, as most quadrupes;[300] some aversely, as all crustaceous animals, lobsters, shrimps, and crevises, and also retromingents, as panthers, tigers, and hares: this is the constant law of their coition, this they observe and transgresse not: onely the vitiositie of man hath acted the varieties hereof;[301] nor content with a digression from sex or species, hath in his own kinde runne thorow the anomalies of venery, and been so bold, not onely to act, but represent to view, the irregular wayes of lust.

CHAPTER XVIII
Of Molls

That molls are blinde and have no eyes, though a common opinion is received with much variety; some affirming onely they have no sight, as Oppianus, the proverbe *Talpa Caecior*, and the word σπαλακία, or Talpitas, which in Hesichius is made the same with Cæcias:[302] some that they have eyes, but no sight, as the text of Aristotle seems to imply, some neither eyes nor sight, as Albertus, Plinie, and the vulgar opinion; some both eyes and sight as Scaliger, Aldrovandus, and some others.[303] Of which opinions, the last with some restriction, is most consonant unto truth: for that they have eyes in their head is manifest unto any, that wants them not in his own, and are discoverable, not onely in old ones, but as we have observed in yong and naked conceptions, taken out of the belly of the dam; and he that exactly enquires into the cavitie of their cranies, may discover some propagation of nerves communicated unto these parts; but that the humors together with their coats are also distinct, (though Galen seeme to affirme it) transcendeth our discovery; for separating these little orbes, and including them in magnifying glasses, wee discerned no more then Aristotle mentions, that is, τῶν ὀφθαλμῶν μέλαινα, that is; *humorem nigrum*, nor any more if they bee broken:[304] that therefore they have eyes we must of necessitie affirme, but that they be comparativly incomplete wee need not to denie: so Galen affirmes the parts of generation in women are imperfect, in respect of those of men, as the eyes of molls in regard of other animals; so Aristotle termes them πηρουμένους, which Gaza translates *oblæsos*, and Scaliger by a word of imperfection, *inchoatos*.[305]

Now as that they have eyes is manifest unto sense, so that they have sight not incongruous unto reason, if wee call not in question the providence of this provision, that is, to assigne the organs, and yet deny the office, to grant them eyes and withold all manner of vision: for as the inference is faire, affirmatively deduced from the action to the organ, that they have eyes because they see, so is it also from the organ to the action, that they have eyes, therefore some sight designed; if we take the intention of nature in every species, and except the casuall impediments, or morbosities in individuals;[306] but as their eyes are more imperfect then others, so do we conceive of their sight, or act of vision; for they will runne against things, and hudling forwards fall from high places; so that they are not blinde, nor yet distinctly see, there is in them no cecity, yet more then a cecutiency;[307] they have sight enough to discerne the light, though not perhaps to distinguish of objects or colours; so are they not exactly blinde, for light is one object of vision; and this (as Scaliger observeth) might be as full a sight as nature first intended;[308] for living in darkenesse under the earth, they had no further need of eyes then to avoid the light, and to be sensible when ever they lost that darkenesse of earth, which was their naturall confinement;[309] and therefore however translators doe render the word of Aristotle, or Galen, that is, *imperfectos*, *oblæsos*, or *inchoatos*, it is not much considerable; for their eyes are sufficiently begun to finish this action and competently perfect, for this imperfect vision.

And lastly, although they had neither eyes nor sight, yet could they not be termed blinde; for blindenesse being a privative terme unto sight, this appellation is not admittible in propriety of speech, and will overthrow the doctrine of privations, which presuppose positive formes or habits, and are not indefinite negations, denying in all subjects but such alone wherein the positive habits are in their proper nature, and placed without repugnancy. So do we improperly say a moll is blinde, if we deny it the organs or a capacity of vision from its created nature; so when the text of John had said, that man was blinde from his nativity, whose cecity our Saviour cured, it was not warrantable in Nonnus to say he had no eyes at all, as he describeth in his paraphrase, and as some ancient fathers affirme, that by this miracle they were created in him;[310] and so though the sence may be accepted, that proverbe must be candidly interpreted which maketh fishes mute, and call them silent which have no voyce in nature.

Now this conceit is erected upon a misapprehension or mistake in the symptomes of vision, men confounding abolishment, diminution and depravement, and naming that an abolition of sight, which indeed is but an abatement. For if vision be abolished, it is called *cæcitas*, or blindnesse, if depraved and receive its objects erroneously, hallucination, if dimished, *hebetudo visus*, *caligatio*, or dimnesse; now instead of a diminution or imperfect vision in the moll, we affirme an abolition or totall privation, in stead of caligation or dimnesse, wee conclude a cecity or blindnesse, which hath beene frequently committed concerning other animals; so some affirme the water rat is blinde, so Sammonicus and Nicander do call the mus-araneus the shrew or ranny, blinde;[311] and because darkenesse was before light, the Ægyptians worshipped the same: so are slow-wormes accounted blinde, and the like we affirme proverbially of the beetle, although their eyes be evident, and they will flye against lights, like many other insects, and though also Aristotle determines, that the eyes are apparent in all flying insects, though other senses be obscure, and not perceptible at all;[312] and if from a diminution wee may inferre a totall privation, or affirme that other animals are blinde which doe not acutely see or comparatively unto others, wee shall condemne unto blindenesse many not so esteemed; for such as have corneous or horney eyes, as lobsters and crustaceous animals, are generally dim sighted, all insects that have *antennae*, or long hornes to feele out their way, as butter-flies and locusts, or their fore legs so disposed, that they much advance before their heads, as may be observed in spiders; and if the ægle were judge, wee might be blinde our selves; the expression therefore of Scripture in the story of Jacob is surely with circumspection, and it came to passe when Jacob was old, and his eyes were dimme, *quando caligarunt oculi*, saith Jerom and Tremellius, which are expressions of diminution, and not of absolute privation.[313]

CHAPTER XIX
Of Lampries

Whether lampries have nine eyes, as is received, we durst refer it unto Polyphemus, who had but one to judge it:[314] an error concerning eyes, occasioned by the errour of eyes, deduced from the appearance of divers cavities or holes on either side, which some call eyes that carelesly behold them, and is not onely refutable by experience, but also repugnant unto reason; for beside the monstrosity they fasten unto nature, in contriving many eyes, who hath made but two unto any animall, that is, one of each side, according to the division of the braine, it were a superfluous and inartificiall act to place and settle so many in one place; for the two extremes would sufficiently performe the office of sight without the help of the intermediate eyes, and behold as much as all seven joyned together; for the visible base of the object would be defined by these two, and the middle eyes although they behold the same thing, yet could they not behold so much thereof as these; so were it no advantage unto man to have a third eye betweene those two he hath already; and the fiction of Argus seemes more reasonable then this;[315] for though he had many eyes, yet were they placed in circumference and positions of advantage.

Againe, these cavities which men call eyes are seated out of the head, and where the gils of other fish are placed, containing no organs of sight, nor having any communication with the braine; now all sense proceeding from the braine, and that being placed (as Galen observeth) in the upper part of the body, for the fitter situation of the eyes, and conveniency required unto sight, it is not reasonable to imagine that they are any where else, or deserve that name which are seated in other parts;[316] and therefore we relinquish as fabulous what is delivered of Sternopthalmi, or men with eyes in their breast;[317] and when it is said by Solomon, A wise mans eyes are in his head, it is to be taken in second sence, and affordeth no objection:[318] true it is that the eyes of animals are seated with some difference, but all whatsoever in the head, and that more forward then the eare or hole of hearing. In quadrupedes, in regard of the figure of their heads, they are placed at some distance, in latirostrous and flat-bild birds they are more laterally seated;[319] and therefore when they looke intently they turne one eye upon the object, and can convert their heads to see before and behinde, and to behold two opposite points at once; but at a more easie distance are they situated in man, and in the same circumference with the eare, for if one foote of the compasse be placed upon the crowne, a circle described thereby will intersect, or passe over both the eares.

The error in this conceit consists in the ignorance of these cavities, and their proper use in nature; for this is a particular disposure of parts, and a peculiar conformation whereby these holes and sluces supply the defect of gils, and are assisted by the conduit in the head; for like cetaceous animals and whales, the lamprey hath a fistula, spout or pipe at the back part of the head, whereat they spirt out water: nor is it onely singular in this formation, but also in many other, as in defect of bones, whereof it hath not one, and for the spine or back-bone, a cartilagineous substance without any spondyles, processes, or protuberance whatsoever;[320] as also in the provision which nature hath made for the heart, which in this animall is very strangely secured, and lyes immured in a cartilage or gristly substance; and lastly, in the colour of the liver, which is in the male of an excellent grasse greene, but of a deeper colour in the female, and will communicate a fresh and durable verdure.

CHAPTER XX
Of Snayles

That snayles have two eyes, and at the end of their hornes, beside the assertion of the people, is the opinion of some learned men; which notwithstanding Scaliger tearmes but imitation of eyes, which Pliny contradicts, and Aristotle upon consequence denyes, when he affirmes that testaceous animals have no eyes at all;[321] and for my owne part after much inquiry, I am not satisfied that these are eyes, or that those black and atramentous spots which seeme to represent them are any ocular reallities;[322] for if any object be presented unto them, they will sometime seeme to decline it, and sometime run against it; if also these black extremities, or presumed eyes be clipped off, they will notwithstanding make use of their protrusions or hornes, and poke out their way as before: againe, if they were eyes or instruments of vision, they would have their originals in the head, and from thence derive their motive and optick organs, but their roots and first extremities are seated low upon the sides of the back, as may be perceived in the whiter sort of snayles when they retract them: and lastly, if wee concede they have two eyes, wee must also grant, they have no lesse then foure, for not onely the two greater extensions above have these imitations of eyes, but also the two lesser below, as is evident unto any, and if they be dextrously dissected, there will be found on either side two black filaments or membranous strings which extend into the long and shorter cornicle upon protrusion; and therefore if they have two eyes, they have also foure, which will be monstrous, and beyond the affirmation of any.

Now the reason why we name these black strings eyes, is because we know not what to call them else, and understand not the proper use of that part, which indeed is very obscure, and not delivered by any, but may probably be said to assist the protrusion, and retraction of their hornes, which being a weake and hollow body, require some inward establishment, to confirme the length of their advancement, which we observe they cannot extend without the concurrence hereof; for if with your finger you apprehend the top of the horne, and draw out this black, and membranous emission, the horne will be excluded no more; but if you clip off the extremity, or onely sindge the top thereof with *aqua fortis*, or other corrosive water, leaving a considerable part behinde, they will neverthelesse exclude their hornes, and therewith explorate their way as before; and indeed the exact sense of these extremities is very remarkable; for if you dip a pen in *Aqua fortis*, oyle of vitriol, or turpentine, and present it towards these points, they will at a reasonable distance, decline the acrimony thereof, retyring or distorting them to avoid it; and this they will nimbly performe if objected to the extremes, but slowly or not at all, if approached unto their rootes.[323]

What hath beene therefore delivered concerning the plurality, paucity, or anomalous situation of eyes, is either monstrous, fabulous, or under things never seene includes good sense or meaning: and so may we receive the figment of Argus, who was an hieroglyphick of heaven, in those centuries of eyes expressing the stars; and their alternate wakings, the vicissitude of day and night;[324] which strictly taken cannot be admitted, for the subject of sleep is not the eye, but the common sense, which once asleep, all eyes must be at rest: and therefore what is delivered as an embleme of vigilancy, that the hare and lion doe sleep with one eye open, doth not evince they are any more awake then if they were both closed; for the open eye beholds in sleepe no more then that which is closed, and no more one eye in them then two in other animals that sleep with both open, as some by disease, and others naturally which have no eye lids at all.

As for Polyphemus although his story be fabulous, the monstrosity is not impossible;[325] for the act of vision may be performed with one eye, and in the deception and fallacy of sight, hath this advantage of two, that it beholds not objects double, or sees two things for one; for this doth happen when the axis of the visive cones, diffused from the object, fall not upon the same plane, but that which is conveyed into one eye, is more depressed or elevated then that which enters the other.[326] So if beholding a candle we protrude either upward or downeward the pupill of one eye, the object will appeare double; but if wee shut the other eye, and behold it but with one, it will then appeare but single, and if we abduce the eye unto either corner, the object will not duplicate, for in that position the axes of the coves remaine in the same plane, as is demonstrated in the opticks, and delivered by Galen, in his tenth *de usu partium*.[327]

Relations also there are of men that could make themselves invisible, which belongs not to this discourse, but may serve as notable expressions of wise and prudent men, who so contrive their affaires, that although their actions be manifest, their designes are not discoverable: in this acception there is nothing left of doubt, and Giges ring remaineth still among us;[328] for vulgar eyes behold no more of wise men then doth the sun, they may discover their exteriour and outward wayes, but their interiour and inward pieces he onely sees, that sees beyond their beings.

CHAPTER XXI
Of the Cameleon

Concerning the chameleon there generally passeth an opinion that it liveth onely upon ayre, and is sustained by no other aliment; thus much is in plaine termes affirmed by Solinus, Pliny, and divers other, and by this periphrasis is the same described by Ovid;[329] all which notwithstanding upon enquiry, I finde the assertion mainly controvertible, and very much to faile in the three inducements of beliefe.

And first for its verity, although asserted by some, and traditionally delivered by others, yet is it very questionable. For beside Ælian, who is seldome defective in these accounts; Aristotle distinctly treating hereof, hath made no mention of this remarkeable propriety;[330] which either suspecting its verity, or presuming its falsity hee surely omitted; for that he remained ignorant of this account it is not easily conceivable, it being the common opinion, and generally received by all men: some have positively denyed it, as Augustinus, Niphus, Stobæus, Dalechampius, Fortunius Licetus, with many more;[331] others have experimentally refuted it, as namely Johannes Landius, who in the relation of Scaliger, observed a chameleon to lick up a flye from his breast;[332] but Bellonius hath beene more satisfactorily experimentall, not onely affirming they feede on flyes, caterpillers, beetles, and other insects, but upon exenteration he found these animals in their bellies;[333] and although we have not had the advantage of our owne observation, yet have we received the like confirmation from many ocular spectators.

As touching the verisimility or probable truth of this relation, severall reasons there are which seeme to overthrow it;[334] for first, there are found in this animall, the guts, the stomack, and other parts officiall unto nutrition, which were its aliment the empty reception of ayre, their provisions had beene superfluous; now the wisdome of nature abhorring superfluities, and effecting nothing in vaine, unto the intention of these operations, respectively contriveth the organs; and therefore where we finde such instruments, wee may with strictnesse expect their actions, and where we discover them not, wee may with safety conclude the non-intention of their operations:[335] so when we observe that oviperous animals, as lizards, frogs, birds, and most fishes have neither bladder nor kidnies, we may with reason inferre they do not urine at all: but whereas in this same kinde we discover these parts in the tortoys beyond any other, wee cannot deny he exerciseth that excretion; nor was there any absurdity in Pliny, when for medicinall uses he commended the urine of a tortoise:[336] so when we perceive that bats have teats, it is not unreasonable to infer they suckle their younglings with milke; but whereas no other flying animall hath these parts, we cannot from them expect a viviparous exclusion, but either a generation of egges, or some vermiparous separation, whose navell is within it selfe at first, and its nutrition after not inwardly dependent of its originall.[337]

Againe, nature is so farre from leaving any one part without its proper action, that she oft-times imposeth two or three labours upon one; so the pizell in animals is both officiall unto urine and to generation, but the first and primary use is generation; for many creatures enjoy that part which urine not, as fishes, birds, and quadrupeds oviparous; but not on the contrary, for the secondary action subsisteth not alone, but in concommitancie with the other;[338] so the nostrills are usefull both for respiration and smelling, but the principall use is smelling; for many have nostrills which have no lungs, as fishes, but none have lungs or respiration, which have not some shew, or some analogy of nostrills: and thus we perceive the providence of nature, that is the wisdome of God, which disposeth of no part in vaine, and some parts unto two or three uses, will not provide any without the execution of its proper office, nor where there is no digestion to be made, make any parts inservient to that intention.

Beside the teeth, the tongue of this animall is a second argument to overthrow this ayrie nutrication, and that not only in its proper nature, but also in its peculiar figure; for indeed of this part properly taken there are two ends; that is, the formation of the voice, and the execution of taste; for the voice, it can have no office in camelions, for they are mute animals, as, beside fishes, are most other sort of lizards: as for their taste, if their nutriment be ayre, neither can it be an instrument thereof; for the body of that element is ingustible, void of all sapidity, and without any action of the tongue, is by the rough artery or weazon conducted into the lungs:[339] and therefore Plinie much forgets the strictnesse of his assertion, when he alloweth excrements unto that animall, that feedeth only upon ayre, which notwithstanding with the urine of an asse, hee commends as a magicall medicine upon our enemies.[340]

The figure of the tongue seems also to overthrow the presumption of this aliment, which according to the exact delineation of Aldrovand, is in this animall peculiar, and seemeth contrived for prey;[341] for in so little a creature it is at the least halfe a palme long, and being it self very slow of motion, hath in this part a very great agility; withall its food being flyes and such as suddenly escape, it hath in the tongue a spongy and mucous extremity, whereby upon a sudden emission, it inviscates and tangleth those insects:[342] and therefore some have thought its name not unsutable unto its nature; the nomination is Greek, χαμαιλέων, that is a little lion, not so much for the resemblance of shape, but affinity of condition, that is for the vigilancy in its prey and sudden rapacity thereof, which it performeth not like the lion with its teeth, but a sudden and unexpected ejaculation of the tongue. This exposition is favoured by some, especially the old glosse upon Leviticus, whereby in the translation of Jerome and the Septuagint, this animall is forbidden;[343] what ever it be, it seems more reasonable then that of Isidore, who derives this name, a *Camelo et Leone*, as presuming herein some resemblance with a camell;[344] for this derivation offendeth the rules of etymology, wherein indeed the notation of names should be orthographicall, not exchanging dipthongs for vowells, or converting consonants into each other.

As for the possibility hereof, it is not also unquestionable, and many wise men are of opinion, the bodies of animalls cannot receive a proper aliment from ayre: for beside that taste being (as Aristotle termes it) a kinde of touch, it is required the aliment should be tangible, and fall under the palpable affections of touch;[345] beside also that there is some sapor in all aliments, as being to be distinguished and judged by the guste, which cannot be admitted in ayre;[346] beside these, I say, if wee consider the nature of aliment, and the proper use of ayre in respiration, it will very hardly fall under the name hereof, or properly attaine the act of nutrication.

And first concerning its nature, to make a perfect nutrition into the body nourished, there is required a transmutation of the nutriment; now where this conversion or aggeneration is made, there is also required in the aliment a familiarity of matter, and such a community or vicinity unto a living nature, as by one act of the soule may be converted into the body of the living, and enjoy one common soule;[347] which indeed cannot be effected by the ayre, it concurring only with our flesh in common principles, which are at the largest distance from life, and common also unto inanimated constitutions; and therefore when it is said by Fernelius, and asserted by divers others, that we are only nourished by living bodies, and such as are some way proceeding from them, that is the fruits, effects, parts, or seeds thereof, they have laid out an object very agreeable unto assimulation;[348] for these indeed are fit to receive a quick and immediate conversion, as holding some community with our selves, and containing approximate disposition unto animation.

Secondly (as is argued by Aristotle against the Pythagoreans) whatsoever properly nourisheth, before its assimulation, by the action of naturall heat it receiveth a corpulency or incrassation progressionall unto its conversion;[349] which notwithstanding it cannot be effected upon the ayre, for the action of heat doth not condense but rarifie that body, and by attenuation, rather then for nutrition, disposeth it for expulsion.

Thirdly (which is the argument of Hippocrates) all aliment received into the body, must be therein a considerable space retained, and not immediatly expelled: now ayre but momentally remaining in our bodies, it hath no proportionable space for its conversion, that being only of length enough to refrigerate the heart, which having once performed, lest being it selfe heated againe, it should suffocate that part, it maketh no stay, but hasteth backe the same way it passed in.[350]

Fourthly, the proper use of ayre attracted by the lungs, and without which there is no durable continuation in life, is not the nutrition of parts, but the contemperation of that fervour in the heart, and the ventilation of that fire alwayes maintained in the forge of life; whereby although in some manner it concurreth unto nutrition, yet can it not receive the proper name of nutriment; and therefore by Hippocrites, *De alimento*, it is termed *Alimentum non Alimentum*, a nourishment and no nourishment;[351] that is in a large acception, but not in propriety of language conserving the body, not nourishing the same, not repairing it by assimulation, but preserving it by ventilation; for thereby the naturall flame is preserved from extinction, and so the individuum supported in some way like nutrition:[352] and so when it is said by the same author, *Pulmo contrarium corpori alimentum trahit, reliqua omnia idem*, it is not to be taken in a strict and proper sense, but the quality in the one, the substance is meant in the other; for ayre in regard of our naturall heat is cold, and in that quality contrary unto it, but what is properly aliment, of what quality soever, is potentially the same, and in a substantiall identity unto it.[353]

[And though the air so entreth the lungs,[354] that by its nitrous spirit, it doth affect the heart, and several ways qualifie the blood; and though it be also admitted into other parts, even by the meat we chew, yet that it affordeth a proper nutriment alone, is not easily made out.]

[Again,[355] some are so far from affirming the air to afford any nutriment, that they plainly deny it to be any element, or that it entreth into mixt bodies as any principle in their compositions, but performeth other offices in the universe; as to fill all vacuities about the earth or beneath it, to convey the heat of the sun, to maintain fires and flames, to serve for the flight of volatils, respiration of breathing animals, and refrigeration of others. And although we receive it as an element, yet since the transmutation of elements and simple bodies, is not beyond great question, since also it is no easie matter to demonstrate that air is so much as convertible into water; how transmutable it is into flesh, may be of deeper doubt.]

And although the ayre attracted may be conceived to nourish that invisible flame of life, in as much as common and culinary flames are nourished by the ayre about them; I confesse wee doubt the common conceit, which affirmeth that aire is the pabulous supply of fire, much lesse that flame is properly aire kindled:[356] and the same before us, hath been denyed by the Lord of Verulam, in his Tract of life and death, and also by Dr. Jorden in his book of Minerall waters:[357] for that which substantially maintaineth the fire, is the combustible matter in the kindled body, and not the ambient ayre, which affordeth exhalation to its fuliginous atomes, nor that which causeth the flame properly to be termed ayre, but rather as he expresseth it, the accention of fuliginous exhalations, which containe an unctuosity in them, and arise from the matter of fuell;[358] which opinion is very probable, and will salve many doubts, whereof the common conceit affordeth no solution.

As first, how fire is stricken out of flints, that is not by kindling the aire from the collision of two hard bodies; for then diamonds and glasse should doe the like as well as flint, but rather from the sulphur and inflamable effluviums contained in them. The like saith Jorden we observe in canes and woods, that are unctuous and full of oyle, which will yeeld fire by frication, or collision, not by kindling the ayre about them, but the inflamable oyle within them:[359] why the fire goes out without ayre? that is because the fuligenous exhalations wanting evaporation recoyle upon the flame and choake it, as is evident in cupping glasses, and the artifice of charcoals, where if the ayre be altogether excluded, the fire goes out; why some lampes included in close bodies, have burned many hundred yeares, as that discovered in the sepulchre of Tullia the sister of Cicero, and that of Olibius many yeares after, neare Padua;[360] because what ever was their matter, either a preparation of gold, or naptha, the duration proceeded from the puritie of their oyle which yeelded no fuligenous exhalations to suffocate the fire; for if ayre had nourished the flame, it had not continued many minutes, for it would have been spent and wasted by the fire: why a piece of flaxe will kindle, although it touch not the flame? because the fire extendeth further, then indeed it is visible, being at some distance from the weeke a pellucide and transparent body, and thinner then the ayre it self:[361] why mettals in their liquation, although they intensly heat the aire above their surface, arise not yet into a flame, nor kindle the aire about them? because their sulphur is more fixed, and they emit not inflamable exhalations: and lastly, why a lampe or candle burneth onely in the ayre about it, and inflameth not the ayre at a distance from it? because the flame extendeth not beyond the inflamable effluence, but closly adheres unto the originall of its inflamation, and therefore it onely warmeth, not kindleth the aire about it, which notwithstanding it will doe, if the ambient aire be impregnate with subtile inflamabilities, and such as are of quick accension, as experiment is made in a close roome, upon an evaporation of spirits of wine and camphir;[362] as subterraneous fires doe sometimes happen, and as Creusa and Alexanders boy in the bath were set on fire by naptha.[363]

Lastly, the element of aire is so far from nourishing the bodie, that some have questioned the power of water; many conceiving it enters not the body in the power of aliment, or that from thence, there proceeds a substantiall supply: for beside that some creatures drinke not at all, unto others it performs the common office of ayre, and serves for refrigeration of the heart, as unto fishes, who receive it, and expell it by the gills;[364] even unto our selves, and more perfect animals, though many wayes assistent thereto, it performes no substantiall nutrition, in serving for refrigeration, dilution of solid aliment, and its elixation in the stomacke, which from thence as a vehicle it conveighs through lesse accessible cavities into the liver, from thence into the veines, and so in a roride substance through the capillarie cavities into every part;[365] which having performed, it is afterward excluded by urine, sweat and serous separations. And this opinion surely possessed the ancients, for when they so highly commended that water which is suddenly hot and cold, which is without all savour, the lightest, the thinnest, and which will soonest boile beanes or pease, they had no consideration of nutrition; whereunto had they had respect, they would have surely commended grosse and turbid streames, in whose confusion at the last, there might be contained some nutriment; and not jejune or limpid water, and nearer the simplicity of its element.[366] [Although, I confess, our clearest waters and such as seem simple unto sense, are much compounded unto reason, as may be observed in the evaporation of large quantities of water; wherein beside a terreous residence some salt is also found, as is also observable in rain water; which appearing pure and empty, is full of seminall principles, and carrieth vitall atomes of plants and animals in it, which have not perished in the great circulation of nature; as may be discovered from several insects generated in raine water, from the prevalent fructification of plants thereby; and (beside the reall plant of Cornerius) from vegetable figurations, upon the sides of glasses, so rarely delineated in frosts.]

All which considered, severer heads will be apt enough to conceive the opinion of this animal, not much unlike unto that of the Astomi, or men without mouthes in Pliny, sutable unto the relation of the mares in Spaine, and their subventaneous conceptions, from the westerne winde;[367] and in some way more unreasonable then the figment of Rabican the famous horse in Ariosto, which being conceived by flame and wind never tasted grasse, or fed on any grosser provender then ayre;[368] for this way of nutrition was answerable unto the principles of his generation; which being not ayrie, but grosse and seminall in the chameleon, unto its conservation there is required a solid pasture, and a food congenerous unto the principles of its nature.

The grounds of this opinion are many, the first observed by Theophrastus, was the inflation or swelling of the body made in this animal upon inspiration or drawing in its breath, which people observing, have thought it to feed upon ayre.[369] But this effect is rather occasioned upon the greatnes of its lungs, which in this animal are very large, and by their backward situation, afford a more observable dilatation, and though their lungs bee lesse, the like inflation is also observable in toads.

A second is the continuall hiation or holding open its mouth, which men observing conceive the intention thereof to receive the aliment of ayre; but this is also occasioned by the greatnes of its lungs, for repletion whereof not having a sufficient or ready supply by its nostrils, it is enforced to dilate and hold open the jawes.

The third is the paucitie of blood observed in this animal, scarce at all to be found but in the eye, and about the heart; which defect being observed, inclined some into thoughts, that the ayre was a sufficient maintenance for these exanguious parts. But this defect or rather paucity of blood, is also agreeable unto many other animals, whose solid nutriment wee doe not controvert, as may bee observed in other sorts of lizards, in frogges, and divers fishes, and therefore an horse-leech will hardly be made to fasten upon a fish, and wee doe not read of much blood that was drawn from frogges by mice in that famous battaile of Homer.[370]

The last and most common ground which begat or promoted this opinion, is the long continuation hereof without any visible food, which some precipitously observing, conclude they eate not any at all. It cannot be denyed it is (if not the most of any) a very abstemious animall, and such as by reason of its frigidity, paucity of blood, and latitancy in the Winter, (about which time the observations are often made) will long subsist without a visible sustentation:[371] but a like condition may bee also observed in many other animals, for lizards and leeches, as we have made triall, will live some months without sustenance, and wee have included snailes in glasses all Winter, which have returned to feed againe in the Spring: now these notwithstanding, are not conceived to passe all their lives without food; for so to argue is fallacious, that is, *A minori ad majus, A dicto secundum quid ad dictum simpliciter*, and is moreover sufficiently convicted by experience, and therefore probably other relations are of the same verity, which are of the like affinity, as is the conceit of the Rhintace in Persia, the Canis Levis of America, and the Manucodiata or bird of paradise in India.[372]

To assigne a reason of this abstinence in animals, or declare how without a supply there ensueth no destructive exhaustion, exceedeth the limits of my intention, and intention of my discourse. Fortunius Licetus in his excellent tract, *De his qui diu vivunt sine alimento*, hath very ingeniously attempted it, deducing the cause hereof from an equall conformity of naturall heat and moisture, at least no considerable exuperancy in either;[373] which concurring in an unactive proportion, the naturall heat consumeth not the moisture (whereby ensueth no exhaustion) and the condition of naturall moisture is able to resist the slender action of heat, (whereby it needeth no reparation) and this is evident in snakes, lizards, snails, and divers other insects latitant many moneths in the yeare; which being cold creatures, containing a weak heat, in a crasse or copious humidity, doe long subsist without nutrition: for the activity of the agent, being not able to overmaster the resistance of the patient, there will ensue no deperdition.[374] And upon the like grounds it is, that cold and phlegmatick bodies, and (as Hippocrates determineth) that old men, will best endure fasting.[375] Now the same harmony and stationary constitution, as it happeneth in many species, so doth it fall out sometime in individualls; for wee read of many who have lived long time without aliment, and beside deceites and impostures, there may be veritable relations of some, who without a miracle, and by peculiarity of temper, have far outfasted Elias.[376] [Which notwithstanding doth not take off the miracle; for that may be miraculously effected in one, which is naturally causable in another. Some naturally living unto an hundred; unto which age, others notwithstanding could not attain without a miracle.]

CHAPTER XXII
Of the Oestridge

The common opinion of the oestridge, struthiocamelus, or sparrow-camell conceives that it digesteth iron; and this is confirmed by the affirmations of many; beside swarmes of others, Rhodiginus in his Prelections taketh it for granted, Johannes Langius in his Epistles pleadeth experiment for it, the common picture also confirmeth it which usually describeth this animall, with an horshooe in its mouth;[377] notwithstanding upon enquiry we finde it very questionable, and the negative seemes most reasonably entertained; whose verity indeed wee doe the rather desire, because hereby wee shall relieve our ignorance of one occult quality; for in the list thereof it is accounted, and in that notion imperiously obtruded upon us: for my owne part, although I have had the sight of this animall, I have not had the opportunity of its experiment, but have received great occasions of doubt, from learned discoursers thereon.

For Aristotle and Oppianus who have particularly treated hereof are silent in this singularity, either omitting it as dubious, or as the comment saith, rejecting it as fabulous;[378] Pliny speaketh generally, affirming onely, the digestion is wonderfull in this animall; Ælian delivereth, that it digesteth stones, without any mention of iron;[379] Leo Africanus, who lived in those countries wherein they most abound, speaketh diminutively, and but halfe way into this assertion, *surdum ac simplex animal est, quicquid invenit, absque delectu, usque ad ferrum devorat*:[380] Fernelius in his second booke *De abditis rerum causis*, extenuates it, and Riolanus in his comment thereof positively denyes it:[381] some have experimentally refuted it, as Albertus Magnus, and most plainly of all other Ulysses Aldrovandus, whose words are these, *Ego ferri frusta devorare, dum Tridenti essem, observavi, sed quæ incocta rursus excerneret*, that is, at my being at Trent, I observed the oestridge to swallow iron, but yet to exclude it undigested againe.[382]

Now beside experiment, it is in vaine to attempt against it by philosophicall argument, it being an occult quality, which contemnes the law of reason, and defends it selfe by admitting no reason at all; as for its possibility, we shall not at present dispute, nor will we affirme that iron ingested, receiveth in the stomack of the oestridge no alteration whatsoever; but if any such there be, we suspect this effect rather from some way of corrosion, then any of digestion; not any liquid reduction or tendance to chilification by the power of naturall heate, but rather some attrition from an acide and vitriolous humidity in the stomack, which may absterse, and shave the scorious parts thereof;[383] so rusty iron crammed downe the throate of a cock, will become terse and cleare againe in its gizard: so the counter, which according to the relation of *Amatus*, remained a whole yeare in the body of a youth, and came out much consumed at last;[384] might suffer this diminution, rather from sharpe and acide humours, then the strength of naturall heate, as he supposeth. So silver swallowed and retained some time in the body will turne black, as if it had beene dipped in *aqua fortis*, or some corrosive water; but lead will remaine unaltered, for that mettall containeth in it a sweet salt and manifest sugar, whereby it resisteth ordinary corrosion, and will not easily dissolve even in *aqua fortis*: so when for medicall uses, wee take downe the filings of iron or steele, we must not conceive it passeth unaltered from us; for though the grosser parts be excluded againe, yet are the volatile and dissoluble parts extracted, whereby it becomes effectuall in deopilations;[385] and therefore for speedier operation we make extinctions, infusions, and the like, whereby we extract the salt and active parts of the medicine, which being in solution, more easily enter the veynes.[386] And this is that the chymists mainely drive at in the attempt of their *aurum potabile*, that is, to reduce that indigestible substance into such a forme as may not be ejected by seidge, but enter the cavities, and lesse accessible parts of the body, without corrosion.[387]

The ground of this conceit is its swallowing downe fragments of iron, which men observing, by a forward illation, have therefore conceived it digesteth them;[388] which is an inference not to be admitted, as being a fallacy of the consequent, that is, concluding a position of the consequent, from the position of the antecedent: for many things are swallowed by animals, rather for condiment, gust, or medicament, then any substantiall nutriment. So poultrey, and especially the turkey, do of themselves take downe stones, and wee have found at one time in the gizard of a turkey no lesse then seven hundred: now these rather concurre unto digestion, then are themselves digested, for we have found them also in the guts, and excrements, but their discent is very slow, for we have given them in paste, stones and final pieces of iron, which eighteene dayes after we have found remaining in the gizard;[389] and therefore the experiment of Langius and others might bee mistaken, whilst after the taking they expected it should come downe within a day or two after: thus also we swallow cherry-stones, but void them unconcocted, and we usually say they preserve us from surfeit, for being hard bodies they conceive a strong and durable heate in the stomack, and so prevent the crudities of their fruit;[390] and upon the like reason do culinary operators observe that flesh boyles best, when the bones are boyled with it: thus dogs will eate grasse, which they digest not: thus camels to make the water sapide do raise the mud with their feet: thus horses will knabble at walls, pigeons delight in salt stones, rats will gnaw iron, and Aristotle saith the elephant swalloweth stones;[391] and thus may also the oestridge swallow iron, not as his proper aliment, but for the ends above expressed, and even as we observe the like in other animals.

[And whether these fragments of iron and hard substances swallowed by the ostrich, have not also that use in their stomacks, which they have in other birds;[392] that is, in some way to supply the use of teeth, by commolition, grinding and compression of their proper aliment, upon the action of the strongly conformed muscles of the stomack; as the honor'd Dr. Harvey discourseth, may also be considered.]

What effect therefore may bee expected from the stomack of an oestridge by application alone to further digestion in ours, beside the experimentall refute of Galen, wee referre it unto the considerations above alledged; or whether there be any more credit to be given unto the medicine of Ælian, who affirmes the stones they swallow have a peculiar vertue for the eyes, then that of Hermolaus and Pliny drawne from the urine of this animall, let them determine who can swallow so strange a transmission of qualities, or beleeve that any bird or flying animall doth urine beside the bat.[393]

CHAPTER XXIII
Of Unicornes Hornes

Great account and much profit is made of unicornes horne, at least of that which beareth the name thereof, wherein notwithstanding, many I perceive suspect an imposture, and some conceive there is no such animall extant: herein therefore to draw up our determinations, beside the severall places of Scripture mentioning this animall (which some perhaps may contend to be onely meant of the rhinoceros) wee are so farre from denying there is any unicorne at all, that wee affirme there are many kinds thereof;[394] in the number of quadrupedes, wee will concede no lesse then five; that is, the Indian oxe, the Indian asse, the rhinoceros, the oryx, and that which is more eminently termed *monoceros*, or *unicornis*: some in the list of fishes, as that described by Olaus, Albertus, and many other:[395] and some unicornes wee will allow even among insects, as those foure kinds of nasicornous beetles described by Muffetus.[396]

Secondly, although we concede there be many unicornes, yet are we still to seeke; for whereunto to affixe this horne in question, or to determine from which thereof we receive this magnified medicine, we have no assurance, or any satisfactory decision: for although we single out one, and antonomastically thereto assigne the name of the unicorne, yet can we not be secure what creature is meant thereby, what constant shape it holdeth, or in what number to be received:[397] for as far as our endeavours discover, this animall is not uniformely described, but differently set forth by those that undertake it: Pliny affirmeth it is a fierce and terrible creature, Vartomannus a tame and mansuete animall:[398] those which Garcias ab Horto described about the cape of Good Hope, were beheld with heads like horses;[399] those which Vartomannus beheld, he described with the head of a deere; Pliny, Ælian, Solinus, and after these from ocular assurance Paulus Venetus affirmeth the feet of the unicorne are undivided, and like the elephants: but those two which Vartomannus beheld at Mecha, were as he describeth footed like a goate:[400] as Ælian describeth, it is in the bignesse of an horse, as Vartomannus of a colt, that which Thevet speaketh of was not so big as an heifer;[401] but Paulus Venetus affirmeth, they are but little lesse then elephants; which are discriminations very materiall, and plainly declare, that under the same name authors describe not the same animall: so that the unicornes horne of the one, is not that of another, although we proclaime an equall vertue in either.

Thirdly, although we were agreed what animall this was, or differed not in its description, yet would this also afford but little satisfaction, for the horne we commonly extoll, is not the same with that of the ancients; for that in the description of Ælian and Pliny was blacke, this which is shewed amongst us is commonly white, none black; and of those five which Scaliger beheld, though one spadiceous, or of a light red, and two inclining to red, yet was there not any of this complexion among them.[402]

Fourthly, what hornes soever they be which passe amongst us, they are not surely the hornes of any one kinde of animall, but must proceed from severall sorts of unicornes; for some are wreathed, some not: that famous one which is preserved at S. Dennis neere Paris, hath awfractuous spires, and chocleary turnings about it, which agreeth with the description of the unicornes horne in Ælian;[403] those two in the treasure of Saint Mark are plaine, and best accord with those of the Indian asse, or the descriptions of other unicornes: Albertus Magnus describeth one ten foote long, and at the base about thirteene inches compasse;[404] and that of Antwerpe which Goropius Becanus describeth, is not much inferiour unto it;[405] which best agree unto the descriptions of the sea-unicornes, for these, as Olaus affirmeth, are of that strength and bignesse, as able to penetrate the ribs of ships; the same is more probable, in that it was brought from Island, from whence, as Becanus affirmeth, three other were brought in his dayes;[406] and we have heard of some which have beene found by the sea side, and brought unto us from America: so that while we commend the unicornes horne, and conceive it peculiar but unto one animall, under apprehension of the same virtue, wee use very many, and commend that effect from all, which every one confineth unto some one, hee hath either seene or described.

Fifthly, although there be many unicornes, and consequently many hornes, yet many there are which beare that name, and currantly passe among us, which are no hornes at all; and such are those fragments, and pieces of *Lapis Ceratites*, commonly termed *Cornufossile*, whereof Boetius had no lesse then twenty severall sorts presented him for unicorns horn:[407] hereof in subterraneous cavities, and under the earth there are many to be found in severall parts of Germany, which are but the lapidescencies, and petrifactive mutations of hard bodies, sometime of horne, of teeth, of bones, and branches of trees, whereof there are some so imperfectly converted, as to retaine the odor and qualities of their originals, as he relateth of pieces of ashe and wallnut.[408] Againe, in most if not all which passe amongst us, and are extolled for precious hornes, wee discover not one affection common unto other hornes, that is, they mollifie not with fire, they soften not upon decoction, or infusion, nor will they afford a jelly, or muccilaginous concretion in either;[409] which notwithstanding wee may effect in goates hornes, sheepes, cows, and harts horne, in the horne of the rhinoceros, the horne of the pristis or sword-fish.[410] [Nor do they become friable or easily powderable by philosophical calcination, that is, from the vapor or steam of water, but split and rift contrary to other horns.] Briefly that which is commonly received, and whereof there be so many fragments preserved in England, is not onely no horne, but a substance harder then a bone, that is, the tooth of a morse or sea-horse, in the midst of the solider part containing a curdled graine, which is not to be found in ivory; this in northerne regions is of frequent use for hafts of knives, or hilts of swords, and being burnt becomes a good remedy for fluxes: but antidotically used, and exposed for unicornes horne, it is an insufferable delusion, and with more veniable deceit, it might have beene practised in harts horne.

[The like deceit may be practised in the teeth of other sea-animals;[411] in the teeth also of the hippopotamus, or great animall which frequenteth the River Nilus: for we reade that the same was anciently used in stead of ivory or elephants tooth. Nor is it to be omitted, what hath been formerly suspected, but now confirmed by Olaus Wormius, and Thomas Bartholinus and others, that those long hornes preserved as pretious rarities in many places, are but the teeth of narhwhales; to be found about Island, Greenland, and other northern regions, of many feet long, commonly wreathed, very deeply fastned in the upper jaw, and standing directly forward, graphically described in Bartholinus, according unto one sent from a Bishop of Island, not separated from the crany. Hereof Mercator hath taken notice in his description of Island: some relations hereof there seem to be in Purchas, who also delivereth that the horn at Windsor, was in his second voyage brought hither by Frobisher. These before the northern discoveries, as unknown rarities, were carried by Merchants into all parts of Europe; and though found on the Sea-shoar, were sold at very high rates; but are now become more common, and probably in time will prove of little esteem; and the bargain of Julius the third, be accounted a very hard one, who stuck not to give many thousand crowns for one.]

[Nor is it great wonder we may be so deceived in this, being daily gulled in the brother antidote bezoar; whereof though many be false, yet one there passeth amongst us of more intolerable delusion; somewhat paler then the true stone, and given by women in the extremity of great diseases, which notwithstanding is no stone, but seems to be the stony seed of some lithospermum or greater grumwell; or the lobus echinatus of Clusius, called also the bezoar nut; for being broken, it discovereth a kernell of a leguminous smell and tast, bitter like a lupine, and will swell and sprout if set in the ground, and therefore more serviceable for issues, then dangerous and virulent diseases.]

Sixtly, although we were satisfied we had the unicornes horne, yet were it no injury unto reason to question the efficacy thereof, or whether those virtues which are pretended do properly belong unto it; for what we observe (and it escaped not the observation of Paulus Jovius many years past) none of the ancients ascribed any medicinall or antidotall virtue unto the unicornes horne;[412] and that which Ælian extolleth, who was the first and onely man of the ancients who spake of the medicall virtue of any unicorne, was the horne of the Indian asse, whereof, saith he, the princes of those parts make boales and drinke therein, as preservatives against poyson, convulsions, and the falling-sicknesse;[413] now the description of that horne is not agreeable unto that we commend; for that (saith he) is red above, white below, and black in the middle, which is very different from ours, or any to bee seene amongst us; and thus, though the description of the unicorne be very ancient, yet was there of old no virtue ascribed unto it, and although this amongst us receive the opinion of the same virtue, yet is it not the same horne whereunto the ancients ascribed it.

Lastly, although we allow it an antidotall efficacy, and such as the ancients commended, yet are there some virtues ascribed thereto by modernes not easily to be received; and it hath surely falne out in this as other magnified medicines, whose operations effectuall in some diseases, are presently extended unto all: that some antidotall quality it may have wee have no reason to deny; for since elkes hoofes and hornes are magnified for epilepsies, since not onely the bone in the heart, but the horne of a deere is alexipharmacall, and ingredient into the confection of hyacinth, and the electuary of Maximilian, wee cannot without prejudice except against the efficacy of this:[414] but when we affirme it is not onely antidotall to proper venomes, and substances destructive by qualities, we cannot expresse; but that it resisteth also sublimate, arsenick, and poysons which kill by second qualities, that is, by corrosion of parts, I doubt we exceed the properties of its nature, and the promises of experiment will not secure the adventure: and therefore in such extremities, whether there be not more probable reliefe from fat and oylie substances, which are the open tyrants of salt and corrosive bodies, then precious and cordiall medicines which operate by secret and disputable proprieties; or whether he that swallowed lime, and dranke downe mercury water, did not more reasonably place his cure in milke, butter, or oyle, then if he had recurred unto pearle and bezoar, common reason at all times, and necessity in the like case would easily determine.

Since therefore there be many unicornes, since that whereto wee appropriate a horne is so variously described, that it seemeth either never to have beene seene by two persons, or not to have beene one animall; since though they agreed in the description of the animall, yet is not the horne wee extoll the same with that of the ancients; since what hornes soever they be that passe among us, they are not the hornes of one but severall animals: since many in common use and high esteeme are no hornes at all: since if they were true hornes, yet might their vertues be questioned: since though we allowed some virtues, yet were not others to be received, with what security a man may rely on this remedy, the mistresse of fooles hath already instructed some, and to wisdome (which is never too wise to learne) it is not too late to consider.

CHAPTER XXIV
That all Animals of the Land, are in their kinde in the Sea

That all animals of the land, are in their kinde in the sea, although received as a principle, is a tenent very questionable, and will admit of restraint; for some in the sea are not to be matcht by any enquiry at land, and hold those shapes which terrestrious formes approach not;[415] as may be observed in the moone fish, or orthragoriscus, the severall sorts of raias, torpedos, oysters, and many more; and some there are in the land which were never maintained to be in the sea, as panthers, hyaenas, camels, sheep, molls, and others which carry no name in icthyologie, nor are to be found in the exact descriptions of Rondeletius, Gesner, or Aldrovandus.[416]

Againe, though many there be which make out their nominations, as the hedg-hog, sea-serpents, and others; yet are there also very many that beare the name of animals at land, which hold no resemblance in corporall configuration; in which account we compute *vulpecula*, *canis*, *rana*, *passer*, *cuculus*, *asellus*, *turdus*, *lepus*, *etc.* wherein while some are called the fox, the dog, the sparrow, or frog-fish, and are knowne by common names with those at land; as their describers attest, they receive not these appellations, as we conceive, from a totall similitude in figure, but any concurrence in common accidents, in colour, condition, or single conformation: as for sea-horses which much confirme this assertion, in their common descriptions, they are but crotesco deliniations which fill up empty spaces in maps, and meere pictoriall inventions, not any physicall shapes:[417] sutable unto those which (as Plinie delivereth) Praxiteles long agoe set out in the temple of Domitius:[418] for that which is commonly called a sea-horse is properly called a morse, and makes not out that shape: that which the ancients named hippocampus is a little animall about six inches long, and not preferred beyond the classis of insects: that they tearmed hippopotamus an amphibious animall, about the river Nile, so little resembleth an horse, that as Mathiolus observeth, in all except the feet, it better makes out a swine: that which they tearmed a lion, was but a kinde of lobster: and that they called the beare, was but one kinde of crab, and that which they named bos marinus, was not as we conceive a fish resembling an oxe, but a skaite or thornbacke, so named from its bignesse, expressed by the Greek word *bous*, which is a prefixe of augmentation to many words in that language.

And therefore although it be not denied that some in the water doe carry a justifiable resemblance to some at the land, yet are the major part which beare their names unlike; nor doe they otherwise resemble the creatures on earth, then they on earth the constellations which passe under animall names in heaven: nor the dog-fish at sea much more make out the dog of the land, then that his cognominall or name-sake in the heavens. Now if from a similitude in some, it bee reasonable to infer a correspondency in all, we may draw this analogie of animalls upon plants; for vegetables there are which carry a neare and allowable similitude unto animals, as we elsewhere declare: wee might also presume to conclude that animall shapes were generally made out in mineralls: for severall stones there are that beare their names in relation to animals parts, as lapis anguinus, conchites, echinites, encephalites, ægopthalmus, and many more, as will appeare in the writers of minerals, and especially in Boetius.[419]

Moreover if we concede, that the animalls of one element, might beare the names of those in the other, yet in strict reason the watery productions should have the prenomination: and they of the land rather derive their names, then nominate those of the sea: for the watery plantations were first existent, and as they enjoyed a priority in forme, had also in nature precedent denominations:[420] but falling not under that nomenclature of Adam, which unto terrestrious animalls assigned a name appropriate unto their natures, from succeeding spectators they received arbitrary appellations, and were respectively denominated unto creatures knowne at land, which in themselves had independent names, and not to bee called after them, which were created before them.

Lastly, by this assertion wee restraine the hand of God, and abridge the variety of the creation; making the creatures of one element, but an acting over those of an other, and conjoyning as it were the species of things which stood at distance in the intellect of God, and though united in the chaos, had several seeds of their creation: for although in that indistinguisht masse, all things seemed one, yet separated by the voyce of God, according to their species they came out in incommunicated varieties, and irrelative seminalities, as well as divided places; and so although we say the world was made in sixe dayes, yet was there as it were a world in every one, that is, a distinct creation of distinguisht creatures, a distinction in time of creatures divided in nature, and a severall approbation, and survey in every one.

[CHAPTER XXV[421]

Concerning the common course of Diet, in making choice of some Animals, and abstaining from eating others

Why we confine our food unto certain animals, and totally reject some others; how these distinctions crept into severall nations; and whether this practice be built upon solid reason, or chiefly supported by custom or opinion; may admit consideration.

For first there is no absolute necessity to feed on any; and if we resist not the streame of authority, and severall diductions from holy Scripture: there was no sarcophagie before the flood;[422] and without the eating of flesh, our fathers from vegetable aliments, preserved themselves unto longer lives, then their posterity by any other. For whereas it is plainly said, I have given you every herb which is upon the face of all the earth, and every tree, to you it shall be for meat; presently after the deluge, when the same had destroyed or infirmed the nature of vegetables, by an expression of enlargement, it is again delivered: every moving thing that liveth, shall be meat for you, even as the green herb, have I given you all things.[423]

And therefore although it be said that Abel was a shepherd, and it be not readily conceived, the first men would keep sheep, except they made food thereof:[424] great expositors will tell us, that it was partly for their skinnes, wherewith they were cloathed, partly for their milk, whereby they were sustained; and partly for sacrifices, which they also offered.

And though it may seem improbable, that they offered flesh, yet eat not thereof; and Abel can hardly be said to offer the firstlings of his flock, and the fat or acceptable part, if men used not to taste the same, whereby to raise such distinctions: some will confine the eating of flesh unto the line of Cain, who extended their luxury, and confined not unto the rule of God. That if at any time the line of Seth eat flesh, it was extraordinary, and only at their sacrifices; or else (as Grotius hinteth) if any such practice there were, it was not from the beginning; but from that time when the waies of men were corrupted, and whereof it is said, that the wickednesse of mans heart was great;[425] the more righteous part of mankind probably conforming unto the diet prescribed in Paradise, and the state of innocency; and yet however the practice of men conformed, this was the injunction of God, and might be therefore sufficient, without the food of flesh.

That they fed not on flesh, at least the faithfull party before the flood, may become more probable, because they refrained the same for some time after. For so was it generally delivered of the golden age and raigne of Saturne; which is conceived the time of Noah, before the building of Babel. And he that considereth how agreeable this is unto the traditions of the Gentiles; that that age was of one tongue: that Saturn devoured all his sonnes but three, that he was the sonne of Oceanus and Thetis; that a ship was his symbole, that he taught the culture of vineyards, and the art of husbandry, and was therefore described with a sickle, may well conceive, these traditions had their originall in Noah.[426] Nor did this practice terminate in him, but was continued at least in many after: as (beside the Pythagorians of old, and Bannyans now in India, who upon single opinions refrain the food of flesh) ancient records doe hint or plainly deliver. Although we descend not so low, as that of Æsclepiades delivered by Porphyrius, that men began to feed on flesh in the raign of Pygmaleon brother of Dido, who invented severall torments, to punish the eaters of flesh.[427]

Nor did men only refrain from the flesh of beasts at first, but as some will have it, beasts from one another. And if we should beleeve very grave conjecturers, carnivorous animals now, were not flesh devourers then, according to the expression of the divine provision for them. To every beast of the earth, and to every fowle of the ayre, I have given every green herbe for meat, and it was so.[428] As is also collected from the store laid up in the Ark; wherein there seems to have been no fleshie provision for carnivorous Animals. For of every kind of unclean beast there went but two into the Ark: and therefore no stock of flesh to sustain them many daies, much lesse almost a year.[429]

But when ever it be acknowledged that men began to feed on flesh, yet how they betook themselves after to particular kindes thereof, with rejection of many others, is a point not cleerly determined. As for the distinction of clean and unclean beasts, the originall is obscure, and salveth not our practice.[430] For no animall is naturally unclean, or hath this character in nature; and therefore whether in this distinction there were not some mysticall intention: whether Moses after the distinction made of unclean beasts, did not name these so before the flood by anticipation: whether this distinction before the flood, were not only in regard of sacrifices, as that delivered after was in regard of food: (for many were clean for food, which were unclean for sacrifice) or whether the denomination were but comparative, and of beasts lesse commodious for food, although not simply bad, is not yet resolved.

And as for the same distinction in the time of Moses, long after the flood, from thence we hold no restriction, as being no rule unto nations beside the Jews in dieteticall consideration, or naturall choice of diet, they being enjoyned or prohibited certain foods upon remote and secret intentions; especially thereby to avoid community with the Gentiles upon promiscuous commensality: or to divert them from the idolatry of Ægypt whence they came, they were enjoyned to eat the Gods of Egypt in the food of sheep and oxen. Withall in this distinction of animals the consideration was hieroglyphicall; in the bosome and inward sense implying an abstinence from certain vices symbolically intimated from the nature of those animals; as may be well made out in the prohibited meat of swine, cony, owl, and many more.

At least the intention was not medicall, or such as might oblige unto conformity or imitation; for some we refrain which that law alloweth, as locusts and many others; and some it prohibiteth, which are accounted good meat in strict and medicall censure: as beside many fishes which have not finnes and scales, the swine, cony and hare, a dainty dish with the ancients; as is delivered by Galen, testified by Martial, as the popular opinion implied, that men grew fair by the flesh thereof: by the diet of Cato, that is hare and cabbage;[431] and the *jus nigrum*, or black broath of the Spartans, which was made with the blood and bowels of an hare.

And if we take a view of other nations, we shall discover that they refrained many meats upon the like considerations. For in some the abstinence was symbolicall; so Pythagoras enjoyned abstinence from fish: that is, luxurious and dainty dishes; so according to Herodotus, some Ægyptians refrained swines flesh, as an impure and sordid animal: which whoever but touched, was fain to wash himself.[432]

Some abstained superstitiously or upon religious consideration: so the Syrians refrained fish and pigeons; the Ægyptians of old, dogges, eeles, and crocodiles; though Leo Africanus delivers, that many of late, doe eat them with good gust: and Herodotus also affirmeth, that the Egyptians of Elephantina (unto whom they were not sacred,) did eat thereof in elder times:[433] and writers testify, that they are eaten at this day in India and America. And so, as Cæsar reports, unto the ancient Britains it was piaculous to taste a goose, which dish at present no table is without.[434]

Unto some nations the abstinence was politicall and for some civil advantage: so the Thessalians refrained storkes, because they destroyed their serpents;[435] and the like in sundry animals is observable in other nations.

And under all these considerations were some animals refrained: so the Jews abstained from swine at first symbolically, as an emblem of impurity; and not for fear of the leprosie, as Tacitus would put upon them.[436] The Cretians superstitiously, upon tradition that Jupiter was suckled in that countrey by a sowe. Some Ægyptians politically, because they supplyed the labour of plowing by rooting up the ground. And upon like considerations perhaps the Phænicians and Syrians fed not on this animall: and as Solinus reports, the Arabians also and Indians. A great part of mankind refraining one of the best foods, and such as Pythagoras himself would eat; who, as Aristoxenus records refus'd not to feed on pigges.[437]

Moreover while we single out severall dishes and reject others, the selection seems but arbitrary, or upon opinion; for many are commended and cryed up in one age, which are decryed and nauseated in another. Thus in the dayes of Mecenas, no flesh was preferred before young asses;[438] which notwithstanding became abominable unto succeeding appetites. At the table of Heliogabalus the combs of cocks were an esteemed service; which country stomacks will not admit at ours.[439] The sumen or belly and dugges of swine with pigge, and sometimes beaten and bruised unto death: the womb of the same animall, especially that was barren, or else had cast her young ones, though a tough and membranous part, was magnified by Roman palats; whereunto nevertheless we cannot perswade our stomacks. How alec, muria, and garum, would humour our gust I know not;[440] but surely few there are that could delight in their cyceon; that is, the common draught of honey, cheese, parcht barley-flower, oyl and wine; which notwithstanding was a commended mixture, and in high esteem among them. We mortifie our selves with the diet of fish, and think we fare coursly if we refrain from the flesh of other animals. But antiquity held another opinion hereof: when Pythagoras in prevention of luxury advised, not so much as to taste on fish. Since the Rhodians were wont to call them clowns that eat flesh: and since Plato to evidence the temperance of the noble Greeks before Troy, observed, that it was not found they fed on fish, though they lay so long near the Hellespont; and was only observed in the companions of Menelaus, that being almost starved, betook themselves to fishing about Pharos.

Nor will (I fear) the attest or prescript of philosophers and physitians, be a sufficient ground to confirm or warrant common practice, as is deducible from ancient writers, from Hippocrates, Galen, Simeon Sethi: and the later tracts of

Nonnus and Castellanus.[441] So Aristotle and Albertus commend the flesh of young hawks: Galen the flesh of foxes about Autumne when they feed on grapes:[442] but condemneth quails, and ranketh geese but with oestriges: which notwithstanding, present practice and every table extolleth. Men think they have fared hardly, if in times of extremity they have descended so low as doggs: but Galen delivereth, that young, fat and gelded, they were the food of many nations: and Hippocrates ranketh the flesh of whelps with that of birds: who also commends them against the spleen, and to promote conception. The opinion in Galens time, which Pliny also followeth, deeply condemned horse-flesh, and conceived the very blood thereof destructive; but no diet is more common among the Tartars, who also drink their blood.[443] And though this may only seem an adventure of northern stomacks, yet as Herodotus tells us, in the hotter clime of Persia, the same was a conviviall dish, and solemnly eaten at the feasts of their nativities: whereat they dressed whole horses, camels and asses; contemning the poverty of Grecian feasts, as unfurnish'd of dishes sufficient to fill the bellies of their guests.

Again, while we confine our diet in severall places, all things almost are eaten, if we take in the whole earth: for that which is refused in one country, is accepted in another, and in the collective judgment of the world, particular distinctions are overthrown. Thus were it not hard to shew, that tigers, elephants, camels, mice, bats and others, are the food of severall countries; and Lerius with others delivers, that some Americans eat of all kindes, not refraining toads and serpents: and some have run so high, as not to spare the flesh of man:[444] a practice inexcusable, not to be drawn into example, a diet beyond the rule and largest indulgence of God.

As for the objection against beasts and birds of prey, it acquitteth not our practice, who observe not this distinction in fishes: nor regard the same in our diet of pikes, perches and eels; Nor are we excused herein, if we examine the stomacks of mackerels, cods, and whitings. Nor is the foulnesse of feed sufficient to justifie our choice; for (beside their naturall heat is able to convert the same into laudable aliment) we refuse not many whose diet is more impure then some which we reject; as may be considered in hogs, ducks, puets, and many more.

Thus we perceive the practise of diet doth hold no certain course, nor solid rule of selection or confinement; some in an indistinct voracity eating almost any, other out of a timerous pre-opinion, refraining very many. Wherein indeed necessity, reason and physick, are the best determinators. Surely many animals may be fed on, like many plants; though not in alimentall, yet medicall considerations: whereas having raised antipathies by prejudgement or education, we often nauseate proper meats, and abhor that diet which disease or temper requireth.

Now whether it were not best to conform unto the simple diet of our fore-fathers, whether pure and simple waters were not more healthfull then fermented liquors; whether there be not an ample sufficiency without all flesh, in the food of honey, oyl, and the several parts of milk: in the variety of grains, pulses, and all sorts of fruits; since either bread or beverage may be made almost of all? whether nations have rightly confined unto severall meats? or whether the common food of one countrey be not more agreeable unto another? how indistinctly all tempers apply unto the same, and how the diet of youth and old age is confounded: were considerations much concerning health, and might prolong our daies, but must not this discourse.]

[CHAPTER XXVI[445]
Of Sperma-Ceti, and the Sperma-Ceti Whale

What sperma-ceti is, men might justly doubt, since the learned Hofmanus in his work of thirty years, saith plainly, *Nescio quid sit.*[446] And therefore need not wonder at the variety of opinions; while some conceived it to be *flos maris*, and many, a bituminous substance floating upon the sea.[447]

That it was not the spawn of the whale, according to vulgar conceit, or nominal appellation phylosophers have always doubted: not easily conceiving the seminal humour of animals, should be inflamable; or of a floating nature.

That it proceedeth from a whale, beside the relation of Clusius and other learned observers, was indubitably determined, not many years since by a sperma-ceti whale, cast on our coast of Norfolk.[*448] Which, to lead on further inquiry, we cannot omit to inform. It contained no less then sixty foot in length, the head somewhat peculiar, with a large prominency over the mouth; teeth only in the lower jaw, received into fleshly sockets in the upper. The weight of the largest

* Near Wells.

about two pound: no gristly substances in the mouth, commonly called whale-bones; only two short finns seated forwardly on the back; the eyes but small, the pizell large, and prominent. A lesser whale of this kind above twenty years ago, was cast upon the same shore.*

* Near Hunstanton.

The description of this whale seems omitted by Gesner, Rondeletius, and the first editions of Aldrovandus; but described in the Latin impression of Pareus, in the Exoticks of Clusius, and the natural history of Nirembergius; but more amply in icons and figures of Johnstonus.[449]

Mariners (who are not the best nomenclators) called it a jubartus, or rather gibbartas. Of the same appellation we meet with one in Rondeletius, called by the French gibbar, from its round and gibbous back.[450] The name gibbarta we find also given unto one kind of Greenland whales: but this of ours seemed not to answer the whale of that denomination; but was more agreeable unto the trumpa or sperma-ceti whale: according to the account of our Greenland describers in Purchas.[451] And maketh the third among the eight remarkable whales of that Coast.

Out of the head of this whale, having been dead divers daies, and under putrifaction, flowed streams of oyl and sperma-ceti; which was carefully taken up and preserved by the coasters. But upon breaking up, the magazin of sperma-ceti, was found in the head lying in folds and courses, in the bigness of goose eggs, encompassed with large flaxie substances, as large as a mans head, in form of hony-combs, very white and full of oyl.

Some resemblance or trace hereof there seems to be in the *physiter* or *capidolio* of Rondeletius;[452] while he delivers, that a fatness more liquid then oyl, runs from the brain of that animal; which being out, the reliques are like the scales of sardinos pressed into a mass; which melting with heat, are again concreted by cold. And this many conceive to have been the fish which swallowed Jonas.[453] Although for the largeness of the mouth, and frequency in those seas, it may possibly be the *lamia*.

Some part of the sperma-ceti found on the shore was pure, and needed little depuration;[454] a great part mixed with fetid oyl, needing good preparation, and frequent expression, to bring it to a flakie consistency. And not only the head, but other parts contained it. For the carnous parts being roasted, the oyl dropped out, an axungious and thicker part subsiding;[455] the oyl it self contained also much in it, and still after many years some is obtained from it.

Greenland enquirers seldom meet with a whale of this kind: and therefore it is but a contingent commodity, not reparable from any other. It flameth white and candent like champhire, but dissolveth not in *aqua fortis*, like it. Some lumps containing about two ounces, kept ever since in water, afford a fresh, and flosculous smell.[456] Well prepared and separated from the oyl, it is of a substance unlikely to decay, and may out last the oyl required in the composition of Mathiolus.[457]

Of the large quantity of oyl, what first came forth by expression from the sperma-ceti, grew very white and clear, like that of almonds or ben. What came by decoction was red. It was found to spend much in the vessels which contained it: It freezeth or coagulateth quickly with cold, and the newer soonest. It seems different from the oyl of any other animal, and very much frustrated the expectation of our soap-boylers, as not incorporating or mingling with their lyes. But it mixeth well with painting colours, though hardly drieth at all. Combers of wooll made use hereof, and country people for cuts, aches and hard tumours. It may prove of good medical use; and serve for a ground in compounded oyls and balsams. Distilled, it affords a strong oyl, with a quick and piercing water. Upon evaporation it gives a balsame, which is better performed with turpentine distilled with sperma-ceti.

Had the abominable scent permitted, enquiry had been made into that strange composure of the head, and hillock of flesh about it. Since the work-men affirmed, they met with sperma-ceti before they came to the bone, and the head yet preserved, seems to confirm the same. The sphincters inserving unto the fistula or spout, might have been examined, since they are so notably contrived in other cetaceous animals; as also the larynx or throtle, whether answerable unto that of dolphins and porposes in the strange composure and figure which it maketh. What figure the stomack maintained in this animal of one jaw of teeth, since in porposes, which abound in both, the ventricle is trebly divided, and since in that formerly taken nothing was found but weeds and a loligo.[458] The heart, lungs, and kidneys, had not escaped; wherein are remarkable differences from animals of the land, likewise what humor the bladder contained, but especially the seminal parts, which might have determined the difference of that humor, from this which beareth its name.

In vain it was to rake for ambergreece in the panch of this Leviathan, as Greenland discovers, and attests of experience dictate, that they sometimes swallow great lumps thereof in the sea; insufferable fetour denying that enquiry. And yet if, as Paracelsus encourageth, ordure makes the best musk, and from the most fetid substances may be drawn the most odoriferous essences; all that had not Vespasians nose, might boldly swear, here was a subject fit for such extractions.[459]]

CHAPTER XXVII[460]

Compendiously of sundry tenents concerning other Animals, which examined prove either False or Dubious

1. And first from times of great antiquity, and before the melodie of syrens, the musicall notes of swans hath been commended, and that they sing most sweetly before their death. For thus we read in Plato *de Legibus*, that from the opinion of metempsychosis, or transmigration of the soules of men into the bodies of beasts most sutable unto their humane condition, after his death, Orpheus the musician became a swan.[461] Thus was it the bird of Apollo the god of musicke by the Greekes, and a hieroglyphick of musick among the Ægyptians, from whom the Greeks derived the conception, hath been the affirmation of many Latines, and hath not wanted assertors almost from every nation.

All which notwithstanding we find this relation doubtfully received by Ælian, as an hearsay account by Bellonius, as a false one by Pliny, expresly refuted by Myndius in Athenæus, and severely rejected by Scaliger, whose words unto Cardan are these. *De Cygni vero cantu suavissimo quem cum parente mendaciorum Græcia jactare ausus es, ad Luciani tribunal, apud quem novi aliquid dicas, statuo.*[462] Authors also that countenance it, speak not satisfactorily of it. Some affirming they sing not till they die; some that they sing, yet die not; some speake generally, as though this note were in all; some but particularly, as though it were only in some; some in places remote, and where we can have no trial of it; others in places where every experience can refute it, as Aldrovand upon relation, delivered, concerning the musicke of the swans on the river of the Thames neer London.[463]

Now that which countenanceth, and probably confirmeth this opinion, is the strange and unusuall conformation of the winde pipe, or vocall organ in this animall:* observed first by Aldrovandus, and conceived by some contrived for this intention: for in its length it far exceedeth the gullet, and hath in the chest a sinuous revolution, that is, when it ariseth from the lunges, it ascendeth not directly unto the throat, but ascending first into a capsulary reception of the breast bone, by a serpentine and trumpet recurvation it ascendeth againe into the neck, and so by the length thereof a great quantity of ayre is received, and by the figure thereof a musicall modulation effected. But to speak indifferently (what Aldrovand himself acknowledgeth) this formation of the weazon, is not peculiar unto the swan, but common also, unto the platea or shovelard, a bird of no musicall throat; and as himselfe confesseth may thus be contrived in the swan to contain a larger stock of ayre, whereby being to feed on weeds at the bottom, they might the longer space detain their heads under water. And indeed were this formation peculiar, or had they unto this effect an advantage from this part: yet have they a knowne and open disadvantage from another, which is not common unto any singing bird wee know, that is a flat bill: for no latirostrous animal (whereof neverthelesse there are no slender numbers) were ever commended for their note, or accounted among those animals which have been instructed to speake.[464]

* This figuration to be found in elkes, and not in common swans.

When therefore we consider the dissention of authors, the falsity of relations, the indisposition of the organs, and the immusicall note of all we ever beheld or heard of, if generally taken and comprehending all swans, or of all places, we cannot assent thereto. Surely he that is bit with a tarantula, shall never be cured by this musicke, and with the same hopes we expect to hear the harmony of the spheres.

2. That there is a speciall proprietie in the flesh of peacocks rost or boiled, to preserve a long time incorrupted, hath been the assertion of many, stands yet confirmed by Austine, *De Civitate Dei*, by Gygas Sempronius, in Aldrovand, and the same experiment we can confirme our selves, in the brawne or fleshy parts of peacocks so hanged up with thred, that they touch no place whereby to contract a moisture; and hereof we have made triall both in the Summer and Winter.[465] The reason some I perceive, attempt to make out from the siccity

and driness of its flesh, and some are content to rest in a secret propriety thereof. As for the siccity of the flesh, it is more remarkable in other animals, as ægles, hawkes, and birds of prey; and that it is a propriety, or agreeable unto none other, we cannot with reason admit: for the same preservation, or rather incorruption we have observed in the flesh of turkeys, capons, hares, partridge, venison, suspended freely in the ayre, and after a yeare and a halfe, dogs have not refused to eat them.

As for the other conceit that a peacocke is ashamed when he looks on his legges, as is commonly held, and also delivered by Cardan, beside what hath been said against it by Scaliger, let them beleeve that hold specificall deformities, or that any part can seeme unhansome to their eyes, which hath appeared good and beautifull unto their makers.[466] The occasion of this conceit, might first arise from a common observation, that when they are in their pride, that is, advance their traine, if they decline their necke to the ground, they presently demit and let fall the same: which indeed they cannot otherwise doe, for contracting their body, and being forced to draw in their foreparts, to establish the hinder in the elevation of the traine, if the foreparts depart and incline to the ground, the hinder grow too weake, and suffer the traine to fall. And the same in some degree is also observeable in turkyes.

3. That storkes are to be found and will onely live in republikes or free states, is a pretty conceit to advance the opinion of popular policies, and from antipathies in nature, to disparage monarchicall government. But how far agreeable unto truth, let them consider who read in Plinie, that among the Thessalians who were governed by kings, and much abounded with serpents, it was no lesse then capitall to kill a storke.[467] That the ancient Ægyptians honoured them, whose government was from all times monarchicall. That Bellonius affirmeth, men make them nests in *France*.[468] And lastly, how Jeremy the prophet delivered himselfe unto his countreymen, whose government was at that time monarchical, *Milvus in Cælo cognovit tempus suum. Turtur Hirundo et Ciconia custodierunt tempus adventus sui.*[469] Wherein to exprobrate their stupiditie, he induceth the providence of storkes. Now if the bird had been unknown, the illustration had been obscure, and the exprobation but improper.

4. That a bittor maketh that mugient noyse, or as we terme it bumping by putting its bill into a reed as most beleeve, or as Bellonius and Aldrovand conceive, by putting the same in

water or mud, and after a while retaining the ayre by suddenly excluding it againe, is not so easily made out.[470] For my own part though after diligent enquiry, I could never behold them in this motion; notwithstanding by others whose observations we have expresly requested, we are informed, that some have beheld them making this noise on the shore, their bills being far enough removed from reed or water; that is, first strongly attracting the aire, and unto a manifest distention of the neck, and presently after with great contention and violence excluding the same againe. As for what others affirme of putting their bill in water or mud, it is also hard to make out. For what may bee observed from any that walketh the fenns, there is little intermission, nor any observable pawse, between the drawing in and sending forth of their breath. And the expiration or breathing forth doth not onely produce a noise, but the inspiration or haling in of the ayre, affordeth a sound that may bee heard almost a flight-shoot.[471]

Now the reason of this strange and peculiar noise, is well deduced from the conformation of the windepipe, which in this birde is different from other volatiles.[472] For at the upper extream it hath no larinx, or throttle to qualifie the sound, and at the other end, by two branches deriveth it selfe into the lunges. Which division consisteth onely of semicircular fibers, and such as attaine but half way round the part; by which formation they are dilatable into larger capacities, and are able to containe a fuller proportion of ayre, which being with violence sent up the weazon, and finding no resistance by the larinx, it issueth forth in a sound like that from cavernes, and such as sometimes subterraneous eruptions, from hollow rocks afford; as Aristotle observeth in a problem of the twenty fifth section, and is observable in pichards, bottles, and that instrument which Aponensis upon that probleme describeth, wherewith in Aristotles time gardiners affrighted birdes.[473]

5. That whelps are blinde nine dayes and then begin to see, is the common opinion of all, and some will be apt enough to descend unto oathes upon it. But this I finde not answerable unto experience; for upon a strict observation of many, I have not found any that see the ninth day, few before the twelfth, and the eyes of some will not open before the fourteenth day. And this is agreeable unto the determination of Aristotle: who computeth the time of their anopsie or invision by that of their gestation;[474] for some saith he do go with their yong, the sixt part of a yeer, a day or two over or under, that is, about sixty

dayes or nine weekes, and the whelps of these see not till twelve dayes; some goe the fifth part of a yeer, that is, seventy-one dayes, and these saith he see not before the fourteenth day. Others doe goe the fourth part of a yeer, that is, three whole months, and these saith hee are without sight no lesse then seventeen dayes: wherein although the accounts be different, yet doth the least thereof exceed the terme of nine dayes which is so generally receaved. And this compute of Aristotle doth generally overthrow the common cause alleadged for this effect, that is, a precipitation or over hasty exclusion before the birth be perfect, according unto the vulgar adage. *Festinans canis cœcos parit catulos*:[475] for herein the whelps of longest gestation, are also the latest in vision. The manner hereof is this. At the first littering their eyes are fastly closed, that is, by coalition or joyning together of the eyelids, and so continue untill about the twefth day, at which time they begin to separate, and may be easily divelled or parted asunder; they open at the inward canthis, or greater angle of the eye, and so by degrees dilate themselves quite open. An effect very strange, and the cause of much obscurity, wherein as yet mens enquiries are blinde, and satisfaction acquirable from no man. What ever it be, thus much we may observe, those animalls are onely excluded without sight, which are multiparous and multifidous, that is, which have many at a litter, and have also their feet divided into many portions; for the swine although multiparous, yet being bisulcous, and onely cloven hoofed, is not excluded in this manner, but farrowed with open eyes, as other bisulcous animals.[476]

6. The antipathy between a toad and a spider, and that they poisonously destroy each other is very famous, and solemne stories have been written of their combats, wherein most commonly the victory is given unto the spider. Of what toades and spiders it is to be understood, would be considered. For the phalangium, and deadly spiders, are different from those we generally behold in England.[477] However the verity hereof, as also of many others, wee cannot but desire; for hereby wee might be surely provided of proper antidotes in cases which require them; but what we have observed herein, wee cannot in reason conceale, who having in a glasse included a toad with severall spiders, wee beheld the spiders without resistance to sit upon his head, and passe over all his body, which at last upon advantage hee swallowed down, and that in few houres to

the number of seven. And in the like manner will toades also serve bees, and are accounted an enemy unto their hives.

7. Whether a lyon be also afraid of a cock, as is related by many, and beleeved by most, were very easie in some places to make tryall. Although how far they stand in feare of that animal, we may sufficiently understand, from what is delivered by Camerarius, whose words in his Symbola are these. *Nostris temporibus in Aula serenissimi Principis Bavariæ, unus ex Leonibus miris saltibus in vicinam cujusdam domus aream sese dimisit, ubi Gallinaciorum cantum aut clamores nihil reformidans, ipsos una cum plurimis gallinis devoravit.*[478] That is, in our time in the court of the Prince of Bavaria, one of the lyons leaped downe into a neighbous yard, where nothing regarding the crowing or noise of the cocks, hee eat them up with many other hens. And therefore a very unsafe defensative it is against the fury of this animal, and surely no better then virginity, or blood royall, which Pliny doth place in cock broth: for herewith, saith he, who ever is anoynted (especially if garlick be boiled therein) no lyon or panther will touch him.[479]

8. It is generally conceived, an earewigge hath no wings, and is reckoned amongst impennous insects by many, but hee that shall narrowly observe them, or shall with a needle put aside the short and sheathie cases on their backe, may extend and draw forth two winges of a proportionable length for flight, and larger then many flyes.[480] The experiment of Pennius is yet more perfect, who with a rush or bristle so pricked them as to make them flie.[481]

9. That wormes are exanguious animalls, and such as have no blood at all, is the determination of philosophy, the generall opinion of scholers, and I know not well to dissent from thence my selfe: if so, surely wee want a proper terme whereby to expresse that humor in them which so strictly resembleth blood: and we refer it unto the discernment of others what to determine of that red and sanguineous humor, found more plentifully about the torquis or carneous circle of great wormes in the Spring, affording in linnen or paper an indiscernable tincture from blood; or wherein that differeth from a veyne, which in an apparent blew runneth along the body, and if dexterously pricked with a lancet emitteth a red drop, which pricked on either side it will not readily afford.

In the upper parts of wormes, there are likewise found certaine white and ovall glandulosities which authors terme egs, and in magnifying glasses, they also represent them: how properly may also bee enquired; since if in them there be distinction of sexes, these eggs are to be found in both. For in that which is presumed to bee their coition that is their usuall complication, or rather laterall adhesion above the ground, dividing suddenly with two knives the adhering parts of both, I have found these egges in either.

10. That flyes, bees, etc. doe make that noise or humming sound by their mouth, or as many beleeve with their wings only, would be more warily asserted, if we consulted the determination of Aristotle, who as in sundry other places, so more expressely, in his booke of respiration, affirmeth this sound to be made, by the allision of an inward spirit upon a pellicle, or little membrane about the precinct or pectorall division of their body.[482] If we also consider that a bee or flye, so it be able to move the body, will buz though its head be off; that it will do the like if deprived of wings reserving the head whereby the body may be the better moved. And that some also which are big and lively will humme without either head or wing.

Nor is it only the beating upon this little membrane, by the inward and connaturall spirit as Aristotle determines, or the outward ayre as Scaliger conceiveth which affordeth this humming noise, but perhaps most of the other parts may also concurre hereto, as will be manifest if while they humme we lay our finger on the backe or other parts; for thereupon will be felt a serrous or jarring motion like that which happeneth while we blow on the teeth of a combe through paper; and so if the head or other parts of the trunke be touched with oyle, the sound will be much impaired, if not destroyed: for those being also dry and membranous parts, by attrition of the spirit doe helpe to advance the noyse: and therefore also the sound is strongest in dry weather, and very weake in rainy season, and toward Winter; for then the ayre is moyst, and the inward spirit growing weake, makes a languid and dumbe allision upon the parts.

11. There is found in the Summer a kind of spider called a tainct of a red colour, and so little of body that ten of the largest will hardly outway a graine; this by country people is accounted a deadly poyson unto cowes and horses, who, if they suddenly dye, and swell thereon, ascribe their death hereto, and will commonly say, they have licked a tainct. Now to satisfie the doubts of men, we have called this tradition unto experiment; we have given hereof unto dogs, chickens,

calves and horses, and not in the singular number, yet never could finde the least disturbance ensue. There must be therefore other causes enquired of the sudden death, and swelling of cattell, and perhaps this insect is mistaken, and unjustly accused for some other; for some there are which from elder times, have been observed pernicious unto cattell, as the buprestis or burstcow, the pityocampe or eruca pinuum, by Dioscorides, Galen and Ætius, the staphilinus described by Aristotle and others, or those red phalangious spiders like cantharides mentioned by Muffetus.[483] Now although the animall may be mistaken and the opinion also false, yet in the ground and reason which makes men most to doubt the verity hereof there may be truth enough, that is the small inconsiderable quantity of this insect. For that a poyson cannot destroy in so small a bulke, we have no reason to affirme. For if as Leo Africanus reporteth, the tenth part of a graine of the poyson of Nubia will dispatch a man in two houres, if the bite of a viper and sting of a scorpion, is not conceived to impart so much, if the bite of an aspe will kill within an houre, yet the impression scarce visible, and the poyson communicated not ponderable, we cannot as impossible reject this way of destruction; or deny the power of death in so narrow a circumscription.

12. Wondrous things are promised from the glow-worme, thereof perpetuall lights are pretended, and waters said to be distilled which afford a lustre in the night; and this is asserted by Cardan, Albertus, Gaudentius, Mizaldus and many others.[484] But hereto we cannot with reason assent: for the light made by this animall depends upon a living spirit, and seems by some vitall irradiation to be actuated into this lustre. For when they are dead they shine not, nor alwayes while they live, but are obscure or light according to the diffusion of this spirit, and the protrusion of their luminous parts, as observation will instruct us; for this flammeous light is not over all the body, but only visible on the inward side, in a small white part neare the tayle. When this is full and seemeth protruded, there ariseth a double flame of a circular figure and emerald green colour, which is discernable in any darke place in the day; but when it falleth and seemeth contracted, the light disappeareth, and the colour of the part only remaineth. Now this light, as it appeareth and disappeareth in their life, so doth it goe quite out at their death. As we have observed in some, which preserved in fresh grasse have lived and shined eighteen dayes, but as they declined their light grew languid, and at

last went out with their lives. Thus also the torpedo which alive hath a power to stupifie at a distance, hath none upon contaction being dead, as Galen and Rondoletius particularly experimented.[485] And this hath also disappointed the mischiefe of those intentions, which study the advancement of poysons, and fancie destructive compositions from aspes or vipers teeth, from scorpions or hornet stings; for these omit their efficacy in the death of the individuall, and act but dependantly on their formes. And thus far also those philosophers concur with us which held the sun and stars were living creatures, for they conceived their lustre depended on their lives; but if they ever dyed their light must perish also.

[It were a notable piece of art to translate the light from the *Bononian* stone into another body;[486] he that would attempt to make a shining water from glow-worms, must make trial when the splendent part is fresh and turgid. For even from the great American glow-worms, and flaming flies, the light declineth as the luminous humour dryeth.]

Now whether the light of animals, which do not occasionally shine from contingent causes, be of kin unto the light of Heaven; whether the invisible flame of life received in a convenient matter, may not become visible, and the diffused ætherial light make little stars by conglobation in idoneous parts of the compositum:[487] whether also it may not have some original in the seed and spirit analogous unto the element of stars, whereof some glymps is observable in the little refulgent humor, at the first attempts of formation: philosophy may yet enquire.

True it is, and we have observed it, that a glow-worme will afford a faint light, almost a dayes space when many will conceive it dead, but this is a mistake in the compute of death, and terme of disanimation; for indeed, it is not then dead, but if it be distended will slowly contract it selfe againe, which when it cannot doe it ceaseth to shine any more. And to speak strictly it is no easie matter to determine the point of death in insects and creatures who have not their vitalities radically confined unto one part; for these are not dead when they cease to move or afford the visible evidencies of life; as may be manifestly observed in flyes, who when they appear even desperate and quite forsaken of their formes, by vertue of the sun or warme ashes will be revoked unto life, and performe its functions againe.

[Now whether this lustre, a while remaining after death, dependeth not still upon the first impression, and light communicated or raised from an inward spirit, subsisting a while in a moyst and apt recipient, nor long continuing in this, or the more remarkable Indian glow-worm; or whether it be of another nature, and proceedeth from different causes of illumination; yet since it confessedly subsisteth so little a while after their lives, how to make perpetual lights, and sublunary moons thereof as is pretended, we rationally doubt, though not so sharply deny, with Scaliger and Muffetus.][488]

13. The wisdom of the pismire is magnified by all, and in the panegyricks of their providence we alwayes meet with this, that to prevent the growth of corne which they store up they bite off the end thereof:[489] and some have conceived that from hence they have their name in Hebrew: from whence ariseth a conceit that corne will not grow if the extreams be cut or broken. What other provision they make for this intention we know not, but herein we finde no security to prevent its germination, as having made tryall in graines whose ends cut off have notwithstanding suddenly sprouted, and according to the law of their kindes, that is the roots of barley and oates at contrary ends, of wheat and rye at the same. And therefore some have delivered that after rainy weather they dry these graines in the sun, which if effectuall, we must conceive to be made in a high degree and above the progression of malt, for that malt will grow this yeare hath informed us, and that unto a perfect ear.

[CHAPTER XXVIII[490]
Of some Others

That a chicken is formed out of the yelk of the egge, was the opinion of some ancient philosophers. Whether it be not the nutriment of the pullet, may also be considered: since umbilical vessels are carried unto it: since much of the yelk remaineth after the chicken is formed: since in a chicken newly hatched, the stomack is tincted yellow, and the belly full of yelk, which is drawn in at the navell or umbilicall vessels towards the vent, as may be discerned in chickens within a day or two before exclusion.

Whether the chicken be made out of the white, or that be not also its aliment, is likewise very questionable: since an umbilical vessell is derived unto it: since after the formation and perfect shape of the chicken, much of the white remaineth.

Whether it be not made out of the grando, gallature, germe or tredde of the egge, as Aquapendente informeth us, doth seem of lesser doubt:[491] for at the blunter end it is not discovered after the chicken is formed; by this also the yelk and white are continued, whereby it may conveniently receive its nutriment from them both.

Now that from such slender materials, nature should effect this production it is no more then is observed in other animals; and even in grains and kernels, the greatest part is but the nutriment of that generative particle, so disproportionable unto it.

A greater difficulty in the doctrine of egges, is, how the sperm of the cock prolificates and makes the ovall conception fruitfull, or how it attaineth unto every egge, since the vitellary or place of the yelk is very high: since the ovary or part where the white involveth it, is in the second region of the matrix, which is somewhat long and inverted: since also a cock will in one day fertilitate the whole racemation or cluster of egges, which are not excluded in many weeks after.

But these at last, and how in the cicatricula or little pale circle formation first beginneth, how the grando or tredle, are but the poles and establishing particles of the tender membrans, firmly conserving the floating parts in their proper places, with many other observables, that ocular Philosopher, and singular discloser of truth, Dr. Harvey hath discovered, in that excellent discourse of Generation;[492] so strongly erected upon the two great pillars of truth, experience and solid reason.

That the sex is discernable from the figure of egges, or that cocks or hens proceed from long or round ones, as many contend, experiment will easily frustrate.

The Ægyptians observed a better way to hatch their egges in ovens, then the Babylonians to roast them at the bottom of a sling, by swinging them round about, till heat from motion had concocted them; for that confuseth all parts without any such effect.

Though slight distinction be made between boiled and roasted egges, yet is there no slender difference, for the one is much drier then the other: the egge expiring less in the elixation or boiling; whereas in the assation or roasting, it will sometimes abate a dragme; that is, threescore grains in weight. So a new laid egge will not so easily be boiled hard, because it contains a greater stock of humid parts; which must be evaporated, before the heat can bring the inexhalable parts into consistence.

Why the hen hatcheth not the egge in her belly, or maketh not at least some rudiment thereof within her self, by the natural heat of inward parts, since the same is performed by incubation from an outward warmth after; why the egge is thinner at one extream? why there is some cavity or emptiness at the blunter end? why we open them at that part? why the greater end is first excluded? why some eggs are all red, as the kestrils; some only red at one end, as those of kites and buzzards? why some egges are not ovall but round, as those of fishes? &c. are problemes, whose decisions would too much enlarge this discourse.

That snakes and vipers do sting or transmit their mischief by the taile, is a common expression not easily to be justified; and a determination of their venoms unto a part, wherein we could never finde it; the poison lying about the teeth, and communicated by bite, in such as are destructive. And therefore when biting serpents are mentioned in the Scripture, they are not differentially set down from such as mischief by stings; nor can conclusions be made conformable to this opinion, because when the rod of Moses was turned into a serpent, God determinately commanded him to take up the same by the taile.

Nor are all Snakes of such empoisoning qualities, as common opinion presumeth; as is confirmable from the ordinary green snake with us, from several histories of domestick snakes, from ophiophagous nations, and such as feed upon serpents.

Surely the destructive delusion of Satan in this shape, hath much enlarged the opinion of their mischief. Which notwithstanding was not so high with the heathens, in whom the Devil had wrought a better opinion of this animall, it being sacred unto the Ægyptians, Greeks and Romans, and the common symbole of sanity. In the shape whereof Æsculapius the god of health appeared unto the Romans, accompanied their embassadors to Rome from Epidaurus; and the same did stand in the Tiberine Isle upon the Temple of Æsculapius.[493]

Some doubt many have of the tarantula, or poisonous spider of Calabria, and that magicall cure of the bite thereof by musick. But since we observe that many attest it from experience: since the learned Kircherus hath positively averred it, and set down the songs and tunes solemnly used for it;[494] since some also affirm the tarantula it self will daunce upon certain stroaks, whereby they set their instruments against its poison; we shall not at all question it.

Much wonder is made of the boramez, that strange plant-animall or vegetable lamb of Tartary, which wolves delight to feed on, which hath the shape of a lamb, affordeth a bloody juice upon breaking, and liveth while the plants be consumed about it. And yet if all this be no more, then the shape of a lamb in the flower or seed, upon the top of the stalk, as we meet with the formes of bees, flies and dogs in some others; he hath seen nothing that shall much wonder at it.

It may seem too hard to question the swiftnesse of tigers, which hath therefore given names unto horses, ships and rivers, nor can we deny what all have thus affirmed; yet cannot but observe, that Jacobus Bontius late physitian at Java in the East Indies, as an ocular and frequent witnesse is not afraid to deny it; to condemn Pliny who affirmeth it, and that indeed it is but a slow and tardigradous animall, and preying upon advantage, and otherwise may be escaped.

Many more there are whose serious enquiries we must request of others, and shall only awake considerations, whether that common opinion that snakes do breed out of the back or spinall marrow of man, doth build upon any constant root or seed in nature; or did not arise from contingent generation, in some single bodies remembered by Pliny or others, and might be paralleld since in living corruptions of the guts and other parts; which regularly proceed not to putrifactions of that nature.

Whether the story of the remora be not unreasonably amplified; whether that of bernacles and goose-trees be not too much enlarged; whether the common history of bees will hold, as large accountants have delivered; whether the brains of cats be attended with such destructive malignities, as Dioscorides and others put upon them.

Whether the fasting spittle of man be poison unto snakes and vipers, as experience hath made us doubt? Whether the nightingals setting with her breast against a thorn, be any more then that she roosteth in thorny and prickly places, where serpents may least approach her? Whether mice may be bred by putrifaction as well as univocall production, as may easily be beleeved, if that receit to make mice out of wheat will hold, which Helmont hath delivered.[495] Whether quailes from any idiosyncracy or peculiarity of constitution, do innocuously feed upon hellebore, or rather sometime but medically use the same; because we perceive that stares, which are commonly said harmlessly to feed on hemlock, do not make good the tradition; and he that observes what vertigoes, cramps, and convulsions follow thereon in these animals, will be of our belief.]

THE FOURTH BOOK

Of many popular and received Tenents concerning Man, which examined, prove either false or dubious

CHAPTER I
Of the erectnesse of Man

That onely Man hath an erect figure, and that for to behold and looke up toward heaven, according to that of the Poet—

> *Pronaque cum spectant animalia cætera terram*
> *Os homini sublime dedit, cælumque tueri*
> *Iussit, & erectos ad sydera tollere vultus,*[1]

is a double assertion, whose first part may be true, if we take erectnesse strictly, and so as Galen hath defined it; for they onely, saith he, have an erect figure, whose spine and thigh bone are carried in right lines, and so indeed of any we yet know, man only is erect;[2] for the thighes of other animals doe stand at angles with their spine, and have rectangular positions in birds, and perfect quadrupedes; nor doth the frog, though stretched out, or swimming, attaine the rectitude of man, or carry its thigh without all angularity: and thus is it also true that man onely sitteth, if we define sitting to be a firmation of the body upon the ischias;[3] wherein if the position be just and naturall the thigh bone lyeth at right angles to the spine, and the leg bone or tibia to the thigh; for others when they seeme to sit, as dogs, cats, or lions, doe make unto their spine acute angles with their thigh, and acute to the thigh with their shanke: Thus is it likewise true, what Aristotle alledgeth in that Probleme; why man alone is ἐξονειρωκτικὸς or suffereth pollutions in the night;[4] that is, because man onely lyeth upon his back, if we define not the same by every supine position, but when the spine is in rectitude with the thigh, and both with the armes lye parallell to the horizon, that a line through their navel will passe through the zenith and centre of the earth, and so cannot other animals lye upon their backs; for though the spine lye parallel with the horizon, yet will their legs incline, and lye at angles unto it; and upon these three divers positions in man wherein the spine can only be at right lines with the thigh, arise those remarkeable postures, prone, supine, and erect, which are but differenced in sight, or inaugular postures upon the back, the belly and the feet.

But if erectnesse be popularly taken, and as it is largely opposed unto pronenesse, or the posture of animals looking downewards, carrying their venters or opposite part to the spine directly towards the earth, it must not be strictly taken;[5] for though in serpents and lizards we may truly allow a pronenesse, yet Galen acknowledgeth that perfect quadrupedes, as horses, oxen, and camels, are but partly prone, and have some part of erectnesse;[6] and birds or flying animals, are so farre from this kinde of pronenesse, that they are almost erect, advancing the head and breast in their progression, and onely prone in the act of their volitation;[7] and if that be true which is delivered of the penguin or *Anser Magellanicus*, and often described in maps about those Straits, that they goe erect like men, and with their breast and belly do make one line perpendicular unto the axis of the earth; it will make up the exact erectnesse of man;[8] nor will that insect come very short which we have often beheld, that is, one kinde of locust which stands not prone, or a little inclining upward, but in a large erectnesse, elevating alwayes the two fore legs, and susteining it selfe in the middle of the other foure; by zoographers called *mantis,* and by the common people of Province, *Prega Dio*, that is, the prophet and praying locust, as being generally found in the posture of supplication, or such as resembleth ours, when we lift up our hands to heaven.

As for the end of this erection, to looke up toward heaven, though confirmed by severall testimonies, and the Greek etymology of man, it is not so readily to be admitted; and as a popular and vaine conceit was anciently rejected by Galen;[9] who in his third, *de usu partium*, determines, that man is erect because he was made with hands, and was therewith to exercise all arts which in any other figure he could not have performed, as he excellently declareth in that place where he also proves that man could have beene made neither quadruped, nor centaur.

[And for the accomplishment of this intention,[10] that is, to look up and behold the heavens, man hath a notable disadvantage in the eyelid; whereof the upper is far greater then the lower, which abridgeth the sight upwards; contrary to those of birds, who herein have the advantage of man: insomuch that the learned Plempius is bold to affirm, that if he had had the formation of the eyelids, he would have contrived them quite otherwise.]

The ground and occasion of this conceit was a literall apprehension of a figurative expression in Plato, as Galen plainely delivers, the effect of whose words is this:[11] to opinion that man is erect to looke up and behold the heavens, is a conceit onely fit for those that never saw the fish uranoscopus, that is, the beholder of heaven; which hath its eyes so placed, that it lookes up directly to heaven, which man doth not, except he recline, or bend his head backward; and thus to looke up to heaven agreeth not onely unto men, but asses; to omit birds with long necks, which looke not onely upwards, but round about at pleasure; and therefore men of this opinion understood not Plato when he said that man doth *sursum aspicere*, for thereby was not meant to gape or looke upward with the eye, but to have his thoughts sublime, and not onely to behold, but speculate their nature with the eye of the understanding.[12]

Now although Galen in this place makes instance but in one, yet are there other fishes, whose eyes regard the heavens, as plane, and cartilagineous fishes, as pectinals, or such as have the apophyses of their spine made laterally like a combe, for when they apply themselves to sleepe or rest upon the white side, their eyes on the other side looke upward toward heaven:[13] for birds, they generally carry their heads erectly like man, and some have advantage in that they move not their upper eyelid; and many that have long necks, and bear their heads somewhat backward, behold farre more of the heavens, and seeme to look above the æquinoxiall circle; and so also in many quadrupeds, although their progression be partly prone, yet is the sight of their eye direct, not respecting the earth but heaven, and makes an higher arch of altitude then our owne. The position of a frogge with his head above water exceedeth these; for therein hee seemes to behold a large part of the heavens, and the acies of his eye to ascend as high as the tropick; but he that hath beheld the posture of a bitour, will not deny that it beholds almost the very zenith.[14]

CHAPTER II
Of the heart

That the heart of man is seated in the left side, is an asseveration which strictly taken, is refutable by inspection;[15]

whereby it appeares the base and centre thereof is in the midst of the chest; true it is that the mucro or point thereof inclineth unto the left, for by this position it giveth way unto the ascension of the midriffe, and by reason of the hollow veine could not commodiously deflect unto the right; from which diversion, neverthelesse wee cannot so properly say tis placed in the left, as that it consisteth in the middle, that is, where its centre resteth; for so doe we usually say a gnomon or needle is in the middle of a diall, although the extreams may respect the north or south and approach the circumference thereof.

The ground of this mistake is a generall observation from the pulse or motion of the heart, which is more sensible on this side; but the reason hereof is not to be drawne from the situation of the heart, but the site of the left ventricle wherein the vitall spirits are laboured, and also the great artery that conveyeth them out, both which are situated on the left, and upon this reason epithems or cordial applications are justly applyed unto the left brest, and the wounds under the fift rib may bee more suddenly destructive if made on the sinister side;[16] and the speare of the souldier that pierced our Saviour, is not improperly described when painters direct it a little towards the left.[17]

The other ground is more particular and upon inspection; for in dead bodies especially lying upon the spine, the heart doth seem to incline unto the left, which happeneth not from its proper site, but besides its sinistrous gravity is drawne that way by the great arterie, which then subsideth & haleth the heart unto it. And therefore strictly taken, the heart is seated in the middle of the chest; but after a carelesse and inconsiderate aspection, or according to the readiest sense of pulsation, wee shall not quarrell if any affirme it is seated toward the left;[18] and in these considerations must Aristotle be salved, when hee affirmeth the heart of man is placed in the left side, and thus in a popular acception may wee receive the periphrasis of Persius when hee taketh the part under the left pappe for the heart;[*19] and if rightly apprehended, it concerneth not this controversie, when it is said in Ecclesiastes, The heart of a wiseman is in the right side, but that of a fool in the left;[20] [for thereby may be implied, that the heart of a wise man delighteth in the right way, or in the path of vertue; that of a fool in the left, or road of vice; according to the mystery of the letter of Pythagoras, or that expression in Jonah, concerning sixscore thousand, that

* Lævâ in parte mæmillæ.

could not discern between their right hand and their left, or knew not good from evil.]

That assertion also that man proportionally hath the largest brain, I did I confesse somewhat doubt, and conceived it might have failed in birds, especially such as having little bodies, have yet large cranies, and seeme to containe much brain, as snipes, woodcocks, &c. but upon triall I finde it very true. The braines of a man Archangelus and Bauhinus observe to weigh four pound, and sometime five and an half; if therefore a man weigh one hundred and forty pounds, and his braine but five, his waight is 27. times as much as his braine, deducting the waight of that five pound which is allowed for it; now in a snype which waighed foure ounces two dragmes, I find the braines to waigh but half dragme, so that the weight of the body (allowing for the brain) exceeded the waight of the brain, sixtie seven times and an half.

CHAPTER III
Of Pleurisies

That Pleurisies are onely on the left side, is a popular tenent, not onely absurde but dangerous. From the misapprehension hereof, men omitting the opportunity of those remedies, which otherwise they would not neglect; chiefly occasioned by the ignorance of anatomie, and the extent of the part affected, which in an exquisite pleurisie is determined to be the skin or membrane which investeth the ribbes, for so it is defined, *inflammatio membranæ costas succingentis*;[21] an inflammation either simple consisting onely of an hot and sanguineous affluxion, or else oedematous, schirrous, erisipelatous according to the predominancy of melancholy, flegme, or choler;[22] The vessells whereby the morbificall matter is derived unto this membrane, are either the ascending branches of the hollow veine, which disperse themselves into the foure upper ribbs, or else the azygos, or *vena sine pari*, whose surcles are disposed unto the other lower;[23] The membrane thus inflamed, is properly called *pleura*, from whence the disease hath its name, and this investeth not onely one side, but overspreadeth the cavitie of the chest, and affordeth a common coat unto the parts contained therein.

Now therefore the *pleura* being common unto both sides, it is not reasonable to confine the inflammation unto one, nor strictly to determine it is alwayes in the side, but sometimes before and behinde, that is, inclining to the spine or brestbone, for thither this coat extendeth; and therefore with equall propriety we may affirme, that ulcers of the lungs, or apostems of the braine doe happen onely in the left side, or that ruptures are confineable unto one side, whereas the peritoneum or rimme of the belly may be broke, or its perforations relaxed in either.[24]

CHAPTER IV
Of the Ring finger

An opinion there is, which magnifies the condition of the fourth finger of the left hand, presuming therein a cordiall relation, that a particular vessell, nerve, veine, or arterie is conferred thereto from the heart, and therefore that especially hath the honour to beare our rings; which was not only the Christian practise in nuptiall contracts, but observed by the heathens, as Alexander *ab Alexandro*, Gellius, Macrobius, and Pierius have delivered, as lately Levinus Lemnius hath confirmed, who affirmes this peculiar vessell to bee an arterie, and not a nerve, as antiquitie conceived it;[25] adding moreover that rings hereon peculiarly affect the heart; that in lipothymis or swoundings he used the frication of this finger with saffron and gold;[26] that the ancient physitians mixed up their medicines herewith; that this is seldome or last of all affected with the gout, and when that becommeth nodous, men continue not long after: notwithstanding all which we remaine unsatisfied, nor can we thinke the reasons alledged sufficiently establish the priviledge of this finger.

For first, concerning the practice of antiquity the custome was not generall to weare their rings either on this hand or finger; for it is said, and that emphatically in Jeremiah, *Si fuerit Jeconias filius Joachim regis Judæ annulus in manu dextrâ meâ, inde evellam eum:* Though Coniah the son of Joachim King of Judah were the signet on my right hand, yet would I pluck thee thence:[27] so is it observed by Pliny that in the portraits of their Gods the rings were worne on the finger next the thumb, that the Romans wore them also upon their little finger, as Nero is described in Petronius:[28] some wore them on the middle finger as the ancient Gaules and Britans, and some upon the forefinger, as is deduceable from Julius Pollux, who names that ring Corionos.

Againe, that the practice of the ancients had any such respect of cordiality or reference unto the heart will much be doubted if we consider their rings were made of iron; such was that of Prometheus who is conceived the first that brought them in use; so, as Pliny affirmeth, for many yeares the senators of Rome did not weare any rings of gold:[29] but the slaves wore generally iron rings untill their manumission or preferment to some dignity; that the Lacedemonians continued their iron rings unto his dayes, Pliny also delivereth; and surely they used few of gold, for beside that Lycurgus prohibited that mettall, we read in Athenæus that having a desire to guild the face of Apollo, they enquired of the oracle where they might purchase so much gold, and were directed unto Cræsus King of Lydia.[30]

Moreover whether the ancients had any such intention, the grounds which they conceived in veyne, nerve, or artery, are not to be justified, nor will inspection confirm a peculiar vessell in this finger: for as anatomy informeth, the basilica veyne dividing into two branches below the cubit, the outward sendeth two surcles unto the thumb, two unto the forefinger, and one unto the middlefinger in the inward side; the other branch of the basilica sendeth one surcle unto the outside of the middlefinger, two unto the ring, and as many unto the littlefingers; so that they all proceed from the basilica, and are in equall numbers derived unto every one: in the same manner are the branches of the axillary artery distributed into the hand, for below the cubit it divideth into two parts, the one running along the radius, and passing by the wrest or place of the pulse, is at the fingers subdivided into three branches, whereof the first conveyeth two surcles unto the thumb, the second as many to the forefinger, and the third one unto the middlefinger; the other or lower division of the artery descendeth by the ulna, and furnisheth the other fingers, that is the middle with one surcle, and the ring and little fingers with two; as for the nerves they are disposed much after the same maner, and have their originall from the brain, and not the heart, as many of the ancients conceived; which is so farre from affording nerves unto other parts, that it receiveth very few it self from the sixt conjugation, or paire of nerves in the brain.

Lastly, these propagations being communicated unto both hands, we have no greater reason to weare our rings on the left, then on the right, nor are there cordiall considerations in the one, more then the other;[31] and therefore when Forestus for the stanching of blood makes use of topicall applications unto the fourth finger, he confines not that practice unto the left, but varieth the side according to the nostrill bleeding:[32] and so in fevers, where the heart primarily suffereth, we apply medicines unto the wrests of either arme; and so we touch the pulse of both, and judge of the affections of the heart by the one as well as the other: and although in indispositions of liver or spleene considerations are made in phlebotomy respectively to their situation; yet when the heart is affected men have thought it as effectuall to bleed on the right as the left;[33] and although also it may be thought, a nearer respect is to be had of the left, because the great artery proceeds from the left ventricle, and so is nearer that arme, it admits not that consideration; for under the channell bones the artery divideth into two great branches, from which trunke or point of division the distance unto either hand is equall, and the consideration answerable.

[All which with many respective niceties,[34] in order unto parts, sides, and veines, are now become of less consideration, by the new and noble doctrine of the circulation of the blood.]

And therefore Macrobius discussing the point, hath alleadged another reason, affirming that the gestation of rings upon this hand and finger, might rather be used for their conveniency and preservation then any cordiall relation;[35] for at first (saith he) it was both free and usuall to weare rings on either hand, but after that luxury encreased, when pretious gems and rich insculptures were added, the custome of wearing them on the right hand was translated unto the left, for that hand being lesse employed, thereby they were best preserved;[36] and for the same reason they placed them on this finger, for the thumb was too active a finger, and is commonly imployed with either of the rest: the index or forefinger was too naked whereto to commit their pretiosities and hath the tuition of the thumbe scarce unto the second joynt:[37] the middle and little finger they rejected as extreams, and too big or too little for their rings, and of all chose out the fourth as being least used of any, as being guarded on either side, and having in most this peculiar condition that it cannot be extended alone and by it selfe, but will be accompained by some finger on either side: and to this opinion assenteth Alexander *ab Alexandro, Annulum nuptialem prior ætas in sinistrâ ferebat, crediderim ne attereretur.*[38]

Now that which begat or promoted the common opinion, was the common conceit that the heart was seated on the left side, but how far this is verified, we have before declared. The Ægyptian practice hath much advanced the same, who unto this finger derived a nerve from the heart, and therefore the priest anointed the same with pretious oyls before the altar; but how weake anatomists they were, which were so good embalmers we have already shewed; and though this reason tooke most place, yet had they another which more commended that practice, and that was the number whereof this finger was an hieroglyphick: for by holding downe the fourth finger of the left hand, while the rest were extended, they signified the perfect and magnified number of six; for as Pierius hath graphically declared, antiquity expressed numbers by the fingers of either hand;[39] on the left they accounted their digits and articulate numbers unto an hundred, on the right hand hundreds & thousands; the depressing this finger which in the left hand implied but six, in the right indigitated six hundred: in this way of numeration may we construe that of Juvenal concerning Nestor.

—mortem
Distulit, atque suos jam dextrâ comptuat annos.[40]

And how ever it were intended, and in this sense it will be very elegant what is delivered of Wisdome, Prov. 3. length of dayes is in her right hand, and in her left hand riches and honour.[41]

As for the observation of Lemnius an eminent physitian, concerning the gowt, how ever it happened in his country, wee may observe it otherwise in ours; that is, that chiragricall persons doe suffer in this finger as well as in the rest, and sometimes first of all, and sometimes no where else;[42] and for the mixing up medicines herewith, it is rather an argument of opinion then any considerable effect, and we as highly conceive of the practice in diapalma, that is in the making of that plaister, to stirre it with the stick of a palme.

CHAPTER V
Of the right and left Hand

It is also suspicious, and not with that certainty to be received, what is generally believed concerning the right and left hand, that men naturally make use of the right, and that the use of the other is a digression or aberration from that way which nature generally intendeth; and truly we do not deny that almost all nations have used this hand, and ascribed a preheminence thereto: hereof a remarkable passage there is in the 48. of Genesis, And Joseph tooke them both, Ephraim in his right hand towards Israels left hand, and Manasses in his left hand towards Israels right hand, and Israel stretched out his right hand and laid it upon Ephraims head, who was the younger, and his left hand upon Manasses head guiding his hands wittingly, for Manasses was the first borne; and when Joseph saw that his father laid his right hand upon the head of Ephraim, it displeased him, and he held up his fathers hand to remove it from Ephraims head unto Manasses head, and Joseph said not so my father, for this is thy first borne, put thy right hand upon his head:[43] And the like appeareth from the ordinance of Moses in the consecration of their priests, Then shalt thou kill the ram, and take of his bloud, and put it upon the tip of the right eare of Aaron, and upon the tip of the right eare of his sonnes, and upon the thumb of the right hand, and upon the great toe of the right foot, and sprinkle the bloud on the altar round about:[44] that the Persians were wont herewith to plight their faith, is testified by Diodorus:[45] that the Greeks and Romans made use hereof, beside the testimony of divers Authors, is evident from their custome of discumbency at their meales, which was upon their left side, for so their right hand was free, and ready for all service;[46] nor was this onely in use with divers nations of men, but was the custome of whole nations of women, as is deduceable from the Amazones in the amputation of their right breast, whereby they had the freer use of their bow:[47] all which doe declare a naturall preheminency and preferment of the one unto motion before the other, wherein notwithstanding in submission to future information, we are unsatisfied unto great dubitation.

For first, if there were a determinate prepotency in the right, and such as ariseth from a constant roote in nature, wee might expect the same in other animals, whose parts are also differenced by dextrality, wherein notwithstanding we cannot discover a distinct and complying account, for we finde not that horses, buls, or mules, are generally stronger on this side; and as for animals whose forelegs more sensibly supply the use of armes, they hold if not an equality in both, a prevalency oft times in the other, as squirrels, apes, and monkeys, and the same is also discernible in parrets, and men observe that the eye of a tumbler is biggest not constantly in one, but in the bearing side.[48]

That there is also in men a naturall prepotency in the right we cannot with constancy affirme, if we make observation in children, who permitted the freedome of both, do oft times confine unto the left, and are not without great difficulty restrained from it: and therefore this prevalency is either uncertainly placed in the laterallity, or custome determines its indifferency: which is the resolution of Aristotle in that Probleme, which enquires why the right side being better then the left, is equall in the senses?[49] because, saith he, the right and left do differ by use and custome which have no place in the senses: and the reason is allowable; for right and left as parts inservient unto the motive faculty are differenced by degrees from use and assuefaction, according whereto the one grows stronger, and oft times bigger then the other;[50] but in the senses it is otherwise; for they acquire not their perfection by use or custome, but at the first we equally heare and see with one eye, as well as with another: and therefore, were this indifferency permitted, or did not institution, but nature determine dextrality, there would be many more Scevolaes then are delivered in story;[51] nor should we wonder at seven thousand in one army, as wee reade concerning the Benjamites.[52] True it is, that although there be an indifferency in either, or a prevalency indifferent in one, yet is it most reasonable for uniformity, and sundry respective uses, that men should apply themselves to the constant use of one, for there will otherwise arise anomalous disturbances in manuall actions, not onely in civill and artificiall, but also in military affaires, and the severall actions of warre.

Secondly, the grounds and reasons alleadged for the right are not satisfactory, and afford no rest in their decision: Scaliger finding a defect in the reason of Aristotle, introduceth one of no lesse deficiency himselfe, *ratio materialis* (saith he) *sanguinis crassitudo simul et multitudo*, that is, the reason of the vigour of this side is the crassitude and plenty of bloud;[53] but this is no way sufficient, for the crassitude or thicknesse of bloud, affordeth no reason why one arme should be enabled before the other, and the plenty thereof, why both not enabled equally: Fallopius is of another conceit, deducing the reason from the azygos or *vena sine pari*, a large and considerable veine arising out of the cava or hallow veine, before it enters the right ventricle of the heart, and placed onely in the right side;[54] but neither is this perswasory, for the azygos communicates no branches unto the armes or legs on either side, but disperseth into the ribs on both, and in its descent doth furnish the left emulgent with one veyne, and the first veyne of the loynes on the right side with another;[55] which manner of derivation doth not conferre a peculiar addition unto either. *Cælius Rodiginus* undertaking to give a reason of ambidexters and left handed men, delivereth a third opinion: men, saith he, are ambidexters, and use both hands alike, when the heat of the heart doth plentifully disperse into the left side, and that of the liver into the right, and the spleene be also much dilated; but men are left handed when ever it happeneth that the heart and liver are seated on the left side, or when the Liver is on the right side, yet so obducted and covered with thick skins, that it cannot diffuse its virtue into the right:[56] which reasons are no way satisfactory; for herein the spleene is injustly introduced to invigorate the sinister side, which being dilated it would rather infirme and debilitate; as for any tunicles or skins which should hinder the liver from enabling the dextrall parts, we must not conceive it diffuseth its virtue by meere irradiation, but by its veines and proper vessels, which common skins and teguments cannot impede, and as for the seate of the heart and liver in one side whereby men become left handed, it happeneth too rarely to countenance an effect so common; for the seat of the liver on the left side is very monstrous, and scarce at all to be met with in the observations of physitians. Others not considering ambidextrous and left handed men, doe totally submit unto the efficacy of the liver, which though it be seated on the right side, yet by the subclavian division doth equidistantly communicate its activity unto either arme, nor will it salve the doubts of observation, for many are right handed whose livers are weakely constituted, and many use the left, in whom that part is strongest; and we observe in apes and other animals, whose liver is in the right, no regular prevalence therein, and therefore the braine, especially the spinall marrow, which is but the braine prolonged, hath a fairer plea hereto, for these are the principles of motion wherein dextrality consists, and are bipartited within and without the crany;[57] by which division transmitting nerves respectively unto either side, according to the indifferency or originall and native prepotency, there ariseth an equality in both, or prevalency in either side; and so may it be made out, what many may wonder at, why some most actively use the contrary arme and leg, for the vigour of the one dependeth upon the upper part of the spine, but the other upon the lower.

And therefore many things are philosophically delivered concerning right and left, which admit of some suspension; that a woman upon a masculine conception advanceth her right leg, will not be found to answer strict observation; that males are conceived in the right side of the wombe, females in the left, though generally delivered, and supported by ancient testimony, will make no infallible account; it happening oft times that males and females doe lye upon both sides, and hermaphrodites for ought we know on either: it is also suspicious what is delivered concerning the right and left testicle, that males are begotten from the one, and females from the other; for though the left seminall veine proceedeth from the emulgent, and is therefore conceived to carry downe a serous and feminine matter, yet the seminall arteryes which send forth the active materials, are both derived from the great artery:[58] beside this originall of the left veine was thus contrived, to avoid the pulsation of the great arterie over which it must have passed to attaine unto the testicle: nor can we easily inferre such different effects from the divers situation of parts which have one end and office; for in the kidneys which have one office, the right is seated lower then the left, whereby it lyeth free, and giveth way unto the liver; and therefore also that way which is delivered for masculine generation, to make a straite ligature about the left testicle, thereby to intercept the evacuation of that part, deserveth consideration; for one sufficeth unto generation, as hath beene observed in semicastration, and oft times in carnous ruptures: beside the seminall ejaculation proceeds not immediately from the testicle, but from the spermatick glandules; and therefore Aristotle affirmes, (and reason cannot deny) that although there be nothing diffused from the testicles, an horse or bull may generate after castration, that is, from the stock and remainder of seminall matter, already prepared and stored up in the prostates or glandules of generation.[59]

Thirdly, although wee should concede a right and left in nature, yet in this common and received account we may aberre from the proper acception, mistaking one side for another, calling that in man and other animals the right which is the left, and that the left which is the right, and that in some things right and left, which is not properly either.[60]

For first the right and left, are nor defined by philosophers according to common acception, that is, respectively from one man unto another, or any constant site in each; as though that should bee the right in one, which upon confront or facing stands athwart or diagonially unto the other, but were distinguished according to the activitie and predominant locomotion upon either side: thus Aristotle in his excellent Tract *de incessu animalium,* ascribeth six positions unto animals, answering the three dimensions;[61] which he determineth not by site or position unto the heavens, but by their faculties and functions, and these are *imum summum, ante retro, dextra et sinistra*: that is, the superiour part where the aliment is received, that the lower extreme where it is last expelled; so hee termeth a man a plant inverted; for hee supposeth the root of a tree the head or upper part thereof, whereby it receiveth its aliment, although therewith it respects the center of the earth, but with the other the zenith; and this position is answerable unto longitude: those parts are anterior and measure profunditie where the senses, especially the eyes are placed, and those posterior which are opposite hereunto; the dextrous and sinistrous parts of the body make up the latitude, and are not certain and inalterable like the other; for that saith hee, is the right side from whence the motion of the body beginneth, that is, the active or moving side, but that the sinister which is the weaker or more quiescent part: of the same determination were the Platonicks and Pythagorians before him, who conceiving the heavens an animated body, named the east the right or dextrous part, from whence began their motion: and thus the Greeks from whence the Latins have borrowed their appellation, have named this hand δεξιά, denominating it not from the site, but office, from δέχομαι, *capio*, that is, the hand which receiveth, or is usually implied in that action.

Now upon these grounds we are most commonly mistaken, defining that by situation which they determined by motion, and give the terme of right hand to that which doth not properly admit it: for first, many in their infancy are sinistrously disposed, and divers continue all their life Ἀριστεροὶ, that is left handed, and have but weak and imperfect use of the right; now unto these that hand is properly the right, and not the other esteemed so by situation: thus may Aristotle bee made out, when hee affirmeth the right claw of crabbes and lobsters is biggest, if we take the right for the most vigorous side, and not regard the relative situation;[62] for the one is generally bigger then the other, yet not alwayes upon the same side: so may it be verified what is delivered by Scaliger in his comment, that palsies do oftnest happen upon the left side if understood in this sense; the most vigorous part protecting it selfe, and protruding the matter upon the weaker and lesse resistive side:[63] and thus the law of Common-weales, that cut off the right hand of malefactors, if philosophically executed, is impartiall, otherwise the amputation not equally punisheth all.

Some are *Ἀμφιδέξιοι*, that is, ambidexterous or right-handed on both sides, which happeneth only unto strong and athleticall bodies, whose heat and spirits are able to afford an ability unto both; and therefore Hippocrates saith, that women are not ambidexterous, that is, not so often as men, for some are found, which indifferently make use of both;[64] and so may Aristotle say, that only man is ambidexter; of this constitution was Asteropæus in Homer, and Parthenopeus the Theban captaine in Statius;[65] and of the same doe some conceive our Father Adam to have been, as being perfectly framed, and in a constitution admitting least defect: now in these men the right hand is on both sides, and that which is the opposite to the one, is not the left unto the other.

Againe, some are *Ἀμφαριστεροὶ*, as Galen hath expressed: that is, ambilevous or left handed on both sides; such as with agility and vigour have not the use of either, who are not gymnastically composed; nor actively use those parts; now in these there is no right hand: of this constitution are many women, and some men; who though they accustome themselves unto either hand, do dexterously make use of neither; and therefore although the politicall advise of Aristotle bee very good, that men should accustom themselves to the command of either hand, yet cannot the execution or performance thereof be generall, for though there bee many found that can use both, yet will there divers remaine that can strenuously make use of neither.

Lastly, these lateralities in man are not onely fallible, if relatively determined unto each others, but made in reference unto the heavens, and quarters of the globe:[66] for those parts are not capable of these conditions in themselves, nor with any certainty respectively derived from us, nor we from them againe. And first in regard of their proper nature, the heavens admit not these sinister and dexter respects, there being in them no diversitie or difference, but a simplicity of parts, and equiformity in motion continually succeeding each other; so that from what point soever we compute, the account will be common unto the whole circularity, and therefore though it be plausible, it is not fundamentall what is delivered by Solinus, that man was therefore a microcosm or little world, because the dimensions of his positions were answerable unto the greater;[67] for as in the heavens the distance of the north and southerne pole, which are esteemed the superiour and inferiour poynts is equall unto the space between the east and west, accounted the dextrous and sinistrous parts thereof; so is it also in man: for the extent of his fathome, or distance betwixt the extremity of the fingers of either hand upon expansion, is equall unto the space between the soale of the foot and the crowne; but this doth but petionarily inferre a dextrality in the heavens, and we may as reasonably conclude a right and left laterallity in the Ark or navall edifice of Noah:[68] for the length thereof was thirty cubits,[69] the bredth fifty, and the height or profundity thirty, which well agreeth unto the proportion of man, whose length, that is a perpendicular from the vertix unto the soal of the foot is sextuple unto his breadth, or a right line drawne from the ribs of one side to another; and decuple unto his profundity, that is a direct line between the breast bone and the spine.[70]

Againe, they receive not these conditions with any assurance or stability from our selves; for the relative foundations and points of denomination, are not fixed and certaine, but variously designed according to imagination. The philosopher accounts that east from whence the heavens begin their motion. The astronomer regarding the south and meridian sun, calls that the dextrous part of heaven which respecteth his right hand, and that is the west. Poets respecting the west assign the name of right unto the north which regardeth their right hand, and so must that of Ovid be explained, *utque duæ dextrâ zonæ totidemque sinistrâ:*[71] but augurs or southsayers turning their face to the East, did make the right in the south, which was also observed by the Hebrews and Chaldæans. Now if we name the quarters of heaven respectively unto our sides, it will be no certaine or invariable denomination; for if we call that the right side of heaven which is seated easterly unto us, when we regard the meridian sun, the inhabitants beyond the equator and southerne tropick when they face us regarding the meridian will contrarily define it; for unto them, the opposite part of heaven will respect the left, and the sun arise to their right.

And thus have we at large declared that although the right be most commonly used, yet hath it no regular or certaine root in nature: since it is most confirmable from other animalls:

since in children it seemes either indifferent or more favourable in the other, but more reasonable for uniformity in action that men accustome unto one: since the grounds and reasons urged for it doe no way support it: since if there be a right and stronger side in nature, yet may we mistake in its denomination, calling that the right which is the left, and the left which is the right: since some have one right, some both, some neither: and lastly, since these affections in man are not only fallible in relation unto one another, but made also in reference unto the heavens, they being not capable of these conditions in themselves, nor with any certainty from us, nor we from them againe.

And therefore what admission we owe unto many conceptions concerning right and left requireth circumspection; that is, how far wee ought to relye upon the remedy of Kiranides, that is the left eye of an hedgehog fryed in oyle to procure sleep, and the right foot of a frog in a deers skin for the gowt; or that to dream of the losse of right or left tooth presageth the death of male or female kindred, according to the doctrine of Metrodorus;[72] what verity there is in that numerall conceit in the laterall division of man by even and odde, ascribing the odde unto the right side, and even unto the left; and so by parity or imparity of letters in mens names determine misfortunes on either side of their bodyes; by which account in Greek numeration Hephæstus or Vulcane was lame in the right foot, and Anniball lost his right eye:[73] and lastly, what substance there is in that auspiciall principle, and fundamentall doctrine of ariolation that the left hand is ominous, and that good things do passe sinistrously upon us, because the left hand of man respected the right hand of the Gods, which handed their favours unto us.[74]

CHAPTER VI
Of Swimming

That men swim naturally, if not disturbed by feare; that men being drowned and sunke, doe float the ninth day when their gall breaketh; that women drowned swim prone but men supine, or upon their backs, are popular affirmations, whereto we cannot assent: and first, that man should swim naturally, because we observe it is no lesson unto others we cannot well conclude; for other animalls swim in the same manner as they goe, and need no other way of motion, for natation in the water, then for progression upon the land;[75] and this is true whether they move *per latera*, that is two legs of one side together, which is tollutation or ambling, or *per diametrum*, which is most generall, lifting one foot before, and the crosse foot behinde, which is succussation or trotting, or whether *per frontem* or *quadratum*, as Scaliger tearmes it, upon a square base of the legs of both sides moving together as frogs, and salient animalls, which is properly called leaping; for by these motions they are able to support and impell themselves in the water, without addition or alteration in the stroake of their legs, or position of their bodies.[76]

But with man it is performed otherwise; for in regard of site he alters his naturall posture and swimmeth prone, whereas hee walketh erect; againe in progression the armes move parallell to the legs and the armes and legs unto each other; but in natation they intersect and make all sorts of angles: and lastly, in progressive motion, the armes and legs doe move successively, but in natation both together; all which aptly to performe, and so as to support and advance the body, is a point of art, and such as some in their young and docile yeares could never attaine. But although it be acquired by art, yet is there somewhat more of nature in it then we observe in other habits, nor will it strictly fall under that definition, for once obtained it is not to be removed; nor is there any who from disuse did ever yet forget it.

Secondly, that persons drowned arise and float the ninth day when their gall breaketh, is a questionable determination both in the time and cause, for the time of floating it is uncertain according to the time of putrefaction, which will retard or accelerate according to the subject and season of the year; for as we have observed cats and mice will arise unequally and at different times, though drowned at the same; such as are fatted doe commonly float soonest, for their bodies soonest ferment, and that substance approacheth nearest unto ayre: and this is one of Aristotles reasons why dead eeles will not float, because saith he, they have but slender bellies, and little fat.[77]

As for the cause it is not so reasonably imputed unto the breaking of the gall as the putrefaction of the body, whereby the unnaturall heat prevailing the putrifying parts do suffer a turgescence and inflation, and becomming airy and spumous affect to approach the ayre, and ascend unto the surface of the water:[78] and this is also evidenced in egges wherof the sound ones sink, & such as are addled swim, as do also those which are tearmed hypenemia or wind-egges, and this is also a way to separate seeds, whereof such as are corrupted and sterill swim; and this agreeth not only unto the seed of plants lockt up and capsulated in their husks, but also unto the sperme and seminall humor of man, for such a passage hath Aristotle upon the inquisition and test of its fertility.[79]

That the breaking of the gall is not the cause hereof experience hath informed us, for opening the abdomen, and taking out the gall in cats and mice, they did notwithstanding arise: and because wee had read in Rhodiginus of a Tyrant, who to prevent the emergencie of murdered bodies did use to cut off their lungs, and found mens minds possessed with this reason, we committed some unto the water without lungs, which notwithstanding floated with the others:[80] and to compleat the experiment, although we tooke out the guts and bladder, and also perforated the cranium, yet would they arise, though in a longer time: from these observations in other animalls, it may not be unreasonable to conclude the same in man, who is too noble a subject on whom to make them expressely, and the casuall opportunity too rare almost to make any. Now if any shall ground this effect from gall or choler, because it is the highest humor and will be above the rest; or being the fiery humor will readiest surmount the water, wee must confesse in the common putrescence it may promote elevation, which the breaking of the bladder of gall so small a part in man, cannot considerably advantage.

Lastly, that women drowned float prone, that is with their bellies downward, but men supine or upward is an assertion wherein the *hoti* or point it selfe is dubious; and were it true the reason alleadged for it, is of no validity.[81] The reason yet currant was first expressed by Pliny, *veluti pudori defunctarum parcente naturâ*, nature modestly ordaining this position to conceale the shame of the dead, which hath been taken up by Solinus, Rhodiginus, and many more:[82] This indeed (as Scaliger tearmeth it) is *ratio civilis non philosophica*, strong enough for morality or rhetoricks, not for philosophy or physicks: for first, in nature the concealment of secret parts is the same in both sexes and the shame of their reveale equall: so Adam upon the taste of the fruit was ashamed of his nakednesse as well as Eve:[83] and so likewise in America and countries unacquainted with habits, where modesty conceales these parts in one sex, it doth it also in the other; and therefore had this been the intention of nature, not only women, but men also had swimmed downwards, the posture in reason being common unto both where the intent is also common.

Againe, while herein we commend the modesty, we condemne the wisdome of nature: for that prone position we make her contrive unto the woman, were best agreeable unto the man in whom the secret parts are very anterior and more discoverable in a supine and upward posture: and therefore Scaliger declining this reason hath recurred unto another from the difference of parts in both sexes, *Quod ventre vasto sunt mulieres plenoque intestinis, itaque minus impletur et subsidet, inanior maribus quibus nates præponderant:*[84] If so, then men with great bellies will float downward, and only Callipygæ and women largely composed behinde, upward.[85] But anatomists observe that to make the larger cavity for the infant, the hanch bones in women, and consequently the parts appendant are more protuberant then they are in men: they who ascribe the cause unto the breasts of women, take not away the doubt, for they resolve not why children float downward who are included in that sex, though not in the reason alleadged: but hereof we cease to discourse lest we undertake to afford a reason of the golden tooth, that is to invent or assigne a cause, when we remaine unsatisfied or unassured of the effect.*

* Of the cause whereof much dispute was made, and at last proved an imposture.

CHAPTER VII
Concerning Weight

That men weigh heavier dead then alive, if experiment hath not failed us, we cannot reasonably grant; for though the triall hereof cannot so well be made on the body of man, nor will the difference be sensible in the abate of scruples or dragmes, yet can we not confirme the same in lesser animalls from whence the inference is good; and the affirmative of Pliny saith that it is true in all:[86] for exactly weighing and strangling a chicken in the scales, upon an immediate ponderation, we could discover no sensible difference in weight, but suffering it to lye eight or ten howres, untill it grew perfectly cold, it weighed most sensibly lighter;[87] the like we attempted, and verified in mice, and performed their trials in scales that would turne upon the eighth or tenth part of a graine.[88]

Now whereas some alledge that spirits are light substances, and naturally ascending do elevate and waft the body upward, whereof dead bodies being destitute contract a greater gravity; although we concede that spirits are light, comparatively unto the body, yet that they are absolutely so, or have no weight at all, wee cannot readily allow; for since philosophy affirmeth that spirits are middle substances between the soule and body, they must admit of some corporiety which supposeth weight or gravity. Beside, in carcasses warme, and bodies newly disanimated while transpiration remaineth, there doe exhale and breathe out vaporous and fluid parts, which carry away some power of gravitation; which though we must allow, we do not make answerable unto living expiration, and therefore the chicken or mice were not so light being dead, as they would have beene after ten houres kept alive, for in that space a man abateth many ounces; nor if it had slept, for in that space of sleepe, a man will sometimes abate forty ounces, nor if it had beene in the middle of Summer, for then a man weigheth some pounds lesse then in the height of Winter, according to experience, and the statick aphorismes of Sanctorius.[89]

Againe, whereas men affirme they perceave an addition of ponderosity in dead bodies, comparing them usually unto blocks and stones, whensoever they lift or carry them, this accessionall ponderancy is rather in appearance then reality;[90] for being destitute of any motion, they conferre no reliefe unto the agents or elevators, which makes us meet with the same complaints of gravity in animated and living bodies, where the nerves subside, and the faculty locomotive seemes abolished, as may be observed in the lifting or supporting of persons inebriated, apoplecticall, or in lipothymies and swoundings.[91]

Many are also of opinion, and some learned men maintaine, that men are lighter after meales then before, and that by a supply and addition of spirits obscuring the grosse ponderosity of the aliment ingested; but the contrary hereof we have found in the triall of sundry persons in different sex, and ages; and we conceave men may mistake if they distinguish not the sense of levity unto themselves, and in regard of the scale or decision of trutination;[92] for after a draught of wine a man may seeme lighter in himselfe from sudden refection, although he be heavier in the balance, from a corporall and ponderous addition;[93] but a man in the morning is lighter in the scale, because in sleepe some pounds have perspired, and is also lighter unto himselfe, because he is refected.

And to speake strictly, a man that holds his breath is weightier while his lungs are full, then upon expiration; for a bladder blowne is weightier then one empty, and if it containe a quart, expressed and emptied it will abate about halfe a graine; and we somewhat mistrust the experiment of a pumice-stone taken up by Montanus, in his comment upon Avicenna, where declaring how the rarity of parts, and numerosity of pores, occasioneth a lightnesse in bodies, he affirmes that a pumice-stone powdered, is lighter then one entire, which is an experiment beyond our satisfaction;[94] for beside that abatement can hardly be avoyded in the trituration;[95] if a bladder of good capacity will scarce include a graine of ayre, a pumice of three or foure dragmes, cannot be presumed to containe the hundreth part thereof, which will not be sensible upon the exactest beames we use:[96] Nor is it to be taken strictly what is delivered by the learned Lord Verulam, and referred unto further experiment;[97] that a dissolution of iron in *aqua fortis* will beare as good weight as their bodies did before, notwithstanding a great deale of waste by a thick vapour that issueth during the working; for we cannot finde it to hold neither in iron, nor copper, which is dissolved with lesse ebullition;[98] and hereof we made trial in scales of good exactnesse, wherein if there be a defect, or such as will not turne upon quarter graines, there may be frequent mistakes in experiments of this nature: but stranger is that, and by the favourablest way of triall we cannot make out what is delivered by *Hamerus Poppius*, that antimony calcin'd or reduced to ashes by a burning glasse, although it emitte a grosse and ponderous exhalation, doth rather exceed then abate its former gravity: whose words are these in his *Basilica Antimonii*, *Si speculum incensorium soli exponatur, ita ut pyramidis luminosæ apex Antimonium pulverisatum feriat, cum multo fumi profusione ad nivis albedinem calcinabitur, et quod mirabile est Antimonii pondus post calcinationem auctum potius quam diminutum deprehenditur*, mistake may be made in this way of trial, when the antimony is not weighed immediately upon the calcination, but permitted the ayre, it imbibeth the humidity thereof, and so repayreth its gravity.[99]

CHAPTER VIII
Of the passage of meate and drinke

That there are different passages for meate and drinke, the meate or dry aliment descending by the one, the drink or moystning vehicle by the other, is a popular tenent in our dayes, but was the assertion of learned men of old, for the same was affirmed by Plato, maintained by Eustathius in Macrobius, and is deducible from Eratosthenes, Eupolis and Euripides:[100] now herein men contradict experience, not well understanding anatomy, and the use of parts; for at the throat there are two cavities or conducting parts, the one the oesophagus or gullet, seated next the spine, a part officiall unto nutrition, and whereby the aliment both wet and dry is conveyed unto the stomack;[101] the other (by which tis conceived the drink doth passe) is the weazon, rough artery, or winde-pipe, a part inservient to voyce and respiration, for thereby the ayre descendeth into the lungs, and is communicated unto the heart; and therefore all animals that breath or have lungs, have also the weazon, but many have the gullet or feeding channell, which have no lungs or winde-pipe; as fishes which have gills, whereby the heart is refrigerated, for such thereof as have lungs and respiration, are not without the weazon, as whales and cetaceous animals.

Againe, beside these parts destin'd to divers offices, there is a peculiar provision for the winde-pipe, that is, a cartiliagineous flap upon the opening of the larinx or throttle, which hath an open cavity for the admission of the ayre; but lest thereby either meate or drinke should descend, providence hath placed the *epiglottis ligula*, or flap like an ivy leafe, which alwayes closeth when we swallow, or that the meate and drinke passeth over it into the gullet, which part although all have not that breathe, as all cetaceous and oviparous animals, yet is the weazon secured some other way; and therefore in whales that breathe, lest the water should get into the lungs, an ejection thereof is contrived by a fistula or spout at the head; and therefore also though birds have no epiglottis, yet can they so contract the rime or chinck of their larinx, as to prevent the admission of wet or dry ingested, either whereof getting in occasioneth a cough, untill it be ejected; and this is the reason why a man cannot drink and breathe at the same time; why if we laugh while we drinke, the drinke flies out at the nostrils, why when the water enters the weazon, men are suddenly drowned; and thus must it be understood, when wee reade of one that dyed by the seed of a Grape, and another by an hayre in milke.

Now if any shall still affirme, that some truth there is in the assertion, upon the experiment of Hippocrates, who killing an hog after a red potion, found the tincture thereof in the larinx; if any will urge the same from medicall practise, because in affections both of lungs and weazon, physitians make use of syrupes, and lambitive medicines;[102] we are not averse to acknowledge, that some may distill and insinuate into the wind-pipe, and medicines may creep downe, as well as the rheume before them; yet to conclude from hence, that ayre and water have both one common passage, were to state the question upon the weaker side of the distinction, and from a partiall or guttulous irrigation, to conclude a full and totall descension.[103]

CHAPTER IX
Of Sneezing

Concerning sternutation or sneezing, and the custome of saluting or blessing upon that motion, it is pretended, and generally beleeved to derive its originall from a disease, wherein sternutation proved mortall, and such as sneezed dyed: and this may seeme to be proved from Carolus Sigonius, who in his History of Italy, makes mention of a pestilence in the time of Gregorie the Great, that proved pernitious and deadly to those that sneezed;[104] which notwithstanding will not sufficiently determine the grounds hereof, and it will evidently appeare, that custome hath an elder æra then this chronologie affordeth.

For although the age of Gregorie extend above a thousand, yet is this custome mentioned by Apuleius in the fable of the fullers wife, who lived three hundred yeers before;[105] by Pliny likewise in that Probleme of his, *Cur Sternutantes salutantur*, and there are also reports that Tiberius the Emperour otherwise a very sowre man, would performe this rite most punctually unto others, and expect the same from others, unto himself;[106] Petronius Arbiter, who lived before them both, and was Proconsul of Bythinia in the raigne of Nero, hath mentioned it in these words, *Gyton collectione spiritus plenus, ter continuò ita sternutavit ut grabatum concuteret, ad quem motum Eumolpus conversus, salvere Gytona jubet.*[107] Cælius Rhodiginus hath an example hereof among the Greeks, far antienter then these, that is, in the time of Cyrus the younger, when consulting about their retreat, it chanced that one among them sneezed, at the noyse whereof, the rest of the souldiers called upon Jupiter Soter;[108] There is also in the Greek Anthologie a remarkeable mention hereof, in an Epigram upon one Proclus, the Latine whereof we shall deliver, as we finde it often translated.

Non potis est Proclus digitis emungere nasum
namque est pro nasi mole pusilla manus,
Non vocat ille Jovem sternutans, quippe nec audit
Se sternutantem, tam procul aure sonat.
Proclus with's hand his nose can never wipe,
His hand too little is his nose to grype;
He sneezing calls not Jove, for why? he heares
himself not sneeze, the sound's so far from's ears.[109]

Nor was this onely an ancient custome among the Greeks and Romanes, and is still in force with us, but is received at this day in remotest parts of Africa; for so we read in Codignus, that upon a sneeze of the Emperour of Monomotapa, there passed acclamations successively through the city.[110]

Now the ground of this ancient custome was probably the opinion the ancients held of sternutation: which they generally conceived to be a good signe or a bad, and so upon this motion accordingly used, a salve or *Ζεῦ σῶσον* as a gratulation for the one, and a deprecation from the other: Now of the wayes whereby they enquired and determined its signality; the first was naturall arising from physicall causes, and consequencies of times naturally succeeding this motion; and so it might be justly esteemed a good signe; for sneezing being properly a motion of the braine, suddenly expelling through the nostrils what is offensive unto it, it cannot but afford some evidence of its vigour; and therefore saith Aristotle in his Problems, they that heare *προσκυνοῦσιν ὡς ἱερὸν*, they honour it as somewhat sacred, and a signe of sanity in the diviner part;[111] and this he illustrates from the practice of physitians, who in persons neere death doe use sternutatories, or such as provoke unto sneezing; when if the facultie arise and sternutation ensue, they conceive hopes of life, and with gratulation receive the signes of safetie; and so is it also of good signality in lesser considerations, according to that of Hippocrates, that sneezing cureth the hickett, and is profitable unto women in hard labour;[112] and so is it of good signality in lethargies, apoplexies, catalepsies, and comas: and in this naturall way it is somtime likewise of bad effects or signes, and may give hints of deprecation; as in diseases of the chest, for therein Hippocrates condemneth it as too much exagitating in the beginning of catarrhs according unto Avicenna as hindering concoction, in new and tender conceptions, (as Pliny observeth) for then it endangers abortion.[113]

The second way was superstitious and augurial, as Cælius Rhodiginus hath illustrated in testimonies, as ancient as Theocritus and Homer; as appears from the Athenian master, who would have retired, because a boatman sneezed, and the testimony of Austine, that the Ancients were wont to goe to bed againe if they sneezed while they put on their shooe;[114] and in this way it was also of good and bad signification; so Aristotle hath a Probleme, why sneezing from noon unto midnight was good, but from night to noon unlucky?[115] So Eustathius upon Homer observes, that sneezing to the left hand was unlucky, but prosperous unto the right; and so as Plutarch relateth, when Themistocles sacrificed in his galley before the battell of Xerxes, and one of the assistants upon the right hand sneezed, Euphrantides the Southsayer presaged the victorie of the Greekes, and the overthrow of the Persians.[116]

And thus wee may perceive the custome is more ancient then commonly is conceived, and these opinions hereof in all ages, nor any one disease to have been the occasion of this salute and deprecation, arising at first from this vehement and affrighting motion of the braine, inevitably observable unto the standers by; from whence some finding dependent effects to ensue, others ascribing hereto as a cause what perhaps but casually or inconexedly succeeded, they might proceed unto forms of speeches, felicitating the good, or deprecating the evil to follow.

CHAPTER X
Of the Jewes

That Jews stinck naturally, that is, that in their race and nation there is δυσωδία or evil savour, is a received opinion, wee know not how to admit; although we concede many questionable points, and dispute not the verity of sundry opinions which are of affinity hereto: we will acknowledge that certaine odours attend on animalls, no lesse then certaine colours; that pleasant smels are not confined unto vegetables, but found in divers animalls, and some more richly then in plants: and though the Probleme of Aristotle enquire why none smells sweet beside the parde? yet later discoveries adde divers sorts of monkeys, the civet cat, and gazela, from which our muske proceedeth:[117]

we confesse that beside the smell of the species, there may be individuall odours, and every man may have a proper and peculiar savour; which although not perceptible unto man, who hath this sense, but weake, yet sensible unto dogges, who hereby can single out their masters in the dark: wee will not deny that particular men have sent forth a pleasant savour, as Theophrastus and Plutark report of Alexander the great, and Tzetzes and Cardan doe testifie of themselves;[118] that some may also emit an unsavoury odour, we have no reason to deny, for this may happen from the qualitie of what they have taken, the fætor whereof may discover it self by sweat and urine, as being unmasterable by the naturall heat of man, nor to be dulcified by concoction beyond an unsavoury condition:[119] the like may come to passe from putrid humors, as is often discoverable in putrid and malignant fevers; and somtime also in grosse and humide bodies even in the latitude of sanity; the naturall heat of the parts being insufficient for a perfect and through digestion, and the errors of one concoction not rectifiable by another: but that an unsavoury odour is gentilitious or national unto the Jews, if rightly understood, we cannot well concede, nor will the information of reason or sense induce it.[120]

For first upon consult of reason, there will bee found no easie assurance for to fasten a materiall or temperamentall propriety upon any nation; there being scarce any condition (but what depends upon clime) which is not exhausted or obscured from the commixture of introvenient nations either by commerce or conquest;[121] much more will it be difficult to make out this affection in the Jewes, whose race how ever pretended to be pure, must needs have suffered inseparable commixtures with nations of all sorts, not onely in regard of their proselytes, but their universall dispersion; some being posted from severall parts of the earth, others quite lost, and swallowed up in those nations where they planted: for the tribes of Ruben, Gad, part of Manasses and Naphthali, which were taken by Assur, and the rest at the sacking of Samaria which were led away by Salmanasser, into Assyria, and after a yeare and half, and arived at Arsereth as is delivered in Esdras, these I say never returned, and are by the Jewes as vainly expected as their Messias:[122] of those of the tribe of Juda and Benjamin, which were led captive into Babylon by Nebuchadnezzar many returned under Zorobabel, the rest remained, and from thence long after upon invasion of the

Saracens, fled as far as India; where yet they are said to remaine, but with little difference from the Gentiles.

The tribes that returned to Judea,[123] were afterward widely dispersed; for beside sixteene thousand which Titus sent to Rome unto the triumph of his father Vespasian, hee sold no lesse then an hundred thousand for slaves;[124] not many yeeres after Adrian the Emperour, who ruined the whole countrey, transplanted many thousands into Spaine, from whence they dispersed into divers countreys, as into France, and England, but were banished after from both: from Spaine they dispersed into Africa, Italy, Constantinople, and the dominions of the Turke, where they remaine as yet in very great numbers, and if (according to good relations) where they may freely speake it, they forbeare not to boast that there are at present many thousand Jewes in Spaine, France, and England, and some dispensed withall, even to the degree of priesthood, it is a matter very considerable, and could they be smelled out, would much advantage, not onely the church of Christ, but also the coffers of princes.

Now having thus lived in severall countreyes, and alwayes in subjection, they must needs have suffered many commixtures, and wee are sure they are not exempted from the common contagion of venerie contracted first from Christians; nor are fornications unfrequent between them both, there commonly passing opinions of invitement, that their women desire copulation with them, rather then their owne nation, and affect Christian carnality above circumcised venery. It being therefore acknowledged, that some are lost, evident that others are mixed, and scarce probable that any are distinct, it will be hard to establish this quality upon the Jews, unlesse we also transferre the same, unto those whose generations are mixed, whose genealogies are Jewish, and naturally derived from them.

Againe, if we concede a nationall unsavourinesse in any people, yet shall we finde the Jewes lesse subject hereto then any, and that in those regards which most powerfully concurre to such effects, that is, their diet and generation; as for their diet, whether in obedience unto the precepts of reason, or the injunctions of parsimony, therein they are very temperate, seldome offending inebrietie or excesse of drink, nor erring in gulosity or superfluity of meats;[125] whereby they prevent indigestion and crudities, and consequently putrescence of humors; they have in abomination all flesh maymed, or the inwards any way vitiated, and therefore eate no meate but of their owne killing. They observe not onely fasts at certaine times, but are restrained unto very few dishes at all times; so few, that whereas Saint Peter's sheet will hardly cover our tables, their law doth scarce permit them to set forth a lordly feast, nor any way to answer the luxurie of our times, or those of our forefathers; for of flesh their law restraines them many sorts, and such as compleate our feasts: that animal, *propter convivia natum*, they touch not, not any of its preparations, or parts so much in request at Roman tables;[126] nor admit they unto their board, hares, conies, herons, plovers, or swans: of fishes, they onely taste of such as have both finnes and scales, which are comparatively but few in number, such onely, saith Aristotle, whose egge or spawne is arenaceous and friable, whereby are excluded all cetaceous and cartilagineous fishes, many pectinall, whose ribs are rectilineall, many costall, which have their ribs embowed, all spinall, or such as have no ribs, but onely a back bone, or somewhat analogous thereto, as eeles, congers, lampries; all that are testaceous, as oysters, cocles, wilks, schollops, muscles, and likewise all crustaceous, as crabs, shrimps, and lobsters;[127] so that observing a spare and simple dyet, whereby they prevent the generation of crudities, and fasting often, whereby they might also digest them, they must be lesse inclinable unto this infirmity then any other nation, whose proceedings are not so reasonable to avoid it.

As for their generations and conceptions, (which are the purer from good dyet) they become more pure and perfect by the strict observation of their law; upon the injunctions whereof, they severely observe the times of purification, and avoid all copulation, either in the uncleannesse of themselves, or impurity of their women;[128] a rule, I feare not so well observed by Christians, whereby not onely conceptions are prevented, but if they proceed, so vitiated and defiled, that durable inquinations, remaine upon the birth, which when the conception meets with these impurities, must needs be very potent, since in the purest and most faire conceptions, learned men derive the cause of pox and meazels, from principles of that nature, that is, the menstruous impurities in the mothers bloud, and the virulent tinctures contracted by the infant, in the nutriment of the wombe.[129]

Lastly, experience will convict it, for this offensive odor is no way discoverable in their synagogues where many are, and by reason of their number could not be concealed; nor is the same discernible in commerce or conversation with such as are cleanly in apparell, and decent in their houses; surely the Viziars and Turkish Bashas are not of this opinion, who as Sir Henry Blunt informeth, doe generally keepe a Jew of their private counsell;[130] and were this true, the Jews themselves do not strictly make out the intention of their law, for in vaine do they scruple to approach the dead, who livingly are cadaverous, or feare any outward pollution, whose temper pollutes themselves. And lastly, were this true, our opinion is not impartiall, for unto converted Jews who are of the same seed, no man imputeth this unsavoury odor; as though aromatized by their conversion, they admitted their scent with their religion, and they smelt no longer then they savoured of the Jew.[131]

Now the ground that begat or propagated this assertion might be the distastfull aversenesse of the Christian from the Jew, from their corruptnesse, and the villany of that fact, which made them abominable and stinck in the nostrils of all men;[132] which reall practise and metaphoricall expression, did after proceed into a literall construction; but was a fraudulent illation;[133] for such an evill savour their father Jacob acknowledged in himselfe, when he said, his sons had made him stinke in the land, that is, to be abominable unto the inhabitants thereof: now how dangerous it is in sensible things to use metaphoricall expressions unto the people, and what absurd conceits they will swallow in their literals, an impatient example wee have in our owne profession, who having called an eating ulcer by the name of a wolfe, common apprehension conceives a reality therein, and against our selves ocular affirmations are pretended to confirme it.

The nastinesse of that nation, and sluttish course of life hath much promoted the opinion, occasioned by their servile condition at first, and inferiour wayes of parsimony ever since; as is delivered by Mr. Sandys, They are generally fat, saith he, and ranck of the savours which attend upon sluttish corpulency:[134] the epithites assigned them by ancient times have also advanced the same; for Ammianus Marcellinus describeth them in such language, and Martiall more ancient, in such a relative expression sets forth unsavoury Bassa,

Quod jejunia Sabbatariorum
Mallem, quam quod oles, olere Bassa.[135]

From whence notwithstanding wee cannot inferre an inward imperfection in the temper of that nation, which was but an effect in the breath from outward observation in their strict and tedious fasting*; and was a common effect in the breaths of other nations, became a proverbe among the Greeks, and the reason thereof occasioned a probleme in Aristotle.[136]

* Jejunia olere.

Lastly, if all were true, and were this savour conceded, yet are the reasons alleadged for it no way satisfactory: Hucherius in his tract *De Sterilitate*, and after him Alsarius Crucius in his medicall epistles, imputes this effect unto their abstinence from salt or salt meats;[137] which how to make good in the present dyet of the Jews we know not, nor shall we conceive it was observed of old, if we consider they seasoned every sacrifice, and all oblations whatsoever, whereof we cannot deny a great part was eaten by the priests; and if the offering were of flesh it was salted no lesse then thrice, that is, once in the common chamber of salt, at the footestep of the altar, and upon the top thereof, as is at large delivered by Maimonides:[138] nor if they refrained all salt, is the illation very urgent; for many there are not noted for ill odors, which eate no salt at all, as all carnivorous animals, most children, many whole nations, and probably our fathers after the Creation; there being indeed in every thing we eate, a naturall and concealed salt, which is separated by digestions, as doth appeare in our teares, sweat and urines, although we refraine all salt, or what doth seeme to containe it.

Another cause is urged by Campegius, and much received by Christians, that this ill savour is a curse derived upon them by Christ, and stands as a badge or brand of a generation that crucified their *Salvator*; but this is a conceit without all warrant, and an easie way to take off dispute in what point of obscurity soever: a method of many writers, which much depreciates the esteeme and value of miracles, that is, therewith to salve not only reall verities, but also non-existences: thus have elder times, not onely ascribed the immunitie of Ireland from any venemous beast, unto the staffe or rod of Patrick, but the long tayles of Kent unto the malediction of Austin.

Thus therefore, although we concede that many opinions are true which hold some conformity unto this, yet in assenting hereto, many difficulties must arise, it being a dangerous point to annex a constant property unto any nation, and much more this unto the Jew; since 'tis not verifiable by observation, since the grounds are feeble that should establish it, and lastly, since if all were true, yet are the reasons alleadged for it, of no sufficiency to maintaine it.

CHAPTER XI
Of Pigmies

By Pigmies we understand a dwarfish race of people, or lowest diminution of mankinde, comprehended in one cubit, or as some will have it, in two foot, or three spans; not taking them single, but nationally considering them, and as they make up an aggregated habitation, whereof although affirmations be many, and testimonies more frequent then in any other point which wise men have cast into the list of fables, yet that there is, or ever was such a race or Nation, upon exact and confirmed testimonies, our strictest enquiry receaves no satisfaction.

I say, exact testimonies, first, in regard of the Authors from whom we derive the account, for though wee meet herewith in Herodotus, Philostratus, Mela, Pliny, Solinus, and many more; yet were they derivative relators, and the primitive Author was Homer; who, not onely intending profit but pleasure, and using often similies, as well to delight the eare, as to illustrate his matter, in the third of his Iliads, compareth the Trojanes unto the Cranes, when they discend against the Pigmies;[139] which was more largely set out by Oppian, Juvenall, Mantuan, and many Poets since; and being onely a pleasant similitude in the fountaine, became a solemne story in the streame, and current still among us.

Againe, many professed enquirers have rejected it; Strabo an exact and judicious Geographer, hath largely condemned it as a fabulous story in the first of his Geographie.[140] Julius Scaliger a diligent enquirer, accounts thereof, but as a poeticall fiction; Ulysses Aldrovandus a most exact Zoographer in an expresse discourse hereon, concludes the story fabulous, and a poetical account of Homer;[141] and the same was formerly conceived by Eustathius his excellent commentator, Albertus Magnus a man oftimes too credulous, herein was more then dubious, for he affirmeth, if any such dwarfes were ever extant, they were surely some kinde of Apes; which is a conceit allowed by Cardan, and not esteemed improbable by many others.[142]

There are I confesse two testimonies, which from their authority admit of consideration. The first of Aristotle, whose words are these, in the eighth of his History of animals, ἐστὶ δὲ ὁ τόπος &c. That is, *Hic locus est quem incolunt Pygmæi, non enim id fabula est, sed pusillum genus, ut aiunt.*[143] Wherein indeed Aristotle playes the Aristotle, that is, the wary and evading assertor; For though with *non est in fabula*, he seem at first to confirme it, yet at the last he claps in, *sicut aiunt*, and shakes the beliefe he put before upon it; and therefore I observe Scaliger hath not translated the first, perhaps supposing it surreptitious, or unworthy so great an assertor: and truely for those bookes of animals, or worke of eight hundred talents, as Atheneus termes it, although it bee ever to be admired, and containe most excellent truths, yet are many things therein delivered upon relation, and some things repugnant unto the history of our senses;[144] as, wee are able to make out in some, and Scaliger hath observed in many more, as he hath freely declared himselfe in his comment upon that peece.

The second testimony is deduced from holy canonicall Scripture; that is, Ezech. 27. verse 11, thus rendred in the vulgar translation, *Sed et Pygmæi qui erant in turribus tuis, pharetras suas suspenderunt in muris tuis per gyrum*:[145] from whence notwithstanding we cannot inferre this assertion; for first the translatours accord not, and the Hebrew word *Gamadim* is very variously rendred: Though Aquila, Vatablus and Lyra will have it Pygmæi, yet in the Septuagint, it is not more then Watchmen; in the Chaldie, Cappadocians; in Symmachus, Medes; Theodotion of old, and Tremellius of late, have retained the textuarie word, and so have the Italian, French, and English translatours, that is, the men of Arvad were upon thy walles round about, and the Gammadims were in thy towers.

Nor doe men onely dissent in the translation of the word, but in the exposition of the sense and meaning thereof, for some by Gammadims understand a people of Syria, so called from the city Gamala; some hereby understand the Cappadocians, many the Medes, and hereof Forerius hath a singular exposition, conceiving the watchmen of Tyre, who might well bee called Pigmies, the towers of that City being so high, that unto men below they appeared in a cubitall stature;[146] others expounded it quite contrary to common acception that is not men of the least, but of the largest size; so doth Cornelius construe *Pygmæi* or *viri cubitales*, that is not men of a cubit high, but of the largest stature, whose height like that of giants is rather to be taken by the cubit then the foot; in which phrase we read the measure of Goliah whose height is said to be six cubits and a span: of affinity hereto is also the exposition of Jerom, not taking Pygmies for Dwarffes, but stout and valiant

Champions;[147] not taking that sense of *πυγμή*, which signifies the cubit measure, but that which expresseth pugills, that is, men fit for combat and the exercise of the fist: Thus can there bee no satisfying illation from this text, the diversity or rather contrariety of expositions and interpretations, distracting more then confirming the truth of the story.

Againe, I say exact testimonies in reference unto its circumstantiall relations so diversly or contrarily delivered; thus the relation of Aristotle placeth above Ægypt towards the head of Nyle in Africa; Philostratus affirmes they are about Ganges in Asia, and Pliny in a third place, that is Geravia in Scythia: some write they fight with cranes, but Menecles in Athenaeus affirmes they fight with partridges, some say they ride on partridges, and some on the backs of rams.[148]

Lastly, I say confirmed testimonies; for though *Paulus Jovius* delivers there are Pygmies beyond Japan, Pigafeta, about the Moluccas, and Olaus Magnus placeth them in Greenland; yet wanting frequent confirmation in a matter so confirmable, their affirmation carrieth but slow perswasion; and wise men may thinke there is as much reallity in the Pygmies of Paracelsus; that is, his non-Adamicall men, or middle natures betwixt men and spirits.

There being thus no sufficient confirmation of their verity, some doubt may arise concerning their possibility; wherein, since it is not defined in what dimensions the soule may exercise her faculties, wee shall not conclude impossibility, or that there might not be a race of Pygmies, as there is sometimes of giants; and so may we take in the opinion of Austine, and his comment Ludovicus; but to beleeve they should be in the stature of a foot or span, requires the preaspection of such a one as Philetas the poet in Athenæus, who was faine to fasten lead unto his feet lest the wind should blow him away, or that other in the same author, who was so little *ut ad obolum accederet,* a story so strange that we might herein accuse the printer, did not the account of Ælian accord unto it, as Causabone hath observed in his learned Animadversions.[149]

Lastly, if any such Nation there were, yet is it ridiculous what men have delivered of them; that they fight with cranes upon the backs of rams or partridges: or what is delivered by Ctesias that they are negroes in the middest of India, whereof the King of that country entertaineth three thousand archers for his guard; which is a relation below the tale of Oberon, nor could they better defend him, then the emblem saith they offended Hercules whilest he slept, that is to wound him no deeper, then to awake him.

CHAPTER XII
Of the great Climactericall yeare, that is sixty three[150]

Certainly the eyes of the understanding, and those of sense are differently deceived in their greatest objects; the sense apprehending them in lesser magnitudes then their dimensions require; so it beholdeth the sunne, the starres, and the earth it selfe; but the understanding quite otherwise, for that ascribeth unto many things far larger horizons then their due circumscriptions require, and receiveth them with amplifications which their reallity will not admit: thus hath it fared with many heroes and most worthy persons, who being sufficiently commendable from true and unquestionable merits, have received advancement from falshood and the fruitfull stocke of fables: thus hath it happened unto the stars and luminaries of heaven, who being sufficiently admirable in themselves have been set out by effects no way dependent on their efficiencies, and advanced by amplifications to the questioning of their true endowments: Thus is it not improbable it hath also fared with number, which though wonderfull in it selfe, and sufficiently magnifyable from its demonstrable affections, hath yet received adjections of admiration from the multiplying conceits of men, and stands laden with additions which its equity will not admit.

And so perhaps hath it happened unto the number 7. and 9. which multiplyed into themselves doe make up 63. commonly esteemed the great climactericall of our lives; for the dayes of men are usually cast up by septenaries, and every seventh yeare conceived to carry some altering character with it, either in the temper of body, minde, or both; but among all other, three are most remarkable, that is 7. times 7. or forty nine, 9. times 9. or eighty one, and 7. times 9. or the yeare of sixty three; which is conceived to carry with it, the most considerable fatality, and consisting of both the other numbers was apprehended to comprise the vertue of either, is therefore expected and entertained with feare, and esteemed a favour of fate to passe it over; which notwithstanding many suspect to be but a panick terrour, and men to feare they justly know not what; and for my owne part, to speake indifferently, I finde no satisfaction, nor any sufficiency in the received grounds to establish a rationall feare...

CHAPTER XIII
Of the Canicular or Dogdayes

Whereof to speake distinctly: among the southerne constellations two there are which beare the name of the dog; the one in 16. degrees of latitude, containing on the left thigh a star of the first magnitude, usually called Procyon or Anticanis, because say some it riseth before the other; which if truly understood, must be restrained unto those habitations, who have elevation of pole above thirty two degrees; mention thereof there is in Horace, who seemes to mistake or confound the one with the other; and after him in Galen, who is willing the remarkablest starre of the other should be called by this name, because it is the first that ariseth in the constellation; which notwithstanding, to speake strictly, it is not, unlesse we except one of the third magnitude in the right paw in his owne and our elevation, and two more on his head in and beyond the degree of sixty; it is also called *canis minor*, though not *canicula*, by which diminitive is meant the greater dog-star: a second and more considerable one there is, and neighbour unto the other in 40. degrees of Latitude, containing 18. starres, whereof that in his mouth of the first magnitude the Greeks call Σέιριος, the Latines *canis major*, and wee emphatically the dog-Starre.

Now from the rising of this starre not cosmically, that is with the sun, but heliacally, that is, its emersion from the rayes of the sunne, the ancients computed their canicular dayes; concerning which there generally passeth an opinion, that during those dayes, all medication or use of physick is to be declined, and the cure committed unto nature, and therefore as though there were any feriation in nature or justitiums imaginable in professions, whose subject is naturall, and under no intermissive, but constant way of mutation; this season is commonly termed the physitians vacation, and stands so received by most men: which conceit however generall, is not onely erroneous, but unnaturall, and subsisting upon foundations either false, uncertaine, mistaken, or misapplied, deserves not of mankinde that indubitable assent it findeth...

THE FIFTH BOOK

Of many things questionable as they are commonly described in pictures

CHAPTER I
Of the Picture of the Pelecan

And first in every place we meet with the picture of the pelecan, opening her breast with her bill, and feeding her young ones with the bloud distilling from her: thus is it set forth not onely in common signes, but in the crest and scucheon of many noble families, hath been asserted by many holy writers, and was an hieroglyphicke of pietie and pittie among the Ægyptians, on which consideration, they spared them at their tables.

Notwithstanding upon enquirie we finde no mention hereof in ancient zoographers, and such as have particularly discoursed upon animals, as Aristotle, Ælian, Plinie, Solinus and many more, who seldom forget proprieties of such a nature, and have beene very punctuall in lesse considerable records: some ground hereof I confesse wee may allow, nor need wee deny a remarkeable affection in pelecans toward their young; for Ælian discoursing of storkes, and their affection toward their brood whom they instruct to flie, and unto whom they redeliver up the provision of their bellies, concludeth at last, that herons and pelecans do the like.[1]

As for the testimonies of ancient fathers, and ecclesiasticall writers, we may more safely conceive therein some emblematicall then any reall storie: so doth Eucherius confesse it to bee the embleme of Christ;[2] and wee are unwilling literally to receive that account of Jerome, that perceiving her young ones destroyed by serpents, she openeth her side with her bill, by the blood whereof they revive and return unto life againe;[3] by which relation they might indeed illustrate the destruction of man by the old serpent, and his restorement by the blood of Christ; and in this sense we shall not dispute the like relations of Austine, Isidore, Albertus, and many more, and under an emblematicall intention, we accept it in coat armour.[4]

As for the hieroglyphick of the Ægyptians, they erected the same upon another story, that is, from earnestly protecting her young, when her nest was set on fire; for as for letting out her blood, it was not the assertion of the Egyptians, but seemes translated unto the pelecan from the vulture, as Pierius hath most plainly delivered *sed quod pelicanum (ut etiam alijs plerisque persuasum est) rostro pectus dissecantem pingunt, ita ut suo sanguine filios alat, ab Ægyptiorum historiâ valde alienum est, illi enim vulturem tantum id facere tradiderunt.*[5]

And lastly, as concerning the picture, if naturally examined, and not hieroglyphically conceived, it containeth many improprieties, disagreeing almost in all things from the true and proper description: for first, whereas it is commonly set forth green or yellow, in its proper colour, it is inclining to white, excepting the extreamities or tops of the wing feathers, which are black:[6] it is described in the bignesse of a henne, whereas it approacheth and sometimes exceedeth the magnitude of a swanne; it is commonly painted with a short bill, whereas that of the pelecan attaineth sometimes the length of two spannes. The bill is made acute or pointed at the end; whereas indeed it is flat and broad, and somewhat inverted at the extreame. It is discribed like fissipedes, or birdes which have their feet or clawes divided; whereas it is palmipedous, or finfooted like swannes and geese, according to the methode of nature, in latirostrous or flat bild birdes, which being generally swimmers, the organ is wisely contriv'd unto the action, and they are framed with fins or oares upon their feet;[7] and therefore they neither light, nor build on trees, if we except cormorants, who make their nests like herons. Lastly, there is one part omitted more remarkeable then any other, and that is the chowle or croppe adhering unto the lower side of the bill, and so descending by the throat; a bagge or sachell very observable, and of capacity almost beyond credit; which notwithstanding, this animall could not want; for therein (as Aristotle, Ælian, and Bellonius since averreth) it receiveth oysters, cochles, sckollops, and other testaceous animals, which being not able to breake, it retaines them untill they open, and vomitting them up, takes out the meat contained.[8] This is that part preserved for a rarity, and wherein (as Sanctius delivers) in one dissected, a negro childe was found.[9]

[A possibility there may be of opening and bleeding their breast;[10] for this may be done by the uncous and pointed extremity of their bill; and some probability also that they sometimes do it, for their own relief, though not for their young ones; that is by nibling and biting themselves on the itching part of their breast, upon fullness or acrimony of blood. And the same may be better made out; if (as some relate) their feathers on that part are sometimes observed to be red and tincted with blood.]

CHAPTER II
Of the Picture of Dolphins

That dolphins are crooked, is not onely affirmed by the hand of the painter, but commonly conceived their naturall and proper figure; which is not onely the opinion of our times, but seemes the beliefe of elder times before us: for beside the expressions of Ovid and Pliny, their pourtraicts in some ancient coynes are framed in this figure, as will appeare in some thereof in Gesner, others in Goltsius, and Lævinus Hulsius in his description of coynes, from Julius Caesar unto Rhodulphus the second.[11]

Notwithstanding, to speake strictly in their naturall figure they are straight, nor have they their spine connexed, or more considerably embowed, then sharkes, porposes, whales, and other cetaceous animalls, as Scaliger plainly affirmeth; *Corpus habet non magis curvum quam reliqui pisces*;[12] as ocular enquiry informeth, and as unto such as have not had the opportunitie to behold them, their proper pourtraicts will discover in Rondeletius, Gesner, and Aldrovandus, and as indeed is deducible from pictures themselves; for though they be drawne repandous, or connexedly crooked in one piece, yet the dolphin that carrieth Arion is concavously inverted, and hath its spine depressed in another.[13]

And therefore what is delivered of their incurvitie, must either bee taken emphatically, that is not really but in appearance; which happeneth, when they leap above water, and suddenly shoot downe againe; which is a fallacy in vision, whereby straight bodies in a sudden motion protruded obliquely downeward, appear unto the eye crooked, and this is the construction of Bellonius:[14] or if it be taken really, it must not universally and perpetually, that is, not when they swimme and remaine in their proper figures, but onely when they leape, or impetuously whirle their bodies any way, and this is the opinion of Gesnerus. Or lastly, it must be taken neither really, nor emphatically, but onely emblematically; for being the hyeroglyphick of celerity, and swifter then other animals, men best expressed their velocity by incurvity, and under some figure of a bowe, and in this sense probably doe heralds also receive it, when from a dolphin extended, they distinguish a dolphin imbowed.

And thus also must that picture be taken of a dolphin clasping an anchor; that is not really, as is by most conceived out of affection unto man, conveighing the anchor unto the ground, but emblematically, according as Pierius hath expressed it, The swiftest animall conjoyned with that heavie body, implying that common morall, *festina lente*, and that celerity should always be contempered with cunctation.[15]

CHAPTER III
Of the Picture of a Grashopper

There is also among us a common description and picture of a grashopper, as may be observed in the pictures of emblematists in the coats of severall families, and as the word *cicada* is usually translated in dictionaries; wherein to speake strictly, if by this word grashopper, we understand that animall which is implied by τέττιξ with the Greeks, and by *cicada* with the Latines, we may with safety affirme the picture is widely mistaken, and that for ought enquiry can informe, there is no such insect in England, which how paradoxicall soever, upon a strict enquiry, will prove undeniable truth.

For first, that animall the French tearme *sauterelle*, we a grashopper, and which under this name is commonly described by us, is named ἀκρίς by the Greekes, by the Latines *locusta*, and by our selves in proper speech a locust; as in the dyet of John Baptist, and in our translation, Proverbs 30, the locusts have no king, yet goe they forth all of them by bands.[16] Againe, between the *cicada* and that wee call a grashopper, the differences are very many, as may bee observed in themselves, or their descriptions in Mathiolus, Aldrovandus, and Muffetus:[17] for first, they are differently cucullated or capuched upon the head and backe, and in the *cicada* the eyes are more prominent;[18] the locusts have *antennae* or long hornes before, with a long falcation or forcipated tayle behinde, and being ordained for saltation, their hinder legs doe far exceed the other.[19] The locust or our grashopper hath teeth, the *cicada* none at all, nor any mouth according unto Aristotle; the *cicada* is most upon trees; and lastly, the note or fritiniancy thereof is far more shrill then that of the locust, and its life so short in Summer, that for provision it needs not recourse unto the providence of the pismire in Winter.[20]

And therefore where the *cicada* must be understod, the pictures of heralds and emblematists are not exact, nor is it safe to adhere unto the interpretation of dictionaries, and we must with candour make out our owne translations: for in the plague of Ægypt, Exodus 10. the word ἀκρίς is translated a locust, but in the same sense and subject, Wisdome 16, it is translated a grashopper, For them the bitings of grashoppers and flyes killed:[21] whereas we have declared before the *cicada* hath no teeth, but is conceived to live upon dew, and the possibility of its subsistence is disputed by Licetus.[22] Hereof I perceive Muffetus hath taken notice, and dissenteth from Langius and Lycostenes, while they deliver, the cicadas destroyed the fruits in Germany, where indeed that insect is not found; and therefore concludeth, *Tam ipsos quam alios deceptos fuisse autumo, dum locustas cicadas esse vulgari errore crederent.*[23]

And hereby there may be some mistake in the due dispensation of medicines desumed from this animall, particularly of diatettigon commended by Ætius in the affections of the kidneys:[24] it must be likewise understood with some restriction what hath been affirmed by Isidore, which is yet delivered by many, that cicades are bred out of cuccow spittle, or woodseare;[25] that is, that spumous frothy dew or exudation or both, found upon plants, especially about the joynts of lavender and rosemary, and observable with us about the latter end of May; for here the true cicada is not bred, but certaine it is, that out of this, some kinde of locust doth proceed; for herein may be discovered a little insect of a festucine or pale green, resembling in all parts a locust, or what we call a grashopper.

Lastly, the word it selfe is improper, and the tearme of grashopper not appliable unto the cicada; for therein the organs of motion are not contrived for saltation, nor are the hinder legges of such extension, as is observable in salient animalls, and such as move by leaping; whereto the locust is very well conformed; for therein the legs behinde are longer then all the body, and make at the second joynt acute angles, at a considerable advancement above their backs.

The mistake therefore with us might have its originall from a defect in our language; for having not the insect with us, we have not fallen upon its proper name, and so make use of a tearme common unto it and the locust, whereas other countries have proper expressions for it; so the Italian calls it cicada, the Spaniard cigarra, and the French cigale; all which appellations conforme unto the originall, and properly expresse this animall. [Whereas our word is borrowed from the Saxon Gærsthopp, which our forefathers, who never beheld the *Cicada*, used for that insect which we yet call a Grashopper.[26]]

CHAPTER IV
Of the Picture of the Serpent tempting Eve

In the picture of Paradice, and delusion of our first parents, the serpent is often described with humane visage, and not unlike unto Cadmus, or his wife, in the act of their metamorphosis, which is not meerly a pictoriall contrivance or invention of the painter, but an ancient tradition and conceived reallity, as it stands delivered by Beda and authors of some antiquity;[27] that is, that Sathan appeared not unto Eve in the naked forme of a serpent, but with a virgins head, that thereby he might become more acceptable, and his temptation finde the easier entertaine; which neverthelesse is a conceit not to bee admitted, and the plaine and received figure, is with better reason embraced.

For first, as Pierius observeth from Barcephas, the assumption of humane shape, had proved a disadvantage unto Sathan;[28] affording not only a suspicious amazement in Eve, before the fact, in beholding a third humanity beside her self and Adam; but leaving some excuse unto the woman, which afterward the man tooke up with lesser reason; that is, to have been deceived by another like her selfe.

Againe, there was no inconvenience in the shape assumed, or any considerable impediment that might disturbe that performance in the common forme of a serpent: for whereas it is conceived the woman must needs be afraid thereof, and rather flye then approach it, it was not agreeable unto the condition of Paradise and state of innocencie therein; if in that place as most determine, no creature was hurtfull or terrible unto man, and those destructive effects they now discover succeeded the curse, and came in with thornes and briars; and therefore Eugubinus (who affirmeth this serpent was a basiliske) incurreth no absurdity, nor need we inferre that Eve should bee destroyed immediatly upon that vision;[29] for noxious animalls could offend them no more in the garden, then Noah in the Arke: as they peaceably received their names, so they friendly possessed their natures: and were their conditions destructive unto each other, they were not so unto man, whose constitutions were antidotes, and needed not feare poysons, who had not incurred mortality. And if (as most conceive) there were but two created of every kinde, they could not at that time destroy either man or themselves; for this had frustrated the command of multiplication, destroyed a species, and imperfected the creation: and therefore also if Cain were the first man borne, with him entred not only the act, but the first power of murther; for before that time neither could the serpent nor Adam destroy Eve, nor Adam and Eve each other, for that had overthrowne the intention of the world, and put its Creator to act the sixt day over againe.

Moreover, whereas in regard of speech, and vocall conference with Eve, it may be thought he would rather assume an humane shape and organs, then the improper forme of a serpent, it implyes no materiall impediment; nor need we to wonder how he contrived a voice out of the mouth of a serpent, who hath done the like out of the belly of a pythonissa, and the trunke of an oake, as he did for many yeares at Dodona.[30]

Lastly, whereas it might be conceived that an humane shape was fitter for this enterprise, it being more then probable she would be amazed to heare a serpent speak; some conceive she might not yet be certaine that onely man was priviledged with speech, and being in the novity of the creation, and inexperience of all things, might not bee affrighted to hear a serpent speak: beside she might be ignorant of their natures who was not versed in their names, as being not present at the generall survey of animalls, when Adam assigned unto every one a name concordant unto its nature; nor is this only my opinion, but the determination of Lombard and Tostatus, and also the reply of Cyrill unto the objection of Julian, who compared this story unto the fables of the Greekes.[31]

CHAPTER V
Of the Picture of Adam and Eve with Navells

Another mistake there may be in the picture of our first parents, who after the manner of their posterity are both delineated with a navell: and this is observable not only in ordinary and stayned peeces, but in the authenticke draughts of Urbin, Angelo, and others;[32] which notwithstanding cannot be allowed, except we impute that unto the first cause, which we impose not on the second, or what we deny unto nature, we impute unto naturity it selfe, that is, that in the first and most accomplished peece, the Creator affected superfluities, or ordained parts without all use or office.[33]

For the use of the navell is to continue the infant unto the mother, and by the vessells thereof to convey its aliment and sustentation: the vessells whereof it consisteth, are the umbilicall veyne, which is a branch of the porta, and implanted in the liver of the infant; two arteries likewise arising from the iliacall branches, by which the infant receiveth the purer portion of bloud and spirits from the mother; and lastly, the urachos or ligamentall passage derived from the bottome of the bladder, whereby it dischargeth the waterish and urinary part of its aliment: now upon the birth when the infant forsaketh the wombe although it dilacerate, and breake the involving membranes, yet doe these vessells hold, and by the mediation thereof the infant is connected unto the wombe not only before, but a while also after the birth:[34] these therefore the midwife cutteth off, contriving them into a knot close unto the body of the infant, from whence ensueth that tortuosity or complicated nodosity we usually call the navell, occasioned by the colligation of vessells before mentioned:[35] now the navell or vessells whereof it is constituted, being a part precedent, and not subservient unto generation, nativity, or parturition, it cannot be well imagined at the creation or extraordinary formation of Adam, who immediately issued from the artifice of God; nor also that of Eve, who was not solemnly begotten, but suddenly framed, and anomalously proceeded from Adam.

And if we be led into conclusions that Adam had also this part, because we behold the same in our selves, the inference is not reasonable; for if we conceive the way of his formation, or of the first animalls did carry in all points a strict conformity unto succeeding productions, we might fall into imaginations that Adam was made without teeth, or that hee ran through those notable alterations in the vessells of the heart, which the infant suffereth after birth: we need not dispute whether the egge or bird were first, and might conceive that dogges were created blind, because we observe they are littered so with us; which to affirm, is to confound, at least to regulate creation unto generation, the first acts of God, unto the second of nature, which were determined in that generall indulgence, encrease and multiply, produce or propagate each other;[36] that is, not answerably in all points, but in a prolonged method according to seminall progression: for the formation of things at first was different from their generation after; and although it had no thing to precede, it was aptly contrived for that which should succeed it: and therefore though Adam were framed without this part, as having no other wombe then that of his proper principles, yet was not his posterity without the same: for the seminalty of his fabricke contained the power thereof, and was endued with the science of those parts whose predestinations upon succession it did accomplish.

All the navell therefore and conjunctive part we can suppose in Adam, was his dependency on his maker, and the connexion he must needs have unto heaven, who was the Son of God, for holding no dependence on any preceding efficient but God, in the act of his production there may bee conceived some connexion, and Adam to have been in a momentall navell with his Maker:[37] and although from his carnallity and corporall existence the conjunction seemeth no nearer then of causality and effect, yet in his immortall and diviner part hee seemed to hold a nearer coherence, and an umbilicality even with God himselfe:[38] and so indeed although the propriety of this part bee found but in some animalls, and many species there are which have no navell at all; yet is there one linke and common connexion, one generall ligament, and necessary obligation of all whatever unto God; whereby although they act themselves at distance, and seem to be at loose, yet doe they hold a continuity with their Maker; which catenation or conserving union when ever his pleasure shall divide, let goe, or separate, they shall fall from their existence, essence, and operations;[39] in briefe, they must retire unto their primitive nothing, and shrinke into their chaos againe.

[They who hold the egge was before the bird, prevent this doubt in many other animals, which also extendeth unto them;[40] for birds are nourished by umbilicall vessels, and the navell is manifest sometimes a day or two after exclusion; the same is probable in all oviparous exclusions, if the lesser part of egges must serve for the formation, the greater part for nutriment. The same is made out in the egges of snakes; and is not improbable in the generation of porwiggles or tadpoles, and may be also true in some vermiparous exclusions; although (as we have observed in the daily progresse in some) the whole maggot is little enough to make a flye, without any part remaining.]

CHAPTER VI

Of the Pictures of Easterne Nations, and the Jews at their Feasts, especially our Saviour at the Passeover

Concerning the pictures of the Jews, and easterne nations at their feasts, concerning the gesture of our Saviour at the Passeover, who is usually described sitting upon a stoole or bench at a square table, in the middest of the twelve, many make great doubt; and though they concede a table jesture will hardly allow this usuall way of session.[41]

Wherein restrayning no mans enquiry, it will appeare that accubation, or lying downe at meales was a gesture used by very many nations.[42] [That the Persians used it,[43] beside the testimony of humane writers, is deducible from that passage in Esther.[44] That when the King returned unto the place of the banquet of wine, Haman was fallen upon the bed whereon Esther was.] That the Parthians used it, is evident from Athenæus, who delivereth out of Possidonius, that their king lay downe at meales, on an higher bed then others.[45] That Cleopatra thus entertained Anthonie, the same author manifesteth when he saith, shee prepared twelve tricliniums.[46] That it was in use among the Greeks, the word triclinium implyeth, and the same is also declareable from many places in the Symposiacks of Plutarke.[47] That it was not out of fashion in the dayes of Aristotle, hee declareth in his Politicks, when among the institutionary rules of youth, he adviseth they might not be permitted to heare iambicks and tragedies before they were admitted unto discumbency or lying along with others at their meales.[48] That the Romanes used this gesture at repast, beside many more is evident from Lipsius, Mercurialis, Salmasius, and Ciaconius who have expresly and distinctly treated hereof.[49]

Now of their accumbing places, the one was called stibadion and sigma, carrying the figure of an halfe moone, and of an uncertaine capacity, whereafter it received the name of hexaclinon, octoclinon, according unto that of Martial,

Accipe Lunata scriptum testudine Sigma
Octo capit, veniat quisquis amicus erit.[50]

Here at the left wing was the principall place, and the most honourable person, if hee were not master of the feast possessed that roome. The other was tearmed triclinium, that is, three beds encompassing a table, as may be seen in the figures thereof, and particularly in the Rhamnusian Triclinium, set down by Mercurialis. The customary use hereof was probably deduced from the frequent use of bathing, after which they commonly retired to bed, and refected themselves with repast; and so that custome by degrees changed their cubiculary beds into discubitory, and introduced a fashion to goe from the bathes unto these.[51]

As for their gesture or position, the men lay downe leaning on their left elbow, their backe being advanced by some pillow or soft substance; the second lay so with his backe towards the first, that his head attained about his bosome; and the rest in the same order: for women, they sat sometimes distinctly with their sexe, sometime promiscuously with men, according to affection or favour, as is delivered by Juvenal, *Gremio jacuit nova nupta mariti*, and by Suetonius of Caligula, that at his feasts he placed his sisters, with whom hee had beene incontinent, successively in order below him.[52]

Againe, as their beds were three, so the guests did not usually exceed that number in every one, according to the ancient lawes, and proverbiall observations to begin with the Graces, and make up their feasts with the Muses: and therefore it was remarkable in the Emperour Lucius Verus, that he lay downe with twelve: which was, saith Julius Capitolinus, *præter exempla majorum*, not according to the custome of his predecessors, except it were at publick and nuptiall suppers.[53] [The regular number was also exceeded in this last supper, whereat there were no lesse than thirteen, and in no place fewer then ten, for, as Josephus delivereth, it was not lawful to celebrate the Passover with fewer than that number.[54]]

Lastly, for the disposing and ordering of the persons: the first and middle beds were for the guests, the third and lowest for the master of the house and his family; he always lying in the first place of the last bed, that is next the middle bed, but if the wife or children were absent, their roomes were supplied by the umbræ or hangers on, according to that of Juvenal, *Locus est et pluribus umbris*:[55] for the guests, the honourablest place in every bed was the first, excepting the middle or second bed, wherein the most honourable guest of the feast was placed in the last place, because by that position he might be next the

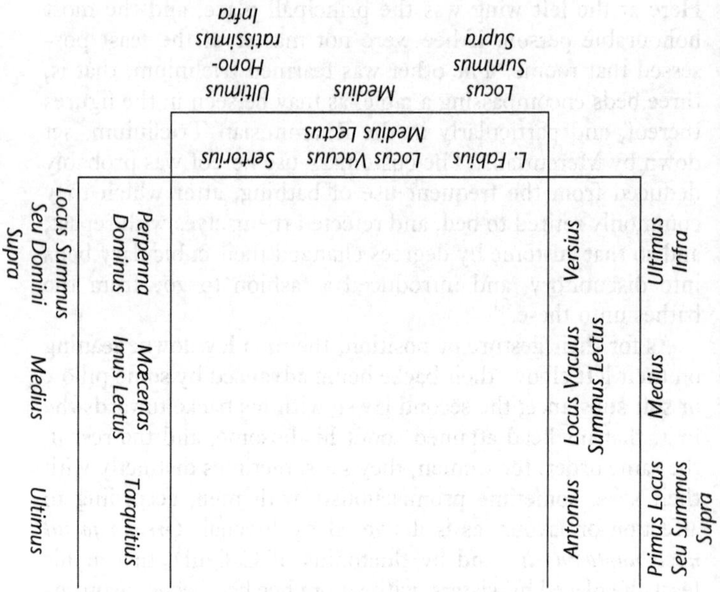

Locus Summus Supra
Medius
Ultimus Honoratissimus Infra
Medius Lectus
L. Fabius
Locus Vacuus
Sertorius
Locus Summus Seu Domini Supra
Medius
Ultimus
Perpenna Dominus
Mæcenas Imus Lectus
Tarquitius
Versius
Locus Vacuus Summus Lectus
Antonius
Ultimus Infra
Medius
Primus Locus Seu Summus Supra

FIG. 4 Image of Seating Plan.

master of the feast; for the master lying in the first of the last bed, and the principall guest in the last place of the second, they must needs be next each other, as this figure doth plainely declare, and whereby wee may apprehend the feast of Perpenna made unto Sertorius, described by Salustius, whose words we shall thus read with Salmasius: *Igitur discubuere, Sertorius inferior in medio lecto, supra Fabius, Antonius in summo, infra scriba Sertorii Versius, alter scriba Mæcenas in imo, medius inter Tarquitium et Dominum Perpennam.*[56]

At this feast there were but seaven; the middle places of the highest and middle bed being vacant, and hereat was Sertorius the Generall and principall guest slaine; and so may wee make out what is delivered by Plutark in his life, that lying on his backe, and raysing himselfe up, Perpenna cast himself upon his stomack;[57] which he might very well do being master of the feast, and lying next unto him, and thus also from this tricliniarie disposure, we may illustrate that obscure expression of Seneca; that the northwinde was in the middle, the north-east on the higher side, and the north-west on the lower; for as appeareth in the circle of the windes, the north-east will answer the bed of Antonius, and the north-west that of Perpenna.[58]

That the custome of feasting upon beds was in use among the Hebrewes, many diduce from the 23 of Ezekiel, Thou sattest upon a stately bed, and a table prepared before it.[59] The custome of discalceation or putting off their shoes at meales, is conceived by some to confirme the same; as by that meanes keeping their beds cleane, and therefore they had a peculiar charge to eate the Passeover with their shooes on, which injunction were needlesse, if they used not to put them off.[60]

That this discumbency at meales was in use in the dayes of our Saviour is conceived probable from severall speeches of his expressed in that phrase, even unto common auditors, as Luke the 14. *Cum Invitatus fueris ad nuptias non discumbas in primo loco*, and besides many more, Matthew the 23. when reprehending the Scribes and Pharisees, hee saith, *Amant protoclisias id est primos recubitus in cœnis, et Protocathedrias sive primas cathedras in Synagogis*:[61] wherein the tearms are very distinct, and by an antithesis do plainly distinguish the posture of sitting, from this of lying on beds.[62] [The consent of the Jews with the Romans in other ceremonies and rites of feasting, makes probable their conformity in this. The Romans washed, were anointed, and wore a cenatory garment: and that the same was practised by the Jews, is deduceable from that expostulation of our Saviour with Simon, that he washed not his feet, nor anointed his head with oyle: the common civilities at festivall entertainments: and that expression of his concerning the cenatory or wedding garment;[63] and as some conceive of the linnen garment of the young man or St. John; which might be the same he wore the night before at the last Supper.]

That they used this gesture at the Passeover, is more then probable from the testimony of Jewish writers, and particularly of Ben-maimon recorded by Scaliger *de emendatione temporum*: after the second cup according to the institution, Exodus 12. the son asketh, what meaneth this service?[64] Then he that maketh the declaration saith, How different is this night from all other nights? for all other nights wee wash but once, but this night twice; all other wee eat leavened or unleavened bread, but this onely leavened; all other we eat flesh roasted, boyled, or baked, but this only roasted; all other nights we eat together lying or sitting, but this only lying along; and this posture they used as a token of rest and security which they enjoyed far different from that, at the eating of the Passeover in Ægypt.

That this gesture was used when our Saviour eate the Passeover, is not conceived improbable from the words whereby the Evangelists expresse the same, that is, ἀναπίπτειν, ἀνακεῖσθαι, κατακεῖσθαι, ἀνακλειθῆναι, which termes do properly signifie this gesture in Aristotle, Athenæus, Euripides, Sophocles, and all humane authors; and the like we meete with in the paraphrasticall expression of Nonnus.[65]

[Lastly,[66] if it be not fully conceded, that this gesture was used at the Passeover, yet that it was observed at the last supper, seems almost incontrovertible: for at this feast or cenatory convention, learned men make more than one supper, or at least many parts thereof. The first was that legall one of the Passover, or eating of the Paschall Lamb with bitter herbs, and ceremonies described by Moses. Of this it is said, that when the even was come he sate down with the twelve. This is supposed when it is said, that the supper being ended, our Saviour arose, took a towel and washed the disciples feet. The second was common and domesticall, consisting of ordinary and undefined provisions; of this it may be said, that our Saviour took his garment, and sate down again, after he had washed the Disciples feet, and performed the preparative civilities of suppers; at this 'tis conceived the soppe was given unto Judas, the originall word implying some broath or decoction, not used at the Passeover. The third or latter part was Eucharisticall, which began at the breaking and blessing of the bread, according to that of Matthew, And as they were eating, Jesus took bread and blessed it.]

[Now although at the Passeover or first supper, many have doubted this reclining posture, and some have affirmed that our Saviour stood; yet that he lay down at the other, the same men have acknowledged, as Chrysostom, Theophylact, Austin, and many more. And if the tradition will hold, the position is unquestionable; for the very triclinium is to be seen at Rome, brought thither by Vespasian, and graphically set forth by Casalius.]

And thus may it properly be made out; what is delivered John 13. *Erat recumbens unus ex Discipulis ejus in sinu Jesu quem diligebat*; Now there was leaning on Jesus bosome one of his disciples whom Jesus loved;[67] which gesture will not so well agree unto the position of sitting, but is naturall, and cannot be avoyded in the laws of accubation;[68] and the very same expression is to be found in Pliny, concerning the Emperour Nerva and Veiento whom he favoured, *Cænabat Nerva cum paucis, Veiento recumbebat propius atque etiam in sinu*;[69] and from this custome arose the word ἐπιστήθιος, that is, a neere and bosome friend: and therefore Causabon justly rejecteth Theophylact, who not considering the ancient manner of decumbency, imputed this gesture of the beloved disciple unto rusticity, or an act of incivility;[70] and thus also have some conceived; it may be more plainly made out what is delivered of Mary Magdalen, Luke 7. That she stood at Christs feet behinde him weeping, and began to wash his feet with teares, and did wipe them with the haires of her head;[71] which actions, if our Saviour sate, she could not performe standing, and had rather stood behinde his back, then at his feet; and thus it cannot be reconciled what is observable in many pieces, and even of Raphaell Urbin, wherein Mary Magdalen is pictured before our Saviour, washing his feet on her knees, which will not consist with the strict description and letter of the text.

Now whereas this position may seeme to be discountenanced by our translation, which usually renders it sitting, it cannot have that illation; for the French and Italian translations expressing neither position of session or recubation, do onely say that he placed himselfe at the table, and when ours expresseth the same by sitting, it is in relation unto our custome, time, and apprehension; and the like upon occasion is not unusuall in our translation; so when it is said Luke 4 πτύξας τὸ βιβλίον, and the Vulgar renders it, *Cum plicasset librum*, ours translateth it, he shut or closed the booke, which is an expression proper unto the paginall books of our times, but not so agreeable unto volumes or rolling bookes in use among the Jews, not onely in elder times, but even unto this day.[72] So when it is said, the Samaritan delivered unto the host two pence for the provision of the Levite;[73] and when our Saviour agreed with the labourers for a penny a day, in strict translation it should be seven pence halfe penny, and is not to be conceived our common penny, the sixtieth part of an ounce;[74] for the word in the originall is δηνάριον, in Latine, *Denarius*, and with the Romans did valew the eight part of an ounce, which after five shillings the ounce amounteth unto seven pence halfe penny of our money.

Lastly, whereas it might be conceived that they eate the Passeover standing rather then sitting, or lying downe, according to the institution, Exodus 12. Thus shall you eate with your loynes girded, your shooes on your feet, and your staffe in your hand;[75] the Jews themselves reply, this was not required of succeeding generations, and was not observed, but in the Passeover of Ægypt, and so also many other injunctions were afterward omitted, as the taking up of the Paschall lambe, from the tenth day, the eating of it in their houses dispersed, the striking of the bloud on the dore posts, and the eating thereof in haste; solemnities and ceremonies primitively enjoyned, afterward omitted, as was also this of station, for the occasion ceasing, and being in security, they applyed themselves unto gestures in use among them.

CHAPTER VII
Of the Picture of our Saviour with Long Hayre

Another picture there is of our Saviour described with long haire, according to the custome of the Jews, and his description sent by Lentulus unto the senate; wherein indeed the hand of the painter is not accusable, but the judgement of the common spectator, conceaving he observed this fashion of his hayre, because he was a Nazarite, and confounding a Nazarite by vow, with those by birth or education.

The Nazarite by vow is declared Numbers 6. and was to refraine three things, drinking of wine, cutting the hayre, and approaching unto the dead, and such a one was Sampson:[76] now that our Saviour was a Nazarite after this kinde, we have no reason to determine, for he dranke wine, and was therefore called by the Pharisees a wine bibber; he approached also the dead, as when he raised from death Lazarus, and the daughter of Jairus.[77]

The other Nazarite was a topicall appellation, and applyable unto such as were borne in Nazareth, a city of Galilee, and in the tribe of Napthali; neither if strictly taken, was our Saviour in this sense a Nazarite; for he was borne in Bethleem in the tribe of Judah; but might receave that name, because he abode in that city, and was not onely conceaved therein, but there also passed the silent part of his life, after his returne from Ægypt, as is delivered by Matthew, And he came and dwelt in a city called Nazareth, that it might be fulfilled which was spoken by the prophet, he shall be called a Nazarene;[78] both which kindes of Nazarites, as they are distinguishable by Zain, and Tsade in the Hebrew, so in the Greeke, by Alpha and Omega; for as

Jansenius observeth, where the votary Nazarite is mentioned, it is written *Ναζαραῖος*, as Leviticus 6. and Lamentations the fourth, where it is spoken of our Saviour, we reade it *Ναζωρεῖος*, as in Matthew, Luke, and John, onely Marke who writ his gospell at Rome did Latinize and wrote it *Ναζαρηνός*.

CHAPTER VIII
Of the Picture of Abraham sacrificing Isaac

In the picture of the immolation of Isaac, or Abraham sacrificing his son, Isaac is described as a little boy, which notwithstanding is not consentaneous unto the authority of expositors, or the circumstance of the text;[79] for therein it is delivered that Isaac carried on his back the wood for the sacrifice, which being an holocaust or burnt offering to be consumed unto ashes, we cannot well conceive the wood a burthen for a boy, but such a one unto Isaac, as that which it typified was unto Christ, that is, the wood or crosse whereon he suffered, which was too heavy a loade for his shoulders, and was faine to be relieved therein by Simon of Cyrene.[80]

Againe, he was so farre from a boy, that he was a man growne, and at his full stature, if we beleeve Josephus, who placeth him in the last of adolescency, and makes him twenty five yeares old; and whereas in the vulgar translation he is termed *puer*, it must not be strictly apprehended, (for that age properly endeth in puberty, and extendeth but unto fourteen) but respectively unto Abraham, who was at that time above sixscore:[81] and therefore also herein he was not unlike unto him who was after led dumbe unto the slaughter, and commanded by others, who had legions at command, that is in meeknesse and humble submission; for had he resisted, it had not been in the power of his aged parent to have inforced; and many at his yeares, have performed such acts, as few besides at any: David was too strong for a lion and a beare, Pompey had deserved the name of Great, Alexander of the same cognomination was Generalissimo of Greece, and Anniball but one yeare after succeeded Asdruball in that memorable warre against the Romanes.[82]

CHAPTER IX
Of the Picture of Moses with Hornes

In many peeces, and some of ancient bibles, Moses is described with hornes; whereof the ground was surely the Hebrew text, in the history of Moses, when he descended from the mount; for therein the originall word being æquivocall, and signifying horned as well as shining, the Vulgar translation hath retained the former; *Qui videbant faciem egredientis Mosis esse cornutam.*[83] But the word in the Septuagint is ἐδοξάσθη, that is his face was glorified, and this passage of the Old Testament is well explaned by another of the New, that is Corinthians 3. wherein it is delivered that they could not stedfastly behold the face of Moses, διὰ τὴν δόξαν τοῦ προσώπου, that is, for the glory of his face. And surely the exposition of one text is best performed by another, men vainly interposing their constructions, where the Scripture decideth the controversie; and therefore some have seemed too active in their expositions, who in the story of Rahab the harlot, have given notice that the word also signifieth an hostesse;[84] for in the Epistle to the Hebrewes, she is plainly tearmed πόρνη, which signifies not an hostesse, but a pecuniary and prostituting harlot, a tearme applyed unto Lais by the Greeks, and distinguished from ἑταίρα, or *amica*, as may appeare in the thirteenth of Athenæus.[85]

And therefore more allowable is the translation of Tremellius, then that of the Vulgar, *Quod splendida facta esset cubis faciei ejus*; or rather as Estius hath interpreted it, *facies ejus erat radiosa*, his face was radiant, and dispersing beames like many hornes and cones about his head;[86] which is also consonant unto the original signification, and yet observed in the peeces of our Saviour, and the Virgin Mary, who are commonly drawne with scintillations, or radiant halos about their head; which after the French expression are usually tearmed, the Glory.

Now if besides this occasionall mistake, any man shall contend a propriety in this picture, and that no injury is done unto truth by this description, because an horn is the hieroglyphick of authority, power and dignity, and in this metaphor is often used in Scripture, the peece I confesse in this acception is harmelesse and agreeable unto Moses. But if from the common mistake, or any solary consideration we persist in this description, we vilifie the mystery of the irradiation, and authorise a dangerous peece conformable unto that of Jupiter Hammon, which was the sunne, and therefore described with hornes; as is delivered by Macrobius; *Hammonem quem Deum solem occidentem Lybies existimant, arietinis cornibus fingunt, quibus id animal valet sicut radiis Sol*:[87] we herein also imitate the picture of Pan, and pagan emblem of nature; and if (as Macrobius and very good authors concede) Bacchus (who is also described with hornes) be the same diety with the sunne, and if (as Vossius well contendeth) Moses and Bacchus were the same person, their descriptions must be relative, or the tauricornous picture of the one, perhaps the same with the other.[88]

CHAPTER X
Of the Scucheons of the Tribes of Israel

We will not passe over the scucheons of the tribes of Israel, as they are usually described in the mappes of Canaan and severall other peeces; generally conceived to be the proper coats, and distinctive badges of their severall tribes.[89] So Ruben is conceived to bear three barres wave, Judah a lion rampant, Dan a serpent nowed, Simeon a sword inpale the point erected, etc. the ground whereof is the last benediction of Jacob, wherein he respectively draweth comparisons from things here represented.[*90]

* Genesis 49.

Now herein although we allow a considerable measure of truth, yet whether as they are usually described, these were the proper cognizances, and coat armes of the tribes, whether in this manner applyed, and upon the grounds presumed, materiall doubts remaine.

For first, they are not strictly made out, from the propheticall blessing of Jacob; for Simeon and Levi have distinct coats, that is a sword, and the two tables, yet are they by Jacob included in one prophesie, Simeon and Levi are brethren, instruments of cruelties are in their habitations. So Joseph beareth an oxe, whereof notwithstanding there is no mention in this prophesie; for therein it is said Joseph is a fruitfull bough, even a fruitfull bough by a well; by which repetition are intimated the two tribes descending from him Ephraim and Manasses; whereof notwithstanding Ephraim beareth an oxe: true it is, that many yeares after in the benediction of

Moses, it is said of Joseph, His glory is like the firstlings of his bullocke;*[91] and so wee may concede, what Vossius learnedly declareth, that the Ægyptians represented Joseph in the symbole of an oxe, for thereby was best implyed the dreame of Pharaoh, which he interpreted, the benefit by agriculture, and provident provision of corne which he performed, and therefore did Serapis beare a bushell upon his head.[92]

* Deuteronomy 33.

Againe, if we take these two benedictions together, the resemblances are not appropriate, and Moses therein conformes not unto Jacob; for that which in the prophesie of Jacob is appropriated unto one, is in the blessing of Moses made common unto others: so whereas Judah is compared unto a lion by Jacob, Judah is a lions whelpe; the same is applyed unto Dan by Moses, Dan is a lions whelpe, he shall leape from Bashan: and also unto Gad, he dwelleth as a lion, and teareth the arme with the crowne of the head.[93]

Thirdly, if a lyon were the proper coat of Judah, yet were it not probably a lyon rampant, as it is commonly described, but rather couchant or dormant, as some heralds and rabins doe determine, according to the letter of the text, *Recumbens dormisti ut Leo*, He couched as a lyon, and as a young lyon, who shall rouse him?

Lastly, when it is said, Every man of the children of Israel shall pitch by his owne standard with the ensigne of their fathers house;† upon enquiry what these standards and ensignes were there is no small incertainty, and men conforme not unto the prophesie of Jacob. Christian expositors are fayne herein to relye upon the rabbins, who notwithstanding are various in their traditions, and confirme not these common descriptions; for as for inferiour ensignes either of particular bands or houses they determine nothing at all, and of the foure principle or legionary standards, that is of Judah, Ruben, Ephraim, and Dan, (under every one whereof marched three tribes) they explaine them very variously. Jonathan who compiled the Thargum, conceives the colours of these banners to answer the pretious stones in the breastplate, and upon which the names of the tribes were engraven. So the standard for the campe of Judah, was of three colours according unto the stones, chalcedony, saphir, and sardonix; and therein were expressed the names of the three tribes, Judah, Isachar, and Zabulon, and in the middest thereof was written,‡ Rise up Lord,[94] and let thy enemies be scattered, and let them that

† Numbers 2.

‡ Numbers 10.

hate thee flye before thee; in it was also the pourtrait of a lyon: the standard of Ruben was also of three colours, sardine, topaz, and amethyst, therein were expressed the names of Ruben, Simeon, and Gad, in the middest was written, Heare, O Israel, the Lord our God, the Lord is one:*[95] therein was also the pourtraiture of a hart. But Abenezra and others beside the colours of the field, do set downe other charges, in Rubens the forme of a man or mandrake, in that of Judah a lyon, in Ephraims an oxe, in Dan's the figure of an aegle.

* Deuteronomy 6.

And thus indeed the foure figures in the banners of the principall squadrons of Israel are answerable unto the cherubins in the vision of Ezechiel, every one carrying the forme of all these:†[96] As for the likenesse of their faces, they foure had the likenesse of the face of a man, they foure had also the face of an ægle, and the face of a lyon on the right side, and they foure had the face of an oxe on the left side, they foure had also the face of an ægle; and conformable hereunto the pictures of the evangelists (whose gospells are the Christian banners) are set forth with the addition of a man or angell, an oxe, a lyon, and an ægle; and these symbolically represent the office of angells, and ministers of Gods will; in whom is required understanding as in a man, courage and vivacity as in the lyon, service and ministeriall officiousnesse, as in the oxe, expedition or celerity of execution, as in the ægle.[97]

† Ezekiel 1.

From hence therefore we may observe that these descriptions the most authenticke of any, are neither agreeable unto one another, nor unto the scuchions in question;[98] for though they agree in Ephraim and Judah, that is the oxe and the lyon, yet doe they differ in those of Dan, and Ruben, as farre as an ægle is different from a serpent, and the figure of a man, hart, or mandrake, from three barres wave, wherein notwithstanding we rather declare the incertainty of armes in this particular, then any way question their antiquity; for hereof more ancient examples there are, then the scucheons of the tribes, if Osyris, Mizraim or Jupiter the Just, were the son of Cham; for of his two sons, as Diodorus delivereth, the one for his device gave a dogge, the other a wolfe; and beside the shield of Achilles, and many ancient Greeks, if we receive the conjecture of Vossius, that the crow upon Corvinus his head, was but the figure of that animall upon his helmet, it is an example of antiquity among the Romans.[99]

CHAPTER XI
Of the Pictures of the Sibylls

The pictures of the sibylls are very common, and for their prophesies of Christ in high esteem with Christians; described commonly with youthfull faces, and in a defined number; common peeces making twelve, and many precisely ten, observing therein the account of learned Varro; that is, Sibylla Delphica, Erythræa, Samia, Cumana, Cumæa, or Cimmeria, Hellespontiaca, Lybica, Phrygia, Tiburtina, Persica.[100] In which enumeration I perceive learned men are not satisfied, and many conclude an irreconcilable incertainty; some making more, others fewer, and not this certaine number; for Suidas though he affirme that in divers ages there were ten, yet the same denomination he affordeth unto more; Boysardus in his Tract of Divination hath set forth the icons of these ten, yet addeth two others, Epirotica, and Ægyptia; and some affirme that prophesying women were generally named Sibylls.[101]

Others make them fewer: Martianus Capella two, Pliny and Solinus three, Ælian foure, and Salmasius in effect but seven, for discoursing hereof in his Plinian Exercitations, he thus determineth; *Ridere licet hodiernos Pictores, qui tabulas proponunt Cumanæ, Cumeæ, et Erythrææ, quasi trium diversarum Sibyllarum; cum una eademque fuerit Cumana, Cumæa, et Erythræa, ex plurium et doctissimorum authorum sententia*:[102] Boysardus gives us leave to opinion there was no more then one; for so doth he conclude, *In tantâ Scriptorum varietate liberum relinquimus Lectori credere, an una et eadem in diversis regionibus peregrinata, cognomen sortita sit ab iis locis ubi oracula reddidisse comperitur, an plures extiterint*: and therefore not discovering a resolution of their number from the pens of the best writers, we have no reason to determine the same from the hand and pencill of painters.[103]

As touching their age, that they are generally described as young women, history will not allow; for the Sibyll whereof Virgill speaketh is tearmed by him *longava sacerdos*, and Servius in his comment amplifieth the same.[104] The other that sold the bookes unto Tarquine, and whose history is plainer then any, by Livie and Gellius is tearmed *Anus*,[*105] that is properly no woman of ordinary age, but full of yeares, and in the dayes of doteage, according to the etymology of

* Anus, quasi Ἄνους, sine mente.

Festus, and consonant unto the history;[106] wherein it is said, that Tarquine thought she doted with old age; which duly perpended, the *Licentia pictoria* is very large, and with the same reason they may delineate old Nestor like Adonis, Hecuba with Helens face, and Time with Absalons head.[107] [But this absurdity that eminent artist Michael Angelo hath avoided, in the pictures of the Cumean and Persian Sibylls, as they stand described from the printed sculptures of Adam Mantuanus.]

CHAPTER XII
Of the Picture describing the Death of Cleopatra

The picture concerning the death of Cleopatra with two aspes or venemous serpents unto her armes, or breasts, or both, requires consideration: for therein (beside that this variety is not excusable) the thing it selfe is questionable; nor is it indisputably certaine what manner of death she dyed. Plutarch in the life of Antonie plainly delivereth, that no man knew the manner of her death; for some affirmed she perished by poyson, which she alwayes carried in a little hollow combe, and wore it in her hayre;[108] beside there were never any aspes discovered in the place of her death, although two of her maids perished also with her, only it was said two small and almost insensible prickes were found upon her arme; which was all the ground that Caesar had to presume the manner of her death. Galen who was contemporary unto Plutarch, delivereth two wayes of her death: that is, that shee killed her selfe by the bite of an aspe, or bit an hole in her arme, and powred poyson therein.[109] Strabo that lived before them both, hath also two opinions, that she dyed by the byte of an aspe, or else a poysonous oyntment.[110]

We might question the length of the aspes which are sometimes described exceeding short, whereas the *chersæa* or land aspe which most conceive she used, is above foure cubits long: their number is not unquestionable; for whereas there are generally two described, Augustus (as Plutarch relateth) did carry in his triumph the image of Cleopatra but with one aspe unto her arme: as for the two pricks, or little spots in her arme, they rather infer the sex, then plurality: for like the viper, the female aspe hath foure, but the male two teeth, whereby it left this impression, or double puncture behinde it.

And lastly, we might question the place; for some apply them unto her breast, which notwithstanding will not consist with the history, and Petrus Victorius hath well observed the same: but herein the mistake was easie, it being the custome in capitall malefactors to apply them unto the breast, as the author *de Theriaca ad Pisonem*, an eyewitnesse hereof in Alexandria, where Cleopatra dyed, determineth: I beheld saith he, in Alexandria, how suddenly these serpents bereave a man of life; for when any one is condemned to this kinde of death, if they intend to use him favourably, that is, to dispatch him suddenly, they fasten an aspe unto his breast, and bidding him walke about, he presently perisheth thereby.[111]

CHAPTER XIII
Of the Pictures of the Nine Worthies

The pictures of the nine worthies are not unquestionable, and to criticall spectators may seeme to containe sundry improprieties:[112] some will enquire why Alexander the Great is described upon an elephant? For indeed, we do not finde he used that animall in his armies, much lesse in his owne person; but his horse is famous in history, and its name alive to this day:[113] beside, he fought but one remarkable battaile, wherein there were any elephants, and that was with Porus King of India; in which notwithstanding, as Curtius, Arrianus, and Plutarch report, he was on horseback himselfe;[114] and if because hee fought against elephants, he is with propriety set upon their backs, with no lesse or greater reason is the same description agreeable unto Judas Maccabeus, as may be observed from the history of the Maccabees;[115] and also unto Julius Caesar, whose triumph was honoured with captive elephants, as may be observed in the order thereof, set forth by Jacobus Laurus:[116] and if also wee should admit this description upon an elephant, yet were not the manner thereof unquestionable, that is, in his ruling the beast alone; for, beside the champion upon their back, there was also a guide or ruler, which sate more forward to command or guide the beast: thus did King Porus ride when hee was overthrowne by Alexander; and thus are also the towred elephants described, Maccab. 2.6.[117] Upon the beasts there were strong towres of wood which covered every one of them, and were girt fast unto them by devices; there were also upon every one of them thirty two strong men, beside the Indian that ruled them.

Others will demand, not onely why Alexander upon an elephant, but Hector upon an horse? Whereas his manner of fighting, or presenting himselfe in battaile, was in a chariot, as did the other noble Trojans, who as Pliny affirmeth were the first inventers thereof; the same way of fight is testified by Diodorus, and thus delivered by Sir Walter Raleigh.[118] Of the vulgar little reckoning was made, for they fought all on foote, slightly armed, and commonly followed the successe of their captaines, who roade not upon horses, but in chariots drawne by two or three horses; and this was also the ancient way of fight among the Britaines, as is delivered by Diodorus, Caesar, and Tacitus;[119] and there want not some who have taken advantage hereof, and made it one argument of their orginall from Troy.

Lastly, by any man versed in antiquity, the question can hardly be avoyded, why the horses of these worthies, especially of Caesar, are described with the furniture of great sadles, and styrrops; for sadles largely taken, though some defence there may be, yet that they had not the use of stirrops, seemeth out of doubt; as Pancirollus hath observed, as Polydore Virgil and Petrus Victorius have confirmed, expresly discoursing hereon;[120] as is observable from Pliny, and cannot escape our eyes in the ancient monuments, medals and triumphant arches of the Romanes. Nor is there any genuine or classick word in Latine to expresse them; for *staphia* or *stapes* is not to be found in authors of antiquity; and whereas the name might promise some antiquity, because among the three small bones in the auditory organ, by physitians termed *incus*, *malleus*, and *stapes*, one thereof from some resemblance doth beare this name; these bones were not observed, much lesse named by Hippocrates, Galen or any ancient physitian; but as Laurentius observeth concerning the invention of the stapes or stirrop bone, there is some contention betweene Columbus and Ingrassias, the one of Sicilia, the other of Cremona, and both within the compasse of this century.[121]

The same is also deduceable from very approved authors: Polybius speaking of the way which Anniball marched into Italy, useth the word βεβηματισται, that is saith Petrus Victorius, it was stored with devices for men to get upon their horses, which ascents were termed *bemata*; and in the life of Caius

Gracchus, Plutarch expresseth as much; for endeavouring to ingratiate himselfe with the people, besides the placing of stones at every miles end, he made at neerer distances certaine elevated places, and scalary ascents, that by the help thereof they might with better ease ascend or mount their horses. Now if we demand how cavalliers then destitute of stirrops did usually mount their horses; Vegetius resolves us, that they used to vault or leape up, and therefore they had wooden horses in their houses and abroad, that thereby young men might enable themselves in this action, wherein by instruction and practice they grew so perfect, that they could vault up on the right or left, and that with their sword in hand, according to that of Virgil:

> *Poscit equos, atque arma simul saltuque superbus*
> *Emicat.*
> And againe:
> *Infrænant alii currus et corpora saltu*
> *Injiciunt in equos.*[122]

And so Julius Pollux adviseth to teach horses to incline, dimit, and bow downe their bodies, that their riders may with better ease ascend them; and thus may it more causally be made out, what Hippocrates affirmeth of the Scythians, that using continuall riding, they were generally molested with the sciatica or hippegowte; or what Suetonius delivereth of Germanicus, that he had slender legs, but encreased them by riding after meales; that is, the humours descending upon their pendulosity, they having no support or suppedaneous stability.[123]

Now if any shall say that these are petty errors and minor lapses not considerably injurious unto truth, yet is it neither reasonable nor safe to contemne inferiour falsities; but rather as betweene falshood and truth, there is no medium, so should they be maintained in their distances, nor the insinuation of the one, approach the sincerity of the other.

CHAPTER XIV
Of the Picture of Jehptha sacrificing his Daughter

The hand of the painter confidently setteth forth the picture of Jephthah in the posture of Abraham, sacrificing his onely daughter;[124] thus indeed is it commonly received, and hath had the attest of many worthy writers; notwithstanding upon enquiry wee finde the matter doubtfull, and many upon probable grounds to have beene of another opinion; conceaving in this oblation not a naturall but a civill kinde of death, and a seperation onely unto the Lord; for that he pursued not his vow unto a literall oblation, there want not arguments both from the text and reason.

For first, it is evident that she deplored her virginity, and not her death; Let me goe up and downe the mountaines, and bewayle my virginity, I and my fellowes.

Secondly, when it is said, that Jephthah did unto her according unto his vow, it is immediately subjoyned, *Et non cognovit virum*, and shee knew no man, which as immediate in words, was probably most neere in sence unto the vow.

Thirdly, it is said in the text, that the daughters of Israel went yearely to talke with the daughter of Jephthah foure dayes in the yeare, which had she beene sacrificed, they could not have done;[125] for whereas the word is sometime translated to lament, yet doth it also signifie to talke or have conference with one, and by Tremellius who was well able to judge of the originall, it is in this sence translated: *Ibant filii Israelitarum ad confabulandum cum filia Jephthaci, quatuor diebus quotannis*: and so it is also set downe in the marginall notes of our translation: and from this annuall concourse of the daughters of Israel, it is not improbable in future ages, the daughter of Jephthah came to be worshipped as a deity, and had by the Samaritans an annuall festivity observed unto her honour, as Epiphanius hath left recorded in the heresie of the Melchidecians.[126]

It is also repugnant unto reason, for the offering of mankinde was against the law of God, who so abhorred humane sacrifice, that he admitted not the oblation of uncleane beasts, and confined his altars but unto five kinds of animals; that is, the oxe, the goat, the sheepe, the pigeon and its kinds:[127] in the cleansing of the leper, there is I confesse, mention made of the sparrow, but great dispute may be made whether it be properly rendred, and therefore the Scripture with indignation, oft times makes mention of humane sacrifice among the Gentiles, whose oblations scarce made scruple of any animall, sacrificing not onely man, but horses, lyons, ægles;[128] and though they come not into holocausts, yet do we read the Syrians did make oblations of fishes unto the goddesse Derceto;[129] it being therefore a sacrifice so abominable unto God, although hee had pursued it, it is not probable the priests and wisedom of Israel would have permitted it, and that not onely in regard of the subject or sacrifice it selfe, but also the sacrificator, which the picture makes to be Jepthah, who was neither priest, nor capable of that office; for he was a Gileadite, and as the text affirmeth, the son also of an harlot; and how hardly the priesthood would endure encroachment upon their function, a notable example there is in the story of Ozias.[130]

Secondly, the offering up of his daughter was not onely unlawfull, and entrenched upon his religion, but had beene a course and progresse that had much condemned his discretion, that is, to have punished himselfe in the strictest observance of his vow, when as the law of God had allowed an evasion; that is, by way of commutation or redemption, according as is determined, Leviticus 27, whereby if she were between the age of five and twenty, shee was to be estimated but at ten shekels, and if between twenty and sixty, not above thirty;[131] a sum that could never discourage an indulgent parent, it being but the value of a servant slain, and the inconsiderable salarie of Judas, and will make no greater noise then three pound fifteen shillings with us;[132] and therefore their conceit is not to be exploded, who say that from the story of Jepthah sacrificing his owne daughter, might spring the fable of Agamemnon, delivering unto sacrifice his daughter Iphigenia, who was also contemporary unto Jepthah; wherein to answere the ground that hinted it, Iphigenia was not sacrificed her self, but redeemed with an hart, which Diana accepted for her.[133]

[Lastly,[134] although his vow run generally for the words, Whatsoever shall come forth, &c., yet might it be restrained in the sense, for whatsoever was sacrificable, and justly subject to lawfull immolation: and so would not have sacrificed either horse or dog, if they had come out upon him. Nor was he obliged by oath unto a strict observation of that which promissorily was unlawfull; or could he be qualified by vow to commit a fact which naturally was abominable. Which doctrine had Herod understood, it might have saved John Baptists head; when he promised by oath to give unto Herodias whatsoever she would ask; that is, if it were in the compasse of things, which he could lawfully grant. For his oath made not that lawfull which was illegall before: and if it were unjust to murder John, the supervenient oath did not extenuate the fact, or oblige the jurer unto it.]

Now the ground at least which much promoted the opinion, might be the dubious words of the text, which containe the sense of his vow; most men adhering unto their common and obvious acception. Whatsoever shall come forth of the doores of my house shall surely be the Lords, and I will offer it up for a burnt offering.[135] Now whereas it is said, *Erit Jehovæ, et offeram illud holocaustum*, the word signifying both *et* and *aut*, it may be taken disjunctively, *aut offeram*, that is, it shall either be the Lords by separation, or else, an holocaust by common oblation, even as our marginal translation advertiseth; and as Tremellius rendreth it, *Erit inquam Jehovæ, aut offeram illud holocaustum*: and for the vulgar translation, it useth often *et* where *aut* must be presumed, as Exodus 21. *Si quis percusserit patrem et matrem*, that is not both, but either.[136] There being therefore two wayes to dispose of her, either to separate her unto the Lord, or offer her as a sacrifice, it is of no necessitie the latter should bee necessary; and surely lesse derogatorie unto the sacred text, and history of the people of God, must bee the former.

CHAPTER XV
Of the Picture of John the Baptist

The picture of John the Baptist, in a camells skin is very questionable, and many I perceive have condemned it; the ground or occasion of this description are the words of the holy Scripture, especially of Matthew and Marke, for Luke and John are silent herein; by them it is delivered, his garment was of camells haire, and had a leatherne girdle about his loynes.[137] Now here it seemes the camels hair is taken by painters for the skinne or pelt with the haire upon it: but this exposition will not so well consist with the strict acception of the words; for Marke 1. It is said, he was ἐνδεδυμένος τρίχας καμήλου, and Matthew 3, εἶχε τὸ ἔνδυμα, ἀπὸ τριχῶν καμήλου, that is, as the vulgar translation, that of Beza, that of Sixtus Quintus, and Clement the eight hath rendred it, *vestimentum habebat e pilis camelinis*; which is as ours translateth it, a garment of camells haire; that is made of some texture of that haire, a course garment, a cilicious or sackcloth habit;[138] sutable to the austerity of his life, and the severity of his doctrine, repentance, and the place thereof the wildernes, his food and diet locusts and wilde hony; agreeable unto the example of Elias, who Kings 1.8. is said to be *vir pilosus*, that is as Junius and Tremellius interpret, *veste villoso cinctus*;[139] answerable unto the habit of the ancient prophets, according to that of Zachary 13.[140] In that day the prophets shall be ashamed, neither shall they weare a rough garment to deceive, and sutable to the cilicious and hairie vestes of the strictest orders of friars, who derive the institution of their monastick life from the example of John and Elias.

As for the wearing of skinnes, where that is properly intended, the expression of the Scripture is plaine, so is it called Hebrews 11. they wandred about ἐν αἰγείοις δέρμασιν, that is in goats skinnes; and so it is said of our first parents, Genesis 3. that God made them χιτῶνας δερμάτινους, *vestes pelliceas*, or coats of skinnes;[141] which though a naturall habit unto all, before the invention of texture, was something more unto Adam, who had newly learned to die; for unto him a garment from the dead, was but a dictate of death, and an habit of mortalitie.

Now if any man will say this habit of John, was neither of camells skinne, nor any course texture of its haire, but rather some finer weave of camelot, grograine or the like, in as much as these stuffes are supposed to be made of the haire of that animall, or because that Ælian affirmeth, that camells haire of Persia, is as fine as Milesians wooll, wherewith the great ones of that place were clothed; they have discovered an habite, not onely unsutable unto his leatherne cincture, and the coursnes of his life, but not consistent with the words of our Saviour, when reasoning with the people concerning John, he saith, What went you out into the wildernes to see, a man clothed in soft raiment? Behold they that weare soft rayment are in kings houses.[142]

CHAPTER XVI
Of the Picture of Saint Christopher

The picture of Saint Christopher, that is a man of a giant like stature, bearing upon his shoulders our Saviour Christ, and with a staffe in his hand, wading thorow the water, is known unto children, common over all Europe, not onely as a signe unto houses, but is described in many churches, and stands Colossus like in the entrance of *Nostre Dame* in Paris.

Now from hence, common eyes conceive an history sutable unto this description, that he carried our Saviour in his minority over some river or water, which notwithstanding wee cannot at all make out; for wee read not thus much in any good author, nor of any remarkable Christopher, before the reigne of Decius, who lived 250 yeares after Christ; this man indeed according unto history suffered as a martyr in the second yeare of that Emperour, and in the Roman calender takes up the 21 of July.

The ground that begat or promoted this opinion was, first the fabulous adjections of succeeding ages, unto the veritable acts of this martyr, who in the most probable accounts was remarkable for his staffe, and a man of a goodly stature.[143]

The second was a mistake or misapprehension of the picture; most men conceiving that an history which was contrived at first but as an emblem or symbolicall fancy, as from the annotations of Baronius upon the Roman Martyrology, Lipellous in the life of Saint Christopher hath observed in these words; *Acta Sancti Christophori à multis depravata inveniuntur; quod quidem non aliunde originem sumpsisse certum est, quam quod symbolicas figuras imperiti ad veritatem successu temporis transtulerint; itaque cuncta illa de Sancto Christophero pingi consueta, symbola potius quam historiæ alicujus existimandum est, esse expressam imaginem*:[144] [that is, the acts of St Christopher are depraved by many: which surely began from no other ground, then, that in process of time, unskilfull men translated symbolicall figures unto real verities: and therefore what is usually described in the picture of St. Christopher, is rather to be received as an emblem, or symbolicall description, then any real history.] Now what emblem this was, or what its signification conjectures are many; Pierius hath set downe one, that is, of the disciple of Christ;[145] for he that will carry Christ upon his shoulders, must relye upon the staffe of his direction, whereon if he firmeth himselfe, he may be able to overcom the billows of resistance, and in the vertue of this staffe like that of Jacob passe over the waters of Jordan: or otherwise thus; he that will submit his shoulders unto Christ, shall by the concurrence of his power encrease into the strength of a gyant, and being supported by the staffe of his holy Spirit, shall not be overwhelmed by the waves of the world, but wade through all resistance.

[Add also the mystical reasons[146] of this pourtract alleadged by Vida and Xerisanus: and the recorded story of Christopher, that before his Martyrdom he requested of God, that where ever his body were, the places should be freed from pestilence and mischiefs, from infection. And therefore his picture or pourtract, was usually placed in publick wayes, and at the entrance of Towns and Churches, according to the received Distick. *Christophorum videas postea tutus eris.*]

CHAPTER XVII
Of the Picture of Saint George

The picture of Saint George killing the dragon, and, as most ancient draughts doe run, with the daughter of a king standing by, is famous amongst Christians; and upon this description dependeth a solemne story, how by this atchievement he redeemed a kings daughter, which is more especially beleeved by the English, whose protector he is, and in which forme and history, according to his description in the English colledge at Rome, he is set forth in the icons or cuts of martyrs by Cevallerius.[147] Now of what authority soever this piece be among us, it is I perceive received with different beliefes: for some men beleeve the person and the story; some the person, but not the story, and others deny both.

That such a person there was, we shall not contend: the indistinction of many in the community of name, or the application of the act of one unto another, have made some doubt there was no such man at all; for of this name we meet with more then one in history, and no lesse then two of Cappadocia, the one an Arrian, who was slain by the Alexandrians in the time of Julian, the other a valiant souldier and Christian martyr, beheaded in the reigne of Dioclesian: and this is the George conceived in this picture, who hath his day in the Romane calender, on whom so many fables are delivered, whose story is set forth by Metaphrastes, and his myracles by Turonensis.[148]

As for the story depending hereon, [some conceive as lightly thereof, as of that of *Perseus* and *Andromeda*; conjecturing the one to be the father of the other; and some too highly assert it. Others with better moderation, doe either entertain the same as a fabulous addition unto the true and authentick story of St. *George*; or else] conceive the literall acception a meere mistake of the symbolicall expression;[149] apprehending that a veritable history, which was but an emblem or peece of Christian posie. And this emblematicall construction hath been received by men who are not forward to extenuate the acts of their saints, as from Baronius, Lipellous the Carthusian hath delivered in the life of Saint George, *Picturam illam St Georgii quâ effingitur eques armatus, qui hastæ cuspide hostem interficit juxta quam etiam virgo posita, manus supplices tendens, ejus explorat auxilium, symboli potius quam historiæ alicujus censenda expressa imago, consuevit quidem ut equestris militiæ miles equestri imagine referri.* [That is, the picture of Saint George wherein he is described like a Curassier or horseman compleatly armed etc. is rather a symbolicall image, then any proper figure.[150]]

Now in the picture of this saint and souldier was implyed the Christian souldier and true champion of Christ; a horseman armed *Cap a pe*, intimating the *panoplia* or compleat armour of a Christian, combating with the dragon, that is, with the divell, in defence of the kings daughter, that is the church of God; and therefore although the history be not made out, it doth not disparage the knights and noble order of Saint George, whose cognisance is honourable in the emblem of the souldier of Christ, and is a worthy memoriall to conforme unto its mystery; nor, were there no such person at all, had they more reason to be ashamed, then the noble order of Burgundy, and knights of the golden fleece, whose badge is a confessed fable.

CHAPTER XVIII
Of the Picture of Jerome

The picture of Jerome usually described at his study, with a clock hanging by him is not to be omitted; for though the meaning bee allowable, and probable it is that industrious father did not let slip his time without account, yet must not perhaps that clocke be set downe to have been his measure thereof: for clocks are automatous organs, and such whereby we now distinguish of time, have found no mention in any ancient writers, but are of late invention, as Pancirollus observeth, and Polydore Virgil discoursing of new inventions whereof the authors are not knowne makes instance in clocks and guns:[151] now Jerome is no late writer, but one of the ancient fathers, and lived in the fourth century, in the reigne of Theodosius the first.

It is not to be denyed that before the dayes of Jerome there were horologies, and severall accounts of time;[152] for they measured the hours not only by drops of water in glasses called *clepsydræ*, but also by sand in glasses called *clepsammia*; there were also from great antiquity, sciotericall or sun dialls, by the shadow of a stile or gnomon denoting the houres of the day: an invention ascribed unto Anaximenes by Pliny;[153] hereof a very memorable one there was in Campus Martius from an obelisk erected, and golden figures placed horizontally about it, which was brought out of Ægypt by Augustus, and described by Jacobus Laurus.[154] And another of great antiquity we meet with in the story of Ezechias; for so it is delivered Kings 2.20,[155] that the Lord brought the shadow backward ten degrees by which it had gone down in the diall of Ahaz; that is, say some, ten degrees, not lines, for the houres were denoted by certaine divisions or steps in the diall, which others distinguished by lines according to that of Persius

Stertimus indomitum quod despumare Falernum
Sufficiat quintâ dum linea tangitur umbrâ.[156]

That is, the line next the meridian, or within an houre of noone.

Of latter yeares there succeeded new inventions, and horologies composed by trochilick or the artifice of wheeles, whereof some are kept in motion by weight, others performe without it: now as one age instructs another, and time that brings all things to ruine perfects also every thing, so are these indeed of more generall and ready use then any that went before them: by the water-glasses the account was not regular; for from attenuation and condensation, whereby that element is altered, the houres were shorter in hot weather then in cold, and in Summer then in Winter; as for sciotericall dialls, whether of the sunne or moon, they are only of use in the actuall radiation of those luminaries, and are of little advantage unto those inhabitants, which for many months enjoy not the lustre of the sun.

It is I confesse no easie wonder how the horometry of antiquity discovered not this artifice, how Architas that contrived the moving dove, or rather the helicoscopie of Archimedes, fell not upon this way;[157] surely as in many things, so in this particular, the present age hath farre surpassed antiquity, whose ingenuity hath been so bold not only to proceed, below the account of minutes, but to attempt perpetuall motions, and engines whose revolutions (could their substance answer the designe) might outlast the examplary mobility, and out measure time it selfe; for such a one is that mentioned by John Dee, whose words are these in his learned Preface unto Euclide:[158] By wheeles strange works and incredible are done: a wondrous example was seen in my time in a certaine instrument, which by the inventer and artificer was sold for twenty talents of gold; and then by chance had received some injury, and one Janellus of Cremona did mend the same, and presented it unto the Emperour Charles the fift. Jeronymus Cardanus, can be my witnesse, that therein was one wheele that moved in such a rate, that in seven thousand yeares onely his owne period should be finished;[159] a thing almost incredible, but how far I keep within my bounds, many men yet alive can tell.

CHAPTER XIX
Of the Pictures of Mermaids, Unicornes, and some Others

Few eyes have escaped the picture of the mermaids; that is, according to Horace his monster, with womans head above, and fishy extremity below:[160] and this is conceived to answer the shape of the ancient syrens that attempted upon Ulysses, which notwithstanding were of another description, containing no fishie composure, but made up of man and bird;[161] the humane mediety variously placed not only above but below, according unto Ælian, Suidas, Servius, Boccatius, and Aldrovandus, who hath referred their description unto the story of fabulous birds, according to the description of Ovid, and the account thereof in Hyginus, that they were the daughters of Melpomene, and metamorphosied into the shape of man and bird by Ceres.[162]

And therefore these pieces so common among us, do rather derive their originall, or are indeed the very descriptions of Dagon, which was made with humane figure above, and fishy shape below; whose stumpe, or as Tremellius and our margin renders it, whose fishie part onely remained, when the hands and upper part fell before the arke.* Of the shape of Atergates, or Derceto with the Phæniceans; in whose fishie and feminine mixture, as some conceive, were implyed the moon and the sea, or the deity of the waters; and therefore, in their sacrifices they made oblations of fishes: from whence were probably occasioned the pictures of nereides and tritons among the Grecians, and such as we reade in Macrobius, to have beene placed on the top of the temple of Saturne.[163]

We are unwilling to question the royall supporters of England, that is, the approved descriptions of the lion and the unicorne; although, if in the lion the position of the pizell be proper, and that the naturall situation; it will be hard to make out their retrocopulation, or their coupling and pissing backward, according to the determination of Aristotle; all that urine backward do copulate πυγηδόν, *clunatim*, or aversly, as lions, hares, linxes.[164]

As for the unicorne, if it have the head of a deere, and the tayle of a boare, as Vartomannus describeth it, how agreeable it is in this picture every eye may discerne:[165] if it be made bisulcous or cloven footed, it agreeth unto the description of Vartomannus, but scarce of any other; and Aristotle supposeth that such as devide the hoofe doe double the horne; they being both of the same nature, and admitting division together.[166] And lastly, if the horne have this situation, and be so forwardly affixed, as is described, it will not be easily conceived, how it can feed from the ground, and therefore we observe that nature in other cornigerous animals, hath placed the hornes higher and reclining, as in bucks;[167] in some inverted upwards, as in the rhinoceros, the Indian asse, and the unicornous beetles; and thus have some affirmed it is seated in this animall.

Wee cannot but observe that in the picture of Jonah and others, whales are described with two prominent spouts on their heads; whereas indeed they have but one in the forhead, and terminating over the windepipe. Nor can we overlooke the picture of elephants with castles on their backs, made in the forme of land castles, or stationary fortifications, and answerable unto the armes of Castile, or Sir John Old Castle; whereas the towres they bore were made of wood, and girt unto their bodies, as is delivered in the books of Maccabees, and as they were appointed in the army of Antiochus.[168]

We will not dispute the pictures of telary spiders, and their position in the web, which is commonly made laterall, and regarding the horizon; although, if it be observed, wee shall commonly finde it downeward, and their heads respecting the center: we will not controvert the picture of the seven stars, although if thereby be meant the Pleiades, or subconstellation upon the back of Taurus, with what congruity they are described, either in site or magnitude, in a cleere night an ordinary eye may discover, from July unto April. We will not question the tongues of adders and vipers, described like an anchor, nor the picture of the flower *de Luce*, though how farre they agree unto their naturall draughts, let every spectator determine.

Many more there are whereof our pen shall take no notice, nor shall we urge their enquiry; we shall not enlarge with what incongruity, and how dissenting from the pieces of antiquity, the pictures of their gods and goddesses are described, and how hereby their symbolicall sence is lost, although herein it were not hard, to be informed from Phornutus, Fulgentius, and Albricus.[169] Whether Hercules be more properly described strangling then tearing the lion, as Victorius hath disputed, nor how the characters and figures of the signes and planets be now perverted, as Salmasius hath learnedly declared: wee will dispence with beares with long tayles, such as are described in the figures of heaven; we shall tolerate flying horses, black swans, hydraes, centaurs, harpies, and satyres; for these are monstrosities, rarities, or else poeticall fancies, whose shadowed moralities requite their substantiall falsities: wherein indeed we must not deny a liberty, nor is the hand of the painter more restrainable then the pen of the poet; but where the real works of nature, or veritable acts of story are to be described, digressions are aberrations; and art being but the imitator or secondary representor, it must not vary from the verity of the example, or describe things otherwise then they truly are or have beene: for hereby introducing false Ideas of things, it perverts and deformes the face and symmetrie of truth.

CHAPTER XX
Of the Hieroglyphicall Pictures of the Egyptians

Certainly of all men that suffered from the confusion of Babel, the Ægyptians found the best evasion; for, though words were confounded, they invented a language of things, and spake unto each other by common notions in nature, whereby they discoursed in silence, and were intuitively understood from the theory of their expresses:[170] for, they assumed the shapes of animals common unto all eyes, and by their conjunctions and compositions were able to communicate their conceptions unto any that coapprehended the syntaxis of their natures.[171] This doe many conceive to have beene the primitive way of writing, and of greater antiquity then letters; and this indeed might

Adam well have spoken, who understanding the nature of things, had the advantage of naturall expressions, which the Ægyptians but taking upon trust upon their owne or common opinion, from conceded mistakes they authentically promoted errors, describing in their hieroglyphicks creatures of their owne invention;[172] or from knowne and conceded animals, erecting significations not inferrible from their natures.

And first, although there were more things in nature then words which did expresse them, yet even in these mute and silent discourses, to expresse complexed significations, they took a liberty to compound and piece together creatures of allowable formes unto mixtures inexistent; and thus began the descriptions of griphins, basilisks, phænix, and many more; which emblematists and heralds have entertained with significations answering their institutions; hieroglyphically adding martegres, wivernes, lion-fishes, with divers others; pieces of good and allowable invention unto the prudent spectator, but are lookt on by vulgar eyes as literall truths, or absurd impossibilities; whereas, indeed they are commendable inventions, and of laudable significations.

Againe, beside these pieces fictitiously set downe, and having no copy in nature, they had many unquestionably drawne of inconsequent signification, nor naturally verfying their intention. Wee shall instance but in few, as they stand recorded by Orus:[173] the male sex they expressed by a vulture, because of vultures all are females, and impregnated by the winde, which authentically transmitted hath passed many pens, and became the assertion of Ælian, Ambrose, Basil, Isidore, Tzetzes, Philes, and others;[174] wherein notwithstanding what injury is offered unto the creation in this confinement of sex, and what disturbance unto phylosophy in the concession of windy conceptions, wee shall not here declare: by two dragmes they thought it sufficient to signifie an heart, because the heart at one yeare weigheth two dragmes, that is, a quarter of an ounce, and unto fifty yeares annually encreaseth the weight of one dragme, after which in the same proportion it yearely decreaseth; so that the life of a man doth not naturally extend above an hundred, and this was not onley a populary conceit, but consentaneous unto their physicall principles, Heurnius hath accounted it, in his *Philosophica Barbarica*.[175]

A woman that hath but one childe, they expresse by a lionesse; for that conceaveth but once: fecundity they set forth by a goate, because but seven dayes old, it beginneth to use coition: the abortion of a woman they describe by an horse kicking a wolfe; because a mare will cast her fole if she tread in the track of that animall.[176] Deformity they signifie by a beare, and an unstable man by an hyæna, because that animall yearely exchangeth his sex: a woman delivered of a female child, they imply by a bull looking over his left shoulder, because if in coition a bull part from a cow on that side, the calfe will prove a female.[177]

All which with many more, how farre they consent with truth, we shall not disparage our reader to dispute; and though some way allowable unto wiser conceits, who could distinctly receive their significations; yet carrying the majesty of hieroglyphicks, and so transmitted by authors, they crept into a beliefe with many, and favourable doubt with most: and thus, I feare, it hath fared with the hieroglyphicall symboles of Scripture, which excellently intended in the species of things sacrifized, in the prohibited meates, in the dreames of Pharaoh, Joseph, and many other passages, are oft times wrackt beyond their symbolizations, and inlarg'd into constructions disparaging their true intentions.[178]

CHAPTER XXI
Compendiously of many questionable customes, opinions, pictures, practises, and popular observations

1. If an hare crosse the high way there are few above threescore that are not perplexed thereat, which notwithstanding is but an auguriall terror, according to that received expression, *Inauspicatum dat iter oblatus Lepus*, and the ground of the conceit was probably no greater then this, that a fearfull animall passing by us portended unto us some thing to be feared;[179] as upon the like consideration the meeting of a fox presaged some future imposture, which was a superstitious observation prohibited unto the Jews, as is expressed in the Idolatry of Maimonides, and is referred unto the sin of an observer of fortunes, or one that abuseth events unto good or bad signes, forbidden by the law of Moses,*[180] which notwithstanding sometimes succeeding, according to feares or desires, have left impressions and timerous expectations in credulous minds for ever.

* Deuteronomy 18.

2. That owles and ravens are ominous appearers, and presignifying unlucky events, as Christians yet conceit, was also an auguriall conception. Because many ravens were seene when Alexander entered Babylon, they were thought to preominate his death;[181] and because an owle appeared before the battaile, it presaged the ruine of Crassus, which though decrepite superstitions, and such as had their nativity in times beyond all history, are fresh in the observation of many heads, and by the credulous and feminine partie still in some majestie among us. And therefore the embleme of superstition was well set out by Ripa, in the picture of an owle, an hare, and an old woman;[182] and it no way confirmeth the auguriall consideration, that an owle is a forbidden food in the law of Moses; or that Jerusalem was threatned by the raven and the owle, in that expression of Esay 34.[183] That it should be a court for owles, that the cormorant and the bitterne should possesse it, and the owle and the raven dwell in it; for thereby was only implyed their ensuing desolation, as is expounded in the words succeeding, he shall draw upon it the line of confusion, and the stones of emptinesse.

3. The falling of salt is an authenticke presagement of ill lucke, nor can every temper contemne it, from whence notwithstanding nothing can be naturally feared: nor was the same a generall prognosticke of future evill among the ancients, but a particular omination concerning the breach of friendship: for salt as incorruptible, was the simbole of friendship, and before the other service was offered unto their guests; which if it casually fell was accounted ominous, and their amitie of no duration.[184] [But whether salt were not only a symbole of friendship with man, but also a figure of amity and reconciliation with God, and was therefore observed in sacrifices; is an higher speculation.]

4. To breake the eggeshell after the meat is out, wee are taught in our childhood, and practise it all our lives, which neverthelesse is but a superstitious relict according to the judgement of Plinie; *Huc pertinet ovorum, ut exorbuerit quisque, calices protinus frangi, aut eosdem coclearibus perforari*, and the intent hereof was to prevent witchcraft; for lest witches should draw or pricke their names therein, and veneficiously mischiefe their persons, they broke the shell, as Dalecampius hath observed.[185]

5. The true lovers knot is very much magnified and still retained in presents of love among us, which though in all

points it doth not make out, had perhaps its originall from Nodus Herculanus, or that which was called Hercules his knot, resembling the snaky complication in the caduceus or rod of Hermes; and in which forme the zone or woollen girdle of the bride was fastened, as Turnebus observeth in his Adversaria.[186]

6. When our cheeke burneth or eare tingleth, wee usually say that some body is talking of us; which is an ancient conceit, and ranked among superstitious opinions by Plinie. *Absentes tinnitu aurium præsentire sermones de se receptum est*, according to that disticke noted by Dalecampius.

Garrula quid totis resonas mihi noctibus auris?
Nescio quem dicis nunc meminisse mei:[187]

which is a conceit hardly to be made out without the concession of a signifying genius, or universall Mercury, conducting sounds unto their distant subjects, and teaching us to heare by touch.

7. When we desire to confine our words we commonly say they are spoken under the rose; which expression is commendable, if the rose from any naturall propertie may be the symbole of silence, as Nazianzene seemes to imply in these translated verses.

Utque latet Rosa Verna suo putamine clausa,
Sic os vincla ferat, validisque arctetur habenis,
Indicatque suis prolixa silentia labris:[188]

and is also tolerable, if by desiring a secrecy to words spoke under the rose, wee onely meane in society and compotation, from the ancient custome in symposiacke meetings, to weare chapletts of roses about their heads;[189] and so we condemne not the Germane custome, which over the table describeth a rose in the seeling; but more considerable it is, if the originall were such as Lemnius and others have recorded; that the rose was the flower of Venus, which Cupid consecrated unto Harpocrates the God of silence, and was therefore an emblem thereof to conceale the prancks of venery, as is declared in this tetrasticke

Est Rosa flos veneris, cujus quo facta laterent
  Harpocrati matris, dona dicavit Amor;
Inde Rosam mensis hospes suspendit Amicis,
  Convivæ ut sub eâ dicta tacenda sciant.[190]

8. That smoake doth follow the fairest is an usuall saying with us, and in many parts of Europe, whereof although there seeme no naturall ground, yet is it the continuation of a very ancient opinion, as Petrus Victorius and Causabon have observed from a passage in Athenæus, wherein a parasite thus describeth himselfe.[191]

To every table first I come,
Whence porridge I am cald by some:
A Capaneus at stares I am,
To enter any roome a ramme;
Like whipps and thongs to all I ply,
Like smoke unto the faire I fly.

9. To set crosse legg'd, or with our fingers pectinated or shut together is accounted bad, and friends will perswade us from it. The same conceit religiously possessed the ancients, as is observable from Pliny. *Poplites alternis genibus imponere nefas olim*;[192] and also from Athenæus, that it was an old veneficious practise, and Juno is made in this posture to hinder the delivery of Alcmæna; and therefore, as Pierius observeth, in the medall of Julia Pia the right hand of Venus, was made extended with the inscription of Venus Genetrix;[193] for the complication or pectination of the fingers was an hieroglyphick of impediment, as in that place he declareth.

10. The set and statary times of payring of nailes, and cutting of haire is thought by many a point of consideration, which is perhaps but the continuation of an ancient superstition:[194] for piaculous it was unto the Romanes to pare their nayles upon the nundinæ observed every ninth day;[195] and was also feared by others in certaine dayes of the weeke, according to that of Ausonius, Ungues Mercurio, Barbam Jove, Cypride Crines; and was one part of the wickednes that filled up the measure of Manasses, when tis delivered hee observed times, Chronicles 2.23.[196]

11. A common fashion it is to nourish haire upon the molls of the face, which is the perpetuation of a very ancient custome, and though innocently practised among us, may have a superstitious originall, according to that of Pliny; *Nævos in facie tondere religiosum habent nunc multi*;[197] from the like might proceed the feares of polling elvelockes or complicated haires of the head, and also of locks longer then the other haire, they being votary at first, and dedicated upon occasion, preserved

with great care, and accordingly esteemed by others, as appears by that of Apuleius; *Adjuro per dulcem capilli tui nodulum.*[198]

12. A custome there is in most parts of Europe to adorn aqueducts, spouts and cisternes with lions heads; which though no illaudable ornament is an Ægyptian continuation, who practised the same under a symbolicall illation; for because the sun being in Leo, the flood of Nilus was at the full, and water became conveyed into every part, they made the spouts of their aqueducts through the head of a lion: and upon some celestiall respects it is not improbable the great mogull or Indian king doth beare for his armes a lion and the sun.

13. Many conceive there is somewhat amisse, and that as we usually say, they are unblest untill they put on their girdle: wherein (although most know not what they say) there are involved unknowne considerations; for by a girdle or cincture are symbollically implied truth, resolution and readinesse unto action, which are parts and vertues required in the service of God: according whereto we finde that the Israelites eat the Paschall lambe with their loynes girded, and the Almighty challenging Job, bids him gird up his loynes like a man;[199] so runneth the expression of Peter, Gird up the loynes of your mindes, be sober and hope to the end;[200] so the high priest was girt with the girdle of fine linnen;[201] so is it part of the holy habit to have our loynes girt about with truth; and so is it also said concerning our Saviour, Righteousnesse shall be the girdle of his loynes, and faithfulnesse the girdle of his reines.*[202] * Esay 1.

Moreover by the girdle the heart and parts which God requires are devided from the inferiour and epithumeticall organs;[203] implying thereby a memento unto purification and cleannesse of heart, which is commonly defiled from the concupiscence and affection of those parts; and therfore unto this day the Jews do blesse themselves when they put on their zone or cincture: and thus may we make out the doctrine of Pythagoras, to offer sacrifice with our feet naked, that is, that our inferiour parts and farthest removed from reason might be free, and of no impediment unto us. Thus Achilles though dipped in Styx, yet having his heele untouched by that water, although he were fortified elsewhere, he was slaine in that part, and as only vulnerable in the inferiour and brutall part of man:[204] this is that part of Eve and her posterity the divel still doth bruise;[205] that is, that part of the soul which adhereth unto earth, and walks in the paths thereof; and in this secondary and symbolicall sense it may be also understood, when the priests in the law washed their feet before the sacrifice; when our Saviour washed the feet of his disciples, and said unto Peter, if I wash not thy feet thou hast no part in me;[206] and thus is it symbollically explainable and implieth purification and cleannesse, when in the burnt offerings the priest is commanded to wash the inwards and legs thereof in water, and in the peace and sin-offerings, to burne the two kidneys, the fat which is about the flancks, and as we translate it the caul above the liver.[207] But whether the Jewes when they blessed themselves,* had any eye unto the words of Jeremy, wherein God makes them his girdle; or had therein any reference unto the girdle, which the prophet was commanded to hide in the hole of the rock of Euphrates, and which was the type of their captivity, we leave unto higher conjecture.

* Jeremiah 13.

14. The picture of the Creator, or God the Father in the shape of an old man, is a dangerous piece, and in this fecundity of sects may revive the Anthropomorphites, which although maintained from the expression of Daniel, I beheld where the Ancient of dayes did sit, whose haire of his head was like the pure woole;[208] yet may it be also derivative from the hieroglyphicall description of the Ægyptians, who to expresse their Eneph, or creator of the world, described an old man in a blew mantle, with an egge in his mouth, which was the embleme of the world. Surely those heathens, that notwithstanding their exemplary advantage in heaven, would endure no pictures of sun or moone, as being visible unto all the world, and needing no representation, do evidently accuse the practise of those pencils, that will describe invisibles. And he that challenged the boldest hand unto the picture of an echo, must laugh at this attempt not onely in the description of invisibility, but circumscription of ubiquity, and fetching under lines incomprehensible circularity.

The pictures of the Ægyptians were more tolerable, and in their sacred letters more veniably expressed the apprehension of divinity; for though they implyed the same by an eye upon a scepter, by an eagles head, a crocodill and the like; yet did these manuall descriptions pretend no corporall representations, nor could the people misconceive the same unto reall correspondencies. So though the cherub carryed some apprehension of divinity, yet was it not conceived to be the shape thereof: and so perhaps because it is metaphorically predicated of God, that he is a consuming fire, he may be harmlesly described by a flaming representation: yet if, as some will have it, all mediocrity of folly is foolish, and because an unrequitable evill may ensue, an indifferent convenience must be omitted; we shall not urge such representments, wee could spare the holy lamb for the picture of our Saviour, and the dove or fiery tongues to represent the holy Ghost.

15. The sun and moone are usually described with humane faces; whether herein there be not a pagan imitation, and those visages at first implyed Apollo and Diana we make some doubt; and wee finde the statua of the sun was framed with rayes about the head, which were the indiciduous and unshaven locks of Apollo.[209] We should be too iconomicall* to question the pictures of the winds, as commonly drawne in humane heads, and with their cheeks distended, which notwithstanding wee finde condemned by Minutius, as answering poeticall fancies, and the gentile discription of Æolus Boreus, and the feigned deities of winds.

* Or quarrelsome with pictures.

16. We shall not, I hope, disparage the resurrection of our Redeemer, if we say the sun doth not dance on Easter day. And though we would willingly assent unto any sympathicall exultation, yet cannot conceive therein any more then a tropicall expression;[210] whether any such motion there were in that day wherein Christ arised, Scripture hath not revealed, which hath beene punctuall in other records concerning solary miracles:[211] and the Areopagite that was amazed at the ecclipse, tooke no notice of this, and if metaphoricall expressions goe so farre, we may be bold to affirme, not onely that one sun danced, but two arose that day:[212] that light appeared at his nativity, and darkenesse at his death, and yet a light at both; for even that darknesse was a light unto the Gentiles, illuminated by that obscurity. That 'twas the first time the sun set above the horizon, that although there were darkenesse above the earth there was light beneath it, nor dare we say that hell was darke if he were in it.

17. Great conceits are raised of the involution or membranous covering, commonly called the silly how, that sometimes is found about the heads of children upon their birth, and is therefore preserved with great care, not onely as medicall in diseases, but effectuall in successe, concerning the infant and others, which is surely no more then a continued superstition; for hereof we reade in the life of Antoninus delivered by Spartianus, that children are borne sometimes with this

naturall cap, which midwives were wont to sell unto credulous lawyers, who had an opinion it advantaged their promotion.[213]

But to speake strictly the effect is naturall, and thus to be conceaved, the infant hath three teguments, or membranous filmes which cover it in the wombe, that is, the corion, amnios, and allantois; the corion is the outward membrane wherein are implanted the veynes, arteries and umbilicall vessels, whereby its nourishment is conveyed: the allantois a thin coat seated under the corion, wherein are received the watery separations conveyed by the urachus, that the acrimony thereof should not offend the skin. The amnios is a generall investment, containing the sudorous or thin serosity perspirable through the skin. Now about the time when the infant breaketh these coverings, it sometime carryeth with it about the head a part of the amnios or neerest coat; which saith Spiegelius, either proceedeth from the toughnesse of the membrane or weakenesse of the infant that cannot get cleare thereof:[214] and therefore herein significations are naturall and concluding upon the infant, but not to be extended unto magical signalities or any other person.

18. That 'tis good to be drunke once a month, is a common flattery of sensuality, supporting it selfe upon physick, and the healthfull effects of inebriation. This indeed seemes plainly affirmed by Avicenna, a physitian of great authority, and whose religion prohibiting wine could lesse extenuate ebriety.[215] But Averroes a man of his owne faith was of another beliefe, restraining his ebriety unto hilarity, and in effect making no more thereof, then Seneca commendeth, and was allowable in Cato;[216] that is, a sober incalescence and regulated æstuation from wine, or what may be conceived betweene Joseph and his brethren, when the text expresseth they were merry, or dranke largely;[217] and whereby indeed the commodities set downe by Avicenna, that is, alleviation of spirits, resolution of superfluities, provocation of sweat and urine may also ensue. But as for dementation, sopition of reason, and the diviner particle from drinke, though American religion approve, and pagan piety of old hath practised, even at their sacrifices; Christian morality and the doctrine of Christ will not allow.[218] And surely that religion which excuseth the fact of Noah, in the aged surprisall of six hundred yeares, and unexpected inebriation from the unknowne effects of wine, will neither acquit ebriosity nor ebriety, in their knowne, and intended perversions.[219]

And indeed, although sometimes effects succeed which may relieve the body, yet if they carry mischiefe or perill unto the soule, we are therein restraineable by divinity, which circumscribeth physick, and circumstantially determines the use thereof. From naturall considerations, physick commendeth the use of venery; and happily, incest, adultery, or stupration may prove as physically advantageous, as conjugall copulation;[220] which notwithstanding must not bee drawne into practise. And truly effects, consequents, or events which wee commend, arise oft times from wayes which all condemne. Thus from the fact of Lot, we derive the generation of Ruth, and blessed nativity of our Saviour;[221] which notwithstanding did not extenuate the incestuous ebriety of the generator. And if, as it is commonly urged, we thinke to extenuate ebriety from the benefit of vomit oft succeeding; Ægyptian sobriety will condemne us, who purgeth both wayes twice a month, without this perturbation: and we foolishly contemne the liberall hand of God, and ample field of medicines which soberly produce that action.

19. A conceit there is that the devill commonly appeareth with a cloven hoofe, wherein although it seeme excessively ridiculous there may be somewhat of truth; and the ground thereof at first might be his frequent appearing in the shape of a goat, which answers that description. This was the opinion of ancient Christians concerning the apparitions of Panites, faunes and satyres, and in this forme we reade of one that appeared unto Antony in the wildernesse. The same is also confirmed from expositions of holy Scripture; for whereas it is said, Thou shalt not offer unto devils, the originall word is *Seghnirim*, that is, rough and hayrie Goats,* because in that shape the devill most often appeared, as is expounded by the Rabbins, as Tremellius hath also explained; and as the word Ascimah, the god of Emath is by some conceived; nor did he onely assume this shape in elder times, but commonly in later dayes, especially in the place of his worship. If there be any truth in the confession of witches, and as in many stories it stands confirmed by Bodinus;[222] and therefore a goat is not improperly made the hieroglyphick of the devill, as Pierius hath expressed it; so might it be the embleme of sin, as it was in the sin offering;[223] and so likewise of wicked and sinfull men, according to the expression of Scripture in the method of the last distribution, when our Saviour shall separate the

* Leviticus 17.

sheep from the goats, that is, the sons of the Lamb from the children of the devill.[224]

20. A strange kinde of exploration and peculiar way of rhabdomancy is that which is used in minerall discoveries, that is, with a forked hazell, commonly called Moses his rod, which freely held forth, will stirre and play if any mine be under it:[225] and though many there are who have attempted to make it good, yet untill better information, we are of opinion with Agricola, that in it selfe it is a fruitlesse exploration, strongly senting of pagan derivation, and the *virgula Divina*, proverbially magnified of old;[226] the ground whereof were the magicall rods in poets; that of Pollas in Homer, that of Mercury that charmed Argus, and that of Circe which transformed the followers of Ulysses;[227] too boldly usurping the name of Moses rod; from which notwithstanding, and that of Aaron were probably occasioned the fables of all the rest; for that of Moses must needs be famous unto the Ægyptians, and that of Aaron unto many other nations, as being preserved in the Arke, untill the destruction of the temple built by Solomon.[228]

21. A practise there is among us to determine doubtfull matters, by the opening of a booke, and letting fall a staffe; which notwithstanding are ancient fragments of pagan divination; the first an imitation of *sortes Homericae*, or *Virgilianæ*, drawing determinations from verses casually occurring. The same was practised by Severus, who entertained ominous hopes of the empire, from that verse in Virgil, *Tu regere imperio populos Romane memento*;[229] and Gordianus who reigned but few dayes was discouraged by another, that is, *Ostendunt terris hunc tantum fata nec ultra esse sinunt.*[230] Nor was this onely performed in heathen authors, but upon the sacred text of Scripture, as Gregorius Turonensis hath left some account, and as the practise of the Emperour Heraclius, before his expedition into Asia minor, is delivered by Cedrenus.

As for the divination or decision from the staffe it is an auguriall relique,* and the practise thereof is accused by God himselfe; My people aske counsell of their stocks, and their staffe declareth unto them. And of this kinde of rhabdomancy was that practised by Nabuchadonosor in that Caldean miscellany,† delivered by Ezekiel, The King of Babylon stood at the parting of the way, at the head of the two wayes to use divination, he made his arrowes bright, he consulted with images, he looked in the liver; at the right hand were the divinations for Jerusalem, that is, as Estius expoundeth it the

* Hosea 4.

† Ezekiel 21.

left way leading unto Rhabbah the chiefe city of the Ammonites, and the right unto Jerusalem, he consulted idols and entrals, he threw up a bundle of arrowes, to see which way they would light, and falling on the right hand he marched towards Jerusalem. A like way of belomancy or divination by arrowes hath beene in request with Scythians, Alanes, Germans, with the Africans and Turks of Algier; but of another nature was that which was practised by Elisha, when by an arrow shot from an easterne window, he presignified the destruction of Syria; or when according unto the three stroakes of Joash, with an arrow upon the ground, he foretold the number of his victories;[231] for thereby the Spirit of God particular'd the same, and determined the stroakes of the king unto three, which the hopes of the prophet expected in twice that number.

We are unwilling to enlarge concerning many other, onely referring unto Christian considerations, what naturall effects can reasonably be expected, when to prevent the ephialtes or night-mare we hang up an hallow stone in our stables; when for amulets against agues wee use the chips of gallowes and places of execution. When for warts wee rub our hands before the moone, or commit any maculated part unto the touch of the dead.[232] Swarmes hereof our learned Selden and criticall philologers might illustrate, whose abler performances our adventures doe but sollicite, meane while we hope they wil plausibly receave our attempts, or candidely correct our misconjectures.

THE SIXTH BOOK

Of sundry common opinions Cosmographicall and Historicall[1]

CHAPTER I

Concerning the beginning of the World, that the time thereof is not precisely to bee knowne, as men generally suppose: Of mens enquiries in what season or point of the Zodiack it began. That as they are generally made they are in vaine, and as particularly applyed uncertain. Of the division of the seasons and foure quarters of the yeare, according to Astronomers and Physitians. That the common compute of the Ancients, and which is yet retained by most, is unreasonable and erroneous. Of some divinations and ridiculous diductions from one part of the yeare to another. And of the providence and wisdome of God in the site and motion of the Sun.

Concerning the world and its temporall circumscriptions, who ever shall strictly examine both extreams, shall easily perceive there is not onely obscurity in its end but its beginning; that as its period is inscrutable, so is its nativity indeterminable: that as it is presumption to enquire after the one, so is there no rest or satisfactory decision in the other. And hereunto we shall more readily assent, if we examine the informations, and take a view of the severall difficulties in this point; which we shall more easily doe, if we consider the different conceits of men, and duly perpend the imperfections of their discoveries.

And first, the Heathens or histories of the Gentiles afford us slender satisfaction, nor can they relate any story, or affixe a probable point to its beginning: for some thereof (and those of the wisest amongst them) are so far from determining its beginning, that they opinion and maintaine it never had any at all; as the doctrine of Epicurus implyeth, and more positively Aristotle in his bookes *de Cœlo* declareth, endeavouring to confirme it with arguments of reason, and those appearingly demonstrative;[2] wherein to speake indifferently, his labours are rationall, and uncontroulable upon the grounds assumed, that is of physicall generation, and a primary or first matter, beyond which no other hand was apprehended:[3] But herein we remaine sufficiently satisfied from Moses, and the doctrine delivered of the creation, that is a production of all things out of nothing, a formation not only of matter, but of forme, and a materiation even of matter it selfe.[4]

Others are so far from defining the originall of the world or of mankinde, that they have held opinions not only repugnant unto chronology but philosophy; that is, that they had their beginning in the soyle where they inhabited, assuming or receiving appellations conformable unto such conceits: so did the Athenians tearm themselves *αὐτόχθονες* or *Aborigines*, and in testimony thereof did weare a golden insect on their heads; the very same name is also given unto the inlanders or midland inhabitants of this island by Cæsar. But this is a conceit answerable unto the generation of the giants, not admittable in philosophy, much lesse in divinity, which distinctly informeth wee are all the seed of Adam, that the whole world perished unto eight persons before the flood, and was after peopled by the colonies of the sonnes of Noah; there was therefore never any Autochthon, or man arising from the earth but Adam, for the woman being formed out of the rib, was once removed from earth, and framed from that element under incarnation. And so although her production were not by copulation, yet was it in a manner seminall: for if in every part from whence the seed doth flow, there be contained the Idea of the whole, there was a seminality and contracted Adam in the rib, which by the information of a soule, was individuated into Eve.[5] And therefore this conceit applyed unto the orginall of man, and the beginning of the world, is more justly appropriable unto its end; for then indeed men shall rise out of the earth, the graves shall shoot up their concealed seeds, and in that great Autumne men shall spring up, and awake from their chaos againe.

Others have been so blind in deducing the originall of things, or delivering their owne beginnings, that when it hath fallen into controversie they have not recurred unto chronologie or the records of time, but betaken themselves unto probabilities, and the conjecturalities of philosophy. Thus when the two ancient nations, that is, Ægyptians and Scythians contended for antiquity, the Ægyptians (as Diodorus and Justine relate) pleaded their antiquity from the fertility of their soyl, inferring that men there first inhabited, where they were with most facility sustained, and such a land did they conceive was Ægypt.[6]

. . .

CHAPTER II

Of mens Enquiries in what season or point of the Zodiack it began, that as they are generally made they are in vaine, and as perticularly uncertaine

Concerning the seasons, that is, the quarters of the yeare; some are ready to enquire, others to determine, in what season, whether in the Autumne, Spring, Winter or Summer the world had its beginning. Wherein we cannot but affirme, that as the question is generally, and in respect of the whole earth proposed, it is most vainely, and with a manifest injury unto reason in any particular determined, because when ever the world had its beginning it was created in all these four. For, as we have else where delivered, whatsoever signe the sun possesseth (whose recesse or vicinity defineth the quarters of the yeare) those four seasons were all actually existent, it being the nature of that luminary to distinguish the severall seasons of the yeare, all which it maketh at one time in the whole earth, and successively in any part thereof. Thus if wee suppose the sunne created in Libra, in which signe unto some it maketh Autumne, at the same time it had beene Winter unto the northern-pole; for unto them at that time the sun beginneth to be invisible, and to shew it selfe againe unto the pole of the south; unto the position of a right Sphere, or directly under the Æquator, it had beene Summer; for unto that situation the sunne is at that time verticall: unto the latitude of Capricorne, or the Winter solstice it had been Spring; for unto that position it had been in a middle point, and that of ascent, or approximation; but unto the latitude of Cancer or the Summer solstice it had been Autumne; for then had it it beene placed in a middle point, and that of descent, or elongation.

And if wee shall take it literally what Moses described popularly, this was also the constitution of the first day: for when it was evening unto one longitude, it was morning unto another; when night unto one, day unto another; and therefore that question whether our Saviour shall come againe in the twilight, as is conceived he arose, or whether he shall come upon us in the night, according to the comparison of a thiefe, or the Jewish tradition, that he will come about the time of their departure out of Ægypt, when they eate the Passeover, and the angell passed by the doores of their houses;[7] this quere I say needeth not further dispute, for if the earth be almost every where inhabited, and his comming (as divinity affirmeth) must needs be unto all, then must the time of his appearance bee both in the day and night: for if unto Jerusalem, or what part of the world soever he shall appear in the night, at the same time unto the Antipodes it must be day, if twilight unto them, broad day unto the Indians; if noone unto them, yet night unto the Americans; and so with variety according unto various habitations, or different positions of the spheare, as will be easily conceived by those who understand the affections of different habitations, and the conditions of Antæci, Perieci, and Antipodes;[8] and so although he appeare in the night, yet may the day of Judgement or Doomesday well retaine that name; for that implyeth one revolution of the Sun, which maketh the day and night, and that one naturall day: and yet to speake strictly, if (as the Apostle affirmeth) we shall be changed in the twinckling of an eye, (and as the Schooles determine) the destruction of the world shall not be successive but in an instant, we cannot properly apply thereto the usuall distinctions of time, calling that twelve houres, which admits not the parts thereof, or use at all the name of time, when indeed the nature thereof shall perish.[9]

But if the enquiry be made unto a particular place, and the question determined unto some certaine meridian; as namely, unto Mesopotamia, wherein the seat of Paradise is presumed, the quæry becomes more seasonable,[10] and is indeed in nature also determinable; yet positively to define that season, there is I conceive no slender difficulty; for some contend that it began in the Spring, as beside Eusebius, Ambrose, Bede, and Theodoret, some few years past Henrico Philippi in his Chronologie of the Scripture: Others are altogether for Autumne; and from hence doe our chronologers commence their compute, as may be observed in Helvicus, Jos. Scaliger, Calvisius and Petavius.

CHAPTER III

Of the Divisions of the seasons and foure quarters of the yeare, according unto Astronomers and Physitians, that the common compute of the Ancients, and which is still retained by some is very questionable

As for the divisions of the yeare, and the quartering out this remarkable standard of time, there have passed especially two distinctions; the first in frequent use with astronomers, according to the cardinall intersections of the zodiack, that is the two æquinoctials and both the solsticial points; defining that time to be the Spring of the yeare, wherein the sunne doth passe from the Æquinox of Aries unto the Solstice of Cancer; the time between the Solstice and the Æquinox of Libra, Summer; from thence unto the solstice of Capricornus, Autumne; and from thence unto the Æquinox of Aries againe Winter. Now this division although it be regular and equall, is not universall; for it includeth not those latitudes, which have the seasons of the year double; as have the inhabitants under the Æquator, or else between the tropicks; for unto them the sunne is verticall twice a yeare, making two distinct Summers in the different points of verticallity. So unto those which live under the Æquator, when the sunne is in the Æquinox it is Summer, in which points it maketh Spring or Autumne unto us; and unto them it is also Winter when the sun is in either tropick; whereas unto us it maketh alwayes Summer in the one: and the like will happen unto those habitations, which are between the tropicks, and the Æquator.

. . .

CHAPTER IV

Of some computation of dayes and diductions of one part of the year unto another

Fourthly, there are certaine vulgar opinions concerning dayes of the yeare and conclusions popularly deduced from certaine dayes of the month; men commonly beleeving the dayes encrease and decrease equally in the whole yeare, which notwithstanding is very repugnant unto truth; for they encrease in the month of March, almost as much as in the two months of January and February; and decrease as much in September, as they doe in July and August: for indeed the dayes encrease or decrease according to the declination of the sun; that is, its deviation northward or southward from the Æquator. Now this digression is not equall, but neare the æquinoxiall intersections, it is right and greater, neare the solstices more oblique and lesser. So from the eleventh of March the vernall Æquinox unto the eleventh of Aprill the sun declineth to the north twelve degrees; from the eleventh of Aprill unto the eleventh of May but 8, from thence unto the 15 of June, or the Summer solstice but 3 and a halfe; all which make 23 degrees and an halfe, the greatest declination of the Sun.

And this inequality in the declination of the sun in the zodiacke or line of life, is correspondent unto the growth or declination of man; for setting out from our infancie we encrease not equally, or regularly attaine to our state or perfection; nor when we descend from our state, and tend unto the earth againe is our declination equall, or carryeth us with even paces unto the grave. For, as Hippocrates affirmeth, a man is hottest in the first day of his life, and coldest in the last;[11] his naturall heate setteth forth most vigorously at first, and declineth most sensibly at last. And so though the growth of man end not perhaps untill 21, yet is his stature more advanced in the first septenary then in the second, and in the second, more then in the third, and more indeed in the first seven yeares, then in the fourteene succeeding:[12] for, what stature we attaine unto at seven yeares, we do sometimes but double, most times come short at one and twenty. And so do we decline againe; for in the latter age upon the tropick and first descension from our solstice, wee are scarce sensible of declination; but declining further, our decrement accelerates, we set apace, and in our last dayes precipitate into our graves.[13] And thus are also our progressions in the wombe, that is, our formation, motion, our birth or exclusion. For our formation is quickly effected, our motion appeareth later, and our exclusion very long after: if that be true which Hippocrates and Avicenna have declared, that the time of our motion is double unto that of formation, and that of exclusion treble unto that of motion; as if the Infant bee formed at 35. dayes, it moveth at 70. and is borne the 210. day, that is, the seventh month; or if it receaves not formation before 45. dayes, it moveth the 90. day, and is excluded in 270. that is, the 9. Month . . .

CHAPTER V
A Digression of the wisdome of God in the site and motion of the Sun

Having thus beheld the ignorance of man in some things, his error and blindnesse in others; that is, in the measure of duration both of yeares and seasons, let us a while admire the wisdome of God in this distinguisher of times, and visible Deity, as some have termed it, the sun; which though some from its glory adore, and all for its benefits admire, we shall advance from other considerations, and such as illustrate the artifice of its Maker; nor doe wee thinke we can excuse the duty of our knowledge, if we onely bestow the flourish of poetry hereon, or those commendatory conceits which popularly set forth the eminency of this creature, except we ascend unto subtiler considerations, and such as rightly understood, convinsively declare the wisdome of the Creator, which since a Spanish physition hath begun, wee will inlarge with our owne deductions;[14] and this we shall endeavour from two considerations, that is, its proper situation, and wisely ordered motion.

And first, we cannot passe over his providence in that it moveth at all; for, had it stood still, and were it fixed like the earth, there had beene then no distinction of times, either of day or yeare, of Spring, of Autumne, of Summer, or of Winter; for these seasons are defined by the motions of the sun; when that approacheth neerest us, wee call it Summer, when furthest off, Winter, when in the middle spaces, Spring or Autumne; whereas remaining in one place these distinctions had ceased, and consequently the generation of all things depending on their vicissitudes; making in one hemisphere a perpetuall Summer, in the other a deplorable and comfortlesse Winter, and thus had it also beene continuall day unto some, and perpetuall night unto others; for the day is defined by the abode of the sun above the horizon, and the night by its continuance below; so should we have needed another sun, one to illustrate our hemisphere, a second to enlighten the other, which inconvenience will ensue, in what site soever we place it, whether in the poles, or the Æquator, or betweene them both; no sphericall body of what bignesse soever illuminating the whole sphere of another, although it illuminate something more then halfe of a lesser, according unto the doctrine of the Opiticks.

His wisdome is againe discernable not onely in that it moveth at all, and in its bare motion, but wonderfull in contriving the line of its revolution; which from his artifice is so effected, that by a vicissitude in one body and light, it sufficeth the whole earth, affording thereby a possible or pleasurable habitation in every part thereof; and that is the line eclyptick, all which to effect by any other circle it had beene impossible. For first, if we imagine the Sun to make his course out of the eclyptick, and upon a line without any obliquity, let it be conceaved within that circle, that is, either on the Æquator, or else on either side (for, if we should place it either in the meridian or Colures, beside the subversion of its course from east to west, there would ensue the like incommodities).[15] Now if we conceave the sun to move betweene the obliquity of this eclyptick in a line upon one side of the Æquator, then would the sunne be visible but unto one pole, that is, the same which was nearest unto it. So that unto the one it would be perpetuall day, unto the other perpetuall night; the one would be oppressed with constant heate, the other with unsufferable cold; and so the defect of alternation would utterly impugne the generation of all things, which naturally require a vicissitude of heate to their production, and no lesse to their encrease and conservation.

. . .

CHAPTER VI
Concerning the vulgar opinion that the earth was slenderly peopled before the Floud

Beside the slender consideration men of latter times doe hold of the first ages, it is commonly opinioned, and at first thought generally imagined, that the earth was thinly inhabited, at least not remotely planted before the floud; so that some conceiving it needlesse to bee universal, have made the deluge particular, and about those parts where Noah built his Arke; which opinion because it is not only injurious to the text, humane history, and common reason, but also derogatory unto that great worke of God, the universall inundation, it will be needfull to make some farther inquisition; and (although predetermined by opinion) whether many might not suffer in the first flood, as they shall in the last flame, that is who knew not Adam nor his offence, and many perish in the deluge, who never heard of Noah or the Arke of his preservation . . .

Now our first ground to induce the numerosity of people before the floud, is the long duration of their lives beyond 7. 8. and 9. hundred yeares, which how it conduceth unto populosity wee shall make but little doubt, if we consider there are two maine causes of numerosity in any kind or species, that is, a frequent and multiparous way of breeding, whereby they fill the world with others, though they exist not long themselves; or a long duration and subsistence, whereby they doe not onely replenish the world with a new annumeration of others, but also maintaine the former account in themselves. From the first cause we may observe examples in creatures oviparous, as birds and fishes; in vermiparous, as flies, locusts, and gnats; in animals also viviparous, as swine and conies; of the first there is a great example in the herd of swine in Galilee, although it were an uncleane beast, and forbidden unto the Jews.[16] Of the other a very remarkable one in Atheneus, in the Isle Astipalea, one of the Cyclades now called Stampalia, wherein from two that were imported, the number so encreased, that the inhabitants were constrained to have recourse unto the oracle of Delphos, for an invention how to destroy them.[17]

Others there are which make good the paucity of their breed with the length and duration of their dayes, whereof there want not examples in animals uniparous: first, in bisulcous or cloven hooft, as camels, and beeves, whereof there is above a million annually slaine in England: It is also said of Job, that he had a thousand yoake of oxen, and six thousand camels; and of the children of Israel passing into the land of Canaan, that they tooke from the Midianites threescore and ten thousand beeves;[18] and of the army of Semiramis, that there were therein 100,000 camels; for solipes, or firme hoofed creatures, as horses, asses, mules, &c. they are also in mighty numbers; so is it delivered that Job had a thousand she asses: that the Midianites lost 61,000 asses: for horses it is affirmed by Diodorus, that Ninus brought against the Bactrians 280,000 horses;[19] after him Semiramis 500,000 horses, and chariots 100,000. Even in creatures sterill and such as do not generate, the length of life conduceth much unto the multiplicity of the species; for the number of mules which live farre longer then their dammes or sires, in countries where they are bred is very remarkable, and farre more common then horses.

For animals multifidous, or such as are digitated or have severall divisions in their feete, there are but two that are uniparous, that is, men and elephants; in whom though their generations be but single, they are notwithstanding very numerous. The elephant (as Aristotle affirmeth) carryeth the young two yeares and conceaveth not againe (as *Edvardus Lopez* affirmeth) in many after;[20] yet doth their age requite this disadvantage, they living commonly one hundred, sometime two hundred yeares. Now although they be unusuall with us in Europe, and altogether unknowne unto America, yet in the two other parts they are abundant, as evidently appeares by the relation of *Garcias ab Horto*, physitian to the Viceroy at Goa; who in his Chapter *de Ebore*, relates that at one venation the King of Siam tooke foure thousand, and is of opinion they are in other parts, in greater number then heards of beeves in Europe. And though this delivered from a Spaniard unacquainted with our northerne droves, may seeme very farre to exceed, yet must we conceave them very numerous, if wee consider the number of teeth transported from one countrey to another, they having onely two great teeth, and those not falling or renewing.

As for man the disadvantage in his single issue is the same with these, and in the latenesse of his generation somewhat greater then any; yet in the continuall and not interrupted time thereof, and the extent of dayes, he becomes at present, if not then any other species, at least more numerous then these before mentioned. Now being thus numerous at present, and in the measure of threescore, fourscore or an hundred years, if their dayes extended unto sixe, seven, or eight hundred, their generations would be proportionably multiplied; their times of generation being not onely multiplyed, but their subsistence continued; for though the great grandchild went on, the Tycho or first originall would subsist and make one of the world, though he outlived all the termes of consanguinity, and became a stranger unto his proper progeny. So by compute of Scripture Adam lived unto the ninth generation, unto the dayes of Lamech the father of Noah; Methuselah unto the yeare of the floud, and Noah was contemporary unto all from Enoch unto Abraham.[21] So that although some dyed, the father beholding so many discents, the number of survivers must still be very great; for if halfe the men were now alive, which lived in the last century, the earth would scarce contain their number; whereas in our abridged and septuagesimall ages, it is very rare and deserves a distich to behold the fourth generation:[22] Xerxes complaint still remaining, and what he lamented in his army, being almost deplorable in the whole world, men seldome arriving unto those yeares whereby Methuselah exceeded nine hundred, and what Adam came short of a thousand, was defined long agoe to be the age of man.[23]

Now although the length of dayes conduceth mainely unto the numerosity of mankinde, and it be manifest from Scripture they lived very long, yet is not the period of their lives determinable, and some might be longer livers, then we account that any were; for, (to omit that conceit of some, that Adam was the oldest man, in as much as he is conceaved to be created in the maturity of mankinde, that is, at 60 (for in that age it is set downe they begat children) so that adding this number unto his 930 he was 21 yeares older then any of his posterity) that even Methuselah was the longest lived of all the children of Adam, we need not grant, nor is it definitively set downe by Moses: indeed of those ten mentioned in Scripture with their severall ages it must be true; but whether those seven of the line of Caine and their progeny, or any of the sons or daughters posterity after them outlived those, is not expressed in holy Scripture;[24] and it will seeme more probable that of the line of Caine, some were longer lived then any of Seth, if we concede that seven generations of the one lived as long as nine of the other. As for what is commonly alledged, that God would not permit the life of any unto a thousand, because (alluding unto that of David) no man should live one day in the sight of the Lord, although it be urged by divers, yet is it me thinks an inference somewhat Rabbinicall, and not of power to perswade a serious examinator.[25]

Having thus made manifest in generall how powerfully the length of lives conduced unto populosity of those times, it will yet be easier acknowledged if we discend to particularities, and consider how many in seven hundred yeares might discend from one man; wherein considering the length of their dayes, we may conceave the greatest number to have beene alive together. And this that no reasonable spirit may contradict, wee will declare with manifest disadvantage; for whereas the duration of the world unto the floud was above 1600 yeares, we will make our compute in lesse then halfe that time; nor will we begin with the first man, but allow the earth to bee provided of women fit for marriage the second or third first centuries; and will onely take as granted, that they might beget children at sixty, and at an hundred yeares have twenty, allowing for that number forty yeares. Nor will we herein single out Methuselah, or account from the longest livers, but make choice of the shortest of any wee finde recorded in the text, excepting Enoch; who after hee had lived as many yeares as there be dayes in the yeare, was translated at 365.[26] And thus from one stock of seven hundred yeares, multiplying still by twenty, we shall finde the product to be one thousand, three hundred forty seven millions, three hundred sixty eight thousand, foure hundred and twenty.

Centurie	1	20.
	2	400.
	3	800.
	4	160,000.
	5	3,200,000.
	6	46,000,000.
	7	1,280,000,000.
The product		1,347,368,420

FIG 5 Calculation of Population before the flood (original illustration from *Pseudodoxia Epidemica*).

Now had wee computed by Methuselah the summe had exceeded five hundred thousand millions; as large a number from one stock as may bee conceaved in Europe; especially if in Constantinople the greatest city thereof, there be no more then Botero accounteth, seven hundred thousand soules, which duely considered, wee shall rather admire how the earth contained its inhabitants, then doubt its inhabitation; and might conceave the Deluge not simply penall, but in some way also necessary; as many have conceaved of translations, if Adam had not sinned, and the race of man had remained upon earth immortall.

. . .

CHAPTER VII
Of East and West

The next shall be of east and west; that is, the proprieties and conditions ascribed unto regions respectively unto those situations, which hath been the obvious conception of philosophers and geographers, magnifying the condition of India, and the easterne countries, above the setting and occidentall climates; some ascribing hereto the generation of gold, pretious stones, and spices, others the civility and naturall endowments of men; conceiving the bodies of this situation to receive a speciall impression from the first salutes of the sunne, and some appropriate influence from his ascendent and oriental radiations. But these proprieties affixed unto bodies, upon considerations deduced from east, west, or those observable points of the sphere, how specious and plausible soever, will not upon enquiry bee justified from such foundations.

For, to speake strictly, there is no east and west in nature; nor are those absolute and invariable, but respective and mutable points, according unto different longitudes, or distant parts of habitation, whereby they suffer many and considerable variations. For first, unto some, the same part will be east or west in respect of one another, that is, unto such as inhabit the same parallel, or differently dwell from east to west; Thus as unto Spaine, Italy lyeth east, unto Italy, Greece, unto Greece Persia, and unto Persia China; so again unto the country of China, Persia lyeth west, unto Persia Greece, unto Greece Italy, and unto Italy Spaine; so that the same country is sometimes east and sometimes west, and Persia though east unto Greece, yet is it west unto China.

. . .

CHAPTER VIII
Of the River Nilus

Hereof uncontroulably and under generall consent many opinions are passant, which notwithstanding upon due examination, do admit of doubt or restriction: it is generally esteemed, and by most unto our dayes received, that the River of Nilus hath seven ostiaries; that is, by seven channells disburdeneth it selfe into the sea; wherein notwithstanding, beside that we finde no concurrent determination of ages past, and a positive and undeniable refute of these present, the affirmative is mutable, and must not be received without all limitation.

For some, from whom wee receive the greatest illustrations of antiquity, have made no mention hereof: So Homer hath given no number of its channells, nor so much as the name thereof in use with all historians. Eratosthenes in his description of Ægypt hath likewise passed them over: Aristotle is so indistinct in their names and numbers, that in the first of

Meteors, he plainly affirmeth the Region of Ægypt, which we esteem the ancientest nation in the world, was a meere gained ground; and that by the setling of mud and limous matter brought downe by the River Nilus, that which was at first a continued sea, was raysed at last into a firme and habitable country. The like opinion hee held of Mæotis Palus, that by the floods of Tanais and earth brought downe thereby, it grew observably shallower in his dayes and would in processe of time become a firme land. And though his conjecture be not as yet fulfilled, yet is the like observable in the River Gihon, a branch of Euphrates and River of Paradise, which having in former ages discharged it selfe into the Persian Sea, doth at present fall short, being lost in the lakes of Chaldea, and hath left between the sea, a large and considerable part of dry land.

...

CHAPTER IX
Of the Red Sea

Contrary apprehensions are made of the Erythræan or Red Sea; most apprehending a materiall rednesse therein, from whence they derive its common denomination; and some so lightly conceiving hereof, as if it had no rednesse at all, are faine to recurre unto other originalls of its appellation, wherein to deliver a distinct account, we first observe that without consideration of colour it is named the Arabian Gulph: The Hebrews who had best reason to remember it, doe call it Zuph, or the Weedy Sea, because it was full of sedge, or they found it so in their passage; the Mahometans who are now lords thereof doe know it by no other name then the Gulph of Mecha a City of Arabia.

...

CHAPTER X
Of the Blacknesse of Negroes

It is evident not only in the generall frame of nature, that things most manifest unto sense, have proved obscure unto the understanding: but even in proper and appropriate objects, wherein we affirme the sense cannot erre, the faculties of reason most often fail us. Thus of colours in generall, under whose glosse and vernish all things are seen, no man hath yet beheld the true nature, or positively set downe their incontroulable causes;[27] which while some ascribe unto the mixture of the elements, others to the graduality of opacity and light; they have left our endeavours to grope them out by twilight, and by darknesse almost to discover that whose existence is evidenced by light. The chymists have attempted laudably, reducing their causes unto sal, sulphur, and mercury; and had they made it out so well in this, as in the objects of smell and taste, their endeavours had been more acceptable: for whereas they refer sapor unto salt, and odor unto sulphur, they vary much concerning colour;[28] some reducing it unto mercury, some to sulphur, others unto salt; wherein indeed the last conceit doth not oppresse the former, and salt may carry a strong concurrence therein. For beside the fixed and terrestrious salt, there is in naturall bodies a *sal niter* referring unto sulphur; there is also a volatile or armoniac salt, retaining unto mercury; by which salts the colours of bodies are sensibly qualified, and receive degrees of lustre or obscurity, superficiality or profundity, fixation or volatility.

Their generall or first natures being thus obscure, there will be greater difficulties in their particular discoveries; for being farther removed from their simplicities they fall into more complexed considerations, and so require a subtiler act of reason to distinguish and call forth their natures. Thus although a man understood the generall nature of coloures, yet were it no easie probleme to resolve, why grasse is green? Why garlick, molyes, and porrets have white roots, deep green leaves, and blacke seeds?[29] Why severall docks, and sorts of rhubarb with yellow roots, send forth purple flowers? Why also from lactary or milky plants which have a white and lacteous juice dispersed through every part, there arise flowers blue and yellow? Moreover beside the specificall and first digressions ordained from the creation, which might bee urged to salve the variety in every species; why shall the marvaile of Peru produce its flowers of different colours, and that not once, or constantly, but every day and variously? Why tulips of one colour produce some of another, and running through almost all, should still escape a blew? And lastly, why some men, yea and they a mighty and considerable part of mankinde, should first acquire and still retaine the glosse and tincture of blacknesse? Which who ever strictly enquires, shall finde no lesse of darknesse in the cause, then blacknesse in the effect it selfe, there arising unto examination no such satisfactory and unquarrellable reasons, as may confirme the causes generally received, which are but two in number; that is the heat and scorch of the sunne, or the curse of God on Cham and his posterity.[30]

The first was generally received by the ancients, especially the heathen, who in obscurities had no higher recourse then nature, as may appeare by a discourse concerning this point in Strabo:[31] by Aristotle it seems to be implyed, in those Problems which enquire why the sun makes men blacke, and not the fire?[32] Why it whitens wax, yet blacks the skin? By the word Æthiops it selfe, applyed to the memorablest nations of negroes, that is of a burnt or torrid countenance: the fancie of the fable infers also the antiquity of the opinion, which deriveth the complexion from the deviation of the sunne, and the conflagration of all things under Phaeton:[33] but this opinion though generally embraced, was I perceive rejected by Aristobulus a very ancient geographer, as is discovered by Strabo;[34] it hath been doubted by severall moderne writers, particularly by Ortelius, but amply and satisfactorily discussed as we know by no man;[35] we shall therefore endeavour a full delivery hereof, declaring the grounds of doubt, and reasons of deniall; which rightly understod, may if not overthrow, yet shrewdly shake the security of this assertion.

And first, many which countenance the opinion in this reason, doe tacitly and upon consequence overthrow it in another: for whilst they make the River Senaga to divide and bound the Moores, so that on the south-side they are blacke, on the other onely tawnie; they imply a secret causality herein from the ayre, place or river, and seem not to derive it from the sunne; the effects of whose activity are not precipitously abrupted, but gradually proceed to their cessations.

Secondly, if we affirme that this effect proceeded, or as we will not be backward to concede, it may be advanced and fomented from the fervor of the sunne; yet doe we not hereby discover a principle sufficient to decide the question concerning other animals; nor doth he that affirmeth the heat makes man blacke, afford a reason why other animalls in the same habitations maintaine a constant and agreeable hue unto those in other parts, as lions, elephants, camels, swans, tigers, estriges; which though in Æthiopia, in the disadvantage of two Summers, and perpendicular rayes of the sunne, doe yet make good the complexion of their species, and hold a colourable correspondence unto those in milder regions. Now did this complexion proceed from heat in man, the same would be communicated unto other animalls which equally participate the influence of the common agent: for thus it is in the effects of cold in regions far removed from the sunne; for therein men are not only of faire complexions, gray eyed, and of light haire, but many creatures exposed to the ayre, deflect in extremity from their naturall colours, from browne, russet and blacke, receiving the complexion of Winter, and turning perfect white; for thus Olaus Magnus relates, that after the autumnall æquinox, foxes begin to grow white;[36] thus Michovius reporteth, and we want not ocular confirmation, that hares and partridges turne white in the Winter; and thus a white crow, a proverbiall rarity with us, is none unto them; but that inseparable accident of Aristotles is separated in many hundreds.[37]

Thirdly, if the fervor of the sunne, or intemperate heat of clime did solely occasion this complexion, surely a migration or change thereof might cause a sensible, if not a totall mutation; which notwithstanding experience will not admit: for negroes transplanted although into cold and flegmaticke habitations continue their hue both in themselves, and also their generations; except they mixe with different complexions, whereby notwithstanding there only succeeds a remission of their tinctures, there remaining unto many descents, a full shadow of their originalls; and if they preserve their copulations entire they still maintaine their complexions, as is very remarkable in the dominions of the Grand Signior, and most observable in the Moores in Brasilia, which transplanted about an hundred years past, continue the tinctures of their fathers unto this day: and so likewise faire or white people translated into hotter countries receive not impressions amounting to this complexion, as hath been observed in many Europeans who have lived in the land of negroes: and as Edvardus Lopes testifieth of the Spanish plantations, that they retained their native complexions unto his dayes.

Fourthly, if the fervor of the sunne were the sole cause hereof in Æthiopia or any land of negroes, it were also reasonable that inhabitants of the same latitude subjected unto the same vicinity of the sunne, the same diurnall arch, and direction of its rayes, should also partake of the same hue and complexion, which notwithstanding they do not; for the inhabitants of the same latitude in Asia are of a different complexion, as are the inhabitants of Cambogia and Java; insomuch that some conceave the negroe is properly a native of Africa, and that those places in Asia inhabited now by Moores, are but the intrusions of negroes ariving first from Africa, as we generally conceave of Madagascar, and the adjoyning islands, who retaine the same complexion unto this day. But this defect is more remarkable in America, which although subjected unto both the tropicks, yet are not the inhabitants black betweene, or neere, or under either, neither to the southward in Brasilia, Chili, or Peru, nor yet to the northward in Hispaniola, Castilia, del Oro, or Nicaraguava; and although in many parts thereof it be confessed there bee at present swarmes of negroes serving under the Spaniard, yet were they all transported from Africa, since the discovery of Columbus, and are not indigenous or proper natives of America.

Fifthly; we cannot conclude this complexion in nations from the vicinity or habitude they hold unto the sun, for even in Africa they be negroes under the southerne tropick, but are not all of this hue either under or neere the northerne. So the people of Gualata, Agades, Garamantes, and of Goaga, all within the northerne tropicks are not negroes, but on the other side about Capo Negro, Cefala, and Madagascar, they are of a jetty black.

Now if to salve this anomaly wee say the heate of the sun is more powerfull in the southerne tropick, because in the signe of Capricorne falls out the perigeum or lowest place of the sun in his excentrick, whereby he becomes neerer unto them then unto the other in Cancer, wee shall not absolve the doubt. And if any insist upon such nicities, and will presume a different effect of the sun, from such a difference of place or vicinity, we shall ballance the same with the concernment of its motion, and time of revolution; and say he is more powerfull in the northerne hemisphere, and in the apogeum;[38] for therein his motion is slower, and so his heate respectively unto those habitations, as of duration so also of more effect. For, though he absolve his revolution in 365 dayes, odde howres and minutes, yet by reason of his excentricity, his motion is unequall, and his course farre longer in the northerne semicircle, then in the southerne; for the latter he passeth in 178 dayes, but the other takes him 187, that is, eleven dayes more; so is his presence more continued unto the northerne inhabitant, and the longest day in Cancer is longer unto us, then that in Capricorne unto the southerne habitator. Beside, hereby we onely inferre an inequality of heate in different tropicks, but not an equality of effects in other parts subjected to the same; for, in the same degree, and as neere the earth he makes his revolution unto the American, whose inhabitants notwithstanding partake not of the same effect. And if herein we seek a reliefe from the dogstarre, we shall introduce an effect proper unto a few, from a cause common unto many, for upon the same grounds that starre should have as forcible a power upon America and Asia, and although it be not verticall unto any part of Asia, but onely passeth by Beach, *in terra incognita*; yet is it so unto America, and vertically passeth over the habitations of Peru and Brasilia.[39]

Sixtly, and which is very considerable, there are negroes in Africa beyond the southerne tropick, and some so far removed from it, as geographically the clime is not intemperate, that is, neere the Cape of Good Hope, in 36 of southerne latitude. Whereas in the same elevation northward, the inhabitants of America are faire, and they of Europe in Candy, Sicily, and some parts of Spaine deserve not properly so low a name as tawny.[40]

Lastly, whereas the Africans are conceaved to be more peculiarly scorched and torrified from the sun, by addition of drinesse from the soyle, from want and defect of water, it will not excuse the doubt. For the parts which the negroes possesse, are not so void of rivers and moisture, as is herein presumed; for on the other side the mountaines of the moone, in that great tract called Zanzibar, there are the mighty rivers of Suama, and Spirito Santo; on this side, the great River Zaire, the mighty Nile and Niger, which doe not onely moysten, and contemperate the ayre by their exhalations, but refresh and humectate the earth by their annuall inundations.[41] Beside, in that part of Africa, which with all disadvantage is most dry, that is, in site betweene the tropicks, defect of rivers and inundations, as also abundance of sands, the people are not esteemed negroes; and that is Lybia, which with the Greeks carries the name of all Africa; a region so desert, dry and sandy, that travellers (as Leo reports) are faine to carry water on their camels, whereof they finde not a drop sometime in 6 or 7 dayes;[42] yet is this countrey accounted by geographers no part of *terra Nigritarum*, and Ptolomy placeth herein the *Leuco Æthiopes*, or pale and tawney Moores.

Now the ground of this opinion might bee the visible quality of blacknesse observably produced by heate, fire, and smoake; but especially with the ancients the violent esteeme they held of the heate of the sun, in the hot or torrid zone; conceaving that part unhabitable, and therefore that people in the vicinities or frontiers thereof, could not escape without this change of their complexions. But how farre they were mistaken in this apprehension, moderne geography hath discovered: and as wee have declared, there are many within this zone whose complexions descend not so low as blacknesse. And if we should strictly insist hereon, the possibility might fall into some question; that is, whether the heate of the sun, whose fervor may swarte a living part, and even black a dead or dissolving flesh, can yet in animals whose parts are successive and in continuall flux, produce this deepe and perfect glosse of blacknesse.[43]

Thus having evinced, at least made dubious, the sunne is not the author of this blacknesse, how and when this tincture first began is yet a riddle, and positively to determine it surpasseth my presumption. Seeing therefore we cannot certainly discover what did effect it, it may afford some piece of satisfaction to know what might procure it: it may be therefore considered, whether the inward use of certaine waters or fountaines of peculiar operations, might not at first produce the effect in question. For, of the like we have records in story related by Aristotle, Strabo, and Pliny, who hath made a collection hereof, as of two fountaines in Bæotia, the one making sheepe white, the other black, of the water of Siberis which made oxen black, and the like effect it had also upon men, dying not onely the skin, but making their haires black and curled.[44] This was the conceit of Aristobulus, who receaved so little satisfaction from the other, or that it might be caused by heate, or any kinde of fire, that he conceaved it as reasonable to impute the effect unto water.

Secondly, it may be perpended whether it might not fall out the same way that Jacobs cattell became speckled, spotted and ringstraked, that is, by the power and efficacy of imagination;[45] which produceth effects in the conception correspondent unto the phancy of the agents in generation, and sometimes assimilates the idea of the generator into a realty in the thing ingendred. For, hereof there passe for currant many indisputed examples; so in Hippocrates wee reade of one, that from the view and intention of a picture conceaved a negroe;[46] and in the history of Heliodore of a Moorish queene, who upon aspection of the picture of Andromeda, conceaved and brought forth a faire one.[47] And thus perhaps might some say it was at the beginning of this complexion, induced first by imagination, which having once impregnated the seed, found afterward concurrent productions, which were continued by climes, whose constitution advantaged the first impression. Thus Plotinus conceaveth white peacocks first came in: thus as Aldrovand relateth, many opinion that from aspection of the snow which lyeth long in northerne regions, and high mountaines, hawkes, kites, beares, and other creatures become white;[48] and by this way Austin conceaveth the devill provided, they never wanted a white spotted oxe in Ægypt, for such an one they worshipped, and called it Apis.[49]

Thirdly, it is not indisputable whether it might not proceed from such a cause and the like foundation of tincture, as doth the black jaundise, which meeting with congenerous causes might settle durable inquinations, and advance their generations unto that hue, which was naturally before but a degree or two below it:[50] and this transmission we shall the easier admit in colour, if we remember the like hath beene effected in organicall parts and figures; the symmetry whereof being casually or purposely perverted, their morbosities have vigorously descended to their posterities, and that in durable deformities.[51] This was the beginning of Macrophali or people with long heads, whereof Hippocrates, *De Aere, Aquis, et Locis*, hath cleerely delivered himself: *Cum primum editus est infans, caput ejus tenellum manibus effingunt, et in longitudine adolescere cogunt; hoc institutum primum hujusmodi, naturæ dedit vitium, successu vero temporis in naturam abiit, ut proinde instituto nihil amplius opus esset; semen enim genitale ex omnibus corporis partibus provenit, ex sanis quidem sanum, ex morbosis morbosum: Si igitur ex caluis calui, ex cæsiis cæsii, et ex distortis, ut plurimum, distorti gignuntur, eademque in cæteris formis valet ratio, quid prohibet cur non ex macrocephalis macrocephali gignantur?*[52] Thus as Aristotle observeth, the deeres of Arginusa had their eares divided, occasioned at first by slitting the eares of deere. Thus have the Chineses little feete, most negroes great lips and flat noses; and thus many Spaniards, and Mediterranean inhabitants, which are of the race of Barbary Moores, (although after frequent commixture) have not worne out the camoys nose unto this day.[53]

[Artificial negroes, or Gypsies acquire their complexion by anointing their bodies with bacon and fat substances, and so exposing them to the sun.[54] In Guinie Moors and others, it hath been observed, that they frequently moisten their skins with fat and oylie materials, to temper the irksom driness thereof from the parching rayes of the sun. Whether this practise at first had not some efficacy toward this complexion, may also be considered.]

Lastly, if wee must still be urged to particularities, and such as declare how and when the seede of Adam did first receave this tincture; wee may say that men became blacke in the same manner that some foxes, squirrels, lions first turned of this complexion, whereof there are a constant sort in divers countries; that some chaughes came to have red legs and bils, that crowes became pyed;[55] all which mutations however they began, depend on durable foundations, and such as may continue for ever. And if as yet we cannot satisfie, but must farther define the cause and manner of this mutation; wee must confesse, in matters of antiquity, and such as are decided by history, if their originals and first beginnings escape a due relation, they fall into great obscurities, and such as future ages seldome reduce unto a resolution. Thus if you deduct the administration of angels, and that they dispersed the creatures into all parts after the flood, as they had congregated them into Noahs Arke before; it will be no easie question to resolve, how severall sorts of animalls were first dispersed into islands, and almost how any into America. How the venereall contagion began in that part of the earth, since history is silent, is not easily resolved by philosophy;[56] for, whereas it is imputed unto anthropophagy, or the eating of mans flesh, the cause hath beene common unto many other countries, and there have beene canibals or men-eaters in the three other parts of the world, if wee credit the relations of Ptolomy, Strabo, and Pliny.[57] And thus, if the favourable pen of Moses had not revealed the confusion of tongues, and positively declared unto us their division at Babell, our disputes concerning their beginning had beene without end, and I feare we must have left the hopes of that decision unto Elias.[58]

And if any will yet insist, and urge the question farther still upon me, I shall be enforced unto divers of the like nature, wherein perhaps I shall receave no greater satisfaction. I shall demand how the camels of Bactria came to have two bunches on their backs, whereas the camels of Arabia in all relations have but one? How oxen in some countries began and continue gibbous or bunch back'd? What way those many different shapes, colours, haires, and natures of dogs came in? How they of some countries became depilous and without any haire at all, whereas some sorts in excesse abound therewith? How the Indian hare came to have a long tayle, whereas that part in others attaines no higher then a scut?[59] How the hogs of Illyria which Aristotle speakes of, became to be solipedes or wholl hoofed, whereas in all other parts they are bisulcous and described cloven hoofed by God himselfe?[60] All which with many others must needs seeme strange unto those, that hold there were but two of the uncleane sort in the Arke, and are forced to reduce these varieties to unknowne originals since.[61]

However therefore this complexion was first acquired, it is evidently maintained by generation, and by the tincture of the skin as a spermaticall part traduced from father unto son, so that they which are strangers contract it not, and the natives which transmigrate omit it not without commixture, and that after divers generations.[62] And this affection (if the story were true) might wonderfully be confirmed, by what Maginus and others relate of the Emperour of Æthiopia, or Prester John, who derived from Solomon is not yet descended into the hue of his countrey, but remaines a mulatto, that is, of a mongrill complexion unto this day.[63] Now although we conceive this blacknesse to be seminall, yet are we not of Herodotus conceit, that is, that their seed is black;[64] an opinion long agoe rejected by Aristotle, and since by sence and enquiry;[65] his assertion against the historian was probable, that all seed was white; that is, without great controversie in viviparous animals, and such as have testicles, or preparing vessels wherein it receives a manifest dealbation:[66] and not onely in them, but (for ought I know) in fishes, not abating the seed of plants, whereof though the skin and covering be black, yet is the seed and fructifying part not so: as may be observed in the seeds of onyons, pyonie, and basill: most controvertible it seemes, in the spawne of frogs, and lobsters, whereof notwithstanding at the very first the spawne is white, contracting by degrees a blacknesse, answerable in the one unto the colour of the shell, in the other unto the porwigle or tadpole, that is, that animall which first proceedeth from it: and thus may it also be in the generation and sperme of negroes; that being first and in its naturals white, but upon separation of parts, accidents before invisible become apparent; there arising a shadow or darke efflorescence in the outside, whereby not onely their legitimate and timely births, but their abortions are also duskie, before they have felt the scortch and fervor of the sun.

CHAPTER XI
Of the Same

A second opinion there is, that this complexion was first a curse of God derived unto them from Cham, upon whom it was inflicted for discovering the nakednesse of Noah.[67] Which notwithstanding is sooner affirmed then proved, and carrieth with it sundry improbabilities. For first, if we derive the curse on Cham, or in generall upon his posterity, we shall benegroe a greater part of the earth then ever was, or so conceived;[68] and not onely paint the Æthiopians, and reputed sons of Cush, but the people also of Ægypt, Arabia, Assyria, and Chaldea; for by his race were these countries also peopled.[69] And if concordantly unto Berosus, the fragment of Cato *De Originibus*, some things of Halicarnasseus, Macrobius, and out of them of Leandro and Annius, wee shall conceive of the travailes of Camese or Cham, wee may introduce a generation of negroes as high as Italy, which part was never culpable of deformity, but hath produced the magnified examples of beauty.[70]

Secondly, the curse mentioned in Scripture was not denounced upon Cham, but Canaan his youngest son, and the reasons thereof are divers;[71] the first, from the Jewish tradition, whereby it is conceived, that Canaan made the discovery of the nakednesse of Noah, and notified it unto Cham. Secondly, to have cursed Cham had been to curse all his posterity, whereof but one was guilty of the fact. And lastly, he spared Cham, because he had blessed him before, cap 9. Now if we confine this curse unto Canaan, and thinke the same fulfilled in his posterity, then do we induce this complexion on the Sidonians, then was the promised land a tract of negroes; for from Canaan were discended the Canaanites, Jebusites, Amorites, Gergezites, and Hevites, which were possessed of that land.

Thirdly, although we should place the originall of this curse upon one of the sons of Cham, yet were it not knowne from which of them to derive it. For the particularity of their discents is imperfectly set downe by accountants, nor is it distinctly determinable from whom thereof the Æthiopians are proceeded. For, whereas these of Africa are generally esteemed to be the issue of Chus, the elder son of Cham, it is not so easily made out. For the land of Chus, which the Septuagint translates Æthiopia, makes no part of Africa, nor is it the habitation of blackmores, but the countrie of Arabia, especially the happy, and stony; possessions and colonies of all the sons of Chus, excepting Nimrod, and Havilah, possessed and planted wholly by the children of Chus, that is, by Sabtah and Raamah, Sabtacha, and the sons of Raamah, Dedan and Sheba, according unto whose names the nations of those parts have received their denominations, as may bee collected from Pliny and Ptolomy; and as wee are informed by credible authors, they hold a faire analogie in their names, even unto our dayes. So the wife of Moses translated in Scripture an Æthiopian, and so confirmed by the fabulous relation of Josephus, was none of the daughters of Africa, nor any negroe of Æthiopia, but the daughter of Jethro, prince and priest of Madian, which was a part of Arabia the stony, bordering upon the Red Sea.[72] So the Queene of Sheba came not unto Solomon out of Æthiopia, but from Arabia, and that part thereof which bore the name of the first planter thereof, the son of Chus. So whether the eunuch which Philip the Deacon baptised, were servant unto Candace Queene of the African Æthiopia, (although Damianus à Goes, Codignus, and the Æthiopick relations averre) is yet by many, and with strong suspicions doubted.[73] So that army of a million, which Zerah King of Æthiopia is said to bring against Asa, was drawn out of Arabia, and the plantations of Chus, not out of Æthiopia, and the remote habitations of the Moores;[74] for it is said that Asa pursuing his victory, tooke from him the city Gerar; now Gerar was no city in or neere Æthiopia, but a place betweene Cadesh and Zur, where Abraham formerly sojourned.[75] Since therefore these African Æthiopians, are not convinced by the common acception to be the sons of Chus, whether they be not the posterity of Phut, or Mizraim, or both, it is not assuredly determined; for Mizraim, he possessed Ægypt, and the east parts of Africa: from Ludym his son came the Lybians, and perhaps from them the Æthiopians:[76] Phut possessed Mauritania, and the westerne parts of Africa, and from these perhaps descended the Moors of the west, of Mandinga, Meleguette and Guinie. But from Canaan, upon whom the curse was pronounced, none of these had their originall, for he was restrained unto Canaan and Syria;[77] although in after ages many colonies dispersed, and some thereof upon the coasts of Africa, and the prepossessions of his elder brothers.[78]

Fourthly, to take away all doubt or any probable divarication, the curse is plainely specified in the text, nor need we dispute it, like the marke of Cain;[79] *Servus servorum erit fratribus suis*, cursed be Canaan, a servant of servants shall he be unto his brethren; which was after fulfilled in the conquest of Canaan, subdued by the Israelites, the posterity of Sem;[80] which prophecy Abraham well understanding, tooke an oath of his servant not to take a wife for his son Isaac out of the daughters of the Canaanites; and the like was performed by Isaac in the behalfe of his son Jacob.[81] As for Cham and his other sons this curse attained them not, for Nimrod the son of Chus set up his kingdome in Babylon, and erected the first great empire, Mizraim and his posterity grew mighty monarches in Ægypt;[82] and the empire of the Æthiopians hath beene as large as either.

Lastly, whereas men affirme this colour was a curse, I cannot make out the propriety of that name, it neither seeming so to them, nor reasonably unto us; for they take so much content therein, that they esteeme deformity by other colours, describing the Devill, and terrible objects white. And if wee seriously consult the definitions of beauty, and exactly perpend what wise men determine thereof, wee shall not reasonably apprehend a curse, or any deformity therein.[83] For first, some place the essence thereof in the proportion of parts, conceiving it to consist in a comely commensurability of the whole unto the parts, and the parts betweene themselves, which is the determination of the best and learned writers: and whereby the Moores are not excluded from beauty; there being in this description no consideration of colours, but an apt connexion and frame of parts and the whole. Others there be, and those most in number, which place it not onely in proportion of parts, but also in grace of colour; but to make colour essentiall unto beauty, there will arise no slender difficulty; for, Aristotle in two definitions of pulchritude, and Galen in one, have made no mention of colour:[84] neither will it agree unto the beauty of animals, wherein notwithstanding there is an approved pulchritude. Thus horses are handsome under any colour, and the symmetry of parts obscures the consideration of complexions; thus in concolour animals and such as are confined unto one colour wee measure not their beauty thereby;[85] for if a crow or black bird grow white, wee generally account it more pretty, and even in monstrosity descend not to opinion of deformity. And by this way likewise the Moores escape the curse of deformity, there concurring no stationary colour, and sometimes not any unto beauty.

The Platonick contemplators reject both these descriptions founded upon parts and colours, or either, as M. Leo the Jew hath excellently discoursed in his Genealogy of Love, defining beauty a formall grace, which delights and moves them to love which comprehend it.[86] This grace say they, discoverable outwardly, is the resplendor and raye of some interiour and invisible beauty, and proceedeth from the formes of compositions amiable; whose faculties if they can aptly contrive their matter, they beget in the subject an agreeable and pleasing beauty, if over ruled thereby, they evidence not their perfections, but runne into deformity. For seeing that out of the same materials, Thersites and Paris, beauty and monstrosity may be contrived, the formes and operative faculties introduce and determine their perfections;[87] which in naturall bodies receive exactnesse in every kinde, according to the first Idea of the Creator, and in contrived bodies the phancie of the artificer: and by this consideration of beauty, the Moores also are not excluded, but hold a common share therein with all mankinde.

Lastly, in whatsoever its theory consisteth, or if in the generall, we allow the common conceit of symmetry and of colour, yet to descend unto singularities, or determine in what symmetry or colour it consisted, were very dangerous; for beauty is determined by opinion, and seems to have no essence that holds one notion unto all; that seeming beauteous unto one, which hath no favour with another, and that unto every one, according as custome hath made it naturall, or sympathy and conformity of minds shall make it seem agreeable. Thus flat noses seem comly unto the Moore, an aquiline or hawked one unto the Persian, a large and prominent nose unto the Romane, but none of all these are acceptable in our opinion. Thus some thinke it most ornamentall to weare their bracelets on their wrests, others say it is better to have them about their ancles; some thinke it most comely to weare their rings and jewells in the eare, others will have them about their privities; a third will not thinke they are compleat except they hang them in their lips, cheeks or noses. Thus Homer to set off Minerva calleth her *γλαυκῶπις*, that is gray or light blew eyed: now this unto us seems farre lesse amiable then the black. Thus we that are of contrary complexions accuse the blacknes of the Mores as ugly: but the spouse in the Canticles excuseth this conceit, in that description of hers, I am black, but comely:[88] and howsoever Cerberus, and the furies of hell be described by the poets under this complexion, yet in the beauty of our Saviour blacknesse is commended, when it is said his locks are bushie and blacke as a raven.[89] So that to inferre this as a curse, or to reason it as a deformity, is no way reasonable; the two foundations of beauty symmetry and complexion, receiving such various apprehensions, that no deviation will bee expounded so high as a curse or undeniable deformity, without a manifest and confessed degree of monstrosity.

Lastly it is a very injurious method unto philosophy, and a perpetuall promotion unto ignorance, in points of obscurity, nor open unto easie considerations, to fall upon a present refuge unto miracles, or recurre unto immediate contrivance from the insearchable hands of God. Thus in the conceit of the evill odor of the Jewes, Christians without a farther research into the verity of the thing, or enquiry into the cause, drawe up a judgement upon them, from the passion of their Saviour.[90] Thus in the wondrous effects of the clime of Ireland, and the freedome from all venomous creatures, the credulity of common conceit imputes this immunity unto the benediction of Saint Patrick, as Beda and Gyraldus have left recorded.[91] Thus the asse having a peculiar marke of a crosse made by a blacke list downe his backe, and another athwart, or at right angles downe his shoulders; common opinion ascribe this figure unto a peculiar signation, since that beast had the honour to beare our Saviour upon his backe. Certainly this is a course more desperate then antipathies, sympathies or occult qualities; wherein by a finall and satisfactive discernment of faith, we lay the last and particular effects upon the first and generall cause of all things, whereas in the other wee doe but palliate our determinations, untill our advanced endeavors doe totally reject or partially salve their evasions.[92]

CHAPTER XII
A Digression concerning Blacknesse

There being therefore two opinions repugnant unto each other, it may not be presumptive or skepticall in me to doubt of both, and because we remaine imperfect in the generall theory of colours, wee shall deliver at present a short discovery of blacknes, wherein although perhaps we afford no greater satisfaction then others, yet shall our attempts exceed any; for wee shall emperically and sensibly discourse hereof, deducing the causes of blacknesse from such originalls in nature, as we doe generally observe things are denigrated by art: and herein I hope our progression will not be thought unreasonable; for art being the imitation of nature, or nature at the second hand; it is but a sensible expression of effects dependant on the same, though more removed causes, and therefore the works of the one, must prove reasonable discoverers of the other.[93] [And though colours of bodies may arise according to the receptions, refraction, or modification of light; yet are there certain materialls which may dispose them unto such qualities.]

And first, things become blacke by a sootish and fuliginious matter proceeding from the sulphur of bodies torrified, not taking *fuligo* strictly, but in opposition unto ἀτμίς, that is any kind of vaporous or madefying excretion, and comprehending ἀναθυμίασις, that is as Aristotle defines it, a separation of moist and dry parts made by the action of heat or fire, and colouring bodies objected.[94] Hereof, in his Meteors, from the qualities of the subject he raiseth three kinds; the exhalations from ligneous and lean bodies, as bones, hair, and the like he calleth καπνός, *fumus*; from fat bodies, and such as have not their fatnesse conspicuous or separated, he tearmeth λιγνύς *fuligo*, as waxe, rosin, pitch, or turpentine; that from unctuous bodies, and such whose oylinesse is evident, he nameth κνίσσα or *nidor*;[95] now every one of these doe blacke the bodies objected unto them, and are to be conceived in the sooty and fuliginous matter expressed.

I say, proceeding from the sulphur of bodies torrified, that is the oily fat and unctuous parts wherein consist the principles of flammability; not pure and refined sulphur, as in the spirits of wine often rectified, but containing terrestrious parts, and carrying with it the volatile salt of the body, and such as is distinguishable by taste in soot; nor vulgar and usuall sulphur, for that leaves none or very little blacknesse, except a metalline body receive the exhalation.

I say, torrified, sindged, or suffering some impression from fire, thus are bodies casually or artificially denigrated, which in their naturalls are of another complexion; thus are charcoales made black by an infection of their own suffitus;[96] so is it true what is assumed of combustible bodies, *Adusta nigra, perusta alba*, black at first from the fuliginous tincture, which being exhaled they become white, as is perceptible in ashes. And so doth fire cleanse and purifie bodies, because it consumes the sulphureous parts, which before did make them foule; and therefore refines those bodies which will never bee mundified by water.[97] Thus camphire of a white substance, by its fuligo affordeth a deepe black. So is pitch blacke, although it proceed from the same tree with rozen, the one distilling forth, the other forced by fire; so of the suffitus of a torch, doe painters make a velvet blacke; so is lampe blacke made; so of burnt harts horn a sable; so is bacon denigrated in chimneyes: so in fevers and hot distempers from choler adust is caused a blacknesse in our tongues, teeth and excretions:[98] so are ustilago, brant corne and trees blacke by blasting, so parts cauterized, gangrenated, siderated and mortified, become black, the radicall moisture, or vitall sulphur suffering an extinction, and smothered in the part affected.[99] So not only actuall but potentiall fire, nor burning fire, but also corroding water will induce a blacknes. So are chimneyes and furnaces generally blacke, except they receive a cleare and manifest sulphur; for the smoak of sulphur will not blacke a paper, and is commonly used by women to whiten tiffanies;[100] which it performeth by an acide vitriolous, and penetrating spirit ascending from it, by reason whereof it is not apt to kindle any thing, nor will it easily light a candle, untill that spirit bee spent, and the flame approacheth the match: and this is that acide and piercing spirit which with such activity and compunction invadeth the braines and nostrills of those that receive it. And thus when Bellonius affirmeth that charcoales, made out of the wood of oxycedar are white, Dr. Jordan in his judicious discourse of minerall waters yeeldeth the reason, because their vapours are rather sulphureous then of any other combustible substance.[101] So we see that Tinby coals will not blacke linnen being hanged in the smoake thereof, but rather whiten it, by reason of the drying and penetrating quality of sulphur, which will make red roses white: And therefore to conceive a generall blacknesse in hell, and yet therein the materiall flames of sulphur, is no philosophicall conception, nor will it consist with the reall effects of its nature.

These are the advenient and artificiall wayes of denigration, answerably whereto may be the natural progresse: these are the waies wherby culinary and common fires doe operate, and correspondent hereunto may be the effects of fire elementall.[102] So may bitumen, coales, jet, blacke lead, and divers minerall earths become black; being either fuliginous concretions in the earth, or suffering a scortch from denigrating principles in their formation: so iron (as metallists expresse it) consisting of impure mercury and combust sulphur, becomes of a darke and sad complexion, whereas other metalls have a vivacity and quicknesse in aspect. So men and other animalls receive different tinctures from constitution and complexionall efflorescences, and descend still lower, as they partake of the fuliginous and denigrating humor. And so may the Æthiopians or negroes become coal-blacke from fuliginous efflorescences and complexionall tinctures arising from such probabilities, as we have declared before.

The second way whereby bodies become blacke, is an atramentous condition or mixture, that is a vitriolate or copperose quality conjoyning with a terrestrious and astringent humidity, for so is *Atramentum scriptorium*, or writing inke commonly made, by copperose cast upon a decoction or infusion of galls.[103] I say, a vitriolous or copperous quality; for vitrioll is the active or chiefe ingredient in inke, and no other salt that I know will strike the colour with galles; neither alom, salgemme, nitre, nor armoniack: now artificiall copperose, and such as we commonly use, is a rough and acrimonious kinde of salt drawne out of ferreous and eruginous earths, partaking chiefly of iron and copper, the blew of copper, the green most of iron:[104] nor is it unusuall to dissolve fragments of iron in the liquor thereof, for advantage in the concretion. I say, a terrestrious or astringent humidity; for without this there will ensue no tincture; for copperose in a decoction of lettuce or mallows affords no black, which with an astringent mixture it will doe, though it be made up with oyle as in printing and painting inke: but whereas in this composition wee use onely nutgalles, that is an excrescence from the oake, therein we follow and beat upon the old receit; for any plant of austere and stipticke parts will suffice, as I have experimented in bistorte, myrobolaus, myrtus brabantica, balaustium, and red-roses: and indeed, most decoctions of astringent plants, of what colour soever, doe leave in the liquor a deep and muscadine red, which by addition of vitrioll descend into a blacke: and so Dioscorides in his receit of inke, leaves out gall, and with copperose makes use of soot.[105]

Now if we inquire in what part of vitriol this atramentall and denigrating condition lodgeth, it will seeme especially to lye in the fixed salt thereof; for the phlegme or aqueous evaporation will not denigrate, nor yet spirits of vitriol, which carry with them volatile and nimbler salt: for if upon a decoction of copperose and gall, be powred the spirits or oyl of vitriol, the liquor will relinquish his blacknes, the gall and parts of the copperose precipitate unto the bottom, and the inke grow cleare again, which indeed it will not so easily doe in common inke, because that gumme is dissolved therein, which hindereth the separation: but colcothar or vitriol burnt, though unto a rednesse containing the fixed salt, will make good inke, and so will the lixivium, or lye made thereof with warme water; but the *terra* or insipide earth remaining, affords no blacke at all, but serves in many things for a grosse and usefull red.[106]

And if we yet make a more exact enquiry, by what this salt of vitriol more peculiarly gives this colour, we shall finde it to be from a metalline condition, and especially an iron property or ferreous participation: for blew copperose which deeply partakes of the copper will doe it but weakly; verdigrise which is made out of copper will not doe it at all; but the filings of iron infused in vinegar, will with a decoction of galles make good inke, without any copperose at all, and so will infusion of loadstone, which is of affinity with iron; and though more conspicuously in iron, yet such a calcanthous or atramentous quality, we will not wholly reject in other metalls, whereby we often observe blacke tinctures in their solutions. Thus a lemmon, quince, or sharpe apple cut with a knife becomes immediatly blacke: and so from the like cause, artichokes, so sublimate beat up with whites of egges, if touched with a knife becomes incontinently black. So *aqua fortis*, whose ingredient is vitriol will make white bodies blacke. So leather dressed with the barke of oake, is easily made blacke by a bare solution of copperose. So divers minerall waters and such as participate of iron, upon an infusion of galles become of a dark colour, and entring upon black. So steele infused, makes not only the liquour duskie, but in bodies wherein it concurs with proportionable tinctures makes also the excretions black. And so also from this vitriolous quality *Mercuries dulcis*, and vitriol vomitive occasion black ejections.[107]

Such a condition there is naturally in some living creatures. Thus that blacke humor by Aristotle named θολός, and commonly translated *atramentum*, may be occasioned in the cuttle.[108] Such a condition there is naturally in some plants, as black-berries, walnut rinds, black cherries, whereby they extinguish inflamations, corroborate the stomacke, and are esteemed, specificall in the epilepsie. Such an atramentous condition there is to bee found sometime in the bloud, when that which some call acetum, others vitriolum, concurs with parts prepared for this tincture. And so from these conditions the Moores might possibly become negroes, receiving atramentous impressions in some of those wayes, whose possibility is by us declared.

Nor is it strange that we affirme there are vitriolous parts, qualities, and even at some distance vitriol it selfe in living bodies; for there is a sowre, stipticke salt diffused through the earth, which passing a concoction in plants, becommeth milder and more agreeable unto the sense, and this is that vegetable vitriol, whereby divers plants containe a gratefull sharpnesse; as lemmons, pomegranates, cherries, or an austere and inconcocted roughnesse, as sloes, medlers and quinces: and that not onely vitriol is a cause of blacknesse, but that the salts of naturall bodies doe carry a powerfull stroake in the tincture and vernish of all things, we shall not deny, if we contradict not experience, and the visible art of dyars, who advance and graduate their colours with salts; for the decoctions of simples which beare the visible colours of bodies decocted, are dead and evanid without the commixtion of alume, argol, and the like;[109] and this is also apparent in chymicall preparations. So cinaber becomes red by the acide exhalation of sulphur, which otherwise presents a pure and niveous white.[110] So spirits of salt upon a blew paper make an orient red. So tartar or vitriol upon an infusion of violets affords a delightfull crimson. Thus it is wonderfull what variety of colours the spirits of saltpeter, and especially, if they be kept in a glasse while they pierce the sides thereof; I say, what orient greens they will project: from the like spirits in the earth the plants thereof perhaps acquire their verdure. And from such salary irradiations may those wondrous varieties arise, which are observable in animalls, as mallards heads, and peacocks feathers, receiving intention or alteration according as they are presented unto the light.[111] Thus saltpeter, ammoniack and minerall spirits emit delectable and various colours; and common *aqua fortis* will in some green and narrow mouthed glasses, about the verges thereof, send forth a deep and gentianella blew.

Thus have we at last drawne our conjectures unto a period; wherein if our contemplations afford no satisfaction unto others, I hope our attempts will bring no condemnation on our selves; (for besides that adventures in knowledge are laudable, and the assayes of weaker heads affords oftentimes improveable hints unto better) although in this long journey we misse the intended end, yet are there many things of truth disclosed by the way: and the collaterall verity, may unto reasonable speculations, requite the capitall indiscovery.

[CHAPTER XIII[112]
Of Gypsies

Great wonder it is not we are to seek in the originall of Æthiopians and natural negroes, being also at a losse concerning the originall of Gypsies and counterfeit Moors, observable in many parts of Europe, Asia, and Africa.

Common opinion deriveth them from Ægypt, and from thence they derive themselves, according to their own account hereof, as Munster discovered in the letters and passe which they obtained from Sigismund the Emperour;[113] that they first came out of lesser Ægypt, that having defected from the Christian rule, and relapsed unto Pagan rites, some of every family were enjoyned this penance to wander about the world; or as Aventinus delivereth, they pretend for this vagabond course, a judgement of God upon their forefathers, who refused to entertain the Virgin Mary and Jesus, when she fled into their countrey.

Which account notwithstanding is of little probability: for the generall stream of writers, who enquire into their originall, insist not upon this; and are so little satisfied in their descent from Ægypt, that they deduce them from severall other nations: Polydore Virgil accounting them originally Syrians, Philippus Bergomas fetcheth them from Chaldæa, Æneas Sylvius from some part of Tartarie, Bellonius no further then Walachia and Bulgaria, nor Aventinus then the confines of Hungaria.[114]

That they are no Ægyptians Bellonius maketh evident: who met great droves of Gypsies in Ægypt, about Gran Cairo, Matærea, and the villages on the banks of Nilus: who notwithstanding were accounted strangers unto that Nation, and wanderers from forreign parts, even as they are esteemed with us.

That they came not out of Ægypt is also probable, because their first appearance was in Germany, since the year 1400. nor were they observed before in other parts of Europe, as is deducible from Munster, Genebrard, Crantsius and Ortelius.

But that they first set out not farre from Germany, is also probable from their language, which was the Sclavonian tongue; and when they wandered afterward into France, they were commonly called Bohemians, which name is still retained for Gypsies. And therefore when Crantsius delivereth, they first appeared about the Baltick Sea, when Bellonius deriveth them from Bulgaria and Walachia, and others from about Hungaria, they speak not repugnantly hereto: for the language of those Nations was Sclavonian, at least some dialect thereof.

But of what nation soever they were at first, they are now almost of all, associating unto them some of every country where they wander, when they will be lost, or whether at all again, is not without some doubt: for unsetled nations have out-lasted others of fixed habitations: and though Gypsies have been banished by most Christian Princes, yet have they found some countenance from the great Turk, who suffereth them to live and maintain publick Stews near the Imperial city in Pera, of whom he often maketh a politick advantage, imploying them as spies into other nations, under which title they were banished by Charles the fift.]

THE SEVENTH BOOK

Concerning many historicall tenents generally received, and some deduced from the history of holy Scripture

CHAPTER I
Of the Forbidden Fruit

That the forbidden fruit of Paradise was an apple, is commonly beleeved, confirmed by tradition, perpetuated by writings, verses, pictures; and some have been so bad prosodians, as from thence to derive the Latine word *Malum*; because that fruit was the first occasion of evill, wherein notwithstanding determinations are presumptuous, and many I perceive are of another beleefe; for some have conceived it a vine, in the mystery of whose fruit lay the expiation of the transgression: Goropius Becanus reviving the conceit of Barcephas, peremptorily concludeth it to be the Indian fig-tree, and by a witty allegory labours to confirme the same.[1] Some fruits we observe to passe under the name of Adams apples, which in common acception admit not that appellation, the one described by Mathiolus under the name of *Pomum Adami*, a very faire fruit, and not unlike a citron, but somewhat rougher chopt and cranied, vulgarly conceived the markes of Adams teeth;[2] another, the fruit of that plant Serapion termeth *Musa*, but the easterne Christians commonly the apples of Paradise;[3] not resembling an apple in figure, and in taste a melon or cowcumber; which fruits although they have received appellations suitable unto the tradition, yet can we not from thence inferre they were this fruit in question; no more then *arbor vitæ*, so commonly called, to obtaine its name from the tree of life in Paradise, or *arbor Judæ*, to bee the same which supplyed the gibbet unto Judas.

Againe, there is no determination in the text, wherein is only particulared that it was the fruit of a tree good for food and pleasant unto the eye, in which regards many excell the apple;[4] and therefore learned men doe wisely conceive it inexplicable, and Philo puts determination unto despaire, when hee affirmeth the same kinde of fruit was never produced since.[5] Surely, were it not requisite or reasonable to have been concealed, it had not passed unspecified, nor the tree revealed which concealed their nakednesse, and that concealed which revealed it; for in the same chapter mention is made of fig-leaves, and the like particulars although they seem uncircumstantiall are oft set downe in holy Scripture; so is it specified that Elias sate under a juniper tree, Absolon hanged by an oake, and Zacheus got up into a sycomore.[6]

And although to condemne such indeterminables, unto him that demanded on what hand Venus was wounded, the philosopher thought it a sufficient resolution to reinquire upon what leg King Philip halted;[7] and the Jews not undoubtedly resolved of the sciatica side of Jacob, do cautelously in their diet abstaine from the sinewes of both;[8] yet are there many nice particulars which may bee authentically determined. That Peter cut off the right eare of Malchus is beyond all doubt. That our Saviour eat the Passeover in an upper roome, we may determine from the text;[9] and some we may concede which the Scripture plainly defines not. That the Dyall of Ahaz was placed upon the west side of the Temple, wee will not deny, or contradict the description of Adricomius.[10] That Abrahams servant put his hand under his right thigh, we shall not question; and that the thiefe on the right hand was saved, and the other on the left reprobated, to make good the method of the last judiciall dismission, we are ready to admit;[11] but surely in vaine we enquire of what wood was Moses rod, or the tree that sweetned the waters; or though tradition or humane history might afford some light, whether the crowne of thorns was made of Paliurus, whether the crosse of Christ were made of those foure woods in the Disticke of Durantes,[*12] or only of oake according unto Lipsius and Goropius, we labour nor to determine; for though hereof prudent symbolls and pious allegories be made by wiser conceivers, yet common heads will flye unto superstitious applications, and hardly avoid miraculous or magicall expectations.

* *Pes cedrus est, truncus cupressus, oliva supremum, palmaque transversum Christi sunt in cruce lignum.*

Now the ground or reason that occasioned this expression by an apple, might be the community of this fruit, and which is often taken for any other. So the goddesse of gardens is termed *Pomona*; so the proverbe expresseth it to give apples unto Alcinous; so the fruit which Paris decided was called an apple; so in the garden of Hesperides (which many conceive a fiction drawne from Paradise) we read of golden apples guarded by the dragon; and to speake strictly in this appellation they placed it more safely then any other; for beside the great variety of apples, the word in Greeke comprehendeth orenges, lemmons, citrons, quinces, and as Ruellius defineth, such fruits as have no stone within, and a soft covering without, excepting the pomegranate.[13]

It hath been promoted in some constructions from a passage in the Canticles, as it runnes in the vulgar translation, *Sub arbore malo suscitavi te, ibi corrupta est mater tua, ibi violata est genetrix tua*;[*14] which words notwithstanding parabollically intended, admit no literall inference, and are of little force in our translation, I raysed thee under an apple tree, there thy mother brought thee forth, there she brought thee forth that bare thee. So when from a basket of Summer fruits, or apples, as the Vulgar rendreth them, God by Amos foretold the destruction of his people, we cannot say they had any reference unto the fruit of Paradise which was the destruction of man;[15] but thereby is declared the propinquity of their desolation, and that their tranquility was of no longer duration then those horary and soon decaying fruits of Summer; nor when it is said in the same translation, *Poma desiderii animæ tuæ discesserunt à te*, the apples that thy soul lusted after are departed from thee, is there any allusion therin unto the fruit of Paradise?[†16] But thereby is threatned unto Babylon, that the pleasures and delights of their palate should forsake them: and we read in Pierius, that an apple was the hieroglyphicke of love, and that the statua of Venus was made with one in her hand.[17]

[*] Canticles 8.

[†] Apocalypse 14.

Since therefore after this fruit curiosity fruitlessesly enquireth, and confidence blindly determineth, we shall surcease our inquisition, rather troubled that it was tasted, then troubling our selves in its decision; this only we observe, when things are left uncertaine men will assure them by determination; which is not only verified concerning the fruit but the serpent that perswaded; many defining the kinde or species thereof. So Bonaventure and Comestor affirme it was a dragon, Eugubinus a basiliske, Delrio a viper, and others a common snake, wherein men still continue the delusion of the serpent, who having deceived Eve in the maine, sets her posterity a worke to mistake in the circumstance, and endeavours to propagate errors at any hand; and those he surely most desireth which either concern God or himself; for they dishonour God who is absolute truth and goodnesse; but for himselfe, who is extremely evill, and the worst we can conceive, by aberration of conceit they extenuate his depravity, and ascribe some goodnesse unto him.

CHAPTER II

That a Man hath one Rib lesse then a Woman

That a man hath one rib lesse then a woman, is a common conceit derived from the history of Genesis, wherein it stands delivered, that Eve was framed out of a rib of Adam; whence 'tis concluded the sex of man still wants that rib our Father lost in Eve;[18] and this is not onely passant with the many, but was urged against Columbus in an anatomy of his at Pisa, where having prepared the sceleton of a woman that chanced to have thirteene ribs of one side, there arose a party that cryed him downe, and even unto oathes affirmed, this was the rib wherein a woman exceeded;[19] were this true, it would autoptically silence that dispute out of which side Eve was framed; it would determine the opinion of Oleaster,[*][20] that she was made out of the ribs of both sides, or such as from the expression of the text maintaine there was a plurality required; and might indeed decry the parabolicall exposition of Origen, Cajetan, and such as fearing to concede a monstrosity, or mutilate the integrity of Adam, preventively conceive the creation of thirteene ribs.[21]

* *Os ex ossibus meis.*

But this will not consist with reason or inspection: for if wee survey the sceleton of both sexes and therein the compage of bones,[22] wee shall readily discover that men and women have foure and twenty ribs, that is, twelve on each side, seven greater annexed unto the sternon, and five lesser which come short thereof, wherein if it sometimes happen that either sex exceed, the conformation is irregular deflecting from the common rate or number, and no more inferrible upon mankinde, then the monstrosity of the son of Rapha, or the vicious excesse in the number of fingers and toes:[23] and although some difference there be in figure, and the female *os inominatum* be somewhat more protuberant, to make a fayrer cavity for the infant, the coccyx sometime more reflected to give the easier delivery, and the ribs themselves seeme a little flatter, yet are they equall in number.[24] And therefore, while Aristotle doubteth the relations made of nations which had but seven ribs on a side, and yet delivereth that men have generally no more then eight; as he rejecteth their history, so can we not accept of his anatomy.[25]

Againe, although we concede there wanted one rib in the sceleton of Adam, yet were it repugnant unto reason and common observation that his posterity should want the same; for we observe that mutilations are not transmitted from father unto son; the blind begetting such as can see, men with one eye, children with two, and criples mutilate in their owne persons, do come out perfect in their generations. For, the seed conveigheth with it not onely the extract and single Idea of every part, whereby it transmits their perfections or infirmities, but double and over againe; whereby sometimes it multipliciously delineates the same, as in twins in mixed and numerous generations. And to speake more strictly, parts of the seed do seeme to containe the Idea and power of the whole; so parents deprived of hands, beget manuall issues, and the defect of those parts is supplyed by the Idea of others.[26] So in one graine of corne appearing similary and insufficient for a plurall germination, there lyeth dormant the virtuality of many other, and from thence sometimes proceed an hundred eares:[27] and thus may bee made out the cause of multiparous productions;[28] for though the seminall materialls disperse and separate in the matrix, the formative operator will not delineat a part, but endeavour the formation of the whole; effecting the same as farre as the matter will permit, and from devided materials attempt entire formations. And therefore, though wondrous strange, it may not be impossible what is confirmed at Lausdun concerning the Countesse of Holland, nor what Albertus reports of the birth of an hundred and fifty, and if we consider the magnalities of generation in some things, wee shall not controvert its possibilities in others;[29] nor easily question that great worke, whose wonders are onely second unto those of the Creation, and a close apprehension of the one, might perhaps afford a glimmering light, and crepusculous glance of the other.[30]

CHAPTER III
Of Methuselah

What hath beene every where opinion'd by all men, and in all times, is more then paradoxicall to dispute; and so that

Methuselah was the longest liver of all the posterity of Adam we quietly beleeve:[31] but that he must needs be so, is perhaps below paralogy to deny.[32] For hereof there is no determination from the text; wherein it is onely particular'd hee was the longest liver of all the patriarchs whose age is there expressed, but that he outlived all others we cannot well conclude. For of those nine whose death is mentioned before the flood, the text expresseth that Enoch was the shortest liver, who saw but three hundred sixty five yeares; but to affirme from hence, none of the rest, whose age is not expressed, did dye before that time, is surely an illation whereto we cannot assent.[33]

Againe, many persons there were in those dayes of longevity, of whose age notwithstanding there is no account in Scripture; as of the race of Caine, the wives of the nine patriarches, with all the sons and daughters that every one begat, whereof perhaps some persons might outlive Methuselah; the text intending onely the masculine line of Seth, conduceable unto the genealogy of our Saviour, and the antediluvian chronology.[34] And therefore we must not contract the lives of those which are left in silence by Moses; for neither is the age of Abel expressed in the Scripture yet is he conceived farre elder then commonly is opinion'd: and if wee beleeve the conclusion of his epitaph as made by Adam, and so set downe by Salian, *Posuit mærens pater cui à filio justius positum foret, Anno ab ortu rerum 130. ab Abele nato 129.* we shall not need to doubt;[35] which notwithstanding Cajetan and others confirme; nor is it improbable, if wee conceive that Abel was borne in the second yeare of Adam, and Seth a yeare after the death of Abel: for so it being said, that Adam was an hundred and thirty yeares old when he begat Seth, Abel must perish the yeare before, which was one hundred twenty nine.

And if the account of Cain extend unto the deluge, it may not bee improbable, that some thereof exceeded any of Seth: nor is it unlikely in life, riches, power and temporall blessings, they might surpasse them in this world, whose lives referred unto the next; for so when the seed of Jacob was under affliction and captivity, that of Ismael and Esau flourished and grew mighty, there proceeding from the one twelve princes, from the other, no lesse then foureteene dukes and eight kings.[36] And whereas the age of Cain and his posterity is not delivered in the text, some doe salve it from the secret method of Scripture, which sometimes wholly omits, but seldome or never delivers the entire duration of wicked and faithlesse persons; as is observable in the history of Esau, and the Kings of Israel and Judah. And therefore, that mention is made that Ismael lived 137 yeares, some conceive he adhered unto the faith of Abraham; for so did others who were not descended from Jacob; for Job is thought to be an Idumean, and of the seed of Esau.

Lastly, (although we rely not thereon) we will not omit that conceit urged by learned men, that Adam was elder then Methuselah, in as much as he was created in the perfect age of man, which was in those dayes fifty or sixty yeares, for about that time wee reade that they begat children; so that if unto 930 we adde sixty yeares, he will exceed Methuselah. And therefore if not in length of dayes, at least in old age he surpassed others; he was older then all who was never so young as any; for though hee knew old age he was never acquainted with puberty, youth, or infancy; and so in a strict account he begat children at one yeare old; and if the usuall compute will hold, that men are of the same age which are borne within compasse of the same yeare, Eve was as old as her husband and parent Adam, and Cain their son coetaneous unto both.

Now that conception that no man did ever attaine unto a thousand yeares, because none should ever be one day old in the sight of the Lord, unto whom according to that of David, a thousand yeares are but as one day, doth not advantage Methuselah;[37] and being deduced from a popular expression, which will not stand a metaphysicall and strict examination, is not of force to divert a serious enquirer; for unto God a thousand yeares are no more then one moment, and in his sight Methuselah lived no neerer one day then Abel, for all parts of time are alike unto him, unto whom none are referable, and all things present, unto whom nothing is past or to come; and therefore, although we be measured by the zone of time, and the flowing and continued instants thereof, do weave at last a line and circle about the eldest; yet can we not thus commensurate the sphere of Trismegistus, or summe up the unsuccessive and stable duration of God.

CHAPTER IV

That there was no Rainebow before the Flood

That there shall no rainebow appeare forty yeares before the end of the world, and that the preceding drought unto that great flame shal exhaust the materials of this meteor, was an assertion grounded upon no solid reason: but that there was not any in sixteene hundred yeares, that is, before the flood, seemes deduceable from holy Scripture, Genesis 9. I do set my bow in the clouds, and it shall be for a token of a Covenant betweene me and the earth. From whence notwithstanding we cannot conclude the nonexistence of the rainebow; nor is that chronology naturally established, which computeth the antiquity of effects arising from physicall and setled causes, by additionall impositions from voluntary determinators. Now by the decree of reason and philosophy, the rainebow hath its ground in nature, and caused by the rayes of the sunne, falling upon a roride and opposite cloud; whereof some reflected, others refracted beget that semicircular variety we generally call the rainebow;[38] which must succeed upon concurrence of causes and subjects aptly prædisposed. And therefore, to conceive there was no rainebow before, because God chose this out as a token of the covenant, is to conclude the existence of things from their signalities, or of what is objected unto the sence, a coexistence with that which is internally presented unto the understanding.[39] With equal reason we may inferre there was no water before the Institution of Baptisme, nor bread and wine before the holy Eucharist.

Againe, while men deny the antiquity of one rainebow, they anciently concede another. For, beside the solary Iris which God shewed unto Noah there is another lunary, whose efficient is the moone, visible onely in the night, most commonly at full moone, and some degrees above the horizon.[40] Now the existence hereof men doe not controvert, although effected by a different luminary in the same way with the other; and probably appeared later, as being of rare appearance and rarer observation, and many there are which thinke there is no such thing in nature. And therefore by casuall spectators they are lookt upon like prodigies, and significations made not signified by their natures.

Lastly, we shall not need to conceive God made the rainebow at this time, if we consider that in its created and predisposed nature, it was more proper for this signification then any other meteor or celestiall appearency whatsoever. Thunder and lightning had too much terrour to have beene tokens of mercy; comets or blazing stars appeare too seldome to put us in minde of a covenant to be remembred often, and might rather signifie the world should be once destroyed by fire, then never againe by water. The galaxia or milky circle had beene more probable; for, (beside that unto the latitude of thirty it becomes their horizon twice in foure and twenty howres, and unto such as live under the equator, in that space the whole circle appeareth) part thereof is visible unto any situation, but being onely discoverable in the night and when the ayre is cleere, it becomes of unfrequent and comfortlesse signification. A fixed starre had not beene visible unto all the globe, and so of too narrow a signality in a covenant concerning all. But rainebowes are seene unto all the world, and every position of sphere; unto our owne elevation it may appeare in the morning while the sunne hath attained about forty five degrees above the horizon, (which is conceived the largest semidiameter of any Iris) and so in the afternoone when it hath declined unto that altitude againe; which height the sun not attaining in Winter, rainebowes may happen with us at noone or any time. Unto a right position of spheare it may appeare three howres after the rising of the sun, and three before its setting; for the sun ascending fifteene degrees an houre, in three attaineth forty five of altitude. Even unto a parallell sphere, and such as live under the pole, for halfe a yeare some segments may appeare at any time and under any quarter, the sun not setting, but walking round about them.

But the propriety of its election most properly appeareth in the naturall signification and prognostick of it selfe; as contayning a mixt signality of raine and faire weather; for being in a roride cloud and ready to drop, it declareth a pluvious disposure in the ayre;[41] but because when it appeares the sun must also shine, there can bee no universall showres, and consequently no deluge. Thus when the windowes of the great deepe were open, in vaine men lookt for the rainebow, for at that time it could not be seene, which after appeared unto Noah.[42] It was therefore existent before the flood, and had in nature some ground of its addition; unto that of nature God superadded an assurance of his promise, that is, never to hinder its appearance, or so to replenish the heavens againe as that we should behold it no more. And thus, without disparaging the promise, it might raine at the same time when God shewed it unto Noah; thus was there more therein then the heathens understood, when they called it the *nuncia* of the gods, and the laugh of weeping heaven[*];[43] and thus may it be elegantly said, I put my bow, not my arrow in the clouds, that is, in the menace of raine the mercy of faire weather.[44]

[*] *Risus plorantis Olympi.*

[Cabalistical heads, who from that expression in Esay,[45] do make a book of heaven, and reade therein the great concernments of earth, do literally play on this, and from its semicircular figure, resembling the Hebrew letter כ Caph, whereby is signified the uncomfortable number of twenty, at which years Joseph was sold, which Jacob lived under Laban, and at which men were to go to war; do note a propriety in its signification; as thereby declaring the dismall time of the deluge. And Christian conceits do seem to strain as high, while from the irradiation of the sunne upon a cloud, they apprehend the mystery of the sunne of righteousness in the obscurity of flesh; by the colours green and red, the two destructions of the world by fire and water; or by the colours of bloud and water, the mysteries of Baptism, and the holy Eucharist.]

Laudable is the custome of the Jews, who upon the appearance of the rainebow, doe magnifie the fidelity of God in the memory of his covenant, according to that of Syracides, Looke upon the rainebow, and praise him that made it.[46] And though some pious and Christian pens have onely symboliz'd the same from the mystery of its colours, yet are there other affections which might admit of theologicall allusions; nor would he finde a more improper subject that should consider, that the colours are made by refraction of light, and the shadows that limit that light; that the center of the sun, the rainebow, and the eye of the beholder must be in one right line; that the spectator must be betweene the sun and the rainebow; that sometime three appeare, sometime one reversed; with many others, considerable in meteorologicall divinity, which would more sensibly make out the epithite of the heathens, and the expression of the son of Syrach, very beautifull is the rainebow, it compasseth the heaven about with a glorious circle, and the hands of the most high have bended it.

CHAPTER V
Of Sem, Ham and Japhet

Concerning the three sons of Noah, Sem, Ham and Japhet, that the order of their nativity was according to that of numeration, and Japhet the youngest son, as most beleeve, as Austin and others account, the sons of Japhet and Europeans need not grant;[47] nor will it so well concord unto the letter of the text, and its readiest interpretations: for, so is it said in our translation,

Sem the father of all the sons of Heber, the brother of Japhet the elder; so by the Septuagint, and so by that of Tremellius; and therefore when the Vulgar reades it, *Fratre Japhet majore*, the mistake, as Junius observeth, might be committed by neglect of the Hebrew accent, which occasioned Jerom so to render it, and many after to beleeve it.[48] Nor is that argument contemptible which is deduced from their chronology; for probable it is, that Noah had none of them before, and begat them from that yeare when it is said hee was five hundred yeares old and begat Sem, Ham, and Japhet; againe, it is said he was sixe hundred yeares old at the flood, and that two yeares after Sem was but an hundred, therefore Sem must be borne when Noah was five hundred and two, and some other before in the yeare of five hundred and one.

Now whereas the Scripture affordeth the priority of order unto Sem, we cannot from thence inferre his primogeniture; for in Sem the holy line was continued, and therefore however borne, his genealogy was most remarkeable.[*] So is it not unusuall in holy Scripture to nominate the younger before the elder;[†] so is it said, that Tarah begat Abraham, Nachor, and Haram; whereas Haram was the eldest. So Rebecca is termed the mother of Jacob and Esau. Nor is it strange the younger should be first in nomination, who have commonly had the priority in the blessings of God, and been first in his benediction. So Abel was accepted before Cain, Isaac the younger, preferred before Ismael the elder,[49] Jacob before Esau, Joseph was the youngest of twelve, and David the eleventh son, and but the caddet of Jesse.[50]

[*] Genesis 11.

[†] Genesis 28.

Lastly, though Japhet were not elder then Sem, yet must we not affirme that he was younger then Cham, for it is plainely delivered, that after Sem and Japhet had covered Noah, he awaked, and knew what his youngest son had done unto him. υἱὸς ὁ νεώτερος, is the expression of the Septuagint, *Filius minor* of Jerome, and *minimus* of Tremellius.[51] And upon these grounds perhaps Josephus doth vary from the Scripture enumeration, and nameth them Sem, Japhet, and Cham, which is also observed by the Annian Berosus; *Noah cum tribus filiis, Semo, Japeto, Chem.* And therefore although in the priority of Sem and Japhet there may be some difficulty, though Cyrill, Epiphanius, and Austin have accounted Sem the elder, and Salian the Annalist, and Petavius the chronologist contend for the same, yet Cham is more plainly and confessedly named the youngest in the text.

[And this is more conformable unto the pagan history and gentile account hereof,[52] unto whom Noah was Saturn, whose symbol was a ship, as relating unto the Ark, and who is said to have divided the world between his three sons. Ham is conceived to be Jupiter, who was the youngest sonne; worshipped by the name of Hamon, which was the Ægyptian and African name for Jupiter, who is said to have cut off the genitals of his father, derived from the history of Ham, who beheld the nakednesse of his, and by no hard mistake might be confirmed from the Text, as Bochartus hath well observed.]

CHAPTER VI

That the Tower of Babel was erected against a second Deluge

An opinion there is of some generality, that our fathers after the flood attempted the tower of Babel to secure themselves from a second deluge. Which however affirmed by Josephus and others, hath seemed improbable unto many who have discoursed hereon.[53] For, (beside that they could not be ignorant of the promise of God never to drowne the world againe, and had the rainebow before their eyes to put them in minde thereof) it is improbable from the nature of the deluge, which being not possibly causable from naturall showres above, or watery eruptions below, but requiring a supernaturall hand, and such as all acknowledge irresistible; wee must disparage their knowledge and judgement in so successlesse attempts.

Againe, they must probably heare, and some might know, that the waters of the flood ascended fifteene cubits above the highest mountaines.[54] Now, if as some define, the perpendicular altitude of the highest mountaines bee foure miles, or as others, but fifteene furlongs, it is not easily conceived how such a structure could bee effected; except wee receive the description of Herodotus concerning the Tower of Belus, whose first tower was eight furlongs higher,[55] and eight more built upon it; except we beleeve the Annian Berosus, or the traditionall relation of Jerome.[56] [Probably it is that what they attempted was fesible, otherwise they had been amply fool'd in the fruitless successe of their labours; not needed God to have hindered them, saying, Nothing will be restrained from them, which they begin to doe.[57]]

It was improbable from the place, that is a plaine in the land of Shinar. And if the situation of Babylon were such at first as it was in the dayes of Herodotus, it was rather a seat of amenity and pleasure, then conducing unto this intention; it being in a very great plaine, and so improper a place to provide against a generall deluge by towers and eminent structures, that they were faine to make provisions against particular and annuall inundations by ditches and trenches, after the manner of Ægypt. And therefore Sir Walter Ralegh accordingly objecteth;[58] if the nations which followed Nimrod, still doubted the surprise of a second flood, according to the opinions of the antient Hebrewes, it soundeth ill to the eare of reason, that they would have spent many yeares in that low and overflowne valley of Mesopotamia. And therefore in this situation, they chose a place more likely to have secured them from the worlds destruction by fire, then another deluge of water, and as Pierius observeth, some have conceived that this was their intention.[59]

Lastly, the reason is delivered in the text. Let us build us a city and a tower, whose top may reach unto heaven, and let us make us a name, lest wee be scattered abroad upon the whole earth, as wee have already began to wander over a part.[60] These were the open ends proposed unto the people, but the secret designe of Nimrod, was to settle unto himselfe a place of dominion, and rule over the rest of his brethren, as it after succeeded, according to the delivery of the text, the beginning of his kingdome was Babel.

CHAPTER VII
Of the Mandrakes of Leah

Wee shall not omit the mandrakes of Leah, according to the history of Genesis.[61] And Reuben went out in the dayes of wheat-harvest and found mandrakes in the field, and brought them unto his mother Leah; then Rachel said unto Leah, Give me, I pray thee, of thy sonnes mandrakes, and she said unto her, Is it a small matter that thou hast taken my husband, and wouldest thou take my sons mandrakes also? And Rachel said, therefore he shall lye with thee this night for thy sonnes mandrakes; from whence hath arisen a common conceit, that Rachel requested these plants as a medicine of fecundation, or whereby she might become fruitfull;[62] which notwithstanding is very questionable, and of incertaine truth.

For first from the comparison of one text with another, whether the mandrakes here mentioned, be the same plant which holds that name with us there is some cause to doubt; the word is used in another place of Scripture*,[63] when the Church inviting her beloved into the fields, among the delightfull fruits of grapes and pomegranats, it is said, the mandrakes give a smell, and at our gates are all manner of pleasant fruits. Now instead of a smell of delight, our mandrakes afford a papaverous and unpleasant odour, whether in the leafe or apple as is discoverable in their simplicity or mixture; the same is also dubious from the different interpretations: for though the Septuagint and Josephus doe render it the apples of mandrakes in this text, yet in the other of the Canticles the Chaldy Paraphrase tearmeth it balsame.[64] R. Solomon, as Drusius observeth, conceives it to be that plant the Arabians named jesemin.[65] Oleaster and Georgius Venetus the lilly;[66] and that the word *Dudaim*, may comprehend any plant that hath a good smell, resembleth a womans breast, and flourisheth in wheat harvest; Junius and Tremellius interpret the same for any amiable flowers of a pleasant and delightfull odour: but the Geneva translators have been more wary then any; for although they retaine the word mandrake in the text, they in effect retract it in the margine, wherein is set downe, the word in the originall is *Dudaim*, which is a kinde of fruit or flower unknowne.

* Canticles 7.

Nor shall we wonder at the dissent of exposition, and difficulty of definition concerning this text, if we perpend how variously the vegetables of Scripture are expounded, and how hard it is in many places to make out the species determined. Thus are we at variance concerning the plant that covered Jonas, which though the Septuagint doth render Colocynthis, the Spanish Calabaca, and ours accordingly a gourd, yet the vulgar translates it Hedera or juice;[67] and, as Grotius observeth, Jerome thus translated it, not as the same plant but best apprehended thereby.[68] The Italian of Diodati and that of Tremellius have named it Ricinus, and so hath ours in the margine; for *palma Christi* is the same with Ricinus. The Geneva translators have herein been also circumspect; for they have retained the originall word *Kikaion*, and ours hath also affixed the same unto the margine: nor are they indeed alwayes the same plants which are delivered under the same name, and appellations commonly received amongst us; so when it is said of Solomon that hee writ of plants from the cedar of Lebanus, unto the hysop that groweth upon the wall, that is from the greatest unto the smallest, it cannot be well conceived our common hysop; for neither is that the least of vegetables, nor observed to grow upon walls;[69] but rather as Lemnius well conceiveth some kinde of the capillaries, which are very small plants and only grow upon walls and stony places;[70] nor are the four species[71] in the holy oyntment, cinnamon, myrrhe, calamus and cassia; nor the other in the holy perfume, frankinsence, stacte, onycha, and galbanum, so agreeably expounded unto those in use with us, as not to leave considerable doubts behinde them; nor must that perhaps be taken for a simple unguent, which Matthew onely tearmeth a pretious oyntment, but rather a composition, as Marke and John imply by pistick nard, that is faithfully dispensed;[72] and as Mathiolus observeth in his epistles, may be that famous composition described by Dioscorides, made of oyle of ben, malabathrum, juncus odoratus, costus, amomum, myrrhe, balsam and nard;[73] which Galen affirmeth to have been in use with the delicate dames of Rome, and that the best thereof was made at Laodicea, from whence by merchants it was conveyed unto other parts; but how to make out that translation concerning the tithe of mint, anise, and cumin, we are still to seek; for we finde not a word in the text that can properly bee rendred anise, the Greeke being ἄνηθον, which the Latines call *Anethum*, and is properly Englished dill.

Againe, it is not deducible from the text or concurrent sentence of comments, that Rachel had any such intention, and most doe rest in the determination of Austine, that she desired them for rarity, pulchritude or suavity;[74] nor is it probable shee would have resigned her bed unto Leah, when at the same time she had obtained a medicine to fructifie her selfe, and therefore Drusius who hath expressely and favourably treated hereof, is so farre from conceding this intention, that he plainly concludeth *hoc quo modo illic in mentem venerit conjicere nequeo*;[75] how this conceit fell into mens minds it cannot fall into mine, for the Scripture delivereth it not, nor can it bee clearely deduced from the text.

Thirdly, if Rachel had any such intention, yet had they no such effect, for she conceived not many yeares after of Joseph; whereas in the meane time Leah had three children, Isachar, Zabulon, and Dinah.[76]

Lastly, although at that time they failed of this effect, yet is it mainly questionable whether they had any such vertue either in the opinions of those times or in their proper nature; that the opinion was popular in the land of Canaan it is improbable, and had Leah understood thus much she would not surely have parted with fruits of such a faculty, especially unto Rachel who was no friend unto her. As for its proper nature, the ancients have generally esteemed it narcotick or stupefactive, and is to be found in the list of poyson set downe by Dioscorides, Galen, Ætius, Ægineta, and severall antidotes delivered by them against it. It was I confesse from good antiquity, and in the dayes of Theophrastus accounted a philtre, or plant that conciliates affection, and so delivered by Dioscorides;[77] and this intent might seem more probable, had they not been the wives of holy Jacob, had Rachel presented them unto him, and not requested them for her selfe.

Now what Dioscorides affirmeth in favour of this effect, that the graines of the apples of mandrakes mundifie the matrix and applied with sulphur stop the fluxes of women, he overthrows by qualities destructive unto conception;[78] affirming also that the juice thereof purgeth upward like hellebore, and applyed in pessaries provokes the menstruous flowes and procures abortion. Petrus Hispanus, or Pope John the twentieth speakes more directly in his *Thesaurus pauperum*; wherein among the receits of fæcundation, he experimentally commendeth the wine of mandrakes given with *Triphera Magna*: but the soule of the medicine may lye in *Triphera magna*, an excellent composition, and for this effect commended by Nicolaus.[79] And whereas Levinus Lemnius that eminent physitian doth also concede this effect, it is from manifest causes and qualities elementall occasionally producing the same; for he imputeth the same unto the coldnesse of that simple, and is of opinion that in hot climates, and where the uterine parts exceed in heat, by the coldnesse hereof they may bee reduced into a conceptive constitution, and crasis accommodable unto generation;[80] whereby indeed we will not deny the due and frequent use may proceed unto some effect, from whence notwithstanding wee cannot inferre a fertiliating condition or property of fecundation: for in this way all vegetables doe make fruitfull according unto the complexion of the matrix;[81] if that excell in heat, plants exceeding in cold doe rectifie it, if it be cold, simples that are hot reduce it, if dry moist, if moist dry correct it, in which division all plants are comprehended; but to distinguish thus much is a point of art, and beyond the method of Rachels or feminine physicke. Againe, whereas it may be thought that mandrakes may fecundate since poppy hath obtained the epithite of fruitfull, and that fertility was hieroglyphically described, by Venus with an head of poppy in her hand; the reason hereof, was the multitude of seed within it selfe, and no such multiplying in humane generation. And lastly, whereas they may well have this quality, since opium it selfe is conceived to extimulate unto venery, and for that intent is sometimes used by Turkes, Persians, and most orientall nations; although Winclerus doth seem to favour the conceit, yet Amatus Lusitanus, and Rodericus a Castro are against it, Garcias ab Horto refutes it from experiment; and they speake probably who affirme, the intent and effect of eating opium, is not so much to invigorate themselves in coition, as to prolong the act, and spinne out the motions of carnality.

CHAPTER VIII
Of the Three Kings of Collein

A common conceit there is of the three kings of Collein, conceived to be the wise men that travelled unto our Saviour by the direction of the star; wherein omitting the large discourses of Baronius, Pineda, and Montacutius, that they might be kings, beside the ancient tradition and authority of many Fathers, the Scripture also implyeth.[82] The gentiles shall come to thy light, and kings to the brightnesse of thy rising. The kings of Tharsis and the Isles, the kings of Arabia and Saba shall offer gifts, which places most Christians and many Rabbines interpret of the Messiah.[83] Not that they are to be conceived potent monarchs, or mighty kings, but toparks, kings of cities or narrow territories, such as were the kings of Sodome and Gomorrah, the kings of Jericho and Ai, the one and thirty which Josuah subdued, and such as some concieve the friends of Job to have been.[84]

But although we grant they were kings, yet can we not bee assured they were three: for the Scripture maketh no mention of any number, and the number of their presents, gold, myrrh and frankinscence, concludeth not the number of their persons;[85] for these were the commodities of their country, and such as probably the Queen of Sheba in one person had brought before unto Solomon; and so did not the sons of Jacob divide the present unto Joseph, but are conceived to carry one for them all, according to the expression of their father, Take of the best fruits of the land in your vessells, and carry downe the man a present:[86] and therefore their number being uncertaine, what credit is to be given unto their names, Gaspar, Melchior, Balthazar? What to the charme thereof against the falling sicknesse? Or what unto their habits, complexions, and corporall accidents, wee must relye on their uncertain story, and authenticke pourtarits of Collein. Lastly, although we grant them kings, and three in number, yet could wee not conceive that they were kings of Collein. For though Collein were the chiefe city of the *Ubii*, then called *Ubiopolis*, and afterwards *Agrippina*, yet will no history informe us there were three kings thereof. Beside these being rulers in their countries, and returning home would have probably converted their subjects; but according unto Munsters report, their conversion was not wrought untill seventy yeares after by Maternus a disciple of Peter.[87] And lastly, it is said that the wise men came from the East; but Collein is seated west-ward from Jerusalem, for Collein hath of longitude thirty foure degrees, but Jerusalem seventy two.

The ground of all was this; these wise men or kings, were probably of Arabia, and descended from Abraham by Keturah, who apprehending the mystery of this starre, either by the spirit of God, the prophesie of Balaam, the prophesie, which Suetonius mentions, received and constantly believed through all the east, that out of Jury one should come that should rule the whole world;[88] or the divulged expectancy of the Jewes from the expiring prediction of Daniel, were by the same conducted unto Judea, returned into their Country, and were after, baptised by Thomas; from whence about three hundred yeares after by Helena the Empresse their bodies were translated to Constantinople, from thence by Eustathius unto Millane, and at last by Renatus the Bishop unto Collein; where they are beleeved at present to remaine, their monuments showne unto strangers, and having lost their Arabian titles, are crowned kings of Collein.

CHAPTER IX
Of the Food of John Baptist, Locusts and Wilde Hony

Concerning the food of John Baptist in the wildernesse, locusts and wilde hony, lest popular opiniatrity should arise, we will deliver the chiefe opinions;[89] the first conceiveth the locusts here mentioned to be that fruit the Greeks name *κεράτιον*, mentioned by Luke in the dyet of the prodigall sonne, the Latins *siliqua*, and some, *panis Sancti Johannis*, included in a broad cod, and indeed of taste almost as pleasant as honey.[90] But this opinion doth not so truly impugne that of the locusts; and might rather call into controversie the meaning of wilde honey.

The second affirmeth they were the tops or tender crops of trees; for so *Locusta* also signifieth: which conceit is plausible in Latin, but wil not hold in Greek, wherein the word is *ἀκρίς*, except for *ἀκρίδες*, we read *ἀκρόδρυα*, or *ἀκρέμονες*, which signifie the extremities of trees; of which belief have divers been; more confidently Isidore Pelusiota, who in his epistles plainly affirmeth they thinke unlearnedly who are of another beliefe; and this so wrought upon Baronius that he concludeth in a newtrality, *Hæc cum scribat Isidorus definiendum nobis non est, et totum relinquimus lectoris arbitrio; nam constat Græcam dictionem ἀκρίδες, et Locustam insecti genus, et arborum summitates significare. Sed fallitur*, saith *Montacutius, nam constat contrarium, Ἀκρίδα apud nullum authorem classicum Ἀκρόδρυα significare.*[91] But above all Paracelsus with most animosity promoteth this opinion, and in his book *de melle*, spareth not his friend Erasmus. *Hoc à nonnullis ita explicatur ut dicant Locustas aut cicadas Johanni pro cibo fuisse; sed hi stultitiam dissimulare non possunt, veluti Jeronymus, Erasmus, et alii prophetæ Neoterici in Latinitate immortui.*[92]

A third affirmeth that they were properly locusts, that is a sheathwinged and six-footed insect, such as is our grashopper; and this opinion seems more probable then the other: for beside the authority of Origen, Jerome, Chrysostome, Hillary, and Ambrose to confirme it, this is the proper signification of the word, thus used in Scripture by the Septuagint, Greeke vocabularies thus expound it;[93] Suidas on the word *ἀκρίς* observes it to be that animall whereon the Baptist fed in the desart, in this sense the word is used by Aristotle, Dioscorides, Galen, and severall humane authors. And lastly, there is no absurdity in this interpretation, or any solid reason why we should decline it; it being a food permitted unto the Jewes, whereof foure kindes are reckoned up among cleane meats.[94] Beside, not onely the Jewes, but many other nations long before and since, have made an usuall food thereof. That the Æthiopians, Mauritanians, and Arabians, did commonly eat them is testified by Diodorus, Strabo, Solinus, Aelian and Plinie; that they still feed on them is confirmed by Leo, Cadamustus and others. John therefore as our Saviour saith, came neither eating nor drinking, that is farre from the dyet of Jerusalem and other riotous places; but fared coursely and poorely according unto the apparrell he wore, that is of camells haire; the place of his abode, the wildernesse; and the doctrine he preached, humilation and repentance.[95]

CHAPTER X
That John the Evangelist should not dye

The conceit of the long living or rather not dying of John the Evangelist is not to be omitted; and although it seem inconsiderable, and not much weightier then that of Joseph the wandring Jew; yet being deduced from Scripture, and abetted by authors of all times, it shall not escape our enquiry.* It is drawne from the speech of our Saviour unto Peter after the prediction of his martyrdome; Peter saith unto Jesus, Lord, and what shall this man do? Jesus saith unto him, If I will that he tarry untill I come, what is that to thee? Follow thou me; then went this saying abroad among the brethren that this disciple should not dye.

* John 21.

Now the apprehension hereof hath been received either grossely and in the generall, that is not distinguishing the manner or particular way of this continuation, in which sense probably the grosser and undiscerning party received it; or more distinctly apprehending the manner of his immortality; that is, that John should never properly dye, but be translated into Paradise, there to remaine with Enoch and Elias untill about the comming of Christ, and should be slaine with them under Antichrist, according to that of the Apocalyps. I will give power unto my two witnesses, and they shall prophesie a thousand two hundred and threescore dayes cloathed in sackcloath, and when they shall have finished their testimony, the beast that ascendeth out of the bottomelesse pit, shall make warre against them, and shall overcome them and kill them.[96] Hereof, as Baronius observeth, within three hundred yeares after Christ, Hippolytus the martyr was the first assertor, but hath been maintained by many since; by Metaphrastes, by Freculphus, but especially by Georgius Trapezuntius, who hath expresly treated upon this text;[97] and although he lived but in the last centurie, did still affirme that John was not yet dead.

As for the grosse opinion that he should not dye, it is unto my judgement sufficiently refuted by that which first occasioned it, that is the Scripture it selfe, and no further of, then the very subsequent verse: yet Jesus said not unto him he should not dye, but if I will that he tarry till I come, what is that to thee? And this was written by John himself whom the opinion concerned, and as is conceived many yeares after when Peter had suffered, and fulfilled the prophesie of Christ.

For the particular conceit the foundation is weake, nor can it bee made out from the text alleadged in the Apocalyps: for beside that therein two persons are onely named, no mention is made of John a third actor in this tragedy; the same is overthrowne by history, which recordeth not onely the death of John, but assigneth the place of his buriall, that is Ephesus a city in Asia minor; whither after hee had beene banished into Patmos by Domitian hee returned in the reigne of Nerva, there deceased, and was buried in the dayes of Trajan, and this is testified by Jerome *De Scriptoribus Ecclesiasticis*, by Tertullian *De Anima*, by Chrysostome, and by Eusebius, in whose dayes his sepulchre was to be seen;[98] and by a more ancient testimony alleadged also by him, that is of Polycrates Bishop of Ephesus, not many successions after John; whose words are these in an epistle unto Victor Bishop of Rome, *Johannes ille qui supra pectus Domini recumbebat, Doctor optimus apud Ephesum dormivit*;[99] many of the like nature are noted by Baronius, Jansenius, Estius, Lipellous, and others.

Now the maine and primitive ground of this error, was a grosse mistake in the words of Christ, and a false apprehension of his meaning; understanding that positively which was conditionally expressed, or receiving that affirmatively which was but concessively delivered; for the words of our Saviour runne in a doubtfull straine, rather reprehending then satisfying the curiosity of Peter; that is, as though he should have said, Thou hast thine owne doome, why enquirest thou after thy brothers? What reliefe unto thy affliction will be the society of anothers? Why pryest thou into the secrets of Gods judgements? If he stay untill I come, what concerneth it thee, who shalt bee sure to suffer before that time? And such an answer probably he returned because he foreknew John should not suffer a violent death, but goe unto his grave in peace; which had Peter assuredly knowne, it might have cast some water on his flames, and smothered those fires which kindled after unto the honour of his master.

Now why among all the rest John only escaped the death of a martyr, the reason is given; because all other fled away or withdrew themselves at his death, and he alone of the twelve beheld his passion on the crosse;[100] wherein notwithstanding, the affliction that he suffered could not amount unto lesse then martyrdome: for if the naked relation, at least the intentive consideration of that passion, be able still and at this disadvantage of time, to rend the hearts of pious contemplators; surely the neare and sensible vision thereof must needs occasion agonies beyond the comprehension of flesh, and the trajections of such an object more sharpely pierce the martyr'd soule of John, then afterward did the nayles the crucified body of Peter.[101]

Againe, they were mistaken in the emphaticall apprehension, placing the consideration upon the words, If I will, whereas it properly lay in these, when I come:[102] which had they apprehended as some have since, that is, not for his ultimate and last returne, but his comming in judgement and destruction upon the Jewes; or such a comming as it might be said, that that generation should not passe before it was fulfilled: they needed not, much lesse need we suppose such diuturnity;[103] for after the death of Peter, John lived to behold the same fulfilled by Vespasian: nor had he then his *nunc dimittis*, or went out like unto Simeon; but old in accomplisht obscurities, and having seen the expire of Daniels prediction, as some conceive, he accomplished his revelation.[104]

But besides this originall, and primary foundation, divers others have made impressions according unto different ages and persons by whom they were received; for some established the conceit in the disciples and brethren, which were contemporary unto him, or lived about the same time with him; and this was first the extraordinary affection our Saviour bare unto this disciple, who hath the honour to bee called the disciple whom Jesus loved.[105] Now from hence they might be apt to beleeve their master would dispence with his death, or suffer him to live to see him returne in glory, who was the onely apostle that beheld him to dye in dishonour. Another was the beliefe and opinion of those times that Christ would suddenly come; for they held not generally the same opinion with their successors, or as descending ages after so many centuries, but conceived his comming would not be long after his passion, according unto severall expressions of our Saviour grossely understood, and as we finde the same opinion not long after reprehended by Saint Paul;* and thus conceiving his comming would not be long, they might be induced to believe his favourite should live unto it. Lastly, the long life of John might much advantage this opinion; for he survived the other twelve, he was aged 22 yeares when he was called by Christ, and 25 that is the age of priesthood at his death, and lived 93 yeares, that is 68 after his Saviour, and dyed not before the second yeare of Trajane. Now having outlived all his fellows, the world was confirmed he might live still, and even unto the comming of his master.

* Thessalonians 2.

The grounds which promoted it in succeeding ages were especially two; the first his escape of martyrdome: for whereas all the rest suffered some kinde of forcible death, we have no history that he suffered any; and men might thinke he was not capable thereof, for so, as history hath related, by the command of Domitian he was cast into a cauldron of burning oyle, and came out againe unsinged.[106] Now future ages apprehending hee suffered no violent death, and finding also the means that tended thereto could take no place, they might bee confirmed in their opinion that death had no power over him, and easily beleeve he might live alwayes who could not be destroyed by fire, and resist the fury of that element which nothing shall resist. The second was a corruption crept into the Latine text, reading for *Si*, *Sic eum manere volo*, whereby the answer of our Saviour becommeth positive, or that he will have it so, which way of reading was much received in former ages, and is still retained in the vulgar translation;[107] but in the Greek and original, the word is ἐάν, signifying *Si* or if, which is very different from οὕτως, and cannot bee translated for it: and answerable hereunto is the translation of Junius and Tremellius, and that also annexed unto the Greeke by the authority of *Sixtus quintus*.

The third confirmed it in ages farther descending, and proved a powerfull argument unto all others following; that in his tombe at Ephesus there was no corps or relique thereof to be found; whereupon arised divers doubts, and many suspitious conceptions, some beleeving he was not buried, some that he was buried, but risen againe; others, that he descended alive into his tombe, and from thence departed after. But all these proceeded upon unveritable grounds, as Baronius hath observed, who alledgeth a letter of Celestine Bishop of Rome, unto the councell of Ephesus, wherein he declareth the reliques of John were highly honoured by that city, and a passage also of Chrysostome in the homilies of the apostles. That John being dead did cures in Ephesus, as though he were still alive. And so I observe that Esthius discussing this point concludeth hereupon, *Quod corpus ejus nunquam reperiatur, hoc non dicerent si veterum scripta diligenter perlustrassent.*[108]

Now that the first ages after Christ, those succeeding, or any other should proceed into opinions so farre devided from reason, as to thinke of immortality after the fall of Adam, or conceit a man in these later times should out-live our fathers in the first, although it seeme very strange, yet is it not incredible, for the credulity of men hath beene deluded into the like conceits, and as Ireneus and Tertullian have made mention, one Menander a Samaritan obtained beliefe in this very point, whose doctrine it was that death should have no power on his disciples, and such as received his baptisme, should receive immortality therewith:[109] 'twas surely an apprehension very strange; nor usually falling either from the absurdities of melancholy or vanities of ambition; some indeed have been so affectedly vaine as to counterfeit immortality, and have stolne their death in a hope to be esteemed immortall; and others have conceived themselves dead: but surely few or none have falne upon so bold an errour, as not to thinke that they could dye at all. The reason of those mighty ones, whose ambition could suffer them to be called gods, would never be flattered into immortality, but the proudest therof, have by the daylie dictates of corruption convinced the impropriety of that appellation. And surely, although delusion may runne high, and possible it is that for a while a man may forget his nature, yet cannot this be durable, for the inconcealeable imperfections of our selves, or their dayly examples in others, will hourely prompt us our corruptions, and lowdly tell us we are the sons of earth.

CHAPTER XI
More compendiously of Some Others

Many others there are which we resigne unto divinity, and perhaps deserve not controversie. Whether David were punished onely for pride of heart in numbring the people, as most doe hold, or whether as Josephus and many maintaine, he suffered also for not performing the commandement of God concerning capitation, that when the people were numbred, for every head they should pay unto God a shekell, we shall not here contend.*[110] Surely, if it were not the occasion of this plague, wee must acknowledge the omission thereof was threatned with that punishment, according to the words of the law. When thou takest the summe of the children of Israel, then shall they give every man a ransome for his soule unto the Lord, that there be no plague amongst them.† Now, how deepely hereby God was defrauded in the time of David, and opulent state of Israel, will easily appeare by the summes of former lustrations.[111] For in the first, the silver of them that were numbred was an hundred talents, and a thousand seven hundred threescore and fifteen shekels; a bekah for every man, that is, half a shekel, after the shekel of the Sanctuary; for every one from twenty years old and upwards, for six hundred thousand, and three thousand and five hundred and fifty men.[112] Answerable whereto wee read in Josephus, Vespasian ordered that every man of the Jews should bring into the Capitoll two dragmas, which amounts unto fifteene pence, or a quarter of an ounce of silver with us, and is equivalent unto a bekah, or halfe a shekell of the Sanctuary.[113] For, an attick dragme is seven pence halfe penny, or a quarter of a shekell, and a didrachmum or double dragme, is the word used for tribute money, or halfe a shekell; and a stater, the money found in the fishes mouth, was two didrachmums, or an whole shekell, and tribute sufficient for our Saviour and for Peter.[114]

* Exodus 30.

† Exodus 38.

We will not question the metamorphosis of Lots wife, or whether she were transformed into a reall statua of salt:[115] though some conceive that expression metaphoricall, and no more thereby then a lasting and durable columne; according to the nature of salt, which admitteth no corruption; in which sense the covenant of God is termed a Covenant of Salt, and it is also said, God, gave the kingdome unto David for ever, or by a covenant of salt.[116]

That Absalon was hanged by the haire of the head, and not caught up by the neck, as Josephus conceiveth, and the common argument against long hair affirmeth, we are not ready to deny.[117] Athough I confesse a great and learned party there are of another opinion; although if he had his morion or helmet on, I could not well conceive it; although the translation of Jerome or Tremellius do not prove it, and our owne seemes rather to overthrow it.

That Judas hanged himselfe, much more that he perished thereby, we shall not raise a doubt.[118] Although Jansenius discoursing the point, produceth the testimony of Theophylact and Euthymius, that he died not by the gallowes, but under a cart wheele;[119] and Baronius also delivereth this was the opinion of the Greeks, and derived as high as Papias, one of the disciples of John, although how hardly the expression of Mathew is reconcilable unto that of Peter, and that he plainely hanged himselfe, with that, that falling headlong he burst asunder in the midst, with many other, the learned Grotius plainely doth acknowledge.[120] And lastly, although as hee also urgeth the word ἀπήγξατο in Mathew, doth not onely signifie suspension, or pendelous illaqueation, as the common picture describeth it, but also suffocation, strangulation or interception of breath, which may arise from griefe, despaire, and deepe dejection of spirit, in which sence it is used in the history of Tobit concerning Sara, ἐλυπήθη σφόδρα ὥστε ἀπάγξασθαι, *Ita tristata est ut strangulatione premeretur*, saith Junius;[121] and so might it happen from the horrour of mind unto Judas. And so doe many of the Hebrewes affirme, that Achitophell was also strangled, that it, not from the rope, but passion.[122] For the Hebrew and Arabick word in the text not onely signifies supension, but indignation, as Grotius hath also observed.

Many more there are of indifferent truths, whose dubious expositions worthy divines and preachers doe often draw into wholesome and sober uses, whereof neverthelesse we shall not speake; with industry we decline such paradoxies, and peaceably submit unto their received acceptions.

CHAPTER XII
Of the cessation of Oracles

That oracles ceased or grew mute at the comming of Christ, is best understood in a qualified sense and not without all latitude; as though precisely there were none after, nor any decay before. For what we must confesse unto relations of Antiquity; some pre-decay is observable from that of Cicero urged by Baronius; *Cur isto modo jam oracula Delphis non eduntur, non modo nostra ætate, sed jam diu, ut nihil possit esse contemptius.*[123] That during his life they were not altogether dumbe, is deduceable from Suetonius in the life of Tiberius, who attempting to subvert the oracles adjoyning unto Rome, was deterred by the lots or chances which were delivered at Preneste; after his death wee meet with many;[124] Suetonius reports, that the oracle of Autium forewarned Caligula to beware of Cassius, who was one that conspired his death.[125] Plutarch enquiring why the oracles of Greece ceased, excepteth that of Lebadia; and in the same place Demetrius affirmeth the oracles of Mopsus and Amphilochus were much frequented in his dayes;[126] in briefe, histories are frequent in examples, and there want not some even to the reigne of Julian.

That therefore wee may consist with history; by cessation of oracles, with Montacutius we may understand their intercision, not absission or consummate desolation;[127] their rare delivery not a totall dereliction: and yet in regard of divers oracles, we may speake strictly, and say there was a proper cessation. And thus may wee reconcile the accounts of times, and allow those few and broken divinations, whereof we reade in story and undeniable authors. For that they received this blow from Christ, and no other causes alledged by the heathens, from oraculous confession they cannot deny; whereof upon record there are some very remarkeable. The first that oracle of Delphos delivered unto Augustus.

Me puer Hebræus Divos Deus ipse gubernans
Cedere sede jubet, tristemque redire sub orcum;
Aris ergo dehinc tacitus discedito nostris.

An Hebrew child, a God all gods excelling,
To hell againe commands me from this dwelling.
Our altars leave in silence, and no more
A resolution e're from hence implore.[128]

A second recorded by Plutarch, of a voyce that was heard to cry unto mariners at the sea, Great Pan is dead; which is a relation very remarkeable, and may be read in his Defect of Oracles. A third reported by Eusebius in the life of his magnified Constantine; that about that time Apollo mourned, declaring his oracles were false, and that the righteous upon earth did hinder him from speaking truth.[129] And a fourth related by Theodoret, and delivered by Apollo Daphneus unto Julian, upon his Persian expedition, that he should remove the bodies about him, before he could returne an answer, and not long after his temple was burnt with lightning.

All which were evident and convincing acknowledgements of that power which shut his lips, and restrained that delusion which had reigned so many centuries.[130] But as his malice is vigilant, and the sins of men do still continue a toleration of his mischiefes, he resteth not, nor will he ever cease to circumvent the sons of the first deceaved, and therefore expelled his oracles and solemne temples of delusion, he runnes into corners, exercising minor trumperies, and acting his deceits in witches, magicians, diviners, and such inferiour seductions. And yet (what is deplorable) while we apply our selves thereto, and affirming that God hath left to speake by his prophets, expect in doubtfull matters a resolution from such spirits; while we say the divell is mute, yet confesse that these can speake; while we deny the substance, yet practise the effect; and in the denyed solemnity maintaine the equivalent efficacy; in vaine we cry that oracles are downe, Apolloe's alter yet doth smoake, nor is the fire of Delphos out unto this day.

Impertinent it is unto our intention to speake in generall of oracles, and many have well performed it. The plainest of others was that recorded by Herodotus and delivered unto Cræsus; who as a tryall of their omniscience sent unto distant oracles, and so contrived with the messengers, that though in severall places, yet at the same time they should demand what Cræsus was then a doing.[131] Among all others the oracle of Delphos onely hit it, returning answer, hee was boyling a lambe with a tortoyse, in a brazen vessell with a cover of the same metall. The stile is haughty in Greeke, though somewhat lower in Latine,

Æquoris est spatium et numerus mihi notus arenæ,
Mutum percipio, fantis nihil audio vocem.
Venit ad hos sensus nidor testudinis acris,
Quæ semel agninâ coquitur cum carne lebete,
Aere infra strato, et stratum cui desuper est æs.
I know the space of sea, the number of the sand,
I heare the silent, mute I understand.
A tender lambe joyned with tortoise flesh,
Thy master King of Lydia now doth dresse.
The sent thereof doth in my nostrills hover
From brazen pot closed with brazen cover.

Hereby indeed he acquired much wealth and more honour, and was reputed by Cræsus as a diety: and yet not long after, by a vulgar fallacie he deceived his favourite and greatest friend to oracles into an irreparable overthrow by Cyrus.[132] And surely the same successe are likely all to have that relie or depend upon him; 'twas the first play he practised on mortallity, and as time hath rendred him more perfect in the art, so hath the inveteratenesse of his malice more ready in the execution. 'Tis therefore the soveraigne degree of folly, and a crime not onely against God, but also our owne reasons, to expect a favour from the divell, whose mercies are more cruell then those of Polyphemus; for hee devours his favourites first, and the nearer a man approacheth, the sooner he is scorched by Moloch. In briefe, his favours are deceitfull and double headed, he doth apparent good, for reall and convincing evill after it, and exalteth us up to the top of the temple, but to humble us downe from it.

CHAPTER XIII
Of the death of Aristotle

That Aristotle drowned himselfe in Euripus as despairing to resolve the cause of its reciprocation, or ebbe and flow seven times a day, with this determination, *Si quidem ego non capio te, tu capies me*, was the assertion of Procopius, Nazianzen, Justine Martyr, and is generally beleeved amongst us;[133] wherein, because we perceive men have but an imperfect knowledge, some conceiving Euripus to be a river, others not knowing where or in what part to place it, wee first advertise, it generally signifieth any strait, fret, or channell of the sea, running betweene two shoares, as Julius Pollux hath defined it, as wee reade of Euripus Hellespontiacus, Pyrrhæus and this whereof we treat, Euripus Euboicus or Chalcidicus; that is, a narrow passage of sea deviding Attica and the Island of Eubæa, now called Golfo de Negroponte, from the name of the island and chiefe city thereof, famous in the warres of Antiochus, and was taken from the Venetians by Mahomet the great.[134]

Now that in this Euripe or fret of Negropont, and upon the occasion mentioned, Aristotle drowned himselfe, as many affirme, and almost all beleeve, we have some roome to doubt. For without any mention of this, we finde two wayes delivered of his death by Diogenes Laertius, who expresly treateth thereof, the one from Eumolus and Phavorinus, that being accused of impiety for composing an hymne unto Hermias, (upon whose concubine he begat his sonne Nichomachus) he withdrew into Chalcis, where drinking poyson he dyed:[135] the hymne is extant in Laertius, and the fifteenth booke of Athenæus.[136] Another by Apollodorus, that he dyed at Chalcis of a naturall death and languishment of stomack, in his sixty three, or great climactericall year; and answerable hereto is the account of Suidas and Censorinus.[137]

Againe, beside the negative of authority, it is also deniable by reason, nor will it be easie to obtrude such desperate attempts unto Aristotle, upon a non ability or unsatisfaction of reason, who so often acknowledged the imbecility thereof; who in matters of difficulty, and such which were not without abstrusities, conceived it sufficient to deliver conjecturalities; and surely he that could sometimes sit downe with high improbabilities, that could content himselfe, and thinke to satisfie others, that the variegation of birds was from their living in the sunne, or erection made by deliberation of the testicles, would not have beene dejected unto death with this;[138] he that was so well acquainted with ἢ ὅτι, and *πότερον*, *utrum*, and *an quia*, as we observe in the queries of his Problemes; with ἴσως and ἐπὶ τὸ πολὺ, *fortasse* and *plerumque*, as is observable through all his workes;[139] had certainely rested with probabilities, and glancing conjectures in this: nor would his resolutions have ever runne into that mortall antanaclasis, and desperate piece of rhetorick, to be compriz'd in that he could not comprehend.[140] Nor is it indeed to bee made out he ever endeavoured the particular of Euripus, or so much as to resolve the ebbe and flow of the sea. For, as Vicomercatus and others observe, he hath made no mention hereof in his workes, although the occasion present it selfe in his Meteors;[141] wherein hee disputeth the affections of the sea: nor yet in his Problemes, although in the twenty third section, there be no lesse then one and forty queries of the sea; some mention there is indeed in a worke on the propriety of elements, ascribed unto Aristotle, which notwithstanding is not reputed genuine, and was perhaps the same whence this was urged by Plutarch, *de placitis Philosophorum*.[142]

Lastly, the thing it selfe whereon the opinion dependeth, that is, the variety of the flux and reflux of Euripus, or whether the same doe ebbe and flow seven times a day, is not incontrovertible; and for my own part, I remaine unsatisfied therein. For, though Pomponius Mela, and after him Solinus, and Pliny have affirmed it, yet I observed Thucydides, who speaketh often of Eubæa, hath omitted it.[143] Pausanias an ancient writer, who hath left an exact description of Greece, and in as particular a way as Leandro of Italy, or Cambden of Great Britaine, describing not only the country townes, and rivers, but hils, springs, and houses, hath left no mention hereof.[144] Æschines in Ctesiphon onely alludeth unto it; and Strabo, that accurate geographer speakes warily of it, that is, ὥς φασὶ, and as men commonly reported. And so doth also Maginus, *Velocis ac varii fluctus est mare, ubi quater in die, aut septies, ut alii dicunt, reciprocantur æstus.*[145] Botero more plainely, *Il mar cresce e cala con un impeto mirabile quatro volte al di, ben che communimente si dica sette volte, etc.*[146] This sea with wondrous impetuosity ebbeth and floweth foure times a day, although it be commonly said seven times, and generally opinion'd, that Aristotle despairing the reason, drowned himselfe therein. In which description by foure times a day, it exceeds not in number the motion of other seas, taking the words properly, that is, twice ebbing and twice flowing in foure and twenty howres; and is no more then what Thomaso Porrcacchi affirmeth, in his description of famous islands, that twice a day it hath such an impetuous floud, as is not without wonder.[147] Livy speakes more particularly, *Haud facile infestior classi statio est et fretum ipsum Euripi non septies die, (sicut fama fert) temporibus certis reciprocat, sed temere in modum venti, nunc huc nunc illuc verso mari, velut monte præcipiti devolutus torrens rapitur.*[148] There is hardly a worse harbour, the fret or channell of Euripus not certainely ebbing or flowing seven times a day, according to common report, but being uncertainely, and in the manner of a winde carried hither and thither, is whirled away as a torrent downe a hill. But the experimentall testimony of Gillius is most considerable of any, who having beheld the course thereof, and made enquiry of millers that dwelt upon its shoare, received answer, that it ebbed and flowed foure times a day, that is, every sixe howres, according to the law of the ocean; but that indeed sometimes it observed not that certaine course.[149] And this irregularity though seldome happening, together with its unruly and tumultuous motion might afford a beginning unto the common opinion; thus may the expression in Ctesiphon be made out; and by this may Aristotle be interpreted, when in his Problemes he seemes to borrow a metaphor from Euripus; while in the five and twentieth section he enquireth, why in the upper parts of houses the ayre doth Euripize, that is, is whirled hither and thither.[150]

Now the ground, or that which gave life unto the assertion, might be his death at Chalcis, the chiefe city of Eubæa, and seated upon Euripus, where tis confessed by all he ended his dayes. That he emaciated and pined away in the too anxious enquirie of its reciprocations, athough not drowned therein, as Rhodiginus relateth some conceived, was a halfe confession thereof not justifiable from antiquity. Surely the philosophy of flux and reflux was very imperfect of old among the Greeks and Latins; nor could they hold a sufficient theory thereof, who onely observeth the Mediterranean, which in some places hath no ebbe, and not much in any part. Nor can we affirme our knowledge is at the height, who have now the theory of the ocean and narrow seas beside. While we referre it unto the Moone, we give some satisfaction for the ocean, but no generall salve for creeks, and seas which know no floud; nor resolve why it flowes three or foure foot at Venice in the bottome of the Golfe, yet scarce at all at Ancona, Durazzo, or Corcyra, which lye but by the way. And therefore old abstrusities have caused new inventions; and some from the hypotheses of Copernicus or the diurnall and annuall motion of the earth, endeavour to salve the flowes and motions of these seas, illustrating the same by water in a boale, that rising or falling to either side, according to motion of the vessell; the conceit is ingenuous, salves some doubts, and is discovered at large by Galilæo in his systeme of the world.[151]

[But whether the received principle and undeniable action of the moon may not be still retained, although in some difference of application, is yet to be perpended; that is, not by a simple operation upon the surface or superiour parts, but excitation of the nitro-sulphureous spirits, and parts disposed to intumescency at the bottom; not by attenuation of the upper part of the Sea, (whereby ships would draw more water at the flow than at the ebb) but inturgescencies caused first at the bottom, and carrying the upper part before them: subsiding and falling again, according to the motion of the moon from the meridian, and languor of the exciting cause: and therefore rivers and lakes who want these fermenting parts at the bottom, are not excited unto æstutations;[152] and therefore some seas flow higher than others, according to the plenty of these spirits, in their submarine constitutions; and therefore also the periods of flux and reflux are various, nor their encrease or decrease equall: according to the temper of the terreous parts at the bottom: who as they are more hardly or easily moved, do variously begin, continue or end their intumescencies.[153]

From the peculiar disposition of the earth at the bottom, wherein quick excitations are made, may arise those agars and impetuous flows in some æstuaries and rivers, as is observable about Trent and Humber in England; which may also have some effect in the boisterous tides of Euripus, not only from ebullitions at the bottom, but also from the sides and laterall parts, driving the streams from either side, which arise or fall according to the motion in those parts, and the intent or remiss operations of the first exciting causes, which maintain their activities above and below the horizon; even as they do in the bodies of plants and animals, and in the commotion of Catarrhes.]

However therefore Aristotle died, what was his end, or upon what occasion, although it be not altogether assured, yet that his memory and worthy name shall live, no man will deny, nor gratefull schollar doubt: and if according to the elogie of Solon, a man may be onely said to be happy after he is dead, and ceaseth to be in the visible capacity of beatitude: or if according unto his owne Ethicks, sence is not essentiall unto felicity, but a man may be happy without the apprehension thereof; surely in that sence he is pyramidally happy, nor can he ever perish but in the Euripe of ignorance, or till the torrent of barbarisme overwhelme all.

A like conceit there passeth of Melesigenes, *alias* Homer, the father poet, that he pined away upon the riddle of the fishermen. But Herodotus who wrote his life hath cleared this point; delivering that passing from Samos unto Athens, he went sicke ashore upon the island Ios, where he dyed, and was solemnly enterred upon the sea side; and so decidingly concludeth, *Ex hac ægritudine extremum diem clausit Homerus in Io, non, ut arbitrantur aliqui, Ænigmatis perplexitate enectus, sed morbo.*[154]

CHAPTER XIV
Of the wish of Philoxenus

That relation of Aristotle and conceit generally received concerning Philoxenus, who wished the neck of a crane, that thereby he might take more pleasure in his meat, although it pass without exception, upon enquiry I finde not onely doubtfull in the story, but absurd in the desire or reason alledged for it. For though his wish were such as is delivered, yet had it not perhaps that end to delight his gust in eating, but rather to obtaine advantage thereby in singing, as is declared by Mirandula.[155] Aristotle (saith he) in his Ethicks and Problemes, accuseth Philoxenus of sensuality, for the greater pleasure of gust in desiring the neck of a crane; which desire of his, assenting unto Aristotle, I have formerly condemned; but since I perceive that Aristotle for this accusation hath beene accused by divers writers; for Philoxenus was an excellent musician, and desired the neck of a crane, not for any pleasure at meate, but fancying thereby an advantage in singing or warbling, and deviding the notes in musick. And indeed, many writers there are which mention a musician of that name, as Plutarch in his booke against usury, and Aristotle himselfe in the eight of his Politicks speakes of one Philoxenus a musician, that went off from the Dorick dytherambicks unto the Phrygian harmony.[156]

Againe, be the story true or false, rightly applied or not, the intention is not reasonable, and that perhaps neither one way nor the other. For, if we rightly consider the organ of taste, we shall finde the length of the neck to conduce but little unto it. For the tongue being the instrument of taste, and the tip thereof the most exact distinguisher, it will not advantage the gust to have the neck extended, wherein the gullet and conveying parts are onely seated, which partake not of the nerves of gustation or appertaining unto sapor, but receive them onely from the sixth payre; whereas the nerves of taste descend from the third and forth propagations, and so diffuse themselves into the tongue. And therefore cranes, hernes, and swans, have no advantage in taste beyond hawkes, kites, and others of shorter necks.[157]

Nor, if we consider it, had nature respect unto the taste in the different contrivance of necks, but rather unto the parts contained, the composure of the rest of the body, and the manner whereby they feed. Thus animals of long legs, have generally long necks; that is, for the conveniency of feeding, as having a necessity to apply their mouths unto the earth. So have horses, camels, dromedaries long necks, and all tall animals, except the elephant, who in defect thereof is furnished with a trunck, without which he could not attaine the ground. So have cranes, hernes, storks, and shovelards long necks; and so even in man whose figure is erect, the length of the neck followeth the proportion of other parts; and such as have round faces, or broad chests and shoulders, have seldome or never long necks. For, the length of the face twice exceedeth that of the neck, and the space betwixt the throat pit and the navell is equall unto the circumference thereof. Againe, animals are framed with long necks, according unto the course of their life or feeding: so many with short legs have long necks, because they feed in the water, as swans, geese, pellicans, and other fin-footed animals. But hawkes and birds of prey have short necks and trussed legs; for that which is long is weake and flexible, and a shorter figure is best accommodated unto that intention. Lastly, the necks of animals doe vary, according to the parts that are contained in them, which are the weazon and the gullet. Such as have no weazon and breathe not, have scarce any neck, as most sorts of fishes, and some none at all, as all sorts of pectinals, soales, thornback, flounders; and all crustaceous animals, as crevises, crabs, and lobsters.

All which considered, the wish of Philoxenus will hardly consist with reason. More excusable had it beene to have wished himselfe an ape, which if common conceit speake true, is exacter in taste then any. Rather some kinde of granivorous bird then a crane, for in this sense they are so exquisite, that upon the first peck of their bill, they can distinguish the qualities, of hard bodies, which the sence of man discernes not without mastication.[158] Rather some ruminating animall, that he might have eate his meate twice over; or rather, as Theophilus observed in Athenæus, his desire had been more reasonable, had hee wished himselfe an elephant, or an horse; for in these animals the appetite is more vehement, and they receive their viands in large and plenteous manner.[159] And this indeed had beene more sutable, if this were the same Philoxenus whereof Plutarch speaketh, who was so uncivilly greedy, that to engrosse the messe, he would preventively deliver his nostrils in the dish.

As for the musicall advantage, although it seeme more reasonable, yet doe we not observe that cranes and birds of long necks have any musicall, but harsh and clangous throats. But birds that are canorous and whose notes we most commend, are of little throats, and short necks, as nightingales, finches, linnets, canary birds and larkes.[160] And truly, although the weazon, throtle and tongue be the instruments of voice, and by their agitations doe chiefly concurre unto these delightfull modulations, yet cannot we assigne the cause unto any particular formation; and I perceive the best thereof, the nightingale hath some disadvantage in the tongue; which is not acuminate and pointed as in the rest, but seemeth as it were cut off; which perhaps might give the hint unto the fable of Philomela, and the cutting off her tongue by Tereus.[161]

CHAPTER XV
Of the Lake Asphaltites

Concerning the lake Asphaltites, the Lake of Sodome, or the Dead Sea, that heavy bodies cast therein sinke not, but by reason of a salt and bituminous thicknesse in the water floate and swimme above, narrations already made are of that variety, we can hardly from thence deduce a satisfactory determination, and that not onely in the story it selfe, but in the cause alledged. For, as for the story men deliver it variously; some I feare too largely, as Pliny, who affirmeth that bricks will swim therein.[162] Mandevill goeth farther, that iron swimmeth, and feathers sinke.[163] Munster in his Cosmography hath another relation, although perhaps derived from the poem of Tertullian, that a candle burning swimmeth, but if extinguished sinketh.[164] Some more moderately, as Josephus, and many other; affirming onely that living bodies floate, nor peremptory averring they cannot sinke, but that indeed they doe not easily descend.[165] Most traditionally, as Galen, Pliny, Solinus and Strabo, who seemes to mistake the lake Serbonis for it;[166] few experimentally, most contenting themselves in the experiment of Vespasian, by whose command some captives bound were cast therein and found to floate as though they could have swimmed: divers contradictorily, or contrarily, quite overthrowing the point. Aristotle in the second of his Meteors speaks lightly thereof, ὥσπερ μυθολογοῦσι, and esteemeth thereof as a fable.[167] Biddulphus devideth the common accounts of Judea into three parts, the one saith he are apparent truths, the second apparent falshoods, the third are dubious or betweene both, in which forme hee ranketh the relation of this lake.[168] But Andrew Thevet in his Cosmography doth ocularly overthrow it; for hee affirmeth, he saw an asse with his saddle cast therein, and drowned.[169] Now of these relations so different or contrary unto each other, the second is most moderate, and safest to be embraced, which saith, that living bodies swim therein, that is, they doe not easily sinke: and this, untill exact experiment further determine, may be allowed, as best consistent with this quality, and the reasons alledged for it.

As for the cause of this effect, common opinion conceives it to bee the salt and bituminous thicknesse of the water. This indeed is probable, and may bee admitted as farre as the second opinion conceadeth. For, certaine it is that salt water will support a greater burden then fresh, and we daylie see an egge will descend in fresh water,[170] which will swimme in brine. But that iron should floate therein, from this cause is hardly granted; for heavy bodies will onely swim in that liquor, wherein the weight of their bulke exceedeth not the weight of so much water as it occupieth or taketh up. But surely no water is heavy enough to answer the ponderosity of iron;[171] and therefore that metall will sinke in any kinde thereof, and it was a perfect miracle which was wrought this way by Elisha.[172] Thus wee perceive that bodies doe swim or sinke in different liquors, according unto the tenuity or gravity of those liquors which are to support them.[173] So salt water beareth that weight which will sinke in vineger, vineger that which will fall in fresh water, fresh water that which will sinke in spirits of wine, and that will swimme in spirits of wine which will sinke in cleere oyle, as wee made experiment in globes of waxe pierced with light sticks to support them. So that although it be conceived an hard matter to sinke in oyle, I beleeve a man should finde it very difficult, and next to flying to swimme therein. And thus will gold swim in quicksilver, wherein iron and other metals sinke; for the bulke of gold is onely heavier then that space of quicksilver which it containeth; and thus also in a solution of one ounce of quicksilver in two of *aqua fortis*, the liquor will beare amber, horne and the softer kinds of stones, as we have made triall in each.

But a private opinion there is which crosseth the common conceit, maintained by some of late, and alledged of old by Strabo, that is, that the floating of bodies in this lake proceeds not from the thicknesse of the water, but a bituminous ebullition from the bottome, whereby it wafts up bodies injected, and suffereth them not easily to sinke.[174] The verity thereof would be enquired by ocular exploration, for this way is also probable; so we observe, it is hard to wade deep in baths where springs arise, and thus sometime are bals made to play upon a spouting streame.

And therefore, untill judicious and ocular experiment confirme or distinguish the assertion, that bodies doe not sinke herein at all we doe not yet beleeve; that they not easily or with more difficulty descend in this then other water we shall already assent: but to conclude an impossibility from a difficulty, or affirme whereas things not easily sinke, they doe not drowne at all; beside the fallacy, is a frequent addition in humane expression, and an amplification not unusuall as well in opinions as in relations; which oftentimes give indistinct accounts of proximities, and without restraint transcend from one unto another. Thus for as much as the torrid zone was conceived exceeding hot, and of difficult habitation, the opinions of men so advanced its constitution, as to conceive the same unhabitable, and beyond possibility for man to live therein. Thus, because there are no wolves in England, nor have beene observed for divers generations, common people have proceeded into opinions, and some wise men into affirmations, they will not live therein although brought from other countries. Thus most men affirme, and few here will beleeve the contrary, that there be no spiders in Ireland; but we have beheld some in that country, and though but few, some cobwebs we behold in Irish wood in England. Thus the crocodile from an egge growing up to an exceeding magnitude, common conceit and divers writers deliver, it hath no period of encrease, but growth as long as it liveth. And thus in briefe, in most apprehensions the conceits of men extend the considerations of things, and dilate their notions beyond the propriety of their natures.

CHAPTER XVI
Of divers other Relations

1. The relation of Averroes and now common in every mouth, of the woman that conceived in a bath, by attracting the sperme or seminall effluxion of a man admitted to bathe in some vicinity unto her, I have scarce faith to beleeve;[175] and had I beene of the jury, should have hardly thought I had found the father in the person that stood by her. Tis a new and unseconded way in history to fornicate at a distance, and much offendeth the rules of physick, which say, there is no generation without a joynt emission, nor onely a virtuall but corporall and carnall contaction. And although Aristotle and his adherents doe cut off the one, who conceive no effectuall ejaculation in women, yet in defence of the other they cannot be introduced:[176] for, as he delivereth, the inordinate longitude of the organ, though in its proper recipient, may be a meanes to improlificate the seed, surely the distance of place, with the commixture of an aqueous body, must prove an effectuall impediment and utterly prevent the successe of a conception.

And therfore that conceit concerning the daughters of Lot, that they were impregnated by their sleeping father, or conceived by seminal pollution received at distance from him, wil hardly be admitted.[177] And therfore what is related of divels, and the contrived delusion of wicked spirits, that they steale the seminall emissions of man, and transmit them into their votaries in coition is much to be suspected, and altogether to be denyed, that there ensue conceptions thereupon, however husbanded by art, and the wisest menagery of that most subtile impostor. And therefore also that our magnified Merlin was thus begotten by the devill, is a groundlesse conception and as vain to think from thence to give the reason of his prophetical spirit. For if a generation could succeed, yet should not the issue inherit the faculties of the devill, who is but an auxiliary and no univocal actor, nor will his nature substantially concurre to such productions.

2. The relation of Lucillius, and now become common, concerning Crassus the grandfather of Marcus the wealthy Roman, that hee never laughed but once in all his life, and that was at an asse eating thistles, is something strange. For, if an indifferent and unridiculous object could draw his habituall austerenesse unto a smile, it will bee hard to beleeve hee could with perpetuity resist the proper motives thereof: for the act of laughter which is a sweet contraction of the muscles of the face, and a pleasant agitation of the vocall organs, is not meerely voluntary, or totally within the jurisdiction of our selves: but as it may be constrained by corporall contaction in any, and hath beene enforced in some even in their death; so the new unusuall or unexpected jucundities, which present themselves to any man in his life, at some time or other will have activity enough to excitate the earthiest soule, and raise a smile from most composed tempers. Certainely the times were dull when these things happened, and the wits of those ages short of these of ours, when men could maintaine such immutable faces, as to remaine like statues under the flatteries of wit, and persist unalterable at all effortes of jocularity. The spirits in hell, and Pluto himselfe, which Lucian makes to laugh at passages upon earth, will plainely condemne these Saturnines, and make ridiculous the magnified Heraclitus, who wept preposterously, and made a hell on earth;[178] for rejecting the consolations of life, he passed his dayes in teares, and the uncomfortable attendments of hell.

3. The same conceit there passeth concerning our blessed Saviour, and is sometimes urged as an high example of gravity. And this is opinioned, because in holy Scripture it is recorded he sometimes wept, but never that he laughed.[179] Which howsoever granted, it will be hard to conceive how he passed his younger yeares and childhood without a smile; if as divinity affirmeth, for the assurance of his humanity unto men, and the concealement of his divinity from the divell, he passed this age like other children, and so proceeded untill he evidenced the same. And surely no danger there is to affirme the act or performance of that, whereof we acknowledge the power and essentiall property; and whereby indeed hee most neerely convinced the doubt of his humanity. Nor need we be afraid to ascribe that unto the incarnate Son, which sometimes is attributed unto the uncarnate Father, of whom it is said, He that dwelleth in the heavens shall laugh the wicked to scorn.[180] For, a laugh there is of contempt or indignation, as well as of mirth and jocosity; and that our Saviour was not exempted from, the ground hereof, that is, the passion of anger, regulated and rightly ordered by reason, the schooles do not deny; and besides the experience of the money-changers, and dove-sellers in the temple, is testified by Saint John when he saith, the speech of David was fulfilled in our Saviour.[*181]

[*] Zelus domus tuæ comedit me.

Now the alogie of this opinion consisteth in the illation; it being not reasonable to conclude from Scripture negatively in points which are not matters of faith, and pertaining unto salvation;[182] and therefore although in the description of the creation there be no mention of fire, Christian philosophy did not thinke it reasonable presently to annihilate that element, or positively to decree there was no such thing at all. Thus whereas in the briefe narration of Moses there is no record of wine before the flood, can we satisfactorily conclude that Noah was the first that ever tasted thereof?[183] And thus because the word braine is scarce mentioned once,[†] but heart above an hundred times in holy Scripture; will physitians that dispute the principality of parts be induced from hence to bereave the animall organ of its priority; wherefore the Scriptures being serious, and commonly omitting such parergies, it will be unreasonable from hence to condemne all laughter, and from considerations inconsiderable to discipline a man out of his nature;[184] for this is by a rusticall severity to banish all urbanity, whose harmelesse and confined condition as it stands

[†] Only in the vulgar Latine Judges 9: 53.

commended by morality, so is it consistent with religion, and doth not offend divinity.

4. The custome it is of popes to change their name at their creation; and the author thereof is commonly said to be *Bocca di Porco*, or swines face, who therefore assumed the stile of Sergius the second, as being ashamed so foule a name should dishonour the chaire of Peter;[185] wherein notwithstanding from Montacutius and others, I finde there may bee some mistake: for Massonius who writ the lives of popes, acknowledgeth he was not the first that changed his name in that Sea;[186] nor as Platina affirmeth, have all his successours precisely continued that custome; for Adrian the sixt, and Marcellus the second, did still retaine their baptismall denominations, nor is it proved, or probable that Sergius changed the name of *Bocca di Porco*, for this was his sirname or gentilitious appellation, nor was it the custome to alter that with the other;[187] but he commuted his Christian name Peter for Sergius, because he would seem to decline the name of Peter the second.[188] A scruple I confesse not thought considerable in other Seas, whose originalls and first patriarchs have been lesse disputed; nor yet perhaps of that reallity as to prevaile in points of the same nature. For the names of the apostles, patriarchs and prophets have been assumed even to affectation; the name of Jesus hath not been appropriate, but some in precedent ages have borne that name, and many since have not refused the Christian name of Emanuel. Thus are there few names more frequent then Moses and Abraham among the Jewes; the Turkes without scruple affect the name of Mahomet, and with gladnesse receive so honourable cognomination.[189]

And truly in humane occurences there ever have beene many well directed intentions, whose rationalities will never beare a rigid examination; and though in some way they doe commend their authors and such as first began them, yet have they proved insufficient to perpetuate imitation in such as have succeeded them. Thus was it a worthy resolution of Godfrey, and most Christians have applauded it, that hee refused to weare a crowne of gold where his Saviour had worne one of thornes. Yet did not his successors durably inherit that scruple, but some were anointed, and solemnely accepted the diademe of regality. Thus Julius Augustus and Tiberius with great humility or popularity refused the name of *Imperator*; but their successors have challenged that title, and retaine the same even in its titularity. And thus, to come neerer our subject, the humility of Gregory the Great, would by no meanes admit the stile of universall Bishop; but the ambition of Boniface his immediate successor made no scruple thereof; nor of more queasie resolutions have beene their successors ever since.

5. That Tamerlane was a Scythian shepheard, from Mr. Knolls and others, from Alhazen a learned Arabian who wrote his life, and was spectator of many of his exploits, wee have reasons to deny:[190] not onely from his birth; for he was of the blood of the Tartarian emperours, whose father Og had for his possession the countrey of Sagathay, which was no slender teritory, but comprehended all that tract wherein were contained Bactriana, Sogdiana, Margiana, and the nation of the Massagetes;[191] whose capitall city was Samarcand; a place though now decayed, of great esteeme and trade in former ages: but from his regall inauguration; for it is said, that being about the age of fifteene, his old father resigned the kingdome, and men of warre unto him. And also from his education; for as the story speakes it, he was instructed in the Arabian learning, and afterward exercised himselfe therein: now Arabian learning was in a manner all the liberall sciences, especially the mathematicks, and naturall philosophy; wherein not many ages before him, there flourished Avicenna, Averrhoes, Avenzoar, Geber, Almanzor and Alhazen cognominall unto him that wrote his history; whose chronology indeed, although it be obscure, yet in the opinion of his commentator, he was contemporary unto Avicenna, and hath left sixteene bookes of opticks, of great esteeme with ages past, and textuary unto our dayes.[192]

Now the ground of this mistake was surely that which the Turkish historian declareth. Some, saith he, of our historians will needs have Tamerlane to be sonne of a shepheard; but this they have said, not knowing at all the custome of their country; wherein the principall revenewes of the king and nobles consisteth in cattell; who despising gold and silver, abound in all sorts thereof. And this was the occasion that some men call them shepheards, and also affirme this prince descended from them. Now, if it be reasonable, that great men whose possessions are chiefly in cattell, should beare the name of shepheards, and fall upon so low denominations, then may wee say that Abraham was a shepheard, although too powerfull for foure kings; that Job was of that condition, who beside camels and oxen had seven thousand sheepe; and yet is said to bee the greatest man in the East.[193] Surely it is no dishonourable course of life which Moses and Jacob have made exemplary, 'tis a profession supported upon the naturall way of acquisition, and though contemned by the Ægyptians, much countenanced by the Hebrewes, whose sacrifices required plenty of sheepe and lambs.[194] And certainely they were very numerous; for, at the consecration of the Temple, beside two and twenty thousand oxen, King Solomon sacrificed an hundred and twenty thousand sheepe; and the same is observable from the daylie provision of his house, which was ten fat oxen, twenty oxen out of the pastures, and an hundred sheepe, beside rowe buck, fallow deere, and fatted fowles.[195] Wherein notwithstanding (if a punctuall relation thereof doe rightly informe us) the grand seignor doth exceed: the daylie provision of whose seraglio in the reigne of Achmet, beside Beeves, consumed two hundred sheepe, lambs and kids when they were in season one hundred, calves ten, geese fifty, hens two hundred, chickens one hundred, pigeons an hundred payre.

CHAPTER XVII
Of some others

1. We are sad when wee reade the story of Belisarius that worthy cheiftaine of Justinian; who, after the victories of Vandals, Gothes and Persians, and his trophies in three parts of the world, had at last his eyes put out by the Emperour, and was reduced to that distresse, that hee beg'd reliefe on the high way, in that uncomfortable petition, *Date obolum Belisario.*[196] And this we do not only heare in discourses, orations and themes, but finde it also in the leaves of Petrus Crinitus, Volateranus and other worthy writers.[197]

But, what may somewhat consolate all men that honour vertue, wee doe not discover the latter scene of his misery in authors of antiquity, or such as have expresly delivered the story of those times. For, Suidas is silent herein, Cedrenus and Zonaras, two grave and punctuall authors, delivering onely the confiscation of his goods, omit the history of his mendication.[198] Paulus Diaconus goeth farther, not onely passing over this act, but affirming his goods and dignities were restored. Agathius who lived at the same time, declareth hee suffered much from the envie of the court, but that hee descended thus deepe into affliction, is not to bee gathered from his pen. The same is also omitted by Procopius a contemporary and professed enemy unto Justinian and Belisarius, and who as Suidas reporteth, did write an opprobrious booke against them both.

And in this opinion and hopes wee are not single; but Andreas Alciatus the civilian in his Parerga, and Franciscus de Cordua in his *Didascalia*, have both declaratorily confirmed the same.[199] Certainely, sad and tragicall stories are seldome drawne within the circle of their verities; but as their relators doe either intend the hatred or pitty of the persons, so are they set forth with additionall amplifications. Thus have some suspected it hath happened unto the story of Oedipus; and thus doe wee conceive it hath fared with that of Judas, who having sinned beyond aggravation, and committed one villany which cannot bee exasperated by all other; is yet charged with the murther of his reputed brother, parricide of his father, and incest with his owne mother, as Florilegus or Matthew of Westminster hath at large related. And thus hath it perhaps befallen the noble Belisarius, who, upon instigation of the Empresse, having contrived the exile, and very hardly treated Pope Serverius, Latin pens, as a judgement of God upon this fact, have set forth his future sufferings: and omitting nothing of amplification, they have also delivered this, which notwithstanding Johannes the Greeke, makes doubtfull, as may appeare from his iambicks in Baronius.[200]

2. That *fluctus decumanus*, or the tenth wave is greater and more dangerous then any other, some no doubt will be offended if we deny; and hereby we shall seeme to contradict antiquity; for, answerable unto the literall and common acception the same is averred by many writers, and plainly described by Ovid,

> *Qui venit hic fluctus, fluctus supereminet omnes,*
> *Posterior nono est, undecimoque prior.*[201]

Which notwithstanding is evidently false, nor can it bee made out by observation either upon the shoare or the ocean, as wee have with diligence explored in both; and surely in vaine wee expect a regularity in the waves of the sea, or in the particular motions thereof, as in its generall reciprocations, whose causes are constant and their effects therefore correspondent; whereas its fluctuations are but motions subservient, which winds, stormes, shoares, shelves, and every interjacency irregulates.[202] With semblable reason wee might expect a regularity in the windes;[203] whereof though some bee statary, some anniversary, and the rest doe tend to determinate points of heaven; yet do the blasts and undulary breaths thereof maintaine no certainty in their course: nor are they numerally feared by navigators.[204]

Of affinity hereto is that conceit of *ovum decumanum*, so called, because the tenth egge is bigger then any other, according unto the reason alledged by Festus, *decumana ova dicuntur, quia ovum decimum majus nascitur.*[205] For the honour wee beare unto the clergy, wee cannot but wish this true; but herein will bee found no more of verity then in the other: and surely few will assent hereto without an implicite credulity, or as Pythagoricall submission unto every conception of number.

For, surely the conceit is numerall, and though not in the sence apprehended, relateth unto the number of ten, as Franciscus Sylvius hath most probably declared. For, whereas amongst simple numbers or digits, the number of ten is the greatest, therefore whatsoever was the greatest in every kinde, might in some sence be named from this number. Now, because also that which was the greatest, was metaphorically by some at first called *Decumanus*, therefore whatsoever passed under this name was literally conceived by others to respect and make good this number.

The conceit is also Latin, for the Greeks to expresse the greatest wave, do use the number of three, that is, the word *τρικυμία*, which is a concurrence of three waves in one, whence arose the proverb, *τρικυμία κακῶν*, or a trifluctuation of evils, which Erasmus doth render, *malorum fluctus decumanus.* And thus, although the termes be very different, yet are they made to signifie the selfe same thing; the number of ten to explaine the number of three, and the single number of one wave the collective concurrence of more.

3. The poyson of Parysatis reported from Ctesias by Plutarch in the life of Artaxerxes, whereby annointing a knife on the one side, and therewith dividing a bird, with the one halfe shee poysoned Statira, and safely fed her selfe on the other, was certainely a very subtile one, and such as our ignorance is well content it knowes not.[206] But surely we had discovered a poyson that would not endure Pandoraes box, could wee be satisfied in that which for its coldnesse nothing could containe but an asses hoofe, and wherewith some report that Alexander the Great was poysoned. Had men derived so strange an effect from some occult or hidden qualities, they might have silenced

contradiction; but ascribing it unto the manifest and open qualities of cold, they must pardon our beliefe, who perceive the coldest and most Stygian waters may be included in glasses, and by Aristotle, who saith, that glasse is the perfectest worke of art, wee understand they were not then to bee invented.

And though it be said that poyson will breake a Venice glasse, yet have wee not met with any of that nature. Were there a truth herein, it were the best preservative for princes, and personages exalted unto such feares: and surely farre better then diverse now in use. And though the best of china dishes, and such as the Emperour himselfe doth use, bee thought by some of infallible vertue unto this effect, yet will they not, I feare, bee able to elude the mischiefe of such intentions. And though also it bee true, that God made all things double, and that if wee looke upon the workes of the most High there are two and two, one against another; that one contrary hath another, and poyson is not without a poyson unto its selfe; yet hath the curse so farre prevailed, or else our industry defected, that poysons are better knowne then their antidotes, and some thereof doe scarce admit of any. And lastly, although unto every poyson men have delivered many antidotes, and in every one is promised an equality unto its adversary; yet doe wee often finde they faile in their effects: Moly will not resist a weaker cup then that of Circe; a man may bee poysoned in a Lemnian dish, without the miracle of John, there is no confidence in the earth of Paul;* and if it bee meant that no poyson could worke upon him, we doubt the story, and expect no such successe from the dyet of Mithridates.

* *Terra Melitea.*

4. A story there passeth of an Indian king, that sent unto Alexander a faire woman fed with aconites and other poysons, with this intent, either by converse or copulation complexionally to destroy him. For my part, although the designe were true, I should have doubted the successe. For, though it be possible that poysons may meet with tempers whereto they may become aliments, and wee observe from fowles that feed on fishes, and others fed with garlick and onyons, that simple aliments are not alwayes concocted beyond their vegetable qualities; and therefore that even after carnall conversion, poysons may yet retaine some portion of their natures; yet are they so refracted, cicurated, and subdued, as not to make good their first and destructive malignities.[207] And therefore the storke that eateth snakes, and the stare that feedeth upon hemlock, though no

commendable aliments, are not destructive poysons.[208] For, animals that can innoxiously digest these poisons become antidotall unto the poyson digested;[209] and therefore whether their breath be attracted, or their flesh ingested, the poysonous reliques goe still along with their antidote, whose society will not permit their malice to be destructive. And therefore also animals that are not mischifed by poysons which destroy us, may bee drawne into antidote against them; the bloud or flesh of storks against the venome of serpents, the quaile against hellebore, and the dyet of starlings against the draught of Socrates. Upon like grounds are some parts of animals alexipharmacall unto others, and some veines of the earth, and also whole regions, not onely destroy the life of venemous creatures, but also prevent their productions.[210] For, though perhaps they containe the seminals of spiders, and scorpions, and such as in other earths by suscitation of the sun may arise unto animation;[211] yet lying under command of their antidote, without hope of emergency they are poysoned in their matrix by those powers, that easily hinder the advance of their originals, whose confirmed formes they are able to destroy.

5. The story of the wandring Jew is very strange, and will hardly obtaine beliefe, yet is there a formall account thereof set downe by Matthew Paris, from the report of an Armenian bishop;[212] who came into this kingdome about foure hundred yeares agoe, and had often entertained this wanderer at his table. That he was then alive, was first called Cartaphilus,*[213] was keeper of the judgement hall, whence thrusting out our Saviour with expostulation for his stay, was condemned to stay untill his returne; was after baptised by Ananias, and by the name of Joseph; was thirty yeares old in the dayes of our Saviour, remembred the saints that arised with him, the making of the Apostles Creed, and their severall peregrinations. Surely were this true, he might be an happy arbitrator in many Christian controversies; but must impardonably condemne the obstinacy of the Jews, who can contemne the rhetorick of such miracles, and blindly behold so living and lasting conversions.

* *Vade quid moraris? Ego vado, tu autem morare donec venio.*

CHAPTER XVIII
More briefly of some Others

Other relations there are, and those in very good authors; which though we doe not positively deny, yet have they not beene unquestioned by some, and as improbable truths doe stand rejected by others. Unto some it hath seemed incredulous what Herodotus reporteth of the great army of Xerxes, that dranke whole rivers dry.[214] And unto the author himselfe it appeared wondrous strange, that they exhausted not the provision of the countrey, rather then the waters thereof. For, as he maketh the account, and Budeus *De Asse* correcting the miscompute of Valla, delivereth it; if every man of the army had had a chenix of corne a day, that is a sextary and halfe, or about two pints and a quarter, the army had daylie expended ten hundred thousand and forty medimnas, or measures containing six bushels.[215] Which rightly considered, the Abderites had reason to blesse the heavens, that Xerxes eate but one meale a day, and Pythius his noble hoste might with lesse charge and possible provision entertaine both him and his army. And yet may all be salved, if we take it hyperbolically, and as wise men receive that expression in Job, concerning Behemoth, or the elephant; Behold, hee drinketh up a river and hasteth not, he trusteth that hee can draw up Jordane into his mouth.[216]

2. That Anniball eate or brake through the Alpes with vinegar, may bee too grossely taken, and the author of his life annexed unto Plutarch affirmeth, onely hee used this artifice upon the tops of some of the highest mountaines.[217] For, as it is vulgarly understood, that hee cut a passage for his army through those mighty mountaines, it may seeme incredible, not onely in the greatnesse of the effect, but the quantity of the efficient: and such as behold them, may thinke an ocean of vinegar too little for that effect. 'Twas a worke indeed rather to be expected from earthquakes and inundations, then any corrosive waters, and much condemneth the judgement of Xerxes, that wrought through Mount Athos with mattocks.[218]

3. The received story of Milo, who by daylie lifting a calfe, attained an ability to carry it being a bull, is a witty conceit, and handsomely sets forth the efficacy of assuefaction.[219] But surely the account had beene more reasonably placed upon some person not much exceeding in strength, and such a one as without the assistance of custome could never have performed that act; which some may presume that Milo without precedent artifice or any other preparative, had strength enough to performe. For, as relations declare, he was the most pancraticall man of Greece, and as Galen reporteth, and Mercurialis in his Gymnasticks representeth, he was able to persist erect

upon an oyled planke, and not to bee removed by the force or protrusion of three men;[220] and if that bee true which Atheneus reporteth, he was little beholding to custome for this ability.[221] For, in the Olympick games, for the space of a furlong, he carryed an oxe of foure yeares upon his shoulders; and the same day hee carried it in his belly; for as it is there delivered he eate it up himselfe: surely he had beene a proper guest at Grandgousiers feast, and might have matcht his throat that eate sixe pilgrims for a salad.*

4. It much disadvantageth the Panegyrick of Synesius,† and is no small disparagement unto baldnesse, if it bee true what is related by Ælian concerning Æschilus, whose balde pate was mistaken for a rock, and so was brained by a tortoise which an eagle let fall upon it.[222] Certainely, it was a very great mistake in the perspicacity of that animall, and some men critically disposed, would perhaps from hence confute the opinion of Copernicus, never conceiving how the motion of the earth below should not wave him from a knock perpendicularly directed from a body in the ayre above.

* In Rabelais.

† Who writ in the praise of baldnesse.

5. It crosseth the proverb, and Rome might well bee built in a day; if that were true which is traditionally related by Strabo; that the great cities Anchiale and Tarsus, were built by Sardanapalus both in one day, according to the inscription of his monument, *Sardanapalus Anacyndaraxis filius, Anchialen et Tarsum unâ die edificavit, Tu autem hospes Ede, Lude, Bibe etc.* which if strictly taken, that is, for the finishing thereof, and not onely for the beginning, for an artificiall or naturall day, and not one of Daniels weeks, that is, seven whole yeares;[223] surely their hands were very heavy that wasted thirteene yeares in the private house of Solomon; it may bee wondred how forty yeares were spent in the erection of the Temple of Jerusalem, and no lesse then an hundred in that famous one of Ephesus. Certainely, it was the greatest architecture of one day, since that great one of sixe; an arte quite lost with our mechanicks, and a work not to be made out, but like the walls of Thebes, and such an artificer as Amphion.[224]

6. It had beene a sight onely second unto the Arke, to have beheld the great Syracusia, or mighty ship of Hiero, described in Atheneus;[225] and some have thought it a very large one, wherein were to be found ten stables for horses, eight towers, besides fishponds, gardens, tricliniums, and many faire roomes paved with agath, and precious stones; but nothing is impossible unto Archimedes, the learned contriver thereof; nor shall

we question his removing the earth, when he findes an immoveable base to place his engine upon it.

7. The relation of Plutarch of a youth of Sparta, that suffered a fox concealed under his robe to teare out his bowels, before he would either by voice or countenance betray his theft;[226] and the other of the Spartan lad, that with the same resolution suffered a coale from the altar to burne his arme; although defended by the author that writes his life, is I perceive mistrusted by men of judgement, and the author with an *aiunt*, is made to salve himself.[227] Assuredly it was a noble nation that could afford an hint to such inventions of patience, and upon whom, if not such verities, at least such verisimilities of fortitude were placed. Were the story true, they would have made the onely disciples for Zeno and the Stoicks, and might perhaps have beene perswaded to laugh in Phaleris his bull.[228]

8. If any man shall content his beliefe with the speech of Balams asse, without a beliefe of that of Mahomets camell, or Livies oxe; if any man make a doubt of Giges ring in Justinus, or conceives hee must bee a Jew that beleeves the Sabbaticall river in Josephus.[229] If any man will say he doth not apprehend how the taile of an African weather out weigheth the body of a good calfe, that is, an hundred pound, according unto Leo Africanus; or desires before beliefe, to behold such a creature as is the ruc in Paulus Venetus, for my part I shall not be angry with his incredulity.

9. If any man doubt of the strange antiquities delivered by historians, as of the wonderfull corps of Antæus untombed a thousand yeares after his death by Sertorius; whether there were no deceipt in those fragments of the Arke so common to bee seene in the dayes of Berosus; whether the piller which Josephus beheld long agoe, Tertullian long after, and Bartholomeus de Saligniaco, and Borchardus long since be the same with that of Lots wife; whether this were the hand of Paul, or that which is commonly showne the head of Peter, if any doubt, I shall not much dispute with their suspicions. If any man shall not beleeve the turpentine tree[230] betwixt Jerusalem and Bethlem, under which the Virgin suckled our Saviour, as she passed betweene those cities; or the figtree of Bethanie shewed to this day, whereon Zacheus ascended to behold our Saviour, I cannot tell how to enforce his beliefe, nor doe I thinke it requisite to attempt it. For, as it is no reasonable proceeding to compell a religion, or thinke to enforce our owne

beliefe upon another, who cannot without the concurrence of Gods Spirit, have any indubitable evidence of things that are obtruded; so is it also in matters of common beliefe; whereunto neither can we indubitably assent, without the cooperation of our sense or reason, wherein consist the principles of perswasion. For, as the habit of faith in divinity is an argument of things unseene, and a stable assent unto things inevident, upon authority of the divine revealer; so the beliefe of man which depends upon humane testimony, is but a staggering assent unto the affirmative, not without some feare of the negative. And as there is required the Spirit of God,[231] and an infused inclination unto the one, so must the actuall sensation of our senses, at least the non opposition of our reasons procure our assent and acquiescence in the other. So when Eusebius an holy writer affirmeth there grew a strange and unknowne plant neere the statue of Christ, erected by his hemarroidall patient in the Gospel, which attaining unto the hemne of his vesture, acquired a sudden faculty to cure all diseases. Although he saith he saw the statua in his dayes, hath it not found in many men so much as humane beliefe;[232] some believing, others opinioning, a third suspecting it might be otherwise. For, indeed in matters of beliefe the understanding assenting unto the relation, either for the authority of the person, or the probability of the object; although there may be a confidence of the one, yet if there be not a satisfaction in the other, there will arise suspensions; nor can we properly believe untill some argument of reason, or of our proper sense convince or determine our dubitations.

And thus it is also in matters of certain and experimented truth: for, if unto one that never heard thereof, a man should undertake to perswade the affections of the loadstone, or that jet and amber attracteth strawes and light bodies, there would be little rhetorick in the authority of Aristotle, Pliny, or any other. Thus, although it be true that the string of a lute or violl will stirre upon the stroake of an unison or diapazon in another of the same kinde; that alcanna being greene, will suddenly infect the nailes and other parts with a durable red; that a candle out of a musket will pierce through an inch board, or an urinall force a naile through a planke, can few or none believe thus much without a visible experiment. Which notwithstanding fals out more happily for knowledge; for these relations leaving unsatisfaction in the hearers, doe stirre up ingenuous dubiosities unto experiment, and by an exploration of all, prevent delusion in any.

CHAPTER XIX
Of some Relations whose Truth we feare

Lastly, as there are many relations whereto we cannot afford our assent, and make some doubt thereof, so are there divers others whose verities we feare, and heartily wish there were no truth therein.

1. It is an unsufferable affront unto filiall piety, and a deepe discouragement unto the expectation of all aged parents, who shall but reade the story of that barbarous queene, who after she had beheld her royall parents ruine, lay yet in the armes of his assassine, and carrouled with him in the skull of her father;[233] for my part, I should have doubted[234] the operation of antimony, where such a potion would not worke; 'twas an act me thinks beyond anthropophagy, and a cup fit to be served up onely at the table of Atreus.[235]

2. While we laugh at the story of Pygmaleon, and receive as a fable that he fell in love with a statua; wee cannot but feare it may bee true, what is delivered by Herodotus concerning the Ægyptian pollinctors, or such as annointed the dead, that some thereof were found in the act of carnality with them;[236] from wits that say 'tis more then incontinency for Hylas to sport with Hecuba, and youth to flame in the frozen embraces of age, we require a name for this: wherein Peronius or Martiall cannot relieve us. The tyranny of Mezentius did never equall the vitiosity of this incubus, that could embrace corruption, and make a mistresse of the grave;[237] that could not resist the dead provocations of beauty, whose quick invitements scarce excuse submission. Surely, if such depravities there be yet alive, deformity need not despaire; nor will the eldest hopes be ever superannuated, since death hath spurres, and carcasses have beene courted.

3. I am heartily sorry and wish it were not true, what to the dishonour of Christianity is affirmed of the Italian, who after he had inveigled his enemy to disclaime his faith for the redemption of his life, did presently poyniard him, to prevent repentance, and assure his eternall death.[238] The villany of this Christian exceeded the persecution of heathens, whose malice

was never so longimanus as to reach the soule of their enemies, or to extend unto the exile of their Elysiums.[239] And though the blindnesse of some ferities have savaged on the dead, and beene so injurious unto wormes, as to disenterre the bodies of the deceased;[240] yet had they therein no designe upon the soule; and have beene so farre from the destruction of that, or desires of a perpetuall death, that for the satisfaction of their revenge they wisht them many soules, and were it in their power would have reduced them unto life againe. It is great depravity in our natures, and surely an affection that somewhat savoureth of hell, to desire the society, or comfort our selves in the fellowship of others that suffer with us; but to procure the miseries of others in those extremities, wherein we hold an hope to have no society our selves, is me thinks a straine above Lucifer, and a project beyond the primary seduction of Hell.

4. I hope it is not true, and some indeed have strongly denyed, what is recorded of the monke that poysoned Henry the Emperour, in a draught of the holy Eucharist.[241] 'Twas a scandalous wound unto Christian religion, and I hope all pagans will forgive it, when they shall reade that a Christian was poysoned in a cup of Christ, and received his bane in a draught of his salvation. Had I believed transubstantiation, I should have doubted the effect;[242] and surely the sinne it selfe received an aggravation in that opinion. It much commendeth the innocency of our forefathers, and the simplicity of those times, whose laws could never dreame so high a crime as parricide: whereas this at the least may seeme to outreach that fact, and to exceed the regular distinctions of murder. I will not say what sinne it was to act it; yet may it seeme a kinde of martyrdome to suffer by it: for, although unknowingly he dyed for Christ his sake, and lost his life in the ordained testimony of his death. Certainely, had they knowne it, some noble zeales would scarcely have refused it, rather adventuring their owne death, then refusing the memoriall of his.

Many other accounts like these we meet sometimes in history, scandalous unto Christianity, and even unto humanity; whose verities not onely, but whose relations honest minds doe deprecate. For of sinnes heteroclitall, and such as want either name or president, there is oft times a sinne even in their histories.[243] We desire no records of such enormities; sinnes should be accounted new, that so they may be esteemed monstrous. They omit of monstrosity as they fall from their rarity; for, men count it veniall to erre with their forefathers, and foolishly conceive they divide a sinne in its society. The pens of men may sufficiently expatiate without these singularities of villany; for, as they encrease the hatred of vice in some, so doe they enlarge the theory of wickednesse in all. And this is one thing that may make latter ages worse then were the former; for, the vicious examples of ages past, poyson the curiosity of these present, affording a hint of sin unto seduceable spirits, and solliciting those unto the imitation of them, whose heads were never so perversely principled as to invent them. In this kinde we commend the wisdome and goodnesse of Galen, who would not leave unto the world too subtile a theory of poysons; unarming thereby the malice of venemous spirits, whose ignorance must be contented with sublimate and arsenick. For, surely there are subtiler venenations, such as will invisibly destroy, and like the basilisks of heaven.[244] In things of this nature silence condemneth[245] history, 'tis the veniable part of things lost; wherein there must never rise a Pancirollus, nor remaine any register but that of hell.*

* Who writ *de Antiquis deperditis*, or of inventions lost.

And yet, if as some Stoicks opinion, and Seneca himselfe disputeth, these unruly affections that make us sinne such prodigies, and even sinnes themselves be animals; there is an history of Africa and story of snakes in these. And if the transanimation of Pythagoras or method thereof were true, that the soules of men transmigrated into species answering their former natures; some men must surely live over many serpents, and cannot escape that very brood whose sire Satan entered; and though the objection of Plato should take place, that bodies subjected unto corruption, must faile at last before the period of all things, and growing fewer in number, must leave some soules apart unto themselves; the spirits of many long before that time will finde but naked habitations; and meeting no assimilables wherein to react their natures, must certainely anticipate such naturall desolations.

Finis.

HYDRIOTAPHIA, URNE-BURIALL, OR, A DISCOURSE OF THE SEPULCHRALL URNES LATELY FOUND IN NORFOLK

HYDRIOTAPHIA,

URNE-BURIALL,

OR,

A Discourse of the Sepulchrall Urnes lately found in

NORFOLK.

Together with

The Garden of CYRUS,

OR THE

Quincunciall, Lozenge, or Net-work Plantations of the Ancients, Artificially, Naturally, Mystically Considered.

With Sundry Observations.

The First Edition.

By *Thomas Browne* D. of Physick.

LONDON,

Printed for *Hen. Brome* at the Signe of the Gun in *Ivy-lane*, 1658.

FIG. 6 Title page from *Hydriotaphia or Urne-Buriall and The Garden of Cyrus* (1658).

To my worthy and honoured friend Thomas le Gros of Crostwick Esquire[1]

When the funerall pyre was out, and the last valediction was over, men took a lasting adieu of their interred friends, little expecting the curiosity of future ages should comment upon their ashes, and having no old experience of the duration of their reliques, held no opinion of such after-considerations.

But who knows the fate of his bones, or how often he is to be buried? Who hath the oracle of his ashes, or whether they are to be scattered?[2] The reliques of many lie like the ruines of Pompey's, in all parts of the earth;[*3] and when they arrive at your hands, these may seem to have wandered far, who in a direct and meridian travell, have but few miles of known earth between your self and the pole.[†]

[*] *Pompeios juvenes Asia, atque Europa, sed ipsum terra tegit Libyes.*

[†] Little directly, but sea between your house and Greenland.

That the bones of Theseus should be seen again in Athens, was not beyond conjecture, and hopeful expectation;[‡4] but that these should arise so opportunely to serve your self, was an hit of fate and honour beyond prediction.[5]

[‡] Brought back by Cimon. Plutarch.

We cannot but wish these urnes might have the effect of theatrical vessels, and great Hippodrome urnes in Rome; to resound the acclamations and honour due unto you.[§] But these are sad and sepulchral pitchers, which have no joyful voices;[6] silently expressing old mortality, the ruines of forgotten times, and can only speak with life, how long in this corruptible frame, some parts may be uncorrupted; yet able to out-last bones long unborn, and noblest pyle among us.[**7]

[§] The great urnes in the Hippodrome at Rome conceived to resound the voices of people at their shows.

[**] Worthily possessed by that true gentleman Sir Horatio Townshend, my honored friend.

We present not these as any strange sight or spectacle unknown to your eyes, who have beheld the best of urnes, and noblest variety of ashes; who are your self no slender master of antiquities, and can daily command the view of so many imperiall faces; which raiseth your thoughts unto old things, and consideration of times before you, when even living men were antiquities; when the living might exceed the dead, and to depart this world, could not be properly said, to go unto the greater number.[††8] And so run up your thoughts upon the ancient of days,[9] the antiquaries truest object, unto whom the eldest parcels are young, and earth it self an infant; and without Ægyptian account makes but small noise in thousands.[‡‡10]

[††] *Abiit ad plures.*

[‡‡] Which makes the world so many years old.

We were hinted by the occasion, not catched the opportunity to write of old things, or intrude upon the antiquary. We are coldly drawn unto discourses of antiquities, who have scarce time before us to comprehend new things, or make out learned novelties.[11] But seeing they arose as they lay, almost in silence among us, at least in short account suddenly passed over; we were very unwilling they should die again, and be buried twice among us.

Beside, to preserve the living, and make the dead to live, to keep men out of their urnes, and discourse of humane fragments in them, is not impertinent unto our profession;[12] whose study is life and death, who daily behold examples of mortality, and of all men least need artificial mementos, or coffins by our bed side, to minde us of our graves.

'Tis time to observe occurrences, and let nothing remarkable escape us; the supinity of elder dayes hath left so much in silence, or time hath so martyred the records, that the most industrious heads do finde no easie work to erect a new Britannia.[*13, 14]

* Wherein M. Dugdale hath excellently well endeavored, and worthy to be countenanced by ingenuous and noble persons.

'Tis opportune to look back upon old times, and contemplate our forefathers. Great examples grow thin, and to be fetched from the passed world. Simplicity flies away, and iniquity comes at long strides upon us. We have enough to do to make up our selves from present and passed times, and the whole stage of things scarce serveth for our instruction. A compleat peece of vertue must be made up from the *Centos* of all ages, as all the beauties of Greece could make but one handsome Venus.[15]

When the bones of king Arthur were digged up, the old race might think, they beheld therein some originals of themselves;[†] unto these of our urnes none here can pretend relation, and can only behold the reliques of those persons, who in their life giving the laws unto their predecessors, after long obscurity, now lye at their mercies.[16] But remembring the early civility they brought upon these countreys, and forgetting long passed mischiefs; we mercifully preserve their bones, and pisse not upon their ashes.[17]

† In the time of Henry the second, Camden.

In the offer of these antiquities we drive not at ancient families, so long out-lasted by them; we are farre from erecting your worth upon the pillars of your fore-fathers, whose merits you illustrate. We honour your old virtues, conformable unto times before you, which are the noblest armoury. And having long experience of your friendly conversation, void of empty formality, full of freedome, constant and generous honesty, I look upon you as a gemme of the old rock, and must professe my self even to urne and ashes.*[18]

* *Adamas de rupe veteri præstantissimus.*

Norwich
May 1 [1658].

Your ever faithfull friend, and servant,

Thomas Browne

FIG. 7 Norfolk Urns, from *Hydriotaphia* (1658).

HYDRIOTAPHIA, URNE-BURIALL

Or, A Brief Discourse of the Sepulchrall Urnes Lately Found in Norfolk

CHAPTER I

In the deep discovery of the subterranean world, a shallow part would satisfie some enquirers; who, if two or three yards were open about the surface, would not care to rake the bowels of Potosi, and regions towards the centre.[*19] Nature hath furnished one part of the earth, and man another. The treasures of time lie high, in urnes, coynes, and monuments, scarce below the roots of some vegetables. Time hath endlesse rarities, and shows of all varieties; which reveals old things in Heaven, makes new discoveries in earth, and even earth it self a discovery. That great antiquity America lay buried for thousands of years;[20] and a large part of the earth is still in the urne unto us.

* The rich mountain of Peru.

Though if Adam were made out of an extract of the earth, all parts might challenge a restitution, yet few have returned their bones farre lower then they might receive them;[21] not affecting the graves of giants, under hilly and heavy coverings, but content with lesse then their owne depth, have wished their bones might lie soft, and the earth be light upon them;[22] even such as hope to rise again, would not be content with centrall interrment, or so desperately to place their reliques as to lie beyond discovery, and in no way to be seen again; which happy contrivance hath made communication with our forefathers, and left unto view some parts, which they never beheld themselves.

Though earth hath engrossed the name yet water hath proved the smartest grave; which in forty dayes swallowed almost mankinde, and the living creation;[23] fishes not wholly escaping, except the salt ocean were handsomely contempered by a mixture of the fresh element.[24]

Many have taken voluminous pains to determine the state of the soul upon disunion;[25] but men have been most phantastical in the singular contrivances of their corporall dissolution:

whilest the sobrest Nations have rested in two wayes, of simple inhumation and burning.[26]

That carnall interment or burying, was of the elder date, the old examples of Abraham and the Patriarchs are sufficient to illustrate;[27] And were without competition, if it could be made out, that Adam was buried near Damascus, or Mount Calvary, according to some tradition.[28] God himself, that buried but one, was pleased to make choice of this way, collectible from Scripture-expression, and the hot contest between Satan and the Arch-angel, about discovering the body of Moses.[29] But the practice of burning was also of great antiquity, and of no slender extent. For (not to derive the same from Hercules) noble descriptions there are hereof in the Grecian funerals of Homer, in the formall obsequies of Patrocles, and Achilles;[30] and somewhat elder in the Theban warre, and solemn combustion of Meneceus, and Archemorus, contemporary unto Jair the Eighth Judge of Israel.[31] Confirmable also among the Trojans, from the funerall pyre of Hector, burnt before the gates of Troy, and the burning of Penthisilea the Amazonean Queen:[*32,33] and long continuance of that practice, in the inward countries of Asia; while as low as the reign of Julian, we finde that the king of Chionia burnt the body of his son, and interred the ashes in a silver urne.[†34,35]

The same practice extended also farre west, and besides Herulians, Getes, and Thracians, was in use with most of the Celtæ, Sarmatians, Germans, Gauls, Danes, Swedes, Norwegians; not to omit some use thereof among Carthaginians and Americans:[‡36] Of greater antiquity among the Romans then most opinion, or Pliny seems to allow.[37] For (beside the old table laws of burning[§] or burying within the city, of making the funerall fire with plained wood, or quenching the fire with wine)[38] Manlius the consul burnt the body of his son: Numa by speciall clause of his will, was not burnt but buried; and Remus was solemnly burned, according to the description of Ovid.[**39]

Cornelius Sylla was not the first whose body was burned in Rome, but of the Cornielian family, which being indifferently, not frequently used before; from that time spread, and became the prevalent practice.[40] Not totally pursued in the highest runne of cremation; for when even crows were funerally burnt, Poppæa the wife of Nero found a peculiar grave enterment.[41] Now as all customes were founded upon some bottome of reason, so there wanted not grounds for this; according to

[*] Q. Calaber lib. I.

[†] Ammianus, Marcellinus, Gumbrates King of Chionia a countrey near Persia.

[‡] Arnoldus Montanis not in Cæs. Commentar. L.L. Guraldus. Kirkmannus.

[§] 12.Tabul. Part. 1, de jure sacro. Hominem mortuum in urbe ne sepelito, neve urito, tom 2. Rogum ascia ne polito, to.4. Item vigeneri Annotat. in Livium. and Alex. ab. Alex. cum Tiraquello. Roscinus cum dempstero.

[**] Ultima prolato subdita flamma rogo. De Fast. lib. 4. cum Car. Neapol. anaptyxi.

severall apprehensions of the most rationall dissolution. Some being of the opinion of Thales, that water was the originall of all things, thought it most equall to submit unto the principle of putrefaction, and conclude in a moist relentment.[42] Others conceived it most natural to end in fire, as due unto the master principle in the composition, according to the doctrine of Heraclitus.[43] And therefore heaped up large piles, more actively to waft them toward that element, whereby they also declined a visible degeneration into worms, and left a lasting parcell of their composition.

Some apprehended a purifying virtue in fire, refining the grosser commixture, and firing out the Æthereall particles so deeply immersed in it. And such as by tradition or rationall conjecture held any hint of the finall pyre of all things; or that this element at last must be too hard for all the rest; might conceive most naturally of the fiery dissolution. Others pretending no natural grounds, politickly declined the malice of enemies upon their buried bodies. Which consideration led Sylla unto this practise; who having thus served the body of Marius, could not but fear a retaliation upon his own; entertained after in the civill wars, and revengeful contentions of Rome.[44]

But as many nations embraced, and many left it indifferent, so others too much affected, or strictly declined this practice. The Indian Brachmans seemed too great friends unto fire, who burnt themselves alive, and thought it the noblest way to end their dayes in fire; according to the expression of the Indian, burning himself at Athens, in his last words upon the pyre unto the amazed spectators, *Thus I make my selfe Immortall*[*].[45]

[*] And therefore the Inscription of his tomb was made accordingly. *Nic. Damasc.*

But the Chaldeans the great idolators of fire, abhorred the burning of their carcasses, as a pollution of that deity. The Persian Magi declined it upon the like scruple, and being only sollicitous about their bones, exposed their flesh to the prey of birds and dogges.[46] And the Persees now in India, which expose their bodies unto vultures, and endure not so much as *feretra* or beers of wood, the proper fuell of fire, are led on with such niceties.[47] But whether the ancient Germans who burned their dead, held any such fear to pollute their deity of Herthus, or the earth, we have no authentick conjecture.[48]

The Ægyptians were afraid of fire, not as a deity, but a devouring element, mercilesly consuming their bodies, and leaving too little of them; and therefore by precious embalments, depositure in dry earths, or handsome inclosure in glasses, contrived the notablest wayes of integrall conservation.[49] And from such Ægyptian scruples imbibed by Pythagoras, it may be conjectured that Numa and the pythagoricall sect first waved the fiery solution.[50]

The Scythians who swore by winde and sword, that is, by life and death, were so farre from burning their bodies, that they declined all interrment, and made their graves in the ayr:[51] And the Ichthyophagi or fish-eating nations about Ægypt, affected the sea for their grave: thereby declining visible corruption, and restoring the debt of their bodies.[52] Whereas the old heroes in Homer, dreaded nothing more than water or drowning; probably upon the old opinion of the fiery substance of the soul, only extinguishable by that element;[53] and therefore the poet emphatically implieth the totall destruction in this kinde of death, which happened to Ajax Oileus.[*54]

The old Balearians had a peculiar mode, for they used great urnes and much wood, but no fire in their burials, while they bruised the flesh and bones of the dead, crowded them into urnes, and laid heapes of wood upon them.[†55] And the Chinois[‡] without cremation or urnall interrment of their bodies, make use of trees and much burning, while they plant a Pine-tree by their grave, and burn great numbers of printed draughts of slaves and horses over it, civilly content with their companies in effigie, which barbarous Nations exact unto reality.[56]

Christians abhorred this way of obsequies, and though they stickt not to give their bodies to be burnt in their lives, detested that mode after death; affecting rather a depositure than absumption,[57] and properly submitting unto the sentence of God, to return not unto ashes but unto dust againe, conformable unto the practice of the patriarchs, the interrment of our Saviour, of Peter, Paul, and the ancient martyrs.[58] And so farre at last declining promiscuous enterrment with pagans, that some have suffered ecclesiastical censures, for making no scruple thereof.[§59]

The Musselman beleevers will never admit this fiery resolution. For they hold a present trial from their black and white angels in the grave; which they must have made so hollow, that they may rise upon their knees.[60]

The Jewish nation, though they entertained the old way of inhumation, yet sometimes admitted this practice. For the men

* Which *Magius* reads ἐξαπόλωλε.

† Diodorus Siculus.

‡ *Ramusius* in *Navigat.*

§ Martialis the Bishop. Cyprian.

of Jabesh burnt the body of Saul.[61] And by no prohibited practice to avoid contagion or pollution, in time of pestilence, burnt the bodies of their friends.[*] And when they burnt not their dead bodies, yet sometimes used great burnings neare and about them, deducible from the expressions concerning Jehoram, Sedechias, and the sumptuous pyre of Asa:[62] And were so little averse from pagan burning,[†63] that the Jews lamenting the death of Cæsar their friend, and revenger on Pompey, frequented the place where his body was burnt for many nights together. And as they raised noble monuments and mausolæums for their own nation,[‡64] so they were not scrupulous in erecting some for others, according to the practice of Daniel, who left that lasting sepulchrall pyre in Echbatana, for the Medean and Persian kings.[§65]

But even in times of subjection and hottest use, they conformed not unto the Romane practice of burning;[66] whereby the prophecy was secured concerning the body of Christ, that it should not see corruption, or a bone should not be broken;[67] which we beleeve was also providentially prevented, from the souldiers spear and nails that past by the little bones both in his hands and feet: not of ordinary contrivance, that it should not corrupt on the crosse, according to the laws of Romane crucifixion, or an hair of his head perish, though observable in Jewish customes, to cut the hairs of malefactors.[68]

Nor in their long co-habitation with Ægyptians crept into a custome of their exact embalming, wherein deeply slashing the muscles, and taking out the brains and entrails, they had broken the subject of so entire a resurrection, nor fully answered the types of Enoch, Eliah, or Jonah, which yet to prevent or restore, was of equall facility unto that rising power, able to break the fasciations and bands of death, to get clear out of the cere-cloth, and an hundred pounds of oyntment, and out of the sepulchre before the stone was rolled from it.[69]

But though they embraced not this practice of burning, yet entertained they many ceremonies agreeable unto Greeke and Romane obsequies. And he that observeth their funerall feasts, their lamentations at the grave, their musick, and weeping mourners; how they closed the eyes of their friends, how they washed, anointed, and kissed the dead; may easily conclude these were not meere pagan-civilities. But whether that mournfull burthen, and treble calling out after Absalom, had any reference unto the last conclamation, and triple

[*] Amos 6.10.

[†] Sueton. in vita. Jul. Cæs.

[‡] As that magnificent sepulchral monument erected by Simon. Mach. 1. 13.

[§] Κατασκεύασμα θαυμασίως πεποιημένον, whereof a Jewish Priest had alwayes the custody unto Josephus his days. *Jos.* Lib. 10. Antiq.

4 *Hydriotaphia,*

hot conteſt between Satan and the Arch-Angel, about diſcovering the body of *Moſes.* But the practice of Burning was alſo of great Antiquity, and of no ſlender extent. For (not to derive the ſame from *Hercules*) noble deſcriptions there are hereof in the Grecian Funerals of *Homer,* In the formall Obſequies of *Patroclus,* and *Achilles*; and ſomewhat elder in the *Theban* warre, and ſolemn combuſtion of *Meneceus,* and *Archemorus,* contemporary unto *Jair* the Eighth Judge of *Iſrael.* Confirmable alſo among the *Trojans,* from the Funerall Pyre of *Hector,* burnt before the gates of *Troy,* And the [b] burning of *Penthiſilea* the *Amazonean Queen*: and long continuance of that practice, in the inward Countries of *Aſia*; while as low as the Reign of *Julian,* we finde that the King of *Chionia* [c] burnt the body of his Son, and interred the aſhes in a ſilver Urne.

The ſame practice extended alſo farre Weſt *, and beſides *Herulians, Getes,* and *Thracians,* was in uſe with moſt of the *Celtæ, Sarmatians, Germans, Gauls, Danes, Swedes, Norwegians*; not to omit ſome uſe thereof among *Carthaginians* and *Americans*:

[b] Q. Calaber. lib. 1.

[c] Ammianus Marcellinus, Gumbrates King of *Chionia* a Countrey near *Perſia.*

* Arnoldus Montanus not in *Caeſ.* Commentar. L. L. Gyraldus. Kirkmannus.

Urne-Buriall. 5

ricans: Of greater Antiquity among the *Romans* then moſt opinion, or *Pliny* ſeems to allow. For (beſide the old Table Laws of burning [d] or burying within the City, of making the Funerall fire with plained wood, or quenching the fire with wine.) *Manlius* the Conſul burnt the body of his Son: *Numa* by ſpeciall clauſe of his Will, was not burnt but buried; And *Remus* was ſolemnly buried, according to the deſcription of *Ovid* [e].

[d] 12. Tabul. part. 1. de jure ſacro. Hominem mortuum in urbe ne ſepelito, neve urito, tom 2. Rogum aſceâ ne polito. to. 4. Item vigeneri Annotat. in Livium. & Alex. ab Alex. cum Tiraquello. Roſcinus cum dempſtero. [e] Ultima prolato ſubdita flamma rogo. De Faſt. lib. 4. cum Car. Neapol. anaptyxi.

Cornelius Sylla was not the firſt whoſe body was burned in *Rome,* but of the *Cornelian* Family, which being indifferently, not frequently uſed before; from that time ſpread, and became the prevalent practice. Not totally purſued in the higheſt runne of Cremation; For when even Crows were funerally burnt, *Poppæa* the Wife of *Nero* found a peculiar grave enterment. Now as all cuſtomes were founded upon ſome bottome of Reaſon, ſo there wanted not grounds for this; according to ſeverall apprehenſions of the moſt rationall diſſolution. Some

B 3 being

FIG. 8 *Hydriotaphia* marginalia.

valediction,[*70] used by other nations, we hold but a wavering conjecture.[71]

* [O Absalom, Absalom, Absalom].

Civilians make sepulture but of the law of nations, others doe naturally found it and discover it also in animals.[72] They that are so thick skinned as still to credit the story of the phœnix, may say something for animall burning;[73] more serious conjectures finde some examples of sepulture in elephants, cranes, the sepulchrall cells of pismires and practice of bees; which civill society carrieth out their dead, and hath exequies, if not interrments.

CHAPTER II

The solemnities, ceremonies, rites of their cremation or enterrment, so solemnly delivered by authours, we shall not disparage our reader to repeat. Only the last and lasting part in their urns, collected bones and ashes, we cannot wholly omit, or decline that subject, which occasion lately presented, in some discovered among us.

In a field of old Walsingham, not many moneths past, were digged up between fourty and fifty urnes, deposited in a dry and sandy soile, not a yard deep, nor farre from one another:[74] not all strictly of one figure, but most answering these described: some containing two pounds of bones, distinguishable in skulls, ribs, jawes, thigh-bones, and teeth, with fresh impressions of their combustion. Besides the extraneous substances, like peeces of small boxes, or combes handsomely wrought, handles of small brasse instruments, brazen nippers, and in one some kind of opale.[†75]

† In one sent me by my worthy friend Dr. Thomas Witherley of Walsingham.

Near the same plot of ground, for about six yards compasse were digged up coals and incinerated substances, which begat conjecture that this was the Ustrina or place of burning their bodies or some sacrificing place unto the *Manes*, which was properly below the surface of the ground, as the *Aræ* and altars unto the gods and heroes above it.[76]

That these were the urnes of Romanes from the common custome and place where they were found, is no obscure conjecture, not farre from a Romane garrison, and but five miles from Brancaster, set down by ancient record under the name of *Brannodunum*.[77] And where the adjoyning towne, containing seven parishes, in no very different sound, but

Saxon termination, still retains the name of Burnham, which being an early station, it is not improbable the neighbour parts were filled with habitations, either of Romanes themselves, or Brittains Romanised, which observed the Romane customs.

Nor is it improbable that the Romanes early possessed this countrey;[78] for though we meet not with such strict particulars of these parts,[79] before the new institution of Constantine,[80] and military charge of the count of the Saxon shore, and that about the Saxon invasions, the Dalmatian horsemen were in the garrison of Brancaster: yet in the time of Claudius, Vespasian, and Severus, we finde no lesse then three Legions dispersed through the province of Brittain.[81] And as high as the reign of Claudius a great overthrow was given unto the Iceni, by the Romane lieutenant Ostorius.[82] Not long after the countrey was so molested, that in hope of a better state, Prasutagus[83] bequeathed his kingdome unto Nero and his daughters; and Boadicea his queen fought the last decisive battle with Paulinus.[84] After which time and conquest of Agricola the lieutenant of Vespasian, probable it is they wholly possessed this countrey, ordering it into garrisons or habitations, best suitable with their securities. And so some Romane habitations, not improbable in these parts, as high as the time of Vespasian, where the Saxons after seated, in whose thin-fill'd mappes we yet finde the name of Walsingham.[85] Now if the Iceni were but Gammadims, Anconians, or men that lived in an angle wedge or elbow of Brittain, according to the originall etymologie, this countrey will challenge the emphaticall appellation, as most properly making the elbow or iken of *Icenia*.[86]

That Britain was notably populous is undeniable, from that expression of Cæsar.[†87] That the Romans themselves were early in no small numbers, seventy thousand with their associats slain by Boadicea, affords a sure account.[88] And though many Roman habitations are now unknown,[89] yet some by old works, rampiers, coynes, and urnes doe testifie their possessions.[90] Some urnes have been found at Castor, some also about Southcreake, and not many years past, no lesse then ten in a field at Buxton, not near any recorded garison.[‡91] Nor is it strange to finde Romane coynes of copper and silver among us; of Vespasian, Trajan, Adrian, Commodus, Antoninus, Severus, etc. But the greater number of Dioclesian, Constantine, Constans, Valens, with many of Victorinus, Posthumius, Tetricus, and the thirty tyrants in the reigne of

† Hominum infinita multitudo est, creberrimaque ædificia fere Gallicis consimilia. Caes. de bello Gal.l.5.

‡ In the ground of my worthy friend Rob. Jegon Esq. wherein some things contained were preserved by the most worthy Sir William Paston, Bt.

Gallienus;[92] and some as high as Adrianus have been found about Thetford, or Sitomagus, mentioned in the itinerary of Antoninus, as the way from Venta or Castor unto London.[*93] But the most frequent discovery is made at the two Casters by Norwich and Yarmouth,[†] at Burghcastle and Brancaster.[‡]

Besides, the Norman, Saxon and Danish peeces of Cuthred, Canutus, William, Matilda,[§] and others, som Brittish coynes of gold have been dispersedly found; and no small number of silver peeces near Norwich;[**94] with a rude head upon the obverse, and an ill formed horse on the reverse, with inscriptions *Ic. Duro. T.* whether implying *Iceni*, *Dutotriges*, *Tascia*, or *Trinobantes*, we leave to higher conjecture.[95] Vulgar chronology will have Norwich Castle as old as Julius Cæsar; but his distance from these parts, and its Gothick form of structure, abridgeth such antiquity.[96] The British coynes afford conjecture of early habitation in these parts, though the city of Norwich arose from the ruines of Venta, and though perhaps not without some habitation before, was enlarged, builded, and nominated by the Saxons. In what bulk or populosity it stood in the old East-angle monarchy, tradition and history are silent. Considerable it was in the Danish eruptions, when Sueno burnt Thetford and Norwich,[††97] and Ulfketel the governour thereof, was able to make some resistance, and after endeavoured to burn the Danish navy.[98]

How the Romanes left so many coynes in countreys of their conquests, seems of hard resolution, except we consider how they buried them under ground, when upon barbarous invasions they were fain to desert their habitations in most part of their empire, and the strictnesse of their laws forbidding to transfer them to any other uses; wherein the Spartans[‡‡99] were singular, who to make their copper money uselesse, contempered it with vinegar. That the Brittains left any, some wonder; since their money was iron, and iron rings before Cæsar; and those of after stamp by permission, and but small in bulk and bignesse;[100] that so few of the Saxons remain, because overcome by succeeding conquerors upon the place, their coynes by degrees passed into other stamps, and the marks of after ages.

Then the time of these urnes deposited, or precise antiquity of these reliques, nothing of more uncertainty. For since the lieutenant of Claudius seems to have made the first progresse into these parts, since Boadicea was overthrown by the forces

[*] From Castor to Thetford the Romanes accounted thirty two miles, and from thence observed not our common road to London, but passed by *Combretonium ad Ansam*, *Canonium*, *Cæsaromagus*, etc. By Bretenham, Coggeshall, Chelmeford, Burntwood, etc.

[†] Most at Caster by Yarmouth, found in a place called East-bloudy-burgh furlong, belonging to Mr Thomas Wood, a person of civillity, industry and knowledge in this way, who hath made observation of remarkable things about him, and from whom we have received divers silver and copper coynes.

[‡] Belonging to that noble gentleman, and true example of worth Sir Ralph Hare Baronet, my honoured Friend.

[§] A peece of Maud the Empress said to be found in Buckenham Castle with this Inscription, *Elle n'a elle.*

[**] At Thorpe.

[††] Brampton Abbas Jorruallensis.

[‡‡] Plut. in vita. Lycurg.

of Nero, and Agricola put a full end to these conquests;[101] it is not probable the countrey was fully garrison'd or planted before; and therefore however these urnes might be of later date, not likely of higher antiquity.

And the succeeding emperours desisted not from their conquests in these and other parts; as testified by history and medall inscription yet extant. The province of Brittain in so divided a distance from Rome,[102] beholding the faces of many imperiall persons, and in large account no fewer then Cæsar, Claudius, Britannicus, Vespasian, Titus, Adrian, Severus, Commodus, Geta, and Caracalla.

A great obscurity herein, because no medall or emperours coyne enclosed, which might denote the date of their enterrments. Observable in many urnes, and found in those of Spittle Fields by London,[*] which contained the coynes of Claudius, Vespasian, Commodus, Antoninus, attended with lacrymatories, lamps, bottles of liquor, and other appurtenances of affectionate superstition, which in these rurall interrements were wanting.[103]

[*] Stowes Survey of London.

Some uncertainty there is from the period or term of burning, or the cessation of that practice. Macrobius affirmeth it was disused in his dayes.[104] But most agree, though without authentick record, that it ceased with the Antonini.[105] Most safely to be understood after the reigne of those emperours, which assumed the name of Antoninus, extending unto Heliogabalus.[106] Not strictly after Marcus; for about fifty years later we finde the magnificent burning, and consecration of Severus;[107] and if we so fix this period or cessation, these urnes will challenge above thirteen hundred years.

But whether this practise was onely then left by emperours and great persons, or generally about Rome, and not in other provinces, we hold no authentick account. For after Tertullian, in the dayes of Minucius it was obviously objected upon Christians, that they condemned the practise of burning.[†108] And we finde a passage in Sidonius,[‡109] which asserteth that practise in France unto a lower account.[110] And perhaps not fully disused till Christianity fully established, which gave the finall extinction of these sepulchrall bonefires.

[†] Execrantur rogos, et damnant ignium sepulturam. Min. in Oct.

[‡] *Sidon. Apollinaris.*

Whether they were the bones of men or women or children, no authentick decision from ancient custome in distinct places of buriall. Although not improbably conjectured, that the double Sepulture or burying place of Abraham,[§] had in it

[§] [Genesis xxiii, 4.]

such intension.[111] But from exility of bones, thinnesse of skulls, smallnesse of teeth, ribbes, and thigh-bones;[112] not improbable that many thereof were persons of minor age, or women. Confirmable also from things contained in them: in most were found substances resembling combes, plates like boxes, fastened with iron pins, and handsomely overwrought like the necks or bridges of musicall instruments, long brasse plates overwrought like the handles of neat implements, brazen nippers to pull away hair, and in one a kinde of opale yet maintaining a blewish colour.

Now that they accustomed to burn or bury with them, things wherein they excelled, delighted, or which were dear unto them, either as farewells unto all pleasure, or vain apprehension that they might use them in the other world, is testified by all antiquity. Observable from the gemme or berill ring upon the finger of Cynthia, the mistresse of Propertius, when after her funerall pyre her ghost appeared unto him.[113] And notably illustrated from the contents of that Romane urne preserved by Cardinall Farnese,[*114] wherein besides great number of gemmes with heads of gods and goddesses, were found an ape of Agath, a grashopper, an elephant of ambre, a crystall ball, three glasses, two spoones, and six nuts of crystall. And beyond the content of urnes, in the monument of Childerick the first,[†115] and fourth king from Pharamond, casually discovered three years past at Tournay, restoring unto the world much gold richly adorning his sword, two hundred rubies, many hundred imperial coyns, three hundred golden bees, the bones and horseshoe of his horse enterred with him, according to the barbarous magnificence of those days in their sepulchral obsequies. Although if we steer by the conjecture of many and Septuagint expression; some trace thereof may be found even with the ancient Hebrews, not only from the sepulcrall treasure of David, but the circumcision knives which Joshua also buried.[116]

Some men considering the contents of these urnes, lasting peeces and toyes included in them, and the custome of burning with many other nations, might somewhat doubt whether all urnes found among us, were properly Romane reliques, or some not belonging unto our British, Saxon, or Danish forefathers.

* *Vigeneri Annot. in 4. Liv.*

† *Chifflet in Anast. Childer.*

In the form of buriall among the ancient Brittains, the large discourses of Cæsar, Tacitus, and Strabo are silent: For the discovery whereof, with other particulars, we much deplore the loss of that letter which Cicero expected or received from his brother Quintus, as a resolution of Brittish customes;[117] or the account which might have been made by Scribonius Largus the physician, accompanying the Emperour Claudius, who might have also discovered that frugall bit[*118] of the Old Brittains, which in the bignesse of a bean could satisfy their thirst and hunger.[119]

* *Dionis excerpta per Xiphilin. in Severo.*

But that the Druids and ruling priests used to burn and bury, is expressed by Pomponius;[120] that Bellinus the brother of Brennus, and king of Brittains was burnt, is acknowledged by Polydorus, as also by Amandus Zierexensis in *Historia*, and Pineda in his *Universa Historia*.[121] That they held that practise in Gallia, Cæsar expresly delivereth.[122] Whether the Brittains (probably descended from them, of like religion, language and manners) did not sometimes make use of burning; or whether at least such as were after civilized unto the Romane life and manners, conformed not unto this practise, we have no historicall assertion or deniall. But since from the account of Tacitus the Romanes early wrought so much civility upon the Brittish stock, that they brought them to build temples, to wear the gowne, and study the Romane laws and language, that they conformed also unto their religious rites and customes in burials, seems no improbable conjecture.[123]

That burning the dead was used in Sarmatia, is affirmed by Gaguinus,[124] that the Sueons and Gothlanders used to burne their princes and great persons, is delivered by Saxo and Olaus; that this was the olde Germane practise, is also asserted by Tacitus.[125] And though we are bare in historicall particulars of such obsequies in this island, or that the Saxons, Jutes, and Angles burnt their dead, yet came they from parts where 'twas of ancient practise; the Germanes using it, from whom they were descended. And even in Jutland and Sleswick in Anglia Cymbrica, urnes with bones were found not many years before us.[126]

‡ Roisold, Brendetiide, Ild tyde.

But the Danish and northern nations[‡] have raised an Æra or point of compute from their custome of burning their dead: some deriving it from Unguinus, some from Frotho the great;[127] who ordained by law, that princes and chief commanders should be committed unto the fire, though the common sort had the common grave enterrment. So Starkatterus that old heroe was burnt, and Ringo royally burnt the body of Harald the king slain by him.[128]

What time this custome generally expired in that nation, we discern no assured period; whether it ceased before Christianity, or upon their conversion, by Ansgarius[129] the Gaul in the time of Ludovicus Pius the sonne of Charles the great, according to good computes;[130] or whether it might not be used by some persons, while for a hundred and eighty years Paganisme and Christianity were promiscuously embraced among them, there is no assured conclusion. About which times the Danes were busie in England, and particularly infested this countrey:[131] where many castles and strong holds, were built by them, or against them, and great number of names and families still derived from them. But since this custome was probably disused before their invasion or conquest, and the Romanes confessedly practised the same, since their possession of this island, the most assured account will fall upon the Romanes, or Brittains Romanized.

However certain it is, that urnes conceived of no Romane originall, are often digged up both in Norway, and Denmark, handsomely described, and graphically represented by the learned physician Wormius,[*132] and in some parts of Denmark in no ordinary number, as stands delivered by authours exactly describing those Countreys.[†] And they contained not only bones, but many other substances in them, as knives, peeces of iron, brasse and wood, and one of Norwaye a brasse guilded Jewes-harp.

Nor were they confused or carelesse in disposing the noblest sort, while they placed large stones in circle about the urnes, or bodies which they interred: somewhat answerable unto the monument of Rollrich stones in England,[‡133,134] or sepulcrall monument probably erected by Rollo, who after conquered Normandy, where 'tis not improbable somewhat might be discovered. Mean while to what nation or person belonged that large urne found at Ashburie,[§135] containing mighty bones, and a buckler;[136] what those large urnes found at little Massingham,[**] or why the Angelsea urnes are placed with their mouths downward, remains yet undiscovered.

[*] Olai Wormii monumenta et Antiquitat. Dan.

[†] *Adolphus Cyprius in Annal. Sleswic. urnis adeo abundabat collis; etc.*

[‡] In Oxfordshire; *Cambden.*

[§] In Cheshire, *Twinus de rebus Albionicis.*

[**] In Norfolk, *Holingshead.*

CHAPTER III

Playstered and whited sepulchres, were anciently affected in cadaverous, and corruptive burials; and the rigid Jews were wont to garnish the sepulchres of the righteous;[*137] Ulysses in *Hecuba* cared not how meanly he lived, so he might finde a noble tomb after death.[†138] Great persons[139] affected great monuments, and the fair and larger urnes contained no vulgar ashes, which makes that disparity in those which time discovereth among us. The present urnes were not of one capacity, the largest containing above a gallon, some not much above half that measure; nor all of one figure, wherein there is no strict conformity, in the same or different countreys; observable from those represented by Casalius, Bosio, and others, though all found in Italy:[140] while many have handles, ears, and long necks, but most imitate a circular figure, in a sphericall and round composure;[141] whether from any mystery, best duration or capacity, were but a conjecture. But the common form with necks was a proper figure, making our last bed like our first; nor much unlike the urnes of our nativity, while we lay in the nether part of the earth,[‡142] and inward vault of our microcosme. Many urnes are red, these but of a black colour, somewhat smooth, and dully sounding, which begat some doubt, whether they were burnt, or only baked in oven or sunne: according to the ancient way, in many bricks, tiles, pots, and testaceous works;[143] and as the word *testa* is properly to be taken, when occurring without addition: and chiefly intended by Pliny, when he commendeth bricks and tiles of two years old, and to make them in the spring.[144] Nor only these concealed peeces, but the open magnificence of antiquity, ran much in the artifice of clay. Hereof the house of Mausolus was built, thus old Jupiter stood in the Capitoll, and the *statua* of Hercules made in the reign of Tarquinius Priscus, was extant in Plinies dayes.[145] And such as declined burning or funerall urnes, affected coffins of clay, according to the mode of Pythagoras, a way preferred by Varro.[146] But the spirit of great ones was above these circumscriptions, affecting copper, silver, gold, and Porphyrie urnes, wherein Severus lay, after a serious view and sentence on that which should contain him.[§147] Some of these urnes were thought to have been silvered over, from sparklings in several pots, with small tinsell

* Mat. 23.

† *Euripides.*

‡ Psa. 63.

'Χωρήσεις τὸν ἄνθρωπον, ὅν ἡ οἰκουμένη οὐκ ἠχώρησεν.'

§ Dion.

parcels; uncertain whether from the earth, or the first mixture in them.

Among these urnes we could obtain no good account of their coverings; only one seemed arched over with some kinde of brickwork. Of those found at Buxton some were covered with flints, some in other parts with tiles, those at Yarmouth Caster, were closed with Romane bricks. And some have proper earthen covers adapted and fitted to them. But in the Homericall urne of Patroclus, whatever was the solid tegument, we finde the immediate covering to be a purple peece of silk:[148] and such as had no covers might have the earth closely pressed into them, after which disposure were probably some of these, wherein we found the bones and ashes half mortered unto the sand and sides of the urne; and some long roots of quich, or dogs-grass wreathed about the bones.[149]

No lamps, included liquors, lachrymatories, or tear-bottles attended these rurall urnes, either as sacred unto the Manes, or passionate expressions of their surviving friends.[150] While with rich flames, and hired tears they solemnized their obsequies, and in the most lamented monuments made one part of their inscriptions.[*151] Some finde sepulchrall vessels containing liquors, which time hath incrassated into gellies.[152] For besides these lachrymatories, notable lamps, with vessels of oyles and aromaticall liquors attended noble ossuaries.[153] And some yet retaining a vinosity[†154] and spirit in them, which if any have tasted they have farre exceeded the palats of antiquity.[155] Liquors not to be computed by years of annuall magistrates, but by great conjunctions and the fatall periods of kingdomes.[‡156] The draughts of consulary date, were but crude unto these, and Opimian wine but in the must unto them.[§157]

In sundry graves and sepulchres, we meet with rings, coynes, and chalices; ancient frugality was so severe, that they allowed no gold to attend the corps, but only that which served to fasten their teeth.[**158] Whether the opaline stone in this urne were burnt upon the finger of the dead, or cast into the fire by some affectionate friend, it will consist with either custome. But other incinerable substances were found so fresh, that they could feel no sindge from fire.[159] These upon view were judged to be wood, but sinking in water and tried by the fire, we found them to be bone or ivory. In their hardnesse and yellow colour they most resembled box, which in old expressions found the epithete[††] of eternall, and perhaps in such conservatories might have passed uncorrupted.[160]

* *Cum lacrymis posuere.*

† Lazius.

‡ About five hundred years. Plato.

§ *Vinum Opimianum annorum centum.* Petron.

** 12. Tabul. l. xi de Jure Sacro. *Neve aurum addito, ast quoi auro dentes vincti erunt, im cum illo sepelire & urere, se fraude esto.*

†† *Plin. Book xvi.* ξύλα ἀσαπῆ

That bay-leaves were found green in the tomb of S. Humbert,[*][161] after an hundred and fifty years, was looked upon as miraculous.[162] Remarkable it was unto old spectators, that the cypresse of the temple of Diana, lasted so many hundred years: The wood of the ark and olive rod of Aaron were older at the captivity.[163] But the cypresse of the ark of Noah, was the greatest vegetable antiquity, if Josephus were not deceived, by some fragments of it in his dayes.[164] To omit the moore-logs, and firre-trees found under-ground in many parts of England; the undated ruines of windes, flouds or earthquakes; and which in Flanders still shew from what quarter they fell, as generally lying in a north-east position.[†]

But though we found not these peeces to be wood, according to first apprehension, yet we missed not altogether of some woody substance; for the bones were not so clearly pickt, but some coals were found amongst them; a way to make wood perpetuall, and a fit associat for metall, whereon was laid the foundation of the great Ephesian temple, and which were made the lasting tests of old boundaries and landmarks;[165] whilest we look on these, we admire not observations of coals found fresh, after four hundred years.[‡] In a long deserted habitation,[§] even egge-shels have been found fresh, not tending to corruption.

In the monument of King Childerick, the iron reliques were found all rusty and crumbling into peeces.[166] But our little iron pins which fastened the ivory works, held well together, and lost not their magneticall quality, though wanting a tenacious moisture for the firmer union of parts, although it be hardly drawn into fusion, yet that metall soon submitteth unto rust[167] and dissolution. In the brazen peeces we admired not the duration but the freedome from rust, and ill savour; upon the hardest attrition, but now exposed unto the piercing atomes of ayre; in the space of a few moneths, they begin to spot and betray their green entrals.[168] We conceive not these urnes to have descended thus naked as they appear, or to have entred their grave without the old habit of flowers. The urne of Philopœmen was so laden with flowers and ribbons, that it afforded no sight of it self.[169] The rigid Lycurgus allowed olive and myrtle.[170] The Athenians might fairly except against the practise of Democritus to be buried up in honey; as fearing to embezzle a great commodity of their countrey, and the best of that kinde in Europe.[171] But Plato seemed too frugally politick, who allowed no larger monument then would contain four heroick verses, and designed the most barren ground for

[*] *Surius*

[†] *Gorop. Becanus in Niloscopio.*

[‡] Of *Beringuccio nella pyrotechnia.*

[§] At Elmeham.

sepulture:[172] though we cannot commend the goodnesse of that sepulchrall ground, which was set at no higher rate then the mean salary of Judas.[173] Though the earth had confounded the ashes of these ossuaries, yet the bones were so smartly burnt, that some thin plates of brasse were found half melted among them:[174] whereby we aprehend they were not of the meanest carcasses, perfunctorily fired as sometimes in military, and commonly in pestilence, burnings; or after the manner of abject corps, hudled forth and carelesly burnt, without the Esquiline port at Rome; which was an affront continued[175] upon Tiberius, while they but half burnt his body,[*176] and in the amphitheatre, according to the custome in notable malefactors;[177] whereas Nero seemed not so much to feare his death, as that his head should be cut off, and his body not burnt entire.[178]

Some finding many fragments of sculs in these urnes, suspected a mixture of bones; in none we searched was there cause of such conjecture, though sometimes they declined not that practise; the ashes of Domitian were mingled with those of Julia, of Achilles with those of Patroclus:[†179] all urnes contained not single ashes; without confused burnings they affectionately compounded their bones; passionately endeavouring to continue their living unions. And when distance of death denied such conjunctions, unsatisfied affections, conceived some satisfaction to be neighbours in the grave, to lye urne by urne, and touch but in their names. And many were so curious to continue their living relations, that they contrived large, and family urnes, wherein the ashes of their nearest friends and kindred might successively be received,[‡] at least some parcels thereof, while their collaterall memorials lay in minor vessels about them.[180]

Antiquity held too light thoughts from objects of mortality, while some drew provocatives of mirth from anatomies,[§181] and juglers shewed tricks with skeletons.[182] When fidlers made not so pleasant mirth as fencers, and men could sit with quiet stomacks while hanging was plaied before them.[**183] Old considerations made few mementos by sculs and bones upon their monuments. In the Ægyptian obelisks and Hieroglyphicall figures it is not easie to meet with bones. The sepulchrall lamps speak nothing lesse then sepulture; and in their literall draughts prove often obscene and antick peeces: where we finde D.M.[††184] it is obvious to meet with sacrificing pateras, and vessels of libation, upon old sepulchrall monuments.[185] In

[*] *Sueton. in vita Tib. et in Amphitheatro semiustulandum, not. Casaub.*

[†] *Sueton. in vita Domitian.*

[‡] S. the most learned and worthy Mr. M. Casaubon upon Antoninus.

[§] *Sic erimus cuncti, etc. ergo dum vivimus vivamus.*

ἀγχόνην παίζειν

[**] A barbarous pastime at feasts, when men stood upon a rolling globe, with their necks in a rope, and a knife in their hands, ready to cut it when the stone was rolled away, wherein if they failed they lost their lives to the laughter of their spectators. Athenæus.

[††] *Diis manibus.*

the Jewish *Hypogæum* and subterranean cell at Rome, was little observable besides the variety of lamps, and frequent draughts of the holy candlestick.[*186] In authentick draughts of Anthony and Jerome, we meet with thigh-bones and deaths heads;[187] but the cemiteriall cels of ancient Christians and martyrs, were filled with draughts of Scripture stories;[188] not declining the flourishes of cypresse, palmes, and olive; and the mysticall figures of peacocks, doves and cocks.[189] But iterately affecting the pourtraits of Enoch, Lazarus, Jonas, and the vision of Ezechiel, as hopefull draughts, and hinting imagery of the resurrection;[190] which is the life of the grave, and sweetens our habitations in the land of moles and pismires.[191]

* *Bosio.*

Gentile inscriptions precisely delivered the extent of mens lives, seldome the manner of their deaths, which history it self so often leaves obscure in the records of memorable persons. There is scarce any philosopher but dies twice or thrice in Laertius; nor almost any life without two or three deaths in Plutarch; which makes the tragicall ends of noble persons more favourably resented by compassionate readers, who finde some relief in the election of such differences.[192]

The certainty of death is attended with uncertainties, in time, manner, places. The variety of monuments hath often obscured true graves: and cenotaphs confounded sepulchres.[193] For beside their reall tombs, many have found honorary and empty sepulchres. The variety of Homers monuments made him of various countreys. Euripides had his Tomb in Attica,[194] but his sepulture in Macedonia.[†195] And Severus found his real sepulchre in Rome, but his empty grave in Gallia.[‡196]

† *Pausan. in Atticis.*

‡ *Lamprid. in vit. Alexand. Severi.*

He that lay in a golden urne[§] eminently above the earth, was not likely to finde the quiet of these bones.[197] Many of these urnes were broke by a vulgar discoverer in hope of inclosed treasure. The ashes of Marcellus were lost above ground, upon the like account.[**198] Where profit hath prompted, no age hath wanted such miners.[199] For which the most barbarous expilators found the most civill rhetorick.[††200] Gold once out of the earth is no more due unto it; what was unreasonably committed to the ground is reasonably resumed from it: let monuments and rich fabricks, not riches adorn mens ashes. The commerce of the living is not to be transferred unto the dead: it is not injustice to take that which none complains to lose, and no man is wronged where no man is possessor.

§ *Trajanus. Dion.*

** *Plut. in vit. Marcelli.*

†† The Commission of the *Gothish* King *Theodoric* for finding out sepulchrall treasure. *Cassiodor.* Var. l. 4.

What virtue yet sleeps in this *terra damnata* and aged cinders, were petty magick to experiment;[201] these crumbling reliques and long-fired particles superannate such expectations:[202] bones, hairs, nails, and teeth of the dead, were the treasures of old sorcerers. In vain we revive such practices; present superstition too visibly perpetuates the folly of our fore-fathers, wherein unto old observation this island was so compleat, that it might have instructed Persia.[*203]

Plato's historian of the other world, lies twelve dayes incorrupted, while his soul was viewing the large stations of the dead.[204] How to keep the corps seven dayes from corruption by anointing and washing, without exenteration, were an hazardable peece of art, in our choisest practise.[205] How they made distinct separation of bones and ashes from fiery admixture, hath found no historicall solution.[206] Though they seemed to make a distinct collection, and overlooked not Pyrrhus his toe.[207] Some provision they might make by fictile vessels, coverings, tiles, or flat stones, upon and about the body.[208] And in the same field, not farre from these urnes, many stones were found under ground, as also by carefull separation of extraneous matter, composing and raking up the burnt bones with forks, observable in that notable lamp of Galvanus.[209] Marlianus,[†210] who had the sight of the *Vas Ustrinum*, or vessell wherein they burnt the dead, found in the Esquiline Field at Rome, might have afforded clearer solution.[211] But their insatisfaction herein begat that remarkable invention in the funerall pyres of some princes, by incombustible sheets made with a texture of *asbestos*, incremable flax, or salamanders wool, which preserved their bones and ashes[‡] incommixed.[212]

How the bulk of a man should sink into so few pounds of bones and ashes, may seem strange unto any who considers not its constitution, and how slender a masse will remain upon an open and urging fire of the carnall composition.[213] Even bones themselves reduced into ashes, do abate a notable proportion.[214] And consisting much of a volatile salt, when that is fired out, make a light kind of cinders. Although their bulk be disproportionable to their weight, when the heavy principle of salt is fired out, and the earth almost only remaineth; observable in sallow, which makes more ashes then oake; and discovers the common fraud of selling ashes by measure, and not by ponderation.[215]

Some bones make best skeletons, some bodies quick and speediest ashes:[§216] Who would expect a quick flame from

* *Britannia hodie eam attonitè celebrat tantis ceremoniis, ut dedisse Persis videri possit. Plin. l.29.*

† *Topographiæ Roma ex Marliano. Erat & vas ustrinum appellatum quod in eo cadavera comburerentur. Cap. de Campa Esquilino.*

‡ To be seen in *Licet. de reconditis veterum lucernis.*

§ Old bones according to Lyserus. Those of young persons not tall nor fat according to Columbus.

hydropicall Heraclitus?[217] The poysoned souldier when his belly brake, put out two pyres in Plutarch.[*218] But in the plague of Athens, one private pyre served two or three intruders;[†219] and the Saracens burnt in large heaps, by the king of Castile, shewed how little fuell sufficeth.[‡220] Though the funerall pyre of Patroclus took up an hundred foot[*], a peece of an old boat burnt Pompey; and if the burthen of Isaac were sufficient for an holocaust, a man may carry his owne pyre.[221]

* *In vita. Gracc.*

† Thucydides.

‡ Laurent. Valla.

* *ἑκατόμπεδον ἔνθα ἢ ἔνθα*

From animals are drawn good burning lights, and good medicines[§222] against burning; though the seminall humour seems of a contrary nature to fire, yet the body compleated proves a combustible lump, wherein fire findes flame even from bones, and some fuell almost from all parts. Though the metropolis of humidity[**] seems least disposed unto it, which might render the sculls of these urnes lesse burned then other bones. But all flies or sinks before fire almost in all bodies: when the common ligament is dissolved, the attenuable parts ascend, the rest subside in coal, calx or ashes.[223]

§ *Sperm. ran. Alb. Ovor.*

** The brain. Hippocrates.

To burn the bones of the king of Edon[††] for Lyme, seems no irrationall ferity;[224] But to drink of the ashes of dead relations,[‡‡225] a passionate prodigality. He that hath the ashes of his friend, hath an everlasting treasure: where fire taketh leave, corruption slowly enters; In bones well burnt, fire makes a wall against it self; experimented in copels, and tests of metals, which consist of such ingredients.[226] What the sun compoundeth, fire analyseth, not transmuteth.[227] That devouring agent leaves almost allwayes a morsell for the earth, whereof all things are but a colonie; and which, if time permits, the mother element will have in their primitive masse again.

†† Amos 2.1.

‡‡ As Artemisia of her Husband Mausolus.

He that looks for urnes and old sepulchrall reliques, must not seek them in the ruines of temples; where no religion anciently placed them. These were found in a field, according to ancient custome, in noble or private buriall; the old practise of the Canaanites, the family of Abraham, and the burying place of Josua, in the borders of his possessions;[228] and also agreeable unto Roman practice to bury by high-wayes, whereby their monuments were under eye: memorials of themselves, and mementos of mortality into living passengers; whom the epitaphs of great ones were fain to beg to stay and look upon them. A language though sometimes used, not so proper in church-inscriptions.[§§229] The sensible rhetorick of the dead, to exemplarity of good life, first admitted the bones of pious men, and martyrs within church-wals;[230] which in

§§ *Siste viator.*

succeeding ages crept into promiscuous practise. While Constantine was peculiarly favoured to be admitted unto the church porch; and the first thus buried in England was in the dayes of Cuthred.[231]

Christians dispute how their bodies should lye in the grave. In urnall enterrment they clearly escaped this controversie: though we decline the religious consideration, yet in cemiteriall and narrower burying places, to avoid confusion and crosse position, a certain posture were to be admitted; which even Pagan civility observed,* the Persians lay north and south, the Megarians and Phoenicians placed their heads to the east: the Athenians, some think, towards the west, which Christians still retain. And Beda will have it to be the posture of our Saviour.[232] That he was crucified with his face towards the west, we will not contend with tradition and probable account; but we applaud not the hand of the painter, in exalting his crosse so high above those on either side; since hereof we finde no authentick account in history, and even the crosses found by Helena pretend no such distinction from longitude or dimension.[233]

* *Kirckmannus de funer.*

To be knav'd[234] out of our graves, to have our sculs made drinking-bowls, and our bones tuned into pipes, to delight and sport our enemies, are tragicall abominations, escaped in burning burials.

Urnall enterrments, and burnt reliques lye not in fear of worms, or to be an heritage for serpents; in carnall sepulture, corruptions seem peculiar unto parts, and some speak of snakes out of the spinall marrow. But while we suppose common wormes in graves, 'tis not easie to finde any there; few in church-yards above a foot deep, fewer or none in churches, though in fresh decayed bodies. Teeth, bones, and hair, give the most lasting defiance to corruption. In an hydropicall body ten years buried in a church-yard, we met with a fat concretion, where the nitre of the earth, and the salt and lixivious liquor of the body, had coagulated large lumps of fat, into the consistence of the hardest castle-soap; whereof part remaineth with us.[235] After a battle with the Persians the Roman Corps decayed in few dayes, while the Persian bodies remained dry and uncorrupted.[236] Bodies in the same ground do not uniformly dissolve, nor bones equally moulder; whereof in the opprobrious disease we expect no long duration.[237] The body of the Marquesse of Dorset seemed sound and handsomely cereclothed, that after seventy eight years was found uncorrupted.*[238] Common Tombs preserve not beyond powder: A firmer consistence and compage of parts might be expected from arefaction, deep buriall or charcoal.[239] The greatest antiquities of mortall bodies may remain in petrified[240] bones, whereof, though we take not in the pillar of Lots wife, or metamorphosis of Ortelius,†[241] some may be older then pyramids, in the petrified reliques of the generall inundation.[242] When Alexander opened the tomb of Cyrus, the remaining bones discovered his proportion, whereof urnall fragments afford but a bad conjecture, and have this disadvantage of grave enterrments, that they leave us ignorant of most personall discoveries.[243] For since bones afford not only rectitude and stability, but figure unto the body; it is no impossible physiognomy to conjecture at fleshy appendencies; and after what shape the muscles and carnous parts might hang in their full consistences.[244] A full spread *Cariola* shews a well-shaped horse behinde, handsome formed sculls, give some analogie of fleshy resemblance.‡[245] A criticall view of bones makes a good distinction of sexes. Even colour is not beyond conjecture; since it is hard to be deceived in the distinction of negro's sculls.§[246] Dantes characters are to be found in sculls as well as faces.**[247] Hercules is not onely known by his foot.[248] Other parts make out their comproportions, and inferences upon whole or parts.[249] And since the dimensions of the head measure the whole body, and the figure thereof gives conjecture of the principall faculties; physiognomy outlives our selves, and ends not in our graves.

Severe contemplators observing these lasting reliques, may think them good monuments of persons past, little advantage to future beings. And considering that power which subdueth all things unto it self, that can resume the scattered atomes, or identifie out of any thing, conceive it superfluous to expect a resurrection out of reliques.[250] But the soul subsisting, other matter clothed with due accidents, may salve the individuality:[251] yet the saints we observe arose from graves and monuments, about the holy city.[252] Some think the ancient patriarchs so earnestly desired to lay their bones in Canaan, as hoping to make a part of that resurrection, and though thirty miles from Mount Calvary, at least to lie in that region, which should produce the first-fruits of the dead. And if according to learned conjecture, the bodies of men shall rise where their greatest reliques remain, many are not like to erre in the topography of their resurrection, though their bones or bodies

* Of Thomas Marquesse of Dorset, whose body being buried 1530, was 1608 upon the cutting open of the cerecloth found perfect and nothing corrupted, the flesh not hardened, but in colour, proportion, and softnesse like an ordinary corps newly to be interred. Burtons descript. of Leicestershire.

† In his Map of Russia.

‡ [re. *Cariola*, that part in the Skeleton of an Horse, which is made by the hanch bones].

§ [for their extraordinary thicknesse].

** The Poet Dante in his view of Purgatory, found gluttons so meagre, and extenuated, that he conceited them to have been in the siege of Jerusalem, and that it was easie to have discovered Homo or Omo in their faces; M being made by the two lines of their cheeks, arching over the eye brows to the nose, and their sunk eyes making O O which makes up Omo. *Parean l'occhiaie anella senza gemme / che nel viso* be after translated by angels into the field of Ezechiels vision, or as some will order it, into the Valley of Judgement, or Jehosaphat.[*253]

degli huomini legge huomo / Ben'havria quivi conosciuto l'emme.

[*] *Tirin.* in Ezek.

CHAPTER IV

Christians have handsomely glossed the deformity of death, by careful consideration of the body, and civil rites which take of brutall terminations.[254] And though they conceived all reparable by a resurrection, cast not all care of enterrment.[255] And since the ashes of sacrifices burnt upon the altar of God, were carefully carried out by the priests, and deposed in a clean field;[256] since they acknowledged their bodies to be the lodging of Christ, and temples of the holy Ghost, they devolved not all upon the sufficiency of soul existence;[257] and therefore with long services and full solemnities concluded their last exequies, wherein to all distinctions the Greek devotion seems most pathetically ceremonious.[†258]

Christian invention hath chiefly driven at rites, which speak hopes of another life, and hints of a resurrection. And if the ancient Gentiles held not the immortality of their better part, and some subsistence after death; in severall rites, customes, actions, and expressions, they contradicted their own opinions: wherein Democritus went high, even to the thought of a resurrection[‡], as scoffingly recorded by Pliny.[259] What can be more expresse than the expression of Phocyllides?[§260] Or who would expect from Lucretius[**261] a sentence of Ecclesiastes? Before Plato could speak, the soul had wings in Homer, which fell not, but flew out of the body into the mansions of the dead; who also observed that handsome distinction of Demas and Soma, for the body conjoyned to the soul and the body separated from it.[262] Lucian spoke much truth in jest, when he said, that part of Hercules which proceeded from Alchmena perished, that from Jupiter remained immortall.[263] Thus Socrates was content that his friends should bury his body, so they would not think they buried Socrates, and regarding only his immortall part, was indifferent to be burnt or buried.[††264] From such considerations Diogenes might contemn Sepulture.[265] And being satisfied that the soul could not perish, grow carelesse of corporall enterrment. The Stoicks who thought the souls of wise men had their habitation about the moon, might make slight

[†] *Rituale Græcum opera J. Goar in officio exequiarum.*

[‡] *Similis reviviscendi promissa Democrito vanitas, qui non revixit ipse. Quæ malum, ista dimentia est; iterari vitam morte.* Pliny 7.55.

[§] Καὶ τάχα δ'ἐκ γαίης ἐλπίζομεν ἐς φάος ἐλθεῖν λείψαν ἀποιχομένων.

[**] *Cedit enim retro de terra quod fuit ante In terram, etc.*

[††] Plato in Phœd.

account of subterraneous deposition; whereas the Pythagorians and transcorporating philosophers, who were to be often buried, held great care of their enterrment.[266] And the Platonicks rejected not a due care of the grave, though they put their ashes to unreasonable expectations, in their tedious term of return and long set revolution.

Men have lost their reason in nothing so much as their religion, wherein stones and clouts make martyrs;[267] and since the religion of one seems madnesse unto another, to afford an account or rationall of old rites, requires no rigid reader; that they kindled the pyre aversly, or turning their face from it, was an handsome symbole of unwilling ministration; that they washed their bones with wine and milk, that the mother wrapt them in linnen, and dryed them in her bosome, the first fostering part, and place of their nourishment; that they opened their eyes towards Heaven, before they kindled the fire, as the place of their hopes or originall, were no improper ceremonies. Their last valediction thrice uttered by the attendants[*268] was also very solemn, and somewhat answered by Christians, who thought it too little, if they threw not the earth thrice upon the enterred body. That in strewing their tombs the Romans affected the rose, the Greeks *amaranthus* and myrtle; that the funerall pyre consisted of sweet fuell, cypresse, firre, larix, yewe, and trees perpetually verdant, lay silent expressions of their surviving hopes:[269] wherein Christians which deck their coffins with bays have found a more elegant embleme. For that tree[270] seeming dead, will restore it self from the root, and its dry and exuccous leaves resume their verdure again; which if we mistake not, we have also observed in fures.[271] Whether the planting of yewe in churchyards, hold not its originall from ancient funerall rites, or as an embleme of resurrection from its perpetual verdure, may also admit conjecture.

* *Vale, vale, nos te ordine quo natura permittet sequamur.*

They made use of musick to excite or quiet the affections of their friends, according to different harmonies. But the secret and symbolicall hint was the harmonical nature of the soul; which delivered from the body, went again to enjoy the primitive harmony of Heaven, from whence it first descended; which according to its progresse traced by antiquity, came down by Cancer, and ascended by Capricornus.[272]

They burnt not children before their teeth appeared, as apprehending their bodies too tender a morsell for fire, and that their gristly bones would scarce leave separable reliques after the pyrall combustion.[273] That they kindled not fire in their houses for some days after, was a strict memoriall of the late afflicting fire. And mourning without hope, they had an happy fraud against excessive lamentation, by a common opinion that deep sorrows disturbed their ghosts.[*274,275]

* *Tu manes ne lœde meos.*

That they buried their dead on their backs, or in a supine position, seems agreeable unto profound sleep, and common posture of dying; contrary to the most naturall way of birth; nor unlike our pendulous posture, in the doubtfull state of the womb. Diogenes was singular, who preferred a prone situation in the grave, and some Christians[†] like neither, who decline the figure of rest, and make choice of an erect posture.[276]

† Russians, etc.

That they carried them out of the world with their feet forward, not inconsonant unto reason: as contrary unto the native posture of man, and his production first into it.[277] And also agreeable unto their opinions, while they bid adieu unto the world, not to look again upon it; whereas Mahometans who think to return to a delightfull life again, are carried forth with their heads forward, and looking toward their houses.

They closed their eyes as parts which first die or first discover the sad effects of death. But their iterated clamations to excitate their dying or dead friends, or revoke them unto life again, was a vanity of affection;[278] as not presumably ignorant of the criticall tests of death, by apposition of feathers, glasses, and reflexion of figures, which dead eyes represent not;[279] which however not strictly verifiable in fresh and warm cadavers, could hardly elude the test, in corps of four or five dayes.[‡280]

‡ [at least by some difference from living Eyes].

That they suck'd in the last breath of their expiring friends, was surely a practice of no medicall institution, but a loose opinion that the soul passed out that way, and a fondnesse of affection from some Pythagoricall foundation,[§] that the spirit of one body passed into another; which they wished might be their own.[281]

§ *Francesco Perucci, Pompe funebri.*

That they powred oyle upon the pyre, was a tolerable practise, while the intention rested in facilitating the ascension; but to place good omens in the quick and speedy burning, to sacrifice unto the windes for a dispatch in this office, was a low form of superstition.

The *archimime* or jester attending the funerall train, and imitating the speeches, gesture, and manners of the deceased, was too light for such solemnities, contradicting their funerall orations, and dolefull rites of the grave.[282]

That they buried a peece of money with them as a fee of the Elysian ferriman, was a practise full of folly.[283] But the ancient custome of placing coynes in considerable urnes, and the present practise of burying medals in the noble foundations of Europe, are laudable wayes of historicall discoveries, in actions, persons, chronologies; and posterity will applaud them.[284]

We examine not the old laws of sepulture, exempting certain persons from buriall or burning. But hereby we apprehend that these were not the bones of persons planet-struck or burnt with fire from Heaven:[285] no reliques of traitors to their countrey, self-killers, or sacrilegious malefactors; persons in old apprehension unworthy of the earth; condemned unto the Tartaras of Hell, and bottomlesse pit of Pluto,[286] from whence there was no redemption.[287]

Nor were only many customes questionable in order to their obsequies, but also sundry practises, fictions, and conceptions, discordant or obscure, of their state and future beings;[288] whether unto eight or ten bodies of men to adde one of a woman, as being more inflammable, and unctuously constituted for the better pyrall combustion, were any rationall practise:[289] or whether the complaint of Perianders wife be tolerable, that wanting her funerall burning she suffered intolerable cold in Hell, according to the constitution of the infernall house of Pluto, wherein cold makes a great part of their tortures;[290] it cannot passe without some question.

Why the female ghosts appear unto Ulysses, before the Heroes and masculine spirits?[291] Why the Psyche or soul of Tiresias is of the masculine gender;* who being blinde on earth sees more then all the rest in Hell;[292] why the funerall suppers consisted of eggs, beans, smallage, and lettuce, since the dead are made to eat Asphodels about the Elyzian medows?†[293] why since there is no sacrifice acceptable, nor any propitiation for the covenant of the grave; men set up the deity of Morta, and fruitlesly adored divinities without ears?[294] it cannot escape some doubt.

* [In Homer].

† [In Lucian].

The dead seem all alive in the humane Hades of Homer, yet cannot well speak, prophesie, or know the living, except they drink bloud, wherein is the life of man.[295] And therefore the souls of Penelope's paramours conducted by Mercury chirped like bats and those which followed Hercules made a noise but like a flock of birds.[296]

The departed spirits know things past and to come, yet are ignorant of things present. Agamemnon foretels what should happen unto Ulysses, yet ignorantly enquires what is become of his own son.[297] The ghosts are afraid of swords in Homer, yet Sybilla tels Æneas in Virgil, the thin habit of spirits was beyond the force of weapons.[298] The spirits put off their malice with their bodies, and Cæsar and Pompey accord in Latine Hell, yet Ajax in Homer endures not a conference with Ulysses:[299] and Deiphobus appears all mangled in Virgils Ghosts, yet we meet with perfect shadows among the wounded ghosts of Homer.[300]

Since Charon in Lucian applauds his condition among the dead, whether it be handsomely said of Achilles, that living contemner of death, that he had rather be a Plowmans servant then Emperour of the dead?[301] How Hercules his soul is in Hell, and yet in Heaven, and Julius his soul in a starre, yet seen by Æneas in Hell, except the ghosts were but images and shadows of the soul, received in higher mansions, according to the ancient division of body, soul, and image or simulachrum of them both.[302] The particulars of future beings must needs be dark unto ancient theories, which Christian philosophy yet determines but in a cloud of opinions. A dialogue between two infants in the womb concerning the state of this world, might handsomely illustrate our ignorance of the next, whereof methinks we yet discourse in Platoes denne, and are but embryon philosophers.[303]

Pythagoras escapes in the fabulous Hell of Dante, among that swarm of philosophers, wherein whilest we meet with Plato and Socrates, Cato is to be found in no lower place then purgatory.[*304] Among all the set, Epicurus is most considerable, whom men make honest without an Elyzium, who contemned life without encouragement of immortality, and making nothing after death, yet made nothing of the king of terrours.[305]

* *Del inferno. cant. 4.*

Were the happinesse of the next world as closely apprehended as the felicities of this, it were a martyrdome to live; and unto such as consider none hereafter, it must be more then death to dye, which makes us amazed at those audacities, that durst be nothing, and return into their chaos again. Certainly such spirits as could contemn death, when they expected no better being after, would have scorned to live had they known any. And therefore we applaud not the judgment of Machiavel, that Christianity makes men cowards,[306] or that with the confidence of but half dying, the despised virtues of patience and humility, have abased the spirits of men, which Pagan principles exalted, but rather regulated the wildenesse of audacities, in the attempts, grounds, and eternall sequels of death; wherein men of the boldest spirits are often prodigiously temerarious. Nor can we extenuate the valour of ancient martyrs,[307] who contemned death in the uncomfortable scene of their lives, and in their decrepit martyrdomes did probably lose not many moneths of their dayes, or parted with life when it was scarce worth the living. For (beside that long time past holds no consideration unto a slender time to come) they had no small disadvantage from the constitution of old age, which naturally makes men fearfull; and complexionally superannuated from the bold and couragious thoughts of youth and fervent years.[308] But the contempt of death from corporall animosity, promoteth not our felicity.[309] They may sit in the orchestra, and noblest seats of Heaven, who have held up shaking hands in the fire, and humanely contended for glory.[310]

Mean while Epicurus lyes deep in Dante's Hell, wherein we meet with tombs enclosing souls which denied their immortalities.[311] But whether the virtuous heathen, who lived better then he spake, or erring in the principles of himself, yet lived above philosophers of more specious maximes, lye so deep as he is placed; at least so low as not to rise against Christians, who beleeving or knowing that truth, have lastingly denied it in their practise and conversation, were a quæry too sad to insist on.

But all or most apprehensions rested in opinions of some future being, which ignorantly or coldly beleeved, begat those perverted conceptions, ceremonies, sayings, which Christians pity or laugh at. Happy are they, which live not in that disadvantage of time, when men could say little for futurity, but from reason. Whereby the noblest mindes fell often upon doubtfull deaths, and melancholy dissolutions; with these hopes Socrates warmed his doubtfull spirits, against that cold potion, and Cato before he durst give the fatall stroak spent part of the night in reading the immortality of Plato, thereby confirming his wavering hand unto the animosity of that attempt.[312]

It is the heaviest stone that melancholy can throw at a man, to tell him he is at the end of his nature; or that there is no further state to come, unto which this seems progressionall, and otherwise made in vaine; without this accomplishment the naturall expectation and desire of such a state, were but a fallacy in nature, unsatisfied considerators would quarrell the justice of their constitutions, and rest content that Adam had fallen lower, whereby by knowing no other originall,[313] and deeper ignorance of themselves, they might have enjoyed the happiness of inferiour creatures; who in tranquility possesse their constitutions, as having not the apprehension to deplore their own natures. And being framed below the circumference of these hopes, or cognition of better being, the wisedom of God hath necessitated their contentment: but the superiour ingredient and obscured part of our selves,[314] whereto all present felicities afford no resting contentment, will be able at last to tell us we are more then our present selves; and evacuate such hopes in the fruition of their own accomplishments.

CHAPTER V

Now since these dead bones have already out-lasted the living ones of Methuselah, and in a yard under ground, and thin walls of clay, out-worn all the strong and specious buildings above it;[315] and quietly rested under the drums and tramplings of three conquests;[316] what prince can promise such diuturnity unto his reliques, or might not gladly say,

Sic ego componi versus in ossa velim.[*317]

Time which antiquates antiquities, and hath an art to make dust of all things, hath yet spared these minor monuments. In vain we hope to be known by open and visible conservatories, when to be unknown was the means of their continuation and obscurity their protection: if they dyed by violent hands, and were thrust into their urnes, these bones become considerable, and some old philosophers would honour them,[†318] whose souls they conceived most pure, which were thus snatched from their bodies; and to retain a stronger[319] propension unto them:[320] whereas they weariedly left a languishing corps, and with faint desires of re-union. If they fell by long and aged decay, yet wrapt up in the bundle of time, they fall into indistinction, and make but one blot with infants.[321] If we begin to die when we live, and long life be but a prolongation of

* *Tibullus.*

† *Oracula Chaldaica cum scholiis Pselii et Phethonis... Vi corpus relinquentium animæ purissimæ.* Βίῃ λιπόντων σῶμα ψυχαὶ καθαρώτεται *[i.e.* καθαρώταται*]*

death; our life is a sad composition; we live with death, and die not in a moment. How many pulses made up the life of Methuselah, were work for Archimedes:[322] common counters summe up the life of Moses his man.[*323] Our dayes become considerable like petty sums by minute accumulations; where numerous fractions make up but small round numbers; and our dayes of a span long make not one little finger.[†]

[*] In the Psalme of Moses.

[†] According to the ancient Arithmetick of the hand wherein the little finger of the right hand contracted, signified an hundred. *Pierius in Hieroglyph.*

If the nearnesse of our last necessity, brought a nearer conformity unto it, there were a happinesse in hoary hairs, and no calamity in half senses.[324] But the long habit of living indisposeth us for dying; when avarice makes us the sport of death;[325] when even David grew politickly cruell; and Solomon could hardly be said to be the wisest of men.[326] But many are too early old, and before the date of age. Adversity stretcheth our dayes, misery makes Alcmenas nights,[‡327] and time hath no wings unto it. But the most tedious being is that which can unwish it self, content to be nothing, or never to have been, which was beyond the male-content of Job, who cursed not the day of his life, but his nativity; content to have so farre been, as to have a title to future being; although he had lived here but in an hidden state of life, and as it were an abortion.[328]

[‡] One night as long as three.

What song the Syrens sang, or what name Achilles assumed when he hid himself among women, though puzling questions[§329] are not beyond all conjecture. What time the persons of these Ossuaries entred the famous nations of the dead,[**330] and slept with princes and counsellours,[††331] might admit a wide solution. But who were the proprietaries of these bones, or what bodies these ashes made up, were a question above antiquarism.[332] Not to be resolved by man, nor easily perhaps by spirits, except we consult the provinciall guardians, or tutellary observators.[333] Had they made as good provision for their names, as they have done for their reliques, they had not so grosly erred in the art of perpetuation. But to subsist in bones, and be but pyramidally extant, is a fallacy in duration.[334] Vain ashes, which in the oblivion of names, persons, times, and sexes, have found unto themselves, a fruitlesse continuation, and only arise unto late posterity, as emblemes of mortall vanities; antidotes against pride, vain-glory, and madding vices. Pagan vain-glories which thought the world might last for ever, had encouragement for ambition, and finding no Atropos unto the immortality of their names, were never dampt with the necessity of oblivion.[335] Even old ambitions had the advantage of ours, in the attempts of their vain-

[§] The puzzling questions of Tiberius unto Grammarians. *Marcel. Donatus in Suet.*

[**] Κλυτὰ ἔθνεα νεκρῶν Hom.

[††] Job.

glories, who acting early, and before the probable Meridian of time, have by this time found great accomplishment of their designes, whereby the ancient Heroes have already out-lasted their monuments, and mechanicall preservations.[336] But in this latter scene of time we cannot expect such mummies unto our memories, when ambition may fear the prophecy of Elias,[*] and Charles the fifth can never hope to live within two Methuselas of Hector.[†337]

And therefore restlesse inquietude for the diuturnity of our memories unto present considerations, seems a vanity almost out of date, and superanuated peece of folly.[338] We cannot hope to live so long in our names, as some have done in their persons, one face of Janus holds no proportion unto the other.[339] 'Tis too late to be ambitious. The great mutations of the world are acted, or time may be too short for our designes. To extend our memories by monuments, whose death we dayly pray for, and whose duration we cannot hope, without injury to our expectations, in the advent of the last day, were a contradiction to our beliefs.[340] We whose generations are ordained in this setting part of time, are providentially taken off from such imaginations.[341] And being necessitated to eye the remaining particle of futurity, are naturally constituted unto thoughts of the next world, and cannot excusably decline the consideration of that duration, which maketh pyramids pillars of snow, and all that's past a moment.

Circles and right lines limit and close all bodies, and the mortall right-lined circle,[‡342] must conclude and shut up all. There is no antidote against the opium of time, which temporally considereth all things; our fathers finde their graves in our short memories, and sadly tell us how we may be buried in our survivors. Grave-stones tell truth scarce fourty years:[§] generations passe while some trees stand, and old families last not three oaks. To be read by bare inscriptions like many in Gruter,[**343] to hope for eternity by Ænigmaticall epithetes, or first letters of our names, to be studied by antiquaries, who we were, and have new names given us like many of the mummies[††344], are cold consolations unto the students of perpetuity, even by everlasting languages.

To be content that times to come should only know there was such a man, not caring whether they knew more of him, was a frigid ambition in Cardan:[‡‡345] disparaging his horoscopal inclination and judgement of himself; who cares to subsist

[*] That the world may last but six thousand years.
[†] Hector's fame lasting above two lives of Methuselah, before that prince was extant.

[‡] *Θ* The character of death.
[§] Old ones being taken up, and other bodies laid under them.
[**] *Gruteri Inscriptiones Antiquæ.*
[††] [which men show in several Countries, giving them what names they please; and unto some the Names of the old Ægyptian kings out of Herodotus].
[‡‡] *Cuperem notum esse quod sim, non opto ut sciatur qualis sim. Card. in vita propria.*

like Hippocrates patients, or Achilles horses in Homer, under naked nominations, without deserts and noble acts, which are the balsame of our memories, the entelechia and soul of our subsistences.[346] To be namelesse in worthy deeds exceeds an infamous history. The Canaanitish woman lives more happily without a name, then Herodias with one.[347] And who had not rather have been the good theef, then Pilate?[348]

But the iniquity of oblivion blindely scattereth her poppy, and deals with the memory of men without distinction to merit of perpetuity. Who can but pity the founder of the pyramids? Herostratus lives that burnt the temple of Diana, he is almost lost that built it;[349] time hath spared the epitaph of Adrians horse, confounded that of himself.[350] In vain we compute our felicities by the advantage of our good names, since bad have equall durations; and Thersites is like to live as long as Agamemnon.[351] Who knows whether the best of men be known? Or whether there be not more remarkable persons forgot, then any that stand remembred in the known account of time? without the favour of the everlasting register,[352] the first man had been as unknown as the last, and Methuselahs long life had been his only chronicle.

Oblivion is not to be hired:[353] the greater part must be content to be as though they had not been, to be found in the register of God, not in the record of man.[354] Twenty seven names make up the first story, and the recorded names ever since contain not one living century.[355] The number of the dead long exceedeth all that shall live. The night of time far surpasseth the day, and who knows when was the Æquinox?[356] Every house addes unto that current arithmetique, which scarce stands one moment. And since death must be the *Lucina* of life, and even pagans could doubt whether thus to live, were to dye.[357] Since our longest sunne sets at right descensions, and makes but winter arches, and therefore it cannot be long before we lie down in darknesse, and have our lights in ashes.[*358,359] Since the brother of death daily haunts us with dying mementos, and time that grows old it self, bids us hope no long duration:[360] diuturnity is a dream and folly of expectation.

* [According to the custome of the Jewes, who place a lighted waxcandle in a pot of ashes by the corps].

Darknesse and light divide the course of time, and oblivion snares with memory, a great part even of our living beings; we slightly remember our felicities, and the smartest stroaks of affliction leave but short smart upon us. Sense endureth no extremities, and sorrows destroy us or themselves. To weep into stones are fables.[361] Afflictions induce callosities, miseries are slippery, or fall like snow upon us, which notwithstanding is no unhappy stupidity.[362] To be ignorant of evils to come, and forgetfull of evils past, is a mercifull provision in nature, whereby we digest the mixture of our few and evil dayes, and our delivered senses not relapsing into cutting remembrances, our sorrows are not kept raw by the edge of repetitions.[363] A great part of antiquity contented their hopes of subsistency with a transmigration of their souls.[364] A good way to continue their memories, while having the advantage of plurall successions, they could not but act something remarkable in such variety of beings, and enjoying the fame of their passed selves, make accumulations of glory unto their last durations.[365] Others rather then be lost in the uncomfortable night of nothing, were content to recede into the common being, and make one particle of the publick soul of all things, which was no more then to return unto their unknown and divine originall again.[366] Ægyptian ingenuity was more unsatisfied, contriving their bodies in sweet consistences, to attend the return of their souls.[367] But all was vanity,[*368] feeding the winde, and folly. The Ægyptian Mummies, which Cambyses or time hath spared, avarice now consumeth.[369] Mummie is become merchandise, Mizraim cures wounds, and Pharaoh is sold for balsoms.[370]

* *Omnia vanitas et pastio venti... νημὴ [i.e. νομὴ] ἀνέμου, βόσκησις ut olim Aquila et Symmachus. v. Drus. Eccles.*

In vain do individuals hope for immortality, or any patent from oblivion, in preservations below the moon:[371] men have been deceived even in their flatteries above the sun, and studied conceits to perpetuate their names in Heaven. The various Cosmography of that part hath already varied the names of contrived constellations; Nimrod is lost in Orion, and Osyris in the Dogge-starre.[372] While we look for incorruption in the heavens, we finde they are but like the earth; durable in their main bodies, alterable in their parts: whereof beside comets and new stars, perspectives begin to tell tales.[373] And the spots that wander about the sun, with Phaetons favour, would make clear conviction.[374]

There is nothing strictly immortall, but immortality; whatever hath no beginning may be confident of no end. All others have a dependent being, and within the reach of destruction, which is the peculiar of that necessary essence that cannot destroy it self;[375] and the highest strain of omnipotency to be so powerfully constituted, as not to suffer even from the power of it self. But the sufficiency of Christian immortality frustrates all earthly glory, and the quality of either state after death, makes a folly of posthumous memory. God who can only destroy our souls, and hath assured our resurrection, either of our bodies or names hath directly promised no duration. Wherein there is so much chance that the boldest expectants have found unhappy frustration; and to hold long subsistence, seems but a scape in oblivion. But man is a noble animal, splendid in ashes, and pompous in the grave, solemnizing nativities and deaths with equall lustre, nor omitting ceremonies of bravery, in the infamy of his nature.

Life is a pure flame, and we live by an invisible sun within us. A small fire sufficeth for life, great flames seemed too little after death, while men vainly affected precious pyres, and to burn like Sardanapalus,[376] but the wisedom of funerall laws found the folly of prodigall blazes, and reduced undoing fires, unto the rule of sober obsequies, wherein few could be so mean as not to provide wood, pitch, a mourner, and an urne.

Five languages secured not the epitaph of Gordianus;[*377,378] The man of God lives longer without a tomb then any by one, invisibly interred by angels, and adjudged to obscurity, though not without some marks directing humane discovery.[379] Enoch and Elias without either tomb or buriall, in an anomalous state of being, are the great examples of perpetuity, in their long and living memory, in strict account being still on this side death, and having a late part yet to act upon this stage of earth.[380] If in the decretory term of the world we shall not all dye but be changed, according to received translation;[381] the last day will make but few graves; at least quick resurrections will anticipate lasting sepultures; some graves will be opened before they are quite closed, and Lazarus will be no wonder.[382] When many that feared to dye shall groane that they can dye but once, the dismall state is the second and living death, when life puts despair on the damned; when men shall wish the coverings of mountaines, not of monuments, and annihilation shall be courted.[383]

* [in Greek, Latine, Hebrew, Ægyptian, Arabick, defaced by Licinius the Emperour].

While some have studied monuments, others have studiously declined them: and some have been so vainly boisterous, that they durst not acknowledge their graves; wherein[†] Alaricus seems most subtle, who had a river turned to hide his bones at the bottome.[384] Even Sylla that thought himself safe in his urne, could not prevent revenging tongues, and stones thrown at his monument.[385] Happy are they whom privacy makes innocent, who deal so with men in this world, that they are not afraid to meet them in the next, who when they dye, make no commotion

† *Jornandes de rebus Geticis.*

among the dead, and are not toucht with that poeticall taunt of Isaiah.*[386]

Pyramids, arches, obelisks, were but the irregularities of vain-glory, and wilde enormities of ancient magnanimity. But the most magnanimous resolution rests in the Christan religion, which trampleth upon pride, and sets on the neck of ambition, humbly pursuing that infallible perpetuity, unto which all others must diminish their diameters, and be poorly seen in angles of contingency.†[387]

Pious spirits who passed their dayes in raptures of futurity, made little more of this world, then the world that was before it, while they lay obscure in the chaos of pre-ordination, and night of their fore-beings. And if any have been so happy as truly to understand Christian annihilation, extasis, exolution, liquefaction, transformation, the kisse of the spouse, gustation of God, and ingression into the divine shadow, they have already had an handsome anticipation of Heaven;[388] the glory of the world is surely over, and the earth in ashes unto them.

To subsist in lasting monuments, to live in their productions, to exist in their names, and prædicament of chymeras, was large satisfaction unto old expectations, and made one part of their Elyziums.[389] But all this is nothing in the metaphysics of true belief. To live indeed is to be again our selves, which being not only an hope but an evidence in noble beleevers; 'tis all one to lye in St Innocents church-yard,‡ as in the sands of Ægypt: ready to be any thing, in the extasie of being ever, and as content with six foot as the moles of Adrianus.§

Lucan

Tabesne cadavera solvat
An rogus haud refert.[390]

* Isa. 14.

† *Angulus contingentiæ*, the least of Angles.

‡ In Paris where bodies soon consume.

§ A stately Mausoleum or sepulchral pyle built by Adrianus in Rome, where now standeth the Castle of St. Angelo.

THE GARDEN OF CYRUS

THE

GARDEN

OF

CYRUS.

OR,

The Quincunciall, Lozenge, or Net-work Plantations of the Ancients, Artificially Naturally, Myſtically Conſidered.

BY

Thomas Brown D. of Phyſick

Printed in the Year, 1658.

FIG. 9 Title page from *The Garden of Cyrus* (1658).

To my worthy and honoured friend Nicholas Bacon of Gillingham esquire.[1]

Had I not observed that Purblinde[*2] men have discoursed well of sight, and some without issue, excellently of generation;[†3] I that was never master of any considerable garden, had not attempted this subject.[4] But the earth is the garden of nature, and each fruitfull countrey a Paradise. Dioscorides made most of his observations in his march about with Antonius; and Theophrastus raised his generalities chiefly from the field.[5]

[*] Plempius, Cabeus, etc.
[†] D. Harvy.

Beside we write no herball, nor can this volume deceive you, who have handled the massiest thereof:[‡6] who know that three folios are yet too little,[§7] and how new herbals fly from America upon us; from persevering enquirers, and old in those singularities,[**] we expect such descriptions. Wherein England is now so exact,[††] that it yeelds not to other countreys.

[‡] Besleri *Hortus Eystetensis*.
[§] Bauhini *Theatrum Botanicum, etc*.
[**] My worthy friend M. Goodier an ancient and learned Botanist.
[††] As in London and divers parts, whereof we mention none, lest we seem to omit any.

We pretend not to multiply vegetable divisions by quincuncial and reticulate plants; or erect a new phytology.[8] The field of knowledge hath been so traced, it is hard to spring any thing new. Of old things we write something new, if truth may receive addition, or envy will have any thing new; since the ancients knew the late anatomicall discoveries, and Hippocrates the circulation.[9]

You have been so long out of trite learning, that 'tis hard to finde a subject proper for you; and if you have met with a sheet upon this, we have missed our intention. In this multiplicity of writing, bye and barren themes are best fitted for invention;[10] subjects so often discoursed confine the imagination, and fix our conceptions unto the notions of fore-writers. Beside, such discourses allow excursions, and venially admit of collaterall truths, though at some distance from their principals.[11] Wherein if we sometimes take wide liberty, we are not single, but erre by great example.[‡‡]

[‡‡] Hippocrates *de superfœtation, de dentitione*.

He that will illustrate the excellency of this order, may easily fail upon so spruce a subject, wherein we have not affrighted the common reader with any other diagramms, then of it self; and have industriously declined illustrations from rare and unknown plants.

Your discerning judgement so well acquainted with that study, will expect herein no mathematicall truths, as well understanding how few generalities and *u finitas*[§§] there are in

[§§] Rules without exception.

nature. How Scaliger hath found exceptions in most universals of Aristotle and Theophrastus.[12] How botanicall maximes must have fair allowance, and are tolerably currant, if not intolerably over-ballanced by exceptions.

You have wisely ordered your vegetable delights, beyond the reach of exception. The Turks who passt their dayes in gardens here, will have gardens also hereafter, and delighting in flowers on earth, must have lilies and roses in Heaven.[13] In garden delights 'tis not easie to hold a mediocrity; that insinuating pleasure is seldome without some extremity.[14] The antients venially delighted in flourishing gardens; many were florists that knew not the true use of a flower; and in Plinies dayes none had directly treated of that subject. Some commendably affected plantations of venemous vegetables, some confined their delights unto single plants, and Cato seemed to dote upon cabbadge;[15] while the ingenuous delight of tulipists, stands saluted with hard language, even by their own professors.*[16]

* *Tulipomania, Narrencruiid, Laurenberg.* Pet. Hondius, *in lib. Belg.*

That in this garden discourse, we range into extraneous things, and many parts of art and nature, we follow herein the example of old and new plantations, wherein noble spirits contented not themselves with trees, but by the attendance of aviaries, fish ponds, and all variety of animals, they made their gardens the epitome of the earth, and some resemblance of the secular shows of old.[17]

That we conjoyn these parts of different subjects, or that this should succeed the other; your judgement will admit without impute of incongruity;[18] since the delightfull world comes after death, and Paradise succeeds the grave. Since the verdant state of things is the symbole of the Resurrection, and to flourish in the state of glory, we must first be sown in corruption. Beside the antient practise of noble persons, to conclude in garden-graves, and urnes themselves of old, to be wrapt up in flowers and garlands.

Nullum sine venia placuisse eloquium, is more sensibly understood by writers, then by readers;[19] nor well apprehended by either, till works have hanged out like Apelles his pictures;[20] wherein even common eyes will finde something for emendation.

To wish all readers of your abilities, were unreasonably to multiply the number of scholars beyond the temper of these times. But unto this ill-judging age, we charitably desire a portion of your equity, judgement, candour, and ingenuity;

wherein you are so rich, as not to lose by diffusion. And being a flourishing branch of that noble family,* unto which we owe so much observance, you are not new set, but long rooted in such perfections; whereof having had so lasting confirmation in your worthy conversation, constant amity, and expression; and knowing you such a serious student in the highest arcanas of nature; with much excuse we bring these low delights, and poor maniples to your treasure.[21]

* Of the most worthy Sir Edmund Bacon prime baronet, my true and noble friend.

Norwich, May 1 [1658]

Your affectionate Friend, and Servant,
Thomas Browne.

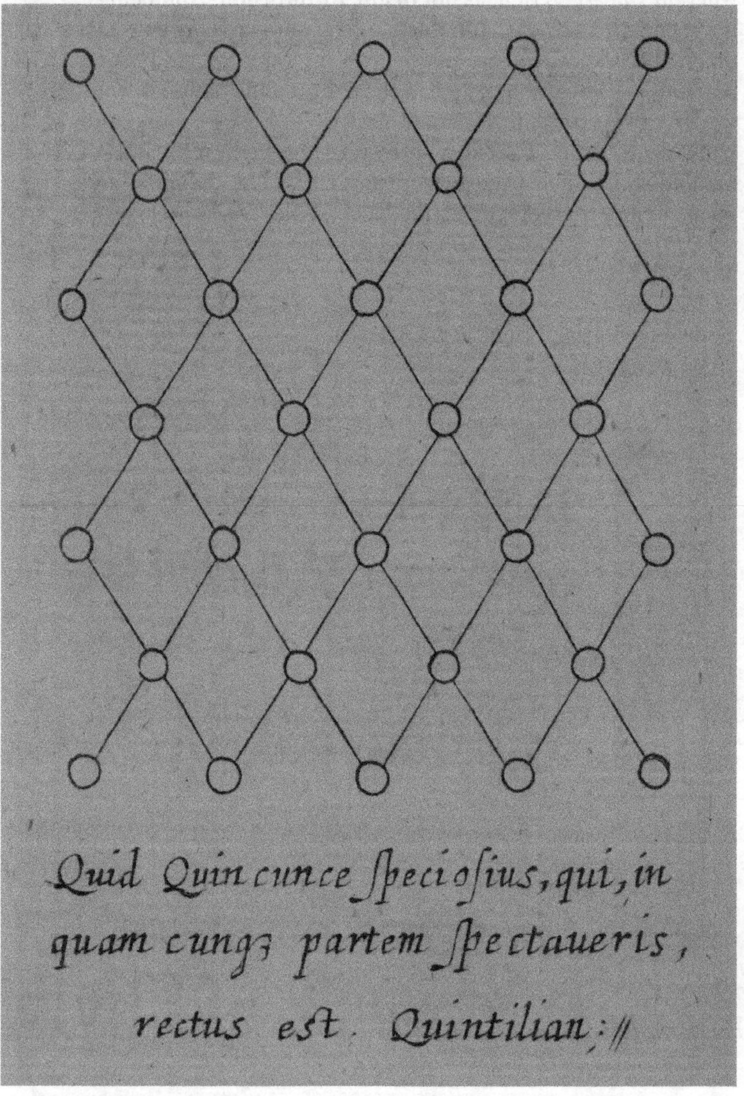
Quid Quincunce speciosius, qui, in
quam cunq; partem spectaueris,
rectus est. Quintilian://

FIG. 10 Quid Quincunce speciosius, qui, in quamcunque partem spectaveris, rectus est?—Quintilian[22]

THE GARDEN OF CYRUS

Or, The Quincunciall, Lozenge, or Net-work Plantations of the Ancients, Artificially, Naturally, Mystically Considered

CHAPTER I

That Vulcan gave arrows unto Apollo and Diana the fourth day after their nativities, according to gentile theology, may passe for no blinde apprehension of the creation of the sunne and moon, in the work of the fourth day; when the diffused light contracted into orbes, and shooting rayes, of those luminaries.[23] Plainer descriptions there are from pagan pens, of the creatures of the fourth day; while the divine philosopher[*24] unhappily omitteth the noblest part of the third;[25] and Ovid (whom many conceive to have borrowed his description from Moses) coldly deserting the remarkable account of the text, in three words,[†26] describeth this work of the third day; the vegetable creation, and first ornamentall scene of nature; the primitive food of animals, and first story of physick, in dietetical conservation.[27]

* Plato in *Timæo.*

† *fronde tegi silvas.*

For though physick may pleade high, from that medicall act of God, in casting so deep a sleep upon our first parent; and chirurgery finde its whole art, in that one passage concerning the rib of Adam, yet is there no rivality with garden contrivance and herbery.[‡28,29] For if Paradise were planted the third day of the creation, as wiser divinity concludeth, the nativity thereof was too early for horoscopie; gardens were before gardeners, and but some hours after the earth.[30]

‡ dissection, in opening the flesh, extraction, in taking out the rib, synthesis in closing up the part again.

Of deeper doubt is its topography, and locall designation, yet being the primitive garden, and without much controversie seated in the east;[§31,32] it is more then probable the first curiosity, and cultivation of plants, most flourished in those quarters. And since the Ark of Noah first toucht upon some mountains of Armenia,[33] the planting art arose again in the east, and found its revolution not far from the place of its nativity, about the plains of those regions. And if Zoroaster were either Cham, Chus, or Mizraim, they were early

§ For some there is from the ambiguity of the word *Mikedem*, whether *ab oriente* or *a principio*.

proficients therein, who left (as Pliny delivereth) a work of agriculture.[34]

However the account of the pensill or hanging gardens of Babylon, if made by Semiramis, the third or fourth from Nimrod, is of no slender antiquity;[35] which being not framed upon ordinary levell of ground, but raised upon pillars, admitting under-passages, we cannot accept as the first Babylonian gardens; but a more eminent progress and advancement in that art, then any that went before it: somewhat answering or hinting the old opinion concerning Paradise it self, with many conceptions elevated, above the plane of the Earth.[36]

Nebuchodnosor whom some will have to be the famous Syrian king of Diodorus, beautifully repaired that city; and so magnificently built his hanging gardens;[*37] that from succeeding writers he had the honour of the first. From whence over-looking Babylon, and all the region about it, he found no circumscription to the eye of his ambition, till over-delighted with the bravery of this Paradise; in his melancholy metamorphosis, he found the folly of that delight, and a proper punishment, in the contrary habitation, in wilde plantations and wanderings of the fields.[38]

* Josephus.

The Persian gallants who destroyed this monarchy, maintained their botanicall bravery. Unto whom we owe the very name of Paradise; wherewith we meet not in Scripture before the time of Solomon, and conceived originally Persian. The word for that disputed garden, expressing in the Hebrew no more then a field enclosed, which from the same root is content to derive a garden and a buckler.

Cyrus the elder brought up in woods and mountains, when time and power enabled, pursued the dictate of his education, and brought the treasures of the field into rule and circumscription.[39] So nobly beautifying the Hanging Gardens of Babylon, that he was also thought to be the authour thereof.

Ahasuerus (whom many conceive to have been *Artaxerxes Longi-manus*) in the countrey and city of flowers,[†40] and in an open garden, entertained his princes and people, while Vashti more modestly treated the ladies within the palace thereof.[41]

† Sushan in Susiana.

But if (as some opinion) King Ahasuerus were Artaxerxes Mnemnon, that found a life and reign answerable unto his great memory, our magnified Cyrus was his second Brother:[‡42] who gave the occasion of that memorable work, and almost miraculous retrait of Xenophon.[43] A person of high spirit and honour, naturally a king, though fatally prevented by the

‡ Plutarch in the life of *Artaxerxes*.

harmlesse chance of post-geniture:[44] not only a lord of gardens, but a manuall planter thereof: disposing his trees like his armies in regular ordination. So that while old Laertas hath found a name in Homer for pruning hedges, and clearing away thorns and bryars;[45] while King Attalus lives for his poysonous plantations of aconites, henbane, hellebore, and plants hardly admitted within the walls of Paradise;[46] while many of the ancients do poorly live in the single names of vegetables; all stories do look upon Cyrus, as the splendid and regular planter.

According whereto Xenophon describeth his gallant plantation at Sardis, thus rendred by Strebæus. *Arbores pari intervallo sitas, rectos ordines, et omnia perpulchrè in Quincuncem directa.*[*47] Which we shall take for granted as being accordingly rendred by the most elegant of the Latines; and by no made term, but in use before by Varro.[†48,49] That is the rows and orders so handsomely disposed; or five trees so set together, that a regular angularity, and through prospect, was left on every side, owing this name not only unto the quintuple number of trees, but the figure declaring that number, which being doubled[50] at the angle, makes up the letter χ, that is the emphaticall decussation, or fundamentall[51] figure.

Xenophon in Oeconomico.

* *καλὰ μὲν τὰ δένδρα εἴη, δι' ἴσου δὲ τὰ πεφυτευμένα, ὀρθοὶ δὲ οἱ στίχοι τῶν δένδρων, εὐδώνια [i.e. εὐγώνια] δὲ πάντα καλῶς*

† Cicero in *Cat. Major.*

Now though in some ancient and modern practice the area or decussated plot, might be a perfect square, answerable to a Tuscan pedestall, and the *quinquernio* or cinque-point of a dye;[52] wherein by diagonall lines the intersection was rectangular;[53] accomodable unto plantations of large growing trees; and we must not deny our selves the advantage of this order; yet shall we chiefly insist upon that of Curtius and Porta,[‡54] in their brief description hereof. Wherein the *decussis* is made within a longilaterall square, with opposite angles, acute and obtuse at the intersection;[55] and so upon progression making a rhombus or lozenge figuration, which seemeth very agreeable unto the originall figure; answerable whereunto we observe the decussated characters in many consulary coynes, and even in those of Constantine and his sons, which pretend their pattern in the sky;[56] the crucigerous ensigne carried this figure, not transversly or rectangularly intersected, but in a decussation, after the form of an Andrean or Burgundian cross, which answereth this description.[57]

‡ Benedict Curtius *de Hortis.* Bapt. porta in *Villa.*

Whereby the way we shall decline the old theme, so traced by antiquity of crosses and crucifixion: whereof some being right, and of one single peece without traversion or transome, do little advantage our subject.[58] Nor shall we take in the mysticall Tau, or the crosse of our blessed Saviour, which having in some descriptions an *empedon* or crossing foot-stay, made not one single transversion.[59] And since the learned Lipsius hath made some doubt even of the crosse of St Andrew, since some martyrologicall histories deliver his death by the generall name of a crosse, and Hippolitus will have him suffer by the sword;[60] we should have enough to make out the received crosse of that martyr. Nor shall we urge the labarum,[61] and famous standard of Constantine, or make further use thereof, then as the first letters in the name of our Saviour Christ, in use among Christians, before the dayes of Constantine, to be observed in sepulchral monuments of martyrs, in the reign of Adrian, and Antoninus;[*62] and to be found in the antiquities of the gentiles, before the advent of Christ, as in the medall of King Ptolomy, signed with the same characters, and might be the beginning of some word or name, which antiquaries have not hit on.[63]

[*] Of Marius, Alexander, *Roma Sotteranea.*

We will not revive the mysterious crosses of Ægypt, with circles on their heads, in the breast of Serapis, and the hands of their geniall spirits, not unlike the characters of Venus, and looked on by ancient Christians, with relation unto Christ.[64] Since however they first began, the Ægyptians thereby expressed the processe and motion of the spirit of the world, and the diffusion thereof upon the celestiall and elementall nature; implyed by a circle and right-lined intersection. A secret in their telesmes and magicall characters among them.[65] Though he that considereth the plain crosse[†66] upon the head of the owl in the Laterane Obelisk, or the crosse[‡] erected upon a picher diffusing streams of water into two basins, with sprinkling branches in them, and all described upon a two-footed altar, as in the Hieroglyphicks of the brasen table of Bembus; will hardly decline all thought of Christian signality in them.[67]

[†] Wherein the lower part is somewhat longer, as defined by Upton *de studio militari*, and *Johannes de Bado Aureo, cum comment. clariss. et doctiss. Bissæi.*

[‡] Casal. *de Ritibus. Bosio nella Trionfante croce.*

We shall not call in the Hebrew Tenupha,[68] or ceremony of their oblations, waved by the priest unto the four quarters of the world, after the form of a cross;[69] as in the peace-offerings. And if it were clearly made out what is remarkably delivered from the traditions of the Rabbins, that as the oyle was powred coronally or circularly upon the head of kings, so the high-priest was anointed decussatively or in the form of a X;[70] though it could not escape a typicall thought of Christ, from mysticall considerators;[71] yet being the conceit is Hebrew, we should rather expect its verification from analogy in that language, then to confine the same unto the unconcerned letters of Greece, or make it out by the characters of Cadmus or Palamedes.[72]

Of this quincunciall ordination the ancients practised much discoursed little; and the moderns have nothing enlarged; which he that more nearly considereth, in the form of its square rhombus, and decussation, with the several commodities, mysteries, parallelismes, and resemblances, both in art and nature, shall easily discern the elegancy of this order.

That this was in some wayes of practice in diverse and distant nations, hints or deliveries there are from no slender antiquity. In the Hanging Gardens of Babylon, from Abydenus, Eusebius, and others, Curtius describeth this rule of decussation.[*73] In the memorable garden of Alcinous anciently conceived an originall phancy, from Paradise, mention there is of well contrived order; for so hath Didymus and Eustachius expounded the emphatical word.[74] Diomedes describing the rurall possessions of his father, gives account in the same language of trees orderly planted.[75] And Ulysses being a boy was promised by his father fourty figge-trees, and fifty rows of vines producing all kinde of grapes.[†76]

* *Decussatio ipsa jucundum ac peramænum conspectum præbuit.* Curt. Hortor.l.6.

† *The Plants being drawn up in ranks, according to* Phavorinus and Philoxenus.

That the eastern inhabitants of India, made use of such order, even in open plantations, is deducible from Theophrastus; who describing the trees whereof they made their garments, plainly delivereth that they were planted κατ᾽ὄρχους, and in such order that at a distance men would mistake them for vineyards.[77] The same seems confirmed in Greece from a singular expression in Aristotle[‡78] concerning the order of vines, delivered by a military term representing the orders of souldiers, which also confirmeth the antiquity of this form yet used in vineall plantations.

‡ συστάδας ἀμπέλων. Polit. 7.

That the same was used in Latine plantations is plainly confirmed from the commending penne of Varro, Quintilian, and handsome description of Virgil.[§79]

§ *Indulge ordinibus, nec secius omnis in unguem Arboribus positis, secto via limite quadret. Georg. 2.*

That the first plantations not long after the floud were disposed after this manner, the generality and antiquity of this order observed in vineyards, and wine plantations, affordeth some conjecture. And since from judicious enquiry, Saturn who divided the world between his three sonnes,[80] who beareth a sickle in his hand, who taught the plantations of vines, the setting, grafting of trees, and the best part of agriculture, is discovered to be Noah,[81] whether this early dispersed husbandry in vineyards, had not its originall in that patriarch, is no such paralogicall doubt.[82]

And if it were clear that this was used by Noah after the floud, I could easily beleeve it was in use before it; not willing to fix to such ancient inventions no higher originall then Noah; nor readily conceiving those aged heroes, whose diet was vegetable, and only, or chiefly consisted in the fruits of the earth, were much deficient in their splendid cultivations;[83] or after the experience of fifteen hundred years, left much for future discovery in botanicall agriculture. Nor fully perswaded that wine was the invention of Noah, that fermented liquors, which often make themselves, so long escaped their luxury or experience; that the first sinne of the new world was no sin of the old.[84] That Cain and Abel were the first that offered sacrifice; or because the Scripture is silent that Adam or Isaac offered none at all.[85]

Whether Abraham brought up in the first planting countrey, observed not some rule hereof, when he planted a grove at Beer-sheba; or whether at least a like ordination were not in the garden of Solomon, probability may contest.[86] Answerably unto the wisedom of that eminent botanologer, and orderly disposer of all his other works. Especially since this was one peece of gallantry, wherein he pursued the specious part of felicity, according to his own description.[87] I made me gardens and orchards, and planted trees in them of all kindes of fruit. I made me pools of water, to water therewith the wood that bringeth forth trees, which was no ordinary plantation, if according to the Targam, or Chaldee Paraphrase, it contained all kindes of plants, and some fetched as far as India; and the extent thereof were from the wall of Jerusalem unto the water of Siloah.[*88]

And if Jordan were but Jaar Eden, that is, the river of Eden, Genesar but Gansar or the prince of gardens; and it could be made out, that the plain of Jordan were watered not comparatively, but causally, and because it was the Paradise of God, as the learned Abramas hinteth, he was not far from the prototype and originall of plantations.[†89] And since even in Paradise it self, the tree of knowledge was placed in the middle of the garden, whatever was the ambient figure, there wanted not a centre and rule of decussation.[90] Whether the groves and sacred plantations of antiquity, were not thus orderly placed, either by *quaternios*, or quintuple ordinations, may favourably

[*] Eccles. 2.

[†] Vetus Testamenti Pharus.

be doubted.[91] For since they were so methodicall in the constitutions of their temples, as to observe the due situation, aspect, manner, form, and order in architectonicall relations, whether they were not as distinct in their groves and plantations about them, in form and species respectively unto their deities, is not without probability of conjecture. And in their groves of the sunne this was a fit number, by multiplication to denote the dayes of the year; and might Hieroglyphically speak as much, as the mysticall statua of Janus[*92] in the language of his fingers. And since they were so criticall in the number of his horses, the strings of his harp, and rayes about his head, denoting the orbes of Heaven, the seasons and moneths of the yeare; witty idolatry would hardly be flat in other appropriations.[93]

[*] Which King Numa set up with his fingers so disposed that they numerically denoted 365 Pliny.

CHAPTER II

Nor was this only a form of practise in plantations, but found imitation from high antiquity, in sundry artificiall contrivances and manuall operations. For to omit the position of squared stones, cuneatim or wedgwise in the walls of Roman and Gothick buildings;[94] and the lithostrata or figured pavements of the ancients, which consisted not all of square stones, but were divided into triquetrous segments, honey-combs, and sexangular figures, according to Vitruvius;[95] the squared stones and bricks in ancient fabricks, were placed after this order. And two above or below conjoyned by a middle stone or Plinthus, observable in the ruines of *Forum Nervæ*, the mausoleum of Augustus, the Pyramid of Cestius, and the sculpture draughts of the larger Pyramids of Ægypt.[96] And therefore in the draughts of eminent fabricks, painters do commonly imitate this order in the lines of their description.

In the laureat draughts of sculpture and picture, the leaves and foliate works are commonly thus contrived, which is but in imitation of the Pulvinaria, and ancient pillow-work, observable in Ionick peeces, about columns, temples and altars.[97] To omit many other analogies, in architectonicall draughts, which art it self is founded upon fives,[†98] as having its subject, and most gracefull peeces divided by this number.

The triumphal oval, and civicall crowns of laurel, oake, and myrtle, when fully made, were pleated after this order. And to omit the crossed crowns of Christian princes; what figure that

[†] Of a structure five parts, *Fundamentum, parietes, Aperturæ, Compartitio, tectum*, Leo. Alberti. Five Columes, *Tuscan, Dorick, Ionick, Corinthian, Compound.* Five different intercolumniations, *Pycnostylos, dystylos, Systylos, Areostylos, Eustylos*. Vitru.

was which Anastatius described upon the head of Leo the third;[99] or who first brought in the arched crown; that of Charles the great, (which seems the first remarkably closed crown,) was framed after this manner;[*100,101] with an intersection in the middle from the main crossing barres, and the interspaces, unto the frontal circle, continued by handsome network-plates, much after this order. Whereon we shall not insist, because from greater antiquity, and practice of consecration, we meet with the radiated, and starry crown, upon the head of Augustus, and many succeeding emperors. Since the Armenians and Parthians had a peculiar royall capp; and the Grecians from Alexander another kinde of diadem. And even diadems themselves were but fasciations, and handsome ligatures, about the heads of princes; nor wholly omitted in the mitrall crown, which common picture seems to set too upright and forward upon the head of Aaron:[102] worne sometimes singly, or doubly by princes, according to their kingdomes; and no more to be expected from two crowns at once, upon the head of Ptolomy.[†103] And so easily made out when historians tell us, some bound up wounds, some hanged themselves with diadems.[104]

* *Uti constat ex pergamena apud Chifflet.*

† Macc. 1.11.

The beds of the antients were corded somewhat after this fashion: that is not directly, as ours at present, but obliquely, from side to side, and after the manner of network; whereby they strengthened the spondæ or bedsides, and spent less cord in the work: as is demonstrated by Blancanus.[‡105,106]

‡ Arist. *Mechan. Quæs.*

And as they lay in crossed beds, so they sat upon seeming crosselegg'd seats: in which form the noblest thereof were framed: observable in the triumphall seats, the *sella curulis*, or *Ædyle Chayres*, in the coyns of Cestius, Sylla, and Julius.[107] That they sat also crosse legg'd many noble draughts declare; and in this figure the sitting gods and goddesses are drawn in medalls and medallions.[§] And beside this kinde of work in retiarie and hanging textures, in embroderies, and eminent needle-works; the like is obvious unto every eye in glass-windows.[108] Nor only in glassie contrivances, but also in lattice and stone-work, conceived in the temple of Solomon; wherein the windows are termed *fenestræ reticulatæ*,[109] or lights framed like nets. And agreeable unto the Greek expression concerning Christ in the Canticles[**], looking through the nets, which ours hath rendered, he looketh forth at the windows, shewing himselfe through the lattesse; that is, partly seen and unseen, according to the visible and invisible side of his nature.[110] To

§ the larger sort of medals.

** Cant. 2.

omit the noble reticulate work, in the chapiters[111] of the pillars of Solomon, with Lillies, and Pomegranats upon a network ground; and the *Craticula* or grate through which the ashes fell in the altar of burnt offerings.[112]

That the networks and nets of antiquity were little different in the form from ours at present, is confirmable from the nets in the hands of the retiarie gladiators, the proper combatants with the secutores.[113] To omit the *conopeion* or gnatnet, of the Ægyptians, the inventors of that artifice: the rushey labyrinths of Theocritus; the nosegaynets, which hung from the head under the nostrils of princes; and that uneasie metaphor of *Reticulum Jecoris*, which some expound the lobe, we the caule above the liver.[114] As for the famous network of Vulcan, which inclosed Mars and Venus, and caused that inextinguishable laugh in Heaven;[115] since the gods themselves could not discern it, we shall not prie into it; although why Vulcan bound them, Neptune loosed them, and Apollo should first discover them, might afford no vulgar mythologie. Heralds* have not omitted this order or imitation thereof, while they symbollically adorn their scuchions with mascles fusils and saltyrs, and while they disposed the figures of ermins, and vaired coats in this quincuncial method.[116]

* [*De armis Scaccatis masculatis, invectis, fuselatis, vide Spelm., Aspilog.*; & *Upton cum erudit. Byssæo.*]

The same is not forgot by lapidaries while they cut their gemms pyramidally, or by æquicrural triangles.[117] Perspective picturers,[118] in their base, horison, and lines of distances, cannot escape these rhomboidall decussations. Sculptors in their strongest shadows, after this order do draw their double haches.[119] And the very Americans do naturally fall upon it, in their neat and curious textures, which is also observed in the elegant artifices of Europe. But this is no law unto the woof of the neat *retiarie* spider, which seems to weave without transversion, and by the union of right lines to make out a continued surface, which is beyond the common art of textury, and may still nettle Minerva the goddesse of that mystery.*[120,121] And he that shall hatch the little seeds, either found in small webs, or white round egges, carried under the bellies of some spiders, and behold how at their first production in boxes, they will presently fill the same with their webbs, may observe the early, and untaught finger of nature, and how they are natively provided with a stock, sufficient for such texture.

* As in the contention between Minerva and Arachne.

The rurall charm against dodder, tetter,[122] and strangling weeds, was contrived after this order, while they placed a chalked tile at the four corners, and one in the middle of their fields, which though ridiculous in the intention, was rationall in the contrivance, and a good way to diffuse the magick through all parts of the area.

Somewhat after this manner they ordered the little stones in the old game of *pentalithismus*, or casting up five stones to catch them on the back of their hand.[123] And with some resemblance hereof, the *proci* or prodigall paramours disposed their men, when they played at *Penelope*.[*124,125] For being themselves an hundred and eight, they set fifty four stones on either side, and one in the middle, which they called Penelope, which he that hit was master of the game.

* In Eustachius.

In chesse-boards and tables we yet finde pyramids and squares, I wish we had their true and ancient description, farre different from ours, or the *chet mat* of the Persians, and might continue some elegant remarkables, as being an invention as high as Hermes the secretary of Osyris, figuring the whole world, the motion of the planets, with eclipses of sunne and moon.[†126,127]

† Plato.

Physicians are not without the use of this decussation in severall operations, in ligatures and union of dissolved continuities. Mechanicks make use hereof in forcipall organs, and instruments of incision;[128] wherein who can but magnifie the power of decussation, inservient to contrary ends, solution and consolidation, union, and division,[129] illustrable from Aristotle in the old *nucifragium* or nutcracker, and the instruments of evulsion, compression or incision;[130] which consisting of two *vectes* or armes, converted towards each other, the innitency and stresse being made upon the *hypomochlion* or fulciment in the decussation, the greater compression is made by the union of two impulsors.[131]

The Roman batalia[‡] was ordered after this manner, whereof as sufficiently known Virgil hath left but an hint, and obscure intimation.[132] For thus were the maniples and cohorts of the *Hastati*, *Principes* and *Triarii* placed in their bodies, wherein consisted the strength of the Roman battle.[133] By this ordination they readily fell into each other; the *Hastati* being pressed, handsomely retired into the intervalls of the *Principes*, these into that of the *Triarii*, which making as it were a new body, might joyntly renew the battle, wherein consisted the secret of their successes. And therefore it was remarkably singular in the battle of Africa, that Scipio fearing a rout from the elephants of the enemy, left not the *Principes* in their alternate distances, whereby the elephants passing the

‡ In the disposure of the Legions in the Wars of the Republike, before the division of the Legion into ten Cohorts by the Emperours. Salmas. in his Epistle *à Mounsieur de Peyresc. et de Re militari Romanorum.*

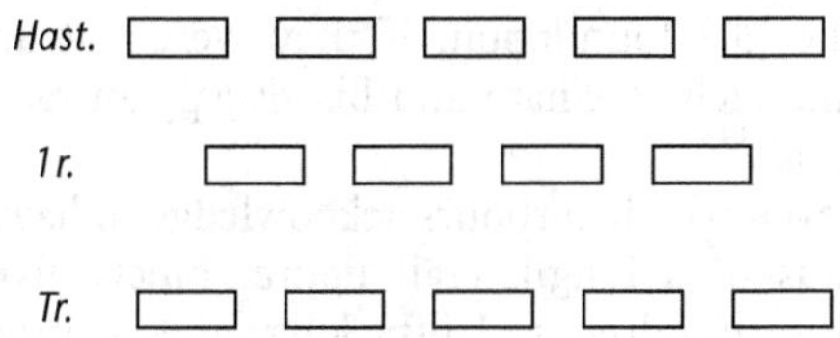

Hast. ▭ ▭ ▭ ▭ ▭

1r. ▭ ▭ ▭ ▭

Tr. ▭ ▭ ▭ ▭ ▭

FIG. 10A

vacuities of the *Hastati*, might have run upon them, but drew his battle into right order, and leaving the passages bare, defeated the mischief intended by the elephants.*[134] Out of this figure were made too remarkable forms of battle, the *cuneus* and forceps, or the sheare and wedge battles, each made of half a rhombus, and but differenced by position. The wedge invented to break or work into a body, the forceps to environ and defeat the power thereof, composed out of the selectest souldiery and disposed into the form of an V, wherein receiving the wedge, it inclosed it on both sides. After this form the famous† Narses[135] ordered his battle against the Franks, and by this figure the Almans were enclosed, and cut in peeces.[136]

The rhombus or lozenge figure so visible in this order, was also a remarkable form of battle in the Grecian cavalry,‡[137] observed by the Thessalians, and Philip king of Macedon, and frequently by the Parthians, as being most ready to turn every way, and best to be commanded, as having its ductors, or commanders at each angle.[138]

The Macedonian Phalanx (a long time thought invincible) consisted of a long square.[139] For though they might be sixteen in rank and file, yet when they shut close, so that the sixt pike advanced before the first ranck,[140] though the number might be square, the figure was oblong, answerable unto the quincunciall quadrate of Curtius.[141] According to this square Thucydides delivers, the Athenians disposed their battle against the Lacedemonians brickwise,[142] and by the same word the learned Guellius expoundeth the quadrate of Virgil,§ after the form of a brick or tile.[143]

And as the first station and position of trees, so was the first habitation of men, not in round cities, as of later foundation; for the form of Babylon the first city was square, and so shall also be the last, according to the description of the holy city in the Apocalpys.[144] The famous pillars of Seth before the floud,

* Polybius; Appianus.

† Agathius, Ammianus.

‡ Aelian. *Tact.*

§ *Secto via limite quadret. Comment. in Virgil.*

had also the like foundation, if they were but antidiluvian obelisks, and such as Cham and his Ægypyian race, imitated after the flood.[145]

But Nineveh which authours acknowledge to have exceeded Babylon, was of a longilaterall figure, ninety five furlongs broad, and an hundred and fifty long, and so making about sixty miles in circuit, which is the measure of three dayes journey, according unto military marches, or castrensiall mansions.[*146,147] So that if Jonas entred at the narrower side, he found enough for one dayes walk to attain the heart of the city, to make his proclamation. And if we imagine a city extending from Ware to London, the expression will be moderate of six score thousand infants, although we allow vacuities, fields, and intervals of habitation as there needs must be when the monument of Ninus took up no lesse then ten furlongs.[148]

* Diod. Sic.

And, though none of the seven wonders, yet a noble peece of antiquity, and made by a copy exceeding all the rest, had its principall parts disposed after this manner, that is, the Labyrinth of Crete, built upon a long quadrate, containing five large squares, communicating by right inflections, terminating in the centre of the middle square, and lodging of the Minotaur, if we conform unto the description of the elegant medall thereof in Agostino.[†] And though in many accounts we reckon grosly by the square, yet is that very often to be accepted as a long sided quadrate, which was the figure of the Ark of the Covenant, the table of the shew-bread, and the stone wherein the names of the twelve Tribes were engraved,[149] that is, three in a row, naturally making a longilaterall figure, the perfect quadrate being made by nine.

† Antonio Agostino *delle medaglie.*

What figure the stones themselves maintained, tradition and Scripture are silent, yet lapidaries in precious stones affect a table or long square, and in such proportion, that the two laterall, and also the three inferiour tables are equall unto the superiour, and the angles of the laterall tables, contain and constitute the *hypothenusæ*, or broader sides subtending.

That the tables of the law were of this figure, general imitation and tradition hath confirmed; yet are we unwilling to load the shoulders of Moses with such massie stones, as some pictures lay upon them, since 'tis plainly delivered that he came down with them in his hand;[150] since the word strictly taken implies no such massie hewing, but cutting, and fashioning of them into shape and surface; since some will have them emeralds, and if they were made of the materials of Mount Sina, not improbable that they were marble:[151] since the words were not many, the letters short of seven hundred,[152] and the tables written on both sides required no such capacity.

The beds of the ancients were different from ours at present, which are almost square, being framed oblong, and about a double unto their breadth; not much unlike the area, or bed of this quincuncial quadrate. The single beds of Greece were six foot, and a little more in length, three in breadth; the giant-like bed of Og, which had four cubits of bredth, nine and a half in length, varied not much from this proportion.[*153] The funeral bed of King Cheops, in the greater Pyramid, which holds seven in length, and four foot in bredth, had no great difformity from this measure;[154] and whatsoever were the bredth, the length could hardly be lesse, of the tyrannical bed of Procrustes, since in a shorter measure he had not been fitted with persons for his cruelty of extension.[155] But the old sepulchral bed, or Amazonian tomb in the market-place of Megara, was in the form of a lozenge; readily made out by the composure of the body.[†156] For the arms not lying fasciated or wrapt up after the Grecian manner, but in a middle distention, the including lines will strictly make out that figure.

* Aristot. *Mechan.*

† Plut. in *vit. Thes.*

CHAPTER III

Now although this elegant ordination of vegetables, hath found coincidence or imitation in sundry works of art, yet is it not also destitute of naturall examples, and though overlooked by all, was elegantly observable, in severall works of nature.[157]

Could we satisfie ourselves in the position of the lights above, or discover the wisedom of that order so invariably maintained in the fixed stars of Heaven; could we have any light, why the stellary part of the first masse, separated into this order, that the girdle of Orion should ever maintain its line, and the two starres in Charles's Wain never leave pointing at the Pole-starre, we might abate the Pythagoricall musick of the spheres, the sevenfold pipe of Pan; and the strange cryptography of Gaffarell in his Starrie Booke of Heaven.[158]

But not to look so high as Heaven or the single quincunx of the Hyades upon the head[159] of Taurus, the triangle, and remarkable Crusero about the foot of the Centaur;[160] observable rudiments there are here of in subterraneous concretions, and bodies in the earth; in the *gypsum* or *talcum rhomboides*, in the *favaginites* or honey-comb-stone, in the *asteria* and *astroites*, and in the crucigerous stone of S. Iago of Gallicia.[161]

The same is observably effected in the julus, catkins, or pendulous excrescencies of severall trees, of wallnuts, alders, and hazels,[162] which hanging all the winter, and maintaining their net-worke close, by the expansion thereof are the early foretellers of the spring, discoverable also in long pepper, and elegantly in the julus of *calamus aromaticus*, so plentifully growing with us in the first palmes of willowes, and in the flowers of sycamore, petasites, asphodelus, and blattaria, before explication.[163] After such order stand the flowery branches in our best spread *verbascum*, and the seeds about the spicous head or torch of *tapsas barbatus*, in as fair a regularity as the circular and wreathed order will admit, which advanceth one side of the square, and makes the same rhomboidall.[164]

In the squamous heads of scabious, knapweed, and the elegant *jacea pinea*, and in the scaly composure of the oak-rose, which some years most aboundeth.[*165,166] After this order hath nature planted the leaves in the head of the common and prickled artichoak; wherein the black and shining flies do shelter themselves, when they retire from the purple flower about it; the same is also found in the pricks, sockets, and impressions of the seeds, in the pulp or bottome thereof; wherein do elegantly stick the fathers of their mother.[†167] To omit the quincunciall specks on the top of the miscle-berry, especially that which grows upon the *tilia* or lime-tree. And the remarkable disposure of those yellow fringes about the purple pestill of Aaron, and elegant clusters of dragons, so peculiarly secured by nature, with an umbrella or skreening leaf about them.

[*] *Capitula squammata quercuum, Bauhini*, whereof though he saith *perraro reperiuntur bis tantum invenimus*, yet we find them commonly with us and in great numbers.

[†] *Antho. Græc. inter Epigrammata.*

The spongy leaves of some sea-wracks, fucus, oaks, in their severall kindes, found about the shoar,[‡] with ejectments of the sea, are over-wrought with net-work elegantly containing this order, which plainly declareth the naturality of this texture;[168] and how the needle of nature delighteth to work, even in low and doubtful vegetations.

[‡] *Especially the porus cervinus Imperari, Sporosa, Bauhini.*

The *arbustetum* or thicket on the head of the teasel,[169] may be observed in this order: and he that considereth that fabrick so regularly palisadoed, and stemm'd with flowers of the royall colour;[170] in the house of the solitary maggot[§171], may finde the seraglio of Solomon, and contemplating the calicular shafts, and uncous disposure of their extremities, so accommodable

[§] [There being a single Maggot found almost in every head].

unto the office of abstersion, not condemne as wholly improbable the conceit of those who accept it, for the herbe borith.*[172,173] Where by the way, we could with much inquiry never discover any transfiguration, in this abstemious insect, although we have kept them long in their proper houses, and boxes. Where some wrapt up in their webbs, have lived upon their own bowels, from September unto July.

* Jeremiah 2.22.

In such a grove doe walke the little creepers about the head of the burre. And such an order is observed in the aculeous prickly plantation, upon the heads of several common thistles, remarkably in the notable palisadoes about the flower of the milk-thistle; and he that inquireth into the little bottome of the globe-thistle, may finde that gallant bush arise from a scalpe of like disposure.[174]

The white umbrella or medicall bush of elder, is an epitome of this order: arising from five main stemms quincuncially disposed, and tollerably maintained in their subdivisions. To omit the lower observations in the seminal spike of mercurie, weld, and plantane.[175]

Thus hath nature ranged the flowers of santfoyne, and French honey suckle; and somewhat after this manner hath ordered the bush in Jupiters beard, or houseleek;[176] which old superstition set on the tops of houses, as a defensative against lightening, and thunder. The like in fenny seagreen or the water souldier;†[177] which, though a militarie name from Greece, makes out the Roman order.

† Stratiotes.

A like ordination there is in the favaginous sockets, and lozenge seeds of the noble flower of the sunne.[178] Wherein in lozenge figured boxes nature shuts up the seeds, and balsame which is about them.

But the firre and pinetree from their fruits doe naturally dictate this position. The rhomboidall protuberances in pineapples maintaining this quincuncial order unto each other, and each rhombus in it selfe. Thus are also disposed the triangular foliations, in the conicall fruit of the firre tree, orderly shadowing and protecting the winged seeds below them.

The like so often occurreth to the curiosity of observers, especially in spicated seeds and flowers, that we shall not need to take in the single quincunx of Fuchsius in the grouth of the masle fearn, the seedie disposure of Gramen Ischemon, and the trunk or neat reticulate work in the codde of the sachell palme.[179]

For even in very many round stalk plants, the leaves are set after a quintuple ordination, the first leaf answering the fifth, in laterall disposition. Wherein the leaves successively rounding the stalke, in foure at the furthest the compass is absolved, and the fifth leafe or sprout, returns to the position of the other fift before it;[180] as in accounting upward is often observable in furze, pellitorye, ragweed, the sproutes of oaks, and thorns upon pollards, and very remarkably in the regular disposure of the rugged excrescencies in the yearly shoots of the pine.[181]

But in square stalked plants, the leaves stand respectively unto each other, either in crosse or decussation to those above or below them, arising at crosse positions; whereby they shadow not each other, and better resist the force of winds, which in a parallel situation, and upon square stalkes would more forcibly bear upon them.

And to omit, how leaves and sprouts, which compasse not the stalk, are often set in a rhomboides, and making long, and short diagonals, doe stand like the leggs of quadrupeds when they goe: nor to urge the thwart enclosure and furdling of flowers, and blossomes, before explication, as in the multiplyed leaves of pionie;[182] and the chiasmus in five leaved flowers, while one lies wrapt about the staminous beards, the other foure obliquely shutting and closing upon each other;[183] and how even flowers which consist of foure leaves, stand not ordinarily in three and one, but two and two crossewise unto the stylus;[184] even the autumnal budds, which awaite the returne of the sun, doe after the winter solstice multiply their calicular leaves, making little rhombuses, and network figures, as in the sycamore and lilac.[185]

The like is discoverable in the original production of plants, which first putting forth two leaves, those which succeed, bear not over each other, but shoot obliquely or crossewise, untill the stalke appeareth; which sendeth not forth its first leaves without all order unto them; and he that from hence can discover in what position the two first leaves did arise, is no ordinary observator.[186]

Where by the way, he that observeth the rudimental spring of seeds shall finde strict rule, although not after this order.[187] How little is required unto effectual generation, and in what diminutives the plastick principle lodgeth, is exemplified in seeds, wherein the greater mass affords so little comproduction.[188] In beanes the leaf and root sprout from the germen, the main sides split, and lye by, and in some pull'd up near the time of blooming we have found the pulpous sides intire or little wasted.[189] In acorns the nebb dilating splitteth the two sides, which sometimes lye whole, when the oak is sprouted two handfuls. In lupins these pulpy sides do sometimes arise with the stalk in a resemblance of two fat leaves. Wheat and rye will grow up, if after they have shot some tender roots, the adhering pulp be taken from them. Beanes will prosper though a part be cut away, and so much set as sufficeth to contain and keep the germen close. From this superfluous pulp in unkindely, and wet years, may arise that multiplicity of little insects, which infest the roots and sprouts of tender graines and pulses.

In the little nebbe or fructifying principle, the motion is regular, and not transvertible, as to make that ever the leaf, which nature intendeth the root; observable from their conversion, until they attain the right position, if seeds be set inversedly.[190]

In vain we expect the production of plants from different parts of the seed, from the same *corculum* or little original proceed both germinations;[191] and in the power of this slender particle lye many roots and sprouts,[192] that though the same be pull'd away, the generative particle will renew them again, and proceed to a perfect plant; and malt may be observed to grow, though the cummes be fallen from it.[193]

The seminall nebbe hath a defined and single place, and not extended unto both extremes. And therefore many too vulgarly conceive that barley and oats grow at both ends; for they arise from one *punctilio* or generative nebbe, and the speare sliding under the husk, first appeareth nigh the toppe.[194] But in wheat and rye being bare the sprouts are seen together. If barley unhulled would grow, both would appear at once.[195] But in this and oat-meal the nebbe is broken away, which makes them the milder food, and lesse apt to raise fermentation in decoctions.[196]

Men taking notice of what is outwardly visible, conceive a sensible priority in the root.[197] But as they begin from one part, so they seem to start and set out upon one signall of nature. In beans yet soft, in pease while they adhere unto the cod, the rudimentall leafe and root are discoverable.[198] In the seeds of rocket and mustard, sprouting in glasses of water, when the one is manifest the other is also perceptible. In muddy waters apt to breed duckweed, and periwinkles, if the first and rudimentall stroaks of duckweed be observed, the leaves and root anticipate not each other.[199] But in the date-stone the first sprout is neither root nor leaf distinctly, but both together; for the germination being to passe through the narrow navell and hole about the midst of the stone, the generative germ is faine to enlengthen it self, and shooting out about an inch, at that distance divideth into the ascending and descending portion.

And though it be generally thought that seeds will root at that end, where they adhere to their originals, and observable it is that the nebbe sets most often next the stalk, as in grains, pulses, and most small seeds, yet is it hardly made out in many greater plants.[200] For in acornes, almonds, pistachios, wall-nuts, and accuminated shells, the germ puts forth at the remotest part of the pulp.[201] And therefore to set seeds in that posture, wherein the leaf and roots may shoot right without contortion, or forced circumvolution, which might render them strongly rooted, and straighter, were a criticisme in agriculture.[202] And nature seems to have made some provision hereof in many from their figure, that as they fall from the tree they may lye in positions agreeable to such advantages.

Beside the open and visible testicles of plants, the seminall powers[203] lie in great part invisible, while the sun findes polypody in stone-wals, the little stinging nettle, and night-shade in barren sandy high-wayes, scurvy-grasse in Greene-land, and unknown plants in earth brought from remote countries.[204] Beside the known longevity of some trees, what is the most lasting herb, or seed, seems not easily determinable. Mandrakes upon known account have lived near an hundred yeares. Seeds found in wilde-fowls gizards have sprouted in the earth. The seeds of marjorane and *stramonium* carelesly kept, have grown after seven years.[205] Even in garden-plots long fallow, and digged up, the seeds of *blattaria* and yellow henbane, after twelve years burial have produced themselves again.[206]

That bodies are first spirits Paracelsus could affirm, which in the maturation of seeds and fruits, seems obscurely implied by Aristotle,[*207,208] when he delivereth, that the spirituous parts are converted into water, and the water into earth, and attested by observation in the maturative progresse of seeds, wherein at first may be discerned a flatuous distension of the husk, afterwards a thin liquor, which longer time digesteth into a pulp or kernell observable in almonds and large nuts.[209] And some way answered in the progressionall perfection of animall semination, in its spermaticall maturation, from crude

* *In met. cum* Cabeo.

pubescency unto perfection. And even that seeds themselves in their rudimentall discoveries, appear in foliaceous surcles, or sprouts within their coverings, in a diaphonous gellie, before deeper incrassation, is also visibly verified in cherries, acorns, plums.[210]

From seminall considerations, either in reference unto one another,[211] or distinction from animall production, the holy Scripture describeth the vegetable creation;[212] and while it divideth plants but into herb and tree, though it seemeth to make but an accidental division, from magnitude,[213] it tacitely containeth the naturall distinction of vegetables, observed by herbarists, and comprehending the four kinds.[214] For since the most naturall distinction is made from the production of leaf or stalk, and plants after the two first seminall leaves, do either proceed to send forth more leaves, or a stalk, and the folious and stalky emission distinguisheth herbs and trees, in a large acception, it compriseth all Vegetables, for the frutex and suffrutex are under the progression of trees,[215] and stand authentically differenced, but from the accidents of the stalk.[216]

The Æquivocall production of things under undiscerned principles, makes a large part of generation, though they seem to hold a wide univocacy in their set and certain originals,[217] while almost every plant breeds its peculiar insect, most a butterfly, moth or fly, wherein the oak seems to contain the largest seminality, while the julus, oak, apple, dill, woolly tuft, foraminous roundles upon the leaf, and grapes under ground make a fly with some difference.[218] The great variety of flyes lyes in the variety of their originals, in the seeds of caterpillars or cankers there lyeth not only a butterfly or moth, but if they be sterill or untimely cast, their production is often a fly, which we have also observed from corrupted and mouldred egges, both of hens and fishes; to omit the generation of bees out of the bodies of dead heifers, or what is stranger yet well attested, the production of eeles in the backs of living cods and perches.[*219]

The exiguity and smallnesse of some seeds extending to large productions is one of the magnalities of nature, somewhat illustrating the work of the creation, and vast production from nothing.[220] The true seeds of cypresse and rampions are indistinguishable by old eyes. Of the seeds of tobacco a thousand make not one grain;[†221] the disputed seeds of harts tongue, and maidenhair, require a greater number.[222] From such

[*] Schoneveldus *de Pisc.*

[†] *Doctissim. Laurenburg hort.*

undiscernable seminalities arise spontaneous productions. He that would discern the rudimentall stroak of a plant, may behold it in the originall of duckweed, at the bignesse of a pins point, from convenient water in glasses, wherein a watchfull eye may also discover the puncticular originals of periwincles and gnats.[223]

That seeds of some plants are lesse then any animals, seems of no clear decision; that the biggest of vegetables exceedeth the biggest of animals, in full bulk, and all dimensions, admits exception in the whale, which in length and above ground measure, will also contend with tall oakes. That the richest odour of plants, surpasseth that of animals may seem of some doubt, since animall-musk, seems to excell the vegetable, and we finde so noble a scent in the tulip-fly, and goat-beetle.*

* The long and tender *capricornus* rarely found, we could never meet with but two.

Now whether seminall nebbes hold any sure proportion unto seminall enclosures, why the form of the germe doth not answer the figure of the enclosing pulp, why the nebbe is seated upon the solid, and not the channeld side of the seed as in grains, why since we often meet with two yolks in one shell, and sometimes one egge within another, we do not oftener meet with two nebbes in one distinct seed: why since the egges of a hen laid at one course, do commonly out-weigh the bird, and some moths coming out of their cases, without assistance of food, will lay so many egges as to outweigh their bodies, trees rarely bear their fruit, in that gravity or proportion: whether in the germination of seeds according to Hippocrates, the lighter part ascendeth, and maketh the sprout, the heaviest tending downward frameth the root; since we observe that the first shoot of seeds in water, will sink or bow down at the upper and leafing end: whether it be not more rational Epicurisme to contrive whole dishes out of the nebbes and spirited particles of plants, then from the gallatures and treddles of egges;[224] since that part is found to hold no seminal share in oval generation, are quæries which might enlarge but must conclude this digression.[225]

And though not in this order, yet how nature delighteth in this number, and what consent and coordination there is in the leaves and parts of flowers, it cannot escape our observation in no small number of plants. For the calicular or supporting and closing leaves, do answer the number of the flowers, especially in such as exceed not the number of swallows egges†[226]; as in violets, stichwort, blossomes, and flowers of one leaf have often

† [Which exceed not five].

five divisions, answered by a like number of calicular leaves; as *gentianella*, *convolvulus*, bell-flowers.[227] In many the flowers, blades, or staminous shootes and leaves are all equally five, as in cockle, mullein and *blattaria*; wherein the flowers before explication are pentagonally wrapped up, with some resemblance of the *blatta* or moth from whence it hath its name:[228] but the contrivance of nature is singular in the opening and shutting of bindeweeds, performed by five inflexures, distinguishable by pyramidicall figures, and also different colours.[229]

The rose at first is thought to have been of five leaves, as it yet groweth wilde among us; but in the most luxuriant, the calicular leaves do still maintain that number. But nothing is more admired then the five brethren of the rose, and the strange disposure of the appendices or beards, in the calicular leaves thereof, which in despair of resolution is tolerably salved from this contrivance, best ordered and suited for the free closure of them before explication.[230] For those two which are smooth, and of no beard are contrived to lye undermost, as without prominent parts, and fit to be smoothly covered; the other two which are beset with beards on either side, stand outward and uncovered, but the fifth or half-bearded leaf is covered on the bare side but on the open side stands free, and bearded like the other.

Besides a large number of leaves have five divisions, and may be circumscribed by a pentagon or figure of five angles, made by right lines from the extremity of their leaves, as in maple, vine, figge-tree: but five-leaved flowers are commonly disposed circularly about the stylus; according to the higher geometry of nature, dividing a circle by five *radii*, which concurre not to make diameters, as in quadrilaterall and sexangular intersections.

Now the number of five is remarkable in every circle, not only as the first sphærical number, but the measure of sphærical motion.[231] For sphærical bodies move by fives, and every globular figure placed upon a plane, in direct volutation, returns to the first point of contaction in the fifth touch, accounting by the axes of the diameters or cardinall points of the four quarters thereof.[232] And before it arriveth unto the same point again, it maketh five circles equall unto it self, in each progresse from those quarters, absolving an equall circle.

By the same number doth nature divide the circle of the sea-starre, and in that order and number disposeth those elegant semi-circles, or dentall sockets and egges in the sea hedge-hogge.[233] And no mean observations hereof there is in the mathematicks of the neatest retiary spider, which concluding in fourty four circles, from five semidiameters beginneth that elegant texture.[234]

And after this manner doth lay the foundation of the circular branches of the oak, which being five-cornered, in the tender annual sprouts, and manifesting upon incision the signature of a starre, is after made circular, and swel'd into a round body: which practice of nature is become a point of art, and makes two problemes in Euclide*[235] But the bramble[236] which sends forth shoots and prickles from its angles, maintains its pentagonall figure, and the unobserved signature of a handsome porch within it.[237] To omit the five small buttons dividing the circle of the ivy-berry, and the five characters in the winter stalk of the walnut, with many other observables, which cannot escape the eyes of signal discerners;[238] such as know where to finde Ajax his name in Delphinium,[239] or Aarons mitre in Henbane.[240]

* *Elem.* 4.

Quincuncial forms and ordinations, are also observable in animal figurations. For to omit the hioides or throat-bone of animals, the *furcula* or merry-thought in birds, which supporteth the *scapulæ*, affording a passage for the windepipe and the gullet, the wings of flyes, and disposure of their legges in their first formation from maggots, and the position of their horns, wings and legges, in their Aurelian cases and swadling clouts:[241] the back of the *cimex arboreus*, found often upon trees and lesser plants, doth elegantly discover the *Burgundian* decussation;[242] and the like is observable in the belly of the *notonecton*, or water-beetle, which swimmeth on its back, and the handsome rhombusses of the sea-poult, or weazell,[243] on either side the spine.[244]

The sexangular cels in the honeycombs of bees, are disposed after this order, much there is not of wonder in the confused houses of pismires, though much in their busie life and actions, more in the edificial palaces of bees and monarchical spirits;[245] who make their combs six-corner'd, declining a circle, whereof many stand not close together, and compleatly fill the area of the place; but rather affecting a six-sided figure, whereby every cell affords a common side unto six more, and also a fit receptacle for the bee it self, which gathering into a cylindrical figure, aptly enters its sexangular house, more nearly approaching a circular figure, then either doth the square or triangle. And the combes themselves so regularly contrived, that their mutual intersections make three lozenges at the bottome of every cell; which severally regarded make three rows of neat rhomboidall figures, connected at the angles, and so continue three several chains throughout the whole comb.

As for the *favago* found commonly on the Sea shoar, though named from an honey-comb, it but rudely makes out the resemblance, and better agrees with the round cels of humble bees.[246] He that would exactly discern the shop of a bees mouth, need observing eyes, and good augmenting glasses;[247] wherein is discoverable one of the neatest peeces in nature, and must have a more piercing eye then mine; who findes out the shape of buls heads, in the guts of drones pressed out behinde, according to the experiment of Gomesius[*248,249] wherein notwithstanding there seemeth somewhat which might incline a pliant fancy to credulity of similitude.

* Gom. *de Sale*.

A resemblance hereof there is in the orderly and rarely disposed cels, made by flyes and insects, which we have often found fastened about small sprigs, and in those cottonary and woolly pillows, which sometimes we meet with fastened unto leaves, there is included an elegant net-work texture, out of which come many small flies.[250] And some resemblance there is of this order in the egges of some butterflies and moths, as they stick upon leaves, and other substances; which being dropped from behinde, nor directed by the eye, doth neatly declare how nature geometrizeth, and observeth order in all things.[251]

A like correspondency in figure is found in the skins and outward teguments of animals, whereof a regardable part are beautiful by this texture.[252] As the backs of several snakes and serpents, elegantly remarkable in the aspis, and the dart-snake, in the chiasmus and larger decussations upon the back of the rattlesnake, and in the close and finer texture of the *mater formicarum*, or snake that delights in ant-hils;[253] whereby upon approach of outward injuries, they can raise a thicker phalanx on their backs, and handsomely contrive themselves into all kindes of flexures: whereas their bellies are commonly covered with smooth semi-circular divisions, as best accommodable unto their quick and gliding motion.

This way is followed by nature in the peculiar and remarkable tayl of the bever, wherein the scaly particles are disposed, somewhat after this order, which is the plainest resolution of the wonder of Bellonius, while he saith, with incredible artifice hath nature framed the tayl or oar of the bever:[254] where by the way we cannot but wish a model of their houses, so much extolled by some describers: wherein since they are so bold as to venture upon three stages, we might examine their artifice in the contignations, the rule and order in the compartitions; or whether that magnified structure be any more then a rude rectangular pyle or meer hovell-building.[255]

Thus works the hand of nature in the feathery plantation* about birds. Observable in the skins of the breast, legs and pinions of turkies, geese, and ducks, and the oars or finny feet of water-fowl: and such a naturall net is the scaly covering of fishes, of mullets, carps, tenches, etc. even in such as are excoriable and consist of smaller scales, as bretts, soals, and flounders.[256] The like reticulate grain is observable in some *Russia* leather.[257] To omit the ruder figures of the ostracion, the triangular or cunny fish, or the pricks of the sea-porcupine.[258]

* Elegantly conspicuous on the insides of the stripped skins of dive-fowl, of the cormorant, goshonder, weasell, loon, etc.

The same is also observable in some parts of the skin of man, in habits of neat textures, and therefore not unaptly compared unto a net: we shall not affirm that from such grounds, the Ægyptian embalmers imitated this texture. Yet in their linnen folds the same is still observable among their neatest mummies, in the figures of Isis and Osyris, and the tutelary spirits in the Bembine table.[259] Nor is it to be over-looked how Orus, the Hieroglyphick of the world is described in a net-work covering, from the shoulder to the foot.[260] And (not to enlarge upon the cruciated character of Trismegistus, or handed crosses, so often occurring in the needles of pharaoh, and obelisks of antiquity) the *Statuæ Isiacæ*, teraphims, and little idols, found about the mummies, do make a decussation or Jacobs crosse, with their armes, like that on the head of Ephraim and Manasses, and this decussis is also graphically described between them.[261]

This reticulate or net-work was also considerable in the inward parts of man, not only from the first *subtegmen* or warp of his formation, but in the netty fibres of the veins and vessels of life;[262] wherein according to common anatomy the right and transverse fibres are decussated, by the oblique fibres; and so must frame a reticulate and quincunciall figure by their obliquations, emphatically extending that elegant expression of Scripture.[263] Thou hast curiously embroydered me, thou hast wrought me up after the finest way of texture, and as it were with a needle.

Nor is the same observable only in some parts, but in the whole body of man, which upon the extension of arms and legges, doth make out a square, whose intersection is at the genitals. To omit the phantastical quincunx, in Plato of the first hermaphrodite or double man, united at the loynes, which Jupiter after divided.[264]

A rudimentall resemblance hereof there is in the cruciated and rugged folds of the *reticulum*, or net-like ventricle of ruminating horned animals, which is the second in order, and culinarily called the honey-comb. For many divisions there are in the stomack of severall animals; what number they maintain in the scarus and ruminating fish, common description, or our own experiment hath made no discovery.[265] But in the ventricle of Porpuses there are three divisions. In many birds a crop, gizard, and little receptacle before it;[266] but in cornigerous animals, which chew the cudd, there are no less then four of distinct position and office.* [267,268]

* [*Magnus venter, reticulum omasus, abomasus*].

The *reticulum* by these crossed cels, makes a further digestion, in the dry and exuccous part of the aliment received from the first ventricle.[269] For at the bottome of the gullet there is a double orifice; what is first received at the mouth descendeth into the first and greater stomack, from whence it is returned into the mouth again; and after a fuller mastication, and salivous mixture, what part thereof descendeth again, in a moist and succulent body, it slides down the softer and more permeable orifice, into the omasus or third stomack; and from thence conveyed into the fourth, receives its last digestion. The other dry and exuccous part after rumination by the larger and stronger orifice beareth into the first stomack, from thence into the *reticulum*, and so progressively into the other divisions. And therefore in calves newly calved, there is little or no use of the two first ventricles, for the milk and liquid aliment slippeth down the softer orifice, into the third stomack; where making little or no stay, it passeth into the fourth, the seat of the *coagulum*, or runnet, or that division of stomack which seems to bear the name of the whole, in the Greek translation of the priests fee, in the sacrifice of peace-offerings.[270]

As for those rhomboidal figures made by the cartilagineous parts of the wezon, in the lungs of great fishes, and other animals, as Rondeletius discovered, we have not found them so to answer our figure as to be drawn into illustration;[271] something we expected in the more discernable texture of the lungs of frogs, which notwithstanding being but two curious bladders not weighing above a grain, we found interwoven with veins not observing any just order. More orderly situated are those cretaceous and chalky concretions found sometimes in the bignesse of a small fech on either side their spine;[272] which being not agreeable unto our order, nor yet observed by any, we shall not here discourse on.

But had we found a better account and tolerable anatomy, of that prominent jowle of the *sperma ceti* whale[*273], then questuary operation,[274] or the stench of the last cast upon our shoar, permitted, we might have perhaps discovered some handsome order in those net-like seases and sockets, made like honey-combs, containing that medicall matter.[275]

* 1652. Described in our *Pseudo. Epidem.* Edit. 3.

Lastly, the incession or locall motion of animals is made with analogy unto this figure, by decussative diametrals, quincunciall lines and angles.[276] For to omit the enquiry how butterflies and breezes move their four wings, how birds and fishes in ayre and water move by joynt stroaks of opposite wings and finnes, and how salient animals in jumping forward seem to arise and fall upon a square base;[277] as the station of most quadrupeds, is made upon a long square, so in their motion they make a rhomboides;[278] their common progression being performed diametrally, by decussation and crosse advancement of their legges, which not observed begot that remarkable absurdity in the position of the legges of Castors horse in the capitol.[279] The snake which moveth circularly makes his spires in like order, the convex and concave spirals answering each other at alternate distances; in the motion of man the armes and legges observe this thwarting position, but the legges alone do move quincuncially by single angles with some resemblance of an V measured by successive advancement from each foot, and the angle of indenture great or lesse, according to the extent or brevity of the stride.[280]

Studious observators may discover more analogies in the orderly book of nature, and cannot escape the elegancy of her hand in other correspondencies. The figures of nails and crucifying appurtenances, are but precariously made out in the *granadilla* or flower of Christs passion:[281] and we despair to behold in these parts that handsome draught of crucifixion in the fruit of the *barbado* pine.[282] The seminal spike of *phalaris*, or great shaking grasse, more nearly answers the tayl of a rattle-snake, then many resemblances in Porta:[283] and if the man *orchis* of Columna be well made out, it excelleth all analogies[†].[284] In young wallnuts cut athwart, it is not hard to

† *Orchis Anthropophora, Fabii Columnæ.*

apprehend strange characters; and in those of somewhat elder growth, handsome ornamental draughts about a plain crosse. In the root of *osmond* or water fern, every eye may discern the form of a half moon, rain-bow, or half the character of Pisces.[285] Some finde Hebrew, Arabick, Greek, and Latine characters in plants; in a common one among us we seem to read, Aiaia, Viviu, Lilil.[286]

Right lines and circles make out the bulk of plants; in the parts thereof we finde helicall or spirall roundles, volutas, conicall sections, circular Pyramids, and frustums of Archimedes;[287] and cannot overlook the orderly hand of nature, in the alternate succession of the flat and narrower sides in the tender shoots of the ashe, or the regular inequality of bignesse in the five-leaved flowers of henbane, and something like in the calicular leaves of *Tutson*.[288] How the spots of *persicaria* do manifest themselves between the sixt and tenth ribbe.[289] How the triangular capp in the stemme or stylus of tuleps doth constantly point at three outward leaves. That spicated flowers do open first at the stalk.[290] That white flowers have yellow thrums or knops.[291] That the nebbe of beans and pease do all look downward, and so presse not upon each other; and how the seeds of many pappous or downy flowers lockt up in sockets after a gomphosis or mortis-articulation, diffuse themselves circularly into branches of rare order, observable in *trapopogon* or goats-beard, conformable to the spiders web, and the radii in like manner telarely inter-woven.[292]

And how in animall natures, even colours hold correspondencies, and mutuall correlations. That the colour of the caterpillar will shew again in the butterfly, with some latitude is allowable. Though the regular spots in their wings seem but a mealie adhesion, and such as may be wiped away, yet since they come in this variety, out of their cases, there must be regular pores in those parts and membranes, defining such exudations.[293]

That Augustus[*] had native notes on his body and belly, after the order and number in the starre of Charles wayne, will not seem strange unto astral physiognomy, which accordingly considereth moles in the body of man, or physicall observators, who from the position of moles in the face, reduce them to rule and correspondency in other parts.[294] Whether after the like method medicall conjecture may not be raised, upon parts inwardly affected; since parts about the lips are the critical seats of pustules discharged in agues; and scrophulous tumours

[*] Suet. in *vit. Aug.*

about the neck do often speak the like about the mesentery, may also be considered.[295]

* [to be observed in white young lambes, which afterward vanisheth].

The russet neck in young lambs*[296] seems but adventitious, and may owe its tincture to some contraction in the womb;[297] but that if sheep have any black or deep russet in their faces, they want not the same about their legges and feet; that black hounds have mealy mouths and feet; that black cows which have any white in their tayls, should not misse of some in their bellies; and if all white in their bodies, yet if black-mouth'd, their ears and feet maintain the same colour, are correspondent tinctures not ordinarily failing in nature, which easily unites the accidents of extremities, since in some generations she transmutes the parts themselves, while in the *Aurelian metamorphosis* the head of the canker becomes the tayl of the butterfly.[298] Which is in some way not beyond the contrivance of art, in submersions and inlays, inverting the extremes of the plant, and fetching the root from the top, and also imitated in handsome columnary work, in the inversion of the extremes; wherein the capitel, and the base, hold such near correspondency.

In the motive parts of animals may be discovered mutuall proportions;[299] not only in those of quadrupeds, but in the thigh-bone, legge, foot-bone, and claws of birds. The legs of spiders are made after a sesqui-tertian proportion, and the long legs of some locusts, double unto some others.[300] But the internodial parts of vegetables, or spaces between the joints, are contrived with more uncertainty; though the joints themselves in many plants, maintain a regular number.

In vegetable composure, the unition of prominent parts seems most to answer the *apophyses* or processes of animall bones, whereof they are the produced parts or prominent explanations.[301] And though in parts of plants which are not ordained for motion, we do not expect correspondent articulations; yet in the setting on of some flowers, and seeds in their sockets, and the lineal commissure of the pulpe of severall seeds, may be observed some shadow of the harmony; some show of the gomphosis or mortis-articulation.[302]

As for the diarthrosis or motive articulation,[303] there is expected little analogy, though long-stalked leaves doe move by long lines, and have observable motions, yet are they made by outward impulsion, like the motion of pendulous bodies, while the parts themselves are united by some kind of symphysis unto the stock.[304]

But standing vegetables, void of motive-articulations, are not without many motions. For beside the motion of vegetation upward, and of radiation unto all quarters, that of contraction, dilatation, inclination, and contortion, is discoverable in many plants. To omit the rose of Jericho, the ear of rye, which moves with change of weather, and the magical spit, made of no rare plants, which windes before the fire, and rosts the bird without turning.[305]

Even animals near the classis of plants, seem to have the most restlesse motions. The summer-worm of ponds and plashes makes a long waving motion; the hair-worm seldom lies still.[306] He that would behold a very anomalous motion, may observe it in the tortile and tiring strokes of gnatworms[*][307].

[*] Found often in some form of redmaggot in the standing waters of cisterns in the summer.

CHAPTER IV

As for the delights, commodities, mysteries, with other concernments of this order, we are unwilling to fly them over, in the short deliveries of Virgil, Varro, or others, and shall therefore enlarge with additional ampliations.[308]

By this position they had a just proportion of earth, to supply an equality of nourishment. The distance being ordered, thick or thin, according to the magnitude or vigorous attraction of the plant, the goodnesse, leannesse, or propriety of the soyle, and therefore the rule of *Solon*, concerning the territory of Athens, not extendible unto all;[309] allowing the distance of six foot unto common trees, and nine for the figge and olive.

They had a due diffusion of their roots on all or both sides, whereby they maintained some proportion to their height, in trees of large radication.[310] For that they strictly make good their profundeur or depth unto their height, according to common conceit, and that expression of Virgil,[†][311] though confirmable from the plane tree in Pliny, and some few examples, is not to be expected from the generallitie[312] of trees almost in any kinde, either of side-spreading, or taproots:[313] except we measure them by lateral and opposite diffusions; nor commonly to be found in minor or hearby plants; if we except sea-holly, liquorish, sea-rush, and some others.[314]

[†] *Quantum vertice ad auras Æthereas, tantum radice ad tartara tendit.*

They had a commodious radiation in their growth; and a due expansion of their branches, for shadow or delight. For trees thickly planted, do runne up in height and branch with no expansion, shooting unequally or short, and thinne upon the neighbouring side. And therefore trees are inwardly bare, and spring, and leaf from the outward and sunny side of their branches.

Whereby they also avoided the peril of συνολεθρισμὸς,[315] or one tree perishing with another, as it happeneth oft-times from the sick effluviums or entanglements of the roots, falling foul with each other.[316] Observable in elmes set in hedges, where if one dieth the neighbouring tree prospereth not long after.

In this situation divided into many intervals and open unto six passages, they had the advantage of a fair perflation from windes, brushing and cleansing their surfaces, relaxing and closing their pores unto due perspiration.[317] For that they afford large effluviums perceptible from odours, diffused at great distances, is observable from onyons out of the earth; which though dry, and kept until the spring, as they shoot forth large and many leaves, do notably abate of their weight.[318] And mint growing in glasses of water, until it arriveth unto the weight of an ounce, in a shady place, will sometimes exhaust a pound of water.

And as they send forth much, so may they receive somewhat in: for beside the common way and road of reception by the root, there may be a refection and imbibition from without;[319] for gentle showers refresh plants, though they enter not their roots; and the good and bad effluviums of vegetables, promote or debilitate each other. So epithymum and dodder, rootlesse and out of the ground, maintain themselves upon thyme, savory, and plants, whereon they hang.[320] And ivy divided from the root, we have observed to live some years, by the cirrous parts commonly conceived but as tenacles and hold-fasts unto it.[321] The stalks of mint cropt from the root stripped from the leaves, and set in glasses with the root end upward, and out of the water, we have observed to send forth sprouts and leaves without the aid of roots, and scordium to grow in like manner, the leaves set downward in water.[322] To omit severall sea-plants, which grow on single roots from stones, although in very many there are side-shoots and fibres, beside the fastening root.

By this open position they were fairly exposed unto the rayes of moon and sunne, so considerable in the growth of vegetables. For though poplars, willows, and severall trees be made to grow about the brinks of Acharon, and dark habitations of the dead;[323] though some plants are content to grow in obscure wells; wherein also old elme pumps afford sometimes long bushy sprouts, not observable in any above-ground: and large fields of vegetables are able to maintain their verdure at the bottome and shady part of the sea; yet the greatest number are not content without the actual rayes of the sunne, but bend, incline, and follow them; as large lists of solisequious and sun-following plants.[324] And some observe the method of its motion in their owne growth and conversion twining towards the west by the south, as bryony, hops, woodbine, and several kindes of bindeweed, which we shall more admire; when any can tell us, they observe another motion, and twist by the north at the antipodes. The same plants rooted against an erect north-wall full of holes, will finde a way through them to look upon the sunne. And in tender plants from mustard seed, sown in the winter, and in a pot[325] of earth placed inwardly against a south-window, the tender stalks of two leaves arose not erect, but bending towards the window, nor looking much higher then the meridian sun. And if the pot were turned they would work themselves into their former declinations, making their conversion by the east. That the leaves of the olive and some other trees solstitially turn, and precisely tell us, when the sun is entred Cancer, is scarce expectable in any climate; and Theophrastus warily observes it;[326] yet somewhat thereof is observable in our own, in the leaves of willows and sallows, some weeks after the solstice. But the great *convolvulus* or white-flower'd bindweed observes both motions of the sunne, while the flower twists æquinoctionally from the left hand to the right, according to the daily revolutions; the stalk twineth ecliptically from the right to the left, according to the annual conversion.[327]

Some commend the exposure of these orders unto the western gales, as the most generative and fructifying breath of Heaven. But we applaud the husbandry of Solomon, whereto agreeth the doctrine of Theophrastus. Arise o north-winde, and blow thou south upon my garden, that the spices thereof may flow out;[328] for the north-winde closing the pores, and shutting up the effluviums, when the south doth after open and relax them; the aromatical gummes do drop, and sweet odours fly actively from them. And if his garden had the same situation, which mapps, and charts afford it, on the east side of Jerusalem, and having the wall on the west; these were the windes, unto which it was well exposed.

By this way of plantation they encreased the number of their trees, which they lost in *Quaternios*, and square-orders, which is a commodity insisted on by Varro,[329] and one great intent of nature, in this position of flowers and seeds in the elegant formation of plants, and the former rules observed in naturall and artificiall figurations.

Whether in this order and one tree in some measure breaking the cold, and pinching gusts of windes from the other, trees will not better maintain their inward circles, and either escape or moderate their excentricities, may also be considered.[330] For the circles in trees are naturally concentricall,[331] parallell unto the bark, and unto each other, till frost and piercing windes contract and close them on the weatherside, the opposite semicircle widely enlarging and at a comely distance, which hindreth ofttimes the beauty and roundnesse of trees, and makes the timber lesse serviceable; whiles the ascending juyce not readily passing, settles in knots and inequalities. And therefore it is no new course of agriculture, to observe the native position of trees according to north and south in their transplantations.

The same is also observable underground in the circinations and sphærical rounds of onyons, wherein the circles of the orbes are ofttimes larger, and the meridionall lines stand wider upon one side then the other.[332] And where the largenesse will make up the number of planetical orbes, that of Luna, and the lower planets excede the dimensions of Saturne, and the higher:[333] whether the like be not verified in the circles of the large roots of briony and mandrakes, or why in the knotts of deale or firre the circles are often eccentricall, although not in a plane, but vertical and right position, deserves a further enquiry.

Whether there be not some irregularity of roundnesse in most plants according to their position? Whether some small compression of pores be not perceptible in parts which stand against the current of waters, as in reeds, bullrushes, and other vegetables toward the streaming quarter, may also be observed, and therefore such as are long and weak, are commonly contrived into a roundnesse of figure, whereby the water presseth lesse, and slippeth more smoothly from them, and even in flags of flat-figured leaves, the greater part obvert their sharper sides unto the current in ditches.[334]

But whether plants which float upon the surface of the water, be for the most part of cooling qualities, those which shoot above it of heating vertues, and why? Whether *sargasso* for many miles floating upon the Western Ocean, or sea-lettuce, and phasganium at the bottome of our seas, make good the like qualities?[335] Why fenny waters afford the hottest and sweetest plants, as calamus, cyperus, and crowfoot, and mudd cast out of ditches most naturally produceth arsmart; why plants so greedy of water so little regard oyl?[336] Why since many seeds contain much oyle within them, they endure it not well without, either in their growth or production? Why since seeds shoot commonly under ground, and out of the ayre, those which are let fall in shallow glasses, upon the surface of the water, will sooner sprout then those at the bottome? And if the water be covered with oyle, those at the bottome will hardly sprout at all, we have not room to conjecture.

Whether ivy would not lesse offend the trees in this clean ordination, and well kept paths, might perhaps deserve the question. But this were a quæry only unto some habitations, and little concerning Cyrus or the Babylonian territory; wherein by no industry Harpalus could make ivy grow: and Alexander hardly found it about those parts to imitate the pomp of Bacchus.[337] And though in these northern regions we are too much acquainted with one ivy, we know too little of another, whereby we apprehend not the expressions of antiquity, the splenetick medicine of Galen[*338,339] and the emphasis of the poet, in the beauty of the white ivy.[†340]

The like concerning the growth of misseltoe, which dependeth not only of the species, or kinde of tree, but much also of the soil. And therefore common in some places, not readily found in others, frequent in France, not so common in Spain, and scarce at all in the territory of Ferrara:[341] nor easily to be found where it is most required upon oaks, lesse on trees continually verdant. Although in some places the olive escapeth it not, requiting its detriment, in the delightfull view of its red berries; as Clusius observed in Spain, and Bellonius about Hierusalem.[342] But this parasiticall plant suffers nothing to grow upon it, by any way of art; nor could we ever make it grow where nature had not planted it; as we have in vain attempted by inocculation and incision, upon its native or forreign stock.[343] And though there seem nothing improbable in the seed, it hath not succeeded by sation in any manner of ground, wherein we had no reason to despair, since we reade of vegetable horns,[‡344] and how rams horns will root about Goa.[345]

* *Galen de med. secundum loc.*

† *Hedera formosior alba.*

‡ *Linschoten.*

But besides these rurall commodities, it cannot be meanly delectable in the variety of figures, which these orders open, and closed do make. Whilest every inclosure makes a rhombus, the figures obliquely taken a rhomboides, the intervals bounded with parallell lines, and each intersection built upon a square, affording two triangles or Pyramids vertically conjoyned; which in the strict quincunciall order doe oppositely make acute and blunt angles.[346]

And though therein we meet not with right angles, yet every rhombus containing four angles equall unto four right,[347] it virtually contains four right in every one. Nor is this strange unto such as observe the naturall lines of trees, and parts disposed in them. For neither in the root doth nature affect this angle, which shooting downward for the stability of the plant, doth best effect the same by figures of inclination; nor in the branches and stalky leaves, which grow most at acute angles; as declining from their head the root, and diminishing their angles with their altitude: verified also in lesser plants, whereby they better support themselves, and bear not so heavily upon the stalk: so that while near the root they often make an angle of seventy parts, the sprouts near the top will often come short of thirty.[348] Even in the nerves and master veins of the leaves the acute angle ruleth; the obtuse but seldome found, and in the backward part of the leaf, reflecting and arching about the stalk. But why ofttimes one side of the leaf is unequall unto the other, as in hazell and oaks, why on either side the master vein the lesser and derivative channels stand not[349] directly opposite, nor at equall angles, respectively unto the adverse side, but those of one part do often exceed the other, as the wallnut and many more deserves another enquiry.

Now if for this order we affect coniferous and tapering trees, particularly the cypresse, which grows in a conicall figure; we have found a tree not only of great ornament, but in its essentials of affinity unto this order. A solid rhombus being made by the conversion of two equicrurall cones, as Archimedes hath defined.[350] And these were the common trees about Babylon, and the east, whereof the ark was made; and Alexander found no trees so accomodable to build his navy;[351] and this we rather think to be the tree mentioned in the Canticles, which stricter botanology will hardly allow to be camphire.[352]

And if delight or ornamentall view invite a comely disposure by circular amputations, as is elegantly performed in hawthorns;[353] then will they answer the figures made by the conversion of a rhombus, which maketh two concentricall circles; the greater circumference being made by the lesser angles, the lesser by the greater.

The cylindrical figure of trees is virtually contained and latent in this order. A cylinder or long round being made by the conversion or turning of a parallelogram, and most handsomely by a long square, which makes an equall, strong and lasting figure in trees, agreeable unto the body and motive parts of animals, the greatest number of plants, and almost all roots, though their stalks be angular, and of many corners, which seem not to follow the figure of their seeds; since many angular seeds send forth round stalks, and sphæricall seeds arise from angular spindles, and many rather conform unto their roots, as the round stalks of bulbous roots, and in tuberous roots stemmes of like figure. But why since the largest number of plants maintain a circular figure, there are so few with teretous or longround leaves;[354] why coniferous trees are tenuifolious or narrowleafed, why plants of few or no joynts have commonly round stalks, why the greatest number of hollow stalks are round stalks; or why in this variety of angular stalks the quadrangular most exceedeth, were too long a speculation; mean while obvious experience may finde, that in plants of divided leaves above, nature often beginneth circularly in the two first leaves below, while in the singular plant of ivy, she exerciseth a contrary geometry, and beginning with angular leaves below, rounds them in the upper branches.

Nor can the rows in this order want delight, as carrying an aspect answerable unto the *dipteros hypœthros*, or double order of columns open above; the opposite ranks of trees standing like pillars in the *cavedia* of the courts of famous buildings, and the porticos of the *templa subdialia* of old;[355] somewhat imitating the *peristylia* or cloyster buildings, and the *exedræ* of the ancients, wherein men discoursed, walked and exercised;[356] for that they derived the rule of columnes from trees, especially in their proportionall diminutions, is illustrated by Vitruvius from the shaftes of firre and pine.[357] And though the interarboration do imitate the *areostylos*, or thin order, not strictly answering the proportion of intercolumniations;[358] yet in many trees they will not exceed the intermission of the columnes in the court of the Tabernacle;[359] which being an hundred cubits long, and made up by twenty pillars, will afford no lesse then intervals of five cubits.

Beside, in this kinde of aspect the sight being not diffused but circumscribed between long parallels and the ἐπισκιασμὸς and adumbration from the branches, it frameth a penthouse over the eye, and maketh a quiet vision:[360] and therefore in diffused and open aspects, men hollow their hand above their eye, and make an artificiall brow, whereby they direct the dispersed rayes of sight, and by this shade preserve a moderate light in the chamber of the eye; keeping the pupilla plump and fair, and not contracted or shrunk as in light and vagrant vision.[361]

And therefore providence hath arched and paved the great house of the world, with colours of mediocrity, that is, blew and green, above and below the sight, moderately terminating the acies of the eye.[362] For most plants, though green above ground, maintain their originall white below it, according to the candour of their seminall pulp, and the rudimental leaves do first appear in that colour;[363] observable in seeds sprouting in water upon their first foliation. Green seeming to be the first supervenient, or above-ground complexion of vegetables, separable in many upon ligature or inhumation, as succory, endive, artichoaks, and which is also lost upon fading in the autumn.[364]

And this is also agreeable unto water it self, the alimental vehicle of plants, which first altereth into this colour;[365] and containing many vegetable seminalities, revealeth their seeds by greennesse;[366] and therefore soonest expected in rain or standing water, not easily found in distilled or water strongly boiled; wherein the seeds are extinguished by fire and decoction, and therefore last long and pure without such alteration, affording neither uliginous coats, gnatworms, acari, hairworms, like crude and common water;[367] and therefore most fit for wholsome beverage, and with malt makes ale and beer without boyling. What large water-drinkers some plants are, the canary-tree and birches in some northern countries, drenching the fields about them do sufficiently demonstrate. How water it self is able to maintain the growth of vegetables, and without extinction of their generative or medicall vertues; beside the experiment of Helmonts tree, we have found in some which have lived six years in glasses.[368] The seeds of scurvy-grasse growing in waterpots, have been fruitfull in the land; and *asarum* after a years space, and once casting its leaves, hath handsomely performed its vomiting operation.[369]

Nor are only dark and green colors, but shades and shadows contrived through the great volume of nature, and trees ordained not only to protect and shadow others, but by their shades and shadowing parts, to preserve and cherish themselves. The whole radiation or branchings shadowing the stock and the root, the leaves, the branches and fruit, too much exposed to the windes and scorching sunne.[370] The calicular leaves inclose the tender flowers, and the flowers themselves lye wrapt about the seeds, in their rudiment and first formations, which being advanced the flowers fall away; and are therefore contrived in variety of figures, best satisfying the intention; handsomely observable in hooded and gaping flowers, and the butterfly bloomes of leguminous plants, the lower leaf closely involving the rudimental cod, and the alary or wingy divisions embracing or hanging over it.[371]

But seeds themselves do lie in perpetual shades, either under the leaf, or shut up in coverings; and such as lye barest, have their husks, skins, and pulps about them, wherein the nebbe and generative particle lyeth moist and secured from the injury of ayre and sunne. Darknesse and light hold interchangeable dominions, and alternately rule the seminall state of things. Light unto Pluto is darknesse unto Jupiter.[*372] Legions of seminall idæas lye in their second chaos and *orcus* of Hippocrates;[373] till putting on the habits of their forms, they shew themselves upon the stage of the world, and open dominion of Jove. They that held the stars of Heaven were but rayes and flashing glimpses of the empyreall light, through holes and perforations of the upper Heaven, took of the natural shadows of stars, while according to better discovery[†374] the poor inhabitants of the moone have but a polary life, and must passe half their dayes in the shadow of that luminary.[375]

* *Lux orco, tenebræ Jovi, tenebræ orco, lux Jovi.* Hippocr. *de diæta.*

† *S. Hevelii Selenographia.*

Light that makes things seen, makes some things invisible, were it not for darknesse and the shadow of the earth, the noblest part of the creation had remained unseen, and the stars in Heaven as invisible as on the fourth day, when they were created above the horizon, with the sun, or there was not an eye to behold them.[376] The greatest mystery of religion is expressed by adumbration, and in the noblest part of Jewish types, we finde the cherubims shadowing the Mercy-seat:[377] life it self is but the shadow of death, and souls departed but the shadows of the living: all things fall under this name. The sunne it self is but the dark *simulachrum*, and light but the shadow of God.[378]

Lastly, it is no wonder that this quincunciall order was first and still affected as gratefull unto the eye: for all things are seen quincuncially; for at the eye the pyramidal rayes from the object, receive a decussation, and so strike a second base upon the retina or hinder coat, the proper organ of vision;[379] wherein the pictures from objects are represented, answerable to the paper, or wall in the dark chamber;[380] after the decussation of the rayes at the hole of the hornycoat, and their refraction upon the christalline humour, answering the *foramen* of the window, and the convex or burning-glasses, which refract the rayes that enter it.[381] And if ancient anatomy would hold, a like disposure there was of the optick or visual nerves in the brain, wherein antiquity conceived a concurrence by decussation.[382] And this not only observable in the laws of direct vision, but in some part also verified in the reflected rayes of sight. For making the angle of incidence equal to that of reflexion, the visuall raye returneth quincuncially,[383] and after the form of a V, and the line of reflexion being continued unto the place of vision, there ariseth a semi-decussation, which makes the object seen in a perpendicular unto it self, and as farre below the reflectent as it is from it above; observable in the sun and moon beheld in water.

And this is also the law of reflexion in moved bodies and sounds, which though not made by decussation, observe the rule of equality between incidence and reflexion; whereby whispering places are framed by ellipticall arches laid sidewise;[384] where the voice being delivered at the *focus* of one extremity, observing an equality unto the angle of incidence, it will reflect unto the *focus* of the other end, and so escape the ears of the standers in the middle.

A like rule is observed in the reflection of the vocall and sonorous line in ecchoes, which cannot therefore be heard in all stations.[385] But happening in woody plantations, by waters, and able to return some words; if reacht by a pleasant and well-dividing voice, there may be heard the softest notes in nature.

And this not only verified in the way of sence, but in animall and intellectuall receptions. Things entring upon the intellect by a pyramid from without, and thence into the memory by another from within, the common decussation being in the understanding as is delivered by Bovillus.[*386] Whether the intellectual and phantastical lines be not thus rightly disposed, but magnified, diminished, distorted, and ill placed in the mathematicks of some brains, whereby they have irregular

* *Car. Bovillus de intellectu.*

apprehensions of things, perverted motions, conceptions, incurable hallucinations, were no unpleasant speculation.[387]

And if Ægyptian philosophy may obtain, the scale of influences was thus disposed, and the geniall spirits of both worlds, do trace their way in ascending and descending pyramids, mystically apprehended in the letter X, and the open bill and stradling legges of a stork, which was imitated by that character.[388]

Of this figure Plato made choice to illustrate the motion of the soul, both of the world and man;[389] while he delivereth that God divided the whole conjunction length-wise, according to the figure of a Greek X, and then turning it about reflected it into a circle; by the circle implying the uniform motion of the first orb, and by the right lines, the planetical and various motions within it.[390] And this also with application unto the soul of man, which hath a double aspect, one right, whereby it beholdeth the body, and objects without; another circular and reciprocal, whereby it beholdeth it self. The circle declaring the motion of the indivisible soul, simple, according to the divinity of its nature, and returning into it self; the right lines respecting the motion pertaining unto sense, and vegetation, and the central decussation, the wondrous connexion of the severall faculties conjointly in one substance. And so conjoyned the unity and duality of the soul, and made out the three substances so much considered by him; that is, the indivisible or divine, the divisible or corporeal, and that third, which was the *systasis* or harmony of those two, in the mystical decussation.[391]

And if that were clearly made out which Justin Martyr took for granted, this figure hath had the honour to characterize and notifie our blessed Saviour, as he delivereth in that borrowed expression from Plato; *Decussavit eum in universo*,[392] the hint whereof he would have Plato derive from the figure of the brazen serpent,[393] and to have mistaken the letter X for T, whereas it is not improbable, he learned these and other mystical expressions in his learned observations of Ægypt, where he might obviously behold the mercurial characters, the handed crosses, and other mysteries not throughly understood in the sacred letter X, which being derivative from the stork, one of the ten sacred animals, might be originally Ægyptian, and brought into Greece by Cadmus of that countrey.[394]

CHAPTER V

To enlarge this contemplation unto all the mysteries and secrets, accomodable unto this number, were inexcusable pythagorisme, yet cannot omit the ancient conceit of five surnamed the number of justice;[395] as justly dividing between the digits, and hanging in the centre of nine, described by square numeration, which angularly divided will make the decussated number;[*396] and so agreeable unto the quincunciall ordination, and rowes divided by equality, and just decorum, in the whole com-plantation; and might be the originall of that common game among us, wherein the fifth place is soveraigne, and carrieth the chief intention.[397] The ancients wisely instructing youth, even in their recreations unto virtue, that is, early to drive at the middle point and central seat of justice.

* • • •
• • •
• • •

Nor can we omit how agreeable unto this number an handsome division is made in trees and plants, since Plutarch,[398] and the ancients have named it the Divisive Number, justly dividing the entities of the world, many remarkable things in it, and also comprehending the general division of vegetables.[†399] And he that considers how most blossomes of trees, and greatest number of flowers, consist of five leaves; and therein doth rest the setled rule of nature; so that in those which exceed there is often found, or easily made a variety; may readily discover how nature rests in this number, which is indeed the first rest and pause of numeration in the fingers, the naturall organs thereof. Nor in the division of the feet of perfect animals doth nature exceed this account. And even in the joints of feet, which in birds are most multiplied, surpasseth not this number; so progressionally making them out in many, that from five in the fore-claw she descendeth unto two in the hindemost;[‡] and so in fower feet makes up the number of joynts, in the five fingers or toes of man.

Not to omit the quintuple section of a cone,[§] of handsome practice in ornamentall garden-plots, and in some way discoverable in so many works of nature; in the leaves, fruits, and seeds of vegetables, and scales of some fishes, so much considerable in glasses, and the optick doctrine;[400] wherein the learned may consider the crystalline humour of the eye in the cuttle fish and loligo.[401]

He that forgets not how antiquity named this the conjugall or wedding number, made it the embleme of the most

† Δένδρον, Θάμνος, Φρύγανον, Πόα, *arbor*, *frutex*, *suffrutex*, *herba*, and that fifth which comprehendeth the *fungi* and *tubera*, whether to be named Ἄσχιον or γύμνον, comprehending also the *conferva marina salsa*, and sea-cords, of so many yards length.

‡ as herns, bitterns and long claw'd fowls.

§ *Elleipsis, parabola, Hyperbole, Circulus, Triangulum.*

remarkable conjunction, will conceive it duely appliable unto this handsome oeconomy, and vegetable combination;[402] may hence apprehend the allegorical sence of that obscure expression of Hesiod[**], and afford no improbable reason why Plato admitted his nuptiall guests by fives, in the kindred of the married couple.[*403]

And though a sharper mystery might be implied in the number of the five wise and foolish virgins, which were to meet the bridegroom,[404] yet was the same agreeable unto the conjugall number, which ancient numerists made out by two and three, the first parity and imparity, the active and passive digits, the materiall and formall principles in generative societies. And not discordant even from the customes of the Romans, who admitted but five torches in their nuptiall solemnities.[†405] Whether there were any mystery or not implied, the most generative animals were created on this day, and had accordingly the largest benediction:[406] and under a quintuple consideration, wanton antiquity considered the circumstances of generation, while by this number of five they naturally divided the nectar of the fifth planet[‡407].

The same number in the Hebrew mysteries and Cabalistical accounts was the character of generation;[§408] declared by the letter *He*, the fifth in their alphabet; according to that Cabalisticall dogma: if *Abram* had not had this letter added unto his name he had remained fruitlesse, and without the power of generation:[409] not onely because hereby the number of his name attained two hundred fourty eight, the number of the affirmative precepts, but because as in created natures there is a male and female, so in divine and intelligent productions, the mother of life and fountain of souls in Cabalisticall technology is called *Binah*; whose seal and character was *He*.[410] So that being sterill before, he recived the power of generation from that measure and mansion in the archetype; and was made conformable unto *Binah*. And upon such involved considerations, the ten of *Sarai* was exchanged into five.[**411] If any shall look upon this as a stable number, and fitly appropriable unto trees, as bodies of rest and station, he hath herein a great foundation in nature, who observing much variety in legges and motive organs of animals, as two, four, six, eight, twelve, fourteen, and more, hath passed over five and ten, and assigned them unto none, or very few, as the *Phalangium monstrosum Brasilianum, Clusii et Jac. De Laet. Cur. poster. Americæ Descript.*, if perfectly described.[412] And for the stability of this number, he shall not want the sphericity of

** πέμπτας *id est nuptias multas Rhodig.*

* Plato *de leg.* 6.

† Plutarch, *Problem Rom* I.

‡ [the lips that Venus has imbued with the quintessence of her own nectar].

§ *Archang. Dog. Cabal.*

** *Jod* into *He*.

its nature, which multiplied in it self, will return into its own denomination, and bring up the reare of the account. Which is also one of the numbers that makes up the mysticall name of God, which consisting of letters denoting all the sphæricall numbers, ten, five, and six; emphatically sets forth the notion of *Trismegistus*, and that intelligible sphere, which is the nature of God.[413]

Many expressions by this number occurre in holy Scripture, perhaps unjustly laden with mysticall expositions, and little concerning our order. That the Israelites were forbidden to eat the fruit of their newly planted trees, before the fifth yeare, was very agreeable unto the naturall rules of husbandry: fruits being unwholsome and lash before the fourth, or fifth yeare.[414] In the second day or feminine part of five, there was added no approbation.[415] For in the third or masculine day, the same is twice repeated; and a double benediction inclosed both creations, whereof the one, in some part was but an accomplishment of the other. That the trespasser[*416] was to pay a fifth part above the head or principall, makes no secret in this number, and implied no more then one part above the principall; which being considered in four parts, the additionall forfeit must bear the name of a fift. The five golden mice had plainly their determination from the number of the princes;[417] that five should put to flight an hundred might have nothing mystically implyed;[418] considering a rank of souldiers could scarce consist of a lesser number. Saint Paul had rather speak five words in a known then ten thousand in an unknowne tongue:[419] that is as little as could well be spoken. A simple proposition consisting of three words and a complexed one not ordinarily short of five.

* Lev. 6:5.

More considerable there are in this mysticall account, which we must not insist on. And therefore why the radicall letters in the Pentateuch, should equall the number of the souldiery of the tribes;[420] why our Saviour in the wildernesse fed five thousand persons with five barley loaves, and again, but four thousand with no lesse then seven of wheat?[421] Why Joseph designed five changes of rayment unto Benjamin?[422] And David took just five pibbles out of the Brook against the Pagan champion?[423] we leave it unto arithmeticall divinity, and theologicall explanation.

Yet if any delight in new problemes, or think it worth the enquiry, whether the critical physician hath rightly hit the nominall notation of quinque;[†424] why the ancients mixed

† τέσσαρα ἕνκε, four and one, or five, *Scalig.*

five or three but not four parts of water unto their wine:[425] and Hippocrates observed a fifth proportion in the mixture of water with milk, as in dysenteries and bloudy fluxes.[426] Under what abstruse foundation astrologers do figure the good or bad fate from our children, in a good fortune, or the fifth house of their celestiall schemes.[*] Whether the Ægyptians described a starre by a figure of five points, with reference unto the five capitall aspects,[†427] whereby they transmit their influences, or abstruser considerations? Why the Cabalisticall doctors, who conceive the whole *Sephiroth*, or divine emanations to have guided the ten-stringed harp of David, whereby he pacified the evil spirit of Saul, in strict numeration doe begin with the *Perihypate Meson*, or si fa ut, and so place the *Tiphereth* answering C sol fa ut, upon the fifth string:[428] or whether this number be oftner applied unto bad things and ends, then good in holy Scripture, and why? he may meet with abstrusities of no ready resolution.

[*] *bona fortuna* the name of the fifth house.

[†] Conjunct, opposite, sextile, trigonal, tetragonal.

If any shall question the rationality of that magick, in the cure of the blind man by Serapis, commanded to place five fingers on his altar, and then his hand on his eyes?[429] Why since the whole comœdy is primarily and naturally comprised in four[‡430] parts, and antiquity permitted not so many persons to speak in one scene, yet would not comprehend the same in more or lesse then five acts?[431] Why amongst sea-starres nature chiefly delighteth in five points? And since there are found some of no fewer then twelve, and some of seven, and nine there are few or none discovered of six or eight? If any shall enquire why the flowers of Rue properly consist of four leaves, the first and third have five? Why since many flowers have one leaf or none,[§] as Scaliger will have it, diverse three, and the greatest number consist of five divided from their bottomes;[432] there are yet so few of two: or why nature generally beginning or setting out with two opposite leaves at the root, doth so seldome conclude with that order and number at the flower? he shall not passe his hours in vulgar speculation.

[‡] protasis, epitasis, catasis, catastrophe.

[§] Unifolium, nullifolium.

If any shall further quæry why magneticall philosophy excludeth decussations, and needles transversly placed do naturally distract their verticities?[433] Why geomancers do imitate the quintuple figure, in their mother characters of acquisition and amission, etc somewhat answering the figures in the lady or speckled beetle?[434] With what equity, chiromantical conjecturers decry these decussations in the lines and mounts of the hand?[435] What that decussated figure intendeth in the medall of Alexander the Great?[436] Why the goddesses sit commonly crosse-legged in ancient draughts, since Juno is described in the same as a veneficial posture to hinder the birth of Hercules?[437] If any shall doubt why at the amphidromicall feasts, on the fifth day after the childe was born, presents were sent from friends, of polipusses, and cuttle-fishes?[438] Why five must be only left in that symbolicall mutiny among the men of Cadmus?[439] Why Proteus in Homer the symbole of the first matter, before he setled himself in the midst of his sea-monsters, doth place them out by fives?[440] Why the fifth years oxe was acceptable sacrifice unto Jupiter?[441] Or why the noble Antoninus in some sence doth call the soul it self a rhombus?[442] He shall not fall on trite or triviall disquisitions. And these we invent and propose unto acuter enquirers, nauseating crambe verities and questions over-queried.[443] Flat and flexible truths are beat out by every hammer; but Vulcan and his whole forge sweat to work out Achilles his armour.[444] A large field is yet left unto sharper discerners to enlarge upon this order, to search out the *quaternios* and figured draughts of this nature,[445] and moderating the study of names, and meer nomenclature of plants, to erect generalities, disclose unobserved proprieties, not only in the vegetable shop, but the whole volume of nature; affording delightful truths, confirmable by sense and ocular observation, which seems to me the surest path, to trace the labyrinth of truth. For though discursive enquiry and rationall conjecture, may leave handsome gashes and flesh-wounds; yet without conjunction of this expect no mortal or dispatching blows unto errour.

But the quincunx[*446] of Heaven runs low, and 'tis time to close the five ports of knowledge;[447] we are unwilling to spin out our awaking thoughts into the phantasmes of sleep, which often continueth præcogitations;[448] making cables of cobwebbes and wildernesses of handsome groves. Beside Hippocrates[†449] hath spoke so little and the oneirocriticall[‡450] masters, have left such frigid interpretations from plants, that there is little encouragement to dream of Paradise it self. Nor will the sweetest delight of gardens afford much comfort in sleep; wherein the dulnesse of that sense shakes hands with delectable odours; and though in the bed[§] of Cleopatra, can hardly with any delight raise up the ghost of a rose.

* *Hyades* near the Horizon about midnight, at that time.

† *De Insomniis.*
‡ *Artemodorus et Apomazar.*

§ Strewed with roses.

Night which pagan theology could make the daughter of Chaos, affords no advantage to the description of order:[451]

although no lower then that masse can we derive its genealogy.[452] All things began in order, so shall they end, and so shall they begin again; according to the ordainer of order and mystical mathematicks of the city of Heaven.

Though Somnus in Homer be sent to rowse up Agamemnon, I finde no such effects in these drowsy approaches of sleep.[453] To keep our eyes open longer were but to act our antipodes.[454] The huntsmen are up in America, and they are already past their first sleep in Persia. But who can be drowsie at that howr which freed us from everlasting sleep? Or have slumbring thoughts at that time, when sleep it self must end, and as some conjecture all shall awake again?

Finis.

CERTAIN

MISCELLANY

TRACTS.

Written by

THOMAS BROWN, K[t],

and Doctour of Physick;

late of *NORWICH*.

LONDON,

Printed for *Charles Mearn*, Bookseller

to his most Sacred Majesty,

MDCLXXXIII.

FIG. 11 Title page from *Certain Miscellany Tracts* (1683).

THE PUBLISHER TO THE READER

The papers from which these Tracts were printed, were, a while since, deliver'd to me by, those worthy persons, the Lady and Son of the excellent authour. He himself gave no charge concerning the manuscripts, either for the suppressing or the publishing of them. Yet seeing he had procured Transcripts of them, and had kept those copies by him, it seemeth probable that he designed them for publick use.

Thus much of his intention being presumed, and many who had tasted of the fruits of his former studies being covetous of more of the like kind; also these tracts having been perused and much approv'd of by some judicious and learned men, I was not unwilling to be instrumental in fitting them for the press.

To this end, I selected them out of many disordered papers, and dispos'd them in to such a method as they seem'd capable of; beginning first with plants, going on to animals, proceeding farther to things relating to men, and concluding with matters of a various nature.

Concerning the plants, I did, on purpose, forbear to range them (as some advised) according to their tribes and families; because, by so doing, I should have represented that as a studied and formal work, which is but a collection of occasional essaies. And, indeed, both this tract, and those which follow, were rather the diversions than the labours of his pen: and because he did, as it were, drop down his thoughts of a sudden, in those little spaces of vacancy which he snatch'd from those very many occasions which gave him hourly interruption; if there appears, here and there, any uncorrectness in the style, a small degree of candour sufficeth to excuse it.

If there be any such errours in the words, I'm sure the press has not made them fewer; but I do not hold my self oblig'd to answer for that which I could not perfectly govern. However, the matter is not of any great moment: such errours will not mislead a learned reader; and he who is not such in some competent degree, is not a fit peruser of these letters. Such these tracts are; but, for the persons to whom they were written, I cannot well learn their names from those few obscure marks which the authour has set at the beginning of them. And these essaies being letters, as many as take offence at some few familiar things which the authour hath mixed with them, find fault with decence. Men are not wont to set down oracles in every line they write to their acquaintance.

There still remain other brief discourses written by this most learned and ingenious authour. Those, also, may come forth, when some of his friends shall have sufficient leisure; and at such due distance from these tracts, that they may follow rather than stifle them.

Amongst these manuscripts there is one which gives a brief account of all the monuments of the cathedral of Norwich.[1] It was written merely for private use: and the relations of the authour expect such justice from those into whose hands some imperfect copies of it are fallen; that, without their consent first obtain'd, they forbear the publishing of it.

The truth is, matter equal to the skill of the antiquity was not there afforded; had a fit subject of that nature offer'd it self, he would scarce have been guilty of an oversight like to that of Ausonius, who, in the description of his native city of Burdeaux, omitted the two famous antiquities of it, Palais de Tutele, and Palais de Galien.

Concerning the authour himself, I chuse to be silent, though I have had the happiness to have been, for some years, known to him. There is on foot a design of writing his life: and there are, already some memorials collected by one of his ancient friends. Till that work be perfected, the reader may content himself with these present tracts; all which commending themselves by their learning, curiosity and brevity, if he be not pleased with them, he seemeth to me to be distemper'd with such a niceness of imagination as no wise man is concern'd to humour.

Thomas Tenison.

THE CONTENTS OF THESE TRACTS

TRACT I

Observations Upon Several Plants Mention'd in Scripture

THE INTRODUCTION

Sir,

Though many ordinary heads run smoothly over the Scripture, yet I must acknowledge, it is one of the hardest books I have met with: and therefore well deserveth those numerous comments, expositions and annotations which make up a good part of our libraries.

However so affected I am therewith, that I wish there had been more of it: and a larger volume of that divine piece which leaveth such welcome impressions, and somewhat more, in the readers, than the words and sense after it. At least, who would not be glad that many things barely hinted were at large delivered in it? The particulars of the dispute between the doctours and our Saviour could not but be welcome to them, who have every word in honour which proceeded from his mouth, or was otherwise delivered by him: and so would be glad to be assured, what he wrote with his finger on the ground: but especially to have a particular of that instructing narration or discourse which he made unto the Disciples after his resurrection, where 'tis said: *and beginning at Moses, and all the Prophets, he expounded unto them in all the Scriptures the things concerning himself.**

* Luke 24:27.

But to omit theological obscurities, you must needs observe that most sciences do seem to have something more nearly to consider in the expressions of the Scripture.

Astronomers find therein the names but of few stars, scarce so many as in Achilles his buckler in Homer, and almost the very same. But in some passages of the Old Testament they think they discover the zodiacal course of the sun: and they also conceive an astronomical sense in that elegant expression of S. James concerning *the father of lights, with whom there is no variableness, neither shadow of turning*:† and therein an allowable allusion unto the tropical conversion of the sun, whereby

† James 1:17.

ensueth a variation of heat, light, and also of shadows from it. But whether the *stellæ erraticæ*, or wandring stars in S. Jude, may be referr'd to the celestial planets, or some meteorological wandring stars, *Ignes fatui, Stellæ cadentes et erraticæ*, or had any allusion unto the impostour Barchochebas, or *Stellæ Filius*, who afterward appeared, and wandred about in the time of Adrianus, they leave unto conjecture.

Chirurgeons may find their whole art in that one passage,[2] concerning the rib which God took out of Adam; that is, their *διαίρεσις* in opening the flesh, *ἐξαίρεσις* in taking out the rib, and *σύνθεσις* in closing and healing the part again.

Rhetoricians and oratours take singular notice of very many excellent passages, stately metaphors, noble tropes and elegant expressions, not to be found or parallel'd in any other authour.

Mineralists look earnestly into the twenty eight of Job, take special notice of the early artifice in brass and iron under Tubal-Cain: And find also mention of gold, silver, brass, tin, lead, iron; beside refining, sodering, dross, nitre, saltpits, and in some manner also of antimony.*[3]

Gemmarie naturalists reade diligently the pretious stones in the holy city of the apocalypse: examine the breast-plate of Aaron, and various gemms upon it, and think the second row the nobler of the four:[4] they wonder to find the art of ingravery so ancient upon pretious stones and signets; together with the ancient use of ear-rings and bracelets. And are pleased to find pearl, coral, amber and crystal in those sacred leaves, according to our translation. And when they often meet with flints and marbles, cannot but take notice that there is no mention of the magnet or loadstone, which in so many similitudes, comparisons, and allusions, could hardly have been omitted in the works of Solomon; if it were true that he knew either the attractive or directive power thereof, as some have believed.

Navigatours consider the ark, which was pitched without and within, and could endure the ocean without mast or sails: they take special notice of the twenty seventh of Ezekiel; the mighty traffick and great navigation of Tyre, with particular mention of their sails, their masts of cedar, oars of oak, their skilfull pilots, mariners and calkers; as also of the long voyages of the fleets of Solomon; of Jehosaphat's ships broken at Ezion-Geber;[5] of the notable voyage and shipwreck of S. Paul, so accurately delivered in the Acts.

* Depinxit oculos stibio. 2 Kings 9:30. Jeremiah 4:30. Ezekiel, 23:40.

Oneirocritical diviners apprehend some hints of their knowledge, even from divine dreams; while they take notice of the dreams of Joseph, Pharaoh, Nebuchadnezzar, and the angels on Jacob's ladder;[6] and find, in Artemidorus and Achmetes, that ladders signifie travels, and the scales thereof preferment; and that oxen lean and fat naturally denote scarcity or plenty, and the successes of agriculture.

Physiognomists will largely put in from very many passages of Scripture. And when they find in Aristotle, *quibus frons quadrangula, commensurata, fortes, referuntur ad leones*, cannot but take special notice of that expression concerning the Gadites; *mighty men of war, fit for battel, whose faces were as the faces of lyons.*[*7]

* 1 Chronicles 12:8.

Geometrical and architectonical artists look narrowly upon the description of the Ark, the fabrick of the temple, and the holy city in the Apocalypse.

But the botanical artist meeting every where with vegetables, and from the figg leaf in Genesis to the star wormwood in the Apocalypse, are variously interspersed expressions from plants, elegantly advantaging the significancy of the text: whereof many being delivered in a language proper unto Judæa and neighbour countries are imperfectly apprehended by the common reader, and now doubtfully made out, even by the Jewish expositour.

And even in those which are confessedly known, the elegancy is often lost in the apprehension of the reader, unacquainted with such vegetables, or but nakedly knowing their natures: whereof holding a pertinent apprehension, you cannot pass over such expressions without some doubt or want of satisfaction in your judgment. Hereof we shall only hint or discourse some few which I could not but take notice of in the reading of holy Scripture.

Many plants are mention'd in Scripture which are not distinctly known in our countries, or under such names in the original, as they are fain to be rendred by analogy, or by the name of vegetables of good affinity unto them, and so maintain the textual sense, though in some variation from identity.

THE OBSERVATIONS

Kikaion

1. That plant which afforded a shade unto Jonah,[*] mentioned by the name of Kikaion, and still retained at least marginally in some translations, to avoid obscurity Jerome rendered *Hedera* or ivy; which notwithstanding (except in its scandent nature) agreed not fully with the other, that is, to grow up in a night, or be consumed with a worm;[8] ivy being of no swift growth, little subject unto worms, and a scarce plant about Babylon.

[*] Jonah 4:6; a Gourd.

Hyssope

2. That hyssope is taken for that plant which cleansed the leper, being a well scented, and very abstersive simple, may well be admitted;[9] so we be not too confident, that it is strictly the same with our common hyssope: the hyssope of those parts differing from that of ours; as Bellonius hath observed in the hyssope which grows in Judæa, and the hyssope of the wall mention'd in the works of Solomon, no kind of our hyssope; and may tolerably be taken for some kind of minor capillary, which best makes out the antithesis with the cedar. Nor when we meet with *Libanotis*, is it to be conceived our common rosemary, which is rather the first kind thereof among several others, used by the ancients.

Hemlock

3. That it must be taken for hemlock, which is twice so rendred in our translation,[†] will hardly be made out, otherwise than in the intended sense, and implying some plant, wherein bitterness or a poisonous quality is considerable.

[†] Hosea 10:4. Amos 6:12.

Paliurus

4. What Tremelius rendreth *spina*, and the vulgar translation *paliurus*, and others make some kind of *rhamnus*, is allowable in the sense; and we contend not about the species, since they are known thorns in those countries, and in our field or gardens among us; and so common in Judæa, that men conclude the thorny crown of our Saviour was made either of *paliurus* or *rhamnus*.

Rubus

5. Whether the bush which burnt and consumed not, were properly a *rubus* or bramble, was somewhat doubtfull from the original and some translations, had not the Evangelist, and S. Paul express'd the same by the Greek word *βάτος* which from the description of Dioscorides, herbarists accept for *rubus*;[10] although the same word *βάτος* expresseth not onely the rubus or kinds of bramble, but other thorn-bushes, and the hipp-briar is also named *κυνόσβατος*, or the dog-briar or bramble.

Myrica

* Canticles 1:14.

6. That myrica is rendred, heath,* sounds instructively enough to our ears, who behold that plant so common in barren plains among us: but you cannot but take notice that *erica*, or our heath is not the same plant with *myrica* or tammarice, described by Theophrastus and Dioscorides, and which Bellonius declareth to grow so plentifully in the desarts of Judæa and Arabia.

Cypress

† Canticles 1:14.

7. That the *βότρυς τῆς Κύπρου*, *botrus Cypri*, or clusters of Cypress,† should have any reference to the cypress tree, according to the original *copher*, or clusters of the noble vine of cyprus, which might be planted into Judæa, may seem to others allowable in some latitude. But there seeming some noble odour to be implied in this place, you may probably conceive that the expression drives at the *Κύπρος* of Dioscorides, some oriental kind of *ligustrum* or *alcharma*, which Dioscorides and Pliny mention under the name of *Κύπρος* and Cyprus, and to grow about Ægypt and Ascalon, producing a sweet and odorate bush of flowers, out of which was made the famous *oleum cyprinum*.

But why it should be rendered camphyre your judgment cannot but doubt, who know that our camphyre was unknown unto the ancients, and no ingredient into any composition of great antiquity: that learned men long conceived it a bituminous and fossile body, and our latest experience discovereth it to be the resinous substance of a tree, in Borneo and China; and that the camphyre that we use is a neat preparation of the same.

Shittah Tree, etc

8. When 'tis said in Isaiah 41. *I will plant in the wilderness the cedar, the shittah tree, and the myrtle and the oil tree, I will set in the desart, the firre tree, and the pine, and the box tree*:* though some doubt may be made of the shittah tree, yet all these trees here mentioned being such as are ever green, you will more emphatically apprehend the mercifull meaning of God in this mention of no fading, but always verdant trees in dry and desart places.

* Isaiah 41:19.

Grapes of Eshcol

9. *And they cut down a branch with one cluster of grapes, and they bare it between two upon a staff, and they brought pomegranates and figgs.*† This cluster of grapes brought upon a staff by the spies was an incredible sight, in Philo Judæus,‡ seem'd notable in the eyes of the Israelites, but more wonderfull in our own, who look onely upon northern vines. But herein you are like to consider, that the cluster was thus carefully carried to represent it entire, without bruising or breaking; that this was not one bunch but an extraordinary cluster, made up of many depending upon one gross stalk. And however, might be parallel'd with the eastern clusters of *margiana* and *caramania*, if we allow but half the expressions of Pliny and Strabo, whereof one would lade a curry or small cart; and may be made out by the clusters of the grapes of Rhodes presented unto Duke Radzivil,§ each containing three parts of an ell in compass, and the grapes as big as prunes.

† Numbers 13:23.

‡ ἄριστος θέα. Philo.

§ Radzivil in his *Travels*.

Ingredients of holy perfume. Stacte, etc

10. Some things may be doubted in the species of the holy ointment and perfume. With amber, musk and civet we meet not in the Scripture, nor any odours from animals; except we take the *onycha* of that perfume for the covercle of a shell-fish called *unguis odoratus*, or *blatta byzantina*, which Dioscorides affirmeth to be taken from a shell-fish of the Indian lakes, which feeding upon aromatical plants is gathered when the lakes are drie.** But whether that which we now call *blatta byzantina*, or *unguis odoratus*, be the same with that odorate one of antiquity, great doubt may be made; since Dioscorides

** Exodus 30:34–35.

saith it smelled like *castoreum*, and that which we now have is of an ungratefull odour.

No little doubt may be also made of *galbanum* prescribed in the same perfume, if we take it for *galbanum* which is of common use among us, approaching the evil scent of *assa fœtida*; and not rather for *galbanum* of good odour, as the adjoining words declare, and the original *chelbena* will bear; which implies a fat or resinous substance, that which is commonly known among us being properly a gummous body and dissoluble also in water.

The holy ointment of stacte or pure myrrh, distilling from the plant without expression or firing, of cinnamon, cassia and calamus, containeth less questionable species, if the cinnamon of the ancients were the same with ours, or managed after the same manner. For thereof Dioscorides made his noble unguent. And cinnamon was so highly valued by princes, that Cleopatra carried it unto her sepulchre with her jewels; which was also kept in wooden boxes among the rarities of kings: and was of such a lasting nature, that at his composing of treacle for the Emperour Severus, Galen made use of some which had been laid up by Adrianus.

Husks eaten by the Prodigal

11. That the Prodigal Son desired to eat of husks given unto swine,* will hardly pass in your apprehension for the husks of pease, beans, or such edulious pulses;[11] as well understanding that the textual word Κεράτιον or Ceration, properly intendeth the fruit of the siliqua tree so common in Syria, and fed upon by men and beasts; called also by some the fruit of the locust tree, and *panis Sancti Johannis*, as conceiving it to have been part of the diet of the Baptist in the desart. The tree and fruit is not onely common in Syria and the eastern parts, but also well known in Apuglia, and the kingdom of Naples, growing along the Via Appia, from Fundi unto Mola; the hard cods or husks making a rattling noise in windy weather, by beating against one another: called by the Italians *carobbe* or *carobbole*, and by the French *carouges*. With the sweet pulp hereof some conceive that the Indians preserve ginger, mirabolans and nutmegs. Of the same (as Pliny delivers) the ancients made one kind of wine, strongly expressing the juice thereof; and so they might after give the expressed and less usefull part of the cods, and remaining pulp unto their swine: which being no gustless or

* Luke 15:16.

unsatisfying offal, might be well desired by the Prodigal in his hunger.

Cucumbers, etc. of Ægypt

12. No marvel is it that the Israelites having lived long in a well watred country, and been acquainted with the noble water of Nilus, should complain for water in the dry and barren wilderness. More remarkable it seems that they should extoll and linger after the cucumbers and leeks, onions and garlick in Ægypt: wherein notwithstanding lies a pertinent expression of the diet of that country in ancient times, even as high as the building of the Pyramids, when Herodotus delivereth, that so many talents were spent in onions and garlick, for the food of labourers and artificers; and is also answerable unto their present plentifull diet in cucumbers, and the great varieties thereof, as testified by Prosper Alpinus, who spent many years in Ægypt.

Forbidden Fruit

13. What fruit that was which our first parents tasted in paradise,* from the disputes of learned men seems yet indeterminable. More clear it is that they cover'd their nakedness or secret parts with figg leaves; which when I reade, I cannot but call to mind the several considerations which antiquity had of the figg tree, in reference unto those parts, particularly how figg leaves by sundry authours are described to have some resemblance unto the genitals, and so were aptly formed for such contection of those parts;[12] how also in that famous statua of Praxiteles, concerning Alexander and Bucephalus, the secret parts are veil'd with figg leaves: how this tree was sacred unto Priapus, and how the diseases of the secret parts have derived their name from figgs.

* Genesis 2:17.

Balsam Oil

14. That the Good Samaritan coming from Jericho used any of the Judean Balsam upon the wounded traveller, is not to be made out,† and we are unwilling to disparage his charitable surgery in pouring oil into a green wound; and therefore when 'tis said he used oil and wine, may rather conceive that he made an *oinelæum* or medicine of oil and

† Luke 10:34.

wine beaten up and mixed together, which was no improper medicine, and is an art now lately studied by some so to incorporate wine and oil that they may lastingly hold together, which some pretend to have, and call it *Oleum Samaritanum*, or Samaritan's Oil.

Pulse of Daniel

15. When Daniel would not pollute himself with the diet of the Babylonians,* he probably declined Pagan commensation, or to eat of meats forbidden to the Jews, though common at their tables, or so much as to taste of their Gentile immolations, and sacrifices abominable unto his palate.

* Daniel 1:12.

But when 'tis said that he made choice of the diet of pulse and water, whether he strictly confined unto a leguminous food, according to the vulgar translation, some doubt may be raised, from the original word *zeragnim*, which signifies seminalia, and is so set down in the margin of Arias Montanus; and the Greek word *spermata*, generally expressing seeds, may signifie any edulious or cerealious grains beside ὄσπρια or leguminous seeds.

Yet if he strictly made choice of a leguminous food, and water instead of his portion from the king's table, he handsomely declined the diet which might have been put upon him, and particularly that which was called the *potibasis* of the king, which as Athenæus informeth implied the bread of the king, made of barley, and wheat, and the wine of Cyprus, which he drank in an oval cup. And therefore distinctly from that he chose plain fare of water, and the gross diet of pulse, and that perhaps not made into bread, but parched, and tempered with water.

Now that herein (beside the special benediction of God) he made choice of no improper diet to keep himself fair and plump and so to excuse the eunuch his keeper, physicians will not deny, who acknowledge a very nutritive and impinguating faculty in pulses, in leguminous food, and in several sorts of grains and corns, is not like to be doubted by such who consider that this was probably a great part of the food of our forefathers before the floud, the diet also of Jacob:[13] and that the Romans (called, therefore, *pultifagi*) fed much on pulse for six hundred years; that they had no bakers for that time: and their pistours were such as, before the use of mills, beat out and cleansed their corn.[14] As also that the athletick diet was of pulse, *alphiton*, *maza*, barley and water; whereby they were advantaged sometimes to an exquisite state of health, and such as was not without danger. And therefore (though Daniel were no eunuch, and of a more fatning and thriving temper, as some have phancied yet) was he by this kind of diet, sufficiently maintained in a fair and carnous state of body, and accordingly his picture not improperly drawn, that is, not meagre and lean, like Jeremy's, but plump and fair, answerable to the most authentick draught of the Vatican, and the late German Luther's Bible.

The Cynicks in Athenæus make iterated courses of lentils, and prefer that diet before the luxury of *Seleucus*. The present Ægyptians, who are observed by Alpinus to be the fattest nation, and men to have breasts like women, owe much, as he conceiveth, unto the water of Nile, and their diet of rice, pease, lentils and white cicers. The pulse-eating Cynicks and Stoicks, are all very long livers in Laertius. And Daniel must not be accounted of few years, who, being carried away captive in the reign of Joachim, by King Nebuchadnezzar, lived, by Scripture account, unto the first year of Cyrus.

Jacob's Rods

16. *And Jacob took rods of green poplar, and of the hazel and the chesnut tree, and pilled white streaks in them, and made the white appear which was in the rods, etc.*[*] Men multiply the philosophy of Jacob, who, beside the benediction of God, and the powerfull effects of imagination, raised in the goats and sheep from pilled and party-coloured objects, conceive that he chose out these particular plants above any other, because he understood they had a particular virtue unto the intended effects, according unto the conception of Georgius Venetus.[†]

Whereto you will hardly assent, at least till you be better satisfied and assured concerning the true species of the plants intended in the text, or find a clearer consent and uniformity in the translation: for what we render poplar, hazel and chesnut, the Greek translateth *virgam styracinam*, *nucinam*, *plataninam*, which some also render a pomegranate: and so observing this variety of interpretations concerning common and known plants among us, you may more reasonably doubt, with what

[*] Genesis 30:37.

[†] G. Venerns *Problem* 200.

propriety or assurance others less known be sometimes rendred unto us.

Lilies of the Field

* Matthew 6:28.

17. Whether in the Sermon of the Mount,* the lilies of the field did point at the proper lilies, or whether those flowers grew wild in the place where our Saviour preached, some doubt may be made: because κρίνον the word in that place is accounted of the signification with λείριον, and that in Homer is taken for all manner of specious flowers: so received by Eustachius, Hesychius, and the scholiast upon Apollonius Rhodius, καθόλου τὰ ἄνθη λείρια λέγεται. And κρίνον is also received in the same latitude, not signifying onely lilies, but applied unto daffodils, hyacinths, iris's, and the flowers of colocynthis.

Under the like latitude of acception, are many expressions in the Canticles to be received. And when it is said *he feedeth among the lilies*, therein may be also implied other specious flowers, not excluding the proper lilies. But in that expression, the lilies drop forth myrrhe, neither proper lilies nor proper myrrhe can be apprehended, the one not proceeding from the other, but may be received in a metaphorical sense: and in some latitude may be also made out from the roscid and honey drops observable in the flowers of martagon, and inverted flowred lilies, and 'tis like, is the standing sweet dew on the white eyes of the crown imperial, now common among us.

And the proper lily may be intended in that expression of 1 Kings 7, that the brazen sea was of the thickness of a hand breadth, and the brim like a lily. For the figure of that flower being round at the bottom, and somewhat repandous, or inverted at the top, doth handsomely illustrate the comparison.

† Canticles 2.

But that the lily of the valley, mention'd in the Canticles,† *I am the rose of Sharon, and the lily of the valleys*, is that vegetable which passeth under the same name with us, that is *lilium convallium*, or the May lily, you will more hardly believe, who know with what insatisfaction the most learned botanists, reduce that plant unto any described by the ancients; that Anguillara will have it be the *Œnanthe* of Athenæus, *Cordus* the *Pothos* of Theophrastus; and Lobelius that the Greeks had not described it; who find not six leaves in the flower agreeably to all lilies, but only six small divisions in the flower, who find it also to have a single, and no bulbous root, nor leaves shooting about the bottom, nor the stalk round, but angular. And that the learned Bauhinus hath not placed in the classis of lilies, but nervifolious plants.[15]

Fitches, Cummin, etc. in Isaiah 28:25

18. *Doth he not cast abroad the fitches, and scatter the cummin seed, and cast in the principal wheat, and the appointed barley, and the rye in their place*: herein though the sense may hold under the names assigned, yet is it not so easie to determine the particular seeds and grains, where the obscure original causeth such differing translations. For in the vulgar we meet with *milium* and *gith*, which our translation declineth, placing fitches for *gith*, and rye for *milium* or millet, which notwithstanding is retained by the Dutch.

That it might be *melanthium*, *nigella*, or *gith*, may be allowably apprehended, from the frequent use of the seed thereof among the Jews and other nations, as also from the translation of Tremellius; and the original implying a black seed, which is less than cummin, as, out of Aben Ezra, Buxtorfius hath expounded it.

But whereas milium or κέγχρος of the septuagint is by ours rendred rye, there is little similitude or affinity between those grains; for milium is more agreeable unto *spelta* or *espaut*, as the Dutch and others still render it.

That we meet so often with cummin seed in many parts of Scripture in reference unto Judæa, a seed so abominable at present unto our palates and nostrils, will not seem strange unto any who consider the frequent use thereof among the ancients, not onely in medical but dietetical use and practice: for their dishes were filled therewith, and the noblest festival preparations in Apicius were not without it: and even in the polenta, and parched corn, the old diet of the Romans, (as Pliny recordeth) unto every measure they mixed a small proportion of lin-seed and cummin-seed.

And so cummin is justly set down among things of vulgar and common use, when it is said in Matthew 23.v.23. *You pay tithe of mint, annise and cummin*: but how to make out the translations of annise we are still to seek, there being no word in the text which properly signifieth annise: the original being ἄνηθον, which the Latins call *anethum*, and is properly englished Dill.

That among many expressions, allusions and illustrations made in Scripture from corns, there is no mention made of oats, so usefull a grain among us, will not seem very strange unto you, till you can clearly discover that it was a grain of ordinary use in those parts; who may also find that Theophrastus, who is large about other grains, delivers very little of it. That Dioscorides is also very short therein. And Galen delivers that it was of some use in Asia minor, especially in Mysia, and that rather for beasts than men: and Pliny affirmeth that the pulticula thereof was most in use among the Germans. Yet that the Jews were not without all use of this grain seems confirmable from the Rabbinical account, who reckon five grains liable unto their offerings, whereof the cake presented might be made; that is, wheat, oats, rye, and two sorts of barley.

Ears of Corn

* Matthew 12:1.

19. Why the Disciples being hungry pluck'd the ears of corn,* it seems strange to us, who observe that men half starved betake not themselves to such supply; except we consider the ancient diet of *alphiton* and *polenta*, the meal of dried and parched corn, or that which was ὠμήλυσις or meal of crude and unparched corn, wherewith they being well acquainted, might hope for some satisfaction from the corn yet in the husk; that is, from the nourishing pulp or mealy part within it.

Stubble of Ægypt

† Exod. 5:7, etc.

‡ Lib. 18. Nat Hist.

20. The inhumane oppression of the Ægyptian task-masters,† who, not content with the common tale of brick, took also from the children of Israel their allowance of straw, and forced them to gather stubble where they could find it, will be more nearly apprehended, if we consider how hard it was to acquire any quantity of stubble in Ægypt, where the stalk of corn was so short, that to acquire an ordinary measure, it required more than ordinary labour; as is discoverable from that account, which Pliny hath happily left unto us.‡ In the corn gather'd in Ægypt the straw is never a cubit long: because the seed lieth very shallow, and hath no other nourishment than from the mudd and slime left by the river; for under it is nothing but sand and gravel.

So that the expression of Scripture is more emphatical than is commonly apprehended, when 'tis said, *the people were scattered abroad through all the land of Ægypt to gather stubble instead of straw*. For the stubble being very short, the acquist was difficult; a few fields afforded it not, and they were fain to wander far to obtain a sufficient quantity of it.

Flowers of the Vine

21. It is said in the Song of Solomon, that *the vines with the tender grape give a good smell.*[*] That the flowers of the vine should be emphatically noted to give a pleasant smell, seems hard unto our northern nostrills, which discover not such odours, and smell them not in full vineyards; whereas in hot regions, and more spread and digested flowers, a sweet savour may be allowed, denotable from several humane expressions, and the practice of the ancients, in putting the dried flowers of the vine into new wine to give it a pure and flosculous race or spirit, which wine was therefore called *οἰνάνθιον*, allowing unto every *cadus* two pounds of dried flowers.[16]

[*] Canticles 2:13.

And therefore, the vine flowering but in the spring, it cannot but seem an impertinent objection of the Jews, that the Apostles were full of new wine at Pentecost when it was not to be found.[†] Wherefore we may rather conceive that the word *γλευκύ* in that place implied not new wine or must, but some generous strong and sweet wine, wherein more especially lay the power of inebriation.

[†] Acts 1:13.

But if it be taken for some kind of must, it might be some kind of *ἀειγλεῦκος*, or long-lasting must, which might be had at any time of the year, and which, as Pliny delivereth, they made by hindring, and keeping the must from fermentation or working, and so it kept soft and sweet for no small time after.

The Olive Leaf in Genesis 8.11

22. When the Dove, sent out of the ark, return'd with a green olive leaf, according to the original: how the leaf, after ten months, and under water, should maintain a verdure or greenness, need not much amuse the reader, if we consider that the olive tree is *ἀείφυλλον*, or continually green; that the leaves are of a bitter taste, and of a fast and lasting substance. Since we also find fresh and green leaves among the olives which we receive from remote countries; and since the plants at the bottom of the sea, and on the sides of rocks, maintain a deep and fresh verdure.

How the tree should stand so long in the deluge under water, may partly be allowed from the uncertain determination of the flows and currents of that time, and the qualification of the saltness of the sea, by the admixture of fresh water, when the whole watery element was together.

And it may be signally illustrated from like examples in Theophrastus and Pliny in words to this effect:* Even the sea affordeth shrubs and trees; in the red sea whole woods do live, namely of bays and olives bearing fruit. The souldiers of Alexander, who sailed into India, made report, that the tides were so high in some islands, that they overflowed, and covered the woods, as high as plane and poplar trees. The lower sort wholly, the greater all but the tops, whereto the mariners fastned their vessels at high waters, and at the root in the ebb; that the leaves of these sea trees while under water looked green, but taken out presently dried with the heat of the sun. The like is delivered by Theophrastus, that some oaks do grow and bear acorns under the sea.

* Theophrast *Hist. Lib* 4. *Cap.* 7, 8. Plin. *Lib.* 13. *cap. ultimo.*

Grain of Mustard-seed in S. Matthew 31:31-2

23. *The kingdom of Heaven is like to a grain of mustard-seed, which a man took and sowed in his field, which indeed is the least of all seeds; but when 'tis grown is the greatest among herbs, and becometh a tree, so that the birds of the air come and lodge in the branches thereof.*

Luke 13:19. *It is like a grain of mustard-seed, which a man took and cast it into his garden, and it waxed a great tree, and the fowls of the air lodged in the branches thereof.*

This expression by a grain of mustard-seed, will not seem so strange unto you, who well consider it. That it is simply the least of seeds, you cannot apprehend, if you have beheld the seeds of *rapunculus*, marjorane, tobacco, and the smallest seed of *lunaria*.

But you may well understand it to be the smallest seed among herbs which produce so big a plant, or the least of herbal plants, which arise unto such a proportion, implied in the expression; *the smallest of seeds*, and *becometh the greatest of herbs*.

And you may also grant that it is the smallest of seeds of plants apt to δενδρίζειν, *arborescere*, *fruticescere*, or to grow unto a ligneous substance, and from an herby and oleraceous vegetable, to become a kind of tree, and to be accounted among the *dendrolachana*, or *arboroleracea*;[17] as upon strong seed, culture and good ground, is observable in some cabbages, mallows, and many more, and therefore expressed by *γίνεται τὸ δένδρον*, and *γίνεται εἰς τὸ δένδρον*, it becometh a tree, or *arborescit*, as Beza rendreth it.

Nor if warily considered doth the expression contain such difficulty. For the parable may not ground itself upon generals, or imply any or every grain of mustard, but point at such a grain as from its fertile spirit, and other concurrent advantages, hath the success to become arboreous, shoot into such a magnitude, and acquire the like tallness. And unto such a grain the kingdom of heaven is likened which from such slender beginnings shall find such increase and grandeur.

The expression also that it might grow into such dimensions that birds might lodge in the branches thereof, may be literally conceived; if we allow the luxuriancy of plants in Judæa, above our northern regions; if we accept of but half the story taken notice of by Tremellius, from the Jerusalem Talmud, of a mustard tree that was to be climbed like a figg tree; and of another, under whose shade a potter daily wrought: and it may somewhat abate our doubts, if we take in the advertisement of Herodotus concerning lesser plants of *milium* and *sesamum* in the Babylonian soil: *milium ac sesamum in proceritatem instar arborum crescere, etsi mihi compertum, tamen memorare supersedeo, probè sciens eis qui nunquam Babyloniam regionem adierunt perquam incredibile visum iri.*[18] We may likewise consider that the word *κατασκηνῶσαι* doth not necessarily signifie making a nest, but rather sitting, roosting, covering and resting in the boughs, according as the same word is used by the Septuagint in other places* as the Vulgar rendreth it in this, *inhabitant*, as our translation, *lodgeth*, and the Rhemish, *resteth* in the branches.

* Daniel 4:9 as Psalms 104:12.

The Rod of Aaron

24. *And it came to pass that on the morrow Moses went into the Tabernacle of witness, and behold the Rod of Aaron for the House of Levi was budded, and brought forth buds, and bloomed blossomes, and yielded almonds.*† In the contention of the tribes and decision of priority and primogeniture of Aaron, declared by the rod, which in a night budded, flowred and brought forth almonds, you cannot but apprehend a propriety in the miracle from that species of tree which leadeth in the vernal

† Numbers 17:8.

germination of the year, unto all the classes of trees; and so apprehend how properly in a night and short space of time the miracle arose, and somewhat answerable unto its nature the flowers and fruit appeared in this precocious tree, and whose original name* implies such speedy efflorescence, as in its proper nature flowering in February, and shewing its fruit in March.

* Shacher from *Shachar festinus fuit* or *maturuit*.

This consideration of that tree maketh the expression in Jeremy† more emphatical, when 'tis said, *what seest thou? And he said, a rod of an almond tree. Then said the Lord unto me, thou hast well seen, for I will hasten the word to perform it.* I will be quick and forward like the almond tree, to produce the effects of my word, and hasten to display my judgments upon them.

† Jeremiah 1:11–12.

And we may hereby more easily apprehend the expression in Ecclesiastes;‡ *when the almond tree shall flourish.* That is when the head, which is the prime part, and first sheweth it self in the world, shall grow white, like the flowers of the almond tree, whose fruit, as Athenæus delivereth, was first called κάρηνον or the head, from some resemblance and covering parts of it.

‡ Ecclesiastes 12:5.

How properly the priority was confirmed by a rod or staff, and why the rods and staffs of the princes were chosen for this decision, philologists will consider. For these were the badges, signs and cognisances of their places, and were a kind of sceptre in their hands, denoting their supereminencies.[19] The staff of divinity is ordinarily described in the hands of gods and goddesses in old draughts. Trojan and Grecian princes were not without the like, whereof the shoulders of Thersites felt from the hands of Ulysses.[20] Achilles in Homer, as by a desperate oath, swears by his wooden sceptre, which should never bud nor bear leaves again; which seeming the greatest impossibility to him, advanceth the miracle of Aaron's Rod. And if it could be well made out that Homer had seen the books of Moses, in that expression of Achilles, he might allude unto this miracle.

That power which proposed the experiment by blossomes in the rod, added also the fruit of almonds; the text not strictly making out the leaves, and so omitting the middle germination: the leaves properly coming after the flowers, and before the almonds. And therefore if you have well perused medals, you cannot but observe how in the impress of many shekels, which pass among us by the name of the Jerusalem shekels, the Rod of Aaron is improperly laden with many leaves, whereas that which is shewn under the name of the Samaritan shekel seems most conformable unto the text, which describeth the fruit without leaves.

The Vine in Gen. 49:11

25. *Binding his foal unto the vine, and his asses colt unto the choice vine.*

That Vines, which are commonly supported, should grow so large and bulky, as to be fit to fasten their juments, and beasts of labour unto them, may seem a hard expression unto many:[21] which notwithstanding may easily be admitted, if we consider the account of Pliny, that in many places out of Italy vines do grow without any stay or support: nor will it be otherwise conceived of lusty vines, if we call to mind how the same authour* delivereth, that the statua of Jupiter was made out of a vine; and that out of one single Cyprian vine a scale or ladder was made that reached unto the roof of the temple of Diana at Ephesus.

* Pliny, lib. 14.

Rose of Jericho

26. *I was exalted as a palm tree in Engaddi, and as a rose plant in Jericho.*†

† Ecclesiasticus. 24:14.

That the rose of Jericho, or that Plant which passeth among us under the denomination, was signified in this text, you are not like to apprehend with some, who also name it the rose of S. Mary, and deliver, that it openeth the branches, and flowers upon the eve of our Saviour's nativity: but rather conceive it some proper kind of rose, which thrived and prospered in Jericho more than in the neighbour countries. For our rose of Jericho is a very low and hard plant, a few inches above the ground; one whereof brought from Judæa I have kept by me many years, nothing resembling a rose tree, either in flowers, branches, leaves or growth; and so, improper to answer the emphatical word of exaltation in the text: growing not onely about Jericho, but other parts of Judæa and Arabia, as Bellonius hath observed: which being a drie and ligneous plant, is preserved many years, and though crumpled and furdled up, yet, if infused in water, will swell and display its parts.[22]

Turpentine Tree in Ecclus. 24:16

27. *Quasi terebinthus extendi ramos*, when it is said in the same chapter, *as a turpentine tree have I stretched out my branches*: it will not seem strange unto such as have either seen that tree, or examined its description:[23] for it is a plant that widely displayeth its branches: and though in some European countries it be but of a low and fruticeous growth, yet Pliny* observeth that it is great in Syria, and so allowably, or at least not improperly mentioned in the expression of Hosea† according to the vulgar translation, *Super capita montium sacrificant, etc. sub quercu, populo et terebintho, quoniam bona est umbra ejus.*[24] And this diffusion and spreading of its branches, hath afforded the proverb of *terebintho stultior*, applicable unto arrogant or boasting persons, who spread and display their own acts, as Erasmus hath observed.

* Terebinthus in Macedonia fruticat, in Syria, magna est. Lib. 13. Plin.

† Hosea. 4:13.

Pomegranate in 1 Samuel 14:2

28. It is said in our translation, *Saul tarried in the uppermost parts of Gibeah, under a pomegranate tree which is in Migron: and the people which were with him were about six hundred men*. And when it is said in some Latin translations, *Saul morabatur fixo tentorio sub malogranato*, you will not be ready to take it in the common literal sense, who know that a pomegranate tree is but low of growth, and very unfit to pitch a tent under it; and may rather apprehend it as the name of a place, or the rock of Rimmon, or Pomegranate; so named from pomegranates which grew there, and which many think to have been the same place mentioned in Judges.‡

‡ Judges 20:45.47. Ch. 21:13.

A Green Field in Wisdom 19:7

29. It is said in the book of Wisedom, *where water stood before, drie land appeared, and out of the red sea a way appeared without impediment, and out of the violent streams a green field*; or as the Latin renders it, *campus germinans de profundo*: whereby it seems implied that the Israelites passed over a green field at the bottom of the sea: and though most would have this but a metaphorical expression, yet may it be literally tolerable; and so may be safely apprehended by those that sensibly know what great number of vegetables (as the several varieties of alga's, sea lettuce, *phasganium*, *conferva*, *caulis marina*, *abies*, *erica*,

tamarice, divers sorts of *muscus*, *fucus*, *quercus marina* and corallins) are found at the bottom of the sea.[25] Since it is also now well known, that the western ocean, for many degrees, is covered with *sargasso* or *lenticula marina*, and found to arise from the bottom of that sea; since, upon the coast of Provence by the Isles of Eres, there is a part of the Mediterranean Sea, called *la Prairie*, or the Meadowy Sea, from the bottom thereof so plentifully covered with plants: since vast heaps of weeds are found in the bellies of some whales taken in the northern ocean, and at a great distance from the shore: and since the providence of nature hath provided this shelter for minor fishes; both for their spawn, and safety of their young ones. And this might be more peculiarly allowed to be spoken of the Red Sea, since the Hebrews named it *Suph*, or the Weedy Sea; and, also, seeing Theophrastus and Pliny, observing the growth of vegetables under water, have made their chief illustrations from those in the Red Sea.

Sycamore

30. You will readily discover how widely they are mistaken, who accept the sycamore mention'd in several parts of the Scripture for the sycamore, or tree of that denomination, with us: which is properly but one kind or difference of *acer*, and bears no fruit with any resemblance unto a figg.

But you will rather, thereby, apprehend the true and genuine sycamore, or *sycaminus*, which is a stranger in our parts. A tree (according to the description of Theophrastus, Dioscorides and Galen) resembling a mulberry tree in the leaf, but in the fruit a figg; which it produceth not in the twiggs but in the trunck or greater branches, answerable to the sycamore of Ægypt, the Ægyptian figg or *giamez* of the Arabians, described in Prosper Alpinus, with a leaf somewhat broader than a mulberry, and in its fruit like a figg. Insomuch that some have fancied it to have had its first production from a figg grafted on a mulberry.

It is a tree common in Judæa, whereof they made frequent use in buildings; and so understood, it explaineth that expression in Isaiah:* *sycamori excisi sunt, cedros substituemus. The bricks are fallen down, we will build with hewen stones: the sycamores are cut down, but we will change them into cedars.*

* Isaiah 9:10.

It is a broad spreading tree, not onely fit for walks, groves and shade, but also affording profit. And therefore it is said that King David appointed Baalhanan to be over his olive trees and sycamores, which were in great plenty;[*] and it is accordingly delivered, that *Solomon made cedars to be as the sycamore trees that are in the vale for abundance.*[†] That is, he planted many, though they did not come to perfection in his days.

[*] 1 Chronicles 27:28.

[†] 1 Kings 10:27.

And as it grew plentifully about the plains, so was the fruit good for food; and, as Bellonius and late accounts deliver, very refreshing unto travellers in those hot and drie countries: whereby the expression of Amos becomes more intelligible, when he said he was an herdsman, and a gatherer of sycamore fruit.[‡] And the expression of David also becomes more emphatical;[§] *he destroyed their vines with hail, and their sycamore trees with frost.* That is, their *sicmoth* in the original, a word in the sound not far from the sycamore.

[‡] Amos 7:14.

[§] Psal. 78:47.

Thus when it is said,[**] *if ye had faith as a grain of mustard-seed, ye might say unto this sycamine tree, Be thou plucked up by the roots, and be thou placed in the sea, and it should obey you*: it might be more significantly spoken of this sycamore; this being described to be *arbor vasta*, a large and well rooted tree, whose removal was more difficult than many others. And so the instance in that text, is very properly made in the sycamore tree, one of the largest and less removable trees among them. A tree so lasting and well rooted, that the sycamore which Zacheus ascended, is still shewn in Judæa unto Travellers; as also the hollow sycamore at Maturæa in Ægypt, where the blessed Virgin is said to have remained: which though it relisheth of the legend, yet it plainly declareth what opinion they had of the lasting condition of that tree, to countenance the tradition; for which they might not be without some experience, since the learned describer of the pyramides[††] observeth, that the old Ægyptians made coffins of this wood, which he found yet fresh and undecayed among divers of their mummies.

[**] Luke 17:6.

[††] D Greaves.

And thus, also, when Zacheus climbed up into a sycamore above any other tree, this being a large and fair one, it cannot be denied that he made choice of a proper and advantageous tree to look down upon our Saviour.

Increase of Seed 100. fold in Matthew 13:23

31. Whether the expression of our Saviour in the Parable of the Sower, and the increase of the seed *unto thirty, sixty and a hundred fold*, had any reference unto the ages of believers, and

measures of their faiths, as children, young and old persons, as to beginners, well advanced and strongly confirmed Christians, as learned men have hinted; or whether in this progressional assent there were any latent mysteries, as the mystical interpreters of numbers may apprehend, I pretend not to determine.

But, how this multiplication may well be conceived, and in what way apprehended, and that this centesimal increase is not naturally strange, you that are no stranger in agriculture, old and new, are not like to make great doubt.[26]

That every grain should produce an ear affording an hundred grains, is not like to be their conjecture who behold the growth of corn in our fields, wherein a common grain doth produce far less in number. For barley consisting but of two *versus* or rows, seldom exceedeth twenty grains, that is, ten upon each στοῖχος, or row; rye, of a square figure, is very fruitfull at forty: wheat, besides the frit and *uruncus*, or imperfect grains of the small husks at the top and bottom of the ear, is fruitfull at ten treble *glumæ* or husks in a row, each containing but three grains in breadth, if the middle grain arriveth at all to perfection; and so maketh up threescore grains in both sides.

Yet even this centesimal fructification may be admitted in some sorts of *cerealia*, and grains from one ear: if we take in the *Triticum centigranum*, or *fertilissimum Plinii*, Indian wheat, and *panicum*; which, in every ear, containeth hundreds of grains.

But this increase may easily be conceived of grains in their total multiplication, in good and fertile ground, since, if every grain of wheat produceth but three ears, the increase will arise above that number. Nor are we without examples of some grounds which have produced many more ears, and above this centesimal increase: as Pliny hath left recorded of the Byzacian field in Africa, *Misit ex eo loco Procurator ex uno quadraginta minus germina. Misit et Neroni pariter tercentum quadraginta stipulos, ex uno grano. Cum centessimos quidem Leontini Siciliæ campi fundunt, aliique, et tota Bœtica, et imprimis Ægyptus.*[27] And even in our own country, from one grain of wheat sowed in a garden, I have numbered many more than an hundred.

And though many grains are commonly lost which come not to sprouting or earing, yet the same is also verified in measure; as that one bushel should produce a hundred, as is exemplified by the corn in Gerar;* *then Isaac sowed in that land, and received*

* Genesis 26:12.

in that year an hundred fold. That is, as the Chaldee explaineth it, *a hundred for one*, when he measured it. And this Pliny seems to intend, when he saith of the fertile Byzacian territory before mentioned, *ex uno centeni quinquaginta modii redduntur*.[28] And may be favourably apprehended of the fertility of some grounds in Poland; wherein, after the account of Gaguinus, from rye sowed in August, come thirty or forty ears, and a man on horseback can scarce look over it. In the sabbatical crop of Judæa, there must be admitted a large increase, and probably not short of this centesimal multiplication: for it supplied part of the sixth year, the whole seventh, and eighth untill the harvest of that year.

The seven years of plenty in Ægypt must be of high increase; when, by storing up but the fifth part, they supplied the whole land, and many of their neighbours after: for it is said, *the famine was in all the land about them*.* And therefore though the causes of the dearth in Ægypt be made out from the defect of the overflow of Nilus, according to the dream of Pharaoh; yet was that no cause of the scarcity in the land of Canaan, which may rather be ascribed to the want of the former and latter rains, for some succeeding years, if their famine held time and duration with that of Ægypt; as may be probably gathered from that expression of Joseph,† *come down unto me [into Ægypt] and tarry not, and there will I nourish you: (for yet there are five years of famine) lest thou and thy houshold, and all that thou hast come to poverty*.

* Genesis 41:56.

† Genesis 45:9–11.

How they preserved their corn so long in Ægypt may seem hard unto northern and moist climates, except we consider the many ways of preservation practised by antiquity, and also take in that handsome account of Pliny; what corn soever is laid up in the ear, it taketh no harm keep it as long as you will; although the best and most assured way to keep corn is in caves and vaults under ground, according to the practice of Cappadocia and Thracia.

In Ægypt and Mauritania above all things they look to this, that their granaries stand on high ground; and how drie so ever their floor be, they lay a course of chaff betwixt it and the ground. Besides, they put up their corn in granaries and binns together with the ear. And Varro delivereth that wheat laid up in that manner will last fifty years; millet an hundred; and beans so conserved in a cave of Ambracia, were known to last an hundred and twenty years; that is, from the time of King Pyrrhus, unto the Pyratick War under the conduct of Pompey.

More strange it may seem how, after seven years, the grains conserved should be fruitfull for a new production. For it is said that *Joseph delivered seed unto the Ægyptians, to sow their land for the eighth year*: and corn after seven years is like to afford little or no production, according to Theophrastus;* *ad sementem semen anniculum optimum putatur, binum deterius et trinum; ultra sterile fermè est, quanquam ad usum cibarium idoneum.*[29]

* Theoph. *Hist.* *l*.8.

Yet since, from former exemplifications, corn may be made to last so long, the fructifying power may well be conceived to last in some good proportion, according to the region and place of its conservation, as the same Theophrastus hath observed, and left a notable example from Cappadocia, where corn might be kept sixty years, and remain fertile at forty; according to his expression thus translated; *in Cappadociæ loco quodam petra dicto, triticum ad quadraginta annos fœcundum est, et ad sementem percommodum durare proditum est, sexagenos aut septuagenos ad usum cibarium servari posse idoneum.*[30] The situation of that conservatory, was, as he delivereth, ὑψηλὸν, εὔπνουν, εὔαυρον, high, airy and exposed to several favourable winds. And upon such consideration of winds and ventilation, some conceive the Ægyptian granaries were made open, the country being free from rain. Howsoever it was, that contrivance could not be without some hazard: for the great mists and dews of that country might dispose the corn unto corruption.

More plainly may they mistake, who from some analogy of name (as if Pyramid were derived from πυρόν, Triticum), conceive the Ægyptian Pyramids to have been built for granaries; or look for any settled monuments about the desarts erected for that intention; since their store-houses were made in the great towns, according to Scripture expression,† *he gathered up all the food of seven years, which was in the land of Ægypt, and laid up the food in the cities: the food of the field which was round about every city, laid he up in the same.*

† Genesis 41:48.

Olive Tree in Romans 11:24

32. *For if thou wert cut out of the olive tree, which is wild by nature, and wert grafted, contrary to nature, into a good olive tree, how much more shall these, which be the natural branches, be grafted unto their own olive tree?* In which place, how answerable to the doctrine of husbandry this expression of S. Paul is, you will readily apprehend who understand the rules of insition or

grafting, and that way of vegetable propagation;[31] wherein that is contrary to nature, or natural rules which art observeth: viz. to make use of cyons more ignoble than the stock, or to graft wild upon domestick and good plants, according as Theophrastus hath anciently observed, and, making instance in the olive, hath left this doctrine unto us;[*][32] *Urbanum sylvestribus ut satis oleastris inserere. Nam si è contrario sylvestrem in urbanos severis, etsi differentia quædam erit, tamen bonæ frugis arbor*[†] *nunquam profecto reddetur*:[33] which is also agreeable unto our present practice, who graft pears on thorns, and apples upon crabb stocks, not using the contrary insition. And when it is said, *how much more shall these, which are the natural branches, be grafted into their own natural olive tree*? This is also agreeable unto the rule of the same authour; ἔστι δὲ βελτίων ἐγκεντρισμὸς ὁμοίων εἰς ὅμοια, *insitio melior est similium in similibus*: for the nearer consanguinity there is between the cyons and the stock, the readier comprehension is made, and the nobler fructification. According also unto the later caution of Laurenbergius;[‡] *arbores domesticæ insitioni destinatæ, semper anteponendæ Sylvestribus.*[34] And though the success be good, and may suffice upon stocks of the same denomination; yet, to be grafted upon their own and mother stock, is the nearest insition: which way, though less practised of old, is now much imbraced, and found a notable way for melioration of the fruit; and much the rather, if the tree to be grafted on be a good and generous plant, a good and fair olive, as the Apostle seems to apply by a peculiar word scarce to be found elsewhere.[§]

[*] De causis Plant. *Lib.*1. *Cap.* 7.

[†] *Καλλικαρπεῖν οὐκ ἕξει.*

[‡] *De horticultura.*

[§] *καλλιέλαιον*, Romans 11:24.

It must be also considered, that the *oleaster*, or wild olive, by cutting, transplanting and the best managery of art, can be made but to produce such olives as (Theophrastus saith) were particularly named Phaulia, that is, but bad olives; and that it was reckon'd among prodigies, for the *oleaster* to become an olive tree.

And when insition or grafting, in the text, is applied unto the olive tree, it hath an emphatical sense, very agreeable unto that tree which is best propagated this way; not at all by surculation, as Theophrastus observeth, nor well by seed, as hath been observed.[35] *Omne semen simile genus perficit, præter oleam, Oleastrum enim generat, hoc est sylvestrem oleam, et non oleam veram.*[36]

'If, therefore, thou Roman and Gentile branch, which were cut from the wild olive, art now, by the signal mercy of God, beyond the ordinary and commonly expected way, grafted into the true olive, the Church of God; if thou, which neither naturally nor by humane art canst be made to produce any good fruit, and, next to a miracle, to be made a true olive, art now by the benignity of God grafted into the proper olive; how much more shall the Jew, and natural branch, be grafted into its genuine and mother tree, wherein propinquity of nature is like, so readily and prosperously, to effect a coalition? And this more especially by the expressed way of insition or implantation, the olive being not successfully propagable by seed, nor at all by surculation.'

Stork nesting on Firre Trees in Psalm 104:17

33. *As for the stork, the firre trees are her house*. This expression, in our translation, which keeps close to the original *Chasidah*, is somewhat different from the Greek and Latin translation; nor agreeable unto common observation, whereby they are known commonly to build upon chimneys, or the tops of houses, and high buildings, which notwithstanding, the common translation may clearly consist with observation, if we consider that this is commonly affirmed of the black stork, and take notice of the description of *Ornithologus* in Aldrovandus, that such storks are often found in divers parts, and that they do *in arboribus nidulari, præsertim in abietibus*; make their nests on trees, especially upon firre trees. Nor wholly disagreeing unto the practice of the common white stork, according unto Varro, *nidulantur in agris*: and the concession of Aldrovandus that sometimes they build on trees: and the assertion of Bellonius,* that men dress them nests, and place cradles upon high trees, in Marish regions, that storks may breed upon them: which course some observe for herns and cormorants with us. And this building of Storks upon trees, may also be answerable unto the original and natural way of building of storks before the political habitations of men, and the raising of houses and high buildings; before they were invited by such conveniences and prepared nests, to relinquish their natural places of nidulation.[37] I say, before or where such advantages are not ready; when swallows found other places than chimneys, and daws found other places than holes in high Fabricks to build in.

* Bellonius *de Avibus*.

Balm in Genesis 43:11

34. *And, therefore, Israel said carry down the man a present, a little balm, a little honey, and myrrhe, nuts and almonds.*[*38] Now whether this, which Jacob sent, were the proper balsam extolled by humane writers, you cannot but make some doubt, who find the Greek translation to be ῥησίνη that is, *resina*, and so many have some suspicion that it might be some pure distillation from the turpentine tree, which grows prosperously and plentifully in Judæa, and seems so understood by the Arabick; and was indeed esteemed by Theophrastus and Dioscorides, the chiefest of resinous bodies, and the word *resina* emphatically used for it.

* Balm, in Genesis 43:11.

That the balsam plant hath grown and prospered in Judæa we believe without dispute. For the same is attested by Theophrastus, Pliny, Justinus, and many more; from the commendation that Galen affordeth of the balsam of Syria, and the story of Cleopatra, that she obtain'd some plants of balsam from Herod the Great to transplant into Ægypt. But whether it was so anciently in Judæa as the time of Jacob; nay, whether this plant was here before the time of Solomon, that great collector of vegetable rarities, some doubt may be made from the account of Josephus, that the Queen of Sheba, a part of Arabia, among presents unto Solomon, brought some plants of the balsam tree, as one of the peculiar estimables of her country.

Whether this ever had its natural growth, or were an original native plant of Judæa, much more that it was peculiar unto that countrey, a greater doubt may arise: while we reade in Pausanius, Strabo and Diodorus, that it grows also in Arabia, and find in Theophrastus, that it grew in two gardens about Jericho in Judæa.[†] And more especially whiles we seriously consider that notable discourse between Abdella, Abdachim and Alpinus, concluding the natural and original place of this singular plant to be in Arabia, about Mecha and Medina, where it still plentifully groweth, and mountains abound therein. From whence it hath been carefully transplanted by the Basha's of Grand Cairo, into the garden of Matarea; where, when it dies, it is repaired again from those parts of Arabia, from whence the Grand Signior yearly receiveth a present of balsam from the Xeriff of Mecha, still called by the Arabians *balessan*; whence they believe arose the Greek appellation balsam. And since these balsam-plants are not now to be found in Judæa, and

† Theophrast. l. 9, c. 6.

though purposely cultivated, are often lost in Judæa, but everlastingly live, and naturally renew in Arabia; they probably concluded, that those of Judæa were foreign and transplanted from these parts.

All which notwithstanding, since the same plant may grow naturally and spontaneously in several countries, and either from inward or outward causes be lost in one region, while it continueth and subsisteth in another, the balsam tree might possibly be a native of Judæa as well as of Arabia; which because de facto it cannot be clearly made out, the ancient expressions of Scripture become doubtfull in this point. But since this plant hath not, for a long time, grown in Judæa, and still plentifully prospers in Arabia, that which now comes in pretious parcels to us, and still is called the balsam of Judæa, may now surrender its name, and more properly be called the balsam of Arabia.

Barley, Flax, etc. in Exodus 9:31

35. *And the flax and the barley was smitten; for the barley was in the ear, and the flax was bolled, but the wheat and the rye was not smitten, for they were not grown up.*[*] How the barley and the flax should be smitten in the plague of hail in Ægypt, and the wheat and rye escape, because they were not yet grown up, may seem strange unto English observers, who call barley summer corn sown so many months after wheat, and beside *hordeum Polystichon*, or big barley, sowe not barley in the winter, to anticipate the growth of wheat.

[*] Linum foliculos germinavit, σπερματίζον.

And the same may also seem a preposterous expression unto all who do not consider the various agriculture, and different husbandry of nations, and such as was practised in Ægypt, and fairly proved to have been also used in Judæa, wherein their barley harvest was before that of wheat; as is confirmable from that expression in Ruth, that *she came into Bethlehem at the beginning of barley harvest*, and staid unto the end of the wheat harvest; from the death of Manasses the father of Judith, emphatically expressed to have happened in the wheat harvest, and more advanced heat of the sun; and from the custom of the Jews, to offer the barley sheaf of the first fruits in March, and a cake of wheat flower but at the end of Pentecost. Consonant unto the practice of the Ægyptians, who (as Theophrastus delivereth) sowed their barley early in reference to their first fruits; and also the common rural practice, recorded by the same authour, *Maturè seritur Triticum, Hordeum, quod etiam maturius seritur*; wheat and barley are sowed early, but barley earlier of the two.

Flax was also an early plant, as may be illustrated from the neighbour country of Canaan. For the Israelites kept the Passeover in Gilgal in the fourteenth day of the first month, answering unto part of our March, having newly passed Jordan: and the spies which were sent from Shittim unto Jericho, not many days before, were hid by Rahab under the stalks of flax, which lay drying on the top of her house; which sheweth that the flax was already and newly gathered. For this was the first preparation of flax, and before fluviation or rotting, which, after Pliny's account, was after wheat harvest.

But the wheat and the rye were not smitten, for they were not grown up. The original signifies that it was hidden, or dark, the Vulgar and Septuagint that it was serotinous or late, and our old translation that it was late sown. And so the expression and interposition of Moses, who well understood the husbandry of Ægypt, might emphatically declare the state of wheat and rye in that particular year; and if so, the same is solvable from the time of the floud of Nilus, and the measure of its inundation. For if they were very high, and over-drenching the ground, they were forced to later seed-time: and so the wheat and the rye escaped; for they were more slowly growing grains, and, by reason of the greater inundation of the river, were sown later than ordinary that year, especially in the plains near the river, where the ground drieth latest.

Some think the Plagues of Ægypt were acted in one month, others but in the compass of twelve. In the delivery of Scripture there is no account, of what time of the year or particular month they fell out; but the account of these grains, which were either smitten or escaped, make the plague of hail to have probably hapned in February: this may be collected from the new and old account of the seed time and harvest in Ægypt. For, according to the account of Radzevil,* the river rising in June, and the banks being cut in September, they sow about S. Andrews, when the floud is retired, and the moderate driness of the ground permitteth. So that the Barley anticipating the wheat, either in time of sowing or growing, might be in ear in February.

* Radzevil's *Travels*.

The account of Pliny is little different.† They cast the seed upon the slime and mudd when the river is down, which commonly happeneth in the beginning of November. They

† Plin. *lib.* 18. cap. 18.

begin to reap and cut down a little before the Calends of April, about the middle of March, and in the month of May their harvest is in. So that barley anticipating wheat, it might be in ear in February, and wheat not yet grown up, at least to the spindle or ear, to be destroyed by the hail. For they cut down about the middle of March, at least their forward corns, and in the month of May all sorts of corn were in.

The turning of the river into bloud shews in what month this happened not. That is, not when the river had overflown; for it is said, *the Ægyptians digged round about the river for water to drink*, which they could not have done, if the river had been out, and the fields under water.

In the same text you cannot, without some hesitation, pass over the translation of rye, which the original nameth *cassumeth*, the Greek rendreth *olyra*, the French and Dutch *spelta*, the Latin *zea*, and not *secale* the known word for rye. But this common rye so well understood at present, was not distinctly described, or not well known from early antiquity. And therefore, in this uncertainty, some have thought it to have been the *typha* of the ancients. *Cordus* will have it to be *olyra*, and *Ruellius* some kind of *oryza*. But having no vulgar and well known name for those grains, we warily embrace an appellation of near affinity, and tolerably render it rye.

While flax, barley, wheat and rye are named, some may wonder why no mention is made of ryce, wherewith, at present, Ægypt so much aboundeth. But whether that plant grew so early in that country, some doubt may be made: for ryce is originally a grain of India, and might not then be transplanted into Ægypt.

Sheaves of Grass, in Psalm 129:6–7

36. *Let them become as the grass growing upon the house top, which withereth before it be plucked up, whereof the mower filleth not his hand, nor he that bindeth sheaves his bosome*. Though the filling of the hand, and mention of sheaves of haye, may seem strange unto us, who use neither handfulls nor sheaves in that kind of husbandry, yet it may be properly taken, and you are not like to doubt thereof, who may find the like expressions in the authour's *de Re rustica*, concerning the old way of this husbandry.

Columella delivering what works were not to be permitted upon the Roman *feriæ*, or festivals; among others sets down, that upon such days, it was not lawfull to carry or bind up hay, *nec fœnum vincire nec vehere, per religiones pontificum licet*.* [39]

* Columella *lib.* 2. cap. 22.

Marcus Varro is more particular; *primum de pratis herbarum cum crescere desiit, subsecari falcibus debet, et quoad peracescat furcillis versari, cum peracuit, de his manipulos fieri et vehi in villam.*† [40]

† Varro *lib.* I. cap. 49.

And their course of mowing seems somewhat different from ours. For they cut not down clear at once, but used an after section, which they peculiarly called *sicilitium*, according as the word expounded by Georgius Alexandrinus, and Beroaldus after Pliny; *sicilire est falcibus consectari quæ fœnisecæ præterierunt, aut ea secare quæ fœnisecæ præterierunt.*[41]

Juniper Tree, in 1 Kings 19:5, etc

37. When 'tis said that Elias lay and slept under a juniper tree, some may wonder how that tree, which in our parts groweth but low and shrubby, should afford him shade and covering. But others know that there is a lesser and a larger kind of that vegetable; that it makes a tree in its proper soil and region. And may find in Pliny that in the temple of Diana Saguntina in Spain, the rafters were made of juniper.

In that expression of David,‡ *sharp arrows of the mighty, with coals of juniper*; though juniper be left out in the last translation, yet may there be an emphatical sense from that word; since juniper abounds with a piercing oil, and makes a smart fire. And the rather, if that quality be half true, which Pliny affirmeth, that the coals of juniper raked up will keep a glowing fire for the space of a year. For so the expression will emphatically imply, not onely the smart burning, but the lasting fire of their malice.

‡ Psal. 120:4.

That passage of Job,§ wherein he complains that poor and half famished fellows despised him, is of greater difficulty; *for want and famine they were solitary, they cut up mallows by the bushes, and juniper roots for meat.* Wherein we might at first doubt the translation, not onely from the Greek text but the assertion of Dioscorides, who affirmeth that the roots of juniper are of a venemous quality. But Scaliger hath disproved the same from the practice of the African physicians, who use the decoction of juniper roots against the venereal disease. The Chaldee reads it *genista*, or some kind of broom, which will be also unusual and hard diet, except thereby we understand the *orobanche*, or broom rape, which groweth from the roots

§ Job 30:3–4.

of broom; and which, according to Dioscorides, men used to eat raw or boiled in the manner of asparagus.

And, therefore, this expression doth highly declare the misery, poverty and extremity of the persons who were now mockers of him; they being so contemptible and necessitous, that they were fain to be content, not with a mean diet, but such as was no diet at all, the roots of trees, the roots of juniper, which none would make use of for food, but in the lowest necessity, and some degree of famishing.

Scarlet Tincture in Genesis 38:28. Exodus 25:4, etc

38. While some have disputed whether Theophrastus knew the scarlet berry, others may doubt whether that noble tincture were known unto the Hebrews, which notwthstanding seems clear from the early and iterated expressions of Scripture concerning the scarlet tincture, and is the less to be doubted because the scarlet berry grew plentifully in the land of Canaan, and so they were furnished with the materials of that colour. For though Dioscorides saith it groweth in Armenia and Cappadocia, yet that it also grew in Judæa, seems more than probable from the account of Bellonius, who observed it to be so plentifull in that country, that it affordeth a profitable commodity, and great quantity thereof was transported by the Venetian merchants.

How this should be fitly expressed by the word *tolagnoth*, *vermis*, or worm, may be made out from Pliny, who calls it *coccus scolecius*, or the wormy berry; as also from the name of that colour called vermillion, or the worm colour; and which is also answerable unto the true nature of it. For this is no proper berry containing the fructifying part, but a kind of vessicular excrescence, adhering commonly to the leaf of the *ilex coccigera*, or dwarf and small kind of oak, whose leaves are always green, and its proper seminal parts acrons.[42] This little bagg containeth a red pulp, which, if not timely gathered, or left to it self, produceth small red flies, and partly a red powder, both serviceable unto the tincture. And therefore, to prevent the generation of Flies, when it is first gathered, they sprinkle it over with vinegar, especially such as make use of the fresh pulp for the confection of *Alkermes*; which still retaineth the Arabick name, from the kermesberry; which is agreeable unto the description of Bellonius and Quinqueranus. And the same we have beheld in Provence and Languedock, where it is plentifully gathered, and called *manna rusticorum*, from the considerable profit which the peasants make by gathering of it.

Oaks, in Genesis 35:4–8, Joshua 24:26, Isaiah 1:29, Ezekiel 27:6, Hosea. 4:13, etc

39. Mention is made of oaks in divers parts of Scripture, which though the Latin sometimes renders a turpentine tree, yet surely some kind of oak may be understood thereby; but whether our common oak as is commonly apprehended, you may well doubt; for the common oak, which prospereth so well with us, delighteth not in hot regions. And that diligent botanist Bellonius, who took such particular notice of the plants of Syria and Judæa, observed not the vulgar oak in those parts. But he found the *ilex*, *chesne verde*, or ever-green oak, in many places; as also that kind of oak which is properly named *esculus*: and he makes mention thereof in places about Jerusalem, and in his Journey from thence unto Damascus, where he found *Montes Ilice, et Esculo virentes*; which, in his discourse of Lemnos, he saith are always green. And therefore when it is said of Absalom,* that his *mule went under the thick boughs of a great oak, and his head caught hold of the oak, and he was taken up between the heaven and the earth*, that oak might be some *ilex*, or rather *esculus*. For that is a thick and bushy kind, in *orbem comosa*, as Dalechampius; *ramis in orbem dispositis comans*, as Renealmus describeth it. And when it is said that *Ezechias broke down the images, and cut down the groves*, they might much consist of oaks, which were sacred unto Pagan deities, as this more particularly, according to that of Virgil,

* 2 Samuel 18:9–14.

—Nemorúmque Jovi quæ maxima frondet
Esculus—[43]

And, in Judæa, where no hogs were eaten by the Jews, and few kept by others, 'tis not unlikely that they most cherished the *esculus*, which might serve for food of men. For the acrons thereof are the sweetest of any oak, and taste like chesnuts; and so, producing an edulious or esculent fruit, is properly named *esculus*.[44]

They which know the *ilex*, or ever-green oak, with somewhat prickled leaves, named πρῖνος, will better understand the irreconcileable answer of the two elders, when the one accused Susanna of incontinency under a πρῖνος, or ever-green oak, the other under a σχῖνος, *lentiscus*, or mastick tree, which are so different in bigness, boughs, leaves and fruit, the one bearing acrons, the other berries: and, without the knowledge hereof, will not emphatically or distinctly understand that of the poet,

Flaváque de viridi stillabant Ilice mella.[45]

Cedars of Libanus

40. When we often meet with the Cedars of Libanus, that expression may be used not onely because they grew in a known and neighbour country, but also because they were of the noblest and largest kind of that vegetable; and we find the Phœnician cedar magnified by the ancients. The cedar of Libanus is a coniferous tree, bearing cones or cloggs; (not berries) of such a vastness, that Melchior Lussy, a great Traveller, found one upon Libanus as big as seven men could compass. Some are now so curious as to keep the branches and cones thereof among their rare collections. And, though much cedar wood be now brought from America, yet 'tis time to take notice of the true cedar of Libanus, imployed in the temple of Solomon; for they have been much destroyed and neglected, and become at last but thin. Bellonius could reckon but twenty eight, Rowolfius and Radzevil but twenty four, and Bidulphus the same number. And a later account of some English travellers[*] that they are now but in one place, and in a small compass, in Libanus.

[*] *A Journey to Jerusalem*, 1672.

Quando ingressi fueritis terram, et plantaveritis in illa ligna Pomifera, auferetis præputia eorum. Poma quæ germinant immunda erunt vobis, nec edetis ex eis. Quarto autem anno, omnis fructus eorum sanctificabitur, laudabilis Domino. Quinto autem anno comedetis fructus.[†] By this law they were injoyned not to eat of the fruits of the trees which they planted for the first three years: and, as the Vulgar expresseth it, to take away the prepuces, from such trees, during that time; the fruits of the fourth year being holy unto the Lord, and those of the fifth allowable unto others. Now if *auferre præputia* be taken, as many learned men have thought, to pluck away the bearing buds, before they proceed unto flowers or fruit, you will readily apprehend the metaphor, from the analogy and similitude of those sprouts and buds, which, shutting up the fruitfull particle, resembleth the preputial part.

[†] Uncircumcised Fruit, in Levit. 19:23.–25.

And you may also find herein a piece of husbandry not mentioned in Theophrastus, or Columella. For by taking away of the buds, and hindring fructification, the trees become more vigorous, both in growth and future production. By such a way King Pyrrhus got into a lusty race of beeves, and such as were desired over all Greece, by keeping them from generation untill the ninth year.

And you may also discover a physical advantage of the goodness of the fruit, which becometh less crude and more wholsome, upon the fourth or fifth years production.

Partition of Plants into Herb and Tree, in Genesis 1:11

41. While you reade in Theophrastus, or modern herbalists, a strict division of plants, into *arbor*, *frutex*, *suffrutex* and *herba*, you cannot but take notice of the scriptural division at the Creation, into tree and herb: and this may seem too narrow to comprehend the classis of vegetables; which, notwithstanding, may be sufficient, and a plain and intelligible division thereof. And therefore in this difficulty concerning the division of plants, the learned botanist, Cæsalpinus, thus concludeth, *clarius agemus si alterâ divisione neglectâ, duo tantùm plantarum genera substituamus, arborem scilicet, et herbam, conjungentes cum arboribus frutices, et cum herba suffrutices*; *frutices* being the lesser trees, and *suffrutices* the larger, harder and more solid herbs.[46]

And this division into herb and tree, may also suffice, if we take in that natural ground of the division of perfect plants, and such as grow from seeds. For plants, in their first production, do send forth two leaves adjoining to the seed; and then afterwards, do either produce two other leaves, and so successively before any stalk; and such go under the name of πόα, βοτάνη, or herb; or else, after the first leaves succeeding to the seed leaves, they send forth a stalk, or rudiment of a stalk before any other leaves, and such fall under the classis of δένδρον or tree. So that, in this natural division, there are but two grand differences, that is, tree and herb. The *frutex* and *suffrutex* have the way of production from the seed, and in other respects the *suffrutices*, or *cremia*, have a middle and participating nature, and referable unto herbs.

The Bay Tree, in Psalm 37:35

42. *I have seen the ungodly in great power, and flourishing like a green bay tree*. Both Scripture and humane writers draw

frequent illustrations from plants. Scribonius Largus illustrates the old cymbals from *cotyledon palustris*, or *umbelicus veneris*. Who would expect to find Aaron's mitre in any plant? Yet Josephus hath taken some pains to make out the same in the seminal knop of *hyoscyamus*, or henbane. The Scripture compares the figure of manna unto the seed of coriander. In Jeremy* we find the expression, *streight as a palm tree*: and here the wicked in their flourishing state are likened unto a bay tree. Which, sufficiently answering the sense of the text, we are unwilling to exclude that noble plant from the honour of having its name in Scripture. Yet we cannot but observe, that the Septuagint renders it cedars, and the Vulgar accordingly, *vidi impium superexaltatum, et elevatum sicut cedros Libani*; and the translation of Tremellius mentions neither bay nor cedar; *sese explicantem tanquam arbor indigena virens*; which seems to have been followed by the last Low Dutch translation. A private translation renders it like a green self-growing laurel.† The High Dutch of Luther's Bible, retains the word *laurel*; and so doth the old Saxon and Island Translation; so also the French, Spanish; and Italian of Diodati: yet his notes acknowledge that some think it rather a cedar, and others any large tree in a prospering and natural soil.

* Jeremiah 10:5.

† Ainsworth.

But however these translations differ, the sense is allowable and obvious unto apprehension: when no particular plant is named, any proper to the sense may be supposed; where either cedar or laurel is mentioned, if the preceding words [*exalted and elevated*] be used, they are more appliable unto the cedar; where the word [*flourishing*][47] is used, it is more agreeable unto the laurel, which, in its prosperity, abounds with pleasant flowers, whereas those of the cedar are very little, and scarce perceptible, answerable unto the firre, pine and other coniferous trees.

The Figg Tree, in S. Mark. 11:13 etc

43. *And in the morning, when they were come from Bethany, he was hungry; and seeing a figg tree afar off having leaves, he came, if haply he might find any thing thereon; and when he came to it, he found nothing but leaves: for the time of figgs was not yet.* Singular conceptions have passed from learned men to make out this passage of S. Mark, which S. Matthew so plainly delivereth;‡ most men doubting why our saviour should

‡ Matthew 21:19.

curse the tree for bearing no fruit, when the time of fruit was not yet come; or why it is said that *the time of figgs was not yet*, when, notwithstanding, figgs might be found at that season.

* Heinsius *in Nonnum.*

Heinsius,* who thinks that Elias must salve the doubt, according to the received reading of the text, undertaketh to vary the same, reading οὗ γὰρ ἦν, καιρὸς σύκων, that is, *for where he was, it was the season or time for figgs.*

† D. Hammond.

A learned interpreter† of our own, without alteration of accents or words, endeavours to salve all, by another interpretation of the same, οὐ γὰρ καιρὸς σύκων, *for it was not a good or seasonable year for figgs.*

But, because men part not easily with old beliefs, or the received construction of words, we shall briefly set down what may be alledged for it.

And, first, for the better comprehension of all deductions hereupon, we may consider the several differences and distinctions both of figg trees and their fruits. Suidas upon the word ἰσχάς makes four divisions of figgs, ὄλυνθος, φήληξ, σῦκον, and ἰσχάς. But because φήληξ makes no considerable distinction, learned men do chiefly insist upon the three others, that is, ὄλυνθος, or *grossus*, which are the buttons, or small sort of figgs, either not ripe, or not ordinarily proceeding to ripeness, but fall away at least in the greatest part, and especially in sharp winters; which are also named συκάδες, and distinguished from the fruit of the wild figg, or *caprificus*, which is named ἐρινεός, and never cometh unto ripeness. The second is called σῦκον, or *ficus*, which commonly proceedeth unto ripeness in its due season. A third the ripe *figg* dried, which maketh the ἰσχάδες, or *carrier*.

Of figg trees there are also many divisions; for some are *prodromi*, or precocious, which bear fruit very early, whether they bear once, or oftner in the year; some are *protericæ*, which are the most early of the precocious trees, and bear soonest of any; some are *æstivæ*, which bear in the common season of the summer, and some *serotinæ*, which bear very late.

Some are biferous and triferous, which bear twice or thrice in the year, and some are of the ordinary standing course, which make up the expected season of figgs.

Again some figg trees, either in their proper kind, or fertility in some single ones, do bear fruit or rudiments of fruit all the year long; as is annually observed in some kind of figg trees in hot and proper regions; and may also be observed in some figg trees of more temperate countries, in years of no great disadvantage, wherein, when the summer-ripe figg is past, others begin to appear, and so, standing in buttons all the winter, do either fall away before the spring, or else proceed to ripeness.

Now, according to these distinctions, we may measure the intent of the text, and endeavour to make out the expression. For, considering the diversity of these trees, and their several fructifications, probable or possible it is, that some thereof were implied, and may literally afford a solution.

And first, though it was not the season for figgs, yet some fruit might have been expected, even in ordinary bearing trees. For the *grossi* or buttons appear before the leaves, especially before the leaves are well grown. Some might have stood during the winter, and by this time have been of some growth: though many fall off, yet some might remain on, and proceed towards maturity. And we find that good husbands had an art to make them hold on, as is delivered by Theophrastus.

The σῦκον or common summer figg was not expected; for that is placed by Galen among the *fructus horarii*, or *horæi*, which ripen in that part of summer, called ὥρα, and stands commended by him above other fruits of that season. And of this kind might be the figgs which were brought to Cleopatra in a basket together with an asp, according to the time of her death on the nineteenth of August. And that our Saviour expected not such figgs, but some other kind, seems to be implied in the indefinite expression, *if haply he might find any thing thereon*; which in that country, and the variety of such trees, might not be despaired of, at this season, and very probably hoped for in the first precocious and early bearing trees. And that there were precocious and early bearing trees in Judæa, may be illustrated from some expressions in Scripture concerning precocious figgs; *calathus unus habebat Ficus bonas nimis, sicut solent esse Ficus primi temporis*; *One Basket had very good figgs, even like the figgs that are first ripe*.* And the like might be more especially expected in this place, if this remarkable tree be rightly placed in some mapps of Jerusalem; for it is placed, by Adrichomius, in or near Bethphage, which some conjectures will have to be the house of figgs: and at this place figg trees are still to be found, if we consult the travels of Bidulphus.

* Jeremiah 24:2.

Again, in this great variety of figg trees, as precocious, proterical, biferous, triferous and always bearing trees, something might have been expected, though the time of common figgs was not yet. For some trees bear in a manner all the year; as may be illustrated from the epistle of the Emperour Julian, concerning his present of Damascus figgs, which he commendeth from their successive and continued growing and bearing, after the manner of the fruits which Homer describeth in the garden of Alcinous. And though it were then but about the eleventh of March, yet, in the latitude of Jerusalem, the sun at that time hath a good power in the day, and might advance the maturity of precocious often-bearing or ever-bearing figgs. And therefore when it is said* that S. Peter stood and warmed himself by the fire in the Judgment Hall, and the reason is added [*for it was cold*]† that expression might be interposed either to denote the coolness in the morning, according to hot countries, or some extraordinary and unusual coldness, which happened at that time. For the same Bidulphus, who was at that time of the year at Jerusalem, saith, that it was then as hot as at midsummer in England: and we find in Scripture, that the first sheaf of barley was offer'd in March.

* S. Mark 14:67. S. Luke 22:55–56.

† S. John 18:18.

Our Saviour therefore, seeing a figg tree with leaves well spread, and so as to be distinguished a far off, went unto it, and when he came, found nothing but leaves; he found it to be no precocious, or always-bearing tree: and though it were not the time for summer figgs, yet he found no rudiments thereof; and though he expected not common figgs, yet something might happily have been expected of some other kind, according to different fertility, and variety of production; but, discovering nothing, he found a tree answering unto the state of the Jewish rulers, barren unto all expectation.

And this is consonant unto the mystery of the story, wherein the figg tree denoteth the Synagogue and rulers of the Jews, whom God having peculiarly cultivated, singularly blessed and cherished, he expected from them no ordinary, slow, or customary fructification, but an earliness in good works, a precocious or continued fructification, and was not content with common after-bearing; and might justly have expostulated with the Jews, as God by the prophet Micah‡ did with their forefathers; *Præcoquas Ficus desideravit Anima mea, my soul longed for*, (or desired) *early ripe fruits, but ye are become as a vine already gathered, and there is no cluster upon you.*

‡ Micah 7:1.

Lastly, in this account of the figg tree, the mystery and symbolical sense is chiefly to be looked upon. Our Saviour, therefore, taking a hint from his hunger to go unto this specious tree, and intending, by this tree, to declare a judgment upon the Synagogue and people of the Jews, he came unto the tree, and, after the usual manner, inquired, and looked about for some kind of fruit, as he had done before in the Jews, but found nothing but leaves and specious outsides, as he had also found in them; and when it bore no fruit like them, when he expected it, and came to look for it, though it were not the time for ordinary fruit, yet failing when he required it, in the mysterious sense, 'twas fruitless longer to expect it. For he had come unto them, and they were nothing fructified by it, his departure approached, and his time of preaching was now at an end.

Now, in this account, besides the miracle, some things are naturally considerable. For it may be question'd how the figg tree, naturally a fruitfull plant, became barren, for it had no shew or so much as rudiment of fruit: and it was, in old time, a signal judgment of God, that *the figg tree should bear no fruit*: and therefore this tree may naturally be conceived to have been under some disease indisposing it to such fructification. And this, in the pathology of plants, may be the disease of φυλλομανία, ἐμφυλλισμός, or superfoliation mention'd by Theophrastus; whereby the fructifying juice is starved by the excess of leaves; which in this tree were already so full spread, that it might be known and distinguished afar off. And this was, also, a sharp resemblance of the hypocrisie of the rulers, made up of specious outsides, and fruitless ostentation, contrary to the fruit of the figg tree, which, filled with a sweet and pleasant pulp, makes no shew without, not so much as of any flower.

Some naturals are also considerable from the propriety of this punishment settled upon a figg tree: for infertility and barrenness seems more intolerable in this tree than any, as being a vegetable singularly constituted for production; so far from bearing no fruit that it may be made to bear almost any. And therefore the ancients singled out this as the fittest tree whereon to graft and propagate other fruits, as containing a plentifull and lively sap, whereby other cyons would prosper: and, therefore, this tree was also sacred unto the deity of fertility: and the statua of Priapus was made of the figg tree.

Olim truncus eram ficulnus inutile lignum.

It hath also a peculiar advantage to produce and maintain its fruit above all other plants, as not subject to miscarry in flowers and blossomes, from accidents of wind and weather. For it beareth no flowers outwardly, and such as it hath, are within the coat, as the later examination of naturalists hath discovered.

Lastly, it was a tree wholly constituted for fruit, wherein if it faileth, it is in a manner useless, the wood thereof being of so little use, that it affordeth proverbial expressions,

Homo ficulneus, argumentum ficulneum,

for things of no validity.

The Palm Tree, in Canticles 7:8

44. *I said I will go up into the palm tree, and take hold of the boughs thereof.* This expression is more agreeable unto the palm than is commonly apprehended, for that it is a tall bare tree bearing its boughs but at the top and upper part; so that it must be ascended before its boughs or fruit can be attained: and the going, getting or climbing up, may be emphatical in this tree; for the trunk or body thereof is naturally contrived for ascension, and made with advantage for getting up, as having many welts and eminencies, and so as it were a natural ladder, and staves, by which it may be climbed, as Pliny* observeth, *palmæ teretes atque proceres, densis quadratísque pollicibus faciles se ad scandendum præbent*, by this way men are able to get up into it. And the figures of Indians thus climbing the same are graphically described in the travels of Linschoten. This tree is often mentioned in Scripture, and was so remarkable in Judæa, that in after-times it became the emblem of that country, as may be seen in that medal of the Emperour Titus, with a captive woman sitting under a palm, and the inscription of *Judæa Capta*. And Pliny confirmeth the same when he saith, *Judæa palmis inclyta*.

* Plin. 13. *cap.* 4.

Lilies, in Cant. 2:1, 2:16

45. Many things are mention'd in Scripture, which have an emphasis from this or the neighbour countries: for besides the cedars, the Syrian Lilies are taken notice of by writers. That expression in the Canticles,† *thou art fair, thou art fair, thou hast doves eyes*, receives a particular character, if we look not upon our common pigeons, but the beauteous and fine ey'd doves of Syria.

† Cant. 4:1.

When the rump is so strictly taken notice of in the sacrifice of the peace offering, in these words, *the whole rump, it shall be taken off hard by the back-bone*,[*] it becomes the more considerable in reference to this country, where sheep had so large tails; which, according to Aristotle, were a cubit broad;[†] and so they are still, as Bellonius hath delivered.

[*] Levit. 3:9.

[†] Aristot. *Hist. Animal. lib.* 8.

When 'tis said in the Canticles, *thy teeth are as a flock of sheep, which go up from the washing, whereof every one beareth twins, and there is not one barren among them*;[‡] it may seem hard unto us of these parts to find whole flocks bearing twins, and not one barren among them; yet may this be better conceived in the fertile flocks of those countries, where sheep have so often two, sometimes three, and sometimes four, and which is so frequently observed by writers of the neighbour country of Ægypt. And this fecundity, and fruitfulness of their flocks, is answerable unto the expression of the psalmist, *that our sheep may bring forth thousands and ten thousands in our streets*.[§] And hereby, besides what was spent at their tables, a good supply was made for the great consumption of sheep in their several kinds of sacrifices; and of so many thousand male unblemished yearling lambs, which were required at their Passeovers.

[‡] Canticles 4:2.

[§] Psal. 144:13.

Nor need we wonder to find so frequent mention both of garden and field plants; since Syria was notable of old for this curiosity and variety, according to Pliny, *syria hortis operosissima*; and since Bellonius hath so lately observed of Jerusalem, that its hilly parts did so abound with plants, that they might be compared unto Mount Ida in Crete or Candia; which is the most noted place for noble simples yet known.

Trees and Herbs not expressly nam'd in Scripture

46. Though so many plants have their express names in Scripture, yet others are implied in some texts which are not explicitly mention'd. In the feast of Tabernacles or Booths, the law was this,[**] *thou shalt take unto thee boughs of goodly trees, branches of the palm, and the boughs of thick trees, and willows of the brook*. Now though the text descendeth not unto particulars of the goodly trees, and thick trees; yet Maimonides will tell us that for a goodly tree they made use of the citron tree, which is fair and goodly to the eye, and well prospering in that country: and that for the thick trees they used the myrtle, which was no rare or infrequent plant among them. And though it groweth but low in our gardens, was not a little tree in those parts; in

[**] Leviticus 23:40.

which plants also the leaves grew thick, and almost covered the stalk. And Curtius Symphorianus[*] in his description of the exotick myrtle, makes it, *folio densissimo senis in ordinem versibus*. The Paschal Lamb was to be eaten with bitterness or bitter herbs, not particularly set down in Scripture: but the Jewish writers declare, that they made use of succory, and wild lettuce, which herbs while some conceive they could not get down, as being very bitter, rough and prickly, they may consider that the time of the Passeover was in the spring, when these herbs are young and tender, and consequently less unpleasant: besides, according to the Jewish custom, these herbs were dipped in the *charoseth* or sawce made of raisins stamped with vinegar, and were also eaten with bread; and they had four cups of wine allowed unto them; and it was sufficient to take but a pittance of herbs, or the quantity of an olive.

[*] Curtius *de Hortis.*

Reeds in Scripture

47. Though the famous paper reed of Ægypt, be onely particularly named in Scripture; yet when reeds are so often mention'd, without special name or distinction, we may conceive their differences may be comprehended, and that they were not all of one kind, or that the common reed was onely implied. For mention is made in Ezekiel[†] of a *measuring reed of six cubits*: we find that they smote our Saviour on the head with a reed,[‡] and put a sponge with the vinegar on a reed, which was long enough to reach to his mouth, while he was upon the cross; and with such differences of reeds, *vallatory*, *sagittary*, *scriptory*, and others, they might be furnished in Judæa: for we find in the portion of Ephraim,[§] *vallis arundineti*; and so set down in the mapps of Adricomius, and in our translation the River Kana, or Brook of Canes. And Bellonius tells us that the River Jordan affordeth plenty and variety of reeds; out of some whereof the Arabs make darts, and light lances, and out of others, arrows; and withall that there plentifully groweth the fine *calamus*, *arundo scriptoria*, or writing reed, which they gather with the greatest care, as being of singular use and commodity at home and abroad; a hard reed about the compass of a goose or swans quill, whereof I have seen some polished and cut with a webb;[48] which is in common use for writing throughout the Turkish dominions, they using not the quills of birds.

[†] Ezekiel 40:5.

[‡] S. Matt. 27:30–48.

[§] Joshua 16:17.

And whereas the same authour with other describers of these parts affirmeth, that the River Jordan, not far from Jerico, is but such a stream as a youth may throw a stone over it, or about eight fathoms broad, it doth not diminish the account and solemnity of the miraculous passage of the Israelites under Joshua; for it must be considered, that they passed it in the time of harvest, when the river was high, and the grounds about it under water, according to that pertinent parenthesis, *as the feet of the priests, which carried the ark, were dipped in the brim of the water (for Jordan overfloweth all its banks at the time of harvest).*[*] In this consideration it was well joined with the great River Euphrates, in that expression in Ecclesiasticus,[†] *God maketh the understanding to abound like Euphrates, and as Jordan in the time of harvest.*

[*] Joshua 3:15.

[†] Ecclesiasticus. 24:26.

Zizania, in S. Matt. 13:24-25 etc

48. *The kingdom of heaven is likened unto a man which sowed good seed in his field, but while men slept, his enemy came and sowed tares (or, as the Greek, zizania) among the wheat.*

Now, how to render *zizania*, and to what species of plants to confine it, there is no slender doubt; for the word is not mention'd in other parts of Scripture, nor in any ancient Greek writer: it is not to be found in Aristotle, Theophrastus, or Dioscorides. Some Greek and Latin fathers have made use of the same, as also Suidas and Phavorinus; but probably they have all derived it from this text.

And therefore this obscurity might easily occasion such variety in translations and expositions. For some retain the word zizania, as the vulgar, that of *Beza*, of *Junius*, and also the Italian and Spanish. The Low Dutch renders it *oncruidt*, the German *oncraut*, or *herba mala*, the French *yuroye* or *lolium*, and the English *tares*.

Besides, this being conceived to be a Syriack word, it may still add unto the uncertainty of the sense. For though this Gospel were first written in Hebrew, or Syriack, yet it is not unquestionable whether the true original be any where extant: and that Syriack copy which we now have, is conceived to be of far later time than S. Matthew.

Expositours and annotatours are also various. Hugo Grotius hath passed the word zizania without a note. Diodati, retaining the word zizania, conceives that it was some peculiar herb growing among the corn of those countries, and not known in our fields. But Emmanuel de Sa interprets it, *plantas semini noxias*, and so accordingly some others.

Buxtorfius, in his Rabbinical lexicon, gives divers interpretations, sometimes for degenerated corn, sometimes for the black seeds in wheat, but withall concludes, *an hæc sit eadem vox aut species, cum zizaniâ apud evangelistam, quærant alii*. But lexicons and dictionaries by zizania do almost generally understand lolium, which we call darnel, and commonly confine the signification to that plant: notwithstanding, since lolium had a known and received name in Greek, some may be apt to doubt, why, if that plant were particularly intended, the proper Greek word was not used for the text. For Theophrastus named lolium αἶρα and hath often mentioned that plant; and in one place saith that corn doth sometimes *loliescere** or degenerate into darnel. Dioscorides, who travelled over Judæa, gives it the same name, which is also to be found in Galen, Ætius and Ægineta; and Pliny hath sometimes latinized that word into *æra*.

* Theophrast. *Hist. Plant.* I. 8.

Besides, lolium or darnel shews it self in the winter, growing up with the wheat; and Theophrastus observed that it was no vernal plant, but came up in the winter; which will not well answer the expression of the text, *and when the blade came up, and brought forth fruit*, or gave evidence of its fruit, the *zizania* appeared. And if the husbandry of the ancients were agreeable unto ours, they would not have been so earnest to weed away the darnel; for our husbandmen do not commonly weed it in the field, but separate the seeds after thrashing. And therefore Galen delivereth, that in an unseasonable year, and great scarcity of corn, when they neglected to separate the darnel, the bread proved generally unwholsome, and had evil effects on the head.

Our old and later translation render *zizania*, tares, which name our English botanists give unto *aracus*, *cracca*, *vicia sylvestris*, calling them tares, and strangling tares. And our husbandmen by tares understand some sorts of wild fitches, which grow amongst corn, and clasp upon it, according to the Latin etymology, *vicia à viciendo*. Now in this uncertainty of the original, tares as well as some others, may make out the sense, and be also more agreeable unto the circumstances of the parable. For they come up and appear what they are, when the blade of the corn is come up, and also the stalk and fruit discoverable. They have likewise little spreading roots, which may intangle or rob the good roots, and they have also tendrils and claspers, which lay hold of what grows near them, and so can hardly be weeded without endangering the neighbour corn.

However, if by *zizania* we understand *herbas segeti noxias*, or *vitia segetum*, as some expositours have done, and take the word in a more general sense, comprehending several weeds and vegetables offensive unto corn, according as the Greek word in the plural number may imply, and as the learned Laurenbergius* hath expressed, *runcare quod apud nostrates weden dicitus, zizanias inutiles est evellere*. If, I say, it be thus taken, we shall not need to be definitive, or confine unto one particular plant, from a word which may comprehend divers: and this may also prove a safer sense, in such obscurity of the original.

* *De Horticultura.*

And therefore since in this parable the sower of the *zizania* is the Devil, and the *zizania* wicked persons; if any from this larger acception, will take in thistles, darnel, cockle, wild strangling fitches, bindweed, *tribulus*, restharrow and other *vitia segetum*; he may, both from the natural and symbolical qualities of those vegetables, have plenty of matter to illustrate the variety of his mischiefs, and of the wicked of this world.

Cockle, in Job 31:40

49. When 'tis said in Job, *let thistles grow up instead of wheat, and cockle instead of barley*, the words are intelligible, the sense allowable and significant to this purpose: but whether the word cockle doth strictly conform unto the original, some doubt may be made from the different translations of it; for the Vulgar renders it *spina*, Tremelius *vitia frugum*, and the Geneva *yuroye* or darnel. Besides, whether cockle were common in the ancient agriculture of those parts, or what word they used for it, is of great uncertainty. For the elder botanical writers have made no mention thereof, and the moderns have given it the name of *pseudomelanthium*, *nigellastrum*, *lychnoeides segetum*, names not known unto antiquity: and therefore our translation hath warily set down [*noisome weeds*] in the margin.

TRACT II

Of Garlands and Coronary or Garland-plants

Sir,

The use of flowry crowns and garlands is of no slender antiquity, and higher than I conceive you apprehend it. For, besides the old Greeks and Romans, the Ægyptians made use hereof; who, beside the bravery of their garlands, had little birds upon them to peck their heads and brows, and so to keep them from sleeping at their festival compotations.[49] This practice also extended as far as India: for at the feast with the Indian King, it is peculiarly observed by Philostratus that their custom was to wear garlands, and come crowned with them unto their feast.

The crowns and garlands of the ancients were either gestatory, such as they wore about their heads or necks; portatory, such as they carried at solemn festivals; pensile or suspensory, such as they hanged about the posts of their houses in honour of their gods, as of Jupiter Thyræus or Limeneus; or else they were depository, such as they laid upon the graves and monuments of the dead. And these were made up after all ways of art, compactile, sutile, plectile; for which work there were *στεφανοπλόκοι*, or expert persons to contrive them after the best grace and property.

Though we yield not unto them in the beauty of flowry garlands, yet some of those of antiquity were larger than any we lately meet with: for we find in Athenæus that a myrtle crown of one and twenty foot in compass was solemnly carried about at the Hellotian Feast in Corinth, together with the bones of Europa.

And Garlands were surely of frequent use among them; for we read in Galen* that when Hippocrates cured the great plague of Athens by fires kindled in and about the city; the fuel thereof consisted much of their garlands. And they must needs be very frequent and of common use, the ends thereof being many. For they were convivial, festival, sacrificial, nuptial, honorary, funebrial. We who propose unto our selves the

* *De Theriaca ad Pisonem.*

pleasures of two senses, and onely single out such as are of beauty and good odour, cannot strictly confine our selves unto imitation of them.

For, in their convivial garlands, they had respect unto plants preventing drunkenness, or discussing the exhalations from wine; wherein, beside roses, taking in ivy, vervain, melilote, etc. they made use of divers of small beauty or good odour. The solemn festival garlands were made properly unto their Gods, and accordingly contrived from plants sacred unto such deities; and their sacrificial ones were selected under such considerations. Their honorary crowns triumphal, ovary, civical, obsidional, had little of flowers in them; and their funebrial garlands had little of beauty in them beside roses, while they made them of myrtle, rosemary, *apium* etc. under symbolical intimations: but our florid and purely ornamental garlands, delightfull unto sight and smell, nor framed according to mystical and symbolical considerations, are of more free election, and so may be made to excell those of the ancients; we having China, India, and a new world to supply us, beside the great distinction of flowers unknown unto antiquity, and the varieties thereof arising from art and nature.

But, beside vernal, æstival and autumnal made of flowers, the ancients had also hyemal garlands; contenting themselves at first with such as were made of horn died into several colours, and shaped into the figures of flowers, and also of *æs coronarium* or *clincquant* or brass thinly wrought out into leaves commonly known among us. But the curiosity of some emperours for such intents had roses brought from Ægypt untill they had found the art to produce late roses in Rome, and to make them grow in the winter, as is delivered in that handsome epigramme of Martial,

At tu Romanæ jussus jam cedere Brumæ
Mitte tuas messes, Accipe, Nile, Rosas.[50]

Some American nations, who do much excell in garlands, content not themselves onely with flowers, but make elegant crowns of feathers, whereof they have some of greater radiancy and lustre than their flowers: and since there is an art to set into shapes, and curiously to work in choicest feathers, there could nothing answer the crowns made of the choicest feathers of some *tomineios* and sun birds.

The catalogue of coronary plants is not large in Theophrastus, Pliny, Pollux, or Athenæus: but we may find a good enlargement in the accounts of modern botanists; and additions may still be made by successive acquists of fair and specious plants, not yet translated from foreign regions or little known unto our gardens; he that would be complete may take notice of these following,

Flos Tigridis.
Flos Lyncis.
Pinea Indici Recchi, Talama Ouiedi.
Herba Paradisea.
Volubilis Mexicanus.
Narcissus Indicus Serpentarius.
Helichrysum Mexicanum.
Xicama.
Aquilegia novæ Hispaniæ Cacoxochitli Recchi.
Aristochæa Mexicana.
Camaratinga sive Caragunta quarta Pisonis.
Maracuia Granadilla.
Cambay sive Myrtus Americana.
Flos Auriculæ Flor de la Oreia.
Floripendio novæ Hispaniæ.
Rosa Indica.
Zilium Indicum.
Fula Magori Garciæ.
Champe Garciæ Champacca Bontii.
Daullontas frutex odoratus seu Chamæmelum arborescens Bontii.
Beidelsar Alpini.
Sambuc.
Amberboi Turcarum.
Nuphar Ægyptium.
Lilionarcissus Indicus.
Bamma Ægyptiacum.
Hiucca Canadensis horti Farnesiani.
Buphthalmum novæ Hispaniæ Alepocapath.
Valeriana seu Chrysanthemum Americanum Acocotlis.
Flos Corvinus Coronarius Americanus.
Capolin Cerasus dulcis Indicus Floribus racemosis.
Asphodelus Americanus.
Syringa Lutea Americana.
Bulbus unifolius.
Moly latifolium Flore luteo.
Conyza Americana purpurea.
Salvia Cretica pomifera Bellonii.

Lausus Serrata Odora.
Ornithogalus Promontorii Bonæ Spei.
Fritallaria crassa Soldanica Promontorii Bonæ Spei.
Sigillum Solomonis Indicum.
Tulipa Promontorii Bonæ Spei.
Iris Uvaria.
Nopolxoch sedum elegans novæ Hispaniæ.

More might be added unto this List; and I have onely taken the pains to give you a short specimen of those many more which you may find in respective authours, and which time and future industry may make no great strangers in England. The inhabitants of Nova Hispania, and a great part of America, Mahometans, Indians, Chineses, are eminent promoters of these coronary and specious plants: and the annual tribute of the King of Bisnaguer in India, arising out of odours and flowers, amounts unto many thousands of crowns.

Thus, in brief, of this matter, I am, etc.

TRACT III

Of the Fishes Eaten by our Saviour With His Disciples After His Resurrection from the Dead

Sir,

I have thought, a little, upon the question proposed by you [viz. What kind of fishes those were of which our Saviour ate with his Disciples after his Resurrection?*] and I return you such an answer, as, in so short a time for study, and in the midst of my occasions, occurs to me.

* S. Joh. 21:9–13.

The books of Scripture (as also those which are Apocryphal) are often silent, or very sparing, in the particular names of fishes; or in setting them down in such manner as to leave the kinds of them without all doubt and reason for farther inquiry. For, when it declareth what fishes were allowed the Israelites for their food, they are onely set down in general which have finns and scales; whereas, in the account of quadrupeds and birds, there is particular mention of divers of them. In the book of Tobit that fish which he took out of the river is onely named a great fish, and so there remains much uncertainty to determine the species thereof. And even the fish which swallowed Jonah, and is called a great fish, and commonly thought to be a great whale, is not received without all doubt; while some learned men conceive it to have been none of our whales, but a large kind of *lamia*.

And, in this narration of S. John, the fishes are onely expressed by their bigness and number, not their names, and therefore it may seem undeterminable what they were; notwithstanding, these fishes being taken in the great lake or sea of Tiberias, something may be probably stated therein. For since Bellonius, that diligent and learned traveller, informeth us, that the fishes of this lake were trouts, pikes, chevins and tenches; it may well be conceived that either all or some thereof are to be understood in this Scripture. And these kind of fishes become large and of great growth, answerable unto the expression of Scripture, *One hundred and fifty three great fishes*;[51] that is, large in their own kinds, and the largest kinds in this lake and fresh water, wherein no great variety, and of the larger sort of fishes, could be expected. For the River Jordan, running through this lake, falls into the lake of Asphaltus, and hath no mouth into the sea, which might admit of great fishes or greater variety to come up into it.

And out of the mouth of some of these forementioned fishes might the tribute money be taken, when our Saviour, at Capernaum, seated upon the same lake, said unto Peter, *Go thou to the sea, and cast an hook, and take up the fish that first cometh; and when thou has opened his mouth thou shalt find a piece of money; that take and give them for thee and me.*[52]

And this makes void that common conceit and tradition of the fish called *faber-marinus*, by some, a Peter or Penny Fish; which having two remarkable round spots upon either side, these are conceived to be the marks of S. Peter's fingers or signature of the money: for though it hath these marks, yet is there no probability that such a kind of fish was to be found in the lake of Tiberias, Geneserah or Galilee, which is but sixteen miles long and six broad, and hath no communication with the sea; for this is a mere fish of the sea and salt water, and (though we meet with some thereof on our coast) is not to be found in many seas.

Thus having returned no improbable answer unto your question, I shall crave leave to ask another of your self concerning that fish mention'd by Procopius,* which brought the famous King Theodorick to his end: his words are to this effect: 'The manner of his death was this. Symmachus and his son-in-law Boëthius, just men and great relievers of the poor, senatours and consuls, had many enemies, by whose false accusations Theodorick being perswaded that they plotted against him, put them to death and confiscated their estates. Not long after his waiters set before him at supper a great head of a fish, which seemed to him to be the head of Symmachus lately murthered; and with his teeth sticking out, and fierce glaring eyes to threaten him: being frightened, he grew chill, went to bed, lamenting what he had done to Symmachus and Boëthius; and soon after died.' What fish do you apprehend this to have been? I would learn of you; give me your thoughts about it.

* *De Bello Gothico, lib.* 1

I am, etc.

TRACT IV

An Answer To Certain Queries Relating to Fishes, Birds, Insects

Sir,

I return the following Answers to your Queries which were these,

1. What fishes are meant by the names, *halec* and *mugil*?
2. What is the bird which you will receive from the bearer? And what birds are meant by the names *halcyon*, *nysus*, *ciris*, *nycticorax*?
3. What insect is meant by the word *cicada*?

ANSWER TO QUERY I

The word *halec* we are taught to render an herring, which, being an ancient word, is not strictly appropriable unto a fish not known or not described by the ancients; and which the modern naturalists are fain to name *harengus*; the word *halecula* being applied unto such little fish out of which they were fain to make pickle; and *halec* or *alec*, taken for the liquamen or liquor it self, according to that of the poet,

—Ego fæcem primus et alec
Primus et inveni piper album—[53]

And was a conditure and sawce much affected by antiquity, as was also *muria* and *garum*.

In common constructions, *mugil* is rendred a mullet, which, notwithstanding, is a different fish from the *mugil* described by authours; wherein, if we mistake, we cannot so closely apprehend the expression of Juvenal,

—Quosdam ventres et Mugilis intrat.[54]

And misconceive the fish, whereby fornicatours were so opprobriously and irksomely punished; for the *mugil* being somewhat rough and hard skinned, did more exasperate the gutts of such offenders: whereas the Mullet was a smooth fish, and of too high esteem to be imployed in such offices.

ANSWER TO QUERY 2

I cannot but wonder that this bird you sent should be a stranger unto you, and unto those who had a sight thereof: for, though it be not seen every day, yet we often meet with it in this country. It is an elegant bird, which he that once beholdeth can hardly mistake any other for it. From the proper note it is called an *hoopebird* with us; in Greek *epops*, in Latin *upupa*. We are little obliged unto our school instruction, wherein we are taught to render *upupa* a *lapwing*, which bird our natural writers name *vannellus*; for thereby we mistake this remarkable bird, and apprehend not rightly what is delivered of it.

We apprehend not the hieroglyphical considerations which the old Ægyptians made of this observable bird; who considering therein the order and variety of colours, the twenty six or twenty eight feathers in its crest, his latitancy, and mewing this handsome outside in the winter;[55] they made it an emblem of the varieties of the world, the succession of times and seasons, and signal mutations in them. And therefore *Orus*, the hieroglyphick of the world, had the head of an hoopebird upon the top of his staff.

Hereby we may also mistake the *duchiphath*, or bird forbidden for food in Leviticus;[*] and, not knowing the bird, may the less apprehend some reasons of that prohibition; that is, the magical virtues ascribed unto it by the Ægyptians, and the superstitious apprehensions which that nation held of it, whilst they precisely numbred the feathers and colours thereof, while they placed it on the heads of their gods, and near their mercurial crosses, and so highly magnified this bird in their sacred Symbols.

[*] Leviticus 11:19.

Again, not knowing or mistaking this Bird, we may misapprehend, or not closely apprehend, that handsome expression of Ovid, when Tereus was turned into an *upupa*, or hoopebird.

> *Vertitur in volucrem cui sunt pro vertice Cristæ,*
> *Protinus immodicum surgit pro cuspide rostrum*
> *Nomen Epops volucri, facies armata videtur.*[56]

For, in this military shape, he is aptly phancied even still revengefully to pursue his hated wife Progne: in the propriety of his note crying out, *pou, pou, ubi ubi*, or *where are you*?

Nor are we singly deceived in the nominal translation of this bird: in many other animals we commit the like mistake. So *gracculus* is rendred a jay, which bird notwithstanding must be of a dark colour according to that of Martial,

> *Sed quandam volo nocte nigriorem*
> *Formica, pice, Gracculo, cicada.*[57]

Halcyon is rendred a king-fisher, a bird commonly known among us,* and by zoographers and naturals the same is named *ispida*, a well coloured bird frequenting streams and rivers, building in holes of pits, like some martins, about the end of the spring; in whose nests we have found little else than innumerable small fish bones, and white round eggs of a smooth and polished surface, whereas the true *alcyon* is a sea bird, makes an handsome nest floating upon the water, and breedeth in the winter.

* *See Vulg. Err. B. 3. c.10.*

That *nysus* should be rendred either an hobby or a sparrow hawk, in the fable of Nysus and Scylla in Ovid, because we are much to seek in the distinction of hawks according to their old denominations, we shall not much contend, and may allow a favourable latitude therein: but that the Ciris or bird into which Scylla was turned should be translated a lark, it can hardly be made out agreeable unto the description of Virgil in his poem of that name,

> *Inde alias volucres minióque infecta rubenti*
> *Crura—*[58]

But seems more agreeable unto some kind of *hæmantopus* or redshank; and so the *nysus* seems to have been some kind of hawk, which delighteth about the sea and marishes, where such prey most aboundeth, which sort of hawk while Scaliger determineth to be a merlin, the French translatour warily expoundeth it to be kind of hawk.

Nycticorax we may leave unto the common and verbal translation of a night raven, but we know no proper kind of raven unto which to confine the same, and therefore some take the liberty to ascribe it unto some sort of owls, and others unto the bittern; which bird in its common note, which he useth out of the time of coupling and upon the wing, so well resembleth the croaking of a raven that I have been deceived by it.

ANSWER TO QUERY 3

While *cicada* is rendered a grashopper, we commonly think that what is so called among us to be the true *cicada*; wherein, as we have elsewhere declared,* there is a great mistake: for we have not the *cicada* in England, and indeed no proper word for that animal, which the French nameth *cigale*. That which we commonly call a grashopper, and the French *saulterelle* being one kind of locust, so rendred in the plague of Ægypt, and, in old Saxon named Gersthop.

* Vulg. Err. B. 5. c.3.

I have been the less accurate in these answers, because the queries are not of difficult resolution, or of great moment: however, I would not wholly neglect them or your satisfaction, as being, Sir,

Yours, etc.

TRACT V

Of Hawks and Falconry, Ancient and Modern

Sir,

In vain you expect much information, *de Re Accipitraria*, of falconry, hawks or hawking, from very ancient Greek or Latine authours; that art being either unknown or so little advanced among them, that it seems to have proceeded no higher than the daring of birds: which makes so little thereof to be found in Aristotle, who onely mentions some rude practice thereof in Thracia; as also in Ælian, who speaks something of hawks and crows among the Indians; little or nothing of true falconry being mention'd before Julius Firmicus, in the days of Constantius, son to Constantine the Great.

Yet if you consult the accounts of later antiquity left by Demetrius the Greek, by Symmachus and Theodosius, and by Albertus Magnus, about five hundred years ago, you, who have been so long acquainted with this noble recreation, may better compare the ancient and modern practice, and rightly observe how many things in that art are added, varied, disused or retained in the practice of these days.

In the diet of hawks, they allowed of divers meats which we should hardly commend. For beside the flesh of beef, they admitted of goat, hog, deer, whelp and bear. And how you will approve the quantity and measure thereof, I make some doubt; while by weight they allowed half a pound of beef, seven ounces of swines flesh, five of hare, eight ounces of whelp, as much of deer, and ten ounces of he-goats flesh.

In the time of Demetrius they were not without the practice of phlebotomy or bleeding, which they used in the thigh and pounces; they plucked away the feathers on the thigh, and rubbed the part, but if the vein appeared not in that part, they opened the vein of the fore talon.

In the days of Albertus, they made use of cauteries in divers places: to advantage their sight they seared them under the inward angle of the eye; above the eye in distillations and diseases of the head; in upward pains they seared above the joint of the wing, and at the bottom of the foot, against the gout; and the chief time for these cauteries they made to be the month of March.

In great coldness of hawks they made use of fomentations, some of the steam or vapour of artificial and natural baths, some wrapt them up in hot blankets, giving them nettle seeds and butter.

No clysters are mention'd, nor can they be so profitably used; but they made use of many purging medicines. They purged with aloe, which, unto larger hawks, they gave in the bigness of a Greek bean; unto less, in the quantity of a *cicer*, which notwithstanding I should rather give washed, and with a few drops of oil of almonds: for the guts of flying fowls are tender and easily scratched by it; and upon the use of aloe both in hawks and cormorants I have sometimes observed bloody excretions.

In phlegmatick causes they seldom omitted stavesaker, but they purged sometimes with a mouse, and the food of boiled chickens, sometimes with good oil and honey.

They used also the ink of cuttle fishes, with smallage, betony, wine and honey. They made use of stronger medicines than present practice doth allow. For they were not afraid to give *coccus baphicus* beating up eleven of its grains unto a lentor, which they made up into five pills wrapt up with honey and pepper: and in some of their old medicines, we meet with scammony and *euphorbium*. Whether, in the tender bowels of birds, infusions of rhubarb, agaric, and *mechoachan* be not of safer use, as to take of agary two drachms, of cinnamon half a drachm, of liquorish a scruple, and infusing them in wine, to express a part into the mouth of hawk, may be considered by present practice.

Few mineral medicines were of inward use among them; yet sometimes we observe they gave filings of iron in the straitness of the chest, as also lime in some of their pectoral medicines.

But they commended unguents of quick-silver against the scab; and I have safely given six or eight grains of *mercurius dulcis* unto kestrils and owls, as also crude and current quick-silver, giving the next day small pellets of silver or lead till they came away uncoloured: and this, if any, may probably destroy that obstinate disease of the *Filander* or back-worm.

A peculiar remedy they had against the consumption of hawks. For, filling a chicken with vinegar, they closed up the bill, and hanging it up untill the flesh grew tender, they fed the hawk therewith: and to restore and well flesh them, they commonly gave them hogs flesh, with oil, butter and honey; and a decoction of cumfory to bouze.[59]

They disallowed of salt meats and fat; but highly esteemed of mice in most indispositions; and in the falling sickness had great esteem of boiled batts: and in many diseases, of the flesh of owls which feed upon those animals. In epilepsies they also gave the brain of a kid drawn through a gold ring; and, in convulsions, made use of a mixture of musk and s*tercus humanum aridum.*

For the better preservation of their health they strowed mint and sage about them; and for the speedier mewing of their feathers, they gave them the slough of a snake, or a tortoise out of the shell, or a green lizard cut in pieces.

If a hawk were unquiet, they hooded him, and placed him in a smith's shop for some time, where, accustomed to the continual noise of hammering, he became more gentle and tractable.

They used few terms of art, plainly and intelligibly expressing the parts affected, their diseases and remedies. This heap of artificial terms first entring with the French artists: who seem to have been the first and noblest falconers in the western part of Europe; although, in their language, they have no word which generally expresseth an hawk.

They carried their hawks in the left hand, and let them flie from the right. They used a bell, and took great care that their jesses should not be red, lest eagles should flie at them.[60] Though they used hoods, we have no clear description of them, and little account of their lures.

The ancient writers left no account of the swiftness of hawks or measure of their flight: but Heresbachius[*] delivers that William Duke of Cleve had an hawk which, in one day, made a flight out of Westphalia into Prussia. And, upon good account, an hawk in this country of Norfolk, made a flight at a woodcock near thirty miles in one hour. How far the hawks, merlins and wild fowl which come unto us with a north-west wind in the autumn, flie in a day, there is no clear account; but coming over sea their flight hath been long, or very speedy. For I have known them to light so weary on the coast, that many have been taken with dogs, and some knock'd down with staves and stones.

[*] *De re Rustica.*

Their perches seem not so large as ours; for they made them of such a bigness that their talons might almost meet: and they chose to make them of sallow, poplar or lime tree.

They used great clamours and hollowing in their flight, which they made by these words, *ou loi, la, la, la*; and to raise the fowls, made use of the sound of a cymbal.

Their recreation seemed more sober and solemn than ours at present, so improperly attended with oaths and imprecations. For they called on God at their setting out, according to the account of Demetrius, τὸν θεὸν ἐπικαλέσαντες, in the first place calling upon God.

The learned Rigaltius thinketh, that if the Romans had well known this airy chase, they would have left or less regarded their circensial recreations.[61] The Greeks understood hunting early, but little or nothing of our falconry. If Alexander had known it, we might have found something of it and more of hawks in Aristotle; who was so unacquainted with that way, that he thought that hawks would not feed upon the heart of birds. Though he hath mention'd divers hawks, yet Julius Scaliger, an expert falconer, despaired to reconcile them unto ours. And 'tis well if, among them, you can clearly make out a lanner, a sparrow hawk and a kestril, but must not hope to find your gier falcon there, which is the noble hawk; and I wish you one no worse than that of Henry King of Navarre; which, Scaliger saith, he saw strike down a buzzard, two wild geese, divers kites, a crane and a swan.

Nor must you expect from high antiquity the distinctions of eyess and ramage hawks, of sores and entermewers, of hawks of the lure and the fist; nor that material distinction into short and long winged hawks; from whence arise such differences in their taking down of stones; in their flight, their striking down or seizing of their prey, in the strength of their talons, either in the heel and fore-talon, or the middle and the heel: nor yet what eggs produce the different hawks, or when they lay three eggs, that the first produceth a female and large hawk, the second of a midler sort, and the third a smaller bird tercellene or tassel, of the masle sex; which hawks being onely observed abroad by the ancients, were looked upon as hawks of different kinds and not of the same eyrie or nest. As for what Aristotle affirmeth that hawks and birds of prey drink not; although you know that it will not strictly hold, yet I kept an eagle two years, which fed upon kats, kitlings, whelps and ratts, without one drop of water.

If any thing may add unto your knowledge in this noble art, you must pick it out of later writers than those you enquire of. You may peruse the two books of falconry writ by that renowned Emperour Frederick the Second; as also the works of the noble Duke Belisarius, of Tardiffe, Francherius, of Francisco Sforzino of Vicensa; and may not a little inform or recreate your self with that elegant poem of Thuanus.* I leave you to divert your self by the perusal of it, having, at present, no more to say but that I am, etc.

* *De Re Accipitraria, in 3 Books.*

TRACT VI

Of Cymbals, etc

Sir,

With what difficulty, if not possibility, you may expect satisfaction concerning the musick, or musical instruments of the Hebrews, you will easily discover if you consult the attempts of learned men upon that subject: but for cymbals, of whose figure you enquire, you may find some described in Baysius, in the comment of Rhodius upon Scribonius Largus, and others.

As for κύμβαλον ἀλαλάζον mentioned by S. Paul, and rendred a *tinckling cymbal*, whether the translation be not too soft and diminutive some question may be made:* for the word ἀλαλάζον implieth no small sound, but a strained and lofty vociferation, or some kind of hollowing sound, according to the exposition of Hesychius, ἀλαλάξατε ἐνυψώσατε τὴν φωνήν. A word drawn from the lusty shout of souldiers, crying ἀλαλά at the first charge upon their enemies, according to the custom of eastern nations, and used by Trojans in Homer; and is also the note of the chorus in Aristophanes ἀλαλαί ἰὴ παιών. In other parts of Scripture we reade of loud and high sounding cymbals; and in Clemens Alexandrinus that the Arabians made use of cymbals in their wars instead of other military musick; and Polyænus in his *Stratagemes* affirmeth that Bacchus gave the signal of battel unto his numerous army not with trumpets but with tympans and cymbals.

* 1 Corinthians 13:1.

And now I take the opportunity to thank you for the new book sent me containing the anthems sung in our Cathedral and Collegiate Churches: 'tis probable there will be additions, the masters of musick being now active in that affair. Beside my naked thanks I have yet nothing to return you but this enclosed, which may be somewhat rare unto you, and that is a Turkish hymn translated into French out of the Turkish metre, which I thus render unto you.

O what praise doth he deserve, and how great is that Lord,
all whose Slaves are as so many Kings!

Whosoever shall rub his eyes with the dust of his feet, shall behold such admirable things that he shall fall into an ecstasie.

He that shall drink one drop of his beverage, shall have his bosome like the ocean filled with gems and pretious liquours.

Let not loose the reins unto thy passions in this world: he that represseth them shall become a true Solomon in the faith.

Amuse not thy self to adore riches, nor to build great houses and palaces.

The end of what thou shalt build is but ruine.

Pamper not thy body with delicacies and dainties; it may come to pass one day that this body may be in hell.

Imagine not that he who findeth riches findeth happiness; he that findeth happiness is he that findeth God.

All who prostrating themselves in humility shall this day believe in Velè, if they were poor shall be rich, and if rich shall become kings. *

* Velè the founder of the Convent.

After the Sermon ended which was made upon a verse in the Alcoran containing much morality, the dervices in a gallery apart sung this hymn, accompanied with instrumental musick, which so affected the ears of Monsieur du Loyr, that he would not omit to set it down, together with the musical notes, to be found in his first letter unto Monsieur Bouliau, Prior of Magny.

Excuse my brevity: I can say but little where I understand but little.

I am, etc.

TRACT VII

Of Ropalic Or Gradual Verses, etc

Mens mea sublimes rationes præmeditatur.[62]

Sir,

Though I may justly allow a good intention in this poem presented unto you, yet I must needs confess, I have no affection for it; as being utterly averse from all affectation in poetry, which either restrains the phancy, or fetters the invention to any strict disposure of words. A poem of this nature is to be found in Ausonius beginning thus,

Spes Deus æterna stationis conciliator.[63]

These are verses *ropalici* or *clavales*, arising gradually like the knots in a ῥοπάλη or clubb; named also *fistulares* by Priscianus, as Elias Vinetus hath noted.* They consist properly of five words, each thereof encreasing by one syllable. They admit not of a spondee in the fifth place, nor can a golden or silver verse be made this way. They run smoothly both in Latin and Greek, and some are scatteringly to be found in Homer; as,

* El. Vinet. *in* Auson.

ὦ μάκαρ Ἀτρείδη μοιρηγενὲς ὀλβιοδαίμον,

Liberè dicam sed in aurem, ego versibus hujusmodi Ropalicis, longo syrmate protractis, Ceraunium affigo.[64]

He that affecteth such restrained poetry, may peruse the long poem of Hugbaldus the monk, wherein every word beginneth with a C penned in the praise of Calvities or baldness, to the honour of Carolus Calvus king of France,

Carmina clarisonæ calvis cantate Camænæ.

The rest may be seen at large in the *Adversaria* of Barthius: or if he delighteth in odd contrived phancies may he please himself with antistrophes, counterpetories, retrogrades, rebusses, leonine verses, etc., to be found in *Sieur des Accords*. But these and the like are to be look'd upon, not pursued, odd works might be made by such ways; and for your recreation I propose these few lines unto you,

Arcu paratur quod arcui sufficit.
Misellorum clamoribus accurrere non tam humanum quam sulphureum est.
Asino teratur quæ Asino teritur.
Ne Asphodelos comedas, phœnices manduca.
Cœlum aliquid potest, sed quæ mira præstat Papilio est.

Not to put you unto endless amusement, the key hereof is the homonomy of the Greek made use of in the Latin words, which rendreth all plain. More enigmatical and dark expressions might be made if any one would speak or compose them out of the numerical characters or characteristical numbers set down by Robertus de Fluctibus.*

* *Tract. 2. Part lib. 1.*

As for your question concerning the contrary expressions of the Italian and Spaniards in their affirmative answers, the Spaniard answering *cy sennor*, the Italian *signior cy*, you must be content with this distich,

Why saith the Italian signior cy, the Spaniard cy sennor?
Because the one puts that behind, the other puts before.

And because you are so happy in some translations, I pray return me these two verses in English,

Occidit heu tandem multos quæ occidit amantes,
Et cinis est hodie quæ fuit ignis heri.[65]

My occasions make me to take off my Pen. I am, etc.

TRACT VIII

Of Languages, and particularly of the Saxon Tongue

Sir,

The last discourse we had of the Saxon tongue recalled to my mind some forgotten considerations. Though the earth were widely peopled before the flood, (as many learned men conceive) yet whether after a large dispersion, and the space of sixteen hundred years, men maintained so uniform a language in all parts, as to be strictly of one tongue, and readily to understand each other, may very well be doubted. For though the world preserved in the family of Noah before the confusion of tongues might be said to be of one lip, yet even permitted to themselves their humours, inventions, necessities, and new objects, without the miracle of confusion at first, in so long a tract of time, there had probably been a Babel. For whether America were first peopled by one or several nations, yet cannot that number of different planting nations, answer the multiplicity of their present different languages, of no affinity unto each other; and even in their northern nations and incommunicating angles, their languages are widely differing. A native interpreter brought from California proved of no use unto the Spaniards upon the neighbour shore. From Chiapa, to Guatemala, S. Salvador, Honduras, there are at least eighteen several languages; and so numerous are they both in the Peruvian and Mexican regions, that the great princes are fain to have one common language, which besides their vernaculous and mother tongues, may serve for commerce between them.

And since the confusion of tongues at first fell onely upon those which were present in Sinaar at the work of Babel, whether the primitive language from Noah were onely preserved in the family of Heber, and not also in divers others, which might be absent at the same, whether all came away and many might not be left behind in their first plantations about the foot of the hills, whereabout the ark rested and Noah became an husbandman; is not absurdly doubted.

For so the primitive tongue might in time branch out into several parts of Europe and Asia, and thereby the first or Hebrew tongue which seems to be ingredient into so many languages, might have larger originals and grounds of its communication and traduction than from the family of Abraham, the country of Canaan and words contained in the Bible which come short of the full of that language. And this would become more probable from the Septuagint or Greek chronology strenuously asserted by Vossius; for making five hundred years between the deluge and the days of Peleg, there ariseth a large latitude of multiplication and dispersion of people into several parts, before the descent of that body which followed Nimrod unto Sinaar from the east.

They who derive the bulk of European tongues from the Scythian and the Greek, though they may speak probably in many points, yet must needs allow vast difference or corruptions from so few originals, which however might be tolerably made out in the old Saxon, yet hath time much confounded the clearer derivations. And as the knowledge thereof now stands in reference unto our selves, I find many words totally lost, divers of harsh sound disused or refined in the pronunciation, and many words we have also in common use not to be found in that tongue, or venially derivable from any other from whence we have largely borrowed, and yet so much still remaineth with us that it maketh the gross of our language.

The religious obligation unto the Hebrew language hath so notably continued the same, that it might still be understood by Abraham, whereas by the Mazorite points and Chaldee character the old letter stands so transformed, that if Moses were alive again, he must be taught to reade his own law.

The Chinoys, who live at the bounds of the earth, who have admitted little communication, and suffered successive incursions from one nation, may possibly give account of a very ancient language; but consisting of many nations and tongues; confusion, admixtion and corruption in length of time might probably so have crept in as without the virtue of a common character, and lasting letter of things, they could never probably make out those strange memorials which they pretend, while they still make use of the works of their great Confutius many hundred years before Christ, and in a series ascend as high as Poncuus, who is conceived our Noah.

The present Welch, and remnant of the old Britanes, hold so much of that ancient language, that they make a shift to understand the poems of Merlin, Enerin, Telesin, a thousand years ago, whereas the Herulian *Pater Noster*, set down by Wolfgangus Lazius, is not without much criticism made out, and but in some words; and the present Parisians can hardly hack out those few lines of the league between Charles and Lewis, the sons of Ludovicus Pius, yet remaining in old French.

The Spaniards, in their corruptive traduction and Romance, have so happily retained the terminations from the Latin, that notwithstanding Gothick and Moorish intrusions of words, they are able to make a discourse completely consisting of grammatical Latin and Spanish, wherein the Italians and French will be much to seek.

The learned Casaubon conceiveth that a dialogue might be composed in Saxon onely of such words as are derivable from the Greek, which surely might be effected, and so as the learned might not uneasily find it out. Verstegan made no doubt that he could contrive a letter which might be understood by the English, Dutch and East Frieslander, which, as the present confusion standeth, might have proved no very clear piece, and hardly to be hammer'd out: yet so much of the Saxon still remaineth in our English, as may admit an orderly discourse and series of good sense, such as not onely the present English, but Ælfric, Bede and Alured might understand after so many hundred years.

Nations that live promiscuously, under the power and laws of conquest, do seldom escape the loss of their language with their liberties, wherein the Romans were so strict that the Grecians were fain to conform in their judicial processes; which made the Jews loose more in seventy years dispersion in the provinces of Babylon, than in many hundred in their distinct habitation in Ægypt; and the English which dwelt dispersedly to loose their language in Ireland, whereas more tolerable reliques there are thereof in Fingall, where they were closely and almost solely planted; and the Moors which were most huddled together and united about Granada, have yet left their *Arvirage* among the Granadian Spaniards.

But shut up in Angles and inaccessible corners, divided by laws and manners, they often continue long with little mixture, which hath afforded the lasting life unto the Cantabrian and British tongue, wherein the Britanes are remarkable, who, having lived four hundred years together with the Romanes, retained so much of the British as it may be esteemed a language; which either they resolutely maintained in their cohabitation with them in Britane, or retiring after in the time of the Saxons into countries and parts less civiliz'd and conversant with the Romans, they found the People distinct, the language more intire, and so fell into it again.

But surely no languages have been so straitly lock'd up as not to admit of commixture. The Irish, although they retain a kind of a Saxon character, yet have admitted many words of Latin and English. In the Welch are found many words from Latin, some from Greek and Saxon. In what parity and incommixture the language of that people stood which were casually discovered in the heart of Spain, between the mountains of Castile, no longer ago than in the time of Duke D'Alva, we have not met with a good account any farther than that their words were Basquish or Cantabrian: but the present Basquensa one of the minor mother tongues of Europe, is not without commixture of Latin and Castilian, while we meet with *Santifica*, *tentationeten*, *Glaria*, *puissança*, and four more in the short form of the Lord's Prayer, set down by Paulus Merula: but although in this brief form we may find some commixture, yet the bulk of their language seems more distinct, consisting of words of no affinity unto others, of numerals totally different, of differing grammatical rule, as may be observed in the dictionary and short Basquensa grammar, composed by Raphael Nicoleta, a priest of Bilboa.

And if they use the auxiliary verbs of *equin* and *ysan*, answerable unto *hazer* and *ser*, to have, and be, in the Spanish, which forms came in with the northern nations into the Italian, Spanish and French, and if that form were used by them before, and crept not in from imitation of their neighbours, it may shew some ancienter traduction from northern nations, or else must seem very strange; since the southern nations had it not of old, and I know not whether any such mode be found in the languages of any part of America.

The Romans, who made the great commixture and alteration of languages in the world, effected the same, not onely by their proper language, but those also of their military forces, employed in several provinces, as holding a standing militia in all countries, and commonly of strange nations; so while the cohorts and forces of the Britanes were quartered in Ægypt, Armenia, Spain, Illyria, etc. the Stablæsians and Dalmatians here, the Gauls, Spaniards and Germans in other countries, and other nations in theirs, they could not but leave many words behind them, and carry away many with them, which might make that in many words of very distinct nations some may still remain of very unknown and doubtfull genealogy.

And if, as the learned Buxhornius contendeth, the Scythian language as the mother tongue runs through the nations of Europe, and even as far as Persia, the community in many words between so many nations, hath a more reasonable original traduction, and were rather derivable from the common tongue diffused through them all, than from any particular nation, which hath also borrowed and holdeth but at second hand.

The Saxons settling over all England, maintained an uniform language, onely diversified in dialect, idioms, and minor differences, according to their different nations which came in to the common conquest, which may yet be a cause of the variation in the speech and words of several parts of England, where different nations most abode or settled, and having expelled the Britanes, their wars were chiefly among themselves, with little action with foreign nations untill the union of the Heptarchy under Egbert; after which time although the Danes infested this land and scarce left any part free, yet their incursions made more havock in buildings, churches and cities, than the language of the country, because their language was in effect the same, and such as whereby they might easily understand one another.

And if the Normans, which came into Neustria or Normandy with Rollo the Dane, had preserved their language in their new acquists, the succeeding Conquest of England, by Duke William of his race, had not begot among us such notable alterations; but having lost their language in their abode in Normandy before they adventured upon England, they confounded the English with their French, and made the grand mutation, which was successively encreased by our possessions in Normandy, Guien and Aquitain, by our long wars in France, by frequent resort of the French, who to the number of some thousands came over with Isabel Queen to Edward the Second, and the several matches of England with the daughters of France before and since that time.

But this commixture, though sufficient to confuse, proved not of ability to abolish the Saxon words; for from the French we have borrowed many substantives, adjectives and some verbs, but the great body of numerals, auxiliary verbs, articles, pronouns, adverbs, conjunctions and prepositions, which are the distinguishing and lasting part of a language, remain with us from the Saxon, which, having suffered no great alteration for many hundred years, may probably still remain, though the English swell with the inmates of Italian, French and Latin. An example whereof may be observ'd in this following,

ENGLISH I.

The first and formost step to all good works is the dread and fear of the Lord of Heaven and Earth, which thorough the Holy Ghost enlightneth the blindness of our sinfull hearts to tread the ways of wisedom, and then leads our feet into the land of blessing.

SAXON I.

The erst and fyrmost stæp to eal gode weorka is the dræd and feurt of the Lauord of Heofan and Eorth, whilc thurh the Heilig Gast onlihtneth the blindnesse of ure sinfull heorte to træd the wæg of wisdome, and thone læd ure fet into the land of blessung.

ENGLISH II.

For to forget his law is the door, the gate and key to let in all unrighteousness, making our eyes, ears and mouths to answer the lust of sin, our brains dull to good thoughts, our lips dumb to his praise, our ears deaf to his gospel, and our eyes dim to behold his wonders, which witness against us that we have not well learned the word of God, that we are the children of wrath, unworthy of the love and manifold gifts of God, greedily following after the ways of the Devil and witchcraft of the world, doing nothing to free and keep ourselves from the burning fire of hell, till we be buried in sin and swallowed in death, not to arise again in any hope of Christ's kingdom.

SAXON II.

For to fuorgytan his laga is the dure, the gat and cæg to let in eal unrightwisnysse, makend ure eyge, eore and muth to answare the lust of sin, ure brægan dole to gode theoht, ure lippan dumb to his preys, ure earen deaf to his Gospel, and ure eyge dim to behealden his wundra, whilc gewitnysse ongen us that wee hœf noht wel gelæred the weord of God, that wee are the cilda of ured, unwyrthe of the lufe and mænigfeald gift of God, gretdiglice felygend æfter the wægen of the Deoful and wiccraft of the weorld, doend nothing to fry and cæp ure saula from the byrnend fyr of Hell, till we be geburied in synne and swolgen in death not to arise agen in ænig hope of Christes kynedome.

ENGLISH III.

Which draw from above the bitter doom of the almighty of hunger, sword, sickness, and brings more sad plagues than those of hail, storms, thunder, bloud, frogs, swarms of gnats and grashoppers, which ate the corn, grass and leaves of the trees in Ægypt.

SAXON III.

Whilc drag from buf the bitter dome of the Almagan of hunger, sweorde, seoknesse, and bring mere sad plag, thone they of hagal, storme, thunner, blode, frog, swearme of gnæt and gærsupper, whilc eaten the corn, gærs and leaf of the treowen in Ægypt.

ENGLISH IV.

If we reade his book and holy Writ, these among many others, we shall find to be the tokens of his hate, which gathered together might mind us of his will, and teach us when his wrath beginneth, which sometimes comes in open strength and full sail, oft steals like a thief in the night, like shafts shot from a bow at midnight, before we think upon them.

SAXON IV.

Gyf we ræd his boc and heilig Gewrit, these gemong mænig othern, we sceall findan the tacna of his hatung whilc gegatherod together miht gemind us of his willan, and teac us whone his ured onginneth, whilc sometima come in open strength and fill seyle, oft stæl gelyc a theof in the niht, gelyc sceaft scoten fram a boge at midneoht, beforan we thinck uppen them.

ENGLISH V.

And though they were a deal less, and rather short than beyond our sins, yet do we not a whit withstand or forbear them, we are wedded to, not weary of our misdeeds, we seldom look upward, and are not ashamed under sin, we cleanse not ourselves from the blackness and deep hue of our guilt; we want tears and sorrow, we weep not, fast not, we crave not forgiveness from the mildness, sweetness and goodness of God, and with all livelihood and steadfastness to our uttermost will hunt after the evil of guile, pride, cursing, swearing, drunkenness, overeating, uncleanness, all idle lust of the flesh, yes many uncouth and nameless sins, hid in our inmost breast and bosomes, which stand betwixt our forgiveness, and keep God and man asunder.

SAXON V.

And theow they wære a dæl lesse, and reither scort thone begond oure sinnan, get do we naht a whit withstand or forbeare them, we eare bewudded to, noht werig of ure agen misdeed, we seldom loc upweard, and ear not offchæmod under sinne, we cleans noht ure selvan from the blacnesse and dæp hue of ure guilt; we wan teare and sara, we weope noht, fæst noht, we craf noht foregyfnesse fram the mildnesse, sweetnesse and goodnesse of God, and mit eal lifelyhood and stedfastnesse to ure uttermost witt hunt æfter the ufel of guile, pride, cursung, swearung, druncennesse, overeat, uncleannesse and eal idle lust of the flæsc, yis mænig uncuth and nameleas sinnan, hid in ure inmæst brist and bosome, whilc stand betwixt ure foregyfnesse, and cæp God and man asynder.

ENGLISH VI.

Thus are we far beneath and also worse than the rest of God's works; for the sun and moon, the king and queen of stars, snow, ice, rain, frost, dew, mist, wind, fourfooted and creeping things, fishes and feathered birds, and fowls either of sea or land do all hold the laws of his will.

SAXON VI.

Thus eare we far beneoth and ealso wyrse thone the rest of Gods weorka; for the sun and mone, the cyng and cquen of stearran, snaw, ise, ren, frost, deaw, miste, wind, feower fet and crypend dinga, fix and yefethrod brid, and fælan auther in sæ or land do eal heold the lag of his willan.

Thus have you seen in few words how near the Saxon and English meet.

Now of this account the French will be able to make nothing; the modern Danes and Germans, though from several words they may conjecture at the meaning, yet will they be much to seek in the orderly sense and continued construction thereof; whether the Danes can continue such a series of sense out of their present language and the old Runick, as to be intelligible unto present and ancient times, some doubt may well be made; and if the present French would attempt a discourse in words common unto their present tongue and the old *Romana Rustica* spoken in elder times, or in the old language of the Francks, which came to be in use some successions after Pharamond, it might prove a work of some trouble to effect.

It were not impossible to make an original reduction of many words of no general reception in England but of common use in Norfolk, or peculiar to the East Angle countries; as, bawnd, bunny, thurck, enemmis, sammodithee, mawther, kedge, seele, straft, clever, matchly, dere, nicked, stingy, noneare, feft, thepes, gosgood, kamp, sibrit, fangast, sap, cothish, thokish, bide owe, paxwax: of these and some others of no easie originals, when time will permit, the resolution may be attempted; which to effect, the Danish language new and more ancient may prove of good advantage: which nation remained here fifty years upon agreement, and have left many families in it, and the language of these parts had surely been more commixed and perplex, if the fleet of Hugo de Bones had not been cast away, wherein threescore thousand souldiers out of Britany and Flanders were to be wafted over, and were by King John's appointment to have a settled habitation in the counties of Norfolk and Suffolk.

But beside your laudable endeavours in the Saxon, you are not like to repent you of your studies in the other European and Western languages, for therein are delivered many excellent historical, moral and philosophical discourses, wherein men merely versed in the learned languages are often at a loss: but although you are so well accomplished in the French, you will not surely conceive that you are master of all the languages in France, for to omit the Briton, Britonant or old British, yet retained in some parts of Brittany, I shall onely propose this unto your construction.

Chavalisco d'aquestes Boemes chems an freitado lou cap cun taules Jargonades, ero necy chi voluiget bouta sin tens embè aquelles. Anin à lous occells, che dizen tat prouben en ein voz L'ome nosap comochodochi yen ay jes de plazer, d'ausir la mitat da paraulles en el mon.

This is a part of that language which Scaliger nameth *Idiotismus Tectosagicus*, or *Langue d'oc*, counter-distinguishing it unto the *Idiotismus Francicus*, or *Langue d'ouy*, not understood in a petty corner or between a few mountains, but in parts of early civility, in Languedoc, Provence and Catalonia, which put together will make little less then England.

Without some knowledge herein you cannot exactly understand the works of Rablais: by this the French themselves are fain to make out that preserved relique of old French, containing the league between Charles and Lewis the sons of Ludovicus Pius. Hereby may tolerably be understood the several tracts written in the Catalonian tongue; and in this is published the tract of falconry written by Theodosius and Symmachus; in this is yet conserved the poem of Vilhuardine concerning the French expedition in the holy war, and the taking of Constantinople, among the works of Marius Æquicola an Italian poet. You may find, in this language, a pleasant dialogue of love: this, about an hundred years ago, was in high esteem, when many Italian wits flocked into Provence; and the famous Petrarcha wrote many of his poems in Vaucluse in that country.

For the word [Dread] in the royal title [Dread Sovereign] of which you desire to know the meaning, I return answer unto your question briefly thus.

Most men do vulgarly understand this word Dread after the common and English acception, as implying fear, awe or dread.

Others may think to expound it from the French word *droit* or *droyt*. For, whereas in elder times, the presidents and supremes of courts were termed sovereigns, men might conceive this a distinctive title and proper unto the king as eminently and by right the sovereign.

A third exposition may be made from some Saxon original, particularly from *driht*, *domine*, or *drihten*, *dominus*, in the Saxon language, the word for *dominus* throughout the Saxon psalms, and used in the expression of the year of our Lord in the decretal epistle of Pope Agatho unto Athelred king of the Mercians, Anno, 680.

Verstegan would have this term *drihten* appropriate unto God. Yet, in the constitutions of Withred King of Kent,* we find the same word used for a lord or master, *si in vesperâ præcedente solem servus ex mandato Domini aliquod opus servile egerit*, *Dominus* (*Drihten*) 80 *solidis luito*. However therefore, though *driht*, *domine*, might be most eminently applied unto the Lord of Heaven, yet might it be also transferred unto potentates and Gods on earth, unto whom fealty is given or due, according unto the feudist term *ligeus à Ligando* unto whom they were bound in fealty. And therefore from *Driht*, *Domine*, Dread Sovereign, may, probably, owe its original.

* V. Cl. *Spelmann* Concil.

I have not time to enlarge upon this subject: 'Pray let this pass, as it is, for a letter and not for a treatise. I am,

Yours, etc.

TRACT IX

Of Artificial Hills, Mounts or Burrows, In many parts of England. What they are, to what end raised, and by what nations

MY HONOURED FRIEND MR. W.D. HIS QUÆRE[66]

'In my last summer's journey through Marshland, Holland and a great part of the fenns, I observed divers artificial heaps of earth of a very large magnitude, and I hear of many others which are in other parts of those countries, some of them are at least twenty foot in direct height from the level whereon they stand. I would gladly know your opinion of them, and whether you think not that they were raised by the Romans or Saxons to cover the bones or ashes of some eminent persons?'

MY ANSWER

Worthy Sir,

Concerning artificial mounts and hills, raised without fortifications attending them, in most parts of England, the most considerable thereof I conceive to be of two kinds; that is, either signal boundaries and land-marks, or else sepulchral monuments or hills of interrment for remarkable and eminent persons, especially such as died in the wars.

As for such which are sepulchral monuments, upon bare and naked view they are not appropriable unto any of the three nations of the Romans, Saxons or Danes, who, after the Britaines, have possessed this land; because upon strict account, they may be appliable unto them all.

For that the Romans used such hilly sepultures, beside many other testimonies, seems confirmable from the practice of Germanicus, who thus interred the unburied Bones of the slain souldiers of Varus; and that expression of Virgil, of high antiquity among the Latins,

——*facit ingens monte sub alto*
Regis Dercenni terreno ex aggere Bustum.

That the Saxons made use of this way is collectible from several records, and that pertinent expression of Lelandus, *Saxones gens Christi ignara, in hortis amœnis, si domi forte ægroti moriebantur; sin foris et bello occisi, in egestis per campos terræ tumulis, quos (Burgos appellabant) sepulti sunt.*[*67]

That the Danes observed this practice, their own antiquities do frequently confirm, and it stands precisely delivered by Adolphus Cyprius, as the learned Wormius hath observed. *Dani olim in memoriam Regum et Heroum, ex terra coacervata ingentes moles, Montium instar eminentes, erexisse, credibile omnino ac probabile est, atque illis in locis ut plurimum, quo sæpe homines commearent, atque iter haberent, ut in viis publicis posteritati memoriam consecrarent, et quodammodo immortalitati mandarent.*[†68] And like monuments are yet to be observed in Norway and Denmark in no small numbers.

* Leland *in Assertione Regis Arthuri.*

† Wormius *in Monumentis Danicis.*

So that upon a single view and outward observation they may be the monuments of any of these three nations: although the greatest number, not improbably, of the Saxons; who fought many battels with the Britains and Danes, and also between their own nations, and left the proper name of burrows for these hills still retained in many of them, as the seven burrows upon Salisbury Plain, and in many other parts of England.

But of these and the like hills there can be no clear and assured decision without an ocular exploration, and subterraneous enquiry by cutting through one of them either directly or crosswise. For so with lesser charge discovery may be made what is under them, and consequently the intention of their erection.

For if they were raised for remarkable and eminent boundaries, then about their bottom will be found the lasting substances of burnt bones of beasts, of ashes, bricks, lime or coals.

If urns be found, they might be erected by the Romans before the term of urn-burying or custom of burning the dead expired: but if raised by the Romans after that period: inscriptions, swords, shields and arms after the Roman mode, may afford a good distinction.

But if these hills were made by Saxons or Danes, discovery may be made from the fashion of their arms, bones of their horses, and other distinguishing substances buried with them.

And for such an attempt there wanteth not encouragement. For a little mount or burrow was opened in the days of King Henry the Eighth upon Barham Down in Kent, by the care of Mr. Thomas Digges and charge of Sir Christopher Hales; and a very large urn with ashes was found under it, as is delivered by Thomas Twinus, *De Rebus Albionicis*, a learned man of that country, *Sub incredibili Terræ acervo, urna cinere ossium magnorum fragmentis plena, cùm galeis, clypeis æneis et ferreis rubigine ferè consumptis, inusitatæ magnitudinis, eruta est: sed nulla inscriptio nomen, nullum testimonium tempus, aut fortunam exponebant*:[69] and not very long ago, as Cambden* delivereth, in one of the Mounts of Barklow Hills in Essex, being levelled there were found three troughs, containing broken bones, conceived to have been of Danes, and in later time we find, that a burrow was opened in the Isle of Man, wherein fourteen urns were found with burnt bones in them; and one more neat than the rest, placed in a bed of fine white sand, containing nothing but a few brittle bones, as having passed the fire; according to the particular account thereof in the description of the Isle of Man.† Surely many noble bones and ashes have been contented with such hilly tombs; which neither admitting ornament, epitaph or inscription, may, if earthquakes spare them, out last all other monuments. *Suæ sunt metis metæ*. Obelisks have their term, and Pyramids will tumble, but these mountainous monuments may stand, and are like to have the same period with the earth.

* Camb. *Brit.* p. 326.

† Published 1656 by Dan. King.

More might be said, but my business, of another nature, makes me take off my hand. I am

Yours, etc.

TRACT X

Of Troas, What place is meant by that Name. Also, of the situations of Sodom, Gomorrha, Admah, Zeboim, in the Dead Sea

Sir,

To your Geographical Queries, I answer as follows.

In sundry passages of the New Testament, in the Acts of the Apostles, and Epistles of S. Paul, we meet with the word Troas; how he went from Troas to Philippi in Macedonia, from thence unto Troas again: how he remained seven days in that place; from thence on foot to Assos, whither the Disciples had sailed from Troas, and there, taking him in, made their voyage unto Cæsarea.

Now, whether this Troas be the name of a city or a certain region seems no groundless doubt of yours: for that 'twas sometimes taken in the signification of some country, is acknowledged by Ortelius, Stephanus and Grotius; and it is plainly set down by Strabo, that a region of Phrygia in Asia minor was so taken in ancient times; and that, at the Trojan War, all the territory which comprehended the nine principalities subject unto the King of Illium, Τροίη λεγομένη was called by the name of Troja. And this might seem sufficiently to salve the intention of the description, when he came or went from Troas, that is, some part of that region; and will otherwise seem strange unto many how he should be said to go or come from that city which all writers had laid in the ashes about a thousand years before.

All which notwithstanding, since we reade in the text a particular abode of seven days, and such particulars as leaving of his cloak, books and parchments at Troas: and that S. Luke seems to have been taken in to the travels of S. Paul in this place, where he begins in the Acts to write in the first person, this may rather seem to have been some city or special habitation, than any province or region without such limitation.

Now that such a city there was, and that of no mean note, is easily verified from historical observation. For though old Ilium was anciently destroyed, yet was there another raised by the relicts of that people, not in the same place, but about thirty furlongs westward, as is to be learned from Strabo.

Of this place Alexander in his expedition against Darius took especial notice, endowing it with sundry immunities, with promise of greater matters at his return from Persia; inclined hereunto from the honour he bore unto Homer, whose earnest reader he was, and upon whose poems, by the help of Anaxarchus and Callisthenes, he made some observations. As also much moved hereto upon the account of his cognation with the Æacides and kings of Molossus, whereof Andromache the wife of Hector was queen. After the death of Alexander, Lysimachus surrounded it with a wall, and brought the inhabitants of the neighbour towns unto it, and so it bore the name of Alexandria; which, from Antigonus, was also called Antigonia, according to the inscription of that famous medal in Goltsius, *Colonia Troas Antigonia Alexandrea, Legio vicesima prima*.

When the Romans first went into Asia against Antiochus 'twas but a κωμόπολις and no great city; but, upon the peace concluded, the Romans much advanced the same. Fimbria, the rebellious Roman, spoiled it in the Mithridatick War, boasting that he had subdued Troy in eleven days which the Grecians could not take in almost as many years. But it was again rebuilt and countenanced by the Romans, and became a Roman colony, with great immunities conferred on it; and accordingly it is so set down by Ptolomy. For the Romans, deriving themselves from the Trojans, thought no favour too great for it; especially Julius Cæsar, who, both in imitation of Alexander, and for his own descent from Julus, of the posterity of Æneas, with much passion affected it, and in a discontented humour,* was once in mind to translate the Roman wealth unto it; so that it became a very remarkable place, and was, in Strabo's time, ἐλλογίμων πόλεων, one of the noble cities of Asia.

* Sueton.

And, if they understood the prediction of Homer in reference unto the Romans, as some expound it in Strabo, it might much promote their affection unto that place; which being a remarkable prophecy, and scarce to be parallel'd in Pagan story, made before Rome was built, and concerning the lasting reign of the progeny of Æneas, they could not but take especial notice of it. For thus is Neptune made to speak, when he saved Æneas from the fury of Achilles.

Verum agite hunc subito præsenti à morte trahamus
Ne Cronides ira flammet si fortis Achilles
Hunc mactet, fati quem Lex evadere jussit.
Ne genus intereat de læto semine totum
Dardani ab excelso præ cunctis prolibus olim,
Dilecti quos è mortali stirpe creavit,
Nunc etiam Priami stirpem Saturnius odit,
Trojugenum posthæc Æneas sceptra tenebit
Et nati natorum et qui nascentur ab illis.[70]

The Roman favours were also continued unto S. Paul's days; for Claudius,* producing an ancient letter of the Romans unto King Seleucus, concerning the Trojan privileges, made a release of their tributes; and Nero elegantly pleaded for their immunities, and remitted all tributes unto them.†

* Sueton.

† Tacit. l. 13.

And, therefore, there being so remarkable a city in this territory, it may seem too hard to loose the same in the general name of the country; and since it was so eminently favoured by emperours, enjoying so many immunities, and full of Roman privileges, it was probably very populous, and a fit abode for S. Paul, who being a Roman citizen, might live more quietly himself, and have no small number of faithfull well-wishers in it.

Yet must we not conceive that this was the old Troy, or re-built in the same place with it: for Troas was placed about thirty furlongs West, and upon the sea shore; so that, to hold a clearer apprehension hereof than is commonly delivered in the discourses of the ruines of Troy, we may consider one inland Troy or old Ilium, which was built farther within the land, and so was removed from the port where the Grecian fleet lay in Homer; and another maritime Troy, which was upon the sea coast placed in the maps of Ptolomy, between Lectum and Sigæum or Port Janizam, southwest from the old city, which was this of S. Paul, and whereunto are appliable the particular accounts of Bellonius, when, not an hundred years ago, he described the ruines of Troy with their baths, aqueducts, walls and towers, to be seen from the sea as he sailed between it and Tenedos; and where, upon nearer view, he observed some signs and impressions of his conversion in the ruines of churches, crosses, and inscriptions upon stones.

Nor was this onely a famous city in the days of S. Paul, but considerable long after. For, upon the letter of Adrianus, Herodes Atticus,* at a great charge, repaired their baths, contrived aqueducts and noble water-courses in it. As is also collectible from the medals of Caracalla, of Severus, and Crispina; with inscriptions, *Colonia Alexandria Troas*, bearing on the reverse either an horse, a temple, or a woman; denoting their destruction by an horse, their prayers for the emperour's safety, and, as some conjecture, the memory of Sibylla, Phrygia or Hellespontica.

* Philostrat. *in Vita Herodis Attici.*

Nor wanted this city the favour of Christian princes, but was made a Bishop's See under the Archbishop of Cyzicum; but in succeeding discords was destroyed and ruined, and the nobler stones translated to Constantinople by the Turks to beautifie their mosques and other buildings.

CONCERNING THE DEAD SEA, ACCEPT OF THESE FEW REMARKS

In the map of the Dead Sea we meet with the figure of the cities which were destroyed: of Sodom, Gomorrha, Admah and Zeboim; but with no uniformity; men placing them variously, and, from the uncertainty of their situation, taking a fair liberty to set them where they please.

For Admah, Zeboim and Gomorrha, there is no light from the text to define their situation. But, that Sodom could not be far from Segor which was seated under the mountains near the side of the lake, seems inferrible from the sudden arrival of Lot, who, coming from Sodom at day break, attained to Segor at sun rising; and therefore Sodom is to be placed not many miles from it, not in the middle of the lake, which against that place is about eighteen miles over, and so will leave nine miles to be gone in so small a space of time.

The valley being large, the lake now in length about seventy English miles, the River Jordan and divers others running over the plain, 'tis probable the best cities were seated upon those streams: but how the Jordan passed or winded, or where it took in the other streams, is a point too old for geography to determine.

For, that the river gave the fruitfulness unto the valley by over watring that low region, seems plain from that expression in the text,† that it was watered, *sicut Paradisus et Ægyptus*, like Eden and the plains of Mesopotamia, where Euphrates yearly

† Genesis 13:10.

overfloweth; or like Ægypt where Nilus doth the like: and seems probable also from the same course of the river not far above this valley where the Israelites passed Jordan, where 'tis said that *Jordan overfloweth its banks in the time of harvest*.

That it must have had some passage under ground in the compass of this valley before the creation of this lake, seems necessary from the great current of Jordan, and from the rivers Arnon, Cedron, Zaeth, which empty into this valley; but where to place that concurrence of waters or place of its absorption, there is no authentick decision.

The probablest place may be set somewhat southward, below the rivers that run into it on the east or western shore: and somewhat agreeable unto the account which Brocardus received from the Sarazens which lived near it, *Jordanem ingredi Mare Mortuum et rursum egredi, sed post exiguum intervallum à Terra absorberi*.

Strabo speaks naturally of this lake, that it was first caused by earthquakes, by sulphureous and bituminous eruptions, arising from the earth. But the Scripture makes it plain to have been from a miraculous hand, and by a remarkable expression, *pluit Dominus ignem et Sulphur à Domino*. See also Deut. 29, *in ardore Salis*: burning the cities and destroying all things about the plain, destroying the vegetable nature of plants and all living things, salting and making barren the whole soil, and, by these fiery showers, kindling and setting loose the body of the bituminous mines, which shewed their lower veins before but in some few pits and openings, swallowing up the foundation of their cities; opening the bituminous treasures below, and making a smoak like a furnace able to be discerned by Abraham at a good distance from it.

If this little may give you satisfaction, I shall be glad, as being, sir,

Yours, etc.

TRACT XI

Of the Answers of the Oracle of Apollo at Delphos to Crœsus King of Lydia

Sir,

Among the Oracles of Apollo[*] there are none more celebrated than those which he delivered unto Crœsus King of Lydia,[†] who seems of all princes to have held the greatest dependence on them. But most considerable are his plain and intelligible replies which he made unto the same king, when he sent his chains of captivity unto Delphos, after his overthrow by Cyrus, with sad expostulations why he encouraged him unto that fatal war by his oracle, saying, *προλέγουσαι Κροίσῳ, ἢν στρατεύηται ἐπὶ Πέρσας, μεγάλην ἀρχήν μιν καταλύσειν*, *Crœsus, if he wars against the Persians, shall dissolve a great Empire*.[‡] Why, at least, he prevented not that sad infelicity of his devoted and bountifull servant, and whether it were fair or honourable for the gods of Greece to be ingratefull: which being a plain and open delivery of Delphos, and scarce to be parallel'd in any ancient story, it may well deserve your farther consideration.

[*] See Vulgar Errors, book 7.12.
[†] Herod. 1.46–47, etc. 90–91.
[‡] Herod. Ibid. 54.

1. His first reply was, *that Crœsus suffered not for himself*; but paid the transgression of his fifth predecessour, who kill'd his master and usurp'd the dignity unto which he held no title.

Now whether Crœsus suffered upon this account or not, hereby he plainly betrayed his insufficiency to protect him; and also obliquely discovered he had a knowledge of his misfortune; for knowing that wicked act lay yet unpunished, he might well divine some of his successours might smart for it: and also understanding he was like to be the last of that race, he might justly fear and conclude this infelicity upon him.

Hereby he also acknowledged the inevitable justice of God; that though revenge lay dormant, it would not always sleep; and consequently confessed the just hand of God punishing unto the third and fourth generation, nor suffering such iniquities to pass for ever unrevenged.

Hereby he flatteringly encouraged him in the opinion of his own merits, and that he onely suffered for other mens transgressions: meanwhile he concealed Crœsus his pride, elation of mind and secure conceit of his own unparallel'd felicity, together with the vanity, pride and height of luxury of the Lydian nation, which the spirit of Delphos knew well to be ripe and ready for destruction.

2. A second excuse was, *that it is not in the power of God to hinder the decree of fate.* A general evasion for any falsified prediction founded upon the common opinion of fate, which impiously subjecteth the power of heaven unto it; widely discovering the folly of such as repair unto him concerning future events: which, according unto this rule, must go on as the fates have ordered, beyond his power to prevent or theirs to avoid; and consequently teaching that his oracles had onely this use to render men more miserable by foreknowing their misfortunes; whereof Crœsus himself held a sensible experience in that dæmoniacal dream concerning his eldest son, *that he should be killed by a spear*, which, after all care and caution, he found inevitably to befall him.

3. In his third apology he assured him that he endeavoured to transfer the evil fate and to pass it upon his children; and did however procrastinate his infelicity, and deferred the destruction of Sardis and his own captivity three years longer than was fatally decreed upon it.

Wherein while he wipes off the stain of ingratitude, he leaves no small doubt whether, it being out of his power to contradict or transfer the fates of his servants, it be not also beyond it to defer such signal events, and whereon the fates of whole nations do depend.

As also, whether he intended or endeavoured to bring to pass what he pretended, some question might be made. For that he should attempt or think he could translate his infelicity upon his sons, it could not consist with his judgment, which attempts not impossibles or things beyond his power; nor with his knowledge of future things, and the fates of succeeding generations: for he understood that monarchy was to expire in himself, and could particularly foretell the infelicity of his sons, and hath also made remote predictions unto others concerning the fortunes of many succeeding descents; as appears in that answer to Attalus,

Be of good courage, Attalus, thou shalt reign
And thy sons sons, but not their sons again.

As also unto Cypselus King of Corinth.

Happy is the man who at my altar stands,
Great Cypselus who Corinth now commands.
Happy is he, his sons shall happy be,
But for their sons, unhappy days they'll see.

Now, being able to have so large a prospect of future things, and of the fate of many generations, it might well be granted that he was not ignorant of the fate of Crœsus his sons, and well understood it was in vain to think to translate his misery upon them.

4. In the Fourth part of his reply, he clears himself of ingratitude which hell it self cannot hear of; alledging that he had saved his life when he was ready to be burnt, by sending a mighty showre, in a fair and cloudless day, to quench the fire already kindled, which all the servants of Cyrus could not do. Though this shower might well be granted, as much concerning his honour, and not beyond his power; yet whether this mercifull showre fell not out contingently or were not contrived by an higher power, which hath often pity upon Pagans, and rewardeth their vertues sometimes with extraordinary temporal favours; also, in no unlike case, who was the authour of those few fair minutes, which, in a showry day, gave onely time enough for the burning of Sylla's body, some question might be made.

5. The last excuse devolveth the errour and miscarriage of the business upon Crœsus, and that he deceived himself by an inconsiderate misconstruction of his oracle, that if he had doubted, he should not have passed it over in silence, but consulted again for an exposition of it. Besides, he had neither discussed, nor well perpended his oracle concerning Cyrus, whereby he might have understood not to engage against him.

Wherein, to speak indifferently, the deception and miscarriage seems chiefly to lie at Crœsus his door, who, if not infatuated with confidence and security, might justly have doubted the construction: besides, he had received two oracles before, which clearly hinted an unhappy time unto him: the first concerning Cyrus.

When ever a mule shall o'er the Medians reign,
Stay not, but unto Hermus fly amain.

Herein though he understood not the Median Mule of Cyrus, that is, of his mixed descent, and from Assyrian and Median parents, yet he could not but apprehend some misfortune from that quarter.

Though this prediction seemed a notable piece of divination, yet did it not so highly magnify his natural sagacity or knowledge of future events as was by many esteemed; he having no small assistance herein from the prophecy of Daniel concerning the Persian monarchy, and the prophecy of Jeremiah and Isaiah, wherein he might reade the name of Cyrus who should restore the captivity of the Jews, and must, therefore, be the great monarch and lord of all those nations.

The same misfortune was also foretold when he demanded of Apollo if ever he should hear his dumb son speak.

O foolish Crœsus who hast made this choice,
To know when thou shalt hear thy dumb son's voice;
Better he still were mute, would nothing say,
When he first speaks, look for a dismal day.

This, if he contrived not the time and the means of his recovery, was no ordinary divination: yet how to make out the verity of the story some doubt may yet remain. For though the causes of deafness and dumbness were removed, yet since words are attained by hearing, and men speak not without instruction, how he should be able immediately to utter such apt and significant words, as Ἄνθρωπε, μὴ κτεῖνε Κροῖσον, *O man slay not Crœsus*,* it cannot escape some doubt, since the story also delivers, that he was deaf and dumb, that he then first began to speak, and spake all his life after.

* Herod. l. 1. 85.

Now, if Crœsus had consulted again for a clearer exposition of what was doubtfully delivered, whether the oracle would have spake out the second time or afforded a clearer answer, some question might be made from the examples of his practice upon the like demands.

So, when the Spartans had often fought with ill success against the Tegeates, they consulted the oracle what God they should appease, to become victorious over them. The answer was, that *they should remove the Bones of Orestes.* Though the words were plain, yet the thing was obscure, and like finding out the body of Moses. And therefore they once more demanded in what place they should find the same; unto whom he returned this answer,

When in the Tegean Plains a place thou find'st
Where blasts are made by two impetuous winds,
Where that that strikes is struck, blows follow blows
There doth the earth Orestes bones enclose.

Which obscure reply the wisest of Sparta could not make out, and was casually unriddled by one talking with a Smith who had found large bones of a man buried about his house; the oracle importing no more than a Smith's forge, expressed by a double bellows, the hammer and anvil therein.

Now, why the Oracle should place such consideration upon the bones of Orestes the son of Agamemnon, a mad man and a murtherer, if not to promote the idolatry of the heathens, and maintain a superstitious veneration of things of no activity, it may leave no small obscurity.

Or why, in a business so clear in his knowledge, he should affect so obscure expressions it may also be wondred; if it were not to maintain the wary and evasive method in his answers: for, speaking obscurely in things beyond doubt within his knowledge, he might be more tolerably dark in matters beyond his prescience.

Though EI were inscribed over the gate of Delphos, yet was there no uniformity in his deliveries. Sometimes with that obscurity as argued a fearfull prophecy; sometimes so plainly as might confirm a spirit of divinity; sometimes morally, deterring from vice and villany; another time vitiously, and in the spirit of bloud and cruelty: observably modest in his civil enigma and periphrasis of that part which old Numa would plainly name,* and Medea would not understand, when he advised Ægeus not to draw out his foot before, untill he arriv'd upon the Athenian ground; whereas another time he seemed too literal in that unseemly epithet unto Cyanus king of Cyprus,† and put a beastly trouble upon all Ægypt to find out the urine of a true Virgin.[71] Sometimes, more beholding unto memory than invention, he delighted to express himself in the bare verses of Homer. But that he principally affected poetry, and that the priest not onely or always composed his prosal raptures into verse, seems plain from his necromantical prophecies, whilst the dead head in Phlegon delivers a long prediction in verse; and at the raising of the ghost of Commodus unto Caracalla, when none of his ancestours would speak,

* Plutarch in Theseus.

† V. Herod.

the divining spirit versified his infelicities; corresponding herein to the apprehensions of elder times, who conceived not onely a majesty but something of divinity in poetry, and as in ancient times the old Theologians delivered their inventions.

Some critical readers might expect in his oraculous poems a more than ordinary strain and true spirit of Apollo; not contented to find that spirits make verses like men, beating upon the filling epithet, and taking the licence of dialects and lower helps, common to humane poetry; wherein, since Scaliger, who hath spared none of the Greeks, hath thought it wisedom to be silent, we shall make no excursion.

Others may wonder how the curiosity of elder times, having this opportunity of his answers, omitted natural questions; or how the old magicians discovered no more philosophy; and if they had the assistance of spirits, could rest content with the bare assertions of things, without the knowledge of their causes; whereby they had made their acts iterable by sober hands, and a standing part of philosophy. Many wise divines hold a reality in the wonders of the Ægyptian magicians, and that those magnalia which they performed before Pharaoh were not mere delusions of sense. Rightly to understand how they made serpents out of rods; froggs and bloud of water, were worth half Porta's magick.

Hermolaus Barbarus was scarce in his wits, when, upon conference with a spirit, he would demand no other question than the explication of Aristotle's *Entelecheia*. Appion the grammarian, that would raise the ghost of Homer to decide the controversie of his country, made a frivolous and pedantick use of necromancy. Philostratus did as little, that call'd up the ghost of Achilles for a particular of the story of Troy. Smarter curiosities would have been at the great elixir, the flux and reflux of the sea, with other noble obscurities in nature; but probably all in vain: in matters cognoscible and framed for our disquisition, our industry must be our oracle, and reason our Apollo.

Not to know things without the arch of our intellectuals, or what spirits apprehend, is the imperfection of our nature not our knowledge, and rather inscience than ignorance in man. Revelation might render a great part of the Creation easie which now seems beyond the stretch of humane indagation, and welcome no doubt from good hands might be a true Almagest, and great celestial construction: a clear systeme of the planetical bodies of the invisible and seeming useless stars unto us, of the many suns in the eighth sphere, what they are, what they contain and to what more immediately those stupendious bodies are serviceable. But being not hinted in the authentick revelation of God, nor known how far their discoveries are stinted; if they should come unto us from the mouth of evil spirits, the belief thereof might be as unsafe as the enquiry.

This is a copious subject, but, having exceeded the bounds of a letter, I will not, now, pursue it farther. I am,

Yours, etc.

TRACT XII

A Prophecy, Concerning the future state of several nations, in a letter written upon occasion of an old prophecy sent to the authour from a friend, with a request that he would consider it

Sir,

I take no pleasure in prophecies so hardly intelligible, and pointing at future things from a pretended spirit of divination; of which sort this seems to be which came unto your hand, and you were pleased to send unto me. And therefore, for your easier apprehension, divertisement and consideration, I present you with a very different kind of prediction: not positively or peremptorily telling you what shall come to pass; yet pointing at things not without all reason or probability of their events; not built upon fatal decrees, or inevitable designations, but upon conjectural foundations, whereby things wished may be promoted, and such as are feared, may more probably be prevented.

THE PROPHECY

When New England shall trouble New Spain.
When Jamaica shall be Lady of the Isles and the Main.
When Spain shall be in America hid,
And Mexico shall prove a Madrid.
When Mahomet's ships on the Baltick shall ride,
And Turks shall labour to have ports on that side.
When Africa shall no more sell out their Blacks
To make slaves and drudges to the American Tracts.
When Batavia the old shall be contemn'd by the new.
When a new drove of Tartars shall China subdue.
When America shall cease to send out its treasure,
But employ it at home in American pleasure.
When the new world shall the old invade,
Nor count them lords but their fellows in trade.
When men shall almost pass to Venice by land,

Not in deep water but from sand to sand.
When Nova Zembla shall be no stay
Unto those who pass to or from Cathay.
Then think strange things are come to light,
Where but few have had a foresight.

THE EXPOSITION OF THE PROPHECY

When New England shall trouble New Spain.

That is, when that thriving colony, which hath so much encreased in our days, and in the space of about fifty years, that they can, as they report, raise between twenty and thirty thousand men upon an exigency, shall in process of time become so advanced, as to be able to send forth ships and fleets, as to infest the American Spanish ports and maritime dominions by depredations or assaults; for which attempts they are not like to be unprovided, as abounding in the materials for shipping, oak and firre. And when length of time shall so far encrease that industrious people, that the neighbouring country will not contain them, they will range still farther and be able, in time, to set forth great armies, seek for new possessions, or make considerable and conjoined migrations, according to the custom of swarming northern nations; wherein it is not likely that they will move northward, but toward the southern and richer countries, which are either in the dominions or frontiers of the Spaniards: and may not improbably erect new dominions in places not yet thought of, and yet, for some centuries, beyond their power or ambition.

When Jamaica shall be the Lady of the Isles and the Main.

That is, when that advantageous island shall be well peopled, it may become so strong and potent as to over-power the neighbouring isles, and also a part of the main land, especially the maritime parts. And already in their infancy they have given testimony of their power and courage in their bold attempts upon Campeche and Santa Martha; and in that notable attempt upon Panama on the western side of America: especially considering this island is sufficiently large to contain a numerous people, of a northern and warlike descent, addicted to martial affairs both by sea and land, and advantageously seated to infest their neighbours both of the isles and the continent, and like to be a receptacle for colonies of the same originals from Barbadoes and the neighbour isles.

When Spain shall be in America hid,
And Mexico shall prove a Madrid.

That is, when Spain, either by unexpected disasters, or continued emissions of people into America, which have already thinned the country, shall be farther exhausted at home: or when, in process of time, their colonies shall grow by many accessions more than their originals, then Mexico may become a Madrid, and as considerable in people, wealth and splendour; wherein that place is already so well advanced, that accounts scarce credible are given of it. And it is so advantageously seated, that, by Acapulco and other ports on the South Sea, they may maintain a communication and commerce with the Indian Isles and territories, and with China and Japan, and on this side, by Porto Belo and others, hold correspondence with Europe and Africa.

When Mahomet's ships in the Baltick shall ride.

Of this we cannot be out of all fear: for, if the Turk should master Poland, he would be soon at this sea. And from the odd constitution of the Polish government, the divisions among themselves, jealousies between their kingdom and republick; vicinity of the Tartars, treachery of the Cossacks, and the method of Turkish policy, to be at peace with the emperour of Germany when he is at war with the Poles, there may be cause to fear that this may come to pass. And then he would soon endeavour to have ports upon that sea, as not wanting materials for shipping. And, having a new acquist of stout and warlike men, may be a terrour unto the confiners on that sea, and to nations which now conceive themselves safe from such an enemy.

When Africa shall no more sell out their blacks.

That is, when African countries shall no longer make it a common trade to sell away their people to serve in the drudgery of American plantations. And that may come to pass when ever they shall be well civilized, and acquainted with arts and affairs sufficient to employ people in their countries: if also they should be converted to Christianity, but especially to Mahometism; for then they would never sell those of their religion to be slaves unto Christians.

When Batavia the old shall be contemn'd by the new.

When the plantations of the Hollanders at Batavia in the East Indies, and other places in the East Indies, shall, by their conquests and advancements, become so powerfull in the Indian territories; then their original countries and states of Holland are like to be contemned by them, and obeyed onely as they please. And they seem to be in a way unto it at present by their several plantations, new acquists and enlargements: and they have lately discovered a part of the southern continent, and several places which may be serviceable unto them, when ever time shall enlarge them unto such necessities.

And a new drove of Tartars shall China subdue.

Which is no strange thing if we consult the histories of China, and successive inundations made by Tartarian nations. For when the invaders, in process of time, have degenerated into the effeminacy and softness of the Chineses, then they themselves have suffered a new Tartarian conquest and inundation. And this hath happened from time beyond our histories: for, according to their account, the famous wall of China, built against the irruptions of the Tartars, was begun above a hundred years before the incarnation.

When America shall cease to send forth its treasure,
But employ it at home for American pleasure.

That is, When America shall be better civilized, new policied and divided between great princes, it may come to pass that they will no longer suffer their treasure of gold and silver to be sent out to maintain the luxury of Europe and other parts: but rather employ it to their own advantages, in great exploits and undertakings, magnificent structures, wars or expeditions of their own.

When the new world shall the old invade.

That is, when America shall be so well peopled, civilized and divided into kingdoms, they are like to have so little regard of their originals, as to acknowledge no subjection unto them: they may also have a distinct commerce between themselves, or but independently with those of Europe, and may hostilely and pyratically assault them, even as the Greek and Roman colonies after a long time dealt with their original countries.

When men shall almost pass to Venice by land,
Not in deep waters but from sand to sand.

That is, when, in long process of time, the silt and sands shall so choak and shallow the sea in and about it. And this hath considerably come to pass within these fourscore years; and is like to encrease from several causes, especially by the turning of the River Brenta, as the learned Castelli hath declared.

When Nova Zembla shall be no stay
Unto those who pass to or from Cathay.

That is, when ever that often sought for northeast passage unto China and Japan shall be discovered, the hindrance whereof was imputed to Nova Zembla; for this was conceived to be an excursion of land shooting out directly, and so far northward into the sea that it discouraged from all navigation about it. And therefore adventurers took in at the southern part at a strait by Waygatz next the Tartarian shore; and sailing forward they found that sea frozen and full of ice, and so gave over the attempt. But of late years, by the diligent enquiry of some Moscovites, a better discovery is made of these parts, and a map or chart made of them. Thereby Nova Zembla is found to be no island extending very far northward; but, winding eastward, it joineth to the Tartarian Continent, and so makes a peninsula: and the sea between it which they entred at Waygatz, is found to be but a large bay, apt to be frozen by reason of the great River of Oby, and other fresh waters, entring into it: whereas the main sea doth not freez upon the north of Zembla except near unto shores; so that if the Moscovites were skilfull navigatours they might, with less difficulties, discover this passage unto China: but however the English, Dutch and Danes are now like to attempt it again.

But this is conjecture, and not prophecy: and so (I know) you will take it. I am,

Sir, etc.

TRACT XIII

Musæum Clausum, *or* Bibliotheca Abscondita: *containing some remarkable Books, Antiquities, Pictures and Rarities of several kinds, scarce or never seen by any man now living*

Sir,

With many thanks I return that noble catalogue of books, rarities and singularities of art and nature, which you were pleased to communicate unto me. There are many collections of this kind in Europe. And, besides the printed accounts of the *Musæum Aldrovandi*, *Calceolarianum*, *Moscardi*, *Wormianum*; the *Casa Abbellita* at Loretto, and *Threasor* of S. Dennis, the *Repository* of the Duke of Tuscany, that of the Duke of Saxony, and that noble one of the emperour at Vienna, and many more are of singular note. Of what in this kind I have by me I shall make no repetition, and you having already had a view thereof, I am bold to present you with the list of a collection, which I may justly say you have not seen before.

The Title is, as above,

MUSÆUM CLAUSUM, OR BIBLIOTHECA ABSCONDITA: CONTAINING SOME REMARKABLE BOOKS, ANTIQUITIES, PICTURES AND RARITIES OF SEVERAL KINDS, SCARCE OR NEVER SEEN BY ANY MAN NOW LIVING

I. Rare and generally unknown Books

1. A poem of *Ovidius Naso*, written in the Getick Language,*[72] during his exile at Tomos, found wrapt up in wax at Sabaria, on the frontiers of Hungary, where there remains a tradition that he died, in his return towards Rome from Tomos, either after his pardon or the death of Augustus.
2. The letter of Quintus Cicero, which he wrote in answer to that of his brother Marcus Tullius, desiring of him an

* *Ab pudet et scripsi Getico sermone Libellum..*

account of Britany, wherein are described the country, state and manners of the Britains of that Age.

3. An ancient British herbal, or description of divers plants of this island, observed by that famous physician Scribonius Largus, when he attended the Emperour Claudius in his expedition into Britany.
4. An exact account of the life and death of Avicenna confirming the account of his death by taking nine Clysters together in a fit of the colick; and not as Marius the Italian poet delivereth, by being broken upon the wheel; left with other pieces by Benjamin Tudelensis, as he travelled from Saragossa to Jerusalem, in the hands of Abraham Jarchi, a famous Rabbi of Lunet near Montpelier, and found in a vault when the walls of that city were demolished by Lewis the thirteenth.
5. A punctual relation of Hannibal's march out of Spain into Italy, and far more particular than that of Livy, where about he passed the River Rhodanus or Rhosne; at what place he crossed the Isara or L'isere; when he marched up toward the confluence of the Sone and the Rhone, or the place where the city Lyons was afterward built; how wisely he decided the difference between King Brancus and his brother, at what place he passed the Alpes, what vinegar he used, and where he obtained such quantity to break and calcine the rocks made hot with fire.
6. A learned comment upon the Periplus of Hanno the Carthaginian, or his navigation upon the western coast of Africa, with the several places he landed at; what colonies he settled, what ships were scattered from his fleet near the Æquinoctial line, which were not afterward heard of, and which probably fell into the trade winds, and were carried over into the coast of America.
7. A particular narration of that famous expedition of the English into Barbary in the ninety fourth year of the Hegira, so shortly touched by Leo Africanus, whither called by the Goths they besieged, took and burnt the city of Arzilla possessed by the Mahometans, and lately the seat of Gayland; with many other exploits delivered at large in Arabick, lost in the ship of books and rarities which the King of Spain took from Siddy Hamet King of Fez, whereof a great part were carried into the Escurial, and conceived to be gathered out of the relations of Hibnu Nachu, the best historian of the African affairs.

8. A Fragment of Pythæas that ancient traveller of Marseille; which we suspect not to be spurious, because, in the description of the northern countries, we find that passage of Pythæas mentioned by Strabo, that all the air beyond Thule is thick, condensed and gellied, looking just like sea lungs.
9. A *sub marine* herbal, describing the several vegetables found on the rocks, hills, valleys, meadows at the bottom of the sea, with many sorts of *alga*, *fucus*, *quercus*, *polygonum*, *gramens* and others not yet described.
10. Some manuscripts and rarities brought from the libraries of Æthiopia, by Zaga Zaba, and afterward transported to Rome, and scattered by the souldiers of the Duke of Bourbon, when they barbarously sacked that city.
11. Some pieces of Julius Scaliger, which he complains to have been stoln from him, sold to the Bishop of Mende in Languedock, and afterward taken away and sold in the civil wars under the Duke of Rohan.
12. A Comment of Dioscorides upon Hyppocrates, procured from Constantinople by Amatus Lusitanus, and left in the hands of a Jew of Ragusa.
13. Marcus Tullius Cicero his Geography; as also a part of that magnified piece of his *De Republica*, very little answering the great expectation of it, and short of pieces under the same name by Bodinus and Tholosanus.
14. King Mithridates his *Oneirocritica*.
    Aristotle, *de Precationibus*.
    Democritus, *de his quæ fiunt apud Orcum, et Oceani circumnavigatio*.
    Epicurus, *de Pietate*.
    A tragedy of *Thyestes*, and another of *Medea*, writ by Diogenes the Cynick.
    King Alfred upon Aristotle, *de Plantis*.
    Seneca's Epistles to S. Paul.
    King Solomon, *de Umbris Idæarum*, which Chicus Asculanus, in his comment upon Johannes de Sacrobosco, would make us believe he saw in the library of the Duke of Bavaria.
15. Artemidori, *Oneirocritici Geographia*.
    Pythagoras, *de Mari Rubro*.

The works of Confutius the famous philosopher of China, translated into Spanish.

16. *Josephus* in Hebrew, written by himself.
17. The commentaries of Sylla the Dictatour.
18. A commentary of Galen upon the plague of Athens described by Thucydides.
19. *Duo Cæsaris Anti-Catones*, or the two notable books written by Julius Cæsar against Cato; mentioned by Livy, Salustius and Juvenal; which the Cardinal of Liege told Ludovicus Vives were in an old library of that city.

Mazhapha Einok, or, the *Prophecy of Enoch*, which Ægidius Lochiensis, a learned eastern traveller, told Peireschius that he had found in an old library at Alexandria containing eight thousand volumes.

20. A Collection of Hebrew epistles, which passed between the two learned women of our age, Maria Molinea of Sedan, and Maria Schurman of Utrecht.

A wondrous collection of some writings of Ludovica Saracenica, daughter of Philibertus Saracenicus a physician of Lyons, who at eight years of age had made a good progress in the Hebrew, Greek and Latin tongues.

II. Rarities in Pictures

1. A picture of the three remarkable steeples or towers in Europe built purposely awry and so as they seem falling. Torre Pisana at Pisa, Torre Garisenda in Bononia, and that other in the city of Colein.
2. A Draught of all sorts of sistrums, crotaloes, cymbals, tympans, etc. in use among the ancients.
3. Large *submarine* pieces, well delineating the bottom of the Mediterranean Sea, the prerie or large sea-meadow upon the coast of Provence, the Coral Fishing, the gathering of Sponges, the mountains, valleys and desarts, the subterraneous vents and passages at the bottom of that sea. Together with a lively draught of *Cola Pesce*, or the famous Sicilian swimmer, diving into the *Voragos* and broken rocks by Charybdis, to fetch up the golden cup, which Frederick, King of Sicily, had purposely thrown into that sea.
4. A moon piece, describing that notable battel between Axalla, General of Tamerlane, and Camares the Persian, fought by the light of the moon.

5. Another remarkable fight of Inghimmi the Florentine with the Turkish galleys by moon-light, who, being for three hours grappled with the Basha Galley, concluded with a signal victory.
6. A delineation of the great fair of Almachara in Arabia, which, to avoid the great heat of the sun, is kept in the night, and by the light of the moon.
7. A snow piece, of land and trees covered with snow and ice, and mountains of ice floating in the sea, with bears, seals, foxes, and variety of rare fowls upon them.
8. An ice piece describing the notable battel between the Jaziges and the Romans, fought upon the frozen Danubius, the Romans settling one foot upon their targets to hinder them from slipping, their fighting with the Jaziges when they were fallen, and their advantages therein by their art in volutation and rolling contention or wrastling, according to the description of Dion.
9. Socia, or a draught of three persons notably resembling each other. Of King Henry the Fourth of France, and a miller of Languedock; of Sforza Duke of Milain and a souldier; of Malatesta Duke of Rimini and Marchesinus the jester.
10. A picture of the great fire which happened at Constantinople in the reign of Sultan Achmet. The Janizaries in the mean time plundring the best houses, Nassa Bassa the Vizier riding about with a cimetre in one hand and a Janizary's head in the other to deter them; and the priests attempting to quench the fire, by pieces of Mahomet's shirt dipped in holy water and thrown into it.
11. A night piece of the dismal supper and strange entertain of the senatours by Domitian, according to the description of Dion.
12. A vestal sinner in the cave with a table and a candle.
13. An elephant dancing upon the ropes with a negro dwarf upon his back.
14. Another describing the mighty stone falling from the clouds into Ægospotamos or the Goats River in Greece, which antiquity could believe that Anaxagoras was able to foretell half a year before.
15. Three noble pieces; of Vercingetorix the Gaul submitting his person unto Julius Cæsar; of Tigranes King of Armenia humbly presenting himself unto Pompey; and

of Tamerlane ascending his horse from the neck of Bajazet.

16. Draughts of three passionate looks; of Thyestes when he was told at the table that he had eaten a piece of his own son; of Bajazet when he went into the iron cage; of Œdipus when he first came to know that he had killed his father, and married his own mother.
17. Of the Cymbrian mother in Plutarch who, after her overthrow by Marius, hanged her self and her two children at her feet.
18. Some pieces delineating singular inhumanities in tortures. The scaphismus of the Persians. The living truncation of the Turks. The hanging sport at the feasts of the Thracians. The exact method of flaying men alive, beginning between the shoulders, according to the description of Thomas Minadoi, in his Persian War. Together with the studied tortures of the French traitours at Pappa in Hungaria: as also the wild and enormous torment invented by Tiberius, designed according unto the description of Suetonius. *Excogitaverunt inter genera cruciatûs, ut largâ meri potione par fallaciam oneratos repentè veretris deligatis fidicularum simul urinæque tormento distenderet.*[73]
19. A picture describing how Hannibal forced his passage over the River Rhosne with his elephants, baggage, and mixed army; with the army of the Gauls opposing him on the contrary shore, and Hanno passing over with his horse much above to fall upon the rere of the Gauls.
20. A neat piece describing the sack of Fundi by the fleet and souldiers of Barbarossa the Turkish Admiral, the confusion of the people and their flying up to the mountains, and Julia Gonzaga the beauty of Italy flying away with her ladies half naked on horseback over the hills.
21. A noble head of Franciscus Gonzaga, who, being imprisoned for treason, grew grey in one night, with this inscription,

    O nox quam longa est quæ facit una senem.[74]

22. A large picture describing the siege of Vienna by Solyman the Magnificent, and at the same time the siege of Florence by the Emperour Charles the Fifth and Pope Clement the Seventh, with this subscription,

Tum vacui capitis populum Phæaca putares?[75]

23. An exquisite piece properly delineating the first course of Metellus his pontificiall supper, according to the description of Macrobius; together with a dish of *pisces fossiles*, garnished about with the little eels taken out of the backs of cods and perches; as also with the shell fishes found in stones about Ancona.
24. A picture of the noble entertain and feast of the Duke of Chausue at the Treaty of Collen, 1673, when in a very large room, with all the windows open, and at a very large table he sate himself, with many great persons and ladies; next about the table stood a row of waiters, then a row of musicians, then a row of musketiers.
25. Miltiades, who overthrew the Persians at the Battel of Marathon and delivered Greece, looking out of a prison grate in Athens, wherein he died, with this inscription,

Non hoc terribiles Cymbri non Britones unquam
Sauromatæve truces aut immanes Agathyrsi.[76]

26. A fair English lady drawn *al negro*, or in the Æthiopian hue excelling the original white and red beauty, with this subscription,

Sed quandam volo nocte Nigriorem.[77]

27. Pieces and draughts in *caricatura*, of princes, cardinals and famous men; wherein, among others, the painter hath singularly hit the signatures of a lion and a fox in the face of Pope Leo the Tenth.
28. Some pieces *a la ventura*, or rare chance pieces, either drawn at random, and happening to be like some person, or drawn for some and happening to be more like another; while the face, mistaken by the painter, proves a tolerable picture of one he never saw.
29. A draught of famous dwarfs with this inscription,

Nos facimus Bruti puerum nos Logona vivum.[78]

30. An exact and proper delineation of all sorts of dogs upon occasion of the practice of Sultan Achmet; who in a great plague at Constantinople transported all the dogs therein unto Pera, and from thence into a little island, where they perished at last by famine: as also the manner of the priests

curing of mad dogs by burning them in the forehead with Saint Bellin's Key.

31. A noble picture of Thorismund King of the Goths as he was killed in his palace at Tholouze, who being let bloud by a surgeon, while he was bleeding, a stander by took the advantage to stab him.

32. A picture of rare fruits with this inscription,

Credere quæ possis surrepta sororibus Afris.[79]

33. An handsome piece of deformity expressed in a notable hard face, with this inscription,

—*Ora*
Julius in Satyris qualia Rufus habet.[80]

34. A noble picture of the famous duel between Paul Manessi and Caragusa the Turk in the time of Amurath the Second; the Turkish Army and that of Scanderbeg looking on; wherein Manessi slew the Turk, cut off his head and carried away the spoils of his body.

III. Antiquities and Rarities of several sorts

1. Certain ancient medals with Greek and Roman inscriptions, found about Crim Tartary; conceived to be left in those parts by the souldiers of Mithridates, when overcome by Pompey, he marched about the north of the Euxine to come about into Thracia.
2. Some ancient ivory and copper crosses found with many others in China; conceived to have been brought and left there by the Greek souldiers who served under Tamerlane in his expedition and conquest of that country.
3. Stones of strange and illegible inscriptions, found about the great ruines which Vincent le Blanc describeth about Cephala in Africa, where he opinion'd that the Hebrews raised some buildings of old, and that Solomon brought from thereabout a good part of his gold.
4. Some handsome engraveries and medals, of Justinus and Justinianus, found in the custody of a Bannyan in the remote parts of India, conjectured to have been left there by friers mentioned in Procopius, who travelled those parts in the reign of Justinianus, and brought back into Europe the discovery of silk and silk worms.

5. An original medal of Petrus Aretinus, who was called *flagellum principum*, wherein he made his own figure on the obverse part with this inscription,

   Il Divino Aretino.

On the reverse sitting on a throne, and at his feet ambassadours of kings and princes bringing presents unto him, with this inscription,

I Principi tributati da i Popoli tributano il Servitor loro.[81]

6. *Mummia Tholosana*; or, the complete head and body of Father Crispin, buried long ago in the vault of the Cordeliers at Tholouse, where the skins of the dead so drie and parch up without corrupting that their persons may be known very long after, with this inscription,

   Ecce iterum Crispinus.

7. A noble *quandros* or stone taken out of a vulture's head.
8. A large ostridges egg, whereon is neatly and fully wrought that famous Battel of Alcazar, in which three kings lost their lives.
9. An *Etiudros Alberti* or stone that is apt to be always moist: usefull unto drie tempers, and to be held in the hand in fevers instead of crystal, eggs, limmons, cucumbers.
10. A small viol of water taken out of the stones therefore called *Enhydri*, which naturally include a little water in them, in like manner as the *Ætites* or *Aëgle* stone doth another stone.
11. A neat painted and gilded cup made out of the *Confiti di Tivoli* and formed up with powder'd egg-shells; as Nero is conceived to have made his *piscina admirabilis*, singular against fluxes to drink often therein.
12. The skin of a snake bred out of the spinal marrow of a man.
13. Vegetable horns mentioned by Linschoten, which set in the ground grow up like plants about Goa.
14. An extract of the inck of cuttle fishes reviving the old remedy of Hippocrates in hysterical passions.
15. Spirits and salt of Sargasso made in the western ocean covered with that vegetable; excellent against the scurvy.
16. An extract of *cachundè* or *liberans* that famous and highly magnified composition in the East Indies against melancholy.

17. *Diarhizon mirificum*; or an unparallel'd composition of the most effectual and wonderfull roots in nature.

Rad. Butuæ Cuamensis.
Rad. Moniche Cuamensis.
Rad. Mongus Bazainensis.
Rad. Casei Bazainensis.
Rad. Columbæ Mozambiguensis.
Gim. Sem. Sinicæ.
Fo. Lim. Lac. Tigridis dictæ.
Fo. seu.
Cort. Rad. Soldæ.
Rad. Ligni Solorani.
Rad. Malacensis madrededios dictæ an. zij.
M. fiat pulvis, qui cum gelatinâ Cornu cervi Moschati Chinensis formetur in massas oviformes.

18. A transcendent perfume made of the richest odorates of both the Indies, kept in a box made of the Muschie stone of Niarienburg, with this inscription,

— —Deos rogato
Totum ut te faciant, Fabulle, Nasum.

19. A Clepselæa, or oil hour-glass, as the ancients used those of water.
20. A ring found in a fishes belly taken about Gorro; conceived to be the same wherewith the Duke of Venice had wedded the sea.
21. A neat crucifix made out of the cross bone of a frogs head.
22. A large agath containing a various and careless figure, which looked upon by a cylinder representeth a perfect centaur. By some such advantages King Pyrrhus might find out Apollo and the nine muses in those agaths of his whereof Pliny maketh mention.
23. *Batrachomyomachia*, or the Homerican battel between frogs and mice, neatly described upon the chizel bone of a large pike's jaw.
24. *Pyxis Pandoræ*, or a box which held the *unguentum pestiferum*, which by anointing the garments of several persons begat the great and horrible plague of Milan.
25. A glass of spirits made of Æthereal salt, hermetically sealed up, kept continually in quick-silver; of so volatile a nature that it will scarce endure the light, and therefore

onely to be shown in winter, or by the light of a carbuncle, or Bononian stone.

He who knows where all this treasure now is, is a great Apollo. I'm sure I am not he. However, I am,

Sir, yours, etc.

Finis.

A LETTER TO A FRIEND, UPON THE OCCASION OF THE DEATH OF HIS INTIMATE FRIEND

A

LETTER

TO A

FRIEND,

Upon occaſion of the

DEATH

OF HIS

Intimate Friend.

By the Learned

Sir *THOMAS BROWN*, Knight,

Doctor of Phyſick, late of *Norwich*.

LONDON:

Printed for *Charles Brome* at the *Gun* at the Weſt-End of S. *Paul's* Church-yard. 1690.

FIG. 12 Title page from *Letter to a Friend* (1690).

To a Friend, upon occasion of the death of his intimate friend

Give me leave to wonder that news of this nature should have such heavy wings, that you should hear so little concerning your dearest friend, and that I must make that unwilling repetition to tell you, *Ad portam rigidos calces extendit*, that he is dead and buried, and by this time no puny among the mighty nations of the dead;[1] for though he left this world not very many days past, yet every hour you know largely addeth unto that dark society; and considering the incessant mortality of mankind, you cannot conceive there dieth in the whole earth so few as a thousand an hour.

Although at this distance you had no early account or particular of his death; yet your affection may cease to wonder that you had not some secret sense or intimation thereof by dreams, thoughtful whisperings, mercurisms, airy nuncios, or sympathetical insinuations, which many seem to have had at the death of their dearest friends: for since we find in that famous story, that spirits themselves were fain to tell their fellows at a distance, that the great Antonio was dead; we have a sufficient excuse for our ignorance in such particulars, and must rest content with the common road, and *Appian* way of knowledge by information. Though the uncertainty of the end of this world hath confounded all humane predictions; yet they who shall live to see the sun and moon darkened, and the stars to fall from heaven, will hardly be deceived in the advent of the last day; and therefore strange it is, that the common fallacy of consumptive persons, who feel not themselves dying, and therefore still hope to live, should also reach their friends in perfect health and judgment. That you should be so little acquainted with Plautus's sick complexion, or that almost an Hippocratical face should not alarum you to higher fears, or rather despair of his continuation in such an emaciated state, wherein medical predictions fail not, as sometimes in acute diseases, and wherein 'tis as dangerous to be sentenced by a physician as a judge.[2]

Upon my first visit I was bold to tell them who had not let fall all hopes of his recovery, that in my sad opinion he was not like to behold a grasshopper, much less to pluck another fig; and in no long time after seemed to discover that odd mortal symptom in him not mention'd by Hippocrates, that is, to lose his own face and look like some of his near relations; for he maintained not his proper countenance, but looked like his uncle, the lines of whose face lay deep and invisible in his healthful visage before: for as from our beginning we run through variety of looks, before we come to consistent and settled faces; so before our end, by sick and languishing alterations, we put on new visages: and in our retreat to earth, may fall upon such looks which from community of seminal originals were before latent in us.

He was fruitlessly put in hope of advantage by change of air, and imbibing the pure aerial nitre of these parts; and therefore being so far spent, he quickly found Sardinia in Tivoli,* and the most healthful air of little effect, where death had set her broad arrow;[†3] for he lived not unto the middle of May, and confirmed the observation of Hippocrates of that mortal time of the year when the leaves of the fig-tree resemble a daw's claw.[‡4] He is happily seated who lives in places whose air, earth, and water, promote not the infirmities of his weaker parts, or is early removed into regions that correct them. He that is tabidly inclined, were unwise to pass his days in Portugal: cholical persons will find little comfort in Austria or Vienna: he that is weak-legg'd must not be in love with Rome, nor an infirm head with Venice or Paris.[5] Death hath not only particular stars in heaven, but malevolent places on earth, which single out our infirmities, and strike at our weaker parts; in which concern, passager and migrant birds have the great advantages; who are naturally constituted for distant habitations, whom no seas nor places limit, but in their appointed seasons will visit us from Greenland and Mount Atlas, and as some think, even from the Antipodes.[§]

* *Cum mors venerit, in medio Tibure Sardinia est.*

† In the King's Forests they set the Figure of a broad Arrow upon Trees that are to be cut down.

‡ *Hippoc. Epidem.*

§ Bellonius *de Avibus.*

Though we could not have his life, yet we missed not our desires in his soft departure, which was scarce an expiration; and his end not unlike his beginning, when the salient point scarce affords a sensible motion, and his departure so like unto sleep, that he scarce needed the civil ceremony of closing his eyes; contrary unto the common way wherein death draws up, sleep lets fall the eye-lids. With what strift and pains we came into the world we know not;[6] but 'tis commonly no easie matter to get out of it: yet if it could be made out, that such who have easie nativities have commonly hard deaths, and contrarily; his departure was so easie, that we might justly suspect his birth was of another nature, and that some Juno sat cross-legg'd at his nativity.[7]

Besides his soft death, the incurable state of his disease might somewhat extenuate your sorrow, who know that monsters but seldom happen, miracles more rarely, in physick.[*] Angelus Victorius gives a serious account of a consumptive, hectical, pthysical woman, who was suddenly cured by the intercession of Ignatius.[†8] We read not of any in scripture who in this case applied unto our Saviour, though some may be contained in that large expression, That he went about Galilee healing all manner of sickness, and all manner of diseases.[‡] Amulets, spells, sigils and incantations, practised in other diseases, are seldom pretended in this;[9] and we find no sigil in the *Archidoxis* of Paracelsus to cure an extreme consumption or *marasmus*, which if other diseases fail, will put a period unto long livers, and at last make dust of all.[10] And therefore the Stoicks could not but think that the firy principle would wear out all the rest, and at last make an end of the world, which notwithstanding without such a lingering period the Creator may effect at his pleasure: and to make an end of all things on earth, and our planetical system of the world, he need but put out the sun.

[*] *Monstra contingunt in medicina Hippoc.*

[†] Strange and rare Escapes there happen sometimes in Physick. *Angeli Victorii Con sultationes.*

[‡] Matth. iv. 25.

I was not so curious to entitle the stars unto any concern of his death, yet could not but take notice that he died when the moon was in motion from the meridian; at which time, an old Italian long ago would persuade me, that the greatest part of men died: but herein I confess I could never satisfie my curiosity; although from the time of tides in places upon or near the sea, there may be considerable deductions; and Pliny hath an odd and remarkable passage concerning the death of men and animals upon the recess or ebb of the sea.[§11] However, certain it is he died in the dead and deep part of the night, when Nox might be most apprehensibly said to be the daughter of Chaos, the mother of Sleep and Death, according to old genealogy;[12] and so went out of this world about that hour when our blessed Saviour entered it, and about what time many conceive he will return again unto it. Cardan hath a peculiar and no hard observation from a man's hand, to know whether he was born in the day or night, which I confess holdeth in my own. And Scaliger to that purpose hath another from the tip of the ear;[**13] most men are begotten in the night, most animals in the day; but whether more persons have been born in the night or the day, were a curiosity undecidable,

[§] *Aristoteles nullum animal nisi æstu recedente expirare affirmat: observatum id multum in Gallico Oceano & duntaxat in Homine compertum, lib.* 2. *cap.* 101.

[**] *Auris pars pendula Lobus dicitur, non omnibus ea pars est auribus; non enim iis qui noctu nati sunt, sed qui interdiu, maxima ex parte. Com. in Aristot. de Animal. lib. I.*

aruspex might have read a lecture upon him without exenteration, his flesh being so consumed that he might, in a manner, have discerned his bowels without opening of him:[*16] so that to be carried *sextâ cervice* to his grave, was but a civil unnecessity; and the complements of the coffin might out-weigh the subject of it.

Omnibonus Ferrarius in mortal dysenteries of children looks for a spot behind the ear;[†] in consumptive diseases some eye the complexion of moals; Cardan eagerly views the nails, some the lines of the hand, the thenar or muscle of the thumb; some are so curious as to observe the depth of the throat-pit, how the proportion varieth of the small of the legs unto the calf, or the compass of the neck unto the circumference of the head: but all these, with many more, were so drowned in a mortal visage and last face of Hippocrates, that a weak physiognomist might say at first eye, this was a face of earth, and that Morta[‡] had set her Hard-Seal upon his temples, easily perceiving what *caricatura* draughts death makes upon pined faces, and unto what an unknown degree a man may live backward.[§]

Though the beard be only made a distinction of sex and sign of masculine heat by Ulmus, yet the precocity and early growth thereof in him, was not to be liked in reference unto long life.[**] Lewis, that virtuous but unfortunate king of Hungary, who lost his life at the Battel of Mohacz, was said to be born without a skin, to have bearded at fifteen, and to have shewn some gray hairs about twenty; from whence the diviners conjectured, that he would be spoiled of his kingdom, and have but a short life: but hairs make fallible predictions, and many temples early gray have out-lived the Psalmist's period.[††17] Hairs which have most amused me have not been in the face or head, but on the back, and not in men but children, as I long ago observed in that endemial distemper of little children in Languedock, called the Morgellons, wherein they critically[‡‡] break out with harsh hairs on their backs, which takes off the unquiet symptoms of the disease, and delivers them from coughs and convulsions.

The Egyptian Mummies that I have seen, have had their mouths open, and somewhat gaping, which affordeth a good opportunity to view and observe their teeth, wherein 'tis not easie to find any wanting or decayed: and therefore in Egypt, where one man practised but one operation, or the diseases but of single parts, it must needs be a barren profession to confine unto that of drawing of teeth, and little better than to have

[*] The Poet *Dante* his Description.

[†] *De morbis Puerorum.*

[‡] *Morta*, the Deity of Death or Fate.

[§] When Mens Faces are drawn with resemblance to some other Animals, the *Italians* call it, to be drawn in *Caricatura.*

[**] *Ulmus de usu barbæ humanæ.*

[††] The Life of a Man is Three-score and Ten.

[‡‡] See *Picotus di Rheumatismo.*

been tooth-drawer unto king *Pyrrhus*, who had but two in his head.* How the Bannyans of India maintain the integrity of those parts, I find not particularly observed; who notwithstanding have an advantage of their preservation by abstaining from all flesh, and employing their teeth in such food unto which they may seem at first framed, from their figure and conformation: but sharp and corroding rheums had so early mouldered those rocks and hardest parts of his fabrick, that a man might well conceive that his years were never like to double or twice tell over his teeth.† Corruption had dealt more severely with them, than sepulchral fires and smart flames with those of burnt bodies of old; for in the burnt fragments of urns which I have enquired into, although I seem to find few incisors or shearers, yet the dog teeth and grinders do notably resist those fires.

* His upper and lower jaw being solid, and without distinct rows of Teeth.

† Twice tell over his Teeth never live to threescore Years.

In the years of his childhood he had languished under the disease of his country, the rickets; after which notwithstanding many I have seen become strong and active men; but whether any have attained unto very great years the disease is scarce so old as to afford good observations. Whether the children of the English plantations be subject unto the same infirmity, may be worth the observing. Whether lameness and halting do still encrease among the inhabitants of Rovigno in Istria, I know not; yet scarce twenty years ago Monsieur du Loyr observed, that a third part of that people halted: but too certain it is, that the rickets encreaseth among us; the small-pox grows more pernicious than the great: the King's purse knows that the King's Evil grows more common. *Quartan Agues* are become no strangers in Ireland; more common and mortal in England: and though the ancients gave that disease very good words‡, yet now that bell makes no strange sound which rings out for the effects thereof.§[18]

‡ *Ἀσφαλέστατος καὶ ῥήϊστος, securissima & facillimæ*, Hippocrat.

§ Pro febre quartana raro sonat campana.

Some think there were few consumptions in the old world, when men lived much upon milk; and that the ancient inhabitants of this island were less troubled with coughs when they went naked, and slept in caves and woods, than men now in chambers and feather-beds. Plato will tell us, that there was no such disease as a catarrh in Homer's time, and that it was but new in Greece in his age. Polydore Virgil delivereth that pleurisies were rare in England, who lived but in the days of Henry the Eighth. Some will allow no diseases to be new, others think that many old ones are ceased; and that such which are esteemed new, will have but their time: however, the mercy of God hath scattered the great heap of diseases, and not loaded any one country with all: some may be new in one country which have been old in another. New discoveries of the earth discover new diseases: for besides the common swarm, there are endemial and local infirmities proper unto certain regions, which in the whole earth make no small number:[19] and if Asia, Africa, and America should bring in their list, Pandoras Box would swell, and there must be a strange pathology.

Most men expected to find a consumed kell, empty and bladder-like guts, livid and marbled lungs, and a withered *Pericardium* in this exuccous corps:[20] but some seemed too much to wonder that two lobes of his lungs adhered unto his side; for the like I had often found in bodies of no suspected consumptions or difficulty of respiration. And the same more often happeneth in men than other animals;[*] and some think, in women than in men: but the most remarkable I have met with, was in a man, after a cough of almost fifty years, in whom all the lobes adhered unto the pleura, and each lobe unto another; who having also been much troubled with the gout, brake the rule of Cardan, and died of the stone in the bladder.[†] Aristotle makes a query, why some animals cough as man, some not, as oxen. If coughing be taken as it consisteth of a natural and voluntary motion, including expectoration and spitting out, it may be as proper unto man as bleeding at the nose; otherwise we find that Vegetius and rural writers have not left so many medicines in vain against the coughs of cattel; and men who perish by coughs dye the death of sheep, cats and lyons: and though birds have no midriff, yet we meet with divers remedies in *Arrianus* against the coughs of hawks. And though it might be thought, that all animals who have lungs do cough; yet in cetaceous fishes, who have large and strong lungs, the same is not observed; nor yet in oviparous quadrupeds: and in the greatest thereof, the crocodile, although we read much of their tears, we find nothing of that motion.

From the thoughts of sleep, when the soul was conceived nearest unto divinity, the ancients erected an art of Divination, wherein while they too widely expatiated in loose and inconsequent conjectures, Hippocrates wisely considered dreams as they presaged alterations in the body,[‡] and so afforded hints toward the preservation of health, and prevention of diseases;[21] and therein was so serious as to advise alteration of diet, exercise, sweating, bathing and vomiting; and also so religious,

[*] So A. F.

[†] *Cardan* in his *Encomium Podagræ* reckoneth this among the *Dona Podagræ*, that they are delivered thereby from the Pthysis and Stone in the Bladder.

[‡] *Hippoc. de Insomniis.*

as to order prayers and supplications unto respective deities, in good dreams unto Sol, Jupiter cœlestis, Jupiter opulentus, Minerva, Mercurius, and Apollo; in bad unto Tellus and the Heroes.

And therefore I could not but take notice how his female friends were irrationally curious so strictly to examine his dreams, and in this low state to hope for the fantasms of health. He was now past the healthful dreams of the sun, moon, and stars in their clarity and proper courses. 'Twas too late to dream of flying, of limpid fountains, smooth waters, white vestments, and fruitful green trees, which are the visions of healthful sleeps, and at good distance from the grave.

And they were also too deeply dejected that he should dream of his dead friends, inconsequently divining, that he would not be long from them; for strange it was not that he should sometimes dream of the dead whose thoughts run always upon death: beside, to dream of the dead, so they appear not in dark habits, and take nothing away from us, in Hippocrates his sense was of good signification*:[22] for we live by the dead, and every thing is or must be so before it becomes our nourishment. And Cardan, who dream'd that he discoursed with his dead father in the moon, made thereof no mortal interpretation: and even to dream that we are dead, was no condemnable fantasm in old *Oneirocriticism*, as having a signification of liberty, vacuity from cares, exemption and freedom from troubles, unknown unto the dead.

* *Hippoc. de Insomniis.*

Some dreams I confess may admit of easie and feminine exposition: he who dream'd that he could not see his right shoulder, might easily fear to lose the sight of his right eye; he that before a journey dream'd that his feet were cut off, had a plain warning not to undertake his intended journey. But why to dream of lettuce should presage some ensuing disease, why to eat figs should signifie foolish talk, why to eat eggs great trouble, and to dream of blindness should be so highly commended, according to the *Oneirocritical* verses of *Astrampsychus* and *Nicephorus*, I shall leave unto your divination.

He was willing to quit the world alone and altogether, leaving no earnest behind him for corruption or aftergrave, having small content in that common satisfaction to survive or live in another, but amply satisfied that his disease should dye with himself, nor revive in a posterity to puzzle physick, and make sad mementos of their parent hereditary. Leprosie awakes not sometimes before forty, the gout and stone often later; but consumptive and tabid Roots sprout more early, and at the fairest make seventeen years of our life doubtful before that age.*[23] They that enter the world with original diseases as well as sin, have not only common mortality but sick traductions to destroy them, make commonly short courses, and live not at length but in figures; so that a sound Cæsarean nativity may out-last a natural birth, and a knife may sometimes make way for a more lasting fruit than a midwife;† which makes so few infants now able to endure the old test of the river, and many to have feeble children who could scarce have been married at Sparta, and those provident states who studied strong and healthful generations;‡ which happen but contingently in mere pecuniary matches, or marriages made by the candle, wherein notwithstanding there is little redress to be hoped from an astrologer or a lawyer, and a good discerning physician were like to prove the most successful counsellor.

* *Tabes maxime contingunt ab anno decimo octavo ad trigesimum quintum*, Hippoc.

† A sound Child cut out of the Body of the Mother.

‡ *Natos ad flumina primum deferimus sævoq; gelu duramus & undis.*

Julius Scaliger, who in a sleepless fit of the gout could make two hundred verses in a night, would have but five plain words upon his tomb.§ And this serious person, though no minor wit, left the poetry of his epitaph unto others; either unwilling to commend himself, or to be judged by a distich, and perhaps considering how unhappy great poets have been in versifying their own epitaphs; wherein Petrarcha, Dante, and Ariosto, have so unhappily failed, that if their tombs should out-last their works, posterity would find so little of Apollo on them, as to mistake them for Ciceronian poets.

§ *Julii Cæsaris Scaligeri quod fuit. Joseph Scaliger in vita patris.*

In this deliberate and creeping progress unto the grave, he was somewhat too young, and of too noble a mind, to fall upon that stupid symptom observable in divers persons near their journey's end, and which may be reckoned among the mortal symptoms of their last disease; that is, to become more narrow minded, miserable and tenacious, unready to part with any thing when they are ready to part with all, and afraid to want when they have no time to spend; meanwhile physicians, who know that many are mad but in a single depraved imagination, and one prevalent decipiency;[24] and that beside and out of such single deliriums a man may meet with sober actions and good sense in Bedlam; cannot but smile to see the heirs and concerned relations, gratulating themselves in the sober departure of their friends; and though they behold such mad covetous passages, content to think they dye in good understanding, and in their sober senses.

Avarice, which is not only infidelity but idolatry, either from covetous progeny or questuary education, had no root in his breast, who made good works the expression of his faith, and was big with desires unto publick and lasting charities;[25] and surely where good wishes and charitable intentions exceed abilities, theorical beneficency may be more than a dream.[26] They build not castles in the air who would build churches on earth; and though they leave no such structures here, may lay good foundations in heaven. In brief, his life and death were such, that I could not blame them who wished the like, and almost to have been himself; almost, I say; for though we may wish the prosperous appurtenances of others, or to be an other in his happy accidents; yet so intrinsecal is every man unto himself, that some doubt may be made, whether any would exchange his being, or substantially become another man.

He had wisely seen the world at home and abroad, and thereby observed under what variety men are deluded in the pursuit of that which is not here to be found. And although he had no opinion of reputed felicities below, and apprehended men widely out in the estimate of such happiness; yet his sober contempt of the world wrought no *Democritism* or *Cynicism*, no laughing or snarling at it, as well understanding there are not felicities in this world to satisfie a serious mind;[27] and therefore to soften the stream of our lives, we are fain to take in the reputed contentations of this world, to unite with the crowd in their beatitudes, and to make our selves happy by consortion, opinion, or co-existimation:[28] for strictly to separate from received and customary felicities, and to confine unto the rigor of realities, were to contract the consolation of our beings unto too uncomfortable circumscriptions.

Not to fear death, nor desire it, was short of his resolution:[*29] to be dissolved, and be with Christ, was his dying ditty. He conceived his thred long, in no long course of years, and when he had scarce out-lived the second life of Lazarus;[†] esteeming it enough to approach the years of his Saviour, who so ordered his own humane state, as not to be old upon earth.

But to be content with death may be better than to desire it: a miserable life may make us wish for death, but a virtuous one to rest in it; which is the advantage of those resolved Christians, who looking on death not only as the sting, but the period and end of sin, the horizon and isthmus between this life and a better, and the death of this world but as a nativity of

[*] *Summum nec metuas diem nec optes.*

[†] Who upon some Accounts, and Tradition, is said to have lived 30 Years after he was raised by our Saviour. *Baronius.*

another, do contentedly submit unto the common necessity, and envy not Enoch or Elias.[30]

Not to be content with life is the unsatisfactory state of those which destroy themselves; who being afraid to live, run blindly upon their own death, which no man fears by experience:[*] and the Stoicks had a notable doctrine to take away the fear thereof; that is, in such extremities to desire that which is not to be avoided, and wish what might be feared; and so made evils voluntary, and to suit with their own desires, which took off the terror of them.

[*] In the Speech of *Vulteius in Lucan*, animating his Souldiers in a great struggle to kill one another. *Decernite Lethum & metus omnis abest, cupias quodcunq; necesse est.* All fear is over, do but resolve to dye, and make your Desires meet Necessity.

But the ancient martyrs were not encouraged by such fallacies; who, though they feared not death, were afraid to be their own executioners; and therefore thought it more wisdom to crucifie their lusts than their bodies, to circumcise than stab their hearts, and to mortifie than kill themselves.

His willingness to leave this world about that age when most men think they may best enjoy it, though paradoxical unto worldly ears, was not strange unto mine, who have so often observed, that many, though old, oft stick fast unto the world, and seem to be drawn like Cacus's oxen, backward with great strugling and reluctancy unto the grave. The long habit of living makes meer men more hardly to part with life, and all to be nothing, but what is to come. To live at the rate of the old world, when some could scarce remember themselves young, may afford no better digested death than a more moderate period. Many would have thought it an happiness to have had their lot of life in some notable conjunctures of ages past; but the uncertainty of future times hath tempted few to make a part in ages to come. And surely, he that hath taken the true altitude of things, and rightly calculated the degenerate state of this age, is not like to envy those that shall live in the next, much less three or four hundred years hence, when no man can comfortably imagine what face this world will carry: and therefore since every age makes a step unto the end of all things, and the Scripture affords so hard a character of the last times; quiet minds will be content with their generations, and rather bless ages past than be ambitious of those to come.

Though age had set no seal upon his face, yet a dim eye might clearly discover fifty in his actions; and therefore since wisdom is the gray hair, and an unspotted life old age; although his years came short, he might have been said to have held up with longer livers, and to have been Solomon's old man.[†] And surely if we deduct all those days of our life which we might

[†] *Wisdom cap. iv.*

wish unlived, and which abate the comfort of those we now live; if we reckon up only those days which God hath accepted of our lives, a life of good years will hardly be a span long: the son in this sense may out-live the father, and none be climacterically old.[31] He that early arriveth unto the parts and prudence of age, is happily old without the uncomfortable attendants of it; and 'tis superfluous to live unto gray hairs, when in a precocious temper we anticipate the virtues of them. In brief, he cannot be accounted young who out-liveth the old man. He that hath early arrived unto the measure of a perfect stature in Christ, hath already fulfilled the prime and longest intention of his being: and one day lived after the perfect rule of piety, is to be preferred before sinning immortality.

Although he attained not unto the years of his predecessors, yet he wanted not those preserving virtues which confirm the thread of weaker constitutions. Cautelous chastity and crafty sobriety were far from him;[32] those jewels were paragon, without flaw, hair, ice, or cloud in him: which affords me an hint to proceed in these good wishes and few Mementos unto you.

Tread softly and circumspectly in this funambulous track and narrow path of goodness:[33] pursue virtue virtuously; be sober and temperate, not to preserve your body in a sufficiency to wanton ends; not to spare your purse; not to be free from the infamy of common transgressors that way, and thereby to ballance or palliate obscure and closer vices; nor simply to enjoy health: by all which you may leaven good actions, and render virtues disputable; but in one word, that you may truly serve God; which every sickness will tell you, you cannot well do without Health. The sick mans sacrifice is but a lame oblation. Pious treasures laid up in healthful days, excuse the defect of sick non-performances; without which we must needs look back with anxiety upon the lost opportunities of health; and may have cause rather to envy than pity the ends of penitent malefactors, who go with clear parts unto the last act of their lives; and in the integrity of their faculties return their spirit unto God that gave it.

Consider whereabout thou art in Cebes his table, or that old philosophical Pinax of the life of man;[34] whether thou art still in the road of uncertainties; whether thou hast yet entered the narrow gate, got up the hill and asperous way which leadeth unto the house of sanity, or taken that purifying potion from the hand of sincere erudition, which may send thee clear and pure a way unto a virtuous and happy life.[35]

In this virtuous voyage let not disappointment cause despondency, nor difficulty despair;[*] think not that you are sailing from Lima to Manillia, wherein thou may'st tie up the rudder, and sleep before the wind; but expect rough seas, flaws, and contrary blasts; and 'tis well if by many cross tacks and verings thou arrivest at thy port. Sit not down in the popular seats and common level of virtues, but endeavour to make them heroical. Offer not only peace-offerings but holocausts unto God. To serve him singly, to serve our selves, were too partial a piece of piety, nor likely to place us in the highest mansions of glory.

[*] Through the Pacifick Sea, with a constant Gale from the East.

He that is chaste and continent, not to impair his strength, or terrified by contagion, will hardly be heroically virtuous. Adjourn not that virtue unto those years when Cato could lend out his wife, and impotent satyrs write satyrs against lust: but be chaste in thy flaming days, when Alexander dared not trust his eyes upon the fair daughters of Darius, and when so many men think there is no other way but Origen's.[†]

[†] Who is said to have castrated himself.

Be charitable before wealth makes thee covetous, and lose not the glory of the mite.[36] If riches increase, let thy mind hold pace with them; and think it not enough to be liberal, but munificent. Though a cup of cold water from some hand may not be without its reward; yet stick not thou for wine and oil for the wounds of the distressed: and treat the poor as our Saviour did the multitude, to the relicks of some baskets.

Trust not to the omnipotency of gold, or say unto it, thou art my confidence:[37] kiss not thy hand when thou beholdest that terrestrial sun, nor bore thy ear unto its servitude. A slave unto Mammon makes no servant unto God: covetousness cracks the sinews of faith, numbs the apprehension of any thing above sense, and only affected with the certainty of things present, makes a peradventure of things to come; lives but unto one world, nor hopes but fears another; makes our own death sweet unto others, bitter unto our selves; gives a dry funeral, scenical mourning, and no wet eyes at the grave.

If avarice be thy vice, yet make it not thy punishment: miserable men commiserate not themselves, bowelless unto themselves, and merciless unto their own bowels. Let the fruition of things bless the possession of them, and take no satisfaction in dying but living rich: for since thy good works, not thy goods, will follow thee; since riches are an appurtenance of life, and no dead man is rich, to famish in plenty, and live poorly to dye rich, were a multiplying improvement in madness, and use upon use in folly.

Persons lightly dip'd, not grain'd in generous honesty, are but pale in goodness, and faint hued in sincerity: but be thou what thou virtuously art, and let not the ocean wash away thy tincture: stand magnetically upon that axis where prudent simplicity hath fix'd thee, and let no temptation invert the poles of thy honesty: and that vice may be uneasie, and even monstrous unto thee, let iterated good acts, and long confirmed habits, make vertue natural, or a second nature in thee. And since few or none prove eminently vertuous but from some advantageous foundations in their temper and natural inclinations; study thy self betimes, and early find, what nature bids thee to be, or tells thee what thou may'st be. They who thus timely descend into themselves, cultivating the good seeds which nature hath set in them, and improving their prevalent inclinations to perfection, become not shrubs, but cedars in their generation; and to be in the form of the best of the bad, or the worst of the good, will be no satisfaction unto them.

Let not the law of thy country be the *non ultra* of thy honesty, nor think that always good enough which the law will make good. Narrow not the law of charity, equity, mercy; joyn Gospel righteousness with legal right; be not a meer Gamaliel in the faith;[38] but let the Sermon in the Mount be thy Targum unto the law of Sinai.

Make not the consequences of vertue the ends thereof: be not beneficent for a name or cymbal of applause, nor exact and punctual in commerce, for the advantages of trust and credit, which attend the reputation of just and true dealing; for such rewards, though unsought for, plain virtue will bring with her, whom all men honour, though they pursue not. To have other bye ends in good actions, sowers laudable performances, which must have deeper roots, motions, and instigations, to give them the stamp of vertues.

Though humane infirmity may betray thy heedless days into the popular ways of extravagancy, yet let not thine own depravity, or the torrent of vicious times, carry thee into desperate enormities in opinions, manners, or actions: if thou hast dip'd thy foot in the river, yet venture not over Rubicon; run not into extremities from whence there is no regression, nor be ever so closely shut up within the holds of vice and iniquity, as not to find some escape by a postern of resipiscency.[39]

Owe not thy humility unto humiliation by adversity, but look humbly down in that state when others look upward upon thee: be patient in the age of pride and days of will and impatiency, when men live but by intervals of reason, under the sovereignty of humor and passion, when 'tis in the power of every one to transform thee out of thy self, and put thee into the short madness.*[40] If you cannot imitate Job, yet come not short of Socrates, and those patient pagans, who tired the tongues of their enemies, while they perceiv'd they spet their malice at brazen walls and statues.

* *Ira furor brevis est.*

Let age, not envy, draw wrinkles on thy cheeks: be content to be envied, but envy not. Emulation may be plausible, and indignation allowable; but admit no treaty with that passion which no circumstance can make good. A displacency at the good of others, because they enjoy it, although we do not want it, is an absurd depravity, sticking fast unto humane nature from its primitive corruption;[41] which he that can well subdue, were a Christian of the first magnitude, and for ought I know, may have one foot already in heaven.

While thou so hotly disclaimst the Devil, be not guilty of diabolism; fall not into one name with that unclean spirit, nor act his nature whom thou so much abhorrest; that is, to accuse, calumniate, backbite, whisper, detract, or sinistrously interpret others; degenerous depravities and narrow-minded vices, not only below S. Paul's noble Christian, but Aristotle's true gentleman.†[42] Trust not with some, that the epistle of S. James is apocryphal, and so read with less fear that stabbing truth, that in company with this vice thy religion is in vain. Moses broke the Tables without breaking of the law; but where charity is broke, the law it self is shattered, which cannot be whole without love, that is the fulfilling of it. Look humbly upon thy virtues, and though thou art rich in some, yet think thy self poor and naked without that crowning grace, which thinketh no evil, which envieth not, which beareth, believeth, hopeth, endureth all things.[43] With these sure graces, while busie tongues are crying out for a drop of cold water, mutes may be in happiness, and sing the Trisagium in heaven.‡

Let not the sun in Capricorn go down upon thy wrath,§ but write thy wrongs in water; draw the curtain of night upon injuries; shut them up in the Tower of Oblivion, and let them be as though they had not been.**[44] Forgive thine enemies totally, and without any reserve of hope, that however, God will revenge thee.

† See Arist. *Ethicks* chapt of Magnanimity.

‡ Holy Holy, Holy.

§ Even when the days are shortest.

** Alluding to the Tower of Oblivion mentioned by Procopius, which was the name of a Tower of Imprisonment among the Persians: whosoever was put therein, he was as it were buried alive, and it was Death for any but to name him.

Be substantially great in thy self, and more than thou appearest unto others; and let the World be deceived in thee, as they are in the lights of heaven. Hang early plummets upon the heels of pride, and let ambition have but an epicycle or narrow circuit in thee. Measure not thy self by thy morning shadow, but by the extent of thy grave; and reckon thy self above the earth by the line thou must be contented with under it. Spread not into boundless expansions either to designs or desires. Think not that mankind liveth but for a few, and that the rest are born but to serve the ambition of those, who make but flies of men, and wildernesses of whole nations. Swell not into actions which embroil and confound the earth; but be one of those violent ones which force the kingdom of heaven.*[45] If thou must needs reign, be Zeno's king, and enjoy that empire which every man gives himself.[46] Certainly the iterated injunctions of Christ unto humility, meekness, patience, and that despised train of virtues, cannot but make pathetical impressions upon those who have well considered the affairs of all ages, wherein pride, ambition, and vain-glory, have led up the worst of actions, and whereunto confusion, tragedies, and acts denying all religion, do owe their originals.

* Matthew xi.

Rest not in an ovation, but a triumph over thy passions; chain up the unruly legion of thy breast; behold thy trophies within thee, not without thee: lead thine own captivity captive, and be Cæsar unto thy self.†

† Ovation a petty and minor kind of triumph.

Give no quarter unto those vices which are of thine inward family; and having a root in thy temper, plead a right and propriety in thee. Examine well thy complexional inclinations.[47] Raise early batteries against those strong-holds built upon the rock of nature, and make this a great part of the militia of thy life. The politick nature of vice must be opposed by policy, and therefore wiser honesties project and plot against sin; wherein notwithstanding we are not to rest in generals, or the trite stratagems of art: that may succeed with one temper which may prove successless with another. There is no community or commonwealth of virtue; every man must study his own œconomy, and erect these rules unto the figure of himself.

Lastly, if length of days be thy portion, make it not thy expectation: reckon not upon long life, but live always beyond thy account. He that so often surviveth his expectation, lives many lives, and will hardly complain of the shortness of his days. Time past is gone like a shadow; make times to come, present; conceive that near which may be far off; approximate thy last times by present apprehensions of them: live like a neighbour unto death, and think there is but little to come. And since there is something in us that must still live on, joyn both lives together; unite them in thy thoughts and actions, and live in one but for the other. He who thus ordereth the purposes of this life, will never be far from the next; and is in some manner already in it, by an happy conformity, and close apprehension of it.

Finis.

CHRISTIAN

MORALS,

BY

S[r] THOMAS BROWN,

Of NORWICH, *M. D.*

And AUTHOR of

RELIGIO MEDICI.

Publiſhed from the Original and Correct Manuſcript of the Author; by *JOHN JEFFERY*, D. D. ARCH-DEACON of NORWICH.

CAMBRIDGE:

Printed at the UNIVERSITY-PRESS, For *Cornelius Crownfield* Printer to the UNIVERSITY; And are to be Sold by Mr. *Knapton* at the Crown in St. *Paul's* Church-yard; and Mr. *Morphew* near Stationers-Hall, *LONDON*, 1716.

FIG. 13 Title page from *Christian Morals* (1716).

To the Right Honourable David, Earl of Buchan, Viscount Auchterhouse, Lord Cardross and Glendovachie, one of the Lord's Commissioners of Police, and Lord Lieutenant of the counties of Stirling and Clackmannan in North Brittain.

My Lord,

The honour you have done our family obligeth us to make all just acknowledgements of it: & there is no form of acknowledgment in our power, more worthy of Your Lordship's acceptance, than this dedication of the last work of our honoured and learned father. Encouraged hereunto by the knowledge we have of Your Lordship's judicious relish of universal learning, and sublime virtue; we beg the favour of your acceptance of it, which will very much oblige our family in general, and her in particular, who is,

My Lord,

Your Lordship's most humble servant,
Elizabeth Littelton.[1]

The Preface

If anyone, after he has read *Religio Medici* and the ensuing discourse, can make doubt, whether the same person was the author of them both, he may be assured by the testimony of Mrs Littelton, Sr. Thomas Brown's daughter, who lived with her father, when it was composed by him; and who, at the time, read it written by his own hand: and also by the testimony of others, (of whom I am one) who read the MS. of the author, immediately after his death, and who have since read the same; from which it hath been faithfully & exactly transcribed for the press. The reason why it was not printed sooner is, because it was unhappily lost, by being mislay'd among other MSS for which search was lately made in the presence of the Lord Archbishop of Canterbury, of which his Grace, by letter, informed Mrs Littelton, when he sent the MS to her. There is nothing printed in the discourse, or in the short notes, but what is found in the original MS of the author, except only where an oversight had made the addition or transposition of some words necessary.

John Jeffery
Archdeacon of Norwich.

PART I

SECTION 1

Tread softly and circumspectly in this funambulatory track and narrow path of goodness:[2] pursue virtue virtuously: leven not good actions nor render virtues disputable. Stain not fair acts with foul intentions: maim not uprightness by halting concomitances, nor circumstantially deprave substantial goodness.[3]

Consider where about thou art in Cebes's table, or that old philosophical Pinax of the life of man:[4] whether thou art yet in the road of uncertainties; whether thou hast yet entered the narrow gate, got up the hill and asperous way, which leadeth unto the house of Sanity, or taken that purifying potion from the hand of sincere erudition, which may send thee clear and pure away unto a virtuous and happy life.[5]

In this virtuous voyage of thy life hull not about like the Ark without the use of rudder, mast, or sail, and bound for no port. Let not disappointment cause despondency, nor difficulty despair. Think not that you are sailing from Lima to Manillia, when you may fasten up the rudder, and sleep before the wind;[6] but expect rough seas, flaws, and contrary blasts, and 'tis well if by many cross tacks and veerings you arrive at the port; for we sleep in lyons' skins in our progress unto virtue, and we slide not, but climb unto it.[7]

Sit not down in the popular forms and common level of virtues. Offer not only peace offerings but holocausts unto God: where all is due make no reserve, and cut not a cummin seed with the Almighty: to serve Him singly to serve ourselves were too partial a piece of piety, not like to place us in the illustrious mansions of Glory.

SECTION 2

Rest not in an ovation but a triumph over thy passions.* Let Anger walk hanging down the head: let Malice go manicled, and Envy fetter'd after thee. Behold within thee the long train of thy trophies, not without thee. Make the quarrelling Lapithytes sleep, and Centaurs within lye quiet.[8] Chain up the

* Ovation a petty and minor kind of triumph.

unruly legion of thy breast. Lead thine own captivity captive, and be Cæsar within thy self.

SECTION 3

He that is chast and continent not to impair his strength, or honest for fear of contagion, will hardly be heroically virtuous. Adjourn not this virtue untill that temper, when Cato could lend out his wife, and impotent Satyrs write Satyrs upon lust:[9] but be chast in thy flaming days, when Alexander dar'd not trust his eyes upon the fair sisters of Darius, and when so many think there is no other way but Origen's.*[10]

* Who is said to have castrated himself.

SECTION 4

Show thy art in honesty, and loose not thy virtue by the bad managery of it. Be temperate and sober, not to preserve your body in an ability for wanton ends, not to avoid the infamy of common transgressors that way, and thereby to hope to expiate or palliate obscure and closer vices, not to spare your purse, nor simply to enjoy health; but in one word that thereby you may truly serve God, which every sickness will tell you, you cannot well do without health. The sick man's sacrifice is but a lame oblation. Pious treasures lay'd up in healthful days plead for sick non-performances: without which we must needs look back with anxiety upon the lost opportunities of health, and may have cause rather to envy than pity the ends of penitent publick sufferers, who go with healthfull prayers unto the last scene of their lives, and in the integrity of their faculties return their spirit unto God that gave it.[11]

SECTION 5

Be charitable before wealth make thee covetous, and loose not the glory of the Mite.[12] If riches encrease, let thy mind hold pace with them, and think it not enough to be liberal, but munificent. Though a cup of cold water from some hand may not be without its reward, yet stick not thou for wine and oyl for the wounds of the distressed, and treat the poor, as our Saviour did the multitude, to the reliques of some baskets.

Diffuse thy beneficence early, and while thy treasures call thee Master: there may be an Atropos of thy fortunes before that of thy life, and thy wealth cut off before that hour, when all men shall be poor;[13] for the justice of Death looks equally upon the dead, and Charon expects no more from Alexander than from Irus.[14]

SECTION 6

Give not only unto seven, but also unto eight, that is unto more than many.* Though to give unto every one that asketh may seem severe advice, yet give thou also before asking, that is, where want is silently clamorous, and men's necessities, not their tongues, do loudly call for thy mercies.†[15] For though sometimes necessitousness be dumb, or misery speak not out, yet true Charity is sagacious, and will find out hints for beneficence. Acquaint thy self with the physiognomy of Want, and let the dead colours and first lines of necessity suffise to tell thee there is an object for thy bounty.[16] Spare not where thou canst not easily be prodigal, and fear not to be undone by mercy. For since he who hath pity on the poor lendeth unto the Almighty Rewarder, who observes no ides but every day for his payments;[17] Charity becomes pious Usury, Christian liberality the most thriving industry, and what we adventure in a cockboat may return in a carrack unto us.[18] He who thus casts his bread upon the water shall surely find it again; for though it falleth to the bottom, it sinks but like the axe of the Prophet, to arise again unto him.[19]

* Ecclesiastes 11:2.

† Luke 6:30.

SECTION 7

If avarice be thy vice, yet make it not thy punishment. Miserable men commiserate not themselves, bowelless unto others, and merciless unto their own bowels. Let the fruition of things bless the possession of them, and think it more satisfaction to live richly than dye rich. For since thy good works, not thy goods, will follow thee; since wealth is an appertinance of life, and no dead man is rich; to famish in plenty, and live poorly to dye rich, were a multiplying improvement in madness, and use upon use in folly.

SECTION 8

Trust not to the omnipotency of gold, and say not unto it Thou art my confidence.[20] Kiss not thy hand to that terrestrial sun, nor bore thy ear unto its servitude. A slave unto Mammon makes no servant unto God.[21] Covetousness cracks the sinews of faith; numbs the apprehension of any thing above sense, and only affected with the certainty of things present makes a peradventure of things to come; lives but unto one world, nor hopes but fears another; makes their own death sweet unto others, bitter unto themselves; brings formal sadness, scenical mourning, and no wet eyes at the grave.[22]

SECTION 9

Persons lightly dipt, not grain'd in generous honesty, are but pale in goodness, and faint hued in integrity.[23] But be thou what thou virtuously art, and let not the ocean wash away thy tincture. Stand magnetically upon that axis, when prudent simplicity hath fixt there; and let no attraction invert the poles of thy honesty.[24] That vice may be uneasy and even monstrous unto thee, let iterated good acts and long confirmed habits make virtue almost natural, or a second nature in thee. Since virtuous superstructions have commonly generous foundations, dive into thy inclinations, and early discover what nature bids thee to be, or tells thee thou mayst be. They who thus timely descend into themselves, & cultivate the good seeds which nature hath set in them, prove not shrubs but cedars in their generation. And to be in the form of the best of the bad, or the worst of the good,[*25] will be no satisfaction unto them.

* *Optimi malorum pessimi bonorum.*

SECTION 10

Make not the consequence of virtue the ends thereof. Be not beneficent for a name or cymbal of applause, nor exact and just in commerce for the advantages of trust and credit, which attend the reputation of true and punctual dealing. For these rewards, though unsought for, plain virtue will bring with her. To have other by-ends in good actions sowers laudable performances, which must have deeper roots, motives, and instigations, to give them the stamp of virtues.[26]

SECTION 11

Let not the law of thy country be the *non ultra* of thy honesty;[27] nor think that always good enough which the law will make good. Narrow not the law of charity, equity, mercy. Join gospel righteousness with legal right. Be not a mere Gamaliel in the faith, but let the sermon in the Mount be thy *Targum* unto the law of Sinai.[28]

SECTION 12

Live by old ethicks and the classical rules of Honesty. Put no new names or notions upon authentick virtues and vices. Think not that morality is ambulatory;[29] that vices in one age are not vices in another; or that virtues, which are under the everlasting seal of right reason, may be stamped by opinion. And therefore though vicious times invert the opinions of things, and set up a new ethicks against virtue, yet hold thou unto old morality; and rather than follow a multitude to do evil, stand like Pompey's Pillar conspicuous by thy self, and single in integrity. And since the worst of times afford imitable examples of virtue; since no deluge of vice is like to be so general, but more than eight will escape;[30] eye well those heroes who have held their heads above water, who have touched pitch, and not been defiled, and in the common contagion have remained uncorrupted.[31]

SECTION 13

Let Age not Envy draw wrinkles on thy cheeks, be content to be envy'd, but envy not. Emulation may be plausible and indignation allowable, but admit no treaty with that passion which no circumstance can make good. A displacency at the good of others because they enjoy it, though not unworthy of it, is an absurd depravity, sticking fast unto corrupted nature, and often too hard for humility and charity, the great suppressors of envy.[32] This surely is a lyon not to be strangled but by

Hercules himself, or the highest stress of our minds, and an atom of that power which subdueth all things unto itself.

SECTION 14

Owe not thy humility unto humiliation from adversity, but look humbly down in that state when others look upwards upon thee. Think not thy own shadow longer than that of others, nor delight to take the altitude of thy self. Be patient in the age of Pride, when men live by short intervals of reason under the dominion of humor and passion, when it's in the power of every one to transform thee out of thy self, and run thee into the short madness. If you cannot imitate Job, yet come not short of Socrates, and those patient pagans who tired the tongues of their enemies, while they perceived they spit their malice at brazen walls and statues.

SECTION 15

Let not the sun in Capricorn* go down upon thy wrath, but write thy wrongs in ashes. Draw the curtain of night upon injuries, shut them up in the Tower of Oblivion and let them be as though they had not been.† To forgive our enemies, yet hope that God will punish them, is not to forgive enough. To forgive them ourselves, and not to pray God to forgive them, is a partial piece of charity. Forgive thine enemies totally, and without any reserve, that however God will revenge thee.

* even when the days are shortest.

† Alluding unto the Tower of Oblivion mentioned by Procopius, which was the name of a Tower of Imprisonment among the Persians; whoever was put therein was as it were buried alive, and it was death for any but to name him.

SECTION 16

While thou so hotly disclaimest the Devil, be not guilty of diabolism. Fall not into one name with that unclean spirit, nor act his nature whom thou so much abhorrest; that is to accuse, calumniate, backbite, whisper, detract, or sinistrously interpret others. Degenerous depravities, and narrow minded vices! Not only below St. Paul's noble Christian, but Aristotle's true gentleman.‡ Trust not with some that the epistle of St. James is apocryphal, and so read with less fear that stabbing truth, that in company with this vice thy religion is in vain.[33] Moses broke the Tables without breaking of the law; but where

‡ See Aristotle's *Ethicks*, chapter of Magnanimity.

charity is broke, the law itself is shattered, which cannot be whole without love, which is the fulfilling of it. Look humbly upon thy virtues, and though thou art rich in some, yet think thy self poor and naked without that crowning grace, which thinketh no evil, which envieth not, which beareth, hopeth, believeth, endureth all things.[34] With these sure graces, while busy tongues are crying out for a drop of cold water, mutes may be in happiness, and sing the *Trisagion* in heaven.*

* Holy, Holy, Holy.

SECTION 17

However thy understanding may waver in the theories of true and false, yet fasten the rudder of thy will, steer straight unto good and fall not foul on evil. Imagination is apt to rove and conjecture to keep no bounds. Some have run out so far, as to fancy the stars might be but the light of the crystalline heaven shot through perforations on the bodies of the orbs. Others more ingeniously doubt whether there hath not been a vast tract of land in the Atlantick Ocean, which earthquakes and violent causes have long ago devoured.[35] Speculative misapprehensions may be innocuous, but immorality pernicious; theorical mistakes and physical deviations may condemn our judgments, not lead us into judgment.[36] But perversity of will, immoral and sinful enormities walk with Adraste and Nemesis at their Backs, pursue us unto judgment, and leave us viciously miserable.[37]

SECTION 18

Bid early defiance unto those vices which are of thine inward family, and having a root in thy temper plead a right and propriety in thee. Raise timely batteries against those strong holds built upon the rock of nature, and make this a great part of the militia of thy life. Delude not thy self into iniquities from participation or community, which abate the sense but not the obliquity of them.[38] To conceive sins less, or less of sins, because others also transgress, were morally to commit that natural fallacy of man, to take comfort from society, and think adversities less, because others also suffer them. The politick nature of vice must be opposed by policy. And therefore wiser honesties project and plot against it. Wherein notwithstanding we are not to rest in generals, or the trite stratagems of art. That may succeed with one which may prove successless with another: there is no community or commonweal of virtue: every man must study his own oeconomy, and adapt such rules unto the figure of himself.

SECTION 19

Be substantially great in thy self, and more than thou appearest unto others; and let the world be deceived in thee, as they are in the lights of Heaven. Hang early plummets upon the heels of Pride, and let ambition have but an epicycle and narrow circuit in thee.[39] Measure not thy self by thy morning shadow, but by the extent of thy grave, and reckon thyself above the earth by the line thou must be contended with under it. Spread not into boundless expansions either of designs or desires. Think not that mankind liveth but for a few, and that the rest are born but to serve those ambitions, which make but flies of men and wilderness of whole nations. Swell not into vehement actions which embroil and confound the earth; but be one of those violent ones which force the Kingdom of Heaven.* If thou must needs rule, be Zeno's king, and enjoy that empire which every man gives himself.[40] He who is thus his own monarch contentedly sways the sceptre of himself, not envying the glory of crowned heads and Elohims of the earth.[41] Could the world unite in the practise of that despised train of virtues, which the divine ethicks of our Saviour hath so inculcated unto us, the furious face of things must disappear, Eden would be yet to be found, and the angels might look down not with pity, but joy upon us.

* Matthew 11.12.

SECTION 20

Though the quickness of thine ear were able to reach the noise of the moon, which some think it maketh in its rapid revolution; though the number of thy ears should equal Argus his eyes;[42] yet stop them all with the wise man's wax, and be deaf unto the suggestions of talebearers, calumniators, pickthank or malevolent delators, who while quiet men sleep, sowing the tares of discord and division, distract the tranquillity of charity and all friendly society.[43] These are the tongues that set the world on fire, cankers of reputation, and, like that of Jonas his gourd, wither a good name in a night.[44] Evil spirits may sit still while these spirits walk about, and perform the business of Hell. To speak more strictly, our corrupted hearts are the factories of the Devil, which may be at work without his presence. For when that circumventing spirit hath drawn malice, envy, and all unrighteousness unto well rooted habits in his disciples, iniquity then goes on upon its own legs, and if the gate of Hell were shut up for a time, vice would still be fertile and produce the fruits of Hell. Thus when God forsakes us, Satan also leaves us. For such offenders he looks upon as sure and sealed up, and his temptations then needless unto them.

SECTION 21

Annihilate not the mercies of God by the oblivion of ingratitude. For oblivion is a kind of annihilation, and for things to be as though they had not been is like unto never being. Make not thy head a grave, but a repository of God's mercies. Though thou hadst the memory of Seneca, or Simonides, and Conscience, the punctual memorist within us, yet trust not to thy remembrance in things which need phylacteries.[45] Register not only strange but merciful occurrences: Let Ephemerides not Olympiads give thee account of his mercies.[46] Let thy diaries stand thick with dutiful mementos and asterisks of acknowledgment. And to be compleat and forget nothing, date not his mercy from thy nativity, look beyond the world, and before the Æra of Adam.

SECTION 22

Paint not the sepulchre of thy self, and strive not to beautify thy corruption. Be not an advocate for thy vices, nor call for many hour-glasses to justify thy imperfections. Think not that always good which thou thinkest thou canst always make good, nor that concealed which the sun doth not behold. That which the sun doth not now see will be visible when the sun is out, and the stars are fallen from Heaven. Meanwhile there is no darkness unto Conscience, which can see without light, and in the deepest obscurity give a clear draught of things, which the cloud of dissimulation hath conceal'd from all eyes. There is a natural standing court within us, examining, acquitting, and condemning at the tribunal of our selves, wherein iniquities have their natural Thetas, and no nocent is absolved by the verdict of himself.[47] And therefore, although our transgressions shall be tryed at the last bar, the process need not be long: for the judge of all knoweth all, and every man will nakedly know himself. And when so few are like to plead not guilty, the assize must soon have an end.[48]

SECTION 23

Comply with some humors, bear with others, but serve none. Civil complacency consists with decent honesty: Flattery is a juggler, and no kin unto Sincerity. But while thou maintainest the plain path, and scornest to flatter others, fall not into self-adulation, and become not thine own parasite. Be deaf unto thy self, and be not betrayed at home. Self-credulity, pride, and levity lead unto self-idolatry. There is no Damocles like unto self opinion, nor any Siren to our own fawning conceptions.[49] To magnify our minor things, or hug ourselves in our apparitions;[50] to afford a credulous ear unto the clawing suggestions of fancy;[51] to pass our days in painted mistakes of ourselves; and though we behold our own blood, to think our selves the sons of Jupiter;* are blandishments of self love, worse than outward delusion. By this imposture wise men sometimes are mistaken in their elevation, and look above themselves. And fools, which are antipodes unto the wise, conceive themselves to be but their *Periœci*, and in the same parallel with them.[52]

* As Alexander the Great did.

SECTION 24

Be not a *Hercules furens* abroad, and a Poltron within thy self.[53] To chase other enemies out of the field, and be led captive by our vices; to beat down our foes, and fall down to other concupiscences; are solecisms in moral schools, and no laurel attends them.[54] To well manage our affections, and wild horses of Plato, are the highest Circenses;[55] and the noblest digladiation is in the theater of ourselves:[56] for therein our inward antagonists, not only like common gladiators, with ordinary weapons and downright blows make at us, but also like retiary and laqueary combatants, with nets, frauds, and entanglements fall upon us.[57] Weapons for such combats are not to be forged at Lipara: Vulcan's art doth nothing in this internal militia:[58] wherein not the armour of Achilles, but the armature of St. Paul, gives the glorious day, and triumphs not leading up into capitols, but up into the highest heavens.[59] And therefore while so many think it the only valour to command and master others, study thou the dominion of thy self, and quiet thine own commotions. Let right reason be thy Lycurgus, and lift up thy hand unto the law of it;[60] move by the intelligences of the superiour faculties, not by the rapt of passion, nor merely by that of temper and constitution.[61] They who are merely carried on by the wheel of such inclinations, without the hand and guidance of sovereign Reason, are but the automatous part of mankind, rather lived than living, or at least underliving themselves.

SECTION 25

Let not fortune, which hath no name in scripture, have any in thy divinity. Let Providence, not chance, have the honour of thy acknowledgments, and be thy Oedipus in contingences.[62] Mark well the paths and winding ways thereof; but be not too wise in the construction, or sudden in the application. The hand of Providence writes often by abbreviatures, hieroglyphicks or short characters, which, like the laconism on the wall, are not to be made out but by a hint or key from that spirit which indited them.[63] Leave future occurrences to their uncertainties, think that which is present thy own; and since 'tis easier to foretell an eclipse, than a foul day at some distance, look for little regular below. Attend with patience the uncertainty of things and what lieth yet unexerted in the chaos of futurity. The uncertainty and ignorance of things to come makes the world new unto us by unexpected emergences, whereby we pass not our days in the trite road of affairs affording no novity; for the novelizing spirit of man lives by variety, and the new faces of things.

SECTION 26

Though a contented mind enlargeth the dimension of little things, and unto some 'tis wealth enough not to be poor, and others are well content, if they be but rich enough to be honest, and to give every man his due: yet fall not into that obsolete affectation of bravery to throw away thy money, and to reject all honours, or honourable stations in this courtly and splendid world. Old generosity is superannuated and such contempt of the world out of date.[64] No man is now like to refuse the favour of great ones, or be content to say unto princes, *Stand out of my sun.*[65] And if any there be of such antiquated resolutions, they are not like to be tempted out of them by great ones; and 'tis fair if they escape the name of hypochondriacks from the genius of latter times, unto whom contempt of the world is the most contemptible opinion, and to be able, like Bias, to carry all they have about them were to be the eighth wise-man. However, the old tetrick philosophers look'd always with indignation upon such a face of things, and observing the unnatural current of riches, power, and honour in the world, and withal the imperfection and demerit of persons often advanced unto them, were tempted unto angry opinions, that affairs were ordered more by stars than reason, and that things went on rather by lottery, than election.[66]

SECTION 27

If thy vessel be but small in the ocean of this world, if meanness of possessions be thy allotment upon earth, forget not those virtues which the great disposer of all bids thee to entertain from thy quality and condition, that is, submission, humility, content of mind, and industry. Content may dwell in all stations. To be low, but above contempt, may be high enough to be happy. But many of low degree may be higher than computed, and some cubits above the common commensuration;[67] for in all states virtue gives qualifications, and allowances, which make out defects. Rough diamonds are sometimes mistaken for pebbles, and meanness may be rich in accomplishments, which riches in vain desire. If our merits be above our stations, if our intrinsical value be greater than what we go for, or our value than our valuation, and if we stand higher in God's, than in the censor's book; it may make some equitable balance in the inequalities of this world, and there may be no such vast chasm or gulph between disparities as common measures determine.[68] The divine eye looks upon high and low differently from that of man. They who seem to stand upon Olympus, and high mounted unto our eyes, may be but in the valleys, and low ground unto his; for he looks upon those as highest who nearest approach his Divinity, and upon those as lowest, who are farthest from it.

SECTION 28

When thou lookest upon the imperfections of others, allow one eye for what is laudable in them, and the balance they have from some excellency, which may render them considerable. While we look with fear or hatred upon the teeth of the viper, we may behold his eye with love. In venomous natures something may be amiable: poysons afford antipoysons: nothing is totally, or altogether uselessly bad. Notable virtues are sometimes dashed with notorious vices, and in some vicious tempers have been found illustrious acts of virtue; which makes such observable worth in some actions of King Demetrius, Antonius, and Ahab, as are not to be found in the same kind in Aristides, Numa, or David.[69] Constancy, generosity, clemency, and liberality have been highly conspicuous in some persons not markt out in other concerns for example or imitation. But since goodness is exemplary in all, if others have not our virtues, let us not be wanting in theirs, nor scorning them for their vices whereof we are free, be condemned by their virtues, wherein we are deficient. There is dross, alloy, and embasement in all human temper; and he flieth without wings, who thinks to find ophyr or pure metal in any. For perfection is not like light center'd in any one body, but like the dispersed seminalities of vegetables at the Creation scattered through the whole mass of the earth, no place producing all and almost all some. So that 'tis well, if a perfect man can be made out of many men, and to the perfect eye of God, even out of mankind. Time, which perfects some things, imperfects also others. Could we intimately apprehend the ideated man, and as he stood in the intellect of God upon the first exertion by creation, we might more narrowly comprehend our present degeneration, and how widely we are fallen from the pure exemplar and Idea of our nature:[70] for after this corruptive elongation from a primitive and pure creation, we are almost lost in degeneration; and Adam hath not only fallen from his Creator, but we ourselves from Adam, our Tycho and primary generator.[71]

SECTION 29

Quarrel not rashly with adversities not yet understood; and overlook not the mercies often bound up in them. For we consider not sufficiently the good of evils, nor fairly compute the mercies of Providence in things afflictive at first hand. The famous Andreas Doria being invited to a feast by Aloysio Fieschi with design to kill him, just the night before, fell mercifully into a fit of the gout and so escaped that mischief.[72] When Cato intended to kill himself, from a blow which he gave his servant, who would not reach his sword unto him, his hand so swell'd that he had much ado to effect his design. Hereby anyone but a resolved Stoick might have taken a fair hint of consideration, and that some mercifull genius would have contrived his preservation. To be sagacious in such intercurrences is not superstition, but wary and pious discretion, and to contemn such hints were to be deaf unto the speaking hand of God, wherein Socrates and Cardan would hardly have been mistaken.[73]

SECTION 30

Break not open the gate of destruction, and make no haste or bustle unto ruin. Post not heedlessly on unto the *non ultra* of folly, or precipice of perdition. Let vicious ways have their tropicks and deflexions,[74] and swim in the waters of sin but as in the Asphaltick Lake, though smeared and defiled, not to sink to the bottom.[75] If thou hast dipt thy foot in the brink, yet venture not over Rubicon.[76] Run not into extremities from whence there is no regression. In the vicious ways of the world it mercifully falleth out that we become not extempore wicked, but it taketh some time and pains to undo our selves.[77] We fall not from virtue, like Vulcan from Heaven, in a day.[78] Bad dispositions require some time to grow into bad habits, bad habits must undermine good, and often repeated acts make us habitually evil: so that by gradual depravations, and while we are but staggeringly evil, we are not left without parentheses of considerations, thoughtful rebukes, and merciful interventions, to recal us unto our selves.[79] For the wisdom of God hath methodiz'd the course of things unto the best advantage of goodness, and thinking considerators overlook not the tract thereof.

SECTION 31

Since men and women have their proper virtues and vices, and even twins of different sexes have not only distinct coverings in the womb, but differing qualities and virtuous habits after; transplace not their proprieties and confound not their distinctions. Let masculine and feminine accomplishments shine in their proper orbs, and adorn their respective subjects. However unite not the vices of both sexes in one; be not monstrous in iniquity, nor hermaphroditically vitious.

SECTION 32

If generous honesty, valour, and plain dealing, be the cognisance of thy family or characteristick of thy country, hold fast such inclinations suckt in with thy first breath, and which lay in the cradle with thee. Fall not into transforming degenerations, which under the old name create a new nation. Be not an alien in thine own nation; bring not Orontes into Tiber;[80] learn the virtues not the vices of thy foreign neighbours, and make thy imitation by discretion not contagion. Feel something of thy self in the noble acts of thy ancestors, and find in thine own genius that of thy predecessors. Rest not under the expired merits of others, shine by those of thy own. Flame not like the central fire which enlighteneth no eyes, which no man seeth, and most men think there's no such thing to be seen. Add one ray unto the common lustre; add not only to the number but the note of thy generation; and prove not a cloud but an asterisk in thy region.[81]

SECTION 33

Since thou hast an alarum in thy breast, which tells thee thou hast a living spirit in thee above two thousand times in an hour;[82] dull not away thy days in slothful supinity and the tediousness of doing nothing. To strenuous minds there is an inquietude in overquietness, and no laboriousness in labour; and to tread a mile after the slow pace of a snail, or the heavy measures of the Lazy of Brazilia, were a most tiring pennance, and worse than a race of some furlongs at the Olympicks.[83] The rapid courses of the heavenly bodies are rather imitable by our thoughts than our corporeal motions; yet the solemn motions of our lives amount unto a greater measure than is commonly apprehended. Some few men have surrounded the globe of the earth; yet many in the set locomotions and movements of their days have measured the circuit of it, and twenty thousand miles have been exceeded by them. Move circumspectly not meticulously, and rather carefully sollicitous than anxiously sollicitudinous. Think not there is a lyon in the way, nor walk with leaden sandals in the paths of goodness; but in all virtuous motions let prudence determine thy measures. Strive not to run like Hercules a furlong in a breath: festination may prove precipitation: deliberating delay may be wise cunctation, and slowness no sloathfulness.[84]

SECTION 34

Since virtuous actions have their own trumpets, and without any noise from thy self will have their resound abroad; busy not thy best member in the encomium of thy self.[85] Praise is a debt we owe unto the virtues of others, and due unto our own from all, whom malice hath not made mutes, or envy struck dumb. Fall not however into the common prevaricating way of self commendation and boasting, by denoting the imperfections of others. He who discommendeth others obliquely commendeth himself. He who whispers their infirmities proclaims his own exemption from them, and consequently says, I am not as this publican, or hic niger[*86], whom I talk of. Open ostentation and loud vainglory is more tolerable than this obliquity, as but containing some froth, no ink, as but consisting of a personal piece of folly, nor complicated with uncharitableness. Superfluously we seek a precarious applause abroad: every good

[*] *Hic Niger est, hunc tu Romane caveto*. Horace.

man hath his plaudite within himself;[87] and though his tongue be silent, is not without loud cymbals in his breast. Conscience will become his panegyrist, and never forget to crown and extol him unto himself.

SECTION 35

Bless not thy self only that thou wert born in Athens;* but among thy multiplyed acknowledgments lift up one hand unto Heaven, that thou wert born of honest parents, that modesty, humility, patience, and veracity lay in the same egg, and came into the world with thee. From such foundations thou may'st be happy in a virtuous precocity, and make an early and long walk in goodness;[88] so may'st thou more naturally feel the contrariety of vice unto nature, and resist some by the antidote of thy temper. As charity covers, so modesty preventeth a multitude of sins; withholding from noon day vices and brazen-brow'd iniquities, from sinning on the house top, and painting our follies with the rays of the sun. Where this virtue reigneth, though vice may show its head, it cannot be in its glory: where shame of sin sets, look not for virtue to arise; for when modesty taketh wing, *Astræa* goes soon after.†

* As Socrates did. Athens a place of learning and civility.

† *Astræa* Goddess of Justice and consequently of all virtue.

SECTION 36

The heroical vein of mankind runs much in the souldiery, and couragious part of the world; and in that form we oftenest find men above men. History is full of the gallantry of that tribe; and when we read their notable acts, we easily find what a difference there is between a life in Plutarch and in Laërtius.[89] Where true fortitude dwells, loyalty, bounty, friendship, and fidelity, may be found. A man may confide in persons constituted for noble ends, who dare do and suffer, and who have a hand to burn for their country and their friend. Small and creeping things are the product of petty souls. He is like to be mistaken, who makes choice of a covetous man for a friend, or relieth upon the reed of narrow and poltron friendship. Pityful things are only to be found in the cottages of such breasts; but bright thoughts, clear deeds, constancy, fidelity, bounty, and generous honesty are the gems of noble minds; wherein, to derogate from none, the true heroick English gentleman hath no peer.

PART II

SECTION I

Punish not thy self with pleasure; glut not thy sense with palative delights; nor revenge the contempt of temperance by the penalty of satiety. Were there an age of delight or any pleasure durable, who would not honour Volupia?[90] But the race of delight is short, and pleasures have mutable faces. The pleasures of one age are not pleasures in another, and their lives fall short of our own. Even in our sensual days the strength of delight is in its seldomness or rarity, and sting in its satiety: mediocrity is its life, and immoderacy its confusion. The luxurious emperors of old inconsiderately satiated themselves with the dainties of sea and land, till, wearied through all varieties, their refections became a study unto them, and they were fain to feed by invention. Novices in true Epicurism! which by mediocrity, paucity, quick and healthful appetite, makes delights smartly acceptable; whereby Epicurus himself found Jupiter's brain in a piece of Cytheridian cheese, and the tongues of nightingales in a dish of onyons.[*91] Hereby healthful and temperate poverty hath the start of nauseating luxury; unto whose clear and naked appetite every meal is a feast, and in one single dish the first course of Metellus;[†92] who are cheaply hungry, and never loose their hunger, or advantage of a craving appetite, because obvious food contents it; while Nero[‡93] half famish'd could not feed upon a piece of bread, and lingering after his snowed water, hardly got down an ordinary cup of Calda.[§94] By such circumscriptions of pleasure the contemned philosophers reserved unto themselves the secret of delight, which the Helluos[95] of those days lost in their exorbitances. In vain we study delight: it is at the command of every sober mind, and in every sense born with us: but Nature, who teacheth us the rule of pleasure, instructeth also in the bounds thereof, and where its line expireth. And therefore temperate minds, not pressing their pleasures until the sting appeareth, enjoy their contentations contentedly, and without regret, and so escape the folly of excess, to be pleased unto displacency.

* *Cerebrum Jovis*, for a delicious bit.

† Metellus his riotous pontificial supper, the great variety whereat is to be seen in Macrobius.

‡ Nero in his flight, Suetonius.

§ *Caldae gelidæque Minister.*

SECTION 2

Bring candid eyes unto the perusal of men's works, and let not Zoilism or detraction blast well intended labours.[96] He that endureth no faults in men's writings must only read his own, wherein for the most part all appeareth white. Quotation mistakes, inadvertency, expedition, and human lapses may make not only moles but warts in learned authors, who notwithstanding being judged by the capital matter admit not of disparagement. I should unwillingly affirm that Cicero was but slightly versed in Homer, because in his work *de Gloria* he ascribed those verses unto Ajax, which were delivered by Hector.[97] What if Plautus in the account of Hercules mistaketh nativity for conception?[98] Who would have mean thoughts of Apollinaris Sidonius, who seems to mistake the river Tigris for Euphrates;[99] and though a good historian and learned bishop of Auvergne had the misfortune to be out in the story of David, making mention of him when the Ark was sent back by the Philistins upon a cart;[100] which was before his time. Though I have no great opinion of Machiavel's learning, yet I shall not presently say, that he was but a novice in Roman history; because he was mistaken in placing Commodus after the Emperour Severus.[101] Capital truths are to be narrowly eyed, collateral lapses and circumstantial deliveries not to be too strictly sifted. And if the substantial subject be well forged out, we need not examine the sparks, which irregularly fly from it.

SECTION 3

Let well weighed considerations, not stiff and peremptory assumptions, guide thy discourses, pen, and actions. To begin or continue our works like Trismegistus of old, *verum certè verum, atque verissimum est*,[*102] would sound arrogantly unto present ears in this strict enquiring age, wherein, for the most part, *probably*, and *perhaps*, will hardly serve to mollify the spirit of captious contradictors. If Cardan saith that a parrot is a beautiful bird, Scaliger will set his wits o'work to prove it a deformed animal. The compage of all physical truths is not so closely jointed, but opposition may find intrusion, nor always so closely maintained, as not to suffer attrition.[103] Many positions seem quodlibetically constituted, and like a Delphian

* In *Tabula Smaragdina.*

blade will cut on both sides.[104] Some truths seem almost falsehoods, and some falsehoods almost truths; wherein falsehood and truth seem almost æquilibriously stated, and but a few grains of distinction to bear down the balance. Some have digged deep, yet glanced by the royal vein; and a man may come unto the pericardium, but not the heart of truth.[105] Besides, many things are known, as some are seen, that is by parallaxis, or at some distance from their true and proper beings, the superficial regard of things having a different aspect from their true and central natures.[106] And this moves sober pens unto suspensory and timorous assertions, nor presently to obtrude them as Sibyl's leaves, which after considerations may find to be but folious apparences, and not the central and vital interiours of truth.[107]

SECTION 4

Value the judicious, and let not mere acquests in minor parts of learning gain thy preexistimation.[108] 'Tis an unjust way of compute to magnify a weak head for some Latin abilities, and to undervalue a solid judgment, because he knows not the genealogy of Hector. When that notable king of France*[109] would have his son to know but one sentence in Latin, had it been a good one, perhaps it had been enough. Natural parts and good judgments rule the world. States are not governed by ergotisms.[110] Many have ruled well who could not perhaps define a commonwealth, and they who understand not the globe of the earth command a great part of it. Where natural logick prevails not, artificial too often faileth. Where nature fills the sails, the vessel goes smoothly on, and when judgment is the pilot, the ensurance need not be high. When industry builds upon nature, we may expect pyramids: where that foundation is wanting, the structure must be low. They do most by books, who could do much without them, and he that chiefly owes himself unto himself is the substantial man.

* Lewis the Eleventh. *Qui nescit dissimulare nescit Regnare.*

SECTION 5

Let thy studies be free as thy thoughts and contemplations: but fly not only upon the wings of imagination; joyn sense unto reason, and experiment unto speculation, and so give life unto embryon truths, and verities yet in their chaos. There is nothing more acceptable unto the ingenious world, than this noble eluctation of truth;[111] wherein, against the tenacity of prejudice and prescription, this century now prevaileth. What libraries of new volumes aftertimes will behold, and in what a new world of knowledge the eyes of our posterity may be happy, a few ages may joyfully declare; and is but a cold thought unto those, who cannot hope to behold this exantlation of truth, or that obscured Virgin half out of the pit.[112] Which might make some content with a commutation of the time of their lives, and to commend the fancy of the Pythagorean metempsychosis; whereby they might hope to enjoy this happiness in their third or fourth selves, and behold that in Pythagoras, which they now but foresee in Euphorbus.[*113] The world, which took but six days to make, is like to take six thousand to make out: mean while old truths voted down begin to resume their places, and new ones arise upon us; wherein there is no comfort in the happiness of Tully's Elyzium,[†114] or any satisfaction from the ghosts of the ancients, who knew so little of what is now well known. Men disparage not antiquity, who prudently exalt new enquiries, and make not them the judges of truth, who were but fellow enquirers of it. Who can but magnify the endeavors of Aristotle, and the noble start which learning had under him; or less than pitty the slender progression made upon such advantages? While many centuries were lost in repetitions and transcriptions sealing up the book of knowledge. And therefore rather than to swell the leaves of learning by fruitless repetitions, to sing the same song in all ages, nor adventure at essays beyond the attempt of others, many would be content that some would write like Helmont or Paracelsus;[115] and be willing to endure the monstrosity of some opinions, for divers singular notions requiting such aberrations.

* *Ipse ego, nam memini, Trojani in tempore belli Panthoides Euphorbus eram.*

† Who comforted himself that he should there converse with the old philosophers.

SECTION 6

Despise not the obliquities of younger ways, nor despair of better things whereof there is yet no prospect.[116] Who would imagine that Diogenes, who in his younger days was a falsifier of money, should in the after course of his life be so great a contemner of metal?[117] Some Negros, who believe the Resurrection, think that they shall rise white.[‡118] Even in this life

‡ Mandelslo.

regeneration may imitate Resurrection, our black and vitious tinctures may wear off, and goodness cloath us with candour. Good admonitions knock not always in vain. There will be signal examples of God's mercy, and the angels must not want their charitable rejoyces for the conversion of lost sinners. Figures of most angles do nearest approach unto circles, which have no angles at all. Some may be near unto goodness, who are conceived far from it, and many things happen, not likely to ensue from any promises of antecedencies. Culpable beginnings have found commendable conclusions, and infamous courses pious retractations. Detestable sinners have proved exemplary converts on earth, and may be glorious in the apartment of Mary Magdalen in Heaven. Men are not the same through all divisions of their ages. Time, experience, self-reflexions, and God's mercies make in some well-temper'd minds a kind of translation before death, and men to differ from themselves as well as from other persons. Hereof the old world afforded many examples to the infamy of latter ages, wherein men too often live by the rule of their inclinations; so that, without any astral prediction, the first day gives the last,*[119] men are commonly as they were, or rather, as bad dispositions run into worser habits, the evening doth not crown, but sowerly conclude the day.

* *Primusque dies dedit extremum.*

SECTION 7

If the Almighty will not spare us according to his merciful capitulation at Sodom,[120] if his goodness please not to pass over a great deal of bad for a small pittance of good, or to look upon us in the lump; there is slender hope for mercy, or sound presumption of fulfilling half his will, either in persons or nations: they who excel in some virtues being so often defective in others; few men driving at the extent and amplitude of goodness, but computing themselves by their best parts, and others by their worst, are content to rest in those virtues, which others commonly want. Which makes this speckled face of honesty in the world; and which was the imperfection of the old philosophers and great pretenders unto virtue, who well declining the gaping vices of intemperance, incontinency, violence and oppression, were yet blindly peccant in iniquities of closer faces, were envious, malicious, contemners, scoffers, censurers, and stufft with vizard vices, no less depraving the ethereal particle and diviner portion of man.[121] For envy, malice, hatred are the qualities of Satan, close and dark like himself; and where such brands smoke, the soul cannot be white. Vice may be had at all prices; expensive and costly iniquities, which make the noise, cannot be every man's sins: but the soul may be foully inquinated at a very low rate, and a man may be cheaply vitious, to the perdition of himself.[122]

SECTION 8

Opinion rides upon the neck of Reason, and men are happy, wise, or learned, according as that empress shall set them down in the register of reputation. However weigh not thy self in the scales of thy own opinion, but let the judgment of the judicious be the standard of thy merit. Self-estimation is a flatterer too readily entitling us unto knowledge and abilities, which others sollicitously labour after, and doubtfully think they attain. Surely such confident tempers do pass their days in best tranquility, who, resting in the opinion of their own abilities, are happily gull'd by such contentation; wherein pride, self-conceit, confidence, and opiniatrity will hardly suffer any to complain of imperfection. To think themselves in the right, or all that right, or only that, which they do or think, is a fallacy of high content; though others laugh in their sleeves, and look upon them as in a deluded state of judgment. Wherein not withstanding 'twere but a civil piece of complacency to suffer them to sleep who would not wake, to let them rest in their securities, nor by dissent or opposition to stagger their contentments.

SECTION 9[123]

Since the brow speaks often true, since eyes and noses have tongues, and the countenance proclaims the heart and inclinations; let observation so far instruct thee in physiognomical lines, as to be some rule for thy distinction, and guide for thy affection unto such as look most like men. Mankind, methinks, is comprehended in a few faces, if we exclude all visages, which any way participate of symmetries and schemes of look common unto other animals. For as though man were the extract of the world, in whom all were *in coagulato*, which in their forms were *in soluto* and at extension;[124] we often observe that men do most act those creatures, whose constitution, parts, and complexion do most predominate in their mixtures. This is a cornerstone in physiognomy, and holds some truth not only in particular persons but also in whole nations.[125] There are therefore provincial faces, national lips and noses, which testify not only the natures of those countries, but of those which have them elsewhere. Thus we may make England the whole earth, dividing it not only into Europe, Asia, Africa, but the particular regions thereof, and may in some latitude affirm, that there are Ægyptians, Scythians, Indians among us; who though born in England, yet carry the faces and air of those countries, and are also agreeable and correspondent unto their natures. Faces look uniformly unto our eyes: how they appear unto some animals of a more piercing or differing sight, who are able to discover the inequalities, rubs, and hairiness of the skin, is not without good doubt. And therefore in reference unto man, Cupid is said to be blind. Affection should not be too sharp-eyed, and love is not to be made by magnifying glasses. If things were seen as they truly are, the beauty of bodies would be much abridged. And therefore the wise contriver hath drawn the pictures and outsides of things softly and amiably unto the natural edge of our eyes, not leaving them able to discover those uncomely asperities, which make oyster-shells in good faces, and hedgehogs even in Venus's moles.[126]

SECTION 10

Court not felicity too far, and weary not the favorable hand of Fortune. Glorious actions have their times, extent and *non ultras*.[127] To put no end unto attempts were to make prescription of successes, and to bespeak unhappiness at the last. For the line of our lives is drawn with white and black vicissitudes, wherein the extremes hold seldom one complexion. That Pompey should obtain the surname of Great at twenty five years, that men in their young and active days should be fortunate and perform notable things, is no observation of deep wonder, they having the strength of their fates before them, nor yet acted their parts in the world, for which they were brought into it: whereas men of years, matured for counsels and designs, seem to be beyond the vigour of their active fortunes, and high exploits of life, providentially ordained unto ages best agreeable unto them. And therefore many brave men finding their fortune grow faint, and feeling its declination, have timely withdrawn themselves from great attempts, and so escaped the ends of mighty men, disproportionable to their beginnings. But magnanimous thoughts have so dimmed the eyes of many, that forgetting the very essence of fortune, and the vicissitude of good and evil, they apprehend no bottom in felicity; and so have been still tempted on unto mighty actions, reserved for their destructions. For Fortune lays the plot of our adversities in the foundation of our felicities, blessing us in the first quadrate, to blast us more sharply in the last.[128] And since in the highest felicities there lieth a capacity of the lowest miseries, she hath this advantage from our happiness to make us truly miserable. For to become acutely miserable we are to be first happy. Affliction smarts most in the most happy state, as having somewhat in it of Bellisarius at beggar's bush, or Bajazet in the grate.[129] And this the fallen angels severely understand, who having acted their first part in Heaven, are made sharply miserable by transition, and more afflictively feel the contrary state of Hell.

SECTION 11

Carry no careless eye upon the unexpected scenes of things; but ponder the acts of Providence in the publick ends of great and notable men, set out unto the view of all for no common *memorandums*. The tragical exits and unexpected periods of some eminent persons cannot but amuse considerate observators; wherein notwithstanding most men seem to see by extramission, without reception or self-reflexion, and conceive themselves unconcerned by the fallacy of their own exemption:[130] whereas the mercy of God hath singled out but few to be the signals of his justice, leaving the generality of mankind to the pedagogy of example. But the inadvertency of our natures not well apprehending this favorable method and merciful decimation, and that he sheweth in some what others also deserve; they entertain no sense of his hand beyond the stroke of themselves.[131] Whereupon the whole becomes necessarily punished, and the contracted hand of God extended unto universal judgments: from whence nevertheless the stupidity of our tempers receives but faint impressions, and in the most tragical state of times holds but starts of good motions. So that to continue us in goodness there must be iterated returns of misery, and a circulation in afflictions is necessary. And since we cannot be wise by warnings, since plagues are insignificant, except we be personally plagued, since also we cannot be punish'd unto amendment by proxy or commutation, nor by vicinity, but contaction; there is an unhappy necessity that we must smart in our own skins, and the provoked arm of the Almighty must fall upon ourselves. The capital sufferings of others are rather our monitions than acquitments.[132] There is but one who dyed salvifically for us, and able to say unto death, hitherto shalt thou go and no farther; only one enlivening death, which makes gardens of graves, and that which was sowed in corruption to arise and flourish in glory: when Death itself shall dye, and living shall have no period, when the damned shall mourn at the funeral of Death, when Life not Death shall be the wages of sin, when the second Death shall prove a miserable Life, and destruction shall be courted.[133]

SECTION 12

Although their thoughts may seem too severe, who think that few ill natur'd men go to Heaven; yet it may be acknowledged that good natur'd persons are best founded for that place; who enter the world with good dispositions, and natural graces, more ready to be advanced by impressions from above, and christianized unto pieties; who carry about them plain and downright dealing minds, humility, mercy, charity, and virtues acceptable unto God and man. But whatever success they may have as to Heaven, they are the acceptable men on earth, and happy is he who hath his quiver full of them for his friends. These are not the dens wherein falsehood lurks, and hypocrisy hides its head, wherein frowardness makes its nest, or where malice, hardheartedness, and oppression love to dwell; not those by whom the poor get little, and the rich sometimes loose all; men not of retracted looks, but who carry their hearts in their faces, and need not to be look'd upon with perspectives;[134] not sordidly or mischievously ingrateful; who cannot learn to ride upon the neck of the afflicted, nor load the heavy laden, but who keep the Temple of Janus shut by peaceable and quiet tempers;[135] who make not only the best friends, but the best enemies, as easier to forgive than offend, and ready to pass by the second offence, before they avenge the first; who make natural Royalists, obedient subjects, kind and merciful Princes, verified in our own, one of the best natured kings of this throne. Of the old Roman emperours the best were the best natur'd; though they made but a small number, and might be writ in a ring. Many of the rest were as bad men as princes; humorists rather than of good humors, and of good natural parts, rather than of good natures: which did but arm their bad inclinations, and make them wittily wicked.

SECTION 13

With what shift and pains we come into the world we remember not; but 'tis commonly found no easy matter to get out of it. Many have studied to exasperate the ways of death, but fewer hours have been spent to soften that necessity. That the smoothest way unto the grave is made by bleeding, as common opinion presumeth, beside the sick and fainting languors which accompany that effusion, the experiment in Lucan and Seneca will make us doubt;[136] under which the noble stoick so deeply laboured, that, to conceal his affliction, he was fain to retire from the sight of his wife, and not ashamed to implore the merciful hand of his physician to shorten his misery therein. Ovid, the old heroes, and the stoicks, who were so afraid of drowning, as dreading thereby the extinction of their soul, which they conceived to be a fire, stood probably in fear of an easier way of death;[*137] wherein the water, entering the possessions of air, makes a temperate suffocation, and kills as it were without a fever. Surely many, who have had the spirit to destroy themselves, have not been ingenious in the contrivance thereof. 'Twas a dull way practised by Themistocles[†138] to overwhelm himself with bulls-blood, who, being an Athenian, might have held an easier theory of death from the state potion of his country; from which Socrates in Plato seemed not to suffer much more than from the fit of an ague.[139] Cato is much to be pitied, who mangled himself with poyniards; And Hannibal seems more subtle, who carried his delivery not in the point, but the pummel of his sword.[‡]

The Egyptians were merciful contrivers, who destroyed their malefactors by asps, charming their senses into an invincible sleep, and killing as it were with Hermes his rod.[140] The Turkish emperour,[§] odious for other cruelty, was herein a

* *Demito naufragium, mors mihi munus erit.*

† Plutarch.

‡ Pummel, wherein he is said to have carried something, whereby upon a struggle or despair he might deliver himself from all misfortunes.

§ Solyman *Turkish history*.

remarkable master of mercy, killing his favorite in his sleep, and sending him from the shade into the house of darkness. He who had been thus destroyed would hardly have bled at the presence of his destroyer; when men are already dead by metaphor, and pass but from one sleep unto another, wanting herein the eminent part of severity, to feel themselves to dye, and escaping the sharpest attendant of death, the lively apprehension thereof. But to learn to dye is better than to study the ways of dying. Death will find some ways to untie or cut the most Gordian knots of life, and make men's miseries as mortal as themselves: whereas evil spirits, as undying substances, are unseparable from their calamities; and therefore they everlastingly struggle under their *angustias*, and bound up with immortality can never get out of themselves.[141]

PART III

SECTION I

'Tis hard to find a whole age to imitate, or what century to propose for example. Some have been far more approveable than others: but virtue and vice, panegyricks and satyrs, scatteringly to be found in all. History sets down not only things laudable, but abominable; things which should never have been or never have been known: so that noble patterns must be fetched here and there from single persons, rather than whole nations, and from all nations, rather than any one. The world was early bad, and the first sin the most deplorable of any. The younger world afforded the oldest men, and perhaps the best and the worst, when length of days made virtuous habits heroical and immoveable, vitious, inveterate and irreclaimable. And since 'tis said that the imaginations of their hearts were evil, only evil, and continually evil; it may be feared that their sins held pace with their lives; and their longevity swelling their impieties, the longanimity of God would no longer endure such vivacious abominations.[142] Their impieties were surely of a deep dye, which required the whole element of water to wash them away, and overwhelmed their memories with themselves;[143] and so shut up the first windows of time, leaving no histories of those longevous generations, when men might have been properly historians, when Adam might have read long lectures unto Methuselah, and Methuselah unto Noah. For had we been happy in just historical accounts of that unparallel'd world, we might have been acquainted with wonders, and have understood not a little of the acts and undertakings of Moses his mighty men, and men of renown of old; which might have enlarged our thoughts, and made the world older unto us. For the unknown part of time shortens the estimation, if not the compute of it. What hath escaped our knowledge falls not under our consideration, and what is and will be latent is little better than non existent.

SECTION 2

Some things are dictated for our instruction, some acted for our imitation, wherein 'tis best to ascend unto the highest conformity, and to the honour of the exemplar. He honours God who imitates him. For what we virtuously imitate we approve and admire; and since we delight not to imitate inferiors, we aggrandize and magnify those we imitate; since also we are most apt to imitate those we love, we testify our affection in our imitation of the inimitable. To affect to be like may be no imitation. To act, and not to be what we pretend to imitate, is but a mimical conformation, and carrieth no virtue in it. Lucifer imitated not God, when he said he would be like the highest, and he imitated not Jupiter, who counterfeited thunder.[144] Where imitation can go no farther, let admiration step on, whereof there is no end in the wisest form of men. Even angels and spirits have enough to admire in their sublimer natures, admiration being the act of the creature and not of God, who doth not admire himself. Created natures allow of swelling hyperboles; nothing can be said hyperbolically of God, nor will his attributes admit of expressions above their own exuperances.[145] Trismegistus his circle, whose center is everywhere, and circumference no where, was no hyperbole. Words cannot exceed, where they cannot express enough. Even the most winged thoughts fall at the setting out, and reach not the portal of divinity.

SECTION 3

In bivious theorems and Janus-faced doctrines let virtuous considerations state the determination.[146] Look upon opinions as thou doest upon the moon, and chuse not the dark hemisphere for thy contemplation. Embrace not the opacous and blind side of opinions, but that which looks most luciferously or influentially unto goodness.[147] 'Tis better to think that there are guardian spirits, than that there are no spirits to guard us; that vicious persons are slaves, than that there is any servitude in virtue; that times past have been better than times present, than that times were always bad, and that to be men it suffiseth to be no better than men in all ages, and so promiscuously to swim down the turbid stream, and make up the grand confusion. Sow not thy understanding with opinions, which make nothing of iniquities, and fallaciously extenuate transgressions. Look upon vices and vicious objects with hyperbolical eyes; and rather enlarge their dimensions, that their unseen deformities may not escape thy sense, and their poysonous parts and stings may appear massy and monstrous unto thee; for the undiscerned particles and atoms of evil deceive us, and we are undone by the invisibles of seeming goodness. We are only deceived in what is not discerned, and to err is but to be blind or dim-sighted as to some perceptions.

SECTION 4

To be honest in a right line*,[148] and virtuous by epitome, be firm unto such principles of goodness, as carry in them volumes of instruction and may abridge thy labour. And since instructions are many, hold close unto those, whereon the rest depend. So may we have all in a few, and the law and the prophets in a rule, the sacred writ in stenography, and the scripture in a nut-shell.[149] To pursue the osseous and solid part of goodness, which gives stability and rectitude to all the rest;[150] to settle on fundamental virtues, and bid early defiance unto mother-vices, which carry in their bowels the *seminals* of other iniquities, makes a short cut in goodness, and strikes not off an head but the whole neck of Hydra.[151] For we are carried into the dark lake, like the Ægyptian river into the sea, by seven principal Ostiaries.[152] The mother-sins of that number are the deadly engines of evil spirits that undo us, and even evil spirits themselves, and he who is under the chains thereof is not without a possession. Mary Magdalene had more than seven devils, if these with their imps were in her, and he who is thus possessed may literally be named *Legion*.[153] Where such plants grow and prosper, look for no champian or region void of thorns, but productions like the Tree of Goa,† and forrests of abomination.

* *Linea Recta brevissima.*

† *Arbor Goa de Ruyz* or *ficus Indica*, whose branches send down shoots which root in the ground, from whence there successively rise others, till one Tree becomes a wood.

SECTION 5

Guide not the hand of God, nor order the finger of the Almighty, unto thy will and pleasure; but sit quiet in the soft showers of Providence, and favorable distributions in this world, either to thy self or others. And since not only judgments have their errands, but mercies their commissions; snatch not at every favour, nor think thy self passed by, if they fall upon thy neighbour. Rake not up envious displacences at things successful unto others, which the wise disposer of all thinks not fit for thy self.[154] Reconcile the events of things unto both beings, that is, of this world and the next: so will there not seem so many riddles in Providence, nor various inequalities in the dispensation of things below. If thou doest not anoint thy face, yet put not on sackcloth at the felicities of others.[155] Repining at the good draws on rejoicing at the evils of others, and so falls into that inhumane vice,* for which so few languages have a name.[156] The blessed spirits above rejoice at our happiness below; but to be glad at the evils of one another is beyond the malignity of Hell, and falls not on evil spirits, who, though they rejoice at our unhappiness, take no pleasure at the afflictions of their own society or of their fellow natures. Degenerous heads! Who must be fain to learn from such examples, and to be taught from the school of Hell.

* Επιχαιρεκακία

SECTION 6

Grain not thy vicious stains, nor deepen those swart tinctures, which temper, infirmity, or ill habits have set upon thee; and fix not by iterated depravations what time might efface, or virtuous washes expunge. He who thus still advanceth in iniquity deepneth his deformed hue, turns a shadow into night, and makes himself a negro in the black jaundice; and so becomes one of those lost ones, the disproportionate pores of whose brains afford no entrance unto good motions, but reflect and frustrate all counsels, deaf unto the thunder of the laws, and rocks unto the cries of charitable commiserators. He who hath had the patience of Diogenes, to make orations unto statues, may more sensibly apprehend how all words fall to the ground, spent upon such a surd and earless generation of men, stupid unto all instruction, and rather requiring an exorcist, than an orator for their conversion.[157]

SECTION 7

Burden not the back of Aries, Leo, or Taurus, with thy faults, nor make Saturn, Mars, or Venus, guilty of thy follies. Think not to fasten thy imperfections on the stars, and so despairingly conceive thy self under a fatality of being evil. Calculate thy self within, seek not thy self in the Moon, but in thine own orb or microcosmical circumference. Let celestial aspects admonish and advertise, not conclude and determine thy ways. For since good and bad stars moralize not our actions, and neither excuse or commend, acquit or condemn our good or bad deeds at the present or last bar, since some are astrologically well disposed who are morally highly vicious; not celestial figures, but virtuous schemes must denominate and state our actions. If we rightly understood the names whereby God calleth the stars, if we knew his name for the Dog-Star, or by what appellation Jupiter, Mars, and Saturn obey his will, it might be a welcome accession unto astrology, which speaks great things, and is fain to make use of appellations from Greek and barbarick systems. Whatever influences, impulsions, or inclinations there be from the lights above, it were a piece of wisdom to make one of those wise men who overrule their stars,[*158] and with their own militia contend with the host of Heaven. Unto which attempt there want not auxiliaries from the whole strength of morality, supplies from Christian ethicks, influences also and illuminations from above, more powerfull than the lights of Heaven.

* *Sapiens dominabitur Astris.*

SECTION 8

Confound not the distinctions of thy life which nature hath divided: that is, youth, adolescence, manhood, and old age, nor in these divided periods, wherein thou art in a manner four, conceive thy self but one. Let every division be happy in its proper virtues, nor one vice run through all. Let each distinction have its salutary transition, and critically deliver thee from the imperfections of the former, so ordering the whole, that prudence and virtue may have the largest section. Do as a child but when thou art a child, and ride not on a reed at twenty.[159] He who hath not taken leave of the follies of his youth, and in his maturer state scarce got out of that division, disproportionately divideth his days, crowds up the latter part of his life, and leaves too narrow a corner for the age of wisdom, and so hath room to be a man scarce longer than he hath been a youth. Rather than to make this confusion, anticipate the virtues of age, and live long without the infirmities of it. So may'st thou count up thy days as some do Adams,[*] that is, by anticipation; so may'st thou be coetaneous unto thy elders, and a father unto thy contemporaries.[160]

[*] Adam thought to be created in the state of man, about thirty years old.

SECTION 9

While others are curious in the choice of good air, and chiefly solicitous for healthful habitations, study thou conversation, and be critical in thy consortion.[161] The aspects, conjunctions, and configurations of the stars, which mutually diversify, intend, or qualify their influences, are but the varieties of their nearer or farther conversation with one another, and like the consortion of men, whereby they become better or worse, and even exchange their natures. Since men live by examples, and will be imitating something; order thy imitation to thy improvement, not thy ruin. Look not for roses in Attalus his garden, or wholesome flowers in a venomous plantation.[†] And since there is scarce any one bad, but some others are the worse for him; tempt not contagion by proximity, and hazard not thy self in the shadow of corruption. He who hath not early suffered this shipwreck, and in his younger days escaped this Charybdis, may make a happy voyage, and not come in with black sails into the port.[162] Self conversation, or to be alone, is better than such consortion. Some school-men tell us, that he is properly alone, with whom in the same place there is no other of the same species. Nabuchodonozor was alone, though among the beasts of the field, and a wise man may be tolerably said to be alone though with a rabble of people, little better than beasts about him. Unthinking heads, who have not learn'd to be alone, are in a prison to themselves, if they be not also with others: whereas on the contrary, they whose thoughts are in a fair, and hurry within, are sometimes fain to retire into company, to be out of the crowd of themselves. He who must needs have company, must needs have sometimes bad company. Be able to be alone. Loose not the advantage of solitude, and the society of thy self, nor be only content, but delight to be alone and single with omnipresency. He who is thus prepared, the day is not uneasy nor the night black unto him. Darkness may bound his eyes, not his imagination. In his bed he may ly, like Pompey and his sons, in all quarters of the earth, may speculate the universe, and enjoy the whole world in the hermitage of himself.[‡][163] Thus the old ascetick

[†] Attalus made a garden which contained only venomous plants.

[‡] *Pompeios Juvenes Asia atque Europa, sed ipsum Terra tegit Libyes.*

Christians found a paradise in a desert, and with little converse on earth held a conversation in Heaven; thus they astronomiz'd in caves, and though they beheld not the stars, had the glory of Heaven before them.

SECTION 10

Let the characters of good things stand indelibly in thy mind, and thy thoughts be active on them. Trust not too much unto suggestions from reminiscential amulets, or artificial *memorandums*. Let the mortifying Janus of Covarrubias be in thy daily thoughts, not only on thy hand and signets.*[164] Rely not alone upon silent and dumb remembrances. Behold not Death's heads till thou doest not see them, nor look upon mortifying objects till thou overlook'st them. Forget not how assuefaction unto any thing minorates the passion from it, how constant objects loose their hints, and steal an inadvertisement upon us.[165] There is no excuse to forget what every thing prompts unto us. To thoughtful observators the whole world is a phylactery, and every thing we see an item of the wisdom, power, or goodness of God. Happy are they who verify their amulets, and make their phylacteries speak in their lives and actions.[166] To run on in despight of the revulsions and pulbacks of such remoras aggravates our transgressions.[167] When Death's heads on our hands have no influence upon our heads, and fleshless cadavers abate not the exorbitances of the flesh; when crucifixes upon men's hearts suppress not their bad commotions, and his image who was murdered for us withholds not from blood and murder; phylacteries prove but formalities, and their despised hints sharpen our condemnations.

* Don Sebastian de Covarrubias writ 3 Centuries of moral emblems in Spanish. In the 88th of the second century he sets down two faces averse, and conjoined Janus-like, the one a gallant beautiful face, the other a death's head face, with this motto out of Ovid's *Metamorphosis*, *Quid fuerim quid simque vide*.

SECTION 11

Look not for whales in the Euxine Sea, or expect great matters where they are not to be found.[168] Seek not for profundity in shallowness, or fertility in a wilderness. Place not the expectation of great happiness here below, or think to find Heaven on earth: wherein we must be content with embryon-felicities, and fruitions of doubtful faces. For the circle of our felicities makes but short arches. In every clime we are in a periscian state, and with our light, our shadow and darkness walk about us.[169] Our contentments stand upon the tops of pyramids ready to fall off, and the insecurity of their enjoyments abrupteth our tranquilities. What we magnify is magnificent, but like to the Colossus, noble without, stuft with rubbidge and coarse metal within.[170] Even the Sun, whose glorious outside we behold, may have dark and smoky entrails. In vain we admire the lustre of any thing seen: that which is truly glorious is invisible. Paradise was but a part of the earth, lost not only to our fruition but our knowledge. And if, according to old dictates, no man can be said to be happy before death, the happiness of this life goes for nothing before it be over, and while we think ourselves happy we do but usurp that name. Certainly true beatitude groweth not on earth, nor hath this world in it the expectations we have of it. He swims in oyl, and can hardly avoid sinking, who hath such light foundations to support him.[171] 'Tis therefore happy that we have two worlds to hold on. To enjoy true happiness we must travel into a very far countrey, and even out of ourselves; for the pearl we seek for is not to be found in the Indian, but in the Empyrean Ocean.[172]

SECTION 12

Answer not the spur of fury, and be not prodigal or prodigious in revenge. Make not one in the *Historia Horribilis*;* flay not thy servant for a broken glass, nor pound him in a mortar who offendeth thee;[173] supererogate not in the worst sense, and overdo not the necessities of evil;[174] humour not the injustice of revenge. Be not stoically mistaken in the equality of sins, nor commutatively iniquous in the valuation of transgressions;[175] but weigh them in the Scales of Heaven, and by the weights of righteous reason. Think that revenge too high, which is but level with the offence. Let thy arrows of revenge fly short, or be aimed like those of Jonathan, to fall beside the mark.[176] Too many there be to whom a dead enemy smells well, and who find musk and amber in revenge. The ferity of such minds holds no rule in retaliations, requiring too often a head for a tooth, and the supreme revenge for trespasses, which a night's rest should obliterate.[177] But patient meekness takes injuries like pills, not chewing but swallowing them down, laconically suffering, and silently passing them over, while angred pride

* A book so entituled wherein are sundry horrid accounts.

makes a noise, like Homerican Mars,*[178] at every scratch of offences. Since women do most delight in revenge, it may seem but feminine manhood to be vindicative. If thou must needs have thy revenge of thine enemy, with a soft tongue break his bones,† heap coals of fire on his head, forgive him, and enjoy it. To forgive our enemies is a charming way of revenge, and a short Cæsarian conquest overcoming without a blow; laying our enemies at our feet, under sorrow, shame, and repentance; leaving our foes our friends, and solicitously inclined to grateful retaliations. Thus to return upon our adversaries is a healing way of revenge, and to do good for evil a soft and melting ultion, a method taught from Heaven to keep all smooth on earth.[179] Common forceable ways make not an end of evil, but leave hatred and malice behind them. An enemy thus reconciled is little to be trusted as wanting the foundation of love and charity, and but for a time restrained by disadvantage or inability. If thou hast not mercy for others, yet be not cruel unto thy self. To ruminate upon evils, to make critical notes upon injuries, and be too acute in their apprehensions, is to add unto our own tortures, to feather the arrows of our enemies, to lash our selves with the scorpions of our foes, and to resolve to sleep no more.[180] For injuries long dreamt on take away at last all rest; and he sleeps but like Regulus, who busieth his head about them.[181]

* *Tu tamen exclamas ut Stentora vincere possis Vel saltem quantum Gradivus Homericus.* Juvenal.

† A soft Tongue breaketh the bones. Proverbs 25. 15.

SECTION 13

Amuse not thy self about the riddles of future things. Study prophecies when they are become histories, and past hovering in their causes. Eye well things past and present, and let conjectural sagacity suffise for things to come. There is a sober latitude for prescience in contingences of discoverable tempers, whereby discerning heads see sometimes beyond their eyes, and wise men become prophetical. Leave cloudy predictions to their periods, and let appointed seasons have the lot of their accomplishments. 'Tis too early to study such prophecies before they have been long made, before some train of their causes have already taken fire, laying open in part what lay obscure and before buryed unto us. For the voice of prophecies is like that of whispering-places: they who are near or at a little distance hear nothing, those at the farthest extremity will understand all. But a retrograde cognition of times past, and things which have already been, is more satisfactory than a suspended knowledge of what is yet unexistent. And the greatest part of time being already wrapt up in things behind us; it's now somewhat late to bait after things before us; for futurity still shortens, and time present sucks in time to come.[182] What is prophetical in one age proves historical in another, and so must hold on unto the last of time; when there will be no room for prediction, when Janus shall loose one face, and the long beard of time shall look like those of David's servants, shorn away upon one side, and when, if the expected Elias should appear, he might say much of what is past, not much of what's to come.[183]

SECTION 14

Live unto the dignity of thy nature, and leave it not disputable at last, whether thou hast been a man, or since thou art a composition of man and beast, how thou hast predominantly passed thy days, to state the denomination. Un-man not therefore thy self by a beastial transformation, nor realize old fables. Expose not thy self by four footed manners unto monstrous draughts, and caricatura representations. Think not after the old Pythagorean conceit, what beast thou may'st be after death. Be not under any brutal metempsychosis while thou livest, and walkest about erectly under the scheme of man.[184] In thine own circumference, as in that of the earth, let the rational horizon be larger than the sensible, and the circle of reason than of sense. Let the divine part be upward, and the region of beast below. Otherwise,' tis but to live invertedly, and with thy head unto the heels of thy antipodes. Desert not thy title to a divine particle and union with invisibles.[185] Let true knowledge and virtue tell the lower world thou art a part of the higher. Let thy thoughts be of things which have not entred into the hearts of beasts: think of things long past, and long to come: acquaint thy self with the *choragium* of the stars, and consider the vast expansion beyond them.[186] Let intellectual tubes give thee a glance of things, which visive organs reach not.[187] Have a glimpse of incomprehensibles, and thoughts of things, which thoughts but tenderly touch. Lodge immaterials in thy head: ascend unto invisibles: fill thy spirit with spirituals, with the mysteries of faith, the magnalities of religion, and thy life with the honour of God; without which, though giants in wealth and dignity, we are but dwarfs and pygmies in humanity, and may hold a pitiful rank in that triple division of mankind into heroes, men, and beasts. For though human souls are said to be equal, yet is there no small inequality in their operations; some maintain the allowable station of men; many are far below it; and some have been so divine, as to approach the *apogeum* of their natures, and to be in the *confinium* of spirits.[188]

SECTION 15

Behold thy self by inward opticks and the crystalline of thy soul.[189] Strange it is that in the most perfect sense there should be so many fallacies, that we are fain to make a doctrine, and often to see by art. But the greatest imperfection is in our inward sight, that is, to be ghosts unto our own eyes, and while we are so sharpsighted as to look thorough others, to be invisible unto our selves; for the inward eyes are more fallacious than the outward. The vices we scoff at in others laugh at us within our selves. Avarice, pride, falshood lye undiscerned and blindly in us, even to the age of blindness: and therefore, to see ourselves interiourly, we are fain to borrow other men's eyes; wherein true friends are good informers, and censurers no bad friends. Conscience only, that can see without light, sits in the *Areopagy* and dark tribunal of our hearts, surveying our thoughts and condemning their obliquities.[190] Happy is that state of vision that can see without light, though all should look as before the creation, when there was not an eye to see, or light to actuate a vision:[191] wherein not withstanding obscurity is only imaginable respectively unto eyes; for unto God there was none; eternal light was ever, created light was for the creation, not himself, and as he saw before the sun, may still also see without it. In the city of the new Jerusalem there is neither sun nor moon;[192] where glorifyed eyes must see by the archetypal sun, or the light of God, able to illuminate intellectual eyes, and make unknown visions. Intuitive perceptions in spiritual beings may perhaps hold some analogy unto vision: but yet how they see us, or one another, what eye, what light, or what perception is required unto their intuition, is yet dark unto our apprehension; and even how they see God, or how unto our glorified eyes the beatifical vision will be celebrated, another world must tell us, when perceptions will be new, and we may hope to behold invisibles.

SECTION 16

When all looks fair about, and thou seest not a cloud so big as a hand to threaten thee, forget not the wheel of things:[193] think of sullen vicissitudes, but beat not thy brains to foreknow them. Be armed against such obscurities rather by submission than fore-knowledge. The knowledge of future evils mortifies present felicities, and there is more content in the uncertainty or ignorance of them. This favour our Saviour vouchsafed unto Peter, when he foretold not his death in plain terms, and so by an ambiguous and cloudy delivery dampt not the spirit of his Disciples.[194] But in the assured fore-knowledge of the deluge Noah lived many years under the affliction of a flood, and Jerusalem was taken unto Jeremy before it was besieged. And therefore the wisdom of astrologers, who speak of future things, hath wisely softned the severity of their doctrines; and even in their sad predictions, while they tell us of inclination not coaction from the stars, they kill us not with Stygian oaths and merciless necessity, but leave us hopes of evasion.[195]

SECTION 17

If thou hast the brow to endure the name of traytor, perjur'd, or oppressor, yet cover thy face when ingratitude is thrown at thee. If that degenerous vice possess thee, hide thy self in the shadow of thy shame, and pollute not noble society. Grateful ingenuities are content to be obliged within some compass of retribution, and being depressed by the weight of iterated favours may so labour under their inabilities of requital, as to abate the content from kindnesses. But narrow self-ended souls make prescription of good offices, and obliged by often favours think others still due unto them: whereas, if they but once fail, they prove so perversely ungrateful, as to make nothing of former courtesies, and to bury all that's past. Such tempers pervert the generous course of things; for they discourage the inclinations of noble minds, and make beneficency cool unto acts of obligation, whereby the grateful world should subsist, and have their consolation. Common gratitude must be kept alive by the additionary fewel of new courtesies: but generous gratitudes, though but once well obliged, without quickening repetitions or expectation of new favours, have thankful minds for ever; for they write not their obligations in sandy but marble memories, which wear not out but with themselves.

SECTION 18

Think not silence the wisdom of fools, but, if rightly timed, the honour of wise men, who have not the infirmity, but the virtue of taciturnity, and speak not out of the abundance, but the well weighed thoughts of their hearts. Such silence may be eloquence, and speak thy worth above the power of words. Make such a one thy friend, in whom princes may be happy, and great councels successful. Let him have the key of thy heart, who hath the lock of his own, which no temptation can open; where thy secrets may lastingly lie, like the lamp in Olybius his urn, alive, and light, but close and invisible.*

* Which after many hundred years was found burning under-ground, and went out as soon as the air came to it.

SECTION 19

Let thy oaths be sacred and promises be made upon the altar of thy heart. Call not Jove to witness with a stone in one hand, and a straw in another, and so make chaff and stubble of thy vows†.[196] Worldly spirits, whose interest is their belief, make cobwebs of obligations, and, if they can find ways to elude the urn of the Prætor, will trust the thunderbolt of Jupiter: and therefore if they should as deeply swear as Osman to Bethlem Gabor;‡ yet whether they would be bound by those chains, and not find ways to cut such Gordian knots, we could have no just assurance. But honest men's words are Stygian oaths, and promises inviolable. These are not the men for whom the fetters of law were first forged: they needed not the solemness of oaths; by keeping their faith they swear, and evacuate such confirmations.§

† *Jovem lapidem jurare.*

‡ See the oath of Sultan Osman in his life, in the addition to Knolls his Turkish history.

§ *Colendo fidem jurant.* Curtius.

SECTION 20

Though the world be histrionical, and most men live ironically, yet be thou what thou singly art, and personate only thy self. Swim smoothly in the stream of thy nature, and live but one man. To single hearts, doubling is discruciating:[197] such tempers must sweat to dissemble, and prove but hypocritical hypocrites. Simulation must be short: men do not easily continue a counterfeiting life, or dissemble unto death. He who counterfeiteth, acts a part, and is as it were out of himself: which, if long, proves so ircksome, that men are glad to pull of their vizards, and resume themselves again; no practice being able to naturalize such unnaturals, or make a man rest content not to be himself. And therefore since sincerity is thy temper, let veracity be thy virtue in words, manners, and actions. To offer at iniquities, which have so little foundations in thee, were to be vitious up hill, and strain for thy condemnation. Persons vitiously inclined want no wheels to make them actively vitious, as having the elater and spring of their own natures to facilitate their iniquities.[198] And therefore so many, who are sinistrous unto good actions, are ambi-dexterous unto bad, and Vulcans in virtuous paths, Achilleses in vitious motions.[199]

SECTION 21

Rest not in the high strain'd paradoxes of old philosophy supported by naked reason, and the reward of mortal felicity, but labour in the ethicks of faith, built upon heavenly assistance, and the happiness of both beings. Understand the rules, but swear not unto the doctrines of Zeno or Epicurus.[200] Look beyond Antoninus, and terminate not thy morals in Seneca or Epictetus. Let not the twelve, but the two tables be thy law:[201] let Pythagoras be thy remembrancer, not thy textuary and final instructer;[202] and learn the vanity of the world rather from Solomon than Phocylides. Sleep not in the dogmas of the peripatus, academy, or porticus. Be a moralist of the Mount, an Epictetus in the faith, and christianize thy notions.[203]

SECTION 22

In seventy or eighty years a man may have a deep gust of the world, know what it is, what it can afford, and what 'tis to have been a man.[204] Such a latitude of years may hold a considerable corner in the general map of time; and a man may have a curt epitome of the whole course thereof in the days of his own life, may clearly see he hath but acted over his fore-fathers, what it was to live in ages past, and what living will be in all ages to come.

He is like to be the best judge of time who hath lived to see about the sixtieth part thereof. Persons of short times may know what 'tis to live, but not the life of man, who, having little behind them, are but Januses of one face, and know not singularities enough to raise axioms of this world: but such a compass of years will show new examples of old things, parallelisms of occurrences through the whole course of time, and nothing be monstrous unto him; who may in that time understand not only the varieties of men, but the variation of himself, and how many men he hath been in that extent of time.

He may have a close apprehension what it is to be forgotten, while he hath lived to find none who could remember his father, or scarce the friends of his youth, and may sensibly see with what a face in no long time oblivion will look upon himself.[205] His progeny may never be his posterity; he may go out of the world less related than he came into it, and considering the frequent mortality in friends and relations, in such a term of time, he may pass away divers years in sorrow and black habits, and leave none to mourn for himself; orbity may be his inheritance, and riches his repentance.[206]

In such a thred of time, and long observation of men, he may acquire a physiognomical intuitive knowledge, judge the interiors by the outside, and raise conjectures at first sight;[207] and knowing what men have been, what they are, what children probably will be, may in the present age behold a good part, and the temper of the next; and since so many live by the rules of constitution, and so few overcome their temperamental inclinations, make no improbable predictions.

Such a portion of time will afford a large prospect backward, and authentick reflections how far he hath performed the great intention of his being, in the honour of his Maker; whether he hath made good the principles of his nature and what he was made to be; what characteristick and special mark he hath left, to be observable in his generation; whether he hath lived to purpose or in vain, and what he hath added, acted, or performed, that might considerably speak him a man.

In such an age delights will be undelightful and pleasures grow stale unto him; antiquated theorems will revive, and Solomon's maxims be demonstrations unto him;[208] hopes or presumptions be over, and despair grow up of any satisfaction below. And having been long tossed in the ocean of this world, he will by that time feel the in-draught of another, unto which this seems but preparatory, and without it of no high value. He will experimentally find the emptiness of all things, and the nothing of what is past; and wisely grounding upon true Christian expectations, finding so much past, will wholly fix upon what is to come. He will long for perpetuity, and live as though he made haste to be happy. The last may prove the prime part of his life, and those his best days which he lived nearest Heaven.

SECTION 23

Live happy in the Elizium of a virtuously composed mind, and let intellectual contents exceed the delights wherein mere pleasurists place their paradise. Bear not too slack reins upon pleasure, nor let complexion or contagion betray thee unto the exorbitancy of delight. Make pleasure thy recreation or intermissive relaxation, not thy Diana, life and profession.[209] Voluptuousness is as insatiable as covetousness. Tranquility is better than jollity, and to appease pain than to invent pleasure. Our hard entrance into the world, our miserable going out of it, our sicknesses, disturbances, and sad rencounters in it, do clamorously tell us we come not into the world to run a race of delight, but to perform the sober acts and serious purposes of man;[210] which to omit were foully to miscarry in the advantage of humanity, to play away an uniterable life, and to have lived in vain.[211] Forget not the capital end, and frustrate not the opportunity of once living. Dream not of any kind of metempsychosis or transanimation, but into thine own body, and that after a long time, and then also unto wail or bliss, according to thy first and fundamental life. Upon a curricle in this world depends a long course of the next, and upon a narrow scene here an endless expansion hereafter.[212] In vain some think to have an end of their beings with their lives. Things cannot get out of their natures, or be or not be in despite of their constitutions. Rational existences in Heaven perish not at all, and but partially on earth: that which is thus once will in some way be always: the first living human soul is still alive, and all Adam hath found no period.

SECTION 24

Since the stars of Heaven do differ in glory; since it hath pleased the Almighty hand to honour the North Pole with lights above the South; since there are some stars so bright, that they can hardly be looked on, some so dim that they can scarce be seen, and vast numbers not to be seen at all even by artificial eyes; read thou the earth in Heaven, and things below from above. Look contentedly upon the scattered difference of things, and expect not equality in lustre, dignity, or perfection, in regions or persons below; where numerous numbers must be content to stand like lacteous or nebulous stars, little taken notice of, or dim in their generations. All which may be contentedly allowable in the affairs and ends of this world, and in suspension unto what will be in the order of things hereafter, and the new systeme of mankind which will be in the world to come; when the last may be the first and the first the last; when Lazarus may sit above Cæsar, and the just obscure on earth shall shine like the sun in Heaven; when personations shall cease, and histrionism of happiness be over;[213] when reality shall rule, and all shall be as they shall be for ever.

SECTION 25

When the Stoick said that life would not be accepted, if it were offered unto such as knew it,* he spoke too meanly of that state of being which placeth us in the form of men. It more depreciates the value of this life, that men would not live it over again; for although they would still live on, yet few or none can endure to think of being twice the same men upon earth, and some had rather never have lived than to tread over their days once more. Cicero in a prosperous state had not the patience to think of beginning in a cradle again.[214] Job would not only curse the day of his nativity, but also of his renascency, if he were to act over his disasters, and the miseries of the

* *Vitam nemo acciperet si daretur scientibus.* Seneca.

dunghil.[215] But the greatest underweening of this life is to undervalue that, unto which this is but exordial or a passage leading unto it.[216] The great advantage of this mean life is thereby to stand in a capacity of a better; for the colonies of Heaven must be drawn from earth, and the sons of the first Adam are only heirs unto the second. Thus Adam came into this world with the power also of another, nor only to replenish the earth, but the everlasting mansions of Heaven. Where we were when the foundations of the earth were lay'd, when the morning stars sang together and all the sons of God shouted for joy,* he must answer who asked it; who understands entities of preordination, and beings yet unbeing;[217] who hath in his intellect the ideal existences of things, and entities before their extances. Though it looks but like an imaginary kind of existency to be before we are; yet since we are under the decree or prescience of a sure and omnipotent power, it may be somewhat more than a non-entity to be in that mind, unto which all things are present.

* Job 38:4, 7.

SECTION 26

If the end of the world shall have the same foregoing signs, as the period of empires, states, and dominions in it, that is, corruption of manners, inhuman degenerations, and deluge of iniquities; it may be doubted whether that final time be so far off, of whose day and hour there can be no prescience. But while all men doubt and none can determine how long the world shall last, some may wonder that it hath spun out so long and unto our days. For if the Almighty had not determin'd a fixed duration unto it, according to his mighty and merciful designments in it, if he had not said unto it, as he did unto a part of it, hitherto shalt thou go and no farther; if we consider the incessant and cutting provocations from the earth, it is not without amazement how his patience hath permitted so long a continuance unto it, how he, who cursed the earth in the first days of the first man, and drowned it in the tenth generation after, should thus lastingly contend with flesh and yet defer the last flames.[218] For since he is sharply provoked every moment, yet punisheth to pardon, and forgives to forgive again; what patience could be content to act over such vicissitudes, or accept of repentances which must have after penitences, his goodness can only tell us. And surely if the patience of Heaven were not proportionable unto the provocations from earth; there needed an intercessor not only for the sins, but the duration of this world, and to lead it up unto the present computation. Without such a merciful longanimity, the heavens would never be so aged as to grow old like a garment;[219] it were in vain to infer from the doctrine of the sphere, that the time might come when *Capella*, a noble northern star, would have its motion in the Æquator, that the northern zodiacal signs would at length be the southern, the southern the northern, and Capricorn become our Cancer. However therefore the wisdom of the Creator hath ordered the duration of the world, yet since the end thereof brings the accomplishment of our happiness, since some would be content that it should have no end, since evil men and spirits do fear it may be too short, since good men hope it may not be too long; the prayer of the saints under the altar will be the supplication of the righteous world. That his mercy would abridge their languishing expectation and hasten the accomplishment of their happy state to come.

SECTION 27

Though good men are often taken away from the evil to come, though some in evil days have been glad that they were old, nor long to behold the iniquities of a wicked world, or judgments threatened by them; yet is it no small satisfaction unto honest minds to leave the world in virtuous well temper'd times, under a prospect of good to come, and continuation of worthy ways acceptable unto God and man. Men who dye in deplorable days, which they regretfully behold, have not their eyes closed with the like content; while they cannot avoid the thoughts of proceeding or growing enormities, displeasing unto that spirit unto whom they are then going, whose honour they desire in all times and throughout all generations. If Lucifer could be freed from his dismal place, he would little care though the rest were left behind. Too many there may be of Nero's mind, who, if their own turn were served, would not regard what became of others, and, when they dye themselves, care not if all perish.[220] But good men's wishes extend beyond their lives, for the happiness of times to come, and never to be known unto them. And therefore while so many question prayers for the dead, they charitably pray for those who are not yet alive; they are not so enviously ambitious to go to Heaven by themselves; they cannot but humbly wish, that the little flock might be greater, the narrow gate wider, and that, as many are called, so not a few might be chosen.[221]

SECTION 28

That a greater number of angels remained in Heaven, than fell from it, the school-men will tell us; that the number of blessed souls will not come short of that vast number of fallen spirits, we have the favorable calculation of others. What age or century hath sent most souls unto Heaven, he can tell who vouchsafeth that honour unto them. Though the number of the blessed must be compleat before the world can pass away, yet since the world itself seems in the wane, and we have no such comfortable prognosticks of latter times, since a greater part of time is spun than is to come, and the blessed roll already much replenished; happy are those pieties, which solicitously look about, and hasten to make one of that already much filled and abbreviated list to come.

SECTION 29

Think not thy time short in this world since the world itself is not long. The created world is but a small parenthesis in eternity, and a short interposition for a time between such a state of duration, as was before it and may be after it. And if we should allow of the old tradition that the world should last six thousand years, it could scarce have the name of old, since the first man lived near a sixth part thereof, and seven Methuselas would exceed its whole duration.[222] However to palliate the shortness of our lives, and somewhat to compensate our brief term in this world, it's good to know as much as we can of it, and also so far as possibly in us lieth to hold such a theory of times past, as though we had seen the same. He who hath thus considered the world, as also how therein things long past have been answered by things present, how matters in one age have been acted over in another, and how there is nothing new under the sun, may conceive himself in some manner to have lived from the beginning, and to be as old as the world; and if he should still live on 'twould be but the same thing.

SECTION 30

Lastly, if length of days be thy portion, make it not thy expectation. Reckon not upon long life: think every day the last, and live always beyond thy account. He that so often surviveth his expectation lives many lives, and will scarce complain of the shortness of his days. Time past is gone like a shadow; make time to come present. Approximate thy latter times by present apprehensions of them: be like a neighbour unto the grave, and think there is but little to come. And since there is something of us that will still live on, join both lives together, and live in one but for the other. He who thus ordereth the purposes of this life will never be far from the next, and is in some manner already in it, by a happy conformity, and close apprehension of it. And if, as we have elsewhere declared, any have been so happy as personally to understand Christian annihilation, extasy, exolution, transformation, the Kiss of the Spouse, and ingression into the divine shadow, according to mystical theology, they have already had an handsome anticipation of Heaven;[223] the world is in a manner over, and the earth in ashes unto them.

Finis.

NOTES

RELIGIO MEDICI

1. *Greedy of life*, from Seneca, *Thyestes*, line 883. The submerged quotation is noted by Browne's early annotator, John Keck (1654), commenting on an early translation of *Religio Medici* into Latin by John Merryweather (1644). On the role of Digby, Ross, and Keck as important guides to the early reception of Browne, see the introductory 'Note on Text and Annotation'.
2. Referring to the effective collapse of censorship and state licensing of the press in the early 1640s.
3. By 1642–3, there was a mounting number of mutual slurs concerning the rights and conduct of both king and parliament.
4. *Incapable of affronts*, too low-born to be insulted; *hopelesse*, with no hope of righting any such affronts.
5. *Importunitie*, continual requests.
6. *c.*1636–7. What other works 'of affinitie' he means is unclear.
7. *Singularitie*, idiosyncrasy; *dissentaneous*, not in agreement with.
8. *Tropicall*, related to tropes.
9. *Maturer discernments*, the wisdom and understanding of age.
10. *Generall scandall of my profession*, i.e. a physician. Keck comments on the proverbial suspicion of the medical trade: 'It is a common speech (but only amongst the unlearn'd sort) *Ubi tres Medici, duo Athei*', i.e. out of every three doctors, two are atheists; Coleridge traces the belief to the fact that 'Ænesidemus and Sextus Empiricus, Sceptics, were both Physicians'; *scandal*, technically, means discrediting religion; *naturall*, on scientific and natural philosophical topics.
11. *Usurpation*, usurping, taking what is not one's right, here the title (*style*) of a Christian.
12. *Font*, by being baptized; *unwary*, here, junior, credulous; *clime*, land, climate.
13. That is, the name of 'Christian' rather than any sub-denomination.
14. *Reformed new-cast religion*, Protestantism, disliking the name on the grounds, presumably, that protesting is not how Browne conceives of his religion. Keck glosses this as 'Lutheran, Calvinist, Zwinglian etc'.
15. *The fathers*, i.e. the patristic writers of the first four centuries of the church.
16. *Sinister*, corrupt; *sinister ends of princes, the ambition and avarice of prelates*, an account of the Reformation as a stripping away of the secular corruption and greed; *prelates*, churchmen.
17. Martin Luther, whose father was involved with mining and smelting.

18. *Desperate resolutions*, glossed by Keck as 'Resolvers', i.e. those who maintain the resolve in Roman Catholicism; *bottome*, hull of ship, or boat in general, hence *new trim'd in the dock*, i.e. Protestantism having stripped away and re-dressed Christianity.
19. *Stand in diameter*, opposite and opposed to.
20. *From them*, from Catholicism.
21. *Improperations*, reproaches; *difference*, used as a verb, differentiate, separate.
22. *Scrupulous*, over-meticulous or anxious.
23. *Pollute themselves*, Israelite laws against entering pagan temples.
24. *Resolved conscience*, i.e. at peace with itself; MS for 'Creator' has 'Maker'.
25. *Holy water and crucifix*, emblematic of Catholic ritual, and liable to idolatry.
26. *Civility of my knee*, genuflecting, likewise seen as Catholic ceremony.
27. [*Textual note:* The sentence is altered from the 1642 publication and Pembroke manuscript: 'I should loose (cut off) mine arme rather then violate a church window, demolish an image or deface the memory of a saint or Martyr'.] With reference to iconoclastic programmes, at their height in the early 1640s, and focusing in particular on removing pictures of the trinity and saints from church windows and decoration.
28. *Elevation*, spiritual uplift.
29. Presumably referring to Browne's time in Catholic Europe, where such processions might take place; *accesse of scorne*, a fit of scorn.
30. *Difference my self nearer*, distinguish more accurately.
31. [*Textual note:* MS and 1642 include: 'No man shall reach my faith unto another Article, or command my obedience unto a Canon more'.] Kenelm Digby concludes 'if I mistake not, this author approveth the Church of England not absolutely, but comparatively with other reformed Churches'. Alexander Ross, considering how readily Browne accepts Catholic ceremony, comments 'this may be indeed *religio Medici*, the religion of the House of *Medicis*, not of the Church of *England*'.
32. *Points indifferent*, not subject to any church rule and not essential to salvation.
33. *Disavouched*, repudiated.
34. *Councell of Trent* (1545–63), Roman Catholic doctrinal council, held in response to the Reformation and codifying Catholic doctrine in a range of areas; *Synod of Dort* (1618–19), council held at Dordrecht in Holland, deliberating in particular on the theology of predestination.
35. *Compute…from Henry the eight*, the assertion that Protestant churches had no apostolic or patristic succession, and therefore were illegitimate, self-ordained churches.

36. [*Textual note:* Some MSS have 'In their quarrel with Pope Paul the first'.] *State of Venice*, The Republic of Venice was excommunicated in 1606 by Pope Paul V (not, as the annotator has it, 'Pope Paul the first').
37. *Temporall prince*, the Papacy claiming both religious and secular jurisdiction of the Vatican territories.
38. *Antichrist*, 1 John 2:18; *whore of Babylon*, Revelation 17:16, both being widely used in Protestant England for the Papacy.
39. *Satyrs*, satires.
40. Keck attributes this idea to Montaigne, though Browne protests in a later manuscript that he had not read Montaigne, 'in a peece of myne published long agoe the learned commentator hath paralleld many passages with others of Mountaignes essays whereas to deale clearly, when I penned that peece I had never read 3 leaves of that Author (& scarce any more ever since)', MS Sloane 1896, f. 20.
41. *Genius*, inclination, talent; *upon a disadvantage*, in unfavourable conditions.
42. *Take up the gauntlet*, accept the challenge.
43. *Oedipus*, who solved the riddle of the Sphinx, i.e. falsehood is found out not by noisy battle, but by establishing a space of inner quiet.
44. *Epicycle*, the smaller orbits and circles of planets in the Ptolemaic system.
45. [*Textual note:* MS, in a later hand, has 'that looseth it selfe in Greece and riseth againe in Cicilie'.]. *Arethusa*, a river that disappears underground and resurfaces overseas, Ovid, *Metamorphoses*, 5. 639–41.
46. *Extirpate*, pluck up, clear.
47. *Metempsychosis*, theory that souls migrate from animal to animal at death.
48. Plato, *Timaeus*, 39c.
49. Diogenes (of Sinope), 4th century BCE, founder of Cynics as an academic school; Timon of Philus, the sceptic philosopher, rather than Timon of Athens, the misanthrope.
50. *Arabians*, Heresy of mortalism. Rejected by Augustine, *De Haeresibus*, 1.83 (Migne, *PL*, 43.46). Ross is aghast that Browne does not think the heresy disproved by philosophy and provides seven philosophical reasons, e.g. 'The soule is a simple substance, not compounded of any principles, therefore can be resolved unto none'.
51. *Last alarum*, the apocalypse.
52. *Backward from*, reluctant to.
53. Origen (*c.*185–254 CE), Patristic theologian. Heresy cited by Augustine, *De Haeresibus*, 1.43 (Migne, *PL*, 42.33–4).
54. *Prayer for the dead*, viewed as a quintessentially Catholic practice in early modern Protestant England.
55. *Inveigle*, deceive, entice.

56. *Lawfull Councels*, Heresies and orthodoxies had been defined at a number of the formative Patristic Christian councils, beginning at Nicea, 325 CE.
57. Satan drew with him a third part of the angels, according to the standard reading of Revelation 12:4.
58. [Texual note: This section was added in the 1643 text.]
59. *Prophecy of Christ*, Matthew 24:11.
60. *Arians*, followers of Arius (250–336 CE), the primary heresy being that Jesus was not co-eternal with God, his status within the Trinity being of a different order from God's divinity. Multiple forms of Arianism sprang up over the centuries.
61. 'disposed', it might be presumed here, should be 'indisposed', but it is left as 'disposed' in all subsequent editions: at a stretch, it might be supposed that the meaning is that schismatics may have their own communities apart from the broader body, though liable to splintering.
62. *Schism…innovation*, the point of reference here is contemporary religious division and schism as much as those of the apostolic era; *complexionally propense*, naturally given to.
63. *Niceties of the schooles*, endlessly more subtle distinctions of philosophy among the scholastic, medieval schools; *expatiate*, discourse upon.
64. *Pia Mater*, membranes surrounding the brain and spinal cord.
65. *Oh altitudo*, either 'O the heights' or 'O the depths' as in Romans 11:33.
66. *Pose my apprehension*, test my understanding; *involved*, convoluted.
67. *Certum est quia impossibile est*, 'it is certain, because it is impossible', Tertullian, *De Carni Christi*, 5.
68. *Christ his sepulchre*, Luke 24:2; *Red Sea*, Exodus 14:15–31.
69. *Christ's patients*, those whom Christ healed.
70. John 20:29.
71. *Mysticall types*, the spiritual typology of the Old Testament history, believed to refer forward to the New Testament.
72. *Sword of faith*, Hebrews 4:12; *buckler*, shield, Ephesians 6:16.
73. *Platonick*, indicating, here, a not strictly rational manner, rather than in relation to Plato.
74. 'A sphere whose centre is everywhere and whose circumference nowhere.'
75. *Anima est angelus hominis, est Corpus Dei*, 'the soul is the angel of man, is the body of God'; *Entelechia;* essence; *Lux est umbra Dei*, 'light is the shadow of God'; *actus perspicui*, 'actual transparency'—i.e. he would as happily be told mysterious, allegorized versions of theological phenomena as attempts to philosophically pin them down, with obfuscatory terms such as *entelechia* and *actus perspicui*. Keck surveys in response a range of 'Ancient Philosophers touching the definition of the Soul. Thales, his was, that it is a Nature without Repose. Asclepiades, that it is an Exercitation of sence: Hesiod, that it is a thing composed of Earth

and Water; Parmenides holds, of Earth and Fire; Galen that it is Heat; Hippocrates, that it is a spirit diffused through the body: some others have held it to be Light; Plato saith, 'tis a Substance moving it self'. Digby peevishly responds: 'I should bee as well contented with his Silence, as with his telling mee it is *Actus perspicui*; unlesse hee explicate clearly to me what those words mean, which I finde very few goe about to do.'

76. *Periphrasis*, using many instead of few words; *adumbration*, foreshadowing, symbolic representation.
77. Genesis 2:4–5. Augustine in *De Genesi ad litteram* (The Literal Meaning of Genesis) explores a range of such contradictions.
78. Genesis 3:14, in which the serpent is cursed to go on its belly, implying, for some, it had previously moved upright. See *Pseudodoxia*, 1.7.
79. *Triall of the pucellage*, re. Deuteronomy 22:13–21 on testing virginity and, should the test fail, the provision of stoning the woman.
80. Genesis 3:16.
81. *Neque enim cum porticus aut me lectulus accepit, desum mihi*, Horace, *Satires*, 1.4.133–4 'for when my couch welcomes me or I stroll in the colonnade, I do not fail myself'.
82. With the one (i.e. wisdom) I amuse my understanding, with the other (i.e. eternity) I confound my understanding; *solecisme*, error, violation of rules; Keck is prompted to consider Boethius and Plato: 'touching the difference betwixt *Eternity* and *Time*, there have been great disputes amongst Philosophers'.
83. *But five days elder*, in the hexameral creation of Genesis, Time comes into being on the first day, humankind on the sixth.
84. Texual note: the Pembroke MS repeats here: 'O! Altitudo!' *Saint Pauls sanctuary*, the inscrutability of God, Romans 11.33.
85. *I am that I am*, Exodus 3:14.
86. *A thousand years*, 2 Peter 3:8.
87. *Deny a priority*, i.e. that one came before the other.
88. *Conceive the world eternall*, Aristotle, *De Caelo*, 1.10 (279b). The 'two eternities' are nature and God.
89. *Triangle, comprehended in a square*, Aristotle, *De Anima*, 2.3 (414b). The square being a more complex and complete form implies the existence of simpler forms, the triangle, just as the sensitive soul is predicated on the existence of the more coarse vegetative soul.
90. *Trinity of soules*, the three souls are different animating aspects of humanity, the vegetative, sensitive, and rational souls. On Browne's differentiating soul, faculty, subject, and substance, Digby says caustically, 'The dint of wit is not forcible enough to dissect such tough matter.'
91. *Pythagoras*, *c.*570–495 BCE. Pythagorean philosophy, as described in Diogenes Laertes and others, was substantially based on the mysteries of numbers.

92. *Beware of philosophy*, Colossians 2:8.
93. *Stenography*, shorthand.
94. The 'abysse of knowledge' is rather wonderfully mis-transcribed in the Pembroke and Landsdowne manuscripts as 'the A.B.C. of knowledge', giving an insight into early modern dictation practice.
95. *Philosophy of Hermes, that this visible world is but a picture of the invisible*, this is Pauline as much as Hermetic; cf. Romans 1:20, 'For the invisible things of him from the creation of the world are clearly seen, being understood by the things that are made'; *pourtract*, portrait; *equivocall*, ambiguous, having more than one meaning.
96. [*Textual note:* 1643 adds the section from 'Wisedome is his most beauteous attribute...' through to 'we stood in feare to know him']. *Solomon*..., 1 Kings 3:10.
97. 'Know thyself', which was inscribed on the temple of the Oracle at Delphi.
98. Moses saw the 'back parts' of God, Exodus 33:23.
99. [*Textual note:* Pembroke MS adds: 'There is no threed or line to guide us in that labyrinth.']
100. [*Textual note:* Pembroke MS has 'impressions' for 'expressions'.]
101. *Sanctum sanctorum*, Exodus 26:33, 'the holy place and the most holy' ('Holy of Holies', Vulgate).
102. [*Textual note:* The poem and everything through to the end of the section was added in the 1643 edition, beginning with 'Therefore'.]
103. See note 106 below, section 14.
104. Avoiding the fate of Icarus, a Renaissance model of presumptuous enquiry.
105. *Lord, Lord*, Matthew 7:21.
106. *Causes*, The four Aristotelian 'causes' or explanations for phenomena are: material (substance), formal (shape and form), efficient (the immediate 'cause' in the modern sense), and final (what purpose the thing exists for). See e.g. Aristotle, *Metaphysics*, 5.2 (1013b); *Physics*, 2.7 (198a). God is the underwriting 'first cause' of all. Keck: 'he speaketh in opposition to the *Manichees*, who held there were *Duo principia*; one from whom came all good, and the other from whom came all evil'.
107. *Profound further*, look more deeply into.
108. *Galen*, Roman physician, 2nd century CE. *De usu partium* (*On the Usefulness of the Parts*), a work combining anatomy and natural theology. Digby describes Galen as Browne's 'Patriarke' or guiding spirit. Franciso Suarez (1548–1617), Spanish Jesuit philosopher, author of *Metaphysicks* (1597).
109. *Natura nihil agit frustra*, 'Nature does nothing in vain'; Aristotle, *Generation of Animals*, 744a line 36 and elsewhere.
110. *Seeds and principles*, i.e. the dormant animating forces of the earth, giving rise to spontaneous generation of animals such as mice, bees, flies, infused by the sun, hence their not being carried in Noah's Ark.

111. Proverbs 6:6–8, reputedly written by Solomon: 'Go to the ant, thou sluggard; consider her ways, and be wise.' Septuagint includes bees in the adage. Spiders found at Proverbs 30:28.
112. *Little Citizens*, the models of animal society providing a template for the human polis.
113. *Regio-Montanus*, Johannes Müller von Königsberg (1436–1476), German astronomer, said to have created flying animal machines; *Cedar*, i.e. there being both vegetative and sensitive souls in the smallest of animals, but only the former in plants, however large. Keck points to Du Bartas' biblical epic *Devine Weekes & Workes* (1578, trans. 1605) as the source of Browne's interest in Regio-Montanus.
114. *Flux and reflux*, the tides; *the encrease of Nile*, its annual flooding of the fertile plains; *conversion of the needle to the North*, magnetism and the compass technology demonstrating it. All of these receive extensive treatment in *Pseudodoxia Epidemica*.
115. *Cosmography*, science of mapping or understanding relations between earth and heavens.
116. *Prodigies*, marvels; *learnes in a compendium*, i.e. man as microcosm, containing or echoing the greater macrocosm.
117. *Two books*, truths to be learned from Scripture and truths from the study of nature.
118. Joshua 10:13, on the sun miraculously standing still in its course as a sign.
119. *Hieroglyphicks*, encoded signs, encompassing natural and religious truths.
120. *Define not with the schooles, the principle of motion and rest*, Aristotle, *Physics*, 2.1 (192b).
121. Exodus 15:25, Moses having led the people into the Wilderness and finding no fresh water.
122. God as *skillful geometrician*, attributed to Plato in Plutarch, *Table Talk*, 8.2. Common in iconography and Jewish traditions.
123. To attribute to nature alone actions that God, as the director of nature, is responsible for.
124. The outward appearance reflecting inner forms is a central Platonic idea. Digby quarrels with Browne over this passage. 'That Logicke which hee quarrelleth at for calling a Toade, or a Serpent ugly, will in the end agree with his; for no body ever tooke them to be so, in respect of the Universe (in which regard, he defendeth their regularity, and Symmetry) but onely as they have relation to us.'
125. [*Textual note:* Several MSS have 'past with approbriation'.]
126. Ross comments: 'It is not their beauty, but their monstrosity and irregularity that makes them remarkable; for the eye is as soon drawn with strange and uncouth, as with beautifull objects; the one to admiration and stupiditie, the other to delight: A woman, as beautifull as

Venus, will not draw so many eyes, as if she were borne with a dogs head, and a fishes taile.'

127. *The chaos*, Genesis 1:2, though sources for imagining the nature of chaos were varied.
128. As a correlate to God as Geometrician, God here works as artist.
129. *Ephemerides*, table of astronomical planetary positions.
130. *Bezo las Manos*, lit. 'I kiss the hands', i.e. a perfunctory salute
131. *Abraham*, Genesis 22:13; *Pharaohs daughter*, Exodus 2:5; *Joseph*, Genesis 37:2–50:26; *convert a Stoick*, i.e. showing that Providence, not chance, directed events.
132. *Rubs*, obstacle or impediment; *doublings*, sudden turns; *wrench*, deceit, guile.
133. *Fougade*, a mine, i.e. the stock of gunpowder. The 'letter' was the advice to Lord Monteagle to avoid Parliament on 5 November, by which means, the plot was discovered.
134. *88,* 1588, the Spanish Armada, driven by storms from the southern shore of England.
135. *Writing upon the wall*, Balshazzar's Feast, Daniel 5:5.
136. *Holland*, gaining full independence from the Hapsburgs, by stages from 1581; *Grand Seignieur*, Ottoman emperor; *throw it into the sea*, i.e. by destroying the Dykes.
137. *Helix*, a screw-shaped spiral curve.
138. *Sortilegies*, casting lots; on saying a prayer before gambling Ross says: 'I think it is profanation, and taking of Gods Name in vaine: For, what doe you pray for? that God would prosper your game, to win your neighbours mony, to which you have no right? If *Abraham* durst scarce intercede to God for the preservation of five populous Cities, how dare you be so bold with him, as to solicite him to assist you in your idle, foolish and sinfull desires, and, in divers respects, unlawfull recreations?' Coleridge, also glossing it as a profanation adds: 'Would Sir T. Brown before weighing two pigs of Lead, *a* and *b* <pray to God> that *a* might weight the heavier? Yet if the result of the Dice be at the time equally believed to be a settled & predetermined Effect, where lies the difference?'
139. *Paint her blind*, traditional emblem of fortune.
140. 'Wise man is out of the reach of fortune', perhaps with reference to Seneca, *Epistles*, 26 'On Old Age and Death'. For the 'strumpet fortune', see *Hamlet* 2.2.489.
141. *Judiciall astrology*, predictive astrology.
142. *Supputation*, reckoning up.
143. *Homers chaine*, in *Iliad*, 8.18–26, by which Zeus suspended the cosmos.
144. *Sorites*, a set of logical propositions or accumulated syllogisms.
145. *Paire of second causes*, providence and fortune.
146. *Advisoes*, counsels, suggestions.

147. *Triumvirate*, three-person government of Rome under Mark Anthony, Octavian, and Lepidus, 43–33 BCE.
148. The final 'reason' in this phrasing is corrected by Denonain and Patrides, following the Norwich manuscript, to 'both unto faith'. All editions in Browne's lifetime, however, keep 'reason'.
149. [*Textual note:* The 1643 edition adds the passage: 'For our endeavours …' through to the end of the section.]
150. *Archidoxis*, Paracelsus' treatise on amulets; *secret sympathies*, sympathies are the natural correspondences between objects, speculatively useful in medicine; *brazen serpent*, Numbers 21:9.
151. *Fire of the altar*, Leviticus 6:13, Maccabees 1:19–36; *Elias*, 1 Kings 18:35–8. Keck points out that this should be Elijah, not Elias; *Naptha*, in Pliny, *Natural History*, 2.108.
152. *Sodom…Gomorrha*, Genesis 19:24–8.
153. *Manna*, the bread that fell from heaven in the wilderness, Exodus 16:4; *Calabria*, Josephus, *Jewish Antiquities*, 3.1.6.
154. *Difference of man from beasts*, Keck cites Lactantius, *de fals Sapienta*, ch. 10, i.e. *Institutes*, 3 (*De Falsa Sapientia*).
155. *Doctrine of Epicurus*, Diogenes Laertius, *Lives*, 10.139.1, where Epicurus is said to argue that the gods pay no attention to humans.
156. *Divinitie of the holy Ghost*, Macedonians, 4th-century sect; *deny our saviour*, referring to contemporary Socinians, as much as patristic heresies.
157. *The three impostors*, 'Moses, Christ and Mahomet', in MS note, *De tribus impostoribus* was an apocryphal statement, attributed to a wide range of writers over several centuries, postulating a grand religious fraud. Both Digby and Keck identify the author as Ochino or Bernardino Tommasino (1487–1564).
158. *Machiavell*, author of *The Prince* (*c.*1514); *Lucian*, Syrian satirist, writing in Greek (*c.*120–180 CE).
159. *Galen*, in *The soul's dependence on the Body*, 3.
160. Browne's note quotes Seneca, *Troades*, 397, 401–2, 378–9, 'There is nothing after death and death itself is nothing'; 'death…destructive to the body and unsparing of the soul'; 'we die wholly, no part of us remains,' though it should be noted that the affairs of *Troades*, the sacrifice of Trojan women, happen at the instigation of a ghost, a part, at least, remaining.
161. *Ælian or Pliny*, writers of fabulous natural histories, frequently the starting points of errors in *Pseudodoxia*; *humane Authors*, classical humanist writers.
162. *Gargantua or Bevis*, François Rabelais' raucous *Gargantua and Pantagruel* (*c.*1495–1553); Sir Bevis of Hampton, medieval romance.
163. *Sampson*, Judges 14:5–16:30.
164. *Catalogue of doubts*, a Baconian phrase in *Advancement of Learning*.

165. *Pigeon* (i.e. dove), Genesis 8:12; *Lazarus*, John 11:44.
166. *Ribbe at the resurrection*, Augustine, *City of God*, 22.14, Genesis 2:21.
167. *Rabbines*, Jewish scholars, rabbis.
168. These queries occur also in *Pseudodoxia*, 3.17, 6.2, 7.2.
169. *Tartaretus de modo Cacandi*, Rabelasian imaginary treatise, attributed to the Sorbonne theologian, Pierre Tartaret, *Of the way to Shit*.
170. *Noah...Deucalion*, version of flood story, Ovid, *Metamorphoses*, 1.376.
171. [*Textual note:* 'forcible' in Pembroke MS changes to 'foesible' in 1643]. *Arke*, Genesis 6:14–22; see too Augustine, *City of God*, 15.27; *foesible*, feasible.
172. *Honest Father*, Augustine, who addresses many of Browne's scriptural difficulties, *City of God*, 16.7.
173. *Triple continent*, Europe, Asia, and Africa.
174. *The mountaines of Ararat*, Genesis 8:4, i.e. where the Ark landed.
175. *Salve*, smooth over a difficulty.
176. [*Textual note:* 'Paradoxe' in 1643, and later editions in Browne's lifetime, is changed in Denonain and other editors to 'postulate'.]
177. *Methusalem*, i.e. Methusaleh, Genesis 5:27.
178. Matthew 27:5, Acts 1:18. [*Textual note:* Pembroke MS differs: 'That Judas hanged himself tis an absurdity & an affirmative that is not expressed in the text, but quite contrarie to the words & their externall construction; with this paradoxe I remember I netled an angrie Jesuite who had that day let this fall in his sermon, who afterwards upon a serious perusal of the text, confessed my opinion & proved a courteous friend to mee a stranger and noe enemy.'.]
179. *Babell...Shinar*, Genesis 11:4, Josephus, *Jewish Antiquities*, 1.4.2.
180. [*Textual note:* Text omitted here in 1643, has in Pembroke MS: 'to instance in one, or two', then in the 1642 unauthorized edition going on: 'as to prove the Trinity from that speech of God in the plural number faciamus hominem, Lett us make man, which is but the common style of princes and men of eminency; hee that shall reade one of his Majesties proclamations, may with the same Logicke conclude there bee two Kings in England.' Pembroke MS alone continues: 'To inferre the obedient respect of wives to their husbands from the example of Sarah, who usually called her husband Lord, which if you examine, you shall finde to be noe more then Seignior, or Mounsieur, which are the ordinarie languages all civill nations use in their familiar compellations, not to their superiors or equals, but to their inferiours also and persons of Lower condition'.]
181. Acts 12:15.
182. *Judgement of Ptolomy*, King of Egypt (283–247 BCE), cited in Josephus, *Jewish Antiquities*, 12.2.
183. *Alcoran*, the Qur'an.
184. [*Textual note:* MS adding 'superfluous repetitions'.]

185. Philo, *Life of Moses*, 2.3.
186. *Zoroaster*, Persian philosopher-magus, known from Plutarch; *writ before Moses*, e.g. Enoch's divine writings, cited sceptically in Augustine, *City of God*, 14.23.
187. *This onely*, i.e. the Scriptures.
188. *Cicero* (*c.*106–43 BCE), Roman orator and political theorist; *library of Alexandria*, great library of Egypt, widely referred to in classical world.
189. [*Textual note:* Pembroke MS adding 'the saying of the Seers and the chronicles of the Kings of Judah'.] *Perished leaves of Solomon*, re. 1 Kings 4:32.
190. *Enochs pillars*, pillars on which all the arts, sciences, and inventions of the antediluvian world were purportedly inscribed. The stone pillar was a back-up, in case the brick pillar should be destroyed by flood, according to Josephus, *Antiquities of the Jews*, 1.70–1 (1.2.3).
191. *Those three great inventions*, gunpowder, printing, and the navigational compass.
192. *Utinam*, lit. 'O that!', i.e. a wish.
193. *Pentateuch*, Genesis, Exodus, Leviticus, Numbers, Deuteronomy—but the Samaritan version contains a number of differences from Septuagint and Masoretic texts.
194. *Rabbinicall Interpretation*, the Talmud.
195. *Ethnick*, heathen.
196. *Promise of Christ*, John 10:16.
197. Christian, Jewish, Muslim, and (classical) pagan.
198. [*Textual note:* Three of the MSS have 'commendation' rather than 'condemation'.]
199. *Aristotle*, on valour as fearlessness, *Nicomachean Ethics*, 3.6–9 (1115a–1117b).
200. *That name*, i.e. martyr.
201. *Councell of Constance* (1414–18); *John Husse* (Hus) (1369–1415), Czech proto-Protestant reformer, burnt to death.
202. *Socrates* (*c.*469–399 BCE); on *the unity of God*, implying that Socrates was martyred for monotheistic beliefs.
203. *Miserable bishop*, Virgil, Bishop of Salzberg (*c.*749–784 CE), investigated for his views on the antipodes, following the Patristic writer Lactantius.
204. *Ceremony, politick points, or indifferency*, all very much live questions in the Laudian context of 1630s, when the imposition of ceremony, and argument that it was 'indifferent', incited much animosity.
205. *Miracles*, the supposition that the era of miracles had finished was a commonplace of the Protestant (but not the Catholic) reformation, and the issue became increasingly doctrinal.
206. *Jesuites*...*in the Indies*, Acosta, *Rerum a Societate Jesu* (1574).
207. *Transmutation*, transubstantiation, one of the key doctrinal differences with Protestantism.

208. *Cana*, John 2:1–10; *Devill…in the wildernesse*, Matthew 4:3.
209. *Work contradictions*, a patristic debate on God's capacity for contradiction, e.g. Jerome, *Letters*, 22.5: 'I will say it boldly, though God can do all things, He cannot raise up a virgin when once she has fallen.'
210. *Question Esdras*, 2 Esdras 4:5.
211. Texual note: This section was added in the 1643 text.
212. *Reliques,…bones…saints*, all traditionally associated with Catholicism.
213. Helena, the mother of Constantine, supposedly discovered the cross of Jesus and gave the nails to her son.
214. *Piæ fraudes*, pious frauds; *Baldwin King of Jerusalem* (1100–18 CE), after first crusade.
215. *Antient of dayes*, Daniel 7:9.
216. *Climacter*, critical period of life.
217. 1 Corinthians 13:8–10 on the cessation of prophecy.
218. Plutarch, *The Obsolescence of Oracles* in *Moralia*, vol. 5; see too *Pseudodoxia*, 7.12, *Miscellany Tracts*, 11.
219. *Dayes of Joshua*, Joshua 10:12–13; *eclipse*, at the Passion, Luke 23:44.
220. *Humane history*, classical history; *chronicle of Hester*, Book of Esther; *Magasthenes*, Greek ethnographer, especially of India (*c.*300 BCE); *Herodotus*, Greek historian (*c.*485–430 BCE).
221. *Justine*, Justinus (2nd–3rd century CE), *Epitome of the Philippic History of Pompeius Trogus*, 36.2.12, 'Sed Aegyptii, cum scabiem et uitiliginem paterentur, responso moniti eum cum aegris, ne pestis ad plures serperet, terminis Aegypti pellunt.'
222. [*Textual note:* 1643 has 'time represents', but MSS and versions after 1645 amend to 'times present represent'.]
223. [*Textual note:* 'as some will have it' added in 1643.] *Of his death also*, Deuteronomy 34:5–8, traditionally written by Moses, including a prophetic account of his own death, according to Philo, *Life of Moses*, 2.51.291.
224. Browne gave evidence to a trial for witchcraft of Amy Denny and Rose Cullender in 1662 (often wrongly stated as 1664, and wrongly spelt as Duny).
225. *Ladder and scale of creatures*, up from animals, to humans and on to angels.
226. Ross: 'A strange kind of Atheisme to deny witches! but is there such a strict relation between witches and spirits, that hee that denies the one, must needs deny the other?' Digby: 'I acknowledge ingenuously our Physicians experience hath the advantage of my Philosophy, in knowing there are witches.' Keck distinguishes between witches 'which proceed upon the principles of Nature' noting 'none have denyed that such there are' and 'Witches which co-operate with the Devil', about which he says: 'there are Divines of great note, and far from any suspition of being irreligious, that do oppose it'.

227. *Legerdemain*, trickery, sleight of hand; *changelings*, who change into animal form.
228. *Transpeciate*, change species; *convert…stones*, Matthew 4:3. See Augustine, *City of God*, 18.18.
229. *Tribe of Dan*, from Genesis 49:17.
230. [*Textual note:* 'detection' rather than 'defection' in MSS, apparently a mistake of the 1642 edition, which was carried over to the authorized 1643 copy. Three of the MSS also have a marginal note on 'maid': 'that lived without meate upon the smell of a rose'.] *Maid of Germany*, Eva Flegan from Mörs, whose fast, it was claimed, lasted from 1597 to *c.*1627.
231. Giovanni Battista Della Porta's *Magiae Naturalis* (1558) was one of many texts on the harnessing of natural rather than demonic magic; see *Pseudodoxia*, 1.10; *actives*, heat and cold; *passives*, moisture and dryness.
232. Paracelsus, *Philosophia Sagax* (1536), 1.3, 'The ascendant star reveals much to those who seek the wonders of nature, the works of God'.
233. *Noble essences…fellow-natures on earth*, i.e. angels. The closeness of humans to angelic essences is asserted in Hebrews 2:7.
234. Plato, *Timaeus*, 34b, 41d on the universal soul; *hermeticall philosophers*, with Paracelsus still in mind; Proclus, *Platonic Theology*, 1.13. Digby mentions Porphyry (*Vita Pythagorae*, 19) but is largely dismissive: 'I doubt, his discourse of an universall Spirit, is but a wilde fansie' he begins, on Browne's mixing of substance and spirit, adding: 'Assuredly one cannot erre in taking this Author for a very fine ingenious Gentleman: but for how deepe a Scholler, I leave them to judge, that are abler then I am.'
235. *Those essences*, souls, unlike bodies, not needing heat for coming into being.
236. Genesis 1:2.
237. Pythagoras' philosophical opinions come second hand, in this case, from Diogenes Laertius, *Lives of Eminent Philosophers*, 8.32; Plato, *Phaedo*, 107d–e. Keck glosses this: 'This appears by *Apuleius* a Platonist, in his book *de Deo Socratis*.'
238. But Matthew 18:10 suggests the existence of guardian angels.
239. *Salve…doubts*, resolve doubts.
240. *Manifest scale of creatures*, bearing some resemblance to the 'chain of being'.
241. [*Textual Note:* Three of the MSS have a marginal note, 'Essentia rationalis immortalis' ('a rational and immortal essence').]
242. *Porphyry*, neo-platonist Philosoher (c.235–305 CE); Digby is unhappy that Browne suggests the difference between angels and men is but '*Porphyries* difference of *Mortality* and immortality' and comments 'If he had applyed himselfe with earnest study, and upon right grounds, to

search out the nature of pure intellects' (i.e. angels) he would have known a good deal more about angelic epistemology.

243. *Numericall*, particular; *formes*, essential nature; *hypostasis*, being (often in relation to a person of the Holy Trinity).
244. *Habakkuk*, in apocryphal *Bel and the Dragon*, 36; *Philip to Azotus*, Acts 8:39–40.
245. Luke 15:10.
246. *That great father*, Augustine, *City of God*, 11.32; *fiat lux*, 'Let there be Light', Genesis 1:3. The hexameral (six-days) creation omits mention of the creation of the angels. Augustine, tentatively, and medieval philosophy after him, plays with the idea that angels are encompassed in the creation of light. Keck, however, rejecting Merryweather's reference to Augustine, considers the 'great Father' to refer to Chrysostom's *Homilies On Genesis*, as Augustine seems hardly to credit the idea he mentions.
247. *Spirituall substance*, a phrase which attracted much comment: Keck: '*Epicurus* was of this opinion, and St. *Aug.* in *Enchirid. ad Laurentium*', i.e. Augustine, *Enchiridion*, 58–60; Ross: 'And if your light may be an Angel, that must needs be an Angell of light. What a skipping Angell will *ignis fatuus* make? The Chandlers and Bakers trades are honourable; those can make lights, which may in time become Angels; these wafers, which in time become gods.' Digby refers his reader and dedicatee to his own forthcoming work on the subject: 'to set downe such Phænomena's of it as I have observed, and from whence I evidently collect the nature of it; were too large a Theame for this place; when your Lordshippe pleaseth I shall shew you another more orderly discourse upon that Subject; wherein I have sufficiently proved it to be a solid Substance and body.'
248. *The best part of nothing*, i.e. having been made *ex nihilo*, out of nothing.
249. *Amphibious*, sharing in the qualities of 'corporall and spirituall', i.e. from amphibians, capable of living on both land and sea.
250. Genesis 1:26.
251. *Microcosme*, a ubiquitous Renaissance trope and idea, that the cosmos is constructed by mirror-like forms, man being duplicated in the celestial realm.
252. *Preferred*, elevated.
253. *Five kinds of existences*, the rude chaos, plants, animals, man, spirits.
254. [*Textual note:* The 'no' here appears in the Pembroke MS, but not the printed text.] Moses' omission of invisible things (including angels) in creation is much commented upon.
255. *Egyptians*, Acts 7:22 and more expansively, the supposition that he encoded the scriptural text with not only literal but 'hieroglyphicall' levels of meaning.

256. *First moveable*, outer celestial sphere in Ptolemaic and scholastic cosmology, the *primum mobile*.
257. Cf. Milton, *Paradise Lost*, 4.677–8, 'Millions of spiritual creatures walk the earth Unseen'.
258. *Corpulency*, physical substance.
259. *Habitation of angels*, Digby, exasperated, says of this series of speculations, 'it putteth me in minde of one of the titles in *Pantagruels* Library', Rabelais' library of nonsense book titles. Ross begins 'This Section consists of divers errours' and goes on to list an extensive series of metaphysical slippages.
260. *Ministring spirits*, Hebrews 1:14.
261. Proverbs 16:4.
262. Genesis 9:9–17, God's swearing so after the flood.
263. Aristotle, *De Caelo*, 1.10 (279b).
264. [*Textual note:* Pembroke MS adds, 'who saw noe futher than the first matter'.]
265. *Decided*, resolved.
266. [*Textual note:* From 'and herein is divinity...' to the end was added in 1643.] Coleridge comments: 'An excellent *Burlesque* on some parts of the Schoolmen, tho' I fear an unintentional one'; *Omneity*, comprising everything; *nullity*, nothingness.
267. [*Textual note:* Sections 36 and 48 (as they appear in this text) are emended from the 1643 text, where the previous section number is repeated, hence subsequent numbers are similarly out of kilter.]
268. Genesis 2:7.
269. *These two affections*, i.e. the properties of incorruptibility and immortality, Plato, *Phaedrus*, 245c–e, Aristotle, *de Anima*, 2.4 (415b).
270. *Auditories*, assemblies.
271. Paracelsus, *De Natura Rerum* (1573), 1; *traduction*, the transmission of the soul from the parent to the child, as opposed to its 'infusion' direct by God—a much-debated question in early modern theories of generation; *antimetathesis*, used in the sense of *chiasmus*, the grammatical structure in which the terms are repeated in reverse; *creando infunditur, infundendo creatur*, 'in creation it is infused, in infusion it is created'.
272. *Equivocall*, ambiguous, with the sense of dubious.
273. This refers, gruesomely, to the deformities that so fascinated early modern Europe.
274. *Inorganicall*, not being specifically located in an organ.
275. *Crasis*, blending.
276. *Cranie*, skull.
277. *All flesh is grasse*, Isaiah 40:6.
278. *Antropophagi,* flesh-eating race, Pliny, *Natural History*, 7.2.
279. *Metempsychosis*, the reincarnation of the soul in different animals.

280. *Lots Wife*, Genesis 19:26; *Nabuchodonosor*, i.e. Nebuchadnezzar, Daniel 4:33, whose hair and nails became like those of wild animals.
281. *Materialled*, embodied.
282. Digby discusses ghosts at length, 'the strange effect which is frequently seen in England, when at the approach of the Murderer, the slaine body suddainely bleedeth afresh'.
283. *Quid fecisti*, 'O Adam, what hast thou done?', 2 Esdras 7:48.
284. *Vespilloes*, night-time body-bearers of the dead.
285. [*Textual note:* 1643 text has 'imagine I could ever dye'.]
286. [*Textual note:* 'defie death' is often replaced by 'desire death', though editions from 1643 to 1656 have the latter, and after the 1659 editions revert to it from 1669. MSS also follow this phrase with 'It is a symptom of melancholy to be afraid of death, yet sometimes to desire it; this latter I have often discovered in my selfe, and think no man ever desired life, as I have sometimes death'.]
287. Digby is uncharacteristically enamoured by the passage: 'I must needs acknowldge that where he ballanceth life and death against one another and considereth that the latter is to bee a kinde of nothing for a moment, to become a pure Spirit within one instant, and what followeth of this strong thought; is extreame handsomely said, and argueth very gallant and generous resolutions in him.'
288. [*Textual note:* MSS have 'too careless' for 'hopeless'.]
289. *30 years old*, the age at which Jesus began his ministry.
290. *Within the bosome of our causes*, i.e. with God.
291. *Secondine*, the afterbirth, though here the body itself, being the afterbirth to the soul.
292. *Ineffable place*, 2 Corinthians 12:4; *ubi*, place.
293. [*Textual note:* Several, but not all of the manuscripts render this: 'nothing else but the perfectest exaltation of God'.]
294. *Philosophers stone*, Ross: 'You see then what a bad Schoole-master the *Philosophers Stone* is, which hath taught so many to make shipwrack of their estates, and you of the soules immortalitie'; *exaltation of gold*, refining into gold.
295. [*Textual note:* Pembroke MS adds: 'I have therefore forsaken those strict definitions of death by privation of life, extinction of naturall heate, separation etc. of soul and body, and have fram'd one in an hermeticall way unto mine own fancie: *est mutatio ultima qua perficitur nobile illud extractum Microcosmi* ['Death is the final change, by which that noble part of the microcosm is perfected'], for to mee that consider things in a naturall and experimental way, man seems to bee but a digestion, or a preparative way unto that last and glorious elixir which lies imprison'd in the chains of flesh. &c.']
296. *Quantum mutatus ab illo!* 'How changed from that (Hector)!' Aeneas, on seeing Hector in Hades, Virgil, *Aeneid*, 2.274.

297. *Progenies*, descendants, children.
298. Cicero, *Tusculan Disputations*, 1.43.
299. Lucan, *Pharsalia*, 7.819; *Cælo tegitur*...'He is covered by the sky, who lacks an urn.'
300. *Envie...crowes*, Cicero, *Tusculan Disputations*, 3.28. The longevity of these birds is suggested in Pliny, *Natural History*, 7.48.
301. [*Textual note:* Several MSS add as marginalia to 'Jubilee': 'The Jewish computation for 50 years' and to 'Saturne': 'The Planet of Saturne makes his revolution once in 30 years'.]
302. The three Holy Roman Emperors are Rudolph II (d.1612), Matthias (d. 1619), and Ferdinand II (d. 1637). The 'grand signiours' are Ahmed I (d. 1617), Mustapha I (who was deposed 1622, d. 1639), Osman II (d. 1622), and Murad IV (d. 1640). The Popes are Leo XI (d. 1605), Paul V (d. 1621), Gregory XV (d. 1623), and Urban VIII (d. 1644). Digby comments: 'What should I say of his making so particular a narration of personall things, and private thoughts of his owne; the knowledge whereof cannot much conduce to any mans betterment? (which I make account is the chiefe end of his writing this discourse).'
303. *Canicular days*, Dog-days, 3 July–11 August, thought to be the most likely time to die; see *Pseudodoxia*, 4.13.
304. *Methuselah*, Genesis 5:27.
305. *Incurvate*, bend, skew.
306. [*Textual note:* The following is in the MSS, and also the 1642 unauthorized edition, but removed from the 1643 copy: 'The course and order of my life would be a very death unto another; I use my selfe to all dyets, humours, aires, hunger, thirst, cold, heate, want, plenty, necessity, dangers, hazards; when I am cold, I cure not my selfe by heate; when sicke, not by physicke; those that know how I live may justly say, I regard not life, nor stand in fear of death.']
307. Cicero, *On Old Age*, 23.84.
308. *Vitiosity*, depravity.
309. *Æsons bath*, restoring his youth, Ovid, *Metamorphoses*, 7:159–294; *threescore*, 60.
310. [*Texual note:* This section was added in the 1643 text.]
311. *Radicall humour*, the juice and fluid of animals or plants, hence 'radical' in the sense of 'root'; *seventie*, traditional biblical length of life, of threescore and ten, Psalms 90:10.
312. *Found themselves*, i.e., base their ideas; *balsome*, preservative essence; *sulphur*, central Paracelsian element.
313. *Glome or bottome*, skein or ball of yarn, referring to the Three Fates, Hesiod, *Theogony*, 221.
314. *Six thousand*, being the apparent date of the end of the world, see *Pseudodoxia*, 6.1.
315. *Antipathies*, malign influences; *occult qualities*, non-material influences.

316. *Construe*, i.e. parse the sentence into its grammatical parts.
317. Lucan, *Pharsalia*, 4.519–20.
318. *Zeno* (of Citium), *c.*300 BCE, founder of stoic school, Diogenes Laertius, book 7.
319. *Cato*, enemy of Caesar, committing suicide in 46 BCE.
320. *Curtius*, rode into chasm as self-sacrifice, Livy, *History of Rome*, 7.6; *Scevola*, soldier, indifferent to death, Livy, *History of Rome*, 2.12; *Codrus*, King of Athens, Cicero, *Tusculan Disputations*, 1.48; *Job*, refusing to take his wife's injunction to 'curse God and die', Job 2:9–10.
321. Cicero, *Tusculan Disputations*, 1.8.
322. *Cæsars religion*, Suetonius, *Julius Caesar*, 87.
323. [*Textual note:* MSS add 'That tyme when the moone is in conjunction and obscured by the Sunne, the Astrologers call *horæ combustæ*'.]
324. *Morall acceptions*, i.e. interpreting the terms in an allegorical (moral) rather than literal sense.
325. *Memento mori*; a reminder of death (lit. 'Remember you will die'); *memento quatuor novissima*, 'Remember the four last things'.
326. *Radamanth*, the judge of the dead, in Greek mythology.
327. Lucan, *Pharsalia*, 7.814–15.
328. [*Textual note:* Altered from 'I beleeve' of all MSS, as well as the pirated 1642 edition.]
329. For example, Psalms 96:13, Acts 10:42, 17:31; 2 Peter 3:7. Ross comments 'It seemes then, that, in your opinion, the Scripture speaks here *mystically*' and gives a series of reasons why 'Christ shall, in a *judiciary* way, come as a *Judge*', including the sheer pleasure of seeing one's enemies damned: 'this visible proceeding will be more satisfactory to the *Saints*, who shall see their desire upon their enemies, and vengeance really executed on those that afflicted them'.
330. See comparable suggestions in *Pseudodoxia*, 1.9.
331. *Convincible and statute madnesse*, liable to lead to conviction for lunacy.
332. See *Pseudodoxia*, 6.1; *denyed unto his angels*, Matthew 24:36. Keck says: 'Lactantius is very positive that the world should last but 6000 years', *De Divino Præmio*, 14.
333. [*Textual note:* MSS 'The Oracle of Apollo'.] *Amphibology*, use of ambiguous terms.
334. Matthew 24:11.
335. [*Textual note:* Pembroke MS adds: 'Those prognosticks of Scripture are obscure; I know not how to construe them'.]
336. Matthew 24:6; Luke 21:9; Mark 13:7.
337. *Signes in the moone*, Luke 21:25; *theefe in the night*, 1 Thessalonians 5:2.
338. *Revelation of Antichrist*, 1 John 2:18; 2 Thessalonians 2:3.
339. [*Textual note:* Added in 1643, 'in our common compute…half of opinion'; the MSS, with slight variations add 'ommitting those ridiculous anagrams' then in the margin 'whereby men labour to prove the Pope

Antichrist from the name making up the number of the Beast...I am half of Paracelsus opinion and think that Antichrist is ...']

340. *Quousque Domine*, Revelation 6:10.

341. i.e. the day of judgement.

342. *Ipsa sui pretium virtus sibi*, a paraphrase of Seneca, *De Vita Beata*, in *Moral Essays*, 9.4.

343. See Seneca, *Epistulae Morales*, 25. Digby is somewhat scathing of the tenor of Browne's argument, 'To bee vertuous for hope of a reward, and through feare of punishment'.

344. *Livery*, the insignia and uniform of a household, or here perhaps, clerical dress.

345. *Impieties*, instances of mocking the gods, committed in the belief that there is no afterlife; Lucian, *The Lover of Lies*; Euripedes, *The Madness of Hercules*; *Julian*, Julian the Apostate (332–363 CE), Roman emperor who rejected the Christianity of his predecessor, Constantine. Keck cites Augustine, on the same topic, *City of God*, 6.16.

346. Isaiah 26:19, Revelation 29:13.

347. *Conversion of the needle*, movement of compass needle, see *Pseudodoxia*, 2.2–3.

348. Augustine, *City of God*, 22:20. Digby: 'But to come to the Resurrection. Methinkes it is but a grosse conception to thinke that every Atome of the present individuall matter of a body; every graine of Ashes of a burned Cadaver, scattered by the wind throughout the world, and after numerous variations changed peradventure into the body of another man; should at the sounding of the last Trumpet be raked together againe from all the corners of the earth, and be made up anew into the same Body it was before of the first man.'

349. *Separation of that confused masse*, i.e. out of the chaos.

350. [*Textual note:* The 1643 edition omits the following, found in the MSS and the 1642 version: 'What is made to be immortall, Nature cannot, nor will the voyce of God, destroy. These bodies that wee behold to perish, were in their created natures immortall, and liable unto death but accidentally and upon forfeit; and therefore they owe not that naturall homage unto death as other creatures, but may be restored to immortality with a lesser miracle, and by a bare and easie revocation of the curse return immortall.']

351. *Mercury*, quicksilver, a liquescent metal; *mortified*, dissolved in caustic substance; *numericall selfe*, an undivided identity.

352. *Schoole philosopher*, scholastic; *sensible Artist*, empirical, with 'artist' having the meaning of scientist. On Browne's idea of form and matter, Ross has a long series of objections, beginning: 'if the forme of the plant be there still, then it is not consumed. Secondly, then Philosophy deceives us, in telling us, that the matter is onely eternall, and the formes perishing. Thirdly, then Art and Nature is all one, both being

able to introduce, or, rather, educe a substantiall forme. Fourthly, then the radicall moisture and naturall heat, without which the forme hath no subsistence in the plant, is not consumed by the fire, but in spight of all its heat, lurkes within the ashes …'

353. [*Textual note:* Pembroke MS: 'revivify' for 'revive'.] Taken up by Digby in *A discourse concerning the vegetation of plants spoken by Sir Kenelme Digby* (1661).
354. Ezekiel 37:1.
355. 1 Corinthians 2:9.
356. *Translated*, conveyed to heaven without dying.
357. *Saint Johns description*, Revelation 21:19–21.
358. *Sensible*, material.
359. 2 Corinthians 12:4.
360. *Empyreall…tenth spheare*, outer Ptolemaic sphere, beyond which was heaven. Ross objects: 'Though it be true, that where Gods presence is, there is *Heaven*; yet wee must not therefore thinke, that there is not a peculiar *ubi* of blisse and happinesse beyond the tenth *Sphere*, wherein God doth more manifestly shew his glory and presence, then any where else, as you seeme to intimate.'
361. [*Textual note:* Pembroke MS has 'or place exempt from the naturall affection of bodies'.]
362. Exodus 33:17; *learning of the Egyptians*, Acts 7:22.
363. *Dives…Lazarus*, parable at Luke 16:19–31; *perspective*, telescope.
364. *Visible species*, image; *Aristotles philosophy*, in *De Anima* 2.7.
365. Revelation 21:8.
366. *Textuarie*, authoritative.
367. [*Textual note:* Three MSS have: 'Calcination a chymicall terme for the reduction of a mineral into powder'.] *Ignition and liquation*, catching fire and melting; *golden calfe*, Exodus 32:20, Deuteronomy 9:21.
368. [*Textual note:* Pembroke MS has: 'neither in its substance, weight or virtue'.]
369. *Vitrification*, reducing to glass by heat.
370. [*Textual note:* 1643 copy leaves out, 'yea and urge Scripture for it', from MSS and 1642 edition.]
371. *Chymicks*, chemists, alchemists; *facetiously* has the sense of 'polished, elegantly' rather than 'flippantly'; *reverberated*, heat forced back upon the glass.
372. *Epitome*, the microcosmic object summing up the macrocosm, usually man.
373. *Compendium of the sixth day*, i.e. man.
374. *Mahomet…heaven*, a sensual paradise, cf. *Pseudodoxia*, 1.3.
375. *Textual note:* From here to the end of the section introduced in 1643 edition.]
376. *Flaming mountaines*, volcanoes.

377. *Legion*, Mark 5:9.
378. *Anaxagoras*, Greek philosopher, 5th century BCE. Keck comments: 'I assure my self that this is false printed, and that instead of *Anaxagoras* it should be *Anaxarchus*; for *Anaxagoras* is reckon'd amongst those Philosophers that maintain'd the Unity of the world, but *Anaxarchus* (according to the opinion of *Epicurus*) held there were infinite Worlds.' It was, more likely, Anaximander whom Browne had in memory; see Augustine, *City of God*, 7.2.
379. *Ubi*, location.
380. *Impassible*, incapable of suffering, not subject to emotion.
381. [*Texual note:* Instead of 'a fine', Pembroke MS has 'a boxe of the eare'.]
382. Cf. Dante, whose Virgil finds in the outer circle of Hell those who were worthy, but unbaptized, *Inferno*, 4.
383. Romans 9:20–1.
384. *Aristotle transgressed the rule of his owne Ethicks*, re *Nicomachean Ethics*, 7.10.1–3, for his friendship with the tyrant, Hermeais. Keck suggests other transgressions: 'Aristotle is said to have been guilty of great vanity in his clothes, of incontinency, of unfaithfulness to his Master Alexander.'
385. *Phalaris his bull*, Brass Bull used by Sicilian tyrant to roast men in, Cicero, *Verrine Orations*, 4.73.
386. *Scepticks*, Keck adds: 'The ancient Philosophers are divided into three sorts, *Dogmatici*, *Academici*, *Sceptici*; the first were those that delivered their opinions positively; the second left a liberty in disputing *pro* & *contra*; the third declared that there was no knowledge of any thing, no not of this very proposition, that there is no knowledge.' See, for instance, Aulus Gellius, *Attic Nights*, 11.5.
387. *Diogenes*, Lucian, *Dialogue of the Dead*, 13, in conversation with Alexander.
388. Annual Venetian ritual marriage; Keck: 'The Duke and Senate yearly on *Ascension-day* use to go in their best attire to the Haven at *Lido,* and there by throwing a Ring into the water, do take the Sea as their spouse.'
389. *Philosopher that threw his money*, Crates the Cynic, in Diogenes Laertius, *Lives of the Philosophers*, 6.87.
390. *Compleat armour*, Ephesians 6:13; *vennie*, a hit in fencing.
391. *Chiron*, wisest of centaurs.
392. 1 Timothy 2:3–4; Matthew 7:14.
393. [*Texual note:* This section was added in the 1643 text.]
394. i.e. 'when hee [had] not subdued'; *Strabo's cloake*, Strabo (*c.*64 bce–24 CE), Greek geographer describing Europe upon the map like a spread chlamys or tunic, *Geographia* 2.5.14; *Alexander*, the Great (356–323 BCE), Keck corrects Browne: 'it is not *Europe*, but the known part of the world that *Strabo* resembleth to a Cloak'.

395. *Peregrinations*, travels; *reformed*, Protestant; *lawfull councells*, with variants, this might include the two councils of Nicaea (325 and 787 CE), three councils of Constantinople (381, 553, 680 CE), two of Ephesus (431 and 449), and Chalcedon (451); *nonage*, youth.
396. *Number of elect*, Matthew 13:20; Revelation 7:4.
397. *Sub-reformists and sectaries*, those who demanded further reform of Protestant churches; *Atomist*, being either atheist materialists or perhaps Adamists, an unlikely sect advocating free love and nakedness; *Familist*, Family of Love, revolutionary mystics.
398. *Reprobated*, destined (or predestined) to hell; *elected*, saved.
399. *Prognostick*, predict; *compasse the earth*, what Satan has been doing before his bet with God, Job 1:7.
400. *Rigid application of the law*, Solomon's sins including idolatry and the introduction of foreign Gods. Alternatively this may be damnation because not baptized, Romans 2:12. Keck: 'St. Aug. upon Psalm 126 and in many other places, holds that Solomon is damned; of the same opinion is Lyra.'
401. [*Textual note:* Norwich MS has 'Law of God'.]
402. *Eye of the needle*, Matthew 19:24.
403. *Little flocke*, Luke 12:32.
404. [*Textual note:* Some MSS have 'how much' instead of 'how little'.]
405. Philippians 2:12.
406. *Beneplacit*, good grace.
407. *Before Abraham was, I am*, John 8:58.
408. *Insolent zeales*, zealots.
409. *Midianites*, Judges 7:4–7.
410. *Mustard seed*, Matthew 17:20.
411. 1 Corinthians 13:13.
412. *Eighth Climate*, a sub-division of latitude.
413. Apparently returning from Ireland, 1629.
414. [*Textual note:* Removing from 1642 copy 'neither plant, animal nor spirit'.]
415. *Hydra*, nine-headed water-monster who, having a head cut off, grew two more.
416. Browne has Proverbs 1:7 in mind.
417. *Mechanickes*, labourers, working class.
418. *Doradoes*, the wealthy (gilded men).
419. *Bias*, in bowls, the predisposition of the ball to run obliquely.
420. *Inoculation…graftes*, inserting the bud of a plant under the bark of another to produce breeds artificially.
421. [*Textual note:* 1678 edition changes to 'I give no almes only to satisfie'.]
422. *His that enjoyned it*, i.e. not for the person begging, but for God. Digby objects: 'Methinkes, he beginneth with somewhat an affected discourse to prove his naturall inclination to Charity which vertue is the intended

Theame of all the remainder of his discourse.' Browne is 'like one in the vulgar throng, that considereth God as a Judge, & as a rewarder or a punisher. Whereas, perfect Charity, is that vehement love of God for his own sake, for his goodnesse, for his beauty, for his excellency that carrieth all the motions of our Soule directly and violently to him.'

423. [*Texual note:* Pembroke MS adding 'buy out of God a faculty to bee exempted from it'.]

424. *Eleemosynaries*, beggars.

425. *Physiognomy*, the study of facial features to determine character, with reference perhaps to Giambattista della Porta, *De humana physiognomonia* (1586).

426. *Signatures*, an inwritten mark, by which properties of an object might be determined.

427. *Phytognomy*, discovering the properties and qualities of a plant from its appearance.

428. *Cals the starres by their names*, Psalms 147:4; *Adam…name*, Genesis 2:19–20.

429. *A la volee*, at random.

430. *Aristotle…booke of physiognomy*, attributed wrongly; *chiromancy*, divination by the hand, palmistry.

431. [*Textual note*: In the two 1642 editions, instead of 1643 'neerer', one has 'never' and the other has 'ever'.]

432. *Vagabond and counterfeit Egyptians*, gypsies, commonly elided in the period with Egyptians.

433. i/j and u/v regarded as interchangeable, hence 24 letters instead of 26.

434. *Portract*, portrait.

435. *Limbe*, limn, draw, sketch.

436. [*Textual note:* Pembroke MS includes: 'I rather wonder how almost all plants being of one color, yet should be all different herein and their severall kinds distinguished in one accident of vert.'] *Copy*, being firstly the painter's model, and secondly the 'form' or ideal pattern.

437. Beggar of parable at Luke 16:20.

438. *Caitif*, vile, base, mean.

439. Digby comments: 'Shall I commend or censure our Author for beleeving so well of his acquired knowledg as to be dejected at the thought of not being able to leave it a Legacy among his friends? Or shall I examine whether it be not a high injury to wise and gallant Princes, who out of the generousnesse and noblenesse of their Nature doe patronize arts and learned men, to impute their so doing to vanity of desiring praise, or to feare of reproach?'

440. [*Textual note:* 1643 seems to mispunctuate 'lawes of charity in all disputes'.]

441. *Βατραχομυομαχία*, 'Battle of the Frogs and Mice', attributed to Homer; Lucian, *The Consonants at Law*, in which a lawsuit is launched over words stolen by one consonant from another.
442. [*Textual note:* MSS and 1642 include 'how many Synods have been assembled and angerly broke up about a line in *Propria quae Maribus*'.]
443. *Priscian*, Latin Grammarian, *c.*500 CE; to 'break Priscian's head' meant poor grammar.
444. *Si foret in terris*... 'Were Democritus still on earth, he would laugh', Horace, *Epistles*, 2.1.194.
445. *Militants*, combatants.
446. *Actius his razor*, Browne's MS Margin: 'That cut a whetsone in two'; Livy, *History of Rome*, 1.36, in which Tarquin challenges the augur to prove himself by doing what Tarquin was thinking, to cut the whetstone.
447. *Basilisco*, cannon, named after the basilisk; see *Pseudodoxia*, 3.7.
448. A misquotation of du Bellay's Sonnet 68 in *Les Regrets* (1558):

> The rebel Englishman and the swaggering Scot,
> The buggering Italian and the mad Frenchman,
> The cowardly Roman and the thief of Gascon,
> The arrogant Spaniard and the drunken German

449. Titus 1:12.
450. Keck considers which bloody thought or action Browne might have in mind: 'I suppose he alludes to that passage in Sueton, in the life of Nero, where he relates that a certain person upon a time, spoke in his hearing these words, When I am dead let Earth be mingled with Fire. Whereupon the Emperour uttered these words, Yea whilst I live.'
451. *Democritus* (*c.*460–370 BCE), Greek Atomist philosopher; *Heraclitus* (*c.*500 BCE), melancholic philosopher of flux.
452. *Prophan'd*, here made available, but also tainted.
453. *Inundation*, flood (of sin).
454. *Reprehension*, reprimand.
455. *Derived*, secondary, i.e. reflected; *trajection of a sensible species*, emission of image; *accidents*, attributes or outward property of something, rather than its essence.
456. *Non occides*, Thou shalt not Kill (Exodus 20:13).
457. *Atropos*, oldest of three Fates, who held and finally cut the threads of each person's life.
458. Genesis 4:8.
459. *Impostures*, i.e. impostors.
460. *Affliction of Job*, Job 4:5.
461. [*Textual note:* Pembroke MS, 'within its owne banks'].
462. *Dimension*, i.e. that anything measureable can be cut.
463. *Engrosse*, absorb.

464. [*Textual note:* Pembroke MS includes 'Nysus and Euralus'.]
465. *Damon and Pythias*, Cicero, *On Duties*, 3.45, being prepared to die for the other; *Achilles and Patroclus*, heroes of the Iliad, the latter's death causing Achilles to rouse himself from his epic sulk.
466. 'Honour thy father and thy mother', Exodus 20:12.
467. [*Textual note:* Pembroke MS adds 'These individuall sypathies are stronger and from a more powerfull hand then those specificall unions.']
468. *Two natures in one person*, Christ as divine and human; *three persons in one nature*, the Trinity.
469. *Story of the Italian*, 'who after he had inveigled his enemy to disclaime his faith for the redemption of his life, did presently poyniard him, to prevent repentance, and assure his eternall death', *Pseudodoxia*, 7.19.
470. *Antipathies*, instinctual dislikes.
471. *Buffet Saint Paul*, 2 Corinthians 12:7; *at sharpe*, i.e. not at play, as in fencing, but with intent to wound.
472. *Battell of Lepanto*, against Turks, 1571, the decisive battle.
473. *Dastards mee*, makes me a coward.
474. *Peccadillo*, small fault.
475. *Our corruption*, i.e. the Fall.
476. *Viciosities*, noun form of 'vicious'.
477. *Lecher that carnald with a statua*, had sex with a statue, Suetonius, *Tiberius*, 43: the Loeb editor apparently could not bring himself to translate this and repeats the two sections in Latin; *spintrian recreations,* sex, esp. anal sex between three or more people.
478. e.g. with Galileo's discoveries, *c.*1610.
479. *Quotidian*, ordinary, daily.
480. [*Textual note:* 'of my self' absent in 1643, but in all MSS and editions from 1645.]
481. [*Textual note:* MSS and 1642 add 'that I detest mine own nature, and in my retired imaginations cannot withhold my hands from violence on my self,'.]
482. i.e. the macrocosm.
483. *Whose rebellions once masters*, i.e. once those rebellions are masters.
484. Ross takes Browne to task sternly: '*You thank God, you have escaped pride, the mortall enemy to charity*. So did the Pharisee thank God, that hee was no extortioner; yet hee went home unjustified. *Pride* is a more subtle sin then you conceive; it thrusts it selfe upon our best actions: as praying, fasting, almes-giving...And have you not pride, in thinking you have no pride?'; *not circumscribed*, 'not' added in editions after 1643.
485. *Toure*, tower; *construction*, i.e. how it is construed, grammatically speaking, or explained.
486. *Six languages*, i.e. six modern languages, not including Latin and some Greek; the list is, probably, French, Italian, Spanish, Portuguese, Dutch, and Danish.

487. *Chorography...topography*, chorography is the description of regions, while topography tends to describe particular places.
488. *Prating*, talk and boast overmuch; *poynters*, the stars in the Great Bear that form a line pointing to the North Star.
489. *Simpled*, collect medicinal herbs; *Cheap-side*, where Browne was brought up, but also the site where London merchants sold herbs.
490. *Opinion of Socrates*, Plato, *Apology*, 21d.
491. *Riddle of the fisherman*, reputed to have told Homer, as Keck puts it, 'this Enigmatical answer, That what they had taken, they had left behind them; and what they had not taken, they had with them'. Having found no fish, they had taken to de-lousing themselves and were instead referring to the lice. Homer, unable to solve the riddle, pined away and died. Keck cites Plutarch and Pliny, *Letters*, 9.36; see *Pseudodoxia*, 7.13.
492. *Aristotle*, see *Pseudodoxia*, 7.13; *flux and reflux*, tides; *Euripus*, strait between Aegean Sea and Greek mainland.
493. *Janus*, double-faced God. Digby is dismissive of such a conclusion that philosophy leads to scepticism: 'It is no small misfortune to him, that after so much time spent, and so many places visited in curious search by travelling after the acquisition of so many languages; after the wading so deepe in Sciences, as appeareth by the ample Inventory and particular hee maketh of himselfe: The result of all this, should bee to professe ingenuously he had studyed enough, onely to become a Sceptike.'
494. Ecclesiastes 8:16–17.
495. [*Textual note:* MSS and 1642 have 'am resolved never to be married twice.']
496. [*Textual note:* Pembroke has: 'The whole woman was made for man.']
497. Genesis 2:21–3.
498. [*Textual note:* MSS and 1642, 'I could wish' instead of 'I could be content'].
499. A much commented upon passage. Keck cites Hippocrates as a 'Physitian long before the Author, that was of the same opinion' and adds 'so of late time was Paracelsus, who did undertake to prescribe a way for the generation of a man without coition'. Ross concludes, 'You let your pen run too much at randome: the way in which Wisdome it selfe hath appointed to multiply mankind, and propagate the Church, cannot be foolish; if it be in your esteem, remember that the foolishnesse of God is wiser then the wisdome of man: for, as great folly as you think coition to be, without it you could not have been; and surely, there had been no other way in Paradise to propagate man.' James Howell in 1645 considers it 'a most unmanly thing'. Digby, addressing the Earl of Dorset, comments: 'But I believe your Lordship will scarcely joyne with him in his wish that wee might procreate and beget Children without the helpe of women or without any conjunction or commerce with that sweete, and bewitching Sex.'

500. Kepler's *Harmonices Mundi* (1619) was the popular scientific revivification of a classical idea.
501. [*Textual note:* MSS and 1642, 'our church music';] *declaime against all church musicke*, as part of the anti-Laudian reforms, church music being seen as a distracting presence from worship.
502. [*Textual note:* MSS and 1643 have 'my maker' in place of 'the first composer'.]
503. *Fit*, canto or section of song.
504. [*Textual note:* Pembroke MS includes 'It unites the ligaments of my frame, takes me to pieces, dilates me out of my self, and by degrees, me thinks, resolves me into Heaven.']
505. Plato, *Phaedo*, 86b–c.
506. Tacitus, *Annals*, 1.1, 'Rome at the outset was a city state under the government of kings.'
507. 'in which I am not tainted by mediocrity', Cicero, *Pro Archia Poeta* (*c.*62 bce), speech in defence of the poet, Archias.
508. *Unchristian desires of my profession*, i.e. more disasters meaning more trade for doctors.
509. *Revolve*, continually think on; *ephemerides, and almanacks*, to predict astrological events; *aspects...conjunctions*, astrological positions of planets.
510. *Husbandman*, farmer.
511. *Holy Ghost*, Matthew 12:31–2, Luke 12:10.
512. *Pils*, i.e. pills.
513. *Magnæ virtutes nec minora vitia*, Plutarch, *Demetrius*, 1.7, 'great natures exhibit great vices, as well as great virtues'.
514. *Antiperistasis*, opposition, contrariness.
515. *Balsams*, naturally soothing ointments.
516. *Deleterious*, destructive.
517. *The man without a navel*, Adam: see *Pseudodoxia*, 5.5. Keck: 'for the Author means *Adam,* and by a Metonymie original sin'.
518. *Nunquam minus solus quam cum solus*, 'Never less lonely than when he was alone', Cicero, *On Duties*, 3.1.1. Digby: 'and how farre from solitude, any man is in a wildernesse; These are (in his discourse) but æquivocall considerations of Good, and of Lonelinesse: nor are they any wayes pertinent to the morality of that part where he treateth of them.'
519. *Dissimilary*, dissimilar; *concourse*, coming together with.
520. [*Textual note:* Pembroke MS has 'and though I seem on earth to stand, on tiptoe in heaven'. From this point down to 'the alphabet of man' is an addition in the 1643 edition.] *Atlas his shoulders*, Atlas, who held up the heavens.
521. *Three hundred and sixty*, i.e. 360.

522. *Before the elements*, Ross comments 'That something must be the soule:' but goes on to argue that this is not possible as we know the body precedes the soul: 'which, though Plato and Origen thought was before the body, yet we know the contrary: for God first made the body, and then inspired it with a soule. To give existence to the soule before the body, can stand neither [with] the perfection of Gods workes in the creation, nor with the dignity and quality of the soule.'
523. Genesis 1:26–7.
524. [*Textual note:* the 1643 edition removes the MSS and 1642 comment: 'I have that in me that can convert poverty into riches, transforme adversity into prosperity: I am more invulnerable than Achilles; Fortune hath not one place to hit me.']
525. *Ruat cœlum Fiat voluntas tua*, 'Though the heavens fall, thy will be done.'
526. [*Textual note:* 1643 leaves out the following (in MSS and 1642):'with this I can bee a king without a crowne, rich without a stiver, in heaven though on earth, enjoy my friend, and embrace him at a distance, when I cannot behold him'.]
527. *Melancholy conceite*, melancholy being a much debated medical term for a spectrum of mental dispositions, from depression to compulsion to madness.
528. [*Textual note:* MSS and 1642 have 'earthie' for 'watery'.]
529. Digby, 'I have much adoe to believe what he speaketh confidently: that hee is more beholding to Morpheus for Learned and rationall, as well as pleasing Dreames; then to Mercury for smart and facetious conceptions; whom Saturne (it seemeth by his relation) hath looked asquint upon in his geniture.'
530. *Galliardize*, revelry.
531. Aristotle, *Of Sleep and Waking*, 1; Galen, *On the Movement of Muscles*, 2.4, on the degree of motion the body undergoes while asleep.
532. *Noctambuloes*, sleep walkers; *Morpheus*, God of sleep and dreams.
533. [*Textual note:* From here to '... discover it,' are added in the 1643 version.]
534. *Themistocles*, This seems to be an error on Browne's part: the story occurs in Frontinus, *Strategematon,* 3.12.2 and is told of Iphicrates, though he is rebuked for cruelty, rather than praised for mercy.
535. *Lucan and Seneca*, both forced to commit suicide by Nero, but allowed to choose their own methods, Tacitus, *Annals*, 15.70, 15.63–4.
536. *Die daily*, 1 Corinthians 15:31.
537. [*Textual note:* 1642 (with varients in the MSS) adds 'it is a fit time for devotion: I cannot therefore lay me downe on my bed without an oration'.]
538. *Centry*, sentry.
539. *Jacob*, on ladder to heaven, Genesis 28:12–15.

540. [*Textual note: Dormitive*, some MSS add 'The name of an extract, wherewith we use to provoke sleep'].
541. Distributive and commutative justice are Aristotelian terms, the former relating to the fair allocation of goods in a community and the latter how an individual ought to be treated in a particular instance, *Nicomachean Ethics*, 5.3; *supererogate*, do more than necessary; *doe unto others*, Luke 6:31, Matthew 7:12.
542. *My starre*, astrological destiny.
543. *To conceive our selves urinals*, a symptom of madness, noted by James Howell, *Epistolæ Ho-Elianæ* (1645), 1.29; *hellebore*, medicine used for insanity, and, according to Horace, as a cure for avarice, *Satires* 2.3.82.
544. *That snow is blacke,* Anaxagoras in Cicero, *Academic Questions*, 2.32 (72); *that the earth moves*, i.e. Copernican theory; *that the soule is ayre, fire, water*, Aristotelian attributions to Diogenes, Democritus, and Hippon, *De Anima*, 1.2.
545. *Subterraneous Idoll*, gold.
546. *That the world adores*, i.e. that which the world adores, gold.
547. i.e. ingesting gold as a medicine: see *Pseudodoxia,* 2.5 (3).
548. *Nicomachean Ethics*, 1.8.
549. [*Textual note:* MSS and 1642 render this: 'I can justly boast I am as charitable as some who have built hospitals, or erected Cathedralls.'] *Mite*, Mark 12:42–4, Luke 21:2–4.
550. [*Textual note:* MSS and 1642: 'when I am reduced to the last tester, I love to divide it with the poore'.]
551. *Peru*, famous for its silver mines.
552. Proverbs 19:17.
553. *Scenicall and accidentall differences*, i.e. in outward appearance.
554. *Centoes*, patched together cloths.
555. *Statists*, political theorists; *forgetting the prophecy of Christ*, Luke 6:20, 'The poore ye shall have always with you,' on which misreading of the text, Coleridge comments 'O for shame!'
556. *Traduction*, infusion.
557. *Call to assize*, call to judgement; *dumbe showes*, mimes.
558. [*Textual note:* Marginal note to Copernicus in some MSS, 'Who holds the Sunne is the centre of the world.']
559. *Crambe*, repetition, a cabbage served twice; *all is vanitie* …, Ecclesiastes 1:14.
560. *Summum bonum*, chief good, *Nicomachean Ethics*, 1.6.
561. *Pliny*, Natural History. See *Pseudodoxia*, 1.8 (5).
562. [*Textual note:* Pembroke MS and 1642: 'mine owne damnation'.]
563. *Politian*, Angelo Poliziano (1454–94), Italian humanist; *Cui quam recta manus, tam fuit et facilis*, 'whose hand was as controlled as it was fluent', said of Giotto, on a bust in Florence Cathedral.

PSEUDODOXIA EPIDEMICA BOOK I

1. *Ex Libris*... 'To cull from books that authors published long ago is very dangerous; true knowledge of the things comes from the things themselves.'
2. *Reminiscentiall*, prompting memory; *colourishing*, to colour in; Plato, *Phaedo*, 72e–76a, the idea, premised on the pre-existence of the soul, that learning and knowledge is remembering the mass of things forgotten.
3. *Tender enquiries*, when young.
4. *Wheeles of heaven*, with reference, at least in part poetical, to a cosmological and theological model of the heavens constructed as a series of crystalline spheres, turning in contrary direction to the earth; *swindge*, or swinge, meaning impetus or whirling motion, also bearing the idea of, variously, 'sway, authority' and its apparent opposite, 'liberty, freedom of action'; *rapt*, an irresistible sweep, force, or current.
5. *Adviso*, piece of advice, information; *decisions*, i.e. resolution of the questions.
6. *Cooperating advancers*, with reference, perhaps, to Baconian programmes of cooperative science; *unequal*, i.e. not equal to the task.
7. *Radicated*, having roots, leading into the image of error as a deep-rooted oak tree; *hardly*, hard, firmly.
8. [*Textual note:* 'twigges... days', in 1650 becomes 'acorns in our younger brows'.]
9. *Requitals*, recompense, reward; *obloquie*, abuse, reproach; *singularities*, distinctiveness, idiosyncrasy, usually used in a negative sense in the era.
10. *Our profession*, i.e. physician.
11. *Importunity*, here, inopportune, time-consuming burden.
12. *Indifferently perpend*, consider without prejudice; *paradoxologie*, habit of indulging in paradoxes; *bee performed upon one legge*, unduly rapid, from Horace, *Satires*, 1.4.10; *smell of oyle*, i.e. of late nights.
13. *Latine republike*, i.e. the 'republic of letters' and the humanist world of intellectual exchange; *ingenuous* carries the meaning 'of free or noble birth' in addition to native and natural to the land. Also sometimes a spelling for *ingenious*; *conceived*, understood.
14. *People*, used in the mildly derogative sense for which Browne usually uses 'vulgar'; *incapable of reduction*, incapable of restoration to a pristine state. 'Reduction' is used, for example, of the rendering of a metal back to its original state; *these weeds,* those needing to be watered and fructified with knowledge are, presumably, those who constitute 'the knowing and leading part of learning'.
15. *Manuduction*, leading or guiding.

16. [*Textual note:* The 1650 edition adds: 'Scipio Mercurij hath also left an excellent Tract in Italian concerning popular errors; but confining himself only unto those in physic, he hath little conduced unto the generality of our doctrine.']
17. James Primrose, *De Vulgi Erroribus in Medicina* (1636); *physick*, medicine; Laurentius Joubertus, *De Vulgi Erroribus* (1579); *inscription*, legend, description on title page.
18. *Andreas*, referred to in Athenaeus, *Deipnosophists*, 7.312e.
19. *Goliah*, Goliath; *pibbles*, pebbles; *scrip*, small satchel or bag, especially for shepherds.
20. *Appertinancies of arts*, belonging or relating to the arts; *receptaries of philosophy*, received notions of philosophy or science.
21. *Naturals*, the natural world and natural history, in particular.
22. *Worthies*, used to signify greatness in any field. The 'advancement of learning' is the title of Francis Bacon's monumental and influential survey of all branches of knowledge.
23. *So many rubbes are levelled*, rubs are obstacles, or hillocks; *the tranquility of axiomes*, generally accepted propositions.
24. *Expurgation*, removing or purging guilt or faults.
25. *More ocular discerners*, 'ocular' touching on ideas of the visual and knowledge arising from experiment.
26. [*Textual note:* 'elenchically' changed from 1658 to 'fallaciously or captiously'.]
27. *Elenchically*, Socratic pursuit of truth by short question and answer.
28. *Traduce*, here, to malign or vilify; *dilucidate*, make clear; *ampliate*, amplify, enlarge.
29. *Desiderated*, required, desired.
30. *Deceptible*, apt to be deceived; *eviction*, demonstration, proof; *more infallible constitutions*, those less prone to error; *ingenerated*, ungenerated, i.e. Adam and Eve; *wounds of constitution*, i.e. the fall and its intellectual consequences; *traductions*, offspring, progenitors; *originalls*, origin.
31. i.e. Adam and Eve 'were grossly deceived'; *gaine upon them*, triumph over them.
32. *Suspition*, suspicion; *circumspection*, caution, heedfulness.
33. *Superstruction*, the upper part of a building, architecturally dependent upon its base, i.e. Eve's dependence on Adam, Eve being the 'fertility of his sleep', taken as a rib from him while he slept.
34. *Traduced*, here, misrepresented.
35. Genesis 2:16-17.
36. *Mendacites*, falsehoods.
37. *Vulgar*, here, vernacular; *Thargum or Paraphrase of Jonathan*, Targum, Aramaic paraphrase and commentary upon the Nevi'im (prophets).
38. *Intellectuals*, powers of reason; *inservient and brutall faculties*, lower animal faculties of the soul.

39. *Inveigled*, cajoled, beguiled; *Saint John*, 1 John 2:16.
40. *Convicted*, convinced; *menace*, threat; *ocular example*, i.e. witnessing; *purposed to mischiefe*, intended harm; *My iniquity* . . . , Genesis 4:13.
41. *Nicities*, subtle distinctions.
42. *Resistibility*, capacity to resist; *schoolman*, medieval scholastic philosopher-theologian.
43. [*Textual note:* Adding from 1650, 'especially if foretasting the fruit, her eyes were opened before his, and she knew the effect of it, before he tasted of it'.]
44. *Relation*, story; *Thalmudist*, Scholar of the Talmud, books of Jewish law, philosophy, and interpretation.
45. *Policie*, shrewdness, design; *conjunction*, sex; *issue*, children; *tentation*, temptation.
46. A syntactical form, 'Whether . . . ' (with no main clause), frequently employed and stemming from Aristotelian *problemata*.
47. *Proposed the world*, a scholastic formulation of 'propose' as presenting a philosophical problem; *his owne resolution*, i.e. secrets not to be explored; *determinations*, resolving of questions; *disquisitions*, topics of diligent investigation.
48. *Deceiveable*, capable of deception; *integrity*, unbroken, unfallen state.
49. A Platonic statement of God's conceptions or ideas as the truth and only partial human perception of such truths; *being the rule he cannot bee irregular*, there being no standard of truth beyond God.
50. Moses being reputed the author of the Pentateuch, the first five books of the Bible from Genesis to Deuteronomy.
51. *Expostulation of God*, 'Where are you?', Genesis 3:9; *pertinacity*, perverse obstinacy; *retirement*, hiding; *infringed the omnisciency*, encroached upon, theologically speaking, the fact of an omniscient God; *causalities, and the essentiall cause*, i.e. God being responsible for the creation of and in scholasticism being the 'cause' of things.
52. *Posterity*, i.e. the human race; *so perpetuated an impayrement*, the post-lapsarian condition; *his conception*, i.e. Adam's; *one tree . . . another*, the first being the fig tree from whose leaves he fashioned clothes, the second being the tree of knowledge, from which Adam and Eve ate the fruit.
53. *Those tormented spirits*, Revelation 6:15–16, 'the kings of the earth, and the great men, and the rich men'; *laid the foundations of the earth*, Job 38:4; *perspicacity*, clarity of sight.
54. *Restlesse spirits*, devils; *Trismegistus his circle*, from Arabic work, translated as *Divine Pymander* (1650). Hermes Trismegistus was seen as a conduit between Mosaic and Egyptian wisdom; *pitch beyond ubiquity*, fly beyond infinity.
55. Genesis 3:12.
56. *The impeachment of his Justice*, impugning or disparaging God's justice.
57. Genesis 3:13.

58. *Extenuating her sinne from that which was an aggravation*, i.e. attempting to mitigate her crime by reference to something that in fact made it worse, that a mere animal's suggestion could prompt her to disobey God.
59. *Consider our degenerated integrities unto some minoration*, reduce the seriousness of our offences in light of our postlapsarian condition; *colourable*, plausible.
60. *Pelagians*, those who hold that humankind can take steps to effect or contribute to their salvation. Pelagius, 4th-century British-Roman theologian, the subject of an influential attack by Augustine.
61. Genesis 4:9.
62. Job 1:7.
63. *Whose cognition is no way deludable*, whose perception cannot be tricked.
64. Matthew 4:1–11; Mark 1:12–13; Luke 4:1–13.
65. *Accompt*, account, reckoning; *calumnies*, false charges.
66. Genesis 4:13.
67. *Expiated*, paid and made amends for, cleansed (by Christ).
68. *Mystically*, Old Testament actions having, typologically and mystically, a New Testament resonance.
69. *Nothing unto them inevident*, i.e. those in heaven do not need to have faith in heaven; *fruition . . . evacuation*, in having the object of faith (heaven) fulfilled, they can dispense with the need for faith.
70. Genesis 4:23.
71. *Illation*, inference, deduction.
72. *Rabbins*, rabbis.
73. *Decollation*, beheading, truncating; *immoderancy*, excess, immoderateness.
74. *Circumscription*, limits, bounds.
75. *Neerely founded*, more immediately based on.
76. *Deceptible*, apt to be deceived.
77. *Unequall*, inadequate, insufficient; *unqualified intellectuals*, mental powers, facilities; *to umpire the difficulty of its dissentions*, to judge between opinions presented.
78. [*Textual note:* 1658 'to speak largely, is a false judgment of things, or an assent unto falsity'.]
79. *Casually*, by accident rather than design.
80. *Having but one eye of sence and reason*, unable to distinguish between what the senses tell us and how reason might correct this; *their figures plaine*, i.e. that sun, moon and stars occupy the same plane or sphere.
81. *Faine*, content, happy; *wasters*, wooded sword, for fencing exercises, or a cudgel.
82. *Rhetorick*, the tropes of oratory and figures of speech, not usually carrying the negative associations given here, as a contrast to logic; *Apologue of Aesope*, fable; *Aesop*, 6th century BCE, slave to whom influential animal fables were attributed; *syllogisme in Barbara*, mnemonic for

recalling basic syllogistic structures and combinations of major and minor premises.

83. *Operable circumstances*, what should be done in a particular case; *prudenciality*, prudence.
84. *Lecture of Holy Scripture,* text of the Bible; *literall sense*, first level of interpretation within the *quadriga*, the fourfold system of reading the Scriptures.
85. *Deuteroscopy*, the levels of the quadriga beyond the literal, i.e. allegoria (mystical or allegorical), analogia or tropologia (moral), aetiologia or anagoga (foreshadowing or salvational); *superconsequencies*, implications; *coherencies*, associations; *figures, or tropologies*, modes of deuteroscopic interpretation; *perswaded by fire*, even burning does not work to convince them that their interpretation is wrong.
86. *Dishonoured into manuall expressions*, made human, anthropomorphized.
87. *Unprovided, or unsufficient*, incapable of; *idolatry*, the chief Old Testament sin, any focus of worship which is not God.
88. *After our image*, whereas in Genesis 1:27, man was made in God's image.
89. *Sensible delusions*, delusions of the senses.
90. *Brutall part of the soule*, animal faculties of the tripartite soul; *the soveraigne facultie*, the rational soul.
91. *They*, i.e. the vices affect man in so far as he deserts his reason.
92. *Mahomet . . . the felicitie of his heaven*, suggesting that the Islamic understanding of heaven was corporeal and sensual.
93. *Beatitude*, here, the turning into spirit.
94. *Doctrine of the one*, relating to a report of the suppression of the Academy in Baghdad; see Henry Blount, *Voyage into the Levant* (1636), p. 84.
95. *Galen*, 2nd century CE, Greek-speaking physician; *nibble at Moses*, in *On the Usefulness of the Parts*, 2; *Apostate Christian*, Emperor Julian, who temporarily reversed the Christianizing of the Roman Empire; *treatie*, discussion of, treatise.
96. *Farraginous*, indiscriminate; *determinations*, their conclusions.
97. *Epithites*, epithets, i.e. of fools.
98. *Orestes*, who avenged the death of his father, Agamemnon, by killing his mother, Clytemnestra. Orestes himself was driven mad by the pursuit of the Erinyes, but later recovered; Pausanias, *Description of Greece*, 3.22.1–3; *Lystrian rabble . . . Paul and Barnabas*, Acts 14:8–9.
99. *Sides of Democritus*, the 'laughing philosopher'; *tumult of Demetrius*, Acts 19:23–41: Demetrius, a silversmith who made icons of Diana, objects to Paul's success in conversion and a riot ensues.
100. *Patience of Job*, proverbial; *meeknesse of Moses*, Numbers 12:3; *mutiny in the wildernesse . . . ear-rings*, Exodus 32; *tenne great miracles*, i.e. the ten plagues, Exodus 7–10.
101. *Impatiencie of Peter*, John 18:10; *staves of the multitude*, Matthew 26:47; *desired of God forgivenes*, Luke 23:34; *triumph*, Matthew 21:8; *Crucifge*, 'Crucify him', Mark 15:13.

102. *Gods peculiar people*, 1 Peter 2:9; *that aphorisme*, 'Vox populi, vox Dei', in a work, for example, by Thomas Scott (1624).
103. *Advenient deception*, from outside.
104. *Subtler devisors*, manipulators.
105. *Ariolation*, *south-saying*, soothsaying. Ariolation is closer to witchcraft; *oblique idolatries*, bordering on idolatry; *cats, lizards, and beetles*, Egypian deities.
106. *Irreproveable*, unreproachable, blameless.
107. *Theudas*, Acts 5:36, with the figure 400; *imposture*, impostor.
108. *That Herod was the Messias*, the Herodians, Matthew 22:16; *David George of Leyden*, (Davis Joris) Dutch Anabaptist, 1501–56.
109. *Aarons brest-plate*, which shone mystically to foretell victory, Josephus, *Antiquities of the Jews*, 3.8.9; on urine in diagnostics, see 'To the Reader'.
110. [*Textual note:* From 'indigitate' to the end of the sentence added in 1650. 1658 changes 'affections' to 'diseases'.] *Seminalitie*, the implanted germ of creation; *the Idea of every part*, the 'Idea' is the quasi-Platonic enfolded quintessence of a seed; *indigitate*, point out, indicate.
111. *Saltimbancoes, quacksalvers, and charlatans*, mountebanks and sellers of quack medicine.
112. *Piazza and Ponte Neufe*, Venetian and Parisian commercial centres, attracting charlatans.
113. *Caballa*, i.e. Kabbalah.
114. [*Textual note:* 1650, 'illumination' for 'infustion'.]
115. *Juglers*, conjurors, tricksters; *geomancers*, divination from earth, or lines; *without infusion*, i.e. of the Holy Spirit, itself liable to being described as 'enthusiasm'.
116. *Legionarie*, vast, also demonic, Mark 5:9.
117. *Statistes and politicians*, terms implying Machiavellian intent; *Ragione di Stato*, reasons of state, as a convenient method of hiding one's real intentions; *the first considerable*, thing to consider; *capitall intention*, the longer-term aims of their designs.
118. *Latitude of sence*, within some parameters.
119. *Cujus alterum* . . . , 'the other name wherof to utter, is counted in the secret mysteries of ceremonies an impious and unlawfull thing', Pliny, *Natural History*, 3.5.65, trans. Holland (1603).
120. *Penates*, household Gods.
121. *Tutelary spirits*, attendant spirits, guardian angels.
122. *Ingannations*, deceptions, fraud.
123. *The first* . . . , i.e. the first misapprehension or 'nearer' cause of error; *secondary relations*, hearing at second hand.
124. John 21:21–3.
125. *Centaurs* . . . *Servius*, in Palæphatus, *De Fabulosis Narrationibus* (trans. 1578), f. 110.

126. *Inconsequent diductions*, illogical deductions, not following from the premises; *fallacious foundations*, false axioms.
127. *Verball and Reall*, Aristotle, *Sophistical Refutations*, 165b.
128. *Æquivocation*, equivocation being associated in the era with Jesuitry and allowing a degree of falsehood to inhabit terms that are, in some other sense, true; *amphibologie*, ambiguous construction; *sintaxis*, syntax.
129. *Doctrine of Pythagoras*, Diogenes Laertius, *Lives of Eminent Philosophers*, Book 8; *involved*, complex.
130. *Abstinence from beanes*, Diogenes, 8.19; Aristoxenus' *Pythagorean Precepts* is a lost work, known by title.
131. *Plutarch*, in *The Education of Children*, 17; Thucydides, *History*, 8.56, 'the councell of the beane' is the phrase in Hobbes' 1629 translation, *Eight bookes of the Peloponnesian Warre* (1629), p. 506.
132. [*Textual note:* 'and might be the original...' to end of sentence, added in 1658.] Aulus Gellius, *Attic Nights*, 4.11, citing Empedocles.
133. This and the following idiomatic phrases are to be found in the account of Pythagoras by Diogenes Laertius, 8.17.
134. [*Textual note:* 1646 has 'understood'.]
135. *Elench*, logical refutation.
136. Genesis 3:4–5.
137. *Brutus... with Tarquine*, Livy, *History of Rome*, 1.51.10. Junius Brutus interpreted the oracle which said he who first kissed his mother should rule Rome. Unlike his competitors, who thought to return home, he fell to the floor and kissed the ground.
138. *Wooden walls*, Herodotus, *Histories*, 7.141, a prophecy of the protection offered by wooden walls, interpreted by Themistocles as being ships; *doubled the altar at Delphos*, Plutarch, *The E at Delphi*, on an ambiguous oracle, enjoining the Greeks to become experts at geometry.
139. *Ironicall*, in a rhetorical sense of dissembling, feigning.
140. *Deductions from metaphors*, reading figures of speech in a literal fashion, i.e. 'reall and rigid interpretations'.
141. Epiphanius, *Adverus Haereses*; *Austin*, i.e. Augustine, who wrote extensively against various heresies; *Prateolus*, Gabriel Dupréau, *De Vitis, Sectis, et Dogmatibus Omnium Haereticorum* (1569).
142. *Inconsequent illations*, conclusions that do not follow from the premise.
143. *Extradictionary*, beyond the verbal; *Aristotle and logicians,* the four fallacies are explained over succeeding paragraphs.
144. *Medium*, in logic, the middle term of a syllogism.
145. Genesis 3:4–5.
146. *Been worthy of death...*, John 18:30.
147. Matthew 4:6.
148. *Proper*, i.e. really (rather than rightly) worshipping symbolic things.
149. *Statue of Belus*, confused with Baal. See Strabo, 1.16.5 and Herodotus, 1.183 on the destruction of the statue.

150. *Accusing*..., Matthew 12:1–14, Luke, 6:1–11.
151. *Pompey the great*, who worked unmolested on successive Sabbaths in filling in the valleys and ditches, in order that he could mount his siege engines, the Jews being permitted only defensive fighting on the sabbath, Josephus, *Wars of the Jews*, 1.7.3.
152. *Use of wine... abolished universities*, see Henry Blount, *Voyage into the Levant* (1636), 84.
153. *Saint Paul*, Colossians 2:8.
154. *Tripudiary divinations*, from the behaviour of birds.
155. *Fallacious illation*, false deduction; *remotion*, removal.
156. *Pharisees*, Luke 5:30, Mark 2:16.
157. *Largely taken*, conceived more generally; *vitious*, depraved, vicious.
158. [*Textual note:* 1646 has 'consequences'.]
159. *Obtruded*, imposed.
160. *From the earth*, Herodotus, *Histories*, 7.161.3; *seminality*, implanted principles of growth.
161. *Alcoran*, Qur'an.
162. *Geber*, 12th-century Andalusian mathematician and astronomer; *Avicenna*, prolific 11th-century physician; *Almanzor*, 10th-century Islamic Córdoban ruler.
163. [*Textual note:* 1650 onwards replaces 'conjunction' with 'copulation'.]
164. Commonplace account of Muslim ideas, this list being lifted from Carolus Clusius, *Exotica* (1605), p. 173.
165. *Scepticall infidelity*, lack of belief.
166. *Promiscuously*, indiscriminately.
167. *Detractory*, disparaging.
168. *Hoc tantum scio quod nihil scio*, 'I know only that I know nothing', Plato, *Apology*, 21b–d.
169. *Acquit the insatisfaction*, exonerate those guilty of chronic, sceptical dissatisfaction.
170. *Zeno*, Zeno of Elea, included in a list of sceptics in Diogenes Laertius, 9.72, on Pyrrho; *Antycera*, Greek city, i.e. Anticyra, reputedly named after Antikyreus, who cured Hercules' madness with the Hellebore of the region; *melancholies*, here, the insane.
171. *Supinity*, inert or inactive idea of inquiry; *purchase*, obtaining by effort.
172. *Palliate*, alleviate the need for.
173. *Sat downe in*, been content with.
174. *Exantlation*, drawing out of a liquid.
175. *In sudore vultus tui*, 'by the sweat of your brow', Genesis 3.19; *exercitations*, efforts; *unthorny place*, thorns being part of the lapsarian curse upon the earth.
176. *Repaire our primarie ruins*, cf. Milton, *Of Education* (1644), 'to repair the ruins of our first parents'.
177. *Flaming swords*, Genesis 3:24; *defected*, been deficient, fallen off.

178. *Transcribed*, reproduced, copied; *satisfaction*, resolving; *the charge*, i.e. the eschatological charge sheet of sins.
179. *Beaten notions*, commonplace errors, already established; *habilities*, abilities.
180. *Magis extra vitia quam cum virtutibus*, 'rather lacking great vice than possessing virtues', Tacitus, *Histories*, 1.49.
181. *Constellated unto knowledge*, born to be knowledgable, astrologically speaking, or deserving a place within the constellations of knowledge.
182. *Worthies*, great men.
183. *Ultimus bonorum*, last good man, Martial, *Epigrams*, 12.36.
184. *Nos numerus sumus*, 'we are but ciphers', Horace, *Epistles*, 1.2.27.
185. *Sedulous*, constant, diligent; *roled the stone*, Sisyphus, for his crimes, was condemned to an eternity of rolling a stone up a hill, at which point it rolled down again, Ovid, *Metamorphoses*, 4.460, Homer, *Odyssey*, 11.593–600.
186. [*Textual note:* 1650 'perfection' replaced by 'measure'.]
187. *Pregnant Minerva*, a ready and fertile wisdom, Minerva being the Roman equivalent of Athena; *teeming constitution*, teeming meaning ready to give birth (to ideas).
188. *Lanthorne... Athens*, Diogenes of Sinope, who paraded with a lantern in daylight, claiming he was unable to find a man, Diogenes Laertius, *Lives*, 6.41.
189. *Execution upon*, damage to; *dictates of antiquities*, this notion of the tyranny of antiquity is so widely repeated as to be a leitmotif of early modern thought. See, for example, Francis Bacon, *Advancement of Learning* (1605), pp. 21–2.
190. *The reasons*, reasoning.
191. *Passe uncontrouled*, without questioning and scrutiny; *become out of the distance of envies*, being too ancient to attract the enmity that contemporary works might.
192. *Hippocrates*, physician, *c.*460–370 BCE, whose works engaged extensively with correcting medical errors of his predecessors; *Galen... Aristotle*, Galen on Aristotle in *On the Usefulness of the Parts*, 6; Aristotle engaging, in turn, with Plato and a wide range of other contemporaries.
193. *Irrefragable*, indisputable.
194. *Horace*, leading Roman poet and satirist, d. 8 CE; *Juvenal*, Roman satirist, late 1st century CE; *Perseus*, Persius, Etruscan satirist, d. 62 CE.
195. *Aristotle... booke of animals* is his *History of Animals*, but the examples come from the pseudo-Aristotelian *Problemata* ('problems'), a work of queries and observations in natural philosophy.
196. *Cough* in *Problemata*, 10.1, 891a; *de re Rustica,* of country things: among those who have 'expresly treated' of them is Varro, who wrote a work of the same name, referenced frequently in *The Garden of Cyrus*.

197. *Juments*, beasts of burdern; *eructation*, belching. Browne commonly doubles up his phrases in such manner, a Latinized and English term side by side; *Columella*, Lucius Collumella, Roman agricultural writer, (*c*.4–70 CE), also wrote a work, *De re rustica*, citing the signs of and remedies to animal indigestion, 6.6.
198. Aristotle, *Problemata*, 10.63 (898b).
199. *Aiunt, ferunt, fortasse*, 'as they have it, they say, perhaps'; *Dioscorides*, Greek physician and author of pharmacopeia (*c*.40–90 CE).
200. *Aelian*, Greek-speaking rhetorician and naturalist (*c*.175–235 CE), author of *On the Nature of Animals*; Athenaeus, *Deipnosophists*.
201. Browne plagiarizes this series of plagiarisms from Claudius Salmasius, *Plinianae Exercitationes* (1629), a fact I lift from Robin Robbins, with barely sufficient acknowledgement; *Justine*, 2nd-century Roman historian, who wrote an 'epitome' of Trogus Pompeius' 44-book *Historiae philippicae et totius mundi origines et terrae situs*; *Julius Solinus*, 4th-century author of *De mirabilibus mundi*; *Lucian*, 2nd-century satiric writer; *Apuleius*, author of the bawdy tale, *The Golden Ass*; *Lucius Pratensis*, i.e. Patrensis, putative originator of the Ass story.
202. *De Nilo*, Diodorus Siculus, 1st century BCE historian, author of the *Library of History*, published with Herodotus by Gottfried Jungermann (1608); Simocrates is Theophylact Simocatta, a 7th century bishop and historian.
203. *Eratosthenes*, geographer, 3rd century BCE; *Timotheus*, i.e. Timosthenes, author of *On Harbours*.
204. *Strabo*, much-cited geographer and historian.
205. [*Textual note:* Sentence from 'To omit . . . Parhenius Chius' added in 1650.] *Clemens Alexandrinus*, second century author of the Christian miscellany, *Stromata*; Pliny, *Natural History* preface, 22.
206. *Virgil*, whose works share little more than genre with the authors described; *Macrobius*, African philosopher, 4th century CE, author of *Saturnalia*; *Pisander*, Athenian politician, 4th century BCE.
207. *Oribasius* (*c*.320–400 CE), physician to Emperor Julian; *Ætius*, Byzantine writer on melancholy, *Ægineta*, i.e. Paul of Aegina, 7th-century Byzantine medical encyclopaedist.
208. *Marcellus Empericus*, 5th-century pharmacological writer and herbalist; *Scriboneus Largus*, 1st-century physician and medical writer.
209. *Fabulous*, in the sense of fable.
210. *Mendacity*, disposition to lie.
211. *Palæphatus*, 4th century BCE, author of *De Fabulosis Narrationibus*, explaining the origins of stories from misinterpretation and mistakes as to their nature. Browne goes on to narrate several, many of which can be found in Ovid's *Metamorphoses*.
212. *Orpheus*, in Palæphatus, 33.
213. *Medea*, Palæphatus, 43.

214. *Cerberus*, Palæphatus, 24, 39.
215. *Briareus*, Palæphatus, 19.
216. *Anthropophagie*, human flesh-eating.
217. *Daedalus* . . . *Niobe* . . . *Acteon* . . . *Diomedes* . . . *Minotaur*, in, respectively, Palæphatus, 12, 8, 6, 7, 2.
218. *Pasiphae*, daughter of the sun, who reputedly had Daedalus construct her a wooden cow, in order to tempt a bull to mate with her; *Domitian*, Roman emperor 81–96 CE, reported in Dio Cassius, *Roman History*, 67; Martial, *Epigrams*, 5.
219. *Nosce teipsum*, 'Know thyself'; *Nosce tempus*, 'Know the times'.
220. *Nihil nimis*, nothing to excess; *Cleobulus*, Greek poet, 6th century BCE.
221. *Salts*, pithy expressions; *Laertius*, Diogenes Laertius, in his *Lives of Eminent Philosophers*; *Lycosthenes*, Conrad Lycosthenes, 16th-century humanist and collector of adages.
222. Erasmus, *Adages* (1500).
223. *Nemo mortalium omnibus horis sapit*, 'No mortal is at all times wise', Pliny, *Natural History*, 7.40.131; *Virtute nil praestantius, nil pulchrius*, 'Nothing is more excellent, more beautiful, than virtue', Seneca, *Moral Letters*, 7.67.16; *Omnia vincit amor*, 'Love conquers all', Virgil, *Eclogues*, 10.69; *Praeclarum quiddam veritas*, 'Truth is a wonderful thing'.
224. *Antonius Guevara*, 16th-century Spanish moralist, *Diall of Princes*, *Reloj de Príncipes* (1529).
225. *Apolonius Thyaneus*, 1st-century CE neo-Pythagorean philosopher.
226. *Euclid*, Axiom 9.
227. *Torrid zone*, equatorial regions.
228. *Empeopled*, populated; *seat of Paradise*, the era engaged busily with trying to find the geographical location of Eden, in, for example, Walter Ralegh, *History of the World* (1617), 1.3.8.
229. *Antipodes*, poles, see 1.7.
230. *Dubitation*, doubt.
231. *Resolved prostration*, a conscious bowing down to antiquity.
232. [*Textual note:* Following the paragraphing of 1650 in this section.]
233. *Topicall probation*, only probable and tentative, investigations from *topi*, or commonplaces; *inartificiall*, an argument constructed without art, or the appropriate building up of logical premises; *asseveration*, emphatic assertion.
234. *Contra negantem principia*, 'against any who denies first principles' (there is no point in arguing); *Ipse dixit*, 'he has spoken' (the matter is settled); *oportet discentem credere*, 'the learner must believe' (what one is told by an authority).
235. *Indoctrinations*, formal teaching; *minority of our intellectuals*, our youthful intellectual state.
236. *Perpensions*, deliberations.

237. *It is of no validity*, i.e. testimony; *mother part*, the part of the quadrivium on which its other arts (music and astronomy) rest.
238. *Dignities*, in rhetoric, a part of elocution equating with 'decorum'. The sense here is mathematical decorum, or appropriate procedures.
239. [*Textual note:* 1650 has 'Geometritians notwithstanding would not recieve'] *Subtendeth*, being opposite to. Pythagoras' theorem, *Euclid*, 1.47.
240. *Probation*, testing, investigation.
241. *Imprecations*, invocations.
242. *That snow was blacke*, attributed to Anaxagoras, Sextus Empiricus, *Outlines of Pyrrhonism*, 1.13; *sea . . . the sweat of the earth*, attributed to Empedocles in Aristotle, *Meteorology*, 2.3 (357a).
243. *Fall upon Melissus*, Aristotle, *Physics*, 1.2 (185a), rejecting Melissus' notion of an infinite universe; *Anaxagoras, Anaximander, and Empedocles*, on the nature of matter, addressed further in the *Physics*, 1.4, 187a–188a; *receptions*, received ideas.
244. *Carry the stroake*, be most influential, i.e. the reasoning is the more important part of the proof.
245. *Comprobation*, proving the truth; *two witnesses*, an axiom both of common and biblical law, in e.g. Deuteronomy 19:15, Corinthians 13:1, John 8:17.
246. *Calumny*, misrepresenting the words or actions of somebody.
247. [*Textual note:* 1650 'unerring' for 'undeceived'.]
248. *Lactantius . . . the earth is plaine*, early and influential Christian Father (*c.*240–320 CE), suggested that the absurdity of antipodean people walking upside down below the earth made a rotund earth nonsensical, *Divine Institutes*, 3.24; *Austin*, i.e. Augustine, *City of God*, 16.9; on which see too Pliny, *Natural History*, 2.65.
249. [*Textual note:* 1646 omits 'not'.]
250. Raymond Sebond, of Toulouse, famous from Montaigne's 'Apology of Raymond Sebonde' in his *Essays*, 2.12. Browne has in mind his *Theologia Naturalis* (*c.* 1484).
251. Hugo Grotius, *De Veritate Religionis Christianae* (1627); *civilian*, i.e. civil lawyer.
252. Aristotle, *History of Animals*, 7.4 (584b), Hippocrates, *Eight Months' Child*, 10. This dispute is noted in Aulus Gellius, *Attic Nights*, 3.16, along with Hadrian's deciding for Hippocrates in a dispute over the inheritance of a woman whose husband had died eleven months previously.
253. This medical genealogy, from Hippocrates to Galen to Avicenna, is, on the whole without pronounced antagonisms to their predecesors. Paracelus (1493–1541), charismatic and innovative physician, on the other hand, is scathing, alleged to have burnt medical books of the ancients at Basel and contemptuous of the medical profession.
254. *Illation*, drawing an inference.

255. *Annihilate many simples*, dispense with many medicinal herbs; *bezoar*, antidote; *ambergris*, waxy secretion of sperm-whale.
256. *Barbara*, rhetorical mnemonic.
257. Basil of Caesarea (*c*.330–379 CE), *De paradiso*, 7; see *Religio Medici*, 1.10.
258. *Tostatus* (*c*.1400–55), Spanish biblical commentator, *Commentaria in Genesim* (1596), f. 299v.
259. *Leonardo Fioravanti*, Italian surgical writer and physician; *pellitory*, non-stinging member of nettle family.
260. *Dove si possa . . .*, 'where one can see the North star'.
261. *Franciscus Sanctius* (1523–1600), Spanish humanist, *Alciats Emblems*, Andrea Alciato (1492–1550), humanist and jurist, whose *Emblemata* (1522) was a phenomenally popular book of moral exemplary emblems; *Avem Philomelam . . .*, 'I can certainly affirm that the nightingale lacks a tongue, if my eyes don't deceive me.'
262. *Pierius . . . Hieroglyphicks*, important work of emblems, by Pierio Valeriano (1477–1558), reputedly based on the discovery of Egyptian hieroglyphics. The example of the scorpion sting is from *Hieroglyphica*, 12.22.
263. *Receite*, prescription; *quartane ague*, fever recurring at four-day intervals; *remedy of Sammonicus*, Rabelais noted satirically the placing of Homer under the pillow for toothache, *Gargantua*, book 2, prologue; *Collyrium*, lotion for the eyes; *Albertus*, Albert the Great, 13th-century natural philosopher.
264. *Nights lodging with Lais*, Lais, courtesan of Corinth, 5th-century BCE; *what is delivered in Kiranides*, a 4th-century collection of magic-medical lore.
265. *Inveigle*, deceive.
266. *Opprobrious*, attended by shame, i.e. of not being able to cure them; *Ars Longa, Vita Brevis*, 'Art is long, life is brief.'
267. *Transcriptive*, copied.
268. *Herodotus*, 5th-century BCE, teller of sweeping world-histories; *Cicero*, *Of the Laws*, 1.1.5; *Historiarum parens*, more commonly *patrem historiae*, the father of history.
269. Dionysius of Halicarnassus, author of *Roman Antiquities*.
270. *Mendaciorum pater*, 'the father of lies', Plutarch, *On the Malignity of Herodotus*, part of his broad-ranging *Moralia*; *Polybius*, 2nd-century Greek historian.
271. *Joachim Camerarius*, German humanist and classical scholar and translator who defended Herodotus in the preface to his 1608 translation; *Stephanus* printed Lorenzo Valla's Latin translation of Thucydides (1588) and offered a prefatory poem in praise of the historian.
272. *Father poet*, Homer; *Ego quae fando . . .*, 'Though it be my business to set down that which is told me, to believe it is none at all of my business', Herodotus, *Histories*, 7.152.

273. *Ctesias the Cnidian*, 5th century BCE, writer of histories of Persia and India. His work was given as a supplement to Herodotus in Camerarius' 1608 translation.
274. *Diodorus*, Diodorus Siculus, 1st-century BCE historian; *read with suspension*, i.e. suspension of belief.
275. Aristotle, *Generation of Animals*, 2.2 (736a); *undervaluing*, derogatory comments on.
276. *Equidem facilius* . . . , 'One could more easily believe Hesiod and Homer in their stories of the heroes than Ctesias, Herodotus, Hellanicus, and other writers of this kind', Strabo, *Geography*, 11.6.3.
277. *Scripsit Ctesias* . . . , 'Ctesias wrote about India and things there that he had not seen himself nor heard from reliable report', Lucian, *True History*, 1.3. Lucian's *True History* (2nd century CE) is a space-travel satire.
278. *Sir John Mandevell*, 14th-century 'travel' writer.
279. *In some acceptions of morality*, i.e. to convey Aesopian or moral meaning.
280. *De mirandis auditionibus* (1557), *De mirabilibus narrationibus*, collected in Meursius' *Historiarum Mirabilium Auctores Graeci* (1622).
281. *Philostratus*, 1st century CE, philosophical biographer of Apollonius.
282. *Dioscorides*, 1st century CE, herbalist (*De Materia Medica*) and physician.
283. Galen, *On the Powers and Mixtures of Simple Remedies*, 6.
284. *Vitex, or Agnus Castus*, Mediterranean flowering plant.
285. *Whores* . . . *experiment of Savine*, shrub used to bring on abortion.
286. These are taken from Pliny, *Natural History*, 25.18.
287. *Oribasius* . . . *Marcellus*, this collection of physicians published in *Medicae Artis principes* (1567).
288. *Plinius Secundus*, i.e. Pliny.
289. *Suetonius*, historian and chronologer, 1st century CE.
290. *Vespasian*, Emperor, 69–79 CE.
291. *Claudius Ælianus* (*c.*170–235 CE), *De Natura Animalium* is a frequent source for book 3 of *Pseudodoxia*, on animals; *Trajan* is in fact an earlier emperor, Browne confusing Ælianus with a military writer of the same name; Claudius Ælianus' writing career coinciding with the reign of Septimius Severus. The *Varia historia* is a miscellany of classical biography and trivia.
292. *Julius Solinus* . . . *Polyhistor*, wide-ranging Latin miscellany (*c.* 3rd century CE).
293. Claudius Salmasius (1588–1653), French humanist scholar, successor to Scaliger at Leiden. Produced a post-regicidal defence of the English monarchy in 1649, which drew Milton's withering scorn.
294. *Athenaeus*, *c.*2nd–3rd century CE; *Deipnosophists*, 15-volume banquet of philosophy and ephemera; *Causabone*, Isaac Casaubon (1559–1614), *Animaduersionum in Athenæi Dipnosophistas* (1600).
295. *Laborious*, painstaking.

296. *De curiositate Aristotelis*, book 13.13, attacking Aristotle's *Historia Animalium*.
297. *Dalecampius*, Jacques d'Alechamp (1513–88), physician.
298. *Nicander*, poet, 2nd century BCE, though many of his works are lost; the surviving corpus is largely medical, on poisons and natural history; *Alexipharmaca* ... *Gorraeus*, i.e. Jean de Gorris, French physician (1505–77).
299. *Grevinus*, Parisian physician and translator of Nicander (1557).
300. *Oppianus*, Oppian, 2nd-century poet.
301. *Cynegeticks or venation*, relating to hunting; *halieuticks or piscation*, related to fishing.
302. *Abating onely*, except for; the following errors come from his *Cynegetica* (*c*.215 CE): *hyaena*, 3.288; *rhinoceros*, 2.560; *antipathy*, i.e. natural hostility, even in this case when dead, 3.282; *murena* (eel) *and the viper*, 1.381 .
303. *Antoninus*, this fact being narrated of Emperor Marcus Aurelius; *stater*, ancient weight or coin.
304. *Philes*, 14th-century Byzantine writer; *Johannes Tzetzes*, 12th-century Byzantine poet, author of *Chiliads* ('Thousands').
305. *Partialitie*, bias; *not to meddle*, not to mention; *miraculous authours* ... *legendary relators*, hagiographers and mythographers.
306. *Hexameron*, a text in which the works of each of six days of creation is elaborated upon in detail, so that weather can be discussed on the second day, astronomy on the fourth, animals on the sixth. St Basil's *Hexameron* (*c*.370 CE) and Ambrose's (*c*.380 CE) are the starting points for a genre that remains alive in the 17th century.
307. *Sutable to*, comparable to; *desumed*, derived.
308. *Epiphanius* ... *Phisiologie*, i.e. *Physiologus*, beast tales, long attributed to the 4th-century Cyprian, Church Father.
309. *Isidore of Sevill*, *c*.560–636 CE.
310. *Albertus* ... *Magnus*, 13th-century Dominican and natural philosopher.
311. *Vincentius Belluacensis*, Vincent of Beauvais, 13th-century French Dominican encyclopaedist; *Gulielmus de Conchis*, 12th-century scholastic philosopher and commentator on Plato; *Hortus Sanitatis*, late 15th-century and richly illustrated botanical miscellany, collected by Jacob Meydenbach; *Bartholomeus Glanvill*, Bartholomeus Anglicus, author of the encylcopaedia, *De proprietatibus rerum* (*c*.1240); *Kiranides*, 4th-century compilation of 'secrets'.
312. *Jeronymus Cardanus*, Cardan (1501–76), mathematician and philosopher, though Browne has in mind his miscellany, *De subtilitate rerum* (1550).
313. *Hoties*, a 'hoti' is a piece of reasoning, or a statement prefaced with 'because'.
314. *Secrets*, popular 'Books of Secrets' ranging from recipes to prescriptions and simples, to spells. Browne's list gives a number of examples: *Alexis*

Pedimont, Girolamo Ruscelli (1500–66), author of medical 'secrets' (1558); *Antonius Mizaldus* (1520–78), doctor and astrologer to Maguerite de Valois, Queen of Navarre; *Trinum Magicum*, collection of plant and alchemy secrets (1630); *abstrucities*, abstruseness, obscurity.

315. *Baptista Porta*, Giambattista della Porta (1535–1615), Italian natural philosopher; *receptary*, collection of medical recipes; *Phylognomy*, i.e. *Phytognomica* (1588); *Villa* (1583), agricultural encyclopaedia; *Naturall Magick* (1558), della Porta's most infamous work.
316. *Sit downe*, rest with, enquire no further.
317. *Diminutive, and pamphlet treaties*, the mechanisms of press licensing in the early part of the civil war having fallen apart; *maintaining*... *typography*, i.e. paying for printers.
318. *Common places*, being a standard early-modern mode of composition, amassing ideas and quotations under headings in commonplace books; *rhapsodies*, planless and formless miscellaneous work.
319. *Enthymemes*, rhetorical term, in which an argument is based on merely probable, rather than demonstrative grounds, with an additional Ciceronian sense of a striking note of paradox.
320. *Phaenix,... salamander, pellican, basilisk*, all occurring as individual chapters, respectively, 3.12, 3.14, 5.1, 3.7.
321. *Every art... hath its owne circle*, i.e. its parameters and mode of acceptable expression.
322. *Sun... Moone*, Genesis 1:16.
323. [*Textual note:* 1672, 'be taken for heresie' replaced by 'be strange'.]
324. *Second in magnitude unto*, i.e. smaller than; *Ptolomy*, i.e. Ptolemy, 2nd-century Egyptian astronomer and geographer, whose writings on the cosmos remained influential, even as the Copernican universe became (quite slowly) the accepted model; *Moses*, presumed author of the Pentateuch.
325. i.e. 2 Chronicles 4:1–3. *Solomon*, who casts an elaborate altar for the temple; *Archimedes*... *Cyclometria* 'The Measurement of a Circle', a fragment on the circle and the use of π.
326. *Largely*, in general terms.
327. *Aristotle*, though a common notion (*Pseudodoxia*, 3.4), in fact, this is not in the *Ethics*.
328. *The beare, the viper*, 3.6, 3.16.
329. *Apologues*, fables; *expiate*, cleanse.
330. *Hieroglyphicall doctrine*, the idea that the Egyptian hieroglyphs contained a condensed and consummate wisdom. This is discussed at various points, e.g. 3.11, 5.20; *Cohabitation*, i.e. the Jewish enslavement in Egypt, prior to the exodus; *learned from the Hebrewes*, this is the idea of the 'Prisca theologia' and the putative writings of Hermes Trismegistus, from where the idea came that similarities between Christian and Egyptian wisdom could be explained by Moses being at the root of both traditions.

331. *Emblematistes, heraldes*, both of them being visual genres, in which meaning was encoded in the image; *first sense... gust of the second*, alluding to the *Quadriga*, or fourfold mode of interpreting Scripture. Browne contrasts the first, literal sense with the three deuteroscopic (allegorical) senses.
332. *Heraiscus,* uncle of Horapollo, according to Damascius, *Philosophical History* (*c*.520 CE); *Cheremon*, in Josephus, *Against Apion*, 1.33; these are other hieroglyphical writings, known to the era primarily via the last figure, Pierio Valeriano, *Hieroglyphica*.
333. *Must rest in the text, and letter*, this being elaborated upon in detail in Book 5 of *Pseudodoxia*, and being particularly the case when the subject matter of the painting was scriptural.
334. *Vaine and idle fictions of the Gentils*, i.e. Greek and Roman myths and legends.
335. *Literary*, i.e. when learning to read.
336. *Cannot avoid their allusions... frigidities of wit*, i.e. forced classicisms.
337. *Galens study*, Roman fire of 192 CE, in which various works of the physician Galen perished.
338. *Were a pregnant wit educated in ignorance*..., not having classical 'intrusions' upon learning, a natural wit could produce more by observing nature.
339. *Permitted unto his proper principles*, i.e. free will.
340. *Oeconomie*, internal constitution.
341. *Efface all tract of its traduction*, all trace of the infusion (traduction) of the 'diviner part' (reason) into humans; *too bold an arithmetic*, i.e. a thing to work out.
342. *Politicall chymera*, political in the sense of manipulative; *chymera*, fire-breathing monster, meaning here a fable.
343. *Guard of individuals*, this being special (rather than general) providence, by which God intervenes directly in human affairs.
344. *Designed*, designated; *inferiour deputations*, to secondary means, such as fate.
345. *Preambulous*, prefatory.
346. *Checke*, contradiction.
347. *Velleities*, act of willing, desiring; *utinam*, strong wish.
348. *Appetible*, attractive, having an appetite to.
349. *His circumvension*, there being many gods; *obtained the former*, i.e. the belief that there is none.
350. *Socrates*, though accounts of his death in Plato and Xenophon contain little sense that it was primarily for his religious views; *Plato and Aristotle*, held to be essentially monotheist.
351. *Apodicticall*, demonstrable.
352. *Their principles*, here, their natural capacities; *Minervaes... Jupiters braines*, in the Greek of which, Zeus, having eaten Metis who was

pregnant by him, gave birth to Athena, fully armed, through his head, Hesiod, *Theogony*, 924–8.

353. *Like the highest*, this characterization of Satan's fall is from Isaiah 14:14.

354. *Play . . . with Moses*, Exodus 7:10–8:18, in which Pharaoh's 'wise men and sorcerers' replicate each trick that Moses performs; *could make good*, here, fake.

355. *Efficacy of the sun*, deemed to be the prerequisite for spontaneous generation.

356. Exodus 8:19, this being the last of Moses' miracles, which the magicians cannot copy.

357. Diogenes Laertius, *Lives of the Philosophers*, 8.4; Ovid, *Metamorphoses*, 15:158–72. This 'transmigration of souls' being metempsychosis.

358. *Abrahams bosome*, Luke 16:22.

359. *Resurrection of Samuel*, whose spirit is summoned up by witchcraft, 1 Samuel 28:11–19.

360. *Endeavoured*, attempted to manipulate.

361. *Skinnes of their owne sacrifices*, Virgil, *Aeneid*, 7.81–94, reports on the interpreters of oracles, sleeping on the skins of sacrificed animals to induce prescient dreams.

362. *Concitation*, stirring up, agitating; *humors*, the four constituent fluids and temperaments of the body, which might be in or out of balance with each other and which were the basis for much of early modern medical theory; *species*, here, with the sense of mental image.

363. *Advanced his deitie*, i.e. Satan's implying that he was himself God.

364. *Jugling*, legerdemain, trickery; *oratour . . . Pythia Phillippised*, the Greek orator Demosthenes (3rd century BCE), who argued that oracles were being used politically, suspecting the Pythian priestess of being in sympathy with Philip of Macedonia, in Plutarch, *Demosthenes*, 20.1; *Ammon unto Alexander*, Alexander became increasingly convinced, on his journey to the Libyan oracle, Ammon, that he was his descendant, reported in Arrian of Nicomedia, *Anabasis*, 3.3–4.

365. *Cræsus*, i.e. Croesus, King of Lydia, tricked by an oracle into battle against the Persians, in Herodotus, *Histories*, 1.53; the God of the oracle, or in Browne's terms, Satan, subsequently just shrugs his oracular shoulders and blames fate, punishing the deeds of Croesus' ancestor, 1.90; *amphibologie*, ambiguity.

366. *advice unto the Spartans*, Nebrus, reputedly descendant from Aesculapius, was called to deal with an outbreak of plague among the Amphictyons.

367. *Caracalla*, Roman emperor (209–217 CE): Herodian, *Roman History*, 4.8.3, gives details of a visit to the God; *Æsculapius*, god of medicine; *kitchin aphorismes*, common medical remedies.

368. *Democritus . . . maggot*, reported by Alexander Trallian, physican, (6th century CE), *Of Medicine*, 1.15; *falling sicknesse*, epilepsy.

369. *Naturall magician*, natural magic meant merely the ingenious utilizing of the properties of nature.

370. *Indagation*, investigation.
371. *Verticity*, tendency of magnet to turn to the pole; *perspicacity*, clarity of discernment.
372. *Inveigled*, beguiled.
373. *That they stand in awe of charmes*, that the devils are really subject to human summons, rather than merely piquing human vanity by pretending such subjugation.
374. *Bitumen, pitch or brimstone*, burnt as fumigant, to drive spirits away; *Hipericon*, Hypericon, i.e. St John's Wort, used for despair and melancholy, presumed to be the devil inducing despair; *fuga Demonis*, 'flee Demons!'; *Josephus*, in *Wars of the Jews*, 7.178, the root proving difficult and dangerous to collect without elaborate rituals, pouring urine or menstrual blood upon it, then hanging the root, or using a dog (who then dies) to drag it out of the ground; *Aelianus*, in *Cynospatus*, 14.27; *Tobias . . . Asmodeus*, in Tobit 8:2.
375. *Pentangle of Solomon*, in the conjuration of devils.
376. *Tetragrammaton*, the letters of the name of God in Hebrew.
377. *Parthian flights*, alluding to strategy of Parthian horsemen, feigning flight, in Horace, *Odes*, 1.19; *ambuscado*, ambush; *tergiversations*, equivocations or pretence of turning one's back on something, in some act of subterfuge.
378. *Indubitate*, cast into doubt.
379. *Anihilates the blessed angels*, if Satan, as fallen angel, does not exist, then neither do the ranks of angels amongst whom he is counted; *last remunerations*, final reckoning or judgement.
380. *Sadduces*, Sadduceeism was equated with a denial of the spirit realm, on the basis of Acts 23:6–9.
381. Plutarch, *Brutus*, 36–7, in which, after seeing an apparition or evil spirit before a battle, Brutus is given an Epicurean philosophy lesson in perception and the plasticity of imagination.
382. *Witches*, Browne presumes the possibility of witchcraft and testified to their medical effects in the trial of two women; *staggereth the immortality*, the heretical doctrine of mortalism, that both body and soul ceased at death, to sleep until the resurrection.
383. Efforts to disturb the biblical canon and replace canonical with apocryphal works.
384. *Valentinus* (*c.*100–16 CE), Gnostic, known via a repudiation by Tertullian; *Arrian*, i.e. *Arius* (*c.*250–336 CE), denied that Christ was co-eternal divinity with God; *Marcion* (85–160 CE), Gnostic who disputed the canon of Christian literature, in particular the canonicity of the Old Testament; *Manes*, i.e. Mani (*c.*216–76 CE), author of Syriac gospel and source of much Patristic ire for his notions of good and evil, hence 'Manichaeism'; *Ebion*, doubtful figure, centre of early Christian Ebionites, reputedly translated the Old Testament; *Julian* (361–3),

Maximinus (305–14), *Dioclesian* (284–305), Roman emperors and, in patristic memory, Christian persecutors.

385. *Saturnes mouth*, in Hesiod, *Theogony*, 497–500, Saturn (Kronos) resolved to eat Zeus, his son, who was substituted by a stone dressed in swaddling clothes.

386. A much recycled list of patristic heretics: *Sabellius* (3rd century CE), anti-trinitarian theologian; *Basilides*, 2nd-century Gnostic; *Priscillian*, 4th-century theologian, executed for heresy and magic practices; *Jovinianus*, known from Jerome's refutation.

387. This group of anti-trinitarians includes *Carpocras* (2nd century), Gnostic, attacked by Irenaeus; *Symmachus* (2nd century), translator, reputedly an Ebionite; *Photinus*, 4th-century bishop.

388. [*Textual note:* 'Abraham' corrected to 'Adam' in 1650.]

389. *Cherinthus* (2nd century), for whom the world was created by angelic creators, with Jesus owning only a temporary divinity.

390. *Theodotus*, Byzantine heretic, for whom Melchisedech, the Abrahamic priest (Genesis 14), was a celestial power.

391. *Paulus Samosatenus*, Bishop of Antioch.

392. *Apollinaris*, Bishop of Laodicea, who denied the human aspect of Christ.

393. *Montanus*, 2nd-century millenarian theologian.

394. [*Textual note:* 'collective' changed in 1650 to 'consectary'.]

395. *Cognation*, natural relationship.

396. *Actives and passives*, natural forces and the objects they act on.

397. *Rainbow in the night*, see, for example, Aristotle, *Meteorology*, 3.2 (372a).

398. *Tragedy of Niceas*, Thucydides, 7.50.4, the Athenian army, worn out and about to flee, are ruinously persuaded by an eclipse to stay and fight.

399. *Indifferencie*, in the sense of impartiality, being unconcerned; *contemporised*, synchronized to.

400. *Two ... moons*, in Pliny, *Natural History*, 2.31–2. Three suns in the London sky were reported by Lilly, *Starry Messenger* (1645), p. 1, 19 November 1644, quoting, oddly perhaps, the 'small, but unparallel'd Piece', *Religio Medici*.

401. *Ephemerides*, tabulation of daily position of heavenly bodies.

402. *Extispicious*, divination from entrails.

403. *Tuscan superstition*, Cicero, *Of Divination*, 1.33.72.

404. *Augustus ... two galls*, when divining to know the outcome of the battle of Actium, Pliny, *Natural History*, 11.75.

405. *Brutus ... blackmore*, Plutarch, *Brutus*, 48, on an Ethiopian cut to pieces because he was thought inauspicious.

406. *Graceus*, Plutarch, *Tiberius Gracchus*, 17.1.

407. *Claudius Pulcher*, Roman consul (249 BCE), Livy, *Roman History*, 19; *Tripudiary Augurations*, divination from sacred birds.

408. *Incircumspection*, heedlessness.

409. *Saul*, who summoned up the ghost of Samuel, 1 Samuel 28:11–19.

410. *Philters*, philtre, a potion or drug, particularly a love potion; *ligatures*, spells causing impotence.
411. *Medicines of the earth*, from Ecclesiasticus 38:4.
412. *Caius the blinde*, from an inscription on the temple of Asclepius, in Dutch antiquarian, Janus Gruterus, *Inscriptiones Antiquae* (1603).
413. *Collyrium*, eye salve.
414. *Aper*... *Julian*... *Lucius*, whose cures are mentioned in the same set of inscriptions.
415. *Nahaman the Syrian*, 2 Kings 5:6–14, the Syrian captain suffering from leprosy, cured by Elisha, but having first to undergo elaborate bathing exercises, in a psychological battle of wills and one-upmanship.
416. *Waters of Jericho*, 2 Kings 2:19–21, Elisha 'healed the water' and drought, by pouring salt in it.
417. *Decoction of wilde gourd*, 2 Kings 4:38, Elisha relieves the dearth at Gilgal, in a manner seen as prefigurative of the feeding of the five thousand in the New Testament; *dulcified*, sweetened.
418. *Ezechias*, 2 Kings 20:1–7, i.e. Hezekiah, whose response to being told he will die pleased God, who instructed Isaiah to pass on a reprieve of the sentence. His disease in the early modern period was usually associated with plague.
419. *Mundificative*, cleansing; *eyes of Tobit*, Tobit 6, the angel Raphael gives medical instructions for the use of a fish's innards.
420. *Efficiencies*, powers.
421. [*Textual note:* 1650, 'indifferent' replaces 'independent'.]
422. *Sun, moone and stars*, a belief that might be derived from, for example, Plato, *Timaeus*, 38e.
423. *Lustrations*, purificatory sacrifices.
424. *Two principles*, antithetical to early Christian heresiography as Manichaeism, but also a casually ubiquitous idea; *Pythagoras*, in Diogenes Laertius, *Lives*, 8.26; *Empedocles*, in Diogenes Laertius, 8.76; *Oromasdes and Arimanius of Zoroaster*, Zoroastrian deities, cited in Diogenes Laertius, 1.8.
425. *Faction of Manes*, the 3rd-century Manichaeus and his followers.
426. *Aristotle*, discussed extensively in *Of the Generation of Animals*, 1.17–23 (721a–731b).
427. *Breake the head of the serpent*, Genesis 3:15.
428. *Xenophanes*, Cicero, *On the Nature of the Gods*, *Academica*, 2.39; *Anaxagoras*, in Cicero, *On the Nature of the Gods*, 2.23.
429. *Nosce teipsum*, 'know thyself', pursing the idea that any pagan oracular voice or deity, however wise and including the Delphic oracle, was a disguise of the devil.
430. *Vespasian*, in Suetonius, *Lives of the Caesars*, Vespasian, 7. Also in Tacitus, *Histories*, 4.81.
431. *Species*, outward or visible forms.

432. *Aristotle*, in for example *On the Heavens*, 2.1 (283b–284a).
433. *in Balneo . . . Ignis Rotae*, terms used in distilling and controlling temperatures, in experimentation and cooking, *in Balneo* being ways of ensuring temperatures do not rise excessively, *ignis rotae* being the method of achieving the maximum possible temperature; *hazard*, threaten.
434. [*Textual note:* 1650 has 'immutable' in place of 'wise'.]

PSEUDODOXIA EPIDEMICA BOOK 2

1. *Sit downe herein*, conclude the matter.
2. In collating his sources of ancient and patristic support for particular errors, Browne's lists often arrive pre-assembled. In relation to mineral theory they include Anselm Boetius de Boodt, *Gemmarum et lapidum Historia* (1609); Bernardus Caesius, *Mineralogia* (1636); Julius Caesar Scaliger, *Exercitationes* (1557); Antonio Brasavola, *In octo libros aphorismorum Hippocratis & Galeni* (1541). His classical sources include Pliny, *Natural History*, 37.9.23; Seneca, *Natural Questions*, 3.25.12; Claudian, *Carmina Minora*, 33–9; Albertus, *De Mineralibus*, 2.2.3. *Crystallus fit gelu . . .*, 'Crystal is made from vigorously congealed ice'.
3. Basil, *Hexameron*, 3.4 (Migne, *PG*, 29.61), 'On the division of the firmament'; Isidore, *Etymologies*, 16.13; *Austin*, i.e. Augustine, *Expositions on the Psalms*, on Psalm 147:17 'who sends his crystal like morsel of bread'; Gregory the Great, *Homilies on Ezekiel*, 1.7.18 (Migne, *PL*, 76.849); Jerome, *On Ezekiel*, 1 (Migne, *PL*, 25.29); Ezekiel 1:22.
4. Diodorus Siculus, *Library*, in fact 2.52.2; Caelius Rhodiginus, *Lectiones Antiquae* (1517); Salmasius, *Plinianae Exercitationes* (1626); *Crystallum esse lapidem . . .* 'Crystal is a stone made from congealed pure water; however, it is not formed by the cold, but by the strength of divine heat'.
5. Gaius Julius Solinus, 3rd century CE, author of *De Mirabilibus Mundi*.
6. *Mathiolus*, Pietro Mattioli, *Commentarii in sex libros Pedacii Dioscoridis* (1565); Dioscorides, *De Materia Medica*. *Putant quidam . . .* 'Certain people believe that ice assimilates and is made into crystal, but they are in error.'
7. Agricola, *De Natura Fossilium* (1558).
8. *Concretion*, hardening and coalescence, in underground mineralogical processes.
9. *Lapidificall principles*, the guiding natural principles by which stones form themselves to certain shapes; *in solutis principiis*, in its unbound origins; *conglaceation*, becoming ice-like or frozen.
10. *Aqua fortis*, corrosive liquid, widely used in experimental and alchemical pursuits, nitric acid.
11. *Induration*, hardening; *imbibition*, absorption.
12. [*Textual note:* The negative is omitted in 1646.]

13. *Salinous*, salty; *circumjacent*, close, allied to.
14. *Diffluency*, fluidity; *amitteth*, loses.
15. *Quick-silver*, mercury; *unctious*, oily, greasy; *incrassation*, thickening.
16. Aristotle, *Generation of Animals*, 2.7 (747a1).
17. *Albuginous*, white of an egg.
18. Paracelsus, *Archidoxis* in *Opera Medico-Chimica* (1603), 6.51; *magistery of wine*, a solution free from impurities.
19. [*Textual note:* This paragraph added in 1650.]
20. *Exsiccation*, drying out, removal of moisture; *expression*, squeezing out; *humectation*, moistening; *siccity*, dryness; *colliquation*, reduction to a liquid; *rectified spirits*, purified by distillation.
21. *Storax* . . . *bdellium*, resinous shrubs.
22. *Calcination*, reduction to a powder by roasting; *factitious*, not naturally produced.
23. *Cornelians*, reddish quartz-stone.
24. *Colliquate*, melt.
25. *Potential calidity*, latent heat.
26. *Attrition*, rubbing against, friction; *calefy*, warm.
27. *Ponderosity*, weight, heaviness.
28. *Congelation*, congealed or frozen matter.
29. [*Textual note:* From here to end of paragraph added in 1650.]
30. *Accidents*, a property or attribute not essential to the substance.
31. *Similary*, the same nature throughout.
32. *Sensibly*, evident, amenable to sensory perception.
33. *Scintillations*, emitting sparks or light; *accension*, kindling, igniting; *effluencies*, the presumed streaming out of particles in electricity or magnetism.
34. *Heliotropes*, a green variety of quartz, sometimes spotted red; *agaths*, semi-transparent, variegated stone (agate).
35. *Some plenty*, quantity.
36. *Lyable*, i.e. liable, subject to; *sublimation*, converting to a solid, by heating first into a vapour.
37. Paracelsus, *De Præparationibus*, 1.3.
38. *Menstruums*, a solvent for metals in alchemical practices; *emolition*, softening; *tincture*, colouring; *Boetius*, de Boodt, *Gemmarum et lapidum Historia* (1609), 2.74; *triturable*, capable of being pulverized; *contrition*, rubbing together; *vitrification*, conversion into glass-like substance; *testified*, demonstrated.
39. [*Textual note:* From here to the end of the paragraph is replaced from 1650 with: 'and a fusion of the salt and earth, which are the fixed elements of the composition, wherein the fusible salt draws the earth and infusible part into one continuum, and therefore ashes will not run from whence the salt is drawn, as bone ashes prepared for the test of metals. Common fusion in metals is also made by a violent heat, acting

upon the volatile and fixed, the dry and humid parts of those bodies; which notwithstanding are so united, that upon attenuation from heat, the humid parts will not fly away, but draw the fixed ones into fluor with them. Ordinary liquation in wax and oily bodies is made by a gentler heat, where the oyl and salt, the fixed and fluid principles will not easily separate. All which, whether by vitrification, fusion or liquation, being forced into fluent consistencies, do naturally regress into their former solidities. Whereas the melting of ice is a simple resolution, or return from solid to fluid parts, wherein it naturally resteth.']

40. *Exhaled*, blown off in a steam.
41. *Stone*, gallstone.
42. *In their continuities*, i.e. when unbroken.
43. *Stibium*, calcined antimony; *murrey*, mulberry colour.
44. Pliny, *Natural History*, 37.9; *circumscription ... contiguities*, i.e. not from external addition of matter or forming, in reaction to the surfaces it touches; *seminall root, and formative principle*, the idea that matter, including minerals, is implanted with a particular impulse to growth.
45. *Circumambiency*, that which surrounds, the physical environment; *conformeth*, which shapes it.
46. *Guttulous*, in drops.
47. [*Textual note:* This sentence replaced in 1650 by 'and so growing greater or lesser according unto the accretion or pluvious aggelation about the mother and fundamental atomes thereof; which seems to be some feathery particle of snow; although snow it self be sexangular, or at least of a starry and many-pointed figure.']
48. Aristotle, *Meteorology*, 1.12 (348a). This reference disappears from subsequent editions of *Pseudodoxia*; *corraded*, worn down.
49. Pliny, *Natural History*, 37.9; *Caramania*, region of Turkey.
50. [*Textual note:* The following sentence added in 1650.] Job 38:30.
51. These medical references are cited from Bernardus Caesius, *Mineralogia* (1636), 'De Crystallo', 3.9.
52. *Difference*, used here to suggest the categorization or differentiation of stones.
53. [*Textual note:* From here to the end of the paragraph is replaced in 1658 by: 'As sensible phylosophers conceive of the generation of diamonds, iris, berils. Not making them of frozen icecles, or from meer aqueous and glaciable substances, condensing them by frosts into solidities, vainly to be expected even from polary congelations: but from thin and finest earths, so well contempered and resolved, that transparency is not hindred; and containing lapidifical spirits, able to make good their solidities against the opposition and activity of outward contraries, and so leave a sensible difference between the bonds of glaciation, which in the mountains of ice about the Northern Seas, are easily dissolved by ordinary heat of the sun, and between the finer legatures of petrification,

whereby not only the harder concretions of diamonds and saphirs, but the softer veins of crystal remain indissolvable in scorching territories, and the negro land of Congor.'] *Lentous*, viscous; *colament*, the product of filtration or percolation; *coadjuvancy*, helping; *concretive spirit*, the force that hardens it into a solid; *Gorgon*, most famously, Medusa, the sight of whom turned viewers to stone.

54. *Lapidificall succity*, a hardening moisture.
55. The absence of minerals from the creation account of Genesis 1, associated with the hexameron, is a widely noted omission; *classis of creatures*, that minerals formed and 'grew' in the earth endows them with the seminal powers of creaturely life. This suggests, though in minimal fashion, an animate view of 'subterranities'; *vivency*, living nature; *seminalities*, implanted principles of growth.
56. *Tralucency*, translucency; *durity*, hardness; *emery*, used for cutting other stones; *turchois*, turquoise.
57. *Diaphanity*, transparency; *continuity... discreted by atomicall terminations*, darker bodies being constituted by their alternating 'atoms' of body with interstices or pores.
58. *Continuated*, being made less porous and hence more transparent in its fabric; *oyled paper*, was used in place of window panes; *umbrosity*, being shady.
59. *Opacus*, opaque.
60. *Superficies*, plane surface.
61. *Crusible*, crucible.
62. *Stirious*, like an icicle; *stillicidious*, formed by drops.
63. *Sperma coeti*, on which, see Book 3.26; *superfluitance*, floating material.
64. *Crystalline humor*, lens.
65. In fact, Psalm 147:17; *vulgar translation*, i.e. the Vulgate, the Latin translation.
66. *Septuagint*, the Greek translation of scripture. Browne gives the AV translation, 'hee casteth forth his ice like morsels'.
67. *Tremellius and Junius*; producers, together with Théodore de Bèze, of a new, 16th-century translation of scriptures into Latin (1579); *Dejicit gelu...* 'He hurls down his ice as if morsels, who will stand in the presence of his cold?'
68. *Synonomy*, i.e. the synonyms; *Austen*, Augustine; *Lyranus*, Nicholas of Lyra, 14th-century exegete.
69. The point of reference and source throughout the chapter is William Gilbert, *De Magnete* (1600).
70. *Vertue*, power, force, a standard co-meaning of virtue, in natural philosophy.
71. *Magellanica*, Strait of Magellan, the southern passageway joining the Atlantic and Pacific.

72. *Center of the universe*, adopting a pre-Copernican model of the universe; *accession*, coming into the presence of, astronomically speaking; *salved*, finding a workable solution to a difficulty; *verticity*, inclination of a needle to turn towards the pole.
73. Psalm 93:1.
74. Job 26:7.
75. Job 38:6.
76. *Anaxagoras, Socrates and Democritus*, Aristotle, *On the Heavens*, 2.13 (294b), citing the three philosophers as believers in the flatness of the earth and the cause of its stability.
77. [*Textual note:* This passage, from 'Now whether the Earth stand still' to the end of the paragraph, disappears after the 1646 edition.] *Xenophanes*... *Thales Milesius*, likewise in Aristotle, *On the Heavens*, 21.3 (194a), Xenophanes positing infinite roots to the earth.
78. *Conversion*, turning, revolving; *dineticall*, relating to rotation.
79. *Effluxions*, the outward flow of atoms by which magnetism is effected; *species of visible objects*, on the idea that sight works by the emission of 'species', or quasi-material images from objects; *congenerous*, of the same kind.
80. *Effluviums*, like effluxions, part of the terminology of corpuscularian magnetism theory; *streated*, narrowed and constrained; *Renatus des Cartes*, René Descartes, *Principles of Philosophy* (1644); Sir Kenelm Digby, *Two Treatises* (1644), 'Of Bodies', Chs. 20–22; *phenomenas*, appearances.
81. *Septentrionate*, point to the north; *Australize*, point to the south.
82. *Equiponderate*, in a state of equilibrium.
83. *Scorious*, the slaggy matter left after smelting a metal from its ore.
84. Gilbert, *De Magnete* (1600), p. 141.
85. *Coition*, coming together.
86. [*Textual note:* Text has 'polarity Iron refrigeration'.]
87. *Graines and circles in trees*, cutting the trunk and observing the difference in distance between circles, for example, Nathaniel Carpenter, *Geographie* (1635), p. 131.
88. *Lyllie*... *cuspis*, northern and southern symbols of compass.
89. *Amits*, loses.
90. [*Textual note:* The following sentence added in 1650.]
91. *Preaction*, its earlier action.
92. *Attenuated*, thinned; *incrassated*, thickened, made more dense.
93. *Alliciency*, the quality of being attractive.
94. *Terrella*, spherical magnet, used as the basis for theorizing the magnetic qualities of the earth.
95. Mark Ridley, *A Short Treatise of Magneticall Bodies* (1613); Henry Brigs, *Arithmetica Logarithmica* (1624).
96. *Vertex*, astronomically, the point directly overhead.

97. *Answerable tract*, equal-sized body of land.
98. *Colombus*, vying for precedence of discovery with the Florentine *Americus Vespucius*.
99. Sebastian Cabot (*c.*1474–1557), Venetian sailor and explorer.
100. *Northerne passage*, a long-standing hope, that to avoid the expense and danger of circumnavigating Africa, a passage to the east could be found north of Russia.
101. *Exuperance*, i.e. exsuperance, superabundance, excess; *rhomb*, rhumb, the angle between points of the thirty-two point compass (11 degrees 15 minutes).
102. *Adjacencyes*, neighbouring land masses.
103. [*Textual note:* Subsequent editions of *Pseudodoxia*, from 1650 on, add to this with an account of the observations of Jesuit scientist, Athanasius Kircherus.] *Carde*, the circular background of a compass, on which the directions are inscribed.
104. *Levinus Lemnius*, physician, in *Occulta Naturae Miracula* (1571), 3.4; *Caelius Calcagninus*, humanist and astronomer (1479–1541); Guido Pancirollus, author of a history of lost things, in use among the ancients, *Res Memorabiles* (1631), 2.2. Browne digests here from the Jesuit astronomer, Juan de Pineda, *Salomon prævius* (1609), 4.15.4.
105. *Hic ventus*... 'Now there is a good wind about the ship, take the rope', a slight mis-rendering of Plautus, the Latin playwright's *Mercator*, line 875; *Ennius*, Roman poet, second century BCE.
106. *Hanno*, Carthaginian explorer and sailor, 5th century BCE; Jonah 1:13.
107. *Salomon*... *Ophir*, 1 Kings 9:28, Ophir, a legendary, though unspecific, source of wealth; the compass, printing, and gunpowder being a common trio of inventions by which the Renaissance proved itself to have outdone the ancients in ingenuity.
108. *Aristotle*... *Alexanders acquirements*, in Pliny, *Natural History*, 8.17.44; *Drake and Candish* (Cavendish), reported among other places in Samuel Purchase, *Purchase His Pilgrimage* (1625), 1.2.
109. *Petrus Peregrinus*, 13th-century writer on magnetism, translated and printed in 1558 by Achilles Gasserus, who worked under the astronomer, Georg Joachim Rheticus.
110. *Paulus Venetus*, 14th-century logician; *Albertus Magnus*, 13th-century Dominican natural philosopher and encylopaedist; *Aristotle*, in Diogenes Laertius, 5.26.
111. *Chalybs præparatus*, ferrous oxide; *crocus martis*, ferric oxide; *fluxes*, menstruation.
112. Descartes, *Priciples of Philosophy* (1644), 4.171, p. 285; *Præterea magnes trahet ferrum*... 'Moreover, the magnet will draw the iron, or rather the magnet and iron mutually approach each other, for there is no dragging in that matter.'

113. Nicholaus Cabeus, *Philosophia Magnetica* (1629), 4.21, p. 346; *Nec magnes trahit proprie*... 'Strictly speaking, the magnet does not draw the iron, nor does the iron call the magnet forth to itself, but both mutually come together with equal effort.'
114. Mark Ridley, *Of Magneticall Bodies and Motions* (1613), p. 83.
115. William Gilbert, *De Magnete* (1600), p. 60.
116. Jean Baptista van Helmont, *Opuscula* (1644), 4.79; Kircher, *Magnes* (1641) p. 75; Licetus, *De Tertio-Quaesitis* (1646), p. 223.
117. *Skiphs*, boats, skiffs; *hoise*, raise aloft.
118. *Alliciency*, attraction.
119. *Austin*, Augustine, *City of God*, 21.4.
120. Galen, *On the Natural Faculties*, 1.14.
121. Aristotle, *De Anima*, 1.2 (405a); Aquinas, *On the Physics of Aristotle*, 7; Scaliger, *Exercitationes* (1557), f. 156v.
122. *Bolary*, clay-like.
123. Pliny and Solinus are cited by Gilbert, pp. 2–3; Ptolemy, *Tetrabiblos* 1.3.13; Plutarch, *Natural Questions,* 2.8.1; Albertus, *De Mineralibus*, 2.2.2; Mattioli, *Commentaires sur Dioscorides* (1572), p. 747; Franciscus Rueus, *De Gemmis*, in Vallesius, *De Sacra Philosophia* (1622), 2.24; Joannes Langius, *Epistolae Medicinales* (1589), 2.18.
124. *Homers Moly*, Homer, *Odyssey*, 10.287–306, in order to resist Circe.
125. Pliny, *Natural History,* 37.15; *Adamas dissidet cum Magnete*... 'Adamas' (or Diamond) 'has so strong an aversion to the magnet, that when it is placed close to the iron, it prevents the iron from being attracted away from itself. Or again, if the magnet is moved towards the iron and seizes it, the "adamas" snatches the iron and takes it away.'
126. Paracelsus, *Opera Medico-Chimica* (1605), 6.210.
127. *Exsiccated*, dried out.
128. [*Textual note:* The following sentence added 1658.]
129. Pliny, *Natural History*, 36.66.
130. [*Textual note:* From 'Beside, vitrification...' to the end of the paragraph is replaced in 1650 with 'True it is that in the making of glass, it hath been an ancient practice to cast in pieces of magnet, or perhaps manganes: conceiving it carried away all ferreous and earthy parts, from the pure and running portion of glass, which the loadstone would not respect; and therefore if that attraction were not rather electrical then magnetical, it was a wondrous effect what Helmont delivereth concerning a glass wherein the magistery of loadstone was prepared, which after retained an attractive quality.']
131. [*Textual note:* From 'But whether the ashes' to the end of the paragraph added in 1650.]
132. Eusebius Nierembergius, *Historia Naturae* (1635), p. 131.
133. Paracelsus, *Archidoxis*, in *Opera* (1605), 6.55; *ordure*, excrement.
134. Michael Sendivogius, *De Sulphure* (1616), 'Angel, teach me law'.

135. Bernardus Caesius, *Mineralogia* (1636), p. 539.
136. Franciscus Rueus, *De Gemmis* (1622), pp. 169–70; Boetius de Boodt, *Gemmarum et Lapidum Historia* (1636), pp. 438–76.
137. Olaus Magnus, *De Gentibus septentrionalibus* (1555), 2.26.12.
138. Pliny, *Natural History*, 36.25.
139. Serapion, *De Simplicibus Medicinis* (1525), f. 187v.
140. *Controled*, checked.
141. Giambattista della Porta, *Natural Magic* (1644), 7.1, p. 288.
142. Dioscorides, *Materia Medica*, 5.130.
143. Galen, *On the Powers and Mixtures of Simple Remedies*, 9.163; *Ætius*, 5th century CE, Byzantine physician; *Paulus Ægineta*, author of 7th-century CE medical compendium; *Oribasius*, physican to Julian the Apostate, 4th century CE.
144. [*Textual note:* From 1650, more on medicinal preparations is included, but omitted here.] *Hæmatites*, iron oxide.
145. Garcias ab Horto, *Aromatum et Simplicium* (1574), 1.56.
146. *Podagrical*, gouty; Ætius, *Tetrabiblos*, 1.2.25.
147. Marcellus Empericus, 5th century CE, Gallic physician, in *De Medicamentis*, 1.63.
148. *Philter*, love potion.
149. Claudian, 4th-century Latin poet, *Carmina Minora*, 29.48.
150. Paracelsus, *De Praeparationibus*, in *Opera* (1605), 6.183; Johann Wecker, *Antidotarium Speciale* (1617), 2.29; Daniel Sennert, *Practica Medicina* (1628), p. 581.
151. *Spruceland*, Prussia; Daniel Beckherus, *De Cultrivoro Prussiaco* (1638), 6.
152. *Magdaleon*, cylindrical, medicinal plaster.
153. Dioscorides, reported by Marbodus, *De Gemmis* (1531), 19.25.
154. Cardan, *De subtilitate* (1560), p. 217.
155. *Menippus*, Lucian, *Icaromenippus*.
156. Taliacotius, *De Curtorum Chiurgia per Insitionem* (1597), 3.9, on grafting.
157. Famianus Strada, *Prolusiones Academicae* (1617), 2.6.
158. *Trithemius*... *Godwin*, reported by John Wilkins, *Mercury* (1641), pp. 145–8.
159. *Unguentum Armarium*, the weapon salve, or powder of sympathy, by which a powder was applied to the weapon that caused a wound and would cure at a distance. Defended by Kenelm Digby among others.
160. *Vulnerary*, used in healing wounds.
161. [*Textual note:* This paragraph appearing in 1650.]
162. Pliny, *Natural History*, 33.20; Pancirollus, *Res Memorabiles*, 1.33.
163. Gilbertus, *De Magnete* (1600), 2.2, p. 48.
164. Cabeus, *Philosophia Magnetica* (1629), 2.17, p. 179.
165. On such rocks, crystals, and compounds, see, for instance, *Pharmacopoeia Londinensis* (1632), along with Gilbertus and Cabeus.

166. *Perspirable*, capable of exhaling; the first edition in fact has 'perspicable', capable of being seen, but this seems to be a printer's erratum.
167. *Obnubilated*, obscured, indistinct.
168. Cabeus, *Philosophia Magnetica* (1629), pp. 192–4.
169. Kenelm Digby, *Treaties of Bodies* (1644), 19.8, p. 173; Descartes, *Principles of Philosophy* (1644), 4.184, p. 293.
170. Gilbert, *De Magnete* (1600), p. 59; *Effluvia illa tenuiora*... 'Those thinner effluvia receive the bodies and encircle them, to which these bodies are united, and then conducted towards the source as if by extended electrical arms, and increasing in strength in relation to their proximity to the source.'
171. Scaliger, *Exercitationes* (1557), f. 163.
172. Pliny, *Natural History*, 37.12.
173. Plutarch, *Table-Talk*, 2.7.1.
174. Levinus Lemnius, *Occulta Naturae Miracula* (1571), 4.10, p. 421; Rueus, *De Gemmis* (1622), p. 172.
175. Jean Baptiste van Helmont, *Opuscula* (1644), 1.44.66.
176. Georgius Melichius, *De Recta Medicamentorum* (1586), p. 281; *pismire*, ant.
177. Albertus, *De Mineralibus*, 2.2.1.
178. Pliny, *Natural History*, 37.15, as translated in text.
179. *Comminuible*, able to be pulverized; *pistillation*, being broken down with a pestle.
180. *Powder of Nicolaus*, Nicholas Myrepsus, *De Compositione Medicamentorum*, in *Medicae Artis Principes* (1567), 2.2.370f.; *stone*, gallstone.
181. *Saxifragous*, stone-breaking.
182. Helmont, *De Lithiasis* (1644), 3.33.
183. *Chylifactory*, digestive; *lapideous*, stony.
184. Bel and the Dragon 27.
185. *Extimulating*, stimulating.
186. Sanctorius, *Commentaria in Artem Medicinalem Galeni* (1630), 3.94.3.
187. [*Textual note:* The following two paragraphs added from 1650.]
188. *Strigments*, scrapings from the skin; *sudorous*, sweaty.
189. *Electuaries*, medical paste; *meseraicks*, mesenteric, of the veins; Browne inserts 'or Lacteal Vessels' in later versions.
190. *Midas*, whose touch turned everything to gold, including his food and wine, Ovid, *Metamorphoses*, 11.100–30.
191. *Wendler*, reputedly produced golden streaks on a hen by feeding it gold.
192. *Dequantitated*, reduced.
193. [*Textual note:* The following brief paragraph added in 1650.]
194. Aristotle, *Problemata*, 25.8 (938b).
195. *Decrepitated*, calcined, to the point of crackling.
196. *Depuration*, removal of impurities.
197. *Exilition*, springing forth.

198. Cardan, *De Subtilitate* (1560), p. 43.
199. *Tonnitrous*, thundery.
200. *Corruscation*, quivering flash of light.
201. [*Texual note:* This paragraph added in 1650.]
202. Vannoccio Biringuccio, *De la pirotechnia* (1559), p. 416.
203. Giambattista della Porta, *Natural Magic* (1644), 12.3, p. 466.
204. Brasavola, *Examen Omnium Simplicium* (1537), p. 488; Cardan, *De Subtilitate*, p. 57.
205. *Iamque pulvis*... 'Recently a powder was discovered which hurls a missile without a deep sound, but not so strongly that it might be able to kill a chicken for example.'
206. [*Textual note:* This paragraph added from 1650.] Girolamo Cataneo, *Dell' Arte Militare* (1584), f. 23r.
207. *Incummiscibility*, inability to remain together.
208. *Hydragyrus*, mercury.
209. *Ebullition*, bubbling, boiling over; *emication*, sparking.
210. Dioscorides, *Materia Medica*, 5.121; Pliny, *Natural History*, 32.11; Solnius, 2.41; Isidore, *Etymologies*, 16.8.1; Rueus, *De Gemmis* (1547), 2.19; *induration*, hardening.
211. *Beguinnus*, Jean Beguin, *Élémens de Chymie* (1624), 2.10.
212. Boetius de Boote, *De Gemmis*, 2.153, p. 305.
213. *Ligneous*, woody in texture; *Johnson*, in Gerard's *Herbal* (1636), 2.458.
214. Pancirollus, *Res Memorabiles* (1631), 2.2, p. 65; Scaliger, *Excertitiones* (1557), f. 136r.
215. *Ramuzius*, Giovanni Battista Ramusio, *Navigationi et Viaggi* (1574), f. 49r.
216. Gonzales de Mendoza, *Historia*... *China* (1585), 1.10.
217. [*Textual note:* From here, to the end of the following paragraph, '... rejected by us' was added in 1672.] Linschoten, *Navigationes in Orientem* (1601), 23.
218. [*Textual note:* Some sections on stones (carbuncle, ægle-stone, and others) added in 1650 and 1672 are omitted.]
219. i.e. epilepsy.
220. Exodus 28:9–12.
221. *Molas*, abnormal swelling of tissue in womb, here meaning fantasy.
222. *Catacresticall*, i.e. catachresis, the improper application of a metaphor.
223. Oswald Croll, *De Signaturis Internis Rerum*, in *Basilica Chymica* (1609); Giambattista della Porta, *Phytognomonica* (1588).
224. Valescus de Taranta, *Philonium Pharmaceuticum* (1523), 4.24, whose strange etymologies are, roughly, 'Diarrhoea is so called because it comes many times in one day. Herisepela as if from 'adhering'; Emorrohois from 'emach' that is 'blood' and 'morrhois', which means 'to die'. Lithargia comes from 'litos' which means 'oblivion', and 'targus': death; Scotomia from 'scotos', which means 'to see' and 'mias', 'a fly'; Opthalmia from the Greek 'opus', which means 'a draught' and 'talmon', which means 'eye';

Paralisis from 'an injury', 'laesio', of 'part' of the body, and Fistula from 'fos', 'sound' and 'stolon' which means 'an emission', as if an emission of sound or the voice.'

225. *Masle*, male.
226. *Empedocles*, in (Pseudo-)Aristotle, *De Plantis*, 1.2 (817a).
227. Mattioli, *Commentarii... Dioscoridis*, in *Opera* (1598), 1.759, 'But this is certainly false and fabulous'.
228. Albertus, *De Vegetabilibus*, 6.2.12.
229. *Cadmus*, Ovid, *Metamorphoses*, 3.101–10; *Jupiter*, Ovid, *Fasti*, 5.493–536.
230. *Eradication*, uprooting; *stridulous*, shrill grating sound; *divulsion*, pulling apart.
231. Pliny, *Natural History*, 25.94.
232. *Napellus, aconite and thora*, poisons.
233. *Circe*, sorceress in *Odyssey*, 10.135, who turned the enchanted sailors into pigs; Dioscorides, 4.75.
234. Homer, *Odyssey*, 10.305–6; moly is the herb by which Odysseus resists Circe.
235. Garcia ab Horto, *Aromatum... Historia* (1567), 1.41.
236. *Torrefaction*, drying out by heat.
237. *Isles of Molucca*, Indonesian archipelago.
238. Garcia, *Historia*, 1.20.
239. *Flosculous*, flower-like.
240. Pliny, *Natural History*, 16.93; Virgil, *Aeneid*, 6.205.
241. The contradictions in this, that mistletoe both 'very commonly' and 'never' grows on holly and bays, for instance, are smoothed out in later editions.
242. Antonio Brasavola, *De Medicamentis Catharticis* (1555), p. 149.
243. *Verulam*, Francis Bacon, *Sylva Slyvarum* (1628), p. 137.
244. *Surcles*, shoots.
245. *Turdus sibi*... 'The thrush shits its own woe', being caught in the birdlime of its own shit.
246. Pliny, *Natural History*, 16.95.
247. *Epilepticall*, inconstant.
248. *Bellonius*, Belon, *Observations*, in Clusius, *Exotica* (1605), p. 143.
249. Ecclesiasticus 24:14.
250. *Simplist*, collector of simples, herbalist.
251. *Glassenbury*, Glastonbury.
252. Mattioli, *Commentarii... Dioscordis*, in *Opera* (1598), 3.135, p. 501; Pliny, *Natural History*, 10.20.
253. Vicomercatus, *In Quatuor Libros Aristotelis Meteorologicorum Commentarii* (1556), 3.1.
254. For fear of divine thunderbolts, in Suetonius, *Augustus*, 90.
255. *Trisulke*, trident; *terebrate*, pierce.

256. *Dipped in Styx*, as was Achilles, *Statius*, Achilleid, 1.133; *Ceneus*, Ovid, *Metamorphoses*, 12.458–531.
257. *Ebriety*, being drunk; Plutarch, *Quaestiones convivales*, 1.6.4.
258. *Glister*, bright light.
259. [*Textual note:* I depart here from the 1646 edition, to include this chapter first included in the 1650 edition, which incorporates some sections (7–9) from the first edition, but also includes new material. Section 1 made its appearance in 1672. Hence subsequent section numbers differ from both the 1646 and 1650 texts.]
260. Johannes Faber, *Animalia* (1651), p.757. [*Textual note:* This paragraph, post-dating microscopic interest in the England of the 1660s, appeared first in 1672.]
261. Scaliger, *Exercitationes* (1557), 161r.
262. Paracelsus, *De Natura Rerum*, in *Opera* (1603), 6.267.
263. Serapion, 12th-century Arabic physician, *De Medicinis Simplicibus* (1525), 2.67, f.132r.
264. Jacobus Hollerius, *De Morbis Internis* (1611).
265. Oribasius, 4th-century Greek medical writer, who left his fragmentary *Collectiones Medicae*.
266. Galen, *On the Powers and Mixtures of Simple Remedies*, 8.18.15.
267. Pliny, *Natural History*, 16.63.
268. Belon, *Observations*, in *Exotica* (1605), 1.2.

PSEUDODOXIA EPIDEMICA BOOK 3

1. Aristotle, *Progression of Animals*, 9 (709a); Diodorus Siculus, *Library of History*, 3.27, on the inhabitants of Ethiopia; Strabo, *Geography*, 16.4.10 on the 'Elephantophagi', tribes of elephant-hunters around the Nile and its tributaries; Ambrose, *Hexameron*, 6.5.31 (Migne, *PL*, 14.253); Cassidorus, *Variae*, 10.30 (Migne, *PL*, 14.235), an excursion in the natural history of the animal occasioned by the presence of wild elephants in the *Via Sacra*. The other sources that inform the chapter are Ulysse Aldrovandi, *De Quadrupedibus Solidipedibus* (1623), 9, who collates Browne's sources, and Pliny, *Natural History*, 8.1.
2. *Inflexion*, bending.
3. *Volatills*, winged creatures.
4. *Arthriticall analogies*, joint-like parts.
5. *Orpheus his harpe*, Ovid, *Metamorphoses*, 11.1.
6. *Decumbence*, rest, lying down.
7. [*Textual note:* Negative omitted in 1646.]
8. Galen, *On the Usefulness of the Parts*, 15.8.
9. *Tyranny*, torture; *Ixion . . . Sisiphus . . . Tantalus*, Ovid, *Metamorphoses*, 4.457–61: three exemplary punishments of Hades, Ixion bound to a wheel turning perpetually, Sisyphus eternally pushing a rock uphill,

and Tantalus standing forever in a pool that receded when he bent to drink and tempted by fruit on branches that pulled away when he reached for them; *Titius*, a giant tied down while vultures ate his liver, Robert Burton, *Anatomy of Melancholy*, 1.4.1.

10. *Mercurialis*, Hieronymus Mercurialis (1530–1606), *De Arte Gymnastica* (1644), 3.3.4.1; Galen, *On the Movement of Muscles*, 2.4.
11. [*Textual note:* This sentence added in 1650.]
12. *Xiphilinus*, an abridgement of Dio Cassius, 61.17.2; Suetonius, *Nero*, 11.2.
13. *Indus qui Elephantem*..., 'the Indian who was managing the animal, thinking that the king was dismounting in the usual manner, ordered the elephant to kneel; when he did so, the rest of the animals also – for so they had been trained – let down their bodies to the ground', Quintus Curtius, *History of Alexander*, 8.14.39.
14. *Pontificem ter genibus*..., 'having genuflected three times, he lowered his body and greeted the pontiff with reverence', Jeronimo Osorio da Fonseca, *De rebus Emmanuelis regis Lusitaniae* (1571), p. 346.
15. *Germanicus*, Pliny, *Natural History*, 8.2; *tricliniums*, Roman dining-room couches.
16. [*Textual note:* This paragraph added 1650.]
17. Polydore Vergil, *Anglica Historia* (1555), 16. This and the following information on the trade in gift-elephants is from Aldrovandi.
18. *Composure*, construction; *bought*, the hollow angle behind the knee; *hough*, the joint in the hind leg of a quadruped; *suffraginous*, in the hocks—the backward-pointing joints—of animals.
19. *à dicto secundum*..., i.e. from a qualified to an absolute statement.
20. *Venation*, hunting. Browne's list of those who assert elephants are hunted by sawing away trees they are asleep against is taken from Johann Eusebius Nieremberg, *Historia Naturae* (1635), pp. 193–4.
21. Oppian, *Cynegetica*, 2.489–550.
22. Pliny, *Natural History*, 8.9.
23. *Averse*, facing backwards; *supersaliency*, leaping up.
24. Aelian, *On Animals*, 2.11; Oppian, *Cynegetica*, 2.540–3; Christobal Acosta, *Aromatum* (1578), 7, an account of the medicines and simples of India; *Achilles horse*, Homer, *Iliad*, 19.404–17, the horse, Xanthus, prophesies Achilles' death.
25. *Serpent*, Genesis 3:1–5.
26. [*Textual note:* Sentence added 1650.]
27. *Solipeds*, animal having an uncloven hoof; Aristotle, *Of the Parts of Animals*, 676b–677a; Pliny, *Natural History*, 11.74.
28. *Absyrtus*, 4th-century CE animal and veterinary writer; *Ruino the Bononian*, Carlo Ruini, *Anatomia del Cavallo* (1603).
29. *Simous*, concave, curving inward.
30. *Extimulates*, provokes, stimulates.

31. *Costive*, constipated.
32. *Flamen*, priest devoted to a particular Roman deity; Pliny, *Natural History*, 28.40.
33. *Our countryman*, Gervase Markham, *Markhams Maister-peece* (1610), 1.63.
34. *Pierius*, Pierio Valeriano (1477–1558), author of *Hieroglyphica* (1556), a work that inaugurated Renaissance emblematic theory, in which meaning, moral and philosophical, might be condensed into a diagrammatic or pictorial form. The work purports to be based on Horapollo, Egyptian priest and the source of hieroglyphic wisdom.
35. *Postillers*, annotators; *Canticles,* Song of Songs, passim; *precept... innocent as doves*, Matthew 10:16; *holy Ghost*, Matthew 3:16, Luke 3:22, at the baptism of Jesus; the list of patristic sources, in Aldrovandi, *de Avibus* (1610), 2.207–8: Cyprian, *On the Unity of the Church*, 1.9 (Migne, *PL*, 4.506); *Austin*, Augustine, *Homilies on the Gospel of John*, 6.3 (Migne, *PL*, 35.1426); Isidore, *Etymologies*, 7.3; *Beda*, Bede, *Homily on the Gospel of Matthew*, 1.3.
36. Aristotle, *History of Animals*, 2.15 (506b), *Fel aliis ventri...* 'some have the gall close to the bladder, others to the gut'; Pliny, *Natural History*, 11.75; Galen, *On Black Bile*, 9.
37. Julius Alexandrinus, *Salubrium* (1575), p. 312; *quinsies*, inflammations of the throat.
38. *Phænigmus or rubifying medicine*, causing the skin to turn red; Galen, *On the Powers and Mixtures of Simple Remedies*, 10.2.25; *famine of Samaria*, 2 Kings 6:25; Josephus, *Antiquities of the Jews*, 9.4.4.
39. *Lixiviated*, infused with alkaline salts, lye; *serosity*, watery and alkaline humors or liquids.
40. *Concupiscible*, desired; *crasis*, constitution and combination of humours.
41. *Paris... Ajax*, the former driven by lust, the latter by bravery and hot-headedness; *Medea*, Ovid, *Metamorphoses*, 7.10–424.
42. *Capillations*, capillary vessels; *lenity*, gentleness; *portract*, portrayal; *holocaust... of Moses*, Exodus 40:29.
43. *Ben Maimon*, Maimonides, *Treatise of Offering Sacrifice*, 6.20–3; *crop*, pouch-like enlargement to the gullet; Leviticus 1:6. Browne takes his references here from Ainsworth, *Annotations* to Leviticus 1:6.
44. *Birds of Venus*, Ovid, *Amores*, 1.2.23.
45. *Illation*, drawing conclusions, inferring.
46. *Tobias*, Tobit 6:1–8; Dioscorides, *Materia Medica*, 2.12; *married couple*, Plutarch, *Advice to the Bride and Groom*, in *Moralia*, 27.
47. Hosea 7:11, 'Ephraim also is like a silly dove without heart' (KJV), silly in the sense of 'misled'. Here and in the following, there are puns on 'columbae'.
48. Jeremiah 25:18, 'He hath forsaken his covert, as the lion: for their land is desolate because of the fierceness of the oppressor, and because of his fierce anger.'

49. Jeremiah 46:16 'made many to fall, yea, one fell upon another: and they said, Arise, and let us go again to our own people, and to the land of our nativity, from the oppressing sword'.
50. *Formicæ sua bilis*... 'They say that even ants and gnats have bile', *Greek Anthology*, 10.49.
51. *Spanish mares*, in Varro, *Res Rustica*, 2.1.19.
52. Aesop, *Fables*, 153, ed. Temple (1998); Aristotle, *Ethics*, but there is no reference to beavers in the Ethics; Aelian, *On Animals*, 6.34; Pliny, *Natural History*, 8.47.109, Solinus, *Collectanea Rerum Memorabilium*, in Arthur Goldings' translation, *The Worthy Works of Julius Solinus Polyhistor* (1587), 22; Juvenal, 12:34–6, 'in imitation of the beaver, who makes himself a eunuch in his wish to escape through the loss of a testicle. That's how well he understands the drugs in his groin.'
53. *Evulsion*, plucking out by force; *tropicall*, i.e. as a trope and rhetorical device.
54. *Sestius*, Sextius Niger (1st century CE); Dioscorides, *Materia Medica*, 2.24.
55. Plutarch, *The Cleverness of Animals*, in *Moralia*, a work on the wisdom and skill of animals.
56. *Fable of Hippomanes*, Hippomenes, who distracted Atalanta in a race by throwing golden apples on the ground.
57. *Absyrtus*, Medea's brother, whose dismembered limbs she cast to delay the chase of her father.
58. *Alogie*, illogical notion, unreasonableness.
59. *Divulsion*, plucking apart.
60. *These parts avelled*, the torn away parts; *cods*, pouches.
61. *Exudate*, exude.
62. *Bellonius*, Pierre Belon, *De Aquatilibus* (1553), 1.4; *Gesnerus*, Conrad Gesner, *De Quadrupedibus Viviparis* (1551), p. 338; *Amatus*, Amatus Lusitanus, *In Dioscoridis de Medica Materia Libros* (1558), p. 258; *Rondeletius*, Guillaume Rondelet, *Libri de Piscibus Marinis* (1555), p. 237; *Mathiolus*, Pietro Mattioli, *Commentarii in VI. libros Pedacii Dioscoridis Anazarbei de Medica materia* (1583).
63. Rondelet, *De Piscibus*, p. 238, 'Beavers have two swellings in their groin area, one on each side, the size of a goose egg. Between these two swellings are the sexual organs pertaining to males or the privy parts of the female; these swellings are not testicles, but the membrane of a concealed sack, in the middle of which is a single passage from which a thick and waxy fluid exudes. The beaver itself often licks this passage with its mouth, sucks out the fluid and afterwards smears the various parts of its body with it, as if with oil. It can certainly be deduced from this information that these swellings are not testicles, because there is no path from them to the male sexual organs, nor any connection by which fluid might be distributed into the passage of the sexual organs and

emitted forth; moreover, because the testicles are found within, I believe that these same swellings pertain to the Moschian animal, from which that odorous pus flows out.'

64. *Emunctories*, organs for conveying waste from body; *garous*, resembling a fermented fish-sauce; *raucide*, rough; *olidous*, having a fetid smell.
65. Dioscorides, *Materia Medica*, 2.24; Galen, *On the Powers and Mixtures of Simple Remedies*, 11.1.15; *Ægineta*, Paulus Aegineta, *De Re Medica* (1567), 7.3; Aetius, *Tetrabiblos*, 1.2.177.
66. Aetius includes information on the Egyptian hieroglyphic and magical traditions; *succedaneous*, acting as substitute for.
67. Pliny, *Natural History*, 32.13 and 8.47; *experiment*, used in the sense of 'observation'.
68. *Illation*, deduction; *office*, use, function.
69. *Orchis*, orchids.
70. Albertus Magnus, *De Animalibus*, 22.tr. 2 (35); Aldrovandi, *De Quadrupedibus Digitatis Vivparis* (1637), p. 265.
71. *Set*, form and structure.
72. Aristotle, *The Progression of Animals*, 8 (708a).
73. *Chely*, chela, prehensile claw.
74. *Ægyptians*, with reference to Valeriano, *Hieroglyphica* (1556), 11; Aristotle, *History of Animals*, 6.30 (579a); Solinus (Polyhistor), *Collectanea Rerum Memorabilium*, trans. Arthur Golding (1587), 38, on the bears of Numidia; Pliny, *Natural History*, 8.54; Aelian, *On Animals*, 2.19; Ovid, *Metamorphoses*, 15.379–81, 'A cub that a she-bear has just brought forth is not a cub, but a scarce-living lump of flesh; but the mother licks it into shape, and in this way gives it as much of a form as she has herself'.
75. *Mathiolus*, Mattioli, *Commentaires sur Dioscoride* (1572), p. 223; *eventerated*, disembowelled.
76. Julius Scaliger, *Exercitationes* (1557), 6.15, 'Rather the bear expels shapeless offspring as she gives birth, if these authors speak the truth, which she afterwards shapes by licking. Nevertheless, in our Alps, hunters captured a pregnant bear and after she had been dissected, a fully formed foetus was found within her.'
77. Aldrovandi, *De Quadrupedibus Digitatis Viviparis* (1637), pp. 120–4.
78. *Exclusion*, bringing to birth; *dilacerates*, tears apart.
79. *Phidias*, Athenian sculptor, the inward Phidias being then the formative powers of the womb.
80. *mirè me* . . . , Psalm 119:73, 'Thy hands have made me and fashioned me' (AV).
81. *Five dayes after*, i.e. the creation, in Genesis 1.
82. Solinus, trans. Golding (1587), 38, 'The thirtieth day liberates the bear's womb, whence it happens that the fruitfulness, which has been cast forth, produces shapeless offspring.'

83. *Passant*, current; *little king*, translating Latin 'regulus'.
84. Psalm 91:13, 'Thou shalt walk upon the asp and the Basilisk' (Douay-Rheims here and in following translations; the AV here and subsequently translates as 'adder' or 'serpent'); Proverbs 23:32, 'But in the end, it will bite like a snake, and will spread abroad poison like a basilisk'; Jeremiah 8:17, 'For behold I will send among you serpents, basilisks, against which there is no charm'; *as ours translate it* . . . *cockatrices*, in AV.
85. This compilation of authorities is taken largely from Gesner, *De Serpentium Natura* (1587), f. 34; Galen (attrib.), *On Theriac to Piso*; Pliny, *Natural History*, 8.33; Solinus, trans. Golding (1587), 39; Aelian, *On Animals*, 3.31; Aetius, *Tetrabiblios*, 4.1.33; *Avicen*, Avicena, *Liber Canonis*, in *Opera* (1608), 2. 215; *Ardoynus*, Santes de Ardoynis, *De Venenis* (1562), p. 262; *Grevinus*, Jacques Grevin, *De Venins* (1568), pp. 105–8.
86. Scaliger, *Exercitationes*, f. 316; *Catoblepas*, Pliny, *Natural History*, 8.32; *Dryinus*, Aetius, *Tetrabiblios*, 4.1.29.
87. *Coronary spots*, circular formation.
88. *Pierius*, Valeriano, *Hieroglyphica* (1556), 14 (p. 102); *heralds*, John Guillim, *Display of Heraldry* (1638), p. 263.
89. Aldrovandi, *Serpentum Historia* (1640), p. 364: 'They commonly counterfeit the form of a basilisk with one similar to a poultry cock: a figure with two feet. In fact, basilisks are not dissimilar to other serpents, save for a white mark as it were on the crown of their heads, from which the name "of kings" was assigned to them.'
90. [*Textual note:* 'and for satisfaction . . . same fishes' added in 1672.]
91. *Priority of vision*, i.e. it poisons if it catches sight of a person before she catches sight of it.
92. *Deleterious*, injurious, noxious.
93. *Torpedoes*, a kind of sting-ray.
94. *Venenation*, poisoning.
95. *Priority of aspection*, first sight; Aristotle, *Sense and Sensibilia*, 437a–438a, on Empedocles' ideas of the sight beam; *Alhazen*, 11th-century Persian philosopher and writer of a book of Optics, in *Opticae Thesaurus* (1572); *Vitello*, i.e. Erazmus Ciolek Witelo, 13th-century optical theorist, *Optica* (1572).
96. [*Textual note:* Editions from 1650 onwards omit from here to the end of the paragraph, replacing it with 'but now sufficiently convicted from observations of the dark chamber', the *camera obscura*.] Browne is relying on Kepler, *Ad Vitellionem Paralipomena* (1604), and Friedrich Risner, *Opticae thesaurus* (1572), largely a version of Alhazen; 5.4; Euclid, *Optics*, preface.
97. *Trodden*, inseminated; *cocks egges*, small yokeless eggs.
98. *Unseconded*, unrepeated.
99. *Livia*, in Pliny, *Natural History*, 10.76.

100. Diodorus Siculus, *Library of History*, 1.74.5.
101. *Castor and Helena*, Hyginius, *Fabulae*, 80.
102. *Ægyptian tradition*, Valeriano, *Hieroglyphica* (1556), 17; *inquinated*, polluted, corrupted.
103. Isaiah 59:5. *Ova aspidum*… 'They hatch cockatrice's eggs, and weave the spider's web: he that eateth of their eggs dieth, and that which is crushed breaketh out into a viper.'
104. Isaiah 14:29.
105. Tremellius, 16th-century Protestant (having converted from Judaism), translator of the Bible into Latin.
106. *Uzziah*, 2 Kings 14–15; *Ezechias*, Hezekiah, 2 Kings 18, 2 Chronicles 29, Isaiah, 33–6.
107. Pliny, *Natural History*, 8.34, 'In Italy it is believed that the sight of wolves is harmful, and that if they look at a man before he sees them, it temporarily deprives him of utterance.'
108. Theocritus, *Idylls*, 14.22–6; Virgil, *Eclogues*, 9.53, 'Even voice itself now fails Moeris, the wolves have seen Moeris first'.
109. Scaliger, *Exercitationes* (1557), f. 453.
110. *Obmutescence*, being made mute.
111. *Mercilesse teeth of wolves*, the wolf and sheep in early modern religious contexts are, almost invariably, Catholic and Protestant, respectively, though ostensibly this is an early church context.
112. Theocritus, *Idylls*, 14.22, 'Can't you speak? Have you seen a wolf?'; *corrivall*, rival in love.
113. *Appellatively*, being made a noun.
114. Explanations from Palaephatus, *De Fabulosis Narrationibus*, published with Hygunis, *Fabularum Liber* (1535).
115. *Chaughes*, chough, jackdaw-like bird.
116. *Nestor,… Artephius, or Methuselah*, all long-lived ancients, Nestor being some 200 years old, according to Ovid, *Metamorphoses*, 12.187; *Artephius*, Arabian alchemist, purportedly 1,025 years old; *Methuselah*, died at 969, Genesis 5:27.
117. Aristotle, *History of Animals*, 6.29 (578b).
118. Scaliger, *Aristotelis Historia de animalibus; Julio Cæsare Scaligero interprete, cum eiusdem commentarijs* (1619), p. 770, 'Many people invent stories concerning the length of its life, yet in fact neither the gestation period nor the growth of its offspring are of such a kind that they present evidence of an animal of great age.'
119. [*Textual note:* Changed in 1650 to 'ten months'.]
120. *Conies*, rabbits.
121. *Salacity… venerie*, being salacious or sexually rapacious.
122. *Dragme*, 1.77 grams; *resolution*, subsequently changed to 'exolution', loss of vigour; *extenuation*, loss of weight; *marcour*, emaciation.
123. *Proper diminution*, actual reduction.

124. [*Textual note:* From 1672 'with the Idea of every one'.]
125. Aristotle, *History of Animals*, 9.5 (611a).
126. Pliny, *Natural History*, 8.50.
127. [*Textual note:* Corrected to '20' in 1650.]
128. *Ulysses his dog*, Homer, *Odyssey*, 22.326; *Athenian mule*, Aristotle, *History of Animals*, 6.24 (577b); John of Times, reputedly living to 300 years old, see George Hakewill, *An apologie* (1627), 3.1.6, pp. 153–4; *assertion of Moses*, Psalm 90:10, the age of man being three score and ten.
129. Aristotle, *History of Animals*, 606a; Pliny, *Natural History*, 8.51.
130. *Æneas*, Virgil, *Aeneid*, 1.184–94.
131. Aelian, *On Animals*, 10.14.
132. Hesiod, *Precepts of Chiron*, 3, in fragment from Plutarch, *The Cessation of Oracles*, 11; Decimus Magnus Ausonius, 4th-century Latin poet.
133. Plutarch, *The Cessation of Oracles*, 11.
134. Pliny, *Natural History*, 7.48, 'Hesiod, who first put forth some observations on this matter, placing many creatures above man in respect of longevity, factiously as I think, assigns nine of our lifetimes to the crow, four times a crow's life to stags, three times a stag's to ravens and for the rest in a more fictitious style in the case of the Phoenix and the nymphs.'
135. *Theophrastus*, according to Cicero, *Tusculan Disputations*, 3.28; Oppian, *Cynegetica*, 2.292, 'that he lives four lives of a crow'; Juvenal, *Satires*, 14.251, 'your long and stag-like old age'.
136. Aristotle, *History of Animals*, 2.15 (506a); Pliny, *Natural History*, 11.74.
137. *Connumeration*, reckoning together.
138. *Cornigerous*, having horns.
139. *Pizzell*, penis; *decidence*, falling off.
140. *Animall of Plato*, in *Timeus* 91b, on the 'unruly and self-willed' desire of the ensouled penis to escape itself.
141. *Art of Taliacotius*, Gasper Taliacotius (1546–99), Italian physician, reported to have surgically re-grafted a nose.
142. *Shoulder of Pelops*; Ovid, *Metamorphoses*, 6.403–11; *limbs of Hyppolitus*, Ovid, *Metamorphoses*, 15.533.
143. *Disanimated*, lacking life.
144. [*Textual note:* Changed in 1650 to 'natural meteorologie'.]
145. *Presention*, powers of prediction.
146. *Prenotion*, foreknowledge.
147. *Conversion*, turning.
148. *Scammonie*, purgative, laxative; *vitall*, living.
149. *Mistion*, mixture.
150. *Fulgour*, luminosity.
151. *Torpedo*, stingrays; *frontalls*, potions applied to forehead, presumably a kind of electrotherapy.
152. *Nidulation*, nesting.
153. *Brumall solstice*, Winter solstice.

154. Pliny, *Natural History*, 8.37; Plutarch, *The Cleverness of Animals*, in *Moralia*, 34 (982c).
155. Athanasius, *Life of St Anthony*, 32 (Migne, *PG*, 26.892).
156. Aelian, *On Animals*, 4.27; Solinus, *Collectanea Rerum Memorabilium*, 15.22; *Mela*, Pomponius Mela, 1st-century Roman geographer, *De Chorographia*, 2.1.1; Herodotus, *Histories*, 3.116.
157. Albertus, *Of Animals*, 23.24 (46); Pliny, *Natural History*, 10.70; Aldrovandi, *Ornithologia*, 10.1.
158. *Michovius*, i.e. Maciej Miechowita, 16th-century Polish geographer, *Tractatus de duabus Sarmatiis* (1517), noted by Aldrovandi, *Ornithologia*, 10.1.
159. Leviticus 11:13; *Tremellius*, Latin translation (1569–79).
160. Origen, *Peri Archon*, 4.2; (*Migne*, *PG*, 11.380).
161. Aldrovandi, *Ornithologia*, 10.1.
162. Virgil, *Eclogues*, 8.27, 'Griffins now shall mate with mares'.
163. Herodotus, *Histories*, 4.13.
164. *Ego vero contra*... 'I affirm to be true, against all the old authors, there are no griffins in the North parts, nor in any part of the world.'
165. *Reservance*, persistence.
166. The phoenix, serving as an emblem of the resurrection, was widely referred to in Christological writings of the Church Fathers: *Cyrill*, Cyril of Jerusalem, 4th-century theologian, *Catechesis*, 18.8 (Migne, *PG*, 33.1025); *Epiphanius*, 4th-century Bishop of Salamis, *Physiologus*, attrib. (Migne, *PG*, 43.173); Ambrose, *Hexameron*, 5.23.79 (Migne, *PL*, 14.238); Tertullian, *de Judicio Domini*, 5.31 (Migne, *PL*, 2.1092), *De Resurrectione Carnis* 13 (Migne, *PL*, 2.811), *Illum dico alitem*... 'I speak of that extraordinary bird of the East, famous on account of a singularity and strange on account of its later life, which, by willingly interring itself, it renews, departing on both the day of its birth and death and returning once more as a Phoenix, where a moment ago there was no bird, once more he is himself, for he is now both another and the same creature.'
167. Job 29:18; AV, 'Then I said, I shall die in my nest, and I shall multiply my days as the sand'; Psalm 92:12, 'The righteous shall flourish like the palm tree', with homophones on 'phoenix'.
168. *Aspection*, viewing, beholding.
169. Herodotus, *Histories*, 2.73.
170. Tacitus, *Annals*, 6.28, reporting how the Phoenix appeared in Egypt, 'But Antiquity is obscure... whence the belief has been held that this was a spurious Phoenix, not originating on the soil of Arabia.'
171. Pliny, *Natural History*, 10.2, 'But no one will doubt that this is false.'
172. *Naturally*, i.e. in terms of natural history.
173. *Herodotus*, in fact Pliny, *Natural History*, 10.50; Aristotle, *History of Animals*, 9.13 (616a); Scaliger, *Aristotelis Historia de animalibus*, 9.20.

174. Plutarch, *Artaxerxes*, in *Lives*, 19.3; *cunningly poysoned*, by smearing the poison only on one half.
175. Julius Caesar Scaliger, *Exercitationes* (1557), p. 233.
176. *Trifistulary*, three-tubed.
177. Lactantius (attrib.), *De Ave Phoenice* (Migne, *PL*, 7.277–84).
178. Ovid, *Metamorposes*, 15.391–407; *Mantuan*, Johannes Baptista Spagnolo, early 16th-century Spanish poet, 'Alfonsus', 5.575–81; *Claudian*, 4th-century Greco-Roman poet, *Rape of Proserpine*, 2.83.
179. Paracelsus, *Azoth sive De Ligno et Linea Vitae*, in *Opera Medica Chimica* (1605), 11.93.
180. Epiphanius, *Physiologus*, 2 (Migne, *PG*, 43.528); Tertullian, *De Resurrectione Carnis* 13 (Migne, *PL*, 2.811).
181. Pliny, *Natural History*, 8.9.
182. *Reviviction*, restoration to life.
183. *Reseminates*, reproduces from seed.
184. *Testaceous*, having a shell; Aristotle, *History of Animals*, 4.11 (539b).
185. *Exanguious*, bloodless; *Vermiparous*, producing young from maggots.
186. *Anatiferous*, producing barnacles, lit. ducks and geese.
187. [*Textual note:* Phrase added in 1650.] Pliny, *Natural History*, 29.9; *Irridere est*... 'It is to joke with mankind to point out remedies that return only after a thousand years.'
188. *Veniable*, pardonable, venial.
189. *Tantum non*, all but.
190. Plutarch, *On Keeping Well*, in *Moralia*, 133 c.20.
191. *Luxurious emperour*, Aelius Lampridius, *Historia Augusta*, 20.6; *phœnicopterus*, flamingo.
192. Julius Caesar Scaliger, *Aristotelis Historia de animalibus* (1619), p. 253, 'Having been disturbed by rustics, (the toad) was induced to deliver its destructive urine in front of the eyes of its persecutor.'
193. Mattioli, *Commentaires sur Dioscoride* (1572), p. 790; *humiditie*, humours and juices of an animal or plant.
194. *Avoid*, void, expel; *serous,* pertaining to serum, or animal fluids.
195. *Exenterats*, disembowels, eviscerates.
196. Aristotle, *History of Animals*, 3.15 (519b).
197. [*Textual note:* From 1658, the rest of this sentence is changed to: 'not because it is emitted aversly or backward, by both sexes, but because it is confounded with the intestinal excretions and egestions of the belly: and this way is ordinarily observed, although possible it is that the liquid excretion may sometimes be excluded without the other.']
198. *Lapideous*, stone-like.
199. *Exosseous*, boneless.
200. *Testaceous*, calcareous, shell-like; Aldrovandi, *De Animalibus Insectis* (1623), p. 280.
201. *Porta*, Giambattista Della Porta, *Magiae Naturalis* (1558), 8.9.
202. *Lapidaries*, Jewellers; *questuary*, interested in making money.

203. Boetius de Boodt, *Gemmarum et Lapidum Historia* (1636), p. 301; *Reperiuntur in agris...*, 'They are found in fields; nevertheless, others in ancient tracts stubbornly assert that these stones and those which have lain hidden for a long time in reed-beds amongst brambles and briars, are produced from the heads of toads.'
204. *Induration*, a hardening; *crany*, skull.
205. *Brassavolus*, Antonio Muso Brassavola, *Examen Omnium Simplicium* (1537), p. 481; Gesner, *De Quadrupedibus Oviparis* (1554), p. 65.
206. [*Textual note:* Subsequent editions, 1658 and 1672, add reports of toadstones from Royal Society sources.] Boetius de Boodt, 2.149, *Ab eo tempore*... 'From that time, I have regarded that which is related concerning the toadstone and its origin as nonsense.'
207. Pliny, *Natural History*, 9.74.
208. *Lentous*, clammy, viscid.
209. Aristotle, *History of Animals*, 5.19 (552b); *Nicander*, 2nd-century BCE poet and physician, in his long poem on poisons, *Alexipharmaca,* line 539; *Serenus Sammonicus*, Quintus Sammonicus Serenus, 2nd century CE, author of medical poem, *Liber Medicinalis*, 8.104; Aelian, *On Animals*, 2.31; Pliny, *Natual History*, 10.86.
210. Sextius, in Pliny, *Natural History*, 29.23; Dioscorides, *Materia Medica*, 2.62; Galen, *On the Powers and Mixtures of Simple Remedies*, 3.4.
211. Mattioli, *Commentaires sur Dioscoride*, 2.56.
212. Amatus Lusitanus, *In Dioscoridis de Medica Materia* (1558), 2.55; *Pierius*, Valeriano, *Hieroglyphica* (1556), 16 (p. 119).
213. Aristotle, *History of Animals*, 5.19 (552b), 'This creature indeed, as they say, entering the fire, puts it out'; *septicall medicine*, poisonous, corrosive.
214. *Moist in the third degree*, in the medical humors.
215. *Hirpini*, central Italian, pre-Roman tribe, who in an annual sacrifice to Apollo walk over burning coals, Pliny, *Natural History*, 7.2.
216. Galen, *On Mixtures*, 3.4.
217. *Aluminous*, made of alum.
218. *Napkins and textures*, cloths, textiles.
219. *Tegument*, coat of an animal.
220. *Corticated and depilous*, with a thick hide, and hairless.
221. *Incremable*, unburnable; Brassavola, *Examen Omnium Simplicium* (1537), p. 160.
222. *Desumed*, borrowed, taken from.
223. *Germanicus his heart*, reputedly not burnable, as he had been poisoned, Pliny, *Natural History*, 11.71; *Pyrrhus his great toe*, which cured illnesses and was unburnable, so preserved in the temple, Pliny, *Natural History*, 7.2.
224. Guido Pancirollus, *Res Memorabiles* (1631), 1.4.

225. Pliny, *Natural History*, 19.4; *Paulus Venetus*, 15th-century Augustinian philosopher, reported in Marco Polo, *Travels*, 2 (1958), p. 59.
226. *Vives*, Augustine, *Of the Citie of God, with the learned comments of Jo. Lod. Vives*, trans J.H. (1620), p. 790.
227. *Snasts*, candle-wicks; *elychinons*, wicks; *plumosum*, mineral with feather-like tufts.
228. Pausanias, *Description of Greece*, 1.26.
229. Nicander, *De Theriaca*, translated to Latin by Jean de Gorris (1557), line 372; Pliny, *Natural History*, 8.35, *Geminum habet caput* . . . 'It has two heads, as if insufficient poison was emitted from one mouth'; Aelian, *On Animals*, 9.23.
230. *Bicipitous*, two-headed; *gemination*, doubling.
231. *Scolopendrae*, relating to centipedes; *farinaceous*, made of flour or meal; *vaginipennous*, with sheath-like wings.
232. Aristotle, *History of Animals*, 8.3 (592b).
233. *Six positions*, in Aristotle, *Of the Progression of Animals*, 2 (704b): above and below, before and behind, right and left.
234. *Geryon or Cerberus*, respectively, three-headed monster and dog.
235. Aristotle, *Of the Parts of Animals*, 3.3–4 (665a).
236. *Geminous births*, conjoined twins; *connascencies*, born at the same time.
237. Petrarch, *De Rebus Memorandi*, in *Opera* (1581), p. 493; *Vincentius*, Vincent of Beauvais, *Speculum Maius* (1591), 1.408, medieval compilation and encyclopaedia; *Scottish history*, George Buchanan, *Rerum Scoticarum Historia* (1624), p. 458.
238. Aldrovandi, *Serpentum Historia* (1640), p. 661.
239. *Inoculate*, engraft.
240. *Quae genus*, lit. 'which genus?', i.e. the chief factor in determining species and distinctions between species; *illation*, inferences from them.
241. Rhodiginus, i.e. Richerius, *Lectiones Antiquae* (1599), 12.14, col. 552, on Nicander, *Theriaca*, 812; *Muffetus*, Thomas Moffet, *Insectorum Theatrum* (1634), p. 200; *Dicitur à Nicandro* . . ., 'Nicander says it is *amphikarēs*, that is 'dicephalus' or two-headed, but wrongly, seeing that, as Aristotle writes, it creeps backwards', scholion on Nicander, *Theriaca* 812b; *Tamen pace* . . ., as translated in text.
242. Herodotus, *Histories*, 3.109; Nicander, *Theriaca*, 128–34; Pliny, *Natural History*, 10.82; Plutarch, *Of Talkativeness*, 508d, 12; Aelian, *On Animals*, 15.16; Jerome, *Epistola ad Praesidium* (Migne, *PL*, 30.187); Basil, *Hexameron*, 9.5 (Migne, *PG*, 29.200); Isidore, *Etymologies*, 12.4.10; Aristotle, *History of Animals*, 5.34 (558a).
243. *Men of Melita*, Acts 28:3–6.
244. *Yee generation of vipers*, Matthew 12:34.
245. Genesis 1:22.
246. Genesis 3:14–16.
247. *Apollonius*, recorded by Philostratus, *Life of Apollonius*, 2.14.

248. Amatus Lusitanus, *In Dioscorides de Medica Materia* (1558), 2.16, *Vidimus nos viperas*…, 'We have seen pregnant vipers give birth while enclosed in small boxes, which after the arrival of their offspring continued (to be) neither dead nor perforated with regards to their flesh'; *Viperas ab impatientibus*… 'We know that it is untrue that vipers are ruptured by their numerous offspring, impatient at the delay, and thus perish, as we have seen young vipers issue forth in the wooden chest of the vendor Vincentius Camerinus, while the parent remained uninjured'.
249. Franciscus Bustamantinus, *De Reptilibus Sacrae Scripturae* (1620), p. 626, *cum vero*…, 'when indeed, I had diligently inquired by myself and through others about these matters and learnt that the viper is kept unharmed during the birth of her offspring'; *seidge*, anus.
250. Herodotus, *Histories*, 3.108.
251. *Superfœtation*, a second conception before delivery.
252. *More nearly*, more closely, exactly.
253. *Secession*, retiring; *latitancie*, hibernation.
254. *Corticated*, tough-skinned.
255. *Candie*, Crete.
256. Nicander, *Theriaca*, 132.
257. *Decollation*, beheading.
258. [*Textual note:* 'two' in 1672.]
259. Horace, *Odes*, 1.13, 'or if a youngster in his passion has left a telltale mark with his teeth on your lips'.
260. *Theophrastus*, Paracelsus; *exesion*, eating its way out; *impletion*, becoming full, with eating.
261. *Dilaceration*, tearing.
262. Pliny, *Natural History*, 10.82, *Cæteri tarditatis*…, 'The remaining ones get so tired of the delay that they burst open their mother's side, so committing matricide.'
263. Aristotle, *History of Animals*, 5.34 (558a); Scaliger, *Aristotelis Historia de animalibus*, 5.29, *sigillatim parit*…, 'She bears her offspring one by one / individually and on a single day sometimes she releases more than twenty young vipers'; *singulos diebus*… 'Each day she bears a single offspring, generally numbering twenty'.
264. *Parit catulos*…, 'She bears her young wrapped in membranes, which are ruptured on the third day; sometimes, it happens that those who are still in the uterus burst forth with gnawed away membranes.'
265. Isidore, *Etymologies*, 12.4.10.
266. *Compellation*, an address, i.e. in Matthew 12:34.
267. Jansenius, *Commentarii in Suam Concordiam* (1624), 13 (1.92); Gregory, *Homiliae in Evangelia*, 20.7 (Migne, *PL*, 76.1163), Jerome, *In Evangelium Matthaei*, 4 (Migne, *PL*, 26.172).

268. [*Textual note:* This paragraph, added in 1672, attests to Browne's ongoing attention to developments in scientific experiment, Francisco Redi's work being described in *Philosophical Transactions* (1665–6), p. 160.]
269. Archelaus, 5th century CE, pupil of Anaxogoras, reported in Pliny, *Natural History*, 8.81; Plutarch, *On Borrowing*, in *Moralia*, 10.4, who in fact refers to hares' repeated copulation only in regard to the charging of excessive interest rates; Philostratus the Elder, *Imagines*, 1.6.6.
270. [*Textual note:* The passage from 'Of the same belief' through to 'denenerous effemination', was added in 1658.]
271. *Empedocles*, in Diogenes Laertius, 8.77; *Tiresias*, Ovid, *Metamorphoses*, 3.322–32.
272. *Restore*, restoration; *Transexion*, changing sex; *Retromingents*, animals urinating backwards.
273. *Congenerous*, of the same kind.
274. *Aracus*, tare; *ægilops*, wild oats.
275. *Serpoile*, wild thyme.
276. Severinus, *In Idea Mediciniae Philosophicae* (1571), p. 139; *equivocall seeds*, whose form or sex is not decided.
277. *Edifie*, grow; *contemning the superintendent forme*, ignoring its original form.
278. *Permansion*, duration.
279. The idea of changes from imperfection to perfection is based on Ambroise Paré, 16th-century physician, *Works* (1634), p. 795, as well as Casper Bauhin, *De Hermaphroditorum Natura* (1614), p. 551.
280. *Impeacheth*, casts doubt on the idea of; *transfeminated*, turned female; *manifesto*, demonstration; Cardan, *De Rerum Varietate* (1557), p. 319.
281. Galen, *On the Usefulness of the Parts*, 16.6.
282. Aristotle, *Generation of Animals*, 4.4 (772b).
283. Plato, *Symposium*, 189d–190d, on the division of primal hermaphrodite humans into halves; *Marcus Leo*, early 16th-century Portuguese philosopher, Leo Hebraeus, *Dialoghi d'Amore*, 3; *suppositum*, individual being.
284. Genesis 1:27.
285. Aristotle, *Generation of Animals*, 1.20 (729a); *spermatize*, produce seed.
286. Aquinas, *Summa Theologica*, 3. Suppl. 81.3.
287. Pliny, *Natural History*, 11.109; Cardan, *De Rerum Varietate* (1559), p. 196.
288. *Superfetation*, conceiving a second time while still pregnant.
289. Aristotle, *History of Animals*, 6.3 (579b); Herodotus, *Histories*, 3.108; Pliny, *Natural History*, 8.81.
290. *Cast*, delivery.
291. *Avidity*, eagerness; *perfection*, conception.

292. *Engrosseth the aliment*, monopolizes the nutrients and food; *Julia*, in Macrobius, *Saturnalia*, 2.5.9; *lading*, taking in cargo onto a ship.
293. *Matrix*, womb; Pliny, *Natural History*, 7.11; *Larissæa*, Hippocrates, *On Epidemics*, 5.11; Plautus, *Amphitryon*, line 1122; Aristotle, *History of Animals*, 7.4 (585a), on Iphicles and Hercules, as cited also by Pliny.
294. *Officiall unto generation*, having that office or purpose; *emunctories*, passages for clearing waste from the body.
295. *Expressed*, forced out; *fœculent*, i.e. feculent, fecal or fetid matter.
296. *Pseudodoxia*, 3.4.
297. Aristotle, *History of Animals*, 6.32 (579b); Scaliger, *Aristotelis Historia de animalibus* (1619), p. 778, *Quod autem aiunt*... 'However, it is false what they say that these animals have the genitals of both sexes, because while it seems that the female reproductive system is under the tail, this opening is merely a similar shape to the feminine genitals and not the true passage.'
298. Pliny, *Natural History*, 8.81.
299. *Dockes*, i.e. the solid fleshy part of their tails.
300. *Postick*, posterior, back.
301. *Vitiositie*, depravity.
302. Oppian, *Cynegetica*, 2.612; *Talpa caecior*, i.e. blinder than a mole, cited in Erasmus, *Adagia*, 1.3.55, who also refers the reader to Hesichius, *Lexicon*.
303. Albertus, *Of Animals*, 22.tr.2 (105); Pliny, *Natural History*, 30.7; Scaliger, *Exercitationes* (1557), f. 322v; Aldrovandi, *De Quadrupedibus Digitatis Viviparis* (1637), pp. 451–5.
304. Galen, *On the Usefulness of the Parts*, 14.6; *humorem nigrum*. 'a black humour', as such from 1658.
305. Galen, *On the Usefulness of the Parts*, 14.6; Aristotle, *History of Animals*, 1.9; Scaliger, *Aristotelis Historia de animalibus* (1619), p. 69.
306. *Morbosities*, abnormal or diseased states.
307. *Cecity*, blindness; *cecutiency*, partial vision, dimness of sight.
308. Scaliger, *Exercitationes*, f. 311.
309. *Sensible*, aware.
310. John 9:1; *Nonnus*, of Panopolis, 5th century CE, Greek poet and later a convert to Christianity, *In Johannem Metaphrasis* (1627), p. 100.
311. Serenus Sammonicus, Roman medical writer of 3rd century CE, *Liber Medicinalis*, 46; Nicander, *Theriaca*, 815.
312. Aristotle, *History of Animals*, 4.7 (532a), 'When the eyes have become dim'.
313. *Jacob*, Genesis 27:1, though the story is of Isaac; *Jerome*, in the Vulgate Bible.
314. *Polyphemus*, the Cyclops in Homer, *Odyssey*, 9.333.
315. *Argus*, having 100 eyes, alternately waking and sleeping, Ovid, *Metamorphoses*, 1.625.

316. Galen, *On the Usefulness of the Parts*, 8.5.
317. *Sternopthalmi*, in for example, Strabo, *Geography*, 1.2.35.
318. *Solomon*, in Ecclesiastes 2:14.
319. *Latirostrous*, broad-billed.
320. *Spondyles*, vertebrae.
321. [*Textual note:* This is one of the relatively few chapters that undergo major revision, indeed a *volta face*, rather than minor additions, particularly in the 1672 edition. This was in large part a response to Henry Power's *Experimental Philosophy* (1664), pp. 36–7, and his microscopic observations, which address Browne's chapter directly. 1672 replaces the entire first two paragraphs as follows: 'Whether snayls have eyes some learned men have doubted. For Scaliger terms them but imitations of eyes; and Aristotle upon consequence denyeth them, when he affirms that testaceous Animals have no eyes. But this now seems sufficiently asserted by the help of exquisite Glasses, which discover those black and atramentous spots or globales to be their eyes. That they have two eyes is the common opinion, but if they have two eyes, we may grant them to have no less then four, that is, two in the larger extensions above, and two in the shorter and lesser horns below, and this number may be allowed in these inferiour and exanguious animals; since we may observe the articulate and latticed eyes in Flies, and nine in some Spiders: and in the great Phalangium Spider of America, we plainly number eight. But in sanguineous animals, quadrupeds, bipeds, or man, no such number can be regularly verified, or multiplicity of eyes confirmed.'] Scaliger, *de Plantis* (1598), p. 67; Pliny, *Natural History*, 9.51; Aristotle, *History of Animals*, 1.9 (491b).
322. *Atramentous*, inky-black.
323. The entire and grisly vivisection disappears in 1672.
324. Ovid, *Metamorphoses*, 1.625.
325. Homer, *Odyssey*, 9.333, 383–94.
326. *Visive*, relating to sight.
327. Galen, *On the Usefulness of the Parts*, 10.12.
328. *Giges ring*, Plato, *Republic*, 2.3.10 (359c), the ring having the power of invisibility.
329. Solinus, in *Works*, ed. Golding (1587), 52; Pliny, *Natural History*, 8.51; Ovid, *Metamorphoses*, 15.411. As often, these and subsequent references are found in collated form in Aldrovandi, *De Quadrupedibus Digitatis Oviparis* (1637), p. 672.
330. Aelian, *On Animals*, 2.14; Aristotle, *History of Animals*, 2.2 (503a).
331. *Augustinus Niphus*, 16th-century commentator on Aristotle, *Expositiones* (1546), p. 42; *Stobæus*, 5th century CE, anthologist; *Dalechampius*, editor of Pliny (1631), p. 151; *Fortunius Licetus*, 17th-century Italian natural philosopher, *De his, qui diu vivunt sine Alimento* (1612), 1.31.
332. *Landius*... in Scaliger, *Exercitationes* (1557), f. 264v.

333. Belon, *Observations*, in Clusius, *Exotica* (1605), p. 105; *exenteration*, removing the entrails.
334. *Verisimility*, verisimilitude, truth.
335. [*Textual note:* After 1658, editions omit 'so when we observe... urine of a tortoise'.]
336. Pliny, *Natural History*, 8.51.
337. *Vermiparous*, worm- or maggot-like production of young.
338. *Concommitancie*, being associated with.
339. *Ingustible,* without taste; *sapidity*, having taste or flavour.
340. Pliny, *Natural History*, 28.29, but an ape, not an ass.
341. Aldrovandi, *De Quadrupedibus*, p. 670.
342. *Inviscates*, makes viscid or sticky.
343. Leviticus 11:30.
344. *Isidore*, in *Etymologiae*, 12.2.18.
345. Aristotle, *On the Soul*, 3.12 (434b).
346. *Sapor*, a quality perceived by taste, e.g. bitterness.
347. *Aggeneration*, an additional production.
348. *Fernelius*, Jean Fernel, 16th-century French physician, *De Abditis Rerum Causis* (1548), 2.7.
349. Aristotle, *On the Senses*, 445a, arguing against the purported Pythagorean belief that some animals are nourished by odour; *corpulency*, body; *incrassation*, thickening; *progressionall unto*, in the process of.
350. Hippocrates, *Of the Heart*, 3.
351. *Contemporation*, blending together; Hippocrates, *De alimento*, 21.
352. [*Textual note:* From here to the end of the paragraph omitted after 1658.] *Individuum*, individual.
353. *De Alimento*, 29; *Pulmo contrarium*..., 'The lungs derive nourishment in a contrary manner to the body, all the remainder do likewise.'
354. [*Texual note:* This brief paragraph added 1672.]
355. [*Textual note:* This paragraph, as introduction to the chapter's discussion of the elements, appears first in 1650.]
356. *Pabulous*, nourishing.
357. *Lord of Verulam*, Francis Bacon, *Historie of Life and Death* (1638), p. 294; Edward Jorden, *Discourse of Naturall Bathes and Minerall Waters* (1632), p. 25.
358. *Fuliginous*, resembling soot; *unctuosity*, oiliness.
359. [*Textual note:* 1646 has 'with them'.] Jorden, *Naturall Bathes*, p. 25; *frication*, chafing, rubbing with hands.
360. *Tullia... Olibius*, in Jorden, *Naturall Bathes*, p. 26.
361. *Weeke*, i.e. wick.
362. *Subtile*, rarified, thin consistency; *accension*, kindling.
363. *Creusa and Alexanders boy*, also in Jorden, *Naturall Bathes*, p. 29.
364. [*Textual note:* 'unto others it performs... gills' removed after 1658 edition, responding to Severinus, *Antiperipatias* (1661), pp. 8, 14.]

365. *Elixation*, boiling, stewing, digestion; *roride*, dewy; the reference to the liver disappears after 1656.
366. [*Textual note:* From here to the end of the paragraph appears from 1650.] *Jejune*, with no nutritive qualities.
367. *Astomi*, who lived on odours, Pliny, *Natural History*, 7.2; *mares in Spaine*, impregnated by wind, Varro, *Res Rustica*, 2.1.19; *subventaneous*, windy, of infertile eggs.
368. Ariosto, *Orlando Furioso*, 15.41.
369. Theophrastus, 3rd century BCE, Athenian philosopher, *De Animalibus quae Colorem Mutant*, frag. 172.4.
370. Pseudo-Homer, *Batrachomyomachia*.
371. *Latitancy*, hibernation; *sustentation*, means of nourishment.
372. *A minori ad majus*... 'From the lesser to the greater. From the qualified statement to the unqualified statement'; *Rhintace*, bird in Plutarch, *Artaxerxes*, 1020e.
373. Fortunius Licetus, *De His, Qui Diu Vivunt sine Alimento* (1612), 3.48–76; *exuperancy*, excess.
374. *Deperdition*, wasting away.
375. Hippocrates, *Aphorisms*, 1.13.
376. [*Textual note:* Final two sentences added 1650.] *Elias*, 1 Kings 19:8, forty days.
377. Rhodiginus, *Lectiones Antiquae* (1599), col. 734; Johannes Langius, *Epistolae Medicinales* (1589), p. 56.
378. Aristotle, *Of the Parts of Animals*, 4.14 (697b); Oppian, *Cynegetica*, 3.482–503.
379. Pliny, *Natural History*, 10.1; Aelian, *On Animals*, 14.7.
380. Leo Africanus, *Geographical History of Africa* (1600), p. 348, *Surdum ac simplex*..., 'It is a deaf and simple creature, that consumes whatever it finds without selection, including even iron.'
381. Jean Fernel, *De Abditis Rerum Causis* (1548); Riolanus, *Opera* (1610), p. 164.
382. Albertus Magnus, *On Animals*, 23.24 (104); Ulysses Aldrovandi, *De Avibus* (1610), p. 300.
383. *Chilification*, converting to chyle, milky pancreatic juices; *vitriolous*, vitriolic; *absterse*, purge, cleanse.
384. *Amatus*, Amatus Lusitanus, *Curationum Medicinalium Centuriae Quatuor* (1556), p. 192.
385. *Deopilations*, removing obstructions.
386. *Extinctions*, chemical tinctures made by immersing hot metals in liquids.
387. *By seidge*, passing out anally.
388. *Forward illation*, a deduction made perversely, falsely.
389. *Gizard*, second, muscular stomach.
390. *Crudities*, the state of being indigestible.
391. *Knabble,* nibble; Aristotle, *Natural History*, 8.26 (605a).

392. [*Textual note:* This paragraph added in 1658.]
393. Galen, *On the Properties of Foodstuffs*, 3.21; Aelian, *On Animals*, 14.7; *Hermolaus*, in Aldrovandi, *De Avibus* (1610), p. 302; Pliny, *Natural History*, 28.18, on the medical uses of urine.
394. *Scripture*, e.g. Numbers 23:22, Deuteronomy 33:17, Job 39:9; Isaiah 37:4.
395. *Olaus*, 16th-century author on Scandinavian lore; Olaus Magnus, *De Gentibus Septentrionalibus* (1555), p. 744; Albertus, *De Animalibus*, 22.tr.2 (106).
396. *Muffetus*, Thomas Moffet, *Insectorum Theatrum* (1634), p. 152.
397. *Antonomastically*, substituting the office or function for the real name.
398. Pliny, *Natural History*, 8.31; *Vartomannus*, apparently a mistake for Aldrovandi, *De Quadrupedibus Solipedibus* (1623), p. 182, Ludovico di Varthema, *Itinerario* (1510); *mansuete*, tame, gentle.
399. Garcias ab Horto, *Aromatum et Simplicium . . . Historia*, in Clusius, *Exotica* (1605), p. 167.
400. Aelian, *On Animals*, 16.20; Solinus, *Collectanea Rerum Memorabilium*, 52.39; *Paulus Venetus*, in Marco Polo, *Travels*, 6.
401. André Thevet, *Cosmographie Universelle* (1575), 1.129r.
402. Aelian, *On Animals*, 16.20; Pliny, *Natural History*, 8.31; *spadiceous*, reddish-brown.
403. *Awfractuous*, anfractuous, sinuous, winding; *chocleary*, spiral.
404. Albertus Magnus, *De Animalibus*, 12.tr.3.7.
405. Goropius Becanus, *Origines Antwerpianae* (1569), p. 1037.
406. *Island*, i.e. Iceland.
407. De Boodt, *Gemmarum et Lapidum Historia* (1636), pp. 425–6.
408. *Lapidescencies*, the results of petrification.
409. *Mucilaginous*, having the moist and viscid condition of plant-mucilage.
410. [*Textual note:* The following sentence added in 1650.]
411. [*Textual note:* This and the following paragraph added in 1650.]
412. Paulus Jovius, *Historiae Sui Temporis* (1550), 1.307.
413. Aelian, *On Animals*, 4.52; *falling-sicknesse*, epilepsy.
414. *Alexipharmacall*, antidote to poison; *electuary*, medicinal paste.
415. Pliny discusses the putative correspondence, *Natural History*, 9.1.2.
416. *Icthyologie*, study of fish; *Rondeletius*, Rondelet, *Universa Aquatilium Historia* (1554), pp. 424–7; Conrad Gesner, *De Piscium et Aquatilium Animantium Natura* (1558), p. 754; Aldrovandi, *De Piscibus* (1623), pp. 156–7.
417. *Crotesco*, grotesque; *deliniations*, i.e. drawings of fantastic animals in the spaces of maps.
418. *Praxiteles*, 4th century BCE, Athenian sculptor; Pliny cites Scopas as the sculptor of sea-creatures in relation to the temple of Domitian, *Natural History*, 36.4.
419. De Boodt, *Gemmarum et Lapidum Historia* (1636), p. 528.

420. Genesis 1:20.
421. [*Textual note:* This chapter appears first in the 1650 text.]
422. *Sarcophagie*, meat-eating.
423. Genesis 1:29; 9:3.
424. Genesis 4:2–3.
425. Hugo Grotius, *Annotata ad Vetus Testamentum* (1644), 1.12, on Genesis 1:20; *wickednesse of mans heart*, Genesis 6:5.
426. On Saturn, Ovid, *Metamorphoses*, 1.89–112.
427. Porphyrius, *De Abstinentia*, 4.15.
428. Genesis 1:30.
429. Genesis 7:2.
430. Leviticus 11 and Deuteronomy 14 contain the rules around clean and unclean animals.
431. Galen, *On the Properties of Foodstuffs*, 3.2; Martial, *Epigrams*, 3.77; *Cato*, in Plutarch, *Cato the Elder*, 23.4.
432. Herodotus, *Histories*, 2.47.
433. Herodotus, *Histories*, 2.69–70.
434. Caesar, *The Gallic Wars*, 5.12; *piaculous*, sinful.
435. Pliny, *Natural History*, 10.31.
436. Tacitus, *Histories*, 5.4.
437. Aulus Gellius, *Attic Nights*, 4.11.
438. *Mecenas*, in Pliny, *Natural History*, 8.68.
439. *Heliogabalus*, 3rd century CE, Roman emperor.
440. *Alec, muria, and garum*, sauces and pickles.
441. This chapter is largely composed via these two works, Ludovicus Nonnus, *Diaeteticon* (1646), and Petrus Castellanus, *De Esu Carnium* (1626).
442. Aristotle, *History of Animals*, 6.7 (564a); Galen, *On the Properties of Foodstuffs*, 3.2.
443. Pliny, *Natural History*, 28.40.
444. Joannes Lerius (Jean de Léry), *Historia Navigationis in Brasiliam* (1586), p. 118.
445. [*Textual note:* This chapter added in 1658 edition.]
446. Caspar Hofmann, *De Medicamentis Officinalibus* (1646), p. 678, 'I do not know what it might be.'
447. *Flos maris*, the flower of the sea.
448. Carolus Clusius, *Exotica* (1605), p. 132.
449. Aldrovandi, *De Cetis* (1623), pp. 263–6.
450. *Gibbous*, convex, humped.
451. Samuel Purchase, *His Pilgrimages* (1625), 3.471.
452. Guillaume Rondelet, *Universa Aquatilium Historia* (1554), p. 485.
453. Book of Jonah.
454. *Depuration*, refining.
455. *Axungious*, lard-like.
456. *Flosculous*, of flowers.

457. Mattioli, *Commentaires sur Dioscoride* (1572).
458. *Loligo*, cuttlefish.
459. *Vespasians Nose*, who, having taxed urinals, was said to be able to bear their smell very well.
460. [*Textual note:* This is Chapter 25 in the 1646 edition.]
461. *Melodie of syrens*, Homer, *Odyssey*, 12.69; Plato, in fact *The Republic*, 10 (620a).
462. Aelian, *On Animals*, 2.32; Pliny, *Natural History*, 10.32; Athenaeus, *Deipnosophists*, Book 9, 393d; Scaliger, *Exercitationes* (1557), p. 232; *De Cygni vero cantu*… 'Concerning the true and most pleasant song of the Swan, which along with Greece, the parent of falsehoods, you have dared to discuss, I assign you to the tribunal of Lucianus, at which you will declare something new.'
463. Aldrovandi, *De Avibus* (1610), p. 9.
464. *Latirostrous*, broad-billed.
465. *Austine*, i.e. Augustine, *City of God*, 21.4.1; Aldrovandi, *Ornitholgia* (1610), p. 15.
466. Cardan, *De Subtilitate* (1560), p. 338; Scaliger, *Exercitationes* (1557), p. 238.
467. Pliny, *Natural Hisory*, 10.31.
468. Belon, *Histoire des Oyseaux* (1555), p. 203.
469. Jeremiah 8:7, 'Yea, the stork in the heaven knoweth her appointed times; and the turtle and the crane and swallow observe the time of their coming.'
470. *Mugient*, lowing, bellowing; Belon, *Histoire*, p. 193; Aldrovandi, *Ornithologia*, p. 166.
471. *Flight-shoot*, how far an arrow would fly.
472. *Volatiles*, collective term for wildfowl.
473. Aristotle, *Problemata*, 25.2 (937b).
474. Aristotle, *History of Animals*, 6.20 (547a); *anopsie*, sightlessness; *invision*, blindness.
475. Erasmus, *Adages* (1629), p. 239, *Festinans canis*…, 'A hasty dog gives birth to blind pups.'
476. *Bisulcous*, cloven-hooved; *farrowed*, brought forth.
477. *Phalangium*, venomous spider.
478. Joachim Camerarius, 16th-century German humanist, *Symbolorum et emblematum* (1595), f. 17v.
479. Pliny, *Natural History*, 29.25.
480. *Impennous*, wingless.
481. Pennius, in Moffet, *Insectorum Theatrum* (1634), p. 171.
482. Aristotle, *On Breathing*, 15 (475a); *allision*, dashing two things together.
483. *Muffettus*, Moffet, *Insectorum Theatrum* (1634), p. 218.
484. Cardan, *De Subtilitate* (1560), p. 284; Albertus, *De Sensu et Sensato*, 1.12; Gaudentius Merula, *Memorabilia* (1556), p. 240.

485. *Torpedo*, stingray; Galen, *On the Powers and Mixtures of Simple Remedies*, 11.1.48; *Rondoletius*, Rondolet, *Universa Aquatilium Historia* (1554), p. 361.
486. [*Textual note:* This paragraph appears first in 1672.]
487. *Idoneous*, suitable; *compositum*, compound.
488. [*Textual note:* This paragraph appears first in 1658.]
489. *Pismire*, ant.
490. [*Textual note:* Chapter added in 1650.]
491. *Aquapendente*, Hieronymus Fabricus of Aquapendente, 16th-century embryologist, *De Formatione Ovi*, in *Opera* (1625), pp. 28–38.
492. [*Textual note:* This appears first in 1658.]
493. *Æsculapius*, from Ovid, *Metamorphoses*, 15.653; Aldrovandi, *Serpentum Historia* (1640), pp. 98–9.
494. *Kircherius*, Jesuit philosopher-scientist, *Magnes* (1641), pp. 865–91.
495. Jean-Baptiste van Helmont, *Ortus Medicinae* (1648), p. 113.

PSEUDODOXIA EPIDEMICA BOOK 4

1. Ovid, *Metamorphoses*, 1.84–6, 'And though all other animals are prone, and fix their gaze upon the earth, he gave to man an uplifted face and bade him stand erect and turn his eyes to heaven'; Aristotle, *Of the Parts of Animals*, 4.10 (686a).
2. Galen, *On the Usefulness of the Parts*, 3.2.
3. *Firmation*, steadying; *ischias*, lowest bones of spine.
4. Aristotle, *Problemata*, 10.16 (892b).
5. *Venters*, abdomen, thorax.
6. Galen, *On the Usefulness of the Parts*, 3.2.
7. *Volitation*, flight.
8. *Penguin*, in Carolus Clusius, *Exotica* (1605), p. 101.
9. Galen, *On the Usefulness of the Parts*, 3.2.
10. [*Textual note:* This paragraph from 1650.]
11. Plato, *Cratylus*, 399c; Galen, *On the Usefulness of the Parts*, 3.3.
12. *Sursum aspicere*, look upwards, contemplate.
13. *Apophyses*, protuberance on vertebrae.
14. *Acies*, line of vision; *bitour*, bittern.
15. *Asseveration*, assertion.
16. *Epithems*, moist external poultice or application.
17. John 19:34.
18. *Aspection*, viewing, beholding.
19. 'In the left region of the breast', Aristotle, *History of Animals*, 2.17 (506b); Persius, *Satires*, 2.53; see also Juvenal, *Satires*, 7.159.
20. [*Textual note:* From here to the end of the paragraph added in 1650.] Ecclesiastes 10:2.

21. *Exquisite*, properly named or carefully ascertained disease; *inflammatio membranæ . . .*, 'An inflammation of the membrane surrounding the ribs'.
22. *Oedematous*, fluid-swollen growth; *schirrous*, hard and tumour-like; *erisipelatous*, subcutaneous infection.
23. *Azygos, or vena sine pari*, unpaired organ; *vena sine pari*, 'a vein without equal'.
24. *Apostems*, abcesses.
25. *Alexander ab Alexandro*, Neopolitan lawyer, *c.*1461–1523; Aulus Gellius, *Attic Nights*, 10.10; Macrobius, *Saturnalia*, 7.8; *Pierius*, Valeriano, *Hieroglyphica* (1556), 36; Levinus Lemnius, *Occulta Naturae Miracula* (1571), p. 178.
26. *Lipothymis or swoundings*, fainting (lipothymy); *frication*, rubbing.
27. Jeremiah 22:24.
28. Petronius, *Satyricon*, 32.
29. Pliny, *Natural History*, 33.6.
30. Athenaeus, *Deipnosophists*, 6.4 (232a).
31. *Cordiall*, relating to the heart.
32. Petrus Forestus, *Observationes et Curationes Medicinales*, in *Opera* (1634), 2.94.
33. *Phlebotomy*, bleeding for therapeutic purposes.
34. [*Textual note:* Paragraph added 1672, with belated reference to William Harvey, *De Motu Cordis* (1628), and the circulation of blood.]
35. Macrobius, *Saturnalia*, 7.13.6.
36. *Insculptures*, engravings.
37. *Pretiosities*, valuable things.
38. Alexander, *Geniales Dies* (1616), f. 80v.
39. *Pierius*, Valeriano, *Hieroglyphica* (1556), 37.
40. Juvenal, *Satires*, 10.248–9, [*Qui per tot saecula*] *mortem* | *distulit . . .*, 'He put off death for so many generations, counted his years by the hundreds' (i.e. on his right hand).
41. Proverbs 3:16.
42. *Chiragricall*, note from 1650 edition, 'Hand-gowty persons'.
43. Genesis 48:13–18.
44. *Moses*, Exodus 29:30.
45. Diodorus Siculus, *Library of History*, 16.43.
46. *Discumbency*, lying down.
47. *Amazones*, a widely known classical story of a military race of women.
48. *Tumbler*, a dog used for baiting rabbits, usually a lurcher.
49. Aristotle, *Problemata*, 958b.
50. *Assuefaction*, becoming accustomed to.
51. *Scevolaes*, left-handed people in Livy, *History of Rome*, 2.13.
52. Judges 20:15.
53. Scaliger, *Aristotelis Historia de animalibus* (1619), 1.15.

54. Gabrielis Fallopius, *Institutiones Anatomicae*, in *Opera* (1600), p. 447.
55. *Azygos*, organs not existing in pairs; *emulgent*, vessels leading from kidneys.
56. *Obducted*, enveloped.
57. *Bipartited*, in two parts; *crany*, cranium.
58. *Serous*, body-fluid, of blood, for instance.
59. Aristotle, *Generation of Animals*, 765a.
60. *Aberre*, from 1650, erre.
61. Aristotle, *Progression of Animals*, 704b.
62. Aristotle, *History of Animals*, 527b and *Progression of Animals*, 714b.
63. Scaliger, *Aristotelis Historia de animalibus* (1619), p. 37.
64. Hippocrates, *Aphorisms*, 7.4.3.
65. Homer, *Iliad*, 21.163; Statius, *Thebaid*, 9.772.
66. *Lateralities*, sidedness.
67. Solinus, *Collectanea rerum memorabilium*, 1.93.
68. *Petionarily*, via an unproven presumption; *Ark*, Genesis 6:15, from Augustine, *City of God*, 15.26.
69. Uncorrected, though the dimensions given in Genesis 6:15 put it at three hundred cubits.
70. *Decuple*, ten times as much.
71. Ovid, *Metamorphoses*, 1.45, 'cut by two zones on the right and two on the left'.
72. Kiranides, *Liber Physico-Medicus* (1638), p. 73; *Metrodorus*, Artemidorus, *Oneirocriticon* (1603), p. 30.
73. *Hephæstus*, Homer, *Iliad*, 18.371.
74. *Ariolation*, divination.
75. *Natation*, floating.
76. Scaliger, *Aristotelis Historia de animalibus* (1619), p. 156; Aristotle, *History of Animals*, 2.1 (498b).
77. Aristotle, *History of Animals*, 8.2 (592a).
78. [*Textual note:* 1646 has 'matter', perhaps a printer's error.] *Turgescence*, swelling.
79. Aristotle, *History of Animals*, 3.22 (523a).
80. Rhodiginus, *Lectiones Antiquae* (1599), col. 442.
81. *Hoti*, piece of reasoning, or the cause in rhetoric.
82. Pliny, *Natural History*, 7.17, 'as if nature spared their modesty after death'; Solinus, *Collectanea*, 1.95; Rhodiginus, *Lectiones Antiquae* (1599), 10.5.
83. Genesis 3:7.
84. Scaliger, *Aristotelis Historia de animalibus*, 8.2, 'Because women have large stomachs that are filled with the intestines; therefore, the stomach is filled up to a lesser degree with air and will sink down. In contrast, men's are emptier and the buttocks of the male sex are of a greater weight.'

85. *Callipygæ*, having shapely buttocks.
86. *In abate of*, deducting; Pliny, *Natural History*, 7.17.
87. *Ponderation*, weighing.
88. Scruple = 20 grains, dragme = 60 grains, grain = 0.064799 g.
89. *Sanctorius*, Italian physician, who weighed himself, his food and waste over a period of some thirty years, *De Statica Medicina Aphorismi* (1634), 1.21.
90. *Accessionall*, additional.
91. *Apoplecticall*, temporarily paralysed; *lipothymies and swoundings*, fainting, swooning.
92. *Trutination*, weighing.
93. *Refection*, refreshment.
94. *Montanus*, Johannes Baptista Montanus, 16th-century anatomist and producer of Greek and Islamic medical texts.
95. *Trituration*, pulverizing, reduction to a powder.
96. *Beames*, measuring pans.
97. *Lord Verulam*, Francis Bacon, *Sylva Sylvarum* (1628), 789, p. 198.
98. *Ebullition*, boiling.
99. Hamerus Poppius, *Basilica Antimonii* (1618), p. 21, 'If a burning hot mirror is exposed to the sun, in such a manner that the summit of the bright pyramid strikes the pulverized Antimony, it will be calcined with an effusion of smoke into the whiteness of snow and, what is even more wondrous, after the calcination, the weight of the Antimony is discovered to have grown rather than diminished.'
100. Plato, *Timeaus,* 70d; Macrobius, *Saturnalia*, 7.15–16.
101. *Officiall unto*, having the office of.
102. *Lambitive*, taken on the tongue.
103. *Guttulous*, dripping.
104. *Carolus Sigonius*, 16th-century humanist antiquarian, *De Regno Italiae* (1591), p. 20.
105. Apuleius, *Golden Ass*, 9.25.
106. Pliny, *Natural History*, 28.5.
107. Petronius, *Satyricon* (1629), 98, p. 29, 'Giton burst with holding his breath, and all at once sneezed three times, so that he shook the bed. Eumolpus turned round at the stir and said "Good day, Giton."'
108. Caelius Rhodiginus (Richerius), *Lectiones Antiquae* (1599), 24.27; *antienter*, more ancient.
109. Greek Anthologie, 11.268 [*Textual note: 'Se sternutantem'* changed from 1650 to '*Sternutamentum*'.]
110. Nicolaus Godignus, *Vita Patris Gonzali Sylveriae* (1612), p. 121.
111. Aristotle, *Problemata*, 33.7 (962a).
112. Hippocrates, *Aphorisms*, 6.13; *hickett*, hiccup.
113. Avicenna, *Liber Canonis*, 3.5.2; Pliny, *Natural History*, 7.6.

114. Rhodiginus, *Lectiones Antiquae* (1599), col. 1145; *Austine*, Augustine, *De Doctrina Christiana*, 2.20.
115. Aristotle, *Problemata*, 33.22 (962b).
116. *Eustathius upon Homer*, from Rhodiginus, *Lectiones Antiquae*, col. 1145–6; Plutarch, *Themistocles*, 8.2.
117. Aristotle, *Problemata*, 8.4 (907b).
118. Plutarch, *Alexander*, 4.3; Cardan, *De rerum varietate* (1557), 8.43.
119. *Fætor*, stench; *dulcified*, sweetened.
120. *Gentilitious*, characteristic of a nation.
121. *Introvenient*, mixing, coming together.
122. *Manasses*, 1 Chronicles 5:26; *Naphthali*, 2 Kings 17:5, 2 Esdras 13:40–5.
123. [*Textual note:* Corrected from 1646 'India'.]
124. Josephus, *Wars of the Jews*, 6.9.3.
125. *Gulosity*, gluttony.
126. *That animal*, pig, Leviticus 11:7; *propter convivia natum*, 'bred for banquets'.
127. Dietary laws from Leviticus 11 and Deuteronomy 14; Aristotle, *History of Animals*, 6.13 (567a).
128. Leviticus 12:2–5 and 15:2–33.
129. *Inquinations*, pollution.
130. Henry Blount, *Voyage into the Levant* (1636), p. 114.
131. *Admitted*, lost.
132. Genesis 34:30.
133. *Illation*, inference.
134. George Sandys, *Relation of a Journey* (1637), p. 148; *ranck*, stink.
135. Ammianus Marcellinus; Martial, *Epigrams*, 4.4, 'the Sabbath fastings of Jewish women . . . I would sooner smell of any of these than of your smell, Bassa.'
136. Aristotle, *Problemata*, 8.7 (908b).
137. Johannes Hucherus, *De Sterilitate* (1610), p. 19; Alsarius Crucius, *De Quaesitis per Epistolam in Arte Medica* (1622), p. 253.
138. *Maimonides*, on Leviticus 2:13.
139. Homer, *Iliad*, 3:2–6.
140. Strabo, *Geography*, 1.2.35.
141. Scaliger, *Aristotelis Historia de animalibus* (1619), p. 914; Aldrovandi, *de Avibus* (1610), p. 140.
142. Albertus Magnus, *De Animalibus*, 7.1.6; Cardan, *De Rerum Varietate* (1557), p. 299.
143. Aristotle, *History of Animals*, 7.12 (597a).
144. Atheneus, *Deipnosophists*, 9 (398e), 800 talents being the sum reputedly given by Alexander the Great towards the work.
145. Ezekiel 27:1, translated in AV as 'the Gammadims were in thy towers: they hanged their shields upon thy walls round about'.
146. *Forerius*, Johann Forster, *Dictionarium Hebraicum Novum* (1564), p. 144.

147. *Goliah*, i.e. Goliath, 1 Samuel 17:4.
148. Aristotle, *History of Animals*, 8.12 (597a); Pliny, *Natural History*, 4.11; Athenaeus, *Deipnosophists*, 9 (390b).
149. *Philetas*, Athenaeus, *Deipnosophists*, 401e. The account of the lead tied to the feet is in Aelian, *Historical Miscellany*, 9.14; *ut ad obolum accederet*, 'that he resembled an obol' (i.e. a small Greek coin).
150. [*Textual note:* This and the following chapter, some 12,000 words in full, are given in brief excerpt.].

PSEUDODOXIA EPIDEMICA BOOK 5

1. Aelian, *On Animals*, 3.23.
2. *Eucherius*, 5th-century Bishop of Lyon, *Formulae Spiritalis Intelligentiae*, 5 (Migne, *PL*, 50.749).
3. Jerome (attrib.), *Epistola ad Praesidium* (Migne, *PL*, 30.187).
4. *Austine*, Augustine, *Enarratio in Psalmum*, 101 (Migne, *PL*, 37.1298); Isidore, *Etymologies*, 12.7.26; Albertus, *De Animalibus*, 23.24 (90); *coat armour*, i.e. coats of arms.
5. *Pierius*, Valeriano, *Hieroglyphica* (1556), 20 (p.146), 'Yet that the Pelican having dissected its own breast thus cuts itself with its beak in such a manner that it nourishes its sons with its own blood, as indeed many others are convinced, is very inconsistent with the history of the Egyptians, for they narrate that the great vulture performs such an act.'
6. [*Textual note:* 'Black' changed to 'brown' in 1672.]
7. *Fissipedes*, with divided feet; *palmipedous*, web-footed; *latirostrous*, broad-beaked.
8. Aristotle, *History of Animals*, 9.10 (614b); Aelian, *On Animals*, 3.20; *Bellonius*, Belon, *Histoire de la Nature des Oyseaux* (1555), 3.2, p. 155.
9. Franciscus Sanctius, *Emblemata* (1573), p. 291.
10. [*Textual note:* This paragraph added 1672.]
11. Ovid, *Metamorphoses*, 2.265; Pliny, *Natural History*, 9.7; Hubert Goltsius, *Caesar Augustus* (1574), plate 68.8; Laevinus Hulsius, *Romanorum Numismatum* (1603), p. 275.
12. Scaliger, *Aristotelis Historia de animalibus* (1619), p. 234, 'Their body has no greater curve than other fish.'
13. *Rondeletius*, Rondelet, *Universa Aquatilium Historia* (1554), p. 459; Gesner, *De Piscium et Aquatilium Animantium Natura* (1558), p. 403; Aldrovandi, *De Cetis* (1623), p. 269; *Arion*, who rode a dolphin, Herodotus, *Histories*, 1.23.
14. Pierre Belon, *De Aquatilibus* (1553), p. 380.
15. *Pierius*, Valeriano, *Hieroglyphica* (1556), 27 (p. 195); *festina lente*, make haste slowly; *cunctation*, delay.
16. *John Baptist*, Matthew 3:4, and see *Pseudodoxia*, 7.9; Proverbs 30:27.

17. Mathiolus, *Commentaires sur Dioscoride* (1572), p. 227; Aldrovandi, *De Animalibus Insectis* (1623), p. 120; Thomas Moffet, *Insectorum... Theatrum* (1634), p. 117.
18. *Cucullated or capuched*, cowled or hooded.
19. *Falcation*, hooked appendage; *forcipated*, pincer-shaped; *saltation*, leaping.
20. *Fritiniancy*, twittering; *providence of the pismire*, Proverbs 6:6–9.
21. Exodus 10:4; Wisdom 16:9.
22. Fortunius Licetus, *De his, qui Diu Vivunt sine Alimento* (1612), 1.72.
23. *Muffetus*, Moffet, *Insectorum* (1634), p. 133, 'I affirm that they were as mistaken as others, insofar as they believed, by a common error, that locusts were cicadas.'
24. *Desumed*, obtained.
25. Isidore, *Etymologies*, 12.8.
26. [*Textual note:* Final sentence added 1672.]
27. *Cadmus*, who is changed, by degrees, into a snake, for a while retaining his human features, Ovid, *Metamorphoses*, 4.571–601.
28. *Pierius*, i.e. Benedictus Pererius, *Commentaria in Genesim* (1622), p. 196.
29. Eugubinus, *Cosmopoeia* (1535), p. 164 and on the basilisk see *Pseudodoxia*, 3.7; the 'thornes and briars' being the result of the fall, Genesis 3:18. [Textual note: syntax of 1646 corrected in 1650.]
30. *Pythonissa*, refers to the Vulgate rendering of the medium consulted by and the cause of Saul's death, 1 Chronicles 10:13; *Dodona*, sacred Greek Shrine, Herodotus, *Histories*, 2:56–7.
31. *Assigned... a name*, Genesis 2:19; Petrus Lombardus, *Sententiae*, 2.21.2; Alphonsus Tostatus, *Commentaria in Genesim* (1596), f. 18r; Cyril of Alexandria, *Contra Julianum* (Migne, *PG*, 76.636).
32. *Urbin*, Raphael; *Angelo*, Michaelangelo. Engravings of their paintings were reasonably widespread.
33. *Naturity*, the creative or regulative power of the natural world.
34. *Dilacerate*, tear apart.
35. *Colligation*, coming together.
36. *Encrease and multiply*, Genesis 1:22.
37. *Momentall*, momentary.
38. *Umbilicality*, intimate, umbilical connection.
39. *Catenation*, links of a chain.
40. [*Textual note:* This paragraph, wonderfully incongruous as it is, was appended from 1658.] The chicken and the egg dilemma appears in Plutarch, *Table Talk* (*Quaestiones Conviviales*), 2.3 (635e–638).
41. *Gesture... jesture*, posture; *session*, sitting.
42. *Accubation*, reclining.
43. [*Textual note:* This and the following sentence added 1650.]
44. Esther 7.
45. Athenaeus, *Deipnosophists*, 153a.

46. Athenaeus, *Deipnosophists*, 147f.
47. Plutarch, *Table Talk*, 1.1.5.
48. Aristotle, *Politics*, 7.17 (1336b).
49. Justus Lipsius, *De Ritu Conviviorum apud Romanos* in *Tractatus* (1609); Hieronymous Mercurialis, *De Arte Gymnastica*, in *Opuscula Aurea* (1644); Salmasius, *Plinianae Exercitationes* (1629); Petrus Ciacconius, *De Triclinio Romano* (1588).
50. Martial, *Epigrams*, 14.87, 'Accept a sigma (semicircular couch) inlaid with crescent tortoise-shell. It takes eight. Let him come, whoever is a friend'; *accumbing*, reclining; *stibadion*, semi-circular couch; *sigma*, C-shaped.
51. Mercurialis, *De Arte Gynmastica*, pp. 25–7; *cubiculary*, belonging to the bedroom; *discubitory*, for use outside the bedroom.
52. Juvenal, *Satires*, 2.120, 'the new bride reclines in her husband's lap'; Suetonius, *Caligula*, 24.1.
53. [*Textual note:* The following sentence from 1650.] *Præter*..., 'Contrary to the example of his ancestors'.
54. Josephus, *Jewish War*, 6.9.3.
55. In fact, Horace, *Epistles*, 1.5.28, 'There is room too, for several shades', i.e. shadows, uninvited guests.
56. *Igitur discubuere, Sertorius*..., 'Therefore, they reclined thus: Sertorius at the lower end of the middle couch, with Fabius above him, while Antonius had been placed at the top of the highest couch and below him the scribe of Sertorius: Versius; another scribe, Maecenas, reclined in the middle position on the lowest couch between Tarquitius at the far end and the Master, Perpenna, at the top end.'
57. Plutarch, *Sertorius*, 26.5.
58. Seneca, *Naturales Questiones*, 5.16.6.
59. Ezekiel 23:41.
60. *Passover*... *injunction*, Exodus 12:11.
61. Luke 14:8, 'When thou art bidden of any man to a wedding, sit not down in the highest room'; Matthew 23:6, '[they] love the uppermost rooms at feasts, and the chief seats in the synagogue'.
62. [*Textual note:* From here, to end of paragraph, added 1650.]
63. Exodus 12:26; Luke 22:14.
64. Scaliger, *De Emendatione Temporum* (1598), p. 534.
65. Nonnus, *In Johannem Metaphrasis*, in *Aristarchus Sacer* (1627), 13.23.
66. [*Textual note:* This and the following paragraph added 1650.]
67. John 13:13.
68. *Accubation*, lying down.
69. Pliny the Younger, *Epistles*, 4.22.4, 'Nerva was dining with a small party where Veiento was his neighbour at table and even leaning on his shoulder.'
70. Notae in Novum, *Novum Testamentum* (1633), p. 442; *decumbency*, reclining.

71. Luke 7:38.
72. Luke 4:20.
73. Luke 10:35.
74. Matthew 20:2.
75. Exodus 12:11.
76. Numbers 6:3–6.
77. John 11:38–44; Mark 5:40.
78. Matthew 2:23.
79. *Isaac*, Genesis 22:6; *consentaneous*, in accordance with.
80. Matthew 27:32; Mark 15:21; Luke 23:26.
81. Josephus, *Antiquities*, 1.13.2.
82. *David*, 1 Samuel 17:34; Plutarch, *Pompey* 12.5.13; *cognomination*, name, i.e. 'the Great'; *Anniball*, i.e. Hannibal, *Polybius*, 15.19.3.
83. *Qui videbant*... 'Who saw that the face of Moses, as he came forth, was horned', Exodus 34:35.
84. *Rahab*, Joshua 2:1; Hebrews 11:31.
85. Athenaeus, *Deipnosophists*, 572b.
86. *Tremellius*, Protestant Latin translation of the Bible.
87. Macrobius, *Saturnalia*, 1.21.19, 'For that reason, they also represent Ammon, the god the Libyans regard as the setting sun, with ram's horns, which are the heart of that animal's power as the rays are of the sun's.'
88. *Tauricornous*, with bull-like horns; Gerardus Vossius, *De Theologia Gentili* (1641), pp. 224–34.
89. *Scucheons*, crests.
90. Genesis 49:1–28; *nowed*, knotted (in heraldry).
91. Deuteronomy 33:17–22; Vossius, *De Theologia Gentili* (1641), p. 216.
92. *Serapis*, Egyptian fertility god.
93. Genesis 49 and Deuteronomy 33.
94. Numbers 10:35.
95. Deuteronomy 6:4.
96. Ezekiel 1:10.
97. The four gospel writers are thus represented with their respective animals on the title page of the King James Bible.
98. *Scuchions*, escutcheons, heraldic shields.
99. Diodorus, *Library of History*, 1.18.1; *shield of Achilles*, Homer, *Iliad*, 18:478–608.
100. Varro, reported in Lactantius, *Divine Institutes*, 1.6.6–8 (Migne, *PL*, 6.140), on the pagan gods. The sybils, though pagan oracles, were co-opted both to monotheism and Christology.
101. *Boysardus*, Boissardus, *De Divinatione* (1616), pp. 198–286, the source for much of the discussion here.
102. Salmasius, *Plinianae Exercitationes* (1629), p. 77, 'It is permitted to ridicule today's painters, who design paintings of the Sibyls of Cumana,

Cumae and Erythea, as if they were three different Sibyls; when, according to the wisdom of many very learned authors, all three were one and the same woman.'

103. Boissardus, *De Divinatione*, p. 197, 'In a great variety of tracts we are allowed the freedom to believe as a reader either that one and the same woman, having travelled about in diverse regions, obtained the cognomen from various places where an oracle was ascertained to have arisen, or several already existed.'
104. Virgil, *Aeneid*, 6.321 'aged priestess'.
105. *Sine mente*, 'without reason'.
106. Livy does not in fact discuss the age of the Sibyls; Aulus Gellius, *Attic Nights*, 1.12.2; Festus, *De Verborum Significatione* (1593), p. 14.
107. [*Textual note:* The final sentence added in 1650.]
108. Plutarch, *Antony*, 86.
109. (Pseudo) Galen, *On Theriac to Piso*, 8.
110. Strabo, *Geography*, 17.1.10.
111. Petrus Victorius, *Variae et Antiquae Lectiones* (1609), 4.22, p. 87.
112. *Nine worthies*, a variable list of great figures, usually including, for instance, Alexander, Julius Caesar, Joshua, David, Judas Maccabeus, with other figures who might be included, Hector, Arthur, or Charlemagne.
113. *His horse*, Bucephalus.
114. Curtius Quintus, *History of Alexander*, 8.14.17; Arrian, *Anabasis of Alexander*, 5.16.4; Plutarch, *Alexander*, 60.4.
115. *Maccebees*, rebellious Jewish army in Apocrypha, 1 Maccabees 6:32–47.
116. Jacobus Laurus, *Antiquae Urbis Splendor* (1612), 51r.
117. In fact, 1 Maccabees 6:37.
118. *Hector*, Homer, *Iliad* , 5.494; Pliny, *Natural History*, 7.56; Diodorus, *History*, 5.21.5; Walter Raleigh, *History of the World* (1617), 2.14.4.
119. Diodorus, *History*, 5.21.5, whose Britons are autochthonous, born from the soil; Caesar, *Gallic War*, 4.24; Tacitus, *Agricola*, 12.
120. Pancirollus, *Res Memorabiles* (1631), 2.274; Polydore Virgil, *De Inventoribus Rerum* (1528), 3.18; Petrus Victorius, *Variae et Antiquae Lectiones* (1609), 37.15.
121. Laurentius, *Historia Anatomica*, in *Opera* (1615), p. 128.
122. Virgil, *Aeneid*, 12.326, 287, 'he calls for horse and arms, with a bound leaps proudly into his chariot' and 'the others rein their chariots or leap on to their horses, [and with drawn swords stand ready]'.
123. Suetonius, *Caligula*, 3.1; *suppedaneous*, placed under the feet for support.
124. *Jephthah*, Judges 11:29–40; *Abraham*, Genesis 22:1–19.
125. Judges 11:40.
126. Epiphanius, *Adversus Haereses*, 35 (Migne, *PG*, 41.973).
127. Leviticus 1:3–14.
128. *Leper*, Leviticus 14:4; on Gentile sacrifices, e.g. Leviticius 18:21, 2 Kings 16:3.

129. *Syrians*, Athenaeus, *Deipnosophists*, 346e.
130. *Gileadite*, Judges 11:1; *Ozias*, i.e. Uzziah, 2 Chronicles 26:16–21.
131. Leviticus 27:1–7.
132. *Salarie of Judas*, Matthew 27:5–8.
133. *Iphigenia . . . redeemed*, Ovid, *Metamorphoses*, 12.28–34.
134. [*Textual note:* This paragraph added 1650.]
135. Judges 11:31.
136. Exodus 21:15.
137. Matthew 3:4; Mark 1:6.
138. *Cilicious*, hair-cloth.
139. 2 Kings 1:8, of Elijah, 'he was an hairy man'.
140. Zechariah 13:4.
141. Hebrews 11:37; Genesis 3:21.
142. Aelian, *On Animals*, 17.34; Matthew 11:7; Luke 7:24.
143. *Adjections*, additions.
144. [*Textual note:* The translation in the text, down to 'real history', was added in 1650.] Caesar Baronius, *Martyrologium Romanum* (1586); Zacharias Lippelous, *Vitae Sanctorum* (1616), 3.264.
145. *Pierius*, Valeriano, *Hieroglyphica* (1556), 15.
146. [*Textual note:* This paragraph added first in 1658.]
147. *Cevallerius*, Giovanni Battista de Cavalleriis, *Ecclesiae Anglicanae Trophaea* (1584), plate 14.
148. Heylyn, *Historie of St George* (1631), 2.1.6.
149. [*Textual note:* From 'some conceive . . ' to ' . . . St. George; or else' added in 1650.]
150. [*Textual note:* Last sentence added in 1650.] 'That picture of St George—in which he is portrayed as an armed knight, who slays his enemy with the point of his spear, next to which a virgin has been placed, stretching out suppliant hands—this image should be assessed as symbolic rather than of any historicity. Indeed it was customary that a soldier of equestrian office be represented with a knightly portrait.'
151. Pancirollus, *Res Memorabiles* (1631), 2.167; Polydore Vergil, *De Inventoribus Rerum* (1528), 3.18, f. 59.
152. *Horologies*, ways of telling the time.
153. Pliny, *Natural History*, 2.78.
154. Jacobus Laurus, *Antiquae Urbis Splendor* (1612), f. 22.
155. *Ezechias*, Hezekiah; 2 Kings 20:11 and Isaiah 38:8.
156. Persius, *Satires*, 3.3, 'We're snoring enough to make the untamed Falernian wine stop fizzing, while the shadow reaches the fifth line.'
157. *Horometry*, measurement of time; *Architas*, who invented a flying mechanical dove, Aulus Gellius, *Attic Nights*, 10.12; *helicoscopie of Archimedes*, spiral, screw-based machine.
158. John Dee, Euclid, *Elements of Geometrie* (1570), Preface.
159. Cardan, *De Subtilitate* (1560), p. 453.

160. Horace, *Ars Poetica*, 4.
161. *Ulysses*, Homer, *Odyssey*, 12.165–200.
162. *Mediety*, intermediate state; Aelian, *On Animals*, 17.23; Ovid, *Metamorphoses*, 5.553–63.
163. Macrobius, *Saturnalia*, 1.8.4.
164. Aristotle, *History of Animals*, 5.2 (539b).
165. *Vartomannus*, Ludovico di Varthema, in Aldrovandi, *De Quadrupedibus* (1623), p. 183.
166. Aristotle, *Of the Parts of Animals*, 3.2.
167. *Cornigerous*, horned.
168. 1 Maccabees 6:37.
169. *Phornutus, Fulgentius, and Albricus*, mythologers, published together with Hyginus, *Fabulae* (1578).
170. *Expresses*, representing by signs.
171. *Syntaxis*, the grammar of nature, or its hieroglyphic representation.
172. *Adam*, who in naming the animals, Genesis 2:19, was understood to have had particular insight into their true nature.
173. *Orus*, i.e. Horapollo, putative Egyptian inventor of hieroglyphic language, rendered into Latin by Valeriano (Pierius), *Hieroglyphica* (1556).
174. Aelian, *On Animals*, 2.46; Ambrose, *Hexaemeron*, 5.20 (Migne, *PL*, 14.233); Basil, *Hexameron*, 8.6 (Migne, *PG*, 29.180); Isidore, *Etymologies*, 12.7.12.
175. *Consentaneous*, in agreement with; Heurnius, *Barbaricae Philosophiae Antiquitates* (1600), p. 203.
176. *Abortion*, miscarriage.
177. Examples from Horapollo, in Valeriano, *Hieroglyphica* (1556), pp. 10–18.
178. [*Textual note:* A chapter 'Of the Picture of Haman hanged' is included here from 1672.] *Dreames of Pharaoh*, Genesis 41:1–7; *Joseph*, Genesis 37:5–10.
179. 'A Hare encountered confers an inauspicious journey (on the traveller).'
180. See also Leviticus 19:26; Maimonides, *De Idolatria* (1641), 11.4, p. 145.
181. *Preominate*, portend, be an omen of.
182. Cesare Ripa, *Iconologie* (1644), 2.170.
183. *Law of Moses*, Leviticus 11:17; *Esay*, Isaiah 34:11.
184. [*Textual note:* Next sentence added in 1650.]
185. Pliny, *Natural History*, 28.4; *veneficiously*, by poison; Jacques Dalechamps, comment in 1634 edition of Pliny, p. 567; 'Such a feeling makes everybody break the shells of eggs or snails after eating them, or else pierce them with their spoon.'
186. Adrianus Turnebus, *Adversaria* (1604), p. 331.
187. Pliny, *Natural History*, 28.5, 'absent people can divine by the ringing in their ears that they are the object of talk'; Dalechamps's 1634 edition of Pliny, p. 568, 'Why does garrulous chatting echo every night to me? I don't know to whom you have remembered me.'

188. Gregory of Nazianzen, *Carmina*, 1.2.1, 'Assuredly the Spring rose lies concealed, enclosed by its husk | In the same way the mouth should bear chains and be curtailed by strong reins, | and declare prolonged silences with its lips.'
189. *Compotation*, drinking together.
190. Levinus Lemnius, *De Plantis Sacris* (1622), pp. 90–1, 'The Rose is the flower of Venus, wherefore her deeds might lie hidden | Amor dedicated the gifts of his mother to Harpocrates | Thereafter the host suspends the rose over the tables of those judged to be friends, | so his guests might know that under the rose all words ought to be silent.'
191. Petrus Victorius, *Variae et Antiquae Lectiones* (1609), 3.21; Causabon, *Animadversiones in Athenaeum* (1600), p. 265; Athenaeus, *Deipnosophists*, 238c.
192. Pliny, *Natural History*, 28.17, 'to cross the knees first in one way, and then in the other'.
193. *Pierius*, Valeriano, *Hieroglyphica* (1556), 35.
194. *Statary*, established, fixed.
195. *Piaculous*, sinful or requiring expiation.
196. 2 Chronicles 33.6.
197. Pliny, *Natural History*, 28.6, 'Many today have scruples about cutting hair from the moles on their faces.'
198. Apuleius, *Golden Ass*, 3.23, 'I swear by the sweet little knot of your hair.'
199. Exodus 12:11; Job 38:3.
200. 1 Peter 1:13.
201. Exodus 39:5.
202. Isaiah 11:5, Ephesians 6:14.
203. *Epithumeticall*, connected with desire, appetite, glossed from 1650 as 'concupiscentiall'.
204. *Achilles*, Statius, *Achilleid*, 1.134.
205. Genesis 3:15.
206. *Washed the feet*, John 13:5–8.
207. Leviticus 1:9–13; Exodus 29:13.
208. Daniel 7:9.
209. *Indiciduous*, not liable to fall.
210. *Tropicall*, i.e. a trope.
211. In Joshua 10:12 and 2 Kings 20:11.
212. *Areopagite*, Dionysius the Areopagite, *Epistles*, 7.2.
213. *Promotion*, i.e. how they promoted cases and causes.
214. Adrianus Spiegelius, *De Formato Foetu*, in *De Humani Corporis Fabrica* (1627), pp. 7–10.
215. Avicenna, *Oeconomiae Librorum Canonis* (1608), p. 180; *ebriety*, drunkenness.
216. Averroes, *Collectanea de Re Medica* (1537); Seneca, *De Tranquillitate Animi*, 17.8; Horace, *Odes*, 3.21, reports Cato's being warmed with wine.

217. *Incalescence*, heating up; *æstuation*, feverish disturbance; *Joseph*, Genesis 43:34.
218. *Dementation*, inducing madness; *sopition*, putting to sleep.
219. *Noah*, Genesis 9:21; *ebriosity*, habitual drunkenness.
220. *Happily*, perhaps; *stupration*, rape.
221. *Lot*, Genesis 19:30–8; Ruth 1:4.
222. Bodin, *De Magorum Daemonomania* (1581), p. 182.
223. *Pierius*, Valeriano, *Hieroglyphica* (1556), 10.
224. Matthew 25:32.
225. *Rhabdomancy*, divination by rod.
226. Georgius Agricola, *De Re Metallica* (1621), p. 26.
227. *Mercury*, Ovid, *Metamorphoses*, 1.715–50; *Ulysses*, Homer, *Odyssey*, 10.237–43.
228. *Moses rod*, Exodus 4:2; *Aaron*, Exodus 7:9–12; *Arke*, Numbers 17:10; *Solomon*, 2 Kings 25:9 and 2 Chronicles 36:19.
229. Severus, *Historia Augusta*, 14.5; Virgil, *Aeneid*, 6.851, 'You, Roman, be sure to rule the world.'
230. Virgil, *Aeneid*, 6.869, 'only a glimpse of him will fate give earth nor suffer him to stay long'.
231. *Elisha . . . Joash*, 2 Kings 13:15–19.
232. *Maculated*, spotted, blemished.

PSEUDODOXIA EPIDEMICA BOOK 6

1. [*Textual note:* This book, which is quite large, is presented only in small extracts. Its subject matter is largely connected with 'chronology', which aimed to determine the age of the earth in precise detail. Browne on the whole doubts the reliability of any such speculation, though not necessarily its value. Included here are indications of the chapter subjects via, by and large, the opening paragraphs. The last three chapters, on blackness, are complete.]
2. Aristotle, *On the Heavens*, 1.3 (270a).
3. *Uncontroulable*, not checkable.
4. *Moses*, as supposed author of the Pentateuch; *materiation*, forming of matter.
5. *Information*, with the sense of forming within.
6. Diodorus Siculus, *Library of History*, 1.10.1–7; Justin, *History of the World, Extracted from Trogus Pompeius*, 2.1.
7. *Theife*, Matthew 24:43, Luke 12:39, 1 Thessalonians 5:2; *departure*, Exodus 12:13.
8. *Antæci*, at the same latitude, on different sides of the equator (or those who dwell there); *Perieci*, at the same latitude, but opposite meridian.
9. *Twinckling of an eye*, 1 Corinthians 15:52.
10. [*Textual note:* Changed to 'reasonable' from 1650.]

11. Hippocrates, *Regimen*, 1.33.
12. *Septenary*, group of seven years.
13. *Decrement*, diminution.
14. *Convinsively*, convincingly; *Spanish physition*, Franciscus Vallesius, *de Sacra Philosophia* (1622), p. 129.
15. *Colures*, meridian of celestial sphere.
16. *Herd of swine*, Mark 5:11; *forbidden unto the Jews*, Leviticus 11:7.
17. Athenaeus, *Deipnosophists*, 9.14 (400d).
18. Job 1:3; Numbers 31:34.
19. Diodorus, *Library of History*, 2.5.4.
20. Aristotle, *History of Animals*, 5.14 (546b).
21. Genesis 5:22–32, 9:28, 11:10–26.
22. *Septuagesimall*, living to 70, i.e. three-score and ten; *distich*, pair of verse lines.
23. *Xerxes complaint*, i.e. that not one of his army would be alive in a hundred years, Herodotus, *Histories*, 7.46.
24. Genesis 4:17–22.
25. Psalm 90:4.
26. Genesis 5:23; *translated*, taken to heaven without dying.
27. *Incontroulable*, indisputable.
28. *Sapor*, related to taste.
29. *Molyes*, moly, a kind of garlic; *porrets*, onions, leeks.
30. *Cham*, Genesis 9:25.
31. Strabo, *Geography*, 15.1.24.
32. Aristotle, *Problemata*, 38.7 (967a).
33. *Phaeton*, Ovid, *Metamorphoses*, 1.748–2.398.
34. Strabo, *Geography*, 15.1.24.
35. Abraham Ortelius, *Theatrum Orbis Terrarum* (1574), map 4.
36. Olaus Magnus, *Historia de Gentibus Septentrionalibus* (1555), p. 634.
37. Referring to Septalius, *In Aristotelis Problemata Commentaria* (1632), 2.55. [*Textual note:* 'Aristotle' is changed to 'Porphyrie' in 1650.]
38. *Apogeum*, apogee, at the greatest distance from the earth.
39. *Beach*, an island off Java in Ortalius' map.
40. *Candy*, Crete.
41. *Contemperate*, temper or cool; *humectate*, moisten.
42. Leo Africanus, *The History and Description of Africa* (1600), p. 33.
43. *Swarte*, darken.
44. Aristotle, *History of Animals*, 3.12 (519a); Strabo, *Geography*, 6.1.13; Pliny, *Natural History*, 31.9.
45. *Jacobs cattell*, Genesis 30:37.
46. *Hippocrates*, who reportedly saved a woman from the charge of adultery by pointing out the picture, reported from Jerome, *Hebraicae Quaestiones in Genesin* (Migne, *PL*, 23.985).
47. Heliodorus, *Aethiopica* (1587), 4.8.

48. *Plotinus*, via Aldrovandi, *Ornithologia* (1610), 2.17.
49. *Austin*, Augustine, *City of God*, 18.5.
50. *Inquinations*, blemishes.
51. *Morbosities*, diseased conditions.
52. Hippocrates, *On Air, Waters and Places*, 14, 'As soon as a child is born they remodel its head with their hands, while it is still soft and the body tender, and force it to increase in length by applying bandages and suitable appliances, which spoil the roundness of the head and increase its length. Custom originally so acted that through force such a nature came into being; but as time went on the process became natural, so that custom no longer exercised compulsion. For the seed comes from all parts of the body, healthy seed from healthy parts, diseased seed from diseased parts. If therefore bald parents have for the most part bald children, grey-eyed parents grey-eyed children, squinting parents squinting children, and so on with other physical peculiarities, what prevents a long-headed parent having a long-headed child?'
53. Aristotle, *History of Animals*, 6.29 (578b); *camoys*, concave.
54. [*Textual note:* Paragraph added 1658.]
55. *Chaughes*, kind of crow.
56. *Venereall contagion*, syphilis.
57. Ptolomy, *Geography*, 7.2, man-eating in the East Indies; Strabo, *Geography*, 4.5.4, on cannibalism in Britain; 7.3.6 on Irish man-eating; Pliny, *Natural History*, 4.12.88 and 7.2.12, on African and Scythian cannibals.
58. *Elias*, who in Rabbinic tradition, would resolve all doubts, with the coming of the messiah.
59. *Scut*, tail-stub of hare or rabbit.
60. Aristotle, *History of Animals*, 2.1 (499b); Leviticus 11:7.
61. *Uncleane . . . Arke*, Genesis 7:2.
62. *Traduced*, transmitted.
63. Giovanni Antonio Maginus, *Geographia* (1617), 2. f 188.
64. Herodotus, *Histories*, 3.101.
65. Aristotle, *History of Animals*, 3.22 (523a).
66. *Dealbation*, whitening, blanching.
67. *Cham . . . Noah*, Genesis 9:22–5.
68. *Benegroe*, blacken, changed to 'denigrate' after 1658.
69. *Cush*, son of Ham, Genesis 10:6.
70. Berosus, *De Antiquitatibus* (1505), 5; Macrobius, *Saturnalia*, 1.7.19.
71. Genesis 9:25.
72. *Wife of Moses*, Numbers 12:1; Exodus 2:16–21.
73. 1 Kings 10; *Damianus à Goes*, in Samuel Purchas, *Purchase His Pilgrimage* (1625), 1.7.5.
74. *Zerah . . . Asa*, 2 Chronicles 14:9.
75. *Abraham*, Genesis 20:1.
76. *Mizraim*, Genesis 10:6, Raleigh, *History of the World* (1617), 1.8.11.

77. *Phut*, Genesis 10:6; *Caanan*, Genesis 10:15–19.
78. *Prepossessions*, former possessions.
79. *Divarication*, disagreement.
80. Genesis 9:25.
81. Genesis 24:3, 28:1.
82. Genesis 10:10–13.
83. *Perpend*, consider.
84. *Pulchritude*, beauty; Aristotle, *Metaphysics*, 13:3 (1078a), *Poetics*, 7.7 (1450b); Galen, *On the Usefulness of the Parts*, 1.9.
85. *Concolour*, of more than one colour.
86. *M. Leo*, Leo Hebraeus, *Dialoghi d'Amore* (1535), 3.
87. *Thersites*, Homer, *Iliad*, 2.216–19.
88. *Canticles*, Song of Songs 1:5.
89. Song of Songs 5:11. The Canticles are understood typologically to refer to Christ and the church.
90. *Jewes*, in *Pseudodoxia*, 4.10.
91. *Beda*, Bede, *Ecclesiastical History*, 1.1; *Gyraldus*, Gerald of Wales, *Topographica Hibernica*, 1.28.
92. *Palliate*, conceal, apply a superficial reasoning to.
93. [*Textual note:* The following sentence added in 1672.]
94. *Fuliginious*, sooty; *torrified*, roasted; *madefying*, moistening.
95. *Ligneous*, wood-like; Aristotle, *Meteorology*, 4.9 (387a).
96. *Suffitus*, fumes.
97. *Mundified*, cleansed.
98. *Adust*, scorched.
99. *Ustilago,* a smutty parasite on grain.
100. *Tiffanies*, a transparent gauze muslin.
101. Edward Jorden, *Discourse of Naturall Bathes and Minerall Waters* (1632), p. 26, on Belon, in Carolus Clusius, *Exotica* (1605), 3.229.
102. *Advenient*, additional.
103. *Atramentous*, inky black.
104. *Eruginous*, bluish-green.
105. Dioscorides, *Materia Medica*, 5.162.
106. *Lixivium*, alkaline soluble extract.
107. *Vitriol vomitive*, solution to induce vomiting.
108. Aristotle, *History of Animals*, 4.1 (524b); *Cuttle*, cuttle-fish.
109. *Evanid*, weak.
110. *Niveous*, snowy lustre.
111. *Salary*, saline.
112. [*Textual note:* Chapter added 1650.]
113. Sebastian Münster, *Cosmographia Universalis* (1550), p. 267.
114. Polydore Vergil, *De rerum Inventoribus* (1528), f. 127; Pierre Belon, *Observations*, in Carolus Clusius, *Exotica* (1605), p. 113.

PSEUDODOXIA EPIDEMICA BOOK 7

1. Goropius Becanus, *Origines Antwerpianae* (1569), pp. 485–505.
2. Pietro Mattioli, *Commentaires sur Dioscoride* (1572), p. 162.
3. Serapion, *De Simplicibus ex Plantis* (1525), f. 134.
4. Genesis 3:6.
5. Philo, *De Opificio Mundi*, 54.
6. *Elias*, 1 Kings 19:4; *Absalon*, 2 Samuel 18:9; *Zacheus*, Luke 19:4.
7. *Venus*, Homer, *Iliad*, 5.335; *King Philip*, Plutarch, *Table Talk*, 9.4.1.
8. *Cautelously*, cautiously.
9. John 18:10; Mark 14:15.
10. 2 Kings 20:11.
11. Genesis 24:2; Luke 23:33.
12. 'These are the woods in the cross of Christ: the foot of the cross was made from cedar, the main shaft from cypress, the highest part from olive wood and the crossbeam from palm.' Lipsius, *De Cruce* in *Opera* (1637), 3.13; Goropius Becanus, *Gallica*, in *Opera* (1580), 4.132–53.
13. Joannes Ruellius, *De Natura Stirpium* (1536), p. 253.
14. Song of Songs, 8:5; *our translation*, i.e. AV.
15. Amos 8:1.
16. Revelation 18:14, 'And the fruits that thy soul lusted after are departed from thee'.
17. *Pierius*, Valeriano, *Hieroglyphica* (1556), 54.
18. Genesis 2:22.
19. Renaldus Columbus, *De Re Anatomica* (1559), p. 60.
20. 'Bone of my bones', Genesis 2:23; Hieronymus Oleaster, *Commentaria in Pentateuchum Mosi* (1588), p. 20; Browne's compilation of sources here comes from Benedictus Pererius, *Commentaria in Genesim* (1622), p. 150; *autoptically*, proved through inspection or observation.
21. Origen, *Contra Celsum*, 4.38.
22. *Compage*, joining together.
23. *Rapha*, 1 Chronicles 20:6.
24. *Os inominatum,* pelvic bone.
25. Aristotle, *History of Animals*, 1.15 (493b).
26. *Manuall*, having hands.
27. *Similary*, homogeneous.
28. *Multiparous*, producing several offspring at once.
29. *Countesse of Holland*, who, having accused a woman with twins of adultery, bore 360 children in a single birthing, Johannes Schenck, *Observationes Medicae* (1609), p. 643.
30. *Crepusculous*, indistinct, of twilight.
31. Genesis 5:26–7.
32. *Paralogy*, false, specious reasoning.

33. *Enoch*, Genesis 5:23; *illation*, inference.
34. Genesis 5.
35. Salian, *Annalium Ecclesiasticorum Veteris Testamenti Epitome* (1635), p. 47, 'A grieving father appointed this, by whose son it was more properly laid down: In the 130th year from the origin of things, 129 from the birth of Abel.'
36. *Captivity*, in Egypt, Exodus 1–13; *princes*, Genesis 25:12–26.
37. Psalm 90:4.
38. *Roride*, dewy.
39. *Signalities*, meanings.
40. *Iris*, rainbow; *efficient*, cause.
41. *Pluvious*, liable to rain; *disposure*, disposition.
42. *Noah*, Genesis 9:13.
43. i.e. messenger of the gods.
44. Genesis 9:13.
45. [*Textual note:* This paragraph added 1650.] Isaiah 34:4.
46. Ecclesiasticus 43:11.
47. Genesis 10:21; *Austin*, i.e. Augustine, *City of God*, 16.3.1.
48. Jerome, in the Vulgate translation.
49. [*Textual note:* 1646 has 'Abraham' instead of Isaac, the error corrected from 1658.]
50. *Abel*, Genesis 4:3; *Isaac*, Genesis 17:19; *Jacob*... *Esau*, Genesis 25:23, 27:1–40; *Joseph*, Genesis, 37:3–11; *David*, 1 Samuel 16:10; *caddet*, cadet, younger brother.
51. *Covered Noah*, Genesis 9:23.
52. [*Textual note:* This paragraph added 1650.]
53. Genesis 9:8–17; Josephus, *Antiquities of the Jews*, 1.4.2.
54. Genesis 7:19.
55. [*Textual note:* Changed in 1650 to: 'whose lowest story was in height and bredth one furlong, and seven more built upon it'.]
56. [*Textual note:* The following sentence added 1650.] Herodotus, *Histories*, 1.181; Berosus, *De Antiquitatibus* (1512), f. 117r.
57. Genesis 11:6.
58. Ralegh, *History of the World* (1617), 1.7.10.3.
59. Pierius, i.e. Benedictus Pererius, *Commentaria in Genesim* (1622), p. 423.
60. Genesis 11:4.
61. Genesis 30:14–16.
62. *Fecundation*, fertility.
63. Song of Songs 7:13.
64. Josephus, *Antiquities of the Jews*, 1.19.7.
65. Johannes Drusius, *De Mandragora* (1632), pp. 101–3.
66. Hieronymi Oleaster, *Commentaria in Pentateuchum Mosi* (1588), p. 122.
67. *Jonas*, Jonah 4:6–10.

68. Hugo Grotius, *Annotata ad Vetus Testamentum* (1644), 2.556.
69. 1 Kings 4:33.
70. Levinus Lemnius, *De Plantis Sacris* (1622), p. 59.
71. [*Textual note:* Changed from 1646 'faire species'.]
72. *Unguent*, ointment; Matthew 26:7, Mark 14:3, John 12:3.
73. Mathioli, *Epistolae Medicinales* (1564), p. 646; Dioscorides, *Materia Medica*, 1.62.
74. *Determination*, conclusion; *Austin*, Augustine, *Contra Faustum Manichaeum*, 22.56 (Migne, *PL*, 42.435); *pulchritude*, beauty; *suavity*, sweetness.
75. *hoc quo modo*... 'I am unable to conclude how this opinion came into the mind', Drusius, *De Mandragora* (1632), p. 102.
76. Genesis 30:23.
77. *Philtre*, love potion.
78. Dioscorides, *Materia Medica*, 4.75; *mundifie*, purify; *fluxes*, menstruation.
79. Petrus Hispanus, *Thesaurus Pauperum*, in Sarapion, *Practica* (1525), f. 266r.
80. *Crasis*, temperature.
81. *Matrix*, womb.
82. Caesar Baronius, *Annales Ecclesiastici* (1623), 1.3–8; Juan de Pineda, *Monarchia Ecclesiastica* (1588), 10.14.2; Richard Montague, *De Originibus Ecclesiasticis* (1636), pp. 166–237.
83. Isaiah 60:3; Psalms 72:10.
84. Genesis 14:2–8; Joshua 8:1; Job 2:11.
85. Matthew 2:11.
86. 1 Kings 10:2; Genesis 43:11.
87. Sebastian Münster, *Cosmographia Universalis* (1550), p. 504.
88. Suetonius, *Vespasian*, 4.5; *Balaam*, Numbers 24:17.
89. Matthew 3:4; Mark 1:6; *opiniatrity*, obstinate adherence to an opinion.
90. Luke 15:16.
91. Quoted from Montague, *De Originibus Ecclesiasticis* (1636), p. 377, 'When Isidorus wrote these things he did not intend them to be defined for us, and we leave the whole matter to the judgement of the reader; for it is undisputed that the Greek word ἀκρίδες signifies both a kind of insect: the locust, and the highest parts of trees.'; 'But he is deceived...for the opposite is well known: in no classical author does Ἀκρίδα, a locust signify Ἀκρόδρυα, fruit tree.'
92. Paracelsus, *De Melle*, in *Opera Medico-Chimica* (1603–5), 7.162, 'This is explained in such a manner by several authors: they say that John ate locusts or crickets as food, but they are unable to disguise their folly – for example Jerome, Erasmus and other deceased modern prophets in Latin.'
93. Cited by Aldrovandi, *De Animalibus Insectis* (1623), p. 173.
94. Leviticus 11:22.

95. Matthew 3:1–4; Mark 1:4–6.
96. Revelation 11:3–7.
97. Baronius, *Annales Ecclesiastici* (1623), 1.135; *Trapezuntius*, George of Trebizond, *Opusculum* (1543), pp. 7–29.
98. Jerome, *De Viris Illustribus*, 9 (Migne, *PL*, 23.623); Tertullian, *De Anima*, 50 (Migne, *PL*, 2.735); Chrysostomus, *Homiliae in Epistolam ad Hebraeos*, 26 (Migne, *PL*, 63.179); Eusebius, *Historia Ecclesiastica*, 3.1.18 (Migne, *PG*, 20.216).
99. *Polycrates*, cited in Jerome's *De Viris Illustribus* (Migne, *PL*, 23.660), 'That John, who reclined on the breast of the Lord, and was the best teacher, fell asleep at Ephesus.'
100. John 19:26, 35.
101. *Trajections*, perceptions, impressions.
102. *Emphaticall*, i.e. where to place the emphasis.
103. *Diuturnity*, duration.
104. Luke 2:25–35; *Simeon*, the '*nunc dimittis*' being Simeon's prayer to be allowed to die in peace; Daniel 12:1.
105. John 21:20.
106. *Domitian*, Roman emperor 81–96 CE.
107. John 22:22.
108. Gulielmus Estius, *Biblia Magna* (1644), 4.475, 'because his body shall never be discovered; they would not say this if they had diligently surveyed the writings of the ancients'.
109. Ireneus, *Contra Haereses*, 1.23.5 (Migne, *PG*, 7.673); Tertullian, *De Anima*, 50 (Migne, *PL*, 2.735).
110. Exodus 30:12; on David, 2 Samuel 24:1–25, 1 Chronicle 21.
111. *Lustrations*, purificatory rites.
112. Exodus 38:25.
113. Josephus, *The Wars of the Jews*, 7.6.6.
114. Matthew 17:27.
115. *Lots wife*, Genesis 19:26.
116. Numbers 18:19; 2 Chronicles 13:5.
117. *Absalon*, i.e. Absalom, 2 Samuel 18:9; Josephus, *Antiquities of the Jews*, 7.10.2.
118. Matthew 27:5.
119. Jansenius, *Commentarii in Suam Concordiam* (1624), 2.244.
120. *Peter*, Acts 1:18.
121. *Illaqueation*, catching in a noose; Tobit 3:10, 'She grieved in such a manner that she was pressed by suffocation.'
122. *Achitophell*, 2 Samuel 17:33.
123. Cicero, *De Divinatione*, 2.57.117, 'Why are Delphic oracles, of which I have just given you examples, not uttered at the present time and have not been for a long time? And why are they regarded with the utmost contempt?'

124. Suetonius, *Tiberius*, 63.1.
125. Suetonius, *Caligula*, 57.3.
126. Plutarch, *The Obsolescence of Oracles*, 5.
127. *Intercision*, interruption; *absission*, cutting off.
128. Quoting from Baronius, *Annales Ecclesiastici* (1623), 1.3.
129. Eusebius, *De Vita... Constantini*, 2.50 (Migne, *PG*, 20.1028).
130. *His lips*, i.e. the Devil's.
131. Herodotus, *Histories*, 1.46.
132. Herodotus, *Histories*, 1.53–6, 86–91.
133. *Euripus*, narrow tidal strait between Greek mainland and island of Euboea; *Si quidem ego...* 'Indeed, if I do not capture you, you will capture me'; Procopius, *Wars of Justinian*, 8.6; Gregory of Nazianzus, *Contra Justinian*, 1.72 (Migne, *PG*, 35.597); Justin Martyr, *Cohortatio ad Graecos*, 36 (Migne, *PG*, 6.305).
134. Julius Pollux, *Onomasticon* (1608), 9.4, p. 421.
135. Diogenes Laertius, *Lives of the Philosophers*, 5.6.
136. Athenaeus, *Deipnosophists*, 696b–d.
137. *Apollodorus*, in Diogenes Laertius, *Lives*, 5.9–10.
138. *Deliberation*, Aristotle, *Problemata*, 4.23 (879a).
139. *Utrum, and An Quia,... fortasse and plerumque*,..., 'whether', and 'or', 'because'...'perhaps' and 'for the most part'.
140. *Antanaclasis*, rhetorical trope of using same word in different senses.
141. Vicomercatus, *In Quatuor Libros Aristotelis Meteorologicorum Commentarii* (1556), 1.171; *Meteors*, Aristotle, *Meteorologica*, 2.1 (353a).
142. *Problemes*, Aristotle, *Problemata*, 23.1–41; Plutarch, *On the opinions of Philosophers*, 3.17.
143. Pomponius Mela, *De Chorographia*, 2.7.
144. Pausanias, *Description of Greece*.
145. Giovanni Maginus, *Geographia* (1617), 2.168; *Velocis ac varii fluctus...* as translated in text.
146. Botero, *Relationi Universali* (1596), f. 150r.
147. Porcacchi, *L'Isole Piu Famose del Mondo* (1576), p. 143.
148. Livy, *History of Rome*, 28.6.9, *Haud facile...*, as in text, quoted in Loeb as: 'But hardly any other anchorage is more dangerous for a fleet. For sudden, squally winds blow down from very high mountains on either shore, and also the Euripus strait itself does not reverse its direction seven times a day at fixed times, as report has it, but with a current that like a wind changes irregularly, now this way, now that, it races along as a torrent dashes down from a steep mountain.'
149. Gillius, *De Bosporo Thracio* (1561), p. 37.
150. Aristotle, *Problemata*, 25.22.
151. [Textual note: the following two paragraphs added 1650] Galileo, *Dialogue concerning the Two Chief World Systems*, 4.
152. *Inturgescencies*, swellings; *æstutations*, boiling, agitating.

153. *Intumescencies*, swelling up.
154. Herodotus (wrongly attributed), *Libellus de Vita Homeri* (1608), 'Homer concluded his final day on the island of Ios from this illness. It is not the case, as some others judge, that he was slain by the perplexity of a Riddle, but rather by disease.'
155. Giovanni Francesco Pico della Mirandola, *Examen Vanitatis Doctrinae Gentium* (1520), 6.19. This is the nephew of the more famous Giovanni Pico della Mirandola.
156. Aristotle, *Politics*, 8.7 (1342b).
157. An account dependent on Galen, *On the Anatomy of the Nerves.*
158. *Granivorous*, feeding on grain.
159. Athenaeus, *Deipnosophists*, Book 1 (6b).
160. *Canorous*, melodious.
161. *Philomela*, Ovid, *Metamorphoses*, 6.424–674.
162. Pliny, *Natural History*, 2.106.
163. John Mandeville, *Travels*, 12.
164. Sebastian Münster, *Cosmographia Universalis* (1550), p. 1005.
165. Josephus, *Wars of the Jews*, 4.8.4.
166. Strabo, *Geography*, 16.2.42.
167. Aristotle, *Meteorology*, 2.3 (359a).
168. William Biddulph, *Travels of Four English Men and a Preacher* (1612), p. 103.
169. André Thevet, *Cosmographie Universelle* (1575), f. 176r.
170. [*Textual note:* All editions have 'salt water', but this is evidently wrong.]
171. *Ponderosity*, weight.
172. *Elisha*, 2 Kings 6:6.
173. *Tenuity*, thinness, in consistency.
174. Strabo, *Geography*, 16.2.42; *ebullition*, maintaining at boiling point.
175. Averroes, *Collectanea de Re Medica* (1537), 1.10, sig. F1v.
176. Aristotle, *Generation of Animals*, 1.19 (726a).
177. *Daughters of Lot*, Genesis 19:30–8.
178. Lucian, *Dialogues of the Dead*, 1.4.
179. John 11:35.
180. Psalm 2:4.
181. John 2:17, Psalm 69:9.
182. *Alogie*, absurdity; *illation*, inference.
183. Genesis 9:21.
184. *Parergies*, secondary or irrelevant matters.
185. Sergius the second (844–7 CE).
186. Richard Montague, *De Originibus Ecclesiasticis* (1636), p. 113; Papirius Massonus, *De Episcopis Urbis* (1586) f. 172v.
187. *Gentilitious*, gentile, i.e. not Christian name, but surname.
188. *Commuted*, exchanged.
189. *Cognomination*, naming.

190. Richard Knolles, *Generall Historie of the Turkes* (1603).
191. See Samuel Purchase, *Purchase His Pilgrimage* (1625), 2.1.8; 4.15.3.
192. Alhazen, *Opticae Thesaurus* (1572).
193. *Abraham*, Genesis 13:2 and 14:1–17; Job 1:3.
194. *Moses*, Exodus 3:1; *Jacob*, Genesis 29:1–10.
195. *Solomon*, 1 Kings 4:23, 8:63.
196. *Date obolum Belisario*, 'Give a penny to Belisarius'.
197. Petrus Crinitus, *De Honesta Disciplina* (1598), p. 236.
198. *Mendication*, begging.
199. Andreas Alciatus, *Parerga*, in *Opera* (1546), 2.303.
200. Baronius, *Annales Ecclesiastici* (1623).
201. Ovid, *Tristia*, 1.2.49, 'Here comes a wave that o'ertops them all—the wave after the ninth and before the eleventh.'
202. *Every interjacency irregulates*, every intervening object makes irregular.
203. *Semblable*, similar.
204. *Statary*, at fixed points; *numerally*, by number.
205. Festus Pompeius, *De Verborum Significatione* (1593), p. 48, 'They are called "tenth eggs", because the tenth egg is found to be of a greater size.'
206. Plutarch, *Artaxerxes*, 19.3.
207. *Cicurated*, rendered harmless or mild.
208. *Stare*, a kind of starling.
209. *Innoxiously*, without evil effects.
210. *Alexipharmacall*, antidote against poison.
211. *Suscitation*, activation, wakening.
212. Matthew Paris, *Historia Maior* (1571), p. 470.
213. 'Go! Why do you delay? I go; however, you delay until I come.'
214. Herodotus, *Histories*, 7.21.
215. Guillaume Budé, *De Asse* (1528), p. 457.
216. Job 40:23.
217. Livy, *History of Rome*, 21.37; Plutarch, appended to *Lives* (1612), p. 1067.
218. *Xerxes*, Herodotus, *Histories*, 7.22.
219. *Assuefaction*, habituation, becoming accustomed to something.
220. *Pancraticall*, skilled, disciplined.
221. Athenaeus, *Deipnosophists*, 412e–413a.
222. Aelian, *On Animals*, 7.16.
223. Strabo, *Geography*, 14.5.9. 'Sardanapallus, the son of Anacyndaraxis, built Anchiale and Tarsus in one day. Eat, drink and be merry, because all things else are not worth this, meaning the snapping of the fingers'.
224. *Amphion*, whose music brought the city into being.
225. Athenaeus, *Deipnosophists*, 206d–207c.
226. Plutarch, *Lycurgus*, 18.1.
227. *Aiunt*, 'They assert.'

228. *Phaleris*, who burnt his enemies alive inside a model bull.
229. *Balams asse*, Numbers 22:28.
230. [*Textual note:* 'Tree' added 1672.]
231. [*Textual note:* Changed in 1650 to 'Word of God, or'.]
232. [*Textual note:* 'not' added 1672.]
233. Rosimund, Lombard queen in Henningus Grosius, *Tragica* (1597), p. 119; *carrouled*, caroused.
234. [*Textual note:* 'doubled' in 1646.]
235. *Anthropophagy*, cannibalism; *Atreus*, who served Thyestes' children to him for dinner.
236. Herodotus, *Histories*, 2.89.
237. *Mezentius*, Virgil, *Aeneid*, 8.485–8; *vitiosity*, defect.
238. *Italian*, in Jean Boden, *Commonweale* (1606), f. 631v.
239. *Longimanus*, far-reaching, long-handed.
240. *Ferities*, savage natures.
241. *Monke*, in 1313, told of Henry VII, Holy Roman Emperor.
242. [*Textual note:* 'I believed' is changed to 'he believed' from 1650.]
243. *Heteroclitall*, deviating from normal rule and standards.
244. *Venenations*, poisonings.
245. [*Textual note:* Changed to 'commendeth' from 1650.]

HYDRIOTAPHIA

1. Thomas Le Gros, family friend. Browne treated his father, Charles Le Gros, and consulted a number of physicians, including Dr Samuel Bave and a 'Dr Rant', about his condition in 1642.
2. *Oracle of his ashes*, knowledge of the future of his ashes.
3. Martial, *Epigrams*, 5.74, 'Asia and Europe cover Pompey's sons, but the Earth of Lybia covers him', going on 'No wonder he is scattered over the whole world. So vast a ruin could not lie in one spot.'
4. Plutarch, *Cimon*, 8.6 reports how the remains of Theseus, who had been treacherously killed, were brought back to Athens after four hundred years, belatedly fulfilling an oracle's command.
5. *These*, i.e. these bones; *hit of fate*, stroke of luck.
6. *Sepulchral pitchers*, funeral urns.
7. *Noblest pyle*, referring to Townshend's home, Raynam Hall, Norfolk.
8. Seleucus talking of the dead Chrysanthus, 'He went over to the majority', Petronius, *Satyricon*, 42.
9. *Ancient of days*, God, Daniel 7:9.
10. There was general scepticism about Egyptian estimates of their own antiquity, being far longer than the presumed date of creation in 4004 BCE.
11. *Coldly drawn*, unwillingly.
12. i.e. physician.

13. William Dugdale, antiquarian, author of *Monasticon Anglicanum* (1655) and correspondent of Browne.
14. *Supinity*, lethargy; *new Britannia*, i.e. following William Camden, whose *Britannia* (1586) inaugurated early modern antiquarian study.
15. *Centos*, patchwork pieces; *Venus*, Roman goddess of love. Wanting to depict the most beautiful form, Zeuxis modelled her on different parts of five women, Cicero, *On Invention*, 2.1. In fact, of Helen, rather than Venus.
16. Presuming the urns to be Roman, and thus exercising Roman law.
17. *Pisse not upon their ashes*, Horace, *Ars Poetica*, 471.
18. 'The finest diamond comes from ancient rock.'
19. Famous for its silver mines and situated in present-day Bolivia. Browne's Sales Catalogue included such works as Antonio de Herrera, *Novus Orbis* (1622).
20. [*Textual note:* (Er) 'thousands of' for (58) 'a thousand'.]
21. *Adam*, made from clay of the earth, or its dust, brought from all corners of the Earth.
22. *Graves of giants*, ancient burial mounds, the giants themselves being both biblical (Genesis 6:4) and 'confirmed' by the occasional finds of dinosaur bones.
23. Genesis 7:17–23.
24. *Contempered*, mixed.
25. *Disunion*, i.e. the separation of the soul and body.
26. *Contrivances*, ingenious methods; *inhumation*, interment.
27. Genesis 25:9.
28. Christianus Adrichomius, *Theatrum terrae sanctae* (1600), p. 29.
29. *Moses*, Deuteronomy 34:6, causing the textual difficulty that the supposed author of the Pentateuch narrated his own death; Jude 1:9: 'Yet Michael the archangel, when contending with the devil he disputed about the body of Moses, durst not bring against him a railing accusation, but said, The Lord rebuke thee.'
30. *Hercules*, cremated his friend Argeus, Kirchmann, *De Funeribus Romanorum* (1625), 1.1; *Patrocles, and Achilles*, Homer, *Iliad*, 23.161–83, *Odyssey*, 24.67–97.
31. *Theban warre*, in Statius, *Thebaid*, 12.60–4 (Roman poet, *c.*45–95 CE); *Jair*, Judges 10:3.
32. Quintus Calaber (Quintus of Smyrna), author of *Posthomerica* (*c.*4th century CE), 1.789–803.
33. *Funerall pyre of Hector*, Homer, *Iliad*, 24.782–804; *Penthisilea*, Queen who fought on the side of Troy and was killed by Achilles.
34. Ammianus Marcellinus (*c.*330–91 CE), Roman historian, author of *Res Gestae*.
35. *As low as*, as recently as; *Julian* (the Apostate), Emperor of Rome who reversed Constantine's acceptance of Christianity, 331–3 CE.

36. This prefaces a series of borrowings and collated references, indebted to Lilio Giraldi, *De Sepulchris* (1539) and Johannes Kirchmann, *De Funeribus Romanorum* (1625), together with Antonio Bosio, *Roma Sotteranea* (1632) and Ole Worm, *Danicorum Monumentorum libri sex* (1643); *Herulians, Getes, and Thracians*, Eastern European nations; *Herulians*, living on the Black Sea, *Getes*, a Dacian or Thracian nation from south-west Europe, modern Romania, see Strabo, *Geography*, 7.3.12.
37. Pliny, *Natural History*, 7.54.187.
38. *Table laws*, the Twelve Tables, a fifth-century BCE codification of Roman law. Browne's source here is Kirchmann, *de Funeribus Romanorum*, 2.20, 3.24.
39. Ovid, *Fasti* 4.856, 'last of all a light was put to the pyre'. *Manlius*, in Livy, 8.7.22, who ordered the beheading of his son for military disobedience; Plutarch, *Numa*, 22.2, buried in two stone coffins, one for him and one for his sacred books; *Remus*, was killed with a shovel for leaping over the low ramparts of Rome. The note refers to Carolus Neapolis, *Anaptyxis ad Fastos P. Ovidii Nasonis* (1638).
40. *Cornelius Sylla*, i.e. Sulla, tyrannical figure given noble burial by Pompey; Plutarch, *Sulla*, 38; *Cornielian family*, Pliny, *Natural History*, 7.54.187, and further in Cicero, *Laws*, 2.22.56.
41. *Poppæa*, Tacitus, *Annals*, 16.6; kicked to death by her husband while pregnant, who eulogized her beauty at her burial. The burning of a talkative crow, killed by a rival, is described by Pliny, *Natural History*, 10.60.122.
42. *Thales*, Greek philosopher, 6th century BCE, discussed by Aristotle, *Metaphysics*, 983b.
43. *Heraclitus*, Greek philosopher, *c.*500 BCE, in Aristotle *Metaphysics*, 983b–984a.
44. *Sylla*, Plutarch, *Sulla*, 10.
45. Nicolas of Damacus, works lost, but cited in Strabo, *Geography*, 15.1, an Indian visitor to Athens who immolated himself because happy and not wishing to suffer misfortune, related in Giraldi, *De sepulchris* and Perucci, *Pompe Funebri* (1639), 7.1; *Brachmans*, Brahmins.
46. *Chaldeans... Persian Magi*, reported in Giraldi, pp. 54–5.
47. Reported in Henry Lord, *A Display of two forraigne sects* (1630), p. 65; Johan Albrecht de Mandelslo, *The Voyages and Travels* (1642); *Persees*, Parsees; *beers*, biers.
48. Discussed in Tacitus, *Germania*, 27.
49. John Greaves, *Pyramidographia* (1646), pp. 43–58.
50. *Pythagoras... Numa*, Plutarch, *Numa*, 1
51. *Scythians*, encompassing in classical and early modern use tribes ranging from Ukraine to India, but primarily areas north of Persia, into southern Russia.

52. *Ichthyophagi*, fish-eaters, in Strabo, *Georgraphy*, 2.5.33; Pausanias, *Descriptions of Greece*, 1.33.
53. *That element*, i.e. water.
54. i.e. utter destruction, *Odyssey*, 4.511.
55. Diodorus Siculus, *Library of History*, 5.18; *Balearians*, of the Balearic Islands.
56. *Chinois*, Chinese; *draughts*, drawings.
57. *Stickt not*, did not scruple to; *depositure*, depositing, being placed; *absumption*, dissolution, destruction.
58. *Sentence of God*, Genesis 3:19, 'unto dust shalt thou return'.
59. Cyprian, *Epistle*, 67.6, who censured Martialis for allowing his sons to be buried with pagans.
60. *Musselman*, Muslim, reported in George Sandys, *A Relation of a Journey* (1615), p. 71.
61. 1 Samuel 31:12–13; but the bones are buried, 31:13.
62. Kings of Israel and Judah; *Jehoram*, Jeremiah 34:5; *Sedechias*, i.e. Zedekiah, 2 Chronicles 16:14; *Asa*, 2 Chronicles 21:19.
63. Suetonius, *Julius Caesar*, 84.5.
64. 1 Maccabees 1:13.
65. 'A wonderfully made work', Josephus, *Antiquities*, 10.11.7; *Echbatana*, capital city of the Medes, in Herodotus, *Histories*, 1.98.
66. *Hottest use*, cruellest practices.
67. Psalms 16:10; with New Testament references at Acts 2:27, 8:35, John 13:31–7.
68. Luke 21:18; *not of ordinary contrivance*, i.e. it was under providential control.
69. Referring first to the pre-Mosaic exile in Egypt: *the types of Enoch, Eliah*, prefiguratively of Jesus; Enoch and Elijah were 'translated' bodily to Heaven, Genesis 5:24 (and Hebrews 6:5), 2 Kings 2:11; *Jonah*, delivered from the body of the whale, Jonah 1:17; *yet to prevent or restore*, to prevent decay and restore to its entirety; *that rising power*, resurrection; *fasciations*, bandages; *cere-cloth*, winding sheet.
70. [*Textual note*: Marginal note in 1658 Quarto.]
71. 2 Samuel 18:33; *conclamation*, shouting together; *wavering conjecture*, uncertainty.
72. *Civilians*, writers on the commonwealth and law; *sepulture*, sepulchre, burial customs.
73. *Thick skinned*, dull-witted; *phœnix*, see *Pseudodoxia*, 3.12.
74. *Walsingham*, north Norfolk, location of shrine and a site of pilgrimage.
75. *Extraneous*, extra, i.e. foreign to the proper contents of urns; *brazen nippers*, brass tweezers, pincers.
76. *Ustrina*, place of cremation; *Manes* (di Manes), gods of underworld and the dead; *Aræ*, altars and shrines to the dead and gods.

77. Browne is wrong in his conjecture as to their Roman origin, though the Roman presence in the region is true enough; *Brancaster*, on north coast of Norfolk, west of Walsingham.
78. *Countrey*, i.e. county, countryside.
79. *Strict particulars*, precise details.
80. *New institution of Constantine*, division of Roman Empire into prefectures, with civil areas of jurisdiction separate from military ones; *Constantine*, Emperor, 306–37 CE.
81. Browne takes his information from William Camden, *Britannia* (1610), pp. 76–7, as well as the *Notitia Dignitatum*, sect. 28, the records of Roman government, listing the presence of Dalmatian horsemen; *Claudius*, Emperor, 41–54 CE; *Vespasian*, 69–79 CE; *Severus*, 193–211 CE.
82. *Iceni*, Norfolk Celts; *Ostorius*, Roman general who defeated the Iceni, Tacitus, *Annals*, 12.31–2.
83. [*Textual Note:* (Er) 'Prasutagus' for (58) 'Prastaagus'.] *Prasutagus*, King of the Iceni, husband of Boadicea.
84. Suetonius Paulinus, Roman general, in Tacitus, *Annals*, 14.33–6; Tacitus, *Agricola*, 16.
85. *Thin-fill'd mappes*, sparsely inhabited.
86. *Gammadims*, Ezekiel 27:11, variously described as inhabitants of Syria or Phoenicia. Thomas Fuller, *Pisgah-sight* (1650), p. 17, wonders whether they were Pigmies, adding, on the basis of Stowe, 'And we know that *Ancona* in *Italy*, and *Elbow-lane* in *London* receive names from the same fashion'; *Anconians*, of Cyprus.
87. Caesar, *Gallic War*, 5.12, 'The multitude of people is numberless, and the buildings countless, like those of the Gauls.'
88. The figure of 70,000 is given in Tacitus, *Annals*, 14.33; *early*, i.e. from an early date.
89. [*Textual note:* (Er) 'unknown' for (58) 'knowne'.]
90. *Rampiers*, ramparts; *possessions*, i.e. possession of the areas.
91. Norfolk towns: *Castor*, i.e. Caistor St Edmunds, *Southcreake*, South of Burnham Market, *Buxton*, North of Norwich.
92. *The thirty tyrants*, i.e. thirty pretenders to the throne of Gallienus (253–68 CE), see the not entirely reliable *Historia Augusta*, vol. 3, pp. 65–151.
93. *Some as high as Adrianus*, as early as Hadrian (117–38 CE); *itinerary of Antoninus*, register of Roman stations, *c.* 3rd century; *Venta*, Norwich.
94. *Cuthred*, King of Wessex, 740–54 CE; *Canutus*, King of Denmark, d.1086; *William*, i.e. the conqueror; *Matilda*, 1102–67, briefly Queen of England, though uncrowned.
95. *Dutotriges, Tascia, or Trinobantes*, Dorset, Sussex, and Essex tribes.
96. *Abridgeth*, i.e. makes a shorter antiquity likely.
97. Brampton Chronicles.
98. *Ulfketel the governour*, *c.*1010.

99. Plutarch, *Lycurgus*, 9.2, though iron, not copper money.
100. *After stamp*, later coinage.
101. *Lieutenant of Claudius*, i.e. Agricola.
102. So far away from Rome.
103. *Lacrymatories*, bottles for tears; *appurtenances*, accessories.
104. *Macrobius*, *c.*400 CE, *Saturnalia*, 7.7.5.
105. *Antonini*, after 161 CE.
106. *Heliogabalus*, d. 222 CE.
107. *Marcus*, Marcus Aurelius, d. 180; *Severus*, Septimius Severus, d. 211.
108. 'They denounce funeral pyres, and condemn cremation,' Minucius Felix, early 2nd-century patristic writer, *Octavius*, 11; *Tertullian* (*c.*160–220), patristic writings on cremation in *On the Resurrection of the Flesh*.
109. Sidonius Apollinaris, *Letters*, 3.3.8: *To his brother-in-law Ecdicius*, though this cremation was in part to disguise the number of soldiers slaughtered by Ecdicius, a slaughter which is the subject of the letter's praise.
110. *Unto a lower account*, to a later date.
111. *Intension*, i.e. intention.
112. *Exility*, smallness.
113. *Finger of Cynthia*, Propertius, *Elegies*, 4.7.9.
114. i.e. an edition of Livy by Blaise de Vigenère. Alessandro Farnese was Pope Paul III (1534–49).
115. Childeric, king of Franks (458–81 CE), whose tomb was found in 1655, containing golden bees and other treasure.
116. *Septuagint expression*, differing from Hebrew in detail of circumcision knives being left in tombs, re Joshua 24:30–1; *sepulcrall treasure of David*, on David's burial and treasure see Josephus, *Antiquities*, 7.15.3.
117. *Letter which Cicero expected*, spoken of in Cicero, *Letters to Quintus*, 2.15.16.
118. Epitome of Dio Cassius by John Xiphilinus, re. Sextus Julius Severus.
119. *Scribonius Largus*, 1st-century physician. Both this and the Letter to Quintus are reimagined in *Musæum Clausum*; *frugall bit of the Old Brittains*. Bean-sized portions in Dio Cassius, 77.12.4.
120. Pomponius, *De Situ Orbis* (*c.*50 CE), 3.2.
121. [*Textual note:* Carter notes that the end of this sentence, after 'Polydorus', printed in the text in 1658, is, in Browne's annotations of *Hydriotaphia*, transferred to the margin.] *Polydorus*, Polydore Vergil, *Anglica Historia* (1555); Amandus Zierexensis, Belgian Hebraist (*c.*1450–1524); Juan de Pineda (*c.*1513–95), Spanish priest and scholar. The latter two references were removed after the first edition.
122. Caesar, *Gallic War*, 6.16.
123. Tacitus, *Agricola*, 21.
124. Robert Gaguin, 15th-century French humanist.

125. *Sueons and Gothlanders*, tribes of Sweden; Saxo Grammaticus, 13th-century Danish chronicler, in *Historia Danica*, 5; Olaus Magnus, 16th-century Swedish historian; Tacitus, *Germania*, 27.
126. *Jutland*, Danish peninsula; *Sleswick*, Schleswig, Denmark/Germany border area.
127. *Unguinus* . . . *Frotho*, Danish kings.
128. *Starkatterus*, Starkad Storverksson; *Ringo*, Sigurd Ring, king of Sweden, both in Saxo Grammaticus, *Historia Danica*, 8.
129. [*Textual note:* (Er) 'Ansgarius' (though the longer 24-line Errata list reads 'Ausgarius') for (58) 'Ausgurius'.] Ansgar, 9th-century French missionary to Denmark.
130. *Ludovicus Pius*, Holy Roman Emperor (814–40).
131. *This countrey*, i.e. county, Norfolk, invaded 866.
132. *Originall*, origin; *Wormius*, Ole Worm, *Danicorum Monumentorum* (1643).
133. i.e. Camden, *Britannia*.
134. *Rollrich stones*, stone circle in Oxfordshire.
135. John Twyne, Tudor humanist.
136. *Buckler*, shield
137. *Playstered*, i.e. plastered; *whited sepulchres*, tombs painted to avoid accidental and polluting contact with the dead, which entailed elaborate purifying rituals, Numbers 19:11–19, but betokening in Mathew 23:29 hypocrisy, beautiful on the outside and putrifying within.
138. Euripides, *Hecuba*, 317–20, 'Yea, for myself, how scant soe'er in life | My fare for daily need, this should suffice: | Yet fain would I my tomb were reverence-crowned | in men's sight'.
139. [*Textual note:* (Er2) 'persons' for (58) 'princes'—not in the errata of the first edition (octavo), but in the quarto of the same year.]
140. Giovanni Battista Casali, *De Urbis ac Romani olim Imperii splendore* (1650); Antonio Bosio, *Roma Sotterranea* (1632), on the Catacombs.
141. *Composure*, shape, composition.
142. Psalm 63:9. Psalm 139:15 has it that 'I was made in secret and curiously wrought in the lowest parts of the earth'.
143. *Testaceous*, of baked clay, earthenware.
144. Pliny, *Natural History*, 35.49.
145. These items of clay or terracotta are compiled from Pliny, *Natural History*: house of Mausolus, 35.49, statues of Jupiter and Hercules, 35.45; *Plinies dayes*, d. 79 CE.
146. *Varro*, 116–27 BCE.
147. Dio Cassius, *Roman History*, 77.15.4, Severus remarking to his own future urn, 'Thou shalt hold a man that the world could not hold.'
148. *Homericall urne of Patroclus*, *Iliad*, 23.254 (though the purple silk belongs in fact to Hector, 24.796); *tegument*, covering.
149. *Quich*, grass.
150. *Lachrymatories*, bottles for tears; *Manes*, gods of underworld.

151. 'laid down with tears'.
152. *Incrassated into gellies*, thickened to jelly.
153. *Ossuaries*, urn, vault, or charnal house.
154. Wolfgang Lazius, Austrian historian.
155. *vinosity*, wine-like flavour or quality.
156. *Republic*, 8.546.
157. *Consulary date . . . Opimian wine*, a vintage of 121 BCE, from the time of the consul, Opimius, that had spent 100 years in the bottle, according to Petronius, *Satyricon*, 34; *in the must*, i.e. not fully fermented.
158. Cf. Cicero, *De Legibus*, 2.24.
159. *Incinerable*, liable to incineration; *sindge*, singe.
160. *Box*, i.e. box-wood tree, not liable to decay; *conservatories*, respositories.
161. Laurentius Surius, *De Probatis Sanctorum Historiis* (1570).
162. *S. Humbert*, French saint, d. 680 CE.
163. *Wood of the ark*, preserving a pot of manna, Exodus 16:31–2; *rod of Aaron*, which blossomed on one side with almonds, Numbers 17:1; the two objects paired at Hebrews 9:4.
164. *Ark of Noah*, Genesis 5:14; Josephus, *Antiquities*, 1.3.5 (92).
165. *Ephesian temple*, Pliny, *Natural History*, 36.21.95: one of the seven wonders.
166. *King Childerick*, d. 481 CE, tomb discovered in 1655.
167. [*Textual note:* (Er) 'rust' for (58) 'rest'.]
168. *Green entrals*, i.e. verdigris, green weathering on brass.
169. *Philopœmen*, Greek military strategist, d. 183 BCE, in Plutarch, *Life of Philopoemen*, 21.3.
170. *Lycurgus*, Spartan legislator, 9th century BCE.
171. *Democritus*, Pythagorean philosopher, in Varro, *Satirae Menippeae*, 81; *honey*, i.e. for preservation; *embezzle*, waste.
172. Plato, *Laws*, 958d–e.
173. *Salary of Judas*, Matthew 27:5–8, see *Pseudodoxia*, 5.14.
174. *Confounded*, confused, mixed.
175. [*Textual note:* 'contrived', instead of 'continued', according to a pen correction to a 1658 edition noted by Carter, though not in Browne's hand. Not in errata]
176. Suetonius, *Tiberius*, 75.3.
177. *Corps*, corpses; *Esquiline port*, Horace, *Satires*, 1.8.14: Roman gate where criminals' bodies and the poor were cast for burning.
178. Suetonius, *Nero*, 49.4.
179. Suetonius, *Domitian*, 17.3; Homer, *Odyssey*, 24.76.
180. *Curious*, anxious.
181. Petronius, *Satiricon*, 34, on presentation of a silver skeleton, 'So we all shall be, after the world below takes us away. Let us then live while it can go well with us.'
182. *Anatomies*, i.e. corpses; *juglers*, tricksters, magicians.

183. Athenaeus, *Deipnosophists*, 4.155.
184. 'To the Gods of the Underworld', Roman funerary inscription.
185. *Literall draughts*, non-allegorical drawings; *obvious*, easy, frequent; *pateras*, dishes for libations.
186. *Hypogæum*, vault.
187. *Anthony and Jerome*, St Anthony, founder of Egyptian monasticism, lived in a tomb, d. 356 CE; St Jerome, translator of Vulgate Bible, visited catacombs, d. 420 CE.
188. *Cemiteriall*, i.e. relating to cemeteries.
189. *Declining*, excluding.
190. *Iterately*, repeatedly; *pourtraits*, portraits; *Enoch*, Genesis 5:24; *Lazarus*, John 11:43–4, *Jonas*, Jonah 1:17; *vision of Ezechiel*, Ezekiel 37:1–14.
191. *Moles and pismires*, i.e. underground; *pismires*, ants.
192. *Laertes*, Diogenes Laertes, 3rd-century author of *Lives of the Philosophers*, one of the primary sources for ancient philosophical biographies; *dies twice or thrice*, i.e. has more than one account of his death; *resented*, felt.
193. *Confounded*, caused confusion with.
194. [*Textual note:* 1658 has 'Africa', though given the marginal note, this seems a printer's error.]
195. Pausanias' 2nd-century geography, *Description of Greece*, 1.2.2.
196. Aelius Lampridius, *Life of Severus Alexander*, 63.3, in the 4th-century Roman collection, *Historia Augusta*.
197. The urn of Trajan, d. 117 CE.
198. Plutarch, *Life of Marcellus*, 30.2–3.
199. *Wanted*, lacked.
200. Cassiodorus, *Variarum*, Book 4.34; the arguments for pillage that ensue, to the end of the paragraph, are the fine 'civil rhetoric' given in Cassiodorus; *expilator*, pillager.
201. *Virtue*, power; *terra damnata*, the residue and superfluous matter of alchemical processes.
202. *Superannate*, grow older than, outlive (the expectations).
203. In fact, Pliny 30.4.13, 'Even today Britain practises magic in awe, with such grand ritual that it might seem she gave it to the Persians.'
204. *Historian of the other world*, in Plato, *Republic*, 10 (614b), Er from Pamphylia revives after twelve days and relates stories told at the crossroads between Heaven and Tartarus.
205. *Exenteration*, removing the entrails; *hazardable*, hazardous; *choisest*, most expert.
206. *Found no historicall solution*, has not been explained by history.
207. *Pyrrhus his toe*, which could not be burnt, *Pseudodoxia*, 3.14, Pliny, *Natural History*, 7.2.
208. *Fictile*, moulded.
209. [*Textual Note:* (Er) Lamp for (58) Lump] *Lamp of Galvanus*, in Fortunius Licetus, *De Lucernis Antiquorum Reconditis* (1621).

210. Bartolemeo Marlianus (1544) is wrongly spelt 'Martianus' in 1658 edition. This and the following marginal note reversal after 1658.
211. *Esquiline Field*, place of Roman executions.
212. *Insatisfaction*, dissatisfaction; *incremable*, incombustible; *salamanders wool*, unburnable flax (see *Pseudodoxia*, 3.14); *incommixed*, unmingled.
213. *Of the carnall composition*, of the body.
214. *Abate a notable proportion*, shink considerably in volume.
215. *Fired out*, burnt out (of the body); *earth almost only*, earth alone; *sallow*, willow-like plant; *ponderation*, weight.
216. Lyserus, *Cultur Anatomicus* (1653).
217. *Hydropicall Heraclitus*, i.e. with dropsy, in Diogenes Laertius, *Lives of the Philosophers*, 9.1.
218. Plutarch, *Tiberius Gracchus*, 13.4–5: the body is said to have dowsed the pyre with its gush of poisoned humoral fluids.
219. Thucydides, *History of the Peloponnesian War*, 2.52.4, the chaos of the plague being such that people stole others' funeral pyres to burn their own dead.
220. *King of Castile*, Ferdinand of Aragon (1452–1516).
221. *Iliad*, 23.164; *Isaac*, Genesis 22; see *Pseudodoxia*, 5.8.
222. Frog-spawn, whites of eggs.
223. *Attenuable*, capable of being made thinner.
224. *Ferity*, barbarous act.
225. Valerius Maximus, *Factorum et Dictorum Memorabilium* 4.6.
226. *Copels*, i.e. cupels, alchemical dish, made of ashes of bone.
227. *Analyseth*, breaks down; *transmuteth*, changes, with a glance at alchemical process.
228. Genesis 23:5–20, 49:29–32; Joshua 24:30.
229. 'Stay, traveller!' Common Roman tomb inscription.
230. *Sensible rhetorick*, carrying the meaning of forceful, but also appealing to the senses.
231. *Constantine*, Roman Emperor, d. 337; *Cuthred*, Wessex king, 740–54.
232. *Beda*, Bede, author of *Ecclesiastical History*, *c.*731 CE.
233. *The painter*, discussing pictures in *Pseudodoxia*, Book 5, Browne commonly uses this definite form without any particular painter being evident in his mind; *Helena*, mother of Constantine, reputedly discovered the cross of Christ in 326 CE; *longitude*, length.
234. [*Textual note:* (Er) 'gnaw'd' for (58) 'knav'd'. Editors differ on which is authoritative.]
235. *Hydropicall*, with swellings of dropsy; *fat concretion*, 'adipocere'; *lixivious*, alkaline consistency of the 'hardest castle-soap'.
236. *Battle with the Persians*, at Amida, 359 CE, reported by Marcellinus, *Res Gestae*, 19.9.
237. *Opprobrious disease*, syphilis (*morbus gallicus*) rotting even dead bodies.
238. *The description of Leicester Shire* (1622), 51–2; *cerecloth*, shroud.

239. *Compage*, holding together; *arefaction*, drying of parts.
240. [*Textual note:* (Er) 'petrified' for (58) 'putrified'. Also later in the sentence.]
241. *Lots wife*, Genesis 19:26; *Ortelius*, drafted a world map (1570), in which there appears a Russian tribe apparently turned to stone.
242. *Generall inundation*, Noah's Flood.
243. *Alexander*, opening tomb of Cyrus the Great (*c.*600–530 BCE), Persian ruler, reported in Arrian of Nicomedia, *Anabasis of Alexander*, 6.29.1–11.
244. *Rectitude*, straightness; *appendencies*, attached (or hanging) parts; *carnous parts*, fleshy parts; *consistences*, the standing of the body, once full growth is attained.
245. In 1658 Quarto edition only.
246. In 1658 Quarto edition only.
247. *Purgatorio*, 23.22, 'The sockets of their eyes were gemless rings; | one who reads *omo* in the face of men, | could easily have recognised the *m*.'
248. *Hercules*, reputedly calculated by Pythagoras, reported in Aulus Gellius, *Attic Nights*, 1.1.
249. *Comproportions*, corresponding sizes.
250. *Scattered atomes*, cf. *Religio Medici*, 1.48.
251. *Accidents*, qualities; *salve the individuality*, i.e. make credible the idea of individual bodily resurrection.
252. Matthew 27:52.
253. Ezekiel 37:1–14; *Valley of... Jehosaphat*, Joel 3:2.
254. *Glossed the deformity*, made its ugliness seem less so; *take of brutall terminations*, take away the animal or brute aspect of death.
255. *Cast not all care*, did not neglect every care.
256. *Deposed*, deposited; *clean field*, Leviticus 4:12, 6:11 on burial rites.
257. *The lodging of Christ*, Romans 8:10; *temples of the holy Ghost*, 1 Corinthians 6:19.
258. *Pathetically*, affecting the emotions.
259. 'Similar also is the vantity [about preserving men's bodies and] about Democritus' promise of our coming to life again—who did not come to life again himself. Plague take it, what is this mad idea that life is renewed by death', Pliny, *Natural History*, 7.55.187–90; *went high*, went so far as.
260. 'We hope that the remains of the dead may return from the earth to the light.' Phocylides, *Sentences*, 103–4, Jewish-Hellenistic pseudo-epigraphia.
261. Lucretius, *On the Nature of Things*, 2.999–1000, 'That which once came from earth, to earth returns back again', echoing Ecclesiastes 12:7.
262. *Before Plato could speak*, Phaedrus 246c–d, Socrates' theory of angels shedding their wings to become earthly; *wings in Homer*, Odyssey 11.222; *Demas and Soma*, the living and dead body.

263. Hercules's mother is Alcmene, his father Jupiter, Lucian, *Hermotius*, 7.
264. Plato, *Phaedo*, 115e.
265. Diogenes Laertius, *Lives of the Philosophers*, on Diogenes the Cynic philosopher, 6.2.
266. *Transcorporating*, metempsychosis of souls, reincarnation from body to body.
267. *Stones and clouts*, relics and cloths.
268. 'Farewell, Farewell, We will follow you in the order that nature permits.'
269. *Larix*, larch.
270. [*Textual note:* (Er) 'tree' for (58) 'he'.]
271. [*Textual note:* (Er) 'furze' for (58) 'fures'.] *Exuccous*, sapless, dry.
272. *Cancer*... *Capricornus*, in Macrobius, *The Dream of Scipio*, 1.12.
273. Juvenal, *Satires*, 15.138, refers to children too young for the pyre.
274. Tibullus, 1.1.67, 'Do thou hurt not my spirit'.
275. *Happy fraud*, a useful delusion.
276. Diogenes Laertius, *Lives of the Philosophers*, 6.2.31, on being buried face down.
277. Pliny, *Natural History*, 7.17.
278. *Discover*, reveal; *iterated clamations*, repeated shouts; *excitate*, arouse.
279. *Apposition of*, placing close to.
280. [*Textual note*: in 1658 Quarto edition only.]
281. *Fondnesse,* foolishness.
282. *Archimime*, Chief mourner-buffoon at funerals, in Suetonius, *Vespasian*, 19.2.
283. *Elysian ferriman*, Charon, who ferried the dead to Hades.
284. *Considerable urnes*, urns of important people.
285. Those hit by lightning were not given full funeral rites; see Marcellinus, *Res Gestae*, 23.5.12–13.
286. [*Textual note:* (Er) 'Pluto' for (58) 'Plato'. Similarly in next paragraph.]
287. *Tartaras*, i.e. Tartarus, underworld of the wicked; *Pluto*, God of the underworld.
288. *In order to*, in regard to.
289. *Eight or ten bodies*, Plutarch, *Table Talk*, 3.4 (651a–b), addressing the relative humoral heat of men and women relates this as the proper cremation ratio; *unctuously*, with an anointing of oil, or as a soothing act.
290. *Perianders wife*, Herodotus, *History*, 5.92, reported in a consultation with the oracle.
291. Homer, *Odyssey*, 11.225–330.
292. *Tiresias*, Homer, *Odyssey*, 10.494–5, Circe's account of Tiresias in Hell. In Hyginus' account (*Fabulae*, 75), Tiresias, upon striking a snake, turned into a woman, but later changed back.
293. *The Downward Journey*, 2. [In 1658 Quarto edition only.]
294. *Propitiation*, atoning for; *Morta*, goddess of death, one of the three fates.

295. *Except they drink bloud*, Homer, *Odyssey*, 11.95–9, 141, respectively Tiresias and Odysseus' mother.
296. *Penelope's paramours*, Homer, *Odyssey*, 24.5–9; *Hercules*, in *Odyssey*, 11.605.
297. *Agamemnon*, Homer, *Odyssey*, 11.440–62.
298. *Afraid of swords*, Homer, *Odyssey*, 11.48, 95; *Sybilla tels Æneas*, Virgil, *Aeneid*, 6.290–4.
299. *Cæsar and Pompey*, Virgil, *Aeneid*, 6.826–7, on the general concord of dead soldiers; *Ajax*, Homer, *Odyssey*, 11.543.
300. *Deiphobus*, Virgil, *Aeneid*, 6.495.
301. *Charon*, Lucian, *Dialogue of the Dead*, 2; *Achilles*, Homer, *Iliad*, 11.487–91.
302. *Hercules*, in *Odyssey*, 11.601–17; *Julius*, deified in Horace, *Odes*, 1.12.46 and seen in Hades, Virgil, *Aeneid*, 6.826–31.
303. *Platoes denne*, i.e. the cave, *Republic*, 7.514–15.
304. Dante, *Inferno*, 4.133–5; *Cato*, Dante, *Purgatorio*, 1.31, 2.119.
305. *King of terrours*, Job 18:14.
306. *Judgment of Machiavel*, in *Discourses*, 2.2.
307. *Extenuate*, lessen.
308. *Complexionally superannuated*, growne old in temperament.
309. *Corporall animosity*, disliking their bodies.
310. *Orchestra*, seats reserved for senators in Roman theatres.
311. *Epicurus*, Dante, *Inferno*, 10.13–15.
312. *Socrates*, Plato, *Phaedo*, on immortality of soul; Cato reads the work and sends a servant to collect a sword for his suicide, Plutarch, *Cato the Younger*, 68.2, 70.1.
313. *Originall*, origin.
314. *Superiour ingredient and obscured part*, the soul.
315. *Methuselah*, Genesis 5:27, lived to the age of 969; *specious*, resplendent.
316. *Three conquests*, i.e. after the Roman: Anglo-Saxon, Viking, and Norman invasions.
317. Tibullus, *Elegy*, 3.2.26, 'Thus, when naught is left of me but bones, would I be laid to rest'; *diuturnity*, long life.
318. 'Thus the Chaldian Oracle with the scholia of Psellus and Plethon . . . the pure souls of those who leave the body by violence'.
319. [*Textual note:* (Er) 'stronger' for (58) 'stranger'.]
320. *Conservatories*, places of preservation; *propension*, attachment, hanging.
321. *Indistinction*, being indistinguishable.
322. *Work for Archimedes*, a mathematical conundrum, equivalent to his numbering every grain of sand.
323. Psalm 90:10, 'The days of our years are threescore and ten.'
324. *Last necessity*, i.e. death; *half senses*, losing our faculties.
325. *Avarice*, greed for life.
326. *David grew politickly cruell*, in his massacres of, for example, Moab (2 Samuel 8:2) and Ammon (1 Chronicles 20:3); *Solomon*, 1 Kings 11:1.

327. *Alcmenas nights*, Zeus lengthened the night to have longer with Hercules' mother.
328. Job 3:1; *to have so farre been*, to have been alive so long.
329. Suetonius, *Tiberius*, 70.
330. Homer, *Odyssey*, 10.526.
331. Job 3:13–15.
332. *Proprietaries*, owners.
333. *Tutellary observators*, guardian angels.
334. *Pyramidally extant*, i.e. in the manner of a mummy.
335. *Atropos*, the eldest of the Fates, who sheared the thread of life.
336. *Meridian of time*, presuming a 6,000-year span, beginning *c.*4000 BCE., the meridian would have been 1000 BCE.
337. Charles V, Holy Roman Emperor (1500–58), whose fame ('hope to live') before the end of the world is so much shorter than that of Hector by two Methuselas (twice 969).
338. *Inquietude*, disquiet.
339. *One face of Janus . . . the other*, i.e. the past and the future, Janus being the God of doorways who looks in both directions (hence January).
340. *We dayly pray for*, in the words, 'thy kingdom come', praying for the end of the world and destruction of monuments.
341. *Setting part of time*, last part.
342. First letter of Greek *thanatos*, death.
343. Jan Gruter, *Inscriptiones Antiquae* (1603), Dutch scholar.
344. In 1658 Quarto edition only.
345. Girolamo Cardano (1501–76), *De Propria Vita*, 9, 'I desire it to be known I exist, not what kind of person I am.'
346. *Hippocrates patients*, 5th century BCE; *Achilles horses*, Homer, *Iliad*, 16.149–54; *naked nominations*, known only by their names; *entelechia*, that which gives form and spirit to substance.
347. *Canaanitish woman*, who gave Christ water, Matthew 15:22–8; *Herodias*, who asked for John the Baptist's head, Matthew 14:3–11.
348. *Good theef*, Luke 23:40.
349. *Herostratus*, arsonist, 356 BCE, whose motive was immortality and whose punishment included the stipulation that his name must not be mentioned. The temple was built by Chersiphron, according to Pliny, 36.21.95.
350. *Adrians horse*, reported by Dio Cassius, *Roman History*, 69.10.2.
351. *Thersites*, Homer, *Iliad*, 2.212–42; *Agamemnon*, chief of Greeks at Troy.
352. [*Textual note:* (Er) The phrase 'without the favour of the everlasting register' is placed in (58) after 'Agamemnon', the errata directing it to its current place.]
353. *Hired*, i.e. one cannot buy off the effects of oblivion.
354. *Register of God*, Revelation 3:5.

355. *Twenty seven names*, before the flood; *not one living century*, i.e. no biblical generation having numbered even a hundred people.
356. *Æquinox*, the half-way point of time *in toto*, and of people.
357. *Lucina of life*, goddess of childbirth, from a lost fragment of Euripedes, quoted in Plato, *Gorgias*, 492e.
358. [*Textual note*: in 1658 Quarto edition only.]
359. *Winter arches*, i.e. arc, astronomically speaking.
360. *Brother of death*, sleep.
361. Perhaps with reference to Niobe's tears for her dead children, who are turned into stone, Ovid, *Metamorphoses*, 6.304–12.
362. *Callosities*, callousness; *stupidity*, stunned state.
363. *Our delivered senses*, our senses, once freed from pain.
364. *Subsistency*, continued existence; *transmigration*, the soul passing into another being at death.
365. *Passed selves*, past selves, within the theory of transmigration.
366. *Recede into the common being*, return to the Platonic world soul.
367. *Sweet consistences*, fragrances in embalming.
368. Ecclesiastes 1:14.
369. *Cambyses*, Persian king, who had Egyptian mummified corpses desecrated, Herodotus, *Histories*, 3.16.
370. *Mummie*, sold as an early modern drug; *Mizraim,* son of Ham, together with *Pharaoh*, as generic figures of Egypt.
371. *Patent*, immunity, freedom; *preservations*, preservatives.
372. *Nimrod is lost in Orion, and Osyris in the Dogge-starre*, putative changes to the names of constellations.
373. *Incorruption in the heavens*, Aristotle, *De Caelo*, 2.1; *perspectives*, telescopes.
374. *Spots . . . about the sun*, sun-spots observed in 1610 by Thomas Harriot; *Phaeton*, who drove and crashed the chariot of his father, the sun, Ovid, *Metamorphoses*, 1.747–2.400.
375. *The peculiar*, the exlusive right.
376. *Sardanapalus*, king of Assyria, besieged for two years at Nineveh, who then set a fire for himself and his entire household, Athenaeus, *Deipnosophists*, 12 (529c), also on his debauched life in Dio Cassius, *Roman History*, 79.
377. [*Textual note*: in 1658 Quarto edition only.]
378. *Gordianus*, briefly emperor, d. 244 CE.
379. *Man of God*, Moses, in Jude 1:9, the archangel Michael contending with the devil over Moses' body.
380. *Enoch and Elias*, both translated bodily to Heaven before death, Genesis 5:24, 2 Kings 2:1.
381. *Decretory term*, in the last judgement; *changed*, re. 1 Corinthians 15:21.
382. *Lazarus*, John 11.
383. *Coverings of mountaines*, Revelation 6:16.

384. In 6th-century Roman historian, Jordanes, *History of the Goths*, 30; *Alaricus*, d. 410 CE.
385. *Sylla*, Sulla, in Dio Cassius, *Roman History*, 78.13.7, Plutarch, *Sulla*, 38, though neither report stones thrown.
386. Isaiah, on Hell.
387. The smallest point at which the circumference of a circle touches its tangent.
388. *Extasis*, ecstasy; *exolution*, release of the soul; *gustation,* tasting; *ingression*, entry; all terms of mystical union with God.
389. *Prædicament of chymeras*, condition of fantasy.
390. Lucan, *Pharsalia*, 7.809–10, 'Whether corruption or the pyre dissolves the corpse does not matter.'

THE GARDEN OF CYRUS

1. This dedicatory letter to Nicolas Bacon on *The Garden of Cyrus* is, in the first edition of 1658, placed at the beginning, before *Urne-Buriall*, together with the letter to Le Gros. Nicholas Bacon was half-brother to Francis Bacon.
2. Dutch physician, Vopiscus Plempius, *Ophthalmographia* (1632); Niccolò Cabeo, Jesuit natural philosopher and commentator on Aristotle.
3. William Harvey, *De Generatione Animalium* (1651).
4. *Purblind*, completely blind; *without issue*, childless.
5. *Dioscorides* (*c.*40–90 CE), Roman physician, author of *De Materia Medica*; *Antonius*, Mark Anthony—the notion that Dioscorides was part of his army is mistaken; *Theophrastus*, *c.* 3rd century BCE, Greek philosopher and writer on botany.
6. Bishop of Nuremburg, Basilus Besler, *Hortus Eystettensis* (1613), a beautifully illustrated herbal.
7. Jean Bauhin and Jean Henry Cherler, *Historia Plantarum* (1650).
8. *Quincuncial*, arrangement of trees in patterns of five, four corners and one in the centre, this being the *leitmotif* of the text; *reticulate*, network; *phytology*, study of plants.
9. With reference to William Harvey's 1628 discovery of the circulation of the blood, apparently anticipated by Hippocrates (*c.*460–370 BCE), Greek physician.
10. *Trite*, simple, childish; *bye*, digressive, in byways; *invention*, in rhetoric, the choice of a topic or theme.
11. *Venially*, without harm; *collaterall*, subordinate or accompanying; *their principals*, their main theme.
12. Julius Caesar Scaliger (1485–1558), Italian physician and scholar, referring to his commentaries on both philosophers.
13. Referring to the presumed physicality of the Islamic heaven.
14. *Mediocrity*, middle way; *insinuating*, subtle or winding penetration.

15. *Venemous vegetables*, Plutarch, *Demetrius*, 20.2, which cites King Attalus' cultivation of poisonous plants as an example of useless endeavours; Cato, *De Agricultura*, 156–7, 'In praise of Cabbage'.
16. Jodicus Hondius (1563–1612), Belgian cartographer.
17. *Secular shows*, grand epochal celebrations, held once in an age.
18. The 'impute' (accusation) of incongruity includes here the incongruous relation between *Urne-Buriall* and *The Garden of Cyrus.*
19. *Nullum sine* . . . , 'No man's ability [in eloquence] has ever been approved without something being pardoned', Seneca, *Moral Letters*, 114.12.
20. *Apelles his pictures*, Pliny, *Natural History*, 35.36.84: the artist would hide behind his paintings to hear what people thought of them, and hearing a shoemaker criticize his shoe changed the painting, but refused to accept his criticism of the leg.
21. *Maniples*, handfuls, offerings.
22. 'What can be more handsome than the quincunx, which presents straight lines whichever way you look', Quintilian, *Institutio Oratoria,* 8.3.9. The quincunx is also translated as *echelon*, when used of troop formations.
23. Gaius Julius Hyginus, *Fabulae*, 140; Genesis 1:14, before which creation there was, apparently, light without a specific source, diffused.
24. Plato, *Timaeus.*
25. *Noblest part of the third*, the production of vegetation.
26. Ovid, *Metamorphoses*, 1.44, 'woods to be clothed in leafage'.
27. *Physick*, medicine; *dietetical conservation*, health by proper diet.
28. Describing the surgery ('chirurgery') of God's creation of Eve.
29. *Pleade high*, argue its esteemed position; *rivality*, rivalry; *garden contrivance*, botanical pharmacy
30. *Gardens were before gardeners*, Adam being born on the sixth day.
31. *Mikedem* is a transliteration of the Hebrew; *ab oriente*, from the east; *a principio*, from the beginning.
32. *Its topography*, i.e. Eden's location.
33. *Mountains of Armenia*, Mount Ararat, Genesis 8:4.
34. *Zoroaster* . . . *Cham*, The identification of pagan figures as a debased historical memory of 'true' biblical history was widespread and frequent across Browne's works; *Zoroaster*, Persian philosopher-prophet, *c.*10th century BCE; *Cham*, *Chus*, i.e. Ham, Cush; *Mizraim*, a son of Ham; *proficients*, experts; Pliny, *Natural History*, 30.1.2 discusses Zoroaster in relation to writings on magic, but not on agriculture.
35. *Pensill*, pensile, hanging; *Semiramis* . . . *Nimrod*, Browne is identifying Nimrod as Ninus, husband (or consort) of the Assyrian queen Semiramis in Diodorus Siculus, *Library of History*, 2.8–9; *Nimrod*, Genesis 10:8–12.
36. *Elevated*, i.e. supposing Eden to be, as in Dante's geography, a raised mountain upon the plain; *with many conceptions*, according to many.

37. Josephus, 10.11.1, Diodorus Siculus, *Library*, 2.10, has it that the hanging gardens were 'built, not by Semiramis, but by a later Syrian king to please one of his concubines'. Browne suggests that this later king was Nebuchadnezzar.
38. *Melancholy metamorphosis*, the madness of Nebuchadnezzar, in Daniel 4:33.
39. Cyrus the elder, Persian King of 6th century BCE, under whom the Persian empire expanded phenomenally.
40. *Ahasuerus*, i.e. Xerxes; *Longimanus*, in Plutarch, *Artaxerxes*, 1.1; *city of flowers*, Esther 1.5–9.
41. *Vashti*, who refused to attend on her drunken husband Xerxes, Esther 1:10.
42. Plutarch, *Artaxerxes*, 1.1; *Artaxerxes Mnemnon*, son of Darius II.
43. *Retrait*, portrait; Xenophon, *Anabasis*, an extensive account of Cyrus the Younger. Cyrus the Elder is dealt with in Xenophon's *Cyropaedia*.
44. *Post-geniture*, being born after.
45. *Old Laertas*, Laertes, in Homer, *Odyssey*, 24:226–31; *found a name*, earned a reputation.
46. *King Attalus*, Plutarch, *Demetrius*, 20.2; *lives*, i.e. is remembered for.
47. Xenophon, *Oeconomicus*, 4.21, 'The trees are planted at regular intervals, in straight rows and everything arranged in beautiful quincuncial regularity'; Strebaeus, i.e. Jacques-Louis d'Estrebay (1481–1550), French writer on rhetoric.
48. Cicero, *On Old Age*, 17.59, praising Xenophon's *Oeconomicus* and the story of Cyrus the Younger showing the quincunical layout of the gardens at Cyrus.
49. Varro, *On Agriculture*, 1.7, on the quincunx as the most efficient use of agricultural land.
50. [*Textual note:* (Er) 'doubled' for (58) 'doubted'.]
51. *Decussation*, crossing of lines; *emphaticall*, implying more than is directly expressed, suggestive and allusive; *fundamentall*, relating to the foundation.
52. *Tuscan pedestall*, Roman adaptation of Doric order of architecture; *dye*, die.
53. [*Textual note:* (Er2) 'rectangular' for (58) 'regular'.]
54. Benedictus Curtius, *Hortorum libri trigentu* (1560); Giambattista della Porta, *Villae* (1592), agricultural compendium.
55. *Decussis*, X-shape; *longilaterall*, form of a long parallelogram.
56. *Consulary coynes*, coins from the Roman Republic; *Constantine*, first Christian emperor of Rome, who saw a cross in the sky while marching on Rome (312 CE), Eusebius, *Life of Constantine*, 1.28.
57. *Crucigerous ensigne*, cross-bearing signal; *Andrean or Burgundian cross*, X-figured cross, used as naval flag of Spain.
58. *Decline the . . . theme*, not engage with—the paragraph is a long instance of *occupatio*, the rhetorical trope by which one mentions a thing by

explaining how one will not mention it; *some being right*, some 'crosses' being upright and made of a single piece; *without traversion or transome*, the cross beam.

59. *Mysticall Tau*, Greek cross-letter 'T'; *empedon*, footrest.
60. Lipsius, *De Cruce* (1593), 1.7; *crosse of St Andrew*, reputedly an Olive Tree, according to *Hippolitus*, i.e. Pseudo-Hippolitus, Fragment 49, in *Ante-Nicene Fathers*, ed. Roberts, vol. 5, Appendix.
61. *Labarum*, the letters X and P, 'chi-rho' Christian symbol ☧.
62. The tomb of Marius under Hadrian and of Alexander under the Antonines.
63. *King Ptolomy*, of Egypt.
64. *Serapis*, A composite Greek-Egyptian deity, instituted under Ptolemy I, Pausanias, *Description of Greece*, 1.18.4.
65. *Telesmes*, talismans.
66. Johannes de Bado Aureo and Nicolas Upton, respectively 14th- and 15th-century heraldic-military writers, published together in 1654 by Sir Edward Bysshe.
67. *Laterane Obelisk*, Egyptian obelisk, transported to Rome by Constantine; *the crosse . . .*, the altar described by Joannes Baptista Casalius (1645) and Antonio Bosio (1632); *brasen table of Bembus*, work of Emblematics; *signality*, meaning.
68. [*Textual note:* (Er2) 'Tenupha' for (58) 'Tenapha']
69. *Tenupha*, Tenufa, a part of sacrificial ceremonies, Ezekiel 48:10.
70. *High-priest*, i.e. in the ceremony of Tenufa.
71. *Typicall thought*, a thought based on typological resemblance.
72. *Characters of Cadmus*, Cadmus, the founder of Thebes, reputed to have taught the Phoenician alphabet to the Greeks, Herodotus, *Histories*, 5.58; *Palamedes*, betrayed by Odysseus in Trojan war, reported to have added a number of Greek letters, according to Stesichorus, *Greek Lyric* (Loeb, v. 3), p. 129.
73. 'The decussation presented a pleasant and lovely appearance', Eusebius, *Chronicles*, 49, citing Abydenus, *History of the Assyrians*. Also Eusebius, *Praeparatio Evangelica*, 9.41; Curtius, *Hortorum* (1650), 6.12.
74. *Alcinous*, Homer, *Odyssey*, 7.112–32, garden of unwithering fruit; *Didymus*, Didymus Chalkenteros (1st century CE) and *Eustachius*, i.e. Eustathius of Thessalonica (12th century) both produced lengthy commentaries on Homer.
75. *Diomedes*, Homer, *Iliad*, 14.123, describing his father's orchards.
76. Homer, *Odyssey*, 24.340–4, described on his homecoming to Ithaca, to establish his identity with his father
77. Theophrastes (d. 285 BCE), *Enquiry into Plants*, 4.4.8; κατ'ὄρχους, in rows.
78. *Politics*, 7.10.5.

79. Virgil, *Georgics*, 2.277–8, 'give the ranks room; yet none the less, when the trees are set, let all the paths, with clear-cut line, square to a nicety'; see Varro, *De Re Rustica*, 1.7.2, on the importance of appearance for profit; Quintilian, *Institutio Oratoria*, 8.3.9, on parallel ornament of rhetoric and quincuncial layout of orchards.
80. [*Textual note:* (Er) 'sonnes' for (58) 'stones'.]
81. *Saturn . . . Noah*, see *Pseudodoxia*, 7.5, referencing Bochart, *Geographia Sacra* (1646), 1.1.1.
82. *Paralogicall*, unreasonable.
83. *Whose diet was vegetable*, on pre-lapsarian vegetarianism, see *Pseudodoxia*, 3.25.
84. *First sinne*, Noah's drunkenness, Genesis 9:21.
85. *Cain and Abel*, Genesis 4:3–5.
86. *Abraham . . . Beer-sheba*, Genesis 21:33, Song of Songs.
87. *Botanologer*, botanist; *specious*, beautiful, not necessarily with the negative connotations later acquired.
88. Ecclesiastes 2:5–6; *Targam, or Chaldee Paraphrase*, interpretation and translations of Aramaic phrases in Bible; *water of Siloah*, Nehemiah 3:15.
89. *Not comparatively, but causally,* not incidently but directly to God's purpose; *Abramas*, Nicholas Abram, Jesuit (1589–1655), *Veteris Testamenti Pharus* (1648), 2.16.
90. *Ambient figure*, the shapes around.
91. *Quaternio*, set of four.
92. Pliny, *Natural History*, 34.16.34.
93. *Criticall*, exact; *his horses*, i.e. the sun's chariot horses; *strings . . . rayes*, i.e. four horses for seasons, seven strings for planets, twelve rays for months of year; *flat*, uninventive.
94. *Cuneatim*, cuneiform, wedge-shaped.
95. *Lithostrata*, overlying rocks; *triquetrous*, three-sided, pyramidal; Vitruvius, *Of Architecture*, 7.1.3–4.
96. *Forum Nervæ, the mausoleum of Augustus, the Pyramid of Cestius*, Roman monuments; *draughts*, drawings.
97. *Laureat draughts*, drawings of laurel patterns; *Pulvinaria,* pillows, couches for reclining.
98. Vitruvius, *On Architecture*, 3.3.
99. *Anastatius*, Anastasius Germonius, *De legatis principum et populorum libri tres* (1627).
100. 'as it appears from a parchment by Chifflet', Jean-Jacques Chifflet, French antiquary (1588–1660).
101. *Charles the Great*, Charlemagne, Frankish king (768–814).
102. *Common picture . . . Aaron*, in Geneva Bible, Exodus 28.
103. *Ptolomy*, Ptolemy VI, King of Egypt (*c.*181–146 BCE).
104. *Bound up wounds*, Justinus, *Epitome*, 15.3.13 (Justin Martyr, 2nd century CE), on Alexander the Great's staunching the bleeding of Lysimachus,

whom he had earlier sent to his death; *hanged themselves*, Plutarch, *Lucullus*, 18.4, on Monimé, the wife of Mithridates, whose attempted suicide by hanging failed, prompting a lament on the uselessness of the crown.

105. Josephus Blancanus *Aristotelis Loca Mathematica* (1615), p. 190.
106. Blancanus, Jesuit astronomer (1566–1624).
107. *Sella curulis*, the cross-legged chairs of the Roman magistery; *Cestius*, Gaius Cestius Epulo, whose pyramid is mentioned earlier in the chapter; *Sylla*, Lucius Cornelius Sulla (138–78 BCE), consul and twice dictator; *Julius*, Caesar.
108. *Retiarie*, net-like; *glass windows*, i.e. with diamond-shaped panes.
109. Rendering the Greek of Ezekiel 41:16 from the Septuagint into Latin.
110. Song of Solomon, 2.9, spoken of the 'beloved' of the text, typologically figured as Christ; *which ours hath rendered*, 'ours' is the AV, which translates 'nets' as lattice.
111. [*Textual note:* (Er) 'chapiters' for (58) 'chapters'.]
112. *Reticulate*, veined in network; *chapiters*, i.e. capitals, on which were carved the lilies and pomegranates; *pillars of Solomon*, 1 Kings 7:17–21, 'nets of checker work, and wreaths of chain work' (AV); *Craticula*, Exodus 27:4, instructions to Moses on the construction of altar and tabernacle.
113. *Retiarie gladiators*, who fought with nets; *secutores*, gladiatorial fighters with daggers.
114. *Conopeion*, mosquito-net; Theocritus, *Idylls*, 21.11, on fishermen's woven equipment and tale of a golden fish; *Reticulum Jecoris*, Leviticus 3:4, on the division of innards during sacrifice.
115. Homer, *Odyssey*, 8.326, Ares and Aphrodite (Mars and Venus) caught in adultery and captured in a net made by the lame god, Hephaestus (Vulcan).
116. *Scuchions with mascles fusils and saltyrs*, heraldic decorative lozenges (muscles, fusils) and diagonals (saltyrs); *ermin*, heraldic tailed spot; *vair*, variegated heraldic colouring. (58) misplaces margin note.
117. *Lapidaries*, jewel-cutters; *æquicrural*, icosceles.
118. [*Textual note:* (C) 'picturers' for (58) 'pictures'.]
119. *Sculptors . . . double haches*, engravers using cross-shading.
120. Ovid, *Metamorphoses*, 6.5–145. Having challenged Minerva to a weaving contest, Arachne attempted to hang herself and turned into a spider.
121. *Woof*, i.e. weft, threads that cross from side to side, at right angles from the warp; *transversion*, crossing athwart; *textury*, weaving.
122. *Dodder*, slender leafless plant, parasitic on flax; *tetter*, white bryony, a strangling vine.
123. *Pentalithismus*, also known as knucklebones, a game whose invention is attributed by Sophocles to Palamedes, Sophocles, *Fragments*, 429.
124. Eustathius of Thessalonica (12th century), Commentary on *Odyssey*.

125. *Proci*, suitors to Penelope.
126. *Phaedrus*, 274c–d, on the Egyptian invention of games, as well as astronomy and other arts, by Theuth, identified by the Greeks as Hermes.
127. *Tables*, backgammon; *continue*, contain; *as high as*, as ancient as.
128. *Mechanicks*, general term for workers; *forcipall organs*, pincers, pliers.
129. *Inservient*, serving.
130. *Nucifragium or nutcracker*, *Quaestiones Mechanicae*, attributed to Aristotle in Blancanus, *Aristotelis loca mathematica* (1615), 185; *evulsion*, extraction.
131. *Innitency*, pressure; *hypomochlion or fulciment*, pivot, fulcrum; *impulsors*, something that compels or forces.
132. Virgil, *Georgics*, 2.279–81. Virgil is describing how best to situate vines on flat or sloped land and uses, as his metaphor, an army ready for war.
133. *Maniples*, subdivision of Roman legion of 120 men; *Hastati*, infantry, set in front line; *Principes*, second line; *Triarii*, best-equipped and usually the wealthiest soldiers, forming the third and rear line. The diagram is taken from Salmasius, *De Re militari Romanorum* (1657).
134. Polybius, *Histories*, 15.12; Livy, *History of Rome*, 30.33, Scipio's strategy against Hannibal at the Battle of Zama, 202 BCE.
135. [*Textual note:* (C) corrects 'Narses' for (58) 'Nasses', though (Er2) has 'nurses'.]
136. *Narses*, general to Justinian I, Byzantine emperor; *Almans*, Germans, defeated in 357 by Julian ('the Apostate').
137. Aelianus Tacticus, Greek-writing military theorist (2nd century CE).
138. *Philip*, 382–336 BCE; *ductors*, leaders.
139. *Long square*, rectangle.
140. [*Textual note:* (Er2) 'first ranck' for (58) 'first'.]
141. *Curtius*, Benedictus Curtius, *Hortorum* (1560), 10.13.
142. Thucydides, *Peloponnesian War*, 6.67.1–3.
143. Vallens Guellius (1575), on Virgil, *Georgics*, 2.278.
144. Revelation 21:16, in which the city is in fact cubed. *Babylon*, Herodotus, *Histories* 1.178.2 on a city fifteen miles squared (120 furlongs squared).
145. *Pillars of Seth*, Josephus, *Jewish Antiquities*, 1.2.3 'that their inventions might not be lost . . . they made two pillars, the one of brick, the other of stone: they inscribed their discoveries on them both, that in case the pillar of brick should be destroyed by the flood, the pillar of stone might remain'; *Cham*, Ham, son of Noah, from whom the Egyptians were thought to descend: see Psalm 105:23 on Egypt as the land of Ham.
146. Diodorus Siculus, *The Library of History*, 2.3.2.
147. *Longilaterall*, rectangular; *castrensiall mansions*, the distance from one camp to another, about twenty miles.
148. *One dayes walk*, Jonah 3:4; *Ware*, *c.*20 miles north of London; *six score thousand infants*, Jonah 4:11, the number of those in Ninevah who

'cannot discern between their right hand and their left hand'; *monument of Ninus*, who founded Ninevah, the monument and much of the city being built by his wife, Semiramis, Diodorus Siculus, *Library*, 2.7–10.

149. *Ark of the Covenant*, Genesis 6:15; *shew-bread*, Exodus 25:23 on the altar and Leviticus 25:5–6 on the ingredients of the bread that was to be present continually; *stone... twelve Tribes*, Exodus 28:17–21 on engraved jewel-stones.

150. *Table of the law*, i.e. ten commandments; *shoulders of Moses*, Exodus 32:15–16.

151. *Mount Sina*, Sinai.

152. [*Textual note:* (Er) 'seven' for (58) 'five'.]

153. *Bed of Og*, Deuteronomy 3:11.

154. *King Cheops*, in Herodotus, *Histories*, 2.125–6. Cheops prostituted his daughter, who in revenge, made the men give her one stone each, from which the pyramid was built.

155. *Tyrannical bed of Procrustes*, a bandit in Greece, who offering hospitality, then laid his captives on an iron bed, racking those who were too short to make them longer, and amputating those too tall for the bed, Apollodorus, *Epitome*, 1.4.

156. Plutarch, *Theseus*, 27.6.

157. *Ordination*, design.

158. *Girdle of Orion... Charles's wain*, constellations, Orion's belt and Ursa Major (Plough, Big Dipper); *Pythagoricall musick*, mathematical and musical harmony of the spheres; *sevenfold pipe of Pan*, Virgil, *Eclogues*, 2.36–7, made of seven uneven Hemlock stalks; *cryptography of Gaffarell*, Jacques Gaffarel (1601–-84), French scholar, author of *Unheard of Curiosities* (1629, trans. 1650), 4.13.

159. [*Textual note:* (Er) 'head' for (58) 'neck'. (C) also has 'head' in some copies and 'front' in others.]

160. *Hyades... Crusero* (Southern Cross), constellations with apparent quincunxes.

161. *Subterraneous concretions*, mineral forms; *favaginites*, honeycomb-shaped; *asteria*, translucent gem; *astroites*, star-stones, with inner glow; *crucigerous*, cross-bearing; *S. Iago of Gallicia*, St James, son of Zebedee, d. 44 CE.

162. *Julus*, catkin with chaffy scales on stalk; *excrescencies*, immoderate growth.

163. *Calamus aromaticus*, sedge, sweet-flag; *petasites*, butterbur, from daisy family; *asphodelus*, herbaceous tufted flowing perennial; *blattaria*, moth mullein, long, spiky, grassy leaf.

164. *Verbascum... tapsas barbatus*, great mullein, rosette-leaved hardy plant; *spicous*, spiky, pointed.

165. Referring to Johan Bauhin, *Historiae Plantarum* (1650) 1.2.86, 'They are rarely found... we have only come upon them twice'.

166. *Squamous*, scaly; *jacea pinea*, a kind of knapweed, thistle-like, lobe-headed, scaly or bract-headed plants.
167. Greek Anthology, 14.58, 'On an Artichoke', 'if you search within my flanks, I have there my mother's father'.
168. *Shoar*, i.e. shore; *ejectments*, jetsam, things cast up by the sea.
169. [*Textual note:* (Er) 'teasel' for (58) 'tearell'.]
170. *Teasel*, dipsacus, long-stemmed, spiny-headed plant; *palisadoed*, spiked.
171. [Browne's additional marginal note.]
172. On the vain use of 'cleansing powder', identified with Borith, used to wash away corruption.
173. *Seraglio of Solomon*, 1 Kings 11:3, with 700 wives and 300 concubines; *calicular*, cup-like; *uncous*, hooked; *disposure*, arrangement; *abstersion*, scouring, purging.
174. *Aculeous*, needle-like; *scalpe*, rind.
175. *Mercurie*, spurge-family; *weld*, *Reseda luteola*, used as a dye; *plantane*, plantaine, banana-like fruit.
176. *Santfoyne*, French grass seed; *Jupiters beard*, dome-headed, pink or red perennial plant.
177. *Fenny seagreen*, Stratiotes aloides, surface-lying pond-weed.
178. *Favaginous*, honeycombed; *flower of the sunne*, sunflower.
179. *Spicated*, spiky; *Fuchsius*, Leonhart Fuchs, *Historia Stirpium* (1542), p. 595; *Gramen Ischemon*, smooth-finger grass; *codde*, seed-sack; *sachell palme*, Manicaria saccifera, large-leafed palm.
180. *Compass is absolved*, the circle being completed.
181. *Pellitorye*, crevice-hugging climbing plant; *ragweed*, ragwort; *pollards*, trees pruned by pollarding, lopping the heads and branches wholesale; *excrescencies*, growths.
182. *Thwart*, run athwart or transversely; *furdling*, furling, curling, explication, unfolding.
183. *Chiasmus*, diagonal arrangement; *staminous*, long-stemmed.
184. *Stylus*, stem.
185. *Calicular*, cup-like.
186. *Observator*, observer, scientifically-speaking.
187. *Spring of seeds*, germinating.
188. *Diminutives*, tiny nubs; *plastick principle*, the animating and internal force driving the processes of nature; *comproduction*, participation, i.e. the parts of the seed seen to serve as nourishment for the nub.
189. *Germen*, seed-vessel.
190. *Fructifying principle*, the seminal or 'fructifying' principle, the quasi-divine impulsive force; *transvertible*, reversible; *inversedly*, inverted, upside-down.
191. *Corculum*, heart.
192. [*Textual note:* (Er2) 'roots and sprouts' for (58) 'roots'.]
193. *Cummes*, sprouting radicles.

194. *Punctilio*, fine point.
195. *Unhulled*, de-husked.
196. *Decoctions*, boiling in water to extract the soluble parts.
197. *Sensible*, perceptible; *priority*, coming first.
198. *Pease*, peas; *cod*, pod.
199. *Duckweed*, surface-lying prolific pond-plant, with barely discernible leaves or roots; *stroaks*, the thin lines of duckweed.
200. *Hardly made out*, difficult to discern.
201. *Accuminated*, pointed.
202. *Criticisme*, a subtlety.
203. [*Textual note:* (Er) 'powers' for (58) 'pores'.]
204. *Seminall powers*, those which generate spontaneously; *polypody*, a kind of multi-fronded fern that grows on walls.
205. *Stramonium*, thorn-apple or jimson weed.
206. *Blattaria*, spiky grass; *yellow henbane*, somewhat poisonous smoking plant, 'English Tabaco', according to John Gerard, *The herball or Generall historie of plantes* (1633), p. 356.
207. Aristotle, *Meteorology*, 4.3, on the process of concoction that allows ripening, with reference to a 1646 commentary by Niccolò Cabeo, Jesuit philosopher
208. *Paracelsus could affirm*, Browne tends to tinge the modal 'could' with a strong element of doubt, particularly where Paracelsus (in *Philosophia Sagax*, 1.3) is concerned.
209. *Flatuous distension*, an airy swelling of the husk.
210. *Rudimentall discoveries*, first showing of the signs of sprouting; *foliaceous*, leaf-like appearance; *surcles*, small shoots; *incrassation*, thickening.
211. [*Textual note:* (58) Octavo has 'one mother', while the quarto has 'one another'.]
212. Genesis 1:11, 'the herb yielding seed, and the fruit tree yielding fruit after his kind, whose seed is in itself'.
213. *Accidental*, based on outward and subsidiary, rather than essential characteristics.
214. *Four kinds*, trees, shrubs, woody-shrubs, and herbs (listed in chapter 5 as *Arbor*, *frutex*, *suffrutex*, *herba*).
215. [*Textual note:* (Er) adds phrase 'in a large acception . . . progression of trees', absent in (58).]
216. *Folious*, abounding in leaves.
217. *Æquivocall production*, spontaneous generation; *univocacy*, oneness, seeming to be produced in a single generative manner.
218. *Foraminous roundles*, porous or perforated spherical shapes.
219. Stephanus Schoneveldt, *Icthyologia* (1624).
220. *Exiguity*, smallness; *magnalities*, wonders, great size.
221. *Rampions*, bellflowers; *one grain*, 30 milligrams.
222. *Disputed seeds*, spores.

223. *Puncticular*, tiny point.
224. *Epicurisme*, in the sense of cultivated taste in eating; *gallatures*, germ of egg; *treddles*, likewise germ, but meaning pellet.
225. *Oval generation*, of the egg.
226. [Browne's additional marginal note].
227. *Gentianella*, felwort; *convolvulus*, flowering bindweed.
228. *Explication*, unfolding.
229. *Inflexures*, an inward curve.
230. *Five brethren*, a medieval riddle of new-born bearded brothers, whose solution is the leaves of the calyx; *disposure*, order; *salved*, finding an explanation or evasion of a difficulty.
231. *Sphærical number*, when multiplied by itself, ending in 5.
232. *Volutation*, rolling; *contaction*, touching, contact; the claim here being that a ball or sphere rolled on a flat surface covers five times its own area before reaching its initial position.
233. *Sea-starre*, starfish; *sea hedge-hogge*, sea-urchin.
234. *Semidiameters*, the radial threads.
235. Euclid, *Elements*, 4.11 and 4.14, both of which relate to describing pentagonal figures within a circle.
236. [*Textual note:* (Er) 'bramble' for (58) 'bryar'.]
237. *Signature*, figure, although signatures also imply some discernible mark of God within the objects of nature.
238. *Signal discerners*, those who can perceive the signs and signatures of the natural world.
239. [*Textual note:* (Er2) 'Delphinium' for (58) 'Gallitricum'.]
240. *Ajax* . . . *Delphinium*, Ajax, out-argued by Ulysses for possession of Achilles' arms, killed himself, and the blood on the ground produced a purple flower inscribed with his name, AIAI. Delphinium is also rendered larkspur, *Metamorphoses*, 13.395–8; *Aarons mitre* . . . *Henbane*, Exodus 28:36–9; Josephus, *Jewish Antiquities*, 3.7.6, 172–8.
241. *Hioides*, hyoid bone, anchoring the thyroid cartilage; *furcula or merry-thought*, wish-bone; *scapulæ*, shoulder-bone; *Aurelian cases*, chrysalis; *clouts*, cloths.
242. *Cimex arboreus*, capsid-family insect.
243. [*Textual note:* (Er) 'weazell' for (58) 'werrell'.]
244. *Notonecton*, water-boatmen, corixids; *sea-poult, or weazell*, weasle.
245. *Sexangular*, hexagonal; *pismires*, ants; *edificial*, stately (building).
246. *Favago*, favago marinus, sand-lines made by honeycomb-worm.
247. *Augmenting glasses*, magnifying glass.
248. Bernardinus Gomesius, *Diascepseon de Sale* (1605), 1.20.
249. *Experiment*, observation.
250. *Rarely*, perfectly; *Cottonary*, cotton-like.
251. *How nature geometrizeth*, rarely a verb, and rarer still an antiquated verb. God as geometrician is met in *Religio Medici*, 1.16.

252. *Teguments*, enveloping cover.
253. *Aspis*, asp; *chiasmus*, patterned by opposites; *mater formicarum*, mother of ants (lit.).
254. *Resolution*, explanation; *wonder of Bellonius*, Pierre Belon, *De Aquatilibus* (1553), p. 29.
255. *Stages*, stories; *contignations*, the joining of a framework of beams; *compartitions*, division of parts in the ground-plan; *pyle*, pile, structure.
256. *Excoriable*, that can be skinned; *bretts*, sprats; *soals*, sole.
257. *Russia leather*, used in bookbinding.
258. *Ostracion*, boxfish; *cunny fish*, skate.
259. *Bembine table*, 1st-century bronze tablet, acquired by the antiquarian Cardinal Bembo in 1527.
260. *Orus*, Horus, Egyptian god and hieroglyphic.
261. *Cruciated character of Trismegistus*, the letter X, reputedly invented by Hermes Trismegistus; *Statuæ Isiacæ*, statues of Isis; *teraphim*, household gods; *Jacobs crosse*, Genesis 48:1, holding his sons, Ephraim and Manasses, who receive a cross-handed blessing.
262. *Subtegmen*, woof of woven matter, here, in the 'veins and vessels of life', being the umbilical cord.
263. *Obliquation*, bent in oblique direction; *expression of Scripture*, Psalm 139:14–15, 'I am fearfully and wonderfully made.'
264. Plato, *Symposium*, 189e–90d.
265. *Scarus and ruminating fish*, the parrot fish; Aristotle, *History of Animals*, 8.2 (591b).
266. *Crop*, pouch-like enlargement of gullet, for partial digestion.
267. [Browne's additional marginal note].
268. *Cornigerous*, horned.
269. *Exuccous*, sapless, without juice.
270. *Runnet*, rennet; *priests fee*, Leviticus 7:31, the breast of the sacrificed animal.
271. *Cartilagineous*, of the cartilage; *wezon*, weasand, gullet; *Rondeletius*, Guillaume Rondelet, *De Piscibus Marinis* (1554), 3.11.
272. *Cretaceous*, chalky; *fech*, vetch, bean-like fruit.
273. *Pseudodoxia*, 3.26.
274. *Jowle*, jaw-bone; *questuary*, money-making. The whale that beached on the Norfolk shore being quickly sold, before there was time for any philosophical anatomy.
275. *Seases*, containers.
276. *Incession*, movement; *diametrals*, relating to the diameter.
277. *Breezes*, gad-flies; *salient animals*, leaping.
278. *Station*, standing-position.
279. *Castors horse*, standing with its two left legs on the ground.
280. *Angle of indenture*, angle of intersection.
281. *Granadilla*, passionflowers, whose stamens are the 'crucifying appurtenances'.

282. *Barbado pine*, banana.
283. *Phalaris*, headed grass; *Porta*, Giambattista della Porta, whose *Phytognomonica* (1588) explores the idea of correspondence.
284. Fabio Colonna, *Minus Cognitorum Stirpium* (1616); *orchis*, orchid.
285. *Half the character of Pisces*, zodiacal symbol.
286. [*Textual note:* (Er) 'Aiaia' for (58) 'Acaia'.]
287. *Helicall*, of the helix; *volutas*, scrolls; *frustums of Archimedes*, the portions of a solid intercepted by two planes, Archimedes, *On Conic Sections*.
288. *Tutson*, tutsan, dense-growing shrub.
289. *Persicaria*, smartweed, pink weed.
290. *Spicated*, spiked.
291. *Thrums*, warp-threads left unwoven; *knops*, tassels.
292. *Pappous*, downy; *gomphosis*, the way in which hard objects, e.g. teeth, are accommodated in a joint, e.g. the jaw, or the joining mechanisms of bones; *mortis-articulation*, fixing in position; *trapopogon or goats-beard*, yellow wild-flower; *telarely*, telary, in the manner of a web.
293. *Mealie*, flour-like; *exudations*, oozing.
294. Suetonius, *Augustus*, 80; *native notes*, birthmark; *Charles wayne*, Big Dipper.
295. *Agues*, violent fevers; *mesentery*, folds of peritoneum.
296. [Browne's additional marginal note].
297. *Adventitious*, accidental, not essential or inherent; *tincture*, colour.
298. *Aurelian*, of butterflies, lepidopterous; *canker*, caterpillar.
299. *Motive*, moving.
300. *sesqui-tertian proportion,* a ratio of 1:1.33r, in Plato, *Timaeus*, 35.
301. *Unition*, joining; *apophyses*, outgrowth.
302. *Commissure*, the seams or joins.
303. *Diarthrosis*, the motion of one bone against another.
304. *Symphysis*, fusion.
305. *Magical spit*, hazelwood, with its natural inter-twists.
306. *Summer-worm*, larva, maggot, gnat-worms.
307. *Tortile*, winding, coiled; *tiring*, pulled, drawn.
308. *Ampliations*, amplification.
309. *Solon*, Athenian politician (*c.* 638–558 BCE), who introduced tree-planting legislation, Plutarch, *Solon*, 23.6.
310. *Large radication*, extensive roots.
311. Virgil, *Aeneid*, 4.445–6, 'as far as it lifts its top to the airs of heaven, so far it strikes its roots down towards hell'.
312. [*Textual note:* (Er) 'generallitie' for (58) 'generation']
313. Pliny, *Natural History*, 12.5, who reports on banqueting in the interior of plane trees and roots of thirty-three cubits, *c.* 15 metres; *tap-roots*, growing vertically downwards.
314. *Hearby plants*, local vegetation; *sea-holly*, coastline thistle-bush; *liquorish*, the root of *Glycyrrhiza glabra*.

315. Infestation and contagion.
316. *Effluviums*, outflow of subtle particles.
317. *Perflation*, blowing through of air.
318. This being part of a philosophical discussion on the material nature of effluvia and smells.
319. *Refection*, refreshment; *imbibition*, drinking in.
320. *Epithymum*, yarn-like purple parasitic plant; *dodder*, hell-bine.
321. *Cirrous*, hairy or filamented; *tentacles*, the pincers by which climbing plants cling.
322. *Scordium*, water germander.
323. *Acharon*, Homer, *Odyssey*, 10.510, Odysseus' instructions for finding the river where his descent into Hades begins.
324. *Solisequious*, turning to the sun.
325. [*Textual note:* (Er) 'pot' for (58) 'plot']
326. *Solstitially*, towards the solstice; *Cancer*, zodiacal sign at summer solstice; Theophrastus, *On Plants*, 1.10.1.
327. *Æquinoctionally*, in the direction of the equinoctial; *ecliptically*, in the direction of the sun's apparent motion.
328. *Husbandry of Solomon*, Song of Songs 4:16; Theophrastus, *On Plants*, 4.1.4.
329. *Quaternios*, square-planted formations; *commodity*, convenient arrangement; Varro, *De Re Rustica*, 1.7.2.
330. *Excentricities*, having its axis not centrally placed.
331. *Concentricall*, with a common centre.
332. *Circinations*, the rounded forms; *meridionall*, markings on a curved body on a plane with the axis.
333. *Planetical orbes*, i.e. seven.
334. *Obvert*, turn towards, though it can also mean turn away from.
335. *Sargasso*, gulf-weed; *sea-lettuce . . . phasganium*, sea-weed.
336. *Arsmart*, smallweed, water-pepper.
337. *Harpalus*, Macedonian, friend of Alexander, Plutarch, *Alexander*, 35.10.
338. Galen, *On the Powers and Mixtures of Simple remedies*, 7.
339. *Splenetick*, given to anger.
340. 'lovelier than pale ivy', Virgil, *Eclogues*, 7.38.
341. *Ferrara*, in Northern Italy.
342. *Clusius . . . Bellonius*, Carolus Clusius, *Rariorum Plantarum Historia* (1601), 1.17.
343. *Inocculation and incision*, inserting the bud of a plant under the bark of another for engrafting.
344. Jan Huyghen van Linschoten, *Discourse of Voyages* (1598).
345. *Sation*, sowing.
346. *Vertically conjoyned*, i.e. at the top; *blunt*, oblique.
347. [*Textual note:* (Er) 'four right' for (58) 'two right', and similarly in the following phrase.]

348. *Parts*, degrees.
349. [*Textual note:* (Er2) 'stand', omitted in (58)]
350. *Equicrurall*, isosceles; Archimedes, *On Conic Sections*.
351. *Alexander*, in Arrian, *Anabasis of Alexandria*, 7.19.4; *accomodable*, suitable.
352. *Canticles*, Song of Songs 1:14; *botanology*, botany; *camphire*, henna.
353. *Circular amputations*, circular topiary.
354. *Teretous*, tapering cylindrical form; *tenuifolious*, narrower, in contrast to teretous leaves.
355. *Dipteros hypœthros*, a roofless building with two rows of columns; *cavedia*, the inner court of a Roman villa; *templa subdialia*, open-air temples.
356. *Peristylia*, cloister; *exedræ*, spacious recessed arcades, in Vitruvius, *On Architecture*, 6.3.7–8.
357. Vitruvius, *On Architecture*, 5.1.3.
358. *Areostylos*, one of the five styles of columns; *intercolumniations*, the spaces between the columns.
359. *Court of the Tabernacle*, Exodus 27:9–11.
360. *Επισκιασμὸς*, shading (in painting, *adumbration*); *penthouse*, subsidiary structure or annex.
361. *Pupilla*, pupil.
362. *Colours of mediocrity*, i.e. not intense.
363. *Candour*, brilliance, whiteness.
364. *Supervenient*, extraneous addition; *ligature or inhumation*, binding up, burying under earth.
365. *Alimental*, nourishing.
366. *Seminalities*, propulsion to growth.
367. *Decoction*, boiling to extract the essence of a substance; *uliginous coats*, oozy or slimy surface cover; *acari*, mites.
368. *Helmonts tree*, Jan Baptista van Helmont, *Ortus Medicinae* (1648), p. 109, on a willow stem in sterilized earth, fed only with rain and distilled water.
369. *Asarum ... its vomiting operation*, an emetic plant.
370. *Radiation*, outward growth.
371. *Cod*, pod; *alary*, pertaining to wings.
372. 'Light for Zeus, darkness for Hades; light for Hades, darkness for Zeus', Hippocrates, *Regimen*, 1.5.
373. *Idæas*, seminal ideas equate to seminal principles, the generative instinct of the created world; *orcus*, the underworld.
374. Johannes Hevelius, Polish Astronomer, published a 1647 atlas of the Moon.
375. *Shadows of stars*, eclipses; *polary*, as at the poles.
376. *Fourth day*, Genesis 1:14–19.
377. *Adumbration*, shadowing, here in the sense of typology, by which the Old Testament figures the New; *cherubims ... Mercy-seat*, Hebrews 9:5, description of the tabernacle.

378. *Simulachrum*, Platonic idea of a copy or image of the insubstantial original form.
379. *Pyramidal rayes*, diagrammatically imagined notion of the light rays from objects reaching the eye as two converging lines and then reversing themselves onto the retina.
380. *Dark chamber*, camera obscura.
381. *Hornycoat*, cornea; *christalline humour*, the lens of the eye; *foramen*, opening, aperture.
382. *Concurrence by decussation*, that the left eye was linked to the right side of the brain and the right eye to the left side.
383. *Incidence*, how a line falls upon a surface; *visuall raye*, on the presumption that sight worked by rays emitted by the eyes and reflected.
384. *Whispering places*, echoing structures.
385. *Stations*, positions.
386. Charles de Bovelle, *De intellectu* (1510), 14.8.
387. *Intellectual and phantastical lines*, on the analogy of the lines of sight, the intellect and fantasy likewise works here, unless corrupted, by the direct quincuncial entry into the brain.
388. *Geniall spirits*, guardian spirits.
389. Plato, *Timaeus*, 36b–d.
390. *Motion of the first orb*, the primum mobile. This places the cross inside a circle and rotates it.
391. Plato, *Timaeus*, 35–7; *systasis*, putting together, union.
392. Justin Martyr, *First Apology*, 60.78, on Plato's prophetic prefigurations of the cross; *notifie*, signify; *Decussavit eum in universo*, 'he placed him cross-ways in the universe'.
393. Numbers 21:8–9. Martyr is arguing for Plato's borrowings from Moses.
394. *Mercurial characters*, referring to Hermes Trismegistus (as Mercury) and the planet sign, ☿; *Cadmus*, legendary founder of Thebes, originator of letters, Herodotus, *Histories*, 5.58.
395. *Pythagorisme*, the seeking of mysterious significance in numbers, undertaken by Pythagoras and his followers.
396. Each dot represents sequentially the numbers 1–9, with 5 in the central position.
397. *Common game*, nine pins, a form of skittles, aiming to knock down the central skittle.
398. Plutarch, *De E Apud Delphos* (*The E at Delphi*), 13–15, as skittish a text as the Garden of Cyrus, exploring the inscription of the fifth letter of the Greek Alphabet—also meaning 'if' and 'you (sg) are'—at Delphi. It contains a significant discussion of why 5 is such an important number.
399. *Entities of the world*, the four elements, together with the aether.
400. *Glasses*, magnifying devices, such as microscopes.
401. *Crystalline humour*, lens; *loligo*, a kind of squid.

402. *Conjugall or wedding number*, Plutarch, *The E at Delphi*, 8, in which it is explained that the beginning of even numbers is 2 and of odd numbers 3, and these are mystically married in 5.
403. Hesiod, *Works and Days*, 802, 'Avoid the fifth days, they are difficult and dread'; Plato, *Laws*, 6.775.
404. *Virgins*, Matthew 25:1.
405. Plutarch, *Roman Questions*, 2.
406. *This day*, the fifth day of creation, Genesis 1:20–3.
407. [Browne's additional marginal note]. Horace, *Odes*, 1.13.
408. Archangelus Burgonovus (1569), a commentary on Pico della Mirandola.
409. Abram renamed Abraham, changing the Cabalistic sum of the letters of his name, Genesis 17:5.
410. *Binah*, in Kabbalah, the second intellectual Sephirah.
411. Sarai renamed Sarah, Genesis 17:15.
412. [*Textual note:* (C) ascribes 'none, or very few . . . if perfectly described' to the margin.] Referring to spiders with two organs of touch, as well as eight legs, Carolus Clusius, *Curae Posteriores* (1611).
413. *Mysticall name of God*, in the Hebrew letters of Yahweh; *Trismegistus*, God is a sphere whose centre is everywhere and circumference nowhere.
414. Leviticus 19:23–5; *lash*, soft and watery.
415. *Second day*, Genesis 1:6–8; *feminine part of five*, with reference again to Plutarch, *The E at Delphi*.
416. On laws of restitution.
417. *Five golden mice*, 1 Samuel 6:4, the 'trespass offering' paid by the Philistines with the return of the Ark.
418. Leviticus 26:8.
419. 1 Corinthians 14:19.
420. *Radicall letters*, consonants of Hebrew words; *souldiery of the tribes*, Numbers 1:46, coming to 603,550.
421. *Barley loaves*, John 6:9–10; *seven of wheat*, Mark 8:5–8.
422. *Joseph*, Genesis 45:22.
423. *Pagan champion*, i.e. Goliath, 1 Samuel 17:40.
424. *Critical physician*, i.e. Julius Caesar Scaliger, *De Causis Linguae Latinae* (1540), on the putative Greek origin (four plus one) of the Latin term for 'five'.
425. *Wine*, Plutarch, *Table Talk*, 3.9.
426. Hippocrates, *Epidemics*, 7.3.
427. Describing the positional relationships of planets.
428. David, 1 Samuel 16:23; *Sephiroth*, emanation of the divine; *Tiphereth*, one of the ten sephiroth; the nature of the emanations from David's harp is discussed by Marin Mersenne, *Quaestiones in Genesim* (1623), p. 1705.
429. *Serapis*, in Janus Gruterus, *Inscriptiones antiquae totius orbis Romani* (1603).

430. *Pratasis, epitasis*... etc., Exposition, development, intensification, dénouement: the four parts of a dramatic poem.
431. *Five acts*, In Horace, *The Art of Poetry*, 189–90.
432. Julius Caesar Scaliger, *Exotericarum Exercitationum* (1615), 177.2.
433. *Magneticall philosophy*, the science surrounding magnetic phenomena, broadly conceived; *distract their verticities*, shift their points (vertices) always to the north, thus never crossing over.
434. *Geomancers*, diviners from earth or lines on page; *amission*, loss; *speckled beetle*, ladybird, ladybug.
435. *Chiromantical conjecturers*, chiromancy being divination from the hand, palm-reading.
436. *Medall of Alexander the Great*, in Agostino, *Diologhi*... *intorno alle medaglie* (1625), p. 140.
437. *Juno*, Ovid, *Metamorphoses*, 9.298; *veneficial*, malign magic.
438. *Amphidromicall*, naming of the child, carrying round the hearth.
439. *Men of Cadmus*, Ovid, *Metamorphoses*, 3.114–26, having planted dragon's teeth, armed men arise from the ground and fight each other, till only five were left.
440. *Proteus*, Homer, *Odyssey*, 4.412–19, Odysseus' instructions on how to defeat Proteus being to seize him while he is sleeping among the seals, whom he numbers out in groups of five.
441. *Fifth years oxe*, Homer, *Iliad*, 2.403.
442. *Antoninus*... *rhombus*, Marcus Aurelius, *Meditations*, 11.12 calls the soul a sphere.
443. *Nauseating crambe verities*, made sick by stale truths.
444. *Flat and flexible truths*, cf. the more positive 'soft and flexible sense' in the preface to *Religio Medici*; *Achilles his armour*, Homer, *Iliad*, 18.468–613.
445. *Quaternios*, Pythagorian tetrad, figuring unity (1 + 2 + 3 + 4 = 10).
446. In March.
447. *Five ports*, five senses.
448. *Præcogitations*, the thoughts we were having before sleep.
449. Hippocrates, *Regimen*, book 4 'Dreams'.
450. *Oneirocritica* or *The Interpretation of Dreams*, 2nd-century Greek work by Artemodorus; *Apomazar* is Ahmed Ibn Sirin, 9th-century Arabic writer on dreams.
451. *Daughter of Chaos*, Hesiod, *Theogony*, 123.
452. *No lower*, no more recently.
453. *Somnus*, Homer, *Iliad*, 2.6–15.
454. *Act our antipodes*, be the inverse of ourselves.

CERTAIN MISCELLANY TRACTS

1. This tract, 'Repertorium, an account of the Tombs of Norwich Cathedral', is not included here.
2. *Chirurgeons*, surgeons.
3. 'She painted her eyes with antimony.'
4. Revelation 21:10–11; Exodus 28:15–21.
5. 1 Kings 9:26–8; 1 Kings 22:48.
6. *Oneirocritical*, interpreting dreams; Genesis 37:5–10, 41:25.
7. *Quibus frons*..., 'Those who possess a commensurate quadrangular forehead are brave: thus it is reported also in relation to lions.'
8. *Scandent*, a climbing plant.
9. *Abstersive*, purgative.
10. Exodus 3:2.
11. *Edulious*, edible.
12. *Contection*, covering up.
13. *Impinguating*, fattening, nutritious.
14. *Pistours*, grinders of corn.
15. *Nervifolious*, leaves with prominent veins.
16. *Flosculous*, flowery.
17. *Oleraceous*, pot-herb.
18. Herodotus, *Histories*, 1.193, 'The millet and sesame grow to a height resembling that of trees, and although I know this full well; nevertheless, I refrain from relating such information in great detail, understanding rightly, that it would seem exceedingly incredible to those who have never visited the Babylonian region.'
19. *Supereminencies*, being supreme.
20. *Iliad*, 2.197–200.
21. *Juments*, beasts of burden.
22. *Ligneous*, woody.
23. *Quasi terebinthus*, Ecclesiasticus 24:16.
24. 'They sacrifice upon the tops of the mountains... under oaks and poplars and elms, because the shadow thereof is good.'
25. *Sensibly*, through the senses.
26. *Centesimal*, hundredfold.
27. Pliny, *Natural History*, 18.21, varying slightly from Browne's text: 'The deputy governor of that region sent to his late Majesty Augustus—almost incredible as it sees—a parcel of very nearly 400 shoots obtained from a single grain as seed... he likewise sent to Nero also 360 stalks obtained from one grain. At all events the plains of Lentini and other districts in Sicily and the whole of Andalusia, and particularly Egypt reproduce at the rate of a hundredfold.'
28. 'It yields 150 *modii* of grain from one.'

29. 'The seed is thought to be best for sowing at a year old, worse at two and three; beyond this it is virtually unfruitful, although it is suitable for using as food.'
30. 'In a certain place of Cappadocia, wheat retains its fecundity for forty years; furthermore, it is reported that it hardens in a manner suitable for sowing and can be preserved for suitable food-related uses for sixty or seventy years.'
31. *Husbandry*, the tending of plants.
32. *Cyons*, scions, shoots for grafting.
33. 'It is sufficient to graft the cultivated olive to forest or wild olives. For if, on the other hand, you should unite the forest olive to the cultivated olives, although there will be a certain difference, nevertheless, it will never truly produce a tree of good fruit.'
34. 'Domestic trees designed for grafting are always to be preferred to those of the forest.'
35. *Surculation*, cutting off shoots for propagation.
36. 'All seed produces a similar offspring, apart from the olive tree, for this produces the wild olive and this is the forest olive tree, not the true olive tree.'
37. *Nidulation*, nest-building.
38. AV has, in fact, 'and their father, Israel'.
39. 1.21.4, 'not to cut hay or bind it or haul it; and it is not permissible either by the ordinances of the priest to be gathered on feast days', Columella goes on 'unless you have first sacrificed a puppy'.
40. 'First, the grass on the hey-meadows should be cut close with the sickle when it ceases to grow and begins to dry from the heat, and turned with the fork while it is drying out; when it is quite dry it should be made into bundles and hauled to the barn.'
41. 'It is to mow with a sickle, that which the mowers have omitted to attend to, or to cut that which the mowers have overlooked.'
42. *Vessicular*, bladder-like; *acrons*, acorns.
43. Virgil, *Georgics*, 2.15–16, The oak 'that spreads its shade for Jove'.
44. *Edulious or esculent*, edible.
45. Ovid, *Metamorphoses*, 1.112, 'and yellow honey was distilled from the verdant oak'.
46. 'We will proceed more clearly, if, with the alternative division having been disregarded, we substitute merely two types of plants: namely the *arbor* ('tree') and *herba* ('herb'), combining *fructices* ('bushes') with trees and *large plants* with that of herbs.'
47. Square bracketing in the original, here and elsewhere in Tracts.
48. *Webb*, nib.
49. *Compotations*, drinking bouts.
50. Martial, *Epigrams*, 6.80.8–9, 'But do thou, bidden now to yield to a Roman winter, send us thy harvests; receive, O Nile, our Roses.'

51. John 21:11.
52. Matthew 17:27.
53. Horace, *Satires*, 2.4.73–4, 'I was the first to serve up wine-lees and caviare', according to Loeb.
54. Juvenal, *Satires*, 10.317, 'even buggery with a mullet, that's the fate of some adulterers'.
55. *Latitancy*, hibernation.
56. Ovid, *Metamorphoses*, 6.672–4, 'Upon his head a stiff crest appears, and a huge beak stands forth instead of his long sword. He is the hoopoe, with the look of one armed for war.
57. Martial, *Epigrams*, 1.115, 'But I want a certain girl, one darker than night, or ant, pitch or crow or cricket'.
58. Virgil, *Ciris*, 505–6, 'then other parts and the legs, coloured with blushing crimson'.
59. *Bouze*, drink.
60. *Jesses*, straps attached to hawk's leg.
61. *Circensial*, pertaining to Roman circus.
62. 'My mind deliberates upon lofty judgements.'
63. Ausonius, *Oratio Consulis Ausonii Versibus Rhopalicis*, 1, 'O Lord, eternal hope and founder of our abode.'
64. 'But I will say freely in your ear, that I fasten the precious stone to a long robe with protracted Ropalic verses of this nature.' Iliad. 3.182
65. Translated, but not in Browne's hand, in MS Sloane, 1827, f.88 as 'She is dead at last, who many made expire | is dust todaye, which yesterday was fire'.
66. William Dugdale. The 1683 edition prints E.D., but this is an error, and the tract echoes their correspondence closely.
67. 'The Saxons, a people ignorant of Christ, were buried in pleasant gardens if, by chance, they died of disease at home, or, if slain in battle abroad, in constructed mounds of earth in the midst of fields (which they called "Burgos").'
68. 'It is entirely credible and probable that the Danes, in memory of Kings and Heroes, formerly erected huge mounds of heaped earth, projecting the likeness of mountains, especially in those places where men often pass to and fro and travel, so that along public roads they might dedicate the memory of the dead to posterity and in a certain manner enjoin it to immortality.'
69. 'From under an incredible heap of earth, an urn of extraordinary size was dug up, which was filled with ash and fragments of huge bones, together with helmets and shields of bronze and iron almost consumed by rust; but no inscription with regards to a name, or testimony of date or fortune was set forth.'
70. Iliad, 20.300–8.
71. To cure the king's eyes.

72. A misquote from Ovid, *Ex Ponto* 4.13.19: *A! pudet et Getico scripsi sermone libellum.* – 'Ah, the shame! I have even written a small tract on the Getan language.'
73. 'Amongst many different types of torture, they devised the following: through deceit certain men were sedated with a large amount of unmixed wine and unexpectedly had their penises bound with cord so that they were tortured simultaneously by the pain from the cord and the need to urinate.'
74. 'O how long is the night that makes one an old man?'—misquotation of Martial, *Epigrams*, 4.7.
75. 'Did you think then that the Phaeacian people were empty-headed?'—quoting Juvenal, *Satires*, 15.23.
76. 'Neither the terrible Cimbri nor Britons, ferocious Sarmatae or the enormous Agathyrsi ever (acted thus)'—quoting Juvenal, *Satires*, 15.124–5.
77. 'But I want that woman who is blacker than the night'—quoting Martial, *Epigrams*, 1.115.
78. 'We fashion the son of Brutus and Lagona as if they were alive'—quoting Martial, *Epigrams*, 9.50.
79. 'Which you might believe were stolen from the African sisters' (i.e. the Hesperides)—quoting Juvenal, *Satires*, 5.152.
80. 'A face just like Julius Rufus appears in the satirists'—half-quotation of Martial, *Epigrams*, 10.99.
81. 'The princes of the tribute-giving people give as tribute their servant.'

LETTER TO A FRIEND

1. '[He] sticks out his stiff heels towards the door', Persius, *Satires*, 3.105.
2. Hippocrates, *Prognostic*, 2.
3. Martial, *Epigrams*, 4.60.5–6, 'when death comes even in Tibur's midst is a Sardinia' (proverbially unhealthy).
4. *Epidemics*, 6.7.9.
5. *Tabidly*, wasted, consumptive; *cholical*, colic, griping pains.
6. *Strift*, striving.
7. Juno gave instructions to the midwife of Hercules' mother, Alcmene, to keep her legs crossed, so as to prevent the birth, Ovid, *Metamorphoses*, 9.273–323.
8. *hectical*, hectic, consumptive; *pthysical*, from phthisis, tuberculosis.
9. *Sigils*, seal, signets.
10. *Marasmus*, wasting-disorder.
11. Pliny, 2.101, 'Aristotle adds that no animal dies except when the tide is ebbing. This has been widely noticed in the Gallic ocean and has been found to hold good at all events in the case of man.'
12. Hesiod, *Theogony*, 212.

13. 'The pendulous part of the ear is called the lobe. Not every ear has this: those who are born at night do not have it, but those born in the day most often do.'
14. Richard Knolles, *Generall Historie of the Turkes* (1603).
15. *Bouffage*, satisfying meal.
16. Dante, *Purgatorio*, 23.28; *aruspex*, haruspex, who divined by examining entrails; *exenteration*, removing entrails.
17. Psalm 90:10.
18. 'The bell rarely tolls for a fourth-day fever.'
19. *Endemial*, endemic.
20. *Kell*, caul, membrane; *exuccous*, dry, juiceless.
21. *On Dreams*, 89 (*Regimen*, book 4).
22. *On Dreams*, 92.
23. Hippocrates, *Aphorisms*, 5.9, 'Consumption occurs chiefly between the ages of eighteen and thirtyfive.'
24. *Decipiency*, desipience, folly.
25. *Questuary*, money-making.
26. *Theorical*, theoretical.
27. *Democritism*, from Democrates, the laughing philosopher.
28. *Contentations*, what brings satisfaction; *existimation*, estimation.
29. Martial, *Epigrams*, 10.47.13, 'don't fear your last day, nor yet pray for it'.
30. *Enoch or Elias*, both 'translated' to heaven, without undergoing death, Malachi 4:5.
31. The Climatical year being 63: see *Pseudodoxia*, 4.12.
32. *Cautelous*, circumspect, cautious.
33. *Funambulous*, rope-walking. Parts of the text from here are also included in *Christian Morals*, and the corresponding notes there are more detailed.
34. *Cebes his table . . . Pinax*, Cebes, disciple of Socrates, purported author of the Pinax (tabula), a painting or series of pictures, depicting the stages of life and learning.
35. *Asperous*, rough, rugged.
36. Luke 21:1–4.
37. Job 31:24.
38. Gamaliel, a Pharisee, who in Acts 5:34 defends Peter's preaching, on the grounds that it will fizzle out, if it has no basis in truth.
39. *Postern of resipiscency*, back entrance to repentance.
40. Horace, *Epistles* 1.2.62, 'Anger is a brief madness.'
41. *Displacency*, displeasure.
42. Aristotle, *Ethics*, 4.5.
43. 1 Corinthians 13.
44. Procopius, *History of the Wars*, 1.5.7.
45. Matthew 11:12.
46. *Zeno's king*, showing self-possession and mastery of the self.
47. *Complexional*, temperamental.

CHRISTIAN MORALS

1. Elizabeth Littleton, Browne's daughter, who jointly edited the work with John Jeffrey, Archdeacon of Norwich.
2. *Funambulatory*, rope-walking. A number of passages, including this opening, are repeated in *A Letter to a Friend*.
3. *Concomitances*, something accompanying or coexisting; *halting*, in the sense of limping, hence 'halting concomitances' are moral qualities that lag behind one's general uprightness.
4. *Cebes's table . . . Pinax*, Cebes, disciple of Socrates, purported author of the Pinax (tabula), a painting or series of pictures, depicting the stages of life and learning, also in *Letter*. [*Johnson:* 'An allegorical representation of the characters and conditions of mankind' which is translated by Mr Collier and added to the meditations of Antonius.]
5. *Sanity*, in the sense of cleanliness rather than being sane.
6. [*Johnson:* Over the pacific ocean, in the course of the ship which now sails from Acapulco to Manilla, perhaps formerly from Lima, or more properly from Callao, Lima not being a sea-port.]
7. [*Johnson:* That is, 'in armour in a state of military vigilance'. One of the Grecian chiefs used to represent open force by the 'lion's skin' and policy by the 'fox's tail'.]
8. A battle between the Lapiths and Centaurs, Ovid, *Metamorphoses*, 12.210–535.
9. [*Johnson:* The censor, who is frequently confounded, and by Pope amongst others, with Cato of Utica.]
10. Eusebius, *Ecclesiastical History*, 6.8.
11. [*Johnson:* With their faculties unimpaired.]
12. Mark 12:42, parable of the widow's mite.
13. *Atropos*, wasting away. [*Johnson:* Atropos is the lady of destiny that cuts the thread of life.]
14. *Irus*, beggar in Homer, *Odyssey*, 18; Charon's fee for ferrying the dead is, it seems, not means-tested.
15. 'Give to every man that asketh of thee.'
16. *Physiognomy*, discerning characteristics from appearance—here, seeing the signs of poverty.
17. [*Johnson:* The ides was the time when money lent out at interest was commonly repaid.] (Horace, *Epodes*, 2.69.)
18. *Cockboat*, the lifeboat on a ship; *carrack*, a galleon.
19. 2 Kings 6:5–7.
20. Job 31:24–7.
21. *Mammon*, God who represents worship of money.
22. *Formal sadness*, i.e. not real.
23. [*Johnson:* Not deeply tinged, not died in grain.]

24. [*Johnson:* That is, with a position as immutable as that of 'the magnetical axis' which is popularly supposed to be invariably parallel to the meridial, or to stand exactly north and south.]
25. Trans. as in text.
26. *Sowers*, sours.
27. *Non ultra,* no further.
28. *Gamaliel*, Pharisee, in Acts 5:39, who prevaricated over Christianity; *Targum* [*Johnson:* A paraphrase or amplification.]
29. *Ambulatory*, shiftable.
30. *Eight*, those of Noah's family who survived the deluge.
31. *Touched pitch*, Ecclesiasticus 13:1.
32. *Displacency*, displeasure.
33. James, one of the fiercest biblical denunciations of mistreating the poor, considered apocryphal by Luther, who objected to its focus on works, not faith.
34. 1 Corinthians 13:2–7, on charity.
35. *Tract of land*, Atlantis.
36. *Theorical*, speculative, theoretical.
37. *Adraste and Nemesis* [*Johnson:* The powers of vengeance.]
38. *Obliquity*, divergence from proper conduct, i.e. one may have less sense of iniquity, in community, but this does not lessen the fault.
39. *Heels of Pride*, flying upwards and needing to be weighted down by 'plummets'. [*Johnson:* An epicycle is a small revolution made by one planet in the wider orbit of another planet. The meaning is 'Let not ambition form thy circle of action, but move upon other principles; and let ambition only operate as something extrinsick and adventitious.']
40. *Zeno's king* [*Johnson:* That is, 'the king of the stoics,' whose founder was Zeno, and who held that the wise man alone had power and royalty.]
41. *Elohims*, the Elohim, itself troublingly plural, is the name of God or gods in the Hebrew Bible.
42. *Argus his eyes*, Ovid, *Metamorphoses*, 1.625–7, Argus, the many-eyed guard of Io, was killed by Hermes on Zeus' instruction, and was subsequently changed into a peacock.
43. [Johnson: Alluding to the story of Ulysses, who stopped the ears of his companions with wax when they passed by the Sirens.] *Delators*, accusers.
44. *Jonas his gourd*, which rose and withered in a night, Jonah 4:6–10.
45. *Phylacteries*, serving as a reminder to keep the law. [*Johnson:* A phylactery is a writing bound upon the forehead, containing something to be kept constantly in mind. This was practised by the Jewish doctors with regard to the Mosaic law.]
46. *Ephemerides not Olympiads*, i.e. mercies over a longer time span. [*Johnson:* Particular journals of every day, not abstracts comprehending several years under one notation. An Ephemeris is a diary, an Olympiad is the space of four years.]

47. *Theta*, letter on Greek ballot used to decide on a sentence of death; *nocent*, guilty person.
48. *Assize*, court session.
49. *Damocles*, sword hanging by the hair of a horse's tale, to illustrate the precarious nature of safety and power, Cicero, *Tusculan Disputations*, 5.61. [*Johnson:* Damocles was a flatter of Dionysious.]
50. [*Johnson:* Appearances without realities.]
51. [*Johnson:* Tickling, flattering. A clawback is an old word for a flatterer. Jewel calls some writers for popery 'the pope's clawbacks'.]
52. *Periœci*, those dwelling at the same latitude, but opposite meridian.
53. *Hercules furens*, mad Hercules; *Poltron*, coward, knave, poltroon.
54. *Concupiscences*, coveting carnal things; *solecisms*, violations.
55. *Wild horses of Plato*, the soul, *Phaedrus*, 246.
56. *Digladiation*, hand-to-hand fight.
57. [*Johnson:* The Retiarius or Laquearius was a prize-fighter, who entangled his opponent in a net, which by some dexterous managements he threw upon him.]
58. [*Johnson:* The Liparean islands, near Italy, being volcanos, were fabled to contain the forges of the Cyclops.]
59. *St. Paul*, Ephesians 6:13–17.
60. *Lycurgus*, law-giver of Sparta.
61. *Rapt*, rapture.
62. *Oedipus*, riddle-solver.
63. *Laconism*, succinctness, i.e. the words inscribed on the wall in Belshazzar's feast, MENE, MENE, TEKEL, UPHARSIN, Daniel 5:5–28; *indited*, inspired the words.
64. *Superannuated*, disqualified by age.
65. [*Johnson:* This was the answer made by Diogenes to Alexander, who asked him what he had to request.] (Plutarch, *Alexander*, 14)
66. *Tetrick*, sour, harsh.
67. *Commensuration*, measuring and comparison of things.
68. *The censor's book* [*Johnson:* The book in which the Census or account of every man's estate was registered among the Romans.]
69. *Demetrius*, dissolute Macedonian king, Plutarch, *Life of Demetrius*; *Antonius*, Mark Anthony; *Ahab*, husband of Jezebel, 1 Kings 16–22; *Aristides*, Athenian statesman, 'the Just'; *Numa*, second Roman king, seen by Livy in positive light; *David*, 1 and 2 Samuel.
70. *Ideated man*, Platonic form and ideal of humankind.
71. *Tycho*, i.e. Tyche, chance or fortune, particularly in generation.
72. In Genoese conspiracy of 1547.
73. [*Johnson:* Socrates, and Cardan, perhaps, in imitation of him, talked of an attendant spirit or genius, that hinted from time to time how they should act.] (Plutarch, *On the Sign of Socrates*, 588d–e)
74. [*Johnson:* The tropic is the point where the sun turns back.]

75. Dead Sea. [*Johnson:* The lake of Sodom; the waters of which being very salt, and therefore very heavy, will scarcely suffer an animal to sink.]
76. *Rubicon*, Apennine river, whose crossing by Julius Caesar was, proverbially, the point of no return.
77. *Extempore*, suddenly.
78. Homer, *Iliad*, 1.592.
79. *Staggeringly*, i.e, by steps.
80. *Orontes into Tiber*, a quasi-xenophobic account of the river confluence, bringing Greek habits to Rome, Juvenal, *Satires*, 3.62ff.
81. *Asterisk*, star.
82. [*Johnson:* The motion of the heart, which beats about sixty times in a minute; or, perhaps, the motion of respiration, which is nearer to the number mentioned.]
83. *Lazy of Brazilia*, the sloth.
84. *Hercules*, third labour, chasing the hind of Ceryneia; *festination*, speed; *cunctation*, procrastination, delay.
85. *Best member*, brain.
86. 'That man is black of heart, of him beware, Good Roman', Horace, *Satires*, 1.4.85.
87. [*Johnson:* Plaudite was the term by which the antient theatrical performers solicited a clap.]
88. [*Johnson:* A ripeness preceding the usual time.]
89. *Plutarch ... Laërtius*, Plutarch writing political and military lives, while Laërtius wrote the lives of philosophers.
90. *Volupia*, Volupta, daughter of Cupid and Psyche.
91. Athenaeus, *Deipnosophists*, 12, 514e; *Cytheridian Cheese*, Diogenes Laertius, *Lives*, 10.11.
92. *Saturnalia*, 3.13.
93. *Life of Nero*, 48.4.
94. 'The server of hot and cold water.'
95. [*Johnson:* Gluttons]
96. [*Johnson:* From Zoilus, the calumniator of Homer.]
97. The mistake is reported in Aulus Gellius, *Attic Nights*, 15.6.
98. Plautus, *Amphitryon*, on the quasi-farcical conception and birth of Hercules to Alcmena, wife of Amphitryon.
99. Apollinaris Sidonius, *Poems*, 9.
100. The ark is returned in 1 Samuel 6, while David's carrying of the ark occurs in 2 Samuel 6.
101. Machiavelli, *The Prince*, 19, in a comment on whether Commodus should have imitated Severus.
102. [*Johnson:* 'It is true, certainly true, true in the highest degree.']
103. *Compage*, structure, construction.
104. *Quodlibetically*, disputatiously, in scholastic fashion; *Delphian blade*, dangerously ambiguous [*Johnson:* The Delphian sword became

proverbial not because it cut on both sides, but because it was used for different purposes.]

105. [*Johnson:* I suppose the main vein of a mine; the integument of the heart.]
106. [*Johnson:* The parallax of a star is the difference between its real and apparent place.]
107. *Sibyl's leaves*, Virgil, *Aeneid*, 3.444.
108. *Acquests*, acquisitions; *preexistimation*, previous opinions.
109. 'He who knows not how to dissemble, does not know how to rule.'
110. [*Johnson:* Conclusions deduced according to the forms of logick.]
111. *Eluctation*, bursting out.
112. *Exantlation*, drawing up, as water from a well.
113. 'I myself (for well I remember it) at the time of the Trojan war was Euphorbus, son of Panthoüs', Ovid, *Metamorphoses*, 15.160–1.
114. Cicero, *On Old Age*, 84.
115. [*Johnson:* Wild and enthusiastic authors of romantick chymystry.]
116. *Obliquities*, aberrations, errors.
117. *Diogenes*, Diogenes Laertius, *Lives of the Philosophers*, 6.20.
118. John Albert de Mandelslo, *Travels into the Indies* (1662), p. 264.
119. 'Our first day fixed our last'.
120. *Capitulation*, God, walking with Abraham, agreed to spare Sodom, if fifty righteous men can be found there, but Abraham barters him down to ten.
121. *Peccant*, culpable; *vizard*, disguised.
122. *Inquinated*, polluted, corrupted.
123. [*Johnson:* This is a very fanciful and indefensible section.]
124. [*Johnson: in coagulato*, 'in a congealed or compressed mass'; *in solute*, 'in a state of expansion and separation'.]
125. *Physiognomy*, exemplified in Giambattista della Porta, *De humana physiognomia* (1586).
126. *Asperities*, roughness.
127. *Non ultras*, no further, limits.
128. [*Johnson:* That is, 'in the first part of our time' alluding to the four quadratures of the moon.]
129. [*Johnson:* The one was reduced to poverty on having his eyes put out, the other while in captivity was placed in an iron cage. 'It may somewhat gratify those who deserve to be gratified, to inform them that both these stories are FALSE.'] See Knolles, *The Generall Historie of the Turkes* (1621), p. 227.
130. See *Pseudodoxia*, 3.7 on ideas of sight by extramission.
131. *Decimation* [*Johnson:* The selection of every tenth man for punishment, a practice sometimes used in general mutinies.]
132. *Monitions*, admonitions; *acquitments*, acquittals.
133. Revelation 21:4.

134. *Perspectives*, magnifying glasses.
135. [*Johnson:* The Temple of Janus amoung the Romans was shut in time of peace and opened at a declaration of War.]
136. [*Johnson:* Seneca, having opened his veins, found the blood flow so slowly, and death linger so long, that he was forced to quicken it by going into a warm bath.]
137. 'Save me from shipwreck, and death will be a boon', Ovid, *Tristia*, 1.2.52.
138. *Themistocles*, 31.
139. *Socrates*, Plato, *Phaedo*, 117–18.
140. *Hermes his rod*, which lulled to sleep, Homer, *Odyssey*, 5.47–8.
141. *Angustias* [*Johnson:* Agonies.]
142. *Longanimity*, long-suffering, forbearance.
143. *Water*, in Noah's flood.
144. *Lucifer*, Isaiah 14:12–15; *Jupiter*, Virgil, *Aeneid*, 6.585–6.
145. *Exuperances*, excess, superabundance.
146. *Bivious theorems* [*Johnson:* Speculations which open different tracks to the mind.]
147. *Luciferously*, luminously.
148. Based on Euclid, 'A straight line is the shortest', most direct route between two points.
149. *Stenography*, short-hand.
150. *Osseous*, bone-like.
151. *Seminals,* seeds.
152. *Ostiaries*, door-keepers, door-ways, i.e. the seven deadly sins. [*Johnson:* Pride, covetousness, lust, envy, gluttony, anger, sloth.]
153. *Legion*, Mark 5:9.
154. *Displacences*, displeasure.
155. *Anoint*... *sackcloth*, the one denoting pride, the other abjection.
156. Glee at the misfortune of others.
157. *Surd*, deaf.
158. Translation as in text.
159. Varying 1 Corinthians 13:11.
160. *Coetaneous*, coming into existence at the same time.
161. *Consortion*, whom one consorts with.
162. *Charybdis*, Whirlpool, or sea monster, on one side of a narrow sea-strait, with Scylla, on the other; *black sails* [*Johnson:* Alluding to the story of Theseus, who had black sails when he went to engage the Minotaur in Crete.], signifying bad news, because he forgot to follow his father's instructions to change his sails to white to signify good news, at which sight, his father, Aegeus, killed himself.
163. Martial, 5.74. 'Asia and Europe cover Pompey's sons, but the Earth of Lybia covers him.'
164. 'See what I was and what I am now.'

165. *Assuefaction*, becoming accustomed, habituation; *minorates*, lessens; *inadvertisement*, lack of attention.
166. *Phylactery*, Jewish box or prayer-fringe, enjoining remembrance of the law.
167. *Remoras*, impediments.
168. *Euxine Sea*, Black Sea, too small and enclosed for whales.
169. [*Johnson:* 'With shadows all round us.' The Perscii are those, who, living within the polar circle, see the sun move round them, and consequently project their shadows in all directions.]
170. *Colossus*, of Rhodes, Pliny, *Natural History*, 34.18.
171. [*Johnson:* Which being but a light fluid, cannot support any heavy body.]
172. Matthew 13:45.
173. [*Johnson:* When Augustus supped with one of the Roman senators, a slave happened to break a glass, for which his master ordered him to be thrown into his pond to feed his lampreys. Augustus, to punish his cruelty, ordered all the glasses in the house to be broken.] Dio, *Roman History*, 54.23; [*Johnson:* Anaxarcus, an ancient philosopher, was beaten in a mortar by a tyrant.], or Diogenes Laertius, *Lives*, 9.27, of Zeno of Elea.
174. *Supererogate*, to pay over and above (i.e. in revenge).
175. *Commutatively*, corrective justice.
176. 1 Samuel 20:20.
177. *Ferity*, brutishness.
178. *Satires*, 13.112–13, 'You're roaring, you poor thing, enough to out-do Stentor, or rather, as loud as Mars in Homer.'
179. *Ultion*, vengeance.
180. *Scorpions*, whips, see 1 Kings 12:14.
181. Regulus, Roman general, whose eyelids were sewn open, Aulus Gellius, *Attic Nights*, 7.4.
182. Presuming a span of world history of 6,000 years.
183. *David's servants*, 2 Samuel 10:4; *Elias*, Revelation 11:3.
184. *Metempsychosis*, transmigration of the soul after death.
185. *Divine particle*, Horace, *Satires*, 2.2.79.
186. *Choragium*, the space in which a choral dance is performed.
187. *Intellectual tubes*, telescopes, a metaphor used metaphorically; *visive*, pertaining to sight.
188. *Apogeum* [*Johnson:* To the utmost point of distance from earth and earthly things.]; *confinium*, limits.
189. [*Johnson:* Alluding to the crystalline humour of the eye], i.e. the lens.
190. *Areopagy*, in Athens, where court appeals were heard.
191. *Actuate*, bring into being, make real.
192. *New Jerusalem*, Revelation 21:23.
193. 1 Kings 18:44.
194. John 21:18–19.

195. *Stygian oaths*, unbreakable oaths, *Iliad*, 15.38.
196. 'The person making the oath would throw the stone away, wishing he too might be cast out if the oath was not kept', Aulus Gellius, *Attic Nights*, 1.21.4, on this being the most sacred of oaths.
197. *Discruciating*, torture.
198. *Elater*, propulsive, elastic force.
199. Vulcan being lame; Achilles, quick to anger.
200. These are the following list, representing aspects of ancient, but pagan and so always suspect, ethical thought.
201. *Twelve . . . tables*, Roman Law; *Two tables*, those of Moses.
202. *Remembrancer . . . textuary*, a reminder of moral injunctions, but not an authoritative one.
203. [*Johnson:* That is, according to the rules laid down in our Saviour's sermon on the mount.]
204. *Gust*, taste.
205. *What a face*, i.e. what kind of face.
206. *Orbity*, bereavement.
207. *Physiognomical*, knowledge from appearance.
208. 'Vanity of Vanities, all is Vanity,' Ecclesiastes 1:2.
209. Acts 19:25.
210. *Rencounters*, skirmishes.
211. *Uniterable*, not to be repeated.
212. *Curricle*, short race-track.
213. *Histrionism*, acting, impersonation.
214. Cicero, *On Old Age*, 23.
215. Job 3:3.
216. *Underweening*, underestimation; *exordial*, relating to exordium, introductory part of composition.
217. *Preordination*, predestined action.
218. Genesis 3:17.
219. Isaiah 51:6.
220. Suetonius, *Nero*, 38. [*Johnson:* Quoting 'When I am dead, let the earth and fire be jumbled together.']
221. Matthew 22:14.
222. Genesis 5:27.
223. [*Johnson:* In his treatise of Urn Burial. Some other parts of these essays are printed in a letter among Browne's posthumous works. Those references to his own books prove these essays to be genuine.]

INDEX

though more have perished by violent deaths in the day; yet in natural dissolutions both times may hold an indifferency, at least but contingent inequality. The whole course of time runs out in the nativity and death of things; which whether they happen by succession or coincidence, are best computed by the natural, not artificial day.

That Charles the Fifth was crowned upon the day of his nativity, it being in his own power so to order it, makes no singular animadversion; but that he should also take King Francis prisoner upon that day, was an unexpected coincidence, which made the same remarkable. Antipater who had an anniversary feast every year upon his birth day, needed no astrological revolution to know what day he should dye on. When the fixed stars have made a revolution unto the points from whence they first set out, some of the ancients thought the world would have an end; which was a kind of dying upon the day of its nativity. Now the disease prevailing and swiftly advancing about the time of his nativity, some were of opinion, that he would leave the world on the day he entered into it: but this being a lingering disease, and creeping softly on, nothing critical was found or expected, and he died not before fifteen days after. Nothing is more common with infants than to dye on the day of their nativity, to behold the worldly hours and but the fractions thereof; and even to perish before their nativity in the hidden world of the womb, and before their good angel is conceived to undertake them. But in persons who out-live many years, and when there are no less than three hundred sixty five days to determine their lives in every year; that the first day should make the last, that the tail of the snake should return into its mouth precisely at that time, and they should wind up upon the day of their nativity, is indeed a remarkable coincidence, which though astrology hath taken witty pains to salve,[*] yet hath it been very wary in making predictions of it.

In this consumptive condition and remarkable extenuation he came to be almost half himself, and left a great part behind him which he carried not to the grave. And though that story of duke John Ernestus Mansfield be not so easily swallowed,[†14] that at his death his heart was found not to be so big as a nut; yet if the bones of a good sceleton weigh little more than twenty pounds, his inwards and flesh remaining could make no bouffage, but a light bit for the grave.[15] I never more lively beheld the starved characters of Dante in any living face; an

[*] According to the Egyptian Hieroglyphick.

[†] *Turkish* History.